THE LATER ROMAN EMPIRE
284–602

THE LATER ROMAN EMPIRE
284-602

A SOCIAL ECONOMIC AND ADMINISTRATIVE
SURVEY

By A. H. M. JONES

Arnold Hugh Martin

VOLUME II

UNIVERSITY OF OKLAHOMA PRESS : NORMAN

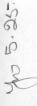

CANISIUS COLLEGE LIBRARY
BUFFALO, N. Y.

VICE CANCELLARIIS ET MAGISTRIS ET SCHOLARIBUS UNIVERSITATUM
OXONIENSIS, BABYLONIENSIS, LONDINIENSIS, CANTABRIGIENSIS;
CUSTODI SOCIIS SCHOLARIBUS CLERICIS ET CHORISTIS COLLEGII
B. V. MARIAE WINTON. IN OXONIA, COMMUNITER NUNCUPATI
NEW COLLEGE, CUSTODI ET SOCIIS COLLEGII OMNIUM
ANIMARUM FIDELIUM DEFUNCTORUM, PRAEPOSITO ET SOCIIS
COLLEGII UNIVERSITATIS APUD LONDINIUM, MAGISTRO ET
SOCIIS COLLEGII B. V. MARIAE, SC. JOHANNIS EVANGELISTAE
ET GLORIOSAE VIRGINIS SC. RADEGUNDAE COMMUNITER
NUNCUPATI JESUS COLLEGE.

Library of Congress Catalog Card Number 64-20762

Original copyright Great Britain, 1964, by Basil Blackwell and Mott, Ltd., Oxford,
England. American edition, manufactured in the United States of America, published
by the University of Oklahoma Press, Publishing Division of the University, Norman,
Oklahoma. First edition 1964.

TABLE OF CONTENTS

VOLUME II

THE LATER ROMAN EMPIRE
284—602

VOLUME II

CHAPTER XX

THE LAND

NO changes in agricultural methods are recorded under the Roman empire. Palladius, who wrote an agricultural manual in the fourth century, lays down the same rules as had Columella in the first. The peasants followed their traditional routine from generation to generation. The main arable crop was wheat, but barley was also grown, more for animal feed than for human consumption: in Egypt and northern Gaul and Illyricum it was brewed into beer, which was the staple drink of the lower classes in those regions. Beans were also a common crop, and flax was extensively grown, especially in the Eastern provinces, for the production of linen. We know little of the technique of arable farming save in the Mediterranean lands, to which the agricultural manuals mainly refer and from which most of our documentary evidence comes. Here, owing to the inadequate rainfall, a laborious technique of dry-farming had to be followed. The land was cropped in alternate years, and frequent ploughing and hoeing was required to break up the soil and keep down weeds and thus conserve moisture. Egypt was an exception: here the inundated land, which was watered and refertilised by the annual flood of the Nile, was cropped every year.[1]

The average yield was low by modern standards. In Egypt it was apparently customary to sow one *artaba* ($3\frac{1}{3}$ *modii*) to the *arura* ($\frac{2}{3}$ acre), and from the scanty evidence it would seem that a tenfold return was normal on good land. This evidence squares with that provided by leases. If land was let on a share of the crop, the tenant and the landlord almost always went fifty-fifty in leases of arable land. If the rent was paid in kind, it was usually five *artabae* to the *arura* or thereabouts. Outside Egypt it was usual to sow more thickly. In Italy Columella recommends 4 *modii* to the *iugerum* ($\frac{5}{8}$ acre) on heavier soils, and 5 on lighter; Palladius prefers 5 to 6. On earlier evidence 6 *modii* to the *iugerum* (nearly twice the Egyptian norm) was the rule in Sicily and in Cyrenaica. We have no data for yields save for much earlier periods. According to

Cicero an eightfold yield was normal in Sicily, a tenfold exceptional. Columella in a pessimistic passage declares that he can scarcely remember when in the greater part of Italy corn yielded fourfold. On Cicero's figures the return in Sicily per acre sown would have been 75 per cent. higher than in Egypt, but in Sicily the land was cropped only every other year. If Columella's statement is to be taken seriously Italian land yielded in alternate years only about two-thirds of what Egyptian land produced every year.[2]

Vines and olives were extensively grown wherever the climate permitted. Wine was the staple drink of all classes in the Mediterranean lands (except Egypt), and was everywhere drunk by the well-to-do. Olive oil was universally used in cooking, and for lighting and for soap. Vines were cultivated not only in the Mediterranean lands but in northern Gaul as far as the valleys of the Seine and the Moselle. Olives were confined to the Mediterranean basin, but were increasingly planted in desert areas, such as eastern Syria, which had hitherto been unproductive. Viticulture was far more profitable than arable farming. In the assessment of land for taxation in Syria 5 *iugera* of vineyard were equated with 20 *iugera* of the best arable. In Egyptian leases the tenant of a vineyard paid two-thirds or even three-quarters of the produce to the landlord. Olives were even more profitable: a little over one *iugerum* planted with mature olive trees was in Syria assessed as equivalent to 5 *iugera* of vineyard or 20 *iugera* of best arable. Various fruit and nut trees—date palms, figs, apples, almonds and pistachios—were also grown and apparently yielded a high profit.[3]

Cattle, sheep, goats and pigs were raised throughout the empire. The cattle were mainly draught animals, for oxen were universally used for ploughing and hauling wagons, but also provided meat and milk, while their hides were valuable for leather. Sheep were mainly raised for their wool, goats mainly for their meat and milk. The animal which provided the greatest part of the meat supply was, however, the pig; pork and, in the winter, ham or bacon was the normal ration of the troops, pork alone was issued to the Roman people. Horses were also reared for the army, the public post and the races and for private use, mules and donkeys for riding and as pack animals. In the Arabian and African deserts camels were bred: they were commonly used as pack animals in many parts of the empire.

We know very little of the organisation of stock farming. There were areas which were noted for the animals which they produced. Spanish and Cappadocian horses were famous, and the wool of certain districts, northern Gaul, Apulia, Phrygia and Asturia, fetched high prices. Here there was probably large-scale production on common pastures or on big ranches; we know of a famous

imperial stud farm, the Villa Palmati, in Cappadocia, which produced race-horses of high repute. The estates of the Roman church
in Sicily evidently included extensive ranches. Gregory the Great
found that they were very unprofitable: 'it is very hard', he wrote
to the rector of the Sicilian patrimony, 'that we spend 60 solidi a
year on our herdsmen, and do not get 60 denarii out of the lands'.
He accordingly ordered that all barren cows and useless bulls
should be sold off, and all the mares except 400, which were to be
hired to the *conductores* of the agricultural estates, while the herdsmen were to be given work as cultivators. We hear also of dairy
farming on a smaller scale. In the Saltus Erudianus in the territory
of Patavium two out of the ten holdings are described as water
meadows (*paludes*) and were evidently let to dairy farmers, for the
tenants in addition to their money rent pay a perquisite of milk, and
nothing else. But to judge by the perquisites (*xenia*) commonly
paid by the tenants of arable holdings in Italy and in Egypt, most
small farmers kept pigs, geese and hens. Many small farmers also
seem to have kept a cow and a few sheep and goats. Most moreover
kept bees; honey often figures among the *xenia*. It was probably
from such small-scale mixed farming that the empire drew much of
its meat, milk and cheese, and most of its eggs, poultry and honey,
all important items in its food supply: in the absence of sugar
honey was greatly in demand.[4]

The paramount importance of agriculture in the economy of the
empire can scarcely be exaggerated. In taxes it provided the vast
bulk of the revenue of the state. The most important of the financial
ministries, the praetorian prefecture, which supplied all the major
needs of the administration, relied entirely on a land tax, which
was exclusively assessed on agricultural land, farm stock and the
rural population. The much less important department of the
sacrae largitiones drew much of its revenue from levies, such as the
vestis, assessed on the same basis, and upon special taxes, such as the
aurum oblaticium and *coronarium*, paid by the main landowning classes,
senators and decurions. The third financial department, the *res
privata*, was fed by the rents of imperial lands. The only taxes not
levied on agriculture were the customs and tolls (*vectigalia*), the
sales tax (*siliquaticum*) instituted by Valentinian III in the West, and
the *collatio lustralis*. The first two bore on all consumers alike:
only the last was assessed directly on trade and industry, and it
produced a negligible amount of revenue, and was abolished
without difficulty by Anastasius.[5]

By far the greatest part of the national income of the Roman empire was, so far as we can estimate, derived from agriculture. Rents formed a major part of the endowments of such corporations as the cities and the churches, and of the incomes of the rentier classes, the senatorial and curial orders, and they also contributed to the incomes of the professional classes. These rents did not all arise from agricultural land, but the proportion which came from urban property was very small. There are in the Liber Pontificalis lists of properties, with their rental value, presented by Constantine and others to eighteen churches in Rome and Italy. The rents total more than 37,000 solidi a year, and were from upwards of 160 named properties, enough to make a fair sample. Nearly 90 per cent. of the whole rent roll comes from agricultural land, and little more than 10 per cent. from urban property of all kinds, houses, gardens, warehouses, baths and bakeries.[6]

The corporate revenues of the cities arose partly from dues and tolls (*vectigalia*) but mainly from their public lands. The churches drew part of their income from offerings (*oblationes*), but became increasingly dependent on the rents of land given or bequeathed to them by benefactors: the offerings, too, were mostly derived in the form of first-fruits from agriculture.[7]

The vast incomes of the Roman senatorial familes, we are told by Olympiodorus, were derived from their estates, and all our other evidence bears this statement out. Those senators, it is true, who took an active part in the administration augmented their unearned incomes with their salaries and with the perquisites of office, and new men who rose into the order made their fortunes by such means. But they invested their profits in land, and increased their estates by grants of land from the crown, and their descendants became great landlords. Decurions were almost necessarily landlords, for a property qualification was required and it was only exceptionally that other forms of property than land were taken into consideration. Decurions sometimes increased their income by professional earnings, especially at the bar, or very occasionally by trade, but the great majority depended for the bulk of their income on agricultural rents.[8]

Many members of the professional classes were also landlords. Many of the privileges granted to higher civil servants, such as immunity from *extraordinaria* and *sordida munera*, presuppose that they owned land. Lower civil servants must also have often possessed substantial landed property. This is implied by the immunity from curial service accorded to the retired *cohortales* of Syria by Diocletian and confirmed by Valens, and by the special rule that in Osrhoene one son of each successive *princeps* of the provincial *officium* was enrolled in the *curia* of Edessa. In the army too both officers and men are often recorded or implied to have had landed property. That barristers commonly owned land is implied by the privilege which *patroni fisci* obtained to continue to plead for their *coloni* after they had retired from practice. We know of professors and doctors who were landlords: Libanius complains of the defiant attitude of some of his tenants, and Flavius Phoebammon, the public doctor of Antinoopolis, had inherited estates situated in two city territories from his father, who had also been a doctor. The immunity from curial service and from *sordida munera* accorded to all professors and doctors implies that these cases were typical.[9]

As early as the reign of Constantius II many of the clergy must have been landowners, for at the council of Ariminum they petitioned the emperor for immunity from land tax. He firmly rejected their plea: 'with regard to clerics who own estates', he wrote to the praetorian prefect, 'your sublime authority will not only prevent their excusing the acreage of other persons, but will cause them to be compelled to pay taxes for the estate which they themselves hold'. We know of several bishops who owned considerable estates, from Pope Damasus, who endowed the church which he built at Rome with two estates bringing in $120\frac{1}{3}$ and 103 solidi a year, to Remigius, bishop of Rheims, whose detailed will we possess. We know too of lower clergy who owned smaller estates. Augustine, replying to critics who declared that some of his clergy had not sold all their goods and adopted a monastic life, according to the rule which he himself had instituted at Hippo, gives some interesting details. Valerius, a deacon, still held some 'little fields' (*agelli*) in common with his brother, a subdeacon at Milevis. Patricius, a subdeacon, held some 'tiny fields' (*agelluli*) in which his mother and sisters had an interest. Faustinus, another deacon, had property in common with a brother. The priest Leporius, who was of a good family, had sold his property, but another priest Barnabas still owned the Fundus Victorianensis, because he was paying off from its proceeds an old debt incurred before his ordination: as he could find no tenant who would pay more than 40 solidi in rent, he ran it by direct labour and sold the crops. At Ravenna in 540 a deacon of the Gothic church sold one-third of a *fundus* to another deacon for 133 solidi, and in 652 a subdeacon of the catholic church owned besides two houses, a bakery and a garden, a farm called the Fundus Carpinianus.[10]

The *navicularii* were by definition landowners; the government paid them freight but expected them to make up their losses and build and maintain their ships from their rents. We meet with

private traders and craftsmen who owned land. An early fourth
century land register from Hermopolis records a number of urban
workers—a builder, a potter, a fuller, three woolworkers, a money
changer and a donkey man—as owning small parcels of land. Sixth-
century deeds from Ravenna reveal a similar situation. In 504
Flavius Basilius, a silversmith (*argentarius*), sold a piece of land for
eighteen solidi: in 541 Isaac, a soapmaker (*saponarius*), bought a
share of a farm for twenty solidi: and in 572 Bonus, a breeches
maker (*bracarius*), gave five-eighths of a farm to the Ravennate
church.[11]

The Hermopolis land register mentioned above shows how many
city dwellers owned land in Egypt in the early fourth century. It
is a list of the landowners resident in the North Fort ward of
Hermopolis and contains about 240 names: this implies nearly
1,000 urban landlords in the four wards into which Hermopolis
was divided. Of the 240 landowners in the North ward seven
between them owned about half the total area, and seven others
about another quarter. These large owners, all above the 250
arura mark, would presumably have been decurions, and so too
might have been six others who owned between 200 and 100 *arurae*
each. This would account for about 80 Hermopolis landlords.
Below come 22 who owned between 30 and 100 *arurae*, 90 who
owned between 10 and 30 *arurae* and 66 with less than 10 *arurae* each.
There must have been well over 700 modest and small landowners,
below the curial class, who were domiciled in the town of Hermopolis and for the most part did not work their own land.[12]

The wide distribution of landed property among the professional
classes and other city dwellers can be accounted for in two ways.
In the first place the professions were largely recruited from the
landowning class. The Codes reveal how many *curiales* went into
the civil service, the army, the law, the church, medicine and
teaching; and at a humbler level peasant proprietors and sons of
veteran allotment holders were conscripted into the army or made
their way into the lower ranks of the civil service. In the second
place land was almost the only safe and permanent form of investment, and successful professional men and merchants and craftsmen, who wished to provide for their old age and for their families,
did so by buying land.

Altogether a high proportion of the land in the empire must
have been owned by absentee landlords. The crown, the cities
and the churches were of necessity absentees. By no means all
senators were domiciled at Rome or Constantinople, but those
who lived in the provinces could not have resided on all their
far-flung estates. Decurions were better able to exercise general

supervision over their farms, but they were legally obliged to reside in town and forfeited their estates if they took up permanent residence on them. Officials and professional men were tied by their work to the towns, and most lawyers and officials to the bigger cities, the provincial, diocesan or imperial capitals. The higher clergy were also from the nature of their duties city dwellers, and the humblest class of landowners, the craftsmen and shop-keepers, were kept busy by their trades in the towns.

Despite the large and growing amount of land owned by land-lords who did not work it themselves the peasant proprietor never became extinct in the Roman empire. That the class declined in numbers is tolerably certain, though it would be difficult to cite much precise evidence for this statement. It might seem at first sight as if the peasant proprietor, who paid only his taxes on his land, stock and family, was in a stronger economic position than the tenant, who had to pay a rent in addition to these, or if his landlord, as was usually the case, paid the taxes, was charged a rent which considerably exceeded the sum due in tax.

It is probable, however, that peasant properties were on the whole smaller than rented farms, and tended to get smaller as from generation to generation they were divided between the heirs. Naturally they varied very greatly in size. The early fourth century land register of the Egyptian village of Theadelphia shows wide divergences. One of the twelve peasants listed owns $58\frac{3}{4}$ *arurae* and two others $47\frac{1}{2}$; but six have very small holdings, $12\frac{7}{8}$, 12, $8\frac{1}{4}$, $3\frac{1}{8}$, $1\frac{3}{8}$ and $1\frac{1}{4}$ *arurae*. The size of leased farms was on the other hand fixed by the landlord of the estate, who would calculate how much land could be conveniently worked by a tenant, and would have no motive for splitting up his farms. A sixth-century rent roll of an estate in the territory of Patavium confirms this hypothesis. It shows, besides a small home farm cultivated by the bailiff (*vilicus*) and two water meadows (*paludes*) leased to dairy farmers, six tenements leased to *coloni* (*colonicae*). One bears the same name as the home farm, and has evidently been carved out of it; the others all have their own names, Candidiana, Valeriaca, Severiaca and the like, derived from some bygone tenant. They are evidently stable traditional units; one is (perhaps temporarily) divided between two *coloni*, most are cultivated by a group of two, three or four *coloni*. The rents are very uniform, ranging from 5 solidi 21 *siliquae* for the largest farm, cultivated by four tenants, to 3 solidi 3 *siliquae* for the smallest. These are substantial rents and imply that the *colonicae* must have been fair-sized farms.[13]

There were, moreover, many disadvantages from which the small man suffered, and these partly counterbalanced his freedom from rent. The regular taxation was in theory uniform for all classes, but the assessment was not always fair: imperial constitutions fulminate against *tabularii* of cities who under-assess the lands of the rich and influential, and throw the resulting burden on the small holders. It was moreover possible for those with influence in high quarters to obtain reduced rates of tax or assessment for their lands, and if cities received rebates of tax or reductions of assessment, it was, Salvian complains, the richer landowners who secured all the relief for themselves. It was, furthermore, the big landowners who profited most from the periodical remission of arrears, which were a regular fiscal practice, for they could keep the tax collector waiting. Even on the score of the regular land tax, then, the peasant proprietor was in fact worse off than his richer neighbours. But in addition to the regular tax there were superindictions, *extraordinaria* and *munera sordida*. From these certain categories of landowners were exempt— besides the crown and the churches, palatine officials of many categories, and from 409 senators of illustrious rank. It would, moreover, appear both from the Codes and from Salvian that in the assessment of *extraordinaria* on a city the local big landlords, the *principales* of the council, contrived to lay the burden on their smaller neighbours.[14]

It was probably, however, not so much the pressure of regular burdens which crushed the peasant freeholders as sudden strokes of misfortune. To meet these the owner of an exiguous holding, living from hand to mouth as he did, could not accumulate any reserve. If there were a succession of bad harvests or his crops were repeatedly ravaged, if his beasts died of disease or were requisitioned and never returned, or carried off by barbarian raiders, he had nothing to fall back upon and unless he mortgaged or sold his land he starved. In similar circumstances a tenant also starved, but the landowner did not have to sell; he was less likely to lose all his crops or his stock, and moreover had reserves of cash to tide him over.

Faced by the inexorable demands of the tax collector in such circumstances the peasant freeholder might abandon his land and seek employment with one of the neighbouring landowners, who, being perennially short of labour, were always glad to take on any man who offered himself as a labourer or tenant. A papyrus from the village of Theadelphia, dating from 332, vividly illustrates such a situation. The disaster in this case was that for several years the water which should have reached the village, which lay at the end of a long canal, had been intercepted by other villages nearer the source. Most of the twenty-five adult males on the census books of the village had vanished, and the three survivors—who incidentally possessed the largest holdings—went in search of them and found some of them in the employ of big landowners in neighbouring territories. A century later Salvian in Gaul lamented the many peasants who 'are driven to flight by the tax collectors and abandon their little holdings because they cannot retain them, and seek out the estates of great men and become the tenants of the rich'.[15]

A less desperate remedy was to sell his land for what it would fetch in such circumstances, or to raise a loan on its security, naturally on exorbitant terms which made foreclosure ultimately inevitable. Justinian found it necessary to give special protection to small holders in Thrace and Illyricum against lenders of money or of corn. He limited the annual rate of interest to one *siliqua* in the solidus (or slightly over 5%) on money loans, and one-eighth (or $12\frac{1}{2}$%) on loans in kind, and enacted that if this were paid with the original debt, the lender must restore the land or stock which he had seized. The lenders were, it appears, mainly officials, probably collectors of taxes or arrears, who made a practice of converting the obligation to the state into a private bond to themselves.[16]

An even commoner resort of a peasant freeholder driven to desperation was to seek the patronage of a powerful person. Patronage is a vague term and seems to cover many different forms of contract, legal or illegal, which prevailed at various periods in various areas. Libanius describes in great detail the form of patronage which was prevalent in Syria in the late fourth century. Here it was used both by villages of freeholders and by villages owned by a landlord, by the former against the tax collector and by the latter against the landlord himself. The villagers would pay a regular bribe to the *dux* of the province to station troops in their village. When the curial *susceptores* arrived to collect the taxes or the landlord or his agent to collect the rents, they were forcibly ejected with the aid of the troops, who had been well entertained by the villagers. If the *susceptores* or the landlord sought legal redress, the *dux* would claim the case for his court, since soldiers were among the defendants, and would give judgment for the villagers.[17]

From a group of constitutions in the Theodosian Code it appears that patronage of a similar type was rampant in the same period in

Egypt. The patrons singled out for censure are persons holding high offices, particularly *duces*, and officials of the military *comes Aegypti*. The clients are peasant freeholders, whose object it is to evade their taxes and other public obligations, and they pay a regular fee to their patrons. Sometimes it is a whole village which takes this step, sometimes individual freeholders, who thereby throw an additional burden on their fellow villagers. Other laws of the same period addressed to the praetorian prefect of the East seem to have been of wider application. They refer to *magistri militum*, *comites*, proconsuls, vicars, Augustal prefects, tribunes and even decurions as exercising patronage.[18]

A law of 415 treats the situation in Egypt in detail. Three commissioners had been appointed to deal with the problem. Their investigations are closed, and no further charges of alleged patronage are to be received if they arose before 397: patrons who took clients under their protection since that date are to be tried before the normal court of the Augustal prefect. Those villages of freeholders (*metrocomiae* or *publici vici*) which had survived were to remain independent, and no outsider was to own land in them, unless acquired before 397, or henceforth to acquire it. The churches of Constantinople and Alexandria were, by a special privilege conceded by the previous praetorian prefect, to retain *metrocomiae* and *publici vici* which had come under their protection, provided that the villagers paid all their taxes and performed all the public functions due from them according to the old rules.[19]

Further clauses of the law, which are unfortunately most obscure, deal with estates (*possessiones*) and their cultivators, who were by local usage known as *homologi coloni*. These were to perform their ancient public functions, like the inhabitants of the *metrocomiae*, whether the estates remained under their old owners or were retained by patrons. The *possessiones* envisaged appear to be estates which had been built up out of village lands by outside landlords and were cultivated by their tenants, who, however, remained on the register of the villagers—this is perhaps the meaning of *homologi*—and were legally liable to share in their obligations to the state. The owners of some such estates, presumably the smaller men, would seem to have sought the patronage of the powerful.[20]

In its earlier stages this oriental form of patronage did not involve the peasant in the loss of his land. The small proprietor in the village paid an annual tribute to his protector, and if his protector was the *magister militum*, the *dux* of the province or the tribune of the local unit, or again the vicar of the diocese for the time being, the relationship was unlikely to become permanent.

These officers were, however, usually landowners on a considerable scale, and might continue their protection not in their official capacity but as men of power and influence; moreover, some villagers and small proprietors sought the patronage of big landowners as such; *curiales* are mentioned in these laws as patrons, and so are the great churches, which had far-flung estates. Such patrons tended to become permanent and their annual tribute to become a rent, until eventually their patronage of the peasants was converted into ownership of the land under some legal form of donation, sale or lease.

The fifth-century emperors continued to legislate against patronage. Marcian issued a constitution, which has not been preserved, annulling contracts of patronage entered into since 437 in the diocese of Thrace, and since 441 in those of Asiana, Pontica, Oriens and Egypt. This law was re-enacted in 468 by Leo, who declared null all contracts of patronage under whatever legal form from the same dates, whether affecting individuals or villages. These two laws dealt only with freeholders who sought to evade payment of their taxes. A later undated law deals also with villages of slaves or free tenants who revolted against their landlords under the protection of a patron. The patrons in this law are of the old type, described by Libanius, who are recompensed by a regular tribute and not, as in Leo's law, by ownership of the land.[21]

In the East the government, in the interest of the revenue, waged periodical campaigns against patronage. It was obliged to condone long-standing violations of the law, and it must have been very difficult to distinguish patronage in its later forms from genuine gifts and sales. One may well doubt whether the government's intervention was very effective, despite the ever severer penalties with which it threatened either party, seeing that normally both parties would maintain a conspiracy of silence.

In the West our information is much more meagre. There are no imperial constitutions on the subject and we have to rely on the rhetorical and rather obscure account of the institution by Salvian. There the patron is a great landlord, who offers his protection to the individual peasant against the tax collector in return for the reversion of the peasant's land on his death. The tragic sequel seems to be rather overdrawn. The sons, according to Salvian, 'though despoiled of their little properties and expelled from their little fields, nevertheless bear the taxation of the property that they have lost. When the possession has left them, the tribute does not . . ., the land-grabbers invade their property and they, poor wretches, pay the taxes for the land-grabbers'. This presumably means not that the sons were physically expelled but that the patron, once securely in possession of the land after the death of the original client, no longer protected his sons, who were now his tenants, from the tax collector's exactions. It is likely enough that patrons did pursue this policy, not wishing to fall foul of the imperial government unnecessarily, but the implication that their tenants gained nothing is almost certainly untrue; they would pay the regular taxes but be spared many additional exactions.[22]

The fact that no imperial legislation against patronage survives in the West does not prove that the practice was rare. The Western government at the time when patronage was becoming rife in the East was falling into the hands of the great territorial magnates who mainly profited by the process, and they are likely to have looked with a blind eye upon it.

Generation after generation peasants abandoned their holdings, sold them to wealthy neighbours, mortgaged them and suffered foreclosure, or surrendered them to patrons in return for protection. To set against this there was very little increase in peasant holdings. The government, it is true, made grants of waste land to veterans in the fourth century. These were on two scales according to a law of Valentinian. Ordinary soldiers received one yoke of oxen and 50 *modii* of seed corn, enough to sow ten or twelve *iugera*; those retired with the rank of *protector* were given two yokes of oxen, and twice as much seed. The author of the De Rebus Bellicis, who addressed his pamphlet to Valentinian, was an enthusiast for this policy, and urged that the term of service should be shortened, partly with a view to increasing the number of these peasant cultivators. The policy seems, however, to have been abandoned shortly afterwards.[23]

Estates, when they came on to the market, seem never to have been broken up. Few peasants probably had enough money laid by to purchase land, and the tenants of the estate were almost certainly too poor to buy their holdings. What was more important, there was always an abundance of rich men eager to snap up any land that was offered for sale. Melania, when she sold her vast estates, found no shortage of wealthy purchasers, who, if they could not find the ready cash with so much land thrown on the market at once, could offer good security. It does not seem to have occurred to this pious lady to offer favourable terms to her tenants.[24]

In these circumstances the number of peasant freeholders must have steadily diminished, particularly from the end of the fourth century, when entire villages were passing into the possession of patrons. It must, however, be emphasised that the evidence which has been cited for the gradual elimination of peasants' properties is also evidence for their continued survival. If the flight of freeholders from their farms and the surrender of their farms by their peasant owners to patrons were common phenomena in Gaul in his day, as Salvian declares, there must still have been a substantial number of small freeholders left in Gaul in the middle of the fifth century. If the activity of moneylenders in Illyricum and Thrace caused grave anxiety to Justinian, there must have been a large number of peasants to mortgage their farms in the sixth century in these areas. Libanius in the later fourth century divided the villages of Syria into two categories, those owned by one landowner, and those divided between many small holders; and Theodoret in the middle of the fifth century still speaks of these two classes of village.[25]

On Asia Minor we have no specific information, but the long and detailed biography of Theodore of Syceon, who spent his whole life ministering in the villages around Anastasiopolis in Galatia during the early seventh century, gives the impression that the villagers were peasant proprietors: no landlord appears in the narrative save the church of Anastasiopolis. In Africa, the classical land of great estates, a group of documents has come to light which show that in the last years of the fifth century Mancian tenures still subsisted. These were not freeholds, it is true. They originated in the policy of the early second century emperors, and probably of other African landlords, of granting perpetual leaseholds to persons, normally their tenants, who brought waste land on their estates into cultivation, and especially planted them with vines, olives or fruit trees. Mancian tenures were subject to a rent in kind, usually one-third of the produce, but they could be left by will or sold by the holder. The documents record the sale of a dozen or so of these tiny holdings, each with a few fruit trees or olives; it is perhaps significant of the trend of the times that all were sold to one purchaser.[26]

It is only in Egypt that we can very roughly measure the decline of the peasant proprietors. Egypt was a somewhat exceptional country in that the fiscal policy of the Ptolemies, continued under the Principate, had discouraged the growth of large estates, or indeed of private property in land. Some land, however, usually of marginal quality, was sold or granted to private owners, and by the Principate there had grown up a small class of substantial landowners, resident in the metropoleis of the nomes, who from the reign of Septimius Severus were enrolled in the city councils. The bulk of the land, however, remained public, and was cultivated by peasants in small holdings on lease from the crown. When

Diocletian finally converted the nomes into cities, the division of the land into public and private was not abolished, but it gradually ceased to be significant and the peasants came to be owners of their customary tenures.

In the early fourth century peasant proprietors were then exceptionally numerous in Egypt. The census register of Hermopolis shows 14,700 *arurae* in the possession of landlords resident in one of the four wards, which implies rather less than 60,000 *arurae* owned by all the inhabitants of Hermopolis; Antinoite citizens also owned 6,700 *arurae*, making a total of about 66,000 *arurae* owned by urban landlords. The territory of Hermopolis must, estimating its area from the map, have comprised about 400,000 *arurae*; that is to say only about one-sixth of the city territory was owned by urban landlords, and the remaining five-sixths by peasant villagers, who were entered on separate registers. The only village on which we have sufficient information, Theadelphia in the Arsinoite territory, yields similar results. The total area of the village was 500 *arurae*, and of this only two holdings, amounting to 30 *arurae*, were in the early fourth century held by urban landlords.[27]

With these figures may be contrasted those relating to the estates of the 'glorious house' of Flavius Apion's heirs in the sixth century. In a comparable area, the combined territories of Oxyrhynchus and Cynopolis, which totalled 280,000 *arurae*, the Apion family alone owned two-fifths, 112,000 *arurae*, and Oxyrhynchus, the capital of a province, certainly contained many other landlords of some substance. But even in the sixth century the peasant proprietor was by no means extinct. We possess a large group of documents from the village of Aphrodito in the territory of Antaeopolis, which show that its peasant freeholders were still maintaining their rights, of which the principal was *autopragia*, the privilege of collecting their own taxes and delivering them direct to the provincial governor, in Justinian's reign and indeed down to the Arab conquest.[28]

Peasant proprietorship was perhaps more strongly rooted and survived more vigorously in Egypt than in most dioceses. But there is evidence which suggests that it was strong in other areas of the Eastern empire. Justinian was able to raise considerable armies from among his subjects, particularly in Illyricum and Thrace and in eastern Asia Minor, whence came the Isaurian regiments. These men were certainly countrymen, and they were not *adscripticii*, the tied tenants of landlords (including the church and the crown), who had been since the early fifth century debarred from military service. They may have included free tenants, but it seems likely that many were freeholders. Justinian's anxiety to protect the free peasants of Illyricum and Thrace against money-lenders is more understandable if they were an important recruiting ground.[29]

For the West there is less evidence for the survival of the peasant freeholder, whereas evidence for absentee landlords, great, middling and small, is abundant. In Italy and Sicily we know of many vast *massae* and *fundi* owned by the crown, the church and senatorial families. In Spain again we know of large senatorial estates, some owned by Italian families, like those of Melania and Pinianus, some by senators of local origin, like Theodosius the *magister militum* or the brothers Didymus and Verinianus, two wealthy young nobles, who, in the early fifth century, raised a private army from the slaves on their estates and maintained it at their own charges. In Africa, too, we have much evidence for large estates owned by the crown, the church, Roman senators like Symmachus, Pammachius and Pinianus, and local magnates such as Gildo; while in Gaul we know of great senatorial landowners like Paulinus of Nola and Sidonius Apollinaris. These big estates must have occupied a large proportion of the total area. We can infer the existence of a large number of more modest estates from the survival of the curial order, which still existed in Visigothic Gaul and Spain in the early sixth century, and is well attested down to the seventh in Italy. In Italy we hear also of small farms or parts of farms owned by other urban residents, officials, soldiers, the minor clergy and merchants or craftsmen, and similar conditions may be postulated elsewhere. As against this we have only the testimony of Salvian for the survival of the peasant freeholder in Gaul, and in Africa the documents which reveal the continued existence of Mancian tenures.[30]

Landlords, both great and small, rarely owned a single con-solidated estate. Their possessions were usually scattered and consisted of a number of farms, some larger, some smaller. The greatest landlord of the empire, the *res privata*, owned besides some large blocks of territory, mostly ancient royal lands, countless estates which had accrued to it by bequest, escheat or confiscation in every province and in almost every city. The great churches, as a result of donations and bequests from emperors and other great benefactors, acquired very far-flung estates. In the fourth century the lands of the Roman church were mostly in Italy, where they were distributed over twenty-five cities, but included also two large groups of estates in Sicily, seven blocks in Africa and two in Achaea, as well as a number of estates in the East at Antioch, Tarsus, Alexandria, Tyre, Cyrrhus and elsewhere. By the time of Gregory the Great the patrimony of St. Peter had grown considerably: it now included lands not only in Italy, Sicily and Africa but in Sardinia and Corsica, Gaul and Dalmatia. The lands of the Great Church of Constantinople were as widely dispersed: its estate office was divided into departments for the dioceses of Thrace, Asiana, Pontica and Oriens, and it is known to have owned lands in Egypt also. The sees of two other imperial capitals, Milan and Ravenna, owned far-flung estates; Ravenna had properties in Bononia, Urbinum, Luca, Forum Cornelii, Ariminum and Agubium, and both are known to have had land in Sicily. Great cities also sometimes possessed civic estates outside their own territories. In the early fourth century Antinoopolis owned four farms with a total area of 520 *arurae* in the territory of Hermopolis, and Zeno restored to Nicaea a number of estates, with a total rental of 400 solidi, which lay in the neighbouring territory of Apamea.[31]

The estates of great private landlords were often scattered over many provinces. Symmachus in his letters mentions twelve villas which he owned in various parts of Italy, and speaks of his lands in Samnium, Apulia, Sicily and Mauretania. The biographer of Melania draws a vivid picture of her making a leisurely progress from Rome to Carthage, systematically selling her estates in Campania, Apulia, Sicily, Africa, Numidia and Mauretania: she also owned lands in Spain, which were at the moment unsaleable owing to the babarian invasions, and even, we are told, in Britain. Senators had many opportunities of acquiring lands in distant provinces. Though they were forbidden to exploit their authority in this way, they married rich heiresses in the provinces which they governed. It was probably as a result of such a marriage that Paulinus owned lands not only near Burdigala, the home of his grandfather Ausonius, but in Achaea and Old and New Epirus: he inherited the latter from his mother, and it is perhaps significant that he was born at Pella and that his father was vicar of Macedonia at that time.[32]

Senators also despite the laws abused their official powers to make advantageous purchases in the provinces, and took advantage of their influence at court to secure grants of property accruing to the crown. An interesting picture of a great property of senatorial proportions, which was mainly built up by purchases and grants from the crown, is given by the very detailed will of a Merovingian royal favourite, Bertram. He was apparently a native of Burdigala, entered the service of King Lothar at Paris, and was promoted to be archdeacon of Paris and then, in 586, bishop of the Civitas Cenomanorum (Le Mans). When Guntram died in 593 he suffered, he complains, great losses in the subsequent troubles but remained steadfastly loyal to Lothar, and when Lothar in 613 became king of all Gaul reaped a rich reward for his loyalty. He seems to have come from a prosperous family of middle rank, inheriting a house at Burdigala and eight villas and one *colonica* in the territory of that city and its neighbour, the Civitas Santonum: some of these properties he originally shared with his brothers, but by outliving them he ultimately concentrated most of the family inheritance in his own hands. To these estates he added a few by legacies or gifts and many more by purchase or by royal grant. He mentions two villas and half a dozen other properties which were left or given to him by private persons, and over twenty-six villas, as well as miscellaneous minor properties such as vineyards, houses and a pine plantation, which he bought out of his own money, besides five villas which he bought from money given him by the king. He also received from the king eleven named villas and two other properties and a house; a half share in the extensive estates of Avitus in the territories of Bituriges, Cadurci, Alba and Agennum; a third share in another great group of villas in Burgundy, formerly the property of Landegesil; and a third share in yet another group in Provence which had belonged to Aureliana. These were free gifts. In addition he was granted, in compensation for losses in the troubles, three named villas and others in the territories of Pictavi, Cadurci and Lemovices from the estate of a lady named Nunciana, who had apparently usurped some of his property. Altogether he names over eighty individual properties, besides five groups of estates. They were distributed over fourteen city territories, from Paris to Bordeaux, apart from the property in Burgundy and Provence. Some of the items were no doubt small: for one he paid only 40 solidi. But of the villas which he bought some were quite substantial—for one he paid 100 solidi, for another 140, and in two cases 300—while one, whose price was 1,000, must have been very large.[33]

This fortune is probably typical of many made by new men of the senatorial order, except that their estates would have been even more widely dispersed. Such great agglomerations were from time to time broken up by division between heirs, and parts of them were added to other agglomerations through the marriages of heiresses. Hence the complexity and dispersion of the average senatorial fortune.

On the gross area of the great senatorial estates we have very little information. In the sixth century the contribution of 'the glorious house' of the Apion family in the Oxyrhynchite and Cynopolite territory to the *embole*, the corn levy for Constantinople, amounted to nearly 140,000 *artabae*. A contemporary document (from another city, Antaeopolis) gives the rate of the levy at approximately 1¼ *artabae* to the *arura*. The Apion estates in this district (they also owned large areas in the Heracleopolite and Arsinoite) would therefore have covered 112,000 *arurae*, about 75,000 acres or 120 square miles.[34]

For other senatorial families we have only the rentals of their estates. The figures are probably net, representing the actual income received after the *actores* had paid the taxes locally. The above-mentioned Apion estates would have yielded, according to the rates of rent and tax normally prevalent in sixth-century Egypt, about 20,000 solidi a year, very nearly 3 *centenaria* of gold. To produce the incomes of 15 *centenaria* enjoyed by Western senators of middling wealth far more than five times 120 square miles would have been needed, for the yield and therefore the rental value of land in Egypt was much higher than in other parts of the empire. The richest Roman senators, whose income was in the range of 40 *centenaria* of gold, must have owned several thousand square miles.

The landed property of lesser men also usually consisted of a group of farms, though these were not as a rule so widely dispersed. We possess a small part of an early fourth century land register from Magnesia on the Maeander. It is an alphabetical list of farms, assessed in *iuga* and *capita*, with the owners' names: the surviving portion covers the letters A and B only. In this we find that Severianus, a tribune, owned five separate farms with these initials, and Paulus, a decurion, four. From another contemporary register we learn that Tatianus, a rich decurion of Tralles, owned fourteen estates, six quite small (under one *iugum*), seven of moderate size (1½ to 6 *iuga*) and one as large as the total holding of his more modest colleague, Latron (17½ *iuga*). Latron's property was formed of four estates, and Critias (with 20 *iuga* in all) owned seven farms. In the Hermopolis register the land of the larger owners is distributed over several of the 18 *pagi* into which the territory of the city was divided. One owner held land in 10 *pagi*, two in 9, and others in 8, 7, or 6; only one large property, actually the largest (1,370 *arurae*), was all in a single *pagus*.[35]

Men of curial status normally owned land only within the territory of their own cities. Sometimes, however, the richer among them had acquired estates in neighbouring cities too. In the early fourth century four prominent decurions of Antinoopolis, a former president, a former *exactor* and two former *curatores*, owned estates in the territory of Hermopolis. Letoius, a very wealthy Antiochene decurion of Libanius' time, is known to have owned a village in the territory of Cyrrhus.

In Gaul in the sixth century bishop Remigius left a most complicated estate, though quite a small one, and all in the territory of Remi. He had inherited from his father and mother lands in the territory of Portus and from his brother Principius other lands in the same place: this estate was apparently called Vacculiacum. He also owned part of another estate called Talpusciacum, part of a third, Casurnicum, 'which came to me by the lot of the division', part of a fourth called Setia, near Laudunum, part of a meadow at Laudunum of which his nephew Lupus owned the rest, some other meadows called Iovia, a field next the mill at Vongum, a holding (*colonica*) called Passiacum, and half a dozen vineyards, including one on the river Subnis, one at Laudunum and a third at Vindonissa which he had planted himself. The will well illustrates the complication of land tenure caused by the division of estates between a number of heirs. Even tiny properties might consist of several separate holdings. A Hermopolitan who owned only nine *arurae* in all had three tenants, one of whom leased four and the others two and a half *arurae* each.[36]

A map of any Roman province, or even *civitas*, showing the boundaries of properties, would thus have been a very complicated jigsaw puzzle. In Italy and the Western provinces the basic unit of ownership was the *fundus*. *Fundi* were fairly stable units with permanent individual names, sometimes descriptive, but most usually derived from a long past owner—Fundus Cornelianus is the typical form. They were naturally not of a standard size. In the lists of estates given by Constantine to the Roman churches there is a *fundus* with as large a rental as 120 solidi, and, at the other end of the scale, another which brought in only 20 solidi. Well over half, however, range between 60 and 40 solidi. The average size of this group of *fundi* is perhaps rather high, for they were grants from the *res privata*, which got most of its land from well-to-do owners. The Ravenna deeds deal on the whole with smaller *fundi*, owned by humble people. Here only one is worth 400 solidi in capital value, which is on the same level as the smallest Constantinian estates, the rest are worth only sums like 120, 72, 48 and even 28 solidi. A *fundus* was not an indivisible unit. Humbler landowners, who owned only one, had to divide it between their heirs, or might sell off a bit if hard up. In the Ravenna deeds most of the transactions are in fractions of *fundi*, a half, a third or even a sixth or an eighth.[37]

Richer men, who owned several *fundi*, had less reason to sub-
divide an individual farm, and the richest, including the crown
and the great churches, who owned many, grouped them into
massae. *Massae* again were not of standard size. The Constantinian
list contains one with a rental of only 115 solidi, less than the
largest *fundus*, but the majority are from 650 to 300 solidi. There
are larger *massae* in the list, of 720, 800, 810 and 1,000 solidi,
and one monster in Sicily with a rental of 1,650. *Massae*
were not necessarily continuous blocks of land, but rather a
group of *fundi* under one management. A large *massa* in the
territory of Signia which was given to a church in Rome in the
sixth century consisted of 31 complete *fundi*, the halves of two
others and a third of another. This strongly suggests that there
were at any rate enclaves in the block: no doubt the three fragmentary *fundi* had already been split before the owners of the
massa acquired them and they had apparently not yet been able to
buy up the odd bits. *Massae* were fairly stable units, which acquired permanent names, usually formed like those of *fundi* from
the name of the original owner, but they might naturally be divided
up again. In 553 a noble but illiterate couple, named Felithan and
Runilo (probably of Gothic descent), gave the church of Ravenna
the half of two *massae*, one in the territory of Urbinum and the
other in that of Luca. King Odoacer, having promised land to
the annual value of 690 solidi to the illustrious Pierius, first gave
him the island of Melita in Dalmatia (200 solidi a year) and lands
to the value of 450 solidi a year from the Massa Pyramitana in the
territory of Syracuse. When Pierius applied for the remaining
40 solidi he was given the Fundus Aemilianus (18 solidi), the rest
of the Fundus Dubli ($15\frac{3}{4}$ solidi) and part of the Fundus Putaxiae
(7 solidi), all out of the same Massa Pyramitana.[38]

Big landowners then as always liked if possible to consolidate
their estates by buying up intervening or adjacent properties.
This is well illustrated by Bertram's will. When Queen Ingoberg
gave half an estate to his church, he bought the other half from
her brother 'so that the estate might come in its entirety into the
possession of the church'. Similarly he bought from the widow
and other heirs of Bobolenus the other half of the Villa Colonia,
of which Bobolenus had given a half share to the church. Bertram
also consolidated his personal estates. Thus he had acquired the
Villa Brea partly by gift from one Daulfus and partly by purchase,
and when King Lothar granted him part of the Villa Tauriaco from
the estate of Nunciana he bought the rest from her sons.[39]

Naturally, therefore, the wealthier and older the family, the
larger tended to be the blocks in which its estates were held. Some

of Melania's estates were vast. Her biographer describes one near Rome which stretched from the sea at one end to the forest at the other, and contained besides a magnificent villa sixty-two hamlets of about four hundred slaves each. In Africa, according to Agennius Urbicus, '*saltus* owned by private persons are as large as the territories of cities; indeed many *saltus* are far larger than territories. Moreover on private *saltus* there is a not inconsiderable plebeian population and villages around the villa like *municipia*'. Melania endowed the church of Tagaste with such an estate, which was larger than that city itself, 'with a villa and many craftsmen, gold, silver and coppersmiths, and two bishops, one of our faith and one of the heretics'. Many African cities were, of course, very small, and African bishops were two a penny, so that this estate need not have been as vast as the hagiographer suggests.[40]

Senatorial estates were not all large. The inheritance of Paulinus' mother was 'dispersed over several cities of Achaea and Old and New Epirus, over which there were scattered, but not at great distances, estates well stocked with numerous cultivators'. In the surviving portion of the land register of Magnesia on the Maeander, the largest estate by far—assessed at 75 *iuga*, more than three times as big as the next largest, one of 21 *iuga* owned by a decurion—is the property of a senator; but three other senators and two ladies of senatorial rank own six quite modest farms. The lands of the Apion family, who had in the sixth century only recently risen to great wealth, consisted of a huge agglomeration of quite small holdings, from hamlets (ἐποίκια) and farms (κτήματα) to little peasant tenements within villages.[41]

In Syria both Libanius and Theodoret classify villages into two contrasted types, those owned by one landlord and those owned by many peasant proprietors, and imperial constitutions imply a similar division in Egypt between the *metrocomiae* and *publici vici* on the one hand and the *possessiones* with their *homologi coloni* on the other. This distinction must be rather schematic, for it is likely that some small holdings survived among or within large estates, and certain that outside landlords often owned land within *metrocomiae*. Some already did so before 397 and though the acquisition of land in free villages by outsiders was prohibited in 415 and again by Leo in 468, it certainly went on: the Apion family held much land so situated in the sixth century. Broadly speaking, however, the picture presented by Libanius, Theodoret and the constitutions is no doubt true to the facts, and probably applied to other regions. In some parts this state of affairs may have been very ancient. The Hellenistic kings of Asia Minor and Syria, no doubt following the precedent of their predecessors, not infrequently granted whole villages of their royal domain to their officials, courtiers and favourites. In other cases it was a recent result of patronage, for patrons often acquired entire villages. The village was in Egypt, and probably elsewhere, a fiscal unit, whose inhabitants were jointly responsible for the taxes, and villages therefore often took joint action in the measures they adopted to protect themselves. But even where large estates were gradually built up in the territory of villages, they often tended to become hamlets (ἐποίκια), no doubt because landlords preferred to house their tenants on the estate. It was probably in this way that most landlords' villages were formed: the large *fundus*, *saltus* or *massa* developed its own village, or even a group of villages and hamlets.[42]

Great landlords managed their estates in a variety of ways. There were broadly three alternatives, to employ agents (*procuratores*, *actores*), to lease their estates on short terms to contractors (*conductores*), or to lease them for terms of lives or in perpetuity to *emphyteuticarii* or *perpetuarii*: these were also in strict law *conductores*, but are often called *possessores*. The three methods were employed in different permutations and combinations by landlords of different types, the crown, the churches and private owners, great and medium. It will be simplest to take some representative examples where our information is fullest.

The greatest of landlords, the *res privata*, had an elaborate managerial hierarchy. For each diocese, or sometimes half diocese, there was a *magister*, later *rationalis*, *rei privatae*. Below him were *procuratores rei privatae*, responsible for a province or two, or for a large nexus of estates which had once belonged to a single owner. Below them again were the *actores dominici* or *rei privatae*. It may be that some of these last actually managed the estates, dealing directly with the tenant cultivators (*coloni*), but normally *conductores* performed this task.[43]

Some imperial estates were leased at short terms (probably the *lustrum* of five years which was standard in Roman law). In that case the *conductor* enjoyed no security of tenure, having to make way for a rival who offered a higher rent unless he were prepared to pay the same figure. On the other hand he was not in practice free to throw up his lease, but might be compelled to renew at the old figure. Leases were sometimes assigned compulsorily; this practice applied particularly to the *fundi iuris reipublicae* and *iuris templorum*, the old civic and sacred lands, which in default of willing lessees were allocated to the decurions who had in old times normally leased them. Already in Constantine's reign, however, a large proportion of imperial land was leased in perpetuity to *emphyteuticarii* or *perpetuarii* (the terms seem to be synonymous in connection with state lands). The practice was convenient for the government, which received a steady, if reduced, income and was spared the trouble of administration, and was also popular with lessees, who gained a secure title, which could be alienated or bequeathed, subject to a fixed rent-charge. More and more imperial land passed into this category as time went on.[44]

The church of Rome had also by the sixth century an elaborate administrative hierarchy. The lands of the Roman see, known collectively as the patrimony of Peter, were divided into regional groups, each known as a patrimony. Overseas we hear of the patrimonies of Gaul, of Africa, of Dalmatia (with which went Praevalitana), and of Sicily, which was sometimes divided into two blocks, administered from Syracuse and Panormus. In Italy there are recorded patrimonies of Apulia, Campania, and Appia, the area south of Rome on the Appian Way. At the head of each patrimony was a *rector*, who was usually one of the minor Roman clergy, a subdeacon, notary or *defensor*, sent out for a term of years. Sometimes a local bishop acted as *rector* temporarily; we find the bishop of Arles managing the Gallic patrimony at times, and the bishop of Syracuse the Sicilian. And sometimes a local layman of high standing undertook the task: thus in Gaul, then ruled by the Merovingian kings, Gregory at first employed the patricians Dynamius and Aregius, no doubt because they could offer efficient protection to the interests of the church.[45]

Under the *rectores* were *actores* or *actionarii*, and below them *conductores*: we happen to know that in Sicily there were 400 *conductores*. The churches were by this time legally entitled to grant emphyteutic leases, but Gregory was chary of them. The bulk of the lands of the Roman see was let on short leases; it had become the practice in Sicily for the agents to demand a fine (*commodum*) for the grant of a lease, but Gregory prohibited this abuse, which led to the *conductores* being too frequently changed. In other churches emphyteutic leases seem to have been common; in the Great Church of Constantinople the clerks at the head office (*chartularii*) who drew up the leases received a commission of 1% on short lets and 2% on emphyteutic grants.[46]

The Apion family, though their estates were concentrated in a small area, also had an elaborate hierarchy of agents. At its head was the 'deputy landlord' (ἀντιγεοῦχος), under whom were a number of chief agents (διοικηταί), and under each of them about ten or a dozen inferior agents (προνοηταί), each of whom managed three or four farms or hamlets and other small holdings in the neighbourhood. The Apions did not use *conductores* at all, the lower grade of agents dealing directly with the tenant cultivators (γεωργοί), who often grouped into gangs under foremen (φροντισταί). Lauricius, former *praepositus sacri cubiculi* of Honorius, managed his Sicilian estates in a very different way. They had fallen heavily into arrears under the tribune Pyrrhus, who had apparently been his principal agent or *procurator*, and on sending out a successor he wrote to his *actores* and his principal *conductores*. He owned three *massae*, the Fadiliana which was leased to Sisinnius for 445 solidi, the Cassitana held under a joint lease by three *conductores*, Eleutherio, Zosimus and Eubulus, for 500 solidi, and the Emporitana, leased by the same Zosimus and a partner named Cuprio for 756 solidi; the last pair also leased the Fundus Anniana, and part of the Fundus Aperae, with rentals of 147 and 52 solidi, and Sisinnius appears to have sublet another *fundus* for 200 solidi. Lauricius thus entrusted his estates to a small group of big *conductores*, and his *actores* cannot have had any direct concern with actual running of the property. For the rest we have little detailed information, but from the legal texts it would appear that most great secular landlords had their *procuratores* and *actores*, and leased their estates to *conductores*, though sometimes the *actores* may have dealt with the *coloni* directly. Private landlords do not seem to have granted emphyteutic leases on any large scale.[47]

The Apions employed free men for their agents. Those of the higher grade (διοικηταί) are often given the title of *comes* and even of *illustris*; this in sixth-century Egypt does not mean very much, for such titles seem to have been given by courtesy to any person of standing, but indicates that they were gentlemen of some substance. The lower grade agents (προνοηταί) were naturally humble folk. We possess the contract of one, Serenus, who was a deacon: he paid twelve solidi for a year's engagement. In the West, and probably in other Eastern provinces, *actores* were commonly slaves or freedmen of the owner. *Procuratores* might also be freedmen or slaves, but landlords often found it convenient to employ persons of higher status who could protect their interests more effectively. An unnamed Constantinopolitan senator in the reign of Arcadius used Antoninus, the metropolitan of Ephesus, to look after his estates in Asia; the arrangement was convenient to both parties, for when Antoninus got into trouble with John Chrysostom, the patriarch of Constantinople, his senatorial employer was able to hold up proceedings against him. The employment of clergy as *procuratores* was sufficiently common for Marcian to suggest to the Council of Chalcedon that the practice should be forbidden. In Africa a council of Carthage had prohibited the clergy from serving as *procuratores* in 349. *Curiales* were also in demand and were forbidden to take such posts, lest by pledging their own lands as security to their employers they should imperil the interests of the treasury, to which these same lands stood as security for the taxes.[48]

Conductores might be slaves, usually of the landlord: Pope Gelasius complains that a certain Ampliatus, a slave of the Roman church, who had been a *conductor* of church lands and owed considerable sums on this account, had had the effrontery to make a will leaving his *peculium* away from the church. More commonly *conductores* were free persons, and persons of substance, seeing that they had to give security for the very considerable sums which they handled. *Curiales* evaded the law which forbade them to be *procuratores* by acting as *conductores*, until this loophole was stopped by Theodosius II in 439. It was also a common practice, noted in a law of the same date, for would-be *conductores* to obtain a sinecure palatine *militia* as *protector*, *domesticus*, *agens in rebus* or the like, so that they could claim *praescriptio fori* against the jurisdiction of the provincial governor or the vicar, or even the praetorian prefect. Persons who had sufficient money and influence to get such posts must have held some position in society. Soldiers were also commonly employed as *conductores*: Justinian complains that despite many laws not only *scholares* but regular soldiers serving under the *magistri militum* and *foederati* neglected their military duties and instead of fighting the enemy turned their arms against the peasants whose rents they collected. The clergy, too, were often employed in this capacity also. In Africa the council of Hippo in 393 prohibited bishops, priests and deacons from serving as *conductores* of great landlords.[49]

The holders of emphyteutic and perpetual leases were no doubt usually rich men; lands so leased were often in bad condition and needed considerable capital outlay, which ruled out the poor man. Moreover, they were a form of investment only slightly less attractive than freehold land. For though they were burdened with a perpetual rent, they were free, if state or church lands, as they usually were, from superindictions, extraordinary levies and *munera sordida*. It is probable that many *emphyteuticarii* and *perpetuarii* were at the same time private landlords on a large scale.

Despite the legal difference in their position a short term *conductor* and an *actor* who directly managed an estate were in practice

in a very similar situation. A *conductor* contracted to pay the owner
a fixed rent; an *actor* was strictly an agent who transmitted the
profits of the estate to the owner, but in fact the owner did not
expect to get more than the sum of the fixed rents of the *coloni*.
Both *conductor* and *actor* made their profit in extra levies and dues
from the *coloni*. Both were primarily rent and tax collectors, but
both had supervisory duties as well. They had to see that all the
holdings were cultivated, reclaim runaway slaves or *coloni*, and
take on new tenants from outside when they were required and if
they were available. They were also responsible for the observation
of the law on the estate: if a deserter were found on it or a pagan
sacrifice were celebrated or a heretical service held or coiners
plied their illicit trade, it was the *actor* or the *conductor* who was
punished unless it could be proved that the owner had connived.
On many estates *actores* and *conductores* probably did little more.
Under more enterprising landlords they maintained and improved
the equipment of the estates. The Apion family were particularly
active and through their hierarchy of agents planted out vineyards,
issued irrigating machinery to their tenants, built and repaired
cisterns and farm buildings, and provided the bricks required,
either by estate labour or by contract.[50]

For the harvest and the vintage a good deal of casual labour was
employed. Some of this was drawn from the local peasant freeholders: John Chrysostom castigates the great landlords of Antioch
for their meanness in paying the peasants who gathered the grapes
a miserable pittance in cash, and not allowing them any of the wine.
Townspeople also helped in the vintage; when King Cavades
invaded Mesopotamia in 502, he captured not only the peasants
but many townsmen from Edessa and Carrhae as well, because
it was the vintage season. In Egypt a reserve of casual labour was
provided by the hordes of monks and hermits who peopled the
neighbouring deserts. According to Rufinus they flocked down
at harvest time, and earned enough not only to keep themselves
for the rest of the year but to have a surplus to distribute in charity.
If, as Rufinus tells us, a monk could make twelve *artabae* of wheat
by his harvest work, this is possible; for twelve *artabae* was a full
year's ration, and monks lived on much less. In Africa the circumcellions, who are described as landless men who went around
the rural homesteads to earn their living, provided a pool of labour
on which the great estates could draw.[51]

Hired labourers seem very rarely to have been employed on a

permanent basis, though one is recorded to have complained: 'I am a hired labourer on the estate of a wicked grasping rich man, and though I have been with him fifteen years, working night and day, he cannot bring himself to give me my pay.' The regular cultivation of the estates was normally carried out either by slaves or by free tenants. Both classes of labour are regarded as normal in the Codes, which contain much legislation on the complicated questions arising out of intermarriage between them, but they give no clue to their relative importance. There were certainly great local and regional variations. In Egypt the papyri prove that agricultural slavery was virtually unknown, and there is no allusion to it in the abundant literary sources for Africa. These two regions, both famous for their teeming peasant population, may have been exceptional. In western Asia Minor and the adjacent islands early fourth century census records give a little information. On the island of Chios of thirteen farms four were cultivated by slaves and *coloni*, and nine by *coloni* only. On the island of Thera the landowner Paregorius, who owned ten farms, totalling 420 *iugera* of arable, 110 *iugera* of vineyard and 580 olive trees, had two rustic slaves only. At Tralles two owners had no slaves, Tatianus, the biggest landlord, had slaves assessed at $7\frac{1}{2}$ *capita* and *coloni* at 58 *capita*, while two others, Critias and Latron, appear to have had about seven or eight times as many *coloni* as slaves. Here the slaves may well have been *vilici* or bailiffs, who supervised the free tenants. In the island of Lesbos on the other hand two farms are recorded with twenty-two and twenty-one slaves respectively together with others where neither slaves nor *coloni* are registered. Here it would seem that some landlords had gangs of slaves with which they worked several farms.[52]

In Italy slaves may have been commoner. On one of Melania's *massae* near Rome there were sixty-two hamlets, each inhabited by about four hundred slave cultivators, if the Latin version of the biography is to be believed. From casual references in the letters of the fifth and sixth century popes it appears that both the Roman church and neighbouring landlords owned agricultural slaves, but *coloni* are also frequently mentioned: the Sicilian estates of the Roman see appear to have been cultivated by free *coloni*. In Spain Orosius speaks of Didymus and Verinianus raising a private army from their agricultural slaves, and the laws of the Visigothic kings and the canons of the Spanish councils often speak of the *servi fiscales* of the state lands and the slaves on the church estates. From Gaul one document, the will of bishop Remigius, records in some detail the number of workers on each farm and vineyard, but unfortunately does not always clearly indicate their status. On the lands which he held in the territory of Portus he had seven free *coloni* (with three women) and one slave. On his other estates, he mentions numerous persons whom he either frees or leaves to his heirs, but he rarely specifies whether they were *coloni* or slaves, and by this date *coloni* like slaves might be bequeathed with the land or granted freedom. The general impression given by the will is of a mixed servile and free population with the latter predominating.[53]

On such tenuous data it is scarcely possible to generalise, but there is no evidence for the extensive use of slave labour except in Italy and Spain. The strong and successful protest of the Roman senate in 397 against the levy of recruits from their lands suggests that even in Italy great estates were for the most part cultivated by free *coloni*, who were alone liable to the normal conscription. There was at the same time a levy of slaves for the army, but these were taken from the senators' town houses.[54]

What is abundantly clear from the Codes is that agricultural slavery was in general hereditary. It was probably in the main a survival from earlier times, when slaves had been very cheap, and many landlords, especially in Italy, had found it convenient and economic to stock their estates with slave labour. By the second century A.D. the price of slaves had risen so greatly that most landlords preferred to divide up their estates and lease them to free tenants; but some owners of large estates had maintained their stock of slaves by breeding.[55]

In the later empire the supply of slaves became somewhat more abundant, and their price correspondingly lower; but they still remained as a rule too scarce and too dear to be employed for agricultural work. On rare occasions when great numbers of barbarian prisoners were thrown on the market, slaves could be bought at bargain prices; after the defeat of Radagaesus his followers were sold off at a solidus apiece. But more often the government, when it made a large haul of barbarian prisoners, preferred not to sell them as slaves, but to distribute them to landlords as *coloni*, thus making them and their descendants eligible for conscription into the army. A Gallic panegyrist of the Caesar Constantius alludes to this practice in vague terms in 297. A constitution of Theodosius II, dated 409, gives details. The captured tribe of the Scyrae were to be distributed to landlords *iure colonatus*; they were not to be converted into slaves by the grantees, or removed from agricultural employment, but were to be permanently attached to their lands: the grantees had a period of five years' grace to make the permanent settlement, within which they could transfer them from one estate to another within the same province, and during that period the new *coloni* were not liable to conscription.[56]

We rarely hear of slaves being bought for agricultural use. A law envisages purchasers or grantees of derelict estates restocking them with slave labour; but this is an exceptional case. When the peasants of Italy were starving the prefect of the city persuaded the senators to subscribe for famine relief by an appeal to their self-interest: 'Do you not see that if these men die we shall have to buy others? How much cheaper it is to feed a cultivator than to buy one! Whence will you make up the loss? Whence will you find the replacements?'[57]

The status of agricultural slaves gradually approximated by law and custom to that of serfs. Slaves registered in the census might not be removed from agricultural employment. Constantine allowed them to be sold to other landowners in the same province, but Valentinian I forbade their sale apart from the land which they cultivated. In Italy Theoderic rescinded this rule, but with this exception it was maintained throughout the empire. Slaves were probably not used as mere labourers but assigned lots of land to cultivate at a rent, as what the classical lawyers called *quasi coloni*: Pope Pelagius, instructing an agent which slaves to choose out of an inheritance part of which had come to the church, insists that he should pick 'men who can maintain or cultivate holdings', and threatens him with his anger if he lets go any 'countrymen who can be *conductores* or *coloni*'.[58]

Agricultural slaves married not only slave women but daughters of free tenants and of peasant proprietors, and reared families. They were commonly allowed to acquire property of their own (*peculia*), and to transmit it to their children: when Ampliatus, a slave of the Roman church, made a will, Pope Gelasius, though he quashed it on the ground that a slave's *peculium* was legally vested in the church, only ordered that his estate should be handed over to his sons. An even stranger case is that of Celerinus, son of a slave woman of the Roman church, who 'to escape his proper state of servitude dared to take to himself the name of a *curialis*'. He was alleged to have retained possession of a piece of land belonging to his first wife, a *colona* of the church, to have deserted his second wife, a slave of the church, and to have in his *peculium* much other property, all of which Pope Pelagius ordered to be restored to the Massa Tarpeiana, to which he belonged.[59]

While agricultural slaves rose to the status of serfs, free tenants gradually sank to a similar status. In the Principate tenants of farms (*coloni*) and of houses (*inquilini*) were free to leave when their leases expired. Under Roman law leases were normally for a term of five years (*lustrum*), and could be continued as an annual tenancy by the tacit consent of both parties. In some parts of the empire, as in Egypt, short tenancies were usual: in others they were in practice lifelong and hereditary. The latter custom was probably commonest on large estates: under Commodus the tenants of imperial lands in Africa speak of themselves as having been born and bred on the estates, and in the early third century imperial tenants in Lydia threaten 'to leave the hearths of our fathers and the tombs of our ancestors' unless their grievances are redressed. Their words show that they were legally free to leave, though long established on their farms and reluctant to abandon them.[60]

The liberty of tenants was probably first restricted by the census of Diocletian, in which every peasant was registered in his village or under his landlord's name on the farm that he cultivated, and by legislation which, for fiscal motives, tied the peasantry to their place of registration, where they paid their *capitatio* and *annona*. But while the rule was introduced in the interests of the state, to facilitate the collection of the *capitatio* and to ensure that the land was cultivated and produced its *annona*, it proved very convenient to landowners, who were short of agricultural labour and welcomed a rule which prevented their tenants from abandoning their farms. It was the interests of landlords, who were after all by and large identical with the official aristocracy who controlled governmental policy, which prevailed.[61]

Originally the whole agricultural population had been tied, freeholders as well as tenants, but landlords had no interest in tying freeholders to their villages, and the rule ceased to be enforced against them save intermittently, as when in the general settlement of Egypt in 415 not only *coloni* but *vicani* were restored to their owners and villages respectively. On the other hand the rights of landlords over their *coloni* were progressively increased. Constantine in 332 allowed landowners to chain *coloni* who were suspected of planning to abscond; in 365 *coloni* were forbidden to alienate their own property without their lord's consent; a few years later it was enacted that landlords (or their agents), and not the public collectors, should levy the taxes of *coloni* registered on their estates; in 396 such *coloni* were debarred from suing their lords except for extracting more than the customary rent.[62]

Moreover the tied tenancy was preserved even when its original *raison d'être*, the *capitatio*, was abolished. When Valentinian remitted the *capitatio* in Illyricum, he ruled that *coloni* might not therefore have freedom of movement but must continue to serve their lords 'non tributario nexu sed nomine et titulo colonorum', and Theodosius, when he extended the remission to Thrace, similarly ruled that the *coloni*, though free from the *capitatio*, 'shall be bound by the rule of origin, and though they appear to be free-born by condition, shall nevertheless be considered as slaves of the land itself to which they are born, and shall have no right of going off where they like or of changing their place, but that the land-owner shall enjoy his right over them with the care of a patron and the power of a master'.[63]

Not all *coloni* throughout the empire were thus tied. Theodosius wrote: 'whereas in other provinces which are subject to the rule of our serenity a law instituted by our ancestors holds tenants down by a kind of eternal right, so that they are not allowed to leave the places by whose crops they are nurtured or desert the fields which they have once undertaken to cultivate, but the landlords of Pales-tine do not enjoy this advantage: we ordain that in Palestine also no tenant whatever be free to wander at his own choice, but as in other provinces be tied to the owner of the farm'. A clue to this anomaly is supplied by a law addressed in 399 to the praetorian prefect of Gaul, which orders that in those provinces 'in which this method of tying the commons by registration is observed', land-lords are to be liable for the public obligations of commoners registered on their estates. It would appear that in some provinces of the Gallic prefecture the rural population was not registered under the estates of which they were tenants, but presumably by villages or other local circumscriptions. In these provinces tenants were probably not tied to their landlords, since registration was the basis of the tied colonate. A similar system of registration may ex-plain the anomalous position in Palestine. In Egypt also, where registration was by villages, there is no trace of the colonate in the papyri in the fourth century; it must have been introduced by the early fifth century (for which the papyrological evidence is weak), for the law of 415 orders the restoration of vagrant *coloni* to their masters.[64]

These large gaps in the colonate system were filled by imperial legislation. But in all provinces there were tenants who were not tied to their landlord. A tenant was registered under his landlord's name only if he possessed no land of his own; if he owned even a tiny plot he was registered in his village. On *massae* and large *fundi* which were villages in themselves the tenants would normally be landless men and therefore entered on the census under their *fundus*. But landlords, as we have seen, also owned many small farms and even plots, and these would often be rented by neigh-bouring peasant proprietors, many of whom owned tiny plots too small to support a family. Such tenants, being registered in their villages, were not legally bound to their landlords. The distinction between tied and free *coloni* would roughly have corresponded to resident and non-resident tenants, for any non-resident tenant would probably own at least a house and garden of his own. Great landlords, who owned large estates, would tend to have tied tenants, lesser landlords, whose holdings were small and scattered, would have free tenants.[65]

Free tenancies also arose in another way. In the original census tenants had been entered by name with their wives (in areas where women were taxed) and their children, including those under taxable age, all with their ages. The idea behind this procedure was that, as the existing taxpayers died or reached the age which gave them immunity, the children would automatically move up into the tax-paying group as they reached the statutory age: the registration and the consequent attachment to the farm was from the beginning assumed to be hereditary. For the system to function properly the census should have been repeated at fixed intervals, but in fact this was not done. From time to time a city or a landowner would ask for a special reassessment, in order to justify a demand for lower taxes, and a *censitor* or *peraequator* would be appointed *ad hoc*, but normally the government based its tax demands on the total recorded in the old census. If *coloni* absconded, the landlord was expected to reclaim them and recover arrears of tax from whoever had harboured them: he remained liable for the full number of tenants registered on his land. If *coloni* were conscripted, he had if possible to make up the deficit from the younger generation, the *adcrescentes* as they were called, and could claim a rebate only if he had none of working age. On the other hand, if he increased his total by taking on a tenant from outside, he no doubt did not add this man to the list.[66]

In practice the registered *coloni* on an estate were thus a hereditary group comprising only the descendants of the *coloni* recorded in the original census. When the group increased the landlord was probably not particular to retain them all, for he wanted only enough men to cultivate his land efficiently; so long as each *colonus* left one son to succeed him, he would be satisfied, and other sons would move elsewhere. But where the group dwindled, the landlord would take on outsiders, and ask no questions. They might be runaway *coloni* from other farms, sons of a neighbour's *coloni*, peasant proprietors who had abandoned their village, or even townspeople who could no longer make a living by their craft or trade. Such men, who had no hereditary connection with the estate, were not tied to it.[67]

With the lapse of time, as on one estate or another the descendants of the original *coloni* fell below the number required and were supplemented by outsiders, free *coloni* became a more and more substantial class, especially on the estates of the lesser landowners: for great landlords could transfer surplus *coloni* from one part of their estates to another where there was a shortage. As free *coloni* became more important, the laws began to make a distinction between them and the tied *coloni*. Down to the third quarter of the fourth century, the imperial constitutions nearly always speak of *coloni* without qualification. They then begin to qualify tied *coloni* by some additional word or phrase. Their terminology is, at first in particular, varied and confused. In the West the word *tributarius* is sometimes used, to denote a *colonus* for whose taxes the landlord is liable. The term *inquilinus* is also not infrequently used, but is apparently not synonymous with *colonus*, probably denoting a man domiciled on an estate but not a lessee of land, a cottager who worked as a labourer or craftsman: but, to quote a law of 396, 'though there is a distinction in name between *inquilini* and *coloni*, as far as matters for claiming their *origo* their condition appears to be indistinguishable and almost identical'. More commonly tied *coloni* are styled *originales* or *originarii*, as being bound by their *origo* to the land.

The Eastern chancery preferred to stress registration on the census, using such phrases as *censibus adscripti*, and eventually coining the word *adscripticius*: the word, in its Greek form ἐνυπό-γραφος, was first to our knowledge used by the emperor Marcian, addressing the Council of Chalcedon, and first appears in the Code in a law of Leo dated 466: it was never used in the West. The two terms *originalis* and *adscripticius* merely express different aspects of the same situation, for the census registered a man where he belonged by birth. Both conceptions are sometimes combined in a single sentence: a law of Valens speaks of '*coloni originales* who are registered in the same places', and in a law of Valentinian I *coloni* and *inquilini* are ordered to return 'to their old homes where they are registered and were born and bred'.[68]

In 419 Honorius applied the rules of *longi temporis praescriptio* to the benefit of *originales* and *inquilini*. Men of this status who had left their land for thirty years and had not been reclaimed became free; women became free after twenty years, and even if reclaimed within this period, might compensate their former master with a substitute. In 449 Valentinian III extended the benefit of this law to *originales* of imperial lands; normally there was no prescription against the rights of the crown. The reason given is an interesting one; high ranking palatine officials had been reclaimed by landlords on the ground that their grandfathers or great-grandfathers had been their *coloni*.[69]

Two years later Valentinian III found that his generosity was being abused by *coloni* who fled from their own landlord and leased a farm from another, pretending to be free men, and after thirty years had their freedom legally confirmed. Worse still, some runaway *coloni* moved from landlord to landlord, until the thirty years were up. He accordingly ruled that an *originarius* who broke his tie with his own lord by thirty years' absence became the *originarius* of his new landlord or of the last of them, if he had kept on the move. Valentinian also noted with indignation that a free man would take a holding and marry an *originaria*, and then move on, abandoning his wife. He ruled that a stranger wishing to marry an *originaria* must make a declaration that he would stay permanently and while remaining otherwise free should be bound by this declaration.[70]

In the Western parts an *originarius* could thus legally shake off his condition only by leaving the land and pursuing some urban occupation for thirty years: as long as he stayed on the land he remained an *originarius*, even if he moved to another estate. On the other hand no free man could become an *originarius*: even if he married an *originaria* and settled on her estate, he retained his personal freedom. It is unlikely that in either case the law was strictly observed. Many *originarii* who left their homes no doubt managed to conceal their status. On the other hand free peasants, according to Salvian, often voluntarily declared themselves *inquilini* or acquired the status by prescription.[71]

In the Eastern parts Honorius' law of 419 was promulgated in the Theodosian Code, but Valentinian III's subsequent legislation was not. Here therefore the rule of thirty years' prescription worked in favour of *adscripticii*. Anastasius applied the rule in the opposite direction, enacting that a free man who leased a farm for thirty years thereby tied himself for life, but remained otherwise free, not subject to the disabilities of *adscripticii*. Justinian interpreted this law as binding the sons of such a tenant, even if they had not lived thirty years on the estate. Justinian also limited and later abolished the right of the *adscripticius* to free himself by thirty years' absence. In 531 he ruled that if the son of an *adscripticius* was allowed by his landlord to absent himself because during the father's lifetime he had no need of his services, and should complete thirty years' absence, he could nevertheless be recalled on his father's death. A year or two later he enacted that the condition of an *adscripticius* was imprescriptable.[72]

In one respect Justinian relaxed the law. Hitherto children of free persons and *adscripticii* had all been *adscripticii*, whether it was their father or their mother that was free. Justinian, regarding *adscripticii* as virtually slaves, was shocked by this breach of the principle of Roman law which declared that the offspring of a free woman was free, and ruled that if an *adscripticius* married a free woman their children should be free; at the same time he prohibited such marriages and allowed landlords to prevent them. The law caused loud and prolonged protest. Justinian had first to explain that it was not retrospective, and children born of such marriages before its enactment could not claim freedom. Dominicus, the praetorian prefect of Illyricum, forwarded protests from the landlords of his prefecture that their estates were being deserted and that they could not pay their taxes. Justinian accordingly interpreted his law as meaning that children of such mixed marriages, while being free, remained *coloni*, and were therefore under Anastasius' law bound by a hereditary tie to their farms. This ruling was promulgated in Illyricum only, but under Justin II the landlords of Africa, through the praetorian prefect of Africa, Theodore, protested that their estates lay desolate owing to the operation of the law, and successfully petitioned that the ruling promulgated in the Illyrican prefecture might be applied to Africa. When Justin was succeeded by Tiberius Constantine the landlords of Africa, headed by the bishop of Carthage, anxiously pressed for confirmation of Justin's ruling.[73]

In the sixth century tenants thus fell into three classes. First there were the *adscripticii*, a hereditary class descended in the main from tenants who had been registered in Diocletian's census as belonging to an estate; in some provinces, such as Palestine and Egypt, where the tied colonate was of more recent origin, they were descended from men who had been tenants when the relevant laws were promulgated. In Egypt they are rarely found even in the sixth century: they are chiefly recorded on the Apion estates, but two are known who belonged to the church of Oxyrhynchus. They are confined to the old consolidated estates (ἐποίκια or κτήματα) and are not found on scattered parcels held in the villages.[74]

Adscripticii were serfs, scarcely distinguishable from agricultural slaves; as Justinian frankly says: 'What difference can be understood between slaves and *adscripticii*, when both are placed in their master's power and he can manumit a slave with his *peculium* and alienate an *adscripticius* with the land?' The status of the two classes had become in fact extraordinarily similar. Slaves were never eligible for military service, but from the early fifth century neither were *coloni adscripticii*. Slaves could not legally own property, but in practice were allowed to enjoy their *peculia* and leave them to their children: *coloni* from 365 were forbidden to alienate their property without their landlord's consent. An owner had always been liable for the tax of his slaves: in 371 landlords were made responsible for collecting the taxes on their *coloni originales*. A slave could not bring a legal action: *coloni* were in 396 debarred from suing their landlords, except for exacting from them more than the customary rent. Slaves could not be ordained without their master's consent: in 409 this rule was applied to *coloni*. The Council of Chalcedon forbade slaves to be received into monasteries without their owners' consent; in 452 Valentinian III enacted the same rule for both slaves and *coloni*, and in 484 Zeno extended the ban on slaves to *adscripticii* in the East. *Coloni* were tied to their holdings. Slaves registered in the census could only be sold with the land.[75]

Next came *coloni* who were tied hereditarily to the land but personally free: that is, they could sue their landlords, alienate their own property as they wished, enlist in the army and take holy orders or enter a monastery without their landlord's permission. They could even, if they acquired land of their own, which demanded all their time and was sufficient to maintain them, throw up their tenancies. These were, or were descended from, men who had leased holdings and settled down on them for over thirty years; they would have been of diverse origin, some descended from peasant freeholders, some from *coloni*, particularly younger sons whom landlords had not wished to retain. After Justinian's law this class was swelled by the sons of *adscripticii* who had married free peasant women.[76]

Lastly there were free men who took short leases and thus retained their freedom of movement. This class is almost ignored in the laws, but the papyri prove that in Egypt at any rate it was still in the sixth century important. We possess over 170 datable leases or fragments of leases, ranging from Diocletian's reign to the Arab conquest, and in over ninety the term of the lease is preserved. Apart from half a dozen life or emphyteutic leases, the great majority (some sixty) are for very short terms, not exceeding seven years and commonly for one year only. In the remainder (some twenty-five) the tenant leases the land 'for as long a period as you wish', that is takes up a yearly tenancy renewable by the consent of both parties: this form of lease is first recorded at the very end of the fourth century and becomes increasingly common. The chronological distribution of the documents is erratic, being largely governed by the accident of survival: of the total datable over fifty are of the late third and the fourth centuries, over a hundred of the sixth and early seventh, but only about ten of the fifth. The figures are not therefore a reliable guide to the number of short-term tenants at any time, but strongly suggest that the class did not decline in the sixth century. In the fourth century, so far as we can judge by the documents, all landlords let their lands on short leases, which were no doubt often renewed. In the fifth automatically renewable yearly tenancies began to come into vogue, but never outnumbered short leases.[77]

It is impossible to estimate the relative importance of these three classes of tenant. Egypt, where the accumulation of great estates began late and there was a strongly established class of peasant proprietors, was perhaps exceptional in the small number of its *adscripticii* and the preponderance of free short-term tenants. In areas like Italy or Africa, where vast *massae* with their villages of *coloni* were already established in Diocletian's time, *originales* or *inquilini* must have been a large group. But the outcry caused by Justinian's law on mixed marriages shows that even in Africa there must have been a large number of free peasant women, daughters of free *coloni* or peasant proprietors, living on or near the great estates. One may suspect that even here *adscripticii*, who were a closed hereditary caste, subject to constant leakage, licit or illicit, and rarely reinforced by new recruits, were a dwindling class.

The Codes, much though they tell us of the legal status of *coloni*, are not very informative about their conditions of work and life. Their rent might take three forms, a money payment, a fixed payment in kind, or a proportion of the crop: mixed rents, partly in kind and partly in money, or of a proportion of the main crop with supplementary payments in cash or kind, are also known. In Italy under the Principate money rents were normal, though Pliny experimented with the share cropping system. In Africa on the other hand share cropping seems to have been usual. In Egypt rents were usually paid as a fixed quantity in kind, though money rents were quite common, especially for vineyards and orchards.[78]

The same kind of regional variation prevailed in the later empire, and within any region there was no fixed practice. A constitution addressed in 366 to the governor of Tripolitania enacts that 'owners of estates shall accept what the land produces and not demand money which the peasants do not dare to hope for, unless the custom of the estate requires this'; but though this may have applied to Tripolitania, it did not to Egypt. Here of the surviving leases about a third provide for a rent in money, a quarter are partiary, and the rest in fixed quantities of produce: no noticeable change takes place from Diocletian down to the Arab conquest, except that in the sixth century it is common to add to the main rent sundry perquisites in kind—cheeses, a basket of fruit, a jar of wine, a sucking pig or the like. The tenants of the Apion family usually paid in wine on vineyards, and on arable partly in gold, partly in wheat. Justinian, laying down rules for the sequestration of the rent when a *colonus* challenged his landlord's title, makes elaborate provision for payment in money or kind or both.[79]

In Italy and Sicily gold rents seem to have been usual in the sixth century. Gregory the Great, wishing to encourage the conversion of Jewish *coloni* of the church, ordered that the rents of converts should be reduced, and suggested that the reduction should be on the scale of one *tremissis* on a rent of one solidus, or one solidus on a rent of three or four. On another occasion he ordered a holding normally leased for $1\frac{2}{3}$ solidi to be granted to a monastery for one *tremissis*. It is significant that when corn was required in Sicily for shipment to Rome, it was bought from the *coloni*: Gregory ordered that on such occasions the agents must pay the market price and not fix an arbitrary valuation. On one occasion he instructed the *rector* of the Sicilian patrimony to spend 50 lb. gold on buying corn from outsiders; the *rector* had this substantial sum of money in hand, drawn presumably from rents, but no corn.[80]

Among the Ravenna papyri there are preserved substantial portions of detailed rentals of two *fundi* in the territory of Patavium, dating from the sixth century. The *coloni* all pay money rents, ranging from 8 solidi 8 siliquae to 3 solidi 3 siliquae. They pay in addition, like many Egyptian tenants, what are styled *xenia* or presents in kind, on one estate pork (from 160 to 80 lb.), geese (two), hens (from 16 to 6) and eggs (ten per hen), on the other geese, hens and eggs on the same scale and also honey (from 130 to 70 lb.). These *xenia* are apparently identical with *excepta et vilicilia* which Gregory mentions as an allowable extra charge on his Sicilian *coloni* and the *excepta praediorum sive accessiones* which Pope Felix allotted in their entirety to the bishop of Ravenna 'on account of the expenses of his household and the presents which are offered to various persons and the banquets which he has to give either for the honour and dignity of his position or for the reception of visitors.'[81]

Besides these minor perquisites most great landlords seem to have taken some proportion of their rents in the staple crops. According to Olympiodorus Roman senators drew about three-quarters of their rents in gold, and the remaining quarter in wheat, wine and oil. Lauricius, in his letters to his *actores* and *conductores* in Sicily, deals only with money, but he gives instructions to his *procurator* to despatch the produce in kind (*species*) to Ravenna or Rome. From many stories of famines it is evident that great landlords held considerable stocks of corn, not only in Rome, but in Antioch, Caesarea and other cities, and these stocks they probably derived from rents in kind.[82]

A constitution of Valens directs that owners of estates should personally or through their *actores* collect the taxes due in respect of their *coloni originales*, but that other *coloni* who owned land of their own and were registered in their own place should pay their taxes direct to the ordinary collector. The second part of the law does not seem to have been mandatory. Egyptian leases frequently contain a clause specifying that all taxes and levies shall fall upon the owner, and Justinian, while regarding it as normal for a free *colonus* to pay his own taxes and get a receipt in his own name, provides for the case where the landlord pays the taxes out of the rent and has the receipt made out to him. The Apion family paid all taxes on their estate, whether the land was cultivated by *adscripticii* or free tenants.[83]

Whether *coloni* normally owed labour services as well as rent is an obscure question. Under the Principate tenants of the great African estates performed labour services on the home farm; the amount varied from six *operae* (presumably days' work) in the year, two in the ploughing season, two in the hoeing and two in the harvest, to twelve, and was a frequent matter of dispute between the *coloni* and the *conductor*. The Codes contain no clear reference to the system. John Chrysostom appears to allude to it in his diatribe against Antiochene landlords who 'impose unceasing and intolerable payments on them (the peasants) and require of them laborious services. . . . What sight could be more pitiable than when, having toiled the whole winter through in frost and rain, spent with work the peasants return with empty hands and even in debt, dreading and fearing more than this ruin and more than hunger the torments inflicted by the bailiffs, the seizures, the demand notes, the arrests, the inescapable forced labour.'[84]

For sixth-century Italy one of the Ravennate rent rolls mentioned above gives more detail. The column containing the descriptions of the holdings and the names of their occupiers is unfortunately missing. The columns containing the rents and *xenia* show one large holding (rent 13 solidi 13 *siliquae*) followed by six others with smaller rents, one at 8 solidi 8 *siliquae*, the rest at 3 or 4. These six smaller holdings also pay weekly work (*pro ebdomada operae*), one, two and three *operae* (presumably a day's work) per week each, in all thirteen *operae*. It is clear that the first holding is the home farm, worked by the *vilicus* with the aid of labour services from the *coloni*.

The *vilicus* would have had two men assisting him every day of the week save one, the *coloni*, if each *colonica* was held by several *coloni*, as on the Saltus Erudianus, would have had to give about one day a week to work on the home farm, a heavy labour service.[85]

On the Saltus Erudianus on the other hand no *operae* are recorded, and the *vilicus* pays one of the lowest rents on the *fundus*. The explanation probably is that the greater part of the original home farm had been let off as a *colonica*, and the *vilicus* cultivated the remainder by himself.[86]

This evidence is a small basis for estimating the importance of *operae* in the colonate, but they suggest that the institution was relatively rare. A system of *operae* would be applicable only to a large *fundus*, with a big home farm and a good number of *colonicae*, and then only if the home farm were not stocked with slave labour. It was probably only on *fundi* where there was a villa where the landlord resided, or had once resided, that there was a home farm to supply his household needs. On many *fundi* the whole area had no doubt from the beginning been divided into *colonicae*, and on many more the home farms were later let off in *colonicae* when they passed into the hands of absentee owners. It is dangerous to argue from silence, but it is significant that among the many abuses which Pope Gregory found to correct on the patrimony of Peter, no mention is made of any connected with labour services, normally a constant source of complaint where they exist. It is also significant that in the abundant documents of the Apion estates— and indeed in the papyri generally—there is no reference to labour services; the agents of the Apion family always deal with rent paying tenants or groups of tenants, and pay wages to any labour that they employ for building or repairs on the estate.[87]

In addition to their rent (with perquisites), their taxes, and labour services, if any, *coloni* were subject to many minor but vexatious exactions from the landlord, or more frequently his agents. When rents and taxes were collected in money a surcharge was made, nominally to compensate for light weight coins. Gregory found that on the estates of the church $73\frac{1}{2}$ solidi were reckoned to the pound instead of 72, a surcharge of half a carat on every solidus: on the Apion estates $\frac{7}{8}$ carat per solidus was the rate. Where corn was being measured either for rent and taxes in kind, or for purchase by the estate, a large 'receipt measure' was used. Gregory found that *modii* of 25 (instead of 16) *sextarii* were in use, and forbade any larger than 18 to be employed. On the Apion estates Serenus the agent agreed to pay his employers 15 *artabae* extra on every 100 in view of the advantage gained by the estate's 'receipt measures'. On the estates of the church, when corn was bought from the *coloni* by the agents, they fixed an arbitrarily low price. *Coloni* on the patrimony of Peter paid substantial fees (Gregory limited them to one solidus) for marriage licences, on what precise legal ground is not known, but presumably they found it worth while to cover themselves against eventual vexatious claims on the ground that they had married outsiders or slaves. In one way or another agents evidently counted on making considerable profits on the side: Serenus the deacon would hardly have paid the Apion estate twelve solidi for one year's appointment as subagent (προνοητής) if he had expected to gain only the salary of a subagent, 2 solidi and 24 *artabae* of wheat (equivalent to another $2\frac{1}{2}$ solidi).[88]

In 325 Constantine enacted that a *colonus*, if his landlord exacted 'more than had been the previous custom, and than had been exacted in earlier times', might apply to any judge, and if he proved his case, the rent would be restored to the old level, and any overpayment refunded. This right of action was expressly preserved for *coloni adscripticii* in 396, and Constantine's law was republished in Justinian's Code. No such rule can have been in force during the inflationary period of the third and early fourth centuries; for agricultural rents, if payable in denarii, would in that case have become nominal. By 325 most rents, if not in kind, must have been reckoned in gold. The rule presumably applied only to a sitting tenant: it certainly did not affect short-term leases such as are recorded in the Egyptian papyri. It was probably not a very effective protection even for the tied *colonus*. It is rather a suspicious circumstance that in one of the Ravennate rent rolls the rents are all multiples of one solidus plus one *siliqua:* it looks as if these rents had all been raised by a *siliqua* in the solidus. Moreover on two holdings an extra 20 *siliquae* has been inserted in smaller letters between 3 solidi and 3 *siliquae*. It is however probable that by and large the rents of tied *coloni* remained at the customary figure, and that landlords made what extra profit they could by extorting perquisites, using special 'receipt measures' and the other similar devices already described.[89]

For the level of rents we have no evidence except from Egypt. There in share cropping leases the division is almost always half and half on arable, the owner paying the taxes, but sometimes getting some extra perquisites. On vineyards and orchards the owner's share is usually two-thirds, sometimes three-quarters. In leases of arable where the rent is payable in kind, a normal rent is five *artabae* to the *arura* (taxes on the owner): there survive six leases at this figure, one at seven, two at six, and two at four. This is evidently for good average land; there are half a dozen leases at much lower figures, ranging from $2\frac{1}{2}$ to 1 *artabae*. Five *artabae* as we have seen is probably roughly equivalent to half the crop. As wheat normally sold at 10 *artabae* to the solidus these figures imply a gold rent of about half a solidus per *arura*. Very few leases survive in which the relevant figures are preserved, and they vary considerably: there are two of slightly over half a solidus (13 and 13½ carats), two of rather under (about 9½ carats), one of as much as 19½ carats (equivalent to 8 *artabae*) and one at as little as 3¼ carats.[90]

In these leases the landlord usually does nothing for his tenant but merely draws the rent. The Apion family on the other hand were progressive landlords, who spent a lot of money on equipping and maintaining their farms, particularly in building cisterns and supplying irrigation machinery and oxen to work it. They expected very much higher rents. From one document it appears that on one estate they demanded one solidus an *arura* for arable and three solidi an *arura* for vineyard. These figures seem very exorbitant even if the *coloni* had all their equipment and seed provided free and contributed only their labour, and in fact the tenants concerned did object, and refused to work the land except on a flat rate of one solidus for arable and vineyard alike. As we cannot calculate their overheads, we cannot tell how much the Apions got net per *arura*, but probably well over the half solidus with which the ordinary landlord was content.[91]

In other parts of the empire rents of arable land must have been substantially lower. In many areas the yield per acre sown was lower, and almost everywhere only half the area could be used each year for growing corn, and the other half lay fallow or yielded only a lighter or less valuable crop. In terms of labour also many more hours of work were required to cultivate the same area by the farming technique practised in other Mediterranean lands. On vineyards and olive yards on the other hand the yield would have been as good in other Mediterranean lands as in Egypt, and the quality and price of the crops in many cases better. On imperial estates in Africa in the second century the tenants usually paid one-third of all crops alike, corn, wine or olives: this flat rate may have been intended to encourage tenants to adopt the more profitable types of cultivation. On these figures the rent of a mixed farm in Africa, one-third of all the produce, would have been about half that of a comparable farm in Egypt, where vineyards and orchards paid two-thirds or three-quarters, and arable half.

It would be unwise to generalise on the condition of the peasantry under the later Roman empire. The kulak was not unknown, not only among free peasants but also among *coloni* and even among agricultural slaves. A good example of an enterprising and prosperous peasant proprietor is Aurelius Sacaon of Theadelphia, many of whose papers have come down to us. He owned a fair-sized holding, more than 20 *arurae*, and leased other land in addition; in 331 he was renting 16 *arurae* from Aurelia Rufina, a lady of senatorial rank who owned land in the village. He also went in for stock farming. In 306 he leased a considerable flock (62 sheep, 13 rams and 59 goats) from two civil servants; the agreement was for five years and was on a *métayage* basis. He eventually in this way built up a flock of his own: in 342 he complained of the theft of 82 of his sheep. Some *coloni* of the *res privata* could afford to buy not only their own holdings but those of their neighbours; the emperor directed that in such a case the land should be sold to the *coloni* jointly, to prevent the rich *colonus* from exploiting the others. Celerinus and Ampliatus, the slaves of the Roman church, one of whom accumulated enough land to pose as a decurion, while the other rose to be a *conductor*, have already been mentioned. Peter, an *originalis* of a *massa* of the Roman see, was appointed a *defensor* of that church.[92]

The legal restrictions on the peasants' freedom must not be exaggerated. Freeholders *de facto* enjoyed full liberty, and so also did free tenants. Tied *coloni* could in the fourth century legally escape from their condition only by joining or being conscripted into the army, and in the fifth century this last loophole was stopped. In spite of the legal position, however, it is fairly evident that many sons of *adscripticii* did, either with the landlord's connivance or by stealth, make their escape into another walk of life, and some did very well. Theodosius II found it necessary to instruct his *magistri militum* not to admit *censibus adscripti* to their *officia*, and Valentinian III allowed thirty years' prescription to extinguish even the claims of the crown because high palatine civil servants were being blackmailed as being descended from *originales*. The church also offered an avenue of escape. *Adscripticii* and slaves could not, it is true, be ordained without their lord's consent, but such consent was often given for them to serve the local church of the estate. Most slaves and *adscripticii* no doubt did not rise above the position of rural parish priests, but some may have found promotion; Justinian ruled that the episcopacy extinguished adscriptician or servile status.[93]

Apart from the lucky few who achieved affluence as farmers or broke their bonds and rose to good positions in church and state there must have been many who lived not too uncomfortably.

The *coloni* of the Saltus Erudianus and its unnamed neighbour evidently kept pigs, geese, fowls and bees on a fair scale, and must have enjoyed a reasonably varied diet. Many of the *coloni* of the Roman church in Sicily apparently owned more valuable stock; for Gregory, having succeeded in recovering from the *conductores* sums illegally extorted from the *coloni*, ordered Peter, the *rector*, to use the money in buying cows, sheep and pigs and distributing them to the poor and indigent *coloni* in each *massa*, of whom he was to draw up a list. We know of *coloni* prosperous enough to own slaves of their own; bishop Remigius inherited one from one of his *originarii* and another from his swineherd.[94]

But taken as a whole the peasantry were an oppressed and hapless class. Enough has been said already of the many ways in which they were exploited by the tax collector, if they were freeholders, and by the landlord's agent if they were tenants. In times of shortage it was they who were the first to suffer. It is significant that on a number of occasions we hear of peasants in a period of bad harvests flocking to the towns to beg for bread. Ambrose comments bitterly on the expulsion of all non-residents from Rome during famines, and tells how one enlightened prefect of the city refused to take this step, protesting to the wealthy aristocrats: 'if so many cultivators are starved and so many farmers die, our corn supply will be ruined for good: we are excluding those who normally supply our daily bread'. Eventually his arguments prevailed, a fund was raised and corn bought for distribution. Libanius tells us of a similar situation at Antioch in 384. 'Famine had filled our city with beggars, some of whom had abandoned their fields, since they had not even grass to eat, it being winter, and some had left their cities'. In this case Eumolpius, the consular of Syria, gave relief from public funds, but Icarius, the *comes Orientis*, refused Libanius' plea for additional help.[95]

At Edessa in the third quarter of the fourth century there was great famine and all the country folk were starving. Ephraim Syrus begged the rich men of the town to subscribe, a fund was raised, bread was distributed and an open-air hospital of 300 beds established in the colonnades of the streets for the bad cases. In the early sixth century there was another famine at Edessa, and once again the country people crowded into town. Demosthenes, the governor of Osrhoene, went up to Constantinople to ask for aid. Meanwhile his deputy, Eusebius, did what he could by releasing grain from the public granaries, but the sufferers had no money to buy the bread, and wandered about the streets scavenging for scraps. At length Demosthenes returned with funds, and distributed a pound of bread per day free to the destitute,

to whom he issued leaden tickets. He also walled in the colonnades and provided straw and mats on which the refugees could
sleep, and organised a hospital service. But despite his efforts there
was a severe outbreak of illness in the spring and many died.[96]

What is particularly significant in these stories is that at a time
when the peasants were reduced to eating grass, corn was available
in the cities, either in the government granaries or in private hands.
If the harvest failed, the tax collector and the landlord extracted his
due, and the peasant had to surrender his crop in kind or sell it to
obtain the necessary cash, even if he was left with nothing to feed
himself and his family.

Such ruthless efficiency was achieved by the use of force. Theodoret tells a story of tax collectors descending on a Syrian village
of peasant proprietors, and when they protest that they cannot pay
the 100 solidi demanded, beating them and putting them in chains;
he makes no comment on this routine procedure. Ammianus
remarks on the stubborn character of the Egyptians: 'among them
a man is ashamed if he cannot display many weals on his body,
earned by refusing his taxes'. Resistance was futile, for behind tax
collector and landlord lay the armed force of the state. In 386
Libanius protested against the grant of military assistance to landowners against their tenants: 'some treat these too like slaves, and
if they do not approve of their extortionate demands upon them, a
few syllables are spoken and a soldier appears on the estate with
handcuffs and the prison receives them in chains'. A century later
great landlords were keeping their own bands of armed retainers
(*bucellarii*) and had their own private prisons.[97]

On the whole the reaction of the peasantry to this kind of treatment was singularly passive. In Africa there was for a time in the
mid-fourth century a resistance movement, inspired by Donatism,
which was widespread among the peasants, against landlords and
moneylenders (no doubt often the same persons), who tended to be
catholics. 'When Axilo and Fasir were called "leaders of the saints"
by these madmen,' writes Optatus, 'no one was allowed to be safe
on his own estates, bonds for debt lost their force, no creditor in
those days had freedom to demand payment, everyone was terrified
by the letters of those who boasted that they were "leaders of the
saints".' In Augustine's day, however, Donatist *coloni* obediently
paid their rents to the catholic senators who were their landlords.[98]

Only in Gaul, and later in Spain, are sustained and widespread
peasant revolts recorded, those of the so-called Bacaudae (probably
a Celtic word). The Bacaudae were already in Diocletian's reign
formidable enough to demand regular and prolonged military
operations by Maximian for their suppression, and their leaders

Aelianus and Amandus were considered important enough to be called usurpers.

In the early fifth century (in 417, 435-7 and 442) there were widespread revolts which had to be suppressed by full-scale military operations. By the middle of the fifth century the movement had spread to northern Spain, where two successive *magistri militum* operated against the Bacaudae of Tarraconensis in 441 and 443, and in 454 the Roman government employed the Visigoths to suppress them. Little enough is known of the character of these movements. Some were no doubt mere jacqueries, and the term Bacaudae was applied to common brigandage, such as was no doubt endemic in the Alpine passes and the Spanish highlands. But in Armorica the movement was more organised. Not only were the Roman officials expelled and landlords expropriated but an army was created and courts of justice set up.[99]

Elsewhere the oppressed peasantry had two resources only if things became intolerable. They could run away and seek employment as *coloni* of some other landlord: or they could buy the support of a powerful patron, a military officer who could employ the armed forces of the state to protect them or a great landlord who could likewise operate the state machine in his interests, or at a pinch defy it with impunity. And in such cases the last state of the peasant was usually worse than the first.

It is generally agreed that there was a decline in agriculture in the later Roman empire, but little attempt has been made to estimate how serious it was, and on its causes debate has been inconclusive, whether it was due to the general exhaustion of the soil, to shortage of agricultural manpower, or, as contemporaries believed, partly to barbarian invasions and depredations but predominantly to over-taxation.

That the area of land under cultivation shrank considerably cannot be doubted. Abandoned lands (*agri deserti*) are a constant theme of imperial legislation from before Diocletian's time to that of Justinian. The problem first appears in the late second century, when the emperor Pertinax issued an edict, inviting all and sundry to cultivate deserted land, whether private or imperial property, in Italy and the provinces, and promising them ten years' immunity from taxes and full ownership. This may have been a temporary crisis, due to the ravages of the great plague which began under Marcus. In the late third century Aurelian decreed that the councils of the cities were to be responsible for the taxes of deserted lands in their territories. Constantine renewed this law, but added that where the councils were not equal to the burden, the tax obligations of abandoned land should be distributed to estates and territories, immunity for three years being granted.[100]

The imperial government was evidently more concerned that the taxes should be paid than that the land should be cultivated. Its methods of achieving this aim remained those employed by Pertinax, Aurelian, and Constantine. The deserted lands might be granted or sold or leased on favourable terms, including a firm title and temporary immunity. They might be compulsorily allocated, with their tax burden, to the governing body of the community in whose territory they lay, which could in its turn either try to get them cultivated or merely raise a supplementary levy on the other landowners to pay the taxes due on them. Or again they might be compulsorily allocated to individual landlords, who made what they could out of them but were responsible for the full tax. These methods could be combined in various ways, and rather different rules were applied to state lands and private lands, but the same general principles were followed throughout the fourth, fifth, and sixth centuries. The one thing which the government was reluctant to do, though occasionally it was forced to make this concession, was to write off deserted lands permanently.

The problem of imperial lands was administratively simpler. The government would offer emphyteutic or perpetual leases, with a few years' initial immunity, insisting that grantees must hold good land of their own to guarantee the rent: in 337 it was enacted that anyone who bought the good private land of an emphyteutic lessee of bad imperial land became responsible for the emphyteutic lease. The emperors also frequently ruled that in any lease, for a term of years or in perpetuity, bad lands must be mixed with good, and that lessees must never be allowed to take productive land only.[101]

In the fourth century the government used private lands deserted by their owners to provide allotments for veterans, and in 368 Valentinian gave a general licence to veterans to cultivate waste lands, forbidding the owners to appear at harvest time and claim *agraticum*. In the same year deserted lands in Italy were sold by auction for what they would fetch and other lands were granted gratis to anyone who would take them, with three years' immunity. In 386 the owners of deserted land were promised remission of arrears and invited to return: if they failed to claim, the land was granted to any applicant who was willing to pay the taxes. A few years later the former owner was allowed to reclaim his land within two years, provided that he indemnified the new occupant for improvements. In 405 a less generous offer was made; the old owners could reclaim their lands only if they paid the arrears, and new applicants had to pay off the arrears by way of purchase price. In 412 the government had to offer better terms. Lands which could not pay their full tax had their assessment reduced, and the former owners or their heirs, or failing them willing neighbours who reoccupied them, were given two years' immunity.[102]

The practice of allocating waste private lands, or the taxes due for them, to the community is frequently attested in the papyri. We possess the proceedings of a lawsuit, held in 340, between two women who had abandoned their property and the villagers of Caranis, where their land was situated. 'What could the *praepositus pagi* do?' says counsel for the villagers. 'Taking thought for his own security and the public revenues at the same time, he went to the village and gave the land to the peasants to cultivate.' There are a number of leases of land by village headmen for the amount of the taxes only or for an exceptionally low rent; these lands had evidently been assigned to the village or city, and are sometimes stated to be 'from insolvent names' on the tax register (ἀπὸ ἀπόρων ὀνομάτων). We also meet with levies 'for insolvent names', made presumably when the land could not be made to yield the necessary revenue. Saint Saba asked Anastasius to remit such an extra levy to Jerusalem. 'The successive *tractatores* and *vindices* of the Palestine revenues,' he explained, 'being pressed for 100 lb. gold which could not be collected from insolvent or difficult names, were forced to impose the payment of this sum on the taxpayers of Jerusalem according to the means of each.' The practice seems to have been known technically in the sixth century as διαγραφή.[103]

The government naturally did not allow a landlord to claim remission of tax on one of his estates if he owned others from which he could pay the tax on the deserted farm. If he asked for relief, he had to allow all his farms to be inspected by a *peraequator*, who decided whether the good land could support the bad. Similarly heirs were obliged to accept bad land with good, or else to renounce the entire estate. The same principle was applied to the territories of cities. When a city requested a *peraequator*, all its territory was inspected and bad land was set off against good. The *peraequator* seems to have achieved this end by allocating deserted estates to neighbouring owners of good land. The practice seems to have been fairly common in the fourth century; Valentinian in 365 stated that 'in Italy the burden of abandoned acreage is imposed on the existing estates and there is no doubt that every tax-payer is oppressed by the addition of the debts of others'.[104]

In 412, however, the principle was laid down that no owner of good land was to be burdened by the arrears or insolvency of others, but was liable only when the deserted land was part of the same property which he held. The rule was later extended to any collection of lands which had once been under common ownership. We possess an edict of the praetorian prefect Demosthenes (521 and 529), issued to the governor of Lydia, which elaborates this principle. In the case involved, probably an actual one, the owner of a group of estates, A, having alienated one of them to an outsider, X, left the rest to his heirs, B, C, D. One of them, D, alienated part of his share to another outsider, Y. Later Y could not pay his taxes and abandoned his land. On whom does the burden fall? First on D, the vendor; then, if he fails, on his co-heirs B and C; and finally, if they fail, on X, the purchaser of an estate originally belonging to A. It is little wonder that vendors of land guaranteed prospective purchasers against ἐπιβολὴ ὁμοδούλων.

The law of 412 remained on the statue book, being incorporated in Justinian's code, but the government seems to have ignored its provisions. Under Anastasius and Justinian we hear not only of ἐπιβολὴ ὁμοδούλων but also of ἐπιβολὴ ὁμοκήνσων, and the latter term can only mean that deserted estates were compulsorily allocated not only to owners of lands which were or had been under the same ownership (ὁμόδουλα), but, if these failed, to owners of lands registered in the same census district (ὁμόκηνσα).[105]

Another principle on which land was allocated to individuals was laid down in 365. If a landowner petitioned the crown for the slaves on a deserted estate or harboured runaway slaves from it, he was made responsible for its taxes. In the sixth century this principle was extended to landlords who received runaway *colon* from deserted estates.[106]

Justinian includes in his routine mandates to provincial governors instructions on how to deal with the lands of owners who disappeared or could not pay their taxes. They are to be assigned by decree of the governor with appeal to the praetorian prefect; the governor may refer the case initially to the prefect if in doubt, the estate being sequestrated in the meanwhile. We have complaints about *agri deserti* from Africa under Justin II and from Sardinia under Maurice. The abandonment of land by its owners thus continued throughout the three centuries which followed Diocletian's accession. How large the total was, and what proportion it bore to the land still cultivated it is more difficult to say, for reliable figures are few.[107]

Julian assigned tax free to the council of Antioch nearly 3,000 *iuga* of uncultivated land; as the territory of Antioch must have comprised well over 60,000 *iuga* the proportion is low, less than 1 in 20. Valens gives precise figures for the *fundi iuris reipublicae* recently confiscated from the cities of the province of Asia; there were 6,736½ fertile *iuga* as against 703 'deserted and now in bad condition and sterile, which are supported by those which we have stated to be fertile'. The proportion is less than 1 in 10. In 395 Honorius wrote off 528,042 *iugera* in Campania as deserted and in bad condition; the area of the province of Campania is not known exactly, but the proportion of deserted land would have been perhaps 1 in 10.[108]

In 422 Honorius wrote off the deserted lands of the *res privata* in Africa Proconsularis and Byzacena. Here he gives precise figures, which are startling. In the Proconsular province there were 5,700 *centuriae* 144½ *iugera* deserted to 9,002 *centuriae* 141 *iugera* in good condition, a proportion of over 1 in 3; in Byzacena 7,615 *centuriae* 3½ *iugera* deserted to 7,460 *centuriae* 180 *iugera* in good condition: more than half the land was deserted. In 451 Valentinian III granted to African landowners expelled by the Vandals the deserted lands of the province of Numidia, which amounted to about 13,000 *centuriae*; here the precise proportion cannot be determined but must have been of the same order as that prevailing thirty years before in the two neighbouring provinces. Finally Theodoret, writing to the praetorian prefect Constantine in 451, gives figures for his city of Cyrrhus. The whole territory comprised 62,000 *iuga* of which 15,000 paid in gold through the *comitiani*, the remainder in kind through the *curiales*. The *comitiani* had got the 2,500 deserted *iuga* in their share transferred to the *curiales* in exchange for 2,500 good *iuga*. The proportion is here 1 in 6.[109]

So far as these scattered figures go, the situation seems to have progressively deteriorated, but had not in the East become disastrous by the middle of the fifth century, with only about one-sixth of the land abandoned. In Africa the loss was already of catastrophic proportions—a third to a half—in the first quarter of the fifth century.

The main objection to the theory of the exhaustion of the soil is that *agri deserti* seem to have been as frequent in Egypt, where fertility was annually renewed by the flood over most of the cultivable area, as in the rest of the empire. It is also significant that the imperial government persisted in believing that deserted lands could be brought back into full production if the occupier were remitted his taxes for a few years and spent some money on improvements. It is even more significant that former owners shared this belief, and would reclaim land that someone else had improved. While it is not unlikely that some land was exhausted by persistent over-cropping, in general the deserted or sterile estates seem to have been suffering from temporary neglect only. The orator who thanked Constantine for his remission of taxes to the Civitas Aeduorum in 311 makes this point clear: it was because the peasants, burdened with debt, could not afford to maintain the drains and cut back the encroaching scrub that once fertile lands had reverted to marsh and maquis.[110]

A more important factor than exhaustion of the soil may have been denudation. In Mediterranean lands, if the forests on the uplands are cut and not replanted or allowed to renew themselves naturally, the heavy seasonal rains wash away the soil. What have been perennial streams, watering the lower areas, become occasional torrents, which often ruin the plains below by covering them with the stones and boulders which they wash down when they are in spate. Denudation went on continuously during antiquity in many areas, and in many has continued to the present day. The ancients regularly cut timber, mainly for ships and for roofs: the large number of timber-roofed churches of basilican form which were built in the late empire must have called for the felling of many large trees. They never thought of replanting forests, and they checked their natural renewal by grazing goats, who eat the young saplings before they have a chance to grow: the well-wooded hills and perennial streams of Mount Athos, where goats have been excluded for a thousand years, are a striking contrast to the arid and rocky landscape of other parts of Greece. Under the Roman empire the innumerable baths must also have contributed to deforestation by their immense consumption of fuel, mostly saplings.

The difficulty is to know how far the process of denudation had gone in the fourth, fifth and sixth centuries. From contemporary authors and from descriptions given by the Arab geographers it would appear that many areas now deforested and denuded were in a flourishing condition not only in the late empire but in the medieval period. Archaeological evidence shows that in areas now utterly treeless large buildings were still being roofed with timber in the sixth century. Some areas were no doubt already suffering from denudation under the later empire, but the bulk of the damage seems to have been done in later ages.

Shortage of manpower is a more plausible explanation for the abandonment of land. Landlords seem to have been perennially short of tenants. They welcomed allocations of barbarian prisoners, and persistently, despite the heavy penalties, harboured runaway *coloni*. The whole course of legislation which tied the *coloni* to their farms confirms this impression; it was at the demand of landlords that the system was maintained and extended. It is a measure of their anxiety to retain their tenants that the Roman senate in 397 vehemently and successfully opposed the conscription of recruits from their estates, and accepted as a preferable alternative a payment of 25 solidi per man. Such figures as there are suggest the same conclusion. The early fourth century census lists from Tralles, Magnesia on the Maeander and Astypalaea record the *iugatio* of farms and the *capitatio* of slaves and *coloni* registered on them. The ratio at Astypalaea and Tralles is 4 *capita* to 3 *iuga*, at Magnesia 7 *capita* to 6 *iuga* if estates which have no *capitatio* are ignored: if they are included in the count, there are only 5 *capita* to 6 *iuga*. The translation of *iuga* into acreage and *capita* into human beings is not certain, but these figures probably represent a labour force, including women and children over fourteen, about half of that, consisting of adult males only, recommended by Cato and Columella—fifteen for a vineyard of 100 *iugera*, eight for an arable farm of 200 *iugera*. The landlords no doubt employed both tenants and casual labour not registered on their estates, but even allowing for this the shortage of agricultural manpower is striking.[111]

Some deserted estates were undermanned; among the improvements which a grantee might make was the restocking of the land with slaves. The landowners of Africa complained to Justin II that as a result of his predecessor's legislation many of their *coloni* had migrated elsewhere, and that these estates had since remained desolate, to the detriment both of the owners and of the treasury. It was reported to Gregory the Great that many of the tenants of the church of Caralis had moved to the lands of private owners, with the result that 'the estates of the church, their own cultivators being occupied elsewhere, are falling into ruin and are incapable of paying their taxes'. But some owners abandoned estates leaving slaves or *coloni* on them, whom neighbouring landlords claimed from the crown as ownerless property or illicitly took over. It would seem that shortage of manpower was not at any rate the sole or main reason for the abandonment of land. It does not appear to have been important until after the great plague of Justinian's reign, which according to Procopius 'swept over the whole world and especially the Roman empire and destroyed the greater part of the peasantry, with the result that estates naturally were deserted'.[112]

Another factor which must have played its part, though we have no means of assessing its importance, was insecurity. The constant pillaging expeditions of the Germans across the Rhine and Danube must have made many landlords in the frontier provinces give up hope, while in the East the raids of the Isaurians in eastern Asia Minor, the Saracens in Syria, the Blemmyes and other nomads in Egypt and Cyrenaica, must have had the same effect. In Africa too the nomads were encroaching; in the reign of Valentinian I they made havoc in Tripolitania, and their activities no doubt contributed to the ruin of Byzacena and Numidia in the early fifth century. The African provinces were also at this time suffering from the attempts of the imperial government to stamp out Donatism; many Donatist peasants must have abandoned their farms and joined the circumcellion bands. Moreover, in 453, when 13,000 *centuriae* were deserted in Numidia, the Vandals had just evacuated that province, and had doubtless taken with them most of the stock and movables. This was doubtless one of the reasons why Africa was in an exceptionally bad case in the second quarter of the fifth century.

Contemporaries generally attribute the phenomenon to heavy taxation. According to Lactantius it was because the resources of tenants were exhausted by Diocletian's exorbitant indictions that fields were deserted and cultivated land went back to scrub. The spokesman of the Civitas Aeduorum similarly attributes the ruin of the land to the poverty of the cultivators, and expects that all will be well as a result of Constantine's reducing the assessment of the city. More significant is the matter-of-fact statement of the lawyer in the Egyptian lawsuit of 340. 'The father of the defendants owned lands in the village of Caranis . . . he cultivated them well and pocketed the profits from them and at the same time paid the public taxes on them to the most sacred treasury . . . but it appears, to make a long story short, that the father of the defendants died leaving as his heirs his daughters, i.e. the defendants, and they, not being able to stand up against the taxes demanded for the same lands, fled.' Conversely when Julian granted 3,000 uncultivated *iuga* to the council of Antioch tax free, both he and they regarded this land as a valuable asset: they, according to Julian, allocated it corruptly to those who least needed it, he granted it to the decurions who were saddled with the most expensive liturgies. Similarly, veterans who received deserted lands tax free were deemed to be well rewarded.[113]

It is assumed throughout the imperial legislation that the deserted lands are owned by landlords, who cultivate them through slaves or *coloni*: it is to be inferred in the Caranis case that the reason why the two daughters could not face the taxes which their father had regularly paid was that he cultivated the land himself, and they had to let it to a tenant.

It would appear then that on some land the taxation was so heavy that the owner could not make a profit on it, or at any rate so little that he could not afford the expenses necessary to keep it in good condition, in particular the maintenance of drainage and irrigation: or that he squeezed his tenants so hard that they could not afford the charges of upkeep. Whether land was cultivated or not depended then on the margin between the gross rent which the landlord could extract from it, and the taxes which he or his tenant had to deduct from the rent.

The rent would obviously depend on the quality of the land and its agricultural use, as olive groves, vineyards, arable or pasture. The tax also in some dioceses varied according to these factors. In Syria there was an elaborate system of classification into olives, 'old' and 'mountain', vineyard, three qualities of arable and pasture. The fiscal unit, the *iugum*, was made up of varying areas of each. Syria seems, however, to have been exceptional. In Asia the only distinction recognised was olives, vineyard, arable and pasture, with no classification by quality. In Egypt taxation was assessed by the *arura*, with differential rates only for vineyards, orchards and the like. In Africa the system was even more rough and ready, land being assessed by the *centuria* of 200 *iugera*, apparently without regard to use or quality, and in Italy the *millena* seems to have been a simple unit of area. In Syria therefore the tax would, in so far as the land was correctly classified, vary with the rental value, while in Africa all land would pay the same tax whether it produced a high or a low rent. This may partly explain why the proportion of deserted land was so much higher in Africa than in Syria.[114]

For taxation in Egypt we possess one document of paramount value, the sixth-century assessment of the city of Antaeopolis. Here the whole tax in corn and in gold, including all supplementary payments, amounts to 61,674 *artabae* of wheat and 10,322 solidi on 51,655 *arurae*, nearly all arable; vineyards come to 2,578½ and gardens to 1,600. This works out at about 1⅕ *artabae* and 4¾ carats per *arura*; if the whole tax be translated into gold 7⅔ carats, or if it be reckoned entirely in wheat 3⅕ *artabae*. If landowners in general paid at this rate they had a small margin between rent and taxes even on good arable, less than two *artabae* per *arura* if the rent was five, or in gold a little over 4 carats, or ⅙ solidus. Enterprising landlords like the Apions, as we have seen, probably extracted a higher rent from their tenants, and it is likely that they paid less tax in gold by avoiding supplementary payments. But poor arable land which was let at 3 *artabae* or less would have involved the owner in a loss if he paid normal taxes. For vineyards, orchards, palms, olives and pasture we cannot judge, as we have no figures.[115]

For the rest of the empire we possess one document only. It deals with the grant by Justinian to the catholic church of Ravenna of the lands which had been held by the Arian church of that city and had been confiscated to the *res privata*. The first part, which appears to enumerate the various estates with their rentals and taxes, is too fragmentary to be intelligible. The summary has however survived intact and reads:

ac sic fieri	sol(idi) n(umero)	$2171\frac{1}{2}$
pensio	sol(idi) n(umero)	$932\frac{1}{2}$
fiunt	sol(idi) n(umero)	1239
in (can)on(e) praefect(orum)	sol(idi) n(umero)	$1153\frac{1}{2}$
in titul(is) largitional(ibus)	sol(idi) n(umero)	$85\frac{1}{2}$

This appears to mean that the gross total of the rents is $2,171\frac{1}{2}$, of which the net rent (*pensio*) is $932\frac{1}{2}$: the remainder, 1,239, is made up of the taxes payable to the praetorian prefect ($1,153\frac{1}{2}$) and those due to the *largitiones* ($85\frac{1}{2}$); and for the payment of these the representatives of the catholic church give a bond. In sixth-century Italy, then, it would appear that taxes absorbed 57% of the gross rental, even on church lands which paid no *superindicta*, *extraordinaria* or *munera sordida*. On poor land which was fully taxed the landlord's margin must have dwindled to nothing.[116]

The figures, then, for what they are worth, support the assertions of the literary authorities up to a point. By the sixth century the taxes on land seem to have been set so high as to make it un-profitable for a landlord who paid full rate to keep low quality land under cultivation: on such land his margin, if any, was so small that he could not afford the expenses necessary to keep it in good condition. The effect of taxation was most disastrous where it was a flat rate on area, and where the amount of marginal land, which was thus overtaxed, was a high proportion of the whole. Both these conditions were fulfilled in Africa; hence the pheno-menal scale on which land was abandoned in Africa, Numidia and Byzacena, especially the last, where the rainfall is lowest and most irregular, and cultivation depends on careful water conserva-tion.

The extent of the evil must not be exaggerated. One must remember that even in the sixth century there must have been vast areas of fertile land which yielded not only the ample revenue which the empire still enjoyed, but provided the large incomes of the senatorial magnates and the great sees, not to speak of countless humbler folk. The demand for land as an investment remained keen. Claimants persistently bombarded the office of the *res privata* with petitions for estates alleged, truly or falsely, to have lapsed to the crown. Land seems always to have found ready purchasers, and the prices recorded are high. Once again most of our figures come from Egypt and are for arable. The lowest figure is 4 solidi for $1\frac{1}{4}$ *arurae*; in another case one *arura* is sold for 4 solidi and in another 8 *arurae* (with $\frac{5}{8}$ of uninundated land) for 40 solidi. The highest price recorded is 6 solidi for one *arura*, in the sixth century, but in this conveyance an exceptionally low tax, half an *artaba* of wheat and $1\frac{1}{2}$ carats in gold, is specified; the land must have been fraudulently assessed. In this last case despite the high price the return on capital is, owing to the low tax, quite high, $6\frac{1}{2}\%$ if the land was let at 5 *artabae* or half shares. Land bought for 4 or 5 solidi, if let at that figure and fully taxed, would yield only $4\frac{1}{2}$ or $3\frac{1}{2}\%$ on capital.[117]

We have one figure only from outside Egypt. In a conveyance dated 539 twenty *iugera* at Faventia in northern Italy are sold for 110 solidi: they are specified to be 'culti optimi arbustali' (*sic*), by which is presumably meant orchard or olive yard. This price, $5\frac{1}{2}$ solidi to the *iugerum* (equivalent to 6 solidi for the *arura*) seems low for land of the type, but we do not know how highly it was taxed. The contrast with Italian land prices under the Principate is instructive. Columella, assessing the profitability of converting arable to vineyard, estimates the cost of the land at 1,000 sesterces the *iugerum*, which is equivalent in gold value to about 17 solidi. He is probably, for the sake of his argument, pitching the price rather high, but the passage implies that one might have to pay as much for good arable land. There were in Columella's day factors which tended to push up the price of Italian land beyond its strictly economic value, for the senatorial and equestrian nobility were still mainly Italian by origin and domicile, and were competing to invest in Italian land the profits they acquired from governing the empire. This no longer applied in Justinian's reign. But the main difference between the first and the sixth century was that in the first Italian land was tax free, and in the sixth it bore the same high taxes as the rest of the empire.[118]

To summarise the problem, it would seem that a considerable and growing proportion of the land was abandoned by landlords during the period of the later Roman empire. The area abandoned probably did not in most areas exceed say 20%, and the land involved was mostly of poor quality. Land of good and average quality continued to yield enough to pay not only taxes but rent, and remained in strong demand, commanding such high prices that the return on investment in land was low, in the range of 4%. There is no evidence that there was general exhaustion of the soil, or that much land had been ruined by denudation, only that marginal land fell back into waste through lack of proper maintenance. The abandonment of land may have sometimes been due to shortage of agricultural labour and in some areas to insecurity, but in the main it was caused by the high and increasing rate of taxation, which reduced the landlord's net rent on marginal land to vanishing point.

The actual fall in agricultural production would not have been so great as the figures of abandoned land suggest, for in the first place this land was the poorest, and in the second place some of it, though booked as *deserta* or *sterilia*, continued to be cultivated by the landlords to whom it was assigned; for even if it yielded no profit, it might be made to produce enough to pay a part at least of the taxes due for it. Finally, we must set against the areas lost to agriculture the hitherto unproductive land which was developed under the later empire. East of Antioch, in what is now desert, there are ruins of scores of well-built and evidently once prosperous villages. They were all built in the fifth and sixth centuries, and there is no trace of earlier occupation. They depended, as their many presses show, on the cultivation of the olive. Here at least agriculture advanced, and it may have done so in other areas where the archaeological evidence has been obliterated by later occupation.[119]

CHAPTER XXI

INDUSTRY, TRADE AND TRANSPORT

THE Roman empire in many ways provided conditions favourable to commerce. It formed a vast common market, stretching from Britain to Egypt, and even when it was administratively divided no political barriers were set up against trade: the embargo which Stilicho placed on merchants from the Eastern parts during the latter part of his rule was quite exceptional. Even when the Western parts were broken up into barbarian kingdoms trade seems to have remained free from political difficulties. In the early seventh century there were still Alexandrian merchants who specialised in the Gallic trade (Γαλλοδρόμοι), and at the other end of the route at Marseilles there were still in the late sixth century regular imports of papyrus, which must have come from Egypt, as well as of oil, which probably came from Africa: wines of central Italy and of Gaza were also imported into Gaul. The Alexandrian merchants who specialised in the Spanish trade (Σπανοδρόμοι) seem still to have continued their activities in the sixth century: we hear of 'Greek' merchants landing at Spanish ports and coming up to Emerita, and the Visigothic kings were liberal to overseas merchants, allowing them to settle their own disputes between themselves according to their own laws, and to employ local men as agents, provided that they did not take them overseas with them.[1]

There were also no currency difficulties to hamper large-scale commerce. Imperial coins wherever minted were legal tender throughout the empire. Retail trade must have been inconvenienced by the chaotic state of the copper currency in the fourth and fifth centuries, and by the growing shortage of silver in the fifth; the situation was improved in the latter part of the fifth century by the issue at Rome and Carthage and later by Anastasius in the East of large copper coins which had a more or less stable relation with the solidus, and also by the renewed issue of silver by the Vandal and Ostrogothic kings—and later by the imperial government in Italy. For large transactions, however, the solidus from the latter part of Constantine's reign provided a reliable and stable medium of exchange. Solidi were accepted not only throughout the empire but in northern Europe, where large numbers have been found, and in the Far East. 'The second sign of the sovereignty which God has granted to the Romans', Cosmas Indicopleustes declared, 'is that all nations trade in their currency, and in every place from one end of the world to the other it is acceptable and envied by every man and every kingdom': and Cosmas, having often sailed to India, could answer for one end of the world at any rate. The Western barbarian kingdoms accepted imperial solidi, and most minted their own on the same standard. Only the gold coins of the Merovingians were lighter and were not acceptable in Italy: Gregory the Great asked the agent of the Gallic estates of the Roman church not to remit his rents in local solidi, but to buy clothes and slaves and despatch them to Rome.[2]

There was an excellent road network, and roads and bridges were maintained by the government at the expense of landowners. Harbour and inland waterways were likewise maintained by the state. Security was, to judge by the many records of travel by sea and land which we possess, on the whole good. It was only in limited areas that brigandage was a serious menace—in Upper Egypt the Blemmyes made travel unsafe in the early fifth century, and in eastern Asia Minor the Isaurians at the same period reduced the towns to a state of siege. Piracy was rife from Diocletian's day onwards in the western ocean, but in the Mediterranean little is heard of it until the Vandals went into the business on a large scale.[3]

Tolls levied were not excessive. Within the empire the standard rates seem to have been 2 per cent. or $2\frac{1}{2}$ per cent. in the fourth century as under the Principate: in the fifth century 5 per cent. is mentioned in Numidia. How frequently they were levied it is difficult to say. In addition to the old imperial inter-provincial customs there were the tolls levied by the cities, which the imperial government took over under Constantine. Laws in the Codes which declare that country people bringing back goods for their own use or for agricultural purposes, or taking in goods for delivery as taxes, are not chargeable with duty, suggest that *octroi* posts at the gates of towns were common, and import and export dues were probably charged at all harbours. These tolls may have been vexatious but were hardly a serious check to commerce. Merchants travelling by sea would presumably have been charged only on the goods which they bought and sold at each port, and not on their whole cargo. Since there was little long-distance trade by land, the local *octroi* dues would have affected only small-scale local traffic.[4]

Valentinian III in 444 imposed on trade another small but vexatious tax, the *siliquaticum*, a levy of one *siliqua* on the solidus (1 in 24) on every sale, payable half by the vendor and half by the purchaser. All sales had to be conducted in the presence of a tax collector, without whose receipt the transaction was invalid, and to make this possible cities were ordered to fix appointed days and places for markets, and no business was permitted except at these. The *siliquaticum*, however, was imposed only on the restricted area which the Western imperial government still controlled in the middle of the fifth century, and survived only in the Ostrogothic kingdom of Italy.[5]

Monopolies are not heard of until the latter part of the fifth century, when Leo and Zeno prohibited them in 473 and 483. The second law forbids the issue of rescripts, pragmatic sanctions or *annotationes* to individuals to have a monopoly of clothing or fish or other kinds of goods, and cancels such rescripts already issued. It also forbids combinations between traders and craftsmen to fix the price of their wares and other such restrictive practices. In Ostrogothic Italy the *monopolium* was associated with the *siliquaticum*, being farmed to the same contractors. It may be conjectured that to facilitate allocation of the *siliquaticum* traders in various classes of goods were licensed, and that they had to pay for the privilege. In the East Justinian, in the interests of public security, created an imperial monopoly in the manufacture of arms: henceforth only the imperial armament factories were to produce them, private armourers were to be drafted into these factories, and the arms produced were to be stored in the imperial armoury, or in the local depots established in certain cities. Justinian also created a *de facto* monopoly of silk fabrics for the imperial factories operated by the *sacrae largitiones*: this he achieved by fixing the price of silk fabrics at a low figure, despite the great rise in the price of raw silk, and thus driving private manufacturers and merchants out of business. He is also alleged by Procopius in the Secret History to have ignored Zeno's law of 483, which he republished in his Code, and granted private monopolies right and left, thereby enormously increasing the cost of living. There is no doubt some germ of truth in this allegation, but like all Procopius' charges against Justinian it is probably greatly exaggerated.[6]

Trade beyond the frontiers of the empire was strictly controlled, mainly for security reasons, and more severely taxed: import and export dues were levied at the rate of $12\frac{1}{2}$ per cent. (*octavae*). In the Eastern empire at any rate foreign trade was subject to the control of the *comites commerciorum*, one for Illyricum, one for Moesia and Pontus, and one for Oriens and Egypt, and had to pass through a few specified places. Thus Clysma (Suez) was at times the sole authorised port for the Red Sea and Indian trade: at others Iotabe, an island at the north end of the gulf of Aqaba, was also a customs station. Under Diocletian land trade with Persia was canalised through Nisibis. In the fifth and sixth centuries it was limited to Callinicum on the Roman side and Nisibis and Artaxata on the Persian. Controlling the Black Sea trade there was a station at Hieron on the Bosporus, while commerce across the Danube was usually limited to a few points: Valens specified two only on the lower Danube in 369 and on the Upper Danube his brother in 371 built a 'burgus cui nomen Commercium, qua causa et factus est'. Various restrictions were placed on exports at various times. Valentinian forbade the export of wine and oil, and Valens of gold, but these restrictions, though preserved in the Code of Justinian, were certainly not observed. Marcian strictly prohibited the export of arms and armour, probably reviving an old rule; iron and bronze had been on the prohibited list in the fourth century.[7]

While conditions were in these ways generally favourable to trade, there were on the other hand important factors which restricted private commerce. In the first place the imperial government, the greatest consumer, made virtually no use of the private merchant, supplying the major needs of its hundreds of thousands of employees by levies in kind upon the producers, by manufacturing some parts of its requirements in state factories, and by conveying the goods thus levied or manufactured to their recipients by means of state transport services.

Transport by sea was the business of the guilds of shippers (*corpora naviculariorum*) controlled by the praetorian prefects or by the *praefecti annonae* of Africa and Alexandria, who were responsible to the praetorian prefects of Italy and the East respectively. They were organised on a diocesan basis: we hear of the guilds of Spain, Africa and Oriens and of the Alexandrian and Carpathian fleets, which represented Egypt and Asiana. Membership of the guilds was hereditary in that it depended on the ownership of land subject to the *navicularia functio*. If *navicularii* alienated such land either by will or bequest, or sale or gift, those who acquired it were obliged to become members of the guild or to contribute to its expenses *pro rata*. This rule applied whatever the status of the new owner, even if the land passed to the *res privata* or to the church: Augustine refused to accept for his church an estate which was burdened with the *navicularia functio* because of the trouble which it brought to its owner. The rule was of course frequently neglected, and periodically the government reclaimed for the guilds lands whose owners refused to contribute: there was no prescription against the *functio* until in 423 fifty years was allowed to count. Periodically also the government renewed the depleted numbers of the guild by compulsorily enrolling persons with sufficient landed wealth.[8]

The *navicularii* were paid freight for the cargoes which they carried: the rate quoted for the *navicularii Orientis* in 334 for conveying corn from Egypt to Constantinople was one solidus per 1,000 *modii* and 1 per cent. of the corn, as for the Alexandrian fleet. As a solidus would buy 30 *modii*, the rate works out at about 4 per cent. of the value of the cargo, one-third of the commercial rate fixed by Diocletian for the same voyage (12 denarii per *modius*, which was worth 100 denarii, that is 12 per cent.). The payment was not indeed expected to cover their costs—Constantine expresses the hope that 'encouraged by all this and spending scarcely anything out of their own property they may diligently make frequent voyages'.

The *navicularii* were mainly compensated in privileges which cost the government nothing, exemption from the guardianship of minors (*tutela*) and from the Lex Julia and Papia Poppaea (which restricted inheritance in certain cases), and above all immunity from curial obligations. They were also exempt from customs, even in respect of goods which they were carrying on their own account. When the *corpus Orientis* was revived in 371, members were also allowed remission of land tax, in corn (and probably other foodstuffs) only, not in garments, horses or such levies, at the rate of 50 *iuga* for each 10,000 *modii* of shipping capacity which they owned; this was for the repair and replacement of their ships.[9]

We chiefly hear of *navicularii* in connection with the shipment of corn from Africa to Rome and from Egypt to Constantinople, but they were also required to ship cargoes to the supply bases of the army (*expeditionales portus*). They were obliged to accept cargoes between 1 April and 10 October, winter navigation being considered too dangerous to be worth while, and were originally allowed two years by Constantine within which to bring back their delivery receipts. In 396, however, it was found that they took advantage of the long delay to trade in the corn that they carried, and the interval was reduced to one year unless they could prove delay by bad weather. Alleged losses due to storms, whether by total wreck, or by spoiling the cargo by water, or by jettison, were carefully investigated, and if they were proved to the satisfaction of the court, the government stood the loss.[10]

Navicularii might be of very varying status. A constitution of 326 envisages their being 'either decurions or plebeians or of some other superior dignity'. When the *corpus Orientis* was reorganised in 371, the praetorian prefect was directed to enrol not only *curiales* and retired officials of the provincial *officia* (*primipilares*) but ex-provincial governors and other *honorati* (excluding former *palatini*): even senators might volunteer. *Navicularii* were not expected to navigate their own ships; in investigations of damage by storms it was normally the skipper (*magister navis*) and sailors who were examined, or in case of total loss their relatives whom the *navicularius* produced in evidence. The *navicularii* were primarily ship-owners, whose business it was to finance the building, repair and operation of their ships: the guilds must also have included many sleeping members, owners of *praedia naviculariorum* who merely paid levies towards the expenses of the guild. By this curious system the government maintained a state merchant fleet financed out of the rents (supplemented by partial remission of taxes) of certain lands. It also reserved the right to charter any privately owned ship of over 2,000 *modii* capacity, whatever the rank of the owner.[11]

The origins of the system can only be conjectured. During the Principate the imperial government encouraged wealthy men to put ships at its disposal by granting them various privileges, including immunity from civic magistracies and liturgies. De-curions and other landowners who might otherwise have been elected to their city councils were thus tempted into the service; it was even found necessary to enact that rich men might not receive immunity unless they put a substantial proportion of their fortunes into shipping. Shippers who joined the service would also have put their profits into land. Since the *navicularii* would have wished to hand on their immunity to their sons, the service no doubt became in general hereditary. It had never, however, in all probability been very profitable, or the lure of immunities would not have been required, and with the inflation of the third century, as the real value of the freights paid sank, it no doubt became a positive burden. By this time, however, the government, unable to dispense with their services, compelled the *navicularii* to carry on, regarding their immunities as an adequate compensation for the losses which they made.[12]

There is less information about inland water transport. There was a state-controlled guild of bargees (*caudicarii*), who carried grain up the Tiber from Ostia to Rome, and another similar guild of boatmen (*lintriones*), whose sixty members supplied the baths of Rome with fuel. King Theoderic created a state fleet of a thousand galleys (*dromones*) for the transport of public corn. These operated mainly by sea, carrying corn round the coasts of Italy, but they also supplemented the *cursus publicus* along the Po, a detachment being based on Hostilia. The ships were built by direct labour, the timber being commandeered—the landowners were compensated only for cypresses and pines felled. They were manned by rowers (*drom-onarii*), levied by the praetorian prefect, who ranked as *milites* and received *annonae*: they might be free men or slaves, either hired from their owners or bought from them and freed. On the Nile we hear of skippers (κυβερνηταί) of public or fiscal boats, but owner skippers (ναυκληροκυβερνηταί) of private boats are commoner. They received the tribute corn from the civic authorities, together with money for freights, and delivered it at the state granaries at Neapolis by Alexandria. The service was probably compulsory; they had to give guarantees that they would perform their function.[13]

For land transport there was a service directly managed by the state through the praetorian prefects and provincial governors, the *cursus publicus*. It consisted of two divisions, the express post, or *cursus velox* (ὀξὺς δρόμος), and the slow wagon post, the *cursus clabularis* (πλατὺς δρόμος). The express post provided saddlehorses (*veredi*) and packhorses for luggage (*parhippi*), light two-wheeled carriages (*birotae*) drawn by three mules, and four-wheeled carts (*raedae*), also drawn by mules, eight in summer and ten in winter. It was intended primarily for the use of officials travelling on government business, especially *agentes in rebus*, but was also used for conveying gold and silver or other valuable goods; Constantine ordered that the copies of the scriptures produced by Eusebius for the churches of Constantinople should be sent up by it. There were strict limits on the weight which might be carried: a horseman might take only 30 lbs., a two-wheeled carriage 200 lbs., a four-wheeled car 1,000 lbs.[14]

The post could be used only by persons to whom a warrant (*evectio*) had been granted, and in theory warrants were issued only for official purposes. They were however freely granted to persons invited to the *comitatus*, and to bishops attending councils convoked by imperial authority. Very high officials, the praetorian prefects and the masters of the soldiers, were given warrants to return to their homes after laying down their posts. It was difficult to enforce the rules. Private persons of sufficiently high status found little difficulty in securing warrants from or through friends in high places. Symmachus thanked Ausonius for 'four warrants which have been enormously convenient for the coming and going of my people' and Stilicho for others for his agents going to Spain to buy horses for his son's praetorship, while Melania travelled with a large retinue from Palestine to Constantinople by the public post though she had no warrant.[15]

For the *cursus clabularis* ox wagons (*angariae*) were used; the maximum load was 1,500 lbs. and the standard team two pairs of oxen. The wagon post was mainly used for carrying the foodstuffs levied for the *annona*, but also for the uniforms and arms destined for the troops, and for timber and building stone for public works. Julian promised as a special concession to the men whom Constantius had summoned from Gaul to the Eastern front that they might use the *cursus* for transporting their baggage and families. This was, however, irregular. A law of 360 allowed troops in transit only two *angariae* per legion for the use of the sick. Provincial governors also were allowed to use it for their tours. Majorian allowed them two *angariae*, one for themselves and one for their *officium*, as well as four riding horses. This service was controlled by warrants, called *tractoriae*. These, too, could be obtained by private persons with sufficient influence. Julian had to forbid the use of the post for carting marble for the erection of private houses, and Symmachus asked the praetorian prefect Vincentius to renew the *tractoriae* given by his predecessor Theodore for the conveyance to Rome of the racehorses which he had bought in Spain.[16]

The maintenance of these services demanded a vast and costly organisation. In the cities along the main roads and at intermediate points between them were maintained posting stations, the larger called *mansiones*, provided with lodging accommodation, the smaller *mutationes*, only with relays of beasts. Some idea of the vast number of the post stations can be gathered from the Antonine Itinerary and the Peutinger Table, but these do not give the full picture, recording only cities and *mansiones* as a rule. A record of his journey kept by a pilgrim who travelled from Burdigala to Jerusalem and back in 333 gives full details for the roads along which he travelled. Between Burdigala and the Italian frontier he passed through 14 cities (as well as one village and one fortress), 11 *mansiones* and 35 *mutationes*. Across the Italian diocese from Segusio to Poetovio he counted 14 cities, 9 *mansiones* and 30 *mutationes*. From thence across Illyricum and Thrace to Constantinople, over 900 miles, cities were scarce—he passed only 14—but 28 *mansiones* filled the gaps between them, and there were 53 *mutationes*. From Chalcedon across Asia Minor to the borders of Cilicia, some 560 miles, there were only 11 cities, but 15 *mansiones* and 28 *mutationes*. From Tarsus to Jerusalem along the coast cities were more frequent; he passed 20 as well as 7 *mansiones* and 21 *mutationes*. On his return journey he took the alternative route across Thrace and Illyricum via Thessalonica to Apollonia. Here again cities were scarce, only 13, to 14 *mansiones* with 32 *mutationes*. Thence he crossed the Adriatic to Hydruntum, and so up to Milan. In Italy cities were thick; he passed through 42, and only 6 *mansiones* with 36 *mutationes*. Stations were, of course, at various distances, but very rarely more than 15 miles apart and often only 8 or 9: the average over the pilgrim's whole journey works out at 10 or 11 miles.[17]

The maintenance of the stations was charged to the revenues of the province in which they lay, and it was the duty of the provincial governor to build or repair them by corvées and levies on the provincial population. Each station was managed by a person styled a *manceps* or contractor; the title was a survival from an earlier age when the post had been farmed. The charge was in some provinces laid on retired officials of the provincial *officium*, or of those of the vicar or *rationalis* of the diocese; even officials of the praetorian prefects might be called upon to serve if they retired before reaching the rank of *cornicularius*. More usually, it would seem, *mancipes* were decurions nominated by the city councils. Valentinian tried to draw upon a higher class, those who had obtained the honorary rank of *comites, praesides* or *rationales*, that is the wealthiest *curiales*, who had thus succeeded in evading their regular duties, and suggested that they might where convenient be put in charge of a group of stations; but this reform was short-lived. *Mancipes* were by a law of 381 to serve for a period not exceeding five years, and were to be rewarded after satisfactory service with the perfectissimate. The office was evidently much disliked both for its exacting duties—a *manceps* was not allowed to leave his post for more than thirty days—and its financial responsibilities.[18]

In the stations were kept an appropriate number of animals; according to Procopius as many as forty horses in each. So high a figure was probably maintained only on frequented routes, for a rule was laid down in 378 that no station was to dispatch more than five (amended in 382 to six) horses per day, except for bearers of imperial letters or holders of warrants marked urgent: not more than one cart per day was to be forwarded. The average working life of beasts was apparently four years, for 25 per cent. of the establishment had to be replaced annually by a levy on the provincials; this levy was probably usually commuted—we find in Egyptian land tax receipts of the early fourth century many payments (in denarii) 'for the account of worn-out public beasts'.[19]

Barley to feed the beasts was provided out of the provincial land tax. A constitution of 365 states that hitherto in the Suburbicarian provinces fodder had been despatched to the several *mutationes* and *mansiones* for the beasts deputed to the public post suddenly and without forethought at the whim of the *tabularii*. The consular Anatolius had remedied this chaos by fixing a regular schedule of deliveries at fixed dates, and allocating them to the various cities with due regard to the distance and difficulty of the journey, and this reform was now to be applied throughout Italy.[20]

Each station had its staff of carpenters to mend the carriages and wagons, of veterinary surgeons, and of grooms (*hippocomi* or *muliones*), the last on the scale of one to three animals. These were hereditary public slaves, provided with rations and clothes, but no wages.[21]

This vast organisation was tremendously expensive to maintain, and very wasteful of manpower, beasts and fodder. The title 'de cursu publico', one of the longest in the Theodosian Code, reveals the anxiety of the government through two centuries to slacken the pressure on the postal services by checking its extravagant use by officials and its illegal usurpation by private persons. The most minute regulations were laid down to prevent the animals being overworked: loads were carefully limited for both horses and wagons, the daily rate of despatch of horses and wagons was fixed: it was even laid down that riders were not to overdrive their horses by the use of 'knotty bludgeons', but only to employ canes or whips, which might have a metal barb. Yet despite its great resources the post could not cope with all demands from its regular establishment and emergency requisitions of horses (*paraveredi*) and ox wagons (*parangariae*) were frequently made.[22]

Efforts were also made to cut down the size of the service. Julian, in addition to curbing the issue of warrants, abolished the *cursus velox* in one province, Sardinia, where, as he said, it hardly justified its demands on the provincials; officials could organise and pay for their own service or use their own animals. An even more drastic cut was made in the reign of Leo, when the praetorian prefect Pusaeus abolished the *cursus clabularis* throughout the diocese of Oriens and in some other regions: when wagons were required for troop movements, for foreign ambassadors, or for carting supplies to the arms factories or arms to the troops, they were to be hired from professional carters. Such a step was by now feasible since most of the taxation in kind had been commuted into gold, and many of the troops were also paid in money. Under Justinian the praetorian prefect John the Cappadocian abolished both the *cursus velox* and the *cursus clabularis* in various districts, including Asiana. Procopius' strictures on this step reveal what an economic burden the post was. In the good old days, he explains, the post had not only provided for the rapid transit of messages, but had been a blessing to the landowners, especially those of the inland districts, since they were able to sell to it their barley and thus obtain money to pay their gold taxes. If the abolition of the post spelt their ruin, as he and John Lydus aver, its barley consumption must have been prodigious.[23]

Both the *sacrae largitiones* and the *res privata* had their own transport services, called *bastagae*. They were staffed by *bastagarii*, who, unlike the public slaves of the *cursus publicus*, were of military status; their reception as recruits into the army was strictly forbidden in 384. They had animals under their charge and were entitled to replacements at the rate of 10 per cent. (raised by Justinian to 20 per cent.) per annum. How these services were related to the *cursus publicus* is obscure, as both the *largitiones* and the *res privata* were entitled to make use of the *cursus* for transporting gold, silver and clothes.[24]

From the time of Diocletian the state manufactured all arms required for the imperial forces in its own factories (*fabricae*). We have a complete list of these as they existed at the turn of the fourth to the fifth centuries. There were fifteen factories in the Eastern parts, general works for the production of shields and arms at Damascus, Antioch, Edessa, Nicomedia, Sardis, Hadrianopolis, Marcianopolis, Thessalonica, Naissus and Ratiaria: at Caesarea of Cappadocia and Antioch and Nicomedia works for heavy cavalry armour (*clibanariae*); at Irenopolis in Cilicia a lance factory and at Horreum Margi a shield factory. In the Western parts there were twenty in all, five in Illyricum, six in Italy, and nine in Gaul, but many of these were more specialised. There were shield works at Aquincum, Carnuntum, Lauriacum, Cremona, Augustodunum and Augusta Trevirorum, arrow factories at Concordia and Matisco, a bow factory at Ticinum, a breastplate works at Mantua, sword factories at Luca and Remi, and one for *ballistae* at Treviri. At Sirmium, Salona, Verona, Argentomagus, Ambiani and Augustodunum there were mixed arms works: the last was the only Western factory to produce heavy cavalry armour. These factories, originally under the direction of the praetorian prefects, had by 390 passed into the hands of the masters of the offices. There were also factories for producing the bronze armour, adorned with silver and gold, worn by officers. These establishments, the workers in which were called *barbaricarii*, were originally, because they handled the precious metals, under the *comes sacrarum largitionum*. In the West they still remained so in the fifth century, when there were three, at Arelate, Remi and Treviri. In the East they passed between 374 and the death of Theodosius the Great to the *magister officiorum*; two establishments are recorded, at Constantinople and Antioch.[25]

The workers in these factories ranked as soldiers. They received rations (*annonae*), and like soldiers were hereditarily tied to their profession; they were branded, for easier identification in case they escaped, as were recruits. Each factory was equated with a regiment, being commanded by a tribune or *praepositus*. The workers held the normal military grades, rising by seniority to become the *primicerius fabricae*, who after two years' service retired with the rank of *protector*. The service was evidently held in good esteem; volunteers who offered themselves had to prove that they were not of curial status. *Fabricenses* seem to have been men of some substance; landlords liked to employ them—illegally—as *procuratores* or *conductores* of their estates. The members of each factory were jointly responsible to the government for any financial default, and in view of this responsibility Theodosius II allocated to them the property of any worker who died intestate without heirs.[26]

The *fabricae* were supplied with iron and other raw materials, such as horn (for making bows), by the praetorian prefects, whose office contained a *scrinium armorum* which handled the necessary levies. Charcoal was also supplied; its production was a *sordidum munus* imposed on landowners. The weight of the arms produced was checked against that of the metal issued; there is a story that Valentinian condemned to death the *praepositus fabricae* who produced a breastplate so highly burnished that it had lost a little weight. Workers were expected to produce a specified number of weapons per month. This at any rate was the rule with the *barbaricarii*. According to a constitution dated 374, it was the rule at Antioch that each worker should in every thirty days make six bronze helmets with cheek pieces, and in the same period decorate eight with silver and gold, whereas at Constantinople the corresponding figures were six and three: the emperor ordered work at Constantinople to be speeded up to Antiochene standards.[27]

The *fabricae* must have been large establishments, for their personnel was a substantial element in the population of the towns in which they were situated. At Hadrianopolis they are mentioned as a leading element in the riots against the Arian council held at that town contemporaneously with the Council of Sardica, and later in 376 as an important part of the force which the magistrates of the city raised to attack the Goths. At Caesarea too the *fabricenses* are recorded to have been prominent in the riots in support of Basil.[28]

The state also operated, through the *comes sacrarum largitionum*, a number of weaving mills, both for woollen and linen fabrics, and dyeworks, to produce uniforms for the troops and the civil service and high quality garments for the court. We have a full list of these establishments for the Western empire in the early fifth century. There were only two linen mills (*linyphia*), at Vienna in Gaul and at Ravenna. Woollen mills (*gynaecia*) were much more numerous. In Italy they existed at Rome, Aquileia, Milan and Canusium with Venusia: in Illyricum at Bassianae, Sirmium and Iovia: in Gaul at Lugdunum, Remi, Treviri, Tornacum and Augustodunum; in Africa at Carthage; and even in Britain at Venta. There were nine dyeing establishments, at Tarentum and Cissa in Italy, at Syracuse in Sicily, at Salona in Dalmatia, at Telo and Narbo in Gaul, in the Balearic isles, at Girba in Tripolitania, and in Africa. There were also a few *gynaecia* and *baphia* in the West under the control of the *res privata*. For the Eastern parts we possess no similar list. We happen to hear of woollen mills at Heraclea of Thrace, Cyzicus, Caesarea of Cappadocia and Tyre, a linen mill at Scythopolis and dyeworks in Phoenicia and Cyprus. There is a single reference, in a law addressed in 344 to the praetorian prefect of Italy, to *calcarienses* or bootmakers; no such factories are recorded in the Notitia Dignitatum for the Eastern or the Western parts.[29]

These factories were managed by *procuratores* and manned by state slaves. During the Great Persecution we hear of Christians being made slaves of the treasury and enrolled in the *linyphia* and *gynaecia*, but by the middle of the fourth century the workers in the state factories had become hereditary groups. They are still called slaves (*mancipia*); the workers in each factory are styled *familiae*, the word used for slave households; and the Senatusconsultum Claudianum was invoked to enslave free women who married them. But it is clear that *de facto* they were free persons bound by a hereditary tie to their trades. In 424 it was even necessary to reclaim purple fishers (*murileguli*) who had illegally obtained codicils of dignities, and in the sixth century the status of a *murilegulus* was often preferred to that of a *curialis*.[30]

These factories were like the *fabricae* quite considerable establishments: the weavers both at Cyzicus and at Caesarea were an important element in the population in the fourth century. We know very little of the way in which they were run, except that each weaving factory was expected to produce a fixed number of garments per year. The workers presumably received rations like the public slaves of the *cursus publicus*.[31]

How they were provided with their raw materials is not clear. Flax and wool were levied in kind from Egyptian villages in the fourth century, and were presumably forwarded to the factories. A law of 395 records that materials (*species*) were compulsorily purchased for the *gynaecium* of Carthage from the *corporati* of the city, and another of 374 distinguishes the *linteones* (of the state factory) from 'the Scythopolitan linenweavers subject to the public levy' (obnoxios Scytopolitanos linyfos publico canoni'). These laws suggest that in some towns the guilds of private weavers had to deliver to the local factory either yarn or fabrics for finishing. The dye works produced their own dyes. The principal task of the *murileguli* or *conchylioleguli* was, as their name suggests, fishing for the murex. Their boats seem to have been maintained on a system similar to that of the *navicularii*, for a law of 424 rules that the possessions of *murileguli* which have come to be held by outsiders by whatever title are to be restored to their original owners, unless the present holders are willing to undertake the service attached to them.[32]

In the early fifth century, when the levy of *vestes* had been commuted to gold, and the troops generally received money allowances for uniform, the factories received cash grants. A law of 423 enjoins that five-sixths of the sum raised by the commuted levy should be distributed in cash to the troops, and the remaining sixth paid to the *gynaecia*, which are to produce uniforms for recruits and private soldiers. The government factories seem at no time to have produced enough clothes to meet more than a small fraction of the state's requirements. Throughout the fourth century there were regular levies of garments in kind, and the law of 423 suggests that by that date the factories produced only a sixth of the uniforms required.[33]

The government claimed a monopoly of marble quarrying, but did not often exercise it. Thus in 320 a general licence was given to all and sundry to quarry marble, and in 363, owing to the high price which marbles were fetching, a similar general licence was issued. In 382 quarries were ordered to pay a tenth of their product to the government, as well as a tenth to the owner of the land. In 393, however, private extraction of marble was prohibited in the interests of the state quarries. Of these there were three of outstanding importance in the East, at Alexandria Troas, at Docimium in Phrygia and in the island of Proconnesus in the Propontis. Little is known of the management of state quarries. In some convict labour was employed. During the Great Persecution many Christians were sent to the quarries of Egypt, including the famous porphyry and granite quarries of the Mons Porphyrites and Mons Claudianus in the Eastern Desert, and condemnation to the mines or quarries (*ad metallum*) remained a standard penalty for humble criminals. In Justinian's day the three great marble quarries were still worked by convicts. In the fourth century the corvée was also used in Egypt, villages being required to send masons, carpenters and labourers to work in the alabaster quarries at Alexandria for periods of from three months to a year.[34]

The organisation of mining is most obscure. Some mines were, at any rate in the fourth century, worked by convict labour; we hear of many Christians being sent to the copper mines of Phaeno in southern Palestine. For the most part, however, the miners (*metallarii*) were free men, bound to their place and trade by a hereditary tie. Gold miners (and gold washers) had to pay to the *largitiones* an annual quantum of gold per head, fixed in 365 at 8 scruples in Illyricum, in Asiana and Pontica at 7 scruples in 392: in addition they had to sell the balance of what they produced to the *largitiones* at 'competent prices' fixed by it, presumably paid in denarii. Valentinian I hoped that these conditions would attract volunteers into the industry, but his expectations were not fulfilled. On the contrary, he and his brother had to conduct a regular hunt for gold miners who had migrated and taken up agricultural work on private and imperial estates, and during the invasion of Thrace in 378 many of them, who were oppressed by the heavy demands of the treasury, fled to the Goths, who welcomed them as expert guides. Further measures to reclaim miners who had transferred themselves to agriculture had to be taken in 424.[35]

The important gold mining areas in the western Balkans were under the control of the *comes metallorum per Illyricum*, and under him there were in the provinces of Macedonia, Inland Dacia, Upper Moesia and Dardania *procuratores metallorum* who collected their dues from the miners: the office was filled by decurions supplied by the city councils. No similar organisation is recorded for the adjacent gold mining areas of the Thracian diocese, or elsewhere. Some gold mining areas (*metallica loca*) were state property, but they might be acquired by private persons, who were bound to carry on production.[36]

Nothing is known of the organisation of the silver mines and very little of copper and iron mining. Basil speaks of the iron producing area of the Taurus, and asks the praetorian prefect, Modestus, to reduce the contribution of iron from its inhabitants. The Codes also mention a contribution of copper (*conlatio aeris*), which might be commuted for gold at a rate of one solidus for 25 lb. This levy is spoken of as being paid by landowners, and from another law it appears that landowners could change over, by the government's permission, from the regular taxation of the *annona* to 'the gold, copper and iron payment' (*auraria aeraria atque ferraria praestatio*). It is difficult to put together any very coherent picture from these scattered hints, but it would appear that the mines were not large-scale enterprises manned by groups of labourers under the management of imperial officials or contractors, but little shafts worked by independent miners, or perhaps small groups. The state owned most of the gold mining areas and monopolised all production of gold, but it only exacted a levy, no doubt sufficient to meet its needs for the mints and arms factories, on the owners of copper and iron mining districts.[37]

The state thus manufactured in its own factories all the arms and armour and a proportion of the uniforms required for the army and the civil service. It produced the marble needed for its public works from its own quarries and also levied a royalty of a tenth in kind from private quarries. It obtained the gold (and probably the silver) required for the mints from its own mines, and levied in kind from the owners of the metalliferous areas the copper and iron needed for the mints and arms factories. In the late third and the fourth centuries it obtained most of its remaining requirements by levies in kind assessed on the land. It secured in this way not only foodstuffs of all kinds, wheat, barley, meat, wine and oil, to feed the troops, the civil service, the population of the capitals, its industrial employees and the personnel of the post, together with the horses of the army and the horses, mules and oxen of the post; but also these animals themselves, and the raw material for the state factories, such as wool and flax for the weaving mills, and charcoal for the mints and arms factories. Public works were also built and repaired by levies of material and labour assessed on the land. Among the *sordida munera* to which landowners were liable are included the provision of craftsmen and labourers, the burning of lime and the supply of timber.[38]

These levies did not necessarily eliminate the private trader. The landowner did not always produce or possess the objects demanded in tax, and in that case he had to buy them. Lactantius complains that Galerius' regular indictions were so exorbitant that landowners had no crops left to sell, to obtain the money wherewith to buy the gold and garments required by his special levies for the *vicennalia*.

For practical convenience also certain levies were commuted: the collectors could not levy horses or uniforms in fractions from smallholders, and preferred to exact money payments and buy them from dealers. The role of the merchants must however have been greatly reduced by the levy system, and the contractor eliminated by the corvée.[39]

As from the late fourth century onwards levies in kind were progressively commuted for gold, and for issues in kind were substituted gold payments, the private trader must have gained by the change. Civil servants and soldiers when they received a cash uniform allowance must have bought their clothes from private dealers, and in so far as their *annona* and *capitus* were paid in gold, they must likewise have bought their food on the market. The corn for Rome and Constantinople was, however, always levied in kind, and in the Eastern empire a sufficient proportion of the land tax was generally paid in kind to supply rations for the field army at any rate. Moreover, when the government required additional foodstuffs it resorted to compulsory purchase (*coemptio*, συνωνή) direct from the landowners, the price of the supplies being deducted from their gold tax, or, if it exceeded the amount of their tax, paid in cash. According to a law of Anastasius this procedure was to be used only in emergencies and required special imperial authorization except in the diocese of Thrace.

In the West, where the taxes had by the middle of the fifth century been entirely commuted to gold, *coemptio* was regularly employed to obtain supplies; it is attested in Italy both under Theoderic and after the reconquest under Justinian. Supplies were sometimes compulsorily purchased from the merchants of the province concerned in addition to the amounts bought from landowners: this was regular in Thrace. In some provinces of Italy (Apulia and Calabria) under Justinian the landowners paid a surtax (*superindicticium*) to be relieved of the burden of *coemptio*, and all the supplies required were compulsorily purchased from the local merchants. The merchants concerned are clearly not importers or exporters, but dealers who bought corn, wine, oil or meat from the landowners and peasants for local sale.[40]

Many large landowners, great senators and the major churches, followed the example of the government on a smaller scale, supplying some of their needs from their own estates. According to Olympiodorus Roman senators took approximately a quarter of their rents in kind—corn, wine and other agricultural produce: we possess a letter from one of them, Lauricius, formerly *praepositus sacri cubiculi* of Honorius, directing the agent of his Sicilian estates 'if a ship can be found which is by good luck sailing for the port of Ravenna at a suitable date, dispatch the produce for the requirements of our house there, and if it happens that you do not find one which is coming to Ravenna, it should be sent to the City (Rome) and stored in our granary'. The church of Ravenna obtained from a group of estates in the neighbourhood (one was at Patavium) dues in pork (3,760 lb.), honey (3,460 lb.), geese (numbers lost), fowls (888), chickens (266) and eggs (8,880); these were allotted to the bishop for hospitality. Gregory the Great obtained the bulk of the corn needed for feeding the Roman poor from the Sicilian estates of the patrimony of Peter (by purchase from the tenants), and cut timber from the south Italian estates to roof a church in Rome. Bertram, bishop of Cenomani, left to his church a pine wood near Burdigala which he had bought together with a pitch works and its hands, so that pitch could be annually delivered to Cenomani for the use of the church. Most landlords seem, like Lauricius, to have relied on commercial shippers to transport their goods, but the church of Alexandria operated not only a fleet of Nile boats, but a small flotilla of seagoing ships, for exporting the surplus corn from its estates and importing its needs from abroad such as timber. This tendency of great landlords to supply their basic needs from their own estates must have diminished the trade in foodstuffs and other raw materials, but for luxuries and for manufactured goods in general the wealthy probably depended on the commercial market.[41]

The state, and to a lesser extent great landlords, thus cut a considerable sector out of the market by supplying their own needs directly. In what remained of the market private commerce was hampered by two important factors, the high cost and slowness of transport and the low purchasing power of the mass of the population.

Diocletian's tariff of prices gives us accurate information on the cost of transport. The authorised charge per mile for a wagon load of 1,200 lbs. is 20 denarii, for a camel load of 600 lbs. 8 denarii, for a donkey load 4 denarii. A *modius* of wheat, which is priced at 100 denarii, weighs 20 lbs., so that a wagon would carry 60 *modii* and a camel 30. A wagon load of wheat, therefore, costing 6,000 denarii, would be doubled in price by a journey of 300 miles, a camel load by a journey of 375 miles. Maritime rates are very much cheaper, especially for long journeys. The charge per *modius* from Alexandria to Rome, some 1,250 miles, is 16 denarii,

from Alexandria to Byzantium 12; the highest rate quoted, from
Syria to Lusitania, is about 26 denarii. It was cheaper to ship
grain from one end of the Mediterranean to the other than to
cart it 75 miles. Against this must be set the risk, very considerable
in ancient conditions, of total or partial loss by shipwreck or
jettison and of spoiling by sea water.[42]

Pack camels and donkeys move at about a man's walking pace,
oxen at about two miles an hour. Land transport was therefore
very slow. Sea transport under favourable weather conditions
was much faster, but contrary winds might cause much delay—
ancient ships could not beat against the wind—and storms might
compel long waits in harbour. Numerous accounts of voyages
illustrate the vagaries of sea travel. Sulpicius Severus' friend
Postumianus sailed from Narbo to Carthage in five days, a good
run, but on the voyage from Carthage to Alexandria was held up
in the Syrtis by bad weather for a week and took another week
to make Alexandria. For his return he found a ship bound with
a cargo for Narbo, and reached Massilia in thirty days. Gregory of
Nazianzus was unwise enough to take a passage on an Aeginetan
ship from Alexandria to Greece in the winter season and was
involved in a bad storm from which they took shelter in Rhodes.
Mark the deacon undertook many voyages for Porphyry, bishop
of Gaza. He sailed in thirteen days from Ascalon to Thessalonica
to settle up Porphyry's estate and returned in twelve, both good
runs. Then he sailed to Constantinople to deliver a letter to John
Chrystostom, taking twenty days: his return voyage was much
speedier, ten days only. Later he accompanied a party of bishops
to Constantinople. They embarked at Caesarea, arrived at Rhodes
in ten days, and at Constantinople in another ten: the return voyage
was again much quicker, only five days to Rhodes, and despite
a storm only another six to Maiuma, the port of Gaza.[43]

Synesius gives a tragi-comic account of a dreadful passage he
endured from Alexandria to Ptolemais. It was a small boat with
only twelve hands; the captain and half the crew were Jews.
The captain was heavily in debt and had sold all the spare gear,
leaving only one sail and one anchor, and the crew were all cripples.
Nevertheless he carried fifty passengers, including a number of
soldiers and about fifteen women; a part of the deck was screened
off with an old sail for their accommodation. In the afternoon a
storm blew up, but as it was Friday, no sooner did the sun set,
than the pious captain abandoned the tiller and despite protests
and threats refused to break the Sabbath till half way through the
night, when, remarking gloomily, 'We are clearly in danger of
death and the Law permits it', he resumed the helm, and managed

next morning to put in on the desert shore. After waiting two days for the storm to abate they put out again, but after two days' run were becalmed. They then ran into another storm which broke their mast, and ran aground in a desolate spot, whence a local fisherman piloted them to a sheltered but equally desolate bay. They had by now run out of provisions and had to catch fish to assuage their hunger. All these adventures occurred on a coasting voyage of less than 600 miles.[44]

It must be remembered, moreover, that during the winter season navigation was normally suspended. Vegetius declares that the seas were absolutely closed for the four months from 11 November to 10 March, and were very dangerous for all the seven months from 22 September to 27 May. The two years' period allowed to *navicularii* for the return voyage from Alexandria to Constantinople shows how incalculable were the hazards of the sea and what very long delays they might sometimes impose. In these circumstances perishable goods could not be objects of long-distance trade.[45]

Merchant ships varied greatly in capacity. The imperial government thought it worth while to charter ships of as small a capacity as 2,000 *modii* for the transport of *annona* from Egypt to Constantinople, which implies that such tiny boats of less than 15 tons (deadweight) must have been quite common. Under the Principate a minimum tonnage of 10,000 *modii* was required for ships in the regular service of the *annona* and a law of Valens suggests that this rule still applied in the fourth century. According to Procopius the fleet assembled to convey Belisarius' army to Africa contained no ship under 3,000 *medimni* (Thucydidean Greek for 18,000 *modii* or about 120 tons), while the largest, in our text, were rated at 50,000 *medimni*; this figure is however certainly corrupt—a ship of this capacity would have been half as large again as the monster ships specially built to carry obelisks—and should perhaps be 5,000 (30,000 *modii*). One of the corn ships belonging to the church of Alexandria is said to have been of two myriads (20,000 *modii* or about 130 tons), and John Moschus speaks of a ship of three and a half myriads (35,000 *modii* or about 230 tons) as being unusually large: the shipper who built it was unable to launch it though he put 300 men on to the job. Elsewhere he records as exceptional a ship of five myriads (330 tons deadweight). This is the largest vessel of which we have reliable record.[46]

Since cartage was so very expensive inland waterways were greatly favoured for heavy transport. The importance of Egypt to the corn supply lay not only in its fertile and regularly watered soil, but in the fact that no part of the country lay far from the

Nile or a navigable canal. The establishment of the *limes* along the Rhine and the Danube was probably dictated as much by logistics as by strategical considerations. In the fourth century the army of the Rhine was supplied by sea and river from Britain, and in the sixth century the army of the lower Danube was evidently supplied from maritime provinces of the Mediterranean via the Bosphorus: this explains the curious group of provinces—Lower Moesia and Scythia on the one hand, the Islands, Caria and Cyprus on the other—which Justinian placed under the *quaestor exercitus*, who was quartermaster of the lower Danube *limes*. The Upper Danube frontier, because it was not easily accessible by water, evidently presented great difficulties of supply. Two units under the *dux* of Raetia were converted into supply trains, and when exemptions from furnishing animals for the post were granted, the requirements of the Raetian *limes* and Illyrian expeditions were expressly excepted.[47]

Grain seems never to have been carted for any considerable distance except by the imperial government, which did not have to count the cost. Commercially the grain trade did not pay by land. In big towns the price of grain was, it is true, substantially higher than in small, because it had to be carried from greater distances. According to Julian wheat was normally sold at Antioch 15 *modii* to the solidus, which was twice the general rate prevailing in Egypt or Africa; he no doubt exaggerated in order to magnify his own achievement in selling wheat at this figure during a shortage, but his statement implies that wheat not infrequently reached this figure in Antioch. But even the higher prices prevailing in the big towns did not attract corn from far. Julian prided himself on having got grain during a famine to Antioch, presumably with the aid of the *cursus publicus*, from Hierapolis, which is not much over 100 miles away, and even from Chalcis, at about half that distance, and he eventually had to fall back on Egyptian supplies. In an inland town, such as Caesarea of Cappadocia, there was little hope if the local crops failed: as Gregory of Nazianzus explains, 'coastal cities support such shortages without much difficulty, as they can dispose of their own products and receive supplies by sea; for us inland our surpluses are unprofitable and our scarcities irremediable, as we have no means of disposing of what we have or of importing what we lack'. It was for this reason that towns had so often to subsidise the import of corn; if there was a local shortage, and corn had to be imported from farther afield, the price had to be artificially reduced.[48]

Conversely, inland regions could not dispose of their surplus corn. Both Procopius and John Lydus complain that when Justinian abolished the *cursus publicus* in various parts—John specifies the diocese of Asia—and the government ceased to buy grain or accept it as tax, 'the unsold crops rotted on the estates, Asia being almost all arable, and the taxpayer was ruined when the tax collectors demanded gold instead of crops, since he could not sell his crops, living far from the sea'. The situation became even worse, he laments, when the military units stationed in the area were moved elsewhere, with the result that 'the taxes were converted to gold, and the crops were ploughed in year by year'.[49]

Long-distance trade in corn was thus commercially profitable only when the corn was grown in areas close to a port or inland waterway, and the market was a large town which lay on the sea or on a navigable river. Wine and oil, being more valuable in proportion to their bulk, were probably more important objects of trade. Special vintages which commanded a high price were always worth transporting, and sometimes ordinary wine was carried some distance overland. In the sixth century Cappadocians, whose country was ill fitted for viticulture, brought wine in bulk from Syria. Africa was still exporting large quantities of oil when the Arabs conquered it in the seventh century, and oil was still being imported to Marseilles in the sixth.[50]

Fruit and vegetables could not travel far owing to the slowness of transport, and big towns seem to have been supplied from their immediate neighbourhood. At Constantinople there was an important guild of market gardeners, who leased suburban estates for the cultivation of vegetables and fruit trees. Justinian had to legislate against their sharp practices: they took over the existing stock at a valuation, and on surrendering the lease were compensated for the stock which they left and for improvements, such as manuring or planting trees. As the valuers were members of the guild, landlords always found that the initial valuation was very low and the final one very high.[51]

Meat could only be transported on the hoof or salted; salt meat was conveyed considerable distances by the government for the use of the troops, and pigs were driven on the hoof from Lucania and cattle from Bruttium to supply the Roman people with pork and beef—losing some 15% or 20% of their weight on the journey. But this was again a government enterprise: we hear of no large-scale private trade in meat. There is one record of long-distance trade in fish. In 615 Bertram, bishop of Cenomani, bequeathed his house at Burdigala to a nephew but stipulated that he must give lodging to the agents of the church of Cenomani who were sent to Burdigala 'pro piscibus ad negotiandum'.[52]

Some of the raw materials of industry must have been transported over considerable distances. Iron and copper, for instance, were universally needed, and were mined in limited areas only. High grade wools, being both easily portable and relatively expensive, were also probably carried long distances. The tariff of Diocletian prices Atrebatic wool (from northern Gaul) at 200 denarii the pound, Tarentine (from Apulia) at 175, Laodicene (from Phrygia) at 150 and Asturian at 100. As against this, 'best medium wool' is tariffed at 50 denarii and 'other wool' at 25. It would clearly be worth while for a merchant to carry the superior wools to distant markets by pack animal.[53]

The imperial government carted valuable marbles considerable distances regardless of cost, and so also did wealthy senators, though they preferred to make illicit use of the public post. Big timber had also to be conveyed over long distances. Gregory the Great, requiring long beams for the church of Peter and Paul, ordered the subdeacon Sabinus, the rector of the patrimony in those parts, to fell twenty trees in Bruttium. Hauling them to the sea was a formidable undertaking, and Gregory asked his namesake the ex-prefect, who leased land in the neighbourhood from the church, the *dux* Arogis, who also owned estates in the area, and the local bishop, Stephanus, all to furnish men and oxen. Egypt, which was destitute of large trees, always had to import timber. Eulogius, patriarch of Alexandria, asked Gregory for timber, offering to pay for it, an offer which was politely refused. He later complained that the timber sent was too short, but Gregory answered that the ship sent to fetch it was too small. It is not known if Eulogius ever got his long beams, as in his last letter on the subject Gregory explains that the ship will not take the timber he had had felled and that he is reluctant to saw it up.[54]

The laws allude to the owners of private quarries transporting marble by sea and selling it; senators were in 376 exempted from customs dues on the marble that they cut from their own quarries. But there is no evidence of any regular trade in building stone or timber. For ordinary purposes local stone or brick was used, and if timber was lacking, builders made do without it. In one of his letters Gregory of Nyssa describes a chapel he has planned. It was an ambitious structure, an octagon with four rectangular chambers and four apses projecting from it, and an inner colonnade of eight columns. He asks a friend to send him some masons skilled in vaulting, and explains apologetically: 'the scarcity of timber induces me to roof the whole building in stone, because there is no building timber in these parts.' And, he adds, skilled freemasons are no use to him, for the local materials are brick and odd stones. In the timberless area south of Damascus buildings were not only roofed with beams of basalt; even doors and windows were made of basalt slabs.[55]

Manufactured articles would bear the cost of transport better, being more valuable in proportion to their bulk and weight, but here we must consider the second factor unfavourable to trade, the poverty of the market. The vast majority of the population of the empire were peasants, whose standard of living was low and whose needs were simple. The working classes in the towns seem to have been as poor, to judge by the difficulty they had in paying a solidus or two every four or five years for the *collatio lustralis*. This meant that the global demand for manufactured goods was very low. Trade in manufactured goods was even more restricted, for the mass of the population could afford only the cheapest and simplest articles, and these were locally produced.

Humble urban craftsmen supplied most of the basic needs of the towns and of the immediately surrounding areas, and where cities were thickly set they probably provided the countryside with manufactured goods. But where cities were widely spaced and their territories large, the needs of outlying villages were supplied by the rural potter and smith, whom Valentinian I declared immune from the *collatio lustralis*, and we may add, by the rural weaver. Libanius in his panegyric on Antioch boasts that in its territory were 'many large and populous villages, with larger populations than not a few cities, which have craftsmen as in towns, and exchange their products with one another through fairs'.[56]

The large village of Aphrodito in the territory of Antaeopolis had a substantial number of craftsmen. A petition to Justinian is signed first by the clergy, eleven priests and a deacon, then by twenty-two principal farmers (κτήτορες), two notaries, the headman of the village, the tax collector and his assistant, and by six headmen of guilds, including the smiths, carpenters, weavers, fullers and boatbuilders and also a wine merchant. A contemporary tax list shows in addition to about one hundred names with no trade specified, presumably peasant proprietors, nine bakers, six butchers, five greengrocers, two millers, three beekeepers, a dyer, eight fullers, four or five linen weavers, a group of wool weavers, three tailors, a group of shoemakers, one potter, three carpenters and two boatbuilders, a group of coppersmiths and five goldsmiths, not to speak of a notary, a letter writer and a barber. The potter must have had quite a big business and employed assistants, for he paid 2,400 wine jars a year as rent for one-third of a pottery to the proprietors, two ladies; he presumably also leased the other two-thirds from the monastery into whose hands they had passed.[57]

A striking example of the dispersal of industry is afforded by the weaving trade. Weaving was a basic and important industry, for even the poorest had to possess some clothes and renew them at intervals, and little clothing was home made. There was some domestic weaving in large households. Pope Pelagius, giving instructions on which slaves are to be picked from an estate part of which had accrued to the church, specified that domestic servants and craftsmen, 'men perhaps who could be useful for wool weaving', are to be rejected in favour of agricultural slaves. Such domestic weaving was, however, not important, and the poor generally bought their clothes from a professional weaver. This point is illustrated by an anecdote told by Augustine. Florentius, a poor cobbler of Hippo, lost his one and only *casula*, and in his distress prayed the Twenty Martyrs to succour him. As he prayed small boys jeered at him, 'as if he had asked the Martyrs for 50 *folles* each wherewith to buy clothes'. He was not granted the 1,000 *folles* which a *casula* would, it is to be inferred, have cost him, but on the sea shore he found a large fish, which he sold to a cook for 300 *folles*. With the money he planned 'to buy wool so that his wife could make up something for him to wear as best she could'. Even a poor cobbler, it would appear, normally bought his clothes ready made.[58]

Clothes are easily portable objects, even more portable than the raw materials out of which they are made, and here if anywhere large-scale manufacture and trade might seem to have been practicable and profitable. The Diocletianic tariff, however, suggests that it was only high quality garments whose production was concentrated in a few towns, whence they were exported to all parts of the empire. The facts are most clearly set out with regard to linen garments. Here five local brands are recognised, of which the most expensive is the Scythopolitan, next the Tarsian, then the Byblian, then the Laodicene, and finally what is called the Tarsian Alexandrian, which means fabrics of Tarsian style produced at Alexandria. Each of these brands is divided into three grades (*formae*). Thus a shirt (στιχή) from Scythopolis cost 7,000, 6,000 or 5,000 denarii according to its grade, while one from Alexandria cost 4,000, 3,000 or 2,000. As compared with these named brands, a military shirt, which would have been substantial if plain, cost according to grade 1,500, 1,250 or 1,000, and shirts 'of rough linen for the use of commoners and slaves' half these prices.[59]

There are similar scales for men's (women's) dalmatics, which range from 10,000 (11,000), to 2,000 (3,000) in the named brands, whereas 'those which are inferior to the above mentioned third grade but are manufactured in more places' are priced at 2,500 to 1,500 (1750), and those 'for the use of commoners and slaves' at 800 (1,000) to 500 (600). Very similar ranges of prices are quoted for half a dozen other garments. Other towns specialised in linen mattresses and bolsters. Antinoopolis and Tralles produced the best only, at 2,750 denarii, Damascus and Cyprus three grades at 1,750, 1,250 and 800: below these named brands come inferior grades at 600, 500 and 400, and those 'for the use of commoners and slaves' at 350, 300 and 250.[60]

It will thus be seen that not only rough clothes, worn by the working classes, but good plain garments at two or three times the price were produced at a large number of places. The famous weaving cities produced only superior garments; even a third-grade Alexandrian imitation of a Tarsian garment was nearly always priced higher than a first-grade garment made elsewhere, and first-grade Scythopolitan fabrics were priced at about four times as much.

The figures for woollen garments are less systematically set out and have not been so well preserved. A 'best indictional cloak' (χλαμύς), which would have been a good serviceable article, is priced at 4,000 denarii, but a Dardanian single cloak at 7,000, and a double one at 12,500. There was a large range of locally named *birri*, of which the Nervian was the dearest (the actual price is lost). There follow the Taurogastric (of unknown provenance) and imitations of Nervian made at Laodicea of Phrygia, both priced at 10,000, Noric and Ripensian at 8,000, those from Britain, Melitomagus and the Argolid at 6,000, Laodicene at 4,500, Canusian at 4,000, Numidian at 3,000, Achaean and Phrygian at 2,000 and African at 1,500. *Fibulatoria* also show a wide range of prices from Raetic at 12,500, through those of Treviri and Poetovio at 8,000 and 5,000, to African at 2,000, while *saga* show even greater contrasts; Gallic garments from Ambiani and Bituriges cost 8,000, African only 500. Most of these garments would seem to be of the luxury class, but the African may well have been cheap enough to command a wide market.[61]

That good plain weaving was very widely practised is suggested by the general levies of garments made for uniforms in every province and city of the empire and assessed like the *annona* on the land, for these garments had to be of decent quality, as the prices of 'military' shirts and 'indictional' cloaks show. Not every village and landowner, it is true, produced garments woven on the spot: many found it more convenient to buy their quota, or commute their obligation, leaving the collector for the city to buy the garments. But the idea of such a general levy would hardly have occurred to the government unless most areas produced the goods required. Moreover in the diocese of Oriens at any rate the levy was a compulsory purchase, and the government in the early fourth entury paid prices according to Diocletian's tariff: thus the village of Caranis in Egypt in 314 received 24,000 denarii for 24 shirts (στιχάρια; they were evidently of the third grade) and 10,000 denarii for 8 cloaks (πάλλια). Such a system of compulsory purchase at prices which had originally been fair would have been a very strange procedure if the articles purchased had not been local products.[62]

The evidence thus far suggests that there was little long-distance trade in clothes except in expensive high-grade garments which were the speciality of a few famous weaving towns. There is, however, one indication that cheap clothes sometimes travelled considerable distances. Where Pinianus adopted the ascetic life he at first wore sackcloth, but his wife Melania saw that he found this too irritating and persuaded him to buy 'natural coloured Antiochenes' ('Αντιοχίσια ἰδιόχροα), which cost only one solidus (or according to the Latin version only two *tremisses*). It would seem then that at Rome cheap workmen's clothes, probably of linen, were imported from Antioch; and it may be conjectured that woollen garments of similar cheap grades were imported from Africa. There probably was then a market for cheap textiles in the largest cities, and a long-distance trade to supply them.[63]

There was also, as we have seen, some seaborne trade in wheat (and also beans), wine and oil to supply the larger maritime towns. Apart from this the objects of trade were luxury or semiluxury articles for which the rich and well-to-do were prepared to pay a price which would cover the cost of transport. They included high quality textiles, the linens and woollens which were the specialities of famous weaving towns, and also silk, which was imported from China regardless of cost and fetched fantastic prices; engraved silver tableware and superior glassware; jewellery and perfumes and unguents, many of these of oriental origin. Among foodstuffs choice brands of wine travelled far; the sweet wines of Gaza were imported into Ostrogothic Italy, Visigothic Spain and Merovingian Gaul. Exotic spices were also much in demand, notably pepper, which after its long journey from Malabar fetched very high prices; Rome must have held large stocks to be able to pay 3,000 lb. to Alaric in 408 as part of the ransom of the city.[64]

There remains the slave trade. Slaves, in so far as they were objects of commerce, may be reckoned as luxury articles, for they were expensive and they were in the main purchased as personal servants. Slaves were, it is true, used on a considerable scale in some areas for agriculture, but such slaves were almost always homeborn. The imperial weaving mills and dyeworks, the mints and the postal service were also manned by slaves, but these again were hereditary groups, and the government neither bought nor sold its workers. Slaves were also sometimes used in private industrial establishments, but not, it would seem, on any large scale. They were more generally employed in posts of confidence, as managers (*actores* and *procuratores*) by landowners and as clerks and agents (πιστικοί) by business men. But the vast majority were personal and domestic servants.[65]

Rich senators kept vast households, if the denunciations of moralists are to be believed. What is more important, slaves were regarded almost as an essential of life by persons of relatively modest means. In his petition to the Council of Chalcedon Athanasius, the nephew of the late patriarch of Alexandria, Cyril, draws a pitiful picture of how Cyril's successor Dioscorus has reduced him to the utmost penury, so that he is forced to beg his bread for himself and the two or three slaves that remain to him. Libanius, urging the council of Antioch to augment the stipends of his four assistant lecturers, represents them as utterly poverty-stricken on their present scales; they do not marry if they are prudent, they have to live in lodgings like cobblers, they owe money to their bakers and have to sell their wives' trinkets to pay the bill. As a climax Libanius declares that they can afford two or three slaves only, who, not belonging to a proper establishment, are insolent to their masters. Slaves seem to have been a regular institution in the army, in which there were exceptionally good opportunities for acquiring them cheap. A law of Constantine suggests that every non-commissioned officer, even of the lowest grade of *circitor*, had his slave batman, and Sulpicius Severus declares that Martin as a private—in the guards, it is true—was so ascetic that he contented himself with one slave only. Aristocratic hermits and monks who kept only a slave or two to look after them were praised for their self-denial.[66]

Many domestic slaves, in large households most no doubt, were home bred, but one category had to be bought. Castration was strictly prohibited within the bounds of the empire. The law was naturally sometimes broken, but in general eunuchs, who were considered essential in all really high-class households, were imported from abroad, mainly from Persia, Armenia and other

Caucasian lands. They were for the most part the product of piracy, kidnapping and tribal wars. In Justinian's time most eunuchs came from the barbarous and still pagan tribe of the Abasgi on the eastern coast of the Black Sea. Their kings made a regular business of seizing the handsomest boys among their subjects and selling them to dealers, killing their parents to eliminate danger of future vengeance. We are not told what alternative source of supply was found when Justinian converted the Abasgi to Christianity and suppressed the eunuch trade with the monarchy, and it may be that his pious action stimulated the increase in the illicit castration of Roman subjects which shocked the old emperor in 558.[67]

Eunuchs had a high scarcity value. The casualty rate in castration was, owing to primitive surgical methods, enormous: according to information submitted to Justinian out of ninety victims only three survived. Justinian for purposes of valuation in certain legal cases put their price at 30 solidi for a boy under 10, 50 for an untrained adult, and 70 for a trained adult. But ordinary slaves were by no means cheap. Justinian's figures are 10 solidi for a child under 10, 20 for an unskilled man or woman, and 30 for a man or woman skilled in any craft; a trained clerk was valued at 50 and a doctor at 60. The few recorded prices confirm these valuations. A Gaulish boy aged 14 was sold at Ascalon in 359 for 18 solidi from one soldier to another. In the early fifth century a man who sold himself to a pair of actors realised 20 solidi, while in the early seventh another, an African collector of customs who was sold to a Jerusalem silversmith, fetched as much as 30 solidi; and this though he was sold incognito not as a clerk but as a general houseboy, who did washing and cooking and waited at table. It is significant also that Roman senators preferred to pay *aurum tironicum* at 5 lb. of silver or 25 solidi per man rather than part with their domestic slaves and *coloni* as recruits. Some lower prices are recorded. Remigius, bishop of Rheims, mentions in his will that he had bought a man named Friaredus for 14 solidi 'to prevent his being killed': in the circumstances he was no doubt sold off cheap. The Council of Matisco in 583 ordained that Jews must surrender their Christian slaves, but compensated them at the rate of 12 solidi each: the compensation in this case is not likely to have been generous. In a late fifth century African document a six-year old boy is sold for one solidus and 700 *folles* (probably equivalent to 3 solidi in all). At Hermopolis 4 solidi were paid in the sixth century for a little black girl, 'Atalous by name, renamed by you (the purchaser) Eutychia, about 12 years of age more or less, an Aloan by race'.[68]

The main lawful source of slaves for the market was the barbarians beyond the frontiers. Prisoners of war did not perhaps often come on the market, as the government preferred to enrol them in the army, or settle them on the land as *laeti* or sell or grant them to landowners as *coloni*, in which status they would still, with their descendants, be liable to military service. But no doubt soldiers often managed to secure prisoners for themselves, and kidnapping and intertribal wars produced a regular flow of barbarian slaves into the empire. Themistius denounces the tribunes and *praepositi* of the frontier forces as being more interested in the slave trade than in their military duties, and Ammianus vividly describes how the *comes* and the *dux* on the lower Danube in 378 exploited the famine among the immigrant Goths, buying their children for a mere song, and selling them all over Thrace. Prices were substantially lower in the frontier areas than in Italy. Symmachus at Rome thought it worth while to ask Flavian, the praetorian prefect of Italy, then presumably in Illyricum, to buy him twenty stable boys, 'since on the frontier slaves are easy to come by and the price is usually tolerable'.[69]

This source was supplemented in various illegal or quasi legal ways. In the strict theory of Roman law the liberty of a Roman citizen was on Roman territory inalienable; he could only become a slave if he were taken beyond the frontiers, and on returning to Roman territory he automatically reacquired his liberty by *postliminium*. There were, however, a number of loopholes in the law. If parents exposed their children they were debarred from later reclaiming them, and those who brought up foundlings could treat them as slaves, until Justinian altered the law and made foundlings free persons. Parents could also sell newborn infants (*sanguinolenti*), but in this case under a law of Constantine had the right of redeeming them later for a fair price. A Visigothic law fixed this at one solidus for each year of their age up to ten, this being deemed the cost of feeding them; ten was the maximum, it being held that after ten the children would have earned their keep by their services.[70]

Parents were forbidden to sell older children or to pledge them for debt, but it is abundantly clear that despite the law they frequently did so. Constantine admitted as much in granting allowances of food and clothing to poor parents, to prevent their selling their children. It is a regular complaint that poor craftsmen and shopkeepers had to sell their children to pay the *chrysargyron*. How little the law was regarded is shown by a constitution of Valentinian III which records that during a famine in Italy in 450 large numbers of people had been driven to sell their children and relatives and specially enacts that they may recover their freedom on repaying the purchasers the price received plus 20%; the typical prices cited, five or ten solidi, suggest that slaves had been obtainable at bargain prices owing to the crisis. Rufinus gives a specific case of a taxpayer who owed 300 solidi to the treasury and had to sell his three children in his attempt to raise this sum, while in a petition from Egypt dated 569 Martha records that her father Menas, having fallen into utter poverty, had pledged her sister for one solidus, and that she had by her trade as a saltfish seller saved up half a solidus to redeem her.[71]

Adults who allowed themselves to be sold did not in strict law prejudice their freedom, but if a person over twenty not only acquiesced in such a transaction but received a part of the price for himself, he became a slave. We know of a few self-sales, but they were made for religious motives; more commonly the transaction was no doubt due to extreme poverty or to debt.[72]

Many thousands of Roman citizens were captured by barbarian raiders from the frontier provinces, and later from the heart of the empire, when the barbarians broke through the defensive ring. Very many such prisoners were redeemed by their relatives and friends, or by the church; bishops were allowed to pawn or sell the church plate for this charitable purpose, and Justinian even permitted the churches of Moesia, which were particularly hard pressed, to alienate real property. But large numbers were sold back into the empire as slaves. Such persons did not technically forfeit their free status but their purchasers could hold them as slaves in pledge until they could refund the price which had been paid for them, either by realising their property or by the help of friends or relatives. Many who had no resources and were sold far from their homes must have fallen into slavery permanently, and in 408 Honorius introduced a more merciful rule that such persons could redeem themselves by five years' service. Even so it is probable that many failed to assert their rights. Theodoret tells a romantic story of a little girl, Maria, who was captured by the Vandals in Africa and sold by them to merchants who sold her in Cyrrhus, together with a faithful slave of her family. The slave told the story, and the local garrison raised a subscription, bought her from her owner and entrusted her to Theodoret. Ten months later news came through that her father Eudaemon was not only alive but held office in the West, and Theodoret arranged for her repatriation. Here all ended happily, but there must have been many helpless persons, especially children, who were not so lucky.[73]

Despite the many sources from which they were drawn it would seem that demand exceeded supply. Slaves were dear in the interior of the empire, though relatively cheap on the frontiers: it would seem that the local market absorbed most near the source of supply. Another indication of the shortage of slaves is the common use of indentured free persons instead of slaves as personal servants. We have a number of contracts of service (παραμονή) from Egypt, in which a free person indentures himself— or is indentured by his parents—to serve for a term of years, specifying sometimes in great detail what board or wages, clothes and perquisites he is to receive, as—to quote an unusually outspoken document—'a resident domestic slave boy'. Such contracts are often made in consideration of a loan or advance of wages.[74]

There were certainly merchants who imported eunuchs and other barbarian slaves and bought Roman captives from the barbarians. Both the black girl Atalous and Maria of Carthage had passed through the hands of slave merchants. In the late sixth century there was a substantial slave trade from Gaul to Italy. Many of the merchants were Jews and Pope Gregory was prepared to tolerate their buying Christians—which was strictly against the law—if they did so on commission on behalf of Christian purchasers, or sold them within forty days of their arrival in Italy. Much of the traffic, however, was by private treaty between one owner and another. The total volume of the trade, catering as it did normally for the wealthy and well-to-do, cannot have been very large.[75]

We may now attempt to draw some picture of the commercial and industrial classes in the empire. In the larger villages, as we have seen, whether those of freeholders or those on the great estates, there were craftsmen—potters, carpenters, smiths, weavers and fullers—who sold their products direct to their customers, and dealers in foodstuffs—bakers, butchers, beekeepers and vegetable sellers. The villagers exchanged their products at rural fairs, and at these they could buy from travelling merchants goods not produced in the district, and sell to them local specialities which would command a good price elsewhere. Theodoret tells a story of such a fair at Immae, a large village in Antiochene territory about twenty-five miles from the city, which attracted merchants in large numbers from all parts: a merchant who had sold all his stock and had his wallet full of gold was murdered as he travelled away. Cassiodorus describes another fair, which seems to have been on a rather larger scale, held on St. Cyprian's day near Consilinum in Lucania. At its stalls could be bought the products of Campania, Bruttium, Apulia and Calabria: it was a notable cattle market, clothes of all kinds were on sale, and boys and girls—the children of needy parents—could be purchased as slaves. Here again local peasants had set upon the merchants as they left and despoiled them. Apollonius the retired merchant (ἀπὸ πραγματευτῶν), who became a monk in the Nitrian desert, was probably such a travelling merchant: knowing no craft whereby he could keep himself, he bought a stock of medicines and dainties, such as grapes, pomegranates, eggs and white bread, and made his living by hawking them round the cells of sick monks.[76]

All peasants had to sell a part of their crops, if freeholders, to buy such household necessities as they did not produce themselves and to pay their money taxes, if tenants, to pay their rent (if not in kind) as well. There were village merchants who bought the local crops and carried them to town: a wine merchant is recorded at Aphrodito and Theodoret tells of a certain Abraham, who, wishing to convert a pagan village of freeholders, rented a house there and set up as a merchant in walnuts, the principal (export) crop of the place. There were also professional carriers, who owned pack animals—donkeys, mules or camels—on which they carried agricultural produce to the cities. Libanius protests against the unfairness of pressing such men to carry builders' rubbish out of the city on their return journey. They were kept waiting all day, their sacks were torn and made filthy with mud, and their beasts worn out by the heavy loads.[77]

The smaller cities did not differ substantially from the larger villages: they too served as markets for the produce of the surrounding countryside, and their craftsmen supplied the needs of the townsfolk and the neighbouring villages. The larger the city the greater was the number and variety of the craftsmen and of the dealers in foodstuffs, wholesale and retail, including corn merchants who bought up and stored the crops and sold them to the local retailers and bakers. Corn merchants and retailers are mentioned at inland cities like Caesarea of Cappadocia, which neither exported nor imported corn, and it was evidently from such local dealers that compulsory purchases of corn were sometimes made by the government.[78]

In the metropoleis of provinces and the other great cities, university towns like Athens or Berytus, or centres of pilgrimage like Jerusalem, there would be dealers in high quality imported goods and superior craftsmen, catering for both the local notables and those of the province, and in some cases for students and pilgrims. Some cities, where there were government arms or clothing factories, or where high quality goods were produced for export, like Scythopolis, Tarsus, Laodicea of Syria and Byblus with their linens, or Mutina, Ambiani, Bituriges, Treviri or Poetovio with their woollens, had a considerable industrial population. Then there were the great ports which handled most of the long-distance trade, usually, like Arles or Ephesus, at the mouth of an important river, along which barges plied collecting agricultural produce; and lesser ports which tapped a smaller area, with their merchants, shipbuilders, sailors and dockers.

Finally, there were the great cities of the empire. Some of these were important primarily as markets. An extreme case is Rome. Here there was a large resident population of wealthy senators and clergy, and a constant flow of visitors, students, pilgrims, litigants, bishops attending councils, literary men giving lectures; and to serve their needs merchants, artists, craftsmen and shopkeepers, dockers, porters and labourers. There was a heavy flow of imports to Rome, and a busy industry to cope with local needs, but it was neither a commercial nor a manufacturing city.

Constantinople seems to have been a rather similar city: Themistius boasts that ships converged on the capital from Asia, Syria and Egypt, bringing in the products of all quarters of the world, but that the only cargo that they carried outward bound was builders' rubbish. Antioch had its two armament factories, and apparently produced cheap linens for export, but Libanius in his great panegyric on the city has very little to say on either trade or industry. He mentions that wine and oil were exported from Antiochene territory, but he praises Seleucia as a port where merchant ships congregated from Europe, Africa and Asia bringing in their finest products, 'since the keen demand attracts merchants' thoughts thither, so that through it we enjoy the products of every land.'[79]

Very different was Alexandria, which was not only an important administrative centre, seat of the Augustal prefect, the *comes Aegypti*, the *praefectus annonae* and the *comes et rationalis summarum Aegypti* with their staffs of officials and barristers; the residence of a patriarch and his numerous clergy; a centre of pilgrimage with its famous shrines of SS. Cosmas and Damian and S. Menas; a university town, celebrated for its school of medicine. It was also a great port, which handled not only the exports of Egypt but the trade with Arabia, East Africa and India. It was also an important industrial town, noted for its linens, its glassware, its papyrus, which supplied the whole empire with writing material, and for many luxury products, such as fine silverware and jewellery and perfumes and unguents made up from oriental imports.[80]

The lowest stratum of the urban population was formed by the casual labourers, who were particularly numerous in the building industry. In the fourth century labour for public works was usually obtained by the corvée system, but the church and private individuals, unless they received an imperial grant, must always have employed hired labour, and by the latter part of the fifth century the state had largely abandoned the corvée. The labourers on a large job must have been a curious mixture if John Moschus' stories are to be believed. Those employed by Ephraem, the *comes Orientis*, in rebuilding Antioch after the disastrous earthquake, included a bishop who found manual labour more tolerable than the cares of his office. Isaurians are also often mentioned among the building labourers at Antioch; these poverty-stricken highlanders were apparently reduced to earning their living by casual labour when they could no longer practise brigandage.[81]

When Anastasius was building the frontier fortress city of Dara, which he had to do quickly in order to present the Persian government with a *fait accompli* before they could object to the breach of treaty, he collected a vast labour force from all quarters by offering very high rates of pay, four carats a day for a man, and eight carats for a man with a donkey. Normally rates were very much lower than this. We hear of labourers in Egypt earning one carat a day, and a monk who, aspiring to buy a beautifully bound copy of the New Testament costing three solidi, took work as a labourer on a cistern which John, the bishop of Jerusalem (516-524), was building got only 5 *folles* a day, which at the current rate of 210 *folles* to the solidus works out at a little over half a carat. Even at this rate, however, a man in full employment could earn 7 solidi a year, about as much as a private soldier got.[82]

Urban craftsmen and shopkeepers were universally organised in guilds (*collegia*): they are commonly called guildsmen (*collegiati*) in the Codes. The guilds were useful to the local and imperial authorities for the collection of the *chrysargyron* and for the imposition of corvées and compulsory services of various kinds (*munera*). Some of the services were for the benefit of the city and directed by the civic authorities; in Majorian's words, the guildsmen had to provide labour services for their native city in rotation under the direction of the *curiales*, and Honorius declares that owing to the flight of the *collegiati* into the country 'the cities robbed of their services have lost the splendour with which in old times they had shone'. The nature of these services is rarely specified in the Codes. The *corporati* of Alexandria had to dredge the river, and it is probable that in Western cities the three guilds of the *dendrofori*, *centonarii* and *fabri* had to provide a fire brigade, as they had under the Principate. Libanius protests against the heavy corvées imposed on the craftsmen and shopkeepers of Antioch, cleaning the drains and re-erecting columns—work which they either had to do themselves or hire labour to perform.[83]

Other services were for the benefit of the imperial government, chiefly in connection with the *cursus publicus*. A law of Valentinian forbids peasants to be pressed into convoying animals (*prosecutio animalium*) and lays this burden on the city guilds, while from Egypt we have nominations of townsmen to perform this duty and also to serve as letter carriers on the *cursus velox*, and as sailors on the public barges which conveyed the *annona* down the Nile. Libanius also records that at Antioch the craftsmen and shopkeepers had to serve and maintain the equipment of the hostelry attached to the local *mansio* of the *cursus publicus*, supplying the beds, tables and tableware and replacing breakages and losses, and serving as cooks, cleaners and attendants.[84]

The guilds were also useful to the local authorities for controlling prices and regulating trade practices for the benefit of the customer—and might be used by their own members to promote their own interests. From the early fourth century, when prices were soaring owing to the rapid depreciation of the denarius, we have a group of declarations by various guilds of Oxyrhynchus—the bakers, brewers, oil sellers, honey dealers, pork butchers, fishmongers and coppersmiths—to the *curator* of the city, stating month by month what prices they would charge. From the year 459 we possess a detailed agreement between the *defensor* of Sardis and the local guild of builders. The latter undertake that their members will not abandon work on a contract, provided that the employer pays the wages mutually agreed, and that they will supply a substitute for any member who wilfully fails to complete a contract, and also, after a period of grace, for a member who is unable to do so owing to sickness. They also guarantee to pay the penalty stipulated in the contract if any member obstructs completion of a contract by another. A law of Zeno, dated 483, which prohibits combinations between dealers to fix prices and between builders and other craftsmen to refuse to work on contracts not completed by their fellows, imposes a fine on the heads of the guilds concerned. The bakers were the guild which most often came into conflict with the authorities. Libanius often protests against the way in which the governor or civic magistrates would fix the price of bread low during a shortage and flog bakers who exceeded it.[85]

Of the structure of industry we know very little. There were some slave establishments owned by well-to-do proprietors. When Libanius' friend Thalassius was refused admission to the senate of Constantinople on the ground that he was a cutler, Libanius indignantly explained that he was no mere artisan, but like Demosthenes owned a factory of slave craftsmen. A law of 383 which permitted the cities of Moesia to enrol on the councils commoners whose wealth consisted in slaves must refer to similar establishments.[86]

But in general industry seems to have been carried on by small independent craftsmen helped by their families and sometimes by apprentices and a few slaves or hired assistants. Caecilianus, one of the *duoviri* of the little African town of Aptungi in 303, seems to have been a prosperous craftsman of this type. He had gone to Zama to buy linen yarn on the day that the edict of persecution arrived, he deposed before a *duovir* of Carthage twelve years later, and giving evidence before the proconsul Aelianus he further deposed: 'He came to me at my house, I was having dinner with my workmen. He came there and stood at the door. "Where is Caecilianus?", he said, "Here," I answered, "what is it?" I said to him. "Is everything all right?" "Yes," he said. I answered him: "If you don't mind having dinner with us, come in and sit down."' Caecilianus must have been a man of some substance to be *duovir*, even of a little town like Aptungi, but he was apparently illiterate— at any rate he employed Ingentius to write his official letters for him when he held the office—and he ate with his workmen, who may have been hired men or slaves, and probably worked with them.[87]

The builders of Sardis were evidently working masons, seeing that sickness was a valid excuse for delay in completing a contract. Most craftsmen seem to have been in a small way: they are classed in the laws as *plebeii*, and only the most prosperous could aspire to the decurionate even in the smallest towns. They plied their trades, as today in the Near East, in little workshops facing on the street; at Antioch they were obliged to keep a lamp burning all night outside their shops to provide street lighting, and Libanius protested that the governor's insistence on tripling these lights had ruined many of them. Others too poor to afford shops worked in stalls between the columns of the street colonnades.[88]

Trades tended to be hereditary, since fathers naturally trained their sons in their own craft, but this was matter of custom not of law, and exceptions are to be found. John of Lycopolis was apprenticed to a carpenter, but his brother was a dyer. From Egypt we have several articles of apprenticeship and contracts of service for a year or term of years, specifying the wages or rations and clothing which the master is to give. From Egypt too we have the record of a dispute between the builders' guild of Oxyrhynchus and one Paul, a linen weaver's apprentice or former apprentice, now working with his master. The linen weavers, Paul's counsel explains, 'are of no small usefulness to the public services, as you, my lord, well know. For they contribute much to the *anabolicum* and there is all the work that they have to do. But despite this pressing need the builders claim to regard them alone as useless. For they are striving to make my client a builder, though he is an unoffending linenweaver. Their attempt is utterly unlawful, for they want to drag him from the trade that he has learned, and to teach him another, that of a builder'. The judge, the *juridicus Aegypti*, upheld Paul's plea, ruling that 'if he has learned the craft and is already in that trade, he is not to be transferred to another craft'. It would appear from counsel's arguments that the builders were claiming that they needed extra manpower, and from the judge's carefully worded ruling that if Paul had not yet passed his apprenticeship he might have been compulsorily drafted into the builders' guild.[89]

From 395 onwards—and particular in the next decade—a number of laws were issued in the Western empire prohibiting *collegiati* from enrolling themselves in the *officia*, enlisting in the army, or migrating to the country and taking up agriculture, and recalling to the guilds those who had thus left them. This legislation was confirmed by Valentinian III, who also forbade *collegiati* to take orders in the church. In the West, then, where the urban guilds were in decay, in order to maintain the civic services which depended on their labour, the government attempted to make the craftsmen and shopkeepers into a hereditary caste. No similar laws were issued by the Eastern emperors, and none of the Western laws were reproduced in Justinian's Code. In the East the guilds of craftsmen and shopkeepers evidently continued to flourish and their membership remained free.[90]

It is unfortunate that we know least of the most important industrial towns, those which produced fine fabrics for export. Something can be gathered from Procopius' rather confused account of how Justinian ruined the silk industry. The raw silk, according to a law of Justinian, was bought from the Persians by the imperial *commerciarii* at the rate of 15 solidi the pound, and was resold by them at the same price to the raw silk merchants (*metaxarii*). The industry was concentrated at Berytus and Tyre, where, according to Procopius, the merchants (ἔμποροι), the superintendents (ἐπιδημιουργοί) and the craftsmen (τεχνῖται) resided. The craftsmen were humble manual workers, who were threatened with starvation when the industry was killed; they were clearly free men, for many of them migrated to Persia. It may be conjectured that they worked as wage earners for the *metaxarii* or for the superintendents, who were presumably either managing agents of the *metaxarii* or entrepreneurs who bought silk from them. Alternatively the *metaxarii* or superintendents may have jobbed out work to the craftsmen on a piece-work basis. Some *metaxarii* seem to have kept the whole business in their hands from start to finish, buying the raw silk and selling the silk garments: such men often resided at Constantinople, which was their principal market.[91]

Whether the structure of the high-grade woollen and linen industries was similar we do not know. Silk, since the raw silk was very expensive and all imported, lent itself particularly to this form of organisation. The fine wools which were used for the best fabrics were also relatively dear. Atrebatic wool cost four times as much as 'best middle' and eight times as much as ordinary wool. The best linen yarn, such as would have been used for the named brands of fabrics, cost 1,200, 960 and 840 denarii a pound according to grade, while ordinary yarn cost from 720 to 450, and coarse yarn only 250 to 72. The weavers in these industries may well have worked for merchants. Ordinary weavers no doubt bought their yarn, as did Caecilianus, and sold their own products. We know of one weaver who rented a piece of land and grew his flax on it; but he was a village weaver of Aphrodito.[92]

Rather superior to the ordinary run of craftsmen were the workers in certain highly skilled trades. Constantine, anxious to encourage these trades, which as a result of the anarchy and impoverishment of the late third century were in decline, exempted them from the personal burdens to which ordinary craftsmen were subject, and this rule was still maintained in the sixth century. The list of exemptions opens with some occupations of professional or semi-professional status—architects, doctors, veterinary surgeons, painters and sculptors. There follow various skilled crafts in the building trade, carvers in stone and marble, makers of mosaics and tessellated floors, plasterers and makers of coffered ceilings, gilders and woodcarvers; metal workers, such as iron smiths, bronze smiths, plumbers, silversmiths and goldsmiths; founders and makers of statuettes; potters and glassworkers; carpenters with inlay workers and ivory carvers; fullers, furriers and purple dyers. Such specialists would mostly have been found in the greater cities, where there was sufficient demand for their products. The building workers were from the nature of their crafts to some extent itinerant. In a letter to the magnificent Isocasius, a sophist, Theodoret, bishop of Cyrrhus, promises to send to him a skilled woodcarver called Gerontius, though he still needs his services for himself: the *clarissimus* Eurycianus, a tribune, also apparently wants Gerontius to decorate his house. Gregory of Nyssa, when he was building his octagonal chapel, wrote to Amphilochius, bishop of Iconium, asking him if he could send him some builders skilled at vaulting. He had made a contract with a gang of thirty freemasons, but they were not the type of mason he needed, and were expensive, costing one solidus (per day for the whole gang?) and their keep. He would prefer a contract which specified the amount of work to be done per day, so that he would not have to pay them for the days they were not working.[93]

The aristocracy of the craftsmen was formed by the goldsmiths, silversmiths, and jewellers, who from the nature of their trade had to carry some stock of expensive goods. Even they, however, did not need to be wealthy men, for they often worked up customers' materials. A charming story is told of a pious apprentice in a goldsmith's shop. A wealthy patrician ordered an elaborate gold cross set with jewels, providing the materials, and the apprentice in his pious zeal added some gold out of his own wages. When the cross was weighed in the presence of the customer and found overweight, he was accused of alloying the metal supplied: the story ends happily with the patrician adopting the apprentice as his son. We also hear of a deacon who worked as a silversmith at Jerusalem. His shop was burgled and he lost 100 pounds of silver, which would have been worth the considerable sum of 400 solidi. But his distress, we are told, was all the greater because much of it was not his own property. It was the ambition of the silversmiths and jewellers of the metropoleis to be enrolled among the *co-hortales* of the provincial *officium*. This seems a humble enough ambition, but Theodosius II indignantly ordered 'every rank and grade to be purged of such contagion'.[94]

Much higher up the social scale were the *argentarii* (ἀργυροπρᾶται) of Constantinople, who from being silversmiths had developed into rudimentary bankers, and received deposits, made loans, and would arrange transfers of money: in a document dated 541 we find Flavius Anastasius, *argentarius* of Constantinople, making a loan of 20 solidi at 8 per cent. to two Egyptians for four months, repayable at Alexandria to his agent Thomas. Justinian exempted them from the general ban against *negotiatores* holding civil service appointments (*militiae*). From his voluminous legislation on this point it appears that the ambition of the *argentarii* of the capital was to buy for themselves or their sons one of the many saleable sinecure offices about the court: these were a form of annuity, carrying a salary, and also gave social distinction and some legal privileges. They varied very considerably in price, from over 2,000 solidi for the post of *protector domesticus* to a mere 250 for a clerkship in the *sacra scrinia*: the Flavius Anastasius mentioned above was content with the fairly modest office of *castrensianus sacrae mensae* or Waiter at the Imperial Table. Difficulties arose when *argentarii* went bankrupt, as they seem, to judge by their numerous petitions to Justinian, to have done fairly frequently. A fraudulent *argentarius* might cheat his creditors by putting all his assets into *militiae* for himself and his relatives, and Justinian ruled that creditors might therefore insist on such *militiae* being sold. On the other hand it was maintained by the *argentarii* that it was unfair that *militiae* bought for their sons out of their wives' fortunes should be thrown into the pool, and this exception Justinian allowed.[95]

Trade is rather difficult to disentangle from industry in the Roman empire, for most craftsmen sold their products direct to customers, and some, like jewellers, were simultaneously skilled workmen and purveyors of imported articles. Nevertheless there were many merchants (*negotiatores*) in the strict sense, who made their living by buying and selling goods. The petty shopkeepers of the towns and the larger villages have been already discussed. Superior to these were the merchants who imported and distributed high-class goods of luxury character, especially the clothiers. Such men normally lived in the larger towns, the provincial and diocesan capitals. In such cities there were customers for quality goods, the vicar or governor with his assessor and higher officials, the barristers of diocesan or provincial bar, the metropolitan and the higher clergy. Moreover many of the provincial nobility made their homes in them, and they served as shopping centres for those of the upper classes who lived in the provincial cities or in country villas. *Honorati* and *curiales* had to attend the annual meeting of the provincial council at the metropolis, and there were also diocesan councils, which gave an opportunity of visiting a great city like Carthage or Thessalonica. Honorius in authorising the revival of the annual council of the Seven Provinces at Arles suggests that a visit to a city where the products of all provinces are on sale may not be unwelcome to the *honorati* and *curiales*. Bishops similarly had to attend the annual provincial synods at the metropolis and in some areas diocesan synods were regularly held, in Africa, for instance, at Carthage. It was to Alexandria that the Egyptian bishop Troilus had come with his thirty pounds of gold to buy an embossed silver dinner service, when John the patriarch shamed him into distributing it to the poor.[96]

These dealers in luxury goods aspired, like the silversmiths and jewellers, to posts in the provincial *officium*. They cannot therefore have been very rich or important persons. We possess some family papers of Aurelius Psates, a purple seller of Panopolis at the end of the sixth century, and of his two sons, Pachymius and John, who succeeded him in the business. Psates owned two houses in Panopolis, and two others in the village of This, where he later settled down. Pachymius bought another house in This, and one floor of a three-storey house in Panopolis. He employed assistants, one of whom indentured himself to serve for two years at the pay of 19 *artabae* of wheat, 9 in the first year and 10 in the second. The family was evidently comfortably off in a modest way.[97]

In the West many of these importers were orientals, natives of the areas from which the bulk of the high quality goods originated; they no doubt maintained trade connections with their old homes and had expert knowledge of the goods they handled. When Procopius of Caesarea was sent by Belisarius to spy out the land in Sicily, he was happy to find a fellow citizen and boyhood friend who had settled as a trader in Syracuse. An inscription dated 602 records Peter of Alexandria, who was a linen merchant at Panormus, the second city of Sicily. A papyrus reveals that George, son of Julian, a silk merchant who left his estate to the church of Ravenna in 552, was a citizen of Antioch.[98]

At Rome in the early fifth century the Greek general dealers (*pantapolae*) aroused the jealousy of the local shopkeepers (*tabernarii*) and they were expelled on the charge of exceeding the statutory prices. In 440 Valentinian III found it necessary to recall them in the interests of the people of Rome. At Ravenna Sidonius Apollinaris regarded it as a paradox that 'the clergy are moneylenders and the Syrians sing psalms', while in the sixth century several local tradesmen, Marinus, the money changer, John the *argentarius*, Peter the *collectarius*, John the Syrian, the *negotiator*, attest Latin documents in Greek, or write out the Latin formulae phonetically in Greek characters.[99]

Even in Merovingian Gaul many of the shopkeepers were Jews and Syrians; King Guntram entering Orleans in 585 was greeted by acclamations in Hebrew and Syriac as well as Latin. Some of the resident oriental merchants were prosperous men. Euphronius, a Syrian *negotiator* of Burdigala, was prepared to pay 200 solidi to save his treasured relics of St Sergius from the rapacity of Gundovald, and Eusebius, a Syrian merchant of Paris, was rich enough to outbid local rivals for the bishopric of the city in 591. Priscus the Jew, who supplied King Chilperic with luxury goods, was evidently a wealthy man.[100]

Itinerant merchants may be divided into two classes, those who traded by land and those who traded by sea. The former included many very humble folk, such as the pedlars who frequented the village fairs. Into this class would fall the veterans who preferred a cash donative to a peasant's holding of land and the humble clerics who earned their living by trade: they were exempt from the *chrysargyron* up to an assessment of 10 or 15 solidi. One would expect to find men of greater substance engaged in the trade beyond the frontiers of the empire. Priscus of Panium met one of these in Attila's camp. He was, he said, a Greek who had settled at Viminacium on the Danube and prospered in trade and married a rich wife. He was wealthy enough to be allotted as a special prize to Onegesius, one of the Hunnic nobles, when the town was captured. Even the merchants engaged in the lucrative luxury trade with Persia seem however to have been relatively modest men. In the fourth century Antoninus, a 'wealthy merchant' ('opulentus mercator') of Mesopotamia, entered the *officium* of the *dux* as a financial clerk and rose to be a *protector*: if so minor a post in the civil service was a step up in the social scale the standard of wealth among Mesopotamian merchants cannot have been high. In the sixth century we hear of two brothers, Elias and Theodore, who served as agents for a merchant in Persia. They were paid at first 5 or 6 solidi a head per year, little more than a common soldier's ration allowance, and were during twenty years' service raised to 10, 20 and finally 30 solidi, perhaps what a senior non-commissioned officer received. They then set up on their own first at Edessa and later at Melitene.[101]

In maritime commerce a distinction must be drawn between the shipper (*navicularius*, ναύκληρος), the captain (*magister*, κυβερνήτης or προναύκληρος) and the merchant (*mercator*, *negotiator*, ἔμπορος, πραγματευτής) or his agent (πιστικός). All these roles might be, and very commonly were, filled by one man, the owner of a vessel which he navigated himself and which he loaded with cargoes which he bought and sold. There were, however, shipowners who did not navigate their own ships. The church of Alexandria owned over a dozen large seagoing vessels. On one occasion the entire fleet was caught in a storm in the Adriatic and had to jettison its cargo, which included dried fruit, clothing, and silver; the loss was estimated at 34 *centenaria* (nearly 25,000 solidi), and the agents and captains (οἱ πιστικοὶ καὶ προναύκληροι) responsible took sanctuary on their return to Alexandria. Other great landowners sometimes owned ships, and it was an abuse which the imperial government prohibited for small owner-masters to sail under the flag of a great man in order to secure privileged treatment. A merchant shipper in a big way might also own a fleet of ships which he operated by agents and captains, and we hear of a quite modest shipper who sent out his one ship under his brother as agent (πιστικός).[102]

Most shippers not only carried their own cargoes, but also merchants with their wares, charging them passage money and freight. The Digest preserves elaborate rules for apportioning the loss between them and the shipper when part of the cargo had to be jettisoned. Hilarion the hermit, when to avoid arrest he took a passage at Paraetonium in Libya for Sicily, was afraid of being recognised by the sailors and merchants on board. John Moschus tells of a jewel merchant, travelling with his slaves, who was nearly murdered by the crew for the sake of his precious wares.[103]

Some shippers and merchants no doubt plied wholesale trade, buying goods in the centres of production and selling them to importers in the centres of consumption, or buying and selling cargoes at one of the big merchants' fairs. There was an annual fair of this kind at Aegae in Cilicia, which lasted, free of toll, for forty days. Even after Vandal piracy had made the Mediterranean unsafe for shipping it was frequented by western merchants, who no doubt bought oriental wares which had come from Persia via Nisibis or Callinicum, as well as products of the region such as the linen fabrics of Cilicia and Syria. Theodoret, anxious to repatriate Maria, the girl who had been sold into slavery at the sack of Carthage, sent her to the bishop of Aegae, confident that he could find a reliable shipper, captain or merchant from the West attending the fair, who would take her back to her father.[104]

But many lesser merchants, particularly those who travelled as supercargoes, hawked their goods retail from port to port. There is a revealing letter from Synesius, in remote Cyrene. He writes to his brother, down at the port of Ptolemais, that he has heard that the Athenian clothing merchant has made his annual call, and asks him to buy three Attic cloaks, and not to delay in case all his best wares should have been sold. Wholesalers also employed travelling salesmen who operated in the same way. Thus in the reign of Heraclius a wealthy Constantinopolitan dealer, perhaps a *metaxarius*, entrusted Jacob, a Jew, with clothing to the value of 2 lb.

gold (144 solidi) and booked him a passage on a ship sailing for Carthage, and perhaps Gaul. Jacob's instructions were to sell the clothes at ports of call, and remit the proceeds back to Constantinople; he received a salary of 15 solidi a year for his services. He actually disposed of all his stock at Carthage, selling them direct to customers, like the Athenian clothier whom Synesius patronised.[105]

A shipper thus made a part of his profit from fares and freight, but he normally carried a cargo of his own. The owner of a large merchant ship, of say 20,000 modii, would have to be a man of some substance, since in addition to his ship he would need working capital to pay his crew and to buy his cargo. The price of ships is not attested, but in the Rhodian Sea Law, which probably dates from the seventh or eighth century, when the value of money had not greatly changed, ships are assessed for average at 50 solidi per 1,000 modii if new, 30 solidi if old. A ship of 20,000 modii would then cost initially about 1,000 solidi, and to load a ship of this capacity even with a cheap cargo like wheat would require about ten pounds of gold.[106]

A shipper, however, rarely depended on his own capital exclusively, preferring to raise nautical loans, which would partially cover him against loss by storm. For such loans, since the creditor stood the risk of losing his money if the ship were wrecked or the cargo jettisoned, the rate of interest was subject to no legal limit, until Justinian in 528 fixed the maximum at 12 per cent. per annum, as against 8 per cent. for ordinary commercial loans and 6 per cent. for private loans.[107]

In 540 he received a petition from two citizens of Constantinople, Peter and Eulogius, who stated that they made their living by the issue of nautical loans: so speculative a business, where so much depended on an intimate knowledge of shippers and their ships, did not appeal to the ordinary investor and was usually conducted by men, often retired sea captains, who specialised in the work. They desired, they said, that the normal practices current in nautical loans should be confirmed by law. The praetorian prefect was ordered to hold an enquiry and summoned a group of shippers, who deposed that practice varied greatly. Sometimes the lender charged 10 per cent. but in addition was entitled to lade the ship (presumably on the return journey) with one modius of wheat or barley per solidus of the loan, free of freight and customs duty. Other lenders charged 12½ per cent. not per annum, but for the duration of the voyage: this worked out to the advantage of the shipper if he was delayed by bad weather but, as a normal round trip was a matter of two or three months, usually paid the lender. The shipper was entitled to 20 days' grace on his return to sell his cargo, but was charged 8 per cent. if he failed to make repayment thereafter. Justinian confirmed these rules, but eight months later revoked the law.[108]

Only 12 per cent. per annum thus remained the rule, and it looks as if on these terms lenders were unwilling to make nautical loans, in which they took the risk of loss, but would only lend on ordinary terms. At any rate in two cases in the later sixth century, at Ascalon and at Tyre, we find that a merchant who has borrowed money and lost his ship is imprisoned by his creditors. Both stories have a romantic ending. At Ascalon there was a brigand imprisoned in the same gaol as the merchant, and he was so touched by the devotion of the merchant's wife that he revealed to her where he had hidden his swag. 'I was a brigand', he said, 'and committed many crimes and murders, and I know that when the governor comes and I am produced, I shall be executed as a murderer. I felt compunction when I saw your virtue. Go to such and such a place by the city wall and dig and take the money you will find there'. The brigand was duly executed, and the merchant's wife dug where he directed her and unearthed a pot of gold, which was more than enough to pay her husband's debts. At Tyre the other merchant's wife tried to make some money by prostituting herself, but her first customer, a wealthy man named Moschus, the local *commerciarius* (controller of foreign trade), struck by her reluctant demeanour, asked her what her trouble was, and learning her story gave her the sum required, which was five pounds of gold.[109]

Neither of these two shippers seems to have been in a very big way of business. Nor was a merchant of Alexandria, who when he sailed for Constantinople, left his wife and little girl in charge of one slave, who unfortunately developed homicidal mania and rushed from the kitchen into the dining room brandishing a knife. The life of John the Almoner, patriarch of Alexandria (611 to 619), tells a strange story of another shipper of this class. He had fallen on evil days, and asked for a loan. John lent him five pounds of gold, with which, added to money of his own, he bought a cargo and set sail. No sooner was he out of Alexandria harbour than he was wrecked; his ship was salvaged but all the cargo lost. John inferred that the money which the shipper had added to the loan came from a tainted source, and lent him ten pounds of gold to buy a second cargo. Again the cargo was lost and this time the ship also perished. John inferred that the ship must also have been tainted and accordingly entrusted him with a ship of two myriads belonging to the church of Alexandria laden with corn. The captain was again involved in a storm which carried him westwards for twenty days, and he eventually found himself in Britain. Luckily there was a famine here, and the chief men of the town where they landed offered to pay a solidus per *modius* for the corn, or alternatively to load the ship with a return cargo of tin.[110]

Another story in the life of John the Almoner introduces a more substantial merchant. This man had loaded his ship and sent it to Africa under his brother's command. He then came to the patriarch and offered him all the rest of his wealth, which amounted to $7\frac{1}{2}$ lb. gold, asking only that he would pray for the life of his son and for the safe return of his ship. In the event the son died and the cargo was lost. The patriarch was greatly relieved when the merchant came to him and told him that it had been revealed to him in a vision that his son would have gone to the bad had he survived, and that but for his charitable gift he would have lost his ship and his crew, including his brother, as well as his cargo.[111]

A story told of an earlier patriarch of Alexandria, Apollinarius (551-569), concerns a much richer merchant. He had been one of the leading citizens of Alexandria and had left his son a great fortune in ships and in gold. The son had been unfortunate, and lost so much by shipwrecks that he was reduced to the utmost poverty. The benevolent patriarch, knowing that he was too proud to accept charity, summoned the church lawyer and instructed him to draw up a bond in which the church of Alexandria acknowledged a loan of 50 lb. gold from the young man's father, and, to add verisimilitude, to crumple and dirty the bond by dipping it in a barrel of meal. This done the lawyer was instructed to go to the young man and intimate to him that for a consideration, say three solidi, he would reveal to him something to his advantage. The young man sadly replied that he had not three solidi in the world, and the lawyer, pretending to be touched with pity, showed him the bond. The 50 lb. of gold set the young man on his feet again, and he was soon richer than his father.[112]

Palladius tells of another Alexandrian merchant, a man in the Spanish trade, who left his two sons 5,000 solidi in cash as well as clothes and slaves. Rufinus records that another, having returned down the Nile with three ships laden with merchandise—probably Arabian, East African and oriental wares transhipped from the Red Sea ports—distributed the profits of this expedition and all his substance to the poor to the amount of 20,000 solidi.[113]

These tales of the hagiographers, which are the only evidence we possess, may not be true, but they are contemporary and typical, and illustrate the scale of wealth which merchants enjoyed. An ordinary merchant who owned one ship usually operated on credit, borrowing sums of the order of 5 lb. of gold (360 solidi) to finance a voyage, and putting in an equivalent sum of his own. Others had a larger reserve, and might still have 500 solidi in hand after loading a ship. Fifty pounds of gold (3,600 solidi) was sufficient working capital to launch a man as one of the leading merchants of Alexandria, and the merchant princes of the greatest commercial city of the empire owned fortunes of 70 or, if Rufinus' figure is to be believed, close on 275 lb. gold. These are substantial sums, but they make a very modest showing beside the fortunes of the great territorial magnates, who enjoyed annual incomes of 1,500 to 4,000 lb. gold.

The figures fall into line with all that we know of the social standing of manufacturers and merchants. There are one or two hints that great men sometimes owned ships or employed agents to trade on their behalf. Honorius forbade 'those who are noble by birth or resplendent with honours or richer in property to ply trade to the detriment of the cities, so that the intercourse of buying and selling may be easier between commoner and merchant'. This law seems to have been little needed. In general senators, *honorati* and even decurions considered industry and trade beneath them. Even the bankers and silk merchants of Constantinople aspired to nothing higher than petty court sinecures. The great majority of *negotiatores* were plebeians, who might, if they acquired enough slaves or bought some land, become eligible for the *curia* of a minor city, and who considered it a distinction to become enrolled in their provincial *officium*.[114]

The best evidence for the poverty of trade and industry is the *collatio lustralis*, the tax which Constantine imposed upon them and which Anastasius abolished. The *collatio* was comprehensive in scope. After 374, it is true, rural craftsmen, a numerous if humble class, were exempted, but rural traders remained liable. The term *negotiator* was widely interpreted, including not only merchants, shopkeepers and craftsmen but moneylenders and prostitutes. Legal immunities were few—painters, veterans and the lower clergy—and though there was some evasion by shippers and merchants who secured the patronage of the great, it was probably less extensive than in the land tax. By universal consent the burden of the tax was very severe. There are many complaints against the severity of the land tax, which was in fact very heavy; but they are surpassed by the laments over the *collatio lustralis*.[115]

Libanius in a pamphlet written not long after 387, the year of the famous Riot of the Statues at Antioch, when the desperate populace, on the announcement of a levy, rose and tore down the imperial images, says: 'I must now speak of what surpassed everything else, that is the intolerable tribute of silver and gold, that makes men shudder at the coming of the dread *quinquennalia*. This tax has a plausible name derived from the merchants, but they use the sea to escape and the sufferers are those whose manual toil scarcely brings them bread. Not even the cobbler escapes. I have often seen them throwing their awls into the air, swearing that that was all they had. But that does not free them from the collectors, who snarl at them and almost bite them. This occasion, your majesty, increases slavery, depriving of their freedom those who are sold by their parents, not that their money boxes may receive the price, but that they may see it going into the hands of the collector'.[116]

During the fourth century the quinquennial incidence of the tax must have added to its terrors, for the average improvident taxpayer would not have saved up for it. But in 410 Anthemius, praetorian prefect of the East, enacted that 'what used to be demanded at one time and on a single demand note should be paid by small, very small contributions, so that the payers will not notice it'. In accordance with this rule the eleven members of an Egyptian guild elected a headman and agreed to pay him 2,000,000 denarii each on the 28th of each month for the *collatio lustralis*. The contribution is not so alarming as it appears, as the solidus at this date probably stood at about 60 or 70 million denarii: they were apparently reckoning on paying about one and a half solidi each at the end of four years.[117]

Nevertheless Zosimus in the fifth century speaks in similar terms to Libanius in the fourth. It was Constantine, he says, who 'imposed the tax of gold and silver on all who pursued trade everywhere, even on keepers of general stores in the cities, down to the poorest, not even exempting the wretched prostitutes from this tax. So that you could see, when the fourth year approached, when this tax had to be paid, moaning and lamentation in every city, and when it came, flogging and torture being laid upon the bodies of those who through utter poverty could not support the loss. And now mothers sold their children, and fathers prostituted their daughters, forced to pay the collectors of the *chrysargyron* from the money they thus earned.'[118]

This terrible tax, which drove the merchants and craftsmen of the empire to desperation, was abolished by so prudent and successful a financier as Anastasius: it apparently yielded about 5 per cent. of the imperial revenue.[119]

CHAPTER XXII

THE CHURCH

AT the Council of Ephesus in 431 the bishops of Cyprus presented a petition. When about to consecrate a new metropolitan of Constantia, they had received a threatening letter from the master of the soldiers of the East, forbidding them to proceed. This letter, they declared, had been inspired by the bishop of Antioch. 'And what was the object of the bishop of Antioch?' asked the council. 'He was trying to lay his hands on our island,' replied one of the Cypriots, 'and to usurp the consecrations for himself, contrary to the canons and the custom which has prevailed from ancient times.' 'So it appears,' the council asked, 'that the bishop of Antioch has not consecrated any bishop in Constantia?' 'From the time of the Holy Apostles,' replied another Cypriot, 'they can never prove that the bishop of Antioch stepped in and held consecrations or had anything to do with the island, or interfered with consecrations there—neither he nor anyone else.' 'The council recalls the canon of the holy fathers assembled at Nicaea which maintained the privileges of each church at that time, in which the city of Antioch is mentioned. Inform the council whether the bishop of Antioch has not the right by ancient custom to hold consecrations among you.' The second Cypriot again spoke up. 'We have already deposed that he has never stepped in or consecrated either in the metropolis or in any other city. The council of our province, acting according to the canons, appoints our metropolitan. We beg your holy council to confirm this by your vote, so that the ancient custom which has prevailed may now prevail, and our province may suffer no innovation from anyone.' The council, after verifying that the last three metropolitans of Constantia had indeed been consecrated by the provincial council, gave provisional judgment in favour of the Cypriots.[1]

This debate is typical of many. In any dispute the canons of the councils and ancient custom are the determining factors. Fundamentally the constitution of the church rested on custom, for in enacting canons councils did not claim so much to legislate as to give their sanction to established custom. Such customs, formally approved by a great council, acquired a stronger and more lasting validity; hence the inquiry of the Council of Ephesus about the Nicene canon, which as generally interpreted gave *prima facie* support to Antiochene claims. But ancient custom was a good enough justification for many anomalies not plainly contrary to any canon. Customs of course grew and changed, disputes arose, and councils were asked to adjudicate. They sometimes accepted ancient customs of recent growth on somewhat slender evidence, sometimes they compromised between two conflicting claims without seriously investigating their historical basis. But they rarely if ever enacted any overt innovation. 'Let the canons prevail,' 'let ancient custom prevail,' were their typical slogans. As in this case bishops were sometimes prone to invoke the aid of the secular arm to enforce their interpretation of the canons and of ancient custom, and the more influential were able to obtain imperial constitutions confirming their claims. But such appeals to the imperial government were always condemned in principle, and on its side the government rarely intervened, except in response to ecclesiastical pressure.

Such being the principles on which it was shaped, the constitution of the church was naturally not a logical or coherent whole. It was full of local or regional variations and abounded in odd anomalies. It grew from the bottom upwards, and it was only gradually that bishoprics were grouped in provinces, and provinces in larger units of church government. Its growth was irregular, depending on the varying success with which greater sees, by gradual encroachments, hardening into custom, established their ascendancy over their lesser neighbours. The process was slow, extending over the fourth and fifth centuries, and until it was completed there was ample room for conflict between the rival great sees in the no man's lands between them.

The basic organisation of the church had been formed long before the Great Persecution. Each Christian community, or church in the narrower sense, was ruled by a bishop whose powers were autocratic. He might consult his clergy or even his whole flock, and in controversial matters perhaps normally did so; but his judgment was final. He ordained his priests, deacons and lower clergy: he could deprive them if they were disobedient to his commands. He admitted new members to the community, and could expel those whose morals or beliefs he condemned. He controlled the revenues and distributed them at his pleasure. He held his office for life, and his people could not depose him.[2]

In his appointment they had some voice. The choice of a new bishop had at least to be approved by the clergy and people of the church which he was to rule, and they might take the initiative in selecting a candidate. But a bishop could be consecrated only by another bishop, and normally the bishops of the neighbourhood acted in concert. The appointment of a bishop was thus dependent upon agreement between the local community and the bishops of the district. The latter could also adjudicate disputes between themselves, or between a bishop and a member of his flock. They could even, in an extreme case, depose a bishop. For these purposes councils of neighbouring bishops were held, at first as occasion arose, then regularly once or twice a year. Such councils served as a check on the autocratic power wielded by one bishop over his church.[3]

The church in the ecclesiastical organisation normally corresponded to the city in the secular administrative scheme. This was only natural, since the city was the unit not only of government but of social life. According to Theodore of Mopsuestia this arrangement was not primitive. 'Originally there were usually only two, or at most three, bishops in each province,' he writes, 'a state of affairs which prevailed in most of the Western provinces until quite recently, and which still may be found in several at the present day. As time went on, however, bishops were ordained not only in cities, but in quite small places where there was really no need of anyone being invested with episcopal authority.' It is very doubtful if Theodore, who wrote towards the end of the fourth century, had any information about the early organisation of the church better than our own, and questionable whether he was well informed about the Western churches of his own day. He may well have been generalising from the well-known anomaly of the province of Scythia, where the bishop of Tomi ruled all the cities.[4]

Such anomalies were survivals of ancient local custom, and do prove that in some places a bishop had in early times a group of cities under his sway. But it would be rash to infer that this was the general practice of the early church. On the contrary the evidence suggests that it was normal in the East, at any rate, to appoint a bishop to each city, however small the Christian community in it might be. When Gregory Thaumaturgus was consecrated bishop of Neocaesarea, about 240, there were only nineteen Christians in his congregation. In the West there was apparently some feeling against multiplying bishoprics to this degree. At the Council of Sardica, it was ruled, on the motion of Hosius of Corduba, 'that it be not lawful to appoint a bishop in a village or small city, for which even one priest alone suffices, in order that the episcopal title and authority be not cheapened. But the bishops of the province, as I said before, ought to appoint bishops in those cities where there have been bishops before, and, if a city be found to have so numerous a congregation as to be held worthy of being a bishopric on its own, let it receive one.' This canon was cited by Pope Leo the Great in a letter to the African bishops, but in Africa conditions were rather peculiar, the cities being so very numerous, and most of them little more than villages. The rule was generally accepted by the fifth century, and already by the fourth in the East, that each city had its bishop, and the exceptions were recognised as anomalies sanctioned by ancient custom.[5]

The major exception, the province of Scythia, has been mentioned above. At the Council of Ephesus in 431 it was deposed that 'an ancient custom has prevailed in the province of Europe that each of the bishops has two or three cities under him, so that the bishop of Heraclea has Heraclea and Panium and Orni and Ganus, four cities in number, and the bishop of Byze has Byze and Arcadiopolis, and similarly the bishop of Coela has both Coela and Callipolis, and the bishop of Sausadia both Sausadia and Aphrodisias.' From the signatures of Chalcedon it appears that the bishop of Mitylene ruled not only the three cities of Lesbos (Mitylene, Methymna and Eresus), but also the neighbouring islands of Tenedos and Porose-lene. There are some other cases known where a small city was subject to a larger neighbour by ancient custom. Mareotes was part of the bishopric of Alexandria: here the anomaly is readily explicable, for Mareotes, though juridically a city, was in fact a rural area with no town of its own. Augustine mentions a small *municipium* near Hippo which, though it had its own decurions, was subject to his episcopal authority.[6]

In other cases anomalies were caused by the creation of new cities by the imperial government. Usually the church followed suit, and the Council of Chalcedon ruled: 'if a city be newly constituted or reconstituted by imperial authority, the arrangement of the ecclesiastical parishes shall follow the civil and public rules.' There were, however, exceptions. When Constantine separated Antaradus (which was predominantly Christian) from Aradus (which was still pagan), one bishop nevertheless continued to rule both the mainland town and the few Christians on the island. It was no doubt for similar reasons that Termessus and the imperial foundations of Iovia and Eudocias, and Isaura and

Leontopolis, were single bishoprics. Conversely at Gaza, when Constantine made its port, Maiuma, into a separate city, two bishoprics were formed, and survived even when Gaza and Maiuma were reunited permanently by Julian.[7]

Bishoprics always tended to proliferate, sometimes for the reasonable causes enunciated by Hosius, more often owing to ecclesiastical controversies, in which rival parties tried to establish their hold on marginal communities by installing one of their adherents as bishop. The Arian party installed the rebel priest Ischyras as bishop of Mareotes to spite Athanasius. The ancient custom of the province of Europe was confirmed at Ephesus because of attempts by sympathisers with Nestorius to consecrate bishops in the non-episcopal towns; a Nestorian got himself made bishop of Tenedos, which traditionally was subject to Mitylene. These particular attempts proved abortive, but new sees were from time to time established and by the end of the fifth century very few cities lacked a bishop. Zeno enacted that, with the exception of Scythia, and of the double see of Isaura and Leontopolis, every city should have its own bishop. It is doubtful if this law was rigidly enforced in defiance of ancient custom, but the exceptions were by now negligible.[8]

Bishoprics were not confined to cities in the legal sense of the word. There were in the first place units of government which were not cities—*saltus, regiones, castra* and independent villages. Here practice varied; sometimes these areas were subject to the ecclesiastical authority of a neighbouring city. Thus Basil, bishop of Caesarea, ruled the *regiones* of central Cappadocia, and the bishops of Nicaea Tottaeum and Doris and the other *regiones* of Bithynia. In Egypt Helearchia was partitioned between the bishops of Phlabonis and Pachnemunis in the fourth century. More usually, however, these areas acquired bishops of their own. In Palestine the four *regiones* of the Jordan valley and the *saltus* of Gerara were independent bishoprics and in Egypt Helearchia had become one by 431. In the province of Arabia, where the village was the normal unit of government, village bishoprics were common.[9]

Bishoprics might also be established in centres of population within a city territory. Bacatha, a village in the territory of Philadelphia of Arabia, had its own bishop, and so had Marathas, a village in the part of the territory of Samosata which lay across the Euphrates. According to Sozomen village bishoprics were common in Cyprus, and as the whole island was divided between its twelve cities, these villages must have been within the city territories. In Cyrenaica we know of five or six villages which were bishoprics in addition to the six cities which constituted the province. Military stations, which, though they might technically lie in a city territory, were probably separately administered and had a life of their own, tended to become bishoprics. Thus in Egypt the fortresses of Philae, Syene and Elephantine, Babylon and Scenae Mandron had their own bishops, and in the eastern desert of Syria a number of military posts, such as Sura, Barbalissus, Resapha, Euaria and Danaba became bishoprics, some being later promoted to be cities. Ecclesiastical controversies encouraged the foundation of village, as of city, bishoprics. Basil of Caesarea consecrated Gregory of Nazianzus bishop of Sasima, a mere posting station, in order to stake his claim to this territory as against Anthimus of Tyana. In Africa Catholics and Donatists in their rival efforts to establish their hold on the rural population consecrated bishops in the countryside. At the conference of Carthage in 411 the catholic bishop Alypius objected: 'it should be put on the record that all these men have been consecrated bishops in villas and estates, not in cities.' Petilian, a Donatist, replied: 'you, too, have many scattered through all the countryside'.[10]

Village bishoprics were always in a small minority, and on the whole their number did not greatly increase. They were less stable than city bishoprics. A city, if it once acquired a bishop, normally remained a see unless it fell into utter decay: Gregory the Great had to suppress a number of old bishoprics in Italy, but this was because the Lombard invasions had reduced the cities to ruin. A village see might more easily lapse or be suppressed. Gindarus, a large village in the territory of Antioch, had its own bishop at the council of Nicaea, but no later bishop of Gindarus is recorded and the see had certainly been suppressed by the time of the Council of Chalcedon. Hydrax and Palaebisca, two villages in Cyrenaica, had in the reign of Valens got a bishop ordained for themselves, but when Synesius on his death asked them to elect a successor, they refused. The old bishop of Erythrum, the village under which they had formerly been, had been slack and they had preferred to have an active man for themselves; now they liked the present bishop of Erythrum and wanted to return to their old allegiance. On the other hand, village bishoprics which grew in importance were often promoted by the imperial government to be cities: Resapha, which was not only a military post, but possessed the shrine of the famous martyrs Sergius and Bacchus, became Anastasiopolis.[11]

The boundaries of a bishopric and a city did not necessarily coincide, and disputes sometimes arose about rural parishes. This obviously might happen when a village bishopric existed within a city territory, or when an extra-territorial area was shared between two bishops of neighbouring cities. But since the evangelisation of the countryside usually took place well after that of the towns, it may sometimes have happened that missionaries from one town unwittingly poached on villages belonging to another. The Council of Chalcedon voted that rural parishes should continue under the bishop to whom they were subject by ancient custom; thirty years' prescription was definitive, disputes of more recent origin were to be referred to the provincial council. Pope Gelasius declared 'it is a well-known old rule that a territory does not make a diocese': ancient custom was to prevail despite negligence or lapse of time, agreement between the parties or orders from above. He also ordered that when a new church was built on an estate, the bishop who had hitherto baptised the inhabitants should consecrate it.[12]

Where a city possessed a large territory its bishop sometimes consecrated 'rural bishops' (χωρεπίσκοποι) to look after parts of it. The institution is very rarely recorded in the Western provinces, and was not apparently very common in the East. The prestige and the powers of 'rural bishops' were progressively reduced. Fifteen attended the Council of Nicaea and signed its canons in their own right: there were half a dozen at Chalcedon, but they signed only as delegates for their bishops. A council held at Antioch not long after Nicaea ruled that they should 'recognise their limitations and administer the churches subject to them and be content with their care and ministry: and ordain readers and sub-deacons and exorcists and be content with their promotion, and not dare to ordain a deacon without the bishop in the city to which they and their territory are subject . . . rural bishops are to be consecrated by the bishop of the city to which they are subject'.[13]

Later in the century the canons of Laodicea declared that 'bishops ought not to be appointed in villages and country districts, but itinerant inspectors (περιοδευταί); those already appointed are to do nothing without the consent of the bishop in the city'. This canon was not generally observed: 'rural bishops' are still recorded in the sixth century. They were probably never very numerous. Basil of Caesarea is said by Gregory Nanzianzen in one of his poems to have had fifty 'rural bishops', and though the figure is certainly poetic licence, Basil, with all the *regiones* of Cappadocia to administer, no doubt had a considerable number. Caesarea was, however, very exceptional in having so large a rural area dependent upon it, and in the ordinary way even great sees probably had one or two rural bishops only, and the great majority had none.[14]

It had, we have seen, been the practice in the third, and even the second, century for the bishops of a district to hold periodic meetings. The Council of Nicaea confirmed and regulated this practice. It enacted that councils of all the bishops of each province should be held twice a year, before Lent and in the autumn, in order to review excommunications enacted by the several bishops and confirm or annul them by common consent. It also ordained that, when a see fell vacant, the new bishop should be consecrated preferably by all the bishops of the province, or, if this were impracticable, by at least three with the written consent of the rest; if unanimity could not be achieved, with that of the majority; and that no bishop be consecrated without the consent of the metropolitan.[15]

By this last term the fathers of Nicaea meant the bishop of the metropolis or capital city of the province, as appears from a canon of the Council of Antioch which further emphasises his authority. 'The bishops in each province ought to recognise that the bishop who presides in the metropolis also undertakes the care of the whole province, because people with business all congregate from everywhere in the metropolis. Whence it is resolved that he should be preferred in honour, and that the other bishops, according to the ancient rule of our fathers which has prevailed, should do nothing without him beyond the affairs which concern their individual sees and the territory subject to them.'[16]

These canons created or confirmed a hierarchy among bishops. The metropolitan had now a certain authority over the other bishops of the province. He presided at the provincial council, and no common action could be taken without his consent: in particular he had thus a veto on the appointment of bishops. The provincial organisation also provided regular machinery for settling disputes between neighbouring bishops, or between bishops and their clergy or people. It also strengthened the control of the bishops over the choice of new colleagues. If the rules were kept, the clergy and people of the city could no longer get the man of their choice consecrated by a bishop acting independently of his colleagues, or even by three, the minimum number which had been required by the Council of Arles. The metropolitan and the majority of the provincial bishops could exercise a complete veto.[17]

The rules laid down at Nicaea were not universally accepted. In the African provinces, except for Proconsularis, where the primacy of Carthage was recognised, it was customary that the senior bishop (by date of consecration) should preside at provincial councils and exercise the authority normally wielded by the bishop of the metropolis. This custom perhaps prevailed in some other Western provinces in the fourth century, but later gave way to the Nicene rule. In Africa it survived down to the sixth century.[18]

The province of the ecclesiastical organisation was in origin the administrative province of the empire, and the ecclesiastical metropolis was its secular capital. As the Antiochene canon suggests, it was practical convenience which suggested the rule: people of the same province often had occasion to meet in its metropolis. In general, except in the special cases of Egypt and Suburbicarian Italy, which will be discussed below, the church in the fourth and fifth centuries conformed its organisation to the changing pattern of the secular provinces. Pope Innocent, it is true, replied to Alexander of Antioch: 'with regard to your question whether, when provinces are divided by imperial decree so that there are two metropoleis, two bishops ought to be called metropolitans, it is not proper that the church of God should be changed in accord with the mutability of worldly needs, or should be subject to the promotions or divisions which the emperor may think fit to make for his own purposes'. In practice the church had more good sense than the pope, and when provinces were divided or reunited followed suit.[19]

It was not until the sixth century that serious divergencies began to arise. The ecclesiastical hierarchy had by then hardened and Justinian refrained from disturbing vested interests. When he reunited Honorias and Paphlagonia, he allowed the metropolitans of Claudiopolis and Gangra to keep their old jurisdictions, and so too with the metropolitans of Amaseia and Neocaesarea when he merged Helenopontus and Pontus Polemoniacus. When he carved a new province of Theodorias out of Syria I and II, he left its cities under Antioch and Apamea for ecclesiastical purposes.[20]

The boundaries of an ecclesiastical province did not always coincide exactly with those of its civil prototype. Philadelphia was in Arabia, but Bacatha, a village bishopric in its territory, belonged to Palestine I. Samosata was in Euphratensis, but its village Marathas in Osrhoene. An even more curious anomaly is recorded in Gaul, where the bishop of Massilia, which was a city of Viennensis, was in the latter part of the fourth century metropolitan of the neighbouring Narbonensis Secunda. The bishops of the latter province, however, became restive, and appealed to a council of Italian bishops held at Turin about 400. The council felt that the violation of the Nicene canons was too flagrant to be ignored, but allowed the existing custom to prevail for the lifetime of the then bishop of Massilia.[21]

The origins of these anomalies are unknown. In other cases conflicts rose out of the ambition of bishops who ruled great cities which were not capitals of provinces. Macarius of Jerusalem, which might be regarded as the mother church of Christendom, apparently felt it rather galling to be a mere provincial bishop, subject to the authority of Eusebius, metropolitan of Caesarea, the capital of Palestine. The Council of Nicaea hedged on this question: 'whereas the ancient custom and tradition has prevailed that the bishop of Aelia be honoured, let him have honorary precedence, saving his own authority to the metropolitan'. A century later Juvenal of Jerusalem was to be more aggressive than Macarius, and to win spectacular success. A similar conflict existed in Viennensis between Vienne, the civil metropolis, and Arles, which was a more important city and moreover claimed to be the oldest see in Gaul, from which its first bishop, St. Trophimus, a disciple of St. Peter, had evangelised the rest of the country. This dispute was also put before the Council of Turin, which gave the rather evasive judgment that 'whichever of them can prove that his city is the metropolis should hold the honour of the primacy over the whole province', but recommended a compromise whereby the two should divide the province amicably. This struggle also had spectacular developments later.[22]

Ambitious prelates often based their claims on imperial grants of the honorary title of metropolis. Two such cases were debated at the Council of Chalcedon. The dispute between Nicomedia and Nicaea is particularly instructive. The rivalry between these two great cities was traditional: since the first century A.D. they had competed for precedence and honorific titles. Now the conflict was extended into the ecclesiastical sphere. The bishop of Nicaea claimed metropolitical jurisdiction over Basilinopolis. His arguments are typical of the confused state of canon law. Basilinopolis had once been a *regio* under Nicaea; Julian or someone had made it a city, it is true, but it had preserved close links with Nicaea—its original council was drawn from that of Nicaea. Then the bishop of Nicaea always had consecrated the bishop of Basilinopolis: this was flatly denied by the bishop of Nicomedia—Nicaea might occasionally have poached, but such usurpations did not constitute good precedents. Finally the bishop of Nicaea admitted that he could have no claim if he were not a metropolitan, but alleged that Nicaea had been made a metropolis by Valentinian and Valens. The imperial institution was produced and read: but the bishop of Nicomedia produced another constitution of the same emperors, addressed to his own city, declaring that the promotion of Nicaea was purely honorary and without prejudice to the rights of Nicomedia.[23]

The other case was more flagrant. Theodosius II had only a year or two before given Berytus the title of metropolis. Eustathius, the bishop of Berytus, on the strength of this document and of a consequential ruling made by a council of bishops at Constantinople, assumed jurisdiction over six cities hitherto subject to the provincial metropolis, Tyre. Called to book at Chalcedon he became very apologetic; he had, he alleged, solicited neither the imperial constitution nor the decision of the bishops at Constantinople. He had acted in perfect good faith, and would willingly submit to the judgment of the great council.[24]

Both these claims were quashed by the Council of Chalcedon, but similar manoeuvres were sometimes crowned with success. The civil metropolis of Pamphylia was Perge, but Side also claimed the same title. At the Council of Ephesus in 431 the bishop of Side signed high on the list as a metropolitan. By 458 he had established his jurisdiction over nearly half the civil province. Resapha, in the fifth century still a see subject to Hierapolis, metropolis of Euphratensis, had by the sixth become metropolitan of an ecclesiastical province of its own. Its promotion was probably due to Anastasius, who raised it to the rank of city, and was no great derogation of the rights of Hierapolis; for the sees which Resapha ruled were all, it would seem, new creations, military stations in the surrounding desert area promoted *ad hoc*.[25]

In its famous sixth canon the Council of Nicaea recognised certain higher jurisdictions. 'Let the ancient customs in Egypt and Libya and Pentapolis prevail, so that the bishop of Alexandria has authority over everything, since this is customary for the bishop in Rome also. And similarly also at Antioch and in the other provinces let their precedence be preserved to the churches.' The objective of this canon was certainly to confirm the traditional rights of Alexandria and the situation here is tolerably clear. No metropolitans of the provinces into which Diocletian and his successors divided Egypt are recorded, and the bishop of Alexandria consecrated, and it would seem virtually appointed, all bishops in the area covered by the old province of Egypt. This was clearly a survival from the pre-Diocletianic régime, when Alexandria had been the metropolis of all Egypt, and reflects the outstanding position which the great city held in the province.[26]

In Pentapolis (Cyrenaica), which had always been a separate province, the bishop of Ptolemais seems to have had the title of metropolitan, but the bishops of Alexandria had already in the third century asserted their authority here also, and by the fourth century they controlled the consecration of the local bishops. Synesius when bishop of Ptolemais conducted the preliminary proceedings at Olbia, a village see of Pentapolis, but he and two local colleagues could not consecrate the candidate whom the people had elected and they had approved: he had to ask Theophilus, the patriarch of Alexandria, for leave to consecrate. The rule was no new one in his day. The consecration of Siderius to Hydrax and Palaebisca in the reign of Valens had, he reported to Theophilus, been uncanonical, though later condoned by Athanasius; he should either have been consecrated at Alexandria, or by three local bishops under instructions from Alexandria.[27]

The authority of the bishop of Alexandria over Egypt and Pentapolis was in fact despotic. During Maximin's persecution four Egyptian bishops protested against Melitius' usurpation of authority because it disregarded 'the honour of our great bishop and father, Peter, on whom, by the hope that we have in our Lord Jesus Christ, we are all dependent'. At Chalcedon the Egyptian contingent declared that they could not sign the dogmatic decisions of the council without the consent of their archbishop— 'the ancient custom has prevailed in the Egyptian diocese that all the bishops obey the archbishop of Alexandria'.[28]

The position of Rome, cited as an analogy by the fathers of Nicaea, was similar. They were clearly not alluding to the general primacy claimed by the bishops of Rome over the whole church, but to their special position in Italy, which the oldest Latin version of the canon makes more explicit—'urbis Romae similis mos est ut in suburbicaria loca sollicitudinem gerat'. In the Suburbicarian provinces of Italy, as in Egypt, there were no metropolitans, and the pope consecrated all bishops: this state of affairs clearly goes back to the pre-Diocletianic period when there were no Italian provinces. But the popes had extended their authority over Sicily also, which, though an old province, had no metropolitan bishop. Sardinia on the other hand, though in the Suburbicarian diocese, had its own metropolitan, the bishop of Caralis, who consecrated the other bishops of the island.[29]

The primacy of Antioch to which the fathers of Nicaea alluded was something much looser and vaguer. The bishop of Antioch was looked up to as their leader by the bishops of all the provinces between the Taurus and the boundary of Egypt—an area which later became the civil diocese of Oriens, but at this date had no official existence, since down to the reign of Valens Oriens included Egypt as well. Bishops from all this area assembled to consecrate a new bishop of Antioch. But all the provinces had their own metropolitans, and it is doubtful whether in the early fourth century the bishops of Antioch had any clearly defined jurisdiction over them. Pope Innocent I in 415 interpreted the Nicene canon as meaning that the bishop of Antioch had the sole right of consecrating bishops in Oriens as did the popes of Rome and Alexandria in the Suburbicarian provinces and in Egypt. But Antioch never claimed such a prerogative. Its bishops, by this time, claimed that metropolitans in the diocese of Oriens must be consecrated by them, but even this right was probably a gradual growth. The bishops of Cyprus, as recorded at the beginning of this chapter, in 431 successfully established their claim that their metropolitan had by ancient custom never been consecrated by the patriarch of Antioch. The Council of Antioch held soon after Nicaea does not seem to recognise any authority higher than that of the metropolitan of a province. When the provincial council could not reach a unanimous verdict on charges brought against a bishop, the metropolitan was to call in bishops from a neighbouring province to resolve the problem; there is no appeal to Antioch, as there was in the fifth century.[30]

It is rather curious, seeing that Caecilian of Carthage attended the Council of Nicaea, that the bishops made no allusion in the sixth canon to the position of his see: they were perhaps unwilling to commit themselves on a topic which the Donatist schism had made controversial. As far back as the third century, as Cyprian's letters show, the bishop of Carthage had enjoyed the same kind of primacy in the African provinces as Antioch enjoyed in Oriens. He summoned councils not only from Africa proper, but from Numidia and even Mauretania, and all the African bishops expected to participate in the consecration of a bishop of Carthage. It was Caecilian's furtive consecration by one neighbouring bishop, before the Numidians had arrived, which fired off the Donatist schism.[31]

The Council of Nicaea did something to clear up the chaos which had hitherto prevailed in the higher levels of church government. It gave its sanction to the provincial organisation under the leadership of the metropolitan bishop, and accorded its recognition to certain larger units of government, Egypt and the Suburbicarian provinces under Alexandria and Rome. It also more vaguely allowed primacy to Antioch and other unnamed sees. But it left many problems unsolved. The rules for the consecration of an ordinary bishop were clear, but what of metropolitans?

Could the bishops of a province consecrate their own metropolitan, as was done in many provinces, or was the sanction of some higher authority required? Disputes between bishops or between a bishop and his clergy or people were to be settled by the provincial council with the consent of the metropolitan. But suppose the provincial council could not agree, or the metropolitan were himself a party to the dispute? There was no ancient custom which regulated such problems, and the way was left open for ambitious holders of great sees to extend their authority.

The next great council, held at Constantinople in 381, did little to resolve these problems. It merely ruled that in the five civil dioceses of the Eastern empire, Thrace, Asiana, Pontica, Oriens and Egypt, the bishops should manage their own affairs and not interfere with those of another diocese. The autocratic powers of Alexandria in Egypt were recognised, and in vaguer terms the precedence of Antioch in Oriens, but in Thrace, Asiana and Pontica no chief bishop was mentioned. The other important pronouncement of the council was that the bishop of Constantinople should have a primacy of honour second to the bishop of Rome, because Constantinople was the New Rome. But no attempt was made to define this honorary primacy, or to accord the bishop any specific rights or authority.[32]

The church had a great belief in the value of councils, but here again there were no accepted rules to determine who might summon them and what jurisdiction they possessed. The Council of Nicaea had, as we have seen, put provincial councils on a regular footing and defined their competence. In some areas larger councils were sanctioned by tradition. The bishops of Rome and Alexandria from time to time summoned councils from the Suburbicarian provinces and from Egypt, and the bishop of Antioch from all the diocese of Oriens. Councils of all the African provinces were regularly held under the presidency of the bishop of Carthage. But elsewhere there were no recognised authorities to convene larger councils.

The imperial government often took the initiative. Only the emperor could summon a general council of the whole church: Constantine had established the precedent at Nicaea, and there was in any case no central ecclesiastical authority which could act. But the emperor also often summoned smaller councils to deal with some problem on which a provincial council was incompetent to decide: Constantine again set the precedent by calling the councils of Rome and Arles to deal with the Donatist controversy and those of Caesarea and Tyre to give judgment on Athanasius. Such *ad hoc* councils were also often convoked by leading bishops, but whether they were summoned by imperial or episcopal initiative, their competence was disputable, and their verdict was frequently challenged by defeated parties who, often truly, alleged that they were packed.[33]

The woeful lack of rules is well illustrated by the tragicomedy which led to John Chrysostom's fall. Theophilus of Alexandria was summoned by the emperor to Constantinople to answer before John various charges brought against him. He arrived with a bevy of Egyptian bishops, received various charges against John, and induced the emperor to issue a summons against him. When John was cited the bishops sitting with him objected: 'You ought to come over to us, so that we can hear your case first. For we have charges against you under seventy heads, involving manifest illegalities, and we are a more numerous synod . . . you are thirty-six from one province, and we forty from different provinces, including seven metropolitans: and it is proper that the lesser should be judged by the more numerous and distinguished according to the canons.'[34]

Of the great sees which profited by this state of anarchy the greatest was Rome. It would be impertinent to attempt to unravel in a few paragraphs the tangled problem of the Roman supremacy. It will suffice to say that from an early date the bishops of Rome claimed a pre-eminent position in the church, and that they consistently claimed it as successors of Peter, the prince of the Apostles. Their primacy in honour was generally admitted not only in the West but in the East, where, however, it was felt to be due to them as bishops of the capital of the empire. But the rest of the empire was less willing to admit the right which the Roman bishops claimed to legislate on doctrine and discipline, and to exercise an appellate jurisdiction throughout the empire. The defeated parties in a dispute naturally appealed to the bishop of Rome, as did Athanasius, if they thought that he could be persuaded to take up their cause, but the verdict of Rome was by no means always accepted.[35]

At the Council of Sardica Hosius endeavoured to get the appellate jurisdiction of Rome universally recognised. If any bishop condemned by his colleagues refused to accept their decision, 'if it please you let us honour the memory of Peter the Apostle, and let the judges write to Julius the bishop of Rome so that the trial can be reviewed by the bishops who are neighbours of the province, if need be, and he himself may appoint those who shall review it'. Again he suggested that if any condemned bishop appealed to Rome, the pope might either order a retrial by neighbouring bishops, or send priests of his own to decide the issue. These proposals were adopted by the council, but in the East they were not recognised and even in the West they received scant attention. In 376 a Roman council under pope Damasus enacted similar rules. In more distant provinces ordinary bishops were to be judged by their metropolitan, but if a metropolitan were himself accused he was to come to Rome for trial, or be tried by judges appointed by the bishop of Rome; similarly there was to be an appeal against a metropolitan's decision either to Rome or to at least fifteen neighbouring bishops. But this same council complained to the emperor about the persistent contumacy of bishops, and Gratian thought it necessary to lend the aid of the secular arm, instructing proconsuls and vicars and the praetorian prefects of Italy and Gaul to arrest bishops who refused to recognise the papal supremacy and send them under escort to Rome or the appropriate council.[36]

For a time the Roman see was rivalled by that of Milan. Milan was at this period the administrative capital of the West, but its ecclesiastical pre-eminence was due less to this fact than to the dominating, not to say domineering, personality of its bishop, Ambrose. His most extraordinary assertion of his authority was to consecrate a bishop of Sirmium in 376. No canon or ancient custom justified this interference of the bishop of Milan in the affairs of a church which lay not only in another province but another diocese. But having thus imposed his ascendancy on Sirmium, which was not only the chief city of Pannonia but claimed to be the 'head of all Illyricum', Ambrose went on to depose two bishops of Dacia. These incidents well illustrate the way in which great prelates exploited the anarchy of the church.[37]

After Ambrose's death the empire of Milan soon crumbled, and even during his lifetime his pretentions in Illyricum were taken over by Rome. Damasus had already established an alliance with Acholius, bishop of Thessalonica, but it was probably his successor Siricius who first formally made the occupant of that great see, the chief city of the Macedonian diocese, his vicar, instructing him that 'none be permitted to presume to consecrate bishops in Illyricum without your consent', and specifying that he should if possible consecrate the bishops himself, or otherwise send bishops of his choice with written instructions to do so. As no canon or ancient custom authorised the pope himself to consecrate bishops in Illyricum, it is difficult to see how Siricius could confer that prerogative on the bishop of Thessalonica. But, despite some resistance by the metropolitans of the provinces, the combined authority of the great city of Thessalonica and of the apostolic see prevailed, and the vicariate of Illyricum, renewed by successive popes in favour of successive bishops of Thessalonica, became an established institution.[38]

In area it corresponded with two civil dioceses of Macedonia and Dacia, which had been transferred by Gratian to Theodosius I, and from 395 became the Illyrian prefecture of the Eastern empire. It was doubtless in order to reinforce their influence in this area, which might easily have drifted into the sphere of Constantinople, that the popes instituted the vicariate. In 421, indeed, Theodosius II, no doubt instigated by Atticus, the bishop of Constantinople, issued a constitution to the praetorian prefect of Illyricum, ordering that in accordance with 'antiquity and the ancient canons of the church' all ecclesiastical disputes throughout all the provinces of Illyricum should be referred to the bishop 'of the city of Constantinople, which rejoices in the prerogative of the old Rome'. However, Pope Boniface protested to Honorius, and Honorius wrote to his nephew, and Theodosius II withdrew the claims of his capital.[39]

The device of the papal vicariate so successfully applied to Illyricum was later extended with less happy results to Gaul. The experiment seems to have been inspired not so much by the desire of the popes to reinforce their authority as by the growing ambitions of the bishops of Arles, who now aspired not only to be metropolitans of Viennensis, but to extend their rule over the two neighbouring provinces of Narbonensis I and II. In 417 Pope Zosimus declared that it was the ancient custom, justified by the pre-eminence of St. Trophimus, that the bishop of Arles should consecrate all bishops in all three provinces, and also gave the present occupant of the see, Patroclus, exclusive authority to issue letters of introduction (*formatae*) to clerics from all parts of Gaul who wished to visit Rome. But Hilary, metropolitan of Narbonensis I, and Proculus, bishop of Marseilles, who was still exercising his anomalous metropolitical authority in Narbonensis II, obstinately refused to recognise the ancient prerogative of Arles alleged by Patroclus, and Popes Boniface and Celestine, evidently perceiving that it did not enhance papal authority to back very disputable claims, tacitly ignored Zosimus' ruling and reasserted the rights of the metropolitans of each province.[40]

Hilary, a later bishop of Arles, tried to revive the primacy of his see, but his interference in the neighbouring provinces so enraged Pope Leo that he deprived him even of his metropolitan rights in Viennensis. The next bishop of Arles, Ravennius, however, got up a petition from the bishops who had formerly owed allegiance to his see. In this petition the claims of St. Trophimus were again elaborated. The secular glories of Arles were also stressed—it had been honoured by Constantine with his name, it had been called by later emperors 'the mother of all the Gauls', it was the seat of the praetorian prefecture of the Gauls, and consuls had inaugurated their office there. Finally the papal records would show that its bishops had the right of consecrating all bishops in the three provinces of Viennensis and Narbonensis I and II and had been accorded authority over all Gaul. The petition was only partially successful. Leo not only ignored the claims of Arles to wider jurisdiction, but took into account the rival claims of Vienne in Viennensis itself. The province was divided, four neighbouring sees being allocated to Vienne and the rest to Arles. Later, in 508, Symmachus accorded to Caesarius of Arles a vicariate extending not only over Gaul but Spain, authorising him to summon councils to settle any problems which might arise and to refer important issues to Rome. He was also to issue letters of recommendation to any of the Gallic or Spanish clergy who wished to visit Rome. This grant was apparently personal and temporary. Before this time Simplicius had made Zeno, bishop of Hispalis, his vicar in Spain, and in 517 Pope Hormisdas gave the same honour to John, bishop of Illici, saving the rights of the metropolitans; he later give a similar vicariate over Baetica and Lusitania to Sallustius of Hispalis.[41]

Meanwhile in the East the bishops of Constantinople were extending their authority. The Council of Constantinople had, as we have seen, in 381 accorded to the New Rome a primacy of honour second only to the old Rome. In practice Constantinople was favourably placed because in none of the three adjacent dioceses of Thrace, Pontica and Asiana was there an outstanding see which already exercised customary authority over it: Ephesus came nearest to this position, but its authority seems to have been confined to the provinces of Asia, Lydia and Caria and its rights had never been formally recognised. In the second place the bishop of Constantinople could readily obtain the backing of the emperor, who naturally favoured the pretentions of his capital, and thus could secure imperial constitutions enforcing his alleged rights. And thirdly bishops, and especially metropolitans, from all parts of the Eastern empire frequently visited Constantinople, and its bishop was thus able at all times to get together a council to lend its authority to his decisions. The so-called 'visiting council' (ἐνδημοῦσα σύνοδος) of Constantinople became a regular institution. The imperial commissioners at Chalcedon raised some doubts as to its status, asking 'if the congress of visitors in the imperial city may be called a council'. Anatolius of Constantinople explained: 'A custom has long prevailed that holy bishops visiting the renowned City should when occasion demands meet about any ecclesiastical business that comes up and decide the several issues and give answers to petitioners. So no innovation has been made on my part and the visiting holy bishops who convened according to custom did not produce a new rule either.'[42]

The story of John Chrysostom's intervention in Asia well illustrates the way in which the authority of the see of Constantinople grew. Eusebius, bishop of Valentinianopolis in Asia, presented a series of charges against his metropolitan, Antoninus of Ephesus, to John before a 'visiting council' comprising twenty-two bishops. John was, according to his biographer, Palladius, reluctant to take up the case, but eventually charged Antoninus, who was present, before the council, which decided that there was a *prima facie* case. John accordingly on its advice sent three of its members to hold a local investigation. But Antoninus bought his accuser off and the case collapsed. Then Antoninus died and the clergy of Ephesus and the bishops of Asia asked John to clear up the scandals of the see. John went down to Ephesus and held a council of seventy bishops from Asia, Lydia and Caria, consecrated a new metropolitan of Ephesus, and deposed several bishops and consecrated others in their place.[43]

John's successors continued to extend their authority. We hear of Atticus visiting Nicaea to consecrate a bishop. He also appointed Silvanus metropolitan of Philippopolis in Thrace and, when Silvanus could not stand the Thracian climate and abandoned his see, later made him bishop of Troas. In this case the people of Troas came spontaneously to Constantinople to ask for a bishop. At Cyzicus the people were more independent. Atticus had to obtain an imperial constitution to enforce his claims, and when his successor Sisinnius on the strength of this document consecrated Proclus bishop of Cyzicus, the Cyzicenes, declaring that the grant had been personal to Atticus, got a local candidate consecrated and refused to accept Proclus. Proclus later became bishop of Constantinople, and as such was asked for a bishop by the people of Caesarea in Cappadocia, and consecrated Thalassius to that great see.[44]

There were therefore ample precedents when the Council of Chalcedon enacted that the bishop of Constantinople should consecrate all metropolitans in the three dioceses of Thrace, Pontica and Asiana. The canon professed to be a mere clarification of the canon of 381, which had given the New Rome primacy next after old Rome: the council 'judged it reasonable that the city honoured with the presence of the emperor and the senate and enjoying equal precedence with the older imperial Rome should also like it be magnified in ecclesiastical affairs, being second after it'. The delegates of the bishop of old Rome lodged a strong protest, and Pope Leo himself refused to recognise the new canon, but in the East it was quietly accepted. The papal delegates suspected that the bishops affected had given their consent under pressure, but when the question was put by the imperial commissioners the bishops all replied that they had signed willingly, and several metropolitans—those of Myra, Amaseia, Gangra, Synnada and Aphrodisias—declared that they themselves had been consecrated by the bishop of Constantinople, some adding that as many as three of their predecessors had also owed their consecration to him.[45]

There was only one dissentient voice, that of Eusebius, the metropolitan of Ancyra, which as the seat of the vicar of Pontica had achieved a certain primacy over the neighbouring provinces. 'I have my story to tell without prejudice to the general view. I have shown in practice that I am far from desiring to consecrate. Peter the holy bishop who has just testified is bishop of Gangra, and I consecrated his predecessor. All the city came to me at Ancyra and brought the resolutions. I answered "I am not one of those who wish to consecrate". They reminded me of those who had previously been consecrated by the bishop of Ancyra, one, two, three of them. I said, "Whatever you say to me I am not going to involve myself in litigation". Then they went and asked the blessed Proclus.' Eusebius, after airing his grievance, allowed the customary rights of his see to lapse.[46]

Ephesus might have caused more trouble, but fortunately there was no bishop of Ephesus at the moment, two rival claimants having both been deposed at an earlier session. There had been argument then as to who should consecrate a new bishop. The imperial commissioners had asked: 'Let the holy council declare where the canons require that the bishop of the holy church of Ephesus be consecrated.' The bishops replied: 'In the province,' and the bishop of Magnesia asserted: 'There have been twenty-six bishops from the holy Timothy to the present day. All were consecrated at Ephesus.' A priest of Constantinople objected: 'The blessed John, bishop of Constantinople, went to Asia and deposed fifteen bishops and consecrated others in their place; and Memnon was confirmed here.' The archdeacon of Constantinople added: 'Castinus was consecrated here too. Heracleides and others were consecrated with the approval of the archbishop here. The blessed Proclus likewise consecrated Basil.' The case was left open at the earlier session and now went by default.[47]

The council also accepted a compromise agreed between

Maximus of Antioch and Juvenal of Jerusalem. The latter had been exploiting the antiquity of his see to challenge the vested rights of Antioch; he had even stated at Ephesus in 431 that 'according to apostolic precedent and tradition' it was the custom that the throne of Antioch itself should be guided and judged by 'the apostolic throne of the church of Jerusalem', and he had actually claimed jurisdiction over the three Palestines, the two Phoenicias and Arabia. He now agreed to split the difference and keep the three Palestines only. With the council's approval the imperial commissioners ratified this settlement, and declared null the various imperial constitutions which the rival parties had obtained to fortify their claims.[48]

The constitution of the church in the Eastern half of the empire underwent one further major change. Justinian, wishing to honour his birthplace, not only made it a city under the style of Justiniana Prima, but gave its bishop the rank of archbishop with authority over all the Dacian diocese, which was withdrawn from the jurisdiction of Thessalonica: later in deference to the protests of Pope Vigilius, he agreed that the archbishop of Justiniana Prima should, like the bishop of Thessalonica, hold his authority as papal vicar. The Eastern parts of the empire were thus divided into six units. The four patriarchs, as they had come to be called, ruled areas of very different size. Constantinople had subject to it three dioceses, Thrace, Pontica and Asiana; Alexandria one, Egypt; Antioch the greater part of Oriens; Jerusalem three provinces carved out of Oriens. Two papal vicars of Thessalonica and Justiniana Prima each ruled a diocese, Macedonia and Dacia respectively. The province of Cyprus alone remained subject to no higher authority. The powers of the various supreme bishops differed. The patriarchs of Constantinople, Antioch and Jerusalem consecrated only the metropolitans of provinces and left to them the consecration of ordinary bishops. The patriarch of Alexandria, by ancient custom, consecrated all bishops under his sway. The papal vicar of Thessalonica, since the days of Pope Leo, himself consecrated only metropolitans, but his consent was necessary for ordinary episcopal consecrations. The vicar of Dacia no doubt followed the same practice.[49]

In the Western parts church government did not achieve even this degree of order. The pope continued to rule the Suburbicarian provinces directly, consecrating all bishops in person or by proxy. In Africa Carthage retained its ill-defined primacy. Here there was no question of the bishop of Carthage consecrating metropolitans, since the senior bishop in each province still exercised metropolitical rights. But though ill-defined the primacy of

Carthage was real, and the African church strongly resented any outside interference. It was generally willing to defer to the judgment of the popes on questions of doctrine and discipline, but preferred to manage its own affairs by frequent councils, held under the presidency of Carthage. When pope Zosimus endeavoured to exercise jurisdiction in the case of Apiarius, the African bishops protested sharply and forbade appeals overseas.[50]

Elsewhere no unit larger than the province developed, and no authority higher than the metropolitan. This was no doubt due to the dominating position of the popes, whose influence steadily grew. There was an increasing tendency to refer all disputes to Rome, and to look to Rome for guidance. The popes on their side preferred in general to deal with metropolitans direct: the vicariate of Thessalonica was designed to meet a special danger. It was safer to allow no see to acquire the degree of authority which Carthage enjoyed and which might tempt it to undue independence.

The revenue from which the churches supported their clergy, maintained their buildings, and distributed charity to the poor, was originally derived entirely from voluntary offerings from the faithful. These offerings (in Latin called *oblationes*, in Greek καρποφορίαι), though later overshadowed by income from endowments, always continued to be an important part of the revenues of the churches, and are frequently mentioned in the sixth century and later. They might be either in kind or in cash. They do not seem to have taken the form of regular first fruits or tithes.[51]

Tithes and first fruits are occasionally mentioned in vague terms, which may imply that they were synonymous with offerings: usually the language seems to be figurative. They are specifically mentioned only twice. John Cassian tells of a pious Egyptian farmer who with his neighbours brought tithes and first fruits of his crops to the abbot of a monastery for distribution to the poor. In Noricum Severinus persuaded people to give tithes for the relief of the poor, ruined by barbarian inroads. It is noteworthy that in both cases the offering was not made to the church of the parish or the city, and appears to have been an additional and exceptional act of piety. In 567 the second Council of Tours urged the faithful in Gaul, as part of a special act of repentance, to give a tenth of all their property to the church. It was not until 585 that the second Council of Matisco ordained that the 'ancient custom', based on scriptural precedent, of paying a regular tithe to the clergy, should be revived, after having, as the bishops admitted, fallen almost entirely into desuetude. Tithe, in fact seems to have been first initiated in Merovingian Gaul in the latter part of the sixth century: it is strange that the clear biblical precedent for it was never exploited earlier.[52]

The offerings of the faithful before that date appear to have been left unregulated, and they were, it would seem, in general really voluntary. An imperial law, probably of Anastasius, gives the first hint that the clergy applied pressure to the faithful. It forbids bishops, rural bishops and itinerant priests to force the laity to pay the 'offerings of the so-called local first fruits or oblations', and 'exact them like a tax', by excommunicating or anathematising those who would not pay or denying them the eucharist or baptism. Whole villages or estates, the emperor had been informed, had been so treated. This must stop; gifts must be voluntary, for the giver might be poor or have had a bad harvest.[53]

Already in the third century the churches had begun, by what legal title is disputed, to acquire property. At first they owned only their places of worship and burial grounds: these are alone mentioned in the letter whereby Gallienus restored the confiscated property of the churches. But Maximin after the Great Persecution restored not only the churches but 'any houses or lands which were heretofore in the ownership of the Christians', and Constantine alludes to gardens and houses in his first edict of restitution: Licinius' edict of Nicomedia clearly distinguishes churches from other property of the Christian community.[54]

From Constantine's time the property of the churches grew rapidly and steadily. He himself set the example by munificent donations of land and houses to the churches of Rome and other Italian cities, and in 321 he expressly legalised bequests to the church. His example was followed by many of his subjects, and, as Christianity spread to the wealthier classes, gifts and bequests became more substantial. The churches received vast properties from pious members of the Roman nobility like Melania, who gave to the see of Tagaste an estate larger than the territory of that city. It also profited from countless small bequests from humble folk, such as are recorded in the Ravenna papyri. It seems to have become almost common form for every will to contain a bequest to the church; even Flavius Pousi, a humble civil servant of the province of Arcadia, who owned nothing except his house, furniture and clothes, left half his house to the church.[55]

The private property of the clergy often swelled ecclesiastical endowments. By a law of 434 the estate of any cleric who died intestate without heirs passed to his church. Apart from this childless bishops often made their church their heir. Gregory Nazianzen left his whole estate, apart from minor legacies, to the church of Nazianzus, and Caesarius bequeathed half his estate to his see of Arles. An African council in 409 regarded this as a moral obligation, anathematising any bishop who left his property to outsiders other than his kin, rather than to his church.[56]

It was often hard to distinguish a bishop's private property from that of his see. Not long after 325 the Council of Antioch ordained that an exact schedule of both must be kept, so that on the bishop's death neither the church should be defrauded nor his heirs put to the trouble of suing for what was their own. It was also often a moot point whether gifts or bequests to a bishop or priest were meant for him personally or for his church. The Council of Carthage in 421 allowed bishops and clergy to dispose as they liked of personal gifts and inheritances, but enacted that they must confer upon their church any lands which they bought. Justinian ruled that a bishop might leave to his heirs or dispose by will only of the property of which he was possessed before his consecration, together with what he might have since inherited from near relatives: the rest was to go to his church. This rather severe rule was enforced in the West by Pope Gregory the Great.[57]

There was always a danger of bishops endowing their poor relations with church property. The Canons of the Apostles, which represent church practice in the East at the end of the fourth century, allow bishops to maintain poor relatives from church funds, but not to alienate church property to them; despite which Ibas of Edessa, if the complaints brought against him by his clergy are true, bestowed not only church revenues but inheritances on his brothers and nephews. There were less reputable reasons for the alienation of church property than the family affection of bishops. In the hotly contested elections to the apostolic see rival candidates bid for the support of influential backers by promises of church lands; under Odoacer and Theodoric this abuse reached scandalous proportions, and these two kings, the Roman senate, and several Roman councils passed stringent rules against it. But the main danger to the estates of the church was that as they grew they attracted the covetous eyes of great men, whose displeasure bishops were afraid to incur or whose favour they wished to gain.[58]

The first imperial law against the alienation of church property was issued by Leo in 470. It applied only to the church of Constantinople, which was particularly subject to pressure from the great, and it absolutely banned all sales, gifts or exchanges. It permitted the church to cede the usufruct of a property to an applicant for a fixed period or for his life, but only on condition that on returning the estate he also gave to the church another of equal value. Anastasius extended the ban to the whole patriarchate of Constantinople, but mitigated it by allowing alienation for reasonable causes under proper control. Sales or mortgages were allowed in order to pay debts, to purchase a more valuable estate, or for urgent repairs, exchanges when a better property was thereby acquired, perpetual emphyteutic leases provided that the rent was not reduced, or when the property was in its present condition valueless. All such transactions had to be registered in the presence of all the clergy of the institution concerned before the *magister census* in Constantinople or the *defensor* in other cities.[59]

Justinian revoked Anastasius' law, and tightened up Leo's, applying it to the whole empire. The ban on sales and gifts had been evaded by the grant of long or even perpetual leases. Justinian absolutely forbade one form of lease, the *ius colonarium*, whereby the tenant virtually bought the estate, holding it in perpetuity subject to a small rent charge. He limited the term of ordinary leases to twenty years, and of emphyteutic leases to three lives (those of the original tenant and his sons and grandsons) and he insisted that in the latter the rent must not be reduced by more than one-sixth. Exchanges were permitted only with the emperor himself, who guaranteed to give in return lands of equal or greater value.[60]

These rules proved excessively rigid. Justinian had soon to allow sales of land to pay arrears of taxes and grants of land to liquidate private debts. The church of Jerusalem obtained a special law to enable it to carry through a very profitable transaction. It had acquired for 380 lb. gold a property bringing in 30 lb. a year. Part of the purchase money had been raised by subscription, but part borrowed, and the debt could readily be paid by selling houses belonging to the church at prices representing fifty times their annual value. Special legislation was also needed for the churches of Moesia and Scythia. As one of their bishops explained, they often received legacies of real property which the testator wished to be sold to raise money for the redemption of prisoners or the relief of the destitute, and such property moreover often consisted of half-ruined houses far from the cities, and vineyards liable to devastation, which could not be profitably let. Later, in 544, Justinian allowed all the churches except that of Constantinople to grant perpetual emphyteutic leases, and even the church of Constantinople was permitted to give perpetual leases of ruinous house property, the tenant paying either a third of the old rents, or half the old rents of such houses as he rebuilt.[61]

There are a number of clauses in Justinian's legislation which betray where the real danger lay. He forbade those holding offices at the capital, and later all those in positions of power, to acquire church lands. He prohibited the issue of personal rescripts authorising those holding offices or at court to do so. The emperor also found that the clause permitting the crown to make exchanges with the churches was exploited by petitioners, who asked the crown to obtain lands in this way and regrant them to themselves.[62]

The contemporary legislation by ecclesiastical councils in the West was somewhat less rigid. According to the rule prevailing in Africa a parish priest might not sell property without the leave of his bishop, and a bishop had to obtain the permission of his priests and of the provincial council. A bishop was allowed by the Council of Agathe in 506 to alienate church property in cases of necessity with the approval of three colleagues. A later council in 517 insisted on the metropolitan's consent, and the Council of Massilia in 533 held that it was contrary to the canons for a bishop to sell property without the leave of the provincial council. On the other hand the Council of Agathe allowed a bishop to free church slaves and grant them land, vineyards or house property up to the value of 20 solidi. He might also grant small and less profitable properties in usufruct, or even sell 'small parcels of land or minute vineyards of little use to the church, situated far from it'.[63]

The rules were evidently rather laxly observed, for many councils enacted that if a bishop did not leave his private estate to his church, he by his will, or his heirs and assigns, must compensate the church for such lands or slaves as he had alienated during his term of office. But in Merovingian Gaul, as in the East, the main threat to the property of the church came from the great. A council held in 535 denounced those who petitioned kings for church lands, and another held at Paris about twenty years later complained bitterly of petitioners 'who have usurped the property of the church by unscrupulous underhand dealing under cover of the royal munificence'.[64]

Church lands enjoyed certain fiscal privileges. With a few very special exceptions, such as Thessalonica, the churches paid the regular land tax, the *canonica inlatio*, but they were exempt from all additional payments, by way of *extraordinaria* or *sordida munera*. This immunity was in 423 curtailed when they were made liable for the repair of roads and bridges.[65]

The churches also from the reign of Constantine received subsidies from the state. According to Theodoret Constantine issued general instructions to all provincial governors to allocate

annual grants in each city for the support of virgins, widows and
the clergy. These grants were cancelled by Julian, but revived
by Jovian, who however reduced them to one-third of their original
amount. The reduced grants were, according to Theodoret, still
paid in his own day, and his statement is confirmed by a law of 451,
which orders the continuance of 'the salaries which have hitherto
been paid from the treasury to the holy churches in various kinds'.
These subsidies are spoken of as *annonae*, and were apparently in
the form of foodstuffs, especially corn. They are not often mentioned either in the legal or the ecclesiastical sources. Athanasius
speaks of the corn which 'had been granted by the father of the
emperors for the assistance of widows separately for Libya and for
some places in Egypt', and the government grant of corn for the
poor in Libya is said to have been sold by Dioscorus and the
money embezzled. This suggests that Constantine's grants were
perhaps not so systematic as Theodoret represents them, but
they must have been very general. They still continued at the
end of the sixth century: Gregory the Great complained to the
praetorian prefect of Italy on the suspension of the government
subsidy (*annonae et consuetudines*) made to the centre for poor relief
(*diaconia*) at Naples.[66]

On the management and distribution of ecclesiastical revenues
we know very little until the late fifth and sixth centuries, and by
that time the financial organisation of the churches had become
exceedingly complex. In early times the position was simple. In
most cities there was one church only, served by a single group of
clergy under the immediate control of the bishop, and he was
responsible for allocating the available funds to the upkeep of the
fabric and the lighting of the building, the distribution of charity
to the poor, and the maintenance of himself and his staff. As the
congregation grew more churches were built in the larger cities;
at Alexandria there were already quite a number—Epiphanius
mentions eight—when Arius began to preach his doctrine. At
Alexandria a priest was permanently allocated to each church—
Arius had that of Baucalis—and at Rome similarly in 341 Athanasius identifies a church as that 'where the priest Vito conducted
the services', while Pope Innocent speaks of the priests in charge
of the several churches.[67]

This practice did not necessarily, however, involve any financial
complications. The additional churches could be, and probably in
early times usually were, regarded as annexes of the principal
church, and they and their clergy maintained out of the common
fund. Sometimes, however, benefactors who built new churches
endowed them with lands for their maintenance. It was indeed

highly desirable that they should do so, as otherwise their munificence might burden the church with maintenance charges which it could not afford, and eventually it was made obligatory. By the end of the fifth century the popes would not license the bishops under their jurisdiction to consecrate a new church unless it had an endowment sufficient to cover its repairs and lighting and the maintenance of its clergy, and in 541 the Council of Orleans laid down the same rule for Gaul, and in 572 the Council of Bracara enacted it for Spain. In the East Justinian enforced the rule by an imperial novel.[68]

A distinction thus grew up between what were called in Latin *tituli*, churches which were financed from the bishop's central fund and served by his clergy, and *parochiae* or *dioeceses*, churches supported by their own endowments. The distinction is clearly brought out by a decision of Pope Pelagius I. John, the bishop of Nola, had asked his leave to sell the plate of the church of Suessula, 'which appears to be a *parochia* of the church of Nola', in order to meet its expenses. The pope deprecated the step, and ruled that Suessula should be made a *titulus* of Nola: priests on the establishment of the Nolan church should be seconded to serve it, and its lands should be cultivated by the men of the Nolan church. In the East Justinian draws a similar distinction between the position when founders have endowed their churches and when 'the church of the city itself supplies salaries both to itself and to other churches'.[69]

Separately endowed churches were sometimes amalgamated with the central group. Constantine according to the Liber Pontificalis settled enormous endowments on each of the basilicas which he built at Rome, but they were later classified as *tituli*, so that their revenues went into the central funds of the papacy. The Roman *tituli* had, however, some separate endowments. In the rules laid down in 502 against the alienation of church property 'all who are or shall be priests of the churches throughout the *tituli* of the city of Rome' were forbidden to alienate 'whatever belongs to the *tituli* or the aforesaid church'. The endowments of the *tituli* were partly estates of the Roman church earmarked for their upkeep, like the Massa Aqua Salvias which Pope Gregory transferred from the *patrimonium Appiae* to the basilica of S. Paul for the maintenance of its lights, partly lands given or bequeathed by private benefactors to a *titulus*, like the Massa Paganicensis given by Flavia Xanthippa to the basilica of S. Maria Dei Genetrix.[70]

At Constantinople Justinian draws a threefold distinction. There was the Great Church, which comprised four churches—St. Sophia, St. Helena, St. Theodore (built by Sporacius, consul in 452), and the Blessed Virgin (built by the Empress Verina)—

but was administered as a single unit and served by one body of clergy. Secondly there were churches 'whose maintenance the Great Church undertakes', which nevertheless had their separate establishments of clergy, as laid down by their founders; and thirdly there were churches 'which do not have their supply and maintenance from the Great Church'. The second category appear to be like the Roman *tituli*, originally independent churches which had been absorbed.[71]

In general the town churches tended to be *tituli*, either because they had initially been built by the bishop from central funds or by subscription, or by subsequent amalgamation. The Council of Orleans in 538 indeed laid down the general rule that gifts bestowed on basilicas in the cities should be at the immediate disposition of the bishop, who should have discretion how much of them he should allocate to the repair or maintenance of the basilica in question, whereas local custom should be observed about the revenues of parishes or basilicas in the villages. Rural churches were on the other hand normally *parochiae*. In villages of peasant proprietors they were generally founded by local initiative; at the village of Libanus the church was built by the joint labour of the inhabitants. On great estates it was normally the owners who built and endowed the churches. They usually no doubt did so from motives of piety. John Chrysostom, who found the great landowners of Constantinople backward in doing their duty, urged them to build churches and endow priests on their estates, if not for Christian zeal, for prudential reasons; the priest would preach obedience to the peasants and prevent unrest. In sixth-century Spain some landowners built churches as a commercial speculation, going fifty-fifty with the priest on the offerings.[72]

There was a similar distinction between the charitable institutions run by the bishops from central funds, and those privately endowed. The churches had from their inception devoted some of their income to the care of the sick, hospitality to strangers, and the maintenance of orphans and widows and of the poor in general. As their wealth increased they built and maintained large numbers of hospitals, orphanages, almshouses and hostels. Sometimes this was done on the initiative of the bishop; Gregory Nazianzen lauds the zeal of Basil, whose charitable institutions added a new quarter to the city of Caesarea. But many private benefactors established and endowed institutions. It is plain from the legislation of Anastasius and Justinian that orphanages, hospitals and almshouses often owned lands of their own from whose rents they were maintained. Cyril of Scythopolis records that Justinian built a hospital of a hundred beds at Jerusalem, and settled on it an annual revenue of 1,850 solidi.[73]

The central fund of the see was originally managed by the bishop himself, but later it became customary, in the East at any rate, for him to appoint one of his priests as manager (οἰκονόμος): this was made the rule by the Council of Chalcedon to avoid the bishop's being involved in any financial scandal. In the West the bishop seems generally to have remained responsible for church finance. In the allocation of the revenues a dividend system was usual, whereby certain proportions of the total revenue were allotted to various purposes. The system seems to have been an old tradition in the Western churches. In Africa it prevailed in the middle of the third century; when Cyprian ordained two confessors as readers, he gave them the status of priests 'so that they may be honoured with the same fees as priests and share in the monthly divisions in equal proportions'. Cyprian also alludes to his own proportion of the church revenue.[74]

The scheme favoured by the popes, which they applied in the Suburbicarian provinces and advocated elsewhere from the end of the fifth century, was to divide all the revenues from rents and offerings (in the cathedral and its *tituli*) into four portions, one for the bishop, one for the clergy (the *cardinales* of the central establishment), one for the repair and lighting of the churches (the cathedral and its *tituli*), and one for the poor. There were local and regional variations. At Ravenna Pope Felix IV ruled that the bishop should have all the extras in kind paid by tenants of the church; the meat, poultry, eggs, cheese, honey and so forth thus provided would help the bishop in his duties of hospitality. In Spain in 572 the Council of Bracara laid down a threefold division, for the bishop, the clergy and the fabric; the special foundations, supplemented by voluntary donations from the bishop and clergy, were presumably deemed sufficient for the poor. In Gaul the Council of Orleans in 511 divided the offerings on the altar half and half between the bishop and his clergy, but reserved all the rents from endowments to the bishop, who was to spend them at his discretion.[75]

The quarter allocated to the clergy was in its turn divided into shares, which varied according to the recipients' grade. The local rules again varied. At Catana the lower clergy claimed that one-third should go to the priests and deacons, and two-thirds to themselves; but the priests and deacons protested that according to the custom of their church they ought to get two-thirds and the rest one-third.[76]

In the East Severus of Antioch alludes to distributions; he declares that aged priests must not be excluded from them. But they evidently played a minor part in clerical incomes; it was probably only the offerings and not the total revenues, as in the

West, which were shared out. It is at any rate plain that by the sixth century it was usual to assign fixed stipends to the various grades of the clergy. This appears from the financial difficulties of the Great Church of Constantinople in the sixth century. Owing to the increase of the clergy above the establishment, Justinian tells us, the church had exceeded its income and run into debt. Severus of Antioch makes the same complaint about his church, and Justinian states that the trouble was general. On the dividend system this difficulty could not arise; the shares of the clergy would have sunk, but the total expended on their stipends would have remained the same. Bishops probably also received fixed stipends. Theodore of Syceon as bishop of Anastasiopolis had an allocation of 365 solidi a year, which is obviously a solidus a day, and not a proportion of the revenue of the see.[77]

The finances of the *parochiae* or *dioeceses* and of the endowed charitable institutions were under the general control of the bishop, but the degree to which he interfered with them in practice varied greatly. In the East Anastasius made the managers of churches and the administrators of institutions, together with the clergy who served in them, responsible even for so serious a step as alienating a part of their endowments in case of urgent need, and only added that the bishop's consent must be obtained if it was the local custom.[78]

In Africa a council enacted in 421 that a priest might not alienate the lands of the church which he served without his bishop's leave. This rule was re-enacted by several sixth-century Gallic and Spanish councils, and in these regions the bishops claimed a tighter control over local endowments, and showed a strong tendency to absorb them. The Council of Orleans in 511 ruled that all lands or slaves given or bequeathed to parishes fell under the bishop's control. This rule had its dangers. The Council of Carpentoratum in 527 had to rule that if the church of the city was adequately endowed, the bishop must allow the rents of property left to parish churches to be used for their repair and the maintenance of their clergy: it did, however, allow poorly endowed bishops to transfer to their own churches the surplus revenues of well-endowed parishes, provided that enough was left for their repair and salary bills. In 545 the fifth Council of Orleans had to pass a special canon to assure King Childebert that the bishop of Lyons would not transfer to his own church the lands with which the king had recently endowed the hostel which had been built in that city. In Spain the third Council of Toledo in 589 denounced those who, when the churches they had built were consecrated, contrary to the canons demanded that the endowments which they had given

to them should not pass under the bishop's control. A later Council
of Toledo, held in 633, explains why they did so. Bishops were
liable, it admitted, to take over the endowment, leaving nothing
for the repairs of the church or the pay of the priests. The council
forbade this abuse, but still insisted that donors must recognise
the bishop's control of the endowment.[79]

The Gallic and Spanish bishops were not only prone on occasion
to pocket the endowments of parochial churches. They also made
a regular claim to a third share in the offerings made in them.
In Gaul the first Council of Orleans laid down this rule in 511.
In Spain it was declared by the Council of Tarraco five years later
to be an ancient custom that the bishop took a third of the parochial
offerings at his annual visitation; it is implied that he was supposed
to devote it to the repair of the local church. The Council of
Bracara in 572 enacted on the contrary that the bishop was not
to take the third of the offerings, which was to be reserved for the
lighting and repair of the church; 'for if the bishop takes that
third part, he has taken away the lights and the sacred fabric'.
The fourth Council of Toledo, however, in 633 allowed the bishops
a third not only of the offerings but of the rents.[80]

We possess very few figures for ecclesiastical revenues earlier
than the sixth century. The wealth of the churches grew enormously between the beginning of the fourth century and the sixth,
but there is no means of estimating how rapid the growth was.
There were at all times great contrasts between the richest and the
poorest sees, and these were probably accentuated with the progress
of time, since the great sees attracted more numerous and larger
benefactions. The church of Rome was already relatively wealthy
in the middle of the third century, when it had, besides its bishop,
46 priests, 7 deacons, 7 sub-deacons, 42 acolytes, 52 exorcists,
readers and doorkeepers, and over 1,500 widows and poor 'all of
whom the grace and bounty of the Lord feeds'. But Constantine's
donations transformed the situation; the rents of the lands which
he gave to the Roman church totalled well over 400 lb. gold.
It is not surprising that fifty years later Pope Damasus lived in so
grand a style that one of the great pagan senators of Rome, Agorius
Praetextatus, could say to him (in jest, it is true): 'Make me bishop
of Rome and I will become a Christian tomorrow.' But Rome was
in a class by itself. Constantine's benefactions to other Italian sees
were on quite a different scale, ranging from about 10 lb. gold a
year for Capua and Naples to about 25 lb. for Albanum; Ostia

also received about 25 lb. from the combined benefactions of the emperor and of Gallicanus. Ammianus Marcellinus points the contrast between the pope and the bishops of the smaller Italian towns, who lived in a very modest style.[81]

According to John Chrysostom the church of Antioch in his day enjoyed a revenue which was comparable with that of one of the wealthier residents of the city, but not of the very richest. Augustine told Albina that 'my paternal estate can hardly be reckoned to be a twentieth part in comparison with the lands of the church which I am now deemed to possess as owner': but Augustine was the son of a poor decurion of a small town, and his see of Hippo was a considerable city. Alexandria must have been a very wealthy see by the 430s, for Cyril was able to lay out 1,500 lb. gold in presents to the court, and soon after to spend another 1,000 lb. gold (not to speak of valuable gifts in kind) for the same purpose: it is true that his archdeacon declared that the church of Alexandria was as a result stripped bare and in debt, but it seems to have recovered from the strain without difficulty. At the beginning of the seventh century John the Almoner on assuming office found 8,000 lb. gold in the patriarchal palace.[82]

In 546 Justinian fixed the consecration fees of bishops on a sliding scale according to their incomes. He placed the five patriarchates in a class by themselves. Below them came sees worth over 30 lb. gold per annum, then those from 30 to 10 lb., from 10 to 5, from 5 to 3, from 3 to 2, and under 2. These figures fairly certainly represent not the total incomes of the sees, but episcopal stipends. We know from a decision given by Pope Felix IV (526-530) that one-quarter of the revenue of the see of Ravenna amounted to 3,000 solidi, over 40 lb. gold. The bishopric of Ravenna thus fell, as one would expect, comfortably within Justinian's first class; for Ravenna was not only a metropolitan see, but probably richer than most, having been the seat of the court, and having thus attracted substantial benefactions from the crown and great personages in governmental circles. We also know that at Anastasiopolis of Galatia I the bishop's stipend in the sixth century was 365 solidi, or just over 5 lb. gold. Anastasiopolis was an unimportant place, formerly the chief town of a *regio* and only recently promoted to city rank: its bishopric falls appropriately about halfway down Justinian's scale. The poorest bishop of whom we know was Musonius of Meloe, a little hill town in Isauria. Cited before Severus of Antioch for usury, he pleaded that he could not make ends meet otherwise: 'By God, what do you care, you who receive the stipends of Antioch, while I have nothing in my city, not so much as six solidi?' His plea was apparently genuine, for he promised to amend his ways on receiving a subsidy of 12 solidi a year from Severus.[83]

There were thus glaring contrasts between episcopal incomes. Musonius got less than a private's pay in the army, but this was probably very exceptional. Even at a second-rate town like Anastasiopolis the bishop was substantially better paid than most professional men: six times what the public doctor got at Antinoopolis, five times what professors of rhetoric or grammar got at Carthage, five times what the judicial assessor of the average magistrate of *spectabilis* grade received. His salary was in fact as high as that which the provincial governors of Helenopontus, Pontus Polemoniacus, Paphlagonia and Honorias had received before Justinian's reforms. A great metropolitan like the bishop of Ravenna drew a salary equal to the highest allocated by Justinian to a *spectabilis*: the Augustal prefect and *dux* of Egypt got 40 lb. gold for his combined offices. The two upper grades in Justinian's scale, which would no doubt include all metropolitans, covered the same salary range as he allotted to his proconsuls, praetors and moderators. A side-light is thrown on the scale on which the great bishops lived by a decision of the Council of Chalcedon. It awarded a pension of 200 *solidi* a year to each of the two rival metropolitans of Ephesus whom it had just deposed, 'by way of subsistence and consolation'. Domnus, ex-bishop of Antioch, got 250 solidi in similar circumstances.[84]

There were as striking differences between the lower clergy. They were graded in orders according to ancient canonical custom. First came priests and deacons, who as servants of the altar stood rather in a class apart. There followed sub-deacons, and the various minor orders, readers, acolytes, singers, exorcists, and doorkeepers. Below these again came such humble fry as gravediggers (*fossores* or *copiatae*) and hospital attendants (*parabalani*). There were also deaconesses, whose principal function was to superintend the baptism of women. The distinction between the orders was primarily liturgical, but they were also grades of seniority, and, within a given church, carried increasing emoluments. In one Italian church deacons were by a strange anomaly better paid than priests, and accordingly refused promotion: Pope Gelasius advised that the salary scales be revised 'so that, convinced by this argument at least, they may try to seek the honour which they had avoided— and profit'.[85]

From the financial point of view the order which a cleric held was much less important than the church to which he belonged. There was a growing distinction between the *cardinales* or *canonici* who were on the roll of the bishop's church, and the clergy of the parishes and institutions. Among the former there were naturally great contrasts according to the wealth and importance of their see, but in general they seem to have been better paid and ranked higher than the latter. In sixth-century Gaul the clergy of 'the church of the city' were apparently reluctant to surrender their places and emoluments when they were appointed to 'dioceses or basilicas situate in any place, i.e. either in the territory or in the city itself', and the Council of Orleans in 538 had to rule that it should be within the bishop's discretion whether he allowed them to retain any part of their emoluments derived from the church of the city. It might even be a financial loss for a priest of a great church to become bishop of a lesser one. Gregory, a priest of Ravenna, was deeply aggrieved when he was in 482 forcibly consecrated to the see of Mutina, and insisted on being compensated by the grant for his life of a Ravennate estate worth 30 solidi a year clear. Among the clergy not on the bishop's roll there was all the difference in the world between the staff of a well-endowed hospital or a martyr's shrine which attracted a great flow of offerings, and the humble priest of a poor rural parish.[86]

In the primitive church the clergy had no doubt to earn their own livings, but by the middle of the third century the higher orders at any rate were deemed to be full-time workers and received salaries adequate to maintain them. The practice varied locally. At Rome Pope Cornelius' letter implies that all the clergy, including the minor orders down to doorkeepers, were paid. At Carthage Cyprian insisted that the higher clergy who served the altar (i.e. priests and deacons) must be full-time and not even act as guardians or trustees under a will, seeing that they shared in the emoluments of the church. The lower clergy, however, might apparently practise trades, and receive only such supplementary payments as they required. At Cirta at the time of the Great Persecution some at any rate of the readers worked for their living; one was a schoolmaster and another a cobbler.[87]

The immunity from the *collatio lustralis* which Constantine granted to clerics, and which a series of fourth and fifth century laws maintained, implies that many of the clergy continued to work at crafts or engage in trade; Basil in one of his letters states that his clergy lived by the former and not the latter. But the clerics concerned were mainly those of the humblest grades: laws of 356 and 360 indeed restrict the immunity to gravediggers (*copiatae*). By the middle of the fifth century clerical trade began to be viewed with disfavour. Valentinian III forbade it in 452, and about the same time the Council of Arles did the like. But many of the minor clergy continued to practise crafts. Severus of

Antioch ruled that the subdeacons of Alexandria ad Issum should not be required to do weekly turns of duty at the bishop's palace, because they received no pay and had to work for their living. Cyril of Scythopolis mentions a deacon of Jerusalem who worked as a silversmith. This is a very exceptional case, for priests and deacons, according to the general practice of the Eastern Church, as set out in the Canons of the Apostles, were salaried: he must have served a very minor parochial church. At Alexandria in the early seventh century we hear of two clerics, one a reader, who worked as cobblers.[88]

By the fifth century at any rate it was well worth while to be a priest or deacon on the establishment of a great see. Theodore, an *agens in rebus* of. twenty-two years' service, who was, as he explained in his petition to the Council of Chalcedon, within sight of 'the privileges of that great corps', accepted a diaconate at Alexandria from Cyril; and from the tone of his petition it is clear that he had no vocation. Marinus the Syrian, Anastasius' great praetorian prefect, asked Severus of Antioch to get the metropolitan of Apamea to ordain one of his relatives as priest; he was a poor relation, but even poor relations of so great a man as Marinus were not paupers. Severus was also asked himself to ordain a protégé of the great eunuch Eleutherius, the *sacellarius*. This kind of thing was, according to Justinian, common in the Great Church of Constantinople and the major sees generally. Under the judgment of Pope Felix IV the sixty clergy of Ravenna received 3,000 solidi between them, that is an average annual stipend of 50 solidi; actually the ten priests and eleven deacons would have received larger stipends, perhaps as much as some 100 solidi each. And this was their income from endowments only, without taking their share of the offerings into account.[89]

By contrast the priest or deacon of a rural parish was usually a very humble person, and often miserably paid. If his church was on a great estate, he was normally a *colonus* and had to pay his *capitatio* like the rest, and find a substitute to work his holding. The endowment of rural parishes was often meagre: Gregory the Great licensed the consecration of churches that had as little as 10, 6 or even 3 solidi a year after payment of tax, and this had to cover the lighting and repair of the church as well as support the priest. He had of course his offerings as well—or two-thirds of them, if as in Spain and Gaul the bishop pocketed a third—but they are unlikely to have been substantial. He was moreover subject to other exactions by his bishop, who was wont to make oppressive claims for hospitality and transport on his annual visitation, and levied a fee called *cathedraticum*, which Pope

Pelagius and two Spanish councils endeavoured to limit to two solidi.[90]

An index to the growing wealth of the church is the emergence of simony and kindred abuses. There had, of course, been isolated cases of simony at all times. In the proceedings before Zenophilus, consular of Numidia, in 320, it was alleged that one Victor had given twenty *folles* to Silvanus, the bishop of Cirta, to be ordained priest, and that four hundred *folles* had been paid for the election of Majorinus as bishop of Carthage. Nor did men always pay money for orders because they were financially profitable. Basil found that his rural bishops were accepting bribes for ordinations, but the motive of the ordinands was to escape military service. Antoninus of Ephesus was alleged to sell consecrations of bishops at a regular tariff according to the revenues of the sees: but when John Chrysostom held an investigation the bishops concerned declared that they had paid for their consecration to escape their curial obligations, and were quite content to be unfrocked when John gave them their money back and promised to persuade the emperor to release them from the *curia*.[91]

Simony does not seem to have become a crying scandal until the middle of the fifth century. The emperor Marcian specially requested the Council of Chalcedon to condemn it, and it duly enacted a canon to that effect. At about the same time in the West the Council of Arles also issued a canon against simony. Thereafter imperial laws and ecclesiastical canons against the abuse became common. Bribery was common at all levels, and with it went the use of influence and intimidation. Candidates for ordination bribed bishops or got patrons to exercise pressure on their behalf; candidates for bishoprics bribed or intimidated the lay and clerical electors; candidates for the papacy bribed their electors on an unprecedented scale.[92]

Some payments became habitual and were eventually sanctioned by custom. Justinian prohibited (except in the Great Church of Constantinople) the payment of what were called *insinuativa* (ἐμφανιστικά), fees demanded by the clergy of a church for the admission of new members, but permitted the customary fees to the assistants of the ordaining bishop—provided that they did not exceed one year's stipend.[93]

He also regulated the consecration fees of bishops (ἐνθρονιστικά). These were an old abuse. At the Council of Chalcedon Eusebius, metropolitan of Ancyra, though accepting the patriarchal dignity proposed for Constantinople, pleaded: 'I beg that the cities may not be ruined on account of consecrations, for if the persons elected by the city are not approved by the provincial council and consecrated in the cities themselves, their property goes to ruin. I speak from experience, as I paid a great sum for my predecessor.' Philip, a priest of Constantinople, objected that this kind of thing was abolished by canon, but Eusebius remained sceptical. 'By God's grace the reputation of the holy archbishop Anatolius is unsullied, but no one is immortal.' Justinian allowed the five patriarchs to pay sums not exceeding 20 lb. gold to the bishops and clergy concerned in their consecration. Those appointed to the wealthiest sees, of an annual value exceeding 30 lb. gold, paid 100 solidi to their consecrator and 200 solidi to his notaries and assistants, and so on down a sliding scale: consecrations to sees worth less than 2 lb. gold were free.[94]

Candidates for bishoprics were apparently allowed reasonable election expenses. In a case tried before Pope Gelasius a certain Eucharistus stated that he had given Faustus, a *defensor* of the church of Ravenna, 63 solidi to spend in connection with his candidature for the see of Volaterrae. He had not been elected and reclaimed the money, but Faustus counterclaimed that he had spent part of the money, $22\frac{2}{3}$ solidi on food and forage for the decurions whom he had produced to support his candidate, and 9 solidi for investigating a false charge (no details are given of this mysterious item). Gelasius allowed the counterclaim and ordered Faustus to repay the balance.[95]

As Christianity spread and the wealth of the church increased, so the numbers of the clergy grew. The see of Rome already had a staff of 154, including 46 priests and seven deacons (a number which the popes considered canonical and never exceeded), in the middle of the third century. But in this Rome was quite exceptional. At Cirta, the capital of Numidia, when on 1 June 302 the *curator* of the city cited the clergy to surrender the scriptures, there appeared at the house where the Christians assembled, besides the bishop, three priests, two deacons, four subdeacons, and half a dozen gravediggers; the *curator* later visited the houses of seven readers, who had failed to present themselves. There were thus a total of sixteen, not counting the gravediggers. Constantine in 326, alarmed by the flood of decurions who took orders in order to escape their curial duties, endeavoured to fix the numbers of the clergy, ordering that none should be ordained save to fill a vacancy caused by death, but this law, if ever enforced, inevitably became a dead letter. No further restrictions were imposed until the Council of Chalcedon enacted that clergy should only be ordained to a particular church.[96]

In 518 a petition against Peter, metropolitan of Apamea in Syria, by the staff of the episcopal church, was signed by 17 priests, over 42 deacons, 3 subdeacons and 15 readers; they thus numbered about 80. The judgment of Pope Felix IV on the revenues of the metropolitan see of Ravenna was signed by 60 persons, including ten priests, eleven deacons, five subdeacons, twelve acolytes, twelve readers and four singers. The patriarchal churches naturally had larger staffs. Justinian ordered that the establishment of the Great Church of Constantinople should be reduced to 60 priests, 100 deacons, 90 subdeacons, 110 readers, 25 singers and 100 doorkeepers—485 persons in all—besides 40 deaconesses; and they served only four of the many churches of the capital.[97]

To these must be added gravediggers and hospital attendants. The latter, the *parabalani*, were at Alexandria reduced to 500 in 416, only to be increased to 600 two years later. At Constantinople there was a body of 950 *decani*, who under a scheme laid down by Constantine provided free burials for the whole city. He gave immunity from taxation to 950 shops on condition that each provided a *decanus*. Anastasius added another 150 shops, and also an endowment of 70 lb. gold a year. Justinian reorganised the service with minute attention to detail. Of the 1,100 shops 800 were to provide a man each, the other 300 to pay a cash commutation. This money, together with Anastasius' endowment (which had apparently dwindled), was to furnish pay not only for the 800 *decani* (182 solidi a month) but for female mourners drawn from various sources (218 solidi a month). The standard funeral was free, but those who wanted more numerous mourners or specially splendid biers had to pay extra.[98]

Many of these clerics were engaged on administrative duties. From the time of the Council of Chalcedon one of the priests in every episcopal church in the East served as general manager of the finances. The popes employed members of their clergy as regional agents in charge of the church lands. There were also sacrists in charge of the church treasures and plate, and keepers of the archives. The charitable activities of the see were conducted by managers of its hospitals, almshouses and hostels. In any episcopal church of any importance there were moreover bodies of notaries, who kept its records, and of *defensores* (ἔκδικοι), who guarded its legal interests and served as clerical policemen. These were recruited from the clergy, holding the grades of lector, sub-deacon, deacon, and priest as they rose in seniority from the bottom of the list to *primicerius notariorum* or *defensorum*.[99]

These figures refer to the staffs of episcopal churches only, and do not take into account the numerous clergy who served in independent charitable institutions, and in urban and rural parochial churches. We have only two figures. When Ibas, bishop of Edessa, told the Council of Chalcedon that his clergy numbered 200 or more, he was probably referring to the total number in his city or see; the staff of the episcopal church of Edessa at this date comprised 14 priests, 37 deacons, 23 subdeacons and one reader. All the clergy of the church of Carthage, according to Victor Vitensis, numbered 500 or more, including boy readers: the cathedral church is unlikely to have had a larger staff than the Great Church of Constantinople, and the figure no doubt represents the total of the clergy in the city.[100]

The clergy enjoyed a number of fiscal and other privileges, mostly granted to them by Constantine or Constantius II. They, or the poorest and humblest grades among them, were, as we have seen, immune from the *collatio lustralis*. They were also exempted with their families and households from the *capitatio*; this privilege was later restricted as the numbers of the rural clergy grew, and each church was allowed only a fixed number of immune places, so that clergy in excess of the quota had to pay poll tax. The clergy were also exempt from billeting and corvées. These privileges mainly affected the humbler sort of clerics. Those who owned land had no immunities; despite representations by the council of Ariminum Constantius II refused to remit either the regular tax or additional levies. The privilege which affected upper-class clergy was immunity from the *curia*, a concession which caused endless conflicts between the government and the church.[101]

It remains to consider how the clergy were appointed and from what classes they were drawn. It was the prerogative of the bishop —except in so far as he delegated his functions to rural bishops— to make all ordinations in his territory. It was also an old rule, affirmed by the Councils of Arles and Nicaea and constantly re-enacted, that clergy might not migrate from the city in which they were first ordained. In theory therefore a bishop had complete control over the appointment and promotion of all clerics in his territory, and conversely all clerics were entirely dependent for their advancement on their bishop: in point of fact the rule against migration was laxly enforced, as its frequent repetition shows.[102]

It was no doubt always the normal rule that a man should take minor orders first, and move up by regular stages to the priesthood. This was certainly the ideal inculcated by the popes in the late fourth and fifth centuries. Siricius ruled that an ordinand must be reader or exorcist for two years and subdeacon for five before going on to the diaconate and that deacons must not be ordained before thirty or priests before thirty-five. Zosimus stiffened these rules; an ordinand must serve five years as reader, then four as subdeacon and five as deacon before reaching the priesthood. Zosimus had, however, to admit that this strict order of promotion was little observed in Gaul or Spain, or even in Africa, where discipline was better enforced.[103]

The rules seem excessively rigid, and would have made the church too like the civil service—which Zosimus cites as a model. They were naturally cherished by the mass of the clergy, who resented persons who possessed influence or were favourites of the bishop being ordained or promoted out of turn. When Peter of Apamea ordained a layman straight to the diaconate, his readers raised a protest and so annoyed the bishop that he blasphemously declared: 'if you do not keep quiet, I will ordain you subdeacons, so that if the Crucified himself came down he could not rescue you from my hands'—the significance of the threat is obscure: perhaps subdeacons at Apamea were, as at Alexandria ad Issum, unpaid and overworked.[104]

Irregular promotions were, however, not uncommon: Cyril of Alexandria made the *agens in rebus* who was deputed to serve him at the Council of Ephesus a deacon. They might be forced on a bishop by external pressure. Pope Felix IV had to warn the clergy of Ravenna that laymen, including monks, must not seek the patronage of great men to obtain orders to which they were not entitled, thus making their bishop appear unfair if he complied or ungracious if he did not. As we have seen Severus of Antioch had great difficulty in refusing a priesthood to a candidate recommended to him by the *sacellarius*, and wrote a piteous letter to one of the other imperial eunuchs, begging him to placate the great man: but he himself backed the candidature of another layman, recommended by Marinus, the praetorian prefect, for a priesthood at Apamea.[105]

Apart from such external pressure and the claims of seniority a bishop had a free hand in appointing and promoting his own clergy, the *cardinales* or *canonici*. In the separately endowed churches he had to consider the wishes of the founder and, when the church was on an estate, those of the landowner, whether he had built the church himself or not. An imperial law of 398 enacted that in a church on an estate only a *colonus* of that estate might be ordained, and another of 409 made the ordination of a *colonus* even on his own estate subject to the landlord's consent. The Council of Arausio in 441 dealt with the rather delicate case when a bishop founded a church, perhaps on an estate of his own, in another bishop's territory. It ruled that the bishop in whose territory the church lay must have control, but he ought to ordain such candidates as the founder bishop presented to him, and accept any already ordained clergy that the founder wished to institute. Justinian enacted that the founder of a church or its patron, who provided its revenue, was not at liberty to present anyone he liked to the bishop to be ordained without question; the bishop was to examine candidates and reject the unworthy. The Council of Orleans in 541 forbade the owners of estates to employ clergy from elsewhere in their churches without the bishop's consent.[106]

Ordinands might be of any age, from infants to men of advanced years. Most candidates were no doubt young men, but some took orders after having completed a secular career, like the retired *memorialis* Euthalius who became a priest at Cyrrhus, and it was not uncommon for parents to dedicate their children in infancy to the church. Siricius and Zosimus made special rules for those who had entered orders in infancy; they were not to be promoted above the grade of reader under twenty however long their service. An interesting example of the variety which prevailed in the age of ordination is provided by the Council of Mopsuestia in 550. Of fifteen aged priests and deacons of that city five had received their first orders at thirty or over (two at thirty-seven or eight), four between fifteen and twenty-four and no fewer than six at ten or under (some at five or six).[107]

Most candidates for orders were volunteers, but by no means all. There are innumerable stories of holy men, monks or hermits, who despite their protests of unworthiness were more or less forcibly ordained by strongminded bishops, usually supported and even pressed on by popular clamour. In other cases compulsion was applied for less worthy motives. There was an embarrassing incident at Hippo when the enormously rich young senator Pinianus came to visit Augustine. The people of Hippo, thinking that he would be a desirable catch owing to his wealth and generosity, clamoured that he be ordained priest forthwith, and the demeanour of the congregation was so threatening that Augustine was almost forced to comply, and only managed to rescue the terrified and unwilling young man by making him swear in public never to accept ordination in any other city. The emperor Majorian found it necessary to legislate against forcible ordinations, allowing the victims to divest themselves of their orders and recover 10 lb. gold as damages from the archdeacon of the church concerned. He states that parents often encouraged such practices in order to get rid of sons whom they disliked and wished to cut out of their inheritance.[108]

By a canon first promulgated by the Council of Nicaea and re-enacted by a number of later councils, a bishop might not leave the see to which he had been consecrated and move on to another. This rule seems to have been fairly well observed; Socrates could only collect a dozen cases of translation in all the Eastern empire over a period of two generations. It was aimed against ambitious careerists, but its strict observance worked hardly for men who like Gregory Nazianzen had been consecrated unwillingly to petty sees which gave no scope for their abilities. It also prevented any promotion from ordinary to metropolitan or patriarchal sees, and meant that men of tried ability and experience were excluded from the most responsible positions in the church.[109]

Bishops stood in a class apart from the ordinary clergy. They were not necessarily chosen from among the clergy of the city—the canon against the migration of clerics to cities other than their own did not apply when the choice of a bishop was being made—and even laymen might be elected. Hosius elicited a canon from the Council of Sardica that a layman must serve as reader, deacon and priest before he became a bishop. This became regular papal policy: Leo directed that in Illyricum metropolitans should be chosen from the priests and deacons of the metropolitical church. Eventually Justinian made an imperial law that only *bona fide* clerics of at least six months' standing might become bishops; the rule was not to be evaded by bestowing the minor orders on the candidate a day or two before his consecration.[110]

This rule was naturally favoured by the clergy, who disliked having an outsider put in over their heads, but the people often thought otherwise. What they wanted was either a really holy man, a monk or hermit, whose intercessions on their behalf would be likely to be effective with the powers above—and such holy men were often not in orders—or a man of position and influence, whose intercessions to the imperial government would be effective. As the people of Hydrax and Palaebisca explained to Synesius, Orion the bishop of Erythrum (under whom they had been) had been 'very mild', and so they had chosen a bishop of their own, Siderius, 'who had come down from the court of the emperor Valens on business connected with the care of lands for which he had petitioned—a man who could do harm to his enemies and good to his friends'.[111]

The popular will often prevailed, and the order laid down by the popes was regularly broken. There are countless instances of monks and hermits being, often much against their will, forced to become bishops. Some were a great success: others, like the unhappy Theodore of Syceon, who ultimately got leave to retire, were quite incapable of handling the administrative work which a bishop had to perform. Ordinary laymen also continued to be consecrated down to the sixth century.[112]

Bishops, like the lower clergy, were on occasion consecrated against their will. Sometimes it was the people of the city who insisted on imposing their will, as in the famous case of Ambrose. Sometimes it was the imperial government which wanted to relegate a powerful subject to a position where he could do no harm; Cyrus, once praetorian prefect of the East and prefect of Constantinople, was made bishop of Cotyaeum when he fell from power. Sometimes it was a strong-minded metropolitan who applied pressure and not always for worthy motives. Bassianus was a wealthy Ephesian who had endeared himself to the people by his charity—he had founded a hospital with seventy beds. According to his own story, which he told to the Council of Chalcedon, Memnon, the bishop of Ephesus, was jealous of him and, wishing to get rid of him, despite his protests consecrated him bishop of the miserable little city of Euaza by violence—'from the third hour to the sixth he exhausted me with blows at the altar, and the holy gospel and the altar were covered with blood'. Bassianus, it may be suspected, had higher ambitions than Euaza; his subsequent career will be told later. The church had no sympathy for bishops who refused to go to the sees to which they were consecrated: the Council of Antioch ordered them to be excommunicated.[113]

Sometimes an aged bishop arranged for his successor to be consecrated during his lifetime: Augustine was made bishop of Hippo in this way by his predecessor Valerian. But the practice was considered irregular and was condemned by a Roman council in 465. The normal procedure was for the clergy and people on the one hand, and the metropolitan and other bishops of the province on the other, to agree on a candidate: when the see was itself a metropolis it was apparently in early times the other bishops of the province who represented the episcopal side; later (in the East) the patriarch's consent was required. The role played by the clergy and people in the proceedings varied greatly according to circumstances. Sometimes they had no ideas of their own and accepted a candidate chosen by the metropolitan or the bishops, or even asked him or them to find a suitable man. When bishop Aeneas died the little Christian community of Gaza could not choose a successor; there were a number of suitable candidates both among the clergy and the laity, but none commanded a majority. So they resolved to send a delegation to their metropolitan, John of Caesarea, to ask him to choose, and he picked on an outsider, Porphyry.[114]

Frequently, and especially in times of acute doctrinal controversy, the bishops took a high hand and consecrated someone of their party in defiance of the wishes of his future flock. This abuse appeared very early. The Council of Ancyra, held before Nicaea, had to deal with cases of bishops whom, though duly consecrated, their cities had refused to receive, and so also had the Council of Antioch, held soon after Nicaea. These homeless bishops were rather a nuisance, being liable to make trouble with the bishops of their native towns, or to take over sees which fell vacant without the leave of their metropolitan and colleagues. The imposition of bishops on unwilling cities was often effected by force, with the aid of troops supplied by the imperial government; after Chalcedon very few orthodox patriarchs of Alexandria took possession of their sees otherwise. Apart from these notorious cases, there was a tendency in the fifth and sixth centuries for patriarchs and metropolitans to ride roughshod over the rights of the cities. Leo had to rebuke the metropolitan of Achaea for doing so, and Sisinnius of Constantinople consecrated Proclus bishop of Cyzicus, only to find that the Cyzicenes had chosen another man.[115]

Usually, however, the people of the city had some say in the election of their bishop. Occasionally they took matters into their own hands by demonstrating with such fervour for the man of their choice that the bishops had to agree. Ambrose and Martin were thus chosen by popular acclamation, and while the former was acceptable to his future colleagues, the latter was not. 'He is a contemptible person,' they objected, 'unworthy of the episcopacy, a man of despicable appearance with dirty clothes and unkempt hair'; but they had to consecrate him.[116]

For a popular candidate to be installed only one bishop was absolutely necessary and one could generally be cajoled or bullied into acting. The story of Bassianus' election to the see of Ephesus was thus told to the Council of Chalcedon by his consecrator, Olympius of Theodosiopolis. 'The clergy of the city of Ephesus itself notified me. "Come to Ephesus," they said, "so that the city can receive a consecration canonically, because the late bishop Basil of holy memory has passed away." When I received this letter, I went, supposing that other reverend bishops had been summoned too. Three days before he was due to enter the church and be enthroned I put up at an hotel and waited for the other bishops, so that there should be a canonical consecration according to custom. I waited one, two, three days at my hotel and no other reverend bishop appeared, and finally some of the reverend clergy came and said to me: "There are not any other bishops here. What's to be done?" "If there are not other reverend bishops here," I replied, "what can I do alone? It is contrary to a strict observance of the canons for one bishop to deal with a church, especially such an important metropolis." While they were talking with me, the building where I was staying was surrounded by an enormous crowd and one Holosericus—that was his name, an official of the *comes*, I think—came in with dagger drawn and he and all the crowd carried me off to the church.'[117]

Popular elections were not always uncontested, and might lead to sanguinary rioting. Ammianus describes the contest between Damasus and Ursinus for the papal throne; after one brawl in the basilica of Sicininus one hundred and thirty-seven corpses were removed. We possess official correspondence between the imperial government and the prefects of the city about the later contest between Boniface and Eulalius; it vividly illustrates the prefect's difficulties in maintaining order in the face of popular passions.[118]

Such tumultuous elections, whether contested or uncontested, were somewhat exceptional. More usually there was an orderly debate. The electoral body is usually described as *clerus et plebs*, but neither body is clearly defined. *Clerus* probably in practice normally meant the priests and deacons of the central episcopal establishment, but at one election Pope Gelasius ordered that the priests and deacons from all the parishes should be convened. *Plebs* might in a small community mean the whole body of the laity. Synesius speaks of the unanimous vote of the whole people at the village see of Olbia, and at another village see, that of Hydrax and Palaebisca, describes how he summoned a mass meeting at which women were present. But in the middle of the fifth century the formula changes to *clerus ordo et plebs* or *clerus honorati ordo et plebs*, and it may be suspected that the common people were in most cities given little opportunity to do more than acclaim a candidate chosen by their betters: the mid fourth-century canons of Laodicea even ordained that 'the mob should not be allowed to make the choice of those to be appointed bishops'. The lay electors were in fact the members of the city council, and the local notables who belonged to the imperial aristocracy.[119]

If the election was unanimous and the candidate acceptable to the consecrators, all went well. If on the other hand either of these conditions was not fulfilled, a deadlock might ensue, and no regular procedure was at first laid down for dealing with such cases. Pope Leo directed his vicar at Thessalonica that the metropolitan of the province should choose the worthier candidate in case of a disputed election. Sidonius Apollinaris tells of two episcopal elections which he witnessed. At Cabillonum there were three candidates, none of them very desirable, a nobleman of dissolute life, a man who based his hopes on his lavish treating of the electorate, and a third who had promised grants of church lands to his backers. The metropolitan rejected all three, and persuaded the meeting to adopt the local archdeacon. At Bituriges there were so many candidates that two benches barely accommodated them, and opinion was quite divided: once again the presiding bishop— in this case Sidonius himself—put forward a man of his own choice.[120]

The mid fifth-century Council of Arles had before this date laid down a procedure for avoiding such difficulties: the bishops were to select three candidates from whom the people were to make their choice. This canon had evidently already become a dead letter, if it was ever observed. In the West no machinery for avoiding disputed elections was in fact ever evolved. In the East the rule was adopted that the clergy, decurions and notables of the city should nominate three candidates, from whom the metro- politan should choose one. This rule was apparently laid down by ecclesiastical authority and confirmed by an imperial law under Anastasius; Severus of Antioch alludes to it as a novel procedure. It was re-enacted by Justinian in 528.[121]

Bishops of important sees are known to have notified the emperor of their consecration. When there was any doubt about the validity of an election, it obviously strengthened one's case to be acknow- ledged by the emperor, and this was probably often the motive. Athanasius, over whose election some doubts were—later, at any rate—raised, wrote promptly to Constantine. Bassianus evidently lost no time in informing Theodosius II of his election at Ephesus, and at the Council of Chalcedon explained that the emperor had accepted it. 'When our most pious emperor heard the news he forthwith confirmed the action taken and forthwith issued a memorandum publicly confirming the bishopric. Afterwards he again sent an imperial letter by Eusebius the silentiary confirming the bishopric.'[122]

There is, however, no sign that official imperial confirmation was required, still less anything in the nature of a congé d'élire. It is indeed remarkable how little the imperial government inter- fered in episcopal elections. Constantine, it is true, when the see of Antioch fell vacant soon after Nicaea, appointed two of his comites to supervise the council of bishops which met to make the election, and when the candidate elected, Eusebius of Caesarea, refused the honour, suggested two names to them. But this action did not become a precedent. The emperors, of course, in periods of controversy, often lent their aid—including the use of troops— to the party which they were at the time backing, but they seem to have left the choice of the bishops whom they should thus assist in occupying their sees to the appropriate ecclesiastical authorities.[123]

The one exception was the see of Constantinople. Theodosius I ordered the bishops assembled for the Council of Constantinople to submit to him a list of suitable candidates from which he could choose: he chose the last name on the list, Nectarius. His successor, John Chrysostom, was picked by Eutropius, Arcadius' chief eunuch, and Nestorius was the choice of Theodosius II. But even in the capital free elections were sometimes allowed. Socrates describes the debates which preceded the election of Sisinnius in 426—he was the people's favourite. After Nestorius' deposition the disputes before Maximian's election were so long drawn out that when he died three years later the emperor served a mandate to the bishops to consecrate his runner-up Proclus. In 449 Theodosius II at first ordered the clergy of Constantinople to produce a list of suitable candidates, reserving the final choice for himself, but later allowed the clergy to choose. Thereafter the emperors probably in effect nominated the patriarchs of their capital. The monks of Constantinople said that Menas was elected 'by the choice and vote of our most pious emperors and of the devout clergy of his most holy church and of Christ-loving men in various ranks and offices of state and of ourselves and all orthodox Christians'. Pope Agapetus, who consecrated him, said more accurately: 'If the choice of the most serene emperors smiled upon him above the rest, yet such was the approval of all the clergy and people that he may be believed to have been chosen by everyone.'[124]

In so far as the emperors did intervene in episcopal elections it was either to secure zealous pastors for their capital or to promote the doctrinal views which they thought to be true. It was left for the Merovingian kings to treat bishoprics as pieces of patronage, and to issue precepts to their bishops to select their ministers and favourites.[125]

The clergy were drawn from almost every class of society. Slaves were excluded from holy orders; they had to be manumitted by their masters before they could be ordained. This was the rule both of the state and of the church. The ordination of slaves was prohibited by Arcadius in 398, by Valentinian III in 452, and by Zeno in 484. Justinian relaxed the rule, allowing slaves to be ordained with their owner's consent; they reverted to him if they abandoned the church. He also ruled that if a slave were ordained without his master's knowledge, he could only be reclaimed within a year.[126]

On the clerical side Pope Leo took a very Roman view on the question. 'Persons whom the merit neither of their birth nor of their character recommends are being freely admitted to holy orders, and those who have not been able to obtain their freedom from their owners are raised to the dignity of the priesthood, as if servile vileness could lawfully receive this honour. . . . There is a double wrong in this matter, that the sacred ministry is polluted by such vile company, and the rights of owners are violated, in so far as an audacious and illicit usurpation is involved.' In the sixth century the first Council of Orleans in 511 ordered that a bishop who ordained a slave without his master's consent should make twofold restitution, and the ban was repeated by the third Council of Orleans in 538, and extended by the fifth in 545 to freedmen, for whose ordination their patron's consent was required.[127]

Similar restrictions were placed on the ordination of *coloni adscripticii* or *originales* in the fifth century. In 409 the imperial government in the East forbade *coloni* to be ordained without their landlord's consent, even to serve on the estate to which they were attached. The laws of Valentinian III and Zeno applied to *coloni* as well as slaves. Justinian again was more liberal, allowing *adscripticii* to be ordained even without their landlord's leave, provided that they served on the estate and did their agricultural work. The church again agreed. Pope Leo ruled that *originales* must not be ordained unless their landlords requested it or at least agreed to it. Pope Gelasius repeated the ban, and so did the third Council of Orleans, citing the authority of the Holy See.[128]

For both slaves and *coloni* who were ordained despite the law Valentinian III laid down rules governing their owner's or landlord's right of recovery. If they had become priests or bishops they could not be reclaimed, and deacons could redeem themselves by surrendering their *peculium* and providing a substitute. Those in minor orders were restored to their masters, unless covered by the rule of thirty years' prescription. The correspondence of Pope Gelasius reveals him enforcing these rules at the instance of indignant owners or landlords.[129]

How many slaves or *coloni* actually took orders with or without their masters' consent we have no means of telling, but probably the majority of the rural clergy on the great estates were drawn from their servile or ascript population. We do not know of any who rose to high office in the church. Justinian enacted that the tenure of the episcopate extinguished servile or ascript condition, but whether this law had more than a theoretical application we do not know.[130]

In the East there was never any ban on the free working population of the towns. The humblest grades of the clergy, the gravediggers and hospital attendants, were recruited from them, and so too no doubt were many of those in minor orders who continued working at their trades. In the West the bakers of Rome were forbidden to take orders in 365, and all members of the Roman guilds in 445. The ban was extended in 452 to the *collegiati* of other cities; Majorian re-enacted the second law. We know of only one individual case of a small trader who took orders, and he does not appear in a favourable light; Albinus in his old profession had bought the plate of a parish church in the territory of Spoletium for a few solidi, and though now in orders refused to part with it though offered a refund of the price.[131]

Very few soldiers or veterans seem to have taken orders. Only two are known to fame. Victricius, who became bishop of Rotomagus in 386, had served in the ranks, only securing his premature discharge with great difficulty from the authorities. Martin, bishop of Tours, had also served as a private in the guards, but he is hardly a typical case, for he had from boyhood resolved to lead a holy life, and was put into the army by his father, an officer, with the object of knocking such nonsense out of him. Otherwise we hear only of those who took orders, usually in the humblest grades of the clergy, to avoid conscription. Basil reproved his rural bishops for ordaining such men for money, and a law addressed to Stilicho alludes to sons of veterans or others liable to service who endeavoured to evade it, or, having been conscripted, to secure their discharge, by becoming clerics or gravediggers.[132]

Some persons of very humble origin certainly rose in the church. The Council of Carthage in 421 passed a canon claiming for the church the lands acquired by men who when they were ordained had owned nothing, and had risen to be priests and even bishops. But individual cases are hard to find. The most striking is that of Aetius. He was the son of a provincial official who misconducted himself and had his property confiscated. Left a penniless orphan with his widowed mother to support, Aetius first worked as a goldsmith, at the same time taking lessons in philosophy. On his mother's death he was able to abandon his trade, and by his brilliance in debate attracted the attention of a professor who in return for domestic service gave him a literary education. Eventually his master became jealous of him and turned him out. For the next few years he led a wandering life, patronised from time to time by various clergy and later practising as a doctor. Eventually one of his clerical patrons became bishop of Antioch and ordained him deacon. He ended his life as a bishop.[133]

To turn to the opposite end of the social scale, senators and other *honorati* do not often seem to have taken orders, and if they did usually became bishops straight away: the case of Paulinus, a wealthy Gallic senator who abandoned his career and sold his estates to pursue a religious life and only became bishop of Nola many years later, is exceptional. It caused a sensation when Ambrose, son of a praetorian prefect and himself consular of Aemilia, was chosen bishop of Milan. A few years later it occasioned surprise when Nectarius, a senator of Constantinople, was, though a layman, put on the short list for the bishopric of Constantinople, and was selected by Theodosius I: his brother Arsacius later occupied the same see.[134]

As the senatorial order expanded and took in men of humbler station, and as the wealth and social position of bishops increased, it no doubt became commoner for senators to condescend to be consecrated. Pope Siricius regarded as an abuse the consecration of those 'who have once gloried in wearing the belt of a secular office' or 'have exulted in secular pomp or have chosen to serve in affairs of state and undertaken the care of worldly matters'. Pope Innocent specifically forbade the ordination or consecration of those who had held *administrationes*. A century later Caesarius of Arles asked Pope Symmachus to renew the ban against former provincial governors. The known instances of such men becoming bishops are not very numerous even in the fifth and sixth centuries. In Gaul Germanus was elected to the see of Autissiodurum by acclamation after having served as provincial governor, and Sidonius Apollinaris, an ex-prefect of the city, was chosen bishop of the Civitas Arvernorum. In the East Chrysanthus, a former vicar of Britain, was made the Novatian bishop of Constantinople, and Thalassius, a former praetorian prefect of Illyricum who was expected to be promoted to the prefecture of the East, was consecrated bishop of Caesarea by Proclus. In the sixth century Ephraem, *comes Orientis*, was elected patriarch of Antioch. These cases all excited comment, and it is to be inferred that it always remained unusual for senators to take orders, even to occupy the great sees.[135]

The great majority of the higher clergy, the urban deacons and priests and the bishops, were drawn from the middle classes, professional men, officials, and above all *curiales*. This was only natural. For these grades a fairly high standard of education was desirable, and literacy essential—the latter ideal seems to have been generally achieved, for we never find a bishop, or the priest or deacon who deputised for him at a council, who could not write his subscription, though some from Mesopotamia could do so only in Syriac. This qualification ruled out most of the lower classes. On the other hand the higher branches of the clerical career offered social and financial advantages which, if negligible to a senator, were attractive to a man of the middle classes.

We hear of few doctors or professors who took orders except for Aetius and Augustine, both somewhat exceptional cases. We know of only one military officer: Mamertinus, the tribune at Favianae in Raetia, whom Severinus inspired into military activity against the barbarian raiders, later became a bishop, presumably when his unit melted away and the province was abandoned. Lawyers on the other hand are frequently mentioned. The Council of Sardica ruled that if a rich man or a practising barrister were thought worthy of a bishopric, he should first serve as reader, deacon and priest for a reasonable time. Pope Innocent's high principles excluded them. 'How many have we learned have been summoned to the episcopacy from those who after receiving the grace of baptism have occupied themselves with practice at the bar and have obstinately persisted in this course?' he wrote to the bishops of Spain. 'Rufinus and Gregory are said to be of that number.' He banned the ordination of those who had after baptism conducted cases in the courts, but his was a lone voice. Apart from Ambrose and Germanus, who had both practised at the bar before obtaining provincial governorships, Augustine's friend Alypius had been three times assessor before he became bishop of Tagaste. Severus of Antioch read for the bar, but did not actually practise; but his biographer Zacharias, bishop of Mitylene, had been a lawyer; and Severus speaks of four lawyers whom he ordained.[136]

Officials met with the disapproval of several popes and councils. Siricius forbade the ordination of anyone who after baptism had held an official post. The Council of Toledo in 401 ruled that anyone who had served after baptism and worn the cloak and belt of the official, even if he had committed no grave sins, should if admitted to the clergy be excluded from the diaconate or higher orders. Pope Innocent protested to the Spanish bishops against the consecration of officials 'who in obedience to the authorities have perforce executed cruel judgments'. Caesarius of Arles asked Pope Symmachus to forbid the ordination of those who had served in provincial offices.[137]

The state was also concerned in this matter. There was probably little objection to higher grade officials taking orders; they were expressly allowed to do so by a law of 466 after completing their term of service. We have already met two palatine civil servants who took orders at or near the end of their careers, Euthalius the ex-*memorialis* who became a priest at Cyrrhus, and Theodore, the *agens in rebus*, who after over twenty years' service (which entitled him to retire with an honorary principate) was ordained deacon of Alexandria.[138]

With *cohortales*, whose service was followed by the financial charge of the primipilate and who were bound to their position by a hereditary tie, the government was more severe. By a law of 361 they might take orders if not liable to the primipilate or similar obligations, or owing anything to the treasury, provided that they received the permission of their chief and colleagues; if they failed to obtain permission, two-thirds of their property passed to their sons or relations, or in default of them to the *officium*. The law of 466 altogether prohibited *cohortales* to take orders even after retirement. Justinian in 531 excluded all *cohortales* from the priesthood—in 546 from the minor orders also—unless they had in childhood entered a monastery, or, by the later law, had been monks for at least fifteen years. He thus in effect allowed only sons of provincial officials to be ordained, and that after they had given clear proof of their vocation. On officials who had actually seen service he held the same views as Pope Innocent. 'It would be improper for a man who has been bred up in severe exactions and the sins that—in all probability—ensue to be at one moment a *cohortalis* and do the harshest things and then be straight away ordained a priest and teach about loving kindness and forgiveness.'[139]

These rules were not rigidly kept; in both his laws Justinian condoned past breaches, and we know of a *cohortalis* who a year or two before the first law became a bishop: Stephen, elected to the see of Larissa in full legal form, chosen by the metropolitan from three candidates submitted by the clergy and people, states in an appeal to Pope Boniface II: 'In my previous secular life I was a provincial official; in this modest career I passed my life humbly.' At the end of the sixth century officials who had not cleared their accounts with the treasury were still taking holy orders, and Maurice had to issue a law once again forbidding these attempts to evade a reckoning.[140]

To judge by the bulk of the imperial legislation on the subject the great majority of the clergy were drawn from the curial order. Men of this class had from the worldly point of view a special incentive in the immunity from curial duties and charges which Constantine in the first ardour of his conversion granted to the clergy. This grant was never withdrawn, but the government strove to counter its deleterious effect on the city councils either by banning the ordination of men of curial family or of fortune up to curial standard, or alternatively by compelling a curial ordinand to surrender his property (or at least two-thirds of it) to a son or other relation who would take his place on the council, or to the council itself. Constantine himself initiated the first policy, his son Constantius II towards the end of his reign introduced the second. In 398 Arcadius tried to revive the absolute ban on the ordination of *curiales* in the East, but evidently without much success, and Valentinian III and Majorian made the same attempt in the West in 439 and in 452, and again in 458: these laws were more severe on clerics in minor orders, who were to be returned to their councils without the option, whereas bishops, priests and deacons who slipped through the net were only compelled to surrender their property or perform their curial duties by deputy. Finally Justinian banned the ordination of *curiales* unless they had, like *cohortales*, either entered a monastery in childhood, or been monks for at least fifteen years.[141]

The laws themselves, which at frequent intervals condoned past breaches wholesale, especially when the offenders had reached the higher orders, and sometimes even made provision for future cases in which the ban should be broken, amply demonstrate that *curiales* despite all the efforts of the imperial government did take orders in large numbers, and frequently managed to keep their property when they did so, at least in the fourth and fifth centuries: by the sixth century the curial order had probably become so depleted that the flow of ordinands from it was much reduced and its members were on the whole humble folk, who found it more difficult to defy or evade the law.

The ecclesiastical authorities at first disliked the imperial legislation, but gradually came to acquiesce in it. Ambrose in 384 complained bitterly that 'if a bishop seeks the privilege of laying aside the curial burden, he has to surrender possession of all the property of his father and grandfather', and in 388-9 protested to Theodosius that 'those who have performed the office of priest or served the church for thirty or any number of years are being dragged away from their sacred office and assigned to the *curia*': it was perhaps in deference to this protest that Theodosius in 390 allowed all *curiales* ordained in or before 388 to keep their property.[142]

Pope Innocent found religious objections to the ordination of *curiales*. To the Spanish bishops he proclaimed that men 'who in obedience to the authorities have executed the orders given to them' and 'have exhibited theatrical shows and games to the people' were unworthy to be bishops. But he added: 'with regard to *curiales* we have to beware lest the same men who have been *curiales* may one day be claimed by their *curiae*—which we frequently see happening'. To Victricius of Rotomagus he took the same equivocal line. 'Moreover some of our brothers often try to ordain *curiales* or those involved in public functions. But later they suffer more sorrow, when some order is made by the emperor to recall them, than they had joy in enlisting them. For it is manifest that in the actual course of their public duties they produce theatrical shows, which are without doubt inventions of the devil, and either preside or are concerned in the exhibition of games.' To Felix of Nuceria he was franker. 'About *curiales* it stands to reason that, although some are to be found of that class who ought to be ordained, still we must beware of them because they are so often reclaimed for the council.'[143]

Justinian endeavoured to justify the ban on moral grounds: like *cohortales*, *curiales* were unsuited by their official duties from preaching the gospel of loving kindness. Later popes accepted the ban on practical grounds. Gelasius in his directions to his bishops forbade them to ordain a *curialis*, and so also did Gregory the Great, 'lest after receiving holy orders he may be compelled to return to his public functions'.[144]

The emperor Constans hoped that the clergy would become a hereditary class, like soldiers, officials or shippers, their sons, as inheriting their father's immunities, carrying on their sacred duties. 'All the clergy ought to be free from curial burdens and all trouble about civic duties, but their sons, if they are not held liable to the *curia*, ought to persevere in the church.' This hope was not fulfilled. There were of course great clerical families which produced bishops over several generations, and no doubt lesser clerical families which produced a succession of priests and deacons. But the clergy never became a caste. Most of the clerics of whom we know either had themselves previously followed a lay career or were the sons of laymen. And we know of sons of clergy who took up a secular career, or at least were trained for it. Chrysanthus, the son of Marcian, a Novatian bishop of Constantinople, became consular of an Italian province and vicar of Britain. The grandfather of Severus, bishop of Antioch, was bishop of Sozopolis, but his father was a decurion.[145]

The rules of clerical celibacy or continence may have had some effect, in areas where they were inculcated or observed, in preventing the clergy from becoming a hereditary caste. It was an old and universal tradition of the church that a man might not marry after ordination to the diaconate, priesthood or episcopate. The Council of Ancyra, shortly after the Great Persecution, allowed deacons to marry if they stated their intention to do so on ordination. Later the law was extended to subdeacons, and only the minor orders, from reader downward, could marry. There was, however, no ban against the ordination of married men or of widowers, and, as a fair number of the clergy took orders late in life, many of them already had children before ordination.[146]

On the sexual life of the married clergy there was a great divergence of opinion. There was a school of thought which held that they ought not to cohabit with their wives. This view was much more strongly held in the West than in the East. Even before the Great Persecution the Council of Illiberis in Spain ordered all the clergy to abstain from their wives, and threatened those who begot children with deprivation. In the East Eusebius advocated continence for priests, but the Council of Nicaea rejected a proposal to enforce it on the clergy, and the Council of Gangra excommunicated laymen who refused to receive communion from a married priest.[147]

In the West it was Pope Siricius (385-99) who first endeavoured to make continence obligatory on bishops, priests and deacons throughout the church. This policy was steadily maintained by his successors, and Leo brought subdeacons within the ban. The lead given by the popes was taken up by episcopal councils in Africa, Spain and Gaul, and by the early fifth century the rule of clerical continence was universally acknowledged in theory throughout the West. Its frequent re-enactment shows that in practice it was difficult to enforce.[148]

In the East Jerome alleged that the churches of the Orient (i.e. the diocese of that name) and Egypt, like those under the Apostolic See, had continent clergy. At about the same date Epiphanius of Cyprus declared that the church did not allow bishops, priests, deacons or even subdeacons to procreate children; but he admitted that the rule was not observed in some areas. In fact both these authors seem to have been guilty of wishful thinking. No Eastern council enjoined continence on the clergy, and the Canons of the Apostles, which reflect contemporary Eastern practice, actually rule that bishops, priests and deacons who put away their wives on the pretext of piety are to be deprived. A bishop might, presumably with her consent, undertake to abstain from intercourse with his wife: it was one of the charges against Antoninus of Ephesus that having done so he had begotten children. In some areas pressure was brought on bishops to make such undertakings: Synesius refused to do so. But according to Socrates it was in his day, the middle of the fifth century, the general rule in the East that even bishops might live a normal married life, and many did beget children. The only exception which he notes was that in Macedonia, Thessaly and Achaea the custom had prevailed of depriving clergy who slept with their wives. He attributes this custom to the influence of Heliodorus, bishop of Tricca in Thessaly: it seems more likely that it was introduced by the popes through their vicars.[149]

Later opinion seems to have hardened about bishops. Justinian forbade the consecration of a man who had a wife living. But he also forbade even a widower who had children or grandchildren to be consecrated and his reasons were prudential. As he put it, a bishop ought to have no other interests to distract him from his duty to his church. Pope Pelagius, when asked to consecrate a married man with children as bishop of Syracuse, interpreted the intention of the law more crudely: he insisted on receiving a bond from the candidate that he would not alienate to his family the lands of the church, or any property he might acquire after consecration.[150]

A general history of the eremitical and monastic movements would lie outside the scope of this book: here only their social and economic aspects can be briefly considered. The founder of the movement was the Egyptian Antony, who retired into the desert in the 270s and during the Great Persecution, about 305-6, organised the numerous disciples who had followed him into a loosely knit community. Such groups of hermits, who lived in separate cells and met only for common worship, were later known as *laurae*. About twenty years later another Egyptian, Pachomius, founded the first *coenobium*, where the monks led a communal life under strict discipline. Both forms of monasticism caught on rapidly in Egypt, and the movement soon spread to Palestine, where the hermit Hilarion organised a *laura* near Gaza in about 330, and a few years later Epiphanius founded another near Eleutheropolis: by the middle years of the century Cyril, bishop of Jerusalem, spoke of 'the regiments of monks'. Rather later, in the latter years of Constantius II, the movement spread to Syria.[151]

In Cappadocia, Armenia and Pontus the monastic life was introduced by Eustathius of Sebaste and popularised by Basil of Caesarea in the 350s and 360s. Further west progress was slower.

One Isaac came from the East to Constantinople in the last years of Valens, and founded a monastery near the city in the early 380s, and an Armenian ex-soldier named John founded another house in Thrace in 386. But when Rufinus, praetorian prefect of the East (392-5), wanted to establish a monastery at Drys in the suburbs of Constantinople, he imported Egyptian monks. On his death they went back to Egypt, and Hypatius, a disciple of John, found the building deserted in 406. Hypatius however soon collected thirty monks, and many other houses were founded about this time.[152]

Athanasius introduced the monastic idea to Gaul and Italy during his exile in the West, but it was slow in catching on. Martin founded the first regular monastery in the West when he became bishop of Tours in 372, and we hear of no others in Gaul until Honoratus established the famous house of Lerins and Cassian two houses at Marseilles in the second decade of the fifth century. In Italy the earliest monastic establishment of which we hear was that which existed under Ambrose's guidance at Milan in the 380s. Augustine seems to have been the first to introduce the monastic life into Africa. But though it made a slow start in the West, by the beginning of the fifth century it had taken root, and thereafter spread rapidly.[153]

These movements had an enormous vogue and many thousands of men became hermits or monks and many thousands of women nuns. No estimate can be made of the total at any date and many of the figures given are no doubt exaggerations, but it may be worth while to quote a few by way of example. The largest figures given are for Egypt, which was not only the home of both the eremitical and monastic movements, but remained their centre and the model to which the rest of the empire looked. Pachomius' original foundation is said to have grown to 1,300 or 1,400, and he also founded other smaller houses of 200 or 300 each. The total inmates of the whole group are stated to have numbered 3,000 before Pachomius' death in 346 and as many as 7,000 at the beginning of the fifth century. Nitria, a favourite haunt of hermits in the desert west of the Delta, is said to have had a population of 5,000, and the four *laurae* of Scetis, a more remote desert settlement, 3,500 inmates. Palladius states that there were 2,000 monks in his day at Alexandria and 1,200 in and about Antinoopolis, as well as twelve convents of women, one of which had sixty inmates. Rufinus declares that there were 5,000 monks in Oxyrhynchus, and another 5,000 in its territory, as well as 20,000 nuns, and 10,000 monks in the Arsinoite; but his figures are very suspect. We hear of some very large monastic houses, one of 800 near the

Red Sea, another of 600 at Thecoa in Palestine. John of Ephesus mentions houses in Mesopotamia of 700 or 750, and one of nearly 1,000 at Amida; but this was formed by amalgamating a number of small houses. Most monasteries were smaller, but the number of houses in a city and its territory might be very large. The signatures to a petition from the monks of Constantinople show 85 monasteries in that city in 518, and 39 across the water in Chalcedon.[154]

Hermits, monks and nuns were drawn indiscriminately from all classes of society from the highest to the lowest, and very little attempt was made by the imperial government to restrict entry into the monastic life. Marcian asked the Council of Chalcedon to forbid the admission of slaves or *adscripticii* to monasteries without their masters' consent. The council issued a canon banning slaves, but took no action about *adscripticii*. Two years later in the West Valentinian III prohibited both classes from becoming monks without their masters' leave, and in 484 Zeno enacted the same rule in the East. Justinian ordered that all applicants of suspect status must pass a three years' probation, and might be reclaimed during that period by their masters. Maurice forbade officials who had not cleared their accounts with the treasury and common soldiers who had not received their discharge to enter monasteries. This seemingly reasonable measure provoked Gregory the Great to the most violent indignation.[155]

It was from the beginning the tradition in Egypt that hermits and monks maintained themselves by the labour of their hands. Many of the hermits wove rush mats, coming down periodically from the desert to the cultivated areas to gather their raw material and to sell their finished products; they also did seasonal agricultural work. Nitria and Scetis were hives of industry, and everyone was expected to work. The Pachomian monasteries were highly organised industrial and agricultural concerns. The monks worked in gangs under foremen at a great variety of trades, as smiths, carpenters, tailors, fullers, tanners, shoemakers, basketmakers, copyists, as well as at agricultural work. The surplus products were sold in the market, and the money devoted to charity.[156]

Even in Egypt hermits and monks received much by way of offerings in kind from the admiring faithful, and monasteries gradually acquired endowments in land and house property by gift and bequest. In Syria it was apparently still customary for hermits and monks to work for their living in the late fourth century, but by the fifth they subsisted almost entirely on charity or on unearned income. Theodoret records as remarkable the régime instituted by Theodosius of Antioch in his monastery near Rhosus. He preached the gospel of work, arguing that monks ought not to be dependent on charity when laymen not only supported their wives and children but paid their taxes and additional levies, and gave their firstfruits to God and alms to beggars. His monks not only cultivated the soil, but wove baskets, mats and sails and dressed hides: he built a little jetty to enable shippers to put in and buy his products.[157]

When Hypatius founded a monastery near Chalcedon in the first decade of the fifth century he maintained the tradition of work. There were not only a steward, a porter, a guestmaster, an infirmarian, a washerman, a man to mend the clothes, another to mind the animals, and a calligrapher to copy books: the monks also worked in the garden and the vineyard and wove hair fabrics, and took weekly turns to do the housework. By the fifth century, however, such industry was exceptional in the East. In the West it seems to have been unknown. John Cassian regretfully contrasts the huge monasteries of Egypt with their thousands of industrious and disciplined monks with the houses of his native Gaul where, because they expected to live on endowments, the monks were few and led idle and irregular lives. An early sixth century Gallic council even forbade abbots to alienate the community's slaves, in case the monks should be compelled to work their land themselves. By this time monasteries both in the East and the West seem normally to have been endowed, and Benedict's renewed insistence on work as well as prayer was a very needful reform.[158]

The eremitic and monastic movements were in some sense a rebellion against the constituted authorities of the church. Monks and hermits set out to live a more strictly Christian life than was possible for the ordinary layman, or for that matter for the ordinary cleric, and as holy men they sometimes thought that they knew better than worldly bishops and were reluctant to submit to their authority. These feelings were generally shared by the laity, which had immense respect for their austere and ascetic lives and reverenced their theological opinions. In doctrinal controversies the bishops who could rally the monks had formidable armies of shock troops at their disposal, and even the imperial government, when it was backing a party which did not command monastic support, found itself in grave difficulties. The emperor Valens had to take very drastic measures against the Egyptian monks, who demonstrated against the Arian bishops whom he favoured: he condemned large numbers to the mines and quarries, deporting them to distant provinces. After the Council of Chalcedon the monks of Palestine raised a regular rebellion against Juvenal, the bishop of Jerusalem, who had changed sides when he saw which way the wind was blowing; troops had to be used to restore order and expel the monophysite bishops whom the monks had installed.[159]

Monks, even if laymen, as they commonly were, were of course subject to normal episcopal jurisdiction and, if they were ordained, came under the closer control of their bishop. There was, however, a conflict of loyalties, to their abbot and to their bishop, and the influence of the former was normally stronger. The emperor Marcian asked the Council of Chalcedon to decree that no one should be permitted to found a monastery without episcopal licence, and that monks should be subject to episcopal authority, and should stay in their monasteries and not cause commotions. The assembled bishops decreed accordingly, no doubt with hearty goodwill. In the West the Councils of Agathe and Orleans and Carthage enacted similar rules in the early sixth century. The third Council of Arles, however, in 455 made a special concession to the famous monastery of Lerins, that the bishop should have authority only over priests and not over lay monks. Caesarius of Arles also secured immunity from episcopal control for the nunnery which he founded. Justinian legislated in great detail on monasteries. Convents of monks and nuns were to be rigorously separated. Monks were to eat together in a common refectory and sleep in a common dormitory. Abbots were to be chosen not by seniority but by merit, and the choice of the community was to be subject to the bishop's approval.[160]

Economically the church was an additional burden, which steadily increased in weight, on the limited resources of the empire. The huge army of clergy and monks were for the most part idle mouths, living upon offerings, endowments and state subsidies. This was something new. In Egypt there had been a full-time professional priesthood of considerable numbers, but Egypt was unique in this. Elsewhere, with a few exceptions of minor importance, pagan priesthoods were part-time offices, generally unremunerated, held by ordinary citizens. The Egyptian temples had possessed large endowments in land, but here again Egypt was exceptional. Some other temples had possessed considerable estates, notably that of Artemis at Ephesus and some others in Asia Minor, but in general the sacred lands of the pagan gods were exiguous, and served only to maintain the fabric of their shrines. Certainly the old gods had never owned a tithe of the vast mass of properties, great and small, whose rents went to support the churches, charitable institutions and monasteries.

A proportion of these rents went to socially useful purposes. Through its almshouses, orphanages, widows' homes and hospitals the churches provided for unfortunates for whom the state did little. But it was only a quarter of the income of each see which went to these purposes, even according to the rules laid down by the popes, and against the specially endowed charitable institutions must be set the far more numerous separate endowments of the monasteries and parochial churches. A good half of the revenues of the churches must have gone to paying the bishops and clergy, and the sum so expended was very considerable. No exact calculations are possible, but by the sixth century, if metropolitans of provinces were, as the figures cited above suggest, paid on the scale of vicars of dioceses, and every city had a bishop, who received on the average the salary of a provincial governor, the episcopate must have cost the empire far more than the administration: while, if the figures we have for the numbers of the lower clergy are at all typical, they must have far outnumbered the civil service. Leaving monks out of account, the staffing of the church absorbed far more manpower than did the secular administration and the church's salary bill was far heavier than that of the empire.

The fluctuating relations between the emperors and the church have already been traced in the first half of this book. The presuppositions on which these relations were based underwent little change. Constantine assumed that, as his pagan predecessors had been responsible for maintaining the *pax deorum*, so it was his duty to ensure that the *summa divinitas* was not 'moved to wrath, not only against the human race, but also against me myself, to whose care he has by his celestial will committed the government of all earthly things'. What chiefly angered the *summa divinitas* was discord in his church, and Constantine therefore had no hesitation in suppressing it. He took expert advice, summoning councils of bishops to decide on the controversies at issue, but he himself took action, expelling from their sees and sending into exile recalcitrant bishops and suppressing dissident sects.[161]

Some emperors were less convinced of the supreme importance of maintaining God's favour, and less conscientious in enforcing the measures requisite for that purpose; some had hesitations as to what beliefs were pleasing to God. But none questioned the basic axiom that victory over the barbarians and the prosperity of the empire were dependent on God's favour, and that it was the emperor's duty to see that he was conciliated. It remained moreover a constant belief that uniformity in doctrine was the prime condition of God's favour. Justinian indeed, in the belief 'that the purity and discipline of priests and their zeal towards our

Lord God Jesus Christ and the continual prayers which they send up to him, give great favour and increase to our empire, whereby we are enabled to conquer the barbarians and gain possession of lands which we formerly did not hold', forbade the clergy to play dice. But the main task of the imperial government was always to suppress heresy and schism.[162]

These beliefs were in principle shared by the leaders of the church. As Nestorius declared when he became bishop of Constantinople: 'Give me the earth purified of heretics, your majesty, and I will give you heaven in return. Subdue the heretics with me, and I will subdue the Persians with you.' That uniformity of doctrine was desirable and that the state ought to suppress dissidents was rarely questioned save by those who were for the time being the victims of repression. Martin protested strongly— and with success—against Maximus when he proposed to use military force against the Priscillianists. Augustine at first wished to win over the Donatists by persuasion, but he soon convinced himself of the necessity of penal laws against them. Socrates expressed disapproval of Nestorius' bigotry. Procopius sympathised with the victims of Justinian's penal legislation. These seem to be the only disinterested voices raised against persecution. The Donatists originally appealed to Constantine to settle their quarrel with the Catholics: it was only when the verdict went finally against them that they evolved the doctrine that the church ought to be independent of the state; 'what has the emperor to do with the church?' Athanasius, Hilary and the homoousian party in the West enunciated a similar doctrine and put forward pleas for religious liberty, when Constantius II was lending his support to their adversaries. They had raised no protest when Constantine had ejected their rivals, and they said nothing about religious freedom when Gratian and Theodosius I banned all beliefs but their own.[163]

Pope Gelasius in reply to Anastasius' demands enunciated the famous doctrine of the two powers: in secular affairs bishops should obey the emperor, in sacred matters the emperors must submit to the judgment of bishops. It is probable that in the abstract all emperors would have subscribed to this formula: Constantius II, it is true, is alleged by Athanasius to have declared, 'what I wish must be regarded as a canon', but if he ever made such a remark it must have been in a moment of pique. But if the principle was admitted, it was a delicate question how the emperor should elicit the judgment of bishops, and how far he could go in interpreting it.[164]

Constantine first referred the Donatist issue to a hand-picked council of bishops, but acquiesced in Miltiades' enlarging the council. On an appeal he summoned a second council, larger but apparently of his own choice, and on a second appeal he judged the issue himself. The Arian controversy he referred to a general council over which he himself presided, and the case of Athanasius to a hand-picked council presided over by an imperial commissioner. He himself pronounced on Athanasius' appeal from this council. Such a technique, whereby the emperor chose the bishops who were to make the decision, and through a lay president guided their discussions, obviously could give the imperial government a considerable *de facto* influence on ecclesiastical decisions. It was freely used by Constantius II and by subsequent emperors.

The practical application of the formula was most difficult in periods when the church was profoundly divided on some doctrinal issue. In such circumstances there was no means of ascertaining what was the judgment of the church. The claim of the popes to define doctrine was not generally accepted, and even general councils did not prove, as Constantine had hoped, infallible. The Council of Ephesus in 449 and the Council of Chalcedon in 451 issued diametrically opposite verdicts, and each was held in abhorrence by a large body of bishops. In such cases the emperors, unless they abdicated their duty of enforcing the true faith, were bound to take a line of their own. In such circumstances they were naturally often swayed by their personal theological beliefs or the opinions of bishops who had their ear, and sometimes by political considerations—the desire to effect a compromise which would bring peace and quiet, or to rally to their support important bodies of malcontents.

It is clear that the formula of Nicaea was regarded as heretical by a large body of opinion in the East. Constantius II himself shared this view, but in reopening the question and getting the church to work out a new formula he was fulfilling the desires of a large and vocal group of bishops. The new formula was solemnly ratified by the Councils of Ariminum, Seleucia and Constantinople, which—if their verdicts had been approved by posterity—would be reckoned as ecumenical. Valens did his imperial duty by enforcing them; Valentinian was highly exceptional in refusing to take sides. Theodosius I, in defiance of the verdict of Ariminum and Seleucia, enacted that all his subjects must accept the doctrines preached by Damasus of Rome and Peter of Alexandria. The Council of Constantinople subsequently confirmed his decision, but he appears to have been guided by his personal convictions, fortified by the advice of Acholius, bishop of Thessalonica, by whom he had recently been baptised.

In the troubled period which followed the Council of Chalcedon, when ecclesiastical opinion was very evenly divided in the East, the decision of doctrinal disputes by imperial edict became increasingly common. Basiliscus rejected Chalcedon outright, Zeno implicitly rejected it in the Henoticon, and Anastasius maintained the Henoticon. Justinian pronounced in favour of Chalcedon, but implicitly corrected its decisions by condemning the Three Chapters. In all these cases the emperors took the initiative, declaring what they considered to be the correct view, and endeavouring to obtain the assent of the principal bishops afterwards; Justinian eventually called a general council to ratify his condemnation of the Three Chapters. Basiliscus and Zeno seem to have been mainly swayed by political considerations in making their choice. Anastasius had strong theological views of his own. Justinian's motives seem to have been mixed: on the one hand he firmly believed that his victories were God's reward to him for suppressing heresy, on the other he laboured to produce a formula which would satisfy both the West, which was to a man Chalcedonian, and Egypt, which was as unanimously monophysite, and being a keen amateur theologian he thought that he could himself find a doctrine pleasing to God and to both parties.

In the judgment of the church the emperors have been praised or blamed according as they supported or opposed the party which was ultimately victorious. But, since they were not endowed with the gift of prophecy, they could not foresee whether they would be remembered as oppressors of the church, or as champions of orthodoxy.

CHAPTER XXIII

RELIGION AND MORALS

DESPITE persistent discouragement paganism took a long time to die. Constantine in the last decade of his reign confiscated the treasures and endowments of the temples, and probably banned sacrifice. Under his sons sacrifices were certainly prohibited, and many temples were demolished. With the accession of Julian the hopes of the pagans rose, only to be dashed by his death less than two years later. Julian's reign did, however, bear some fruit, in that pagan cult was tolerated by his successors until in 391 Theodosius I issued the first of a series of laws which progressively banned not only sacrifice but all pagan ceremonies. The temples were closed and many of them demolished.[1]

Pagan worship was never thereafter legal, but the laws were laxly enforced and from time to time had to be re-enacted. In 407, in response to representations by the catholic bishops of Africa, Honorius issued a constitution which should by this date have been hardly necessary, confiscating the endowments of temples and ordering cult images to be removed and altars demolished. In 415 he reiterated this law, and extended it to other dioceses. In the East the penalties against the pagan cult were re-enacted by Theodosius II in 423 and 435, by Marcian in 451, by Leo in 472, and by Anastasius, who even at this late date had to prohibit bequests for the maintenance of pagan rites.[2]

During the fourth century pagans suffered no disabilities provided that they refrained from the exercise of their cult. Honorius debarred them from any *militia* or *dignitas*, but in 409 was forced to revoke the ban by a strongminded German general, Generid, who refused otherwise to take up the command to which he had been appointed. Seven years later Theodosius II imposed the same ban on the East. In 468 Leo, by a law which confined admission to the bar to orthodox Christians, excluded pagans from the legal profession. Finally Justinian prohibited them from holding chairs as professors, and subjected them to

the same legal disabilities as he imposed upon Jews and heretics—
incapacity to make wills, to receive inheritances or bequests, or to
testify in court. In 529 he even ordered all pagans to accept
baptism under penalty of confiscation and exile.[3]

This legislation is enough to prove that there were still in the
sixth century a considerable number of pagans in the Eastern parts.
But we have other and more circumstantial evidence. John of
Ephesus was appointed in 542 official missionary to the pagans in
the provinces of Asia, Caria, Lydia and Phrygia. He tells us that
with a staff of priests and deacons he laboured for several years,
demolishing temples, destroying altars and cutting down sacred
trees. He baptised 80,000 persons, and built for them 98 churches
and 12 monasteries. Even in this district, in the heart of the empire,
the cult of the heathen gods was being overtly carried on in
Justinian's reign on so wide a scale. A generation later Heliopolis
in Phoenicia was still a predominantly pagan city, where the Christians were a poor and oppressed minority. Tiberius Constantine
instituted a severe persecution there in 578, in the course of which
it was revealed that pagan rites were secretly celebrated in many
cities, including Antioch and Edessa; in the latter town a group of
prominent persons, including the governor of the province, were
caught red-handed holding a sacrifice to Zeus. In some places
paganism survived the Arab conquest. In 830 the people of
Carrhae, a city always notorious for its devotion to the old gods,
were threatened with massacre by the Caliph unless they abandoned
their religion for Islam or one of the tolerated faiths and only
saved themselves by professing themselves to be Sabians. To this
day the heretical sect of the Nusairi in the mountains between the
upper Orontes and the sea profess doctrines which clearly derive
from the Neo-Platonic paganism of the later empire.[4]

In the West also overt pagan cult survived into the sixth and
seventh centuries. In Italy itself Pope Gregory ordered the bishop
of Tarracina to suppress, if necessary with the aid of the local
vicecomes, the worship of sacred trees. In Sicily the bishop of
Tyndaris reported to him that he was unable to stop pagan worship
since it enjoyed the protection of the notables. In Sardinia Gregory
had to undertake a missionary campaign against the pagans, who
paid a regular *douceur* to the governor to turn a blind eye on their
cult. From Spain we have a tract of Martin of Bracara, written
about 575, denouncing the heathen practices of the rural population: they seem harmless enough, burning candles and making
offerings to trees and springs and rocks, holding feasts on pagan
festivals such as New Year's Day, and keeping Thursday, the
day of Jupiter, as a holiday instead of Sunday. A few years later

the third Council of Toledo in 589 declared that 'the sacrilege of idolatry is rooted in almost the whole of Spain and Gaul' and ordered bishops with the aid of the civil governors to take active steps against it. In Gaul a series of councils, in 533, 541, 567, 585 and 625, denounced pagan practices such as the worship of trees and fountains. Gallus, the uncle of Gregory of Tours, demolished a temple near Cologne, where offerings were still regularly made, and Gregory spoke with a hermit who had overturned and destroyed an image of Diana near Trier which was still being worshipped.[5]

Paganism was not so much a religion as a loosely-knit amalgam of cults, myths and philosophical beliefs of varying origins and even more varying levels of culture. A certain superficial unity was given to it by the identification, often on very slender grounds, of local gods and goddesses with those of the Greco-Roman pantheon: there was some reciprocal borrowing of myths, cult practices, symbols and forms of representation. But its main strength lay in the fact that it incorporated everywhere ancient cults, hallowed by tradition and fortified by local loyalty. At the same time it had something to offer to all sorts and conditions of men. For countrymen there were rites and ceremonies to promote fertility and to avert pests. For those who craved for communion with the divine and an assurance of a future felicity there were the mystery cults of Isis, Mithras or the Great Mother. To intellectuals paganism was a somewhat misty pantheism, in which the multifarious gods were aspects or emanations of the divine Unity, and their myths and cults allegories and symbols of an esoteric truth hidden from the vulgar.

The old gods made their strongest appeal to two very different strata of society, the most aristocratic and cultivated classes on the one hand, and the peasantry on the other. The old senatorial families of Rome remained predominantly pagan down to the early fifth century. Their sentiments are eloquently expressed in Symmachus' plea for the altar of victory. In their minds the traditional religion was intimately linked with pride in the glorious history of Rome: 'this worship made the world subject to my laws,' pleads the ancient city to the young emperor, 'these rites repelled Hannibal from my walls and the Gauls from the Capitol'. For the cultured classes throughout the empire, whose minds were steeped from childhood in the study of the ancient poets, orators and philosophers, paganism was associated with the great heritage of classical literature and learning which they so highly prized. The teaching profession in particular long remained predominantly pagan. Down to the early fifth century most of the great rhetors and philosophers, Libanius, Himerius, Themistius, Hypatia, clung to the old religion. Zacharias of Mytilene gives a vivid picture of university life at Alexandria at the end of the fifth century. Several of the professors and a considerable number of the students were pagans, and frequented a secret temple at Menuthis nearby, a building covered with hieroglyphs and housing a huge assortment of idols of dogs, cats, and monkeys in wood, bronze and stone. At Berytus, too, where Zacharias went on to study law, a number of the students practised magical rites in secret. At Athens the professors remained pagans until Justinian's law deprived them of their chairs.[6]

In the West the upper classes seem to have abandoned the old religion by the latter part of the fifth century. In the East even after Justinian's penal legislation many of the aristocracy, while outwardly conforming, not only retained their old beliefs but continued to celebrate the cult in secret. In 529 many persons of high station, including Thomas the quaestor, Asclepiodotus, a former prefect, and Phocas, a patrician, were denounced and convicted. At a second purge in 546 many senators, grammarians, sophists, lawyers and doctors were punished. In 578 under Tiberius Constantine there was another round-up of pagans in high places, arising out of the incident at Edessa mentioned above.[7]

Peasants in all ages have been intensively conservative, and Christianity from its earliest days had been a predominantly urban religion, whose missionaries travelled from town to town, neglecting the intervening countryside. It is not therefore surprising that in most parts of the empire the rural population remained pagan long after the towns were mostly Christian. Martin of Tours in the last quarter of the fourth century found many flourishing village temples in his diocese and was active in destroying them. In the Alps the Anauni of the territory of Tridentum were still untouched by Christianity in the last years of the fourth century, and lynched a Cappadocian priest who ventured to build a church in one of their villages. Two generations later Maximus of Turin urged his congregation not to connive at pagan rites on their estates, where temples, altars and images still survived.[8]

In the East John Chrysostom similarly appealed to the great landowners of Constantinople to convert the pagan tenants of their estates, and to build churches and endow priests to serve them. In Syria hermits did much to convert the countryside in the late fourth and early fifth centuries. Theodoret tells how Abram settled in the pagan village of Libanus, and by successfully intervening on behalf of the inhabitants with the tax collectors won such popularity that the whole village was converted and built a church and elected him their priest. Theodoret himself spoke with peasants near Gabala who had been weaned from paganism by the hermit Thalalaeus, whose prayers had expelled the local god from his temple.[9]

Paganism lingered yet later among the nomadic populations on the fringe of the empire. The Arab tribes of the Syrian desert began, it is true, to be converted even in the fourth century, when in Valens' reign the Saracen queen Mavia demanded as a condition of renewing her treaty with the Roman government that a local hermit of renown, named Moses, should be consecrated bishop for her tribe. The process continued in the fifth century. Aspebetus, a pagan sheikh who had migrated from the Persian zone and been appointed phylarch of the federate Saracens of Arabia, was converted with all his tribe by the hermit Euthymius, who cured his son, and another bishopric 'of the encampments' was established. But the Nobades of Nubia and the Blemmyes of the Eastern desert of Egypt remained pagans in the sixth century, enjoying by treaty the right of annually borrowing the image of Isis from the temple of Philae, until Justinian closed the temple and removed the statue to Constantinople: he later succeeded in converting the Nobades to Christianity. Justinian also closed the temple of Ammon at Augila which the nomads of Libya had hitherto frequented, and built instead a church of the Virgin. Further west the nomad Moorish tribes of Tripolitania, Africa, Numidia and Mauretania were still pagan when Justinian reconquered these regions from the Vandals. On the northern frontiers many of the East German tribes were converted in the fourth century, including the Goths and the Vandals, but the Franks on the Rhine remained pagans till the days of Clovis.[10]

But if broadly speaking it is true that the rural areas of the empire and its barbarian fringe longest remained pagan, there were many local exceptions. Not only were there some rural areas that were early Christianised; there were also some towns which long remained obstinately pagan. In Africa Christianity was widely diffused over the countryside as early as the third century, but the towns of Calama, Madaura and Sufes were apparently still predominantly pagan in the early fifth. Replying to a fulsome letter from the council of Madaura Augustine suggests that before invoking the aid of a bishop they might adopt the Christian faith. At Calama the populace, in defiance of the law of 407, provocatively celebrated a pagan festival, and when the local clergy tried to intervene, beat them up, killing one, and attacked the church: these disorders were connived at by the notables of the town and probably, Augustine suggests, promoted by them. At Sufes the destruction by the Christians of an image of Hercules led to a riot in which sixty of them were killed: here again the council, according to Augustine, gave support to the pagans.[11]

In Mesopotamia Edessa had been converted in the early third century, but its neighbour Carrhae remained pagan till the end of Roman rule and even later. Antioch was already in Julian's reign a thoroughly Christian city; at Apamea the citizens vigorously defended their temples under Theodosius I, and the bishop had to hire gladiators to overpower them. Heliopolis is spoken of as a pagan town under Valens; it still was so, as we have seen, under Tiberius Constantine. Maiuma, the port of Gaza, was already predominantly Christian in Constantine's reign, but Gaza itself remained pagan nearly a century later; under Constantius II it had only one Christian decurion. In the reign of Arcadius the temples still functioned openly despite Theodosius I's penal laws, and it was only by obtaining a special order from Constantinople that the bishop of the tiny Christian community was able to get them demolished.[12]

Paganism was not a heroic faith, and could boast few martyrs. At Alexandria a devoted band, led by a philosopher, Olympius, occupied the Serapeum when it was threatened with destruction in Theodosius' reign, and stood a regular siege. At Gaza and Raphia in Palestine, at Petra and Areopolis in Arabia, and at Apamea in Syria, the pagans put up a fight for their temples at the same period, but in general the official ban on pagan worship seems to have been submissively accepted. Nevertheless passive resistance was widespread and prolonged, and pagans were prepared to pay, if not to suffer, for their faith.[13]

There were still some, as the severe penal legislation against apostates shows, who deserted Christianity for the old religion. The first extant law against apostates was issued by Theodosius in 381: it deprived them of the right of making wills. Two years later their disabilities were increased both by Theodosius and by Gratian. In 391 Honorius deprived them of any rank which they had inherited or earned. As late as 426 Valentinian III found it necessary to re-enact the penalties against apostates. These measures imply that the spirit of paganism was not yet crushed. Even in the reign of Zeno the pagans of the East still cherished hopes that the old gods would come into their own again. When Illus raised his rebellion, Zacharias of Mitylene tells us, the pagans of Caria celebrated sacrifices, encouraged by an oracle which declared that the allotted span of Christianity was terminated, and that the reign of the old gods was to be restored.[14]

Despite the ruthless measures taken by Hadrian during and after the great rebellion of Barcochbar a considerable Jewish population survived in Palestine. In Jerusalem and Judaea proper the Jews seem to have been completely exterminated, but Galilee, with the two cities of Tiberias and Sepphoris (or Diocaesarea), remained solidly Jewish. Epiphanius tells the interesting story of Joseph, a Jewish convert, who in the reign of Constantine endeavoured to build churches in Tiberias, Sepphoris, Nazareth and Capernaum. With imperial support he managed to convert a derelict temple of Hadrian into a church at Tiberias, and built a small church at Sepphoris, but local opposition proved too strong, and he ultimately retired to Scythopolis. There was a serious Jewish revolt in Galilee under Gallus Caesar, who as a penal measure destroyed Diocaesarea.[15]

A strong Samaritan community also survived in Palestine. Its centre was at Neapolis, by the national sanctuary of Shechem, but Samaritans were numerous in Caesarea and Scythopolis also. They rebelled in the reign of Marcian, and plundered and destroyed the churches of the area. A more serious revolt broke out in 529, when one Julianus, described as a brigand, was proclaimed emperor and celebrated chariot races at Neapolis: a hundred thousand people are said to have been killed in the course of its suppression. Towards the end of Justinian's reign there was yet another rebellion, whose centre was at Caesarea, in which both Jews and Samaritans joined.[16]

The great majority of the Jewish people, however, lived scattered throughout the empire, and beyond its boundaries in Persia and the Arab kingdoms along the Red Sea coast. There is evidence for considerable Jewish communities in many cities both of the Eastern and the Western parts. The Jews of the dispersion seem to have been mostly urban, and are frequently mentioned as traders, but there were some on the land. Libanius possessed an estate, probably near Antioch, which was cultivated by Jewish tenants, and Pope Gregory found that there were Jews among the *coloni* of the church lands in Sicily. Samaritans are less frequently mentioned outside Palestine, but a group is recorded in Upper Egypt, and Cassiodorus mentions their synagogue at Rome: Gregory also speaks of them at Catana and Syracuse in Sicily.[17]

The Jewish community throughout the empire was until 429, when the line died out, subject to a succession of hereditary patriarchs, who resided at Tiberias; the hereditary principle had its disadvantages, as the patriarchate sometimes devolved on children, and some patriarchs exploited their office for their own profit, selling appointments to the highest bidder. The patriarchs nominated all the clergy of the synagogues, who are styled in the codes by a variety of titles, priests (*hiereis*), elders (*maiores, presbyteri*), heads of the synagogue (*archisynagogi*), or finally fathers (*patres*) or patriarchs (*patriarchae*). They were assisted by a body of *apostoli*, who were sent out to the provinces to inspect the synagogues and exercise disciplinary control over them, and to collect the dues, described by Epiphanius as first fruits and tithes, by the laws as crown gold, which they paid to the patriarchate. The patriarch was normally accorded high official rank by the imperial government. He is alluded to as *illustris* in laws of 392 and 396-7, and as *spectabilis* in 404. In 415 Gamaliel was deprived of the honorary prefecture which had been bestowed upon him; but this was a penalty for exceeding his powers, and he was allowed to retain the rank which he had held before the supreme honour of the prefecture was conferred.[18]

Jewish worship had been not only recognised but protected by the pagan empire, and this recognition and protection was on the whole maintained by the Christian emperors despite the increase in antisemitism which Christianity produced. A number of laws declare that synagogues are not to be burned or sacked, and enact that, if such incidents have occurred, the buildings are to be restored and the loot returned, unless they have been consecrated to Christian use, in which case monetary compensation is to be paid. By the early fifth century however, the erection of new synagogues had been prohibited—it was one of the charges against the patriarch Gamaliel that he had broken this rule—and this regulation was re-enacted in 423 and 438. The repair of existing synagogues was, however, expressly authorised. The Samaritans appear to have enjoyed similar toleration until Justinian in 529 demolished their synagogues, thus provoking the revolt of Julianus.[19]

Worship was not to be interrupted, though the Jews on their side were warned to refrain from provocative rites, such as the ceremonial burning of the cross at the feast of Aman. In the sixth century the synagogue at Tarracina was suppressed because it was adjacent to a church, and the Jewish chanting offended Christian ears, but a new site was allocated to the congregation. Even Justinian made no attempt to suppress Jewish worship, or even to regulate it, except in one particular case. There was in his day a division of opinion in the Jewish communities, some wishing the scripture to be read in Greek, as had probably been the common practice, and others insisting on the exclusive use of Hebrew. Petitions were made to the emperor by the rival parties and Justinian, hoping that the Jews, if they listened to the scriptures in the vulgar tongue, might be convinced by the prophecies of Christ which they contained, authorised the use of Greek (or Latin when that was the normal language of the congregation) when the community concerned desired it. He recommended the Septuagint, but allowed the version of Aquila (although his translation of some key passages was less favourable to Christian interpretation). He further took the opportunity of prohibiting the teaching of the Deuterosis (probably the Talmudic commentaries) as being unscriptural.[20]

Synagogues were exempt from billeting, and their staffs enjoyed an immunity from curial charges similar to that accorded to the Christian clergy, if more limited; by a law of Constantine only two or three persons from each synagogue enjoyed the privilege. This immunity was withdrawn in the West in 383. In the East it was confirmed in 397, but may have been revoked two years later; it certainly no longer existed in Justinian's day. It was forbidden to take legal proceedings against Jews on the Sabbath. Religious jurisdiction over Jews was exercised by the patriarch or his deputies, who had the power of expelling disobedient members from the community: in a law of 392 provincial governors were forbidden to bring pressure on the Jewish authorities to readmit those whom they had expelled. The Jewish authorities had moreover a recognised voluntary jurisdiction in civil disputes. Disputes between Jews could be referred to them by consent of the parties, and their judgments were in such cases enforced by the imperial authorities. The patriarch Gamaliel exercised his jurisdiction even in cases between Jews and Christians; but this was another of the reasons why he was deprived of his honorary prefecture, and the practice was henceforth forbidden. The Jewish authorities also fixed prices for Jewish traders, and provincial governors were forbidden to appoint controllers for them.[21]

Against these privileges, which were an inheritance from the pagan empire, are to be set a growing series of disabilities. Intermarriage between Jews and Christians was declared by Theodosius to be tantamount to adultery and subjected to the same penalties: the rule was reproduced in Justinian's Code. Constantine forbade Jews to circumcise their slaves, and declared slaves thus treated to be free. His son Constantius II made the circumcision of a slave a capital offence, and furthermore forbade Jews to buy slaves of any religion but their own. This rule was somewhat relaxed by Honorius in 415 and by Theodosius II in the East two years later.

Jews were permitted to retain Christian slaves provided that they did not interfere with their religion, and to inherit them on the same condition: the acquisition of Christian slaves by purchase or gift was still forbidden to Jews. Justinian forbade the possession of Christian slaves by Jews, freeing the slave and fining the owner 30 lb. gold.[22]

A letter of Julian to the Jewish community reveals that under Constantius II the Jews had been subjected to vexatious special levies (*discriptiones*). Julian forbade the practice and destroyed the records, and thereafter the Jews were not made the victims of any special fiscal extortion. Nothing is heard even of the poll tax of two *denarii* imposed by Vespasian, which probably lapsed during the third century inflation. In 399, when relations were very strained between the Eastern and Western governments, Stilicho ordered that the dues collected from the synagogues of Honorius' dominions should no longer be transmitted to the patriarch, a subject of Arcadius, but be confiscated to the imperial treasury: but this law was revoked five years later. On the lapse of the patriarchate in 429 these dues were permanently assigned to the *largitiones*. The collection in the East was enforced by the *palatini*, and any sums which came from the West were to be likewise confiscated.[23]

During the Principate few Jews except renegades seem to have entered the imperial service, or even to have taken any part in municipal life, save in predominantly Jewish cities like Tiberias: no doubt they feared to incur ritual pollution, or to be forced to break the sabbath—for which reason the Roman government exempted them from military service. It thus came about that Jews, since they had never served on city councils, claimed immunity from membership of the *curia* when this became a burden rather than an honour. This claim was naturally challenged by the cities, and Constantine, in response to a petition from the council of Agrippina, expressly disallowed it. Early in Honorius' reign the Jews of Apulia and Calabria appear to have made a concerted attempt to secure exemption on the basis of a constitution of Arcadius. Their claim was denied, and a year later the Eastern government also reasserted the liability of Jews to the *curia*.[24]

From the fourth century Jews appear to have entered municipal life and the imperial service in increasing numbers. We know of very few specific examples, it is true. At Magona in the Balearic Isles we happen to hear that in 418 a father of the synagogue, Caecilianus, was *defensor civitatis*, and the leading rabbi, Theodorus, occupied an even more prominent position, having held all the local offices, including that of *defensor*, and being now patron of the city. Another practising Jew, Lectorius, had recently been governor of the province and obtained the rank of *comes*. Better evidence of the infiltration of Jews into public life is to be found in the legislation forbidding it. In 404 Honorius expelled Jews (and Samaritans) from the *agentes in rebus*, and in 418 from the army. By the same law he debarred them for the future from all branches of the civil service—the palatine ministries and the *agentes in rebus* are specially mentioned—while allowing those already enrolled to complete their careers. Jews were, however, expressly permitted to practise at the bar.[25]

The Eastern government followed suit in 438 with a severer law, debarring Jews and Samaritans from all *dignitates* and *militiae*, including even the lowly post of *defensor civitatis*; they were not, however, relieved of the onerous service of the *cohortalini*, nor yet from the *curia*. By the law of Leo, which declared that only ortho-dox Christians might be barristers, Jews were also excluded from the legal profession. This remained the law under Justinian, who sharpened it by adding to the list of prohibited posts that of *curator* or *pater civitatis*, and by depriving Jews and Samaritans of the meagre privileges which still attached to curial rank while holding them to its onerous obligations.[26]

Except for their exclusion from the public service and the bar the Jews thus incurred no serious civil disabilities until the reign of Justin. He applied to them (and to Samaritans) the same penal laws which he enacted against pagans and heretics. Like them they were debarred from making wills or receiving inheritances, from giving testimony in a court of law, or indeed from performing any legal act.[27]

In the relative toleration accorded to Jews down to the reign of Justinian the imperial government was undoubtedly fighting a rearguard action against the mounting pressure of public opinion. Antisemitism was widespread at least as far back as the reign of Augustus, and in places where the Jewish community was large, such as Alexandria, there were frequent explosions of popular violence. Christianity added theological animus to the general dislike of the Jews, and the numerous diatribes against them, in the form of sermons or pamphlets, which Christian leaders produced, must have fanned the flames. It is surprising, indeed, that the emperors, most of whom shared the popular view, maintained such moderation in their legal enactments: the language of Con-stantine, for instance, in his laws, and even more in his letter on the date of Easter, is strangely at variance with his quite restrained and fair-minded enactments. The Jewish community certainly had some influence, particularly as long as the patriarchate existed to voice its views. There is some evidence for this in the fact that several laws which reassert Jewish privileges are addressed to the community or its official representatives, and are presumably in response to petitions and delegations. But the attitude of the emperors seems to have been mainly inspired by respect for the established law. The Jews had since the days of Caesar been guaranteed the practice of their ancestral religion and the government shrank from annulling this ancient privilege.[28]

The responsible heads of the church normally followed the same line. Ambrose, who by spiritual terrors bullied Theodosius I into revoking his just decision that the bishop of Callinicum should rebuild the synagogue which he had burned down, and would not even allow the emperor to compensate the Jews from the treasury, appears to have been exceptional in his bigotry. There were bishops who took the lead in anti-Jewish outrages, but generally these were due to the mob or to fanatical monks. In the sixth and early seventh centuries a number of episcopal councils in Merovingian Gaul and the Visigothic kingdom passed a series of canons about the Jews, but for the most part these merely insisted on the enforcement of the existing legal bans on Jews' holding public office or circumcising or acquiring Christian slaves: in the last case reasonable compensation was given for the loss of the slaves. The only novelties are a prohibition of chanting at Jewish funerals (alleged to be an innovation) and the confinement of Jews to their houses during Eastertide. Gregory the Great's attitude to the Jews was strictly fair. While scrupulous to enforce the laws against Jews' acquiring Christian slaves, he paid proper compensation and made allowance for the difficulties of Jewish slave dealers who were commissioned to buy Christian slaves by persons in authority. On the other hand he was insistent that synagogues must not be destroyed and that compensation must be given when this took place. And he set his face against the baptism of Jews under threats of force.[29]

Forcible mass baptisms had occurred sporadically as early as the beginning of the fifth century. In 418 Severus, bishop of Iammona in the Balearic Isles, encouraged by the arrival of relics of St. Stephen, marched his flock across to the neighbouring city of Magona, and, having burned down their synagogue, persuaded 540 Jews to accept baptism. But such measures first came into prominence towards the end of the sixth century in the barbarian kingdoms of the West. In 576 Avitus, bishop of Arverni, again taking advantage of the terror produced by the burning of the local synagogue, laid before the Jewish community the alternatives of baptism or exile. Five hundred submitted, the remainder migrating to Marseilles. In 583 King Chilperic ordered the baptism of a large number of Jews at Paris. In 591 the bishops of Narbo and Arelate were reproved by Pope Gregory for forcibly baptising the Jewish inhabitants of their cities. In Spain King Sisebut (612-20) ordered all the Jews of his kingdom to receive baptism. The first Roman emperor to enforce baptism on the Jews was Heraclius.[30]

The Jews and Samaritans were the only minority who reacted to persecution with active hostility. They rose in rebellion several times, and when under Phocas and Heraclius the Persians invaded Syria and Palestine they seized the opportunity to burn the churches, loot the houses of the Christians and force them to deny their faith or massacre them. They alone openly rejoiced at the calamities of the empire and welcomed its fall. We have contemporary evidence that the Jews of Palestine exulted when the Roman commander Sergius was overwhelmed and killed by the Arab invaders at the end of Heraclius' reign.[31]

From the earliest times there had been periodic divisions of opinion among Christians, and these conflicts had been resolved by the expulsion of such minority groups as refused to conform to the general consensus of the church. Many of these groups had died out, but a substantial number survived as dissident sects or heresies, which often in their turn split into smaller groups. Constantine was distressed to find that besides the catholic church there were a number of other bodies which, while claiming to be Christian, maintained theological views which the catholic church had condemned, or which refused on other grounds to communicate with it. He strove to reconcile some of them to the church, and, when his efforts proved unavailing, endeavoured to suppress them all by administrative action, confiscating their churches and forbidding their religious meetings.[32]

From this time onwards the imperial government normally, if not very persistently, penalised dissidents in various degrees, but heresies and schisms nonetheless continued to proliferate. Under Constantine himself, and despite his utmost efforts, the Donatists seceded in Africa, and while his attempts to heal the Arian controversy were temporarily successful, the dispute broke out again after his death, and the final condemnation in 381 of the various schools of thought which rejected the homoousian doctrine led to the formation of new groups of sectaries. It does not appear that these sects had much following within the empire, but unfortunately the Goths were converted during the period when Arian views were in the ascendant in the East, and they and other East German tribes clung obstinately to their Arian faith.

The next serious controversy was between the Monophysites and the Dyophysites. Monophysism obtained no foothold in the Latin-speaking church, but in the East opinion was very evenly divided. After many hesitations and changes of front, the imperial government eventually, two generations after Chalcedon, came down on the Dyophysite side, but the vast majority of Egyptians and a substantial number of people in Syria, as well as smaller groups elsewhere, refused to accept this decision, and formed dissident churches.

The Donatists were always strong in Africa, and at times outnumbered the catholics. The Arian Goths, Burgundians and Vandals formed substantial minorities in Italy, southern Gaul, Spain and Africa. In Egypt Monophysites were in an overwhelming majority, and in Syria they were very numerous. With these exceptions the heretical and schismatic sects seem to have been numerically negligible. Some were geographically widespread. Manichees, for instance, were to be found not only in the East, but in Italy and in Africa, where they were especially strong. Marcionites, according to Epiphanius, were to be found not only in Egypt and the Thebaid, Arabia, Palestine, Syria and Cyprus, but also in Italy. But the majority of the sects were confined to limited regions. Some were and always had been strictly local. Donatists did not exist outside Africa, nor Melitians outside Egypt. Others had never spread much beyond their home lands; Priscillianism for instance does not seem to have penetrated beyond Spain. Others again which once had a wide vogue had shrunk: Montanism, which had in the second and third centuries invaded Africa, was by the fifth restricted to its original homeland in Phrygia and some adjacent provinces, and the Novatians survived only in north-western Asia Minor. In general the Latin-speaking half of the empire was less troubled by heresies than the East. Western Christians were not on the whole interested in the metaphysical controversies which produced so many dissident groups in the East, and apart from the Donatists, the Priscillianists and the Pelagians, produced few heresies of their own. The Eastern provinces on the other hand pullulated with queer eccentric sects, many of them of very ancient origin.[33]

If the heretical sects were for the most part small, they were extremely numerous. It is scarcely possible from the evidence at our disposal to estimate how many sects existed at any given time. Epiphanius towards the end of the fourth century wrote a learned and scholarly work on the heresies, of which he enumerated 60. Philastrius, bishop of Brixia, in a very uncritical summary, brought the total up to 128. Augustine, who used both their books, nevertheless reduced the figure to 87. Theodoret, in a well-informed little treatise, brought down the total still further to 56. All these figures are, as Augustine remarks in the introductory letter to his work, somewhat arbitrary, as the authors differed as to what exactly constituted a heresy. Moreover all four works are— or profess to be—historical, and include extinct, and perhaps mythical, heresies of the past; nor do they draw any clear line between organised sects and aberrant opinions. Imperial constitutions which enumerate the sects which they penalise are perhaps a safer guide, but they often increase the total by the use of synonymous names: on the other hand none of them gives an exhaustive list. A constitution of Theodosius II yields 23 names, two or three of which are synonyms; Justinian in his version of the same law adds another eleven, a few of which are again merely verbal variants.[34]

The distinctive doctrines and practices of the sects were many and various. Some, like the Arians, Macedonians and Monophysites, differed from the catholic church on some purely metaphysical point of theology. The Quartodecimans were peculiar only in celebrating Easter on the Jewish Passover, the fourteenth day of Nisan. Other sects had broken off on disciplinary issues. The Novatians, or as they called themselves, the Pure ($\varkappa\alpha\theta\alpha\varrho o\iota$), had objected to the reconciliation of those who had sacrificed in the Decian persecution, holding that those who committed a mortal sin after baptism must remain for ever excommunicate. The Donatists similarly refused to receive back those who had surrendered the scriptures in the Diocletianic persecution, and regarded the catholic hierarchy as polluted because, as they alleged, Caecilian of Carthage had been consecrated by a *traditor*. The Melitians in Egypt split off on similar grounds, and later the Luciferians refused to communicate with the catholic church because it readmitted Arians.

Other sects differed more radically from the norm. The Manichees, though regarded by the imperial government and the church as Christians, might almost be classified as a separate religion. They taught a dualist view of the universe probably derived from Zoroastrianism, and while accepting Christ regarded the doctrine of their own prophet Mani as the final revelation. They preached an extreme asceticism, which was however practised only by a select inner group, the *Electi*, the ordinary believers or *Auditores* being allowed to live more or less normal lives. There were many other smaller sects, which, though historically unconnected with Mani-chaeism, and mostly older than it, held a basically similar dualistic view of the universe, and preached similar extreme ascetic practices on the ground that all material things were evil. Prominent among them were the Marcionites, founded in the reign of Hadrian by Marcion, who rejected the Old Testament and taught that its God, the demiurge who had created the material world, was evil; and the Montanists, who followed the teaching of Montanus, Priscilla and Maximilla, prophets who had arisen in Phrygia in the second century. These and many other sects, some of much later origin, were usually teetotallers and vegetarians, and condemned all sexual intercourse as sinful: some, like the followers of Eustathius condemned by the Council of Gangra, went so far as to encourage women to abandon their husbands and children and put on male attire, and even condemned private property and incited slaves to leave their masters.

We need not believe all the fantastic doctrines and grotesque practices which catholic writers attributed to the sectarians. The allegation that the Montanists pricked an infant all over to obtain blood for their sacramental ceremony, and reverenced their victim as a martyr if it died, and as a saint if it survived and grew up, is a variant of a libel brought against all Christians in the early centuries, and later transferred to the Jews. One may have one's doubts about the Ophitae, who revered the serpent as the giver of wisdom to mankind, and kept a tame snake in a box, releasing it on to the altar to sanctify the bread at the communion. Epipha-nius is himself somewhat sceptical about the Adamians, who, he had been informed from several sources, worshipped stark naked, and very sensibly provided their churches, or paradises, with cloakrooms and hypocausts.[35]

But there certainly were very curious communities on the lunatic fringe of Christianity. Theodoret personally met an aged Marcionite who had all his life washed his face in his own spittle, to avoid using water, the creation of the demiurge. Augustine records from personal knowledge the practices of the Abelonii, a sect which survived to his own day in a village of his own city of Hippo. They held that marriage and continence were obligatory on all believers. Each couple adopted a boy and girl, who on the death of both foster parents, succeeded to the family farm and in turn adopted a boy and a girl. There was never any difficulty, Augustine tells us, in maintaining the sect, as neighbouring villages were always ready to provide children to be adopted in the certainty of ultimately acquiring a farm.[36]

The penalties inflicted on heretics varied in severity according to the general policy of the government from time to time, and according to the opprobrium in which the various sects were held. Normally their churches were confiscated, their religious meetings banned, and any building or estate, in which their meetings were held, forfeited to the crown. Sometimes their clergy were specially penalised; in 392 a fine of 10 lb. gold was imposed on all heretical clergy, and Montanist bishops, priests and deacons were in 415 threatened with deportation. At the same period in Africa the policy was introduced of inflicting crushing fines, graded according to the offender's rank, on all Donatists who refused to reconcile themselves to the catholic church. Members of the more objectionable sects were from time to time declared incapable of making wills or of taking inheritances. This disability was inflicted on the Manichees in 381, and again in 407 and 445 in the West, and in 428 in the East. It was also imposed in 389 on the Eunomians, an extreme Arian sect, to be revoked in 394, reimposed and again revoked in 395, yet again remitted in 399, having been apparently re-enacted meanwhile, and finally reimposed in 410.[37]

Heretics were also from time to time debarred from the public service, or at any rate from its higher branches. This penalty was imposed by Theodosius I on all heretics, and in 395 Arcadius ordered his master of the offices to conduct a purge of the palatine ministries; Honorius took the same step in 408. The more detested sects, such as Manichees, Eunomians and Montanists, were later excluded from all grades of the public service, civil or military, except the *cohortales* and the *limitanei*. Leo, as we have seen, excluded all but orthodox Christians from the bar.[38]

The death penalty was very rarely invoked. Manichees had been subjected to it by Diocletian some years before he began the persecution of the Christians. Theodosius I in 382 imposed it not on the Manichees proper, but on three extremist sects which he regarded as even more sinister variants of Manicheism, the Encratites, the Hydroparastatae (who used water instead of wine in the communion) and the Saccophori. In 510 Manichees were subjected to the death penalty by Anastasius, and this remained the law under Justinian, who tightened up the legislation against heretics generally, reinforcing the ban on the public service and extending it to all sects, and debarring all heretics from taking inheritances or bequeathing their estates to any but orthodox heirs.[39]

Despite these penal laws the heretical sects stubbornly survived. The Donatists, though they seemed to have been crushed by the systematic campaign waged against them in the early fifth century by the combined forces of the catholic church and the imperial government, raised their heads again. At the end of the sixth century Pope Gregory received alarming reports from Africa that they were rebaptising catholics in large numbers and even seizing catholic churches, and he felt it necessary not only to stimulate the African bishops to action, and to demand governmental support from the praetorian prefect of Africa, but to send a delegation of bishops to Maurice himself to enlist his aid. The Donatists were, it is true, a large sect with wide popular backing, but the parallel sect in Egypt, the Melitians, who never achieved any widespread success even in the early fourth century, nevertheless survived. They still existed in the time of Theodoret, who notes that they had introduced instrumental music (that of the old Egyptian sistrum) and dancing into their services. A document of 512 reveals a monk who describes himself as formerly Melitian, now orthodox, selling a monastery near Arsinoe to a Melitian priest. The sect still flourished a century after the Arab conquest.[40]

Our sources, which are almost entirely hostile and controversial, tell us very little of the inner life of the heretical sects, and it is difficult to gauge their social composition. The majority of the sectaries seem to have been humble people, and many of them were countryfolk. Procopius speaks of the victims of Justinian's campaign against the heresies as being in general simple peasants; the Montanists of Phrygia, who rather than submit, shut themselves up in their churches and set fire to them, were certainly so. Theodoret, too, records that in the territory of Cyrrhus he had converted, risking considerable personal danger, eight villages of Marcionites, one of Arians and one of Eunomians; he implies that the town was free of heresy. A document inserted in the acts of the Council of Ephesus gives an interesting glimpse of a little group of sectaries at Philadelphia in Lydia. It is a copy of the recantations of 19 Quartodecimans and 5 Novatians (the majority of whom had adopted the Quartodeciman Easter in the reign of Valens). Only four are villagers; the rest are from the town, but half of them are illiterate. They include, however, a decurion and a barrister. This perhaps gives a not untypical cross-section of the more respectable sects. We know more about Donatism than about most. Here it is clear that the great majority were simple folk, who did not even know Latin; Augustine had often to ask for an interpreter to argue with them, and was short of Punic-speaking clergy to take charge of converts. Most of them were country people from the estates, villages and little rural towns; it was from this class that the extremist wing of the Donatists, the circumcellions, were drawn. But the Donatist church had also among its leaders men of standing and culture, barristers like

Petilian or professors like Cresconius, who could keep their end up in learned controversy with Augustine himself. It is significant, too, that the sliding scale of fines imposed on Donatist recusants is graded for *illustres*, *spectabiles*, *clarissimi*, *sacerdotales* and *principales* as well as for decurions, *negotiatores* and plebeians.[41]

We also know something of the Novatians in Asia Minor, thanks to Socrates, who took a sympathetic interest in their affairs. Here again the majority were simple rustics, Phrygians and Paphlagonians, and the rigid tenets of the sect appealed to them, as Socrates explains, because they were naturally rather puritanical: they were not addicted to theatres or horse races, and held irregular sexual relations in abhorrence. It was the rank and file of the country Novatians who in Valens' reign, at a congress held at Pazus, a remote village near the source of the Sangarius, adopted the fundamentalist view of the Quartodecimans about the date of Easter. The congress was not attended by the four chief Novatian bishops, those of Constantinople, Nicaea, Nicomedia and Cotiaeum, who generally regulated the worship of the sect. They evidently disliked the reactionary movement among the rural Novatians, and a schism threatened, but was averted by another council, where the bishops with unusual good sense agreed to differ, declaring the date of Easter a matter of indifference.[42]

The Novatians of Constantinople were evidently more sophisticated than their Phrygian and Paphlagonian brothers, and included men of rank and learning. Marcian, who became their bishop in 385, had previously been a palatine civil servant, and had acted as tutor to Valens' daughters. His successor, Sisinnius, was a highly cultivated man, a pupil of the great pagan philosopher Maximus, under whom Julian had studied, a subtle controversialist whom the Arian Eunomius dared not face, and the author of many literary works, whose style Socrates considered too ornate and poetic. He moved in the best senatorial circles, and was rather a dandy, wearing white instead of the usual episcopal black, and was a celebrated wit. Socrates records a number of his repartees, and one is worth quoting. Asked why, being a bishop, he took two baths a day, he replied: 'Because I have not time for a third.' Later Novatian bishops of Constantinople were severer characters, but kept up the aristocratic and scholarly traditions of the see. Paul was a Latin scholar, a distinction rare in fifth-century Constantinople, and Chrysanthus, Marcian's son, had been a consular in Italy and vicar of Britain, and was in the running for the prefecture of the city when he was consecrated. He ordained a distinguished rhetorician, Ablabius, who later became Novatian bishop of Nicaea.[43]

It is difficult to make any generalisation which is both true and significant about the religious temper of an age, but it may at least be asserted with some confidence that the later Roman empire was intensely religious. Sceptics and rationalists, if they existed, have left no mark on history and literature. All, pagans, Jews and Christians alike, believed, and it would seem believed intensely, in supernatural powers, benevolent and malign, who intervened actively in human affairs; all were anxious to win their aid and favour, or to placate or to master them, as the case might be. This had probably always been true of the great mass of the population: by the fourth, and indeed probably by the third century, the educated minority, who had in the late Republic and early Principate ceased to believe in the gods, had become religious once more. Epicureanism, the rationalist and materialist school of philosophy, seems to have died out by Julian's time, and was regarded by him with almost as much disfavour as Christianity. The dominant philosophical school, Neoplatonism, was deeply impregnated with religion.[44]

Pagan intellectuals were usually monotheists or pantheists, believing in one ineffable divinity who ruled or permeated the universe; but such beliefs were not incompatible with a deep reverence for and attachment to the old traditional deities. Philosophers regarded the gods as aspects of or emanations from the supreme divinity, and believed that their myths and rites were divinely inspired and appointed, and possessed an esoteric symbolic significance.

Of the beliefs of the ordinary pagan we know little. He no doubt believed in all the gods, and in the various contingencies of life might make prayers and vows and offerings to the appropriate deity, to Asclepius in sickness or Pan on a desert journey. But he normally paid his devotion to some particular god or group of gods. Some were devotees of one or more of those deities, like Isis or Mithras, who had acquired fame throughout the empire, as not only giving success in this life, but promising bliss beyond the grave. But the great majority of simple pagans probably concentrated their devotions on the local god or gods who protected their city or village. The people of Carthage worshipped Caelestis, the Heavenly Goddess, those of Alexandria Serapis, those of Ephesus their own Artemis of the Ephesians, who, though she might be theoretically identified with other goddesses of the same name, was in the minds of her citizens a local deity, the patroness of their city.

Christians worshipped the one God, but believed in an infinite multitude of evil demons, among whom they generally classified the pagan gods. These demons were considered to be powerful and dangerous. They often lurked in desecrated temples, but might be found anywhere, and frequently took possession of human beings. To judge by the biography of Theodore of Syceon the peasants of central Asia Minor in the sixth century led an utterly demon-ridden existence. In several cases farmers inadvertently removing a rock or digging into a mound released swarms of demons who took possession not only of them but of their neighbours and their animals, and the saint had to be summoned to drive the evil spirits into their lair again and seal them in. This biography is somewhat exceptional in its preoccupation with demons, but the whole hagiographical literature of the age is permeated with the belief in their ubiquitous presence.

The austere monotheism of the early Christian church did not long satisfy the religious needs of the multitude of converts who flowed in from Constantine's reign onwards. There rapidly grew up a cult of the martyrs, which was soon extended to other holy men, the patriarchs and prophets of the Old Testament, the apostles and evangelists, and hermits and ascetics of more modern times.

It is very difficult to trace the stages in the growth of this cult. The churches had naturally always cherished the memory of their martyrs, had reverenced their graves and commemorated the anniversaries of their deaths. After the Peace of the Church chapels, called in the West *memoriae*, and sometimes regular churches, were built over their tombs, and their commemorations came to be popular festivities, celebrated on a grand scale and attended by a vast concourse of worshippers. How early their prayers were invoked it is impossible to say, but the practice was a natural corollary of the belief that they had passed straight to heaven, and could not only hear their suppliants' requests but present them to God himself. In the doctrine of the church, as officially taught, this was the limit of their powers. They played in the heavenly sphere a role analogous to that played on earth by the great men of the court, through whom petitions could be more efficaciously brought to the emperor's notice than if they were directly addressed to him; in the language of the day the same terms were applied to both heavenly and earthly patrons, whose *suffragia* were sought. In answer to critics, pagan and Christian, the leaders of the church firmly maintained that martyrs and saints were not worshipped. But in less guarded moments, when they were pronouncing panegyrics at their festivals, they attributed to them the power of fulfilling the prayers of their suppliants, and encouraged a devotion which it is difficult to distinguish from worship.[45]

The bodies of the martyrs soon acquired a kind of magical power. Shortly after the Great Persecution a Carthaginian lady named Lucilla was reproved by Caecilian, the archdeacon of Carthage, for carrying a martyr's bone upon her person and kissing it before communion: she may have cherished it as a memento, but more probably she regarded it as a charm. A clearer case is the transfer of S. Babylas' corpse from Antioch to Daphne by Gallus Caesar (350-4); this was done with the object of expelling the pagan gods from the famous shrine, and was, we are told, effective, silencing the oracle of Apollo. By this time the cult and its attendant miracles must have been in full swing. It was only a few years later that Hilary asserted that 'the tombs of the apostles and martyrs proclaim Him (Christ) by the working of miracles', and Basil, bishop of Caesarea (370-8), in a panegyric on St. Mamas, speaks of the miracles wrought at his shrine as a commonplace.[46]

Saints and martyrs evidently satisfied a deep popular craving, and the demand for their bodies was insatiable. It was supplied by the miraculous discovery of the tombs either of forgotten martyrs or of well-known figures of the apostolic age or of Old Testament times. The most famous and best attested case is the discovery by Ambrose in 386 of the bodies of SS. Gervasius and Protasius, which is described by himself and by two contemporaries, his biographer Paulinus and Augustine. It is difficult to attribute a deliberate hoax, as some have done, to a man of Ambrose's character, but the fact remains that the names of the two martyrs were unknown until Ambrose, impelled as he says by a sort of premonition, ordered the floor of a church to be taken up and discovered their skeletons with an abundance of blood. Ambrose later discovered another pair, Vitalis and Agricola, at Bononia, and yet another in a garden at Milan. But he was not the first to make such discoveries. Pope Damasus (366-84) is recorded to have searched for and found many bodies of saints at Rome.[47]

Martin, who became bishop of Tours about 372, visited a martyr's shrine which had been consecrated by his predecessor in a place nearby. The saint's name was uncertain and there was no firm tradition about his passion, and Martin, with a critical sense unusual for the age, had doubts. Standing before the grave he prayed for a revelation, and there appeared a sinister wraith which confessed that he had been in fact a brigand, executed for his crimes and reverenced by a vulgar error.[48]

An African council held in 401 expressed similar doubts. It decreed that chapels should be consecrated only when there was an authentic corpse or relic, or a genuine tradition that a martyr had lived or suffered on the spot, and condemned 'the altars which are being established everywhere through the dreams or vain so-called revelations of anybody and everybody'. Such scepticism was, however, very rare, and discoveries of the bodies of saints, usually revealed in dreams, went on unabated through the fifth and sixth centuries in both East and West. One of the most celebrated and best documented took place at the Palestinian village of Caphargamala in 415. We possess the statement circulated by the discoverer, the local priest Lucian. Gamaliel appeared to him three times in a dream and revealed to him where the bodies of himself and his son, of Nicodemus, and, most precious of all, of the protomartyr S. Stephen, were to be found: and found they were, neatly labelled.[49]

The bodies of contemporary saints were as much sought after as those of the ancient martyrs, apostles and prophets. Antony, who died in 356, so disliked the idea of his body becoming an object of cult, that he charged the two disciples who were with him when he died to keep the place of his burial a secret. The corpse of Hilarion, who died in Cyprus in 371, was soon after his death surreptitiously removed by one of his disciples and brought back to Palestine, where it became the object of a cult which flourished in Sozomen's day. In Syria Theodoret records that shrines were built for several celebrated hermits in anticipation of their death, and describes the battles between rival villages for possession of their corpses. Particularly vivid is his eyewitness account of the neighbouring villagers waiting to pounce upon the body of the hermit Jacob, who lived on a mountain four miles from Cyrrhus. So persistent were they that the saint, who was suffering from acute diarrhoea, was put to great embarrassment until Theodoret with great difficulty succeeded in driving them away at nightfall. During a later illness citizens and soldiers from Cyrrhus by a display of force frightened the local villagers away and carried the saint, who was in a coma, to the town. He recovered, however, and was still living when Theodoret wrote.[50]

In the West there was some sentiment against moving corpses from their original places of burial. In the East there seems to have been no such feeling, and the bodies of saints were frequently translated. It was thus that Constantinople, poor in native martyrs, was able to acquire a collection of relics which rivalled that of Rome; Constantius II began the process as early as 356, when he secured the body of S. Timothy, and in the following year those of S. Andrew and S. Luke. In the East corpses were also frequently dissected and distributed to various places. This practice was obviously open to abuse, and soon led to a traffic in dubious relics of which Augustine complained: for the churches of the West, though reluctant to disturb their own martyrs' graves, had no qualms in acquiring relics from the East.[51]

The saints and martyrs, as Theodoret boasts, replaced the pagan gods: their shrines superseded the temples and their feasts the old festivals. Like the old gods, they cured the sick, gave children to barren women, protected travellers from perils of sea and land, detected perjurors and foretold the future. Some acquired widespread fame for some special power. SS. Cyrus and John, the physicians who charged no fee, were celebrated for their cures, and their shrine at Canopus, near Alexandria, was thronged by sufferers from all the provinces, as in the old days had been the temple of Asclepius at Aegae. But the main function of the saints and martyrs in the popular religion of the day was to replace the old gods as local patrons and protectors. S. Martin became for Tours and S. Demetrius for Thessalonica what Serapis had been for Alexandria and Artemis for Ephesus.[52]

This is not to say that the pagan gods ever became saints. There is no case where such a transformation is recorded, and it is on the face of it most unlikely that Christians, who believed that the pagan gods were malignant demons and were taught to avoid any contact with their rites as pollution, would have adopted them into their religion. Martyrs were sometimes translated to pagan sanctuaries, as was S. Babylas to Daphne, or later SS. Cyrus and John to Canopus, but with the intent of exorcising the old gods. Christian festivals were sometimes celebrated on old pagan feast days, but with the deliberate idea of providing a counter-attraction. Occasionally myths of the pagan gods and heroes came to be attached to Christian saints, but the figures to which such myths were attached were often genuine martyrs.[53]

The cult of the saints and martyrs was undoubtedly a popular movement, but it was not confined to the vulgar. From the beginning it was welcomed and promoted by the leaders of the church, including its greatest intellectual figures. The pagan Julian sneered at 'old women who grovel round tombs', and was controverted by Gregory of Nazianzus and later by Cyril of Alexandria. Faustus the Manichee objected: 'You have transformed idols into martyrs and honour them in the same way', and was rebuffed by Augustine. The only orthodox Christian who is recorded to have raised his voice against the cult of martyrs was an obscure Aquitanian priest named Vigilantius. He protested that 'we almost see the rites of the pagans introduced into the churches under the pretext of religion, ranks of candles are lit in full daylight, and everywhere people kiss and adore some bit of dust in a little pot, wrapped in a precious fabric'; and he argued that 'the souls of the apostles and martyrs rest in the bosom of Abraham or in a place of refreshment or under the altar of God' and mocked at the idea that they 'loved their ashes and hovered about them, and were always on the spot in case they could not hear any suppliant who came in their absence'. His work is only known to us because some neighbouring priests, shocked by his impiety, sent a copy to Jerome, who refuted it in a more than usually vitriolic pamphlet.[54]

From what has already been said it is evident that the religion of the age was riddled with superstition. The common man had always believed in magic and divination, and astrology, owing to its pseudo-scientific character, was often accepted by the most enlightened. All these practices (except for the consultation of established oracles and of the officially recognised *haruspices* and *augures* of the Roman state) were criminal offences in the law of the Principate, but they were nevertheless widespread and often openly tolerated. Christians naturally regarded magic and divination as sinful, since they involved the invocation of pagan gods or demons, but they believed in their efficacy. Astrology they endeavoured to discredit on rational grounds, since the fatalistic view which it presupposed was contrary to the doctrine of free will and human responsibility: but it is doubtful whether their arguments had much effect on popular belief.

Towards the end of the third century the belief in and practice of magic penetrated to the most exalted intellectual circles. Plotinus and Porphyry had been sceptical and disapproving of theurgy, as it was called. Porphyry's successor Iamblichus, who flourished about the turn of the century, openly defended it, and is reputed to have performed feats of levitation and to have evoked spirits. The great philosophers at whose feet Julian sat regarded theurgy as the consummation of their wisdom: Maximus had great powers —he is recorded to have elicited a smile from a statue and to have caused the torch it carried to burn—and it was his miracles that won Julian's devout adherence.[55]

Christian miracles followed slightly in the wake of pagan. Down to about the middle of the fourth century Christian literature is reasonably free from the miraculous element. With the growth of the cult of the martyrs a flood of miracles begins. Augustine was particularly interested in contemporary miracles, and with a view to giving them greater publicity, instituted a system whereby the beneficiary wrote a brief narrative (*libellus*), which was subsequently read out in church and filed for future reference: the same practice was introduced in the neighbouring towns of Uzalis and Calama. We possess the actual text of one of these *libelli*, incorporated among Augustine's works, and it was from this source that he culled the miracles which he catalogues in the City of God. We also possess a contemporary account of the miracles performed at Uzalis, drawn up from *libelli* on the instruction of the bishop Euodius.[56]

These documents show that miracles were very frequent occurrences; Augustine recorded seventy at Hippo in less than two years. They are mostly cures, with a few resurrections from the dead, and some revelations of future events. What is most noticeable about them is their magical character. The result is practically always achieved by physical contact with the martyr's shrine, either directly or through some object, usually a piece of cloth, which has been laid upon the tomb. Thus the proprietor of a vineyard at Uzalis, going to his cellar, finds that his entire vintage, 200 jars of wine, is utterly undrinkable. He tells his slave to draw a little wine from each jar into a flagon, and leave it for the night in S. Stephen's shrine. Next day the flagon is brought back, and a little poured from it into each jar, and the entire contents of the cellar forthwith acquire a superb quality. Such silly stories had no doubt always been believed by the common herd, but it is a sign of the times that a man of the intellectual eminence of Augustine should attach importance to them.[57]

One of Augustine's letters is very revealing of the growth of credulity. A scandal had arisen among his clergy. A priest named Boniface had accused a junior cleric named Spes of making improper advances to him, and Spes had retorted by turning the charge against him. It was a case of one man's word against another's, and Augustine saw no means of getting at the truth, though he clearly suspected Spes. Meanwhile the retention of the offender, whichever he was, among the clergy caused scandal to the church, and the promotion of either was blocked until the slur could be removed. Augustine's solution was to send them both to Italy, to swear to their stories before the shrine of S. Felix of Nola. For, he observes, though God is everywhere present, particular types of miracle occur in some places and not in others. He was not aware that any African shrine detected perjurors; on the other hand he knew of a case at Milan when a thief who had perjured himself had been compelled to confess. S. Felix apparently had this power, and Augustine had friends there who would send a reliable report of the result. It is difficult to believe that in the second century any judge would have thought of solving a conflict of evidence by recourse to an oracle.[58]

Another notable feature of the age was the profound and widespread interest in dogmatic controversies. That ordinary people felt passionately on these questions is amply proved by the long series of riots and commotions which they provoked, and the stubborn resistance offered to the penal laws against heretics by thousands of humble Christians. How far the mass of the people understood the often very subtle metaphysical points involved may be open to doubt, but it would seem that popular interest in these controversies, which to us seem so arid, was intense. Gregory of Nyssa gives an amusing picture of Constantinople in the final stage of the Arian controversy: 'If you ask about your change, the shopkeeper philosophises to you about the Begotten and the Unbegotten; if you enquire the price of a loaf, the reply is: "The Father is greater and the Son inferior": and if you say, "Is the bath ready?" the attendant affirms that the Son is of nothing.' Ordinary people, that is, at least learned the stock arguments and catchwords, and enjoyed argumentation.[59]

Some theologians felt the need of presenting their doctrines in popular form to attract the masses. Arius composed a poem in a popular metre, entitled Thaleia, with this intent. Athanasius has preserved an extract from this work. It begins: 'God himself then is ineffable to all. He alone has no equal, none like him or of the same glory. We call him ingenerate because of him that is generate by nature; we hymn him as without beginning because of him who has a beginning; we revere him as everlasting because of him that is born in time.' If the Thaleia was, as Athanasius alleged, sung in the bars of Alexandria, the lower orders in that city must have had a strong taste for theology. Augustine also composed a 'Psalm against the Party of Donatus', 'wishing that the case of the Donatists should come to the knowledge of the very lowest classes and of utterly ignorant and uninformed persons, and stick in their memory as far as in me lay'. It is a fairly simple and straightforward ballad, most of it devoted to the history of the schism, with a refrain at the end of each verse. 'All who rejoice in peace now judge the truth.' It is written in a rough jingle, 'so that needs of metre should not force me to use any words unfamiliar to the vulgar'. Often doctrinal propaganda was not on so high a level as this, but consisted of simple slogans. Even the most ignorant monophysite could proclaim his faith by adding to the

Trisagion the words 'who was crucified for us', and the chanting of the refrain provoked many bloody riots.[60]

It has often been argued that the passions ostensibly evoked by doctrinal controversies were in reality the expression of national sentiment or of social movements. Such theories are scarcely susceptible of proof or of refutation but they are plausible in a very limited number of cases only. It is likely that the Germanic tribes clung to Arianism rather because it was their tribal cult, than from any intellectual conviction of its truth. Theoderic's tolerant policy in Italy seems to have been based on the idea that the Goths and the Romans should live together in peace and mutual respect, but that each should keep to their own function and preserve their separate institutions and faiths. The doubtless apocryphal story that he executed a catholic deacon for conversion to Arianism suggests that this at any rate was the popular impression produced by his policy.[61]

Other Arian kings, however, did not regard their faith as the exclusive national religion of their tribesmen, but endeavoured to force it on their Roman subjects; and it is hard to see what motive they had, save a fanatical conviction that catholicism was a heresy displeasing to God. The Germans certainly believed that their doctrine was, and could be demonstrated to be, correct: the Vandal king Huneric staged a set debate between his clergy and the catholics. Sidonius Apollinaris makes an interesting remark about the Visigothic king Euric, so fanatical a persecutor that 'one might doubt whether he is the leader of his tribe or of his sect'. 'His mistake is,' says Sidonius, 'that he believes that success is vouchsafed to him in his plans and policies in virtue of his religion, whereas really he obtains it in virtue of earthly good fortune.' In other words Euric believed that God rewarded him with victory for his zeal in suppressing the heresy of his Roman subjects.[62]

Apart from the Germans there are only four areas where national sentiment can be plausibly alleged as the basis for heresy or schism, Africa, Egypt, Syria and Armenia. The Donatists were confined to Africa. They frequently challenged the right of the imperial government to interfere in religious affairs and resisted its agents by armed violence. They gave their support to the two African pretenders, Firmus and Gildo, and some of them are alleged by Augustine in 417 to have compromised with Arianism in an attempt 'to conciliate the Goths, since they have some power'. The reference is probably to the federate troops under the command of the tribune Boniface, who later married an Arian wife and allowed his daughter to receive an Arian baptism, doubtless with the same end in view. Finally the Donatists drew their main support from the Punic or Berber speaking population.

These are the facts, and they hardly justify the assertion that Donatism was essentially an expression of African national feeling. Donatism was in fact confined to Africa, but its adherents upheld that they were the one surviving fragment of the catholic church, which had elsewhere gone astray: it is significant that they for long maintained a bishop in Rome. That they were frequently in revolt against the imperial government was because the government usually persecuted them: they were perfectly willing to co-operate with Julian, who granted them toleration, and with such pro-consuls and vicars as favoured their cause. Their adherence to local pretenders who promised them support was in the circum-stances perfectly natural; Firmus and Gildo were not national leaders, but pretenders to the imperial throne, and in backing them the Donatists were hoping for an imperial government in sympathy with their church. Nor was there anything treasonable in their ingratiating themselves with the federates operating in the area. There is no evidence that they welcomed or supported the Vandals.

Nor is there anything very significant in the adherence of the Punic and Berber speaking population to the Donatist cause. Any church which included the peasant masses was bound to have a majority of them, and the Donatists took no pride in the fact. Their leaders were Latin speaking, their literature was in Latin, and so are the inscriptions even of the country churches.[63]

The Africans never, so far as we know, possessed any national sentiment. The Egyptians in times past had cherished their national traditions. Under the later Ptolemies there had been serious native revolts, and native Pharaohs had established their rule over parts of the country for considerable periods. Even under Roman rule there was in the reign of Marcus Aurelius a formidable popular uprising in the Delta which may well have been inspired by nationalism. One of its leaders was a priest, and it is certain that the 'Prophecy of the Potter', a strongly xenophobic document which foretold the destruction of the foreign city of Alexandria, was in circulation at this period and even later. There is, however, no sign that Egyptian nationalism survived the third century, and it is likely to have died with the old Egyptian religion, with which it was closely linked. Certainly there was from the fourth century onwards no hostility to Alexandria, which became on the contrary the acknowledged spiritual centre of Egypt.[64]

The Egyptians undoubtedly showed great solidarity in the doctrinal conflicts of the fourth, fifth and sixth centuries. They stubbornly maintained their loyalty to the homoousion throughout the prolonged controversy which followed the Council of Nicaea, and they were as united and as intransigent in the monophysite cause after Chalcedon. They fiercely resisted the attempts of the imperial government to impose upon them bishops whom they considered to be heretical, but this does not seem to have involved any hostility to the empire as such. There were no attempts at political rebellion, and in periods when the imperial doctrine coincided with their own they were perfectly content.[65]

Egyptian doctrinal solidarity seems to be the result of the immense prestige of the Alexandrian church, and the highly centralised organisation of the patriarchate. The people of Egypt took great pride in the high repute of Alexandria for theological learning, and had very little opportunity of hearing other views. They were in turn homoousians and monophysites partly because they had been taught no other doctrine, but mainly because these were the faiths of their great popes Alexander and Athanasius, Cyril and Dioscorus. It was probably for this reason that they obstinately refused any compromise which did not expressly anathematise Chalcedon, the council which had condemned Dioscorus.

Egyptian hostility to the doctrine of Chalcedon was probably enhanced by the fact that the council had given primacy in the East to Constantinople, the upstart see whose pretentions the patriarchate of Alexandria had always resented and often successfully crushed. It was doubtless for similar reasons that monophysitism was strong at Ephesus, whose bishop the Council of Chalcedon had deposed and whose see it had robbed of its quasi-patriarchal status and subjected to Constantinople.[66]

Monophysitism became by accident the national faith of the Armenians in much the same way as Arianism became that of the German tribes. The Armenian kingdom had been early converted to Christianity and had created what may truly be called a national church. In the middle decades of the fifth century the Armenians were involved in a struggle with their Persian overlords, who were endeavouring to impose Zoroastrianism upon them, and took no part in the Councils of Ephesus and Chalcedon. As late as 506 they were unaware of the issues involved, and learned of them only from monophysite refugees from Mesopotamia, where the Persian government supported the Nestorians. The Armenians naturally accepted the views of their fellow victims. They condemned Nestorius and Chalcedon and approved 'the letter of Zeno, blessed emperor of the Romans', that is, the Henoticon, which was at that time the official orthodoxy of the empire. When Justin and Justinian reversed the imperial attitude, the Armenians were apparently not consulted and clung to their old faith. They remained friendly with Rome and solicited and obtained her aid against the Persians, but steadfastly refused to change the doctrine to which they were traditionally attached.[67]

Outside Egypt and Armenia monophysitism ultimately survived only in Syria and Mesopotamia. It cannot, however, be called the national faith of those areas. There was always a large body of Chalcedonians in Syria, and of Nestorians in Persian Mesopotamia. Moreover in the late fifth and sixth centuries monophysitism had a considerable following in other parts of the Eastern empire. For the first few decades after Chalcedon Palestine was strongly monophysite; the monks denounced the traitor Juvenal, who had signed the Chalcedonian creed, and set up a rival patriarch in his place. At Thessalonica the papal commissioners who came in 519 to receive the bishop into communion were greeted by riots; shortly before 2,000 citizens had crowded to be baptised before the monophysite faith was abandoned. In Justinian's reign the great monophysite leader James Baradaeus in his many journeys visited Cappadocia, Cilicia, Isauria, Pamphylia, Lycaonia, Phrygia, Lycia, Caria, Asia, Cyprus and the islands of the Aegean. Of the twenty-nine sees to which he consecrated bishops thirteen were in Egypt, seven in Syria and Mesopotamia, and nine in Asia Minor. John of Ephesus mentions monophysite communities in many cities of Asia Minor, and notes in particular the flourishing churches of Pamphylia.[68]

It would seem in fact as if for a century and more after Chalcedon monophysitism was as widely diffused, and in as haphazard a fashion, as had been Arianism. It was perhaps stronger in Syria; but it survived there and died elsewhere, because in Syria it enjoyed toleration under the Arabs and in Asia Minor it eventually succumbed to persecution.

The linguistic question is relevant neither in Egypt nor in Syria and Mesopotamia. In Egypt translations of the scriptures into Coptic were made in the fourth century, if not earlier, for the benefit of the masses who knew no Greek, and much theological and hagiographical literature was translated long before the Egyptian church went into permanent schism. Greek on the other hand was the language of educated Christians, whether orthodox or monophysite. It was only when Greek died out after the Arab conquest that Coptic became the exclusive language of the national monophysite church, while the orthodox patriarchate of Alexandria, which was virtually a foreign mission from Constantinople, naturally used Greek.

In the Antiochene patriarchate the position was somewhat

different, since Syriac not only was the language of the people in Syria and Palestine, but in Mesopotamia remained in continuous use as a literary language. It was used by Christian writers of all persuasions in Mesopotamia from the third century onwards. In Syria and Palestine the liturgy or at least parts of it were translated into Syriac for the benefit of humble folk as early as the third century, but Christian literature, whether orthodox or monophysite, was written in Greek. Here again Greek died out after the Arab conquest, and Syriac became the exclusive language of the local monophysite church, with the result that the works of the great monophysite leaders of the sixth century, originally written in Greek, survive only in Syriac translations. Here too the orthodox patriarchate became a virtual dependency of Constantinople and therefore maintained the use of Greek.

The only religious conflict which can be associated with a social struggle is the Donatist controversy. According to Optatus the circumcellion bands in the middle of the fourth century established a reign of terror over the propertied classes. 'No one could be safe on his estates: the bonds of debtors lost their force, no creditor at that time could recover his money.' Rich men travelling through the country were hustled out of their chariots and compelled to run behind while their slaves drove. Augustine brings similar charges against the circumcellions. Peasants were encouraged to defy their landlords, and slaves not only to desert but to menace their masters. 'What owner was not compelled to fear his own slave if he resorted to their patronage? Who could exact payment from those who consumed his stores or from his debtors, if they appealed for their aid and defence? Under the terror of clubs and fire and instant death the accounts of the worst slaves were destroyed so that they could escape to freedom. The bonds of debtors were extorted and given back to them.'[69]

It is likely enough that the peasants who formed the circumcellion bands were glad to take advantage of the religious struggle to intimidate and beat up landlords and moneylenders who happened to be catholics and to champion their fellow sectaries against them. But these incidents were only part of a wider campaign of terrorism, in which the principal incidents were the seizure of catholic churches and the kidnapping and maltreatment of catholic clergy. There is no evidence that landlords in general were attacked. There were plenty of Donatist landowners, who would hardly have remained faithful to the cause if they had been subject to such treatment. And there is evidence that catholic landowners were not molested if they allowed their tenants freedom of worship. Augustine in a fulsome letter to the great senator Pammachius congratulates him on his courage in urging his tenants in the Donatist stronghold of Numidia to join the catholic church, and expresses the wish that other senators may be encouraged to do the same. Evidently their Donatist tenants were quietly paying their rents to these Italian senators and would only cause trouble if their religion were interfered with.[70]

In all religious conflicts the upper classes tended for prudential motives to conform to government policy. They had more to lose by opposition: they were more likely to be denounced, their property might be confiscated, they might lose their posts. The lower classes were more stubborn; flogging and torture were familiar incidents to them, and had not the same terror as they had for their social superiors. In the persecutions the vast majority of upper-class Christians seem to have lapsed; the martyrs and confessors were mostly men of humble station. The same seems to have been true when the empire became Christian and persecution was turned against the dissidents. Hence in most heretical sects the majority tended to be humble people. Only among the Donatists, so far as we know, did this circumstance give to a religious struggle some features of a class war. In general, it would seem, the religious struggles of the later empire were in reality what they appeared to be. Their bitterness demonstrates the overwhelming importance of religion in the minds of all sorts and conditions of men.

It is even more difficult to generalise about morals than about religion. It is possible to record the ideals set forth by philosophers and theologians, and to describe the precepts of moralists and preachers. It is much more difficult to assess the codes of behaviour which ordinary men in various walks of life accepted as binding upon them, and next to impossible to estimate how far men lived up to these codes.

There was much in common between the moral ideals preached by pagan philosophers and Christian theologians. Both alike proclaimed the equality of men, by the law of nature and in the sight of God respectively. The philosophers were as insistent on love of one's fellow men (φιλανθρωπία) as Christians of love of one's neighbour. The pagan Libanius regarded forgiveness of one's enemies as a divine and typically Athenian virtue. Both philosophers and divines preached contempt for wealth and power, both alike advocated temperance and chastity. There were, however, differences in emphasis in the pagan and Christian ideals. The philosophers taught that wealth was indifferent, and that its loss should be borne with equanimity: Christians preached that riches were a positive hindrance to salvation, and the better way was to give away all one's possessions to the poor. Pagans held marriage in high esteem. Christians set up celibacy and virginity as the ideal, and gave only a grudging approval to marriage as a concession to weaker vessels.[71]

In their practical precepts there was also much in common between paganism and Christianity. Despite their common belief in the equality of men both accepted slavery as a matter of course, and contented themselves with urging slaves to be obedient and dutiful, and masters to be kind. But once again there were differences of emphasis. Liberality was part of the pagan code. The rich were expected to spend their money lavishly for the benefit of their fellow citizens, subscribing to public buildings, maintaining the gymnasia and baths, buying corn for distribution at a fair price in time of famine, and above all providing games and other entertainments. The standard of generosity expected was high, and there were men who reduced themselves to poverty by their benefactions. This kind of liberality reached its apogee in the second century A.D. but the spirit survived in pagan circles down to the end of the fourth century at any rate: Libanius' letters are full of the praises of wealthy pagans who have impoverished themselves in the service of their cities.[72]

The church frowned on such forms of liberality. The principal object to which it was devoted, the games, were in its view sinful, and the motive was vainglory. 'It is prodigality', declares Ambrose 'to exhaust one's own fortune for the sake of popularity, as do those who squander their patrimony on giving horse races or even theatrical entertainments and gladiatorial shows and wild beast hunts in order to outshine the productions of their predecessors.'[73]

On the other hand, the church laid an immense emphasis on charity to the poor, and particularly to widows, orphans, strangers, and the sick. The poor were not altogether neglected in the pagan code, as the alimentary benefactions of the second century testify, but the Christians set a new standard. The best witness to their generosity is Julian, who allocated an annual grant of 30,000 *modii* of wheat and 60,000 *sestarii* of wine to his pagan high priest of Galatia, and instructed him: 'A fifth of this sum is to be spent on the poor who serve the priests, and the rest distributed by us to strangers and beggars. For it is a disgrace that no Jew is a beggar, and the impious Galilaeans feed our people in addition to their own, whereas ours manifestly lack assistance from us. Teach the pagans also to subscribe to such services, and the pagan villages to offer first fruits to the gods, and accustom the pagans to beneficence of this kind.'[74]

Christian charity was not limited to almsgiving to the poor. Christians built churches, and maintained and endowed their clergy, and supported thousands of monks. The duty extended to a much wider social circle than did pagan liberality; even the humblest were urged to contribute their mite. On the whole it is probable, though no figures can be adduced, that more people gave away a larger proportion of their wealth in Christian than in pagan society: otherwise the rapid growth of the immense wealth of the churches is unaccountable. Many motives contributed to the strength of the movement. Vainglory no doubt played its part, particularly in the erection of churches—as in pagan times benefactors were far more willing to put up a new building which would commemorate their name than to make provision for repairs. But the most cogent motive was the desire to save one's soul, for the church taught that almsgiving, together with prayer and fasting, won remission for sin. In particular this motive accounts for the flood of testamentary bequests to the church.[75]

In sexual relations the teaching of the church was more exacting than the pagan code. Both the Christian and the Greco-Roman moral code condemned homosexuality: Libanius is as passionate in denouncing the vice, which was apparently very prevalent at Antioch, as is his contemporary John Chrysostom. It may be suspected, however, that average pagan opinion was more lax than Christian. Both alike abhorred incest, but there were areas of the empire where marriages between close kin were normal and approved. In Egypt brother and sister marriage was traditional and commonly practised at any rate down to the early third century A.D. It was tolerated by the Roman government, being forbidden only to Roman citizens, presumably Egyptians who had received the citizenship. After the Constitutio Antoniniana the Roman rules against incest should have been universally enforced, but apparently they were not. Diocletian was shocked to find that owing to ignorance of the law many of his subjects were contracting incestuous unions, and in a constitution redolent of religious emotion peremptorily prohibited practices so beastly and so offensive to the immortal gods. In Egypt, whether under the pressure of Roman law or of Christian teaching, brother and sister marriages seem to have ceased by the fourth century. Among the rural population of Osrhoene and Mesopotamia incestuous marriages were still common in the sixth century, even among the clergy: Justinian, after ordering an investigation, had to condone past offences.[76]

Since the reign of Augustus adultery, that is intercourse between a married woman and anyone but her husband, and *stuprum*, intercourse between a man and any free woman other than his wife, or a registered prostitute, had been criminal offences, visited by severe penalties on both parties. Breaches of chastity by women were strongly condemned by public opinion. The offences of men seem to have been more lightly regarded, but the lawyers held that in trying a case of adultery the judge should enquire whether the husband led a chaste life: for it was 'most inequitable that a husband should exact chastity from his wife, when he does not practise it himself'. Divorce on the other hand was permissible under Roman law at the wish of either party, and the husband might remarry forthwith, the wife after a year's delay. Though there were probably not many who went as far as the couple cited by Jerome, who had each had twenty-two previous spouses, divorce seems to have been frequent; on the other hand scores of pagan tombstones record with pride long and happy marriages. Concubinage, a regular union between an unmarried man and a slave or freedwoman, was recognised by law and regarded as perfectly respectable. Prostitution was also recognised by law, and, while brothel keepers and prostitutes were despised as a degraded class, recourse to them was not condemned by public opinion.[77]

The standards taught by the church were much more rigorous. All intercourse outside marriage was declared sinful, though there was some hesitation about concubinage. Augustine declared uncompromisingly against it, but his attitude apparently evoked surprise and indignation from his flock, and the Council of Toledo in 400 ruled that an unmarried man might have one concubine, thus conforming to the classical law. It was generally agreed that divorce was permissible only for adultery, but Augustine by a rather casuistical argument equated idolatry with adultery, and avarice with idolatry, and concluded that any grave sin justified divorce. On the question whether divorced persons might remarry there was a division of opinion. Origen states that some bishops in his day allowed it, and though he thought them wrong he did not presume to condemn them. The Council of Arles in 314 evidently disapproved of it, advising young men who had divorced adulterous wives to refrain from a second marriage if possible. Epiphanius at the end of the fourth century considered remarriage after a lawful divorce, for adultery or other grave sin, quite normal. Augustine, after prolonged thought, decided that it was forbidden, and so advised his flock. But he admitted that the texts were very obscure, and therefore regarded the second marriage of divorced persons as a venial sin. An African council in 407 subjected to penance all husbands or wives who had been divorced by their spouses if they subsequently remarried. A Gallic council in 465 excommunicated husbands who married again if they had divorced their first wives for reasons other than adultery. But on one point all Christians were agreed, that marriage was indissoluble except for adultery.[78]

The Christian emperors tightened up the laws of divorce, but not in an entirely Christian sense. Constantine enacted that a woman might legitimately divorce her husband only if he were a murderer, poisoner or tomb robber. If she did so for any other cause, such as drunkenness, gambling or sexual offences, she lost her dowry and was deported. A man might divorce his wife for adultery, poisoning or procuring, and if he did so for other reasons had to restore her dowry and was debarred from a second marriage. It may be noted that the illegitimate divorce, though the guilty party was penalised, was valid, so that the divorced party could remarry. Honorius in 421 reformed the law, distinguishing three kinds of divorce, that for a crime, that for bad character and that without reasons alleged. In divorces of the first class a wife, if she proved her case, recovered her dowry and was allowed to remarry after five years; a husband could remarry forthwith. In those of the second class a man who divorced was allowed to marry again after two years but a woman was debarred from remarriage. In those of the third class the penalties were the same as under Constantine's law, deportation for a woman, celibacy for a man.[79]

Since divorce under the old legal forms had been rendered so difficult, many couples dissolved their marriage by consent. This was forbidden by Theodosius II in 439, but he at the same time abolished all the penalties for divorce, and went back to the classical law. His constitution was received in the West in 448, but Valentinian III four years later revoked it, going back to the law of 421. Theodosius II also had second thoughts in 449. He allowed divorce for a long list of crimes, ranging from treason to stealing cattle, and for various marital offences, such as, in the case of a man, wife beating or introducing loose women into the home, and in the case of a woman, going to the games or the theatre or spending a night away without her husband's leave. A man who divorced his wife in these circumstances could marry again forthwith; a woman kept her dowry and could remarry after a year. But divorces without due cause remained valid; a woman who thus divorced her husband was not allowed to marry again within five years, a man merely forfeited the dowry. As a result of this law the dissolution of marriages by consent reappeared: the law of 439 was apparently evaded by one party sending the other a formal document of divorce (*repudium*). Anastasius in 497 cleared up an ambiguity by ruling that if a husband divorced his wife with her consent, she did not have to wait five years but might remarry after the year laid down by the classical law.[80]

Justinian legislated extensively on marriage, revising in various ways the legitimate causes of divorce. In 542 he made a drastic change. He prohibited divorce by consent, and ordered that a woman who divorced her husband without cause should be placed in a nunnery for life. Under this law a husband in like case suffered only pecuniary damages, but in 548 he too was relegated to a monastery. The prohibition of divorce by consent caused much discontent, and within a year of its author's death, Justin II, besieged by petitions from couples who, though they had no lawful cause for divorce, found married life intolerable, regretfully revoked it. We possess the contract of divorce of an Egyptian couple who took advantage of Justin II's law three years later. Aurelius Theodore, a baker, and Aurelia Amaresia, daughter of a merchant, both of Antinoopolis, declare: 'We were in time past joined to one another in marriage and community of life in fair hopes and with a view to the procreation of legitimate children, thinking to maintain a peaceful and seemly married life with one another for the whole time of our joint lives; but on the contrary we have suffered from a sinister and wicked demon which attacked us unexpectedly from we know not whence, with a view to our being separated from one another.' After which they get down to business details, abandoning all reciprocal claims and specifying that either party may make a second marriage.[81]

This record of legislation shows how impotent was the church to change accepted moral standards even on a matter on which it felt so strongly as the sanctity of marriage. Constantine and his successors in making divorce more difficult were evidently actuated by Christian ideals, and were probably subjected to clerical pressure: the African council which in 407 prohibited the remarriage of all persons who had been divorced resolved to petition the emperor for an imperial law to that effect. But the imperial government never ventured to impose any such general ban, and on the whole tended to relax the drastic rules against divorce enacted by Constantine: even Justinian allowed remarriage after divorce for a wide range of causes. But the most significant fact is the survival of divorce by consent throughout the three centuries which followed Constantine's law. It was apparently despite the church's teaching quite common among Christians.

Asterius of Amaseia in one of his sermons castigates his congregation 'who change your wives like your clothes, and build new bride chambers as often and as casually as stalls at a fair'.[82]

The church's condemnation of fornication had rather more effect, if not in diminishing it, at any rate in rescuing prostitutes. Constantine, it is true, took prostitution for granted and levied the *collatio lustralis* from it as from other trades: he moreover assimilated barmaids to prostitutes, ruling that they should be neither subject to the penalties of the *Lex Julia de adulteriis* nor protected by it. It was not until the fifth century that any legislation was introduced against prostitution, and it was apparently due to the initiative of a pious layman, Florentius, twice praetorian prefect of the East. In 428 he inspired a law authorising prostitutes who wished to abandon their trade to appeal to bishops, provincial governors or *defensores* of cities, and empowering these authorities to free them from their fathers or owners or employers. In 439 he secured the issue of a constitution freeing all prostitutes in Constantinople and expelling brothel keepers from the city; he recompensed the treasury for the resulting loss of revenue out of his own fortune. It was evidently by this time felt to be a scandal that a Christian government should draw profit from immorality, and twenty or thirty years later Leo enacted a general prohibition of prostitution and abolished the tax upon it.[83]

Needless to say the prohibition was ineffective. In 529 Theodora made a vigorous attack on the problem in the capital. She made the brothel keepers declare on oath how much they had paid for their girls, and having established that five solidi was the average price, bought up all the prostitutes and put them in a former imperial palace, which she converted into the Convent of Repentance; according to the malicious Procopius many of the girls found their new life so depressing that they flung themselves out of the windows. Six years later Justinian received private information, which was verified by an enquiry conducted by the praetors, that prostitution was again rampant in the capital. In a constitution which he issued as a result of this enquiry he gives some details of the trade. Agents toured the provinces and allured girls, sometimes younger than ten years of age, into their clutches by offering them fine clothes and shoes: once in the city they were made to sign contracts and provide sureties for their observance, or kept imprisoned in brothels.[84]

To turn to a minor issue, the church viewed the baths with displeasure. Mixed bathing it naturally condemned as an incitement to sin, but it also disapproved of bathing in general. 'He who has once been bathed in Christ has no need of a second bath', wrote

Jerome. Augustine allowed nuns to go to the baths only once a month, unless by doctor's orders. Pious Christians had doubts even about this. The Palestinian hermit Barsenuphius was asked: 'Since I am ill, and my doctor has ordered me to take baths, is it a sin?' He replied: 'Bathing is not absolutely forbidden to a man in the world, when need demands. So if you are ill and need it, it is not a sin. But if a man is healthy, it cossets and relaxes his body and conduces to lust.' In this sphere the church's censure was utterly ignored save by a puritanical minority. The baths remained a great social institution among rich and poor alike. Even the clergy did not always conform to the church's teaching; bishop Sisinnius, it will be remembered, shocked his Novatian congregation by bathing twice a day.[85]

Christian writers consistently and unanimously condemn the games in all their forms. They had a special objection to gladiatorial shows and wild beast hunts as being organised murder. They had an even stronger objection to theatrical displays, both because they enacted pagan myths and because they were normally suggestive and indecent. But all games, including chariot races, came under the church's condemnation as being frivolous distractions and because they were by origin celebrated in honour of pagan gods and were still associated with pagan festivals. Not only actors and actresses but charioteers were refused baptism unless they renounced their profession and excommunicated if they resumed it.[86]

Here the church secured one victory. Constantine prohibited gladiatorial shows in 326, and in the Eastern parts, where they were a Roman importation and had never been very common, the law seems to have been effective. Libanius in his autobiography recalls with nostalgic melancholy 'those single combats in which fell or conquered men who, one could say, were disciples of the three hundred at Thermopylae': though he did not watch the show and was sickened by the sight of blood, he could not as a good pagan condemn gladiators. He is speaking of the Antiochene Olympia of 328 and implies that he had seen none since. In the West gladiatorial games continued until the reign of Honorius, when an Eastern hermit, Telemachus, sacrificed his life to stop them, leaping into the arena and thrusting himself between the contestants. Wild beast hunts, however, which might be just as murderous, went on; the puritanical and economical Anastasius banned them in 499, but they were soon revived.[87]

Anastasius also banned the mime a few years later, with equal lack of success. One form of theatrical entertainment, the *maiuma*, which Christian opinion particularly condemned for its licentious character, was occasionally prohibited by the imperial government, but never, it would seem, for long. In 396 Arcadius conceded 'that the pleasure of the *maiuma* should be restored to the provincials, on condition that decency is preserved and modesty is maintained with chaste morals'. Three years later he felt obliged to prohibit 'the filthy and indecent spectacle of the *maiuma*'; but Justinian's Code preserves only the former law.[88]

The evidence is overwhelming that Christians of all classes from the richest to the poorest took a passionate interest in all forms of games, wild beast hunts, the mime and the *maiuma*, and above all chariot races. Not even all the clergy were resolute against them. When, in about 430, Leontius the prefect announced that he was going to revive the Olympia in the theatre of Chalcedon, a local abbot, Hypatius, raised the cry of idolatry—though he had no idea what happened at the Olympia—and asked Eulalius the bishop of Chalcedon to protest. But Eulalius told Hypatius to mind his own business.[89]

In the de Gubernatione Dei Salvian denounces his Christian contemporaries on three main counts, the laxity of their sexual morals, their passionate addiction to the games, and their heartless oppression of the poor. The first two charges seem to be justified, the last is borne out by much factual and detailed evidence in the Codes and in the canons of the councils, in the letters of laymen and ecclesiastics, in the speeches of Libanius and the sermons of bishops, in the biographies of saints and in the papyri. There were many good Christians who were charitable to the poor, but many more who abused their wealth and position to exploit their necessities, lending them money at usurious rates of interest, enslaving them when they were starving, juggling with the assessments to throw on them more than their due of taxation, extorting from them extra perquisites beyond their lawful rent and cheating them by the use of false measures. It is difficult to assess whether in these matters the general level of morals was lower than it had been under the pagan empire, but it seems to have been no higher. Pliny the younger reveals himself in his letters as a more considerate landlord than were the rectors of the patrimony of St. Peter under Gregory the Great.

In some aspects of morals it is possible to trace a decline. The Codes give a very strong impression that brutality increased. In dealing with slaves, and from the middle of the second century onward the lower orders generally, the Roman administration had always been brutal. Torture was freely used to obtain evidence and extract confessions, flogging was arbitrarily inflicted, and the penalties for crime were often savage. Under the Christian emperors flogging and torture seem to have been used more and more as a matter of course, and were extended to classes hitherto exempt from them. Savage penalties, such as burning alive, were applied to a wider range of offences by successive emperors.

Official extortion and oppression and judicial corruption seem also to have increased. The Roman administration had never been free of these evils, but there was certainly a marked decline, which appears to be progressive, from the relatively high standards attained in the second and early third centuries. A definite decline in public morality can be traced in the sale of offices, which from being an exceptional abuse became a standard practice. It lay at the root of extortion and corruption, which concurrently became accepted as normal.

It is strange that during a period when Christianity, from being the religion of a small minority, came to embrace practically all the citizens of the empire, the general standards of conduct should have remained in general static and in some respects have sunk. If the moral code taught by the church was not notably higher than that of pagan philosophy, it was preached with far more vigour to a far wider audience, and was backed by the sanction of eternal punishment in the next world. In all the churches of the empire Christians received regular exhortation in sermons; there was a flood of homiletical literature; and sinners were disciplined by penance and excommunication.

One reason for the church's failure may have been that it set its standards too high, and insisted too strongly that any major lapse entailed eternal damnation. It had built up its code when it was a small exclusive society of the elect. When after the Peace of the Church it became mingled with the world, its demands became intolerable. This is the main explanation of the tremendous appeal made by the eremitic and monastic life. Some Christians sought the solitude of the desert to achieve a higher spiritual life. They yearned by mortifying the flesh and devoting their whole life to the study of the scriptures, meditation and prayer to obtain an intimate mystical knowledge of God. There survives a large body of devotional literature which gives psychological guidance to such aspirants. The vast majority of monks and hermits, however, had a simpler and lowlier ambition, to shun the distractions and temptations of the world and thus to make it possible for themselves to escape eternal damnation.

In one passage John Chrysostom affirms that it is perfectly

possible for a Christian to live an ordinary life and save his soul. 'Where now are those who say that it is impossible for a man to preserve his virtue living in the midst of a city, and that withdrawal and life in the mountains is essential, and that a man who is head of a household and has a wife and looks after his children and slaves cannot be virtuous?' He hastily adds, 'not that I discourage withdrawal from cities or forbid life in the mountains and deserts', and his general tone is very different. He stresses the temptations and distractions of secular life and paints an idyllic picture of the peace and quiet enjoyed by the monks. The cities, he declares, are so evil 'that those who wish to be saved are forced to seek the desert' and he urges all his flock not only to send their sons to the desert but to go there themselves en masse. John is exceptionally enthusiastic on this theme, but most Christian writers advocate the monastic life not as a special vocation for the spiritually minded but as a means of salvation for the ordinary men and women. When the emperor Maurice forbade serving soldiers and officials indebted to the treasury to enter monasteries, Pope Gregory could scarcely bring himself to execute this decree. 'I am terribly frightened by this constitution, I confess to your majesty, for by it the way to heaven is closed to many, and what has hitherto been lawful is now prohibited. For there are many who can live a religious life even in secular garb. And there are some who unless they leave everything can in no way be saved before God.'[90]

Countless earnest Christians, who despaired of saving their souls in the world, flocked to the deserts or crowded into monasteries. Many others, who had the means to do so, lived austere and secluded lives of prayer and meditation within their own homes, as did the noble ladies with whom Jerome corresponded. The great majority of ordinary Christians, who had their families to keep and their livings to earn, and could not bring themselves to make the great renunciation, placed their hopes of salvation in the sacrament of baptism, which washed away all sin.

This is the explanation of the apparently common practice of postponing baptism to the last minute. This habit is denounced in sermons and pamphlets by Basil of Caesarea, Gregory of Nazianzus and Gregory of Nyssa. There were no doubt, as these authors say, cynics who wished to indulge themselves and then to win salvation by a deathbed baptism. But there were probably more who were afraid that they would not be able to keep to the straight and narrow path, and preferred to be on the safe side.[91]

Late baptism was apparently by this time generally considered to be wrong, since offenders alleged specious excuses, such as a desire to be baptised in Jordan. It is very difficult to estimate how common the practice was. Infant baptism was already common in the early third century, and children in Christian families were no doubt generally baptised early owing to parental anxiety for their salvation. But down to the end of the fourth century we know of a number of pious Christians who postponed their baptism till late in life. The case of Constantine is well known. It is more remarkable that his son, Constantius II, who was brought up as a Christian and was morbidly pious, was not baptised until shortly before his death. Theodosius I, a convinced Christian from a Christian family, was in his middle thirties when he received baptism, and only received it then because he was seriously ill. Ambrose was still a catechumen, though he came of a very pious family, when he was elected bishop of Milan, and his brother Satyrus was baptised only shortly before his death. An inscription records that Junius Bassus, who died during his prefecture of the city at the age of forty-two, 'went to God a neophyte'. Another inscription commemorates a humbler Roman, a man of exemplary virtues, who died a neophyte at the same age in 396.[92]

In the fifth century we hear no more of late baptisms. Infant baptism was probably by now normal for children of Christian parentage, though there were local variations of practice. Zacharias of Mitylene explains that Severus was still a catechumen when he went to Alexandria as a student, because it was the custom in his country, Pisidia, not to baptise until the beard began to grow. But it is significant that Zacharias thought Severus' case required explanation; and even in Pisidia youths received baptism before they embarked on the hazards of adult life.[93]

A baptised Christian who fell into serious sin had a second chance in the sacrament of penance. In the Western church the primitive rigours of penance were maintained down to the sixth century. It was a humiliating and exacting process. Penitents had to wear a distinctive garb and stand or kneel in special parts of the church. They were excluded from the eucharist, and had to perform extra fasts and to refrain from carnal pleasures. All this they might have to do for as much as ten or twelve years, in the case of the worst sins, before they were reconciled. Many people naturally shrank from the ordeal, but there were other reasons for deferring penance as long as possible. It was granted once and once for all. There was no assurance of forgiveness if one sinned after penance, and to avoid the risk of sin the church imposed a severe discipline on penitents for the rest of their lives. They might not marry and must observe continence if already married: Pope Leo conceded with some hesitation that a young man who had received penance

owing to fear of death might be excused if he subsequently married
to avoid the greater sin of fornication. They might not engage in
trade, nor practise at the bar nor serve in the army or the civil
service. To the ordinary man, with his living to earn and his family
to keep, penance was impracticable until he could retire on his
savings, and most people preferred to postpone it until their
deathbeds, when the church would take their intention on trust
and give them absolution—though if they recovered they had to
undergo the full rigours. Preachers like Augustine or Caesarius
deprecated postponing penance until the very last moment, but it is
clear that the latter at any rate did not expect it to be undertaken
except by the elderly.[94]

Owing to the very exacting standards demanded by the church,
especially in sexual morals, many Christians despaired of leading a
sinless life. In the fourth century many, if they had not been
baptised in childhood, remained catechumens all their days, relying
on a last minute baptism to secure salvation. In the fifth and sixth
centuries, when most people were baptised in infancy or at any rate
as adolescents, they relied on deathbed penance. In these circumstances many who started with the best intentions may have come
to feel that having sinned once or twice it did not matter if they
sinned again: the final result would be the same.

In the Eastern churches the primitive discipline of penance
seems to have been relaxed from the end of the fourth century.
The rot began, according to Socrates and Sozomen, when Nectarius, bishop of Constantinople under Theodosius I, owing to a
scandal, abolished the penitentiary priest, whose office it had been
to hear confessions and order the appropriate penance. Henceforth
sinners were left to fix their own penance at their own discretion,
and it seems to have followed that penance, instead of being a
solemn rite enacted once for all, might be repeated as often as
required. The repetition of penance also crept in towards the
end of the sixth century in the West: it was severely condemned
as a pernicious innovation by the third Council of Toledo in 589.
But it may be questioned whether it was not a healthy development,
which enabled the average man to try again after lapses from
virtue.[95]

The special decline in the civic virtues may be due to other
causes also. The churches during the first three centuries of their
existence had been societies consisting in the main of humble
persons, and had included few who exercised authority. The
moral teaching of the church had therefore naturally been directed
to the life of the ordinary man, and the code of ethics which it
developed was concerned with his problems. Pagan philosophers

down to the end of the fourth century produced countless works on the virtues and duties of kings. Christian writers have nothing to say on this topic, and but little on the duties of the citizen. For the most part they are content to repeat a few texts inculcating obedience to the authorities and payment of one's taxes.

In the second place the church had in its early days lived in expectation of the second coming of Christ, and as this hope faded had fixed its eyes on the life of the world to come. Christians regarded themselves as sojourners on this earth and unconcerned with its problems. Some regarded the imperial government as satanic, the majority accepted it as ordained of God, but all alike viewed it as an external power alien to themselves.

It was difficult for Christians to adjust their ideas when under Constantine the government became Christian, and they did so only very slowly and with imperfect success. One can sense the bewilderment of the bishops assembled at Arles in 314 in the seventh canon which they enacted. 'About governors who being of the faithful advance to a governorship, it was resolved that when they are promoted they shall receive ecclesiastical letters of communion with the reservation that wherever they administer, the bishop of the place shall keep an eye on them, and when they begin to act contrary to the rules of the church, then they shall be excluded from communion.' The bishops evidently felt that the imperial service was almost incompatible with membership of the church, and that if a baptised Christian took a government post he was highly suspect and only retained his membership during good behaviour.[96]

The church had never had to face the moral problems of a Christian placed in a position of secular authority, and on some very elementary points it was still in doubt almost a century after Constantine's conversion. The question was put to Ambrose whether a Christian judge who passed a death sentence should be excommunicated. He replied that he himself did not excommunicate in such a case, but he clearly had qualms. 'You will be excused if you do it, you will be praised if you do not . . . I know that many pagans often boast that they have brought back their axe unstained with blood from a provincial government. If pagans do this, what should Christians do?' The same question was put to Pope Innocent I: 'What about those who after baptism have held administrative posts and have either merely applied torture or have even pronounced a capital sentence?' Innocent replied that there was no ancient rule, but that as 'these powers had been granted by God and the sword had been permitted for the punishment of the guilty', those who wielded it were not blameworthy.[97]

The teachers of the church offered no inspiring advice to a Christian governor. They urged him not to oppress widows and orphans and not to pervert justice, but beyond such somewhat negative counsels they did not go. With regard to soldiers the attitude of Christian teachers was similarly hesitant and negative. Even in the fourth century some Christians held that Christianity was incompatible with military service: Basil held that a soldier who killed a man in the course of duty was guilty of murder and must be excommunicated. This extreme view found little support, but the church offered no positive message to soldiers: it was content with reiterating the advice of John the Baptist that they refrain from extortion and be content with their pay.[98]

The church long maintained the suspicious attitude of the Council of Arles to all forms of government service. An early papal letter declares: 'It is manifest that those who have acquired secular power and administered secular justice cannot be free from sin. For when the sword is unsheathed or an unjust sentence is pronounced or torture is applied for the requirements of the cases, or they devote their care to preparing games, or attend games prepared for them—they are making a large claim, not if they aspire to a bishopric, but if having undergone penance for all this they are allowed, after a certain time has elapsed, to approach the altar.' Pope Siricius and his successors debarred from holy orders all who after baptism had held administrative posts, or served in the army or the civil service, or had even practised as barristers. In the same spirit those who had performed penance and received absolution were forbidden to return to their posts. Government service, if not in itself sinful, was so perilous, so liable to lead to acts of extortion or cruelty, that it unfitted a man for the service of God and should not be risked by those who had no further opportunity of having their sins remitted. Many Christian writers adopt the same attitude. Augustine is somewhat exceptional in asking Caecilianus, who holds some public office, why he is still a catechumen, 'as if the faithful, the more faithful and the better they are, cannot administer the state the more faithfully and the better'. Paulinus of Nola writes in a very different tone, urging his correspondents to resign from their posts or abandon the official careers which they contemplated in order to take up a Christian life. 'Ye cannot serve two masters,' he quotes, 'that is the one God and Mammon, in other words Christ and Caesar.'[99]

In the pagan scheme of morality the service of the state in peace and war was a noble activity, and even philosophers, though they might prefer a life of contemplation, were in duty bound to undertake it. A whole literature was devoted to the virtues required of a ruler, piety, justice, courage, temperance, self-control, and above all love of his fellow men. It is of course true that the majority of pagans in positions of authority did not live up to these ideals, but at any rate men of high character were encouraged to devote themselves to the service of the state. Good Christians on the other hand were made to feel that they were, if not sinners, falling short of the highest ideals, if they entered public service. Many good men preferred to live a life of retirement or take holy orders, and many that did take up an official career must have felt that having thus committed themselves to a sinful life, they might as well be hanged for a sheep as a lamb.

CHAPTER XXIV

EDUCATION AND CULTURE

CULTURALLY the Roman empire fell into two halves, the Latin-speaking West and the Greek-speaking East. The boundary was sharply defined. In Africa it lay in the desert separating the Romanised Punic cities of Tripolitania from the Greek cities of the Pentapolis. In Europe Greece and Macedonia and Epirus were Greek speaking, as were the four provinces of Thrace south of the Haemus range, together with the cluster of old Greek cities on the Black Sea coast as far as the mouth of the Danube. North and west of this line, in the dioceses of Dacia and Pannonia, and in the Danubian provinces of Thrace, Latin prevailed. There seem to have been no surviving enclaves of Greek in the West; Sicily and southern Italy had been Latinised by the end of the third century. Conversely the Roman colonies in the East had long been assimilated by their Greek environment.

The linguistic boundary in Europe, it may be noted, did not coincide with either the political or the ecclesiastical frontiers. The Eastern emperors always had some Latin-speaking subjects in Moesia Inferior and Scythia, and from 395 ruled the Dacian diocese, while in the fourth century some Western emperors ruled the diocese of Macedonia. The patriarch of Constantinople controlled a few Latin-speaking sees on the lower Danube, while the pope established his jurisdiction over the Greek churches of Macedonia, Epirus, Greece and Crete.

The linguistic cleavage grew sharper from the third century onwards. In the Ciceronian and Augustan ages cultivated Romans had been as much at home in Greek as in Latin. With the growth of a Latin literature and the development of an educational system based upon it, Greek inevitably fell into the background, but even in the latter part of the second century Marcus Aurelius wrote his intimate diary in Greek.

By the fourth century things had changed. Greek was still a regular part of the school curriculum, and not only the sons of aristocratic families but boys from humble middle class homes like Augustine learnt from the *grammaticus* to construe Homer and Menander. But Greek was not continued at a higher level under the rhetor, and most boys never got beyond a rather elementary stage. Augustine admits that he hated Greek at school, and he never seems to have mastered the language, preferring to read Greek authors in translations, sometimes painfully verifying a passage with the aid of the dictionary. An aristocrat like Paulinus, Ausonius' grandson, brought up by Greek slaves, was able to read Homer and Plato when he was only five years old, but even aristocrats do not seem to have kept up their Greek in later life. So cultivated a nobleman as Symmachus had to rub up his Greek to help his son with his lessons. 'While my son is being initiated into Greek letters,' he writes to a friend, 'I have joined his studies afresh like a schoolfellow. Parental affection bids us become boys again, so that shared labours may instil the charm of literature into our children.'[1]

In the fifth century boys in aristocratic homes still learnt Greek. In Gaul Sidonius Apollinaris remembered enough to read Menander to his son in the 460s. In Africa Fulgentius, who was born in 467, learnt to pronounce Greek with a perfect accent thanks to his mother's care, knew his Homer by heart, and read most of Menander; but in later life, his biographer admits, he lost the habit of either speaking or reading the language. It may be doubted, however, whether Greek continued to form part of the regular curriculum taught in the schools. Even at the end of the fourth century competent teachers of Greek were evidently hard to find in the Western provinces. Gratian, though he ordained that Greek and Latin grammarians should be appointed in every provincial capital in the Gallic prefecture, at the same time expressed doubts whether a worthy candidate could be found for the post of Greek grammarian even at Trier, then the imperial capital.[2]

There were of course some scholars in the West who made a serious study of Greek, pagans like Agorius Praetextatus, who read the Greek philosophers, and Christians like Jerome and Rufinus, who wished to know the scriptures in the original and to study the works of Eastern theologians. In Italy there were still a few such scholars in the sixth century, Boethius for instance, Cassiodorus and Dionysius Exiguus; but their number was always very limited, and even men of learning relied for the most part on Latin translations of Greek works. These were produced in large numbers throughout the fourth, fifth and sixth centuries to meet the needs of an educated public to whom Greek literature had become a closed book. But the number of translators capable of performing this work was small, and it is significant that two of the more celebrated, John Cassian and Dionysius Exiguus, were immigrants from the bilingual province of Scythia.[3]

The Greeks never ceased to look upon the Romans as barbarians: they regarded their own language and literature as supreme, and despised that of Rome. Latin was no part of the regular educational curriculum in the East, and Latin literature, whether secular or religious, was not read. An anecdote told by Cassian is significant. An Italian who became a monk in Egypt could write Latin book hand, but had no other skill. Wishing to provide him with work, his kindly abbot declared that he had a brother in the civil service well versed in Latin, to whom he wished to send a holy book. This was a pious fraud; the Latin book 'would be of no use or profit, since everybody in these parts is completely ignorant of that language'.[4]

Broadly speaking it is true to say that Greeks learnt Latin only from interested motives. Some few authors of Eastern origin wrote in Latin in order that their works might reach high senatorial society in Rome, with the curious result that the last of the Latin historians was Ammianus of Antioch, and the last of the Latin poets Claudian of Alexandria. But most Greeks learnt Latin from motives of a more crudely materialistic kind. In the fourth century Latin was the official language of the empire even in the Eastern parts, and a knowledge of the language was, if not essential, a useful asset to a man who aspired to rise in the administration, the army, or the law.

It is not easy to determine how far Latin was effectively used in the administration of the Eastern empire. The Roman government had from the beginning communicated with its Greek subjects in Greek. Laws and edicts were promulgated in an official Greek translation; letters and rescripts to Eastern provinces, cities and individuals were drafted in Greek; proceedings in the courts were conducted in Greek. In effect therefore Latin was used for very limited purposes only. Imperial constitutions were drafted in Latin, as well as in Greek, by the quaestor and his clerks: this was still so in Justinian's day, though by that time the master text was in Greek, and the Latin a translation, often inaccurate. Latin was also used down to the fifth century for internal records and inter-departmental correspondence in the higher levels of the administration. The papyri show that even in the fourth century Greek was almost exclusively used in the provincial offices and in that of the Augustal prefect, Latin being preserved only in the record of judicial proceedings. Even there it is used only in the formal

heading giving the date and place of the trial and the names of
the judge and of the parties and their counsel, and for indicating
the speakers in the course of the proceedings—'Flavius Hesychius
v.p. praeses dixit'. In the praetorian prefecture of the East, however, it was only Cyrus, prefect in 439-41, who abolished the use of
Latin, and John Lydus, who strongly deplored the change, has
preserved a number of the old Latin formulae which had been in
use until that date.[5]

In the army Latin was more persistent. Under Constantius II
the official letter from Flavius Valacius, *dux* of Egypt, to Flavius
Abinnaeus, *praepositus* of Dionysias, is in Latin, and Flavius
Abinnaeus drafted his petition to the emperor, protesting against
his dismissal, in that language. Under Anastasius a formal letter
from the *comes* of the Thebaid to the tribune of Hermopolis is in
Latin. Even in the early sixth century then, it would appear,
clerks in the military offices had to have enough Latin to understand and draft formal administrative communications.[6]

In the law Latin was still important in the fourth century. Not
that it played any significant part either in court proceedings or
in the drafting of legal documents. By an old rule the formal
written judgment had to be in Latin, until in 397 the use of Greek
was permitted even for this purpose. By another old rule the wills
of Roman citizens had to be drawn in Latin. It is not known when
this rule was relaxed, but it was certainly before 439. But even
while these rules remained in force it only meant that the notaries
and clerks of the court had to know how to write out certain
more or less stereotyped formulae. Even barristers, if they were
prepared, as many were, to take their law from a jurisconsult,
needed no Latin; they spoke in court in Greek, and imperial
constitutions were cited in their Greek versions.[7]

Nevertheless for a real legal training, such as was increasingly
demanded of barristers, Latin was necessary. The sources of the
law, the works of the old jurisconsults and the standard collections
of imperial constitutions, were all in Latin, and the teaching of
law at Berytus and Constantinople seems to have been conducted
in Latin until the end of the fourth century at any rate: Libanius
links Latin and law as the twin enemies of Greek higher education.
It is not certain when Latin was replaced by Greek as the language
of instruction at Berytus, but two early fifth century professors,
Cyril and Patricius, wrote text books and commentaries in Greek.
For a really scholarly knowledge of law Latin of course remained
necessary until Justinian's day, since the bulk of the legal literature
remained untranslated. But when the Institutes, the Digest and
the Code, with subsequent Novels, became the sole sources of law,

they were forthwith translated into Greek, and Latin ceased to be essential even for the academic lawyer.[8]

In the fourth century then a rather rudimentary knowledge of Latin was required of notaries and of civil servants in the judicial branches of the provincial *officia*, in the military *officia*, and in the praetorian prefectures and the palatine ministries. A competent grasp of the language was needed by jurisconsults and by barristers who were not content to be mere orators. A full rhetorical training in Latin was essential only for the clerks of the *sacra scrinia* who drafted imperial pronouncements. But at this period Latin might still be socially useful to aspirants to high office. Some of the emperors who ruled at Constantinople came from the West and were more at home in Latin than in Greek: Constantine, though he could speak Greek fluently enough, preferred to read the dissertations on the faith, which Eusebius of Caesarea sent to him, in a Latin translation. These emperors often promoted to high offices of state Westerners, whose native language was Latin. Rufinus, the Aquitanian barrister appointed praetorian prefect of the East by Theodosius I, apparently knew little or no Greek—at any rate he told Libanius that he had to have his letters translated to him. A Latin-speaking Greek might then stand a better chance of gaining the ear of the emperor or his influential friends.[9]

In the fifth century the usefulness of Latin declined. It ceased to be necessary for barristers, notaries or civil servants, except in the military offices and the *sacra scrinia*. With the final division of the empire the court became exclusively Greek in language and culture. Latin became a learned language needed only by academic lawyers and legal draftsmen.

Elementary Latin must have been widely taught in the East in the fourth century: among the papyri of Egypt are many Greco-Latin *abecedaria* and vocabularies, and texts of Virgil's *Aeneid* and Cicero's *Catilinarians* with word for word Greek translations in parallel columns. Higher teaching must have been harder to come by; wealthy Antiochene parents, according to Libanius, sent off their sons to Berytus or even to Italy to learn Latin and law.[10]

It seems probable, however, that a full Latin education in both grammar and rhetoric was always available at the imperial capital. Lactantius was professor of Latin at Nicomedia under Diocletian, and in the state university of Constantinople, inaugurated in 425, ten chairs were established of Latin grammar—as many as of Greek—and three chairs of Latin rhetoric—as against five of Greek. The large number of Latin professorships was no doubt inspired less by practical needs than by motives of prestige—Latin was the language of the Romans, and Constantinople the second Rome. These chairs were sometimes occupied by distinguished Latinists from the West: the great grammarian, Priscian, from the Mauretanian Caesarea, taught at Constantinople in the early sixth century. But the local candidates for the professorships were not always of such high calibre. John Lydus, to judge by his surviving works, was no profound Latinist—he had learnt Latin with a view to becoming a *memorialis*—but Justinian deemed him worthy of one of the grammarians' chairs.[11]

The linguistic cleavage between East and West accentuated and prolonged doctrinal controversies. Latin and Greek theologians spoke different languages both in the literal and in the figurative sense of the words. Unable to read one another's works, they thought along different lines, and developed different technical vocabularies. Even in the early fourth century Constantine found it difficult to find anyone to explain to him the complexities of the Eastern heresies. Strategius, an Antiochene, who, owing to his mastery of both Greek and Latin, was able to perform this function, made his fortune by it, rising to be a *comes* and ultimately praetorian prefect of the East. In the last stages of the Arian controversy agreement between Basil and his school and Damasus and Ambrose was long postponed because Latin-speaking theologians could not understand the difference between οὐσία and ὑπόστασις, both rendered *substantia* in the dictionaries. When Pope Leo's delegates at Ephesus could contribute nothing to the discussion, except an occasional '*contradicitur*', and had to fall back on an interpreter to make any longer statement, real understanding between the Eastern and Western churches was difficult.[12]

Within their respective zones Latin and Greek were the sole languages of administration and law, and with a very few minor exceptions, of literature, secular and Christian, and of polite intercourse: they were, indeed, almost the only written languages. East of the Euphrates, in Osrhoene and Mesopotamia, Syriac had survived, not only as a spoken, but as a written language, and it was adopted by the local churches as the language of the liturgy. Not only were the scriptures and many Greek theological works translated into Syriac, but a considerable mass of original literature, mostly chronicles and hymns, was produced from the fourth century onwards. Syriac enjoyed in this area the status of a literary language. It was taught in the schools of grammar and rhetoric, as were Latin and Greek, and it was possible in Osrhoene and

Mesopotamia for an educated man to know no Greek: even bishops from that area sometimes subscribe to councils in Syriac.[13]

In Egypt the indigenous language did not maintain a continuous literary tradition, and failed to achieve the same status as did Syriac. Under the Principate the demotic script was less and less used, and seems to have died out before the end of the third century: Egyptian thus became a mere peasant *patois*. During the third century the Greek alphabet, with the addition of a few demotic characters, was adapted for writing Coptic. But even when it thus again became literate, it remained the language of the lower classes only. No educated Egyptian deigned to write in Coptic, and Coptic literature, apart from translations, was confined to popular lives of the saints.[14]

In the Latin zone no indigenous language even achieved literacy, and the only rival to Latin was Gothic. When the Goths were converted to Christianity in the latter part of the fourth century, the scriptures were translated into their language, a special alphabet, mostly derived from Greek, being devised to write it. The language and alphabet continued to be used by the Gothic church, but it would seem as if only the clergy learned to write their native tongue. The Gothic kings invariably used Latin for administrative and legal purposes. Even the clergy appear often to have preferred Latin. In a deed dated 551, whereby the Gothic church of Ravenna surrendered some property to a creditor, all the clergy, who numbered eighteen, appended their subscriptions. Of the ten who were literate, six subscribed in Latin and only four in Gothic.[15]

Though the documents make it clear that Greek and Latin were, with these minor exceptions, the only written languages, it is much more difficult to estimate how far they were the normal speech of the mass of the people. There were of course areas where they were indigenous or had long superseded the native tongues. Latin was the only language of Italy, and probably had ousted Celtic, Ligurian and Iberian in southern Gaul and in eastern and southern Spain.

The survival of Welsh and Cornish implies that Celtic was still the dominant language in Britain when it was lost to the empire in the fifth century. There is evidence for the survival of Celtic in Gaul at the same period. Sulpicius Severus in the Dialogus represents Gallus, a disciple of Martin of Tours, as apologising to the Aquitanian Postumianus for the rusticity of his Latin, and Postumianus replies: 'Talk in Celtic or in Gallic, if you prefer, so long as you talk about Martin.' The jesting allusion implies that Celtic was a living language in central Gaul when Sulpicius wrote. Nor is there any reason to doubt that when Jerome stated that the dialect of the Galatians of Asia Minor closely resembled that spoken around Trier he was speaking from personal knowledge.[16]

The survival of Basque demonstrates that Iberian still flourished in the mountains of northern Spain throughout the period of Roman rule, and Severus of Minorca, writing in 418, speaks of 'a very fine hail which the inhabitants of that island call "albigistinum" in their native language'.[17]

For Africa the evidence is fuller and more explicit. Augustine frequently alludes to Punic as the language of the people. On several occasions he used a Punic interpreter to conduct arguments with Donatists, especially circumcellions, and when he established an episcopal see at Fussala, a country town in his own diocese, he looked out for a Punic speaker to fill it. From words which Augustine quotes it is clear that the language which he calls Punic was Phoenician, which had survived in the coastal areas from the days of the Carthaginian domination of Africa. The survival of Berber in modern Algeria shows that inland the old indigenous language continued to be spoken.[18]

For Illyricum there is no contemporary evidence, and we have to rely entirely on the evidence of survival. On the one hand the wide currency of Vlach, especially in the northern Balkans, suggests that Latin must have been the dominant language of the Danubian provinces. On the other hand Albanian represents the indigenous Illyrian tongue, which must have prevailed in the mountains of Dalmatia.

In the Eastern half of the empire Greek was spoken not only in Greece proper, Macedonia, Epirus and the islands of the Aegaean, but in the western districts of Asia Minor, where Lydian and Carian had long been extinct, and along most of its southern coast, in Lycia, Pamphylia and Cilicia, and in Cyprus. In Thrace, however, the native language survived. John Chrysostom states that the scriptures were translated into Thracian and Gregory of Nyssa speaks of Thracian as a living tongue: even in the sixth century the services in the monastery of the Bessi in Palestine were conducted in their native language.[19]

In the interior of Asia Minor also native languages persisted. Jerome states that the Galatians still spoke Celtic in his day, and in the middle of the sixth century Cyril of Scythopolis tells of a Galatian monk in Palestine who was struck dumb, and who, on recovering his speech, could at first talk only in Galatian. Basil of Caesarea in one of his sermons alludes to Cappadocian as a language familiar to all his hearers. In the latter part of the sixth century we are told of a Lycaonian, who knew no Greek; when he was miraculously cured at the shrine of S. Martha at Antioch, he glorified God in his own language, while his companion, who did know Greek, interpreted his story to the wondering crowd. At the same period an Isaurian who had returned from Antioch to his native town was cured of paralysis, and all the people, seeing the miracle, cried aloud in their own tongue. For northern and north-eastern Asia Minor evidence is lacking, but it seems likely that in these remote and backward areas the native languages survived.[20]

For Syria and Palestine the evidence is much more abundant, and it is clear that Syriac was the normal language of the peasantry and of the lower classes in the towns. John Chrysostom in one of his sermons speaks of the country folk who came into Antioch on the Sunday before Palm Sunday as 'a people divided from us in language, but agreeing with us in faith'. Publius, a decurion of Zeugma, who founded a monastery in the desert, at first had Greek speaking disciples only. Later Syriac-speaking peasants wished to join the community, and Publius, remembering the text 'Go teach all nations', felt obliged to admit them. But the Greek and Syriac-speaking monks lived separately, meeting only for divine worship, which they each celebrated in their own tongues. Many of the famous hermits of the Syrian desert knew no Greek: Macedonius, known to the people as Gubba, when he went into Antioch to intercede for the city after the Riot of the Statues, spoke to the imperial commissioners through an interpreter. Theodoret, on meeting the hermit Thalalaeus, was at first surprised to find that he spoke Greek; it later transpired that he was a Cilician by origin. In Palestine one of the martyrs in the Diocletianic persecution was Procopius, a reader of the church of Scythopolis, whose function it was to translate the service into Syriac for the benefit of the humbler members of the congregation. The hermit Hilarion, when he visited Elusa, was greeted by the townsfolk in Syriac. When Porphyry, bishop of Gaza, was perplexed as to how to demolish the solidly built temple of Marnas, a small boy was inspired to instruct him in Greek; miraculously, as it appeared, for it was found that neither the boy nor his mother could speak the language.[21]

From Egypt the evidence is fullest and most instructive. The papyri would at first sight suggest that Greek was the normal language used by all classes in town and country alike. Not only are all administrative documents, even those addressed to or proceeding from village headmen and tax receipts issued to peasants, written in Greek, but so are all leases, contracts and other business documents, down to the loan of a *solidus* or two and yearly tenancies of two or three *arurae*. The vast majority of private letters, even from the humblest folk, are written in Greek.

A closer study of the papyri shows that the first impression is misleading. The legal documents were written by professional notaries, who often also wrote the subscriptions and affidavits of the parties, who are declared to be illiterate, or to 'write slowly'—they could presumably just spell out their names in Greek. Many administrative documents were also written by professional scribes, and a study of the hands in which private letters are written, and a comparison of the texts of the letters with their signatures, shows that a very large number of them also are the productions of professional letter writers.[22]

The papyri thus prove that a high proportion of the humbler ranks of society, both rural and urban, were illiterate in Greek. Other evidence suggests that they could not speak the language either. In a trial held in 340 the headman of the village of Caranis addresses the court through an interpreter. When at the end of the fourth century a party of Greek visitors was touring the Egyptian monasteries, one of their hosts, the abbot Apollonius, picked out three of his monks who knew both Greek and Egyptian to escort them to their next objective, 'so that they might both interpret for us, and also edify us by their conversation'. In the sixth century the government yielded so far as to post some public notices in Coptic as well as in Greek.[23]

It may be conjectured that similar conditions prevailed in many parts of the empire. There seems to have been a sharp cultural cleavage between the upper classes, who had not only received a literary education in Latin and Greek, but probably spoke one or other of these languages, and the mass of the people, who were not only illiterate, but spoke in a different tongue. From the evidence cited above it is clear that many of the common people, not only peasants but townspeople, had no knowledge of Greek or Latin. On the other hand many of the upper classes evidently could not speak the language of the people. Augustine knew a few words of Punic, but could not conduct an argument in it, and seems to have found some difficulty in finding among his clergy men who knew Punic. In one of his sermons he translates a Punic proverb into Latin, 'since not all of you know Punic'. In the Egyptian courts the judges and advocates, though local men, could not understand evidence given in Egyptian. There must, it is clear, have been a fairly large number of people who were bilingual, notaries and scribes, professional interpreters for the courts, bailiffs and agents who acted as intermediaries between landlords and their tenants and labourers. Many of the rural clergy must also have been bilingual; in Egypt they often acted as scribes for their humble parishioners.[24]

The extent of Hellenisation and Latinisation in the various parts of the empire is very difficult to gauge, and naturally varied very greatly from district to district, and from town to town. In general it was the rural areas, the villages and the remote country towns which were least Latinised or Hellenised. In the larger cities it is likely that many or most of even the lower classes spoke Latin or Greek: Augustine would not have written his Psalm against the Donatists in simple colloquial Latin unless 'the very humblest masses and the altogether uneducated simple folk' in Hippo and the larger cities of Africa had been Latin speaking.[25]

On the whole it would seem, however, that in large parts of the empire it was only a thin upper crust which was Latinised or Hellenised. The evidence of survival is here particularly suggestive. In Syria and Egypt Greek does not seem to have outlived the end of Roman rule by more than about a century. It was maintained by the Arabs as their administrative language until the middle of the eighth century, but when the caliphs ordered the use of Arabic in the government offices it quickly died out. Syriac and Coptic, on the other hand, were adopted by the local monophysite churches as their liturgical and literary languages, and continued to flourish down to the late middle ages. In central and eastern Asia Minor the native languages were ultimately ousted by Greek, but after several more centuries under a Greek-speaking government and church: in the sixth century, as the evidence cited above shows, the native languages were still alive, and may well have been dominant.

In the Western parts of the empire also it is on the whole in areas which continued after the fall of the empire to be ruled by Latin-speaking governments that the Romance languages have prevailed. In Africa Latin disappeared, but Berber has survived to the present day. In Britain, where the Celtic population set up its own government after the collapse of Roman rule, Celtic and not Latin survived, and in similar circumstances in north-eastern Spain Basque has prevailed, as has Albanian in Dalmatia. The final victory of Latin over Celtic and Iberian in Gaul and Spain may well have been achieved under the Merovingian and Visigothic kings.

When therefore we speak of the culture of the empire, we must remember that it was the culture of a very small minority. In many areas the bulk of the population could not understand either of the languages which were the vehicles of culture, and throughout the empire the peasants and the labourers, the craftsmen and the shopkeepers who formed the majority of the urban population were for the most part illiterate.

Education fell into three stages, the primary school which taught the three Rs, the grammar school, and the school of rhetoric. The primary schoolmaster was a very humble personage. In the Diocletianic tariff his scale of pay is fixed at 50 denarii a month per pupil, as against the 200 and 250 allocated to the grammarian and the rhetorician respectively, and he was denied the immunities and privileges which they received. Seeing that in the tariff craftsmen are given daily wages of 50 or 60 denarii, plus their keep, it is clear that a primary schoolmaster would have had to have a large class in order to live on the same scale as a mason or a carpenter.[26]

Primary schools must have existed not only in cities but also in some villages, to produce the rural notaries and letter writers, clergy, agents and clerks, but we hear little of them. Theodoret talks of a catholic priest named Protogenes, who was exiled by Valens to Antinoopolis, and found to his distress that most of the population were pagans. He opened a school, which seems to have been primary, since the syllabus included shorthand, and by using biblical texts as exercises he instructed his pupils in the Christian faith. John of Ephesus tells of two holy men, Simeon and Sergius, who settled in a village near Amida, and earned their living by keeping a school in which they taught thirty or forty infants and boys. Such schools taught reading and writing and arithmetic: Augustine in his Confessions recalls his boredom as a small boy, chanting the dreary tables—'unum et unum, duo: duo et duo, quattuor'. Instruction was in Latin or Greek only, except in Egypt and Mesopotamia (and probably Syria), where Coptic and Syriac were also taught.[27]

These schools were attended by the children of middle class parents and by some poor boys; among the aristocracy the first stage of education seems generally to have been given by a private tutor, usually a slave. Higher education was for all practical purposes reserved to members of the upper and middle classes, roughly from decurions upwards. Not only could few poor parents afford to keep their children idle when they might have been earning, but the fees were four or five times as high as at an elementary school. Moreover grammatical and rhetorical schools were not to be found in every city—Augustine received his elementary education at his home town of Tagaste, but his father had to send him to Madaurus for his grammar and rhetoric. A boy might therefore have had to be boarded at some distance from home for several years, and a slave had to be provided to serve as his *paedagogus*. In these circumstances it is not surprising that only an exceptionally brilliant and ambitious poor boy could achieve a higher education, as did Aetius, who paid for his education by acting as his professor's personal servant.[28]

Unlike elementary education, which received no encouragement from the state, and was left entirely to private enterprise, higher education was favoured and subsidised. The state maintained a number of chairs at Rome and Constantinople, whose occupants were paid salaries from public funds, and most important cities had municipal chairs maintained from the civic revenues. Grammarians and rhetors who held these official posts enjoyed many privileges, originally granted under the Principate and carefully maintained by later emperors, including exemption from military service, billeting and all *sordida munera*, and, most important of all, immunity from curial obligations.[29]

It is difficult to say how many cities maintained official professors, for we naturally hear most of municipal chairs at the greatest cities, such as Milan and Carthage in the West, and Athens, Nicomedia or Antioch in the East. A law of Gratian orders that chairs of rhetoric and of Greek and Latin grammar should be established from state funds in the most populous cities, by which are apparently meant the provincial *metropoleis*, throughout the Gallic prefecture; which would seem to imply that in some provinces even the capital cities had hitherto lacked endowed chairs. On the other hand in the East, apart from the exceptional case of Athens, we know of municipal chairs at Nicaea and at Gaza, which were not capitals of provinces.[30]

There were no universities in the mediaeval or modern sense of the word, corporate institutions which provided regular courses of instruction, held examinations and granted degrees. There were however a number of what may be loosely called university towns, which had an established reputation as centres of higher education, where the celebrated teachers tended to congregate, and whither students flocked from all quarters of the empire. Besides the two capitals there were, for instance, in the West Carthage and Bordeaux, in the East Alexandria and above all Athens. But higher teaching was by no means confined to such centres, and a celebrated teacher like Libanius might make Antioch a serious rival to them as long as he lived; he drew pupils not only from Syria and Palestine but from many provinces of Asia Minor.[31]

The length of the course was fluid. Three years seems to have been normal for the rhetorical stage, but a serious student with ambitions to become a professor himself might go on studying for far longer. There were no formal examinations or degrees. Students demonstrated their talents by the public declamations which they delivered as part of their training, and the nearest thing to a degree was a letter of recommendation from the professor under whom one had studied.[32]

Some university towns had their specialities over and above the normal course of grammar and rhetoric. Alexandria was celebrated for mathematics, astronomy and medicine; Athens, with its ancient endowed chairs of the various schools, was the acknowledged centre of philosophical studies, though philosophy was also taught at Rome and Constantinople. The two capitals also provided instruction in law, but the great centre of legal studies was Berytus. In this field teaching was more systematically organised. There was a regular four year course, with a set syllabus for each year, and students who had completed it to their professor's satisfaction obtained a formal certificate, which in the late fifth century became an official qualification for being called to the bar. In these specialised fields, as in the normal literary course, the more celebrated centres of study enjoyed no monopoly until Justinian prohibited the teaching of law except at Rome, Constantinople and Berytus.[33]

At Constantinople Theodosius II in 425, when he greatly increased the number of official salaried professors, gave to them the monopoly of higher education in the capital. This was a unique privilege. In all the other cities of the empire, including Rome, and in Constantinople at an earlier date, it was free to anyone to open a grammatical or rhetorical school, and many grammarians and rhetors ran successful schools, either in rivalry with the official professors in the greater cities, or in cities which lacked official chairs.[34]

Such private schools seem to have existed in quite small places. Libanius wrote to Paeoninus, who taught rhetoric at Tavium, a minor city of Galatia, recommending to him a pupil of his own who proposed to open a school, probably of grammar, in the same town. Ausonius tells of a barrister of Burdigala named Dynamius, who having been involved in a scandal in his native city, migrated to the little Spanish city of Ilerda, where he became a successful teacher of rhetoric under the assumed name of Flavinius. Augustine started his teaching career by opening a private school in his home town of Tagaste, and having built up a reputation, moved first to Carthage and then to Rome. It was not until he was thirty that the city council of Milan, on the advice of Symmachus, prefect of the city of Rome, appointed him to their official chair. Libanius was encouraged to open a school at Constantinople by a friend, who promised him an audience of forty young men from the best families: his friend let him down, but he opened his school none the less, and soon, as he proudly boasts, had over eighty pupils. Feeling, as may be imagined, often ran high between the established professors and young freelance teachers who threatened to out-shine them and steal their pupils. Libanius' success brought him the bitter enmity of the two official rhetors of Constantinople, who with the aid of Limenius, a newly appointed governor, made the city too hot to hold him.[35]

The Roman and Constantinopolitan chairs were filled by the senates of the two capitals, the civic chairs by the councils of the cities. Julian, who was not only keenly interested in higher educa-tion, but anxious to secure that men with the right religious views should be chosen, ordered that all appointments should be sub-mitted to him for his personal approval, but this rule seems to have fallen into desuetude after his death. The Eastern emperors, however, often intervened in the appointment of professors in Constantinople. There was naturally keen competition among grammarians and rhetors for the salaried posts, and equally keen competition among the cities to secure outstanding men for their chairs.[36]

The subsequent career of Libanius well illustrates both the bitter rivalries between the professors and the intrigues in which they indulged, and also the strong interest which the councils took in the appointments. By the time he was hounded out of Constantinople Libanius had established his reputation as a teacher, and he had no difficulty in securing a post. He would have gone to Nicomedia, but that his enemy, Limenius, used his official powers to prohibit him. He was, however, allowed to accept an official invitation from Nicaea. Soon afterwards he received a second official invitation from Nicomedia, and this time no obstacles were put in his way. Nicomedia already had one official rhetor, but he had been so rude to the council that they decided to bring in Libanius to undermine him.

Libanius soon drew all his pupils away from him, and he retaliated by bringing a charge of murder against Libanius. He even went to Cappadocia and persuaded Philagrius, the vicar of Pontica, who happened to have been an old fellow student of his at Athens, to summon Libanius to Nicaea for trial. Luckily Philip, the praetorian prefect, now appeared on the scene, and Philagrius was afraid to proceed with the plot under his superior's eye. Instead a public competition was arranged between Libanius and his rival,

in which the former achieved such a resounding victory that
Philip arranged for an imperial decree to be issued summoning
him to the capital. Libanius was now appointed to one of the
official chairs at Constantinople by decree of the senate, confirmed
by the emperor.

Some years later Libanius received what he considered to be
the supreme honour of his academic career. The council of
Athens invited him to fill one of their chairs, which had always
hitherto been reserved for men already teaching in the city.
But Libanius hankered after his native Antioch, where he ultimately
obtained the official chair and spent the rest of his life.[37]

Grammarians and rhetors were naturally drawn mostly from the
upper ranks of society, for if an ordinary rhetorical education
was expensive, the course of training required to make a success
as a teacher was very much more costly. It was normally very
prolonged. Libanius was already twenty-two, having studied
rhetoric for seven years, when he went as a student to Athens, and
he spent another three years there before he ventured to open a
school himself. Moreover it was almost essential to complete
one's education at one of the great university towns, or at any
rate under some celebrated professor whose fees would be high.
Augustine's father, Patricius, a modest decurion of a little African
town, found considerable financial difficulty in sending his son to
complete his rhetorical studies at Carthage, and was only enabled
to do so by the aid of a wealthy fellow townsman, who recognised
Augustine's promise.[38]

Though the cost of training was high the rewards seem to have
been adequate. A beginner might have a hard time building up
his class; even Libanius, despite the successes he had achieved
at Constantinople and Nicomedia, started at Antioch with only
fifteen pupils. If he were less adventurous, and took a post as
assistant to an established teacher, he might earn a meagre living;
Libanius draws a pitiful picture of his four assistants, who had
to share one professorial salary between them and could not
afford to marry or to keep more than a couple of slaves apiece.
But once he achieved an established chair a grammarian was at
least assured of modest comfort. The scale of salaries laid down
by Gratian in Gaul was 24 *annonae* (equivalent to about 100 solidi)
for a rhetor, and 12 for a grammarian, with higher rates—30 and
20 *annonae* respectively for rhetor and grammarian—at the imperial
capital of Trier. These salaries, no doubt suggested by Ausonius,
a professor himself, were perhaps exceptionally high. At Carthage
Justinian allocated 70 solidi to rhetors and grammarians alike.[39]

The official salary was, however, the smaller part of a successful professor's income, which came mainly from fees paid by his pupils or their parents. Libanius was surprised and annoyed with Gerontius of Apamea, who insisted on an official salary: 'When a man has a class of rich pupils, why should he look elsewhere?' We have no figures for fees, which no doubt varied according to the celebrity of the teacher, but they seem to have been considerable. Libanius, whilst teaching at Nicomedia, was robbed by one of his slaves of 1,500 solidi: he must have put by this sum in less than eight years.[40]

A teacher's income from fees was, of course, somewhat precarious. There was keen competition for pupils, which at Athens took the form of organised kidnapping. Each professor's band of pupils lay in wait for new arrivals at the Piraeus and Sunium, and forcibly abducted them and enrolled them in his class without regard for their preferences. Brawls between rival gangs often required the intervention of the proconsul from Corinth. Elsewhere we do not hear of open violence being used, but rivalry was as keen, and a brilliant newcomer might lure away an established teacher's pupils, as did Libanius at Constantinople, at Nicomedia and at Antioch. Even when a teacher had attracted a class, he was not sure of his fees. As the academic year drew to a close, and fees were due to be paid, classes would melt away. Such dishonesty according to Augustine was rife at Rome, and Libanius complains of it at Antioch, and advises his fellow teachers to insist on formal contracts with their pupils or their parents.[41]

Eloquence and literary culture were immensely respected in the Roman world, and professors enjoyed a social standing higher than that which their birth or wealth would normally have won them. Symmachus considered it natural that an Athenian philosopher who had opened a school in Rome should be elected to the senate. At Constantinople the professors after twenty years' service received a *comitiva primi ordinis* with rank of ex-vicars. Distinguished teachers were accorded yet more elevated official rank; Libanius was offered codicils of a quaestor by Julian and of a praetorian prefect by Theodosius I.[42]

Despite the difference in language the aims and technique of higher education were identical in East and West. The theoretical aim was a general education (ἐγκύκλιος παιδεία), comprising grammar, rhetoric, dialectic, arithmetic, geometry, music and astronomy, and culminating in philosophy. In actual practice only the first two of these subjects were seriously studied, and education was almost entirely linguistic and literary. It was based on a rather limited range of classical authors. In Latin Virgil and Terence, Sallust and Cicero were the standard four. In Greek the range was somewhat wider, including Homer, selected plays of the Attic tragedians and comedians, Thucydides, and Demosthenes and selected orations of the other Attic orators. But it may be suspected that this rather limited curriculum was often curtailed. At Gerasa under Anastasius and Justinian poetasters could be found to write dedicatory inscriptions for churches in quite tolerable Homeric hexameters, but their efforts at iambic trimeters do not even scan.[43]

The aim of the system was first to teach correct classical (in Greek, Attic) diction, secondly to instil appreciation of the form and content of classical literature, and thirdly, and most important by far, to inculcate the rules of rhetoric, and thus to train its subjects to compose and deliver elegant and flowery orations. The first task became increasingly arduous as the spoken languages diverged progressively in pronunciation, grammar, syntax, and vocabulary from their classical prototypes. It was achieved by learning by rote declensions, paradigms and grammatical rules (and the exceptions to them), by exercises involving the application of these rules, and by a minute grammatical analysis of the classical texts read in class. Literary appreciation was instilled by memorising the recognised poetical and rhetorical tropes, and once again by a minute stylistic analysis of the texts. Appreciation of the content of the classics in practice meant the explanation of the mythological, historical and geographical allusions in the texts read. The grammatical stage of a liberal education was thus an exacting grind of memorising rules and writing exercises, and then of going through classical authors line by line, and word by word, while the teacher expounded and commented on them. Many boys evidently found the process extremely tedious, and their attention was maintained by the use of the cane.

The rhetorical stage was more interesting, for there were not only rules to learn and texts to analyse, but compositions to be written and recited. Not that the theses set for such competitions were of any great interest. No real topic of contemporary life was ever admitted. The themes of political speeches were based on mythology or ancient history, those of forensic speeches not on real legal issues, but on imaginary and usually fantastic problems. Typical political theses, culled from Libanius' Declamations, are an ambassadorial speech of Menelaus to the Trojans, reclaiming Helen, or, slightly more up to date, 'After Chaeronea Philip sends promising to give back 2,000 prisoners if Demosthenes is handed over to him: Demosthenes asks to be surrendered.' A typical forensic speech from the same collection is: 'There was a law that with a tyrant his sons should be killed, and another law that a tyrannicide could claim any boon he wishes. A woman kills her husband who is a tyrant and asks for her sons as her boon.'[44]

This system of education had its obvious defects. It included neither mathematics nor science, and only very scrappy fragments of geography, history or philosophy. What little geography the average man learnt was derived from commentaries on the place names occurring in the ancient authors, and bore very little relation to the world in which he lived. His history was likewise derived from literary allusions, or from collections of anecdotes suitable for adorning speeches. Of philosophy he learned little but the names of the great philosophers, and brief summaries of their lives and doctrines. The learning that he acquired was a jumble of miscellaneous lore, mainly mythological and antiquarian, but containing odd pieces of history, geography, philosophy and natural—or more often unnatural—history. A learned man was one who, like Macrobius or Cassiodorus, had accumulated a large stock of such curious information.

On the other hand the standard education enabled men to read their classics with enjoyment and appreciation, and to express themselves fluently, if not always clearly; for the straining after effect which a rhetorical training encouraged tended to produce a style that was turgid and bombastic or cryptically epigrammatic. Any educated man could readily turn off tolerable verses for an epitaph or an epithalamium, and could write an elegantly phrased letter, spiced with a few literary or mythological allusions. The more talented might aspire to the more serious task of a panegyric in prose or verse.

The upper classes of the empire were in this sense highly cultured, and many of them spent much of their ample leisure in reading the classics or one another's compositions, and in themselves composing prose or verse. The art of letter-writing in particular was highly developed. To judge by the surviving collections most educated men must have devoted much of their time to writing letters to a very large circle of correspondents, not with any practical end in view, but as a social convention. A large proportion of the letters preserved contain no information and solicit none, but are merely elegant compositions, which, if they came from a celebrated figure like Symmachus or Libanius, were treasured by their recipients as masterpieces and shown round to a circle of admiring friends.

It might have been expected that the church would have rejected an educational system which was based on the pagan classics and permeated with pagan mythology. There was a fundamentalist current in Christian thought which regarded the study of the classics as sinful. Even highly cultured Christians sometimes had qualms. Augustine as a bishop roundly condemned the literature which he had taught as a professor, and Jerome has revealed his scruples in his account of his famous dream; standing before the Heavenly Judge, 'asked my condition, I replied that I was a Christian: "You lie," said he who sat in judgment, "you are a Ciceronian, not a Christian. Where your treasure is, there is your heart also." '[45]

This rigorist current of thought finds expression in the Canons of the Apostles, which though not official was widely accepted as authoritative in the Eastern churches in the fourth, fifth and sixth centuries. It expressly commands all the faithful to abstain from all pagan books, and declares that the scriptures contain all that is necessary not only for salvation but for culture. 'Do you want history? There is the Book of Kings. Eloquence and poetry? The Prophets. Lyric? The Psalms. Cosmology? Genesis. Law and ethics? The glorious law of God.' Such sentiments were from time to time expounded in the West also down to the end of the sixth century. Gregory the Great was deeply shocked to hear that a Gallic bishop, Desiderius, actually taught grammar, and wrote to reprove him, 'because one mouth cannot contain the praises of Christ together with the praises of Jupiter'. Desiderius' sin was particularly flagrant because he was a bishop, but Gregory felt that even laymen should refrain from the classics: 'and consider for yourself how grave a sin it is for a bishop to recite what is unseemly even for a religious layman'.[46]

The average educated Christian had no such scruples, and even the strictest fundamentalists had to admit that though it was a sin for an adult to read the classics for pleasure, boys had to learn them at school. As Jerome points out, priests who 'abandon the gospels and prophets, and read comedies, sing the amatory words of bucolic verses, and cling to Virgil, make what is for boys a necessity a deliberate sin for themselves.'[47]

Tertullian, who had held the same view, had declared that though Christian boys could not avoid learning the classics at school, it was sinful for a Christian to teach the pagan authors. In this view he was exceptional. From the third century onward we know of many pious Christians who were distinguished teachers, and when

Julian, on the somewhat specious ground that Christians could not honestly expound the pagan poets and philosophers, debarred them from the teaching profession, his action aroused a greater storm of protest than any of his other anti-Christian measures.[48]

Julian ordered Christian professors 'to go to the Christian churches and expound Matthew and Luke'. The reaction of two of them, Apollinaris, a grammarian of Laodicea in Syria, and his son of the same name, who was a rhetor in the same city, is interesting and instructive. Between them they rewrote the scriptures in classical forms. To replace Homer, the father composed an epic poem in twenty-four books covering the historical books of the Old Testament from the creation to the reign of Saul, and converted other books into Euripidean tragedies, Menandrian comedies and Pindaric odes. The son rewrote the New Testament in the form of Platonic dialogues. But their labour, Socrates tells us, was wasted, for as soon as Julian died, Christian teachers returned to the pagan classics.[49]

This story well illustrates the immensely strong hold which classical literary culture had on the educated classes of the empire. To mix in polite society, and to make his way in the world, whatever profession he adopted, a man had to know his pagan authors, and to Christian parents of the upper classes it was unthinkable to deprive their sons of the standard course of education, whatever its spiritual dangers. It was not only correct diction and style that were essential; the works of the Apollinares were, so Socrates assures us, models of style, and provided examples of all the modes of composition taught in the schools; it was the genuine classics, with all the pagan gods and myths, which were necessary to make a cultivated man.

The educational system was undoubtedly an obstacle to the spread of Christianity among the upper classes. Men who had been through the grammatical and rhetorical mill found the Greek and Latin translations of the scriptures intolerable: as Jerome confesses, after a diet of Cicero and Plautus, 'if at length I returned to myself, and began to read a prophet, the uncouth diction jarred'. This in itself, in an age which set such immense store on verbal elegance, was a serious matter. But even more important was the fact that to an educated man all the glories of his classical heritage were intimately connected with the pagan gods and myths.[50]

Nevertheless so strong was the tradition that the church was powerless to modify it. Throughout the fourth, fifth and sixth centuries the schools maintained their syllabus unchanged, and Christian boys continued to memorise the genealogies of pagan gods and the amours of Zeus. Nor did the church make any signi-

ficant attempt to create schools of its own. There were classes
for catechumens in which the bishop or one of his priests gave
elementary instruction in Christian doctrine and morals to converts.
Provision was made in monasteries for teaching their letters to
illiterate postulants and to child oblates. But such monastic schools
in general catered only for future monks: Basil indeed contemplated
receiving boys not destined for the religious life, but there is no
evidence that parents sent their sons to monasteries; in the West
they apparently sometimes sent their daughters to nunneries.[51]

In the sixth century in Italy, Spain and Gaul, when the secular
educational system was breaking down, it would seem that the
church was forced to make arrangements for maintaining a supply
of literate clergy. The second Council of Toledo in 527 ordered
all bishops to provide on church premises a school for the instruction of children destined for the priesthood, and two years later
the second Council of Vaison instructed all parish priests to teach
their unmarried readers the psalms and the scriptures with a view
to providing successors for themselves.[52]

The instruction given in monastic, episcopal and parochial
schools was not only reserved for future monks and clergy but was
of the most elementary kind, merely reading and writing sufficient
to spell out and copy the scriptures. Only outside the sphere of
Greek and Roman culture in Mesopotamia did there exist Christian
schools of a higher grade, which gave a grammatical and rhetorical
education based on the Syriac scriptures. Augustine indeed drafted
a syllabus for a similar educational course in Latin, but it remained
in the realm of theory. Cassiodorus, inspired by the example of
the Syriac church, not only composed a syllabus, but founded a
monastery at Vivarium, where he put it into practice, but this lone
venture did not outlive its author.[53]

The leading features of the literary culture of the later Roman
empire are its conservatism, its uniformity, and its widespread
geographical diffusion. The educational system taught men not
only to venerate the classical authors but to regard them as models
to be imitated, and a contemporary poet or author was the more
highly esteemed the closer he approximated to the ancients. No
higher praise could be given to a Latin poet than to say that he
equalled or even surpassed Virgil, or to a Greek orator than to
declare him a modern Demosthenes: and such praises were to be
taken in the literal sense that their objects reproduced the diction
and style of their models.

Based on the same classics and an identical technique, the educational system produced a literary culture which was throughout each linguistic zone completely uniform. There were no regional schools of literature. Whether he lived and wrote in Gaul, Africa, or Illyricum, in Thrace, Cappadocia or Egypt, the training of every aspirant to literary fame was identical, and the exemplars which he strove to emulate the same.

This uniform culture was, moreover, remarkably widely diffused. There were, of course, literary centres, such as Rome in the West or Athens in the East, whose supremacy was generally recognised, and outlying areas of the empire where culture was relatively backward. Pacatus, delivering a panegyric on Theodosius I before the Roman senate, professes to fear that 'in view of their inborn and hereditary oratorical skill, the rude and unpolished roughness of my Transalpine speech may not disgust' his audience, and one of the speakers in Sulpicius Severus' dialogues modestly declares: 'when I reflect that I, a Gaul, am going to talk to Aquitanians, I fear that my rather rustic diction may offend your too urbane ears'.[54]

These are somewhat insincere rhetorical compliments. Symmachus corresponds with men living in Gaul and Spain on terms of perfect equality, and professes to derive as much pleasure from their letters as they did from his; and Libanius writes to inhabitants of remote cities of Armenia or Arabia with the evident assurance that his classical reminiscences and mythological allusions will be appreciated and savoured. It is indeed remarkable how many of the leading literary figures of the later empire, especially in the East, come from regions which under the Principate had been regarded as backwaters. The great philosopher, Themistius, was of Paphlagonian origin. Cappadocia, whose barbaric Greek Philostratus had scorned, produced in the fourth century a rich crop of distinguished authors, and not only from Caesarea, which had long been recognised as a Hellenic oasis in the Cappadocian desert, but from backwoods towns like Nazianzus. Even in Egypt, where culture had been practically confined to Alexandria, the minor cities of the Nile Valley now produced historians like Olympiodorus of Thebes and poets like Nonnus of Panopolis.

The literary output of the age was large, but not on the whole distinguished. There were many versifiers of varying degrees of competence, from Dioscorus, the notary of the Egyptian village of Aphrodito, who wrote reams of doggerel hexameters in the reign of Justinian, to the great nobleman Sidonius Apollinaris, whose verse panegyrics on Avitus, Majorian and Anthemius are, if uninspired, technically respectable and replete with mythological learning. There were, however, few that could rank as poets. Some of Ausonius' occasional verse has charm, and Claudian's panegyrics and invectives have rhetorical power and many felicitous lines: Nonnus' great epic, the Dionysiaca, has its admirers. Religious poetry is no better. A number of notable hymns were written by diverse authors, from Arnobius and Prudentius in the fourth century to Venantius Fortunatus in the sixth: but most religious verse—Gregory Nazianzen's voluminous poems for instance, in Greek, and in Latin, Paulinus of Nola's many poetical tributes to S. Felix—is of the same rather pedestrian quality as secular verse.[55]

The rhetorical set pieces which were the most highly esteemed prose productions of the age are for the most part vapid and turgid in the extreme. When, however, they have something to say, orators can say it cogently and eloquently; despite his involved and often obscure style Libanius speaks well on themes that move him. Christian oratory has a much greater range of themes and of style. Some sermons, especially those delivered on the great festivals, are as rhetorical in the worst sense as their secular counterparts; encomia of martyrs in particular are closely modelled on the standard panegyric and share its vices. There were on the other hand some good Christian orators, like John Chrysostom, who used rhetorical techniques to advantage in exposition and exhortation. There were other preachers like Augustine, who, though fully trained orators, deliberately adopted a simple and matter-of-fact style better adapted to their humbler hearers. And there were naturally uneducated or half-educated preachers who aspired to a lofty style. The sermons of the age show one charac-teristic which seems to be almost universal: they are mostly very dull.

The other literary form which was highly esteemed, the letter, is usually very jejune and artificial; but here again writers who are normally dull can achieve distinction when they have something to say. Symmachus' letters are mostly elegant nothings, but his appeal for the Altar of Victory is sincere and moving, and Sidonius Apollinaris can be a good *raconteur* and describe a scene vividly. Many of the collections of letters which we possess were not intended to be literature, and are none the worse for that. A curious example of the epistolary form is the Variae of Cassiodorus, who wrote official letters on behalf of the Gothic kings so replete with rhetorical tropes and antiquarian and mythological allusions that they were regarded as literary masterpieces.

History enjoyed a great vogue in the Eastern parts. The contri-bution of the West was very meagre in this field. In the fourth century Aurelius Victor wrote thumbnail biographies of the emperors and Eutropius a very brief Breviarium from the Foundation of the City; this was an elegant summary for gentlemen who had not the patience to plough through Livy. In the early fifth century Sulpicius Severus wrote a similar elegant summary of sacred history from Adam for cultured Christians, and Orosius a Historia contra Paganos, a work of propaganda. Apart from this there are only crude and meagre annalistic chronicles.

The East on the other hand produced many competent and some great historians. In the fourth century Ammianus of Antioch continued and emulated Tacitus, and if he falls far short of his model in artistry, excels him in breadth of view and impartiality of judgment. In the sixth Procopius of Caesarea took Thucydides as his model in recording the wars of Justinian. He is in a different class from his exemplar but is nevertheless a very sound and conscientious military historian. Besides these great names there was a succession of very competent and workmanlike historians who between them covered the whole period from Constantine to the death of Maurice. Of their works only two have survived intact, Agathias' continuation of Procopius' wars, and Theophylact's narrative of the reign of Maurice. We have probably not missed much by the loss of Eunapius, if we can fairly judge his quality from his epitomator Zosimus. But to judge by their surviving fragments many of the others, such as Olympiodorus, Priscus and Menander wrote sound and interesting histories of their times.

Eusebius of Caesarea was a great scholar, whose command of his voluminous and scattered documentary material is remarkable. His Ecclesiastical History is by any standards a great work. His successors were not of the same calibre, but several of them, such as Socrates and Evagrius, were learned and competent.

The historians so far mentioned wrote for the educated public. But history evidently appealed to a lower stratum of society; for there were popular historians like John Malalas who wrote in vulgar Greek and catered for the tastes of the common man, describing minutely the personal appearance and manners of the emperors and filling their pages with picturesque anecdotes and social scandal.

Biography also had a great vogue. The pagan Eunapius wrote the Lives of the Sophists in a very highflown rhetorical vein. There are countless lives of saints and collections of anecdotes at every literary level, from turgid and pretentious encomia to simple and unadorned tales for the edification of the vulgar.

Scholarship, as was natural in so religious an age, was mainly concentrated on theological studies. Much of the vast output was inevitably mediocre and derivative. In bulk the greatest part by far of the theological literature of the period consists of commentaries on the scriptures. Most of these follow too faithfully the tradition of the secular *grammaticus*, explaining the text line by line and word by word and commenting on obscurities with much pedantic learning; the authors are also very prone to far-fetched allegorical interpretations and rather trite moralising. Against the many mediocrities, however, can be set a few great men, most notably Jerome, whose encyclopaedic learning and exacting scholarship raised scriptural studies to a level not surpassed for many centuries.

In theology in the narrower sense much of the literature is again repetitive and derivative, but in the East a series of great theologians, heretical and orthodox, formulated Christian doctrine in philosophical terms, and worked out a solution of the problem of the Trinity which has satisfied the church ever since: while the West produced at least one great Christian thinker, Augustine, whose theories have profoundly influenced all subsequent ages.

In philosophy the West produced no great original thinker, but in the East there was a succession of distinguished philosophers, from Iamblichus in the early fourth century to Simplicius, Damascius and John Philoponus in the reign of Justinian: all except the last, who was converted late in life, were pagans. Their works were mostly commentaries on Plato, Aristotle and the other classical philosophers, but they were by no means all mere commentators, who slavishly accepted the doctrines of the great masters. Most were Platonists, who developed and refined the ideas of the Platonic school. For this reason they were often critical of Aristotle and did not hesitate to contradict his most fundamental views. Their attacks were mostly based on internal inconsistencies in the Aristotelian system, but they also made use of scientific knowledge gained since Aristotle's day by observation or experiment: John Philiponus anticipated Galileo in knowing that heavier bodies do not fall faster than lighter, and applied this knowledge to confuting Aristotle's cosmography.

These philosophers were familiar with the scientific experiments and discoveries of the Hellenistic age, including steam power, but it did not occur to them to try to put this knowledge to practical use. The only inventor of the later Roman empire was an unknown man who addressed a little treatise to Valentinian and Valens; he was evidently a man of little education, probably a military officer. His inventions include two ingenious scythed chariots, two pieces of artillery, a portable pontoon bridge, and most ambitious of all a warship propelled by three pairs of paddlewheels, operated by oxen.[56]

Apart from rhetors, grammarians and lawyers we know little of the professional classes and their training. Doctors—those, that is, who held official appointments—enjoyed the same immunities and privileges as professors, and seem to have ranked socially more or less on a par with them. The aristocracy of the profession was formed by the court physicians (*archiatri sacri palatii*), who normally enjoyed the rank of *comes* of the first or second class, and were often rewarded with an administrative post; we know of one who became *comes thesaurorum*, and of another who rose to be a vicar. They were a highly privileged group, enjoying special exemption from all the normal burdens of their elevated rank, including the *gleba senatoria*.[57]

Next came the public doctors of Rome, instituted by Valentinian I, one for each of the regions of the city save two. Their posts were evidently lucrative, for the government had to lay down stringent rules against those who sought to obtain them by the interest of the great.[58]

Below these came the public doctors whom many cities maintained. The public doctors received salaries which no doubt varied with the importance of the city. At Carthage Justinian provided for five doctors, the senior of whom received 99 solidi, the second 70 and the other three 50 each. We happen to know from his will that Flavius Phoebammon, public doctor of Antinoopolis, metropolis of the Thebaid, drew 60 solidi per annum in the latter part of the sixth century. He seems incidentally to have been quite comfortably off, owning properties, partly inherited, partly acquired by himself, not only in Antinoopolis, but in the neighbouring Hermopolite territory. Public doctors also took fees from their patients. This is to be inferred from the code of professional conduct laid down by Valentinian I for the newly instituted *archiatri* of Rome. Seeing that they received salaries from the public funds, they were, he demanded, 'honestly to attend the poor, rather than basely to serve the rich', and they were authorised to accept what patients whom they had cured offered them for their services, but not to demand fees from those in a critical condition. Besides the public doctors there were no doubt private practitioners who lived by fees alone, but we know little of them.[59]

The little that we know of a doctor's life is derived mainly from the papyri and from hagiography. The former suggest that their principal activity was signing medical certificates for the use of the courts and the administration, the latter that their fees were exorbitant and their cures few. Both impressions are no doubt unjust.[60]

Medicine was taught at an academic level at Alexandria. It was here that Caesarius, brother of Gregory Nazianzen, obtained the qualifications that won him the post of court physician to Constantius II. But the average doctor probably received his training from the public doctor of his native town or the capital of his province: it is assumed in the Code that the public doctors of the cities normally took pupils, and that teaching was one of their official duties. Flavius Phoebammon records in his will that his father before him had been a public doctor, and it is likely that sons often received their training from their fathers, and that the profession tended, like so many others, to be hereditary.[61]

Surveyors (*geometrae*), engineers (*mechanici*) and architects were also professional men, belonging to the upper ranks of society. Architects appear to have ranked lowest; in Diocletian's tariff a teaching architect is only to charge 100 denarii a month for each pupil, very little more than the fee of 75 denarii which teachers of mathematics and shorthand were entitled to demand. A surveyor, on the other hand, could charge 200 denarii, the same as a grammarian. Nevertheless architects were drawn from the educated class: when Constantine, alarmed at the shortage of architects, ordered that young men should be encouraged to learn the art by the grant of immunity for their parents and scholarships for themselves, he stipulated that candidates should be of about eighteen years of age, and should already have received a liberal education.[62]

Engineers, who appear in fact to have been a superior grade of architects, who planned large buildings involving complicated structural problems, ranked the highest. Cyriades, who was concerned with the erection of a bridge and a basilica at Rome when Symmachus was prefect of the city, was a *clarissimus comes*. Isidore the younger of Miletus, who was responsible for the repair of Santa Sophia after the earthquake in 558, and for many others of Justinian's public works, is styled *magnificentissimus et illustris* on an inscription recording his work at Chalcis in Syria. Thanks to Agathias we have more intimate information about Anthemius of Tralles, the great engineer who shared with the elder Isidore of Tralles the responsibility for Santa Sophia. He came of a family of five talented brothers; Olympiodorus was a distinguished barrister, Metrodorus a celebrated grammarian, Dioscorus and Alexander both doctors; the former practised in his home town, the latter had the distinction of receiving an appointment at Rome. Anthemius himself was evidently an engineer of no mean order, with a remarkable knowledge of mathematics and physics, as appears not only from his architectural achievements but from his scientific practical jokes. He carried on a feud with a distinguished barrister named Zenodotus, whose house was in the same block as his own, and being defeated in a law suit, revenged himself by producing artificial thunder and lightning and earthquakes in Zenodotus' appartments. The earthquake was particularly ingenious, involving the use of steam pressure, and was so convincing that Zenodotus fled in terror, and, rushing to the palace, caused great mirth by asking everyone what damage their houses had sustained.[63]

Architects, engineers and surveyors enjoyed the social standing which they were accorded because their arts were based on a theory which could only be acquired by way of a literary education. Painters and sculptors on the other hand, ranked with mosaicists as superior craftsmen. A figure painter (*pictor imaginarius*) under Diocletian's tariff received 150 denarii a day with his keep, as against 75 denarii for a wall painter, and 60 for a mosaicist, and 50 for an ordinary mason or carpenter; the privileges accorded to painters by Valentinian I, which include immunity from the poll tax for themselves and their families and slaves, show that they were classified as plebeians.[64]

The troubled period of the mid-third century, when monumental building and the production of statuary and other works of art almost came to a standstill, nearly broke the tradition of skilled craftsmanship. Constantine in one of his laws complained that he needed a large number of architects, but that none existed, and he gave instructions for young men to be encouraged to learn that art. In another law he granted immunities to a whole range of skilled craftsmen, sculptors, painters, mosaicists, cabinet-makers, gold and silver smiths, and the like, so that they might have 'leisure to learn their arts', and might 'both themselves become more skilled, and train their sons'. That such measures were urgent is amply demonstrated by the very low standard of technical skill displayed even in important monuments, such as Constantine's own triumphal arch at Rome, which were built in that period.[65]

The shortage of men trained in the old traditions meant that humble craftsmen had to apply their simple techniques to more ambitious compositions, and in certain arts, notably sculpture, the result was that a more primitive, but often more vigorous, style emerged. In other arts, such as floor mosaics, the breach was less noticeable, for private houses continued to be built throughout the most troubled periods. Here there is a remarkable continuity; the same patterns go on generation after generation, and if pictorial designs become less common and floral and geometrical designs are more favoured, this is probably due to lack of skill rather than to a change of taste. In architecture the most notable feature of late Roman provincial buildings is their extremely slovenly technique. There was throughout the period such an immense quantity of worked stone available from the demolition of pagan temples and other now superfluous public buildings that new stone cutting was scarcely ever required: the columns, entablatures and doors of the average urban church are reused pieces of the time of the Principate, and the walls are a patchwork of old blocks; only the mosaic floors and the marble revetment of the walls and the timber roofs with their coffered ceilings were the products of contemporary craftsmanship.

Skilled masons and carvers must have found little employment except under the imperial government, especially in the three great imperial marble quarries, which continued to produce capitals and other ornamental members. Here a tradition of fine craftsmanship was built up again and new forms of architectural decoration were evolved which came to flower in the age of Justinian.

In the provinces there was very little monumental building done under the later empire. Most cities were already over-supplied with grand public buildings, and it was generally only on the occasion of a great fire or earthquake, or destruction by the enemy, that architects were given an opportunity. The major exception to this rule is churches, many thousands of which were built during this period. The response of architects to this new demand was not very interesting. Nearly all churches were built on a simple standardised plan, based on the basilica, which can be dignified, but is often dull. A few churches like the cathedral of Bostra and St. George's at Gerasa have interesting circular plans, but these are very rare exceptions to the general rule. Nearly all were timber roofed and presented no structural problems.

It was again only in the employment of the imperial government that *mechanici* were given the opportunity to plan more ambitious buildings, and in particular to experiment with the problems of vaulting on a monumental scale. At Constantinople there developed a school of architects which ultimately under Justinian produced the masterpiece of S. Sophia.

In the visual arts, as in literature, there was a remarkable degree of uniformity throughout the empire. In their humbler forms there were of course regional idioms. There were local styles in the tombstones of the poor, and in common pottery and metal ware. There were local techniques of building, dictated by the materials available and by age-old tradition. In Africa walls continued to be built with stone uprights at intervals and rubble filling in between; in Syria, where timber was very scarce, roofs were made of stone slabs laid on transverse arches. For farm buildings and humbler houses various districts had their traditional plans, adapted to the climate and to the local building materials. In the villages, which rarely possessed monuments of an earlier age whose decorative members could be reused, churches built by local masons often follow a regional style, derived from the local domestic architecture.

In the arts which catered for the upper classes, on the other hand, there was little variation from one end of the empire to the other. Mosaic pavements in Britain and in Syria used basically the same repertory of patterns and pictorial designs. Silver plate found in all parts of the empire is so similar that experts cannot distinguish its place of manufacture. The town houses and villas of the rich, the baths and churches in the cities, in every province follow the same designs and are ornamented in the same style.

The games, despite the thunders of the church, retained a central place in the life of the empire. They were indeed, with the baths, generally regarded as essentials of civilised life. Suspension of the games and closing of the baths was a drastic penalty meted out only in the most serious cases of disorder, like the famous Riot of the Statues at Antioch. After the disastrous barbaric invasions of Gaul at the beginning of the fifth century, the first request of the city of Treviri to the imperial government, when order was temporarily restored, was for chariot races. Salvian regarded this as criminal frivolity—but he condemned all games on moral and religious grounds. It might be regarded rather as a heroic resolve to maintain civilisation in the direst extremities.[66]

The passion for the games pervaded all classes of the population. For the fervour of the commons the sanguinary riots in which the rivalry of the Blues and the Greens often found expression are sufficient testimony. But they appealed equally to the educated classes. Augustine confesses to his craze for the mimes when a young man at Carthage, and tells of the hold which the chariot races and the gladiatorial games gained on his younger friend Alypius. Libanius constantly rates the councillors of Antioch for thinking of nothing but horses, charioteers, bears and mimes;

when they sent a delegation to the emperor, he complains, their requests were for such frivolities, to the neglect of the serious needs of the city. The production of games was the only liturgy which was sometimes undertaken without reluctance, and councillors often endangered their fortunes by their extravagant expenditure. Though in public Libanius was severe—and the games seem really to have bored him—he took infinite pains to make the shows given by his relatives and friends an outstanding success, writing to all his influential friends, vicars of dioceses or governors of provinces, to provide wild beasts and whip up hunters and athletes and facilitate their journeys by the grant of postal warrants.[67]

The types of games varied somewhat in East and West. In the Hellenistic East games of the traditional Greek form, athletic (including chariot races) and musical (including drama), were well established before Roman rule. The Roman favourites were chariot races, gladiatorial shows, wild beast hunts and the drama. Under Greek influence athletic games were introduced later in the West, but they were never widespread. Conversely gladiatorial shows and wild beast hunts spread under Roman influence to the East. Wild beast hunts caught on, but gladiatorial shows enjoyed only a limited popularity.

Gladiators were as under the Principate either prisoners of war and convicts, or free men who voluntarily signed on: a law of 357 forbids givers of shows to solicit soldiers or palatine officials to enter the profession. Gladiatorial games were abolished by Constantine in the East and by Honorius in the West, but wild beast hunts continued to flourish in both halves of the empire. They were, according to Libanius, the most popular item in any show—people would rise at dawn to go to the theatre or the races, but for the sake of the beast hunts, they would queue all night, 'deeming the paving stones softer than their beds'—and the producers of the Syriarchic games at Antioch spared neither trouble nor expense to get unfamiliar beasts from as far afield as Mount Ida in the Troad. The Syriarchic festival was, of course, an exceptionally big show, but even lesser towns indulged in their spectacles. Once when the council of Antioch refused to put on a wild beast hunt at the governor's request, to shame them he called in the show about to be produced at the neighbouring little city of Beroea. The expense of these spectacles was heavy. The beasts had to be caught and transported long distances. They were consequently rather dear; in the Edict of Diocletian an 'African lion (first grade)' is priced at 150,000 denarii (equivalent to about 50 solidi), and even an 'African lioness (second grade)' cost

100,000 denarii (over 30 solidi). The hunters—who were apparently professionals and were often sought from other provinces —had to be paid, and the beasts had to be fed. In one of his letters Libanius complains bitterly that after his nephew had spent all his cash (and borrowed from his friends) to collect beasts and hunters, an imperial ban had been laid on killing beasts, and the games postponed, with the result that he would have to sell his lands to feed them.[68]

Athletic competitions still continued in the fourth century. In 376 Gratian welcomed the revival of *gymnici agones* in Africa, presumably at Carthage, and athletic contests continued to form part of the Antiochene Olympia till the end of the century. They seem indeed to have grown in popularity there. In his young days, according to Libanius, they had been rather an exclusive affair, given in a small arena before a select audience. But the arena had been doubled and tripled in size by successive *agonothetae* and the vulgar crowd admitted. A constitution of Diocletian, which limited the immunity from the *curia* traditionally given to victors in the major games, shows that in his day athletes were still, as under the Principate, drawn from the upper classes. Technically amateurs, though in practice often professionals, they seem in Libanius' day to have been still unpaid, for he speaks of *agonothetae* attracting them from distant provinces like Asia by the offer of supplementary prizes. After the fourth century there is no mention of athletic games, but Justinian's republication of Diocletian's constitution on athletic victors implies that they continued.[69]

Chariot races enjoyed ever-increasing popularity. Star charioteers were eagerly sought for—and no doubt paid high salaries— by the decurions who gave the games, and the aid of magicians was also commonly invoked. For the big races horses were bought from distant provinces. Libanius writes of a friend who trained two teams—the gift of the emperor—in Bithynia for the Olympia at Antioch, and Symmachus mentions an Antiochene mission buying race horses in Spain. Breeding and training horses for the games was reckoned the heaviest of all the liturgies, and those who undertook it at Antioch received leases of civic lands to compensate them.[70]

Throughout the empire, both in the two capitals and in the provinces, the rivalry of the Blues and Greens was intense. The nature of these two 'factions' is obscure. Under the Principate there were at Rome four *factiones*, the Reds, Whites, Blues and Greens. They were companies or guilds which furnished chariots to the magistrates who gave the games, each *factio* providing one chariot for each race. They were apparently recompensed mainly by prize money, but the losing *factiones* presumably got some payment. The organisation was extended to other cities of the empire, and naturally acquired special importance at Constantinople when it became a second capital.[71]

There were still four colours at Constantinople in the fifth century, but only two, the Blues and the Greens, counted for anything: Anastasius only favoured the Reds so that he could chastise the Blues and Greens with impartial severity. Under the later empire the *factiones* no longer seem to have normally supplied the horses: all givers of games of whom we know from the emperor and the great senators of Rome down to humble decurions bought or bred their own horses. The *factiones* at Rome, however, had their own stables in which they kept horses which they received, either as their due or as free gifts, from the emperor and the consuls and praetors. From these stables they perhaps furnished teams to the more indigent or parsimonious senators, especially no doubt those who did not organise their own games but delegated the business to the *censuales*. The chariots, however, still continued to run under the colours of the *factiones*, who supplied the charioteers and other personnel required. By the sixth century the *factiones* had come to include the dancers of the mimes, the keepers of the wild beasts, and probably all members of the entertainment professions.[72]

Each *factio* had its 'fans' (στασιῶται), young men who cut their hair in a peculiar fashion and wore a distinctive style of clothes, like the modern Teddy Boy. They were the leaders in the riots which the games so frequently provoked, and according to Procopius exercised a reign of terror in every city of the empire. But apart from these enthusiasts every man and woman in the empire from the emperor and empress downwards was either a Blue or a Green. As Procopius explains: 'The populace in every city has from time immemorial been divided into Blues and Greens, but it is only recently that for the sake of those names and of the positions in which they stand to watch they lavish their money, expose their persons to the most cruel tortures and are willing to die a dreadful death. They fight with their opponents, not knowing what the struggle is about, though they understand full well that, even if they defeat their adversaries in the fight, their fate will be to be put into prison forthwith and after the extremest tortures to be executed. The enmity which they feel towards their neighbours is irrational, but it persists without end for all time. It overrides the bonds of kinship or friendship, even if those who quarrel about these colours are brothers or the like. They care for

nothing human or divine beside victory in this contest, whether a
sacrilege is committed against God or the laws or the constitution
are overturned by domestic or foreign foes. Though they may
lack the necessities of life and their fatherland may be in
the direst straits, they do not bother if their "faction" is going
to gain an advantage: for that is the name they give to their fellow
enthusiasts. Even women share in this contagion, not only
supporting their husbands, but if it so happens opposing them—
though they never go to the theatres and have no other motive.
In short I can only describe it as a psychopathic condition.'[73]

Jerome tells a curious tale of how on one occasion a race was
run under colours other than the Blues and Greens. Italicus,
a Christian decurion in the strongly pagan city of Gaza, was appointed to produce one chariot, his opposite number being a
wealthy pagan, one of the *duoviri* of the town. Italicus, despairing
of his chances, especially as his rival had retained the services of a
celebrated magician, appealed to the hermit Hilarion to bless his
team and charioteer and stable. Hilarion at first reproved him for
his frivolity, but eventually, convinced that Italicus was merely
fulfilling his lawful duty in producing the chariot, he gave his
blessing. These facts became generally known, and excitement
rose in Gaza as the test of the two religions approached. The race
was run amidst cries of 'Victory to Marnas!' and 'Victory to
Christ!' Italicus' chariot won, and many pagans were converted.[74]

The drama had by the fourth century—and probably long before
—given way to the mime, which was apparently a kind of ballet.
The themes continued to be drawn from Greek mythology, a
fact which exacerbated Christian dislike of the theatre, but reconciled Libanius to its low intellectual level. The actors or dancers,
both male and female (*scaenici, scaenicae*), though many of them
were popular idols, were a despised class, very strongly reprobated
by Christian sentiment and excluded from membership of the
church unless they left the stage. The Christian emperors were
torn between their secular duty of keeping up the supply of
entertainers for their subjects and their Christian duty of at least
permitting actors and actresses to save their souls. Actors and
actresses could make a deathbed repentance and be received into
the church, but the provincial governor, or in his absence the
curator of the city, had in such cases to verify that they really were
in extremis, as, if they recovered, they could not be recalled to the
stage. Daughters of theatrical families might refuse to go on the
stage, and were excused so long as they behaved unexception-
ably. Actresses might even abandon their profession if they

wished to be received into the church, but if they afterwards returned to the stage were condemned to it without reprieve.[75]

One form of theatrical entertainment came under particular reprobation, the *maiuma*: very little is known of it, save that the spectacle was aquatic, and, in Christian eyes, highly licentious. It nevertheless continued to flourish. Many small theatres or odea were adapted for it by making arrangements for flooding the orchestra, and in 535 the city of Gerasa recorded by an inscription a celebration of the festival in a small theatre, near a reservoir outside the town, which was apparently specially built for it.[76]

The games included other forms of entertainment. As might have been expected in an age so addicted to rhetoric, they were feasts of oratory: Libanius wrote his immense panegyric on Antioch for the Olympia of 360 and regularly produced an oration for subsequent celebrations. The Olympia also included a vast banquet, at which the chairman of the games was expected to give a present to every guest. But this last extravagance was abandoned in Libanius' lifetime.[77]

A Roman citizen of the upper classes must have found himself at home wherever he travelled. The cities which he visited and the houses in which he stayed would have presented a very similar appearance to those he left behind. Social habits varied little, if at all: everywhere the baths offered the same amenities, and the theatre, the circus and the amphitheatre provided the same entertainments. Everywhere within his own linguistic zone he would find the same language spoken, and the same literature read, quoted and discussed.

This uniformity of cultural environment must have contributed to the sense of solidarity which certainly existed. There is no trace of regional separatism in the higher ranks of Roman society. Some provinces had their proverbial characteristics; Gauls were gluttons, Cappadocians stupid, and Ammianus calls almost every Pannonian a brutal boor. Conversely a man might be proud of his province, and laud its beauties or write up its history and antiquities. But such local distinctions and local loyalties amounted to very little. Augustine, as an African, might feel some sentimental sympathy for the cause of Dido, but basically he felt himself to be a Roman, and the sack of Rome moved him to his depths. The election of Avitus as emperor has been interpreted as an expression of the national sentiment of the Gallic aristocracy. If Sidonius Apollinaris was a typical senator, and there is every indication that he was, no such sentiment existed. The most that can be said is that the Gallic senators may have felt that they were as good as the Italians, and took the opportunity offered by the anarchy in Italy after the Vandal sack of Rome to elect one of themselves as emperor. Neither Avitus nor any of his following showed the slightest inclination to create a separate Gallic empire.

That the upper classes of the Western parts should have felt themselves to be Romans is not surprising. For centuries they had spoken Latin, and for generation after generation they had been brought up on Roman literature. No indigenous Gallic, Spanish or African traditions survived, and what little they knew of their past history of their own peoples was derived from Roman sources. It is ironic that a Gallic senator desirous of writing the history of his own country applied to the Roman Symmachus for guidance, and was recommended to read Livy, Caesar's Commentaries, and Pliny's German Wars—which were in fact the only sources available. With this cultural background it was inevitable that educated Western provincials should have come to regard themselves as Romans, and to take pride in the imperial traditions of Rome.[78]

It is more surprising that the same sentiment prevailed in the Eastern parts, where the language was Greek, and where education was based on the Greek classics. The cultured classes in the East were proud of their Hellenic heritage, and treasured the historical and mythological traditions of their cities. But here also centuries of Roman rule had eliminated any traces of political separatism. By the fourth century, if not earlier, the Greek-speaking inhabitants of the Eastern provinces felt themselves to be what they had legally been since 212 A.D., Roman citizens.

There is scarcely any sign of alienation between the Greek and Latin halves of the empire, even after they had been politically separated for generations. Arvandus, praetorian prefect of the Gauls, in a letter to the king of the Visigoths spoke contemptuously of Anthemius as 'the Greek emperor'; but he was a traitor, condemned as such by his fellow senators. When Ricimer called Anthemius an 'excitable Galatian' ('Galatam concitatum'), he may have been trying to create prejudice against him as an oriental, but if so he was unsuccessful; the senate and people of Rome, we are told, stood firm on Anthemius' side. The mass of the Africans and Italians welcomed the armies of Justinian, and if they came to detest his fiscal agents there is no sign that they resented being governed by Greeks.[79]

If we know something of the sentiments of the upper classes from the literature which they produced, we have little clue to the feelings of the humbler strata of the population, many of whom still spoke their indigenous languages and were scarcely touched by Roman culture. To their barbarian conquerors they were Romans. In the laws of the Visigothic, Ostrogothic, Burgundian and Frankish kings their non-German subjects, whether in Gaul, Italy or Spain, are called *Romani*, and a Moorish chief, who in the sixth century ruled a part of the former province of Mauretania Caesariensis, styled himself 'rex Maurorum et Romanorum'. In the East the inhabitants of the provinces which they conquered were called *Rumi* by the Arabs. It seems likely that even a Syriac or Celtic speaking peasant would have called himself a Roman, and, if he cherished no strong feelings of loyalty to Rome, was not animated by any hostile feelings towards her as an alien oppressor.[80]

The revolts of Britain and Armorica may have had some national character, but the evidence is too slight to form a definite conclusion. According to Zosimus, when in 408 the forces of the usurper Constantine were engaged in Spain, the attacks of barbarians from across the Rhine 'drove the inhabitants of the island of Britain and some of the provinces of Gaul to the necessity of revolting from the Roman empire and living on their own, no longer obeying their laws: and the people of Britain took up arms and fought for themselves and freed their cities from the attacking barbarians. And the whole of Armorica and other provinces of Gaul imitated the Britons and freed themselves in this way, expelling the Roman governors and establishing their own independent state.'[81]

It is to be noted that this movement was directed against a usurper, and that Honorius gave it his blessing, 'writing letters to the cities in Britain, urging them to defend themselves'. Despite Zosimus' emphatic words it would seem that the Britons and north-western Gauls were not rebelling against the empire, but were driven to self-help against the barbarians by the inaction of a usurper.[82]

Ten years later in 417 Exuperantius was crushing an uprising in Armorica in which slaves had reduced their masters to subjection. There were further risings of Bacaudae in Armorica in 435-7 and in 442. There is, however, no reason to connect these peasant revolts with the movement of 408, and they were probably social revolutions. The cities of Britain and Armorica were left very much to their own devices in the last years of Valentinian's reign, and became practically independent, but there is no sign that they wished to break away. The Britons appealed for aid to Aetius in or after 446, and the Armoricans fought with the Roman army against Attila in 451.[83]

A clue to the sentiments of the Egyptians is given by the history written by John, Bishop of Niciu, about two generations after the Arab conquest. As a monophysite Copt he might be expected to display some national pride in Egypt and the Egyptians, and some hostility to the Roman empire. In fact he writes from an imperial standpoint, giving no special emphasis to Egyptian affairs, except that he is better informed on them. He naturally condemns those emperors who had lapsed from the orthodox (that is, monophysite) faith, and especially those like Justinian and Heraclius who had been persecutors. But he gives high praise to the pious Anastasius and even to Tiberius Constantine, who merely tolerated monophysitism. He does not rejoice in the Arab conquest as a delivery from the Roman yoke, but laments it as a chastisement inflicted by God upon the empire for the heresy of Heraclius.[84]

CHAPTER XXV

THE DECLINE OF THE EMPIRE

THE sack of Rome by Alaric in 410 caused a tremendous shock to Christians and pagans alike. Jerome, when he heard the news in Bethlehem, declared: 'When the brightest light on the whole earth was extinguished, when the Roman empire was deprived of its head, when, to speak more correctly, the whole world perished in one city, then "I was dumb with silence. I held my peace, even from good, and my sorrow was stirred".' Only a decade earlier Claudian had written: 'There will never be an end to the power of Rome,' and Ammianus had believed that 'as long as there are men Rome will be victorious and will increase with lofty growth'. The fall of Rome spelt the fall of the empire; it even meant the end of the world. A century before Lactantius had written: 'The fall and ruin of the world will soon take place, but it seems that nothing of the kind is to be feared as long as the city of Rome stands intact. But when the capital of the world has fallen . . . who can doubt that the end will have come for the affairs of men and for the whole world? It is that city which sustains all things.'[1]

To pagans the explanation of the catastrophe was only too obvious. The misfortunes of the empire had increased with the growth of Christianity. The final disaster had come only a few years after Theodosius the Great had closed the temples and banned the worship of the gods. It was plain that the ancient gods by whose favour Rome had climbed to universal power had withdrawn their protection and were chastising the faithless Romans who had abandoned their worship.[2]

The Christians made several answers, none of them very convincing. Orosius in his Historia contra Paganos set out to prove that the history of Rome while she still worshipped the gods had been one uninterrupted series of disasters, and that with the barbarians in Spain and Gaul exterminating one another and vying to take service under the empire, things were now at last taking a turn for the better. This was too perverse to carry conviction to any reasonable man. Despite occasional misfortunes Rome had been

victorious and had won a great empire under the old dispensation.
Things did not get better, but went from bad to worse, and Salvian
a generation later took a quite different line in his de Gubernatione
Dei. The disasters of the empire, he argued, were the chastisement
inflicted by God on the Romans for their sins, their loose sexual
morals, their oppression of the poor, and their addiction to the
games. By contrast, reviving the legend of the noble savage, he
pictured the barbarians as perhaps uncouth but chaste, austere and
righteous. The refugees whose homes had been plundered and
burnt, the free men who had been carried off and sold into slavery,
the sacred virgins whom the Vandals had raped by the score,
cannot have found Salvian's arguments very convincing.

Augustine in the City of God used both these arguments, but
his main theme was different. It was true, he admitted, that in the
civitas terrena pagan Rome had prospered and the history of the
Christian empire had been calamitous. But what did the things of
this world matter in comparison with the spiritual world, the
civitas Dei? To the Christian earthly disasters were indifferent, they
were even to be welcomed as sent by God to discipline and purify
the faithful. This world was only a vale of tears, and true blessed-
ness was to be found in the life of the spirit here on earth, and in
all its fullness in the world to come.

In the eighteenth century the debate on the fall of the empire
was resumed, and it has gone on ever since. Rationalists like
Gibbon saw religion as a primary cause of its decline, but in a very
different way from the pagan and Christian controversialists of the
fifth century. Christianity in his view sapped the morale of the
empire, deadened its intellectual life and by its embittered controversies undermined its unity. Other historians, according to the
temper of their times, have emphasised the empire's military decline,
its political or social weaknesses, or its economic decay.

All the historians who have discussed the decline and fall of the
Roman empire have been Westerners. Their eyes have been fixed
on the collapse of Roman authority in the Western parts and the
evolution of the medieval Western European world. They have
tended to forget, or to brush aside, one very important fact, that
the Roman empire, though it may have declined, did not fall in
the fifth century nor indeed for another thousand years. During
the fifth century, while the Western parts were being parcelled out
into a group of barbarian kingdoms, the empire of the East stood
its ground. In the sixth it counter-attacked and reconquered
Africa from the Vandals and Italy from the Ostrogoths, and part
of Spain from the Visigoths. Before the end of the century, it is
true, much of Italy and Spain had succumbed to renewed barbarian

attacks, and in the seventh the onslaught of the Arabs robbed the empire of Syria, Egypt, and Africa, and the Slavs overran the Balkans. But in Asia Minor the empire lived on, and later, recovering its strength, reconquered much territory that it had lost in the dark days of the seventh century.

These facts are important, for they demonstrate that the empire did not, as some modern historians have suggested, totter into its grave from senile decay, impelled by a gentle push from the barbarians. Most of the internal weaknesses which these historians stress were common to both halves of the empire. The East was even more Christian than the West, its theological disputes far more embittered. The East, like the West, was administered by a corrupt and extortionate bureaucracy. The Eastern government strove as hard to enforce a rigid caste system, tying the *curiales* to their cities and the *coloni* to the soil. Land fell out of cultivation and was deserted in the East as well as in the West. It may be that some of these weaknesses were more accentuated in the West than in the East, but this is a question which needs investigation. It may be also that the initial strength of the Eastern empire in wealth and population was greater, and that it could afford more wastage; but this again must be demonstrated.

In one respect, however, the Eastern empire was demonstrably better placed than the Western. It was strategically less vulnerable, and was down to the end of the fifth century subjected to less pressure from external enemies. This suggests that the simple but rather unfashionable view that the barbarians played a considerable part in the decline and fall of the empire may have some truth in it. External pressures and internal weaknesses of course interacted. The enfeeblement of the empire no doubt encouraged the barbarians to win easy spoils. The devastations of the barbarians impoverished and depopulated the frontier provinces, and their unceasing pressure imposed on the empire a burden of defence which overstrained its administrative machinery and its economic resources. But directly or indirectly, it may be plausibly argued, barbarian attacks probably played a major part in the fall of the West.

During the first two centuries of the Principate the empire held its own against the barbarians with very little trouble. There was a serious crisis under Marcus Aurelius, and from the reign of Severus Alexander the imperial armies found increasing difficulty in beating off attacks across the frontier. How far was this due to increasing barbarian pressure? We know next to nothing of what was happening in the forests and marshes of Germany and the steppes of eastern Europe, but it is observable that in these areas there were long periods of relative stability, broken only by perennial border wars, and other periods of widespread restlessness. Trouble generally started when a tribe, whether because it had outgrown the means of subsistence in its homeland, or because it was hard pressed by aggressive neighbours, or lured by stories of richer lands far away which might be plundered or occupied, decided to abandon its home and start on trek. Such a movement had a snowball effect. Other tribes were excited and joined the adventure: others again were displaced and forced to migrate elsewhere; unless the movement was nipped in the bud, it tended to proliferate over a wider and wider area.

Some such movement probably produced the violent irruption of Gallic tribes into Italy in the fifth and fourth centuries B.C. and into the Balkans and Asia Minor in the third. The Cimbri and Teutones, whose migrations caused such turmoil at the end of the second century B.C., are certainly a case in point. Caesar was able to check a movement of the Helvetii before it gathered way. Then for two centuries northern Europe was quiescent. We do not know what caused the disturbance of the Quadi and Marcomanni which gave Marcus Aurelius so much trouble, but in the third century we know from their national legends of the great trek of the Goths and other East German tribes from their homes round the Baltic. They and the tribes that they set in motion broke into the empire and were only beaten back after long struggles by the great Illyrian emperors of the late third century, and barbarian pressure on the Rhine and Danube remained heavy during the fourth.

From the third quarter of the fourth century there appears a new disturbing force, the Huns. Their advent produced panic and turmoil throughout the German tribes. Fleeing before them the Visigoths sought refuge within the empire and the Ostrogoths trekked westward. It was without doubt the pressure of the Huns, direct or indirect, that caused waves of Germanic tribes to flood into Italy under Radagaesus and to sweep over the Rhine a few years later. The Hunnic kingdom itself grievously afflicted the empire until it broke up in 454, and in the wake of the Huns came other Asiatic tribes, such as the Avars, who in their turn set in motion the Slavs.

It is impossible to measure numerically the strength of the attacking forces. Contemporaries certainly often grossly exaggerated the numbers of the barbarian hordes, and on the meagre and for the most part unreliable evidence available it would seem that a tribal group such as the Vandals or the Visigoths could not put into the field more than twenty or thirty thousand fighting men. To modern ears such figures seem negligible, but in relation to the size of the armies which the empire could muster at any given point they were formidable. Moreover it must be remembered that the empire had to defend itself against a considerable number of such groups, and that some major disasters, such as the great breakthrough on the Rhine in 407, were the result of a combined movement of several tribes. The difficulties of the defence were increased by the anarchic state of the barbarian world. The movements of the barbarians were entirely unpredictable; at any point along hundreds of miles of frontier there might at any moment flood a swarm of warriors which far outnumbered the troops immediately available. Moreover the gaps in the front line were always filled by newcomers; scarcely had the power of the Huns been broken when the Avars appeared in the West, and less than twenty years after Justinian's army had finally cleared the Ostrogoths out of Italy the Lombards swarmed in.[3]

Though we cannot gauge the numbers involved, we can, if we compare the narratives of two historians who wrote on a similar scale—Tacitus and Ammianus—sense the change between the first and the fourth century A.D. In the Annals there are occasional border disturbances, but on the whole the frontier armies have very little to do except when an aggressive commander carries the war into enemy territory. In the pages of Ammianus we see Constantius II, Julian, Valentinian and Valens constantly engaged in repelling an attack here or conducting a punitive expedition there, and if for a moment their backs are turned, the barbarians forthwith break in. And except for the last book, Ammianus' history describes the period before the impact of the Huns pushed the German tribes westwards and redoubled the pressure on the Roman frontier.

The Persian empire under the Sassanid dynasty was certainly a more formidable enemy than had been the Parthian empire in the first two and a half centuries of the Principate. It was probably, when it put its full strength into play, more formidable than any but the largest concentrations of German tribes; the largest Roman armies on record were mustered against Persia.[4]

On the other frontiers the barbarians were a nuisance rather than a menace, but everywhere the pressure seems to have increased. In the diocese of Africa, where we hear of very little fighting under the Principate after the annexation of Mauretania by Claudius, the Moorish tribes became increasingly aggressive from the end of the third century and by the sixth were a constant menace. Cyrenaica, which had been ungarrisoned under the early empire, suffered from heavy raids in the fifth century. In Upper Egypt, which had been adequately protected by half a dozen auxiliary units, a much larger garrison found it difficult to cope with growing activity of the Nobadae and Blemmyes. Even in the interior of the empire the Isaurian highlanders, who had given no trouble since the early first century, from the late third were a constant menace to the surrounding provinces.

The brunt of the barbarian attack fell for obvious reasons on the West. In the fourth century the Western emperor was generally responsible for the defence of the whole length of the Rhine and Danube frontier, except for the last 300 miles of the Danube's course. Even in the fifth century, when the Eastern emperor took over the Dacian and Macedonian dioceses, the Western emperor still had more than twice as long a frontier to guard. This put a constant heavy strain on the resources of the West, and moreover presented it with a very difficult strategic problem. It was beyond the resources of the Western empire to contain a simultaneous attack on the Rhine and the upper Danube, and when the front line was breached by such a double assault, as it was in the early fifth century, there was no satisfactory second line of defence. The Eastern emperor had less front to cover, and therefore less constant wear and tear on his resources, and if the lower Danube was breached, as it often was, could and did hold the enemy at the Straits. The defence of his capital, indeed, forced him to hold this line at all costs, and adequate forces were always kept in reserve to guard Constantinople. In the West the defence of Rome absorbed troops which might from a purely strategical point of view have been better employed guarding the Pyrenees or the straits of Gibraltar, and the result was that when the Rhine frontier was breached the barbarian invaders surged on almost unchecked into Spain, and a few years later were able to cross into Africa.

The Eastern emperor was, it is true, responsible for the defence of the empire against the Persians, and when Persia was aggressive this was a heavy burden. But the Persian kings had their own troubles, dynastic disputes, internal rebellions and the barbarian pressure on their own northern frontier, and they generally preferred to keep the peace with Rome. There was a brief Persian war under Diocletian in 297-8. There were prolonged, but not continuous, hostilities from the accession of Constantius II in 337 to the defeat of Julian's great expedition in 363. Thereafter, apart from some rather desultory fighting in Armenia under Valens and two brief wars under Theodosius II in 421-2 and 440-2, there was peace until in 502 Cavades attacked Anastasius.

In the 240 years which passed between the accession of Diocletian and that of Justinian there was thus a state of war between
Rome and Persia for less than forty, and in most of those forty years
there were no hostilities, but truces, official or unofficial, during
which negotiations were pursued. Moreover when peace was
arranged, there was genuine peace: Persia was a civilised power
which normally kept its bond and could control its subjects. For
most of the fourth century therefore and nearly all the fifth the
empire did not have to worry about its Eastern frontier. From
the beginning of the sixth century Persia, under a series of vigorous
and aggressive kings, Cavades (488-531), Chosroes I (531-79) and
Hormisdas IV (579-90) exercised heavy pressure on the empire,
but there were long spells of peace, from 507 to 527, from 531 to
540, from 562 to 577 and from 590 to 602, and between 545 and
562 there were a series of truces, partial or complete, and little
fighting of importance. Nevertheless the strain was severe, and
partly accounts for the débâcle which followed the death of Maurice.

All things considered it would appear that on all fronts the
empire was exposed to much greater pressure from the middle of
the third century, and that this pressure became yet more intense
with the advent of the Huns, and did not thereafter relax. It is
also plain that the Western empire bore much more than its fair
share of the burden and was much less favourably placed to make a
recovery when its first line of defence was broken. Within twenty-
five years of the great break-through on the Rhine, Italy was en-
circled by barbarian kingdoms in Gaul, Spain and Africa, and the
struggle became hopeless. The Eastern emperors always had the
resources of Asia Minor, Syria and Egypt on which to draw, and
could always hold any tribes that crossed the Lower Danube at
bay until they tired of ravaging Thrace and Illyricum and moved
on to less devastated areas. In this way the strength of the East
contributed to the troubles of the West. The Visigoths under
Alaric moved West into Italy, having exhausted the possibilities of
Illyricum, and so did the Ostrogoths under Theoderic. Even
Attila tired of ravaging the Balkans and ultimately marched against
the West. They all realised that Constantinople was too tough a
nut to crack.

Some critics have stressed the evil consequences of the division
of the empire, particularly after 395, and have urged that if its
whole resources had been pooled the Western fronts could have
been held. It is true enough that during Stilicho's ascendancy

friction between the Eastern and the Western governments materially aided Alaric's ambitions, and that thereafter the Eastern emperors only gave spasmodic help to the West. A few regiments were sent by Theodosius II to Honorius' aid in Italy; the usurper John was crushed and Valentinian III installed; three expeditions were sent against the Vandals in Africa, the last on a very big scale, and Anthemius was furnished with some troops by Leo. Much more might have been done if one emperor had ruled the whole empire, but it is doubtful whether one man could have effectively controlled both the East and the West in the political and military conditions of the time, when communications were so slow and crises so frequent and so sudden. Whenever by any chance the control of the empire did devolve upon a single ruler, he always in fact delegated the government of a part to a colleague or colleagues, equal or subordinate to himself. When Constantine had eliminated all his rivals, he divided the administration of the empire between his sons and nephews as Caesars. When Constantius II moved west to attack the usurper Magnentius, he left the East in charge of the Caesar Gallus, and when he moved east again he entrusted the defence of the Gauls to the Caesar Julian. When Valentinian was elected the army forthwith demanded that he appoint a colleague. Theodosius I left his elder son Arcadius in charge of the East when he marched west against successive usurpers, and divided the empire at his death between his two sons. It seems to have been regarded as axiomatic that two emperors at least were required to cope with the dangers which threatened on the Rhine, the Danube and the Euphrates.

It is moreover arguable that the resources of the Eastern parts might have been exhausted, and the West have none the less been lost. When Justinian did reconquer Africa and Italy he seems to have found them a heavy burden, and though Africa ultimately proved to be an asset under Heraclius, Italy was a constant drain on the empire's resources. Nor did the Western dioceses find unitary government an unmixed blessing. The emperors at Constantinople naturally gave the Eastern and Danube fronts priority, and starved Italy and Africa of troops and money.

The constitution of the empire has been criticised for its failure to provide a clear rule for the succession to the throne, and thus permitting, if not encouraging, usurpations. For the third century the charge has some substance, but from the time of Diocletian the college of emperors provided the continuity required. When a member of the college died, his colleague or colleagues appointed his successor: they could also nominate their successors in advance. Only if the college became extinct did the choice of an emperor devolve upon the senate and the army. From Constantine onwards the hereditary principle was *de facto* followed. It evidently accorded with the sentiment of the army and made for stability, though it produced minorities and incompetent rulers. Unfortunately dynasties were short-lived: those of Constantine and Valentinian I lasted only two generations, those of Theodosius and Justin I three. Nevertheless these families built up a certain tradition of loyalty.

It is true that the empire too often dissipated its strength in civil wars, but in this respect its record from the fourth century was far better than it had been in the third. Diocletian maintained internal peace for twenty years, broken only by two revolts—those of Carausius in Britain and of Domitius Domitianus in Egypt. After his death there was an orgy of civil wars until Constantine finally conquered Licinius in 324. Thereafter the record of the Eastern parts is strikingly good. Apart from the rather feeble attempt of Procopius to challenge Valens there was no rebellion until the reign of Zeno, who lacked both dynastic and personal prestige. He had to face three revolts, those of Basiliscus, Marcian and Illus' protégé Leontius. He mastered them all, but left Anastasius the task of reducing the Isaurians to obedience: Anastasius later, by his unpopular religious policy, supplied a pretext for the rebellion of Vitalian. After this there was no attempt at usurpation until the mutiny which brought Phocas to the throne.

In the East not only were legitimate emperors rarely challenged but when an emperor had not already designated his successor, an election was held in a constitutional manner, and its result accepted. The record of the West is by no means so good. Constantine II and Constans fought one another, Magnentius murdered Constans, Julian usurped the title of Augustus, Magnus Maximus rebelled against Gratian and Arbogast put up Eugenius against Valentinian II. Under Honorius there was a crop of tyrants— Attalus, Constantine and Jovinus, and after his death John. After the death of Valentinian III emperors were set up and deposed with bewildering rapidity. In Africa there were a series of local pretenders—Firmus, Gildo, Heraclian, Boniface.

All these usurpations provoked civil wars, some minor, some of major importance. Several involved the forces of the East; Theodosius the Great had to subdue Maximus and Eugenius, Theodosius II John, and in all three cases the struggle was severe and the losses heavy, especially to the Western armies, which were defeated. It is hard to see why rebellions were so much more rife in the West than in the East. One reason may be that in the West the incompetence of a feeble emperor was more glaringly revealed because he had greater difficulties to face. The disasters of Honorius' reign invited usurpers to take over the defence of the empire; his equally feeble brother and nephew did not have their incompetence put to the test. But probably the principal reason for the greater stability of the Eastern empire was that monarchy was more deeply rooted there, and respect for royal authority had a longer tradition behind it. The Greek East had lived under kings from time immemorial, and had promptly hailed Augustus and his successors as kings.

Apart from usurpations, which were due to the ambition of individuals, some modern historians have seen a growth of regional or national sentiment in the later empire, and a tendency of outlying provinces to break away from the empire. The evidence for such a view is very tenuous. There is the alleged revolt of Britain and Armorica in 408, which was more probably an attempt at self help, when the emperor, who incidentally was the usurper Constantine, failed to do his duty and protect his subjects from the barbarians. There is the election of Avitus by the senators of Gaul; but Avitus had no intention of founding an *imperium Galliarum*, but promptly marched to Rome. The revolts of Firmus and Gildo have also been regarded as nationalist risings because their leaders came of a Moorish princely family. But there is nothing in the history of the family which suggests that its members were not merely ambitious careerists. Gildo aided the Roman government to crush his brother Firmus, and was himself subdued by his brother Mascazel.[5]

The only other evidence adduced for the theory is the virulence and stubbornness of certain regional heresies, notably Donatism in Africa and monophysitism in Egypt and Syria. That local loyalty played a large part in the devotion of many Africans to the Donatist cause and of most Egyptians to the monophysite faith may be granted; the case of Syria is much more disputable. It is also true that the Donatists and monophysites execrated those emperors who persecuted them, and violently resisted attempts to impose catholic or orthodox bishops upon them. This resistance certainly imposed an additional burden upon the imperial armies; very few orthodox patriarchs of Alexandria could be installed or hold their own without the backing of several regiments of troops. But evidence is entirely lacking that either sect envisaged secession from the empire, or gave welcome or support to the empire's enemies. If the Donatists had supported the Vandals, we should certainly have heard of it from Victor Vitensis and the other African catholics who told of the tribulations of the faithful under the Vandal kings. We know from Coptic sources that the Persian invaders of Egypt under Heraclius were remembered not as liberators but as scourges of God, and John of Niciu took a similar view of the Arabs. The only religious minority which showed active hostility to the Roman government was the Jews, and they seem to have been goaded into opposition only by Justinian's ruthless measures. The Jews of Naples were the backbone of the city's resistance to Belisarius, and the Jews of the East took advantage of the Persian invasion under Phocas to turn upon their Christian oppressors and rejoiced in the defeat of Heraclius' armies by the Arabs.[6]

The army of the later empire has been criticised on many counts. On two at any rate the imperial government cannot be accused of negligence. In the first place it enormously increased the size of the army. Reliable figures are lacking, but it is certain that Diocletian increased numbers very substantially, and it seems likely that before the end of the fourth century the army was twice as large as it had been in the second. This was no mean achievement, but the recruitment of so large a force, despite the free use of barbarian soldiers, put a heavy strain on the manpower of the empire, while its maintenance greatly overtaxed its economic resources. In the second place, in order to meet the requirements of a situation where mobility was essential, the imperial government greatly increased the proportion of cavalry to infantry. This change added substantially to the expense of maintenance: for the fodder of a horse cost as much as the rations of a man.

How far these huge forces were used to the best advantage is questionable, but the general strategic principle was sound. Under the Principate the whole army had been evenly distributed round the frontier and there was no reserve. If a major crisis developed or if offensive operations were undertaken, a temporary concentration of troops was formed by withdrawing detachments from the quiet sectors of the front. In the relatively peaceful conditions which prevailed under the Principate such a system was possible; its success indeed is a proof that pressure on the frontier cannot have been heavy. When pressure increased in the third century the defence of the empire broke down. Diocletian, still clinging to the old strategy, endeavoured to restore the situation by greatly strengthening the frontier forces, but even an army of double the size could not have manned the frontier in sufficient force to hold the much heavier and more frequent attacks which the empire had now to face. Constantine was certainly wise in developing the imperial *comitatus* into a substantial mobile reserve, which could be rushed to any sector which had been breached.

Successive emperors increased the size of the *comitatus*, but its unity was not maintained after Constantine's death. The division of the field army into several groups was partly a consequence of the political division of the empire, but it was also dictated by sound strategic reasons. The empire was too large and communications were too slow for a single reserve to cover all the fronts, and it proved necessary to create regional reserves for the Rhine, the upper and the lower Danube and the Eastern frontier, in addition to the central reserves at the disposal of the emperors. The system was sound enough in principle, but it was in the fifth century carried to excess in the West, where regional reserves were formed for Africa, Spain and Britain, and became too rigid in the East, where the army of Oriens, which for the long periods of peace with Persia had little work to do, does not seem to have been used for the pressing needs of the Danube front. In both East and West moreover the regiments of the field army tended increasingly to be used for garrison duty in the interior and ceased to be mobile.

By withdrawing the best units from the frontier to serve in the *comitatus* Constantine somewhat weakened the *limitanei* from their peak strength under Diocletian, but the frontier armies at the end of the fourth century remained considerably more numerous than they had been under the Principate, when they formed the sole defence of the empire. They could no longer be expected to withstand major attacks, but they remained essential if the provinces were to be protected against constant small-scale raids. Without them the barbarians would have extended their ravages further and further into the interior, and the empire would have been destroyed by gradual attrition.

On the quality of the imperial armies it is difficult to judge. Vegetius repeatedly laments their degeneracy in his day, but he was an antiquarian and a *laudator temporis acti*. As all readers of Tacitus know, the Roman army of the Principate was not impeccable. The troops sometimes mutinied; they sometimes panicked and fled before the enemy; they were very prone to ravage a friendly countryside and to sack Roman towns when occasion offered. Discipline was slack in legions stationed in towns, and the men were allowed to neglect their military duties and follow civil avocations. Centurions used their authority to extort money from their men. Nevertheless the army of the Principate was on the whole a very efficient force. Similar abuses flourished in the army of the later empire, almost certainly on a larger scale, but it does not necessarily follow that its fighting quality was seriously impaired,

In two respects the later Roman army was superior to that of
the Principate. In the first place it was on the whole better officered.
Under the Principate both commanders of regiments and generals
of armies had been in the main civilians holding temporary commissions, and few of them remained long enough in their posts to
acquire experience. In the later empire most officers were professional soldiers. Regimental commanders were not uncommonly
promoted from the ranks, and generals were usually chosen from
officers who had proved their ability in command of regiments.
In the second place the later Roman army was remarkably obedient
to its commanders, and did not exploit its position to hold the
government to ransom. Though much worse off than under the
Principate the troops never tried to extort an increase of pay or
even a larger donative from the government: the rates of both
remained static for over three centuries. It was only when under
Justinian their pay fell into long arrears that some units mutinied
or deserted, and the military rebellions under Maurice were provoked by his attempts to reduce pay and make the conditions of
service more onerous.[7]

The *limitanei*, having become second-class troops, certainly
declined in efficiency. They received recruits of inferior quality
and were too often commanded by officers whose main objective
was to make money. It was among them that administrative abuses
were rampant, and the government found it difficult to maintain
their numbers and discipline. Their deterioration has however
been greatly exaggerated by modern historians, and in the sixth
century the government not only thought it worth while to maintain them on the Danubian and Eastern fronts, but tried to recreate
them in the reconquered provinces of Africa.[8]

The field army, on the other hand, received the best recruits
and officers of better quality. To judge by its battle record it remained a tolerably efficient fighting force. Under good leadership
Roman armies could still defeat barbarian hordes which far outnumbered them, as the victories of Stilicho over Alaric and Radagaesus and of Belisarius over the Vandals and Ostrogoths amply
demonstrate.

Both in antiquity and in modern times the emperors have been
severely criticised for relying to excess on German troops and
German officers. Stilicho, after his fall, was denounced as a traitor.
Synesius, in his address to Arcadius, enlarges on the folly of en-
trusting the defence of the flock to the very wolves who raven
against it, and eloquently urges the formation of an exclusively
national army of Roman citizens.

A study of the history of the empire suggests that both criticisms are ill-founded. Some German generals were politically ambitious and like Stilicho or Gainas held, or aspired to hold, supreme power under a faineant emperor, or even, like Arbogast and Ricimer in the West or Aspar in the East, put up puppet emperors; some like the last named coveted the purple for their sons. But generals of Roman birth, like Constantius or Aetius or Illus, did the like, and no career officer of German origin—as opposed to tribal chieftains like Alaric and the two Theoderics who extorted high military commands from the government—is ever known to have betrayed the interests of the empire to his countrymen. The same applies to the rank and file. There is no hint in our sources that Germans recruited into the regular army and properly administered and disciplined were ever unreliable. The trouble was caused when, from the time of Theodosius the Great, barbarian tribes which had forced their way into the empire were given the status of federates. The Roman government was perhaps unwise in inviting refugee tribes to settle within the empire, as did Marcian after the fall of the Hunnic empire, but in general it was making the best of a bad job when it tried to use as federates tribes which had broken in and which it had not the strength to expel or destroy.[9]

An attempt has been made to prove that the fall of the empire in the West was due to the decay of trade and industry. The argument runs that in the early Principate Italy had flourished by manufacturing and exporting products such as Arretine ware to the provinces. Later such products were manufactured locally in the provinces, and Italian industry decayed and trade withered away. Finally the provincial industries, unable to expand beyond the frontiers, themselves decayed. It is difficult to see the force of this argument, assuming that the facts were as alleged. There never had been a large-scale export trade beyond the frontier; imports had always been paid for mainly in coin, and their volume was hardly significant in relation to the wealth of the empire. In so far as industry was decentralised within the frontiers of the empire there was no net loss: what Italian manufacturers lost, provincial manufacturers gained. If, as would appear, goods could be as cheaply and efficiently made in the provinces as in Italy, there was in fact a net saving in that the costs of transport were eliminated. Trade in manufactured articles may have declined, as did trade in certain agricultural products; as viticulture was extended to new areas, the wine trade must have declined. But trade is not a good thing in itself; it adds to the community's wealth only in so far as it supplies areas with goods which they lack or can only produce at high cost.[10]

In fact it is very doubtful whether there ever had been any large-scale inter-provincial trade. The evidence suggests that the production of one commodity of basic importance, clothing, had always been decentralised. Workaday clothes for the poor and sound medium fabrics suitable for army uniforms seem always to have been woven locally in every city and indeed village, and it was only silk and very high-quality woollens and linens that were manufactured in a limited number of towns and exported to distant markets.[11]

There continued to be a brisk trade in such high-grade fabrics down to the seventh century from end to end of the Mediterranean, and there is no sign that the demand for other luxury goods diminished, or that supply fell off. There may have been some contraction of the market for medium priced and cheap goods owing to the impoverishment of the peasantry and the urban working class and the lower strata of the *curiales*. But the decline of trade and industry, in so far as there was a decline, was a result and not a cause of a general economic recession. Finally it was of very marginal importance. Even in the Eastern parts, where their importance was admittedly greater and their decay less marked, trade and industry made a minute contribution to the national income.[12]

That there was some recession in the major industry of the empire—agriculture—cannot be disputed. The laws about *agri deserti* prove that land once cultivated was being abandoned from the third century to the sixth, and the few figures available show that in some areas where conditions were particularly unfavourable, such as Africa, the loss by the fifth century was enormous, up to 50 per cent., and that in others which there is no reason to think exceptional it amounted to some 10 per cent. or 15 per cent. The decline may have been in some areas due to exhaustion of the soil by overcropping, in others to the progress of denudation: sometimes it may have been due to lack of labour. Some of the loss was attributable to the direct pressure of the barbarians, whose continual razzias made cultivation unprofitable if not impracticable in the exposed border provinces. The principal cause of the progressive abandonment of land was, however, as contemporaries held, the heavy and increasing load of taxation, which on land of marginal value absorbed so much of the rent that landlords could make no profit, and might incur a loss. In so far as the high taxation was caused by the heavy military expenditure of the empire, the decline of agriculture was thus indirectly caused by barbarian pressure.[13]

The extent of the decline must not be exaggerated. Taken as a whole the area was not very large, and the loss in yield was less, since it was the least productive land that was abandoned, and moreover much land officially registered as uncultivated continued to be worked by landlords or local authorities responsible for the taxes, in order that the product should at least help to cover them. Against the areas abandoned must also be set some areas which were brought under cultivation for the first time during the same period. It must be emphasised that there was no general agricultural decline; land of good and medium quality continued to pay high taxes, yield high rents and command high prices.

Depopulation has been regarded as a major factor in the decline of the empire. Unfortunately our information is so vague, and facts and figures are so sparse that it is impossible to calculate what the population of the empire was at any date, or how much it declined, if, as is very probable if not certain, it did decline. All we can do is to note certain demographic trends, and speculate about their causes.[14]

The population of the empire undoubtedly was, and always had been, very small by modern standards. Figures for the *annona* suggest that the inhabitants of Rome numbered between half and three-quarters of a million in the early fourth century and that Constantinople had reached about the same figure in the sixth. Alexandria, the third city of the empire, was to judge by its *annona* half the size of Constantinople in the sixth century. Libanius gives the figure of 150,000 and John Chrysostom 200,000 for Antioch, probably the fourth city of the empire. These figures for the largest towns, however, even if they were reliable, are not of much use in estimating a population which was predominantly rural, and figures for the rural population are even more difficult to find. At the end of the first century the population of Egypt, excluding Alexandria, numbered, according to a reliable source, seven and a half millions, and it was certainly not greater under the later empire. For the Civitas Aeduorum in the reign of Constantine we have a precise figure: the number of *capita* registered in a recent census was, according to a contemporary local orator, 32,000. The orator's words clearly imply that this figure included women, but not young children (by analogy with other parts of the empire we may exclude those under twelve or fourteen). We must then add half as much again for the children, reaching a total of about 50,000. Unfortunately we do not know whether the Gallic *capitatio* included the urban as well as the rural population. The Civitas Aeduorum was one of the larger of the hundred and twenty cities of Gaul: the exact extent of its territory at this date is not certain but has been plausibly calculated at one forty-eighth of the area comprised between the Rhine, the Alps, the Pyrenees and the Atlantic ocean. The total rural population of this area, perhaps its total population, would then have been less than two and a half millions.[15]

We know something of the age distribution of the population from tombstones. Their evidence is incomplete, for they exclude the very poor, who could not afford tombstones; women also are less well recorded than men, and on children the evidence is so incomplete as to be useless. There are minor variations between different areas and between town and country, but broadly speaking the same pattern emerges everywhere, and there is no significant difference between the Principate and the later empire. This pattern is markedly different from that of modern European countries, and coincides very closely with that of India at the beginning of this century. The death-rate was uniformly high at all ages from ten, below which we have no adequate data; judging by modern analogies the infant and child death-rate would have been very much greater than that of adults. The female death-rate was substantially higher than the male, especially in the child-bearing years. Thus in Africa, of 100 boys of ten 85 survived to 22, 74 to 32, 58 to 42, 47 to 52, and 36 to 62. For girls the corresponding percentages were 73, 54, 47, 39 and 28. A population with so high a death-rate would have required a very high birth-rate even to maintain its numbers, and modern populations of a similar structure have in fact very high birth rates.[16]

Though it is at first sight startling that the population of the Roman empire should have been similar to that of India fifty years ago, it is on reflection not unnatural. Conditions were basically similar. The Roman empire was a country of peasants, who lived near subsistence level. Their resistance to disease must have been weakened by chronic malnutrition. Medical science was primitive and doctors few. The threat of famine was always near.

Such populations are normally very resilient, rapidly recovering from any but the severest checks caused by massacres, famines or epidemics. They tend generally to increase up to the maximum number that the country can support at subsistence level. The ceiling is fixed naturally not only by the gross amount of food available, but by its distribution; if more than the minimum is consumed by some sections of the population, the number which can be supported at subsistence level will be reduced.

There are many indications that there was a chronic shortage of manpower in the later empire. It must have been for this reason that the government forbade workers in essential industries—miners, armourers, weavers and dyers in the state factories, and above all agricultural workers—to leave their occupations, reclaimed them when they strayed from them, and compelled their children to follow their fathers' occupation. The labour shortage is most manifest on the land. It is plain that landlords were perennially short of tenants to cultivate their land. They were always ready to accept barbarian prisoners of war as *coloni*. They would rather pay 25 or 30 solidi, more than the normal price of a slave, than give up a *colonus* as a recruit to the army. They hunted down their *coloni* when they escaped, and despite all penalties they welcomed fugitive *coloni* from other estates. The laws tying *coloni* to the soil were never relaxed, but were, on the contrary, tightened. Anastasius tied free tenants to their farms if they stayed more than thirty years. When Justinian declared the son of a free woman by a *colonus adscripticius* to be free, he was bombarded by protests from landowners, who declared that their estates were being deserted. The shortage of labour on the land was not, so far as we can see, due to a movement from the country to the towns: the movement was rather in the opposite direction. *Coloni* normally, the laws imply, moved to another farm if they left their own. Miners and urban craftsmen often had to be reclaimed from the land.[17]

This of course does not necessarily mean that the population shrank. A labour shortage may be caused either by a decline in the supply or by an increase in the demand for manpower, and in the later empire there were greater demands for manpower by the church, the civil service and above all the army. It may seem absurd to suggest that an army of 650,000 men could have strained the manpower resources of an empire which stretched from the Western Ocean to the Euphrates, especially as a substantial number of the recruits were barbarians from outside the frontiers; and as compared with those of the army the demands of the civil service and the church were negligible. But it must not be forgotten how sparsely inhabited the vast area of the empire was by modern standards. Increase of the demand may therefore have made a significant contribution to the labour shortage from which the later Roman empire suffered.

There is however proof that the population did sink. As we have seen progressively less land was cultivated, and less food must therefore have been produced. The empire never either imported foodstuffs or produced a surplus for export. Since consumption per head could hardly sink for the mass of the population, who were already near subsistence level, the population must have grown smaller. There was moreover an increasing maldistribution of the diminishing quantity of food which was produced. Soldiers enjoyed ample rations—their consumption was perhaps twice as much as that of poor peasants—and civil servants and most of the clergy were at least as well fed. As the army, the civil service and the clergy increased in numbers, the proportion of the total amount which was left for the mass of the population sank, and their numbers must have sunk correspondingly.

The reasons for the decline are more difficult to determine. There was a great plague under Marcus Aurelius, which recurred from time to time during the third century: outbreaks are recorded under Gallus in 251, under Gallienus about 261, and under Claudius in 271. It is probable that this plague had spent its force by Diocletian's reign. No other great plague is recorded—and such events are noted even in the baldest chronicles—until the bubonic plague which swept the empire in Justinian's reign from 542 onwards.[18]

There were of course many local disasters which reduced the population. Barbarian raiders sometimes massacred the inhabitants, but more often they carried them off; and though many such prisoners no doubt died in exile, more were ransomed or sold as slaves within the empire. Barbarian devastation produced famines, which were followed by epidemics. Famines also occurred from natural causes, droughts or invasions of locusts, and these too were often followed by epidemics. Modern analogies, however, suggest that a population of the type of that of the Roman empire should have had a very high birth rate, and ought to have recovered rapidly from such temporary and local losses.

One is driven to the conclusion that the population dwindled because, when they had paid their rent and taxes and other exactions, the peasantry had not enough left to rear sufficient children to counterbalance the very high death-rate. What evidence we have supports this hypothesis. We know that the land tax which the peasant proprietor paid had reached over a third of his gross product by Justinian's reign, and that the rents paid by the tenant farmer were substantially more, in Egypt at least half. Poor parents were often driven to infanticide. In 315 Constantine ordered the publication throughout Italy of a law 'which may withhold the hands of parents from murder'; any parent who produced 'a child which he could not rear because of poverty' was to be forthwith issued with food and clothing, 'since the raising of a newborn infant does not admit delay'. The sale of newborn infants had become so common that, contrary to the principles of Roman law, it was officially permitted by Diocletian's day, and the poor, despite the law, commonly sold or pledged their older children. The practice is alluded to by Constantine in another alimentary law, and is frequently mentioned in hagiographical tales and in the papyri. Cassiodorus states that there was a regular market for peasants' children at a great fair in southern Italy.[19]

Perhaps the most significant sign, however, of the poverty of the peasantry, and of the reason for it, is the fact that in times of famine they flocked to the towns for bread, and were often fed from stocks held by the government or the landowners. So ruthless and efficient was the collection of rents and taxes that, however poor the crop, the quantity due to the state and the landlords was carried off to town, and the peasants might be left with little or nothing for their own needs.[20]

How many children died of malnutrition or deficiency diseases we have no means of estimating, but the record of nine complete peasant households preserved in the early fourth-century census lists of western Asia Minor suggests that few children survived and also that the general mortality rate was high and that men married late in life. There is only one fair-sized family, a man (aged 65) with a wife and three sons and one daughter, ranging from 6 to 14. A widower of 56 has two sons under four years of age, he also keeps a woman of 48 and a boy of three, labelled orphans or foundlings. A couple aged 30 have a three-years-old son and keep two other boys, one apparently a nephew. An older couple (aged 60 and 52) have a son and a daughter. A widow has an adult son and a daughter of eleven. A widow of 20 has a baby girl of two. A widower has one son of 11, and another, aged 40, a son of 20; he also keeps a woman of 30, perhaps a sister, perhaps a second wife. Finally there is a bachelor of 20, living alone.[21]

The condition of the urban poor, though they were much more lightly taxed, was no better. They too were frequently, almost regularly, it would seem, driven to sell their children to pay the *collatio lustralis*. They too in times of shortage had to be supplied with cheap bread at the expense of the city authorities. It seems unlikely that they could have reared large families, and in towns, as the statistics drawn from tombstones show, the general rate of mortality was substantially higher than in the country. Though in some parts of the West, notably Italy and Gaul, there was an exodus of urban workers to the countryside, the reason was not that the population of the towns had grown, but that urban industry was on the decline and there was not enough employment even for a shrinking number of workers.

Neither the poverty of the peasantry and the urban working class, nor the decline of the population, must be exaggerated,

There were many prosperous peasants and craftsmen, and many more who led a tolerable existence. It would, however, appear that as a whole they could not rear enough children to maintain the population against the very high death-rate prevailing. The population fairly certainly sank, but if the decrease may be measured by the amount of land abandoned, it was not in most areas catastrophic.

The basic economic weakness of the empire was that too few producers supported too many idle mouths. This state of affairs was in part an inheritance from the Principate, in part imposed by increasing barbarian pressure, in part again due to the incompetence of the government, in part finally to the new religion which the empire adopted.

The later empire inherited a number of extravagances from the more prosperous days of the Principate. It still provided a free ration of bread (and of pork in season) to 120,000 citizens of Rome: the number was only about half that of the *plebs frumentaria* under the Principate, but Constantine instituted a similar free issue to 80,000 citizens of Constantinople, and here the number of beneficiaries was subsequently increased. A few major provincial cities enjoyed a similar privilege, Alexandria, Antioch and perhaps Carthage; the first of these received it from Diocletian.[22]

Another body of idle consumers inherited from the Principate was the senatorial order. Though numerically small it was immensely rich, and absorbed a disproportionate share of the national income. Each senator directly maintained an army of slaves to minister to his wants, and indirectly employed a great number of artists, craftsmen and merchants to supply him with luxury goods. The later emperors made little attempt to reduce the wealth of the senatorial order by special taxation, and weakly granted it fiscal privileges. They also vastly increased the numbers of the order, and lavishly enriched its members, old and new, by allowing them to make huge illicit profits from the offices which they held, and by bestowing upon them extravagant gifts of gold and land. The huge and ever-growing wealth which the aristocracy enjoyed was in the main derived from the estates which they inherited, bought or received as gifts from the crown, and was a direct charge on the peasantry.[23]

Under the Principate the local aristocracies of the cities had constituted a second class of rentiers, far larger numerically but individually much less wealthy than the senatorial order. This class shrank both in numbers and in wealth under the later empire, as its richer members moved up into the senatorial aristocracy and its poorer members sold their estates, usually to the imperial aristocracy, while others found their way into the civil service, the church or the professions. The land which the curial aristocracy had held under the Principate thus partly went to swell the estates of the senatorial order and partly provided unearned incomes to the professional middle class, while part was still held by the surviving *curiales*. It still contributed to the maintenance of economically idle mouths, whatever its vicissitudes.[24]

The later empire also inherited from the Principate a professional standing army and civil service. It doubled the size of the former and vastly expanded the latter. For these increases in the number of idle mouths the pressure of the barbarians was largely responsible, directly or indirectly. The empire was obliged to maintain far larger armed forces, and the increased strain put on its fiscal and administrative system by the maintenance of a much bigger army goes far to explain the expansion of the civil service. It must be admitted, it is true, that the government did not make the most efficient use of its military expenditure, allowing too much of it to be absorbed by the peculations of the officers, and wasting too many troops on internal security. It must also be admitted that it allowed the numbers of the civil service to expand beyond the real needs of the administration, and its emoluments, licit and illicit, to grow inordinately. Nevertheless, however efficiently the government had used its resources, it would have been obliged to burden the economy of the empire with a greatly increased army to resist the barbarians, and a larger civil service to administer it and provide for its multifarious requirements.

Finally the Christian church imposed a new class of idle mouths on the resources of the empire. The pagan gods had, it is true, owned some land, whose revenue helped to maintain their temples and to support their cult, but except in Egypt and at a few famous shrines its amount was small, and nowhere outside Egypt did a large body of endowed priests exist. The Christian church from the time of Constantine accumulated ever-growing endowments in land, and from their rents and from the firstfruits of the faithful maintained an increasing number of full-time stipendiary clergy. By the sixth century the bishops and clergy had become far more numerous than the administrative officers and civil servants of the empire, and were on the average paid at substantially higher rates. In addition to the clergy there were many thousands of monks and hermits. Not all of these were idle mouths. The inmates of the Pachomian houses of Egypt produced a surplus, and many monks and hermits just earned their keep. But a large number lived on the alms of the peasantry, and as time went on more and more monasteries acquired landed endowments which enabled their inmates to devote themselves entirely to their spiritual duties.[25]

None of these classes was economically productive. All of them drew the bulk of their incomes in one form or another from the land, by way of rents, the land tax or firstfruits. Most of them enjoyed a standard of living higher than that of the peasantry. Some, like the richer senators and the best-endowed bishops, had vast revenues; even the humblest, common soldiers, lower civil servants, the lesser clergy and the monks were for the most part substantially better off than the peasantry. The burden proved too heavy for agriculture to bear. The higher rate of taxation led to the progressive abandonment of marginal land once cultivated, and many of the peasants, after paying their rents or taxes, had too little food left to rear their children, and the number of the producers thus slowly shrank.

In estimating the burden one must remember that the Roman empire was technologically as backward as medieval Europe, and in some important aspects more so. Spinning was done with the primitive distaff and spindle, weaving on hand looms. Pottery was turned on the wheel, metal work hammered out on the anvil. In agriculture so simple a device as the wheelbarrow had not been invented; since the horse collar had not been discovered, the ox, a very slow beast, was used for ploughing. The crops were reaped by hand with the sickle; Palladius indeed mentions a reaping machine propelled by oxen, which was already known to Pliny, but it was very wasteful of grain, and was only used on the great Gallic estates, where weather conditions might make speed essential.[26]

Some other mechanical devices, invented in the first century B.C. or earlier, were more commonly used in the later empire. The Apions supplied wheeled machines by the score to their tenants for raising water; these were probably sakkias, driven by oxen, which saved the long hours of human labour required by the shaduf (still commoner than the sakkia in Egypt). Water mills for grinding grain, still a curiosity in the reign of Augustus, had become more common during the third century: Diocletian, in his tariff, fixed prices for the construction of hand, donkey, horse and water mills (250, 1250, 1500 and 2000 denarii respectively), and Palladius in his handbook on agriculture recommends the last. Rome, which was in the first and probably the second centuries dependent on donkey mills, had, by the fourth century, gone over to water mills. Nevertheless, to judge by paucity of archaeological remains and of allusions in literature, and the absence of any rules on water rights in the law, water mills cannot have been very common. In the Mediterranean area suitable streams with a perennial even flow are not very common; at Rome waterpower was obtained from the aqueducts and the Tiber was only harnessed by an ingenious device, invented by Belisarius, when the aqueducts were cut by the Goths during the siege of 537-8. In most towns the bakers probably used donkey mills, and in the countryside the hand quern was still widely employed, as archaeology testifies.[27]

But the greatest incubus on the empire was the primitive means of transport. Food, clothing and arms had to be carried to the great armies on the frontier, often for hundreds of miles, and except in so far as inland waterways could be utilised all this vast load had to be hauled by slow moving ox wagons.

All this meant that the amount of human labour required to feed, clothe and supply with his household needs one idle mouth was very large. The Romans have been criticised for their uninventiveness and lack of enterprise. The economic situation clearly demanded labour saving devices, for there was a manifest shortage of manpower, whether slave or free. The anonymous inventor of the oxen driven paddle-boat seems to have been conscious of this; for he boasts that it will be effective 'without the assistance of any large crew', and he also claims that his artillery could be operated by two men only. There existed moreover a fund of theoretical scientific knowledge, on steam power for instance, which was familiar to philosophers and to learned *mechanici* like Anthemius of Tralles.[28]

It is however hardly reasonable to single out the Roman empire for criticism on this score. Until the scientific and industrial revolution which began in the eighteenth century mechanical invention had been in all civilisations excessively rare, and the Romans do not compare unfavourably with the Chinese, the Indians, or with medieval Christendom or Islam. It is only by a rare combination of economic stimulus, scientific knowledge and technological skill—and, it may be added, the genius of an inventor—that practicable inventions are made and exploited. In some ways the social structure of the empire was unfavourable to invention. The skilled workers were humble craftsmen without education, who naturally followed the tradition of their trade. The bias of education was overwhelmingly literary, and its products were mostly uninterested in scientific knowledge: the church condemned scientific thought as worldly vanity. It was only in medicine and in military and civil engineering that educated practitioners existed. It is perhaps significant that highly efficient siege engines were developed and that water power was exploited for sawing marble.[29]

The social regimentation of the empire has been severely criticised as conducive to apathy and inertia and destructive of enterprise. It is true that the imperial government persistently strove by legislation and coercive measures to tie certain classes, with their children, to their occupations. The tied classes fell into two main groups. There were those whose labour or personal services were primarily required; these included soldiers, agricultural workers, urban craftsmen, miners, the workers in the state factories and the public post. There were others whose capital assets, that is in general their land, were earmarked for certain purposes: these included the *navicularii*, the bakers and butchers of Rome, and the decurions. In these cases the servitude was sometimes, as with the *navicularia functio*, legally attached to the land, and fell on whoever acquired it; sometimes, as with decurions, was legally hereditary. In practice the obligation normally went in all cases from father to son, since the land generally passed by inheritance.

The distinction between the two groups is not always absolutely clear cut. Decurions owed *munera personalia* as well as *munera patrimonalia*, and were only in rare cases allowed to perform the former by deputy. The property of *fabricenses* and *conchylioleguli* was tied, since it served the government as a guarantee fund, from which it could recover in cases of malfeasance or peculation. Lower civil servants were required for clerical work, but their property was also tied for the same reason as was that of *fabricenses*.

The origins of these tied classes and the reasons for their creation are usually obscure. In some cases the government was merely enforcing its legal rights. The weavers and dyers in the state factories, the workers in the mints, the postal personnel and some grades of lower civil servants, such as the *Caesariani*, were by origin and remained technically state slaves. The state naturally used its proprietary rights over them and their children to conserve its labour force. Soldiers, and civil servants and *fabricenses*, who ranked as *milites*, had of course always been obliged to complete their term of service until legally discharged and could be punished for desertion. In extending the obligation to their sons Diocletian was making universal and compulsory a very old and widespread custom of hereditary service.[30]

In other cases, such as the *navicularii* and the Roman bakers and butchers, privileges had in the past been given to capitalists who invested their wealth in certain occupations useful to the state, and the imperial government came to regard these privileges as imposing an obligation on their holders. It was in this spirit that Constantine justified the conscription of veterans' sons: 'because of the privileges granted to their fathers we do not allow the sons of veterans to be idle'. In the same spirit Constans in 349 enacted: 'all the clergy ought to be free from curial burdens and all the trouble of civil functions, but their sons, if they are not held liable to the *curia*, ought to persevere in the church'. This attempt to make the clergy a hereditary caste was not however pursued.[31]

Decurions had, during the Principate, been in practice a largely hereditary class, since they comprised the richest landowners in each city, and their estates normally passed by inheritance to their sons. Membership of the *curia* was already by the early third century compulsory for any qualified person duly nominated unless he could claim a legal exemption. Diocletian and his successors did no more than tighten up the rules by restricting the exemptions, and thus gradually cutting off most legal avenues of escape.[32]

It is more difficult to see on what principles the government tied down urban craftsmen, miners and the agricultural population. It can only be said that in all civilisations miners have usually been a hereditary group, and peasant proprietors have clung to their holdings and passed them on to their sons. There is also evidence that under the Principate the tenants of large states went on holding their farms from generation to generation. In Egypt at any rate the Roman government, already in second century, held that it had the right to order peasants to return to their own place and cultivate the soil.[33]

It would seem that under the Principate society was largely static: on the whole men of all classes followed their father's way of life. There was some degree of social mobility but the government, except in very rare cases, felt no need to check it. From the reign of Diocletian onwards, on the other hand, the emperors were constantly endeavouring to hold certain classes, whose work or whose wealth was essential to the state, to their normal and hereditary functions. The inference is that on the one hand there was a manpower shortage, which encouraged mobility of labour, and on the other hand that the burden on the propertied groups increased and that they sought to evade it.

What little evidence there is suggests that these conditions existed. The wars and plagues of the third century must have reduced the population and at the same time there was the increased demand for men by the army. The resulting shortage of agricultural manpower evidently tempted tenants to move in hopes of better conditions elsewhere, and attracted miners and other industrial workers to the land. In the second place the great inflation must have eaten away the profit margin of such classes as the *navicularii* who were paid in money. The increasing burden of levies in kind, which the collapse of the currency and the growth of the army entailed, must have made the life of the curial class which collected them much more onerous. At the same time the expansion of the administrative machine offered tempting avenues of escape to men of this class.

The government reacted, as most governments do in times of crisis, to the simplest expedient—the use of its powers of coercion to compel the existing workers and property owners to go on performing their essential functions. That the system was from the beginning made hereditary was inevitable. It was the simplest and most obvious course, and any alternative would have been administratively highly complicated. It conformed to the traditional social pattern; the emperors no doubt felt that they were merely preventing deviations from the natural rule. In some cases, that of the decurions, for instance, and of the peasantry, it was based on the ancient principle of *origo*, which was fundamental in Roman law. Once the system was established it tended to be perpetuated, and in some cases extended and in many made more rigid, from the mere force of inertia. The government came to regard it as in itself desirable, and to continue to enforce it when it was no longer necessary; it filled in gaps and stopped up loopholes for the sake of tidiness, and regarded the man who did not fit into the system, the *vagus*, as an undesirable anomaly. But in many spheres the stringency which had dictated the system remained, and any relaxation of it produced alarming results. The laws of Valentinian I and Theodosius I continuing to tie the *coloni* of Illyricum and Thrace after the abolition of the *capitatio*, and the strong reaction against Justinian's law freeing the sons of *coloni* married to free women, show that agricultural manpower was still very short in the late fourth and even in the sixth century.

The theoretical extent and the actual effectiveness of the restrictive legislation have often been exaggerated. The conscription of the sons of soldiers and veterans seems to have been dropped at the end of the fourth century. Constantine ruled that all sons of civil servants should go into their fathers' offices, but the rule was never applied except to the lowest grade, the *cohortales*. Urban craftsmen were not tied to their trades in the West until the end of the fourth century, and were never tied in the East. Diocletian tied all the rural population to the land, but the rule very soon ceased to be applied to peasant proprietors, and came to be limited to *adscripticii* or *originales*, the descendants of tenants originally registered on an estate; it was only at the end of the fifth century that free tenants became tied by thirty years' prescription. There were, moreover, some legal loopholes. *Adscripticii* could, until the early fifth century, legally join the army, and could generally be ordained, at any rate with their masters' consent. Decurions were not debarred from certain professions—medicine, teaching and the law—and could generally take orders provided that they surrendered most of their property: they were also rarely excluded from the higher branches of the government service.

In practice the enforcement of the laws was very lax and unsystematic. Soldiers and *fabricenses* were branded, but there was no system of identity papers whereby those who left their lawful occupations could be traced, and very little attempt was made to verify systematically the antecedents of those who joined any service. The enforcement of the law was left to informers, whose object was usually to extort blackmail rather than to reclaim delinquents, or to interested parties: it was the duty of landlords to trace and reclaim their vagrant *coloni* and of cities to recall errant decurions to the *curia*. All that the government did was to issue laws and order occasional purges and roundups. At long intervals the swollen staff of a palatine ministry would be checked, and *curiales* and *cohortales* expelled (unless they had been for a long time in the service): from time to time there would be a call-up of sons of veterans, and they would be drafted into the army (unless they were already too old for active service).[34]

The laws themselves, by their constant reiteration of the same prohibitions and their frequent condonation of past offences, show how impossible it was without any police to enforce the rules. They also, by their constant denunciation of corrupt practices, show how easy it was to bribe the officials to turn a blind eye. We know too from casual references of a surprisingly large number of cases where the rules were broken with impunity.

In any stable society, however free, the rate of social mobility is low. The average man is content to remain in the station of life in which he was born, and very often to follow the same trade as his father. On the other hand even in the most rigid societies some able and ambitious men succeed in breaking through the legal or social barriers. There was a marked tendency in the later Roman empire for the free professions to become hereditary by the spontaneous desire of their members. We know of many clerical families which produced bishops generation after generation, and of military families which produced a succession of generals. We know of doctors who were sons of doctors and of professors who were sons of professors. Lawyers and higher civil servants sought and obtained from the government preference for their sons, who wished to go to the bar or to the ministry where their fathers had spent their lives. But while the forces which made for social stability were so strong, we know of far more men who rose from humble origins to the highest positions in the state under the later empire than under the Principate. The laws may have been irksome to some ambitious men who were unlucky or lacked the drive to elude them, but they were evidently no serious obstacle to men of ability and determination.[35]

Other historians have attributed the decline of the empire to the gradual elimination of the 'bourgeoisie' or 'middle class', by which term they mean the curial order. It is not clear why the destruction of this class, if and in so far as it was destroyed, should have adversely affected the economic life of the empire. The *curiales* were not, and never had been, creators of wealth. They were rentiers, landlords who were often absentees and did not on the whole, so far as we know, take any active interest in their estates. They were, many of them, men of culture and education, and in so far as they gave their unpaid services to the government and contributed to its cost, fulfilled a useful social role: but they did not increase the wealth of the empire.

It is in fact very questionable whether this class was in any real sense eliminated. The curial order was certainly diminished very greatly in numbers and wealth over the centuries, but this was very largely because *curiales* became senators, *honorati*, civil servants, lawyers and clergy. Some families certainly were crushed by the financial strain, and had to sell their lands, usually to their richer neighbours, and there was thus some tendency for the great landlords to increase their estates at the expense of the lesser. But there always remained a substantial middle class, who mostly owned land. The only difference was that they bore different official titles, and that many of them were in the professions and supplemented their unearned income, with salaries and fees.[36]

The imperial government was very conscious of the abuses of the administrative machine. The Codes are full of laws which endeavour to combat the venality and extortion of provincial governors and officials and to curb the inordinate growth of the bureaucracy. This very fact perhaps makes us exaggerate the extent of the evil, but it cannot be doubted that there was a marked deterioration from the days of the Principate.

Even in its best days the imperial civil service was not impeccable; the few records that we possess reveal that some governors were dishonest and brutal, and inscriptions and papyri show that officials were often guilty of minor extortion from the provincials. Nevertheless respectable standards were in general maintained. The bulk of the routine work of the administration, including the collection of the taxes, was delegated to the cities, and this made it possible to keep the imperial service small and select. A conscientious emperor could pick his men and keep his eye on their conduct, and, since promotion usually depended on a good record, governors and procurators, if they wished for a successful career, had to avoid scandals. They were moreover very liberally paid, and thus had less temptation to make money by illicit means. A tradition was thus built up.[37]

This happy state of affairs was largely dependent on the fact that the imperial civil service was subjected to very little strain. The army was small and largely recruited by voluntary enlistment; the taxes were moderate and normally paid without effort; and the city councils did most of the work without complaint. Much heavier strains were imposed on the administration in the third century. The local gentry, who had regarded it as an honour, or at least a social obligation, to serve on the city councils, now tried to evade service, and the imperial government had to compel them to perform their administrative functions. The taxes, supplemented by frequent levies in kind, became more difficult to exact from a population diminished by plague and impoverished by constant wars. Under these strains the traditional code of the second century seems to have broken down. What was required in governors and procurators was ruthless efficiency rather than scrupulous probity. At the same time the inflation of the currency drastically reduced the real value of their salaries. They had increased opportunities for corruption and extortion, and strong temptation to exploit them.

Diocletian's great expansion of the army redoubled the pressure on the administration. Its numbers had to be increased if it was to levy the men and the supplies required. The rapid expansion of the service must have involved some dilution of quality, and, while under the tetrarchy four emperors could select their men and maintain some control over them, when the whole empire was ruled by two emperors or even one, it was no longer easy for the central government to exercise much discrimination in appointments or to keep a close check on the conduct of the men appointed. Salaries, moreover, remained very low as compared with those of the Principate. It is clear from Constantine's legislation that he was shocked by the corruption and extortion which prevailed among provincial governors, but he was evidently unable to restore respectable standards of probity.

It would appear that a governorship was, except by a few exceptionally scrupulous men, regarded as a financial prize. The best evidence for this is the system of *suffragia*, which first comes to our notice under Constantine and, despite the efforts of successive reforming emperors, proved an ever-spreading and ineradicable evil. It was taken over by the crown under Zeno, who sold posts officially for the benefit of the treasury, and had by his time extended to the second grade of the administrative service, the *spectabiles iudices*. Justinian at a considerable financial sacrifice abolished imperial *suffragia*, but they soon crept back and were prevalent under Maurice.[38]

Not all the men who paid large sums for an appointment were primarily interested in the financial aspect of the deal. Many wished to raise their social status, and in particular to escape from the *curia*. But a large number must have wanted to make money, and even those who did not probably expected to recover their costs. *Suffragia*, moreover, set up a vicious spiral. As the price of office rose by competitive bidding, governors increased their illicit profits, and, as the average profit of a governorship went up, prices rose. By the sixth century an honest man could not serve except at a heavy financial loss.

Many forms of extortion no doubt became traditional perquisites which excited no comment, but there is ample evidence that the corruption of justice in the provincial courts did cause grave discontent, and that fiscal extortion and other forms of blackmail went beyond the bounds accepted by contemporary opinion. Justinian seriously believed that the capacity of the provincials to pay their taxes was gravely impaired by the illicit exactions of governors.[39]

The military administration suffered less from corruption. Commissions, particularly in the *limitanei*, were often obtained by *suffragium*, but were for the most part awarded by merit or seniority, and the purchase of posts never became systematic. *Duces* and tribunes supplemented their meagre pay by various forms of peculation. Some grossly exploited their position by intercepting the arms, remounts, uniforms, rations and donatives of their troops, but these were exceptions. Most made certain deductions, which eventually became customary, from the rations of their men, and kept their units under strength, appropriating the pay and allowances of men who were dead or who had been granted indefinite leave. These abuses of course reduced the effective strength of the army, but they came to be regularised and standardised. The eventual result was that officers' salaries, which were in the fourth century very low, came by the fifth century to be supplemented by certain recognised perquisites.[40]

In the civil service proper the officials increased their meagre pay by tips or fees (*sportulae*). Litigants had to pay fees to the officials of the court at every stage of the judicial procedure, applicants for posts or grants or privileges had to tip the clerk who handled their petitions, taxpayers had to pay various forms of commission to the financial officials concerned in the collection of the revenue. Constantine endeavoured to abolish these *sportulae*, but under his successors they were condoned and regulated. In so far as they were controlled and standardised they were not a serious abuse: it was not unreasonable that litigants should pay what amounted to court fees and petitioners the equivalent of stamp tax, while the fiscal *sportulae* could be justified as a surcharge to cover the costs of collection. The trouble was that, when fees were standardised, additional tips soon came to be expected, and *sportulae* thus tended always to increase, and that the distinction between fees and bribes tended to be blurred: for more substantial payments officials were willing to put through illegal transactions.[41]

Diocletian greatly increased the number of *officia* by his multiplication of the provinces and creation of the dioceses. He must also have enlarged the praetorian prefectures to enable them to cope with the additional work which he imposed upon them, especially the elaborate annual calculation of the indiction. The provincial and diocesan staffs did not increase substantially thereafter, but the central ministries continued to grow. This was partly the result of growing centralisation. The emperors, justifiably mistrusting the honesty and efficiency of their administrative officers in the dioceses and provinces, allowed them less and less initiative and imposed upon them ever stricter control and audit; and the central ministries, which profited from this policy in greatly increased fees, constantly encroached on the functions of the diocesan and provincial staffs. The praetorian prefectures and the palatine offices had necessarily to be enlarged to cope with the increased volume of work which was concentrated upon them. But this was not the only cause for the inflation of the central ministries. The emperors lavishly rewarded *palatini* and *praefectiani* for their services by grants of privileges and honours, and the fees which could be earned in the central offices grew steadily more substantial. The result was a constant pressure, which proved irresistible, of applicants for places: by the middle of the fifth century posts in the most highly favoured ministries had come to command a price. The emperors tried hard to check the inflation of numbers by laying down maximum establishments, but supernumerary clerks always accumulated.[42]

Excessive centralisation involved an immense volume of clerical labour and slowed up the processes of government. Nor did it achieve its object of checking corruption. The emperors and their ministers were so snowed under with papers that they signed them without reading them, and the clerks of the central ministries could thus put through for those prepared to pay for them illegal grants of lands, privileges, titles and immunities. The high courts of justice were so clogged with appeals, the delays so interminable and the fees so high, that the victims of injustice in the lower courts were denied redress unless they had very long purses. The fees of the central financial officials added substantially to the burden of taxation in the Western parts, as much, it would seem, as 25 per cent. in the last days of the empire.[43]

The number of officials became unnecessarily inflated, but was not vast in relation to the size of the empire. There were less than 12,000 *cohortales* in all the provincial *officia* and approximately half that number in the diocesan *officia*. The military offices were all very modest; *magistri militum* had 300 officials each, *duces* 40. There were probably under 5,000 military officials all told. The praetorian and urban prefectures may have employed about 5,000 clerks. Of the palatine ministries the largest recorded was the *agentes in rebus* with 1,248 members; the *largitiones* had 546 or 446 clerks, the *res privata* 300, the *sacra scrinia* 130, and there were only 33 silentiaries and 30 active notaries. The total for each emperor would thus have been about 2,500, that is 5,000 for both parts of the empire. These figures refer to established posts only and take no account of supernumeraries. The grand total of regular officials was thus not much in excess of 30,000, not an extravagant number for an empire which stretched from Hadrian's Wall to beyond the Euphrates. The direct expense imposed on the state was small, since supernumeraries were not paid and the pay of established officials was modest, not to say meagre.[44]

The great officers of state had considerable opportunities for making money on the side. Being in close contact with emperors they could successfully press for grants of land and money, and could exact *suffragia* from aspirants to lesser offices. Most no doubt exploited such opportunities, and many probably took bribes in other circumstances also. Sulpicius Severus accuses the *magister officiorum* Macedonius of accepting money from Priscillian, and Cyril gave large sums to the master of the offices and the quaestor of the day—but did not attempt to corrupt the praetorian prefect. Ministers are not in general mentioned in the sanctions of laws, which assume that their *officia* are guilty of breaches of the law. This is probably a polite fiction. In a law prohibiting *petitiones*, addressed to the praetorian prefect, Theodosius II threatens the quaestor and *comes rei privatae* with his condign wrath if they nevertheless promote them, and Leo in a law against monopolies again threatens the quaestor and all the palatine ministers if they support petitions for them. The high officers of state do not seem, however, on the whole to have been as systematically corrupt as the lower grades of the administration. Some, like Rufinus and John of Cappadocia, made enormous fortunes by very dubious practices, but they were exceptions whose excesses excited remark.[45]

The most depressing feature of the later empire is the apparent absence of public spirit. The motive forces seem to be, on the one hand, compulsion, and on the other, personal ambition in its cruder forms, the desire to rise in the social scale and to get rich quick. Under the Principate decurions had been inspired by pride in their cities and a laudable ambition to win the approbation of their fellow citizens. In the later empire the government had to compel them not to shirk their duties. In the second century there seems to have been a certain tradition of public service among senators and members of the equestrian order. Under the later empire the majority appear to have been interested only in the rank and wealth which offices bestowed upon their holders. The spirit of public service was not, it is true, entirely lacking. Many of the emperors were devoted public servants, who worked hard both to increase the efficiency of the administration and to protect their subjects from oppression. Many, too, of their chief ministers had the interests of the empire at heart. Some, like Anthemius, who virtually governed the Eastern parts in the early fifth century, received high praise from contemporaries for their wise and just rule. Others, who, like John the Cappadocian, were execrated for their rapacity and brutality, and certainly did not neglect their opportunities for self-enrichment, were nevertheless efficient public servants, who did much to improve the finances of the empire and to eliminate waste and peculation. Others, again, like Symmachus, though lacking energy and initiative, performed their functions with honesty and diligence. But even among the great ministers of the empire there were many who used their offices only to enrich them-selves and distribute patronage to their relations and friends, and at the lower levels of the administration the general standard was, as the government often admitted, deplorably low. The only way to secure honest provincial governors, Marcian publicly declared, was to appoint men who did not wish to serve. This is a pessimistic, not to say cynical, doctrine. No one, it implies, ever applied for a post save for self-interested motives; the context implies the desire to make money. The emperor does not envisage the possibility that anyone might wish to earn an honest livelihood by conscientious work, much less have the disinterested desire to serve the state to the best of his ability.[46]

Even more striking evidence of the lack of public spirit is the inertia of the civil population, high and low, in the face of the barbarian invasions.

The upper classes were proud of being Romans and valued Roman civilisation. They rejoiced in the victories of the empire over the barbarians and were shocked and dismayed by its defeats. They certainly had no desire to fall under barbarian rule. We know of two men only who can be called traitors. Arvandus, praetorian prefect of the Gauls from 464 to 468, and Seronatus, probably vicar of the Seven Provinces shortly after, no doubt despairing of the empire, collaborated with the Visigoths. Both were indicted by their fellow countrymen, Arvandus by the diocesan assembly of Gaul, Seronatus by the Civitas Arvernorum, and were brought to trial at Rome and condemned.[47]

The loyalty of the upper classes was, however, of a very passive character. A handful only raised resistance movements. The only large scale concerted movement was that of the British and Armorican cities in 408. In 397 Valentinus, a notable of Selge, raised a force of slaves and peasants which successfully withstood Tribigild's Goths. A few years later Synesius of Cyrene organised and armed a band of peasants against the Austuriani. In 532 Pudentius raised his province of Tripolitania against the Vandals and with the aid of a small body of imperial troops ejected them. In 546 Tullianus, a magnate of Lucania and Bruttium, organised a large force of rustics to assist the imperial armies against Totila.[48]

More usually those who could fled to safer places. According to Orosius, when the barbarians overran Spain in 409, the majority of the Romans—he is clearly thinking of the upper classes—acted on the text, 'when they persecute you in one city flee to another', often bribing barbarians to escort them and carry their baggage. Possidius gives us a vivid and contemporary picture of the flight from the Vandals when they invaded Mauretania and Numidia in 437. When the Vandals occupied Africa Proconsularis and Byzacena in 442, there was again a large emigration of upper-class Romans. Next year Valentinian III declared a moratorium on debts owed by African refugees, who appear to have been persons of substance, and licensed African lawyers to plead in the Italian courts. Even in Syria bishop Theodoret was embarrassed at the demands for hospitality made by once wealthy African refugees. Many landowners and *honorati* fled to Numidia and the two Mauretanian provinces, and in 451 were allotted 13,000 *centuriae* of deserted land in the former, and all imperial lands in the latter, together with the estates belonging to the bakers' guilds of Rome.[49]

The panic in Spain and Africa was somewhat exceptional, for these provinces had never seen a barbarian for generations. We hear of no similar exodus from Gaul or Illyricum, and even in Spain and Africa many of the upper classes stayed behind, whether they could not get away or did not wish to do so we do not know. Under the barbarian kings they grumbled but made the best of things: soon many were collaborating with the barbarian kings, acting as their ministers and governors. Orosius goes a little further. After the first orgy of pillage the barbarians, he says, treated the provincials kindly, 'so that there are now some Romans to be found among them who prefer poverty and freedom among the barbarians to the burden of tribute among the Romans'. Even this guarded statement is suspect, for Orosius is most anxious to prove that even the horrors of the invasion of Spain, then fresh in men's minds, were not so bad as the disasters of the pagan empire. An even more biassed and unreliable witness, Salvian, goes further. In Gaul, he asserts, governmental oppression of the provincials was so outrageous that 'many of them, persons of good family and liberal education, flee to the enemy, to avoid death inflicted by public persecution, seeking Roman humanity among the barbarians because they cannot endure barbarian inhumanity among the Romans'. Some victim of extortion may have fled in desperation, but there is no evidence to support Salvian's improbable assertion.[50]

Rather lower down the social scale townsmen occasionally took the initiative against the barbarians. In 376 the magistrates of Adrianople armed the townspeople and the workers in the local arms factory and made an attack on the Goths. In 443 the citizens of Asemus sallied out against a party of Huns and captured them and recovered their booty and prisoners. Inspired by their bishop, Sidonius Apollinaris, the Arverni defended their city against the Visigoths for five years from 471–5. In many cities no doubt the townspeople manned the walls, or assisted the garrison in the task, but in Mesopotamia and Syria quite a number did not risk resistance to Chosroes but bought immunity from captivity and pillage with large money payments.[51]

But once again, if townsmen were not very active in resisting the barbarians, we know of no city which threw open its gates to welcome them. When Justinian's armies arrived in Africa and Sicily and Italy, on the other hand, with the solitary exception of Naples, where there was a strong Gothic garrison and a party in the town preferred to play for safety, the towns readily opened their gates to the imperial forces, greeted them with enthusiasm, and even asked to be occupied. We know of only one townsman who preferred life among the barbarians, the Greek merchant from Viminacium whom Priscus met at Attila's court, who justified his strange choice by a denunciation of Roman taxation and injustice.[52]

Salvian declares that the peasants were so oppressed under Roman rule and so well treated in the Visigothic kingdom, that 'the one wish of all the Romans there is that they may never be obliged to pass under Roman jurisdiction; the one unanimous prayer of the Roman common people there is that they may be allowed to live the life they lead with the barbarians'. The facts do not bear him out. On the very few occasions that they were given a lead by their landlords or other local magnates the peasantry fought against the barbarians. But under similar leadership they fought in civil wars which can have meant little or nothing to them: Didymus and Verinianus, two young Spanish senators, who were related to Honorius, raised an army of slaves from their estates to fight the usurper Constantine. Peasants would also, under similar stimulus, fight for the barbarians. When Tullianus raised his force of rustics to fight for the empire, Totila mobilised a peasant army to fight for the Ostrogoths, and the two bodies of Italian peasants slaughtered each other in a bloody battle. Later the senators under Totila's control, on his instructions, sent agents to order their tenants in Tullianus's force to go back to their farms, and they obediently and no doubt gladly did so. On our evidence the peasantry were in general apathetic and docile: of any spontaneous action on either side there is scarcely any trace. Synesius praises the courage and initiative of a village in Cyrenaica, which, led by a deacon, beat off the Austuriani. On the other hand many miners in Thrace, Ammianus tells us, joined the Goths in 376, because they could not endure the burden of the taxes; it is perhaps relevant that there had recently been a roundup of miners who had taken up farming. Slaves are twice recorded to have joined the invading hordes. Many rallied to the Goths before the battle of Adrianople and again when Alaric was at the gates of Rome. But these slaves were certainly in the first case and probably in the second recently enslaved barbarians, who naturally sought refuge with their fellow tribesmen.[53]

The passive inertia displayed by the civil population, high and low alike, was no new phenomenon: we hear of no resistance movements under the Principate. It was probably in large part due to the fact that for generations the population had been accustomed to being protected by a professional army. The civil population was in fact, for reasons of internal security, forbidden to bear arms. More important than this legal prohibition was the attitude of mind which it reflected. Citizens were not expected to fight, and for the most part they never envisaged the idea of fighting.

The Roman empire seems never to have evoked any active patriotism from the vast majority of its citizens. Most of them no doubt were indifferent but even those who admired the empire felt no call to devote themselves to its service. Their attitude was well expressed by Aelius Aristides' great panegyric on Rome, and symbolised by the official cult of Rome and Augustus. Rome was to them a mighty and beneficent power which excited their admiration and gratitude, but the empire was too immense to evoke the kind of loyalty which they felt to their own cities. They revered the emperor as a saviour and benefactor, who with his legions defended their cities against the barbarians, and by his wisdom, humanity and justice promoted their peace and prosperity, but they did not regard him as a leader whom they must serve. Rome was eternal, and the emperor was a god, who needed no assistance from his worshippers.

Under the later empire the same attitude persisted. The regular army was expected to defend the empire, and it was only in a most desperate emergency, when Radagaisus and his hordes had broken into Italy, that the government appealed to the provincials to join up as temporary volunteers 'for love of peace and country'. It was still in theory illegal for civilians to own or bear arms. Only when Gaiseric was threatening to invade Italy was this rule relaxed and the provincials urged to arm themselves in order to resist Vandal landings. Justinian tightened up the ban on arms by making their manufacture a strict imperial monopoly; but he did provide the cities with armouries, controlled by the *patres civitatum*. Nor did the fundamental attitude of the provincials to the empire change. The emperor was no longer a god, but he was the vicegerent of God, entrusted by him with the task of governing and defending the empire. His subjects were taught to render unto Caesar the things that are Caesar's, that is, to pay their taxes and obey the authorities; but they were not exhorted to devote themselves to the empire's service.[54]

Christianity has been accused on the one hand of sapping the empire's morale by its otherworldy attitude, and on the other hand credited with giving the empire new spiritual energy and reforming it by its moral teaching. Neither allegation seems to have much substance. There is little to show that pagan worship promoted a patriotic spirit; the gods were, it is true, regarded as the patrons and protectors of the Roman state, so long as they were not offended by the breach of certain moral rules and were duly placated with sacrifices, but they do not seem to have inspired patriotic devotion. Constantine and his successors and their Christian subjects carried over the same attitude to the one God whom they worshipped. God in their eyes was the mighty power who would give victory and prosperity to the empire, provided that he was properly appeased by his worshippers. His demands were, it is true, more exacting than those of the old gods, since he required not only ritual acts, but correct belief about his own nature, and the standard of morality which he expected from his devotees was markedly higher. But for the vast majority of ordinary men Christianity caused no fundamental change of attitude.

To the ordinary man likewise the moral teaching and the otherworldly doctrine of Christianity seems to have made little practical difference. In some respects moral standards declined, and most people continued to devote their energies to the goods of this world. The average Christian does not seem to have worried greatly about the fate of his soul until he feared that death was near, and then hoped to win access to heaven by the rituals of baptism or penance. In the meanwhile he pursued his worldly ends with no more, and sometimes less, regard for moral principles than his pagan forebears.

There was, of course, a minority who took the Christian message seriously to heart, and regarding the things of the world as of no account, devoted themselves to achieving eternal life in the world to come. Many thousands withdrew into the desert or into monasteries and spent the rest of their lives striving by austerities and prayer to gain salvation; many were drawn, often against their will, into the service of the Church as priests and bishops.

Quantitatively the loss to the state was probably not significant. Numerous as the clergy, monks and hermits were, their withdrawal cannot have seriously accentuated the manpower shortage from which the empire suffered, nor can the fact that the majority of them were celibate have contributed much to the shrinkage of the population. Qualitatively the loss was more serious. It was men of high moral character who were most drawn to the spiritual life, and were thus lost to the service of the state. In the pagan empire such men had regarded the public service as one of the principal duties of the good man and citizen. Under the new dispensation they were taught that a public career was, if not sinful, so fraught with spiritual danger that it should be eschewed. The service of the state tended to be left to ambitious careerists, and

Christianity thus paradoxically increased the corruption of the government.[55]

It may be asked whether the Eastern parts suffered less from any of the weaknesses discussed above than did the West. In some respects the East was at a disadvantage. Christianity prevailed earlier in the Eastern parts and obtained a more thorough hold. Monks and clergy were more numerous and more richly endowed, and thus a heavier burden on the economy. Theological controversy was more widespread and more embittered, and the repression of heresy demanded a greater use of force and provoked more hostility. In so far as the otherworldly attitude which Christianity inculcated weakened public morale, the East should have been more gravely affected. In most matters no significant distinction can be traced. The most serious losses in the area of cultivation are recorded in Africa, but *agri deserti* were a problem common to both halves of the empire. The rules tying *coloni* to the soil and *curiales* to their cities were even more rigid in the East than in the West. The East was, it is true, more politically stable and dissipated less of its strength in civil wars, but as against this it was obliged on a number of occasions to waste its resources on suppressing Western usurpers.

In two ways, however, the East seems to have been stronger and healthier than the West. In the first place the Eastern provinces were probably initially richer and more populous than the Western. It is very difficult to substantiate this statement, but it must be remembered that Macedonia and Greece, Asia Minor, Syria and Egypt had been settled and civilised lands for many centuries when they were incorporated in the empire, while many parts of the West, Britain, northern Gaul, north-western Spain, and the Danubian provinces, had been barbarous and undeveloped even after their annexation. The resources of the Eastern lands had long been fully exploited and their population had swelled. In the north-western provinces much of the potentially best land was probably woodland and waste, forest or swamp. It is significant that Aquitania is more highly praised for its agricultural wealth by Salvian than northern Gaul, and that supplies had to be carted all the way from Aquitania to Châlons and even to Paris to feed Constantius II's and Julian's armies. It is even more significant that Sicily, Sardinia and above all Africa were still under the later empire regarded as the granaries of the Western empire. For these countries, with their mountainous terrain and scanty and irregular rainfall, can never have been highly productive, however intensively they were cultivated, and their yield would have been far exceeded by that of Britain, Gaul and the Danubian lands, had the resources of these regions been fully exploited. From the meagre figures available it would appear that the African diocese, the richest in the Western parts, produced only a third or a quarter of the revenue that Egypt, its richest diocese, yielded to the Eastern government.[56]

This picture is rather difficult to believe when one looks at the present state of affairs, when north-western Europe is intensively cultivated and densely populated, and north Africa (with the exception of Egypt, whose natural wealth has in all ages remained indestructible), Syria, Anatolia and the Balkans are derelict after long centuries of neglect and misgovernment. Progressive denudation has by now reduced their water supplies and washed away much of their good soil, but even now they could produce far more than they do, and the archaeological remains show that they were far more extensively cultivated in Roman times.

A rough index to the geographical distribution of wealth under the Roman empire is provided by the ruins of ancient monuments; for under the Principate all cities expended as much as they could afford on public buildings. The survival of ancient buildings is of course largely a matter of chance, and their chances are far better in areas which have subsequently become derelict than in those which have remained in continuous occupation and prospered. Whole cities survive in the deserts of Africa and Syria and in the more desolate parts of Asia Minor, but virtually nothing at continuously occupied sites like Antioch or Alexandria. Nevertheless the distribution of ruins is suggestive. In all northern western Europe—Britain, northern Gaul, north-western Spain and the Danubian lands—no monumental buildings survive except at the imperial capital of Trier, and the buildings which excavation has revealed are mostly on a modest scale. By contrast Narbonensis, eastern and southern Spain, Italy, north Africa, Syria and Palestine, Asia Minor and the southern Balkans can boast of many, and the largest and most magnificent are in the Eastern parts. In these areas, furthermore, where the Roman buildings have disappeared, Roman columns, capitals and other architectural members have been freely reused in the medieval mosques and churches. It is hard to find a Roman column in north-western Europe, and it is likely the medieval builders found few.[57]

The Eastern Empire was thus probably from the start richer than the Western, the greater part of which was still underdeveloped. The distribution of wealth was also probably more even in the East. This again is difficult to substantiate, but the few facts and figures that we possess strongly suggest that the senators of Rome were far wealthier than those of Constantinople and owned far more extensive estates. There were probably more medium landowners in the East, and fairly certainly more peasant proprietors, notably in Egypt, eastern Asia Minor, Thrace and Illyricum. The explanation of this appears to be historical. The Roman aristocracy in the West had begun to accumulate wealth far earlier, and in some Western lands, such as Gaul, there had already existed a landowning aristocracy before the Roman conquest. In the East an imperial aristocracy only began to accumulate wealth in the fourth century, and in some provinces, notably Egypt, the system of land tenure had protected the peasant proprietor.[58]

The greater number of small freeholders, since taxes came to less than rent, meant that a higher proportion of the yield of agriculture remained in the hands of the cultivators in the East than in the West. By and large the peasantry were better fed and probably reared more children. It also meant that the state secured a higher proportion of the agricultural surplus, for peasant proprietors and small landowners paid full rate of tax, while the great senatorial landlords, apart from the legal exemptions which they enjoyed, could evade taxation.

The existence of an ancient wealthy aristocracy in the West also had important political effects. The Roman aristocracy from the reign of Constantine became ever more influential, and by the fifth century almost monopolised the higher administrative posts. These great noblemen were naturally tender to the interests of their own class, and were on the whole inefficient administrators. In the East, on the other hand, hereditary nobles did not dominate the administration, and the highest posts were often filled by men who had risen by ability, and being dependent on the emperor's favour, gave priority to the interests of the government. The result was that the fiscal privileges of the great owners were curbed, and also that there was less wastage in the administration: it is highly significant that the perquisites of the officials who collected the taxes were fifty or sixty times greater in the West than in the East.[59]

The East then probably possessed greater economic resources, and could thus support with less strain a larger number of idle mouths. A smaller part of its resources went, it would seem, to maintain its aristocracy, and more was thus available for the army and other essential services. It also was probably more populous, and since the economic pressure on the peasantry was perhaps less severe, may have suffered less from population decline. If there is any substance in these arguments, the Eastern government should have been able to raise a larger revenue without overstraining its resources, and to levy more troops without depleting its labour force.

It is impossible to check this hypothesis for the crucial period, the fourth century, in which both halves of the empire were territorially intact. In the fifth and sixth centuries the Eastern government commanded a larger and more buoyant revenue than the Western. It could spend very large sums on lavish blackmail to the barbarians and on ambitious military operations without running into serious financial difficulties. Leo's expedition against the Vandals, followed by Zeno's reckless expenditure, did indeed temporarily exhaust the treasury, but Anastasius was quickly able to restore the empire's finances, and it was not until the reign of Maurice that the strain of the protracted Persian and Avar wars caused a serious financial crisis. It was also able to raise large armies from its own subjects and did not make excessive use of barbarian troops.

The Western government on the other hand was almost bankrupt by the end of Valentinian III's reign and had virtually abandoned conscription, relying almost entirely on barbarian federates. The collapse of the West was however by no means entirely attributable to its internal weaknesses, for the government had by now lost to the barbarians many of the provinces on which it had relied for revenue and recruits, and those which it still controlled had suffered so severely from the ravages of the barbarians that they had to be allowed remission of taxation.

Of the manifold weaknesses of the later Roman empire some, the increasing maldistribution of wealth, the corruption and extortion of the administration, the lack of public spirit and the general apathy of the population, were to a large extent due to internal causes. But some of the more serious of these weaknesses were the result, direct or indirect, of barbarian pressure. Above all the need to maintain a vastly increased army had far-reaching effects. It necessitated a rate of taxation so heavy as to cause a progressive decline in agriculture and indirectly a shrinkage of population. The effort to collect this heavy taxation required a great expansion of the civil service, and this expansion in turn imposed an additional burden on the economy and made administrative corruption and extortion more difficult to control. The oppressive weight of the taxation contributed to the general apathy.

The Western empire was poorer and less populous, and its social and economic structure more unhealthy. It was thus less able to withstand the tremendous strains imposed by its defensive effort, and the internal weaknesses which it developed undoubtedly contributed to its final collapse in the fifth century. But the major cause of its fall was that it was more exposed to barbarian onslaughts which in persistence and sheer weight of numbers far exceeded anything which the empire had previously had to face. The Eastern empire, owing to its greater wealth and population and sounder economy, was better able to carry the burden of defence, but its resources were overstrained and it developed the same weaknesses as the West, if perhaps in a less acute form. Despite these weaknesses it managed in the sixth century not only to hold its own against the Persians in the East but to reconquer parts of the West, and even when, in the seventh century, it was overrun by the onslaughts of the Persians and the Arabs and the Slavs, it succeeded despite heavy territorial losses in rallying and holding its own. The internal weaknesses of the empire cannot have been a major factor in its decline.

NOTE ON THE MAPS

THE maps are intended to be diagrammatic and do not pretend to be geographically exact. Geographical exactitude is indeed often unattainable, for many provincial boundaries are only approximately known, and some are purely conjectural; and the precise location of many minor cities and military stations is uncertain.

The evidence for Maps I, II and VI is listed and set out in tabular form in Appendix III. The geographical arrangement of the British provinces is conjectural (based on J. C. Mann, *Antiquity*, xxxv (1961), 317–20).

Map III is based on the Notitia Dignitatum (*occ.* ix, xi, xii, *or.* xi, xiii, xiv). As regards treasuries and factories it is incomplete for the Eastern parts, where complete lists are lacking and only casual information is available (see ch. XIII, n. 44, ch. XXI, nn. 25, 29).

Map IV is also based on the Notitia Dignitatum (*occ.* v-vii, xxiv-xlii, *or.* v-ix, xxviii-xlii); the material is tabulated in Appendix II, Tables V, VI, X-XV. Both for lack of space and because many of their stations are unidentified, the units of the *limitanei* have been more or less arbitrarily packed within their areas. The number of units of various types in each army group is, however, correct, and the general distribution of the armed forces truly presented.

For the evidence for Map V see pp. 712–18. In Britain a few conjectural cities have been added to make up Gildas' total (see ch. XIX, n. 7). Gaul is based on the Notitia Galliarum (see ch. XIX, n. 2), Africa on the lists of bishoprics (ch. XIX, n. 8), the Eastern parts on Hierocles and Georgius Cyprius (ch. XIX, n. 2). The detailed location of the cities in Africa and some of the more crowded provinces of the East is arbitrary, but approximately the correct number of cities has been placed in each province, so that the relative density of cities in the different areas is truly presented.

Map VII is based on the conciliar lists and episcopal *notitiae* (see ch. XXII, n. 8). For the patriarchates and papal vicariates see pp. 883–94.

LIST OF MAPS

1069

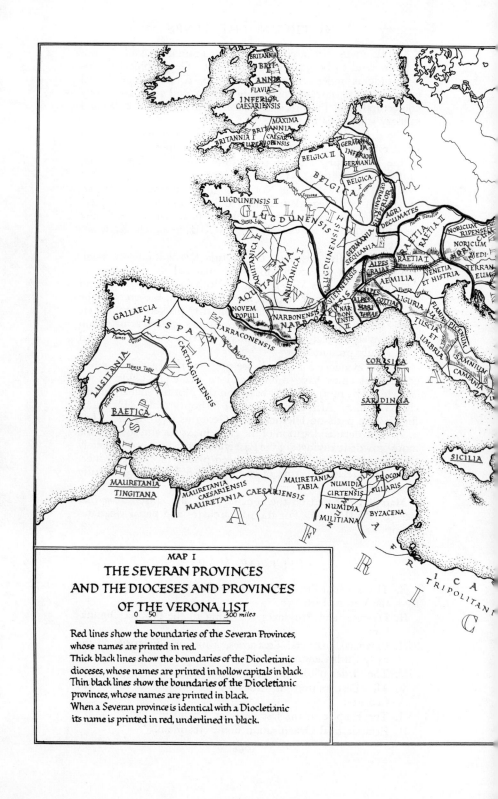

MAP I

THE SEVERAN PROVINCES
AND THE DIOCESES AND PROVINCES
OF THE VERONA LIST

0   50   300 miles

Red lines show the boundaries of the Severan Provinces,
whose names are printed in red.
Thick black lines show the boundaries of the Diocletianic
dioceses, whose names are printed in hollow capitals in black.
Thin black lines show the boundaries of the Diocletianic
provinces, whose names are printed in black.
When a Severan province is identical with a Diocletianic
its name is printed in red, underlined in black.

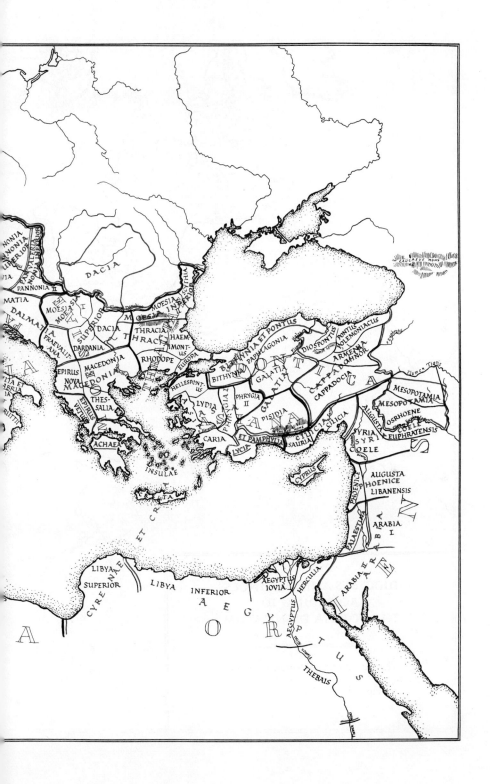

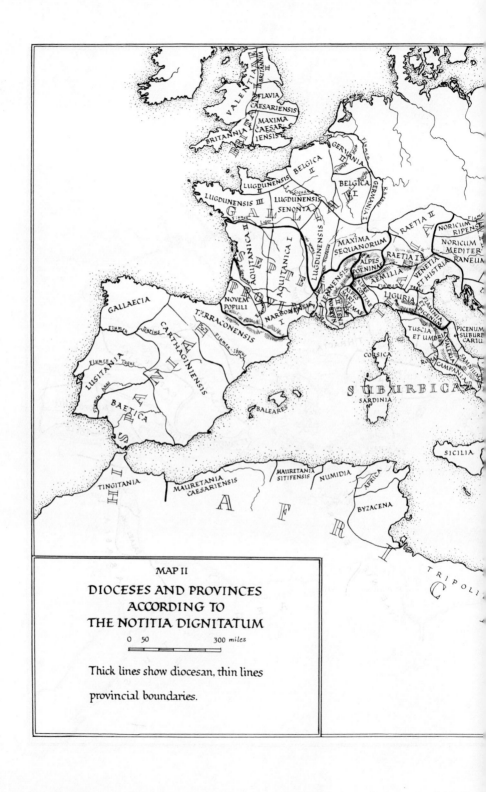

MAP II

DIOCESES AND PROVINCES
ACCORDING TO
THE NOTITIA DIGNITATUM

0   50   300 miles

Thick lines show diocesan, thin lines

provincial boundaries.

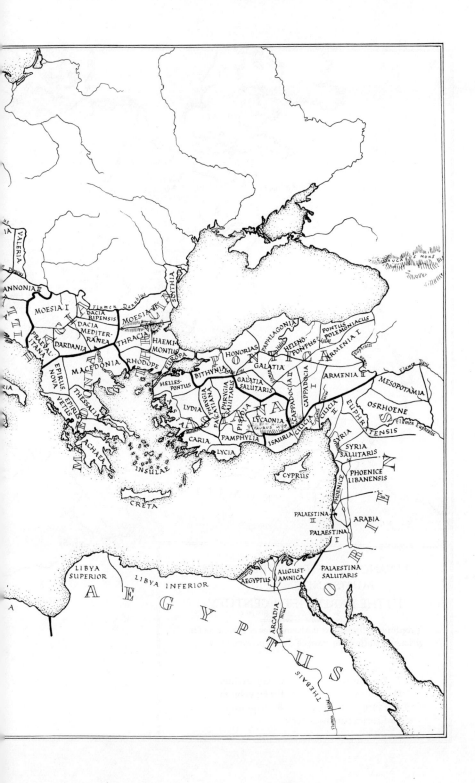

MAP III

FINANCIAL DISTRICTS, TREASURIES
MINTS AND FACTORIES

IN THE EARLY FIFTH CENTURY

0   50   300 miles

A continuous line shows the boundaries of the sacrae largitiones, a dotted line those of the res privata.

T = Thesaurus   G Gynaecium
M = Moneta   L Linyphium
F = Fabrica   B Baphium
Fb Fabrica barbaricariorum

F. Carnuntum
Flumen Danubias
Savaria
Aquincum
TRIP.
iscia
ONIA II
G
MATIA
Sirmium
SAVIA
G Bassiana
F. Horreum Margi
GF
F. Ratiaria
Salona
F. Naissus
DACIA
THRACIAE
F. Marcianopolis
Flumen Danubias
T. Philippopolis
MACEDONIA
PONTICA
Thessalonica
Hadrianopolis Constantinopolis
MF
MG
Heraclea
MFE
MF
Nicomedia
Flumen Lycus
Euphrates
Nicaea
MG Cyzicus
ASIANA
FG
Caesarea
F. Irenopolis
F. Sardis
F. Edessa
Flumen Maeander
TAURUS
Flumen Euphrates
Antiochia
MFB
Cyprus
Z
Tyrus
F. Damascus
G
LL
Scythopolis
ORIENS
Alexandria
M
AEGYPTUS
CAUCASUS MONS

The information is complete for the Western parts but partial
only for the thesauri, gynaecia, linyphia and baphia for the
Eastern parts.

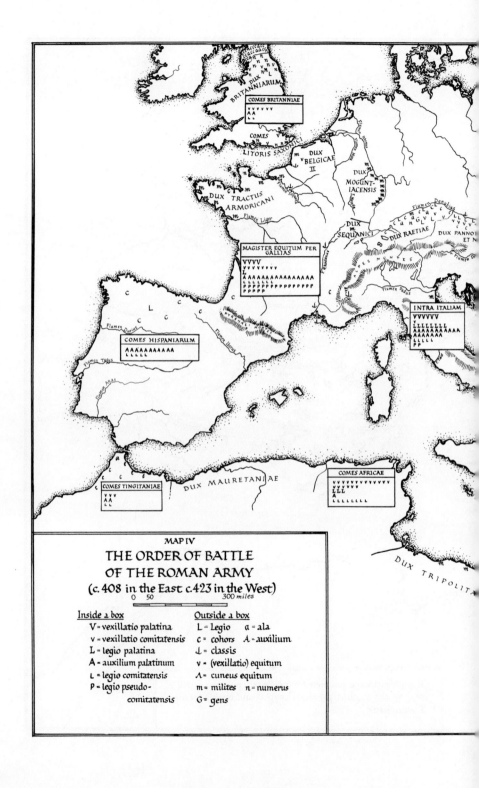

MAP IV
THE ORDER OF BATTLE
OF THE ROMAN ARMY
(c. 408 in the East c. 423 in the West)

0   50   300 miles

Inside a box	Outside a box	
V = vexillatio palatina	L = Legio	a = ala
v = vexillatio comitatensis	c = cohors	A = auxilium
L = legio palatina	⌐ = classis	
A = auxilium palatinum	v = (vexillatio) equitum	
ʟ = legio comitatensis	ʌ = cuneus equitum	
P = legio pseudo-	m = milites n = numerus	
comitatensis	G = gens	

Labels on map: DUX BRITANNIARUM · COMES BRITANNIAE · COMES LITORIS SAXONICI · DUX BELGICAE II · DUX MOGUNTIACENSIS · DUX TRACTUS ARMORICANI · DUX SEQUANICI · DUX RAETIAE · DUX PANNONIAE ET N · MAGISTER EQUITUM PER GALLIAS · INTRA ITALIAM · COMES HISPANIARUM · COMES AFRICAE · COMES TINGITANIAE · DUX MAURETANIAE · DUX TRIPOLITA

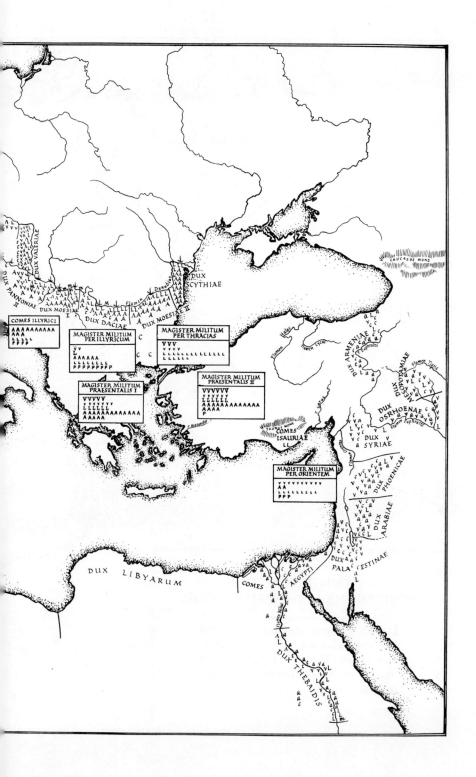

DUX VALERIAE

DUX PANNONIAE II

CAUCASUS MONS

DUX SCYTHIAE

DUX MOESIAE I

DUX DACIAE

DUX MOESIAE II

Flumen Danuvius

Flumen Halys

Flumen Lycus

DUX ARMENIAE

Euphrates

DUX MESOPOTAMIAE

Flumen Tigris

COMES ILLYRICI
A A A A A A A A A
A A A
L L L L
P P P P

**MAGISTER MILITUM
PER ILLYRICUM**
V V
V
A A A A A A
L L L L L L L
P P P P P P P P P

**MAGISTER MILITUM
PER THRACIAS**
V V V V
V V V V
L L L L L L L L L L L L
L L L L L

**MAGISTER MILITUM
PRAESENTALIS II**
V V V V V
V V V V V V
L L L L L L
A A A A
P

DUX OSRHOENAE

Flumen Euphrates

**MAGISTER MILITUM
PRAESENTALIS I**
V V V V V V V
V V V V V V V
L L L L L L
A A A A A A A A A A A A A A
A A A A A

DUX SYRIAE

TAURUS MONS

Flumen Maeander

**COMES
ISAURIAE**
L L

DUX PHOENICAE

**MAGISTER MILITUM
PER ORIENTEM**
V V V V V V V V V V
A A
L L L L L L L
P P P

DUX ARABIAE

DUX LIBYARUM

COMES

AEGYPTI

DUX PALAESTINAE

Flumen Nilus

DUX THEBAIDIS

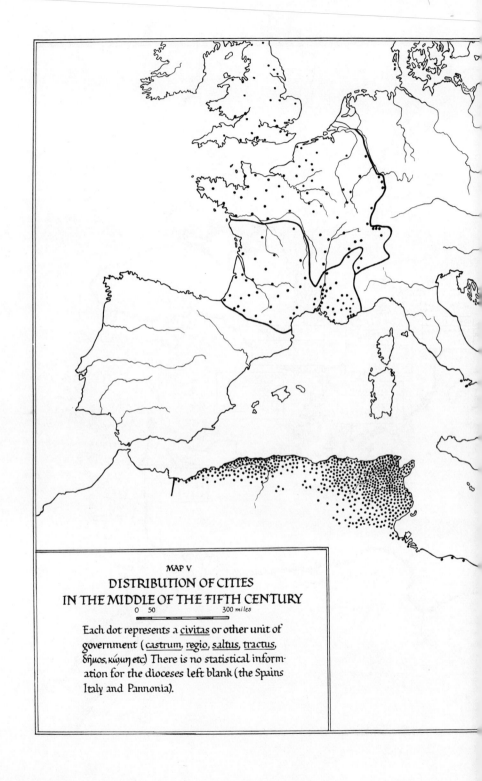

MAP V

DISTRIBUTION OF CITIES
IN THE MIDDLE OF THE FIFTH CENTURY

0   50   300 miles

Each dot represents a <u>civitas</u> or other unit of
government (<u>castrum</u>, <u>regio</u>, <u>saltus</u>, <u>tractus</u>,
δῆμος, κώμη etc) There is no statistical inform-
ation for the dioceses left blank (the Spains
Italy and Pannonia).

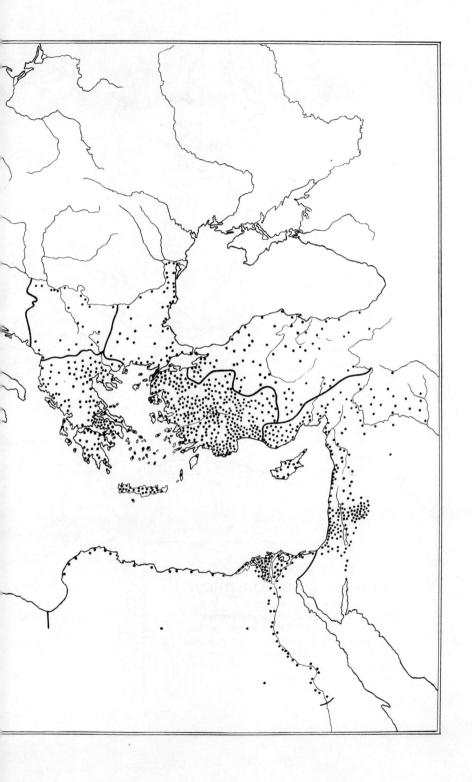

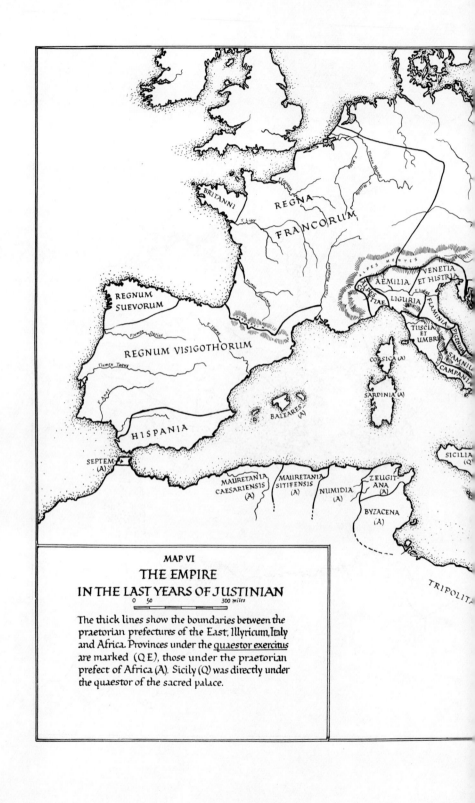

BRITANNI

REGNA

FRANCORUM

T. Liger

Flumen Garumna

Flumen Rhodanus

ALPES MONTES

REGNUM
SUEVORUM

Flumen Durius

T. Iberus

AEMILIA

VENETIA
ET HISTRIA

COTTIAE

LIGURIA

FLAMINIA

PICENUM

REGNUM VISIGOTHORUM

Flumen Tagus

TUSCIA
ET
UMBRIA

CORSICA (A)

SAMNIUM

CAMPANIA

F. Anas

SARDINIA (A)

HISPANIA

BALEARES
(A)

SICILIA
(Q)

SEPTEM
(A)

MAURETANIA
CAESARIENSIS
(A)

MAURETANIA
SITIFENSIS
(A)

NUMIDIA
(A)

ZEUGIT-
ANA
(A)

BYZACENA
(A)

TRIPOLITA

MAP VI

THE EMPIRE
IN THE LAST YEARS OF JUSTINIAN

0   50   300 miles

The thick lines show the boundaries between the
praetorian prefectures of the East, Illyricum, Italy
and Africa. Provinces under the quaestor exercitus
are marked (Q E), those under the praetorian
prefect of Africa (A). Sicily (Q) was directly under
the quaestor of the sacred palace.

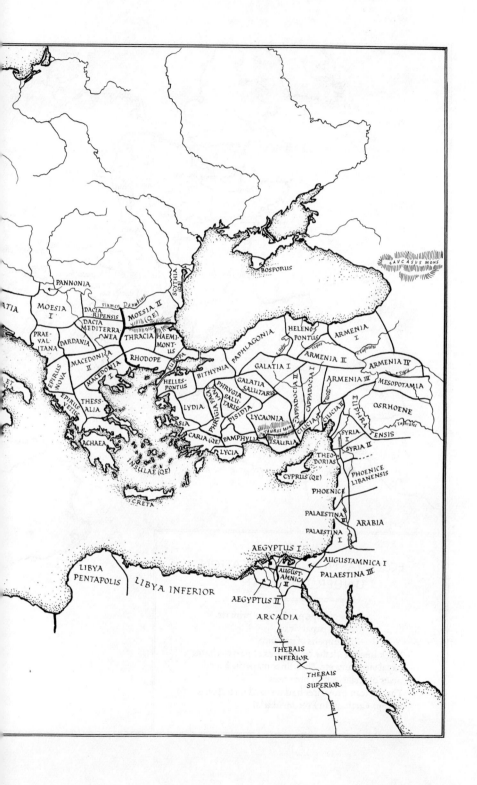

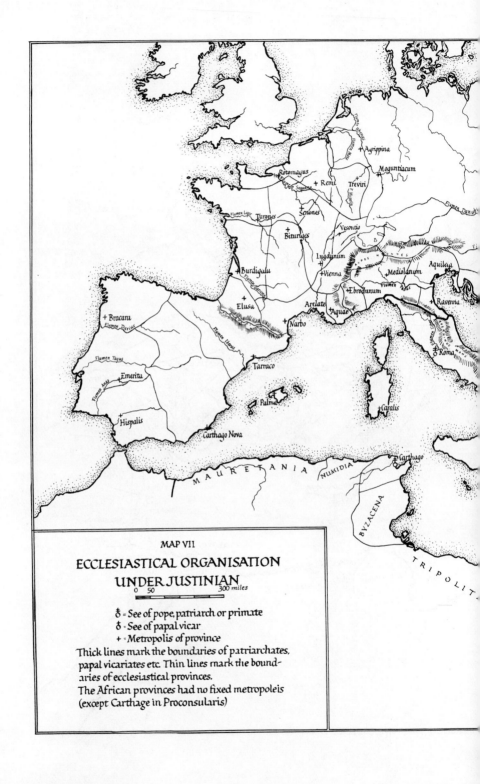

MAP VII

ECCLESIASTICAL ORGANISATION
UNDER JUSTINIAN
0   50   300 miles

ꝺ = See of pope, patriarch or primate
ꝺ = See of papal vicar
+ = Metropolis of province

Thick lines mark the boundaries of patriarchates,
papal vicariates etc. Thin lines mark the boundaries of ecclesiastical provinces.

The African provinces had no fixed metropoleis
(except Carthage in Proconsularis)

CAUCASUS MONS

+ Sirmium
+ Viminacium
Flumen Danubius
+ Tomi
Ratiaria
+ Marcianopolis
§ Iustiniana
Prima
Neocaesarea
+ Amaseia
Scupi
Philippopolis
+ Hadrianopolis
+ Gangra
+ Sebaste
Scodra
Stobi
Traianopolis
Constantinopolis
+ Claudiopolis
Melitene
Flumen Tigris
+ Amida
Dyrrachium
Heraclea
Nicomedia
+ Ancyra
Thessalonica
Cyzicus
Pessinus
+ Caesarea
Larissa
Synnada
+ Antiochia
Tyana
+ Anazarbus
+ Edessa
Nicopolis
Sardis
Iconium
Hierapolis
Ephesus
+ Laodicea
Tarsus
+ Resapha
Corinthus
Aphrodisias
Perge
Side
Seleucia
§ Antiochia
+ Apamea
Rhodius
Myra
Constantia
Damascus
Gortyna
Tyrus
+ Bostra
Caesarea
§ Scythopolis
§ Hierosolyma
Ptolemais
Alexandria
Petra

NOTES

I. THE PRINCIPATE (pp. 1–19)

As this introductory chapter is merely a résumé of well-known material I have given authorities only for a few isolated facts and figures which the reader might like to verify, and for some controversial views.

1. A. Momigliano (*Secondo Contributo alla Storia degli Studi Classici*, 105–44) has to my mind conclusively demonstrated that there is no valid reason for doubting that the *Historia Augusta* could have been written at the date its authors profess to have written it. On the positive side I would add that, as Mommsen (*Ges. Schr.* VII. 302 ff.) long ago observed, the administrative terminology of the authors precisely fits this period. For example there are *duces* and very rarely a *magister militum*, but usually the praetorian prefect is commander in chief; there is no quaestor or *magister officiorum*, but the *magister memoriae* is still the chief secretary (see ch. XII, n. 3).

2. My statistics do not agree with those of P. Lambrechts (*La composition du sénat romain* (117–92), Antwerp, 1936, (193–284), Budapest, 1937), but this work is now obsolete. My figures are derived from an unpublished thesis of my former pupil J. Morris of University College, London, which comprises an exhaustive prosopography of senators and their provenance when known.

3. The titles first appear in inscriptions at the end of the second century (e.g. *ILS* 1455) but were generally current much earlier (e.g. Suet. *Claudius*, 24).

4. PIUS' ACCUMULATED BALANCE: Cassius Dio, LXXIV. 8. MARCUS' AUCTIONS: SHA, *Marcus*, 17.

5. HADRIAN'S ARREARS: *ILS* 309. MARCUS' ARREARS: Cassius Dio, LXXI. 32.

6. Galen, *de probis pravisque alimentorum succis* (Ed. Kühn, VI. 749). I am indebted for this reference to Dr. David Woollam of Emmanuel College.

7. TRIBUTUM SOLI: *Dig.* L. XV. 4 (the *forma censualis*), Appian, *Syriaca*, 50 (1% of the assessment). TRIBUTUM CAPITIS: *Dig.* L. XV. 3 (age limits in Syria); it was certainly a polltax in Egypt (Wilcken, *Grundzüge*, 189), and a polltax is recorded in Macedonia and Greece (*IG* XII. v. 724, 946, 'Aϱχ. Δελτ., 1916, p. 148). *Dig.* L. XV. 8 §7 suggests that *tributum soli* and *capitis* were the two standard direct taxes. Where movable property (such as ships, Tac. *Ann.* XIII. 51) was assessed is not known.

8. See my *Greek City*, 140–3.

9. SC DE GLADIATORIBUS: *FIR* I². 49. TERGESTE: *ILS* 6680.

10. PERTINAX'S RESERVE: Cassius Dio, LXXIII. 5. SEVERUS AND THE ARMY: Herodian, III. viii. 4.

11. CARACALLA'S INCREASE OF PAY AND ITS COST: Herodian, IV. iv. 7, Cassius Dio, LXXVIII. 36. CARACALLA AND THE VICESIMA HEREDITATUM: Cassius Dio, LXXVII. 9.

12. For my views on the *Constitutio Antoniniana* see my *Studies in Roman Government and Law*, ch. VIII.

13. MACRINUS REDUCES THE VICESIMA HEREDITATUM: Cassius Dio, LXXVIII. 12. HIS RESTRICTION OF PAY INCREASES: ib. LXXVIII. 28, 36.

14. THE SENATORIAL COUNCIL OF STATE: Herodian, VI. i. 2.

15. See n. 2.

16. Aur. Victor, *Caes.* xxxiii. 34, xxxvii. 5, 6; see C. W. Keyes, *The rise of the equites in the third century of the Roman Empire* (Princeton, 1915).

17. MARCUS AND THE MARCOMANNI: Cassius Dio, LXXI. 15. PERTINAX AND THE LAND: Herodian, II. iv. 6. PROBUS AND THE BARBARIANS: SHA, *Probus*, 18. AURELIAN AND THE LAND: *CJ* XI. lix. 1.

18. AURELIAN'S CURRENCY REFORM: *Econ. Hist. Rev.* 1953, 297–8; my interpretation is confirmed by C. H. V. Sutherland in *JRS* LI (1961), 94–5. THE FOLLIS: *JRS* XLIX (1959), 34 ff.; my conjecture that the *follis* was worth 12,500 denarii under Diocletian has since been proved correct by P. *Beatty Panop.* 2, line 302, when 4 *folles* are equated with 33 talents (= 49,500 denarii) + 500 denarii.

19. *Econ. Hist. Rev.* 1953, 295–6, 299.

20. BLACK MARKET IN AUREI: *CIL* XIII. 3162; for the old ratio of *denarius* to *aureus* see Cassius Dio, LV. 12 § 4, and T. V. Buttrey's analysis of this passage in *JRS* LI (1961), 40–5. AURUM CORONARIUM: Cassius Dio, LXXVII. 9.

21. RISE IN PRICES AND WAGES: P. *Oxy.* 1414.

22. For the Egyptian evidence see S. L. Wallace, *Taxation in Egypt* (Princeton, 1938). It is one of the unsolved mysteries of history that so useful a tax as the *vicesima hereditatum* had ceased to exist by the fourth century.

23. DIOCLETIAN'S EDICT: *ILS* 642. The most recent study of the *annona* problem is D. van Berchem, 'L'annone militaire dans l'empire Romain au IIIᵉ siècle', *Mém. Soc. Nat. Ant. de France*, 8ᵐᵉ série, Tome X (1937), 117–202.

24. INDICTIONES: Pliny, *Paneg.* 29, Cassius Dio, LXXVII. 9, *Dig.* XIX. i. 13 §6, XXVI. vii. 32 §6, XXXIII. ii. 28. Cf. *CJ* X. xvi. 2, 260, 3, 249. PAYMENTS FOR ANNONA: *Sb* 7181 (220 A.D.), P. *Kalen*, 9 (240 A.D.); FOR CLOTHING: P. *Oxy.* 1414. The problem is discussed by van Berchem (see n. 23), but a thorough study based on the papyri is a *desideratum*.

25. For pay and deductions see P. *Gen. Lat.* 1 (reprinted in M. McCrum and A. G. Woodhead, *Documents of the Flavian Emperors* (Cambridge, 1961), no. 405).

26. THE MAGISTER MEMORIAE'S SALARY: Pan. Lat. IX. 11; for the Augustal prefect and the *dux* of Libya see p. 397.

II. DIOCLETIAN

In chapters II to IX I have not thought it necessary to give full documentation for the political and military narrative, as I am covering the same ground (more rapidly) as a number of more learned historians; O. Seeck, *Geschichte des Untergangs der antiken Welt* (Berlin, 1897–1921) for the period from A.D. 284 to 476, J. B. Bury, *A history of the Later Roman Empire* (London, 1923) for A.D. 395 to 565, A. Piganiol, *L'empire chrétien* (325–95) (Paris, 1947), E. Stein, *Histoire du bas-empire*, vol. I (284–476) (Paris, 1959, translation and revision by J. R. Palanque), vol. II (476–565) (Paris, 1949). The same applies to church history, where the story is more fully told in *Histoire de l'église* (A. Fliche, B. Martin), vol. III, *De la paix Constantinienne à la mort de Théodose* (by J. R. Palanque, G. Bardy, P. de Labriolle, Paris, 1947), vol. IV, *De la mort de Théodose à l'avènement de Grégoire le Grand* (by P. de Labriolle, G. Bardy, L. Bréhier, G. de Plinval, Paris, 1945).

There is no full scale modern biography of Diocletian. W. Seston has never completed his *Dioclétien et la Tétrarchie* (Paris, 1940), of which only the first volume has appeared. There are exhaustive and useful articles by G. Costa in the *Dizionario Epigrafico* and by W. Ensslin in Pauly-Wissowa (s.v. Valerius Diocletianus). Apart from the general works mentioned above, there is a full account of the reign in the *Cambridge Ancient History*, XII, chapters ix, x, xi and xix.

1. Arcadius Charisius and Hermogenian are usually placed after 331 A.D. because both (Arcadius in *Dig.* I. xi. 1 §1 and Hermogenian in *Dig.* IV. iv. 17) know of the inappellable jurisdiction of the praetorian prefect, affirmed in that year by *CTh* XI. xxx. 16. But both (Arcadius in *Dig.* L. iv. 18 §26 and Hermogenian in *Dig.* L. iv. 1 §1) speak of *decaproti*, who appear to have been abolished in 307–8 in favour of *praepositi pagorum* (see my *Greek City*, p. 333, n. 106), and neither in their exhaustive treatment of *munera* mention the latter office. The wording of *CTh* XI. xxx. 16, a proconsulibus et comitibus et his qui vice praefectorum cognoscunt, sive ex appellatione sive ex delegato sive ex ordine iudicaverint, provocari permittimus . . . a praefectis autem praetorio, qui soli vice sacra cognoscere vere dicendi sunt, provocari non sinimus, ne iam nostra contingi veneratio videatur, suggests that Constantine's object was to affirm that appeals were allowed from *vice sacra iudicantes*, except for the praetorian prefects. It may be that the title *vice sacra iudicans* originally meant that the holder's judgments were like the emperor's inappellable, and that this title was originally given to the praetorian prefects only. When the title was more widely granted appeals were allowed, and Constantine in this law made this plain, reaffirming the old inappellability of the prefects only.

2. For the date and composition of the Notitia Dignitatum see App. II.

3. The vexed question of the date of Diocletian's *dies imperii* has now been settled by P. *Beatty Panop.* 2, lines 162, 170, etc. Maximian's dates remain highly problematical, but there is no doubt that he was appointed first Caesar and then Augustus. Eutropius, the only literary authority to record the fact (IX. 20, 22), is wrong in making Maximian continue as Caesar until 293, but a few inscriptions (e.g. *ILS* 616) record him as Caesar; since he issued no coins as such the period in which he was Caesar must have been very brief.

4. THE CAESARS: Aur. Victor, *Caes.* xxxix. 24–5, Eutrop. IX. 22. Despite Seston's ingenious arguments (*op. cit.* pp. 88 ff.) I find it hard to disbelieve the contemporary evidence of Pan. Lat. VIII. 3 that both were created simultaneously on 1 March.

5. Lact. *Mort. Pers.* xviii, xix, Aur. Victor, *Caes.* xxxix. 48, xl. 1, Eutrop. IX. 27, X. 1, 2.

6. ADORATIO A PERSIAN CEREMONIAL: Aur. Victor, *Caes.* xxxix. 2, 4, Eutrop. IX. 26. SECLUSION: SHA, *Aurelianus*, 43.

7. For collegiality see pp. 325–6. The division of the empire in 293 is described by Aur. Victor, *Caes.* xxxix. 30 and Praxagoras (*FHG* IV, p. 2). That Diocletian was in Illyricum and Thrace throughout 293 and 294 is proved by the subscriptions of the Code (see pp. 495–7 of Krüger's edition). Lactantius (*Mort. Pers.* xvii) represents Diocletian as leaving for Rome after starting the persecution in the spring of 303, and returning to Nicomedia next year 'aestate peracta per circuitum ripae Istricae': he had already reached Durostorum by 8 June 303 (*CJ* v. lxxiii. 4) and was back in Nicomedia by 27 August 304 (*CJ* III. xxviii. 26).

8. Lact. *Mort. Pers.* vii. 4, provinciae quoque in frusta concisae. BYZACENA: *AE* 1908, 197. SITIFENSIS: *CIL* VIII. 8924, 20215. NUMIDIA C. AND M.:

ILS 631–3, 651, CIL VIII. 5526, 7965. TRIPOLITANIA: ILS 9352, IRT 577, CIL VIII. 22763. THE EGYPTIAN PROVINCES: J. Lallemand, Bull. Ac. Roy. Belg. (Cl. lettres et sc. mor. et pol.) 5 sér. XXXVI (1950), 387–95. CARIA: ILS 635. INSULAE: CIL III. 450, AE 1947, 57, CJ III. xxii. 5, 294. PISIDIA: ILS 8932, 9480. SCYTHIA: ILS 4103. NORICUM DIVIDED: ILS 4197. LUGDUNENSIS DIVIDED: CTh XI. iii. 1, 313 (S). VIENNENSIS: CIL XII. 1852.

9. See my article, 'The date and value of the Verona list', JRS XLIV (1954), 21–9, and add CIL VIII. 18905, which shows Numidia reunited in 314.

10. ACTA MARCELLI: Anal. Boll. XLI (1923), 260 ff. AURELIUS LITUA: ILS 628; Cornelius Octavianus appears to have dealt with the rebel Bavares 'et in priori praesidatu et post in ducatu' (ILS 9006). FORTRESSES BUILT BY PRAESIDES: AE 1931, 82 (Britain), ILS 640 (Maxima Sequanorum), AE 1942–3, 81, cf. ILS 5786 (Numidia), CIL VIII. 8712 (Sitifensis), ILS 9352 (Tripolitania), 6886 (Caesariensis), CIL III. 14149, AE 1895, 182 (Arabia), CIL III. 6661 (Libanensis).

11. VALERIUS CONCORDIUS: CIL XIII. 3672 (v.p.). CARAUSIUS: Eutrop. IX. 21. DUCES OF SCYTHIA: ILS 4103 (v.p.); IN VALERIA: CIL III. 10981 (v.p.); IN NORICUM: ILS 664 (v.p.); IN ILLYRICUM: FIR I². 93, line 24; OF EGYPT, etc.: AE 1934, 7–8 (v.p.); OF AFRICA, ETC.: ILS 2774, cf. 9006. For later ducatus covering several provinces see Not. Dig. Or. xxxiii, xxxviii, Occ. xxxii, xxxiv, xxxv, xxxvii, xl.

12. See JRS XLIV (1954), 24 ff. I have noted the following praesides of Diocletianic date who are styled v.p.; IGR I. 789–92, 1511–2, IRT 577, ILS 618, 628, 635, 640, 644, 4495, 9352, CIL II. 4104, 5140, III. 223, 307, 450, 480, 6661, 14156, VI. 1641, VIII. 2573–5, 2660, 4325, 8474, 21447–9, 23179, AE 1908, 107, 1917–8, 30, 1920, 15, 1930, 114, 1942–3, 81, 1956, 34; also prefects of Egypt, P. Oxy. 71, 888, 1456, 1503, 2187.

13. The administrative set up of Egypt under Diocletian has been vividly illuminated by P. Beatty Panop., which shows ὁ ἐπίτροπος τῆς κατωτέρω Θηβαίδος arranging all financial affairs and mentions ὁ ἐπίτροπος τῆς ἀνωτέρω Θηβαίδος fulfilling similar functions (1, lines 79, 187, 2, line 180), while ὁ ἡγούμενος τῆς Θηβαίδος appears only as a judge (1, lines 143, 272, 347, cf. 126) or as concerned with forts (1, lines 77, 385, 404) and the manufacture of arms (1, lines 213, 342). In 316 an ἐπίτροπος τῆς Ἑπτανομίας is recorded at the same time as a ἡγεμὼν τῆς Ἑρχουλίας (P. Oxy. 2113–14): these procurators of subdistricts are not later continued. For the financial responsibility of proconsuls under Constantine see CTh XI. i. 2+vii. 1, 313 (S), XI. xvi. 1, 319, I. xii. 2, 319.

14. Lact. Mort. Pers. vii. 4.

15. For Diocletian's insistence on fair assessments see the edict of Optatus (P. Cairo Isid. 1, Sb 7622); on jurisdiction, CJ III. iii. 2, 294.

16. Italy appears as officially one diocese not only in the Verona list but in the Notitia Dignitatum (Occ. i. 52–60, 90–7, ii. 6, 10–27), though by that time the vicarius urbis Romae was long established. A vicarius of the praefectus urbi is very occasionally mentioned (Zos. II. 9, ILS 1214, 792, Chron. Min. I. 67, 68) and elaborate theories have been formulated (most recently by Chastagnol, La Préfecture Urbaine à Rome, 26–42, who cites the earlier literature) on his relation with the vicarius of the praetorian prefect in urbe Roma. The meagre evidence does not seem to me to justify these theories: so far as we know the vicarius of the urban prefect was merely his temporary deputy (as certainly in Chron. Min. I. 67, 68). The vicarius urbis is first recorded with that title in ILS 1214, vicario

praeff. praetorio bis, in urbe Roma et per Mysias, but *ILS* 619 records 'Septimius Valentio v.p. a.v. praeff. praett. cc. vv.' at Rome in 293–6.

17. EARLY VICARS: *ILS* 619, 1214 (cited in n. 16; Urbs Roma and Moesia), *Acta Marcelli, Anal. Boll.* XLI (1923), 260 ff. (Spain), *AE* 1942–3, 81, *IRT* 464, Aur. Victor, *Caes.* xl. 17, Eus. *HE* x. 6 (Africa), *ILS* 1218 (Italy), *P. Oxy.* 1469, *CJ* XI. l. 1 (325), *CTh* XII. i. 12, 325, II. xxxiii. 1, 326 (S), Eus. *V. Const.* I. 31 (Oriens), *CTh* XI. vii. 2, 319 (Britain). A number of others are recorded in the Codes without their dioceses (e.g. *CJ* VII. xxii. 3, 314; VIII. x. 6, 321, IX. xxxiv. 3, 320, *CTh* II. vii. 1, 314, II. xv. 1, 319). For the military duties of early *vicarii* see the *Acta Marcelli* and *AE* 1942–3, 81. The equestrian rank of vicars is attested by *ILS* 619, *IRT* 464 and (of later date) *ILS* 1214, 1218, Aug. *Ep.* 88 §4, *CIL* II. 2203, *P. Oxy.* 1469. The constitutional position of proconsuls is described by Eunapius (*V. Soph.* VII. 5) and also emerges from *Not. Dig. Or.* ii, xxiv, where Asia is omitted from the lists of provinces under the disposition of the praetorian prefect of the East and the vicar of Asiana, and *Occ.* ii, xx, where Africa is similarly omitted. The later established proconsul of Achaea was subject to the praetorian prefect of Illyricum (*Not. Dig. Or.* iii. 8).

18. Lact. *Mort. Pers.* vii. 4. I know of the following diocesan *rationales* under Diocletian and Constantine: Africa, *CIL* VIII. 7043, *ILS* 1218, Eus. *HE* x. 6 §1, *CTh* x. i. 2, 319, xix. 1, 320; Numidia and Mauretania, *CIL* VIII. 7008–9, 7067; Gaul, *ILS* 1214, rationalis vicarius per Gallias; Spain, *CTh* x. xi. 1, rationali[bus] Hispaniarum, 317; Tres Provinciae, *CTh* II. xxv. 1, 325 (S), XII. vi. 2, 325 and vii. 1, 325; Urbs Roma, *ILS* 1218, *CTh* XI. xxx. 14, 327; Asiana, *ILS* 6091; Egypt, *P. Oxy.* 1410, τοῦ διασημ(οτάτου) καθολ(ικοῦ) ἐπαρχείας Αἰγύπτου καὶ Λιβύης, *CIL* III. 17, *P. Oxy.* 1204, 1260, 2187, *P. Merton*, 90, *PSI* 302, *P. Harris*, 160, *P. Vind.* 14, *Sb* 4295, *P. Beatty Panop.* 1, lines 64, 90; 2, lines 12, 23, *P. Flor.* 54. There are a large number of *rationales* recorded at Rome (*CIL* VI. 1120a, 1121, 1132, 1145, 1701 a, b); they may have been *rationales urbis Romae*, but some may have been *rationales* of the (Western) empire. Practically all the above are styled v.p.

19. Diocesan *magistri rei privatae* are rarely recorded. I can cite *P. Beatty Panop.* 1, lines 160, 205, 227 (298), *CTh* x. i. 4, ad Dometium Dracontium magistrum privatae rei Africae, 320, *CIL* III. 18, Val. Epiphanius v.p. mag. privat. Aeg. et Lib. (Constantine). *Magistri (rei privatae)* are often coupled with *rationales (rei summae)*, e.g. in Lact. *Mort. Pers.* vii. 4, Firm. Mat. *Math.* IV. xxi. 9, *CJ* III. xxii. 5, 294, *CTh* x. i. 2, 319, XII. i. 14 (326–54).

20. A proconsul of Crete is still recorded under Diocletian (*AE* 1933, 101, 1934, 259), and a *v.c. legatus Augusti* in Phoenice (*AE* 1939, 58). A ληγᾶτος of Moesia II appears in the *Acta Dasii* (*Anal. Boll.* XVI (1897), 11–5). DECIMUS: *ILS* 607, 2291, 3091. MAXIMIANUS: *ILS* 2292, 5786–7. CONSTANTIUS: Anon. Val. I. CONCORDIUS: *CJ* IX. ix. 27, 295, *CIL* XIII. 3672. Cf also Octavianus, *ILS* 9006 (cited in n. 10).

21. DUCES AND IUDICES: Pan. Lat. x. 3, qui iustitiam vestram iudices aemulentur, qui virtutis vestrae gloriam duces servent. FLAVIANUS: *CIL* VIII. 4325. MEN OF LIBERAL EDUCATION: Pan. Lat. IX. 5, 15, VI. 23.

22. ASCLEPIODOTUS AND HANNIBALIANUS: *ILS* 8929, SHA, *Probus*, 22, Aur. Victor, *Caes.* xxxix. 42, Eutrop. IX. 22. VOLUSIANUS: Aur. Victor, *Caes.* xl. 18. POMPEIANUS: Pan. Lat. XII. 8, cf. IV. 25. For the functions of the praetorian prefects see pp. 371–2, 448 ff., 479 ff. For the two financial departments and the secretariats see pp. 412 ff., 367–8.

23. SICORIUS PROBUS: Petr. Patr. 14. The *magister studiorum* is last recorded in *ILS* 1214, which is also the only evidence for *a consiliis sacris*.

24. For Asclepiodotus see n. 22. EUMENIUS: Pan. Lat. IX. 6, 11. Gallus had a praetorian prefect and a quaestor (Amm. XIV. i. 10, vii. 9, 12), appointed by Constantius. So also had Julian (Amm. XVII. iii. 4, XX. viii. 14, ix. 5), but Ursulus, Constantius' *comes sacrarum largitionum*, controlled the *largitiones* in Julian's dominions (Amm. XXII. iii. 7).

25. SALARY OF MAGISTER MEMORIAE: Pan. Lat. VI. 11, trecena illa sestertia quae sacrae memoriae magister acceperam. For the allowances of *duces* etc. see p. 397.

26. Lact. *Mort. Pers.* vii. 4. For the numbers of *officia* see pp. 592-4.

27. Zos. II. 34. The latest substantial contribution to the problem of the army is D. van Berchem, *L'Armée de Dioclétien et la Réforme Constantinienne*, Paris, 1952.

28. LANCIARII: *ILS* 2781, Val. Thiumpo qui militavit in leg. XI Cl., lectus in sacro comit. lanciarius, deinde protexit annis V, missus, pref. leg. II Hercul., 2782, Martino . . . qui vixit ann. XXXVIII, in prima Minerbes mil. ann. V, in und. ann. IIII, in lanciaria ann. V, in pr. ann. V, 2045, Val. Tertius militi corti X pretorie qui vixit annis XXXVI mes. III dies XV, militabit legione Mesiaca annis V, inter lanciarios annis XI, in pretoria ann[is . . .]. COMITES: *P. Oxy.* 43R, col. ii, 17, 24, 27. The Lanciarii Seniores are the senior palatine legion in the East (*Not. Dig. Or.* v. 42), the Comites Seniores the senior palatine vexillation in both East and West (*Not. Dig. Or.* vi. 28, *Occ.* vi. 43). ACTA MAXIMILIANI: G. Krüger, *Ausgewählte Märtyrerakten*, 86-7.

29. Opt. *App.* I, *ad init.*

30. The usurper Magnentius was commander of Ioviani and Herculiani (Zos. II. 42); cf. also Soz. VI. 6, Zos. III. 30, Vegetius, I. 17, where their origin is given. Their Seniores rank highest among the palatine legions of the West (*Not. Dig. Occ.* v. 145-6) and their Iuniores next after the Lanciarii in the East (*Not. Dig. Or.* v. 43-4). The Equites Promoti Seniores are the highest ranking palatine vexillation in the East (*Not. Dig. Or.* v. 28), and the second highest, after the Comites Seniores, in the West (*Not. Dig. Occ.* vi. 44).

31. On the origins of the *protectores* see Stein, *Bas-Empire*, I. 57-8. DIOCLETIAN: Aur. Victor, *Caes.* xxxix. 1, domesticos regens, SHA, *Carus*, 13, domesticos tunc regentem. VALERIUS VINCENTIUS: *ILS* 2779. PROTECTORES IN EGYPT: *P. Oxy.* 43R, col. ii, 7, col. iv, 18-20.

32. For Thiumpus see n. 28.

33. ACTA SERGII ET BACCHI: *Anal. Bol.* XIV (1895), 375 ff. SCUTARII: Lact. *Mort. Pers.* xix. 6, statim scutarius, continuo protector, mox tribunus, postridie Caesar, *CTh* XIV. xvii. 9, 389, annonas civicas in urbe Constantinopolitana scholae scutariorum et scutariorum clibanariorum divi Constantini adseruntur liberalitate meruisse. For the later history of the *scholae* see pp. 613-4.

34. For the Constantinian additions to the *comitatus* see pp. 97-8. THE EGYPTIAN EXPEDITIONARY FORCE: *P. Oxy.* 43R, col. ii, 21-3, col. iv, 11, col. v, 12-13, 23-4, cf. *Not. Dig. Or.* xxviii. 14, 15, for V Macedonica and XIII Gemina; xxxi. 43, for ala II Hispanorum.

35. *CJ* VII. lxiv. 9 (293-305), veteranis qui in legione vel vexillatione militantes post vicesima stipendia honestam vel causariam missionem consecuti sunt, honorum et munerum personalium vacationem concessimus, x. lv. 3 (286-93), veteranis ita demum honorum et munerum personalium vacatio iure conceditur

si post vicesimum annum militiae quam in legione vel vexillatione militaverunt, honestam vel causariam missionem consecuti esse ostendantur. unde cum te in cohorte militasse commemoras, intellegis supervacuo vacationem tibi velle flagitare, FIR I². 93, 311, quo tam legionarii milites quam etiam equites in vexillationibus constituti Inlyriciani sicuti similes labores militiae suae sustinent ita etiam provisionis nostrae similibus commodis perfruantur. In the Notitia this distinction is still observed in most provinces of the East in so far as *alae* and *cohortes* are on the *laterculum minus* (*Not. Dig. Or.* xxviii. 23, xxxi. 42, xxxii. 32, etc.).

36. EQUITES DALMATAE COMIT.: *ILS* 664, 2792. LANCIARII: *Not. Dig. Or.* viii. 44, ix. 36, *Occ.* v. 152, 259, 260 (= vii. 58, 59, 82). For Aurelian's Moorish and Dalmatian cavalry see Zos. I. 52, and for their distribution in the Notitia App. II, Table X.

37. For the strength of various classes of units see pp. 680–2 and for the analysis of the Notitia which follows see App. II, Tables IX–XIV.

38. Lact. *Mort. Pers.* vii. 2. BARBARIAN UNITS: *Not. Dig. Or.* xxviii. 25–6, 33, 43, xxxi. 46, 51, 55–6, 61–3, 66–7, xxxii. 35–7, 41, xxxiii. 31–2, xxxvi. 33–4, 36. For the *laeti* see p. 620.

39. For the later system of conscription see pp. 615–6. PROTOSTASIA: *CJ* x. xlii. 8 (293–305), lxii. 3 (286–93). TEMONARIUS: *Acta Maximiliani* (see n. 28). SEVERITY OF CONSCRIPTION: Lact. *Mort. Pers.* vii. 5, haec quoque tolerari non possunt quae ad exhibendos milites spectant.

40. Lact. *Mort. Pers.* vii. 3, adeo maior esse coeperat numerus accipientium quam dantium ut enormitate indictionum consumptis viribus colonorum desererentur agri et culturae verterentur in silvam.

41. For the currency see pp. 438–9.

42. THE EDICT ON PRICES: Lact. *Mort. Pers.* vii. 6, 7; the best text is in Tenney Frank, *Economic Survey of Ancient Rome*, v. 310–421: there is an important additional fragment in *AE* 1947, 148–9.

43. The best account of the *capitatio* is A. Déléage, *La capitation du bas-empire*, Macon, 1945. See also my article, 'Capitatio and iugatio', *JRS* xlvii (1957), 90 ff. For the quinquennial cycle see L. Amundsen, *Ostraca Osloensia*, pp. 64–8, and for the first indiction of 312, E. H. Kase, *A papyrus Roll in the Princeton Collection*, pp. 25–31. EDICT OF OPTATUS: *P. Cairo Isid.* 1 (=*Sb* 7622).

44. The Syrian census inscriptions are collected in Déléage, op. cit., 152–7, the Egyptian declarations, ibid. 48 ff., the inscribed census records of Asiana, ibid. 164 ff.; cf. my article, 'Census records of the later Roman Empire', *JRS* XLIII (1953), 49 ff. THE CENSUS OF PONTICA: Lact. *Mort. Pers.* xxiii. 1–6; OF GAUL: Pan. Lat. V. 5.

45. SYRIAN SCHEDULE: *Leges saeculares*, 121 (FIR II². pp. 795–6). ASIANIC SCHEDULE: *JRS* XLIII (1953), 49–50. CENTURIAE: *CTh* XI. i. 10, 365, xxviii. 13, 422, Val. III, *Nov.* xxxiv, 431. MILLENAE: *CIL* x. 407, Val. III, *Nov.* v §4, 440, Maj. *Nov.* vii §16, 458, Just. *App.* vii §26, 554.

46. *JRS* XLIII (1953), 50–1.

47. POLLTAX ON RURAL POPULATION ONLY: *CJ* XI. lv. 1 (290), ne quis ex rusticana plebe quae extra muros posita capitationem suam detulit et annonam congruam praestat ad ullum aliud obsequium devocetur, *P. Cairo Isid.* 1 (= *Sb* 7622); ON URBAN POPULATION IN ASIA MINOR: Lact. *Mort. Pers.* xxiii. 2, hominum capita notabantur, in civitatibus urbanae ac rusticae plebes adunatae; IN EGYPT: *PSI*

163, 302, 462, 780; REMITTED IN ASIANA: *CTh* XIII. x. 2, 311 (S), plebs urbana, sicut in orientalibus quoque provinciis observatur, minime in censibus pro capitatione sua conveniatur, sed iuxta hanc iussionem nostram inmunis habeatur, sicuti etiam sub domino et parente nostro Diocletiano seniore Augusto eadem plebs urbana inmunis fuerat.

48. SEVERUS' CENSUS AT ROME: Lact. *Mort. Pers.* xxvi. 2. AFRICA: *CTh* XIII. iv. 4, 374. GAUL: Pan. Lat. v. 5–6, 11–2, *CTh* XII. i. 36, 343, XI. xxiii. 2, 362, XIII. x. 4. 368, 6, 370.

49. *CJ* XI. lv. 1 (290); Arcadius Charisius, *Dig.* L. iv. 18 §8, qui annonam suscipit vel exigit vel erogat et exactores pecuniae pro capitibus; Lact. *Mort. Pers.* xxiii. 6, post hoc pecuniae pro capitibus pendebantur; for the Egyptian poll tax see above n. 47.

50. *FIR* I². 93, 311, *CTh* VII. xx. 4, 325. For further details see *JRS* XLVII (1957), 88 ff.

51. TAXATION OF ITALY: Aur. Victor, *Caes.* xxxix. 31, hinc denique parti Italiae invectum tributorum ingens malum; cf. Lact. *Mort. Pers.* xxvi. 2 for the *capitatio*. The *ius Italicum* was conferred on Constantinople (*CTh* XIV. xiii. 1, 370, *CJ* XI. xxi. 1, 421), but as appears from Soz. VII. 9 this merely meant that τὰ συμβόλαια κατὰ τὰ νόμιμα τῶν ἐν 'Ιταλίᾳ 'Ρωμαίων ἐκρίνετο. For Justinian's abolition of the distinctions between Italian and provincial lands see *CJ* VII. xxv. 1 (530–1), xxxi. 1, 531, xl. 1, 530, *Inst.* II. vi. pr.

52. For *capitula* see pp. 615–6. COMMUTATION FOR ANIMALS: E. H. Kase, *A Papyrus Roll in the Princeton Collection*, I. 11–4, 21–4, II. 12–20. PAYMENT FOR CLOTHING: *P. Cairo Isid.* 54; for the later system see *CTh* VI. vi. 3, 377.

53. PUBLIC WORKS AND THE CORVÉE: Lact. *Mort. Pers.* vii. 8–10. QUARRIES: *Chr.* I. 391. See also ch. XXI, n. 34.

54. FABRICAE: Lact. *Mort. Pers.* vii. 9, cf. *P. Beatty Panop.* 2, lines 213–6, 342–6 (conscription of craftsmen πρὸς τὴν τῆς φάβρικος ἐργασίαν and πρὸς ἐργασίαν περικεφαλέων καὶ λωρίκων κνημίδων. GYNAECIA AND LINYPHIA: Eus. *V. Const.* II. 34. For the organization of the factories see pp. 834–7.

55. For the *cursus publicus* see pp. 830–4 and for the *pastus primipili*, p. 459. Arcadius Charisius cites 'cursus vehicularis sollicitudo, item angariarum praebitio' as personal *munera*, and 'agminales equi vel mulae et angariae atque veredi' as patrimonial (*Dig.* L. iv. 18 §§4, 21, 29, cf. §10 for building *mansiones*).

56. Lact. *Mort. Pers.* vii. 3.

57. Pan. Lat. v. 6–7. Aur. Victor, *Caes.* xxxix. 32, pensionibus inducta lex nova: quae sane illorum temporum modestia tolerabilis in perniciem processit his tempestatibus. Them. *Or.* VIII. 113 c.

58. On my theory of the development of the tied colonate see my article, 'The Roman Colonate', *Past and Present*, XIII (1958), 1–13. EDICT OF THE PREFECT OF EGYPT: *Chr.* I. 202. LETTER OF THE PRAEPOSITUS PAGI: *P. Cairo Isid.* 126. THEADELPHIA: *P. Thead.* 16, 17.

59. For the census registers see *JRS* XLIII (1953), 49 ff.

60. On the *curiales* see my *Greek City*, 192 ff. LAWS OF DIOCLETIAN: *CJ* x. xxxii. 6, 293 (illiteracy), 12, 293, lix. 1 (286–93, *infamia*), xxxii. 13 (293–305, Protus), xxxiii. 1 (286–93), lviii. 1 (293–305, freedmen).

61. BAN ON MILITARY SERVICE: *CJ* XII. xxxiii. 2 (286–93).

62. OFFICERS EXCUSED: *CJ* x. xlviii. 2 (286–93), *CTh* VII. ii. 1, 313.

63. AURELIUS PLUTARCHUS: *P. Oxy.* 1204.

64. CONSTANTINE'S LAW: *CTh* XII. i. 4, 317. LICINIUS' LAW: *CTh* XII. i. 5, 317.

65. For the great persecution see *CAH* XII. ch. xix, and the bibliography on pp. 789–96. THE CHURCH OF NICOMEDIA: Lact. *Mort. Pers.* xii. 3–5. ADAUCTUS: Eus. *HE* VIII. 11. CHRISTIAN DUOVIRI, FLAMINES AND SACERDOTES: *C. Ilib.* can. 2, 3, 55, 56.

66. THE INTERRUPTED SACRIFICE: Lact. *Mort. Pers.* x, cf. *Div. Inst.* IV. 27 §§4–5.

67. THE FIRST EDICTS: Lact. *Mort. Pers.* xii, xiii, Eus. *HE* VIII. 2, Mart. *Pal.* pr. That Christian meetings were prohibited appears from the *Acta Saturnini* (*Studi e Testi*, LXV (1935), 49 ff.). CONSTANTIUS: Lact. *Mort. Pers.* xv. 7, cf. the Donatist petition in Opt. I. 22; Eusebius (*HE* VIII. 13 and *V. Const.* I. 16) exaggerates his favour to the Christians.

68. SECOND AND THIRD EDICTS: Lact. *Mort. Pers.* xiv, xv. 2, Eus. *HE* VIII. 6, *Mart. Pal.* pr. and 1 §4. FOURTH EDICT: Eus. *Mart. Pal.* 3 §1. Among the Western acts of the martyrs I know of only one of reputable appearance (*Acta Crispinae*, Krüger, *Ausgewählte Märtyrerakten*, 29) which speaks of an imperial order of general sacrifice. There are a few cases where a Roman governor ordered a recalcitrant Christian to sacrifice (Aug. *c. Cresc.* III. 30, Donatus respondit: scis quantum me quaesivit Florus ut turificarem, *Acta Eupli*, *Studi e Testi*, XLIX (1928), 47 ff., where the order to sacrifice may be an apocryphal addition), but these are not proof of any general edict, for sacrifice was a test normally applied to accused Christians and may have been ordered by governors in individual cases. As against this must be set the fact that the whole Donatist controversy hinged on *traditio*, the surrender of the Scriptures under the first edict, and charges of sacrifice did not arise. It is incredible, if the African bishops had been imprisoned and forced to sacrifice, that the council of Cirta (Aug. *c. Cresc.* III. 30) should have concerned itself only with accusations of *traditio* and that the council of Arles (*C. Arel.* I, can. 13) should have legislated on charges of *traditio* only. In the East, on the contrary, the sin of *traditio* was completely overshadowed by that of sacrifice, and the canons (see n. 76) deal only with Christians who had sacrificed.

69. MAXENTIUS: Eus. *HE* VIII. 14, Aug. *Brev. Coll.* III. 34, *ad Don. post Coll.* 17. MAXIMINUS' EDICTS: Eus. *Mart. Pal.* 4 §8, 9 §2.

70. Lact. *Mort. Pers.* xxxiii–xxxv, Eus. *HE* VIII. 17, IX. 1.

71. Lact. *Mort. Pers.* xxxvi, Eus. *HE* IX. 2 ff. For Lycia-Pamphylia see *OGI* 569.

72. ANULLINUS AND THE MAGISTRATES OF TIGISIS: Aug. *Brev. Coll.* III. 25. BRIBERY OF OFFICIALS: Peter of Alexandria, can. xii (*PG* XVIII. 500). BOGUS TORTURES: *C. Anc.* can. 1.

73. Any judgement on this question is subjective, but it can hardly be an accident that genuine martyr acts are so rare in the West outside Africa: Euplus in Sicily is the only case of which I know. In Africa we have an absolutely genuine record of abject *traditio* at Cirta in Opt. *App.* I. 17b–19a, and less certain charges of *traditio* and evasion in Aug. *Brev. Coll.* III. 28 and *C. Cresc.* III. 30.

74. For Egypt Eusebius, who was an eyewitness, gives an impressive picture in *HE* VIII. 9; for the Egyptian convicts sent to Palestine and elsewhere see Eus. *Mart. Pal.* 8 §§1, 13; 11 §6. For Egyptian stubbornness, Amm. XXII. xvi. 23.

75. PROCOPIUS: Eus. *Mart. Pal.* 1. For other voluntary martyrs in Palestine see Eus. *Mart. Pal.* 3 §3, 4 §8.

76. SCALES OF PENANCE: *PG* XVIII. 467–508 (Peter of Alexandria), *C. Anc.* can. 1–9. For the Donatists and Melitians see pp. 954–5.

III. CONSTANTINE (pp. 77–81)

The latest scholarly work on Constantine is J. Vogt, *Constantin der Grosse und sein Jahrhundert*[2], Munich, 1960, which contains a bibliography of the abundant modern literature; cf. the same author's article 'Constantinus der Grosse' in the *Reallexicon für Antike und Christentum* (1956). I have set out my own view of Constantine in full in my popular work, *Constantine and the Conversion of Europe*[2], New York, 1963, which though it gives no references cites the major documents in translation *in extenso*.

1. For the documents in the *Vita Constantini* see *J. Eccl. Hist.* v (1954), 196–200. Vogt has to my mind successfully vindicated the authenticity of the *Vita* itself in *Röm. Mitt.* LVIII (1943), 198 ff., *Mélanges Grégoire* I (1949), 593 ff., *Historia* II (1953–4), 463 ff. and *Hermes* LXXXI (1953), 111 ff.

2. A peculiarly baffling group of laws is that addressed *ad vv. cc. PPO* (*CTh* VI. xxvii. 1, VII. xiii. 1, xxi. 2, VIII. iv. 5, vii. 4, 5, 6, XII. i. 14, 18). Both Mommsen and Seeck regarded them as parts of a single law, because they all deal with cognate topics, and the consulships look suspiciously like various corruptions of one imperial consulship (it should however be noted that the day and month are quite different in each); Mommsen decided for 353 as the real date, Seeck for 326. Both overlooked the fact that VI. xxvii. 1 grants immunity from the *curia* after *twenty* years' service to 'largitionales et officiales comitum rerum privatarum', while VIII. vii. 6 gives immunity from the *curia* after *twenty-five* years' service to 'largitionalibus comitatensibus et officialibus rationalis rerum privatarum'. Since they prescribe a different rule and give a different title to the chief of the *res privata* they cannot be parts of the same law. I suspect that these laws are derived from a file of imperial rulings on the question of decurions and *militiae* kept in the office of one of the praetorian prefects, and that the redactors of the Code took the date of the file to be that of the laws which it contained: in which case they are all of uncertain date.

3. Pan. Lat. VI. 2–3.

4. Eus. *V. Const.* I. 28, Lact. *Mort. Pers.* xliv.

5. The inscription of the arch (*ILS* 694) must have been composed or at any rate approved by Constantine. GRANTS TO THE CHURCH: Eus. *HE* x. 5 §§15–17, 6, 7. The quotation is from the last passage.

6. THE EDICT: Lact. *Mort. Pers.* xlviii, Eus. *HE* x. 5 §§1–14. Licinius' monotheist prayer (Lact. *Mort. Pers.* xlvi. 6) bears a remarkable resemblance to the prayer which Constantine later ordered his pagan soldiers to use (Eus. *V. Const.* IV. 20) and may well have been suggested by him to his colleague. Lactantius declares that an angel dictated the prayer to Licinius in a dream, thus putting him on a par with Constantine, and Eusebius in the opening words of *HE* IX. 9 couples Constantine and Licinius together as equally servants of God.

7. *CTh* VII. xx. 2, 326 (S), adclamatum est: Auguste Constantine, dii te nobis servent.

8. COINS OF SOL: *Num. Chron.* 1957, 32–3. SUNDAY: *CTh* II. viii. 1, 321, diem solis veneratione sui celebrem.

9. For the origins and early history of the Donatist schism see W. H. C. Frend, *The Donatist Church*, 3–24, 141–68. Constantine in his letter to Caecilian (Eus. *HE* x. 6) assumes the latter's opponents to be in the wrong, and orders that his bounty should be reserved for the clergy listed by Hosius. THE DONATIST PETITION: Aug. *Ep.* 88 §2. CONSTANTINE'S LETTER TO MILTIADES: Eus. *HE* x. 5 §§18–20. THE COUNCIL OF ROME: Opt. I. 23–4. CONVOCATION OF THE COUNCIL OF ARLES: Eus. *HE* x. 5 §§21–4, Opt. *App.* III.

10. Opt. *App.* III. *ad fin.*

11. The decision of the Council of Arles is given in its letter to the pope (Opt. *App.* IV), and Constantine's rejection of the Donatists' appeal in his letter to the council (Opt. *App.* V). The investigation whereby Felix was cleared of *traditio* is in Opt. *App.* II, and that in which the Donatist bishop Silvanus was convicted of *traditio* in Opt. *App.* I. For Constantine's first abandonment of the persecution see Opt. *App.* IX, X.

12. It appears from Them. *Or.* IV. 58b, that Constantine laid out the walls of Constantinople at the same time that he declared Constantius II Caesar, that is in 324: the formal dedication of the site took place on 3 November of that year (*Chron. Min.* I. 233, 643). *CTh* XIII. v. 7, 334, pro commoditate urbis quam aeterno nomine iubente deo donavimus; the second quotation is from Eus. *V. Const.* III. 48. CHURCHES AND SCRIPTURES: ibid. IV. 36 (a letter of Constantine). I prefer this evidence to the spiteful and confused statement of Zosimus (II. 31) that Constantine built temples to Rhea and the Fortune of Rome: the alleged temples were doubtless halls for the exhibition of statues (note that the statue of Rhea was altered from its original form as a cult image).

13. Soc. I. 16. The statement is usually doubted, but Socrates declares that the constitution conferring the title was publicly engraved in the Strategion and Alexander, Bishop of Byzantium, is styled bishop of New Rome in a document of 324 (*Nachr. Ges. Gött. Wiss.* 1905, 272–9). The prefecture of Constantinople was inaugurated in 359 (Soc. II. 41, *Chron. Min.* I. 239), and prior to that date a proconsul is mentioned at Constantinople in 343 (Ath. *Apol. de fuga*, 3), 355 (Them. *Or.* ed. Dindorf, p. 502) and 356 (*CTh* VI. iv. 8, 9). It is generally assumed that this proconsul was governor of the city only, but the passage in Athanasius implies that he had authority over Aenus and Trajanopolis, cities of Rhodope. I am inclined to think that Constantine united two or more of the provinces of Thrace and gave their governor the higher title of proconsul. An earlier stage in the process may be recorded in *ILS* 1240, when Aradius Proculus is *consularis provinciae Europae et Thraciae* soon after 324 (for the date cf. *ILS* 6111); 'Thracia' in this inscription cannot denote the province of Thrace, which was not contiguous to Europa, but probably means 'the rest of the diocese of Thrace' or 'other provinces of the Thracian diocese'. Europa had earlier been under an equestrian *praeses* (*IGR* I. 789–91). Themistius' statement (*Or.* IV. 55b), Κωνσταντίνου ἐστὶ γέννημα καὶ θρέμμα ἡ γερουσία, no doubt means that Constantine gave the title of senate to the council of his city, but Anon. Val. 30, ibi etiam senatum instituit secundi ordinis; claros vocavit, is decisive that this 'senate' was not coordinate with the Roman senate. Constantius II implies that the *senatus Constantinopolitanus* only bore Constantine's name and was not his creation, when he says (Them. *Oratio Constantii*, 23b): οὕτως γὰρ ἂν

καὶ τῷ θειοτάτῳ πατρὶ πράττοιμεν κεχαρισμένα τὴν ἐπώνυμον αὐτοῦ βουλὴν ἀνθεῖν τε καὶ θάλλειν τοῖς μεγίστοις τῶν ἀγαθῶν παρασκευάζοντες. Zosimus' statement (III. 11) that Julian ἔδωκε μὲν τῇ πόλει γερουσίαν ἔχειν ὥσπερ τῇ 'Ρώμῃ must be an error. For the magistracies see *CTh* VI. iv. 5+6, in which Constantius II appears to establish the praetorship for the first time in 340.

14. THE INAUGURATION: *Chron. Min.* I. 233, 643. Zosimus' strictures on Constantine's jerry building (II. 32) are borne out by Themistius (*Or.* III. 47c). GRANTS OF IMPERIAL LAND: Th. II, *Nov.* v. 1 §1, 438, valuerit igitur in fundis patrimonialibus sitis per Asianam diocesim, sitis per Ponticam . . . lex divae memoriae Constantini, quae aedes per Constantinopolitanam urbem sacratissimam dominos exigebat. For the corn doles see pp. 696–7.

15. For the dates of the proclamation of the Caesars see *Chron. Min.* I. 232, 234–5. Crispus' rule in Gaul is clearly proved by Pan. Lat. IV. 3, 17, 36–7 (the speech was delivered in 321). Constantine Caesar's Gallic command is attested only by his title Alamannicus, which he held by 331 (*ILS* 6091); his Danubian command by Anon. Val. 31. Constantius' rule in Gaul is proved by Julian, *Or.* I. 11d, 12a, and his transfer to the East by ibid. 13b. For the later divisions of the empire see Eutrop. x. 6, eo tempore res Romana sub uno Augusto et tribus Caesaribus, quod numquam alias, fuit, cum liberi Constantini Galliae, Orienti Italiaeque praeessent, Anon. Val. 35, ita ut Gallias Constantinus minor regebat, Orientem Constantius, Africam Illyricum et Italiam Constans, ripam Gothicam Dalmatius tuebatur, *Epit. Caes.* xli. 20, hi singuli has partes regendas habuerunt: Constantinus iunior cuncta trans Alpes, Constantius a freto Propontidis Asiam atque Orientem, Constans Illyricum Italiamque et Africam, Dalmat[ius Dac]iam, Thraciam, Macedoniamque et Achaiam.

16. CONSTANTINE'S LETTER TO SAPOR: Eus. *V. Const.* IV. 9–13. On Hannibalianus see *Klio* XXIX (1936), 102 ff.

17. For the beginning of the Arian controversy see *Hist. de l'Église*, III. 69–81. The documents are published in H. G. Opitz, *Athanasius Werke*, III. i. nos. 1–16.

18. CONSTANTINE'S LETTER TO ALEXANDER AND ARIUS: Eus. *V. Const.* II. 64–72. THE COUNCIL OF ANTIOCH: Opitz, op. cit. no. 18; that Hosius presided is demonstrated by H. Chadwick, *JTS* 1958, 292–304.

19. Opitz, op. cit., no. 20.

20. For the council of Nicaea see *Hist. de l'Église*, III. 81–95. Constantine's responsibility for the homoousion is demonstrated by Eusebius' letter to the church of Caesarea (Soc. I. 8, Theod. *HE* I. 12, Gelasius, II. 35).

21. THE MELITIANS: Ath. *Decr. Nic.* 36, Soc. I. 9, Theod. *HE* I. 9, Gelasius, II. 34. THE NOVATIANS AND PAULIANISTS: *C. Nic.* can. 8, 19. THE LAPSED: *C. Nic.* can. 11, 12. EASTER: Eus. *V. Const.* III. 17–20, Soc. I. 9, Theod. *HE* I. 10, Gelasius, II. 37. On the organization of the church see pp. 880 ff.

22. The quotation is from Constantine's letter to the church of Alexandria (Ath. *Decr. Nic.* 38, Soc. I. 9, Gelasius, II. 37). EDICT AGAINST HERETICS: Eus. *V. Const.* III. 64–5. THE NOVATIANS: *CTh* XVI. v. 2, 326. CONSTANTINE AND ARIUS: Soc. I. 25–6, Soz. II. 27. I follow E. Schwartz, *Nachr. Ges. Gött. Wiss.* 1911, 380 ff. in postulating a second session of Nicaea, to which Eusebius and Theognius addressed a letter preserved in Soc. I. 14, Soz. II. 16, Gelasius, III. 13.

23. For this very obscure period see *Hist. de l'Église*, III. 97–113. In general I follow the version of E. Schwartz in *Nachr. Ges. Gött. Wiss.* 1911, 367–426,

to whose documentation must be added *P. Lond.* 1913–4 (published by H. I. Bell, *Jews and Christians in Egypt*) on the abortive council of Caesarea.

24. IMMUNITY OF THE CLERGY: Eus. *HE* x. 7, *CTh* xvi. ii. 1, 313, 2, 313 (S), 7, 330, Opt. *App.* x. 37a; limited by *CTh* xvi. ii. 6, 326, 3, 326 (S).

25. GRANT TO CAECILIAN: Eus. *HE* x. 6. For later regular grants see pp. 898–9.

26. SUBSIDY FOR BUILDING CHURCHES: Eus. *V. Const.* ii. 46. ROME AND ITALY: *Lib. Pont.* xxxiv. CIRTA: Opt. *App.* x.

27. THE HOLY PLACES: Eus. *V. Const.* iii. 25–43, 51–4. At Constantinople Socrates (1. 16) mentions S. Irene and the Holy Apostles but curiously omits S. Sophia. NICOMEDIA AND ANTIOCH: Eus. *V. Const.* iii. 50.

28. RENTALS OF CHURCH LANDS: *Lib. Pont.* xxxiv. BEQUESTS TO THE CHURCH LEGALIZED: *CTh* xvi. ii. 4, 321.

29. MANUMISSION: *CTh* iv. vii. 1, 321. EPISCOPAL JURISDICTION: *Sirm.* 1, 333.

30. CONSTANTINE'S SERMONS: Eus. *V. Const.* iv. 29. PROPAGANDA IN THE ARMY: ibid., iv. 18–21.

31. ABLABIUS' HUMBLE ORIGIN: Lib. *Or.* xlii. 23, Eunap. *V. Soph.* vi. 3; a Christian, Ath. *Fest. Ep.* iv, 332 (*PG* xxvi. 1379), *Sirm.* 1, 333. JOSEPH: Epiph. *Adv. Haer.* xxx. 11–12. ORCISTUS: *ILS* 6091, quibus omnibus quasi quidam cumulus accedit quod omnes ibidem sectatores sanctissimae religionis habitare dicuntur. MAIOUMA: Soz. ii. 5, v. 3, Eus. *V. Const.* iv. 38. ANTARADUS: Soz. ii. 5, Eus. *V. Const.* iv. 39, Hierocles, 716. 6–7, *A.C.Oec.* ii. v. 44. INTERESTED CONVERSIONS: Eus. *V. Const.* iv. 54.

32. I have argued my case for Constantine's changing attitude to paganism in *Atti del X Congresso Internazionale di Scienze Storiche* (1955), 267–71. EDICT OF TOLERATION: Eus. *V. Const.* ii. 48–60. CONSTITUTION OF CONSTANS: *CTh.* xvi. x. 2, 341. This constitution implies that Constantine's law had become a dead letter, in the West at any rate, as does Firmicus Maternus' appeal to Constantine's sons to abolish the pagan cult (*de Errore Profanarum Religionum*, 16, 24), which may have provoked Constans to action.

33. DEMOLITION OF THE THREE TEMPLES: Eus. *V. Const.* iii. 55–6, 58, Soc. 1. 18, Soz. ii. 5. CONFISCATION OF TEMPLE TREASURES: Eus. *V. Const.* iii. 54; *Laud. Const.* 8, Lib. *Or.* xxx. 6, 37, lxii. 8, Julian, *Or.* vii. 228b, Anon. *de rebus bell.* ii. 1; the date is given as 331 in Jerome's Chronicle (edicto Constantini gentilium templa subversa sunt). For the temple lands see p. 416.

34. CELIBACY: *CTh* viii. xvi. 1, 320, Eus. *V. Const.* iv. 26. ABDUCTION: *CTh* ix. xxiv. 1, 320 (S). DIVORCE: *CTh* iii. xvi. 1, 331. BASTARDS: *CTh* iv. vi. 2, 336. GLADIATORS: *CTh* xv. xii. 1, 325, Eus. *V. Const.* iv. 25. ALIMENTARY GRANTS: *CTh* xi. xxvii. 1, 315, 2, 322.

35. For Constantine and the Jews see pp. 944 ff.

36. The three quotations are from Eus. *V. Const.* ii. 28; Pan. Lat. xii. 2; Eus. *Laud. Const.* 1 ad fin.

37. *ILS* 705, aedem quoque Flaviae, hoc est nostrae, gentis ut desideratis magnifico opere perfici volumus, ea observatione perscripta, ne aedis nostro nomini dedicata cuiusquam contagiosae superstitionis fraudibus polluatur, cf. Aur. Victor, *Caes.* xl. 28, tum per Africam sacerdotium decretum Flaviae genti.

38. The quotation is from Opt. *App.* vii.

39. Constantine's letter to Pope Miltiades (Eus. *HE* x. 5 §§18–20) reads very

much like an instruction to a delegate judge, and from his letter to Chrestus, bishop of Syracuse (ibid. §§21–2), it appears that he chose the members of the council of Arles. From Eus. *V. Const.* III. 59 and 62 it appears that two imperial *comites* attended the council of Antioch. The *comes* Dionysius was in charge of the council of Tyre (Eus. *V. Const.* IV. 42, Ath. *Apol. c. Ar.* 72, 78–81); for his officials see Ath. *Apol. c. Ar.* 8, πῶς δὲ σύνοδον ὀνομάζειν τολμῶσι, ἧς κόμης προὐκάθητο καὶ παρῆν σπεκουλάτωρ καὶ κομεντάριος ἡμᾶς εἰσῆγεν ἀντὶ διακόνων τῆς ἐκκλησίας.

40. ARLES: Opt. *App.* v. NICAEA: Soc. I. 9, Eus. *V. Const.* III. 20. JERUSALEM: Ath. *Apol. c. Ar.* 84, *de Synodis*, 21. ANTIOCH: Eus. *V. Const.* III. 60–2.

41. *C. Ant.* can. 11, 12. These canons, traditionally ascribed to the Council of the Encaenia in 341, were enacted by the earlier council of Antioch, held not long after Nicaea, described by Eusebius in *V. Const.* III. 60–2 (see *Nachr. Ges. Gött. Wiss.*, 1911, 389–400, *JTS* 1948, 27–35).

42. THE MAGISTRI MILITUM: Zos. II. 33. Of the earliest *magistri* known Flavius Sallustius, *magister peditum*, was consul in 344 with Flavius Leontius, praetorian prefect, as his colleague (*Chr.* I. 464); Flavius Sallia, *magister equitum*, was consul in 348 with Flavius Philippus, praetorian prefect (*BGU* 405), while in 347 Vulcacius Rufinus, praetorian prefect, was colleague of Flavius Eusebius, who in 360 is styled 'ex consule et ex magistro equitum et peditum' (*CTh* XI. i. 1). COMITATENSES: Zos. II. 34, *CTh* VII. xx. 4, 325.

43. DIVITENSES AND TUNGRICANI: *Not. Dig. Occ.* v. 147–8, Amm. XXVI. vi. 12, XXVII. i. 2 (365), *ILS* 2346, Val. Genialis miles legionis secunde Divitensium Italice (tomb at Rome), 2777, Florio Baudioni, viro ducenario, protectori ex ordinario leg. II Ital. Divit. . . . Val. Vario optio leg. II Italice Divit. (tomb at Spoletium); it is a plausible conjecture that these soldiers from the Rhine died in Italy having come there in Constantine's army.

44. See App. II, Table VIII.

45. Pan. Lat. XII. 3, vix enim quarta parte exercitus contra centum milia armatorum hostium Alpes transgressus es. The same author (ibid. XII. 5) states that Constantine's army was under 40,000. The only other figures available are those of Zosimus (II. 15), who assigns 98,000 to Constantine and 188,000 (of which 80,000 in Italy) to Maxentius. If these figures are of any value, they must represent the total forces of either party. The orator's 100,000 for Maxentius' army of Italy would then be a pardonable exaggeration of 80,000, and Constantine's expeditionary force would have been well under 40,000 (or he used over a quarter of his troops).

46. BONITUS: Amm. XV. v. 33, licet patris quoque Boniti praetenderet fortia facta, Franci quidem, sed pro Constantini partibus in bello civili acriter contra Licinianos saepe versati. BARBARIAN CONSULS: Amm. XXI. x. 8, tunc et memoriam Constantini, ut novatoris turbatorisque priscarum legum et moris antiquitus recepti, vexavit, eum aperte incusans quod barbaros omnium primus adusque fasces auxerat et trabeas consulares; insulse nimirum et leviter, qui cum vitare deberet id quod infestius obiurgavit brevi postea Mamertino in consulatu iunxit Nevittam nec splendore nec usu nec gloria horum similem quibus magistratum amplissimum detulerat Constantinus. These German consuls cannot be identified and must have taken Roman names.

47. LEGIONS IULIA ALPINA: *Not. Dig. Occ.* v. 248, 257–8 (= vii. 35, 34, 60). GALLIA RIPARENSIS: *Not. Dig. Occ.* xlii. 13–17. LEGION IULIA ALEXANDRIA: *Not. Dig. Or.* viii. 51. For dynastic titles of the Flavian house in the frontier units see App. II, Tables X–XII.

48. See App. II, Table XII.

49. *CTh* VII. xiii. 7, 375, and VII. xiii. 1; the latter is one of the laws addressed *ad praefectos praetorio* discussed above in n. 2. CONSTANTINE'S GOTHIC AND SARMATIAN WARS: Anon. Val. 31–2.

50. On the relation of the *magistri* and *duces* see pp. 375–6. ABOLITION OF THE PRAETORIAN GUARD: Aur. Victor, *Caes.* xl. 25, Zos. II. 17. PRAETORIAN PREFECTS LOSE MILITARY FUNCTIONS: Zos. II. 33; for recruitment, *annonae* and the *fabricae* see ch. XII, nn. 8, 14, and for combined military and civil commands see p. 373. THE DUX OF EGYPT: *ILS* 701.

51. Zos. II. 33. Constantine's prefects have been the subject of a vast controversy, summarized (with references to the earlier literature) by Ensslin in *PW* XXII. 2428–31, but the evidence, mainly laws whose dates are dubious, is to my mind too tenuous to justify any but the most tentative conclusions. That there were only two prefects, Petronius Annianus (Constantine) and Julius Julianus (Licinius), between 313 and 317 is proved by *ILS* 8938 and Opt. *App.* VIII.; the same pair still hold office without a third colleague in *AE* 1938, 85, which is dedicated to a Caesar (probably Crispus in the original version); but perhaps Crispus was not given a command and assigned a praetorian prefect directly he was proclaimed Caesar.

52. Menander is connected with Africa by *CTh* IV. xiii. 3, 321 (mention of Legio III Augusta), XI. xxvii. 2, 322 (proconsules praesidesque et rationales per universam Africam), cf. VIII. v. 4, 320 (S), super qua re proconsules, rectores provinciarum, praefectos vehiculorum adque omnes qui cursui publico praesunt admoneri conveniet. ARADIUS PROCULUS: *ILS* 1240–1. Felix is styled praetorian prefect in *CTh* XII. i. 21, 335 (complaints of *Afri curiales*), *Sirm.* 4, 336 (posted at Carthage, to instruct governors 'per diocesim sibi creditam'); he is addressed without title in XIII. iv. 1, 334 (posted at Carthage, acting 'in provinciis Africanis'), v. 6, 334 (posted at Carthage). Gregorius is addressed as praetorian prefect in XI. i. 3, 336, and without title in IV. vi. 3, 336 (read at Carthage; reference to *gynaecium* of Carthage); he was addressed by Donatus as 'Gregori, macula senatus et praefectorum' (Opt. III. 3). There are no other clear indications that a praetorian prefect was responsible for a region, for in *CTh* XI. xxvii. 1, Ablabius, who is instructed to take action 'per omnes civitates Italiae', is not styled *PPO* and may well have been a vicar or *comes*.

53. INSCRIPTION OF TUBERNUC: *AE* 1925, 72; literature cited in *PW* XXII. 2430. TIBERIANUS: Jerome, *Chron.*, Tiberianus . . . praefectus praetorio Gallias regit (A.D. 336). PACATIANUS: *CTh* XIV. iv. 1, 334 (on the *suarii* of Rome), VIII. ix. 1, 335 (on the *decuriae* of Rome). ABLABIUS: *ILS* 6091 (foundation of Orcistus, c. 326), Zos. II. 40 (killed at Constantinople in 337), Eunap. *V. Soph.* VI. 3 (*PPO* of Constantius). Gregorius is last recorded in *CTh* III. i. 2, 4 Feb. 337. EVAGRIUS: *CTh* XII. i. 22, 336; there is no evidence to indicate where he functioned at this date.

54. AUXENTIUS: Suidas, s.v. Αὐξέντιος. MARIANUS: Eus. *V. Const.* IV. 44 (Index). For the notaries see pp. 572 ff.

55. HERACLIANUS: *CTh* XVI. x. 1, 320. PROCULEIANUS: *CTh* XI. ix. 1, 323. MARTINIANUS: Joh. Lydus, *Mag.* II. 25, *Epit. Caes.* xli. 6. For the functions of the *magister officiorum* see ch. XII, nn. 6–8.

56. AGENTES IN REBUS: Aur. Victor, *Caes.* xxxix. 44–5, *CTh* VI. xxxv. 3 §3, 319. The *curiosus* of Egypt: Ath. *Apol. c. Ar.* 75. On the organization and functions of the *agentes in rebus* see pp. 578 ff.

57. QUAESTOR: Zos. V. 32. The earliest known are Montius, Gallus' quaestor in 353 (Amm. XIV. vii. 12, Soc. II. 34, Soz. IV. 7, Philostorgius, III. 28), and Taurus, quaestor to Constantius II in 354 (Amm. XIV. xi. 14, *AE* 1934, 159, v.c. Tauro comiti ordinis primi quaestori sacri palatii). For the duties of the office see ch. XII, n. 3.

58. PRIVILEGES OF PALATINI: CTh VI. xxxv. 1, 314 (*munera sordida et personalia*), 3, 319 (*munera* and the *curia*), 4, 321 (*munera sordida*), xxxvi. 1. 326 (S) (*peculium castrense*). These privileges were retained if *palatini* were promoted to *dignitates* (*CTh* VI. xxxv. 2, 319, 3, 319, 5, 328). For the grades in the palatine offices see p. 584.

59. On the *comitiva* see pp. 333–4. Eusebius speaks of the three orders (*V. Const.* IV. 1), κομήτων δ' οἱ μὲν πρώτου τάγματος ἠξιοῦντο, οἱ δὲ δευτέρου, οἱ δὲ τρίτου, and the titles first appear on inscriptions of Constantine's reign. *CTh* XII. i. 26, 338, speaks of 'ex comitibus cuiuslibet ordinis . . . honorarios'.

60. See pp. 333–4, 412, 427.

61. The *comites* Acacius and Strategius were in charge of the council of Antioch (Eus. *V. Const.* III. 62) and the *comes* Dionysius presided at Tyre (Ath. *Apol. c. Ar.* 78–81). For the general functions of *comites provinciarum* see *CTh* I. xvi. 6, 331, praefectis praetorio et comitibus qui per provincias constituti sunt provincialium nostrorum voces ad nostram scientiam referentibus, 7,331, conquerendi vocem omnibus aperimus apud comites provinciarum aut apud praefectos praetorio, cf. XI. xxx. 16, 331, for appeals 'a proconsulibus et comitibus et his qui vice praefectorum cognoscunt'. The constitutions addressed to them deal with a great variety of legal and administrative topics. OCTAVIANUS: *CTh* IX. i. 1, 316, XII. i. 4, 317. TIBERIANUS: *CTh* XII. v. 1, 325 (S), i. 15, 327, *CJ* VI. i. 6, 332. SEVERUS: *CTh* VIII. xii. 5, XI. xxxix. 2, 333, VIII. xviii. 3, 334, *AE* 1935, 4. ACACIUS: *CTh* XI. iii. 2, 327. TERTULLIANUS: *CTh* II. xxvi. 1, 330. LOLLIANUS: *ILS* 1224; Firmicus Maternus (*Math.* I, *proem* 7) proves that he held the office under Constantine. The origins of the *comitiva Orientis* are obscure. Glanville Downey (*A study of the Comites Orientis and the Consulares Syriae*, diss. Princeton, 1939) puts faith in Malalas, 218–9, who dates the establishment of the office on a permanent footing very precisely in 335, and regards the *comes* as a deputy of the praetorian prefect for the supply of the eastern army. Against this view of his functions may be set the fact that he had no *cura epistularum* but did have an *a libellis* (*Not. Dig. Or.* xxii. 40), which suggests he originally had no financial functions, but did handle complaints of the provincials (see p. 593). There is no certain holder of the office earlier than Malalas' Felicianus (Lollianus may well have been his successor). The *comes* Acacius who was present at the council of Antioch and was directed to destroy the pagan temple of Mamre (Eus. *V. Const.* III. 52–3, 62) may, as Downey suggests, have been a special commissioner for religious affairs. The latest known *vicarii Orientis* are Dracilianus (Eus. *V. Const.* III. 31, *CTh* II. xxxiii. 1, 325) and Maximus (*CTh* XII. i. 12, 325, *CJ* XI. l. 1). The earliest *comes rei militaris* known to us is Gratian, the father of Valentinian I (see ch. IV, n. 26).

62. Most of the Constantinian *comites* known to us were senators (e.g. *ILS* 1213, 1216–8, 1223, 1227–8; *AE* 1935, 4), but three *comites provinciarum* were *perfectissimi*, Tertullianus (*CTh* II. xxvi. 1) and Acacius and Strategius (Eus. *V. Const.* III. 62), and Caelius Saturninus became a *comes* before being adlected to the senate (*ILS* 1214). The lower grades of the *comitiva* were always open to non-senators. On the patriciate see ch. XV, n. 28.

63. Eus. *V. Const.* IV. 1. SATURNINUS: *ILS* 1214. NONIUS VERUS: *ILS* 1218.

64. SENATORS AS PRAEFECTI ANNONAE AND VIGILUM: *ILS* 700, 707; AS PRAESIDES: *ILS* 1240, 6111, 5699, *CIL* II. 2635. For the title *consularis* see *JRS* XLIV (1954), 27–8. CONSULARIS AQUARUM ETC.: *ILS* 1223–4. PROCONSUL OF ACHAEA: *ILS* 1217, C. Vettio Cossinio Rufino c.v. praefecto urbi, comiti Augg. nn., corr. Camp., corr. Tusciae et Umbriae, corr. Venitiae et Histriae, cur. alvei Tiberis et cloacarum sacrae urbis, cur. viae Flaminiae, proconsuli provinciae Achaiae sortito, pontifici dei Solis, auguri, salio Palatino, ordo populusque Atinas quod in correctura eius, quae sevissimam tyrannidem incurrerat, nullam iniuriam sustinuerit, patrono dignissimo, Firm. Mat. *Math.* II. 29, de exilio raptus in administrationem Campaniae primum destinatus est, deinde Achaiae proconsulatum, post vero ad Asiae proconsulatum et praefecturam urbi Romae (referring to the same man). From the inscription it appears that Rufinus was *corrector Campaniae* (in which Atina lay) under Maxentius. He was prefect of the city from 20 Aug. 315 to 4 Aug. 316 (*Chron. Min.* I. 67), having previously been proconsul of Achaea. This office he can only have held between Constantine's final victory over Licinius late in 314 and August 315. Firmicus Maternus omits the Italian offices held, probably under Constantine, between the correctorship of Campania and the proconsulate of Achaea, and adds, evidently out of order, the proconsulate of Asia. This he cannot have held before 324; it is odd that he should have held a second proconsulate after his prefecture of the city, but it was no doubt an emergency post-war appointment. Cf. *CIL* III. 6103, *IG* v. i. 538, *BSA* XXIX. 53, no. 80, for earlier *correctores*. Constantine probably also created a fourth proconsulate at Constantinople (see above, n. 13).

65. ARADIUS PROCULUS: *ILS* 1240. SEPTIMIUS ACINDYNUS: *CIL* II. 4107. MAESIUS LOLLIANUS: *ILS* 1224. Proculus and Lollianus were evidently from the Roman magistracies and priesthoods which they held of established senatorial families. Acindynus, later praetorian prefect of the East in 335 and consul in 340, owned a villa at Bauli in Campania (Symm. *Ep.* I. 1).

66. *CTh* XI. iii. 2, 327, Acacio comiti Macedoniae; as all other *comites provinciarum* ruled dioceses, this must mean that Macedonia was by now a separate diocese. For the amalgamation of provinces see *JRS* XLIV (1954) 21 ff. and *App.* III.

67. COMPULSORY PURCHASE OF GOLD: *P. Beatty Panop.* 2, lines 215–21, *P. Oxy.* 2106. GOLD AND SILVER SURCHARGES: *P. Oxy.* 1653, *P. Merton*, 31, *P. Cairo*, 57049 (*Chron. d'Égypte*, 1952, 247), *P. Thead.* 33, *CTh* XI. ix. 2, 337, si quis fundum vel mancipia ob cessationem tributorum vel etiam ob vestium auri argentique debitum quae annua exactione solvuntur occupata . . . comparaverit. GOLD RENT ON IMPERIAL LAND: *CTh* XI. xvi. 1, 318 (S), XII. vi. 2, 325.

68. For the confiscation of the temple treasures see above, n. 33. The quotation is from Anon. *de rebus bell.* II. 1.

69. For the amalgamation of *capitatio* and *iugatio* see *JRS* XLVII (1957), 88–94. STIPENDIUM ET DONATIVUM IN DENARII: *P. Oxy.* 1047. WHEAT PRICES: *Ed. Diocl.* i. 1, *P. Lond.* 1914, *P. Oxy.* 85. GOLD PRICES: *P. Oxy.* 1430, *PER* 187, 37, *SPP* xx. 96, 81 (in ascending order of price).

70. GOLD PAYMENT TO NAVICULARII: *CTh* XIII. v. 7, 334. For later commutation see pp. 460–1.

71. *Epit. Caes.* xli. 16, decem annis praestantissimus, duodecim sequentibus latro, decem novissimis pupillus ob profusiones immodicas nominatus; Eutrop. x. 7. sicut in nonnullos amicos dubius, ita in reliquos egregius, nihil occasio-

num praetermittens quo opulentiores eos clarioresque praestaret; Eus. *V. Const.* IV. 1, οὐδέ τις ἐλπίσας ἀγαθῶν τυχεῖν τοῦ προσδοκηθέντος ἠστόχησεν, ἀλλ' οἱ μὲν χρημάτων οἱ δὲ κτημάτων περιουσίας ἐτύγχανον, cf. IV. 54; Amm. XVI. viii. 12, namque ut documenta liquida prodiderunt proximorum fauces aperuit primus omnium Constantinus, sed eos medullis provinciarum saginavit Constantius.

72. LICINIUS' FISCALITY: Eus *HE* x. 8 §12, *V. Const.* I. 55, Aur. Victor, *Caes.* xli. 3, *Epit. Caes.* xli. 8–10, and especially Julian, *Or.* I. 8b, ἐπεὶ δὲ ἀπάντων κύριος κατέστη (sc. Constantine), ὥσπερ ἐξ αὐχμοῦ τῆς ἀπληστίας τοῦ δυναστεύσαντος (sc. Licinius) πολλῆς ἀπορίας χρημάτων οὔσης καὶ τοῦ πλούτου τῶν βασιλείων ἐν μυχοῖς συνειλημμένον, τὸ κλεῖθρον ἀφελὼν ἐπέκλυσεν ἀθρόως τῷ πλούτῳ πάντα. For the temple treasures see above, n. 33, and for the *collatio lustralis* and *glebalis*, pp. 431–2.

73. The civic *vectigalia* had certainly been confiscated by the end of Constantius II's reign, since Julian restored them (Amm. xxv. iv. 15, vectigalia civitatibus restituta cum fundis). I am inclined to assign their confiscation to Constantine because the *largitionales urbium singularum* first appear in his reign (*CTh* VI. xxxv. 3, 319), for it is hard to see why *largitionales* should have been required in individual cities except to manage the local *vectigalia*. It also seems probable that *CTh* IV. xiii. 1, 321, refers to the civic *vectigalia*, since no other *vectigalia* are likely to have existed in the province of Aemilia and in *CTh* IV. xiii. 2 and 3, 321, local *octroi* dues in Africa appear to be under imperial control. For the later history of the civic *vectigalia* see pp. 732–3. INCREASE OF THE INDICTION: Them. *Or.* VIII. 113c.

74. For death bed baptism see pp. 980–1.

IV. THE HOUSE OF CONSTANTINE (pp. 112–15)

The sons of Constantine have not attracted biographers, but Julian has inspired many, the best of which is J. Bidez, *La vie de l'empéreur Julien*, Paris, 1930. There is also a useful collection of sources for his reign, J. Bidez and F. Cumont, *Iuliani Imperatoris epistulae et leges*, Paris, 1922.

1. Zos. II. 40–1, Eutrop. x. 9. For the date of the proclamation of the three Augusti, see *Chron. Min.* I. 235.

2. Zos. II. 42–5, Eutrop. x. 9, Aur. Victor, *Caes.* xli. 22–5, xlii. 1–9, *Epit. Caes.* xli. 22–5, xlii. 1–3. MAGNENTIUS A LAETUS: Julian, *Or.* I. 34a, τῆς ἀπὸ Γερμανῶν λείας λείψανον.

3. Zos. II. 51–2, Eutrop. x. 12, *Epit. Caes.* xlii. 4–8.

4. LAWS AGAINST SACRIFICE: *CTh* XVI. x. 2, 341, 5, 353, 4, 356 (S), 6, 356. CLOSURE OF TEMPLES: *CTh* XVI. x. 4, 356 (S). DEMOLITION OF TEMPLES: *CTh* XVI. x. 3, 342 (S), Lib. *Or.* LXII. 8, ὁ μὲν γὰρ (sc. Constantine) ἐγύμνωσε τοῦ πλούτου τοὺς θεούς, ὁ δὲ (sc. Constantius II) καὶ κατέσκαψε τοὺς ναούς, *Ep.* 724. THE ALTAR OF VICTORY: Amb. *Ep.* 18 §32.

5. *Hist. de l'Église*, III. 115–21.

6. Ibid. III. 123–30.

7. Ibid. III. 135–6.

8. THE JEWISH REVOLT: Soc. II. 33, Soz. IV. 7. THE ISAURIANS: Amm. XIV. ii. ANTIOCH: Amm. XIV. vii. 1–6. THE FALL OF GALLUS: Amm. XIV. vii. 9 ff., xi. SILVANUS: Amm. XV. v.

9. JULIAN CAESAR: Amm. XV. viii. 1–17.

10. *Hist. de l'Église*, III. 142–50.

11. Ibid. III. 150–76.

12. PRIVILEGES OF THE CLERGY: *CTh* XVI. ii. 8, 343, 10, 346 (S), 14, 356 (S), 15, 359. Lands belonging to the church seem to have been allowed immunity by the last law. This interpretation is supported by *CTh* XI. i. 1, 360 (S), where church lands again appear to be immune from regular taxation.

13. The immunity of the clergy from the *curia* is reaffirmed in *CTh* XVI. ii. 11, 342 (S) by Constantius and in law 9 (349) by Constans. The new rule of the surrender of property is first mentioned in *CTh* XII. i. 49, 361, which modifies an earlier enactment which has not survived.

14. Amm. XVII. iii.

15. Amm. XVI. v. 14, 15.

16. Amm. XX. iv, v, viii, ix, XXI. v, viii, ix, x, xv.

17. TOLERATION FOR HERETICS: Bidez and Cumont, op. cit. nos. 43–5. STATE GRANTS TO CHURCHES STOPPED: Soz. V. 5, Theod. *HE* I. 11, IV. 4. IMMUNITY OF CLERGY CANCELLED: *CTh* XII. i. 50, 362, Julian, *Ep.* 11. PAGAN CULT RESTORED: Bidez and Cumont, no. 42. The restoration of the temple lands is to be inferred from *CTh* v. xiii. 3, x. i. 8, 364.

18. SACRIFICE AT PAY PARADES: Greg. Naz. *Or.* IV. 82–4. THE IMPERIAL PORTRAIT: ibid. 80–1. LAVISH SACRIFICES: Amm. XXV. iv. 17.

19. HIGH PRIESTS: Julian, *Frag. Ep.*, *Ep.* 49, 62, 63.

20. PROFESSORS: Julian, *Ep.* 42, Amm. XXII. x. 7, XXV. iv. 20, Greg. Naz. *Or.* IV. 100 ff. THE APOLLINARES: Soc. III. 16, Soz. V. 18.

21. ALEXANDRIA: Julian, *Ep.* 10, Amm. XXII. xi. 3–11, Soc. III. 2 and 3, Soz. V. 7. ARETHUSA: Greg. Naz. *Or.* IV. 88–91, Soz. V. 10. GAZA: Soz. V. 9. MERUS: Soc. III. 15, Soz. V. 11. CAESAREA: Soz. V. 4. EDESSA: Julian, *Ep.* 43.

22. TEMPLES: Lib. *Ep.* 724, 757, 763, 819, 1364.

23. Greg. Naz. *Or.* IV. 57 ff.

24. PURGE OF THE COMITATUS: Amm. XXII. iv, Lib. *Or.* XVIII. 130 ff., cf. II. 58; *CTh* VI. xxiv. 1, 362, and xxvii. 2, 363, imply reductions in the *protectores* and *agentes in rebus*. CURSUS PUBLICUS: Lib. *Or.* XVIII. 143–5, *CTh* VIII. v. 12–16, 362–3. CURIAE: Amm. XXII. ix. 12, XXV. iv. 21, Lib. *Or.* XVIII. 146–8, *CTh* XII. i. 52–4, 362.

25. For the *magistri militum* of this period see Ensslin, *Klio*, XXIV (1931), 102 ff. The names known to us are few, but under Constans in the West we have Flavius Sallustius (344) followed by Vetranio (350) as *magister peditum*, and Flavius Sallia as *magister equitum* (348), and under Constantius in the East Eusebius as *magister equitum* and *peditum* (successively?) and Hermogenes (342) and Bonosus (347) as *magister equitum*. HERMOGENES IN THRACE: Soc. II. 13, Soz. III. 7.

26. GRATIAN: Amm. XXX. vii. 2, comes praefuit rei castrensi per Africam, unde furtorum suspicione contactus digressusque multo postea pari potestate Britannum rexit exercitum. His commands may perhaps be associated with

the Donatist disorders in Africa, and the troubles in Britain implied by Amm. XXVII. viii. 4, XXVIII. iii. 8. The significance of the title *comes rei militaris* is obscure. It evidently covered a wide range of commands. In Ammianus we meet with *comites* who command all the troops of a diocese, such as Marcianus (XXI. xii. 22, dispersum per Thraciam militem contra vim subitam cito coactum adventare Succorum confinia, comite Marciano ducente), Julius (XXVI. vii. 5, Iulius comes per Thracias copiis militaribus praesidens) and Lupicinus (XXXI. iv. 9) in Thrace, and Equitius in Illyricum (XXVI. v. 2, tunc et Equitius Illyriciano praeponitur exercitui nondum magister sed comes): Lucillianus, whom Ammianus calls 'comes qui per illas regiones rem curabat castrensem, agensque apud Sirmium', he later styles *magister equitum* (XXI. ix. 5 and 7) and the rank of Januarius ('curantem summitatem necessitatum castrensium per Illyricum') is not stated (XXVI. i. 5). Prosper *comes* acts *pro magistro equitum* in command of the army of the East (XIV. xi. 5, XV. xiii. 3). In Julian's Persian expedition the *comites* Procopius and Sebastian command a force of 30,000 men (XXIII. iii. 5, XXVI. vi. 2). These are important officers, ranking very little below *magistri*. At the other end of the scale we have the *comes* Severinus, 'qui apud Cabillona Divitensibus praesidebat et Tungricanis' (XXVII. i. 2), and several *comites* in charge of such a relatively minor operation as the siege of Aquileia (XXI. xii. 3).

These *comites rei militaris*, whose responsibility varies so greatly, have one feature in common, that they command *comitatenses*. Some of the later *comites* recorded in the Notitia fall into the same pattern. Those of Spain, Illyricum and Britain (*Not. Dig. Occ.* vii. 40, 118, 153, 199) were certainly commanders of regional groups of *comitatenses*, like the earlier *comites* of Thrace and Illyricum, and so too no doubt were the mysterious *comes Italiae* and *comes Argentoratensis* (see App. II). But in the Notitia we find two other types of *comes rei militaris*. The *comes Tingitaniae* commands both the local *limitanei* and also regiments of *comitatenses* (*Not. Dig. Occ.* vii. 135, 206, xxvi) and so does the *comes Africae* (ibid. vii. 140, 179, xxv: in my view most of his *comitatenses* are upgraded *limitanei* but they include some genuine regiments of the field army, nos. 141–5, see App. II). Finally there are three *comites rei militaris*, those of the Saxon shore, Isauria and Egypt (*Not. Dig. Occ.* xxviii, *Or.* xxviii, xxix), who command *limitanei* only and appear to differ from *duces* only in title; the superior rank of the first two is particularly anomalous as they command very small forces.

I would suggest that *comites rei militaris* of the mixed type (Africa and Tingitania) arose from the reinforcement of a local army of *limitanei* by *comitatenses* to meet an emergency. The *dux* might then be superseded temporarily by a *comes*, or alternatively the *dux* might be, also temporarily, given the higher rank of *comes*.

We may perhaps trace this development in Isauria. The *comes* Castricius operating against the Isaurian rebels in 353 (Amm. XIV. ii. 14) probably had *comitatenses* under his command as well as the local troops (XIV. ii. 20). Later in 359 'Lauricius adiecta comitis dignitate missus est rector' to Isauria (XIX. xiii. 2, cf. *ILS* 740, Bassidius Lauricius v.c. com. et praeses; he is called ὁ τῶν κατ' Ἰσαυρίαν στρατιωτῶν ἡγούμενος in Soc. II. 39). I would conjecture that before the Isaurian revolt the (*dux et*) *praeses* of the province had commanded the local garrison of *limitanei*, that to suppress the revolt a *comes rei militaris* with reinforcements of *comitatenses* took over, and after this the (*dux et*) *praeses* retained some regiments of the field army and was given the additional title of *comes*.

Some of these emergency commands were transitory. In 368 we meet with 'Charietto tunc per utramque Germaniam comes' (Amm. XXVII. i. 2) but such a command never appears later. Gratian's *comitiva* in Britain seems to have lapsed by 368, for no *comes Britanniarum* is mentioned in Amm. XXVII. viii. 1, to be later revived (*Not. Dig. Occ.* xxix). Gratian's other post of *comes Africae* became permanent (*CTh* VII. i. 4, cf. Amm. XXI. vii. 4, for Cretio in 351, and *CTh* VIII. vii. 13, Amm. XXVII. ix. 1, for Romanus). Here, as we have seen, the local army was stiffened with *comitatenses*. In Isauria the change was not permanent, for in 382 there was a *dux et praeses Isauriae* (*CJ* IX. xxvii. 1; the text in *CTh* IX. xxvii. 3, which gives *Sardiniae* for *Isauriae*, is surely corrupt). In the Notitia he is styled *comes rei militaris per Isauriam et praeses*, but evidently had recently been a *dux* (*Not. Dig. Or.* xxix. 6 and 18), and after this the title *comes* appears to become fixed (*CJ* XII. lix. 10, 466, Just. *Nov.* xxvii, 535). The variation in the title suggests that it had some real significance, and it is a possible explanation that the commander in Isauria lost the rank of *comes* because the reinforcements from the *comitatus* were withdrawn, and regained it when they returned; in the absence of a *Distributio Numerorum* for the East we cannot say whether the *comes Isauriae* at that time commanded any *comitatenses*.

There is a similar variation of title in Egypt. The *dux Aegypti* became a *comes* between 384 and 391 (*CTh* XI. xxx. 43, XVI. x. 11). He remained a *comes* until 466 (*CJ* XII. lix. 10, and in the interval *CTh* XI. xxiv. 3, 395, *Not. Dig. Or.* xxviii, *CTh* VI. xiii. 1, 413, xxviii. 8, 435), but from 468 the title is *dux* again (*CJ* I. lvii. 1, II. vii. 13, and still in Just. *Ed.* xiii).

There remains the *comes litoris Saxonici*. The post is first mentioned in 368 (Amm. XXVII. viii. 1, Nectaridum, comitem maritimi tractus). On the analogy of the other cases I would conjecture that it was originally an emergency command, and that the *comes* was assigned a mixed army comprising some of the *limitanei* of Britain and some *comitatenses*; the latter had been withdrawn by the time the *Distributio Numerorum* was drawn up, but the title was anomalously preserved.

I offer this as a possible interpretation of the evidence, but it may be that I attribute to the Roman government a consistency in the use of titles which it did not possess. It is not impossible that the title of *comes rei militaris*, though it may have originated in the way that I suggest, may in later times have been in some cases retained from inertia or in others arbitrarily bestowed on *duces* merely as an honour. I would however urge that the bestowal of so high a rank on so minor a command as that of Isauria requires explanation.

For the *magistri* under Constantius II after 351 see Ensslin, *Klio*, XXIV (1931), 107 ff. The *magistri peditum* were Silvanus, Barbatio, Ursicinus and Agilo, the *magister equitum in praesenti* Arbetio. Ursicinus was *magister equitum per Orientem* for most of the period, in Gaul the *magistri equitum* were Marcellus, Severus and Lupicinus. In Illyricum Lucillianus was *magister* at the end of the reign, but as some subsequent commanders were only *comites* it would seem that the command was not fully established (see above for references). The title *praesentalis* is not attested until the Notitia Dignitatum (*Or.* v, vi, *Occ.* v, vi).

27. Amm. XX. iv. 4, illud tamen nec dissimulare potuit nec silere, ut illi nullas paterentur molestias qui relictis laribus transrhenanis sub hoc venerant pacto ne ducerentur ad partes umquam transalpinas, XX. iv. 10–11, 'nos quidem ad orbis terrarum extrema ut noxii pellimur et damnati, caritatis vero nostrae Alamannis denuo servient, quas captivitate prima post internecivas liberavimus pugnas', quo textu ad comitatum perlato lectoque Iulianus contemplans rationabiles querelas cum familiis eos ad orientem proficisci praecepit, clavularis cursus facultate permissa.

28. *CTh* VIII. i. 10, 365, actuariis palatinorum et comitatensium numerorum senas annonas, senum etiam capitum, pseudocomitatensium etiam quaternas

annonas et quaternum capitum. . See App. II, Tables V–VI. The rule is more strictly observed in the infantry, where the praesental armies contain only one unit of *pseudocomitatenses* (*Or.* vi. 68–9), and in the regional armies there are only one palatine legion (*Or.* ix. 21–2) and eight *auxilia*, mostly in the newly formed army of Illyricum (*Or.* vii. 35–7, ix. 23–9). In the cavalry there are only three *vexillationes palatinae* in the regional armies (*Or.* viii. 24–7) but thirteen *vexillationes comitatenses* in the praesental armies (*Or.* v. 33–40, vi. 34–40). In the West the picture is less clear, but among the cavalry there is only one *vexillatio comitatensis* stationed in Italy, and the senior palatine legions and *auxilia* are all in Italy.

29. For the first mention of *pseudocomitatenses* see above n. 28, and for the origins of the regiments so called see App. II, p. 357.

30. On the praetorian prefects at this date the latest contribution is Palanque, *Historia* IV (1955), 257–63. The detailed list is in parts highly conjectural, but the fact of the three prefectures is attested by *ILS* 8944, set up shortly after Constantine II's fall by 'Ant. Marcellinus et Dom. Leontius et Fab. Titianus, vv. cc. praeff. praet.' Of these Titianus is proved to have ruled Gaul by Jerome's Chronicle and Leontius the East by the subscriptions of *CTh* IX. xxi. 5, 343, XI. xxxvi. 6, 342, and XII. i. 35, 343. The succession of praetorian prefects of the East after Gallus' death, Musonianus, Hermogenes and Elpidius, is firmly attested by Ammianus (XV. xiii. 1, XIX. xii. 6, XXI. vi. 9). The only known *praefecti praetorio Illyrici* are Anatolius and Florentius (Amm. XIX. xi. 2, XXI. vi. 5) and in 365 there are three prefects only (Amm. XXVI. v. 5, et orientem quidem regebat potestate praefecti Sallustius, Italiam vero cum Africa et Illyrico Mamertinus, et Gallicas provincias Germanianus).

31. For Eusebius see especially Amm. XVIII. iv. 3. ARSACIUS: Ath. *Hist. Ar.* 10. HESYCHIUS: Ath. *Apol. c. Ar.* 36, *Hist. Ar.* 15. EUTHERIUS: Amm. XVI. vii. 2, XX. viii. 19. HILARIUS: *CSEL* LXV. 171. For the organization of the *cubicularii* see pp. 567–8.

32. For the silentiaries see pp. 571–2. EUSEBIUS THE DECURIO: Ath. *Apol. c. Ar.* 56.

33. HILARIUS AND DIOGENIANUS: Ath. *Hist. Ar.* 48, cf. 81, *Apol. Const.* 24. ENVOYS TO SAPOR: Amm. XVII. v. 15, xiv. 3. DECENTIUS: Amm. XX. iv. 2. PAULUS: Amm. XIV. v. 6, XIX. xii. 1, XXII. iii. 10. GAUDENTIUS: Amm. XVII. ix. 7, XXI. vii. 2, XXII. xi. 1.

34. FELIX: Amm. XX. ix. 5. The other persons mentioned are all stated to have won their promotion by σημείων ἡ τεχνή by Libanius (*Or.* XLII. 23–5). For Taurus see ch. XI, n. 28, for Datianus, ch. XI, n. 29, and for Philippus, *Historia* IV (1955), 229–33. DOMITIANUS: Amm. XIV. vii. 9. ELPIDIUS: Amm. XXI. vi. 9. DULCITIUS: Lib. *Or.* XLII. 24, *ILS* 751.

35. HUMBLE ORIGINS: Lib. *Or.* XLII. 23–5. Libanius' diatribes against the notaries (ὑπογραφεῖς) are to be found in *Or.* XVIII. 131–4; cf. 149, 158, LXII. 10 ff., cf. 51, II. 44 ff. JULIAN'S PURGE: Lib. *Or.* II. 58.

36. APODEMIUS: Amm. XIV. xi. 19, 23, XV. i. 2, v. 8, XXII. iii. 11. GAUDENTIUS: Amm. XV. ii. 8; I assume his identity with Gaudentius the notary (see above n. 20), as promotion from *agens in rebus* to *notarius* was regular, see p. 579. For the role of the *agentes in rebus* as secret police (which was, I believe, a passing phenomenon) see pp. 581–2.

37. See p. 579.

38. CTh VIII. vii. 8, 365, proves that officials of the praetorian prefecture then retired with the rank of *cornicularius*, and that the post of *princeps* was therefore otherwise occupied. CTh I. xv. 11, 380 proves the same for the offices of the *comes Orientis* and of vicars, and Symm. *Rel.* 42 (384–5) for the urban prefecture. The later extension of the system is shown by the Notitia Dignitatum.

39. CTh I. ix. 1, 359, gives the stages of promotion as *biarchia, centena, ducena* and then *principatus*. RUFINUS: Amm. xv. iii. 8, xvi. viii. 3.

40. PURGE OF THE AGENTES IN REBUS BY CONSTANTIUS: CTh I. ix. 1, 359; BY JULIAN: Lib. *Or.* II. 58, XVIII. 135–41, cf. CTh VI. xxvii. 2, 363. For the later strength of the corps see CTh VI. xxvii. 23, 430, CJ XII. xx. 3 (457–70).

41. PURGE OF THE DOMESTICI: CTh VI. xxiv. 1, 362.

42. BISHOPS AND THE CURSUS PUBLICUS: Amm. XXI. xvi. 18, CSEL LXV. 64; cf. Lib. *Or.* XVIII. 143–5 for the general abuse of the post and Julian's reform.

43. PROVINCIAL GOVERNORS AND EVECTIONES: CTh VIII. v. 5, 354. JULIAN'S SYSTEM: CTh VIII. v. 12, 362, modified by 13, 362. The details of the system are set out in the Notitia for the Eastern parts, where at the end of each chapter the number of warrants issued to the magistrate in question is given.

44. Amm. XXI. xvi. 17, nec provinciarum indemnitati prospexit cum multiplicatis tributis et vectigalibus vexarentur. LAW AGAINST SUPERINDICTIONS: CTh XI. xvi. 7 and 8, 356. FLORENTIUS: Amm. XVII. iii. Julian is praised for his moderate taxation by Ammianus (xxv. iv. 15, indicta sunt tributorum admodum levia) and Eutropius (x. 16, in provinciales iustissimus et tributorum quatenus ferri posset repressor), and even Ambrose (*de ob. Val. Jun.* 21) and Gregory Nazianzen (*Or.* IV. 75) admit this in his favour. They may be referring to Julian's reduction of the taxes of Gaul when he was Caesar or to his diminution of the *aurum coronarium* (see p. 430), for from the evidence of Themistius (*Or.* VIII. 113c) and Libanius (*Or.* XVIII. 282) it is plain that the regular taxes of the whole empire were not reduced.

45. See ch. XIX, n. 44.

46. Amm. xxv. iv. 15, vectigalia civitatibus restituta cum fundis; see pp. 732–3 for later developments.

47. Amm. XVI. viii. 11–3; for *petitio* see pp. 422–3.

48. THE PRAETORS: CTh VI. iv. 5+6, 340, 8+9, 356. THE PREFECT OF THE CITY: Soc. II. 41, καὶ τότε τὸν ἔπαρχον τῆς Κωνσταντινουπόλεως κατέστησεν, Ὀνώρατον ὄνομα, τὴν ἀνθυπάτων παύσας ἀρχήν, *Chron. Min.* I. 239. THE LAW OF 361: CTh I. vi. 1+xxviii. 1+VI. iv. 12+13+VII. viii. 1+XI. i. 7+xv. 1+xxiii. 1 + XII. i. 48+XIII. i. 3+XV. i. 7.

49. CTh VI. iv. 11, 357, si quos in urbe Roma perfunctos esse claruerit magistratibus, ad nulla editionum genera devocentur. urbis autem Romae curiam callide declinantes clarissimo praeditos nomine per Achaiam Macedoniam totumque Illyricum iussimus quaeri raro vel numquam sedem dignitatis propriae frequentantes, quibus locorum grata confinia possint esse iucunda, ut carens mora longinquae peregrinationis debeat dignitas concupisci. For an actual case of the transfer of a senator from Rome to Constantinople see Lib. *Ep.* 251–2 (Olympius of Antioch). NUMBERS UNDER CONSTANTIUS: Them. *Or.* XXXIV. xiii.

50. For Acindynus see ch. III, n. 65, and for Philippus etc. n. 34 above. STRATEGIUS MUSONIANUS: Amm. xv. xiii. 1–2.

51. Aco Catullinus was *PU* 342–4 and consul 349; his daughter, who married Agorius Praetextatus, alludes to her noble ancestry (*ILS* 1259, cf. 1260). The nobility of Placidus and Lollianus is attested by their Roman magistracies and priesthoods (*ILS* 1223–5, 1231). For the family of Rufius Volusianus see Seeck, *Symmachus*, clxxiv ff. Maecilius Hilarianus' career as *corrector* of Lucania and Bruttium (*CTh* IX. xix. 1+XII. i. 3, 316) and proconsul of Africa (*CIL* VIII. 1179, 12524) makes it likely that he was a senator by birth. Vulcacius Rufinus was brother of Galla, who married Constantius, the half brother of Constantine (Amm. XIV. xi. 27); his origin is not known, but if he was not a noble by birth he was probably given senatorial rank early in life: for his career see *ILS* 1237. Examples of *vicarii* of senatorial birth are Aco Catullinus (*CTh* XII. i. 24, 26, 338), Crepereius Madalianus (*ILS* 1228, cf. 707), Julius Eubolida (*CTh* VIII. x. 2, 344, *ILS* 1233), Clodius Octavianus (*ILS* 1253, cf. 756) and Symmachus, the father of the orator (*ILS* 1257). FACUNDUS AND ARSENIUS: *CTh* VI. iv. 15, 359.

52. For Taurus, Felix and Domitian see above n. 34. NEMESIANUS: *Sb* 1005, Νεμεσιανὸς . . . ἀπὸ καθολικῶν [Αἰγύπ]του καὶ ἀπὸ ἡγεμόνων . . . καὶ καθολικὸς ὢν τ[ῆς] διοικήσεως, *CTh* XII. i. 30, Nemesiano comiti, 340 (the law deals with the *res privata*), XI. vii. 5, 345, Nemesiano v.p. com. larg. CONSISTORY OF 362: *CTh* XI. xxxix. 5, pars actorum aput imperatorem Iulianum Augustum Mamertino et Nevitta conss. x Kal. April. Constantinopoli in consistorio: adstantibus Iovio viro clarissimo quaestore, Anatolio magistro officiorum, Felice comite sacrarum largitionum. On the other hand in 356 the *magister officiorum* and the *comes sacrarum largitionum* are spoken of as *clarissimi* (*CTh* VIII. v. 8 and XI. xvi. 7).

53. SILVANUS: *Amm.* XV. v. 11, 16 (a Frank), 33 (tribune of the Armaturae). AGILO: Amm. XIV. x. 8 (an Alaman), XX. ii. 5 (promoted direct from tribune of the Gentiles and Scutarii). NEVITTA: Amm. XXI. x. 8 (a barbarian). VICTOR: Amm. XXXI. xii. 6 (a Sarmatian). HORMISDAS: Amm. XVI. x. 16, cf. XXIV. ii. 11 (a Persian). GOMOARIUS: Amm. XXI. viii. 1 (formerly tribune of the Scutarii).

54. VALENTINIAN AND EQUITIUS: Amm. XXVI. i. 4–5. Another general, Eusebius, if he was the father of the empress Eusebia and of Eusebius and Hypatius, was a Macedonian (Julian, *Or.* III. 106c ff., 110a). GRATIAN: Amm. XXX. vii. 2–3. ARBETIO: Amm. XV. ii. 4, XVI. vi. 1. JOVIAN: Amm. XXV. v. 4, cf. Zos. III. 30 for Varronianus' office and Amm. XXV. x. 13 for Jovian's age.

55. MAGISTRI MADE CONSULS: Sallustius, *Chr.* I. 464; Eusebius, *CTh* XI. i. 1 (he is styled *comes* as consul in *P. Oxy* 1190); Salia, *BGU* 405; Nevitta, Amm. XVII. vi. 3, XXI. viii. 1, x. 8; Arbetio, Amm. XV. iv. 1, viii. 17. CONSTANTIUS AND DUCES: Amm. XXI. xvi. 2.

56. CURIALES AND EQUESTRIAN RANK AND THE COMITIVA: *CTh* XII. i. 26, 338, 36, 343, 41, 353, 42, 354, 44, 358; laws 24 and 25, 338, 27, 339, and 34, 342, which speak in general terms of *honores* or *dignitates*, probably also refer to equestrian posts or the *comitiva*. CURIALES AND THE SENATE: *CTh* XII. i. 29, 340, 42, 354, 14 and 15 (of uncertain date), 48, 361.

57. THE ARMY: Julian, *Ep.* 38, Lib. *Or.* XVIII. 166–8, Greg. Naz. *Or.* IV. 64. GAZA ETC.: Soz. V. 9, 10, Greg. Naz. *Or.* IV. 86 ff. BEROEA: Julian, *Ep.* 27.

1. ELECTION OF JOVIAN: Amm. XXV. v. PERSIAN TREATY: Amm. XXV. vii. 9.

2. ELECTION OF VALENTINIAN: Amm. XXVI. i.; Zosimus (III. 36) puts the offer of the throne to Salutius here, but Ammianus' account is to be preferred. My character sketch is largely derived from Ammianus' obituary notice in XXX. viii, ix. Valentinian's refusal to sacrifice under Julian is probably historical, since it is alluded to by Ambrose (*de ob. Val. Jun.* 55, adest pater qui militiam sub Iuliano et tribunatus honores fidei amore contempsit). Socrates' version (IV. 1) that he offered his resignation but that Julian refused it is the most likely: it is compatible with Ambrose's words and with the silence of Ammianus, who would hardly have ignored the incident if Valentinian had been cashiered or exiled, as alleged by later Christian writers (e.g. Orosius, VII. xxxii. 2, Soz. VI. 6).

3. PROCLAMATION OF VALENS: Amm. XXVI. iv. 3. That he was only a *protector domesticus* under Julian is stated by Socrates (IV. 1); he was promoted to *tribunus stabuli* by his brother shortly before his elevation to Augustus (Amm. XXVI. iv. 2). His character sketch is in Amm. XXXI. xiv.

4. The previous career of Procopius is given in Amm. XXVI. vi. 1 (cf. XVII. xiv. 3, XXIII. iii. 5). His revolt is recounted in Amm. XXVI. vi–x.

5. GOTHIC WAR: Amm. XXVII. v, Zos. IV. 10–11; the peace terms are given by Them. *Or.* x. 135 bcd. PERSIAN AFFAIRS: Amm. XXVII. xii, XXX. i, ii.

6. THE ALAMANS: Amm. XXVII. x, XXVIII. ii. 1–9, v, XXIX. iv, XXX. iii. BRITAIN: idem, XXVII. viii, XXVIII. iii. TRIPOLITANIA: idem, XXVIII. vi. FIRMUS: idem, XXIX. v. EXECUTION OF THEODOSIUS: Orosius, VII. xxxiii. 7, Jerome, *Chron.* s.a. 376.

7. THE QUADI AND SARMATIANS: Amm. XXIX. vi. 1–16, XXX. v. DEATH OF VALENTINIAN: Amm. XXX. vi. PROCLAMATION OF GRATIAN: Amm. XXVII. vi; he comments on the fact that Valentinian appointed his son not Caesar but Augustus, technically his equal colleague, from the start, see §16, in hoc tamen negotio Valentinianus morem institutum antiquitus supergressus non Caesares sed Augustos germanum nuncupavit et filium, benivole satis, nec enim quisquam antehac adscivit sibi pari potestate collegam praeter principem Marcum qui Verum adoptivum fratrem absque diminutione aliqua auctoritatis imperatoriae socium fecit. PROCLAMATION OF VALENTINIAN II: Amm. XXX. x, Zos. IV. 19; Zosimus links Equitius with Merobaudes as one of the principal promoters of the proclamation. His statement that the empire was divided between Gratian and Valentinian II, the former taking the Gallic prefecture and the latter Illyricum, Italy and Africa, is untrue (see Palanque, *REA* XLVI (1944), 59 ff.).

8. REMIGIUS: Amm. XV. v. 36, Remigio etiam tum (355) rationario apparitionis armorum magistri, XXVII. ix. 2 (magister officiorum, 368). LEO: XXVI. i. 6, Leo, adhuc sub Dagalaifo magistro equitum rationes numerorum militarium tractans exitialis postea magister officiorum, XXX. ii. 10 (succeeds Remigius as *magister officiorum*); he was in the interval a notary (XXVIII. i. 12). MAXIMINUS: Amm. XXVIII. i. 5–6, 41. FESTUS: Amm. XXIX. ii. 22, Lib. *Or.* i. 156 (ignorant of Greek).

9. MODESTUS: Seeck, *Die Briefe des Libanius*, 213–18. TATIAN: *ILS* 8844, cf. *JTS* 1954, 224–7 for the creation of the diocese of Egypt. VULCACIUS RUFINUS: Amm. XXVII. vii. 2. PETRONIUS PROBUS: Amm. XXVII. xi. 1; for his career see below n. 58.

10. EQUITIUS: Amm. XXVI. i. 6 (Pannonian), v. 3 (*comes*), v. 11 (*magister*). THEODOSIUS: Pan. Lat. II. 4 (his son a native of Spain), Amm. XXVIII. iii. 9 (promoted *magister equitum* after his British campaign). For the other *magistri* see Ensslin, *Klio*, XXIV (1931), 123 ff.

11. Amm. XXVIII. i.

12. Symm. *Or.* IV, Amm. XXI. xvi. 1.

13. VALENTINIAN'S LAW OF PRECEDENCE: *CTh* VI. vii. 1+ix. 1+xi. 1+xiv. 1+xxii. 4, 372, alluded to by Gratian, *CTh* VI. v. 2, 384, caelestis recordationis Valentinianus genitor numinis nostri singulis quibusque dignitatibus certum locum meritumque praescripsit.

14. A law of Gratian, *CTh* VI. x. 2+xxvi. 2, 381, orders 'notariorum primicerios . . . non solum vicariis anteponi sed etiam proconsulibus aequari'. The implication is that they were already graded above *vicarii*. The same law grants equality with *vicarii* to *tribuni et notarii* and to the *proximi scriniorum* and *magistri dispositionum*, who are styled *clarissimi viri*. It is to be inferred that all these were already *consulares* and were moved up one grade. LIBANIUS' COMPLAINTS: Lib. *Or.* II. 43–6, LXII. 10–16, *Ep.* 1224. The social transformation of the *notarii* must have begun in Constantius II's reign, seeing that Procopius, a relative of Julian, was serving in the corps in 358 (Amm. XVII. xiv. 3). In 371 Theodorus, a man of ancient family and good education, had risen to be *secundicerius notariorum* (Amm. XXIX. i. 8).

15. On these titles see O. Hirschfeld, *Die Rangtitel der römischen Kaiserzeit* (*Kleine Schriften*, 657–71) and Ensslin s.v. 'spectabilis', *PW* III A, 1552–68, Berger s.v. 'illustris', *PW* IX. 1070–85.

16. VALENS' LETTER TO FESTUS: Bruns, *Fontes Iuris Romani*[7], 97b. THE INCREASE OF THE SENATE: Them. *Or.* XXXIV. xiii.

17. RULE ABOUT CHILDREN: *CTh* XII. i. 57, 364, nemo ad ordinem senatorium ante functionem omnium munerum municipalium senator accedat . . . in locum suum scilicet filiis subrogatis, si eos successio familiae ad exsequendam universae legis nostrae mentem docebitur adiuvare; 58, 364, qui curiali ortus familia ante completa munera patriae senator factus est, fructu careat, quousque muneribus absolvatur; quibus expletis si velit sumptuosum ordinem senatorium vitare, renuntiet dignitati; si permanserit, liberos quos post ediderit habeat senatores, praetores iam quaestoresque, non muneri decurionum obnoxios; 69, 365, universi qui praematura cupiditate senatorios coetus honoribus patriae praetulisse noscuntur, habeant quidem incolumem statum senatoriae dignitatis, verum fungantur his honoribus quos patriae nondum reddiderunt. quin etiam liberos suos indicent quos ante senatoriam dignitatem quisque suscepit. The rule was applied to all senators, whether of curial origin or not, by *CJ* XII. i. 11, 377, senator [vel alius clarissimus] privatos habeat filios, editos quippe antequam susciperet dignitatem (the bracketed works are probably an interpolation of Justinian). VALENS' LAW: *CTh* XII. i. 74, 371; by *CTh* XII. i. 73, 373 (S), Valentinian reaffirmed the rule that decurions could obtain senatorial rank only by an *administratio* or a palatine *militia*.

18. For the early history of the *defensor* see ch. XIX, n. 31.

19. *CTh* I. xxix. 1, 368 (S), admodum utiliter edimus ut plebs omnis Inlyrici officiis patronorum contra potentium defendatur iniurias. super singulas quasque praedictae dioeceseos civitates aliquos idoneis moribus quorumque vita anteacta laudatur tua sinceritas ad hoc eligere curet officium. INSTRUCTIONS

TO SENECA: *CTh* I. xxix. 2+VIII. xv. 4; as the name of the place at which this law was given is uncertain we cannot be sure which emperor issued it, nor to which of the consulates of Valentinian and Valens it belongs. VALENS' LAW: *CTh* I. xxix. 5, 370 (given at Hierapolis).

20. *CTh* I. xxix. 1, 3, 4, 368 (S).

21. SUSCEPTORES AND PRAEPOSITI HORREORUM: *CTh* XII. vi. 5, 6, 7, 9, cf. VIII. iii. 1, vii. 8 (all 364–5). SUSCEPTORES VESTIS: *CTh* XII. vi. 4, 365. CURSUS PUBLICUS: *CTh* VIII. v. 23, 365.

22. *CTh* XII. vi. 9, 365, susceptores specierum idcirco per Illyrici provincias ex officialium corpore creari praecepimus quod cognitum est illos et re et fide idoneos haberi quam eos, qui in curia suscipere consueverint. verum in provinciis Africae tua sinceritas hoc ab his officium iubeat amoveri atque eos susceptores specierum annonariarum manere, quos ad hanc necessitatem vetus consuetudo constringit, maxime cum, si susceptores de curia dati aliquid vel neglegentia vel fraude decoxerint, ad redintegrationem specierum, sicuti moris est, ordo qui creaverit possit artari. For the alleged difficulty in filling the posts see *CTh* XII. vi. 5, 365, sed quoniam praeses Ciliciae adseruit deesse ex his corporibus quibus possit haec sollicitudo committi, ne in praesens tempus fisci nostri seu publica emolumenta vacillent, excellentia tua, ubi eos deesse perviderit, quos susceptores ac praepositos creari scitis prioribus iusseramus, vetustum morem consuetudinemque sectabitur, scilicet ut ex eo ordine constituantur ex quo ante consueverant ordinari; also *CTh* VIII. v. 26, 365, cursus mancipes clavularii ex quo genere hominum debeant ordinari, apertissima lege decrevimus. quorum si praedictae numerus functioni non potuerit occurrere, curiales ad hoc munus sunt vocandi. For corrupt evasion by those liable see *CTh* XII. vi. 5, 365, nam si qui per gratiam fuerint praetermissi, necesse habet exigere publica commoditas ultionem. nec enim dubium est eos officiales qui nunc diversis officiis obsecundant plurimos praetermittere.

23. VALENS' LETTER TO EUTROPIUS: *FIR* I², 108. THE THIRD: *CTh* IV. xiii. 7, xv. i. 18, 374. For the civic lands and taxes see pp. 732–3.

24. Amm. XXX. ix. 1, XXXI. xiv. 2.

25. Them. *Or.* VIII. 112–13. Amm. XXXI. xiv. 3.

26. The abolition of *capitatio* in Illyricum is implied by *CJ* XI. liii. 1, 371 (cf. the similar law about Thrace, *CJ* XI. lii. 1). The story of Valentinian and Iphicles is told in Amm. XXX. v. 4–10. FISCAL OPPRESSION IN AFRICA: Zos. IV. 16.

27. GOLD MINERS: *CTh* X. xix. 3, 365, 5, 370 (S), 6, 369, 7, 370, 9, 378.

28. In *CTh* XIII. i, *de lustrali collatione*, laws 1 (356), 4 (362), 6 (364) and 8 (370) speak of gold and silver, but 9 (372), 11 (379), 15 (386), 17 (399), 18 (400), 19 (403), 20 (410) and 21 (418) all mention gold only: only in *CTh* I. v. 14 (405) is silver spoken of as part of the *collatio lustralis* after 370. The tax was known as the *pensio auraria* in Ostrogothic Italy (Cass. *Var.* II. 26, 30) and was paid in gold under Anastasius (Josh. Styl. 31).

29. VALENTINIAN'S MILITARY DISCIPLINE: Amm. XXX. v. 3, ix. 1. VALENS' CARE FOR THE TROOPS: Them. *Or.* VIII. 116ab, x. 136ab, 138bc. The following units in the Notitia can be attributed to Valens in the field armies: *Not. Dig. Or.* v. 56, Tertii Sagittarii Valentis, vii. 46, Secunda Felix Valentis Thebaeorum, viii. 52–3 (cf. 20–2), Augustenses, Valentinianenses, Gratianenses. He also probably reinforced the army of Oriens with units withdrawn from the areas ceded by Jovian to Persia (see App. II). Among the *limitanei* he can be credited with

the following: *Not. Dig. Or.* xxxi. 36, legio I Valentiniana, 39, legio II Valentiniana, xxxiv. 35, ala II Felix Valentiana, 42, cohors II Gratiana, xxxvii. 29,
30, ala I Valentiana, ala II Felix Valentiniana, xxxviii. 37, cohors II Valentiana.

30. SONS OF VETERANS: *CTh* VII. i. 5, 364, 8, 364 (S), xxii. 7, 365, 8, 372. REFORM
OF THE CONSCRIPTION: *CTh* VII. xiii. 7, 375; section 1 of this law shows that the
levy was annual. For an explanation of the system see pp. 615–16. TAX EXEMP-
TIONS FOR RECRUITS: *CTh* VII. xiii. 6, 370, 7 §3, 375. ALLOTMENTS TO VETERANS:
CTh VII. xx. 8, 364.

31. REDUCTION OF HEIGHT: *CTh* VII. xiii. 3, 367. EXEMPTION OF RES PRIVATA:
CTh VII. xiii. 2, 370. The commutation of recruits is mentioned in this law
(domum nostram ad exhibenda tironum corpora per eas provincias, a quibus
corpora flagitantur, nolumus perurgueri: ceterum sinimus conveniri, in quibus
pretia postulantur) and in *CTh* VII. xiii. 7 §1: the latter passage implies that in
the same province recruits might be levied in one year and gold in another.
RECRUITS FROM THE SUBURBICARIAN PROVINCES: *CTh* VII. xiii. 3+4, 367.
RECRUITS FROM EGYPT: *Chr.* 1. 466–7, 469 (dated by *ILS* 8947). AURUM
TIRONICUM FROM EGYPT: *P. Lips.* 34 v, 61.

32. CONFISCATION OF TEMPLE LANDS: *CTh* V. xiii. 3, X. i. 8, 364. JOVIAN'S
EDICT: Them. *Or.* v. Valentinian's edict is referred to in *CTh* IX. xvi. 9, 371,
testes sunt leges a me in exordio imperii mei datae, quibus unicuique quod
animo inbibisset, colendi libera facultas tributa est. NOCTURNAL SACRIFICES:
CTh IX. xvi. 7, 364, Zos. IV. 3. HARUSPICINA: *CTh* IX. xvi. 9, 371. On the
position under Valens the evidence is conflicting. According to Theodoret
(*HE* v. 21) pagan rites, including sacrifice, flourished unchecked. According
to Libanius (*Or.* xxx. 7) sacrifice was at first allowed but later prohibited owing
to a conspiracy (νεωτέρων τινῶν συμβάντων) but incense was still permitted. It
may well be as the result of the Theodore incident (Amm. xxix. i) that stringent
laws were issued against divination and magic, and that it became dangerous
to offer sacrifices, which were associated with these activities.

33. MANICHEES: *CTh* XVI. v. 3, 372. REBAPTISM: *CTh* XVI. vi. 1, 373. VALEN-
TINIAN'S RELIGIOUS IMPARTIALITY: Soz. VI. 7, Amm. xxx. ix. 5.

34. DAMASUS AND URSINUS: Amm. XXVII. iii. 12–15. AGORIUS PRAETEXTATUS:
Jerome, *c. Joh. Hierosol.* 8. VALENTINIAN'S CONSTITUTION: *CTh* XVI. ii. 20, 370.

35. Paul. *V. Amb.* 6–9.

36. *CTh.* XII. i. 59+XVI. ii. 17, 364, XVI. ii. 19, 370, 21, 371.

37. VALENS' EDICT: Soz. VI. 12.

38. VALENS AND BASIL: Greg. Naz. *Or.* XLIII. 48–54, Theod. *HE* IV. 19. VALENS
AND PETER: Theod. *HE* IV. 22.

39. Amm. XXXI. iii, iv. 1–8.

40. LUPICINUS AND MAXIMUS: Amm. XXXI. iv. 9–11. The Goths enrolled in
the army of Oriens are mentioned in XXXI. xvi. 8, those sent to Adrianople in
XXXI. vi. 1.

41. THE OSTROGOTHS: Amm. XXXI. iv. 12–13, v. 1–3. THE MASSACRE: idem,
XXXI. v. 4–7. ADRIANOPLE: idem, XXXI. vi. 1–4. SLAVES AND MINERS: idem, XXXI.
vi. 5–6.

42. Amm. XXXI. vii–xiii.

43. THE SARACENS: Amm. XXXI. xvi. 5–6, Soc. v. 1, Soz. VII. 1. JULIUS: Amm.
XXXI. xvi. 8, Zos. IV. 26.

44. The transfer of the two dioceses is mentioned only by Soz. VII. 4, Ἰλλυρίους καὶ τὰ πρὸς ἥλιον ἀνίσχοντα τῆς ἀρχῆς Θεοδοσίῳ ἐπιτρέψας, but is confirmed by Theodosius' residence at Thessalonica during the first two years of his reign.

45. CONSCRIPTION: *CTh* VII. xiii. 8, 9, 380, 10, 381, 11, 382. SONS OF VETERANS: *CTh* VII. xxii. 9, 10, 380. ENROLMENT OF BARBARIANS: Zos. IV. 30–1.

46. The date is given by *Chron. Min.* I. 243, ipso anno universa gens Gothorum cum rege suo in Romaniam se tradiderunt die V non. Oct. The settlement is described in Them. *Or.* XVI. 211, XXXIV. xx–xxiv; cf. also Pan. Lat. II. 22, dicamne ego receptos servitum Gothos castris tuis militem, terris sufficere cultorem? Synesius severely criticises the settlement (*de Regno*, 14–15). He stresses the folly of introducing into the empire νεότητα πολλὴν ἑτερότροφον ἔθεσιν ἰδίοις χρωμένην (ch. 14) and blames Theodosius for his weakness in making the Goths allies and giving them land (ch. 15, καὶ συμμάχους ἐποίει καὶ πολιτείας ἠξίου καὶ μετεδίδου γερῶν καὶ γῆς τι ἐδάσατο τοῖς παλαμναίοις Ῥωμαϊκῆς. That the main settlement was in Moesia and Scythia appears from Zos. IV. 34, and from the fact that Alaric's first move was from τὰ τῆς Θράκης ἄνω μέρη (Philostorgius, XII. 2, cf. Zos. V. 5). The allusion to Macedonia in Them. *Or.* XXXIV. xxiv is puzzling; presumably some other bands of Goths were settled there. The use of the word ὁμωροφίους in the same passage suggests that the Goths were settled as *hospites* on the system later used in the West (see pp. 248–53).

47. The number 20,000 depends on Jordanes, *Get.* 145.

48. Zos. IV. 35. Claudian, *de IV cos. Hon.* 623 ff., cf. *in Eutrop.* II. 153 ff. for the Gruthungi settled in Phrygia.

49. See my *CERP*, 224–6 and 444–5, n. 15.

50. GRATIAN'S CHARACTER: *Epit. Caes.* xlvii. 4–6. REVOLT OF MAXIMUS: Zos. IV. 35.

51. Justina is spoken of as the power behind the throne in Paul. *V. Amb.* 11–2, Rufinus, *HE* II. 15, Soc. V. 11, Soz. VII. 13, Zos. IV. 43, 47. RECOGNITION OF MAXIMUS: Zos. IV. 37. Theodosius' visit to Italy is an inference (doubtful in view of the many inaccuracies of the Code) from *CTh* XII. i. 107, which was addressed from Verona on 31 Aug. 384 to Cynegius, praetorian prefect of the East. The date of the retrocession of Dacia and Macedonia to the Western empire is the subject of a vast literature, see Stein, *Bas-Empire* I. 520, n. 5. It is proved by *CTh* I. xxxii. 5 that they belonged to the West in 386, but in *CTh* VI. ii. 14, 384, Theodosius grants immunity from the *gleba* to senators of Constantinople from both the Thracian and Macedonian dioceses.

52. MAXIMUS' CONFISCATIONS: Pan. Lat. II. 25–6, Sulp. Sev. *Dial.* III. 11. PRAISE OF MAXIMUS: Sulp. Sev. loc. cit. and *Dial.* II. 6, vir omni vita merito praedicandus, si ei vel diadema non legitime, tumultuante milite, impositum repudiare vel armis civilibus abstinere licuisset, Orosius, VII. xxxiv. 9, Maximus, vir quidem strenuus et probus atque Augusto dignus, nisi contra sacramenti fidem per tyrannidem emersisset. FALL OF MAXIMUS: Zos. IV. 42–6.

53. PROCLAMATION OF ARCADIUS: *Chron. Min.* I. 244. ARBOGAST AND EUGENIUS: Zos. IV. 53–4, Soz. VII. 22, Joh. Ant. 187. PROCLAMATION OF HONORIUS: *Chron. Min.* I. 298.

54. BARBARIAN TROOPS UNDER THEODOSIUS AND MAXIMUS: Pan. Lat. II. 32, Amb. *Ep.* 24 §§ 4 and 8; UNDER THEODOSIUS AND EUGENIUS: Zos. IV. 57–8, Orosius, VII. xxxv. 11–12, 19, Soc. V. 25, Soz. VII. 24, Greg. Tur. *HF* II. 9.

55. See App. II, Tables I–II for Theodosian units. To Gratian may be

reasonably attributed two *auxilia palatina*, the Gratianenses Jun. and Valentinianenses Jun. (*Not. Dig. Occ.* v. 189, 190). The Gratianenses Sen., who have much higher seniority (ibid. v. 181), may have been raised by Valentinian I. The Felices Valentinianenses (ibid. v. 208) seem to have suffered a penal loss of seniority (see App. II); they might belong to Gratian or Valentinian II.

56. BAUTO AND ARBOGAST FRANKS: Zos. IV. 33, Amb. *Ep.* 24 § 8, Paul. *V. Amb.* 30. Of Theodosius' *magistri* only Timasius (Joh. Ant. 187) and Abundantius (Zos. v. 10, ἀπὸ τῆς ἐν τῇ Θρᾳκίᾳ Σκυθίας) are definitely attested to have been Romans, and only Modares (Zos. IV. 25) a Goth. BACURIUS: Rufinus, *HE* I. 10, II. 33. For the other generals see Ennslin, *Klio*, xxiv (1931), 131 ff.

57. For Ausonius and his family see the fully annotated family tree in Schenkl, *Ausonius*, MGH (*AA*) v, p. xiv. For Syagrius see Seeck, *Symmachus*, MGH (*AA*) vi, p. cix.

58. The prefectures of Petronius Probus are a much discussed problem. He certainly held four prefectures (*ILS* 1267-8), of which the first, under Valentinian I, was of Italy, Illyricum and Africa (*ILS* 1265). He is recorded (Soc. v. 11, Soz. VII. 13) as praetorian prefect of Italy (and presumably Illyricum and Africa) in 383 at the time of Maximus' revolt and in 387 at the time of Maximus' invasion of Italy; these must be the third and fourth prefectures. He was also at some time prefect of the Gauls (*ILS* 1266-8, *CJ* VII. xxxviii. 1), presumably in 380, when he is recorded as praetorian prefect (*CTh* VI. xxxv. 10). The inscription *ILS* 1266 must be muddled. AGORIUS PRAETEXTATUS: *ILS* 1258-9, cf. Amm. XXII. vii. 6 (proconsul of Achaea), XXVII. ix. 8 (prefect of the city), *CTh* VI. v. 2 (praetorian prefect). NICOMACHUS FLAVIANUS: *ILS* 2947-8; he may have been prefect for the first time in 383 (*CTh* VII. xviii. 8 and IX. xxix. 2), unless the date of this law is wrong; his prefecture in 391-2 is well attested in the Code, and under Eugenius by Paul. *V. Amb.* 26, Rufinus, *HE* II. 33, Soz. VII. 22.

59. EUTROPIUS: *magister memoriae* in the dedication of his Breviarium; *procos. Asiae*, Amm. XXIX. i. 36. TATIAN: *ILS* 8844. NEOTERIUS: notary, Amm. XXVI. v. 14. Cynegius' Spanish origin is inferred from *Chron. Min.* I. 245 (his widow takes his corpse from Constantinople to Spain); *magister scrinii*, Lib. *Or.* XLIX. 3. RUFINUS: a Gaul, Claudian, *in Ruf.* I. 123 ff.; career, Zos. IV. 51-2; the transfer of the *fabricae* is attested by *CTh* X. xxii. 3 (addressed to Rufinus as *magister officium* in 390; contrast the previous law addressed in 388 to the praetorian prefect).

60. PRECEDENCE: *CTh* VI. vi. 1, 382, vii. 2, 380, ix. 2, 380, xxii. 5, 6, 381, and especially VI. xxii. 7, 383. COMITES CONSISTORIANI: *CTh* VI. ix. 2, 380; the *magister officiorum* is *spectabilis* in 378 (VIII. v. 35) but *illustris* in 384 (Symm. *Rel.* 34, 38, 43). NEW PROCONSULATES: SPAIN: Sulp. Sev. *Chron.* II. 49. CAMPANIA: *ILS* 1262-3, 5702, 8984. PALESTINE: *CTh* XI. xxxvi. 28, 383, xxx. 42, 384, X. xvi. 4, 385.

61. NOTARIES: *CTh* VI. x. 2, 381, 3, 381. PROXIMI SCRINIORUM: *CTh* VI. xxvi. 2, 381, 4, 386. PRINCIPES AGENTIUM IN REBUS: *CTh* VI. xxvii. 5, 386, 6, 390. REDUCTION OF THE GLEBA: *CTh* VI. ii. 15, 393.

62. DECURIONS: *CTh* XII. i. 90, 383, 111, 386, 118, 387, 122, 390, 129, 392, 130 and 132, 393; cf. Lib. *Or.* XLIX. 5, 6.

63. REMISSION OF GLEBA: *CTh* VI. ii. 14, 384. REMISSION OF CAPITATIO: *CJ* XI. lii. 1. THEODOSIUS' EXPENDITURE: Pan. Lat. II. 13, Zos. IV. 33, *Epit. Caes.* xlviii. 9, Lib. *Or.* II. 58. THE RIOT AT ANTIOCH: Zos. IV. 41, Soz. VII. 23, Theod.

HE v. 20, Lib. *Or*. XIX–XXIII, Joh. Chrys. *Hom. ad pop Ant*.; for the tax involved see R. Browning, *JRS* XLII (1952), 14–5.

64. GRATIAN'S DECREE OF TOLERATION: Soc. v. 2, Soz. VII. 1; he refers to it in *CTh* XVI. v. 5, antiquato rescripto quod apud Sirmium nuper emersit. THE ROMAN COUNCIL AND GRATIAN'S REPLY: Mansi, III. 634, *Coll. Avell*. 13. LAW AGAINST HERETICS: *CTh* XVI. v. 5, 379; law 4 is probably misdated, see *Rev. Hist.* CLXVIII (1931), 87–90.

65. PONTIFEX MAXIMUS: Zos. IV. 36. THE ALTAR OF VICTORY (382): Amb. *Ep.* 17.

66. THE ALTAR OF VICTORY (384): Symm. *Rel.* 2, Amb. *Ep.* 17, 18, 57. THE ARIAN BASILICA: Amb. *Ep.* 20, 21, Paul. *V. Amb.* 12–13, Rufinus. *HE* II. 15–16, Soz. VII. 13, *CTh* XVI. i. 4, 386.

67. Sulp. Sev. *Chron.* II. 46–51, *Dial.* III. 11.

68. THEODOSIUS' BAPTISM: Soc. v. 6, Soz. VII. 4.

69. THEODOSIUS' LAWS ON THE FAITH: *CTh* XVI. i. 2, 380, v. 6, 381. DEPOSITION OF DEMOPHILUS: Soc. v. 7, Soz. VII. 5.

70. CHOICE OF NECTARIUS: Soz. VII. 8. The council is described in Soc. v. 8, Soz. VII. 7–9. The canons referred to are the second and third.

71. *CTh* XVI. i. 3, 381.

72. THEODOSIUS' LAWS AGAINST HERETICS: *CTh* XVI. v. 6–24, 381–94; of these nos. 7, 9 and 18 are against Manichees and 9 also against the Encratites. LAWS AGAINST APOSTATES: *CTh* XVI. vii. 1, 381, 2, 383, 3, 383, 4, 391, 5, 391.

73. DECURIONS AND THE CHURCH: *CTh* XII. i. 104, 383, 115, 386, 121, 390, cf. Amb. *Ep.* 40 § 29. Ambrose complained of the same rule to Valentinian II in 384 (*Ep.* 18 § 13). DEACONESSES AND WIDOWS: *CTh* XVI. ii. 27, 28, 390.

74. PROTECTION OF THE JEWS: *CTh* XVI. viii. 8, 392, 9, 393. CALLINICUM INCIDENT: Amb. *Ep.* 40, 41, Paul. *V. Amb.* 22–3.

75. LAWS OF 381 AND 385: *CTh* XVI. x. 7, 381, si qui vetitis sacrificiis diurnis nocturnisque velut vesanus ac sacrilegus incertorum consultorem se immerserit fanumque sibi aut templum ad huiuscemodi sceleris executionem adsumendum crediderit vel putaverit adeundum, proscribtione se noverit subiugendum, cum nos iusta institutione moneamus castis deum precibus excolendum, non diris carminibus profanandum, 9, 385, si quis mortalium ita faciendi sacrificii sumat audaciam, ut inspectione iecoris extorumque praesagio vanae spem promissionis accipiat uel, quod est deterius, futura sub execrabili consultatione cognoscat. acerbioris etenim inminebit supplicii cruciatus eis qui contra vetitum praesentium vel futurarum rerum explorare temptaverint veritatem. While these laws are specifically directed against divination, their menaces are so vaguely worded that it is understandable that Libanius states the legal position as he does in *Or.* xxx. 8, cf. 17. For the continuation of some form of public pagan cult see *CTh* XII. i. 112, 386. In *CTh* XVI. x. 8, 382, Theodosius orders that a temple in Osrhoene be kept open 'neque huic rei obreptivum officere sinimus oraculum': evidently a petition for its closure had been granted. The last sentence of the law' 'ne illic prohibitorum usus sacrificiorum huius occasione aditus permissus esse credatur', is ambiguous; are all sacrifices forbidden, or only prohibited sacrifices, i.e. those for the purpose of divination?

76. DESTRUCTION OF TEMPLES: Lib. *Or.* xxx. 8 ff. CYNEGIUS' TOUR: Zos. IV. 37, *Chron. Min.* I. 244, Theod. *HE* v. 21, cf. Soz. VII. 15.

77. DESTRUCTION OF THE SERAPEUM: Rufinus, *HE* II. 23–30, Soc. v. 16, Soz. VII. 15, Theod. *HE* v. 22, Eunap. *V. Soph.* VI. 11; the date is uncertain, being

given as 389 by Marcellinus and 391 by the Gallic chronicle (*Chron. Min.* I. 650, II. 62). Evagrius and Romanus, the Augustal prefect and *comes Aegypti* under whom the temple was destroyed, were in office in June, 391 (*CTh* XVI. x. 11), but they may have been so two years earlier. The law addressed to them has no bearing on the destruction of the Serapeum, and might be earlier or later than it.

78. *CTh* XVI. x. 10, 11, 391, 12, 392.

79. EUGENIUS' PAGAN REACTION: Amb. *Ep.* 57, Paul. *V. Amb.* 26, 31, Soz. VII. 22, Rufinus, *HE* II. 33. Cf. the contemporary Christian pamphlets cited by Piganiol, *Empire chrétien*, 226, n. 105.

80. THE MASSACRE OF THESSALONICA: Amb. *Ep.* 51, Paul. *V. Amb.* 24, Rufinus, *HE* II. 18, Soz. VII. 25, Theod. *HE* v. 17-18. The law is *CTh* IX. xl. 13, 390.

VI. THE HOUSE OF THEODOSIUS (pp. 173-7)

For the first part of the period covered by this chapter there is a detailed study, E. Demougeot, *De l'unité à la division de l'empire romain*, Paris, 1951, and for the relations of the empire with the Huns E. A. Thompson, *A history of Attila and the Huns*, Oxford, 1948.

1. THEODOSIUS II'S PIETY: Soc. VII. 22, cf. the dedicatory epistle of Sozomen's Ecclesiastical History. On Pulcheria and Galla Placidia see Ensslin in *PW* XXIII. 1954-63, XX. 1910-31. Pulcheria's power is praised by Sozomen (IX. 1) and reviled by Eunapius (fr. 87). For Galla Placidia's dominance see Proc. *BV* I. iii. 14-36, *Chron. Min.* II. 22, 78, Joh. Ant. 201. 3.

2. *Not. Dig. Occ.* v, vi, vii. 111-14, xxv. 37-42, xxvi. 21-4, xxviii. 22-5, xxix. 6-9, xxx. 20-3, xxxi. 32-4, xxxv. 35-8, xxxvi. 6-9, xxxvii. 30-3, xl. 57-60, xli. 26-9, cf. *CTh* I. vii. 3, 398, sicut clarissimis viris comitibus et ducibus diversarum provinciarum et limitum, ita et viro spectabili comiti per Africam principes et numerarii ex officio magisteriae potestatis mittantur.

3. JACOBUS: Claudian, *Epigr.* 50. VINCENTIUS: Zos. v. 32. For Stilicho's title see *ILS* 797, 1277.

4. STILICHO'S FALL: Zos. V. 32-4. VARANES AND TURPILIO: idem, v. 36. TURPILIO AND VIGILANTIUS: idem, v. 47, cf. 48. FALL OF OLYMPIUS: idem, v. 46.

5. VALENS AND ALLOBICH: Zos. v. 48; Valens is called στρατηγὸς ἑκατέρας δυνάμεως in Olymp. 13. CONSTANTIUS IN GAUL: Orosius, VII. xlii. 1-3, Soz. IX. 13-4; patrician in 415, *Chron. Min.* I. 467, cf. *ILS* 8992, 801. For the use of the title see pp. 343-4. CONSTANTIUS' MARRIAGE AND CORONATION: Olymp. 34.

6. CASTINUS: *Chron. Min.* I. 469-71. FELIX: *ILS* 1293, *Chron. Min.* I. 471-3, II. 21-2, Jch. Ant. 201. AETIUS AND THE HUNS: Greg. Tur. *HF* II. 8, Philostorgius, XII. 14. He is described as *comes* in 425 (Philostorgius, loc. cit.) and in 428 (*Chron. Min.* I. 472, describing his operations in Gaul). He was made *magister militum* (under Felix as patrician) in 429 (*Chron. Min.* I. 472). BONIFACE: *Chron. Min.* I. 473-4, II. 22, Joh. Ant. 201.

7. For a hostile account of Stilicho see Orosius, VII. xxxviii, cf. xlii. 2, Constantio comiti huius belli summa commissa est. sensit tunc demum respublica et quam

utilitatem in Romano tandem duce receperit et quam eatenus perniciem per longa tempora barbaris comitibus subiecta tolerarit. CONSTANTIUS FROM NAISSUS: Olymp. 39. AETIUS FROM DUROSTORUM: Jordanes, *Get*. 176. ALLOBICH: Zos. V. 48. ULFILAS: Soz. IX. 14. GAISO: *CTh* VII. xviii. 16, 413. SIGISVULT: Val. III, *Nov*. vi. 1, ix, 440; he is first mentioned in Africa in 427 (*Chron. Min*. 1. 472, Aug. *Coll. cum Maximino*, 1) and was consul in 437.

8. We know the full career of only one of Honorius' praetorian prefects, thanks to Claudian's *Pan. Mallio Theodoro cos*.: he was an advocate from Milan, and was governor of an African province, consular of Macedonia (or vicar?), *magister epistularum* (or quaestor?), *comes sacrarum largitionum*, praetorian prefect of the Gauls and then of Italy. Hadrianus was an Alexandrian (Claudian, *Epigr*. 21) and served as *CSL* and *mag. off*. before becoming *PPO It*. John was a notary in 394 (Paul. *V. Amb*. 31) and had risen to be *primicerius* in 408 (Zos. v. 40); he was *mag. off*. under Attalus (Soz. IX. 8) before becoming *PPO It*. in 412–3. Of the rest little is recorded (see Sundwall, *Weströmische Studien*, for their careers), but only one, Valerius Messalla, is known to have been an aristocrat (Rut. Nam. *de red. suo*, 1. 267 ff.). For Valentinian's noble prefects see Sundwall, op. cit. The early career of Petronius Maximus is given in *ILS* 809, that of Faustus in *ILS* 1283. Nicomachus Flavianus was consular of Campania and proconsul of Asia before becoming *PU* and *PPO It*. (*ILS* 2948). Albinus was *PU* 'vitae flore puer' (Rut. Nam. *de red. suo*, 1. 466 ff.) and is not known to have held any lower office. Volusianus was proconsul of Africa as 'puer' and quaestor 'primaevus' (Rut. Nam. *de red. suo*, 1. 171–3) before being *PU* and *PPO It*.

9. RUFINUS AND EUTROPIUS: Zos. V. 1–10.

10. *Not. Dig. Or*. v–ix. It is noteworthy that only one of the *praesentales* and the *magister militum per Orientem* had established civil servants (*officium cardinale*), and the other three were served by soldiers seconded from their regiments; this must have been a temporary arrangement and suggests that Theodosius had left behind only the *magister* of Oriens and one praesental *magister*, and that the other three commands were hastily improvised.

11. REVOLT OF GAINAS: Zos. V. 13–22, Soc. VI. 6, Soz. VIII. 4, Syn. *de Prov*., Claudian, *in Eutrop*. II.

12. ANTHEMIUS: Soc. VII. 1; he was *CSL* in 400 (*CTh* I. x. 5) and *mag. off*. in 404 (*CTh* VI. xxvii. 14, X. xxii. 5, XVI. iv. 4), and is recorded as *PPO* from 405 (*CTh* VII. x. 1) to 414 (*CTh* IX. xl. 22), as patrician in 406 (*CTh* IX. xxxiv. 10) and 408 (*CTh* XII. xii. 14). PULCHERIA AUGUSTA: *Chron. Min*. II. 71. Helio is recorded as *mag. off*. from 414 (*CTh* XIII. iii. 17) to 427 (*CTh* VII. viii. 14, XIII. iii. 18), and no other *magister* is known until Paulinus in 430 (*CTh* VI. xxvii. 23), Helio is called patrician in *CTh* VI. xxvii. 20 (426) and VII. viii. 14 (427), and crowned Valentinian III (Olymp. 46).

13. VALERIUS: Malalas, 355, *CTh* VI. xxviii. 8, VII. viii. 16. CYRUS: Suidas, *s.v.* Κῦρος, Malalas, 361–2: he is first recorded as *PPO* in 439 (Th. II, *Nov*. xviii) and last in 441 (Th. II, *Nov*. v. 3, *CJ* I. lv. 10); his fall is attributed to Chrysaphius in *V. Dan*. 31. For the story of the intrigues which led to the fall of Pulcheria and Eudocia we are dependent on Theophanes, A.M. 5940 (cf. Malalas, 356–8, for Eudocia). Theophanes' date (447–8) must be wrong, for Eudocia retired to Palestine, never to return, in 443 (see Bury, *Later Roman Empire*[2], 229, n. 5, 230, n. 5). Chrysaphius' power is attested by Priscus (7, Χρυσαφίῳ τῷ βασιλέως ὑπασπιστῇ, οἶα δὴ τὰ μέγιστα δυναμένῳ, and in *A.C.Oec*. II. i. 216, and by later authors such as John of Antioch (194) and Malalas (363).

Nomus' power and his friendship with Chrysaphius are attested by Priscus (13, συνεπέμπετο δὲ 'Ανατολίῳ Νόμος οὐ διὰ τὸ μέγεθος τῆς τύχης μόνον, ἀλλὰ ὡς καὶ τῷ Χρυσαφίῳ εὔνους ὤν), Theodore Lector (cited in *A.C.Oec.* II. vi. 5, Χρυσάφιος καὶ οἱ περὶ Νόμον τὸν ὕπατον ἐκθύμως τῷ Εὐτυχεῖ προσκείμενοι πείθουσι Θεοδόσιον κελεῦσαι σύνοδον γενέσθαι κατὰ τὴν Ἔφεσον), and the petition of Cyril's nephews (*A.C. Oec.* II. i. 216, τῷ τῆς ἀνοσίας μνήμης Χρυσαφίῳ οὐ μὴν ἀλλὰ καὶ τῷ μεγαλοπρεπεστάτῳ καὶ ἐνδοξοτάτῳ Νόμῳ τότε τὰ τῆς οἰκουμένης ἐν χερσὶν ἔχοντι πράγματα). While master of the offices he was given additional functions, control of the *limitanei* (Th. II, *Nov.* xxiv, 443) and the restoration of civic lands to the cities, the praetorian prefect, whose proper business it was, being ordered to act 'una cum viro inlustri magistro officiorum, cuius administratio probatissima nobis est' (Th. II, *Nov.* xxiii, 443). Theod. *Ep.* (PG) 110, τοῦ μεγαλοπρεπεστάτου σπαθαρίου καὶ τοῦ ἐνδοξοτάτου ἀπὸ μαγίστρων.

14. See ch. XV, n. 68.

15. DECURIONS AND THE SENATE: *CTh* XII. i. 159, 398, 180, 416, 183, 418, 187, 436, Th. II, *Nov.* xv. 1, 439, xv. 2, 444. All these are Eastern laws. The one Western law (XII. i. 155, 397) allows decurions who are *clarissimi* or *spectabiles* to remain in the senate, with children born to them after their promotion, and frees all sons of *illustres* from curial duties. Actual cases of sons of *curiales* who had held illustrious offices are cited in two laws of Leo (*CJ* x. xxxii. 61, 63).

16. EXECUTION OF FRAVITTA: Eunap. 85-6. FLORENTIUS AND SAPRICIUS: *CTh* I. viii. 1, 415. LUPIANUS: *CTh* XII. i. 175, 412. HYPATIUS: *CTh* I. vii. 4, 414, VIII. i. 15, 415. CONSTANS: *CTh* VII. xvii. 1, 412.

17. PERSIAN WAR (421-2): Soc. VII. 18, 20. EXPEDITION AGAINST JOHN: Olymp. 46. AFRICAN EXPEDITION (431): Proc. *BV* I. iii. 35-6. PRAESENTALES IN 441: Th. II, *Nov.* vii. 4. EXPEDITION AGAINST THE VANDALS (441): *Chron. Min.* I. 478; Theophanes (A.M. 5941) adds two other Germans; Germanus was not one of the regular *magistri* but was given the rank of *magister militum inter agentes* for the occasion (*CJ* XII. viii. 2). APOLLONIUS: *CJ* XII. liv. 4, Apollonio magistro militum praesentali et Anatolio magistro militum per Orientem (linked by Seeck with *CJ* I. xlvi. 3, 443); Apollonius was a friend of Zeno, the Isaurian *magister militum per Orientem* (Priscus, 18). ANATOLIUS: Priscus, 13, τὸν μὲν 'Ανατόλιον τῶν ἀμφὶ βασιλέα ἄρχοντα τελῶν (449). PLINTHAS: Soc. v. 23, Soz. VII. 17, Priscus, 1. JOHN THE VANDAL: *Chron. Min.* II. 80, cf. Joh. Ant. 206. ARNEGISCLUS: *Chron. Min.* II. 80, 82, Jordanes, *Rom.* 331, cf. Joh. Ant. 206. AGINTHEUS: Priscus, 8 (p. 78). PROCOPIUS: Soc. VII. 20, *CTh* VII. iv. 36, 424, Sid. Ap. *Carm.* II. 68 ff. DIONYSIUS: *A.C.Oec.* I. i. pars vii. 119-20, Priscus, 1 (a Thracian). ANATOLIUS: Th. II, *Nov.* iv, 438, Proc. *BP* I. ii. 12, *CJ* XII. liv. 4 (see above). ZENO: Priscus, 8 (p. 94), cf. 12, 13, 14, Joh. Ant. 199. Ardaburius and Areobindus seem from Socrates' language (VII. 18) to have been the *praesentales* in 421-2, Vibianus and Procopius being *magistri militum Orientis*. Ardaburius after commanding the expedition against John in 425 (Olymp. 46) and holding the consulship in 427 disappears from our record and may have soon died. He was probably succeeded as *praesentalis* by his son Aspar, who commanded the Vandal expedition of 431 (Proc. *BV* I. iii. 35-6). Areobindus and Aspar were certainly the two *praesentales* in 441 (Th. II, *Nov.* vii. 4). Areobindus may have retired soon after, if Apollonius was *praesentalis* in 443, as suggested above; he did not die till 449 (*Chron. Min.* II. 83). Aspar continued *praesentalis* till his assassination by Leo in 471.

18. For the family relationships of the German generals see *PW*, *s.v.* Ariovindus, Ardaburius, Plinthas. An interesting record of the group is a silver dish,

celebrating Aspar's consulship, and depicting Aspar, his father Ardaburius, Plinthas, and Aspar's son Ardaburius (later consul in 447), who is recorded as praetor (*ILS* 1299). For the intermingling of Romans and Germans see the family tree of the descendants of Valentinian I in Nicephorus, *Opuscula Historica* (ed. Teubner, pp. 103–4).

19. EASTERN AID FOR HONORIUS: Zos. VI. 8. For the other Eastern expeditions to the West see above n. 17.

20. Stilicho's guardianship of both the sons of Theodosius is attested by contemporary, but perhaps biassed, western authors (Amb. *de ob. Theod.* 5, Claudian, *in Ruf.* II. 4–6, *de III cos. Hon.* 157–8, *de IV cos. Hon.* 430–3, *de cos. Stil.* II. 53–60), and by later Eastern historians (Olymp. 2, Zos. v. 4). For eastern Illyricum see Demougeot, op. cit. 143 ff.

21. The main authority for these events is Claudian, *in Ruf.* II (Stilicho's Thessalian campaign, the return of the Eastern army and Rufinus' death), and *de IV Cos. Hon.* 459–83 (Stilicho's Peloponnesian expedition). For a detailed reconstruction see Demougeot, op. cit. 146–73. DESERTERS AND RECRUITS: *CTh* VII. xviii. 9, 396. ALARIC MAGISTER MILITUM OF ILLYRICUM: Claudian, *in Eutrop.* II. 214–18, *de bello Getico*, 535–9.

22. The principal sources are Claudian, *de bello Gild.*, Orosius VII. xxxvi, Zos. v. 11. RECRUITS: *CTh* VII. xiii. 12–14, 397, Symm. *Ep.* VI. 58, 62, 64. THE EXPEDITIONARY FORCE: Claudian, *de bello Gild.* 415–23 (seven units named), Orosius, VII. xxxvi. 6 (5,000 men). GILDO MAGISTER UTRIUSQUE MILITIAE PER AFRICAM: *CTh* IX. vii. 9, 393. COMITIVA OF AFRICA RESTORED: *CTh* I. vii. 3, 398. BATHANARIUS: *CTh* IX. xlii. 18, 401, Zos. v. 37.

23. Demougeot, op. cit. 267 ff. The main source is Claudian, *de bello Getico* and *de VI cos. Hon.*

24. Zos v. 26, Orosius, VII. xxxvii. VOLUNTEERS AND SLAVES: *CTh* VII. xiii. 16, 17, 406. ENROLMENT OF 12,000 BARBARIANS: Olymp. 9.

25. STILICHO AND ILLYRICUM: Olymp. 3, Soz. VIII. 25, IX. 4. THE INVASION OF GAUL AND THE BRITISH TYRANTS: Zos. VI. 2, 3, Orosius, VII. xxxviii. 3, xl. 3, 4. ALARIC'S BLACKMAIL: Zos. v. 29.

26. CONSTANS IN SPAIN: Zos. VI. 4, Orosius, VII. xl. 7. THE FALL OF STILICHO: Zos. v. 31–4.

27. Zos. v. 35–42.

28. Zos. v. 44–51.

29. Zos. VI. 6–13, Soz. IX. 8, 9.

30. DEATH OF ALARIC: Jordanes, *Get.* 156–8. ATHAULF MOVES TO GAUL: Jordanes, *Get.* 158–61. EVENTS IN SPAIN: Zos. VI. 5, Orosius, VII. xl. 7–10, xlii. 4, Soz. IX. 12, 13, Olymp. 16.

31. BRITAIN AND ARMORICA: Zos. VI. 5, cf. 10; Rut. Nam. *de red. suo,* I. 213–16.

32. Orosius, VII. xlii. 1–5, Olymp. 16, Soz. IX. 13–5.

33. Olymp. 17, 19–21, 24, Orosius, VII. xliii. 1, *Chron. Min.* I. 467; for the Alans see Paul. Pell. *Euch.* 377–85.

34. Hydatius, 49, 60, 63, 67–8 (*Chron. Min.* II. 18–19), Olymp. 31.

35. For the settlement of the Goths in Aquitania see n. 65. BACAUDAE: Rut. Nam. *de red. suo,* I. 213–16.

36. *Chron. Min.* I. 471–2, 475–7, 660.

37. SETTLEMENTS: *Chron. Min.* I. 660 (cited in n. 66). BACAUDAE: *V. Germani*, 28, 40.

38. Hydatius, 71, 74, 77, 86, 89, 90 (*Chron. Min.* II. 20–1).

39. *Chron. Min.* II. 21–7.

40. HERACLIAN: Orosius, VII. xlii. 10–14. BONIFACE: *Chron. Min.* I. 471–2. The story of Boniface's invitation of the Vandals (Proc. *BV* I. iii. 25, Jordanes, *Get.* 167–9) is now generally rejected in view of the silence of Augustine and Possidius (see Stein, *Bas-empire*, I. 575, for the modern literature). THE VANDAL INVASION: Poss. *V. Aug.* 28. SETTLEMENT OF 435: *Chron. Min.* I. 474, Isid. *Hist. Vand.* 74.

41. CAPTURE OF CARTHAGE: *Chron. Min.* I. 477. SETTLEMENT OF 442: *Chron. Min.* I. 479, Victor Vit. I. 13. For the territorial arrangements in 435 and 442 see Courtois, *Les Vandales et l'Afrique*, 170, 174–5.

42. On this vexed question I side with Bury and Stein; for the literature see Stein, *Bas-Empire*, I. 580, n. 61. The sources are Zos. VI. 10 (Honorius' letter to the British cities), *V. Germani*, 12–18 (Germanus' first visit, cf. *Chron. Min.* I. 472 for the date), ibid. 25–7 (Germanus' second visit), *Chron. Min.* I. 660 (the Saxon conquest of 442), Gildas, *de excidio et conquestu Britanniae*, 20 (the appeal to Aetius).

43. This very conjectural reconstruction is mainly based on the self-contradictory data of the Notitia Dignitatum (see App. II, pp. 355–7). For the *comes Illyrici* see Zos. V. 46, and for Chariobaudes, Zos. V. 32.

44. For this paragraph also see App. II. ASTERIUS: *Chron. Min.* II. 20. There is no clearly attested *magister per Gallias* until Cassius about 428 (*V. Hilarii*, vi §9). The *magistri utriusque militiae* operating in Spain are Asturius in 441–3, Merobaudes in 443 and Vitus in 446 (*Chron. Min.* II. 24; Asturius' title is confirmed by *ILS* 1300). A *comes Hispaniarum*, Mansuetus, reappears in 453 (*Chron. Min.* II. 27). I base my belief that the Spanish command was temporarily upgraded on my restoration of Honorius' letter to the troops of Spain (*Estudios de Edad Media de la Corona de Aragon, sec. de Zaragoza*, I, 1945, 268–9), sent 'cum Savinianus patricius qu(o)dam tempore erede (sic) praelatus in Hispaniam profectus est ob infestationem diversarum gentium barbararum: Honorius imperator gloriosus, perpetuus triumfator, semper a(u)gustus universis militibus nostris, < Ascariis > senioribus, iunioribus, < Sagittariis Neruiis, > Speculatoribus, < Exculcatoribus iunioribus, Tubantibus, Felicibus senioribus, Invictis senioribus, Victoribus iunioribus, Invictis iunioribus > [ac] Brita(n)nicis gaude(a)t(i)s sanctissimi co(m)militones nostri communium remuneratione meritorum, et omnes iuxta exultatione gaude(a)t(i)s. hi(c) enim maxime est splendor inlustris qui pari cunct(o)s luce perfu(n)dit. a(d) vos quo(que) magnific(i) comites [h]ac magistri utriusque militi(a)e ad similitudine(m) < Galliarum sunt provisione > nostr(a)e clementi(a)e constituti. constituta si(n)t vobis stipendia Galli(c)an(o)rum, qu(a)e const(antia)e vestr(a)e porreximus ut e(or)undem (una) esset forma virtutis quibus ex(c)ellens una devotio est. proinde instructis sim(ul at)que nobis cuncta subdita sunt in (Hi)spania, et ampli< fi >cat< ionem annonarum > congru(a)m et dignitatis augmentum qu(a)e serenitas nostra (vestris) praestiterit usibus gratanter agnosc(e)mus. ut ubi (otio) vivendi degendique tempus extiterit omni alacritate atque virtute (o)b(l)atis (h)ospitiis obsequamini; qua propter fore quidem confidimus ut (mun)eris resoluti(o) incitet potius quam restinguat ardorem. opt(a)mus conmilitones nostros per multos annos (b)ene agere. et alia manu. bene ualete.

45. ULDIN: Soz. IX. 5, cf. *CTh* v. vi. 3, 409, for the Scirae. AUSTURIANS: Syn. *Catastasis* I. ISAURIANS: Joh. Chrys. *Ep.* 13 (garrison at Cucusus), 14 (garrison at Caesarea), 15 (Arabissus), cf. also 61, 69, 70, 72, 74–6, 120, 127, 131, 135, Theod. *Hist. Rel.* x, Jerome, *Ep.* 114, Philostorgius, XI. 8. COMES DIOECESEOS PONTICAE: *CTh* VI. xiii. 1, 413.

46. PERSIAN WAR: Soc. VII. 18–20. HUNNIC WAR: *Chron. Min.* II. 75; the terms of a previous treaty are mentioned in the negotiations of 434 (Priscus, 1), and this seems an appropriate date for the first treaty.

47. SUPPRESSION OF JOHN: Olymp. 46. AFRICAN EXPEDITION: Proc. *BV* I. iii. 35–6. TREATY WITH THE HUNS: Priscus, 1.

48. AFRICAN EXPEDITION: *Chron. Min.* I. 478, Theophanes, *A.M.* 5941. PERSIAN WAR: *Chron. Min.* II. 80. HUNNIC WAR AND TREATY: *Chron. Min.* II. 80–1, Theophanes, *A.M.* 5942, Priscus, 2, 3, 5.

49. HUNNIC WAR: *Chron. Min.* II. 82; the new clause in the treaty is mentioned in Priscus, 7. CHRYSAPHIUS' PLOT: Priscus, 7–8. THE NEW TREATY: Priscus, 14.

50. The story of Honoria is told in Joh. Ant. 199 and referred to in Priscus, 16. For Attila's invasion of the West we are mainly dependent on Jordanes, *Get.* 180 ff.

51. Victor Vit. I. 1.

52. BURGUNDIANS: Jerome, *Chron.* 373, Orosius, VII. xxxii, 11: when they were almost exterminated by the Huns, 20,000 (fighting men?) are said to have been killed (*Chron. Min.* I. 475, II. 23). GOTHS: Eunap. 42. It has been argued from Ammianus, XXXI. xii. 3, incertum quo errore procursatoribus omnem illam multitudinis partem quam viderunt in numero decem milium esse firmantibus, that the Gothic host at Adrianople must have been not greatly in excess of 10,000. But Ammianus clearly indicates that the scouts' estimate was wildly wrong. As appears from the following narrative the Goths were not yet concentrated and the scouts no doubt saw one group only. VISIGOTHS IN 393: Jordanes, *Get.* 145.

53. BURGUNDIANS: Olymp. 17, *Chron. Min.* I. 467 (west of the Rhine), Soc. VII. 30 (east of the Rhine). ALANS: Orosius, VII. xliii. 14, *Chron. Min.* II. 17 ff. (in Spain), Olymp. 17 (with the Burgundians), Paul. Pell. *Euch.* 377–85 (with the Visigoths), *Chron. Min.* I. 660 (settled at Valentia and in Gallia ulterior); the latter are probably Goar's group, mentioned in *V. Germani*, 28, and later found at Orleans (Jordanes, *Get.* 194).

54. ALANS JOIN THE VANDALS: *Chron. Min.* II. 19, cf. the official title of the later Vandal kings (Victor Vit. II. 39, III. 3). THE FEDERATES AND SLAVES JOIN ALARIC: Zos. V. 35 and 42 (giving the total 40,000).

55. Radagaesus' horde is put at 400,000 by Zosimus (V. 26) and at 200,000 by Orosius (VII. xxxvii. 4, cf. *Chron. Min.* II. 68 and Jordanes, *Rom.* 321); Augustine says 100,000 were killed at Faesulae (*Civ. Dei*, V. 23). These figures are not wholly incredible, seeing that the 12,000 men enrolled by Stilicho in his forces were a very small proportion of the survivors (Olymp. 9, Zos. V. 26) and that the remaining captives were so numerous that they were sold off at one solidus a head (Orosius, VII. xxxvii. 16), as against the normal price of 20 solidi for an adult male (see ch. XXI, n. 68). The tribes which crossed the Rhine are said by Orosius to have comprised the Sueves, Vandals (two tribes, the Asdings

and the Silings) and Alans, and many others with them (VII. xl. 3; in VII. xxxviii. 3 he adds the Burgundians).

56. For this and the following paragraphs see App. II, pp. 357–8.

57. THE THIRTY REGIMENTS AT FAESULAE: Zos. v. 26. DISPERSION OF THE ROMAN FORCES: Zos. v. 36, ἢ πολεμεῖν αἱρούμενον πάντα συναγαγεῖν ὅσα στρατιωτῶν τάγματα ἦν, cf. 35, οἱ ταῖς πόλεσιν ἐνιδρυμένοι στρατιῶται, 45, τοὺς στρατιώτας πάντας, ἱππέας τε καὶ πεζούς, ὅσοι κατὰ τὰς πόλεις ἦσαν.

58. Stilicho's withdrawal of troops from the Gallic army is described in Claudian, de bello Getico, 400 ff.

59. See App. II, pp. 357–8.

60. SENATORIAL RESISTANCE TO CONSCRIPTION: CTh VII. xiii, 13 and 14, 397, cf. Vegetius, I. 7, indicti possessoribus tirones per gratiam aut dissimulationem probantium tales sociantur armis quales domini habere fastidiunt.

61. HUNS USED AGAINST RADAGAESUS: Zos. v. 26, Orosius, VII. xxxvii. 12; summoned in 409, Zos. v. 50; obtained by Aetius for John, Greg. Tur. HF II. 8, Philostorgius, XII. 14, Chron. Min. I. 471, 658; by Aetius again in 433, Chron. Min. I. 473, 658; used by Aetius against the Burgundians, Chron. Min. I. 475, by Litorius against the Visigoths, Chron. Min. I. 475–6, II. 23.

62. Sarus first appears as a dux Gothorum serving under Stilicho against Radagaesus (Orosius VII. xxxvii. 12), then in 408 as στίφους βαρβάρων ἡγούμενος still under Stilicho (Zos. v. 30). He then turned against Stilicho (Zos. v. 34); he is described as τῶν ἄλλων συμμάχων προέχων and massacred Stilicho's bodyguard μετὰ τῶν ὑπ' αὐτὸν τεταγμένων βαρβάρων. In 410 he was at large in Picenum with 300 followers, having quarrelled with Honorius (Zos. VI. 13, Olymp. 3, Soz. IX. 9). He took service under Honorius again, but again quarrelled with him and ended his life in Gaul with only a score of followers (Olymp. 17). He may have been the leader of one of the groups of Goths who deserted Alaric after Verona (Claudian, de cos. VI Hon. 250–3). ENROLMENT OF PRISONERS: Zos. v. 26, Olymp. 9. FEDERATES NEARLY 30,000 IN 408: Zos. v. 35. FOEDERATI AND DEDITICII: CTh VII. xiii. 16, 406, praecipue sane eorum servos, quos militia armata detentat, foederatorum nihilo minus et dediticiorum. FEDERATES MADE INTO REGULARS: Orosius, VII. xl. 7, cum barbaris quibusdam qui quondam in foedus recepti atque in militiam allecti Honoriaci vocabantur.

63. For the Huns in Gaul see above n. 61. For the Goths in Spain, Chron. Min. II. 19, 20, 24, 28 ff. CONSCRIPTION: Val. III, Nov. vi. 1, 440 (a levy of recruits from landowners and a round-up of deserters), cf. v, 440 (exemption for citizens of Rome), vi. 2, 443 (a new levy of recruits from senators and other landowners in the Suburbicarian provinces). On the other hand in Val. III, Nov. vi. 3, 444, the levy is commuted for money. THE ROMAN ARMY MUSTERED AGAINST ATTILA: Jordanes, Get. 191, hi enim adfuerunt auxiliares: Franci, Sarmatae, Armoriciani, Liticiani, Burgundiones, Saxones, Ripari, Olibriones, quondam milites Romani, tunc vero iam in numero auxiliarium exquisiti, aliaeque nonnullae Celticae vel Germanicae nationes.

64. Val. III, Nov. xv, 444, ut ipso experimento non modo his qui novis sacramentis obligantur, sed ne veteri quidem exercitui quae ab exhaustis aegerrime conferuntur ad victum vel ad vestitum posse praeberi; quos nisi indigna et pudenda armato homini negotiatio aluerit, vix possunt a famis periculo et a frigorum pernicie vindicari.

65. Alaric's most extravagant demand (Zos. v. 48) was χρυσίον μὲν ἔτους ἑκάστου δίδοσθαί τι ῥητὸν καὶ σίτου τι χορηγεῖσθαι μέτρον, οἰκεῖν δὲ αὐτὸν ἅμα τοῖς σὺν αὐτῷ πᾶσι Βενετίας ἄμφω καὶ Νωρικοὺς καὶ Δελματίαν. He later reduced this to (Zos. v. 50) μόνους ἄμφω Νωρικούς, ἐν ταῖς ἐσχατιαῖς που τοῦ Ἴστρου κειμένους συνεχεῖς τε ὑφισταμένους ἐφόδους καὶ εὐτελῆ φόρον τῷ δημοσίῳ εἰσφέροντας, καὶ σῖτον ἐπὶ τούτοις ἔτους ἑκάστου τοσοῦτον ὅσον ἀρκεῖν ὁ βασιλεὺς οἰηθείη. Athaulf certainly did not receive any land and his only complaint was that the corn which had been stipulated was not provided (Olymp. 20, 21). Wallia is stated to have received 600,000 *modii* of corn (Olymp. 31); if this was an annual allowance it would feed 15,000 men. SETTLEMENT OF THE VISIGOTHS: *Chron. Min.* I. 469, Constantius patricius pacem firmat cum Vallia data ei ad habitandum secunda Aquitanica et quibusdam civitatibus confinium provinciarum. Philostorgius (xii. 4) says that the Goths made their treaty σιτήσεσί τε δεξιωθέντες καὶ μοῖράν τινα τῆς τῶν Γαλατῶν χώρας εἰς γεωργίαν ἀποκληρωσάμενοι. The grant both of *annonae* and of land seems improbable; perhaps the *annonae* were a temporary grant, until the next harvest. For the later system of *hospitalitas* see pp. 248–53.

66. THE ALANS: *Chron. Min.* I. 660 §440, deserta Valentinae urbis rura Alanis quibus Sambida praeerat partienda traduntur; §442, Alani quibus terrae Galliae ulterioris cum incolis dividendae a patricio Aetio traditae fuerunt, resistentes armis subigunt et expulsis dominis terrae possessionem vi adipiscuntur. THE BURGUNDIANS: ibid. §443, Sapaudia Burgundionum reliquis datur cum indigenis dividenda. For Honorius' letter see above n. 44. THE OLIBRIONES: Jordanes, *Get.* 191 (cited in n. 63).

67. See App. II, Table XV.

68. NUMBER OF GAINAS' GOTHS: Zos. v. 19, Syn. *de Prov.* II. 2. GAINAS DISPERSES THE REGULAR TROOPS: Zos. v. 18.

69. THE SCIRAE: *CTh* v. vi. 3, 409, cf. Soc. IX. 5. THRACIAN RECRUITS: Pall. *Dial.*, p. 57.

70. THE UNIGARDI: Syn. *Catastasis* I, II, *Ep.* 78. COMPLAINTS OF RUA AND ATTILA: Priscus, 1, 2, 3, 5, 6, 14. THE ISAURIANS: Priscus, 6, 8 (p. 94).

71. LIMITANEI: Th. II, *Nov.* iv, 438, xxiv, 443.

72. WALLS OF ANTHEMIUS: Soc. VII. 1, *CTh* xv. i. 51, 413; STRENGTHENED BY CYRUS: *Chron. Pasch.* 583; BY CONSTANTINE: *ILS* 823, *Chron. Min.* II. 82.

73. TAX REMISSIONS: *CTh* XI. xxviii. 7, 413, 12, 418 (Suburbicarian provinces), Val. III, *Nov.* i. 2, 440 (Sicily), xiii, 445 (Numidia and Mauretania).

74. LEVY ON RENTS: *CTh* XI. xx. 3, 405 (S); ON GRANTEES OF IMPERIAL LANDS: *CTh* XI. xx. 4, 423. SILIQUATICUM: Val. III, *Nov.* xv (444).

75. FISCAL PRIVILEGES CURBED: Val. III, *Nov.* iv, 440, x, 441.

76. SORDIDA MUNERA: Val. III, *Nov.* x §3, 441.

77. REMISSIONS OF ARREARS: Val. III, *Nov.* i. 1, 438, 3, 450.

78. REMISSIONS OF ARREARS: *CTh* XI. xxviii. 9, 414; cf. 10, 415; 16, 433. LEVY ON GRANTEES OF IMPERIAL LANDS: *CTh* XI. xx. 5, 424.

79. ANTIOCHUS' LAW: *CTh* XI. xx. 6, 430. The levy of 443 is mentioned by Priscus, 5, δασμὸν εἰσπραττομένους καὶ τοὺς κατὰ χρόνον τινὰ τὴν βαρυτάτην κουφισθέντας τῆς γῆς ἀποτίμησιν εἴτε δικαστῶν κρίσει εἴτε βασιλέων φιλοτιμίαις, and in Th. II, *Nov.* xxvi, 444.

80. LEVY ON SENATORS: Priscus, 5, συνεισέφερον δὲ ῥητὸν χρυσίον καὶ οἱ ἐν τῇ γερουσίᾳ ἀναγεγραμμένοι ὑπὲρ σφῶν αὐτῶν ἀξίας.

81. See ch. XIII, nn. 137–8.

82. See p. 439.

83. Val. III, *Nov.* xiii, 445, hunc tributi modum ab his magnitudo tua sperandum esse cognoscat, ut retractis septem partibus octavam . . . possessor agnoscat, pro qua octava omnibus titulis ad unum redactis . . . quattuor milia ducentos tantum solidos et mille ducentas militares annonas et ducentum capitum Numida provincialis exsolvat, §3 has autem militares annonas cum provinciales pro longinqui difficultate itineris in adaeratione persolverint, unius annonae adaeratio quattuor per annum solidis aestimetur, §5, Mauri vero Sitifenses . . . pro omnibus titulis totius annonae nomine quinque milia solidorum et quinquaginta capitum in annonis ducis consueto tempore annua functione dependant, pro octava parte soluturi quod tributum erit, Maj. *Nov.* ii. §3, 458, et quia totum pro remedio possessoris serenitas nostra constituit, quem tributorum gratia solvendorum fruges suas sub opportunitate vendentem volumus per temporis intervalla refoveri, trina per annum vice singularum indictionum quantitas speranda solvatur et quadrimenstruis inlationibus annuae functionis celebretur exactio.

84. See ch. XII, n. 64, XVI, n. 5, XVII, nn. 47–8, XIII, n. 120

85. PAGANS EXCLUDED FROM IMPERIAL SERVICE: Zos. V. 46, *CTh* XVI. V. 42, 408, X. 21, 416. ARCADIUS AND GAZA: *V. Porph.* 41; earlier he (or rather his ministers) had enacted laws against sacrifices, pagan priests and temples, *CTh* XVI. X. 13, 395, 14, 396, 16, 399. THEODOSIUS II'S ANTI-PAGAN LAWS: *CTh* XVI. X. 22, 23 and 24, 423, 25, 435. Honorius' earlier laws (*CTh* XVI. X. 15, 17 and 18, 399), while maintaining the ban on sacrifice, protect the temples and maintain the festivals. LAW OF 407: *Sirm.* 12; of 415, *CTh* XVI. X. 20.

86. *Hist. de l'Église*, IV. 79–128. There is a useful collection of documents relating to the Pelagian controversy in *PL* XLV. 1679–1792.

87. On Augustine and the Donatists, see W. H. C. Frend, *The Donatist Church*, 227 ff., G. G. Willis, *St. Augustine and the Donatist Controversy*.

88. The story of the election of Boniface is told in the interesting series of documents *Coll. Avell.* 14–37.

89. The dossier of the Apiarius case is contained in *Cod. Can. Eccl. Afr. ad init.* and 127–38 (*C. Carth.* VI, VII).

90. See pp. 888–9.

91. See pp. 889–90.

92. Leo, *Ep.* 12.

93. See pp. 890–1.

94. *Hist. de l'Église*, IV. 129–48. We have a first-hand account of Chrysostom's career in Palladius, *Dialogus*, and full narratives in Soc. VI. 2–23, VII. 25, 45, Soz. VIII. 2–28; also a summary of the acts of the Council of the Oak in Photius, *Bibliotheca*, 59 (*PG* CIII. 105–13).

95. *Hist. de l'Église* IV. 163–96. The acts of the first Council of Ephesus and the documents relating to the controversy which preceded and followed it are printed in *A.C.Oec.* I.

96. *Hist. de l'Église*, IV. 211–24. The acts of the second Council of Ephesus survive in a Syriac translation (English translation in S. G. F. Perry, *The Second Council of Ephesus*, 1881). Part of the acts of that council and of the proceedings antecedent to it were cited at Chalcedon and are preserved in its acts (see *A.C.Oec.* II. vi. 115, for a list of the relevant passages).

1. MARCIAN'S PREVIOUS CAREER: Evagr. II. 1; Theodosius named him according to Malalas, 367, and *Chron. Pasch.* 589. APPOINTMENT OF ARDABURIUS: Priscus, 20.

2. EXECUTION OF CHRYSAPHIUS: *Chron. Min.* II. 83, Malalas, 368. REFUSAL OF TRIBUTE TO ATTILA: Priscus, 15. SETTLEMENTS OF BARBARIANS: Jordanes, *Get.* 265–7. Theoderic Strabo and his Goths are first recorded in Jordanes, *Get.* 270; he was, according to Theophanes, A.M. 5964, Aspar's brother-in-law, but in A.M. 5970, nephew of Aspar's wife.

3. ABOLITION OF THE FOLLIS: *CJ* XII. ii. 2. THE PRAETORSHIP: *CJ* I. xxxix. 2, 450. THE CONSULSHIP: *CJ* XII. iii. 2 (451). REMISSION OF ARREARS: Marc. *Nov.* ii, 450. THE RESERVE: Joh. Lydus, *Mag.* III. 43.

4. For this and the following paragraphs see *Hist. de l'Église*, IV. 224–40. The acts of Chalcedon and the documents relating to it are printed in *A.C.Oec.* II.

5. Leo's accession is described in Const. Porph. *Cer.* I. 91; he is there described as *comes* and tribune of the Mattiarii. He is called Aspar's nominee in Jordanes, *Rom.* 335, Proc. *BV* I. v. 7, Priscus, 20, Candidus, 1; his earlier service under Aspar is attested only by Zonaras, XIII. 25, κτησέων αὐτοῦ, ὡς λέγεται, προνοούμενον, and Theophanes, A.M. 5961, κουράτωρα αὐτῶν ὄντα.

6. Jordanes, *Get.* 270–1, Priscus, 28, *Chron. Min.* II. 92.

7. QUARRELS OF LEO AND ASPAR: Candidus, 1, Priscus, 35.

8. *V. Dan.* 55. For the Excubitors see ch. XVII, n. 117.

9. *V. Dan.* 65. THE EXPEDITION AGAINST THE VANDALS: Proc. *BV* I. vi.

10. BIRTH OF LEO II: *V. Dan.* 66. PATRICIUS CAESAR: Theophanes, A.M. 5961.

11. ANAGAST: Joh. Ant. 206.2. ARDABURIUS AND THE ISAURIANS: Candidus, 1.

12. MURDER OF ASPAR AND REVOLT OF OSTRYS: Candidus, 1, Malalas, 371–2, Theophanes, A.M. 5963–4. REVOLT OF THEODERIC STRABO: Malchus, 2.

13. Jordanes, *Get.*, 283–7.

14. *CJ* XII. lix, 10 §5 (471–2).

15. COST OF THE VANDAL EXPEDITION: Candidus, 2, Joh. Lydus, *Mag.* III. 43, Proc. *BV* I. vi. 2. LEO'S CONFISCATIONS: Malchus, 2a.

16. LEO II CROWNS ZENO: Malalas, 376, Candidus, 1, *V. Dan.* 67. Leo II had already been crowned by his father (Const. Porph. *Cer.* I. 94).

17. REBELLION OF BASILISCUS: Candidus, 1, Joh. Ant. 210, *V. Dan.* 68–9, Malchus, 7, 8, Theophanes, A.M. 5967–9. THE ENCYCLICAL: Evagr. III. 4. There is a vivid account of the riots which followed in *V. Dan.* 70–85. Basiliscus was forced to recant in an Antencyclical (Evagr. III. 7).

18. Malchus, 11, 14, 15.

19. Malchus, 15, 16.

20. Malchus, 17, 18.

21. Malchus, 18.

22. Joh. Ant. 211. 2–5.

23. THE HENOTIKON: Evagr. III. 14.

24. ILLUS MADE MAGISTER MILITUM PER ORIENTEM: Malalas, 387–8. THEODERIC MADE PRAESENTALIS: *Chron. Min.* II. 92. DEATH OF RECITACH: Joh. Ant. 214.3. ILLUS' NEGOTIATIONS: Joh. Ant. 214.2.

25. MISSION OF LEONTIUS: Josh. Styl. 14. ZENO DISMISSES ILLUS: Joh. Ant. 214.1.
VERINA PROCLAIMS LEONTIUS: Joh. Ant. 214.2, Malalas, *Exc. de Insid.* 35.

26. JOHN THE SCYTHIAN: Malalas, 389, Theophanes, A.M. 5976. THEODERIC
KEPT BACK: Joh. Ant. 214.4; his troops nevertheless took part in the expedition
(Joh. Ant. 214.6); the Rugians are mentioned in both passages. THE SATRAPIES:
Proc. *Aed.* III. i. 24–6; the *comes Armeniae* (*CJ* I. xxix. 5, Proc. *Aed.* III. i. 14–15)
does not appear to have existed under Leo (*CJ* XII. lix. 10 §5).

27. THEODERIC: *Chron. Min.* II. 93, Jordanes, *Get.* 291–2, Joh. Ant. 214.7,
Proc. *BG* I. i. 10–12, II. vi. 16. COTTOMENES: Joh. Ant. 214.6. The Isaurian
subsidy was abolished by Anastasius; John of Antioch gives the figure 1,400 lb.
gold (*Exc. de Insid.* 100), Evagrius (III. 35) makes it 5,000 lb.

28. ZENO'S FINANCIAL POLICY: Malchus, 6 (Erythrius), 9 (Sebastianus); for his
system of *suffragia* see pp. 394–5.

29. ACCESSION OF ANASTASIUS: Const. Porph. *Cer.* I. 92: his rank is given as
decurion of the silentiaries in Zach. Myt. *Chron.* VII. 1. LONGINUS' AMBITION:
Evagr. III. 29.

30. Joh. Ant. *Exc. de Insid.* 100, Malalas, *Exc. de Insid.* 37, Theophanes, A.M.
5985–8.

31. BULGARS: Marcell. com. 493, 499 (*Chron. Min.* II. 94–5), Theophanes,
A.M. 5994. THE LONG WALL: Evagr. III. 38, Proc. Gaz. *Pan.* 21, Just. *Nov.*
xxvi. pr., 535.

32. Josh. Styl. 18–23, 48–53, Proc. *BP* I. vii, *Aed.* III. ii. 4–8.

33. Josh. Styl. 54, 70, 77, Proc. *BP* I. viii. 1–5.

34. Proc. *BP* I. viii, ix. DARA: Proc. *BP* I. x. 13–17, *Aed.* II. i. 4–10, Zach. Myt.
Chron. VII. 6.

35. WILD BEAST FIGHTS AND MIMES: Josh. Styl. 34, 46, Proc. Gaz. *Pan.* 15, 16.
EUPHEMIUS AND THE CORONATION: Evagr. III. 32.

36. For a contemporary account of the proceedings against Macedonius see
Zach. Myt. *Chron.* VII. 8.

37. Events at Jerusalem are vividly described in Cyr. Scyth. *V. Sabae,* 56.

38. *Chron. Min.* II. 97–8, Malalas, 407–8.

39. Joh. Ant. *Exc. de. Insid.* 103, Malalas, 402–6, Theophanes, A.M. 6005–7,
Chron. Min. II. 98–9. The most detailed account is that of John of Antioch,
who gives the figure of 50,000 for Vitalian's force (πολεμικῶν τε καὶ ἀγροίκων
ἀνδρῶν) and 80,000 for Hypatius' army. Vitalian's post is nowhere defined. He
is called *comes* in Victor Tonnennensis (*anno* 510, *Chron. Min.* II. 194), and that
he was *comes foederatorum* is inferred from John's statement that his original
grievance was about τῶν καλουμένων φοιδερατικῶν ἀννωνῶν, and that he next
intrigued with the regular troops (τοῖς περὶ τὴν Σκυθίαν καὶ Θρᾴκην πληροῦσι
τάγματα). His men are described as Huns in John (Malalas adds Goths).

40. The correspondence between Anastasius and Hormisdas is in *Coll. Avell.*
107 ff.

41. MARINUS: Joh. Lydus, *Mag.* III. 36, 46, 49, Zach. Myt. *Chron.* VII. 9, Malalas,
400, Cyr. Scyth. *V. Sabae,* 54. He instituted the *vindices* (Joh. Lydus, *Mag.*
III. 46, 49); cf. Just. *Ed.* xiii §15 (reorganization of the civic finances of Alexandria by Potamo, the *vindex,* under Anastasius, ἡνίκα Μαριανὸς (*sic*) ὁ τῆς ἐνδόξου
μνήμης ἐπ' αὐτῷ τὰ πράγματα ἔπραττε). POLYCARP: Joh. Lydus, *Mag.* III. 36. JOHN
THE PAPHLAGONIAN: Malalas, 400.

42. The name of the praetorian prefect who issued the edict limiting tax *sportulae* to one *siliqua* per *iugum* (Zachariä von Lingenthal, *'Ανέκδοτα*, 271, no. xiii) is not given, but this edict is among a series issued by Zoticus, Eustathius and Constantine, who all held office under Anastasius. MILITARY PAY: *CJ* XII. xxxvii. 16. FEES OF LIMITANEI: *SEG* IX. 356 (Libya), cf. the Syrian and Palestinian inscriptions giving elaborate schedules of payments relating to the *limitanei* (Wadd. 2033, *Princeton Exp. Syria*, 20, 562, Alt, *Die griechischen Inschriften der Palaestina Tertia*, 1–4). RETURNS OF MILITARY STRENGTH: *CJ* I. xlii. 1, 2.

43. For *χρυσοτέλεια τῶν ἰούγων* and *συνωνή* see ch. XIII, n. 120. MOVEMENTS OF TROOPS: *CJ* I. xxix. 4. TROOPS FOR SPECIAL DUTIES: *CJ* XII. xxxvii. 17, 19.

44. For the *vindices* see above, n. 41 and ch. XIII, n. 111.

45. See pp. 443–4.

46. PARCA SUBTILITAS: *CJ* II. vii. 25 pr., 519. THE ARMY: Priscian, *Pan.* 204–5, cf. Josh. Styl. 54, and Joh. Ant. *Exc. de Insid.* 103, for the numbers. PUBLIC WORKS: Proc. Gaz. *Pan.* 7, 18–20, Joh. Lydus, *Mag.* III. 47, Malalas, 406, 409, Josh. Styl. 87 (Edessa), 89 (Batnae), Zach. Myt. *Chron.* VII. 6 (Dara).

47. Anastasius insisted that all reductions or remissions of taxation must be personally approved by himself (*CJ* x. xvi. 13, 496); he almost yielded to a request of Saba on behalf of Jerusalem, but was checked by Marinus (Cyr. Scyth. *V. Sabae*, 54). REMISSIONS IN MESOPOTAMIA: Josh. Styl. 39, 42 (locusts), 66, 78, 92 (cost of the army), 99 (Amida, Edessa). RANSOM OF PRISONERS: Marcell. com. 517 (*Chron. Min.* II. 100).

48. For the *collatio lustralis* and the *patrimonium* see pp. 424–5 (ch. XIII, n. 36). CAPITATIO HUMANA ET ANIMALIUM: Joh. Ant. *Exc. de Insid.* 103, *τῆς ὑπὲρ τῶν ζώων εἰσφορᾶς τετάρτην περιελὼν μοῖραν τοῦ Βιθυνῶν τε καὶ 'Ασιανῶν ἔθνους*, Joh. Lydus, *Mag.* III. 47, *ὅτι δὲ μόνος αὐτὸς μετὰ Κωνσταντῖνον τὴν τῶν ψυχῶν ἐκούφισε δασμολογίαν, εἰ καὶ μὴ πᾶσαν, οὐδὲ γὰρ ἔφθασε.*

49. Proc. *HA* xix. 7.

VIII. THE FALL OF THE WESTERN EMPIRE (pp. 240–2)

1. Joh. Ant. 201, cf. Sid. Ap. *Ep.* II. 13.

2. AVITUS MAGISTER MILITUM: Sid. Ap. *Carm.* VII. 375–8; ELECTED EMPEROR: ibid. 489 ff.; AT ROME: Joh. Ant. 202. RICIMER IN SICILY: *Chron. Min.* II. 29, Sid. Ap. *Carm.* II. 360 ff. (a Sueve). REMISTUS: *Chron. Min.* I. 304. FALL OF AVITUS: Joh. Ant. 202, Greg. Tur. *HF* II. 11.

3. On the complex problem of Majorian's accession see Stein, *Bas-Empire*, I. 596, n. 49.

4. Stein, op. cit. I. 377–80.

5. Stein, op. cit. I. 380–2.

6. ANTHEMIUS: Sid. Ap. *Carm.* II. 67–93 (father Procopius), 94–5 (maternal grandfather Anthemius), 199–209 (*mag. mil.* and *cos.*), 193–7, 481–2 (husband of Euphemia). RICIMER MARRIES HIS DAUGHTER: Sid. Ap. *Ep.* I. 5 §10.

7. Proc. *BV* I. vi.

8. Stein, op. cit. 391-3.

9. Joh. Ant. 209.1, Ennod. *V. Epiph.* 343-9.

10. Joh. Ant. 209.2. ORESTES' SERVICE UNDER ATTILA: Priscus, 7, 8 (pp. 78, 84), Anon. Val. 38.

11. C. E. Stevens, *Sidonius Apollinaris and his age,* 207-11.

12. BASILIUS: Maj. *Nov.* ii, vi, vii, 458, Sev. *Nov.* i, 463, ii, 465; cf. Sid. Ap. *Ep.* 1. 9. The law on the *laeti* is Sev. *Nov.* ii, 465.

13. Proc. *BG* 1. i. 1-8, Anon. Val. 37-8, Jordanes, *Get.* 242-3.

14. Malchus, 10; for the *regalia* see Anon. Val. 64.

15. On Odoacer's constitutional position see *JRS* LII (1962), 126-30.

16. THE VANDALS: Victor Vit. 1. 13. THE VISIGOTHS IN SPAIN: *Chron. Min.* II. 32, Nepotianus Theuderico ordinante Arborium accepit successorem, cf. II. 281 for Roman resistance. THE SUEVES SUBDUED BY THEODERIC: Jordanes, *Get.* 229-34, *Chron. Min.* II. 28-9; for their continued resistance see *Chron. Min.* II. 29-35. THE VASCONES: Joh. Biclar. 581 (*Chron. Min.* II. 216), Leovegildus rex partem Vasconiae occupat et civitatem quae Victoriacum nuncupatur condidit. VISIGOTHIC CONQUEST OF BOURGES AND AUVERGNE: Jordanes, *Get.* 237-8; OF MARSEILLES, ARLES, ETC.: Proc. *BG* 1. xii. 20, *Chron. Min.* I. 309, 665. SYAGRIUS: Greg. Tur. *HF* II. 18, 27.

17. SICILY: Victor Vit. I. 14. DALMATIA: *Chron. Min.* I. 311, 313. NORICUM: *V. Severini,* 44, Joh. Ant. 214-7.

18. Anon. Val. 50-57.

19. See *JRS* LII (1962), 126-30.

20. THE SIRMIUM WAR: Jordanes, *Get.* 300-1, *Chron. Min.* II. 96, 160, Ennod. *Pan.* 277 ff., cf. Cass. *Var.* III. 23 for Pannonia Sirmiensis under Theoderic's rule.

21. CLOVIS CONQUERS SYAGRIUS AND THE VISIGOTHS: *Greg. Tur. HF* II. 27, 37. THEODERIC IN GAUL: *Chron. Min.* II. 223, 282 ff. GESALIC AND AMALARIC: Proc. *BG* 1. xii. 43-6. TAXES AND DONATIVES IN SPAIN: Proc. *BG* 1. xii. 47-8, cf. Cass. *Var.* v. 35, 39. THEUDIS: Proc. *BG* 1. xii. 50-4; for the government of Spain see Cass. *Var.* v. 35, 39, addressed to Ampelius, v.i., and Livvitit, v.s.

22. JUDICIAL SPORTULAE UNDER THE GERMAN KINGS: Cass. *Var.* IX. 14, *Lex Burg. prima const.* 7, and the law of king Theudis of the Visigoths 'de litium expensis et commodis iudicum et executorum' (*MGH* (*Leg.*) I. i. 467-9). FALSE MEASURES: Cass. *Var.* v. 39, XI. 16, XII. 16. INTERPRETIA IN COMMUTATION: Cass. *Var.* II. 26, *Consensus de fisco Barcinonensi* (Mansi, x. 473). EXTRA FEES FOR COLLECTORS: Cass. *Var.* XI. 8.

23. For Frankish crown lands see Greg. Tur. *HF* v. 48 (fiscalis vinitor), VI. 45 (familias multas de domibus fiscalibus), and for grants therefrom, ibid. v. 3, villas vero quas ei rex a fisco in territorio Sessionico indulserat abstulit, VIII. 21, ablataeque sunt ei deinceps omnes res quas in Arverno de fisci munere promeruerat, IX. 38, X. 19, tu ab eodem possessionum fiscalium praedia meruisti? . . . villas vero quas memoras per istius regis chartas emerui, *V. Patrum* I. 5, where the abbot Lupicinus refuses a grant of land, but accepts a 'praeceptionem ut annis singulis trecentos modios tritici eiusdemque mensurae numero vinum accipiant et centum aureos ad comparandum fratrum indumenta, quod usque nunc a fisci ditionibus capere referuntur'. For lavish grants of lands see the will of Bertram bishop of Le Mans (pp. 782-3). For grants of church lands, see below, n. 69.

24. GAISERIC'S CONFISCATIONS: Victor Vit. I. 13–14, Proc. BV I. v. 11–17. VICTORIANUS: Victor Vit. III. 27. COMPENSATION OF AFRICAN REFUGEES: Val. III, Nov. xxxiv, 451.

25. Victor Vit. I. 13, disponens quoque singulas quasque provincias sibi Bizacenam, Abaritanam atque Getuliam et partem Numidiae reservavit, exercitui vero Zeugitanam vel Proconsularem funiculo hereditatis reservavit, cf. II. 39, III. 4, in sortibus Vandalorum, Proc. BV I. v. 12, καὶ ἀπ' αὐτοῦ κλῆροι Βανδίλων οἱ ἄγροι οὗτοι ἐς τόδε καλοῦνται τοῦ χρόνου, 14, καὶ τὰ μὲν χωρία ξύμπαντα, ὅσα τοῖς τε παισὶ καὶ τοῖς ἄλλοις Βανδίλοις Γιζέριχος παραδεδώκει, οὐδεμιᾶς φόρου ἀπαγωγῆς ὑποτελῆ ἐκέλευσεν εἶναι, cf. II. xiv. 8–10. GORDIANUS: V. Fulg. 4; in V. Fulg. 28 and 39 we meet with other Roman landowners, one described as 'provinciae Byzacenae primarius', the other as 'inter suos nobilissimus civis' (of Ruspae).

26. On the system of hospitalitas see F. Lot, Rev. Belge de philol. et de l'histoire, VII (1928), 975 ff. and the earlier literature there cited. ROMAN HOSPITALITAS: CTh VII. viii. 5, 398 (the rule of the third is also alluded to in tit. cit., 16, 435, Th. II, Nov. xxv, 444 and CJ XII. xl. 10). The earliest definite allusions to the sharing of land are in reference to the settlements of the Alans and Burgundians in 440 and 443 (Chron. Min. I. 660, cited in ch. VI, n. 66). Cf. also Chron. Min. II. 232, Burgundiones partem Galliae occupaverunt terrasque cum Gallis senatoribus diviserunt (in 456). No doubt the system was applied in the settlement of the Visigoths in Aquitania (see ch. VI, n. 65) and it may even go back to their earlier settlement in Thrace (see ch. V, n. 46).

27. ODOACER: Proc. BG I. i. 4–5, 8. THEODERIC: Proc. BG I. i. 28, Cass. Var. II. 16, iuvat nos referre quemadmodum in tertiarum deputatione Gothorum Romanorumque et possessiones iunxit et animos (Liberius), I. 18, si Romani praedium, ex quo deo propitio Sontii fluenta transmisimus, ubi primum Italiae nos suscepit imperium, sine delegatoris cuiusquam pittacio praesumptor barbarus occupaverit, etc. NO GOTHS IN APULIA AND CALABRIA: Proc. BG I. xv. 3. TERTIAE AS A TAX: Cass. Var, I. 14, et ideo praecelsa magnificentia tua (Faustus, PPO. It.) quod a Cathaliensibus inferebatur genere tertiarum faciat annis singulis in tributaria summa persolvi; nec post super hac parte patiantur supplices aliquam quaestionem. quid enim interest quo nomine possessor inferat dummodo sine imminutione quod debetur exsolvat? ita et illis suspectum tertiarum nomen auferimus, et a nostra mansuetudine importunitates competentium submovemus, II. 17, munificentiam nostram nulli volumus exstare damnosam, ne quod alteri tribuitur alterius dispendiis applicetur, et ideo praesenti auctoritate cognoscite, pro sorte quam Butilani presbytero nostra largitate contulimus nullum debere persolvere fiscalis calculi functionem, sed in ea praestatione quanti se solidi comprehendunt de tertiarum illationibus vobis noveritis esse relevandos. There is an entry 'de titulis tertiarum' in P. Dip. 138. SORS BARBARI: P. Dip. 115.

28. THE ALANS: Chron. Min. I. 660 (cited in ch. VI, n. 66).

29. Ennod. Ep. IX. 23, Cass. Var. II. 16.

30. Cass. Var. I. 19, et ideo praesenti vobis iussione praecipimus ut Adrianae civitatis curialium insinuatione suscepta quicumque Gothorum fiscum detractat implere eum ad aequitatem redhibitionis arctetis, IV. 14, is solvat tributum qui possessionis noscitur habere compendium. atque ideo praesenti tibi auctoritate delegamus ut Gothi per Picenum sive Tuscias utrasque residentes te imminente cogantur exsolvere debitas functiones. These letters might refer to lands

acquired by Goths by purchase, marriage, etc., but they are framed in such general terms that they probably include the Gothic *sortes*. In *Var.* II. 17, it might be inferred from the vague language used that the *sors* granted to the priest Butilas was immune from tax, but if so it was no doubt a special case. In *Var.* V. 14, antiqui barbari qui Romanis mulieribus eligerint nuptiali foedere sociari quolibet titulo praedia quaesiverunt fiscum possessi caespitis persolvere et superindictitiis oneribus parere cogantur, it is, I think, implied that the barbarians settled in Savia before Gothic rule did not pay land tax on their allotments, and that Theoderic, while respecting their vested interest, made them pay on lands acquired through marriage with provincial women. In *Var.* II. 16, Theoderic is made to say of Liberius, 'censum non addendo sed conservando protendens', and 'sensimus auctas illationes, vos addita tributa nescistis'.

31. *Lex Burg.* 57, Burgundionis libertus, qui domino suo solidos XII non dederit ut habeat licentiam sicut est consuetudinis quo voluerit discedendi nec tertiam a Romanis consecutus est, necesse est ut in domini familia censeatur. I take this to be an early law, issued while the Burgundians were still under Roman administration, and to mean that the freedman of a Burgundian gained full freedom if he either paid his master the customary 12 solidi, or if the Roman government made him an independent warrior by allotting him a *sors*.

32. *Lex Vis.* x. ii. 1 (= *Cod. Euric.* 277), sortes Gothicae et tertiae Romanorum quae intra L annos non fuerint revocatae nullo modo repentantur, cf. x. i. 8, ne de duobus partibus Gothi aliquid sibi Romanus praesumat aut vindicet, aut de tertia parte Romani Gothus sibi aliquid audeat usurpare aut vindicare, 16, ut si Goti de Romanorum tertiam quippiam tulerint, iudice insistente Romanis cuncta reforment. iudices singularum civitatum, vilici atque praepositi tertias Romanorum ab illis qui occupatas tenent auferant et Romanis sua exactione sine aliqua dilatione restituant ut nihil fisco debeat deperire, *Lex Burg.* 54. 1, licet eodem tempore quo populus noster mancipiorum tertiam et duas terrarum partes accepit eiusmodi a nobis fuerit emissa praeceptio, ut quicumque agrum cum mancipiis seu parentum nostrorum seu nostra largitate perceperat, nec mancipiorum tertiam nec duas terrarum partes ex eo loco in quo ei hospitalitas fuerat delegata requireret . . . qui agris et mancipiis nostra munificentia potiuntur, de hospitum suorum terris contra interdictum publicum praesumpsisse docentur, sine dilatione restituant; it is clear that the grant of two thirds of the land and one third of the slaves had taken place in the reign of the king who issued this law (probably Gundobad), and that when the grant was made the Burgundians were already settled as *hospites*, and had some of them received additional grants of land from the present king and his parents. If the Burgundians had originally received one third of the land (without slaves), the grant meant in effect a second third of the land and one third of the slaves. This would account for the curious anomaly, which so greatly exercised Lot (see above n. 26), between the proportion of land and of slaves.

33. INALIENABILITY OF SORTES: *Lex Burg.* 1, ut patri etiam antequam dividat de communi facultate et de labore suo cuilibet donare liceat, absque terra sortis titulo adquisita, de qua prioris legis ordo servabitur, 14, his vero puellis quae se Deo voverint et in castitate permanserint, si duos fratres habuerint, tertiam iubemus ut portionem de hereditate patris accipiat, hoc est, de ea tantum terra quam pater eius sortis iure possidens mortis tempore dereliquit. SALE OF SORTES: *Lex Burg.* 84, quia agnovimus Burgundiones sortes suas nimia facilitate distrahere . . . ut nulli vendere terram suam liceat nisi illi qui alio loco sortem aut possessionem habet, ut quisque habens alibi terram necessitatem

habet in comparando quam Burgundio venalem habet nullus extraneus Romano hospiti praeponatur. SORTES TAX FREE: *Lex Vis.* x. i. 16 (cited above in n. 32).

34. *Cod. Euric.* 276, si quodcumque ante adventum Gothorum de alicuius fundi iure remotum est et aliqua possessione aut venditione aut donatione aut divisione aut aliqua transactione translatum est, id in eius fundi adque a Romanis antiquitus probatur adiunctum iure consistat. *Lex Burg.* 55, quotiens de agrorum finibus qui hospitalitatis iure a barbaris possidentur inter duos Romanos fuerit mota contentio, hospites eorum non socientur litigio sed Romanos in iudicio contendentes expectentur, ut cuius barbari hospes evicerit cum ipso postmodum de re obtenta habeat rationem.

35. WOODLAND: *Lex Burg.* 54, quoniam sicuti iamdudum statutum est medietatem silvarum ad Romanos generaliter praecipimus pertinere, cf. 67, *Lex Vis.* x. i. 9, de silvis quae indivisae forsitan residerunt, sive Gothus sive Romanus sibi eas adsumserit, fecerit fortasse culturas, statuimus ut, si adhuc silva superest unde paris meriti terra eius cui debetur portioni debeat compensari, silvam accipere non recuset. CLEARINGS AND VINEYARDS: *Lex Burg.* 13, 31, 54.2, *Lex Vis.* x. i. 6, 7, 9 (cited above). HOMESTEAD AND ORCHARDS: *Lex Burg.* 54, similiter de curto et pomariis circa saramannos conditione servata, id est, ut medietatem Romani aestiment praesumendam.

36. Extra grants are mentioned in *Lex Burg.* 54 (cited above in n. 32), 55, sane si ex eiusdem agri finibus quem barbarus ex integro cum mancipiis publica largitione perceperit fuerit contentio cepta, licebit ei . . . Romano iure contendere, cf. *extrav.* xxi. 14.

37. *Lex Burg. extrav.* xxi. 12, de Romanis vero hoc ordinavimus ut non amplius a Burgundionibus qui infra venerunt requiratur quam ad praesens necessitas fuerit, medietas terrae. alia vero medietas cum integritate mancipiorum a Romano teneatur.

38. Of Odoacer we know that Basilius was his praetorian prefect (Symmachus, *Ep.* 6 §4), Andromachus his master of the offices (*FIR* III.[2] 99), Cassiodorus (the father of the author) his *comes rei privatae* and *comes sacrarum largitionum* (Cass. *Var.* I. 4) and Pierius his *comes domesticorum* (Anon. Val. 53); also Marcianus, v.c. notarius, presumably a member of the imperial corps of notaries (*FIR* III.[2] 99). For Theoderic we have ample evidence from Cassiodorus' *Variae*, analysed by Mommsen (*Ges. Schr.* VI. 387 ff.) and Ensslin (*Theoderich der Grosse*, 175 ff.). The most important documents are the *formulae* for the appointment to the various offices (*Var.* VI. 3, 5–8, 15–17, 20, 21, VII. 2 for those mentioned in this paragraph). VICAR OF THE GAULS: Cass. *Var.* III. 16, 17. PREFECT OF THE GAULS: ibid. VIII. 6, XI. 1 §16.

39. For Rome see ch. XVIII, n. 55. For the part played by the Roman nobility see J. Sundwall, *Abhandlungen zur Geschichte des ausgehenden Römertums*, 84 ff.

40. P. Grierson, *JRS* xlix (1959), 73–80.

41. LAND TAX: Cass. *Var.* II. 25–6, IV. 14, VII. 45, IX. 10–11, XI. 7, XII. 2, 26; *augmenta* are mentioned in IX. 9–10, *superindicta* in I. 26, V. 14. BINA ET TERNA: ibid. III. 8, VII. 20–2, cf. ch. XIII, n. 137. AURARIA: Cass. *Var.* II. 26, 30. SILIQUATICUM AND MONOPOLIUM: ibid. II. 4, 12, 26, 30, III. 25–6, IV. 19, V. 31. COEMPTIO: ibid. II. 26, 38 (from merchants), XII. 5, 14, 22–3, 26 (against rebate of tax). Cf. also Ennod. *V. Epiph.* 358 (*coemptio* under Odoacer). Boeth. *Consol.* I. 4 (complaints of oppressive *coemptio* under Theoderic).

42. In the proem of the Edict (*FIR* II.[2] pp. 684 ff.) Theoderic makes the reserva-

tion: 'salva iuris publici reverentia et legibus omnibus cunctorum devotione servandis', and at the end he speaks of his Edict as 'quae ex novellis legibus ac veteris iuris sanctimonia pro aliqua parte collegimus'. There is a substantive change of law in §142. On the question of Theoderic's legislative powers see *JRS* LII (1962), 129.

43. PRAEPOSITUS: Anon. Val. 82, Triwane praeposito cubiculi, cf. Boeth. *Consol.* I. 4, Ennod. *Ep.* IX. 21. CUBICULARII: *CIL* XI. 310, vir sbl. Seda ignucus et cubicularius regis Theoderici. MAIORES DOMUS: Symmachus, *Ep.* 5 §7 (= *MGH* (*AA*) XII. 429), Cass. *Var.* X. 18. SILENTIARIES: Proc. *HA* XXVI. 27–8; the 'ex silentiario sacri palatii' who died at Rome in 519 (*CIL* VI. 32003) was presumably a pensioner. From Cass. *Var.* VI. 13, 'formula magistri scrinii quae danda est comitiaco quando permilitat', it appears that members of the 'officium quod nostris iussionibus speciali sollicitudine famulatum est' were called *comitiaci*. In *Var.* II. 28 (an actual application of this formula) the recipient is called 'ex principe nostri officii', and VII. 31 speaks of the *princeps cardinalis* of the *officium comitiacum* of Ravenna and his *vicarius* at Rome. From VII. 21–2, it appears that there were *scriniarii officii nostri*; from VII. 25, that the *principes* of the *comes Dalmatiae* were seconded 'ex officio nostro'. In IV. 40 a summons to the king's court is executed *per officium nostrae sedis*, and in I. 8 (cf. IV. 5), I. 27, II. 10, V. 6, *comitiaci* act as the king's *executores* (cf. IV. 5, VIII. 27, for more general administrative tasks). Mommsen (*Ges. Schr.* VI. 407 ff.) and Stein (*Bas-empire*, II. 122–3) held that the *comitiaci* were the *agentes in rebus* under another name, but I prefer the view that they were the officials of the *magisterium militum praesentale*. The head of the *agentes in rebus* was the *adiutor*, that of the *officium magistri militum* the *princeps*. There were no *scriniarii* among the *agentes in rebus*, but there were in the military offices (implied by the *primiscrinii* of *Not. Dig. Or.* V. 72, VI. 75, VIII. 59, IX. 54, *Occ.* VI. 89). The *principes* of *comites rei militaris* were supplied from the *officia* of the *magistri militum*, not from the *agentes in rebus* in the West (*Not. Dig. Occ.* XXV. 38, XXVI. 22, etc.). The title *comitiaci* would be odd for the *agentes in rebus*, who were under the *magister officiorum*; for though he was a *comes* he was never known as such, but was the *magister* par excellence. On the other hand the *magistri militum* were often known as *comites* (see p. 105) and according to John Lydus their officials were called *comitiani* (*Mag.* II. 7, οἱ μὲν γὰρ λεγόμενοι στρατηλάται τὴν τῶν κομίτων ἔχουσιν ἐκ τῆς ἀρχαιότητος καὶ μόνην τιμήν. ταύτῃ καὶ κομιτιανοὺς τοὺς δευτεροστρατηλατιανοὺς ἡ παλαιότης οἶδε). The *agentes in rebus* still existed in the Ostrogothic kingdom, and supplied *principes* for the *officia* of the praetorian prefects (Cass. *Var.* XI. 35), and urban prefect (ibid. VI. 6). SAIONES: as messengers, Cass. *Var.* IX. 10; as *executores*, ibid. II. 13, III. 20, IV. 32, 39, VIII. 24, IX. 14; assigned to support civil administrators, ibid. II. 4, IV. 47, IX. 18, XII. 3; control the post, ibid. V. 5; enforce revenue collection, ibid. IV. 14; claim treasure trove, ibid. IV. 34; levy men and timber for the fleet, ibid. V. 19, 20; *tuitio*, ibid. IV. 27–8, VII. 39, 42; call up Goths, ibid. I. 24, cf. V. 27; transport and supply of troops, ibid. V. 10, 23; cf. also III 48. VIII. 27 for other miscellaneous commissions. *Saiones* and *comitiaci* were sometimes employed in pairs, e.g. Cass. *Var.* VIII. 27, cf. III. 20, VII. 39.

44. The only evidence for Odoacer is *FIR* III.² 99, where the details of the estates already granted to Pierius by the king are given 'viri sublimis comitis et vice domini nostri Arborii . . . suggestione': the title *vice domini* was used for the agents of private landowners (*Ed. Theod. epil.*, Greg. *Ep.* IX. 83, cf. ch. XX, n. 47, for the similar Greek term ἀντιγεοῦχος). For the functions of

the *comes rei privatae* see Cass. *Var.* VI. 8. The *comites patrimonii* whose names are known are Bergantinus (VIII. 23, IX. 3), Julianus (I. 16), Senarius (IV. 3, 4, wrongly styled *CRP* in IV. 7, 13) and Wilia (V. 18–20, IX. 13). For their management of estates in Italy see Cass. *Var.* V. 18–20 (raising men and cutting timber on royal lands near the Po for the fleet; IV. 15 probably concerns this operation), I. 16 (*conductores* in Apulia), VIII. 23 (grant of *massae* to Theodahad), IX. 3 (goldmining on the *massa Rusticiana*); cf. Ennod. *Ep.* VI. 10 for a dispute between the *comes patrimonii* and the *conductor* of an estate. They had officials called *chartarii* (Cass. *Var.* VIII. 23, IX. 3, XII. 4, cf. Ennod. *Ep.* VII. 1, a dispute 'inter Bautonem regiae domus conductorem et Epiphanium cartarium'). SICILY: Cass. *Var.* IV. 7, Just. *Nov.* cix, 537, nam publicas eiusdem insulae functiones sub iurisdictione viri excellentissimi comitis sacri patrimonii per Italiam esse antiqua consuetudo tradidit, cuius auctoritate tam exactio quam inlatio earum procederet; for Odoacer's acquisition of Sicily, see Victor Vit. I. 14. SPAIN: Cass. *Var.* V. 39, exactorum quoque licentia fertur amplius a provincialibus extorqueri quam nostro cubiculo constat inferri; cf. Proc. *BG* I. xii. 47–8. DALMATIA: Cass. *Var.* IX. 9, per quartam indictionem quod a vobis augmenti nomine quaerebatur illustrem virum comitem patrimonii nostri nunc iussimus removere. SAVIA: ibid. V. 14, si hoc quod tabularius a cubiculo nostro suscepit rationabiliter non docetur expensum, ab iniusto retentatore reddatur . . . domestici comitis Gothorum necnon et vicedomini aliqua dicuntur provincialibus concinnatis terroribus abstulisse. Theoderic evidently subsidised the administration of Savia from his *cubiculum*; I interpret the second phrase as *domestici* of the *comes Gothorum* (the military governor) and of the *vicedominus* (the provincial agent of the *comes patrimonii*). PANNONIA: ibid. IV. 13 (payment by Senarius to Colossaeus for his army). In Cass. *Var.* IX. 13, Wilia is directed to increase the emoluments of the *domestici* 'qui destinatis comitibus obsequuntur'; the *comites* referred to are probably those of Dalmatia, Savia and Pannonia.

45. SCHOLARES AND DOMESTICI: Proc. *HA* xxvi. 27–8; the *domestici* of Cass. *Var.* I. 10, who complain about their pay were presumably pensioners. Odoacer had active *comites domesticorum* (Anon. Val. 53) but in the *Variae* there is no formula for the office, but only for the *comitiva domesticorum vacans*, which was used for bestowing the lowest grade of the illustrate (VI. 11, cf. II. 15–16, VIII. 12). MUSTER OF GOTHS (WITH ARMS AND HORSES): Cass. *Var.* I. 24; the arms were presumably supplied from the *fabricae* (ibid. VII. 18–19). GEPIDS: ibid. V. 10–11. For garrisons see next note. ANNONAE: ibid. II. 5, III. 41–2, IV. 13, V. 10–11, 13, 23, XII. 5. MUSTERS FOR DONATIVE: ibid. V. 26–7; *millenarii* are mentioned in V. 27, the donative also in IV. 14, V. 36, VIII. 26.

46. ODOACER'S MAGISTRI MILITUM: Anon. Val. 51, 54. ATHALARIC'S PATRICII PRAESENTALES: Cass. *Var.* VIII. 9–10, XI. 1. DUCES OF FIELD ARMIES: ibid. III. 42, IV. 17, V. 30, 33; the *dux* Ibba of IV. 17 is styled *comes* in Jordanes, *Get.* 302. DUX RAETIARUM: Cass. *Var.* I. 11, VII. 4. COMES DALMATIARUM: ibid. VII. 24–5, IX. 8–9 (with Savia), cf. I. 40, III. 26, IV. 9; for Savia see also IV. 49, V. 14. COMES PANNONIAE: ibid. III. 23–4, IV. 13. COMITES PROVINCIARUM: ibid. VII. 1; I see no reason to limit this formula to the frontier provinces. COMES CIVITATIS OF NAPLES: ibid. VI. 23–5; cf. Syracuse, ibid. VI. 22, IX. 11, 14. OTHER COMITES CIVITATIS: ibid. VII. 26–8; for *comites* of individual cities see III. 34 (Massilia), IV. 45, X. 29 (Ticinum), VII. 16 (Insulae Curicta et Celsina), *V. Caes.* I. 48 (Arelate). COMITES GOTHORUM PER SINGULAS CIVITATES: Cass. *Var.* VII. 3; these *comites* are often identified with the *comites diversarum civitatum* of VII. 26–8, but their functions are described in very different terms.

47. The members of the Visigothic royal household are first recorded among the signatories of the later councils of Toledo (from *C. Tol.* VIII of 653 onwards). *Rectores* or *iudices provinciarum* are frequently mentioned in the *interpretationes* of the Breviarium of Alaric (which I cite from the Theodosian Code), e.g. *CTh* I. xvi. 11, 14, xxii. 2, II. I. 4, 5, 8, 9, iv. 2, III. vi. 1, xi. 1, XI. vi. 1, vii. 20, xi. 1, xxx. 15, Val. III, *Nov.* xix; they still appear in *Lex. Vis.* XII. i. 2, of 589. For their *praetoria* and *annonae* see *CTh* I. xxii. 4, *Lex. Vis.* XII. i. 2, quia nostra recordatur clementia quod dum iudices ordinamus nostra largitate eis compendia ministramus. For their *officiales* see *CTh* I. xvi. 7, xxii. 1, II. i. 8, IX. i. 15, XI. xi. 1; for *consiliarii*, etc., I. xxxiv. 1, 2, omnes iudices evidenter agnoscant nullum in provincia sibi commissa de eadem de qua venit provincia vel de alia regione sibi cancellarium vel domesticum fortasse coniungere nisi qui ei publice civium electione fuerit deputatus. TABULARII: *CTh* VIII. ii. 5, sive in solida provincia sive per singulas civitates tabularii fuerint ordinati, hoc est qui rationes publicas tractant, ingenui a provincialibus ordinentur, *Lex Vis.* XII. i. 2, comperimus quod numerarii vel defensores annua vice mutentur, qua de causa detrimentum nostris non ambigimus populis evenire, ideoque iubemus ut numerarius vel defensor qui electus ab episcopis vel populis fuerit commissum peragat officium. The *numerarii* of the *comes patrimonii* were not elected but nominated by their chief (*Consensus de fisco Barcinonensi*, Mansi, x. 473).

48. AURARIA: *CTh* XIII. i. 13. VECTIGALIA: *CTh* IV. xiii. 1, vectigalia sunt quae fisco vehiculorum subvectione praebentur, hoc est aut in litoreis locis navibus aut per diversa vehiculis merces deportant, cuius rei conductelam apud strenuas personas triennio esse praecipit, et continuo hanc exactionem aliis iterum permittendam qui maiorem summam praestationis obtulerint, Cass. *Var.* v. 39 (transmarinorum canon, telonei canon). THE LAND TAX: *CTh* XI. i. 15, ista lex hoc praecipit, ut in inferendo publicis horreis tritico, quod debetur, possessor pro rata canonis sui tribus inlationibus, id est quaternis mensibus, singulas debitorum partes adceleret; iii. 5, xxvi. 2 (*publici libri, polyptychi*, cf. Cass. *Var.* v. 39), vi. 1, xvi. 11 (*superindicta*), vii. 20, XII. vi. 20, 22, XVI. ii. 2 (*exactores*). For the civic *tabularii* see *CTh* VIII. ii. 5 cited in n. 47.

49. DOMUS DOMINICAE: *CTh* II. i. 11, x. i. 2, iv. 2; FISCALES: II. xxv. 1. ORDINATOR: II. i. 5, X. i. 2. ACTOR: II. i. 11, vi. 5, X. iv. 1, 2, *C. Tol.* III, can. 18, actores fiscalium patrimoniorum. CONDUCTORES REGIAE DOMUS: Cass. *Var.* v. 39. COMES PATRIMONII: *Lex Vis.* XII. i. 2, 589, comitem patrimonii aut actores fisci nostri, *Consensus de fisco Barcinonensi*, Mansi, x. 473. *Servi fiscales* seem to have been a numerous class in Visigothic Spain. They are mentioned in *C. Tol.* III, can. 8, clericos ex familia fisci nullus audeat a principe donatos expetere, can. 15, si qui ex servis fiscalibus fortasse ecclesias construxerint easque de sua paupertate ditaverint, *Lex Vis.* v. vii. 16 (forbidden to alienate *mancipia sua aut terras* to free persons, but only to other *servi fiscales*, or to give them to the church; if they wish to endow a church they must sell their slaves and land to other slaves of the crown and use the money they receive for the purpose), XII. i. 2 (disputes between *privati* and *servi fiscales* not to be judged by the *actor fisci*, but by the *rector provinciae* or *iudex territorii*).

50. DEFENSOR: *CTh* I. xxix. 6, *Lex Vis.* XII. i. 2 (elected); *CTh* III. xxx. 6 (*officium*); *CTh* II. i. 8, iv. 2 (jurisdiction). The *defensor* still existed in 589 (*Lex Vis.* XII. i. 2), but in this law jurisdiction belongs to the courts 'rectoris provinciae vel iudicis territorii'. The *iudex territorii* is also mentioned in *Lex Vis.* VI. iv. 4, VII. v. 1, iudicibus vicinis territorii illius, IX. i. 6, iudici vel vicario proxime civitatis vel territorii, x. i. 16, iudices singularum civitatum; he is

coupled with the *comes civitatis* in III. vi. I, VII. i. 5, ad comitem civitatis vel iudicem in cuius est territorio constitutus. He is alluded to simply as *iudex* in many laws which couple the *comes civitatis* with the *iudex*, II. i. 13, III. iv. 17, IV. ii. 14, VI. i. 1, VII. iv. 2, VIII. iv. 26, 29, IX. i. 20. Both the *comes* and the *iudex* existed by Euric's time (*Cod. Euric.* 322, vel ad comitem civitatis aut iudicem). Other early references to *comites civitatis* are Sid. Ap. *Ep.* VII. 2 and *C. Narb.* can. 4, 9. The *comes civitatis* does not appear in the Breviarium, but may be alluded to in such periphrases as 'ille . . . ad cuius ordinationem is respicit qui militat vel arma tenuerit' (*CTh* II. I. 2) or 'illis qui armatis praeesse noscuntur' (ibid. II. i. 9), substituted for the *iudices militares* of the Code. There is a mention of the *iudex territorii* in the Breviarium, *CTh* III. xi. 1, de his iudicibus qui provincias administrant vel etiam his quibus civitates vel loca commissa sunt. The *comes civitatis* assists the *iudex* in arresting Goths in *Lex Vis.* VII. iv. 2; in III. iv. 17 he flogs the *iudex* if the latter does not enforce the law. JOINT JURISDICTION IN CRIMINAL CASES: *Lex Vis.* VII. iv. 5. CASES REFERRED TO THE KING: *Lex Vis.* II. i. 13, *CTh* IX. xl. 10.

51. THE MUSTER: *Lex Vis.* IX. ii. 1–5; *millenarii* are referred to in *Cod. Euric.* 322, but not in a military context.

52. THE DONATIVE: Proc. *BG* I. xii. 48. GARRISONS: *Lex Vis.* IX. ii. 6. This law makes no allusion to a *dux provinciae*, who might have been expected to command the permanent garrisons. The office is attested under Euric (Greg. Tur. *HF* II. 20, Euricus autem Gothorum rex Victorium ducem super septem civitates praeposuit anno quarto decimo regni sui, cf. *V. Patr.* 3, and Sid. Ap. *Ep.* VII. 17, where he is styled *comes*). The *vir illustris* Vincentius who is called *dux provinciae nostrae* by the bishops of Tarraconensis in 464 (Hilarus, *Ep.* 14) was also probably an officer of Theoderic; he is mentioned ten years later as *Hispaniarum dux* and *quasi magister militum* under Euric (*Chron. Min.* I. 665). 'Claudius Lusitaniae dux' is mentioned by Joh. Biclar. 589, and a 'provinciae dux nomine Argimundus' in 590 by the same chronicler (*Chron. Min.* II. 218–9). The *dux provinciae* is also mentioned in later Visigothic laws (*Lex Vis.* II. i. 18, 19).

53. CODICILLI OF RANK: Cass. *Var.* VI. 2, formula patriciatus, 10, formula qua per codicillos vacantes proceres fiunt, 11, formula illustratus vacantis, 12, formula comitivae primi ordinis, VII. 37, formula spectabilitatis, 38, formula clarissimatus; cf. II. 2, 3, IX. 22, 23, for the consulate, and ch. XV, n. 23, for admission to the senate. SENATORS UNDER THE VISIGOTHS: *CTh* II. xxxiii. 3 (equated with 'senatorio genere nati'), 4, IX. xl. 10 (changed to 'maiores personae aut alicuius dignitatis viri'), Marc. *Nov.* iv. HONORATI: *CTh* I. xx. 1, honorati provinciarum, id est ex curiae corpore, IX. xix. 1, curiae dignitate privabitur, id est ut honoratus esse non possit. CURIAL OBLIGATIONS AND PROPERTY: *CTh* III. i. 8, v. ii. 1, x. iii. 2, XII. i. 1, 12, 19, 20, 55, 124, 170, Th. II, *Nov.* ix, xv. 1, xxii. 1, 2, Val. III, *Nov.* xxxv, Maj. *Nov.* vii.

54. PRAEPOSITUS REGNI: Victor Vit. II, 15, 43. ROMAN OFFICIALS AT COURT: ibid. II, 10, ut nostrae religionis homines in aula eius constituti neque annonas neque stipendia solita potirentur, 23, ut nemo in eius palatio militaret neque publicas ageret actiones nisi sese Arianum fecisset. IUDICES PROVINCIARUM: ibid. III. 13. PROCONSUL: ibid. III. 27. PROCURATORS: ibid. I. 45 (Felix), 48 (Saturus), *V. Fulg.* 5–6.

55. MILLENARII: Victor Vit. I. 30, Vandalus de illis quos millenarios vocant, cf. the χιλίαρχοι of Proc. *BV* I. v. 18. For revolts of the Moors under the Vandals see Proc. *BV* I. viii. 2, 5, 7, 14–29, ix. 3.

56. *Lex Burg. prima const.* 5, optimates consiliarii domestici et maiores domus nostrae, cancellarii etiam, Burgundiones quoque et Romani civitatum et pagorum comites vel iudices deputati, omnes etiam et militantes. Cf. 2, habito consilio comitum et procerum nostrorum, and law 74, sed nunc ex ipso eodemque titulo cum optimatibus populi nostri adtentius universa tractantes generalitatem praedictae legis placuit temperari. The *consiliarii* and *maiores domus* are also mentioned in *extrav.* xxi. 14 (cited in n. 57). PUERI OR WITTISCALCI: *Lex Burg.* 76.

57. The two *comites* are mentioned in *Lex Burg. prima const.* 5 (cited in n. 56), 13, nullam causam absente altero iudice vel Romanus comes vel Burgundio iudicare praesumat, *extrav.* xxi. 11, omnes comites tam Burgundionum quam Romanorum, cf. law 49, locorum comites atque praepositi, 50, singulorum locorum iudices, 76, 79 (*comites* as judges), *extrav.* xxi. 14, si quicumque aliquid loco munificentiae petere voluerit cum literis comitis sui veniat, et consiliarii aut maiores domus qui praesentes fuerint ipsas literas comitis ipsius accipiant et suas literas ex nostra ordinatione ad illius iudicis faciant cuius territorio res illa quae petitur tenetur et hoc eis concedant ut diligenter et fideliter inquirant si sine peccato dari potest. It is not clear to me whether the *iudices deputati* are identical with these *comites civitatum* or judges appointed for special cases; they are mentioned in *prima const.* 5 (cited in no. 56), 7, 12, laws 81, 90. NOTARII: *Lex Burg. prima const.* 7. MILITANTES: ibid. 5 (cited in n. 56).

58. COMITES PALATII: Greg. Tur. *HF* v. 18, ix. 12, 30, *Virt. Mart.* iv. 6. DOMESTICI: Greg. Tur. *HF* IV. 3, VI. 11, VII. 15, IX. 19, X. 5, 15, 28, *Virt. Mart.* i. 25. MAIORES DOMUS: Greg. Tur. *HF* VI. 9, 45, VII. 27–8, 43, IX. 30, *Virt. Mart.* iv. 6–7. REFERENDARII: Greg. Tur. *HF* v. 3, 28, 42, 45, VI. 28, VIII. 39, IX. 23, 33, 38, X. 19, 31, *Virt. Mart.* i. 25, iii. 17, *Glor. Conf.* 93. In *HF* v. 3, the referendary is described as 'qui anolum regis Sygiberthi tenuerat', and in *HF* x. 19 as giving his *subscriptio* to royal grants; he is concerned with taxation in *HF* v. 28. Other officials of whom we hear are *thesaurarii* (*HF* v. 39, VII. 4), *cancellarii* (*Virt. Mart.* iv. 28), *camerarii* (*HF* IV. 7, 26, VI. 45) and *comites stabuli* (*HF* v. 39, 48, IX. 38, X. 5).

59. BELGICA II: *MGH* (*Ep.*) III. 113; cf. Greg. Tur. *Virt. Jul.* 32. RECTOR PROVINCIAE: Greg. Tur. *HF* IV. 43 (Jovinus and Albinus), VI. 7, 11 (Dynamius), VIII. 43 (Nicetius); Jovinus and Albinus are called *ex praefectis* in VI. 7, 11, and Mummolus is styled *praefectus* in VI. 35, VII. 15. *Comites civitatum* are recorded in Gregory *passim*; for their judicial duties see especially *HF* v. 48, *V. Patrum*, 7 §1, 8 §3, for the taxes, *HF* VI. 22, VII. 23, IX. 30, X. 21, for military affairs, *HF* IV. 30, VI. 41, VII. 29, 42. See also the *formula* of the office in *MGH* (*Leg.*) v. 47–8.

60. CHILDEBERT'S DISCRIPTORES: Greg. Tur. *HF* IX. 30; for another case of out of date registers see *HF* X. 7.

61. CHILPERIC'S LEVIES: Greg. Tur. *HF* v. 28, 34, cf. VI. 28. TAXATION OF FRANKS: ibid. III. 36 (Parthenius), VII. 15 (Audo). The church normally paid tax; for special remissions see *HF* III. 25, X. 7, and for a special levy, *HF* IV. 2.

62. MILITARY LEVIES: Greg. Tur. *HF* v. 26, VI. 19, VII. 24, VIII. 30, cf. n. 59 for the role of the *comes civitatis*. PATRICII: ibid. IV. 24, 30, 42, v. 13; Nicetius is also styled *patricius* in IX. 22. *Duces* are recorded *passim* in Gregory as commanders of armies in the field: for *duces* in command of groups of cities see *HF* VI. 31, VIII. 18, 26, 42, IX. 7 (with *comites civitatis* under him).

63. EURIC: Sid. Ap. *Ep.* VII. 6. The Breviarium was drawn up 'adhibitis sacerdotibus et nobilibus viris' and received the approval 'venerabilium episcoporum vel electorum provincialium nostrorum' (*MHG* (*Leg.*) I. i. 466). Councils of catholic bishops were frequently held (Agathe, 506, Tarraco, 516, Gerunda, 517, Ilerda, 523, Valentia, 524, Toledo, 531, Barcino, 540) and at the Second Council of Toledo (531) the bishops thanked the king, 'qui innumeris annis regni eius ea quae ad cultum fidei perveniunt peragendi nobis licentiam praestat' (Mansi, VIII. 787). The conversion of Visigoths is celebrated in the Third Council of Toledo.

64. Stein, *Bas-empire* II. 185–9.

65. Odoacer's intervention is cited in the acts of Symmachus' council of 502 (*MGH* (*AA*) XII. 445–7). For Theoderic's intervention see Stein, *Bas-empire*, II. 134–42; the main sources are *Lib. Pont.* liii and the acts of Symmachus' councils (*MGH* (*AA*) XII. 399–455).

66. Victor Vit. I, passim.

67. Victor Vit. II. 23 (bishops and civil servants), 26 ff. (deportation of the clergy to the south), 39, 52 ff. (the council), III. 2–14 (the penal laws), 20 ff. (deportation of the clergy to Corsica).

68. Courtois, *Les Vandales et l'Afrique*, 299–304.

69. ROYAL GIFTS OF LAND: *C. Aurel.* I, can. 5, de oblationibus vel agris quos domnus noster rex ecclesiis suo munere conferre dignatus est, *C. Aurel.* V, can. 15 (endowment of a hospital at Lyons by Childebert). GRANTS OF IMMUNITY: Greg. Tur. *HF* III. 25, X. 7 (Auvergne), IX. 30 (Tours). USURPATION OF CHURCH LANDS: Greg. Tur. *Virt. Mart.* i. 29, *C. Arvern.* I, can. 5, qui reiculam ecclesiae petunt a regibus, *C. Paris.* III, can. I, competitoribus . . . qui facultates ecclesiae sub specie largitatis regiae improba subreptione pervaserint, *C. Turon.* II, can. 24. AWARD OF BISHOPRICS TO ROYAL MINISTERS: Greg. Tur. *HF* IV. 18 (Austrapius *dux*), VI. 7 (Jovinus *rector provinciae*), VIII. 22 (Gundegisil *comes civitatis*), IX. 23 (Charimeres *referendarius*); a suspiciously large number of referendaries became bishops (*HF* V. 42, 45, VIII. 39, X. 31).

70. LAWS AGAINST BARBARIAN HOSPITES: *Lex Vis.* X. i. 16, *Lex Burg.* 54, Cass. *Var.* I. 18; AGAINST CORRUPT JUDGES: *Lex Theudi* (*MHG* (*Leg.*), I. i. 467–9), *Lex Burg. prima const.*

71. For the persistence of old abuses see above n. 22. PLUNDERING BY GOTHIC TROOPS: Cass. *Var.* V. 26, illud tamen necessario commonentes ut venientium nullus provenire possit excessus, nec possessorum segetes aut prata vastetis; though they received *annonae* Gothic armies on the march seem always to have looted the countryside and the provincials were regularly compensated for their losses (see Cass. *Var.* II. 8, III. 38, IV. 36, V. 13, XII. 5). TUITIO: Cass. *Var.* VII. 39, 42; cf. IV. 27 for the attempted murder by a *saio* of the person whom he was appointed to protect.

For the reign of Justin I there is a detailed study in A. A. Vasiliev, *Justin the First, An introduction to the epoch of Justinian*, Cambridge, Mass. 1950. For the reign of Justinian the most important works are C. Diehl, *Justinien et la civilisation byzantine au VIᵉ siècle*, Paris, 1901, and the massive work of B. Rubin, *Das Zeitalter Iustinians*, of which the first volume only has appeared (Berlin, 1960).

1. JUSTIN'S EARLY CAREER: Proc. *HA* vi. 1–16. HIS ELECTION: Const. Porph. *Cer.* 1. 93, Malalas, 410–11, Marcell. com. 519 (*Chron. Min.* II. 101).

2. Stein, *Bas-empire*, II. 223–35.

3. GERMANUS: Proc. *BV* II. xvi. 1 ff., *BG* III. xl. 5–6 (the Antae), 9 (character). Justinian's full name was Flavius Petrus Sabbatius Justinianus (*ILS* 1307). He is already styled *comes* in April, 519 (*Coll. Avell.* 162). VITALIAN: Malalas, 411–2, *Chron. Min.* II. 101. JUSTINIAN BECOMES MAG. MIL PRAES.: *ILS* 1307, *Chron. Min.* II. 196. Cf. Proc. *BP* I. xi. 16, xii. 21.

4. PERSIAN AFFAIRS: Proc. *BP* I. xi, xii. JUSTINIAN'S CORONATION: Const. Porph. *Cer.* I. 95. JUSTIN'S DEATH: Malalas, 424.

5. Even Procopius (*HA* xii. 27, xiii. 28–32) has to admit that Justinian was abstemious and worked very late.

6. Justinian speaks of Latin as ἡ πάτριος ἡμῶν φωνή in *Nov.* xiii. pr., cf. vii. 1, xv pr., xxii. 2, xxx. 5, lxix. pr., cxlvi §1; for his antiquarianism see also *Nov.* xxiv. pr., xxv. pr., xli, xlviii. pr.

7. ABROGATION OF LAW ON SENATORS AND ACTRESSES: Proc. *HA* ix. 51, *CJ* v. iv. 23 (520–3). Justinian acknowledges Theodora's aid in *Nov.* viii §1, 535. For Theodora and John see Proc. *BP* I. xxv.

8. MAGISTER MILITUM PER ARMENIAM: *CJ* I. xxix. 5, Proc. *Aed.* III. i. 16. NEW DUCES: Proc. *Aed.* III. i. 28–9, ii. 1, iii. 14, vi. 17, 26. DUX OF CIRCESIUM: Proc. *Aed.* II. vi. 9. DUX OF PALMYRA: Malalas, 426.

9. SITTAS AND BELISARIUS JUSTINIAN'S δορύφοροι: Proc. *BP* I. xii. 21. Sittas's nationality is inferred from his name, Belisarius' origin is given in Proc. *BV* I. xi. 21.

10. The main sources for the Nika rebellion are Proc. *BP* I. xxiv, Malalas, 473–7, and *Exc. de Insid.* 46, Marcell. com. 532 (*Chron. Min.* II. 103). JOHN THE CAPPADOCIAN'S ORIGIN: Joh. Lydus, *Mag.* III. 57. Tribonian first appears as *magisteria dignitate inter agentes decoratus* in 528 (*CJ const.* Haec, Summa).

11. Proc. *BP* I. xxii. 1–8.

12. DEBATE ON THE VANDAL WAR: Proc. *BV* I. x. 1–20. BELISARIUS' FORCE: ibid. I. xi. 1–21.

13. ORGANISATION OF AFRICA: *CJ* I. xxvii. 1, 2, 534. THE LAND: Proc. *BV* II. xiv. 8–10, Just. *Nov.* xxxvi, 535. THE CHURCH: Just. *Nov.* xxxvii, 535, Proc. *BV* II. xiv. 12–14.

14. VANDAL REGIMENTS: Proc. *BV* II. xiv. 17–18. BELISARIUS' TRIUMPH: ibid. II. ix.

15. CONQUEST OF SICILY: Proc. *BG* I. v. 1–7, 12–16.

16. Proc. *BG* I. vi.

17. REINFORCEMENTS: Proc. *BG* I. xxvii. 1–2, II. v. 1.

18. NARSES' ARMY: Proc. *BG* II. xiii. 16–18.

19. REINFORCEMENTS TO SOLOMON: Proc. *BV* II. ix. 23–4. REVOLT OF STOTZAS: ibid. II. xiv. 7 ff.

20. GERMANUS: Proc. *BV* II. xvi–xviii. SOLOMON: ibid. II. xix ff.

21. Stein, *Bas-empire*, II. 305–10.

22. Proc. *BG* II. xxix.

23. See pp. 477–8.

24. See pp. 478–9, and for Tribonian's career, Stein, *Bas-empire*, II. 404–7.

25. The first law addressed to John is *CJ* VI. xxvii. 5 of 30 April 531, and the last *Nov.* lix of May 541. SUFFRAGIA: Just. *Nov.* viii, 535; see pp. 394–5. MANDATA: ibid. xvii, 535. DEFENSORES: ibid. xv, 535.

26. PRAETOR OF THRACE: Just. *Nov.* xxvi, 535. QUAESTOR EXERCITUS: Joh. Lydus, *Mag.* II. 28–9, Just. *Nov.* xli, 536. PRAETOR POPULI: ibid. xiii, 535. See also p. 692. QUAESITOR: Just. *Nov.* lxxx, 539: see also p. 692.

27. CHANGES IN ASIA MINOR: Just. *Nov.* viii §§2, 3, xxiv, xxv, xxviii, xxix, 535, xxx, xxxi, 536.

28. Just. *Nov.* viii §5 (*comes Orientis*), xxvii (Isauria), 535, cii (Arabia), ciii (Palestine), 536, *Ed.* iv (Phoenice).

29. Just. *Ed.* xiii; for the date see *Chron. d'Égypte*, 1955, 112–21 and for the missing chapters M. Gelzer, *Studien zur Byzantinischen Verwaltung Aegyptens*, 21 ff.

30. See pp. 483–4.

31. Procopius gives a full account of Justinian's building activity in his *Aedificia*.

32. ANASTASIUS' RESERVE SPENT: Proc. *HA* xix. 7–8, Joh. Lydus, *Mag.* III. 51. TAXATION IN AFRICA: Proc. *BV* II. viii. 25. SICILY: Just. *Nov.* civ, 537. PRAETORIAN PREFECT OF ITALY: Proc. *BG* I. xx. 19–20 (Fidelius), II. xxi. 40 (Reparatus), II. xxii. 24 (Athanasius), III. vi. 9 (Maximinus).

33. ARREARS IN AFRICA: Proc. *BV* II. xvi. 5, xxvi. 12.

34. On John see Proc. *BP* I. xxiv. 12–15, *HA* xxi. 1–2, Joh. Lydus, *Mag.* III. 57 ff. THE ἀεϱικόν: Proc. *HA* xxi. 1–3; this tax is mentioned in *P. Vars.* 32, *P. Iand.* 102, but its precise character is unknown.

35. CURSUS PUBLICUS: Proc. *HA* xxx. 1–11, Joh. Lydus, *Mag.* III. 61. SCHOLAE REDUCED: Proc. *HA* xxiv. 18–20. PAY OF SCHOLARES AND DOMESTICI DOCKED: Proc. *HA* xxiv. 21–6.

36. LIMITANEI: Proc. *HA* xxiv. 12–14. BEROEA: Proc. *BP* II. vii. 37. DONATIVE: Proc. *HA* xxiv. 27–9, cf. Val. III, *Nov.* xiii, *CJ* I. xxvii. 1, 2.

37. DISCUSSORES: Proc. *HA* xxiv. 1–11 (military), ch. XIX, n. 106 (civil).

38. The principal laws on the ordination and discipline of the clergy are *CJ* I. iii. 41, 528, 44, 530, 47, 531, Just. *Nov.* vi, xvi, 535 (and cxxxvii, 565); on monks, *CJ* I. iii. 43, 529, 46, 530, Just. *Nov.* v, 535, lxxix, cxxxiii, 539 (and cxxiii, 546); on church property, *CJ* I. ii. 24, 530, Just. *Nov.* vii, 535, xlvi, 536, lv, 537 (and cxx, 544).

39. COMPULSORY BAPTISM OF PAGANS: *CJ* I. xi. 10. PURGE OF PAGANS: Malalas, 449. For John of Ephesus see ch. XXIII, n. 4. MANICHEES: Malalas, 423. MONTANISTS: Proc. *HA* xi. 23.

40. *CJ* I. v. 12, 527, 13–16, 18, 19, 529, 20, 530, 21, 531, Just. *Nov.* xlv, 537. SYNAGOGUES IN AFRICA: Just. *Nov.* xxxvii, 535. SAMARITANS: *CJ* I. v. 17, Proc. *HA* xi. 24–30, Malalas, 445–6, 487.

41. Stein, *Bas-empire*, II. 376–8. THE COLLOQUY: *A.C.Oec.* IV. ii. 169–84. THE EDICT AND THE POPE'S AGREEMENT: *CJ* I. i. 6–8, 533–4.

42. Stein, *Bas-empire*, II. 380–91.

43. THE PLAGUE: Proc. *BP* II. xxii, xxiii, Agathias, v. 10, *Chron. Min.* II. 213–14, 238.

44. The Persian war from the renewal in 541 is described in Proc. *BP* II. THE TRUCE OF 545: ibid. II. xxviii. 7–11.

45. TOTILA'S 5,000 MEN: Proc. *BG* III. iv. 1. HIS LAND POLICY: ibid. III. vi. 5–8. WALLS OF NAPLES DEMOLISHED: ibid. III. viii. 10.

46. BELISARIUS' 4,000 RECRUITS: Proc. *BG* III. x. 1–2. ALEXANDER: ibid. III. i. 28–33. ILLYRIAN TROOPS GO HOME: ibid. III. xi. 13–15.

47. BELISARIUS' LETTER: Proc. *BG* III. xii. 3–10. REINFORCEMENTS UNDER JOHN: ibid. III. xiii. 20. FALL OF ROME: ibid. III. xx.

48. REINFORCEMENTS UNDER VALERIAN: Proc. *BG* III. xxvii. 1–3. Belisarius held the office of *comes stabuli* during his second Italian command (Proc. *HA* iv. 39, cf. *BG* III. ix. 23): reappointed *magister militum orientis*, *BG* IV. xxi. 1.

49. DAGISTHAEUS: Proc. *BP* II. xxix. 10 ff. BESSAS: Proc. *BG* IV. ix. 4 ff. TRUCE OF 551: ibid. IV. xv. 1–3.

50. GERMANUS' PREPARATIONS: Proc. *BG* III. xxxix. 9–20.

51. NARSES' PREPARATIONS: Proc. *BG* IV. xxvi. 5–16.

52. BUSTA GALLORUM: Proc. *BG* IV. xxix–xxxii. MONS LACTARIUS: ibid. IV. xxxv: the terms given to the remnant of the Ostrogoths are in §§33–8. FIGHTING AGAINST THE FRANKS: Agathias, I and II. 1–14.

53. PRAGMATIC SANCTION: Just. *App.* vii, 554.

54. GRANT OF LANDS OF GOTHIC CHURCH TO RAVENNA: *P. Ital.* 2; cf. Agnellus, *Lib. Pont. Eccl. Rav.* 85. GOTHIC LANDOWNERS: *P. Ital.* 7 (557), 13 (553).

55. NARSES' TITLE: Just. *App.* vii §27, 554, *ILS* 832. For the frontier defences see Stein, *Bas-empire*, II, 612–13, and for the civil administration ch. x, n. 29. Pelagius II wrote a letter to John, *comes patrimonii* (*PL* LXIX. 416), presumably of Italy.

56. Stein, *Bas-empire*, II, 560–3.

57. SERGIUS: Proc. *BV* II. xxii, xxiii. AREOBINDUS: ibid II. xxiv–xxvii. JOHN: ibid. II. xxviii ff. His exploits are described in great detail in Corippus' *Johannis*. MOORISH REVOLT IN 563: Malalas, 495–6.

58. INVASION OF 544: Proc. *BG* III. xi. 15; of 548, ibid. III. xxix. 1–3; of 550–1, ibid. III. xl. 1–7, 30–45; of 559, Malalas, 490, *Chron. Min.* II. 205, Agathias, v. 11 ff., Theophanes, A.M. 6051. THE AVARS: Joh. Eph. *HE* VI. 24, Menander, 9, *Chron. Min.* II. 205.

59. Menander, 11.

60. Just. *Nov.* clvii, 542, dealing with conditions in Osrhoene and Mesopotamia, is addressed to Lazarus, *comes Orientis*. VICAR OF PONTICA: Just. *Ed.* viii, 548. BIOCOLYTES: Just. *Nov.* cxlv, 553. The vicar of Thrace does not appear in the Notitia of Just. *Nov.* viii, and must therefore have been abolished before 535, probably by Anastasius when he instituted the vicariates of the Long Walls. A vicar of Thrace reappears in 576 (*BCH* VI (1882), 186; cf. also *AE* 1938, 12, 138), and the restitution of the office was no doubt due to Justinian, who restored the other vicariates.

61. REVENUE COLLECTION: Just. *Nov.* cxxviii, 545. LOCI SERVATORES: ibid. cxxxiv, 556.

62. Peter is attested as *CSL* in 542 (Just. *Ed.* vii §6), *PPO Or.* in 543–6 (Just. *Nov.* cxviii–cxx, cxxiii–cxxv, cxxviii, cxxx, cxxxi), *CSL* again c. 546 in Proc. *HA* xxii. 33 (cf. Just. *Ed.* xi, 559, where he is styled ἀπὸ κομήτων τῶν θείων λαργιτιόνων τὸ δεύτερον), *PPO* again in 554–62 in Just. *Nov.* cxxxiv, clix, *Ed.* xi, Malalas, 491. His career is described in Proc. *HA* xxii. 3–38.

63. Just. *Nov.* cxxviii, cxxx, 545.

64. See ch. XXI, n. 6.

65. MONOPOLIES: Proc. *HA* xx. 1–5, xxvi. 18 ff., 36–9. SUFFRAGIA: ibid. xxii. 7–9, cf. Just. *App.* vii §12.

66. Justinian's later laws on the church are *Nov.* cxx, 544, cxxxi, 545, cxxiii, 546, cxxxvii, 565; on synagogue services, *Nov.* cxlvi, 553. PURGE OF PAGANS IN 562: Malalas, 491. For the story of the Three Chapters see Stein, *Bas-empire*, II, 632–83.

67. JAMES BARADAEUS: Joh. Eph. *V. SS. Or.* xlix.

68. Evagr. IV. 39.

69. Barbarians were more used in the West than in the East; the army in Lazica at the end of Justinian's reign was still almost entirely Roman (Agathias, III. 20). Procopius gives a detailed description of Justinian's fortifications in Thrace and Illyricum in *Aed.* IV; in ch. iv are long lists of forts built or repaired in the interior, as far from the Danube as Epirus and Thessaly.

70. PELAGIUS: *PL* LXIX. 404–5 (to the bishop of Arles), 417 (to the praetorian prefect of Africa).

71. For the Western regiments see ch. XVII, nn. 119, 121.

72. Agathias, V. 13.

73. Just. *Nov.* cxlviii pr., 566.

X. THE SUCCESSORS OF JUSTINIAN (pp. 304–5)

The history of this period is covered by the *Cambridge Medieval History*, II. ix. In P. Goubert, *Byzance avant l'Islam*, there is a detailed study of the Persian wars and negotiations (Tome I, *Byzance et l'Orient*, Paris, 1951) and of relations with the Franks (Tome II, i, *Byzance et l'Occident*, Paris, 1955).

1. The accession of Justin II is voluminously described by Corippus, *de Laudibus Justini*. For the fate of the other Justin see Evagr. V. 1–2. Justin II is first recorded as *cura palatii* in 551, Vigilius, *Ep. Encycl.* (PL LXIX. 53). Tiberius, then a notary, was introduced to Justin, then *cura palatii*, in 562 (*V. Eutych.* 66–7).

2. THE AVAR EMBASSY: Menander, 14, Joh. Eph. *HE* VI. 24; also rhetorically described in Corippus, *de Laudibus Justini*. THE SARACEN AND PERSIAN EMBASSIES: Menander, 15–17.

3. Menander, 24–9, Paulus, *HL* I. 27.

4. Paulus, *HL* II. 7–14, 25–7.

5. AFRICA AND SPAIN: *Chron. Min.* II. 212–13. PERSIA: Menander, 36, Theoph. Byz. 3, Joh. Epiph. 2, Joh. Eph. *HE* II. 18–21, Evagr. v. 7.

6. Theoph. Byz. 3–4, Joh. Epiph. 2–5, Joh. Eph. *HE* VI. 2–6, Evagr. v. 8–10, Theoph. Sim. III, 9–11.

7. Justin's madness and Tiberius' nomination are fully described by Joh. Eph. *HE* III. 2–5; cf. also ibid. v. 13, Evagr. v. 11–13, Joh. Epiph. 5, Theoph. Sim. III. 11. TRUCE WITH PERSIA: Menander, 37–8, Theoph. Sim. III. 11.

8. THE EDICT OF UNION: Evagr. v. 4, Joh. Eph. *HE* I. 19. THE PERSECUTION: Joh. Eph. *HE* I. 33 ff., II. 1–14. SUFFRAGIA: Just. *Nov.* cxlix, 569, cf. clxi, 574 for the rapid revival of *suffragia*. WINE DUTY AND PAYMENT FOR BREAD RATION: Joh. Eph. *HE* III. 14; as the bread ration was worth only about a solidus a year, the fee cannot have been annual.

9. Tiberius is praised for his toleration by Joh. Eph. *HE* III. 21. HIS EXTRAVAGANCE: Evagr. v. 13, Joh. Eph. *HE* III. 11 and 14 (abolition of Justin's taxes), v. 20. SUFFRAGIA: Evagr. v. 13, Just. *Nov.* clxi, 574. REMISSION OF TAXES: Evagr. v. 13, Just. *Nov.* clxiii, 575. That this remission was actually made is proved by *P. Oxy.* 1907, λόγος κουφισμοῦ τοῦ τετάρτου μέρους (for one of the other cities of Arcadia, not Oxyrhynchus itself, for which the figures are far too low, see p. 436). It gives the normal tax as 25372½ *artabae* of wheat and 2297 solidi 10½ carats in gold (including commutation of barley and *sportulae* of officials), of which 300 solidi were not eligible for the remission. One quarter of the wheat (6343 *artabae* 5 *choenices*) is valued at 735 solidi 6 carats, and one quarter of the net gold tax comes to 499 solidi 8½ carats; the total rebate is added up to 1234 solidi 14½ carats. This accords with the provisions of the law, whereby taxes in kind, including the ἐμβολή, were to be paid in full, but the taxpayers received a rebate for a quarter of their value in gold.

10. AVAR SUBSIDY: Menander, 63 (*ad init.*). WAR WITH THE SCLAVENI: ibid. 48.

11. FALL OF SIRMIUM: Menander, 63–6, Joh. Eph. *HE* VI. 30–3. SCLAVENE INVASION: Joh. Eph. *HE* VI. 25.

12. DEATH OF ALBOIN AND CLEPH: Paulus, *HL* II. 28–31. THE DUCES: ibid. II. 32, cf. III. 13, 33 for Faroald and Zotto. ROMAN EMBASSIES: Menander, 49, 62.

13. THE TRUCE: Menander, 39–40, Joh. Eph. *HE* VI. 8, Theoph. Sim. III. 12. For subsequent operations and negotiations see Menander, 41–3, 46, Joh. Eph. *HE* VI. 9–13. BUILD UP OF FORCES: Evagr. v. 14, Theophanes, A.M. 6074, Theoph. Sim III. 12, Joh. Eph. *HE* VI. 14.

14. Evagr. v. 19, Joh. Eph. *HE* VI. 14, 27–8, Theoph. Sim. III. 15–18.

15. Menander, 47, 50, 54–5, Joh. Eph. *HE* VI. 21–3. For Tiberius' death and Maurice's accession see Joh. Eph. *HE* v. 13.

16. Paulus, *HL* III. 17.

17. Paulus, *HL* III. 16, 18, 22, 28–9, Greg. Tur. *HF* VIII. 18, IX. 25, *MGH* (*Ep.*) III. 145–7 (two letters of the exarch Romanus). Other correspondence between the Franks and the imperial government about the Lombards are to be found ibid. 138–53.

18. Theoph. Sim. I. 3–8, II. 10–18.

19. Theoph. Sim. I. 9, 12–15, II. 1–10, 18, III. 1–3, Evagr. VI. 3–6, 9.

20. Theoph. Sim. III. 4–8, Evagr. VI. 10–13.

21. Theoph. Sim. IV. 1–16, v. 1–15, Evagr. VI. 16–19, Joh. Epiph. 1.

22. DEATH OF AUTHARI: Paulus, *HL* III. 35.

23. These events are well described (with full reference to the sources) in F. Homes Dudden, *Gregory the Great*. II. 6–17, 21–42. For the Theodosiaci see Greg. *Ep*. II. 45.

24. VENAFRUM: Greg. *Ep*. I. 66, VI. 11. CROTON: ibid. II. 40, VII. 23. AUXIMUM: ibid IX. 99–100.

25. Greg. *Ep*. I. 8, II. 44, 48, III. 20, IX. 60. Cf. also I. 15, 51, II. 19, 37, 42, III. 13, VI. 9.

26. C. Diehl, *Études sur l'administration byzantine dans l'exarchat de Ravenne* (568–751), Paris, 1888, is still the basic work on the subject. The title of exarch first appears in 584 (Pelagius II, *Ep*. I, see next note). For his powers see Diehl, op. cit. 168–81. The evidence there cited does not prove that he officially issued their codicils to military officers, though he certainly appointed them *de facto*, nor that he had any special powers over the civil administration, though like most military officers of the period (and earlier) he tended to intervene. One may suspect that a new title was invented to distinguish the supreme *magister militum* from the many *duces* who by now bore that title.

27. ROME: Pelagius II, *Ep*. I, quia ita hic coangustata est respublica ut nisi deus piissimi in corde principis inspiraverit ut insitam sibi misericordiam suis famulis largiatur et super illam dioecesim vel unum magistrum militum vel unum ducem dignetur concedere in omni sumus angustia destituti quia maxime partes Romanae omni praesidio vacuatae videntur, et exarchus scribit nullum nobis posse remedium facere quippe qui nec ad illas partes custodiendas se testatur posse sufficere. No regular *dux* or *magister militum* of Rome appears in Gregory's letters. NAPLES: Greg. *Ep*. II. 45, de Neapolitana vero urbe excellentissimo exarcho instanter imminete . . . valde insidiatur eidem civitati, in qua si celeriter dux non mittitur, iam omnino inter perditas habeatur, IX. 17, 53, 65, 124, 162 (Maurentius mag. mil.), X. 5 (Gudiscalco duci Campaniae), XIV. 10 (Guduin duci Neapolim). For Istria and Ariminum the only early evidence is Greg. *Ep*. IX. 160 (*mag. mil.*), I. 56 (*dux*).

28. Greg. *Ep*. IX. 53, 121 (Misenum), 174, cf. 112 (Sipontum), 200, 205 (Hydruntum). At Naples Gregory (*Ep*. II. 34) took it upon himself to appoint a tribune, and at Centumcellae (I. 13) the tribune Zemarchus was succeeded by his widow in his *comitiva* (whose duties appear to have been mainly financial). Cf. also IX. 71, comes castri Aprutiensis.

29. PRAETORIAN PREFECT: Greg. *Ep*. I. 22, 35–6, III. 28 (George), X. 8 (John): cf. the earlier prefect Aurelian in *P. Ital*. 4–5, B. VII. 12, VIII. 4. VICAR OF THE CITY: Greg. *Ep*. X. 8, *Dial*. III. 10, IV. 52. VICAR OF ITALY: Greg. *Ep*. IX. 103. IUDEX CAMPANIAE: ibid. III. 1 (cf. I. 66). IUDEX SAMNII: ibid. II. 38; the praetor of Sicily is frequently mentioned (I. 2, II. 30, X. 12, XI. 4, 8). PALATINI REI PRIVATAE: ibid. IX. 72; in *Ep*. XIII. 26, Gregory speaks sarcastically of a *palatinus* 'qui quasi comes privatarum dici vult'. PALATINI SACRARUM LARGITIONUM: ibid. I. 13, IX. 113, *P. Dip*. 120 (572). NUMERARII: Greg. *Ep*. IX. 63, 130, *P. Ital*. 22, lines 36, 51, 55; we also hear of *scriniarii gloriosae sedis* (*P. Ital*. 6, lines 7, 38) and *exceptores gloriosae sedis eminentissimi praefecti* (*P. Ital*., 22, lines 10, 52). PREFECT OF THE CITY: Greg. *Ep*. IX. 116–17; the *comes formarum* is implied by XII. 6. There was still a *comes patrimonii per Italiam* (Greg. *Ep*. IX. 239).

30. EXARCH: Greg. *Ep*. I. 59, 72–3, IV. 7, IX. 9, cf. VI. 59, VII. 3. PRAETORIAN PREFECT: Greg. *Ep*. IV. 32 (Pantaleon), X. 16, XI. 7 (Innocentius). The last letter

alludes to the *iudices* of the provinces; the *praeses* of Sardinia is mentioned in
IX. 195, XI. 12.

31. Theoph. Sim. V. 16, VI. 1-6.

32. Theoph. Sim. VI. 7-11, VII. 1-5.

33. Theoph. Sim. VII. 10-15.

34. Theoph. Sim. VIII. 1-7.

35. Theoph. Sim. VIII. 8-9.

36. Theoph. Sim. VIII. 9-11.

37. *Doctrina Iacobi*, iv. 2.

38. Ibid. iii. 9.

39. Ibid. v. 16.

XI. THE GOVERNMENT (pp. 321-3)

1. QUOD PRINCIPI PLACUIT, ETC.: *Inst.* I. ii. 6, cf. *Dig.* I. iv. 1 pr. For
Constantine's conception of his divine right see especially Opt. *App.* III, ex
quibus forsitan commoveri possit summa divinitas non solum contra humanum
genus sed etiam in me ipsum, cuius curae nutu suo caelesti terrena omnia
moderanda commisit. The same idea is expressed throughout Eus. *Laud.
Const.*, particularly in the elaborate and to the modern reader almost
blasphemous analogy drawn between the relation of the Father to the Son,
and the Son and the emperor in the second chapter. *Sacer* came to mean simply
'imperial', σάκρα became the ordinary Greek for an imperial constitution,
e.g. *A.C.Oec.* I. i. pars ii. 80, iii. 31-2, v. 119, etc. For sacrilege see *CTh* I. vi.
9, VI. v. 2, xxiv. 4, xxix. 9, xxxv. 13, VII. iv. 30, viii. 10, etc.

2. *CJ* I. xiv. 4, digna vox maiestate regnantis legibus alligatum se principem
profiteri: adeo de auctoritate iuris nostra pendet auctoritas. et re vera maius
imperio est submittere legibus principatum, et oraculo praesentis edicti quod
nobis licere non patimur indicamus. Greg. *Ep.* XI. 4, cf. XIII. 34, hoc namque
inter reges gentium et reipublicae imperatores distat, quod reges gentium
domini servorum sunt, imperatores vero reipublicae domini liberorum.
Cf. Amb. *Ep.* 21 §9, leges enim imperator fert quas primus ipse custodiat.

3. Gregory Nazianzen states in plain language the various ways in which an
emperor might be legitimately created in *Or.* IV. 46, ἢ χρόνος ἢ ψῆφος βασιλέως
ἢ τῆς συγκλήτου βουλῆς, ὡς τὸ πάλαιον, κρίσις. Maj. *Nov.* i, 458, imperatorem
me factum, patres conscripti, vestrae electionis arbitrio et fortissimi exercitus
ordinatione cognoscite. For Leo, Anastasius and Justin see below, n. 7.

4. For Diocletian see ch. II, nn. 3, 4. For Constantine see ch. III, n. 15, IV, n. 1.
CONSTANTIUS II: Zos. II. 45, *Chron. Min.* I. 238, Aur. Victor, *Caes.* xlii. 8 (Gallus),
Amm. xv. viii. 1-17 (Julian).

5. THE USURPER CONSTANTINE: Zos. VI. 4, 13. THE USURPER BASILISCUS:
Candidus, 1. THEODOSIUS II AND VALENTINIAN III: Olymp. 46. Anthemius
was crowned as Augustus at Rome 12 April, 467 (*Chron. Min.* I. 305, II. 158),
but died on 11 July 472 (*Chron. Min.* I. 306), having reigned 5 years, 3 months
and 18 days (Joh. Ant. 209); he must therefore have been made Caesar on

25 March 467. LEO AND PATRICIUS: Candidus, 1, Malalas, 371–2. ZENO AND
BASILISCUS: Candidus, 1. For Justin II and Tiberius see ch. X, n. 7. Leo
also made his grandson Leo II Caesar before finally making him Augustus
(Const. Porph. *Cer.* I. 94).

6. VALENS: Amm. XXVI. iv. 3. Gratian: idem, XXVII. vi. 4–16; Ammianus
stresses the innovation, 'in hoc tamen negotio Valentinianus morem institutum
antiquitus supergressus non Caesares sed Augustos germanum nuncupavit et
filium benivole satis'. VALENTINIAN II: Amm. XXX. x. 4–6, Zos. IV. 19. THEO-
DOSIUS I: *Chron. Min.* I. 243. ARCADIUS AND HONORIUS: Zos. IV. 57, 59, *Chron.
Min.* I. 244, 298. THEODOSIUS II: *Chron. Min.* I. 299, II. 67.

7. Amm. XXV. v. 1, principio lucis secutae, quae erat quintum Kalendas Julias,
hostibus ex omni latere circumfusis, collecti duces exercitus, advocatisque
legionum principiis et turmarum, super creando principe consultabant,
XXVI. i. 3, progresso Nicaeam versus exercitu, quae in Bithynia mater est
urbium, potestatum civilium militiaeque rectores magnitudine curarum
adstricti communium, interque eos quidam spe vana sufflati, moderatorem
quaeritabant diu exploratum et gravem, XXVI. ii. 2, in unum quaesito milite
omni, progressus Valentinianus in campum permissusque tribunal ascendere
celsius structum comitiorum specie, voluntate praesentium secundissima ut vir
serius rector pronuntiatur imperii. For the later mention of the officers of
state or the palace see Const. Porph. *Cer.* I. 91, αὗται εὐχαὶ τοῦ παλατίου·
αὗται ἐντεύξεις τοῦ στρατοπέδου· αὗται εὐχαὶ τῆς συγκλήτου· αὗται εὐχαὶ τοῦ λαοῦ (Leo),
92, ὅτι καὶ πρὸ τῶν ὑμετέρων αἰτήσεων ἐκελεύσαμεν τοῖς ἐνδοξοτάτοις ἄρχουσι καὶ τῇ ἱερᾷ
συγκλήτῳ μετὰ κοινῆς τῶν γενναιοτάτων (ἐξερκίτων) δοκιμασίας ἄνδρα ἐπιλέξασθαι . . .
τοὺς ἐνδοξοτάτους ἄρχοντας καὶ τὴν ἱερὰν σύγκλητον, συντρεχούσης καὶ τῆς τῶν γενναιοτάτων ἐξερκίτων ψήφου . . . βουλευόμενοι μετὰ τῶν εὐδόξων ἀρχόντων καὶ τῆς ἱερᾶς συγκλήτου, συντρεχούσης καὶ τῆς τῶν γενναιοτάτων ἐξερκίτων συναινέσεως . . . τῶν ὑπερ-
φυεστάτων πρωτευόντων καὶ τῆς ἐνδοξοτάτης συγκλήτου ἡ ἐκλογὴ καὶ τῶν δυνατῶν στ-
ρατοπέδων τοῦ τε καθωσιωμένου λαοῦ ἡ συναίνεσις (Anastasius), *Coll. Avell.* 141,
proinde sanctitati vestrae per has sacras declaramus epistolas, quod primum
quidem inseparabilis Trinitatis favore, deinde amplissimorum procerum sacri
nostri palatii et sanctissimi senatus necnon electione fortissimi exercitus, ad
imperium nos licet nolentes ac recusantes electos fuisse atque firmatos (Justin I).

8. See ch. VIII, nn. 1, 2, 3, 5, 6, 10, 11. PETRONIUS MAXIMUS: Joh. Ant. 201. 6.
AVITUS: Sid. Ap. *Carm.* vii. 571 ff. Nepos' nomination by Leo is recorded only
in Jordanes, *Rom.* 338, but implied in Malachus, 10.

9. See ch. VII, nn. 1, 5, 16, IX, nn. 1, 4, X, n. 1.

10. All constitutions in the codes and novels are headed by the names of the
whole imperial college: the name of a colleague subsequently condemned as
a 'tyrant' was deleted, but Licinius' name has occasionally survived, e.g. *CJ*
VII. xvi. 41 and Aug. *Ep.* 88 §4, *c. Cresc.* III. 81. Even a personal letter like
that of Constantius Caesar to Eumenius (Pan. Lat. IX. 14) was headed by the
names of all four tetrarchs (ibid. 15 §2, 'in his imperatorum et Caesarum
litteris'). Conversely Anullinus proconsul of Africa addresses his letter to
Constantine 'Auggg. nnn.' (Aug. *Ep.* 88 §2), Symmachus addresses his *relationes*
as prefect of the city to Valentinian II, Theodosius and Arcadius (except for
three personal letters to Valentinian II, Symm. *Rel.*, 13, 14, 43), the younger
Symmachus as prefect of the city addresses Honorius and Theodosius II (*Coll.
Avell.* 14, 16, 34); and so do private petitioners (*Coll. Avell.* 2, 17). Cf. also
A.C.Oec. I. i. pars iii. 3, 10, 28, 32, 47, 63, 65; v. 7, vii. 78, 157, *Chr.* I. 6 (letters
and petitions to Theodosius II addressed to him and Valentinian III). For the

praetorian prefects see Opt. *App.* VIII, 'Petronius Annianus et Iulianus Domitio Celso vicario Africae' (praetorian prefects of Constantine and Licinius), Mansi, IV. 446, exemplar edicti propositi a Palladio pp. Iunius Quartus Palladius, Monaxius, et Agricola iterum, praefecti praetorio, edixerunt, *A.C.Oec.* I. iii. 38 (cf. I. i. pars iii. 69 for the Greek version), Flavius Anthemius Isidorus, Flavius Bassus, et Flavius Simplicius Reginus, praefecti, edixerunt, Just. *Nov.* clxvi: Φλάβιος Θεόδωρος Πέτρος Δημοσθένης, ὁ μεγαλοπρεπέστατος ἔπαρχος τῶν ἱερῶν πραιτωρίων καὶ ἀπὸ ἐπάρχων τῆς βασιλίδος πόλεως καὶ ἀπὸ ὑπάτων, Φλάβιος Φαῦστος καὶ Φλάβιος Στέφανος Φλαβίῳ Ὡρταλίνῳ τῷ λαμπροτάτῳ ὑπατικῷ Λυδίας, *IGC* 240 and 281 bis, [Φλ. Ἰο]υλειανὸς Πρίσκος [. . . . .] ὁ μεγαλοπρεπ' ἔ[παρ]χος τῶν [ἱερῶν] πρετορίων, Φλ. Βοήθιος, Φλ. Ἰωάννης.

11. For usurpers seeking recognition from a legitimate colleague see Lact. *Mort. Pers.* xxv (Constantine), Amm. xx. viii. 2-17 (Julian), Zos. IV. 37 (Maximus), 55 (Eugenius), v. 43 (Constantine III).

12. See ch. V, nn. 1, 2 (Salutius), VI, n. 5 (Constantius III), VIII, n. 2 (Avitus), X, n. 14 (Maurice). For Petronius Maximus' earlier career see *ILS* 809, Val. III, *Nov.* i. 2, iii, iv, vii. 1, x, 439-41, Sid. Ap. *Ep.* II. 13.

13. *MGH* (AA) XII. 425, aliquando Aspari a senatu dicebatur ut ipse fieret imperator, qui tale refertur dedisse responsum, 'timeo ne per me consuetudo in regno nascatur.' For the popular clamour against an Arian Caesar, see Zonaras, XIV. 1, *V. Marcelli*, 34 (*PG* CXVI. 741-4).

14. EUGENIUS AND JOHN: Soc. v. 25, VII. 23. ATTALUS: Zos. v. 44, 46, VI. 7. Olybrius is called a noble senator by Procopius (*BV* I. v. 6) and Evagrius (II. 7). MAJORIAN: *Chron. Min.* I. 305. GLYCERIUS: Joh. Ant. 209. For Marcian and Leo see ch. VII, nn. 1, 5.

15. GALERIUS, SEVERUS AND MAXIMIN: Lact. *Mort. Pers.* ix. 1, xviii. 12-3, xix. 6; Constantius is of course for obvious reasons declared to be of noble birth. THEODOSIUS: Amm. XXIX. vi. 15. For Tiberius see ch. X, n. 7, and for Anthemius, ch. VIII, n. 6. Julius Nepos was nephew of the patrician Marcellinus (*Chron. Min.* II. 91) and *magister militum Dalmatiae* in 473 (*CJ* VI. lxi. 5).

16. JOVIAN: Amm. XXV. v. 4. EQUITIUS AND VALENTINIAN: idem, XXVI. i. 4, 5. For Anastasius and Justin see ch. VII, n. 29, ch. IX, n. 1.

17. SILVANUS: Amm. XV. v. VETRANIO: Zos. II. 43. MAGNENTIUS: idem, II. 42. MAXIMUS: idem, IV. 35, Orosius, VII. xxxiv. 9. CONSTANTINE III: Orosius, VII. xl. 4. PHOCAS: Theoph. Sim. VIII. 7. THEODORE: Amm. XXIX. i. 8. Other very humble candidates for the throne were Maximianus, the domestic of Aetius, son of an Egyptian merchant, who was a rival of Petronius Maximus (Joh. Ant. 201. 6), and Theocritus, the domestic of Amantius, the *praepositus sacri cubiculi*, who was to have succeeded Anastasius (Malalas, 410, *Chron. Min.* II. 101).

18. ROUTINE CONSULTATION OF THE SENATE OF CONSTANTINOPLE: *V. Mel.* (G), 44, Proc. *HA* xiv. 7, 8. SENATE CONDEMNS STILICHO: Zos. v. 11; GILDO: Claudian, *de cos. Stil.* I. 326-32; VITALIAN: Joh. Ant. *Exc. de Insid.* 103. DEBATE ON ALARIC: Zos. v. 29; cf. also VI, 12, ἐπὶ τούτοις Ἄτταλος καταλαβὼν τὴν Ῥώμην συνάγει τὴν γερουσίαν, καὶ βουλῆς προτεθείσης ἅπαντες μὲν ὡς εἰπεῖν ἐδοκίμαζον καὶ βαρβάρους χρῆναι μετὰ τῶν στρατιωτῶν εἰς τὴν Λιβύην ἐκπέμψαι. Here again the senate was compelled to ratify an unpopular decision.

19. LEO AND ASPAR: *V. Dan.* 55. ZENO AND THE THEODERICS: Malchus, 11. Other votes of the Constantinopolitan senate are recorded in Zos. IV. 43-4 (war with the usurper Maximus), v. 20 (the appointment of Fravitta as *magister militum*), Candidus, 1, μετὰ τελευτὴν Λέοντος ὁ παῖς Λέων Ζήνωνα τὸν πατέρα

συναισέσει τῆς βουλῆς βασιλέα ἔστεψε. It was suggested that the tangled issues of the Council of Ephesus should be judged at Constantinople εἴτε ἐπὶ τοῦ εὐσεβεστάτου βασιλέως δέοι εἴτε ἐν κονσιστορίῳ εἴτε ἐπὶ τῆς ἱερᾶς συγκλήτου (*A.C.Oec.* I. i. pars iii. 37, cf. I. iv. pars ii. 63 for the Latin version); cf. *A.C.Oec.* I. iv. pars ii. 80, omni amico Christi consistorio sive senatui, 65, omnem senatum ⟨et⟩ qui erant in consistorio (but the latter is a mistranslation of I. i. pars vii. 77, ὅλον τὸ κονσιστόριον). Anastasius brought the question of the *collatio lustralis* before the senate (Evagr. III. 39), but probably only to announce its abolition.

20. JULIUS' PLAN: Zos. IV. 26. THE SENATE AND ALARIC: Zos. V. 40 ff., VI. 6–7.

21. LEGAL FORCE OF SENATUS CONSULTA: *Dig.* I. ii. 2 §9, iii. 9, cf. Gaius, I. 4, confirmed by *CJ* I. xvi. 1, 384, quamvis consultum senatus perpetuam per se obtineat firmitatem, *Inst.* I. ii. 5, senatus consultum est, quod senatus iubet atque constituit. nam cum auctus est populus Romanus in eum modum, ut difficile sit in unum eum convocare legis sanciendae causa, aequum visum est senatum vice populi consuli. For the citation of the imperial *oratio* see *Dig.* II. xv. 8 pr., XXIV. i. 23, XXVII. ix. 1 §1, XL. xv. 1 §3. THE LAW OF CITATIONS: *CTh* I. iv. 3+IV. i. 1+V. i. 8+VIII. xiii. 6+xviii. 9+10+xix. 1+*CJ* I. xiv. 2 +3+xix. 7+xxii. 5+VI. xxx. 18, 426. Other constitutions on private law addressed to the senate include *CTh* VIII. xviii. 1, 315 (S), IX. xiii. 1, 365, *CJ* VI. xxx. 22, 531, II. xliv. 4+III. xxxviii. 12+V. iv. 24+VI. xxv. 7, 530. Constitutions on the codification of the law are also addressed to the senate, *CTh* I. i. 5, 429, and Justinian's 'Haec', 'Cordi' and 'Tanta'.

22. *CTh, Gesta Senatus.*

23. *CJ* I. xiv. 8, 446, humanum esse probamus, si quid de cetero in publica vel in privata causa emerserit necessarium, quod formam generalem et antiquis legibus non insertam exposcat, id ab omnibus antea tam proceribus nostri palatii quam gloriosissimo coetu vestro, patres conscripti, tractari et, si universis tam iudicibus quam vobis placuerit, tunc allegata dictari et sic ea denuo collectis omnibus recenseri et, cum omnes consenserint, tunc demum in sacro nostri numinis consistorio recitari, ut universorum consensus nostrae serenitatis auctoritate firmetur.

24. THE ALTAR OF VICTORY: Amb. *Ep.* 17, 18, 57, Symm. *Rel.* 3. Constitutions addressed to the senate on the privileges of the order are *CTh* XV. xiv. 4, 326, I. xxviii. 1+ VII. viii. 1+XI. i. 7+XV. 1+xxiii. 1+XII. i. 48+XIII. i. 3+ XV. i. 7, 361, IX. i. 13, 376, X. xix. 8, 376, *CJ* III. xxiv. 2 (376), *CTh* VI. ii. 17+18, 397, I. vi. 11+II. i. 12, 423, *CJ* X. xxxii. 63 (471–4); on the praetorship, *CTh* VI. iv. 5+6, 340, 8+9, 356, 10, 356, 11, 357, 14+15, 359, 16, 359, 12+13, 361, 19, 372, 22+23, 373, 24, 376, 25, 384, 31, 397, Th. II, *Nov.* xv. 1, 439; on the corn supply of Rome, *CTh* XIII. v. 27+ix. 5+XIV. xv. 3, 397; on the buildings of Rome, *CTh* XV. i. 19, 376; on the *haruspices*, *CTh* IX. xvi. 9, 371.

25. Symm. *Rel.* 8, *CTh* XV. ix. 1+*CJ* I. xvi. 1, 384.

26. Marc. *Nov.* v pr., 455, nuper cum de testamento clarissimae memoriae feminae Hypatiae, quae inter alios virum religiosum Anatolium presbyterum in portione manifesta bonorum scripsit heredem, amplissimo senatu praesente tractaret pietas mea, Just. *Nov.* lxii, 1 §2, 537, et quia magna utilitas ex iudicandi sinceritate reipublicae nostrae cedit, quaedam autem causae post appellationes iudicibus porrectas in sacrum nostri numinis consistorium inferuntur et a nostris proceribus examinantur, idcirco nobis ⟨placuit⟩ non solum iudices nostros, sed etiam senatores ad examinandas lites in consultationibus conve-

nientes una cum aliis florentissimis nostris proceribus litium facta trutinare, et quemadmodum, si quando silentium ob alia una cum conventu fuerit nuntiatum, omnes colliguntur et proceres et senatores, ita et nunc, quando silentium tantummodo propter alicuius causae examinationem pronuntietur, etsi non addatur conventus vocabulum, tamen eos convenire et omnes consedentes quod eis visum fuerit sub sacrosanctorum evangeliorum praesentia et statuere et ad nostram referre scientiam et augustae maiestatis dispositionem expectare: a solis senatoribus, sed ab utroque ordine, huiusmodi litibus exercendis.

27. In *CTh* VI. xxx. 1, 379, and 4, 378 (S), *comites consistoriani* denote the *comites sacrarum largitionum* and *rei privatae*. The term is used to cover all four offices in *CTh* VII. viii. 3, 384, eos, qui ex praefectis summum sibi fastigium dignitatis agendo pepererunt, et ex magistris equitum ac peditum, quos decursi actus inlustrat auctoritas, adque ex comitibus consistorianis, qui participantes augusti pectoris curas agendo claruerunt, ex praepositis quoque sacri cubiculi, quos tanta et tam adsidua nostri numinis' cura inter primas posuit dignitates, and *CJ* II. xii. 25, 392, quicumque praetorianae vel urbanae praefecturae sublimissimae fastigium vel magisterium militare vel consistorianae comitivae insignia meruerit dignitatis vel proconsulare ius dixerit aut vicarii fuerit administratione subfultus. The quaestor, *magister officiorum* and *comes sacrarum largitionum* are present at a consistory in *CTh* XI. xxxix. 5, 362, pars actorum habitorum aput imperatorem Iulianum Augustum Mamertino et Nevitta conss. X Kal. April. Constan(tin)op(oli) in consistorio: adstante Iovio viro clarissimo quaestore, Anatolio magistro officiorum, Felice com(ite) sacrarum largitionum; the quaestor in Amm. XXVIII. i. 25, qui cum intromissi in consistorium haec referrent, negantem Valentinianum se id statuisse et calumnias perpeti clamitantem moderate redarguit quaestor Eupraxius; the *comes sacrarum largitionum* in Amm. XVI. viii. 7, spretis, qui prohibebant, perrupit intrepidus ingressusque consistorium ore et pectore libero docuit gesta. The praetorian prefect has been denied a seat on the ground that he is never styled *comes*. Amm. XIV. vii. 11 is ambiguous, for the fact that the newly appointed praetorian prefect Domitianus was 'rogatus ad ultimum admissusque in consistorium' may mean that he was invited to take his seat or that he was received, like an ambassador. That the military officers were members is deduced from their title *comes*; Arbetio, *magister equitum in praesenti*, takes part in the consistory of Amm. XV. v. 8 and the two *magistri praesentales*, Bauto and Rumoridus, in that of Amb. *Ep.* 57 §3. For the *comes domesticorum* see *CJ* XII. xvi. 1, 415, decuriones nostri palatii post emensum fideliter obsequium postque deposita sacramenta militiae electionem habeant, sive ex magistro officiorum velut agentes dignitatem consequi a nostra maiestate maluerint, sive inter vires illustres comites domesticorum, videlicet inter agentes, taxari, ut tam in adoranda nostra serenitate quam in salutandis administratoribus et reliquis praedicti honoris privilegiis nec non in nostro consistorio his honor omnifariam observetur.

28. It appears from *CJ* XII. xvi. 1 (cited in n. 27) that titular (and therefore presumably real) ex-masters of the offices and *comites domesticorum* were members of the consistory by 415. Examples of men made *comites consistoriani* after a vicariate or proconsulship are *ILS* 1240, L. Aradio Val. Proculo—praesidi provinciae Byzacenae, consulari provinciae Europae et Thraciae, consulari provinciae Siciliae, comiti ordinis secundi, comiti ordinis primi, proconsuli provinciae Africae—comiti iterum ordinis primi intra palatium, praefecto urbi, *ILS* 1254, Fl. Sallustio v.c. cons. ordinario, praef. praet., comiti consistorii, vicario urbi Romae, vicario Hispaniarum, vicario quinq. provinciarum,

ILS 1255, Saturninio Secundo v.c. praesidi provinciae Aquitanicae, magistro memoriae, comiti ordinis primi, proconsuli Africae, item comiti ordinis primi intra consistorium et quaestori, praef. praetorio iterum; after a *consularitas*, *ILS* 1225, Mavortii. Fl. Lolliano v.c.q.k. praet. urb., curat. alvei Tiberis et operum maximorum et aquarum, cons. Camp., comiti intra pal[atium] et [v]ice sa[cra iudicanti, comiti] Ori[entis]. . . . *ILS* 1237, Vulcacio Rufino v.c., cons. ordin., prae[f.] praetorio, comiti per Orientem, Ae[g]ypti et Mesopotamiae, per [e]asdem vice sacra iudicanti, comiti ordinis primi intra consistorium, Numidiae consulari, *ILS* 1243, Memmio Vitrasio Orfito v.c.,—praef. urbi, non multo interposito tempore iterum praef. urbi, proconsuli Africae, comiti ordinis primi, item comiti intra consistorium ordinis primi, legato petitu senatus populiq. Romani, comiti ordinis secundi, consulari provinciae Siciliae; after the prefecture of the city, *ILS* 1232, . . . [comiti Ori]entis v.s. iudicanti, procons. prov. Africae et v.s. iudicanti, praef. urbis et v.s. iudicanti, iterum comiti ord. primi intra palatium, praef. praet., consuli ord. By the sixth century the Augustal prefect and proconsuls were made *comites consistoriani* as a regular rule, but by this time the title had no practical significance (Const. Porph. *Cer.* I. 85). RETIRED DUCES: *CTh* VI. iv. 28, 396, qui ducatum administrarunt ad editionem vel nominationem praeturae pertineant praeter eos, qui gravissimam armatae militiae sollicitudinem longa temporum serie pertulerunt et eos, qui sacri consistorii nostri arcanis interesse meruerunt. hos enim a praeturae munere alienos esse censemus. It seems likely that *comites rei militaris* were automatically members of the consistory, if only nominal ones. PALATINE OFFICIALS: *ILS* 1244, Fl. Eugenio v.c., ex praefecto praetorio, consuli ordinario designato, magistro officiorum omnium, comiti domestico ordinis primi omnibusque palatinis dignitatibus functo. CONSTANTIUS' COMITES: Ath. *Hist. Ar.* 22, καὶ γὰρ καὶ τοὺς κόμητας αὐτοῦ πεποίηκε γράψαι, Πολέμιον, Δατιανόν, Βαρδίωνα, Θάλασσιον, Ταῦρον καὶ Φλωρέντιον, οἷς καὶ μᾶλλον πιστεύειν ἦν. For Taurus' career see *AE* 1934, 159, v.c. Tauro comiti ordinis primi quaestori sacri palatii patricia dignitate praef. praet. per Italiam atque Africam, Amm. XIV. xi. 14 (quaestor in 354), XXI. vi. 5 (praetorian prefect in 360), Lib. *Or.* XLII. 24–5 (notary). Thalassius was at court in 351 (Zos II. 48) and appointed praetorian prefect to Gallus (Amm. XIV. i. 10). Florentius was made praetorian prefect to Julian in 357 (Amm. XVI. xii. 14). Polemius was consul in 338 but is not known to have held any office; he was probably, like Datianus (see n. 29), an imperial favourite. Bardio is otherwise unknown (a German general?).

29. NUMMIUS ALBINUS: *ILS* 1238, Triturrii. M. Nummio Albino v.c. quaestori candidato, praetori urbano, comiti domestico ordinis primi et consuli ordinario iterum, Nummius Secundus eius. DATIANUS: Lib. *Or.* XLII. 24–5 (a notary of humble origins), Ath. *Hist. Ar.* 22 (see n. 28, an important *comes* in 346), Philostorgius, VIII. 8 (a patrician and an influential man in 364); he obtained but thought it wiser to renounce the extraordinary privilege of immunity from taxation (*CTh* XI. i. 1, 360 (S); he was already patrician at this date, having been consul in 358).

30. Amm. XV. v. 5–8.

31. Amm. XV. v. 18–22.

32. THE PETITION OF THE GOTHS: Eunap. 42, ἐντεῦθεν ἀναφέρεται μὲν ἐπὶ τὸν βασιλέα ἡ γνῶσις· πολλῆς δὲ ἀντιλογίας γενομένης, καὶ πολλῶν ἐφ' ἑκάτερα γνωμῶν ἐν τῷ βασιλικῷ συλλόγῳ ῥηθεισῶν, ἔδοξε τῷ βασιλεῖ; cf. Amm. XXXI. iv. 4. THE ALTAR OF VICTORY: Amb. *Ep.* 57 §3, lecti sunt mei libelli in consistorio, aderat amplissimus honore magisterii militaris Bauto comes et Rumoridus et ipse eiusdem

dignitatis. THE ARIAN BASILICA: Amb. *c. Aux.* 29, de imperatore vult invidiam commovere, dicens indicare debere adulescentem catechumenum, sacrae lectionis ignarum, et in consistorio indicare, quasi vero superiore anno quando ad palatium sum petitus, cum praesentibus primatibus ante consistorium tractaretur, cum imperator basilicam vellet eripere, ego tunc aulae contemplatione regalis infractus sum, *Ep.* 21 §20, dignanter igitur, imperator, accipe quod ad consistorium venire non potui. The consistory also dealt (or was asked to deal) with the problems of the Council of Ephesus (*A.C.Oec.* 1. i. pars vii. 74, καὶ ἐπὶ τῆς ὑμετέρας εὐσεβείας καὶ ἐπὶ τοῦ λαμπροῦ κονσιστορίου, 79, ἐπὶ τοῦ εὐσεβεστάτου βασιλέως καὶ τοῦ λαμπροῦ κονσιστορίου, 80, ἢ ἐπὶ τοῦ εὐσεβεστάτου βασιλέως ἢ ἐπὶ τοῦ λαμπροῦ κονσιστορίου, 1. iv. pars ii. 162, in consistorio et coram piissimo et amico Christi imperatore nostro): cf. also n. 19.

33. THE QUADI: Amm. XXX. vi. 2–3. AMBROSE AND MAXIMUS: Amb. *Ep.* 24 §§2–3.

34. ADMINISTRATIVE QUESTIONS: *CTh* I. xxii. 4, 383, pars actorum habitorum in consistorio Gratiani A. Gratianus A. dixit. det operam iudex, ut praetorium suum ipse componat. ceterum neque comiti neque rectori provinciae plus aliquid praestabitur, quam nos concessimus in annonis seu cellariis. PETITIONS: *Sirm.* 3, 384, denique lectis in consistorio precibus, quibus episcopalis pietas aliquid postulans refragatur. DELEGATIONS: Amm. XXVIII. i. 25 (see n. 27), vi. 9, venerunt in comitatum legati, aditoque principe, verbis, quae perpessi sunt, ostenderunt: obtulerunt decreta, textum continentia rei totius. quibus lectis cum neque relationi officiorum magistri faventis Romani flagitiis, nec contraria referentibus crederetur promissa disceptatio plena dilata est eo more, quo solent inter potiorum occupationes ludi potestates excelsae.

35. *CTh* XII. xii. 4, 364, 10, 385, quotienscumque ex diversis provinciis ad sacrum mansuetudinis nostrae comitatum legationes, quas instruxere decreta, necesse erit commeare, in auditorio quidem celsitudinis tuae universa tractentur, sed ita, ut nullum finem capiat ordo gestorum inlibataque rerum decisio singularum nostro auditui sententiaeque servetur, ita ut deinceps excellentia tua, cum in consistorio mansuetudinis nostrae secundum consuetudinem ex decretis petitiones legatorum de nostris scriniis recitantur, motum proprii arbitrii ratione decursa sententiis, quas pandimus, referat.

36. Amm. XXX. v. 8–10.

37. LARGESSES: Amm. XVI. v. 11, inductis quadam sollemnitate agentibus in rebus in consistorium ut aurum acciperent, inter alios quidam ex eorum consortio, non ut moris est pansa chlamyde sed utraque manu cavata suscepit, et imperator 'rapere' inquit 'non accipere sciunt agentes in rebus'. APPOINTMENTS: *CJ* XII. viii. 2 (441), omnes privilegia dignitatum hoc ordine servanda cognoscant, ut primo loco habeantur ii, qui in actu positi illustres peregerint administrationes: secundo venient vacantes, qui praesentes in comitatu illustris dignitatis cingulum meruerint: tertium ordinem eorum prospicimus, quibus absentibus cingulum illustris mittitur dignitatis: quartum honorariorum, qui praesentes a nostro numine sine cingulo codicillos tantum honorariae dignitatis adepti sunt: quintum eorum quibus absentibus similiter sine cingulo mittuntur illustris insignia dignitatis. That these appointments were made in consistory is proved by the passages from Peter the Patrician cited in n. 39.

38. THE LIMITANEI: Th. II, *Nov.* xxiv §5, 443, id autem curae perpetuae tui culminis credimus iniungendum, ut tam Thracici, quam Illyrici, nec non etiam Orientalis ac Pontici limitis, Aegyptiaci insuper, Thebaici, Lybici quemadmodum se militum numerus habeat, castrorumque ac lusoriarum cura

procedat, quotannis mense Ianuario in sacro consistorio significare nobis propria suggestione procures, ut, uniuscuiusque tam industria quam desidia nostris auribus intimata, et strenui digna praemia consequantur, et in dissimulatores competens indignatio proferatur. For legislation see above n. 23.

39. LAWS READ IN CONSISTORY: *CJ* I. ii. 22, xiv. 12, II. lv. 4, IV. i. 12, xxxiv. 11, v. xii. 31, xxx. 5, VI. iv. 3, xxx. 19, xlii. 30, lxi. 6, VII. xiv. 13, 14, VIII. liii. 34, XI. xlviii. 20. RECEPTION OF PERSIAN ENVOYS: Const. Porph. *Cer.* I. 89-90; ch. 87-8 deal with the reception of envoys from a Western Augustus, precedents from two generations before which Peter may have recorded for antiquarian interest, or may have thought useful in case of a possible re-establishment of the Western Empire. APPOINTMENT OF THE COMES ADMISSIONUM: Const. Porph. *Cer.* I. 84, ὁ κόμης τῶν ἀδμηνσιόνων ἐπὶ σιλεντίου γίνεται, καὶ καθημένου τοῦ βασιλέως ἐν κονσιστωρίῳ, πολλάκις δὲ καὶ εἰς ἱππικὸν ἀνιὼν ποιεῖ αὐτὸν ἐν τῷ μεγάλῳ τρικλίνῳ, ἐν ᾧ τόπῳ δέχεται τοὺς ἄρχοντας; OF THE COMITES SCHOLARUM AND THE CURAE PALATII: ibid. I. 84, τοὺς δὲ κόμητας σχολῶν ἢ κουροπαλάτας ἐὰν βουληθῇ ἐν κονσιστωρίῳ προαγαγεῖν, ὡς ἐπὶ τῶν ἄλλων προαγαγῶν καὶ τούτους ποιεῖ· ὡς ἐπὶ πολὺ δὲ κατέσχεν ἔθος ἰδίᾳ ἐν τῷ κουβουκλείῳ γίνεσθαι αὐτοὺς καὶ πρὸ ἀρίστου καὶ δείλης, ὡς ἂν δόξῃ τῷ βασιλεῖ; OF THE AUGUSTAL PREFECT: ibid. I. 85, τὰ μανδάτα δίδεται τῇ πρὸ μιᾶς σιλεντίου, καὶ τὸν αὐγουστάλιον ᾿Αλεξανδρείας ἔπαυσεν. καὶ μετὰ τὸ γενέσθαι πάντα τὰ ἐξ ἔθους δίδωσιν αὐτῷ κωδικέλλια; OF PROTECTORES, PROTECTORES DOMESTICI AND CANDIDATI: ibid. I. 86 . . . νῦν δὲ προβατωρείαν ποιεῖ ὁ δεσπότης, καὶ προσάγει αὐτὸν ὁ δηκουρίων ἀτραβατικὸν φοροῦντα χλανίδιν, ἢ ἐν κονσιστωρίῳ μετὰ τὸ πάντα πραχθῆναι, ἢ ἀνιόντος αὐτοῦ εἰς τὸ ἱππικὸν ἵσταται ἐμπρὸς τοῦ δέλφακος, . . . καὶ ταῦτα μὲν ἡ συνήθεια· ὁ μέντοι εὐσεβὴς ἡμῶν δεσπότης πολλάκις καὶ ἐν φερίαις καὶ ἔσω καθήμενος ἐκέλευσεν γενέσθαι πάσας ταύτας τὰς στρατίας καὶ δίχα σιλεντίου.

40. For the distinction between the formal reception of envoys and the actual negotiations see Const. Porph. *Cer.* I. 89-90. For the report on the *limitanei* note that *CJ* I. xxxi. 4 omits 'mense Ianuario in sacro consistorio' from Th. II, *Nov.* xxiv. ANASTASIUS AND THE CONSISTORY: Zach. Myt. *Chron.* VII. 7-8.

41. PROCERES PALATII: *CJ* I. xiv. 8, 446 (cited in n. 23), cf. Const. Porph. *Cer.* I. 91-2, *Coll. Avell.* 141 (cited in n. 7), and especially Const. Porph. *Cer.* I. 92, οἱ δὲ ἥκοντες, τεθέντων σκαμνίων πρὸ τοῦ δέλφακος, ἐκάθισαν, καὶ ἤρξαντο βουλεύεσθαι περὶ τοῦ ὀφείλοντος γενέσθαι, καὶ πολλὴ φιλονεικεία μεταξὺ αὐτῶν ἐκινήθη. ὁ δὲ πραιπόσιτος Οὐρβίκιος εὐφυέστερον ἐδήλωσεν αὐτοῖς, ὅτι καλῶς ποιεῖτε τῇ αὐγούστῃ παρέχοντες τὴν αὐθεντείαν, ἵνα αὐτὴ ἐπιλέξηται, ὃν ἂν βουληθείη . . ., καὶ ὀψὲ ἐδόθη τά μανδάτα σιλέντιον καὶ κομέντον, καὶ τῇ ἑξῆς προῆλθον πάντες ἀπὸ λευκῶν χλανιδίων, καὶ ἐδέχθησαν ἐν τῷ κονσιστωρίῳ.

42. *A.C.Oec.* II. i. 334-5, iii. 407-9. For the status of the *praepositus sacri cubiculi* see *CTh* VI. viii. 1, 422.

43. Th. II, *Nov.* vii. 2, 440, 3, 440, 4, 441.

44. *CTh* XI. vii. 17, 408, 18, 409.

45. For Justina, Pulcheria and Galla Placidia see ch. V, n. 51, ch. VI, n. 1. EUTROPIUS: Zos. v. 8-12, Claudian, *in Eutrop.* I. 170 ff., II. 58 ff., *V. Porph.* 26. For Chrysaphius see ch. VI, n. 13.

46. ARBOGAST: Zos. IV. 53, Joh. Ant. 187, Soz. VII. 22. For Stilicho and the *magisterium militiae* see ch. VI, n. 2.

47. VALENTINIAN III AND ARBOGAST: Zos. IV. 53-4. FALL OF STILICHO: Zos. V. 32-4. MURDER OF AETIUS: Joh. Ant. 201. 2.

48. See ch. VI, nn. 9-13.

49. For Aspar and Marcian see ch. VII, nn. 1, 2, Aspar and Leo, ch. VII, nn. 5, 7, 8, 10–12.

50. TITLE OF PATRICIAN: *ILS* 801, 8992 (Constantius), 1293, 1298 (Felix), Val. III, *Nov.* xxxiii (Aetius), *ILS* 813, 1294, Maj. *Nov.* i, xi (Ricimer). CONSTANTIUS AND THE URBAN PREFECT: *Coll. Avell.* 29–32. AETIUS AND THE ROMAN SEE: Val. III, *Nov.* xvii §4, 445; AND THE ROMAN PORK SUPPLY: Val. III, *Nov.* xxxvi pr., 452, non miramur inter bellicas curas et obstrepentes lituos ordinatione magnifici viri parentis patriciique nostri Aetii formam publicae dispositionis in meliorem statum fuisse mutatam, cuius sollicitudini facillimum effectum praestitit amplitudinis vestrae in aeternum consulens laudanda provisio, quae sacrae urbis privilegiis et administrantis providentia et optimi civis affectione subvenit, cf. also Val. III, *Nov.* i, 3 §4, 450, utrum mitti debeat inspector publicus tractatus ante deliberet sublimis viri parentis patriciique nostri, nec non magnifici viri praefecti praetorio, qui communionis utilitate virtutum suarum magnitudinem nobiscum pervigiles et cogitant et tuentur: cum aulicis potestatibus pro sua moderatione disponant, si iusta necessitas cogit, qualis persona mittatur.

51. For Stilicho and the military offices see ch. VI, n. 2. NOMUS AND THE LIMITANEI: Th. II, *Nov.* xxiv, 443, cf. *Nov.* xxiii §2, 443, where the enforcement of a law on civic lands is entrusted to Apollonius, praetorian prefect of the East, 'una cum viro inlustri magistro officiorum, cuius administratio probatissima nobis est'. THE MASSACRE OF STILICHO'S MEN: Zos. V. 32.

52. *V. Porph.* 26–7.

53. Ibid. 37–41.

54. Ibid. 42–51.

55. *A.C.Oec.* I. iv. pars ii. 224–5.

56. EUSEBIUS: Amm. XVIII. iv. 3. MARINUS AND THE VINDICES: Joh. Lydus, *Mag.* II. 46, 49; AND SABA: Cyr. Scyth. *V. Sabae*, 54 (this incident proves that *vindices* were instituted some time before). For the dates of Marinus' prefecture see Bury, *Later Roman Empire*, I². 470.

57. *CJ* I. xiv. 3, 426, leges ut generales ab omnibus aequabiliter in posterum observentur quae vel missa ad venerabilem coetum oratione conduntur vel inserto edicti vocabulo nuncupantur, sive eas nobis spontaneus motus ingesserit sive precatio vel relatio vel lis mota legis occasionem postulaverit. Cf. Just. *Nov.* ii pr., 535, καὶ τοῖς πρὸ ἡμῶν νενομοθετηκόσι Ῥωμαίοις τῆς ἀεὶ νομοθεσίας ἀφορμὴν ἡ τῶν ἀναφυομένων πραγμάτων ἐδίδου ποικιλία, καὶ ἡμεῖς, τὸ νομοθετικὸν ἅπαν κατακοσμήσαντες τῆς πολιτείας μέρος, τὴν ὅλην σχεδὸν ἐπανόρθωσιν ποτὲ μὲν ἐπὶ ταῖς τῶν δεομένων προσαγγελίαις, ποτὲ δὲ ἐπὶ ταῖς δικαστικαῖς ζητήσεσιν ἐποιησάμεθα· καί πολλούς γε τῶν νόμων ἐντεῦθεν τοῖς ὑπηκόοις τοῖς ἡμετέροις ἐγράψαμεν.

58. For Justinian's legal reforms see pp. 477–9. ANTIOCHUS: *CTh* I. v. 5, 429, 6, 435, Th. II, *Nov.* i, 438. For the legal reform of 426 see above n. 21 (the law of citations).

59. Marc. *Nov.* v, 455 (repealing *CTh* XVI. ii. 20), Just. *Nov.* xiv, 535, xli, 537, lxxiii, lxxvi, 538, lxxxviii, xci, 539, cviii, 541.

60. Marc. *Nov.* iv, 454, Maj. *Nov.* ix, 459. Cf. also *Sirm.* 1, 333, *CJ* VI. lxi. 5, 473, Just. *Nov.* cxii, 541, cxv, 542, pervenit ad scientiam nostrae serenitatis, quod [cum] inter Eustathium virum reverentissimum Tloae civitatis episcopum et Pistum diaconum ecclesiae Telmissenae fuisset causa commota, processit a rectore provinciae definitiva sententia, contra quam appellatio est porrecta.

iudices igitur, apud quos appellatio ventilabatur, dubitantes ad nostram clementiam retulerunt. A curious *relatio* is that of the emperor Anthemius to his senior colleague Leo (Anth. *Nov.* ii-iii, 468).

61. Just. *Nov.* clxii, 539: ἐπύθετο ἡμῶν ἡ σὴ ἐνδοξότης περί τινων ἀμφισβητουμένων παρὰ τῶν ἐλλογιμωτάτων τῆς παρὰ ᾽Ιλλυριοῖς ἀγορᾶς τῆς δίκης ἀγωνιστῶν, ἅπερ ἔφησας ἡμετέρας διακρίσεως δεῖσθαι, ὥστε μὴ διηνεκῶς στασιάζεσθαι, *CJ* II. iii. 30, 531, de quaestione tali a Caesariensi advocatione interrogati sumus; cf. also *CJ* VI. xxxviii. 5, 532, suggestioni Illyricianae advocationis respondentes decernimus familiae nomen talem habere vigorem.

62. LEONIUS AND PELAGIA: Val. III, *Nov.* xxi. 1, 446, 2, 446. GREGORIA, MARTHA AND THECLA: Just. *Nov.* ii, 535, clv, 533, clviii, 544. ARISTOCRATES: Just. *Nov.* clx (undated). ANDREW: Just. *Nov.* cliii, 541. Other laws provoked by private petitions are Val. III, *Nov.* viii. 1, 440, 2, 441, Anth. *Nov.* i, 468, Just. *Nov.* xciii, 540, cxxxv (undated), clix, 555.

63. BOTTOMRY LOANS: Just. *Nov.* cvi, 540, repealed by cx, 541. ARGENTARII: Just. *Nov.* cxxxvi, 535, *Ed.* vii, 542, ix (undated). CURIALES: Just. *Nov.* ci, 539. There are general references to litigants in Just. *Nov.* i, 535, liii, 537, xciv, xcviii, 539.

64. VINDICES: Joh. Lydus, *Mag.* III. 46, 49. THE CURRENCY: Malalas, 400. SILIQUATICUM: Val. III, *Nov.* xv, 444. ABOLITION OF THE COLLATIO LUSTRALIS: Evagr. III. 39.

65. Th. II, *Nov.* xviii, 439, fidem de exemplis praesentibus mereantur historiae, et omni dehinc ambiguitate liberetur antiquitas, quae nobis summos viros praetulisse rem publicam facultatibus indicavit, cum virum illustrem Florentium, praefecturae praetorianae administratione subfultum, cernamus non iam cum maiorum laudibus, sed cum suis magnis in rem publicam meritis praeclari animi aemula virtute certantem existimationem rei publicae non solum consilio suo ac providentia, sed etiam devotione ac munificentia pudendae turpitudinis labe atque ignominia liberasse. nam cum lenonum calliditate damnabili circumventam veterum videret incuriam, ut sub cuiusdam lustralis praestationis obtentu corrumpendi pudoris liceret exercere commercium, nec iniuriam sui ipsam quodammodo ignaram cohibere rem publicam, pio circa omnium verecundiam proposito mansuetudini nostrae amore pudicitiae castitatisque suggessit ad iniuriam nostrorum temporum pertinere, si aut lenones in hac liceret urbe versari, aut eorum turpissimo quaestu aerarium videretur augeri. ac licet nos illud adverteret execrari etiam cessante vicaria oblatione vectigal, tamen, ne ullum ad aerarium incommodum perveniret, propriam possessionem obtulit, ex cuius reditibus possit accedere, quod praedictum pessimum genus consueverat pensitare. Cf. *CTh* xv. viii. 2, 428.

66. Amb. *Ep.* 40 §4, praesertim cum etiam imperatoribus non displiceat suo quemque fungi munere, et patienter audiatis unumquemque pro sua suggerentem officio, imo corripiatis si non utatur militiae suae ordine.

67. MAGISTER OFFICIORUM: *CTh* VII. viii. 8, 405, Th. II, *Nov.* vi, 438 (*fabricae*), xxv, 444 (*metata*), xxi, 441 (*scholae*), Val. III, *Nov.* xxviii, 449 (*agentes in rebus*), xxx, 450 (*lampadarii*). COMES SACRARUM LARGITIONUM: *CTh* VI. xxx. 8, 385, Val. III, *Nov.* vii. 3, 447 (*palatini*), xxiv, 447 (*collatio lustralis*), Th. II, *Nov.* xvii. 1, 439, suggestionem viri illustris comitis sacrarum largitionum Marcellini, vicem agentis viri illustris comitis rerum privatarum, admodum comprobamus (*petitiones*). COMES REI PRIVATAE: Th. II, *Nov.* v. i, 438, xix, 440 (*res dominica*), Maj. *Nov.* v, 458 (*caduca*), Just. *Nov.* cxxxix (535-6) (incest); cf. Val. III, *Nov.*

i. 3 §7, 450. MAGISTRI MILITUM: Th. II, *Nov.* vii. 4, 441. PRAEFECTUS PRAETORIO:
Th. II, *Nov.* vii. 1, 439, 2, 440 (*praescriptio fori*); xiii, 439 (*supplicatio*); v. 2, 439,
3, 441 (*fundi limitotrofi*); xx, 440 (*adluviones*); Val. III, *Nov.* vii. 1, 440, 2, 442,
Just. *Ed.* ii (531-5) (tax collection), Val. III, *Nov.* i. 1, 438, 2, 440, iv, 440,
Marc. *Nov.* ii, 450, cf. Th. II, *Nov.* xxvi, 444, referring to the 'dispositio
amplissimae recordationis Antiochi' and the law 'quae ad viri inlustris et
consularis Florentii suggestionem emissa est' (remissions); Val. III, *Nov.* ii. 2,
442, Th. II, *Nov.* x. 1, 439 (advocates); Marc. *Nov.* iii, 451 (civic lands); Th.
II, *Nov.* viii, 439 (ships); ix, 439, xv. 1, 439, 2, 444, xxii. 1, 442, Just. *Nov.*
xlv, 537, cli (*curiales*); *Sirm.* 11, 412 (fiscal privileges of the church); *CJ* I. l. 2,
427 (acting provincial governors); *CTh* VIII. iv. 29, 428 (*cohortales*). Cf. also
CTh I. viii. 1, 415, Just. *Nov.* xxxv, 535, for *suggestiones* of the quaestor touching
military commissions issued *de minore laterculo* and the number of his *adiutores*.
Magistrates of course also made routine administrative *suggestiones* when permission or action by the emperor was required, e.g. *CTh* VIII. i. 10, 365 (*mag.
mil.*), v. 13, 362 (*CSL*), x. ix. 2, 395 (*CRP*), XI. xxx. 41 (*CRP, CSL*), XIV. vi.
3, 365 (*iudices* at Rome). *CJ* I. xxix. 4, XII. xxxv. 17, 472 (*mag. mil.*).

68. *CTh* xv. v. 4, 424, Th. II, *Nov.* iv, 438.

69. *CTh* XII. i. 33, Rufino comiti Orientis, 342, quoniam sublimitas tua suggessit; VIII. iv. 4, Antonio duci Mesopotamiae, 349, iuxta suggestionem vicarii
Mesopotamiae (the second *Mesopotamiae* is a dittography of the first); VII. i. 4,
ad Cretionem v. c. com. 350, quamvis omni tempore opera dari debuerit,
ne sacramentis militaribus spretis otio traderentur qui nec stipendiorum
numero nec contraria corporis valetudine quiete perfrui debent, tamen prudentiae tuae prosecutione admissa, quae apud nos verbis facta est, praecipimus,
ut, qui ante stipendia emensa vel integra corporis valetudine otio mancipati
sunt, restituantur pristinis numeris. Cf. Amm. XXXI. vii. 4 for Cretio *comes
Africae*. Cf. also *CTh* VII. iv. 12, 364, in provinciis statione militum adfici
possidentes Ursicini comitis suggestione cognovimus.

70. Val. III, *Nov.* xxii, 446, officium sedis celsitudinis tuae, sine quo necessitates
publicae nequeunt expediri, per infortunia multa iam saucium, medicinam
nostrae curationis exposcit, quae dudum potuisset adhiberi, si suggestio similis
ante manasset. Just *Nov.* xx pr., 536, congregatisque et apud tuam celsitudinem
et gloriosissimum nostrum quaestorem saepius et his, qui ex sacris scriniis appellationibus ministrant, et qui ex tuae sedis officio, novissime ad quandam formam
causa perducta est, quam ex non scripto ad nos deduxistis. Cf. also *CJ* XII.
xix. 15, 527, certae quidem sunt dispositiones nostri numinis quas super
adiutoribus viri illustris pro tempore quaestoris nostri palatii, quorum obsequio
res agitur quaestoria, dedimus. quarum prima quidem ad supplicationem
eorundem adiutorum emissa, etc. Val. III, *Nov.* xxviii, 449, suggestionem
sequentes agentum in rebus scholae, *CJ* XII. xxi. 8, 484, multis devotissimae
scholae agentum in rebus aditionibus permoti. QUARREL OVER COMMISSIONS:
CTh I. viii. 1, 415, viro illustri quaestore Eustathio suggerente cognovimus
per innovationem quorundam a minore laterculo praeposituras fuisse sublatas,
2, 424, 3, 424.

71. *CTh* I. xii. 5, 396, officium Hellesponti consularis aeternae recordationis
patrem serenitatis nostrae adiit et expositis suis incommodis, quibus a vicarianis
apparitoribus urgebatur, oravit sub tuae sublimitatis agere potestate, xv. xi. 2,
417, praesidalis officii Eufratensis deploratione comperimus eos qui trans-
ductioni ferarum a duciano officio deputantur, etc.

72. E. A. Thompson, *A Roman Reformer and Inventor* (Oxford, 1952).

73. Syn. *de Regno*, 14, 15. Libanius' *Orations* xxx (on the temples), xxxiii (against Tisamenus), xlv (on prisoners), xlvi (against Florentius), xlvii (on patronage), xlix (on the city councils), l (on corvées), li, lii (on lobbying governors), are all addressed to the emperor.

74. IRON LEVY: Basil, *Ep.* 110. ASSESSMENT OF CYRRHUS: Theod. *Ep.* (*PG*) 42–7. THE SAMARITANS: Just. *Nov.* cxxix, 551. BISHOPS AS WATCH-DOGS: *CJ* I. iv. 22, 529, Just. *Nov.* lxxxvi. 1, 539.

75. For the senate see above n. 24. EPIPHANEIA: *CTh* vii. iv. 25, 398, quoniam clementia nostra poscenti Epifanis ordini consensit, ut Novembri mense novellum vinum militi praeberetur. HERACLEA: Th. II, *Nov.* xxiii, 443, quapropter cum voti causa per Heracleotanam civitatem transitum faceremus, petitionibus civium eiusdem maxima sumus cum miseratione commoniti, qui tam murorum suorum quam aquaeductus nec non etiam aliorum operum publicorum, utpote longo tempore neglectorum, curam fieri oportere nostris provisionibus flagitarunt. et quoniam saepe ab una civitate vel homine postulatum remedium generalem solet formam correctionis adferre, horum desideriis annuentes, liberalitatem nostram ad omnes provincias ducimus propagandam. Cf. *CJ* I. xl. 6, 385, civitas Rhodiorum iniuriam suam non tam decenter quam sero conquesta est.

76. *CTh* xi. vii. 18, 409, recens conditae legis in hac parte auctoritate sequestrata quae ritu vetustatis neglecto palatina munera dignitatis intempestiva legatorum Achivorum admonitione abstulerat; xi. i. 33, 424: id ab unaquaque provincia censuimus expetendum, quod ab isdem nuper esse promissum tua sublimitas indicavit. ut vero nullus de cetero ad possessiones eorum, quod maxime reformidant, inspector accedat, Macedonum reliqui exemplum secuti mediae quantitatis, ut obtulisse noscuntur, tributa suscipiant. sed Achivi, qui protestati sunt nihil a se ultra tertiam partem posse conferri, illud exsolvant, ad quod se indubitanter fore idoneos pollicentur; xi. i. 34, 429, quae pietatem nostram viri spectabilis Bubulci comitis et legati decernere coegit eloquium; xii. i. 186, 429, legatio proconsularis provinciae per Bubulcum spectabilem virum comitem curiales pro aliis, qui nec in eodem territorio possident, deflevit adstringi, quod ab obnoxiis saepe debetur devotissimi quique cogantur exsolvere, Val III, *Nov.* xiii, 445, Numidarum et Maurorum Sitifensium nuper acta legatio, quam Palladius vir spectabilis comes et . . . tribunus vir clarissimus, et Maximinus vir laudabilis sacerdotalis probabiliter executi sunt, huius legis praeceptum de nostra perennitate promeruit.

Other allusions to provincial delegations are *CTh* xi. vii. 4, ad Afros, 327, 'quoniam subclamatione vestra merito postulastis', Sev. *Nov.* ii, 465, Just. *Nov.* cxlv, 553.

77. HERACLIAN: *CTh* IX. xl. 21, honoratis et provincialibus Africae, 413. The law addressed to the province of Byzacena is *CTh* v. xv. 16+x. x. 9+xi. xix. 3+xii. i. 59+60+xvi. ii. 17. Cf. vii. iv. 26+viii. v. 63+xi. i. 29, provincialibus provinciae proconsularis, 401.

78. *CJ* II. vii. 13, 468: petitionem virorum disertissimorum advocatorum Alexandrinae splendidissimae civitatis, quam de fori sui matricula et fisci patrono obtulerunt, merito admittentes hac sanctione decernimus, 24, 517, petitiones virorum disertissimorum fori praesidalis secundae Syriae provinciae advocatorum cum competenti moderatione censuimus admittendas et iubemus, 20, 497, suggestionem viri illustris comitis privatarum et proconsulis Asiae duximus admittendam, per quam nostrae serenitatis auribus intimavit fori sui advocatos communi petitione magnopere postulasse.

79. *CTh* XIII. v. 16+ix. 3, naviculariis Afris, 380, XIII. v. 36+37+ix. 6, naviculariis per Africam, 412.

80. For the *argentarii* see above n. 63. LECTICARII: Just. *Nov.* xliii pr., 536, adeuntes autem qui collegiorum sunt felicissimae nostrae huius regiae civitatis, quorum praecipue nobis cura est, nostram docuerunt potestatem, magnam et importabilem se sustinere vexationem. COLLECTARII AND MANCIPES SALINARUM: Symm. *Rel.* 29, 44. Laws confirming the privileges of the *corporati urbis* and regulating the *naviculariI amnici* and the distribution of oil are suggested by the prefect of the city in Val. III, *Nov.* xx, 445, xxix, 450, *CTh* XIV. xvii. 15, 408. Honorius addressed a constitution directly to the *decuriales*, *CTh* XIV. i. 4, 404.

81. Symm. *Ep.* i. 17.

82. TYMANDUS AND ORCISTUS: *ILS* 6090, 6091. APHRODITO: *P. Cairo*, 67019, αὐτόπρακτος καὶ αὐτοτελὴς τῶν εὐσεβῶν καὶ δημοσίων φόρων . . . ἐχόντων τὸ προνόμιον αὐτῶν ἀπὸ θείου τύπου τοῦ τῆς θείας λήξεως Λέοντος, cf. pp. 407-8.

83. Laws protecting peasants are *CTh* XI. x. 1, 369, xi. 1, 368, *CJ* XI. xlviii. 5 (365-6), l. 1 (325). For *coloni*, see pp. 799-801.

84. THE GREEK SHOPKEEPERS: Val. III, *Nov.* v, 440, Graecos itaque negotiatores, quos pantapolas dicunt, in quibus manifestum est maximam inesse multitudinem magnamque in emendis vendendisque mercibus diligentiam, ulterius non patimur sacrae urbis habitatione secludi, licet eos dissensio et maxima invidia tabernariorum magis quam venerabilis urbis Romae utilitas a negatione submoverit. LAW AGAINST COMBINATIONS: *CJ* IV. lix. 2, 483. THE GARDENERS: Just. *Nov.* lxiv, 538, πολλαὶ πανταχόθεν ἡμῖν μέμψεις ἐκ χρόνου πολλοῦ κατὰ τῶν τῆς εὐδαίμονος ταύτης πόλεως καὶ τῶν αὐτῆς προαστείων κηπουρῶν προσφέρονται, δυσχεραινόντων ἁπάντων πρὸς τὴν αὐτῶν κακουργίαν.

85. *CTh* VII. xx. 1, 2, 326 (S).

86. MUTINIES: Amm. xx. iv (Julian), Zos. v. 32-4 (Stilicho), Proc. *BG* i. i. 2-8 (Odoacer), Theoph. Sim. III. 1-4, VIII. 17-8 (Maurice). For the donative see pp. 624, 670.

87. *C. Sard.* can. 7.

88. DONATISTS: *Cod. Can. Eccl. Afr.* 93-4, cf. *CTh* XVI. v. 38+vi. 3, vi. 4+5, v. 37, v. 39, 405; *Cod. Can. Eccl. Afr.* 99, cf. *CTh* XVI. v. 41, 43, 407; *Cod. Can. Eccl. Afr.* between can. 106 and 107, Aug. *Ep.* 97, cf. *CTh* XVI. v. 44, 45, 408, ii. 31, v. 46-7, 409; *Cod. Can. Eccl. Afr.* 107, cf. *CTh* XVI. v. 51, 410. PAGANS: *Cod. Can. Eccl. Afr.* 58, cf. *Sirm.* 12, 407. MANICHEES: Val. III, *Nov.* xviii, 445, superstitio paganis quoque damnata temporibus, inimica publicae disciplinae et hostis fidei Christianae, ad excidium sui clementiam nostram non immerito provocavit. Manichaeos loquimur, quos execrabiles et toto orbe pellendos omnium retro principum statuta iudicarunt. nec dissimulationem crimina nuper detecta patiuntur. quae enim et quam dictu audituque obscoena in iudicio beatissimi papae Leonis coram senatu amplissimo manifestissima ipsorum confessione patefacta sunt? *Sirm.* 10, 420, forbidding the clergy to have housekeepers, was enacted on the instance of a bishop, and *Sirm.* 2, 405, on deposed bishops, on that of a council of bishops.

89. *CTh* XVI. ii. 15, 360, in Ariminensi synodo super ecclesiarum et clericorum privilegiis tractatu habito usque eo dispositio progressa est, ut iuga, quae videntur ad ecclesiam pertinere, a publica functione cessarent inquietudine desistente: quod nostra videtur dudum sanctio reppulisse; it would appear from *CTh* XI. i. 1, 360 (S), that the council's petition was granted for a brief

period. IMMUNITY OF THE CHURCH OF THESSALONICA: *CTh* XI. i. 33, 424, sacrosancta Thessalonicensis ecclesia civitatis excepta, ita tamen, ut aperte sciat, propriae tantummodo capitationis modum beneficio mei numinis sublevandum nec externorum gravamine tributorum rem publicam ecclesiastici nominis abusione laedendam. On decurions, see pp. 745–6, 925–6. On *episcopalis audientia*, see p. 480. On *praescriptio fori*, see pp. 491–2, Just. *Nov.* lxxxiii, 539, on this topic, was evoked by a petition of the patriarch of Constantinople. Other ecclesiastical petitions led to modifications of the laws against alienation of church lands, Just. *Nov.* xl, 535, lxv, 538; another petition was rebuffed, Just. *Nov.* clvi (undated).

90. On provincial councils see pp. 763–6.

91. TAX REMISSIONS: *CTh* XI. xxviii. 5, 410, i. 33, 424, Val. III, *Nov.* xiii, 445. TAX COLLECTION: *CTh* XI. xix. 3, 364, VII. iv. 26, XI. i. 29, 401. CROWN LANDS AND INFORMERS: *CTh* IX. xxxiv. 5, 338, X. x. 9, 364, 10, 365, 19, 387. APPEALS, ETC.: *CTh* XI. xxx. 15, 329, xxx. 32+xxxvi. 15, 365 (S). OTHER ABUSES: *CTh* VIII. iv. 2, 315, v. 63, 401.

92. *CTh* XVI. viii. 3, decurionibus Agrippiniensibus, 321; XII. i. 29, ordini civitatis Constantinae Cirtensium, 340; 41, ordini Carthaginiensium, 353; 42, ordini Caesenatium, 354; XII. i. 60+XVI. ii. 17, ad Byzacenos, 364; VII. i. 6+ XII. i. 64, Mauris Sitifensibus, 368.

93. On the varying privileges and disabilities of officials see ch. XVI. COHORTALES OF SYRIA: *CTh* VIII. iv. 11, 365. VICARIANI OF PONTICA: *CTh* I. xv. 11. 380.

94. THE CUBICULARII: *CTh* X. x. 32, 425, 34, 430. THE PALATINI: Val. III, *Nov.* vii. 1, 440, 2, 442.

95. See pp. 509–10.

96. *CTh* VII. xiii. 12, 13, 14, 397. Symm. *Ep.* VI. 58, 62, 64.

97. Val. III, *Nov.* i. 3, 450; Val. III, *Nov.* xv, 444, proclaims the bankruptcy of the treasury.

XII. THE ADMINISTRATION (pp. 366–8)

1. On the numbers of the *scholae* see p. 613, on the numbers of the ministries see pp. 571, 573, 576, 583, 585.

2. Even *praefectiani* all received *capitum* (fodder allowances), see *CJ* I. xxvii. 1 §§22 ff., 534. On the *mensores* see pp. 582–4. *CTh* VI. xxxvi. 1, 326 (S), sed nec alieni sunt a pulvere et labore castrorum, qui signa nostra comitantur, qui praesto sunt semper actibus, quos intentos eruditis studiis itinerum prolixitas et expeditionum difficultas exercet.

3. MAGISTER MEMORIAE: SHA, *Claudius*, 7, extat ipsius epistola missa ad senatum legenda ad populum—hanc autem ipse dictasse perhibetur, ego verbo magistri memoriae non requiro, SHA, *Carus*, 8: Julius Calpurnius, qui ad memoriam dictabat, talem ad praefectum urbis super morte Cari epistulam dedit, Petr. Patr. 14, ὅτι Γαλέριος καὶ Διοκλητιανὸς εἰς Νίσιβιν συνῆλθον, ἔνθα κοινῇ βουλευσάμενοι στέλλουσιν εἰς Περσίδα πρεσβευτὴν Σικόριον Πρόβον ἀντιγραφέα

τῆς μνήμης. The Scriptores Historiae Augustae do not know of the quaestor and regard the *magistri officiorum* as the chief imperial secretaries (e.g. *Pesc. Niger*, 12, *Alex. Sev.* 31-2, *Gallienus*, 17). QUAESTOR: Zos. v. 32, ὁ τὰ βασιλεῖ δοκοῦντα τεταγμένος ὑπαγορεύειν, ὃν κοαίστωρα καλεῖν οἱ ἀπὸ Κωνσταντίνου δεδώκασι χρόνοι. The earliest known quaestors are Montius (of Gallus Caesar in 353, Amm. XIV. vii. 12, Soc. II. 34, Soz. IV. 7, Philostorgius, III. 28), Taurus (of Constantius II in 354, Amm. XIV. xi. 14), and Leontius (of Gallus Caesar in 354, Amm. XIV. xi. 14). DUTIES OF THE QUAESTOR: *Not. Dig. Or.* xii, *Occ.* x, sub dispositione viri illustris quaestoris: leges dictandae, preces, Symm. *Ep.* I. 23: quaestor es, memini; consilii regalis particeps, scio; precum arbiter, legum conditor, recognosco, Cass. *Var.* VI. 5 (formula), *V. Porph.* 50, τῇ δὲ ἑξῆς μετεπέμψατο τὸν κυαίστορα καὶ ἡμᾶς, λέγει δὲ αὐτῷ· λάβε τὸν χάρτην τοῦτον καὶ κατὰ τὴν δύναμιν αὐτοῦ διατύπωσον θεῖον γράμμα. DUTIES OF MAGISTRI SCRINIORUM: *Not. Dig. Or.* xix, magister memoriae adnotationes omnes dictat et emittit et precibus respondet. magister epistolarum legationes civitatum, consultationes et preces tractat. magister libellorum cognitiones et preces tractat. magister epistolarum graecarum eas epistolas quae graece solent emitti aut ipse dictat aut latine dictatas transfert in graecum. *Occ.* xvii omits the *magister epistolarum Graecarum*. For the work of the quaestor and *magistri scriniorum* in connection with petitions and rescripts see Val. III, *Nov.* xix, 445, Th. II, *Nov.* XVII. 2, 444, *CJ* IV. lix. 1, 473, I. xxiii. 7, 477, I. xii. 8, ὁσάκις ἐξ ἔθους κατὰ τὰς μεγάλας ἑορτὰς ἐν τῇ ἁγιωτάτῃ μεγάλῃ ἐκκλησίᾳ ἢ καὶ ἐν ἄλλαις ἐκκλησίαις προΐεμεν, ἐπιτρέπομεν τῷ ἐνδοξοτάτῳ ἡμῶν κοιαίστωρι τὰς αἰτήσεις τῶν δεομένων δέχεσθαί τε καὶ εἰς ἡμᾶς φέρειν. It is not clear why Benivolus, the *magister memoriae*, instead of the quaestor, was directed to draft *CTh* XVI. i. 4, 386 (Ruf. *HE* II. 16). On the judicial functions of the quaestor see pp. 505-6.

4. LEGAL WORK OF SCRINIA: *CTh* I. xvi. 3, 319, XI. xxx. 32, 365 (S), 34, 364, 54, 395, 65, 415. OTHER DUTIES: Symm. *Rel.* 24, per vices mensium singulorum ad perennitatis vestrae scrinia senatus et populi acta mittuntur, *CTh* VI. ii. 13, 383 (*professiones* of senators, cf. Symm. *Rel.* 46), VII. iv. 24, 398, XI. i. 13, 365 (arrears of *annona* from Africa), XIV. ix. 1, 370 (reports on students at Rome), XII. xii. 10, 385 (requests of provincial delegations), *CJ* XI. xliii. 11 (517) (permits for drawing domestic water supply from aqueducts). PROBATORIAE: *CTh* VIII. vii. 21, 426 (officials of *PPO*, *procos.*, *com. Or.*, *praef. Aug.* and vicars), 22, 426 (officials of *PU*), 23, 426 (*thesaurenses*), *CJ* I. xxxi. 5, 527 (*scholares*), XII. xx. 3 (457-70) (*agentes in rebus*), XII. lix. 9 (470) (*memoriales, agentes in rebus*, etc.), 10 (472) (Notitia showing distribution of all *probatoriae* between the three *scrinia*), XII. xxxv. 17 (472) (all soldiers), cf. also Just. *Nov.* xxv §1, xxvi §2, xxvii §1, 535 (officials of the *praetor Lycaoniae, praetor Thraciae* and *comes Isauriae*).

5. See ch. XVI, n. 23.

6. EARLIEST MAGISTRI OFFICIORUM: *CTh* XVI. x. 1, 320, de qua ad Heraclianum tribunum et magistrum officiorum scribseras, XI. ix. 1, 323, litterae missae ad Proculeianum tribunum et magistrum officiorum, Joh. Lydus, *Mag.* II. 25, *Epit. Caes.* xli, Zos. II. 25 (Martinianus under Licinius); Joh. Lydus, *Mag.* II. 25 (Palladius under Constantine from 324); Ath. *Apol. Const.* 3, *ILS* 1244 (Eugenius under Constans). DUTIES OF MAGISTER OFFICIORUM: *Not. Dig. Or.* xi, *Occ.* ix, Joh. Lydus, *Mag.* II. 26, οὐ μόνον γὰρ τὰς τῶν ἐθνῶν πρεσβείας ὑφ' ἑαυτῷ τελούσας ὁ μάγιστρος ἔχειν πιστεύεται, τόν τε δημόσιον δρόμον καὶ πλῆθος ἐμβριθὲς τῶν πάλαι μὲν φρουμενταρίων νῦν δὲ μαγιστριανῶν, τήν τε τῶν ὅπλων κατασκευὴν καὶ ἐξουσίαν, ἀλλ' ἔτι καὶ τὴν τῶν πολιτικῶν πραγμάτων, Priscus, 7, πασῶν γὰρ τῶν βασιλέως

βουλῶν ὁ μάγιστρος κοινωνός, οἷα δὴ τῶν ἀγγελιαφόρων καὶ ἑρμηνέων καὶ στρατιωτῶν τῶν ἀμφὶ τὴν βασιλείαν φυλακὴν ὑπ᾽ αὐτὸν ταττομένων, Cass. *Var*. VI. 6.

7. The administrative and disciplinary control of the *magister* over the various palatine *scholae* and *officia* is shown by the following laws, all addressed to him: Th. II, *Nov*. xxi, 441, *CJ* I. xxxi. 5, 527, Cass. *Var*. VI. 6 §1, ipse insolentium scholarum mores procellosos moderationis suae prospero disserenat (*scholae palatinae*); *CTh* I. viii. 1, 415, 3, 424, VI. xxvi. 6, 396, 11, 397, 17, 416, *CJ* I. xxx. 3, 492, XII. xix. 7, 8 (444), 9 (457–70), 10 (470), 11 (492–7), 12, 14, 15 (527) (*sacra scrinia*); *CTh* VI. xxxiii. 1, 416 (*decani*); *CTh* VI. xxxiv. 1, 405 (*mensores*); Val. III, *Nov*. xxx, 450 (*lampadarii*); *CTh* I. ix. 2, 386, 3, 405, VI. xxvii. 3, 380, 4, 382, 7, 395, 8, 9, 396, 11, 399, 14, 404, 15, 412, 17, 416 (S), 18, 416, 19, 417, 20, 426, 23, 430, xxviii. 8, 435, xxix. 6, 381, 8, 395, Val. III, *Nov*. xxviii, 449, *CJ* XII. xx. 3, 5 (457–70), xxi. 6 (444) (*agentes in rebus*); *CTh* VII. xii. 2, 378 (S), XVI. iv. 4, 404, V. 29, 395, 42, 408, *CJ* XII. xxxiii. 5, 524 (palatine offices in general). From *CJ* XII. vii. 2 (474) and Just. *Nov*. x, 535, it appears that he had (in the fifth and sixth centuries at any rate) a similar control over the *notarii* and the *referendarii* who were drawn from them. His jurisdiction extended over a wider field (see ch. XIV, n. 46).

8. On the *cursus publicus* see below, n. 74. The great majority of the laws on *metata* are addressed to the *magister*; *CTh* VII. viii. 2, 368, 3, 384, 4, 393, 5, 398, 8, 405 (S), 14, 427, 15, 433 (S), 16, 435, XIII. iii. 15, 393, Th. II, *Nov*. xxv, 444, *CJ* XII. xl. 9, 444, 10 (450–55), 11 (Zeno). AUDIENCES: Ath. *Apol. Const*. 3, Cass. *Var*. VI. 6 §2: per eum senator veniens nostris praesentatur obtutibus: ammonet trepidum, componit loquentem, sua quin etiam verba solet inserere, ut nos decenter omnia debeamus audire. aspectus regii haud irritus promissor, collocutionis nostrae gloriosus donator, aulici consistorii quasi quidam lucifer. RECEPTION OF EMBASSIES: Amm. XXVI. v. 7, Priscus, 26, Corippus, *Laud. Just*. III. 231 ff., Cass. *Var*. VI. 6 §4: per eum exteris gentibus ad laudem rei publicae nostrae ordinatur humanitas et nolentes redeunt, quos maerentes exceperit; per eum quippe nobis legatorum quamvis festinantium praenuntiatur adventus, Const. Porph. *Cer*. I. 87–90 (Peter the patrician on the reception of envoys from a Western Augustus and a Persian king). The *magister* sometimes served as ambassador to negotiate treaties: Theophanes, A.M. 6022 (Hermogenes), Proc. *BP* I. ix. 24 (Celer), *BG* IV. xi. 2, Menander, 11 (Peter), Theoph. Sim. III. 15 (Theodore). FABRICAE: Joh. Lydus, *Mag*. II. 10, III. 40. John is mistaken in thinking that the change was made after Rufinus' fall, for he already controlled the factories when *magister officiorum* in 390 (*CTh* x. xxii. 3). The praetorian prefect supplied the raw materials (*CTh* x. xxii. 2, *PPO Or*., 388, cf. Joh. Lydus, *Mag*. III. 5) and the rations of the workers (*Cass. Var*. VII. 19), but the *magister* henceforth ran the factories (*Not. Dig. Or*. xi. 18–39, *Occ*. ix. 16–39, *CTh* x. xxii. 4, *mag. off*., 398, 5, *mag. off*., 404, Th. II, *Nov*. vi, 438, ut viri inlustris atque magnifici magistri officiorum suggestio nostrae clementiae patefecit, *CJ* XI. x. 6 and 7 (467–72), XII. xx. 5 (457–70), Just. *Nov*. lxxxv, 539). The *barbaricarii* were under the *comes sacrarum largitionum* in the West (*Not. Dig. Occ*. xi. 74–7), and in the East in 374 (*CTh* x. xxii. 1, *CSL*, 374) but later under the *magister* (*Not. Dig. Or*. xi. 45, *CJ* XII. xx. 5, *mag. off*. (457–70), in unoquoque scrinio fabricarum et barbar[icari]orum). LIMITANEI: Th. II, *Nov*. xxiv, 443.

9. See pp. 412 ff.

10. Gallus Caesar is recorded to have had a praetorian prefect (Thalassius and Domitian, Amm. XIV. i. 10, vii. 9), a *magister equitum* (Amm. XIV. ii. 20), a

quaestor (Montius and Leontius, Amm. xiv. vii. 12, xi. 14) and a *comes domesticorum* (Lucilianus, Amm. xiv. xi. 14). Julian Caesar had a praetorian prefect (Florentius, Amm. xvi. xii. 14, etc.), a *magister equitum* (Marcellus, Severus, Lupicinus, Amm. xvi. vii. 1, x. 21, xviii. ii. 7), a quaestor (Nebridius, Amm. xx. ix. 5), a *magister officiorum* (Pentadius and Felix, Amm. xx. viii. 19, ix. 5), a *comes domesticorum* (Excubitor, Amm. xx. iv. 21) and a *praepositus sacri cubiculi* (Eutherius, Amm. xvi. vii. 2). For Ursulus see Amm. xxii. iii. 7, cum enim Caesar in partes mitteretur occiduas omni tenacitate stringendus, nullaque potestate militi quicquam donandi delata, ut pateret ad motus asperior exercitus, hic idem Ursulus datis litteris ad eum, qui Gallicanos tuebatur thesauros, quicquid posceret Caesar procul dubio iusserat dari.

11. See ch. XII, nn. 51-3, ch. IV, n. 30. I should perhaps take the opportunity of saying that I do not believe in the hypothesis, accepted by most scholars, that on occasion two prefects administered a zone in collegiate fashion. I emphasize the word hypothesis, for there is no hint of such an arrangement in any ancient author, or in the language of any law. The hypothesis has been invented to account for the fact that the dates in the Codes seem at times to show two prefects simultaneously in one zone. But the dates in the Code are notoriously unreliable and many have to be corrected to produce any semblance of order; I would prefer to correct more and have thus eliminated one collegiate prefecture ('The career of Flavius Philippus', *Historia* IV (1955), 229-33). It must also be remembered that before 395 at any rate the zones of the prefects were not rigidly fixed and for instance one of a pair of prefects may have governed Africa with Italy and the other Illyricum, or one Illyricum with Italy and the other Africa. We also do not allow for the fact that at times of faction and crisis prefects might be appointed, dismissed and reappointed with great rapidity. The only good evidence for a double prefecture is the curious duplication of posts in the praetorian prefecture of the East (see ch. XVI, n. 61). This may have arisen from the amalgamation of two *officia*; I would conjecture that late in Constantine's reign there may have been a praetorian prefect attached to Constantine himself and another to Constantius Caesar, and that on Constantine's death their *officia* were combined.

12. For the prefecture of Italy and Gaul under Odoacer and Theoderic see ch. VIII, n. 38. PREFECTURE OF AFRICA: *CJ* i. xxvii. 1, 534. QUAESTURA EXERCITUS: Just. *Nov.* xli, 536.

13. Praetorian prefects who held military commands are Asclepiodotus under Constantius Caesar (Aur. Victor, *Caes.* xxxix. 42, Eutrop. ix. 22), Anullinus under Severus (Zos. ii. 10), Rufius Volusianus and Pompeianus under Maxentius (Aur. Victor, *Caes.* xl. 18, Zos. ii. 14, Pan. Lat. xii. 8). The inappellability of the prefect was confirmed by Constantine in 331 (*CTh* xi. xxx. 16), but was probably older (see ch. II, n. 1).

14. MAGISTRI MILITUM: Zos. ii. 33, Joh. Lydus, *Mag.* ii. 10, iii, 40. On the financial and judicial functions of the prefects see pp. 448 ff., 479 ff. All the laws about recruiting in *CTh* vii. xiii (*de tironibus*) are addressed to the prefects (or vicars, etc.) except 2, 12, 14 (CRP, on tenants of imperial lands), 15 (PU, on a *collatio iuniorum* from *honorati*), 18 (*mag. mil.*, on exemption of military officers from a *collatio iuniorum*), 19 (CSL, on recruits in the *scholae*; was the CSL acting *mag. off.*?) and 20 (CRP, on *aurum tironicum*; was the CRP acting CSL?). All the laws on military supply in *CTh* vii. iv. (*de erogatione militaris annonae*) are likewise addressed to the prefects (or vicars, etc.) except 10 (PU, on *protectores* at Rome), 12, 18 (*mag. mil.*, on abuses committed by soldiers) and 34

and 36 (*mag. mil.*, on commutation of officers' rations). See also Zos. II. 32–3, Amm. XIV. vii. 11, 'proficiscere', inquit (sc. Domitianus, Gallus' praetorian prefect), 'ut praeceptum est, Caesar, sciens quod si cessaveris, et tuas et palatii tui auferri iubebo prope diem annonas', Cass. *Var.* VI. 3, quando palatium sua provisione sustentat, servientibus nobis procurat annonas, Amm. XIV. x. 4, unde Rufinus ea tempestate praefectus praetorio ad discrimen trusus est ultimum. ire enim ipse compellebatur ad militem, quem exagitabat inopia simul et feritas, et alioqui coalito more in ordinarias dignitates asperum semper et saevum, ut satisfaceret atque monstraret, quam ob causam annonae convectio sit impedita, xx. iv. 6, (Julian) redire ad se praefectum hortatus est, olim Viennam specie annonae parandae digressum. All laws on the post in *CTh* VIII. v (*de cursu publico*) are addressed to the prefects (or vicars, etc.) except 19, 22, 32, 55 (PU), 49 (*mag. off.*), 56 (*mag. mil.*), 57 (*dux*); also in the corresponding title in *CJ* XII. 1. In the Ostrogothic kingdom the *magister officiorum* took over the administration of the post; Cass. *Var.* VI. 6 §3, veredorum quin etiam opportunam velocitatem, quorum status semper in cursu est, diligentiae suae districtione custodit, ut sollicitudines nostras, quas consilio iuvat, beneficio celeritatis expediat, v. 5 §4, quam summam protinus exactam, sicut iam anterioribus edictis constitutum est, per officium magisteriae dignitatis cursui proficere debere censemus. In the titles *de operibus publicis* (*CTh* XV. 1, *CJ* VIII. xi) and *de itinere muniendo* (*CTh* XV. iii) all the laws are addressed to the praetorian prefects except those referring to the capitals, which go to the prefects of the city, and *CTh* XV. i. 13 (*dux*, on frontier fortifications) and 32 (*CSL*, on use of civic revenues): there was a *scrinia operum* in the praetorian prefectures of Illyricum (*Not. Dig. Or.* iii. 26, *CJ* XII. xlix. 12), Oriens (Joh. Lydus, *Mag.* III. 5) and Africa (*CJ* I. xxvii. 1 §36), cf. also Just. *Nov.* cxxviii §18, 545, τοὺς σκρινιαρίους τῶν ἔργων τοὺς ὑπὸ τοὺς ἐπάρχους τῶν ἱερῶν πραιτωρίων τελοῦντας.

15. For the appointment of governors see below, n. 52. JURISDICTION OVER GOVERNORS: *CTh* I. v. 9, 389, si quos iudices corpore marcentes et neglegentes desidiae somniis oscitantes, si quos servilis furti aviditate degeneres vel similium vitiorum labe sublimitas tua reppererit involutos, in eos vindictam publicae ultionis exaggeret et amotis vicarios subroget, ut ad nostrae mansuetudinis scientiam non crimina sed vindicta referatur (for the appointment of acting governors cf. *CJ* I. l. 2, 427, eos qui praeceptione principali seu vestrae sedis amplissimae tueri locum rectorum provinciarum noscuntur), *CTh* I. v. 10+ vii. 2, 393, de ordinario iudice semper inlustris est cognitio praefecturae, licet militari viro ab eo facta fuerit iniuria, Cass. *Var.* VI. 3, delicta provinciarum iudicum punit. CIRCULARIZATION OF LAWS: *Sirm.* 4, 9, 11, 12, 16, Th. II, *Nov.* iii, Val. III, *Nov.* xxiii, xxvi, Marc. *Nov.* ii, iii. For the range of the praetorian prefect's responsibilities see the list of his *suggestiones* in ch. XI, n. 67.

16. On the *magistri militum* and *comites rei militaris* see ch. III, n. 42, ch. IV, n. 25–6. COMITES DOMESTICORUM: *Not. Dig. Or.* xv, *Occ.* xiii. Diocletian is said to have commanded the *domestici* before his accession (Aur. Victor, *Caes.* xxxix. 1). The earliest *comites* known are Latinus under Constantius (Amm. XIV. x. 8) and Lucilianus under Gallus Caesar (Amm. XIV. xi. 14), both in 354. The earliest known *comes domesticorum equitum* is Athaulf, appointed by Attalus in 409 (Soz. ix. 8), but the distinction between the two *comites* is very rarely made in inscriptions, laws or authors (only in *ILS* 1305, *CJ* II. vii. 25, XII. xvii. 3 and the Notitia), and the change may have been made earlier. PROMOTION OF COMITES DOMESTICORUM: Barbatio (Amm. XIV. xi. 19 and XVI. xi. 2), Dagalaifus (Amm. XXI. viii. 1 and XXVI. v. 9), Richomer (Amm. XXXI. vii. 4 and *CTh* VII. i. 13), Stilicho (*ILS* 1277–8), Allobich (Zos. v. 47–8),

Castinus (Greg. Tur. *HF* II. 9, *Chron. Min.* I. 470, II. 20), Boniface (Aug. *Ep.* 220 §7, *Chron. Min.* I. 473), Aetius (*Greg. Tur.* II. 8), Zeno (*V. Dan.* 55, 65), Philoxenus (*ILS* 1308), cf. *CTh* xv. xi. 1, Mauriano com. dom. et vices agenti mag. mil. 414. TRIBUNI SCHOLARUM: *CTh* vi. xiii. 1, 413, praepositos ac tribunos scholarum, qui et divinis epulis adhibentur et adorandi principis facultatem antiquitus meruerunt, inter quos tribunus etiam sacri stabuli et cura palatii numerantur, si primi ordinis comitivam cum praepositura meruerint et casu ad altiora non pervenerint, deposito sacramento inter eos qui comites Aegypti vel Ponticae dioeceseos fuerint, quorum par dignitas est, haberi praecipimus. sin absque honore comitivae cuiuslibet scholae regimen fuerint nancti, absolutos militia inter eos qui duces fuerint provinciarum numerari iubemus. PROMOTION OF TRIBUNI SCHOLARUM: Silvanus (Amm. xv. v. 2 and 33), Agilo (Amm. xx. ii. 5), Gomoarius (Amm. xxi. viii. 1 and xx. ix. 5), Equitius (Amm. xxvi. i. 4 and v. 3 and 11), Arinthaeus (Amm. xv. iv. 10 and xxvii. v. 4), Malarich (Amm. xv. v. 6 and xxv. viii. 11, x. 6). CURA PALATII: *CTh* xi. xviii. 1, 412 (S), vi. xiii. 1 (cited above), Cass. *Var.* vii. 5, Const. Porph. *Cer.* i. 84. Known holders of the office are Apollinaris under Gallus Caesar (Amm. xiv. vii. 19), Saturninus under Constantius II (Amm. xxii. iii. 7), Rumitalca under Procopius (Amm. xxvi. viii. 1), Equitius under Valens (Amm. xxxi. xii. 15), Aetius under John (Greg. Tur. *HF* ii. 8), Consentius under Avitus (Sid. Ap. *Carm.* xxiii. 430–1), the future emperor Justin II (Evagr. v. 1) and Baduarius under Justin II (Corippus, *Laud. Just.* ii. 285). This office is not to be confused with the much inferior *curae palatiorum* on the staff of the *castrensis* (*Not. Dig. Or.* xvii. 5, *Occ.* xv. 6). TRIBUNUS STABULI: *CTh* xi. xviii. 1, 412 (S), vi. xiii. 1 (cited above): for the *stratores* and their duties see ch. XVII, n. 37. Known holders of the office are Agilo under Constantius II (Amm. xiv. x. 8), Sintula under Julian Caesar (Amm. xx. iv. 3), the future emperor Valens under his brother (Amm. xxvi. iv. 2), Constantianus and Cerealis under Valentinian I (Amm. xxviii. ii. 10, xxx. v. 19), Valerianus under Valens (Amm. xxxi. xiii. 18), Stilicho (*ILS* 1278), Aetius under Marcian (*A.C.Oec.* ii. i. 334), Areobindus (*ILS* 1303), Jordanes (*V. Dan.* 49), Constantianus (Proc. *BG* i. vii. 26) and Belisarius (Proc. *HA* iv. 39).

17. See the table of provinces and dioceses in App. III. Under Diocletian there survived only the proconsuls of Africa and Asia; Constantine added Achaea and apparently Europe (abolished by Constantius II); in the 380s there were for a brief period proconsuls of Campania, a Spanish province and Palestine: see *JRS* XLIV (1954), 27–9. Justinian abolished the proconsulate of Africa (*CJ* i. xxvii. 1 §12) but created proconsuls of Cappadocia, Armenia I and Palestine I (Just. *Nov.* xxx, xxxi §1, ciii). Under Diocletian there were *correctores* of the Italian provinces, Sicily and Achaea, but most of these were later upgraded to *consulares* (Achaea to proconsul): see *JRS* as above. In the Notitia there are only three *correctores* in the West (*Not. Dig. Occ.* i. 78–83, xix. 7–9, xliv), and two in the East (*Not. Dig. Or.* i. 126–8), both of recent creation (see App. II): from *CTh* xii. i. 133 it appears that in 393 Tripolitania had a *corrector* temporarily (cf. *CTh* xi. xxx. 59 and *Not. Dig. Occ.* i. 100, xx. 13). For *praesides* and *consulares* see *JRS* XLIV (1954), 24 ff. PRAETORS: Just. *Nov.* xxiv (Pisidia), xxv (Lycaonia), xxvi (Thrace), xxix (Paphlagonia), civ (Sicily). MODERATORS: Just. *Nov.* xxviii (Helenopontus), cii (Arabia), *Ed.* iv (Phoenice Libanensis). COMITES: Just. *Nov.* viii §2, (Phrygia Pacatiana), §3 (Galatia I), xxxi §1 (Armenia III). PRAEFECTUS AEGYPTI: *CTh* xvi. ii. 11, 342, (S), xv. i. 8 + 9 (362); thereafter *praefectus Augustalis* (*JTS* 1954, 224–7). On the institution of *duces* see ch. II, n. 11. In the Notitia military and civil government is

united in Isauria and Arabia (*Not. Dig. Or.* xxix, xxxvii) and in Mauretania Caesariensis (*Not. Dig. Occ.* xxx). In Isauria the union seems to have been permanent, though it was only Justinian who formally amalgamated the offices of *comes* and *praeses* (Just. *Nov.* xxvii). In Arabia it was temporary; the province had a separate *praeses* under Justinian (Just. *Nov.* viii, notitia 39, cii). Other temporary unions are Tripolitania, *IRT* 565, Fl. Nepotiano v.p. com. et praesidi provinc. Trip. . . . rei etiam militaris peritissimo . . . quod barbarorum insolentiam exercito scientiae militaris adtriberit, quod limitis defensionem tuitionemque perpetuam futuris etiam temporibus munitam securamque ab omni hostili incursione praestiterit, *CTh* xii. i. 133, duci et correctori limitis Tripolitani, 393) and Egypt (*CJ* ii. vii. 13, duci Aegyptiaci limitis et praefecto Augustali, 468, i. lvii. i, duci et praefecto Augustali, 469, Priscus, 22, Evagr. ii. 5, iii. 22) and the Upper Thebaid (Hierocles, 731). For Justinian's changes see ch. IX, n. 27–9.

18. On the dioceses see ch. II, n. 16, 17 (Diocletian), ch. III, n. 66 (Macedonia), ch. V, n. 9 (Egypt); also the table of provinces and dioceses in App. III. The two dioceses of Macedonia and Dacia are under the disposition of the praetorian prefect of Illyricum (*Not. Dig. Or.* iii. 4–6) but there is only a vicar of Macedonia (ibid. i. 34; his chapter is missing). Under the praetorian prefect of Italy there are the three dioceses of Italia, Illyricum and Africa (*Not. Dig. Occ.* ii. 5–8) but there are only vicars of Urbs Roma, Italia and Africa (ibid. i. 23–6, xix, xx, but no chapter for the vicar of Italia). Under the praetorian prefect of the Gauls only three dioceses, Hispaniae, Septem Provinciae and Britanniae are shown (*Not. Dig. Occ.* iii. 1–4) and all the provinces of Gaul are enumerated under Septem Provinciae (ibid. iii. 14–31, xxii). That in Julian's day as Caesar there was no *vicarius* of the diocese of Gaul is shown by Amm. xvii. iii. 6, inusitato exemplo id petendo Caesar inpetraverat a praefecto ut secundae Belgicae multiformibus malis oppressae dispositio sibi committeretur ea videlicet lege, ut nec praefectianus nec praesidalis apparitor ad solvendum quemquam urgeret. There were no *vicariani* who might have intervened.

19. See ch. IX, nn. 27–8, 60.

20. On the financial and judicial duties of a provincial governor see pp. 414, 434, 450, 479. Laws are often addressed to provincial governors on the post (*CJ* i. xl. 4, 335, *CTh* viii. v. 24, 365, 25, 365, 27, 365, 29, 368) and on public works (*CTh* xv. i. 8+9, 362, 17, 365) and their activity in this sphere is frequently mentioned (*CTh* xv. i. 2, 3, 14–6, 18, 20–1, 31, 34–5, 37, iii. 6); cf. also Symm. *Ep.* ii. 27: videlicet ut sub actorum confectione vel tuorum, ni adhuc retines potestatem, vel vicariae praefecturae, quae tibi poscenti aequa non deerit, diligentiae tuae ratio digeratur, quae possit ostendere, quot numero animalia conlocaris, et quo apparatu instruxeris mansiones, et quantum in titulis fiscalibus exigendis tua cura promoverit. A full description of a governor's duties is given in Just. *Nov.* xvii, and in abbreviated form in the Novels establishing the praetorship of Pisidia, etc. (see above n. 17).

21. On the judicial duties of vicars see p. 481; on their general powers of supervision, *CTh* i. xiv. 2, 395, praefectus Augustalis ordinariorum sub se iudicum examinandi flagitia ac super his referendi, non amovendi vel puniendi habeat potestatem; on their financial duties, *CTh* i. xiv. 1, praef. Aug. 386, per Thebaidem atque Augustamnicam provincias officium tuum et officia iudicum competentium omnia tributa exigere suscipere postremo compellere iubemus, xv. 6, 372, 15, 400, virum spectabilem vicarium septem provinciarum reliqua praeteriti temporis exigere iubemus, recentia vero debita

ordinarios iudices maturare decernimus, quibus tamen vicarium convenit imminere, 17, 401. Other laws allot special financial duties, e.g. the *patrimoniales fundi* to the *comes Orientis* (*CTh* I. xiii. 1, 394), the *largitionales tituli* and the *vectigalia* of Carthage to the vicar of Africa (*CTh* I. xv. 9, 378, 10, 379).

22. Asia does not appear in the lists of provinces under the disposition of the praetorian prefect of the East or the vicar of Asiana (*Not. Dig. Or.* ii, xxiv), nor Africa under the praetorian prefect of Italy or the vicar of Africa (*Not. Dig. Occ.* ii, xx); cf. Eunap. *V. Soph.* VII. 5. Constitutions circularized: *CTh* I. xv. 12, omnibus vicariis, 386, VIII. i. 12, omnibus rectoribus provinciarum, 382, XI. vi. 1, ad proconsules, vicarios omnesque rectores, 382, Maj. *Nov.* iii, universis rectoribus provinciarum, 458: *CTh* VI. xxxi. 1, VII. xx. 1, XII. i. 71, are clearly copies of such circulars. Just. *Nov.* xxxii and xxxiv are two copies, addressed in 535 to the governors of Haemimontus and Moesia II, of a law 'quam primo quidem in Thraciam et totas eius provincias, in praesenti autem in Illyricianas patrias direximus' (Just. *Nov.* xxxiii, *PPO Illyr.*, 535). Apart from answers to judicial *relationes* the following laws addressed to provincial governors contain local allusions: *CJ* VII. xvi. 41 (316), *CTh* VIII. iv. 11, 365, IX. xxvii. 3, 382, XXX. 4, 365, XII. i. 61, 364, Just. *Nov.* xxi, 536, lxv, 538. JULIAN'S LAW: *CTh* XII. i. 55, 363.

23. On the administration of the capitals see ch. XVIII, Symm. *Rel.* 17, *CTh* I. vi. 7, 376. Constitutions addressed to *praefecti annonae, praefecti vigilum* and *consulares aquarum* are listed in Mommsen's edition of *CTh*, pp. ccii, cciii.

24. *Duces* are not said to be under the disposition of the *magistri militum* in *Not. Dig. Or.* vii, viii, ix, but were in fact under their control, as appears from *CTh* VII. xvii. 1, mag. mil. Thrac. 412, Th. II, *Nov.* iv, 438, xxiv §1–3, 443, *CJ* XII. lix. 8 (467–70), illustribus scilicet ac magnificis viris magistris militum consuetudine ac potestate, si qua ad limites aliquos Orientis Thraciarum et Illyrici ex longo tempore hactenus optinuit, reservata. In 483 Illus as *magister militum per Orientem* was given the exceptional privilege of appointing *duces* (Theophanes, A.M. 5972). In the fourth century frontier posts were built on the orders of the *magistri militum*; *ILS* 762 (cf. *AE* 1941, 12), disponente Equitio v.c. comite mag. equitum peditumque, curante Augustiano v.c. comite ord. pr. et duce Val. limitis, and *ILS* 773–5. JUSTINIAN'S CHANGES: *CJ* I. xxix. 5, Proc. *Aed.* III. i. 16 (Armenia), Proc. *BV* II. xxii. 1, 4, xxviii. 43–5, *ILS* 831 (Africa), *ILS* 835 (Spain); in Italy Justinian does not seem to have formally established a *magisterium*, but Narses was left as commander in chief when the conquest had been completed. The western hierarchy is set out in *Not. Dig. Occ.* v. 125–143; the *magister equitum per Gallias* receives his *princeps* and *numerarii* from the *officia* of the *praesentales* (ibid. vii. 112, 118) like the *comites* and *duces*.

25. For the diocesan *rationales*, etc., see pp. 412–14, 428–9. Their waning importance is indicated by the fact that nineteen constitutions are addressed to them down to 357 and none thereafter (*CJ* III. xxvi. 7, X. x. 1, *CTh* II. xxv. 1, V. xiii. 2, IX. iii. 1, X. i. 2, 7, viii. 1, 2, 4, X. 5, XI. 1, xviii. 1, xix. 1, XI. vii. 5, XXX. 14, XII. i. 30, vi. 2, vii. 1). They are not mentioned in the codes after 400 except in *CTh* XI. xxx. 68, 429 and Val. III, *Nov.* vii. 2, 442.

26. CONSTITUTIONS ADDRESSED TO COMITES REI MILITARIS: *CTh* VI. xxviii. 8, VII. i. 4, VIII. vii. 13, IX. xlii. 18, XI. xxiv. 3, XVI. v. 56, x. 11; those addressed to *duces* are listed in Mommsen's edition of *CTh*, p. cci; those addressed to *rationales (summarum)* and *magistri rei privatae* on pp. ccii, cciii.

27. *CTh* I. vii. 2, Addaeo com. et magistro utriusque militiae, 393, corrector quidem provinciae Augustamnicae ob inlatam duci contumeliam ut cum officio suo condemnaretur meruit, a sede autem sublimitatis tuae usurpari iudicii pars ista non debuit, quia semper de ordinario iudice illustris est cognitio praefecturae. DIONYSIUS AND THE GOVERNOR OF CYPRUS: *A.C.Oec.* I. i. pars vii. 119-20.

28. For *probatoriae* see above n. 4 and for *militia* in the civil service and the army see ch. XVI and XVII. CODICILLI: *CTh* VI. vii. 1, 372 (for praetorian and urban prefects and *magistri militum*), IX. xxvii. 1, 380 (for *iudices*), XIII. xi. 11, 406 (for *peraequatores* and *discussores*), XV. xiv. 8, 389 (for *dignitates* in general), *CJ* I. xxvii. 1 §§18-19, 534 (for provincial governors), I. xlix. 1 §2, 479 (for provincial governors, vicars, etc., *comites rei militaris* and *duces*), Just. *Nov.* xvii pr. 535, placuit etiam omnibus iudicibus nostris qui minores vel medias administrationes gerunt, sive inter correctores sive inter consulares sive inter spectabiles ordinentur, non solum codicillos praestare sed etiam mandata dare, Const. Porph. *Cer.* I. 84, καὶ ἐπιδίδωσιν αὐτῷ ὁ βασιλεὺς τὰ κωδικέλλια τοῦ κόμητος τῶν ἀδμηνσιόνων, 85, τὰ μάνδατα δίδεται τῇ πρὸ μιᾶς σιλεντίου καὶ τὸν Αὐγουστάλιον Ἀλεξανδρείας ἔπαυσεν, καὶ μετὰ τὸ γενέσθαι πάντα τὰ ἐξ ἔθους δίδωσιν αὐτῷ κωδικέλλια. *Codicilli* were also used to convey equestrian or senatorial rank and honorary offices, see ch. XV, nn. 18, 20. That they were issued through the *primicerius notariorum* appears from Just. *Nov.* viii, notitia, where the main fees go to him and his *adiutor*. *Epistula* is sometimes used as a mere literary variant for *codicillus*, e.g. *CTh* VI. xxii. 5, 381, omnes qui extra palatium constituti codicillis proconsularibus vel epistulis vicariorum vel insignibus consularium emendicatis atque adsimulaticiis vestiuntur, 7 §1, 383, seu epistolas ex vicariis sive ex proconsulibus seu . . . ex praefectis meruerint codicillos, XV. xiv. 8, 389, omnes qui tyranni usurpatione provecti cuiuslibet acceperunt nomen inlicitum dignitatis, codicillos adque epistolas et promere iubemus et reddere. *Epistula* is more normally—and perhaps correctly—used for inferior posts, e.g. *CJ* II. vii. 23 §2, 509, eos clarissimorum notariorum inseri consortio tribunorum, sacras solitas epistulas sine quadam suffragii solutione percepturos, 25 §1, 519, sacras insuper epistulas quibus adprobantur viri clarissimi tribuni praetoriani et notarii, Paul. *V. Amb.* 43, faceretque falsas epistulas tribunatus, *CTh* VIII. v. 23, 365, codicillis comitivae et praesidatus aut rationum epistulis (but this may be literary variation only). *Epistulae* were also used for appointments to civic posts (see ch. XIX, nn. 30, 35) and issued to veterans, both officers and other ranks; *CTh* VII. xxi. 1, si qui ex protectoribus vel ex praepositis vel ex tribunis epistulas reportaverint, VIII. vii. 2, 3, ex protectoribus epistulas, VII. xx. 4 §1, 325, post emeritae missionis epistulas, VIII. vi. 1, 365, nemini ex his qui ex castrensibus muniis absoluti ad domum redeunt post labores tractoria praebeatur a sacro separata iudicio, sed unusquisque in epistulis nostris quibus ad aevi reliqui testimonium singulos sequimur viaticum conficiendi itineris consequatur.

29. The word *dignitas* is sometimes used of *protectores* and *domestici*, e.g. *CTh* VII. xxi. 2 (326-54), ad honores protectoriae dignitatis, 3, 396, quicumque ex protectoribus aut domesticis honorarias missiones meruerint, sub hac norma penes eos dignitas maneat), and Julian appointed Leontius a *domesticus* by *epistula* (Julian, *Ep.* 22, ἐπιτρέψαντες οὖν σοι τὴν τῶν ὅπλων χρῆσιν ἀπεστείλαμέν τε πανοπλίαν, ἣ τέως τοῖς πεζοῖς ἁρμόττει . . . ἐγκατελέξαμέν τέ σε τῷ τῶν οἰκείων συντάγματι). But the service is more often called *militia* (*CTh* VI. xxiv. 5, 392, 6, 395, 7, 414, 9, 416) and this was apparently strictly correct; Justinian insisted on the issue of a *probatoria* to those who adored the sacred purple

(Const. Porph. *Cer.* I. 86, δομεστικοὶ δὲ καὶ προτίκτορες οὕτως· πάλαι μὲν ἀπὸ προσκυνήσεως μόνης ἦν ἡ στρατεία αὐτῶν, νῦν δὲ προβατωρείαν ποιεῖ ὁ δεσπότης). For the notaries see pp. 572–5

30. See ch. V, nn. 13–4, XV, n. 12.

31. For the provinces see App. III. For posts under the *comites largitionum* and *rei privatae* and *praefectus urbi* see *Not. Dig. Occ.* xi, xii, iv. For numbers of regiments see App. II, Table XV.

32. *Chron. Min.* I. 66–9. There is a list of the prefects of the city of Rome from 312 to 458 in Seeck, *Reg.* 475–6, and in Sundwall, *Weströmische Studien*, 24–6, a fuller list from 395 to 476. There is now a more complete list in A. Chastagnol, *Les fastes de la Préfecture de Rome au Bas-Empire*, Paris, 1962. He shows 129 appointments in 133 years (290–423) and a normal tenure of under one year.

33. The latest list of praetorian prefects is that of Ensslin in *PW* XXII A, 2495–2501 (based on previous lists there cited). The praetorian prefects of the East known from the Codes and Novels are listed in Seeck, *Reg.* 475; the three additional ex-prefects of 451 are Eugarus, Parnasius and Constantinus (*A.C.Oec.* II. i. 334–5). Another example of the incompleteness of our information is Florentius, who is recorded on 13 April 449 as ὁ μεγαλοπρεπέστατος ἀπὸ ἐπάρχων πόλεως καὶ ἀπὸ ἐπάρχων πραιτωρίων τὸ ἔκτον (*A.C.Oec.* II. i. 149, 176). He is known to have been *PU Const.* in 422 (*CTh* VI. viii. 1), *PPO Or.* 21 April 428 to 27 March 429 (*CTh* xv. viii. 2, *CJ* I. xix. 8), and again from 31 January 438 to 26 November 439 (Th. II, *Nov.* iii, *CJ* IX. xxvii. 6), and again on 11 February 445 (*CJ* I. iii. 22); this date was rejected by Seeck as being between Hermocrates on 29 November 444 (Th. II, *Nov.* xxvi) and Taurus 17 February 445 (*CJ* I. ii. 11 and x. xlix. 2), but probably records a brief term of office. We are still left with two prefectures unaccounted for.

34. Ensslin has compiled a list of *magistri militum* down to 395 and of the Western *magistri* to 476 in *Klio* XXIV (1931), 102–47, 467–502; for Areobindus and Aspar see ch. VI, n. 17. A. E. R. Boak gives a list of *magistri officiorum* in *The Master of the Offices in the later Roman and Byzantine Empires* (Univ. of Michigan Studies, Humanistic Series, XIV, 1924), 148–51.

35. The list of proconsuls in A. C. Pallu de Lessert, *Fastes des provinces Africaines*, Paris, 1896, is nearly complete: add Iuniorinus Polemius (*AE* 1949, 28), Flavius Rhodinus Primus (*CIL* VIII. 1873 + 14279, 24044) and Rufius Volusianus (Rut. Nam. *de red. suo* I. 167–73). There is a short complete run of *praefecti Augustales* between 379 and 393 in Cantarelli, *La serie dei prefetti di Egitto*, 39–40 (nos. 125–140), showing an average tenure of under a year. The *duces* of Egypt are Valacius in 339–40 (Ath. *Hist. Ar.* 12) and 344 (*Chr.* I. 464), Felicissimus in 346 (*Chr.* I. 179) and 350 (Ath. *Hist. Ar.* 51, *Apol. Const.* 10), Syrianus in 356 (Ath. *Hist. Ar.* 81, *Apol. Const.* 22, 24, *Apol. de Fuga*, 24), Sebastianus in 358 (Ath. *Hist. Ar.* 59, 72, *Apol. de Fuga*, 6, F. Larsow, *Die Festbriefe des Heiligen Athanasius*, 37), Artemius in 360 (Larsow, op. cit. 37), Theophilus in 362 (Julian, *Ep.* 50), Victorinus in 364 and 366 (*CTh* XII. xii. 5, Larsow, op. cit., 42) Trajanus in 367–8 (Larsow, *op. cit.*, 44–5).

36. Larsow, op. cit., 26–46, E. Schwartz, *Ges. Schr.* III. 15–26, L. Cantarelli, *La serie dei prefetti di Egitto*, 23–36 (nos. 99–124).

37. Great nobles include Anicius Paulinus (*ILS* 1220–1, *pc. As.*, *PU*), Anicius Auchenius Bassus (*ILS* 1262, *pc. Camp.*, *PU*), and Petronius Probus (*ILS* 1265 ff., *pc. Afr.*, *PPO*); cf. Avianius Symmachus (*ILS* 1257, *pf. annonae, vic. U.R.*,

PU) and in the fifth century Auxentius Draucus (*ILS* 1284, *vic. U.R., PU*) and Rufius Volusianus, who 'primaevus meruit principis ore loqui, rexerat ante puer populos pro consule Poenos' (Rut. Nam. *de red. suo,* I. 172–3), that is, was proconsul of Africa as a boy and quaestor as a youth. More normal careers (omitting minor offices in Rome) are *ILS* 1231 (*corr. Ven., com. Or., PPO,* later *PU*), 1237 (*cons. Num., com. Or., PPO*), 1243 (*cons. Sic., pc. Afr., PU*), 8985 (*cons. Camp., pc. As., PU*). Rather longer are *ILS* 1224 (*cons. Camp., com. Or., pc. Afr.,* later *PU*), 1227 (*corr. Flam., cons. Sic., pc. Afr., PU*), 1228 (*corr. Flam., cons. Bith., pc. Afr.*), 1258 (*corr. Tusc., cons. Lus., pc. Ach., PU, PPO*). Even longer are *ILS* 1240 (*pr. Byz., cons. Eur., cons. Sic., pc. Afr., PU*) and 1256 (*corr. Tusc., cons. Camp., vic. U.R., pc. Afr.*), *AE* 1955, 150 (*corr. Flam., corr. Venet., cons. Belg.* I, *vic. Hisp., procos. Afr.*), *ILA* 456 (post correcturas et consularem dignitatem Achaiae Asiae iterum et Africae IIII procos.) MAXIMINUS: Amm. XXVIII. i. 5, 6, 41. TATIAN: *ILS* 8844, cf. *JTS* v (1954), 224–7; he is last recorded as *CSL* in 377 and first recorded as praetorian prefect in 388 (*CTh* VIII. vii. 14, XVI. iv. 2). A very long career of a new man is *ILS* 1214 (Caelius Saturninus).

38. PETRONIUS MAXIMUS: *ILS* 809, qui primaevus in consistorio sacro tribunus et notarius meruit nono decimo aetatis anno, sacrarum remunerationum per triennium comes, post praef. urbis anno et sex mensibus, hasque omnes dignitates intra vicesimum quintum adsecutus aetatis annum. ANICIUS ACILIUS GLABRIO FAUSTUS: *ILS* 1283, quaestori candidato, praetori tutelari, comiti intra consistorium, tertio praefecto urbi utriusque imperii iudicii sublimitato, praefecto praetorio Italiae Africae et Inlyirici. RUFIUS PRAETEXTATUS POSTUMIANUS: *ILS* 1285, quaestor candidatus, praetor urbanus, tribunus et notarius praetorianus, praefectus urbi secundo, consul ordinarius. JUNIUS QUARTUS PALLADIUS: *AE* 1928, 80, not. et tri. com. sacrar. larg. praef. praetorii per annos sex Illyrici Italiae et Africae, consuli ordinario; he has been identified with the Palladius who was proconsul of Africa in 410 (*CTh* VI. xxviii. 7, IX. xxxviii. 12), but this must be wrong as the inscription would not omit so honourable an office. ANTHEMIUS: Joh. Lydus, *Mag.* III. 50. MARINUS AND JOHN: Joh. Lydus, *Mag.* III. 36, 46, 57. AGILO: Amm. XX. ii. 5, Agilone ad eius locum immodico saltu promoto ex Gentilium et Scutariorum tribuno. According to Sid. Ap. *Carm.* II. 75 ff. the noble Procopius, after serving as envoy to Persia as a youth, was straightway appointed *magister militum per Orientem,* while his son Anthemius was appointed *comes rei militaris* on the Danube as soon as he had finished his literary education, and soon after *magister militum* (ibid. 193 ff.): cf. also Proc. *BV* II. xxiv. 1, ἐν τούτοις δὲ βασιλεὺς ἄλλον ἐς Λιβύην στρατηγὸν ᾿Αρεόβινδον ξὺν στρατιώταις ὀλίγοις τισὶν ἔπεμψεν, ἄνδρα ἐκ βουλῆς μὲν καὶ εὖ γεγονότα, ἔργων δὲ πολεμίων οὐδαμῶς ἔμπειρον. It was also usual for emperors to appoint their relatives as *magistri militum,* e.g. Leo and his brother-in-law Basiliscus, Anastasius and his nephews Pompeius and Hypatius, Justin and his nephews Germanus and Justinian, Justinian and his nephews Marcianus and Marcellus and his cousin Germanus with his two sons, Justin and Justinian (see Stein, *Bas-Empire,* indices, under these names).

39. Of twenty-two *duces* mentioned by Ammianus only three are heard of again, Sebastianus who rose to *comes* under Julian and *magister* under Valens (Amm. XXIII. iii. 5, XXXI. xi. 1, xiii. 18), Serenianus, who was already *ex duce* in 353 (XIV. vii. 7) and was made *comes domesticorum* by Valens in 364 (XXVI. v. 3), and the future emperor Theodosius (XXIX. vi. 15). Nearly all *duces* mentioned in the Codes and in inscriptions are otherwise unknown. The same applies to the vast majority of provincial governors.

40. Symm. *Rel.* 17, melius urbi vestrae in posterum consuletis si legatis invitos, Marc. *Nov.* i pr., 450, sciens quippe felicem fore rem publicam si a nolentibus et actus publicos repulsantibus regeretur.

41. Lib. *Ep.* 959, μίαν εὑρίσκει καταφυγὴν ζώνην τε καὶ τὸ ἄρξαι· καὶ δακρύων ἅμα δεῖταί μου θαρρῆσαι πέμψαι πρὸς σὲ τὴν τοῦτο ποιήσουσαν ἐπιστολήν· πάντως δὲ αὐτὸν ἀγαπήσειν ἅπαν τὸ διδόμενον, ἅπαν γὰρ ἕξειν τὴν αὐτὴν ἀσφάλειαν, ὥσπερ αὖ καὶ χρόνον ἅπαντα, κἂν μὴν οὗτος ᾖ.

42. Tac. *Ann.* I. 80. Lib. *Or.* LIX. 164, ἀεὶ δὲ τοὺς προτέρους ὑπάρχους ἀναπαύοντες ἐν τῷ μέρει δευτέρους ἑτέρους πρὸς τὰς διοικήσεις ἄγουσι. καὶ πάνυ γε εἰκότως, εἴτε γὰρ ἐπίπονόν τι τὸ χρῆμα τῆς ἀρχῆς, οὐκ ἀξιοῦσι διηνεκεῖ φορτίῳ τοὺς αὐτοὺς ἐπιτρίβεσθαι, εἴτε τινὸς εὐδαιμονίας μετέχον, πολλοὺς εἰς μετουσίαν τῆς εὐδαιμονίας καλοῦσιν. PROBUS: Amm. XXVII. xi. 2–3: et licet potuit, quoad vixit, ingentia largiendo, et intervallando potestates adsiduas, erat tamen interdum timidus ad audaces, contra timidos celsior, ut videretur cum sibi fideret, de cothurno strepere tragico, et ubi paveret, omni humilior socco, atque ut natantium genus elemento suo expulsum haut tam diu spirat in terris, ita ille marcebat absque praefecturis, quas ob iurgia familiarum ingentium capessere cogebatur, numquam innocentium per cupiditates inmensas, utque multa perpetrarent impune, dominum suum mergentium in rem publicam. Amm. XXIX. iii. 6, Africanus causarum in urbe defensor adsiduus, post administratam provinciam ad regendam aliam adspiravit, cuius suffragatori magistro equitum Theodosio id petenti, subagresti verbo pius respondit imperator: 'abi' inquit 'comes, et muta ei caput, qui sibi mutari provinciam cupit' et hoc elogio perit homo disertus ad potiora festinans ut multi. *CTh* IX. xxvi. 4, 416, si quis proconsularem aut vicarianam potestatem vel consularitatis fasces aut vexilla praesidalia atque in discussionibus comitivas vel officia principatus contra definitionem nostram iterare temptaverit, fisco eius omne patrimonium sociari decernimus. ACACIUS: Lib. *Ep.* 1449. NEON: Theod. *Ep.* (Azema), 37, 39, 40.

43. MARCELLIANUS: Amm. XXIX. vi. 3. THEODOSIUS: Amm. XXIX. vi. 15. When any details are given *duces* in Ammianus have previous military experience: e.g. Cassianus (XVI. ix. 2), Valentinus (XVIII. iii. 5), Pusaeus (XXIV. i. 9), Maurus (XXV. i. 2). NARSES: Proc. *BG* II. xiii. 16.

44. Procopius (*HA* xx. 15) declares that Justinian's predecessors had nearly all appointed men learned in the law as quaestors, and admits that even under Justinian Tribonian and Constantine (*HA* xx. 20) had this qualification. For advocates as *magistri scriniorum* see *ILS* 4152, Aedesius v.c. causarum non ignobilis Africani tribunalis orator, et in consistorio principum item magister libellorum et cognitionum sacrarum, magister epistularum, magister memoriae (cf. Amm. xv. v. 4); as quaestors, Cass. *Var.* I. 12, v. 3–4, viii. 18–19, x. 6–7. For rhetors as *magistri scriniorum* and quaestors, Eunap. *V. Soph.* XVIII (Nymphidianus), Auson. III. 15–36 (Ausonius), Soc. v. 25 (Eugenius), Proc. *HA* xx. 17 (Junillus, an eminent Latinist). For the general promotion of barristers see ch. XIV, n. 97. POLYCARPUS AND MARINUS: Joh. Lydus, *Mag.* III. 36, ηὐξήθη δὲ λοιπὸν τὰ τῶν σκρινιαρίων ἀπὸ τῆς Ζήνωνος βασιλείας τοσοῦτον, ὅσον τὰ τῆς τάξεως ἔληξε· πολλῶν μὲν γὰρ ἄλλων καὶ Πολυκάρπου δὲ ἀπ' αὐτῶν εἰς τὴν ἀρχὴν ἁρπασθέντος ὑπὸ τῷ Ἀναστασίῳ, εἶτα καὶ Μαρίνου τὴν ὅλην ἀναζωσαμένου τῶν πραγμάτων διοίκησιν, ὃς καὶ αὐτὸς εἰς τῶν τῆς Συρίας σκρινιαρίων ἐτύγχανε (cf. *CJ* v. xxx. 4, x. xxxii. 66, XII. xvi. 5 for Polycarpus). JOHN THE CAPPADOCIAN: Joh. Lydus, *Mag.* III. 57. Leo and Remigius started as financial clerks, but were rather inappropriately promoted to *magister officiorum*, an office which involved no financial work (Amm. XXVI. i. 6, XXX. ii. 10; xv. v. 36, XXVII. ix. 2).

45. For promotion of notaries see ch. pp. 127-8. AGENTES IN REBUS: *CTh* VI. xxvii. 13, 403, si post principatus officium nulla ulterioris honoris fuerint administratione perfuncti, xxviii. 2, 380, agentes in rebus, si principatus sorte deposita forsitan provinciae gubernacula isdem non evenerint. SILENTIARIES: *CTh* VI. xxiii. 2, 423, 3, 432. SACRA SCRINIA: *CTh* VI. xxvi. 14 §2, 412 (S); cf. on *palatini* in general, Symm. *Ep.* v. 76, Bonoso optimo viro et post militiam palatinam geminae administrationis integritate conspicuo, *CTh* VI. xxxv. 3, 319, etiam si quis ad diversas administrationes post obsequia palatina pervenerit, 5, ad universos palatinos, 328, ab his qui post impleta officia fidelis obsequii administrationes publicas meruerunt, 9, 380, agentem in rebus aliumve palatina dignitate subfultum, qui vel post administratam provinciam honorati auctoritate fulcitur vel testimonii nostri adsertione confidit frequenter super dignitate sua. ARCHIATRI: *CTh* XIII. iii. 15, 393, qui egerunt administrationes aut earum honore fungentur vel dimissi e palatio testimonialium suffragio munientur, 16, 414, seu indepta administratione seu accepta testimoniali meruerint missionem. CAESARIUS: Greg. Naz. *Or.* VII. 6-10, 13, 15.

46. *CTh* XII. i. 14, 326-54, dudum lege promulgata sanxit nostra clementia ut filii comitum et praesidum et rationalium magistrorumque privatae, qui tamen ex origine curialium descendunt, ordinibus necterentur. nunc praecipimus ut qui perfuncti muneribus idonei reperti sint iudicio clementiae nostrae accedere ad honores praecepti ad honestas promotiones perveniant. RHETORS: Amm. XXVII. ix. 6, Asiae vicarius ea tempestate Musonius advertisset, Athenis Atticis antehac magister rhetoricus, cf. Symm. *Ep.* I. 20, iter ad capessendos magistratus saepe literis promovetur, Lib. *Ep.* 1222 (Acacius' post is λόγων καρπός and his son's is λόγων πατρῴων καρπός); see also n. 44 above. POETS: Lib. *Or.* I. 225, (Icarius, *comes Orientis*) τὴν ἀρχὴν ἆθλον εἶχεν ἐπῶν, Lib. *Ep.* 77: Ἀνδρόνικος ὁ ποιητὴς οὕτω διέθηκε πρὸς αὐτὸν τὰς μέχρις Αἰθιόπων πόλεις, ὡς εἰκὸς ἦν Ἀνδρόνικον τοιοῦτον ἀφιέντα μέλι. καίτοι τὸ τῆς μητρὸς αὐτὸν καὶ τὸ τῆς πόλεως πάθος διεκώλυσε μὴ πάντα δεῖξαι τὰ ἀγάλματα τῆς ψυχῆς, ἀλλ' ὅμως οἷς ἠδυνήθη δεῖξαι δέδωκε τοῖς ἀνθρώποις εἰκάζειν περὶ τῶν οὐ φανέντων. ἐχαρίζετο δὲ ἡμῖν οὐ μᾶλλον διὰ τῶν ἐπῶν ἢ τῶν ἐπαίνων οἷς ἐχρῆτο κατὰ σοῦ λέγων τὸν μὲν βασιλέα τιμᾶν σε πᾶσιν οἷς εἶχεν, εὑρῆσθαι δὲ οὐδὲν οὐδέπω τῆς σῆς ἀξίας ἐγγύς. ἐμοῦ δὲ αὐτῷ παραινοῦντος μὴ διωθεῖσθαι τὰς διδομένας ἀρχὰς ὡς ἐνὸν ἄρχειν τε ὁμοῦ καὶ ἄδειν, ἀλλ' ἐγώ φησιν εἰμὶ δώσων ἐμαυτὸν Θεμιστίῳ μαθητὴν κάλλιον ἡγούμενος τοῦ πολλῶν ἄρχειν, Joh. Lydus, *Mag.* III. 42: Κύρου γάρ τινος Αἰγυπτίου, ἐπὶ ποιητικῇ ἔτι καὶ νῦν θαυμαζομένου, ἅμα τὴν πολίαρχον ἅμα τὴν τῶν πραιτωρίων ἐπαρχότητα διέποντος καὶ μηδὲν παρὰ τὴν ποίησιν ἐπισταμένου, . . .

47. For barbarians and Romans in military posts see ch. IV, nn. 53, 54, ch. V, nn. 10, 56, ch. VI, nn, 3-7, 16-18. ALYPIUS: Amm. XXIII. i. 2, XXIX. i, 44. CHRYSANTHUS: Soc. VII. 12. FESTUS: Amm. XXIX. ii. 22, cf. Lib. *Or.* I. 156 for his ignorance of Greek. RUFINUS: Zos. IV. 51 ff., Claudian, *in Ruf.* I. 137, 171-2; cf. Lib. *Ep.* 865 (no Greek). VADOMARIUS THE ALAMAN DUX OF PHOENICE: Amm. XXI. iii. 5. MUNDERICH THE THURINGIAN DUX OF ARABIA: Amm. XXXI. iii. 5. PREFECTS OF EGYPT: F. Larsow, *Die Festbriefe des heiligen Athanasius*, 26-46, E. Schwartz, *Ges. Schr.* III. 15-26.

48. PRAETORIAN PREFECTS OF GAUL: Sundwall, *Weströmische Studien*, 8 ff. LAW AGAINST NATIVES: *CJ* IX. xxix. 3, 380 (S), I. xli. 1, Syn. *Ep.* 73. ELECTION OF PROVINCIAL GOVERNORS: Just. *App.* vii. 12, 554, *Nov.* cxlix §1, 569, ἵνα τοίνυν μὴ ξένοι τινὲς ἐπεισπηδῶντες ταῖς ἐπαρχίαις ἀδικοῖεν αὐτάς, ἡμεῖς τε συχναῖς ταῖς κατ' αὐτῶν ἐνοχλοίμεθα προσελεύσεσι, προτρέπομεν τοὺς ἑκάστης ἐπαρχίας ὁσιωτάτους ἐπισκόπους κτητόρων τε καὶ οἰκητόρων τοὺς ἄγοντας τὰ πρωτεῖα διὰ κοινῆς δεήσεως

ἀναφέρειν ἐπὶ τὸ ἡμέτερον κράτος τοὺς αὐτοῖς ἐπιτηδείως ἔχειν πρὸς τὴν ἀρχὴν τῆς αὐτῶν ἐπαρχίας νομιζομένους.

49. PANNONIANS: A. Alföldi, *A conflict of Ideas in the Later Roman Empire*, 13-17. Theodosius I's praetorian prefect Cynegius was a Spaniard (see ch. V, n. 59). For Constantius II and Constans see pp. 133-4.

50. For the promotion of *tribuni scholarum* and *duces* see nn. 16 and 39. AUSONIUS: Auson. III. 25-36. SITTAS AND BELISARIUS: Proc. *BP* I. xii. 21, xiii. 9, xv. 3. JOHN: Joh. Lydus, *Mag.* III. 57.

51. AURELIUS VICTOR: Amm. XXI. x. 6. SUFFRAGATORES: *PL* XVII. 58, nam ideo ad regem per tribunos aut comites itur, quia homo utique est rex et nescit quibus debeat rempublicam credere. ad deum autem, quem utique nihil latet (omnium enim merita novit), promerendum, suffragatore non opus est sed mente devota.

52. PRAETORIAN PREFECTS AND GOVERNORS: Lib. *Ep.* 1224 (Salutius), 871 (Tatian), βασιλέως μὲν γὰρ τὸ δοῦναι τὸ γραμματεῖον, σὺ δ' ὃν λαβεῖν ἄξιον διδάσκεις, cf. 563, 1426, 1489; Syn. *Ep.* 73, Theod. *Ep.* (Azema) 39, *CJ* IX. xxvii. 6 pr., 439, sancimus eiusmodi viros ad provincias regendas accedere qui honoris insignia non ambitione vel pretio, sed probatae vitae et amplitudinis tuae solent testimonio promoveri, ita sane ut quibus hi honores per sedis tuae vel nostram fuerint electionem commissi, iurati inter gesta depromant se pro administrationibus sortiendis neque dedisse quippiam neque daturos umquam postmodum fore; cf. also Theod. *Ep.* (Azema) 39. SYMMACHUS: Symm. *Rel.* 17; *CTh* I. vi. 9, ad Symmachum, 385, disputari de principali iudicio non oportet; sacrilegii enim instar est dubitare an is dignus sit quem elegerit imperator.

53. THEODOSIUS: Amm. XXIX. iii. 6. MAXIMINUS: Amm. XXIX. vi. 3. For Pannonians under Valentinian and Valens, see n. 49. MAXIMINUS: Amm. XXVIII. i. 5. FESTUS: Amm. XXIX. ii. 22. AQUITANIANS UNDER GRATIAN: K. F. Stroheker, *Der senatorische Adel im spätantiken Gallien*, 26 ff.

54. Among Libanius' letters which directly solicit offices for his friends are *Ep.* 1224, 1260, 1426, 1443, 1449, 1474, 1489, 1510.

55. *CTh* VII. xxi. 2, 326-54, si quis de paganis vel decurionibus ambierit ad honores protectoriae dignitatis, nec tempus nec stipendia ei post hanc legem computanda sunt; hoc et circa eos qui ad praeposituras ambitu pervenerint custodiri praecipimus, VI. xxiv. 3, 365 (S), sicuti variis itineribus protectorum domesticorum schola comprehensos ad eam venire perspicimus, ita etiam sportularum diversa esse debebit insumptio. grave enim admodum est viros post emensum laborem, qui nullius rei cupidiores fuere quam gloriae, huiuscemodi erogationibus fatigari. eos tamen penitus solummodo inter quinos et denos sportularum nomine primatibus distribuere praecipimus. eos autem qui vel suffragio vel potentium gratia sacram purpuram adorare pervenerint, quinquagenos solidos volumus insumere, VII. xx. 13, 407 (S), oportet inter eos qui ambitio ac suffragiis ad tribunatus praepositurasque perveniunt et eos qui labore periculis atque ordine militiae decurso huiusmodi dignitates acceperint esse discretionem. ABINNAEUS: P. Abinn. 1.

56. CONSTANTINE: *CTh* VI. xxii. 1, 324 (S), si qui tamen bonorum virorum suffragio nulla data pecunia vel provinciae legatione suscepta nostris sunt obtutibus illustrati . . . qui vero coemptis procurationum administrationibus post lucra de fisco captata vacationem meruerunt. JULIAN: Amm. XX. v. 7,

'ut autem rerum integer ordo servetur, praemiaque virorum fortium maneant incorrupta, nec honores ambitio praeripiat clandestina, id sub reverenda consilii vestri facie statuo, ut neque civilis quisquam iudex nec militiae rector, alio quodam praeter merita suffragante, ad potiorem veniat gradum, non sine detrimento pudoris eo, qui pro quolibet petere temptaverit, discessuro'; xxii. vi. 5, unde velut aequitate ipsa dictante lex est promulgata, qua cavetur nullum interpellari suffragatorem super his quae eum recte constiterit accepisse; *CTh* 11. xxix. 1, 362, foedis commentis quae bonorum merito deferuntur quidam occupare meruerunt et cum meruissent in republica quolibet pacto versari, repetendam sibi pecuniam quam inhoneste solverant impudentius atque inhonestius arbitrantur: alii etiam quae tunc donaverant vel potius proiecerant ob inmeritas causas, invadenda denuo crediderunt. sed quia leges Romanae huiusmodi contractus penitus ignorant, omnem repetendi eorum quae prodige nefarieque proiecerunt copiam prohibemus. qui itaque repetere nititur vel repetisse convincitur, et quod dedit apud suffragatorem eius manebit vel extortum restituet et alterum tantum fisci viribus inferre cogetur. For 'fumum vendere' see SHA, *Ant. Pius*, 11, *Heliogab.* 10, *Alex. Sev.* 36. Mamertinus (Pan. Lat. iii. 19 ff.) gives a lurid account of *suffragia* under Constantius II, and his verdict is borne out by the praises given by Ammianus to Valentinian I (xxx. ix. 3, nec imperante eo provinciam nummularius rexit, aut administratio venumdata) and by Themistius to Valens (Or. viii. 117a, τοιγαροῦν σπάνιν ἐποίησας σπουδαρχούντων. καὶ οὐ πρόκειται νῦν ἀρχῶν ἀγορά, οὐδὲ προκηρύττονται αἱ τῶν ἐθνῶν ἐπιτροπεῖαι ὥσπερ τὰ ὤνια). THEODOSIUS I: *CTh* II. xxix. 2, 394, si qui desideria sua explicare cupientes ferri sibi a quoquam suffragium postularint et ob referendam vicem se sponsione constrinxerint, promissa restituant cum ea quae optaverint consequantur; si artibus moras nectent, ad solutionem debiti coartandi sunt. sed si quid eo nomine in auro vel argento vel in ceteris mobilibus datum fuerit, traditio sola sufficiat . . . quod si praedia rustica vel urbana placitum continebit, scriptura quae ea in alium transferat emittatur, sequatur traditio corporalis et rem fuisse completam gesta testentur.

57. RUFINUS: Claudian, *in Ruf.* I. 180, ambitos a principe vendit honores, Zos. v. 1. EUTROPIUS: Claudian, *in Eutrop.* I. 196 ff. THEODOSIUS I: Zos. IV. 28. PULCHERIA: Eunap. 87. LAW OF 439: *CJ* IX. xxvii. 6 (cited in n. 52). Themistius praises Valens because σπάνιν ἐποίησας σπουδαρχούντων, καὶ οὐ πρόκειται νῦν ἀρχῶν ἀγορά, οὐδὲ προκηρύττονται αἱ τῶν ἐθνῶν ἐπιτροπεῖαι ὥσπερ τὰ ὤνια (Or. viii, 117a); it is implied that offices were sold under Constantius II. We do not hear much of *suffragia* in the west in the fifth century, but they are regarded as a matter of course by Sidonius Apollinaris (*Ep.* v. 16, namque ille iam pridem suffragium dignitatis ineundae non solvit in lance sed in acie, aerariumque publicum ipse privatus non pecuniis sed manubiis locupletavit).

58. Malchus, 9, καὶ χρηστῆς ἂν βασιλείας ἔτυχον Ῥωμαῖοι, εἰ μὴ Σεβαστιανὸς ὁ τότε παραδυναστεύων ἦγεν αὐτὸν ὅπη ἐβούλετο, καπηλεύων ὥσπερ ἐξ ἀγορᾶς ἅπαντα καὶ μηδὲν ἄπρατον ἐῶν ἐν τῇ βασιλέως αὐλῇ διαπράττεσθαι, ἀλλὰ τὰς μὲν ἀρχὰς ἀπεδίδοτο πάσας, ἰδίᾳ μὲν ἑαυτῷ ἰδίᾳ δὲ λαμβάνων τῷ βασιλεῖ τὰ τιμήματα . . . εἰ δέ τινι ἀρχὴν τῶν περὶ αὐτὸν ὄντων ἐχαρίσατο Ζήνων, ὥσπερ πολιτοκάπηλος, αὐτὸς ταύτην ὀλίγου παρ' ἐκείνου λαμβάνων, ἄλλοις παρεῖχε τοῦ πλείονος, Ζήνωνι δὲ τὰ κλέμματα παρέχων, 12, ὅτι τὸν ἄρχοντα Αἰγύπτου ἐπὶ μόλις χρυσίου λίτρας ν' ἐκπεμπόμενον, ὥσπερ εὐδαιμον-εστέρας γενομένης ἢ πρόσθεν, ἐπὶ πεντακοσίαις ὁμοῦ λίτραις ἀπέστειλεν.

59. Just. *Nov.* viii, iusiurandum, ὄμνυμι δὲ τοὺς αὐτοὺς ὅρκους ὡς οὐδενὶ παντελῶς οὔτε δέδωκα οὔτε δώσω προφάσει τῆς δεδομένης μοι ἀρχῆς οὐδὲ προφάσει προστασίας, οὔτε ἐπηγγειλάμην οὔτε ὡμολόγησα ἐκ τῆς ἐπαρχείας πέμπειν οὔτε πέμψω, οὐδὲ προφάσει

δεσποτικοῦ suffragiou οὔτε τοῖς ἐνδοξοτάτοις ἐπάρχοις οὔτε τοῖς ἄλλοις πανευφήμοις ἀνδράσι τοῖς τὰς ἀρχὰς ἔχουσιν οὔτε τοῖς περὶ αὐτοὺς καθεστῶσιν. cf. proem, πῶς γὰρ ἂν ἴσχυον οἱ συντελεῖς, τῶν τε ἔκ τινος χρόνου βεβασιλευκότων ἀεί τι κερδαίνειν ἐκ τῆς ἐπὶ ταῖς ἀρχαῖς προαγωγῆς βουλομένων, εἰκότως τε τούτοις ἀκολουθούντων καὶ τῶν ἐνδοξοτάτων ὑπάρχων, ἔκ τε τῆς ἐντεῦθεν ἀδικίας, ταῖς τε ἔξωθεν ζημίαις ταῖς τε νενομισμέναις εὐσεβέσιν ἐπαρκεῖν εἰσφοραῖς; and §§1 and 7.

60. Just. *Nov.* viii pr., ἐσκοπήσαμεν γὰρ ὅτιπερ, εἰ καὶ πόρος οὐ μικρὸς ἐλαττοῦται τῇ βασιλείᾳ, ἀλλ᾽ οὖν τῶν ἡμετέρων ὑποτελῶν ἐπίδοσιν μεγάλην λαμβανόντων, εἴπερ ἀζήμιοι παρὰ τῶν ἀρχόντων φυλάττοιντο, ἥ τε βασιλεία τό τε δημόσιον εὐθηνήσει χρωμένη ὑπηκόοις εὐπόροις . . . ἢ οὐ πᾶσίν ἐστι φανερόν, ὅτιπερ ὁ χρύσιον διδοὺς καὶ οὕτω τὴν ἀρχὴν ὠνούμενος οὐκ αὐτὸ δίδωσι μόνον ὅσον προφάσει τῶν καλουμένων ἐπενοήθη suffragion, ἀλλὰ καὶ ἕτερον ἔξωθεν προσεπιθήσει πλεῖον προφάσει τῆς τῶν ἄλλων τῶν τὴν ἀρχὴν ἢ διδόντων ἢ μνηστευόντων θεραπείας; xxviii §4, ταῦτα ἡμᾶς ἐδυσώπησεν οὐ μόνον τοῖς ἐντεῦθεν κέρδεσιν ἀπειπεῖν, ἀλλὰ καὶ οἴκοθεν προσδαπανῆσαι μεγάλα, καὶ εἴ που τισὶν ὤνιον παρὰ τῶν πρὸ ἡμῶν τὸ τῆς ἀρχῆς ἐδίδοτο σχῆμα, τοῦτο ἐξωνήσασθαι καὶ ἐλευθέρους τοὺς ἡμετέρους ἀφεῖναι συντελεῖς τοῦ τοιούτου δασμοῦ καὶ οἴκοθεν ἀντεισαγαγεῖν τὴν παραψυχὴν τοῖς λαμβάνουσι, ἵνα καὶ τούτοις μεταδῶμεν ἐλευθερίας, xxix §2, ἡμεῖς γὰρ κἀνταῦθα τοὺς ἡμετέρους ὑποτελεῖς ἐξωνησόμεθα καὶ τοῖς κομιζομένοις ἐξ ἔθους προφάσει τοῦ καλουμένου σουφραγίου δώσομεν αὐτοί, τοῦτο ἐκ τῶν φόρων αὐτοῖς τῶν τῆς ἐπαρχείας ἐπιδίδοντες διὰ τοῦ θρόνου τοῦ σοῦ, Ed. iv §1, καὶ τὸ τοῦ μοδεράτωρος αὐτῇ δοῦναι σχῆμα καὶ σιτήσεις αὐτῇ ἄχρι δέκα λιτρῶν ἀφορίσαι χρυσίου, αὐτοῦ μὲν μηδέν τῷ δημοσίῳ παρέχειν ὀφείλοντος προφάσει τῆς τοιαύτης προαγωγῆς, τοῦ δὲ τὸ Φοινίκης σκρίνιον τρακτεύοντος δέκα μόνας χρυσίου λίτρας ἐτησίας διδόντος ἀπὸ τοῦ κανόνος τῆς αὐτῆς ἐπαρχίας τῷ κατὰ καιρὸν περιβλέπτῳ πριμικηρίῳ τῶν λαμπροτάτων τριβούνων νοταρίων, ὑπὲρ τῆς πρῴην αὐτῷ δεδομένης δωρεᾶς, ὅπερ καὶ βενεφίκιον ὀνομάζεται.

61. Proc. *HA* xxi. 9-19, Just. *App.* vii. 12, 554, *Nov.* cxlix, 569, clxi, 574, Greg. *Ep.* v. 38: sed rem mihi sacrilegam nuntiavit: quia hi qui in ea idolis immolant iudici praemium persolvunt, ut hoc eis facere liceat. quorum dum quidam baptizati essent et iam immolare idolis deseruissent, adhuc ab eodem insulae iudice etiam post baptismum illud praemium exigitur, quod dare prius pro idolorum immolatione consueverant. quem cum praedictus episcopus increparet, tantum se suffragium promisisse respondit, ut nisi de causis etiam talibus impleri non possit.

62. Just. *Nov.* viii pr.

63. *CTh* i. xxii. 4, 383, ceterum neque comiti neque rectori provinciae plus aliquid praestabitur quam nos concessimus in annonis seu cellariis, vii. iv. 32 (see n. 64). *Cellaria* are also mentioned in remissions of arrears, *CTh* xi. xxviii. 9, 414, 16, 433, Marc. *Nov.* ii §1, 450, also in *CTh* xi. i. 6, 354; these laws may refer to supplies for the *comitatus*. According to *Chron. Pasch.* 540, Vetranio after his abdication received from Constantius II ἀννώνας καὶ κελλαρικὰ δαψίλως. The bishops at the Council of Ariminum were given *annonas et cellaria* (Sulp. Sev. *Chron.* ii. 41) JULIAN: Amm. xvi. v. 3, denique cum legeret libellum adsidue, quem Constantius ut privignum ad studia mittens manu sua conscripserat, praelicenter disponens, quid in convivio Caesaris inpendi deberet: fasianum et vulvam et sumen exigi vetuit et inferri, munificis militis vili et fortuito cibo contentus. IMAGINARY LISTS: SHA, *Claudius*, 14, *Aurelianus*, 9, *Probus*, 4; cf. *SPP* xx. 75 (payments of barley for the *annona* of the governor, and of wine, meat, vegetables and fruit εἰς τὸ κελλαρικόν).

64. Symm. *Ep.* iv. 19, Flavianus vir inl. commune pignus diu eluctatus fortunae aspera, sed divi principis beneficio in tranquillum reductus, solvere salarium

patris iussus est, taxatione pretiorum graviter aggerata, neque census exilis tanto oneri convenit. *CTh* vii. iv. 32, 412, procuratores curiarum annonarum et cellariensium specierum gratia minime fatigentur quas in dignitatibus constituti, id est rectores provinciarum et comites, solent accipere. nam cum adaerationis aestimatio prius per centum et viginti capita exactione solidi teneretur, per sexaginta recens redegit aviditas exindeque iam nutrita licentia ad tredecim tributarios non dubitavit artare, procuratore damnum quo ipse subditus fuisset provincialibus infligente. ideoque per cornicularium cuius-cumque provincialis officii hanc sollicitudinem inpleri conveniet, ita ut nulla ab eodem exactionis molestia provincialibus inferatur. sed erogandas species ex horreis publicis et cellariensium nomine aurum ex titulo manifesto eidem delegatum pro erogationis qualitate suscipiat, etiam pretium his qui adaerare voluerint depensurus iuxta nundinationem quae aut foro rerum venalium continetur aut amplissimae praefecturae est culmini deputata, *CJ* i. lii. 1, 439, omnibus tam viris spectabilibus quam viris clarissimus iudicibus qui per pro-vincias sive militarem sive civilem administrationem gerunt . . . in praebendis solaciis annonarum hic fixus ac stabilis servabitur modus, ut ea pro annonis et capitu dignitati suae debitis pretia consequantur quae particularibus delega-tionibus soleant contineri. Just. *Nov.* viii §§2, 3, 5, xxiv. notitia, xxv. notitia, xxvi. notitia, 535, ὑπὲρ ἀννωνῶν καὶ καπιτατιόνων καὶ λοιπῆς παραψυχῆς.

65. Just *Ed.* xiii §3, 539, οὐδὲ γὰρ ἡμεῖς ἐκ τοῦ δημοσίου αὐτῷ ταύτην μόνην δώσομεν τὴν παραψυχήν, ἣν μέχρι νῦν ὁ περίβλεπτος Αὐγουστάλιος ἔχει, τὰς πεντήκοντα μὲν ἀννόνας καὶ τὰ πεντήκοντα κάπιτα, §18, λήψεται δὲ καὶ αὐτὸς τὰς ἀφωρισμένας αὐτῷ σιτήσεις, ὑπὲρ μὲν τῶν ἐν εἴδει ἀννονῶν ἐνενήκοντα καὶ καπίτων ἑκατὸν εἴκοσι νομίσματα χίλια πέντε τέταρτον, ὑπὲρ δὲ τῶν ἐν χρυσῷ ἀννονῶν πεντήκοντα καὶ καπίτων πεντήκοντα νομίσματα τετρακόσια. I regard the *annonae* 'in gold' as the basic salary, and those 'in kind' as perquisites, see ch. XVII, n. 84. Just. *Nov.* xxix §2, 535, σίτησιν μὲν λαμβάνων ἣν ἑκατέρα πρώην εἶχεν ἀρχή, συνιοῦσαν εἰς χρυσοῦς ἑπτακοσίους εἴκοσι πέντε, xxiv §1 and notitia, xxv §1 and notitia.

Justinian's salaries are as follows:

Praefectus praetorio Africae	100 lb.	(= 7,200 solidi)	*CJ* i. xxvii. 1 §21
Praefectus et dux Augustalis	40 lb.	(= 2,880 solidi)	Just. *Ed.* xiii §3
Proconsul Palaestinae	22 lb.	(= 1,584 solidi)	Just. *Nov.* ciii §1
(with assessor and *officium*)			
Dux Tripolitanae		1,582 solidi	*CJ* i. xxvii. 2 §20
Dux Byzacenae		,,	,, §23
Dux Numidiae		,,	,, §26
Dux Mauretaniae		,,	,, §29
Dux Sardiniae		,,	,, §32
Proconsul Cappadociae	20 lb.	(= 1,440 solidi)	Just. *Nov.* xxx §6
Dux Libyae (unaltered)		1,405¼ solidi	Just. *Ed.* xiii §18
Moderator Arabiae	15 lb.	(= 1,080 solidi)	Just. *Nov.* cii §2
Praetor Pisidiae		800 solidi	,, xxiv not.
Praetor Lycaoniae		,,	,, xxv not.
Praetor Thraciae		,,	,, xxvi not.
Comes Isauriae		,,	,, xxvii not.
Moderator Helenoponti		725 solidi	,, xxviii §3
Praetor Paphlagoniae		,,	,, xxix §2
Moderator Phoenicae Lib.	10 lb.	(= 720 solidi)	Just. *Ed.* iv §1
Quaesitor	10 lb.	,,	Just. *Nov.* lxxx §8

Praetor plebis (with assessor) 10 lb.	720 solidi	Just. *Nov.* xiii §3
Comes Armeniae III	700 solidi	„ xxxi §1
Consulares in Africa	448 solidi	*CJ* I. xxvii. 1 §40

66. *CTh* II. xxix. 2 (cited in n. 56), Lib. *Or.* XLVIII. 11, πρῴην τις ἐνεχθεὶς χορηγὸς ἐγγυητὴν καταστήσας ἀπέδρα. πῶς οὖν ὑμεῖς; τὸν μὲν ἐγγυητὴν ἀδικοῦντα οὐδέν, ἐξηπάτητο γάρ, καθείρξαντες εἴχετε, καὶ ὁ θυμὸς πολὺς καὶ αἱ ἀπειλαὶ δειναὶ καὶ διασπώμεθα τὸν ἄνθρωπον ἦσαν οἱ λέγοντες, μικρὸν δὲ ὕστερον τὸν ἐξεγγυηθέντα ἠκούομεν ἀρχὴν πριάμενον τῆς πατρῴας οἰκίας ἀγρὸν αὐτῇ προστεθεικότα συλλέγειν τὴν τιμὴν τοῖς ἐπὶ τῆς ἀρχῆς κακοῖς. BORROWING: Just. *Nov.* viii pr., 535, καὶ τοῦτο τὸ χρυσίον οὐκ οἴκοθεν ἴσως παρέχειν ἀλλὰ δεδανεισμένον, καὶ ἵνα δανείσασθαι δυνηθείη ζημιούμενον, καὶ συλλογίζεσθαι κατ' αὐτὸν ὅτι προσῆκόν ἐστι τοσοῦτον ἐκ τῆς ἐπαρχίας λαβεῖν ὁπόσον διαλύσει μὲν αὐτῷ τὰ ὀφλήματα, κεφάλαιά τε καὶ τόκον, καὶ τὰς ὑπὲρ αὐτοῦ τοῦ δανείσασθαι ζημίας, cf. xxviii §4, Lib. *Or.* IV. 20–2, Proc. *HA* xxi. 13, Syn. *Ep.* 72, 73, 100, πάντως δὲ συχνοῖς ἐντεύξῃ τοῖς δεῦρο ἀφικνουμένοις, καὶ εἰ μηδέσιν ἄλλοις ἀλλὰ τοῖς ἄρξουσιν ἡμῶν καὶ τὴν ἐλάττω καὶ τὴν μείζω καὶ τὴν Αἰγυπτίων ἀρχήν· οὓς οὐκ εἰκὸς ἀγνοεῖσθαι διὰ τὴν ἀκολουθίαν τῶν δανειστῶν.

67. Malchus, 12 (cited in n. 58), Just. *Ed.* iv §1 (cited in n. 60).

68. *CTh* IX. xxviii. 1, 392, *CJ* IX. xxviii. 1, 415, iudices, qui tempore administrationis publicas pecunias subtraxerunt, lege Iulia peculatus obnoxii sunt et capitali animadversioni eos subdi iubemus. A case of peculation is mentioned in Val. III, *Nov.* i. 3 §6, Sardiniam ab hoc excipi placuit quoniam apud nonnullos calliditate quadam maxima pars pecuniae resedit, quam exactam publicis oportuit erogationibus adplicari, but it is not stated who had pocketed the money. For extortion in tax collection see pp. 457–8, 467–8.

69. JUDICIAL CORRUPTION: *CTh* IX. xxvii. 5, 383, 6, 386, Marc. *Nov.* i pr., 450, Just. *Nov.* viii pr., 535. THE GOVERNOR OF SARDINIA: Greg. *Ep.* v. 38 (cited in n. 61). For laxity against heretics, see below, n. 84.

70. SALES AND GIFTS: *CTh* VIII. xv. 5, 368, 6, 380, 8, 397, Val. III, *Nov.* xxxii, 451, *CJ* I. liii. 1, 528. MARRIAGES: *CTh* III. vi. 1, 380, xi. 1, 380. Gregory Nazianzen (*Or.* XLIII. 56) recounts how Basil foiled the matrimonial pressure of the governor's assessor on a wealthy lady.

71. Theod. *Ep.* (Azema) 37, 39, 40. Other warm commendations of governors include Greg. Naz. *Ep.* 154, Lib. *Ep.* 780, 1261.

72. *CJ* I. xlix. 1, 479.

73. On the perquisites of military officers see pp. 644–5. For *petitio* by the great see Amm. XVI. viii. 11, Olymp. 23.

74. See ch. XVI, n. 34 (*agentes in rebus*), XVI, n. 19 (*notarii*), XVII, n. 165 (*domestici*), XVII, n. 118 (*scribones*), XVI, n. 15 (*silentiarii*), XVI, n. 8 (*cubicularii*). MITTENDARII: *CJ* I. xxvii. 1 §30, PPO Afr. 534, *CTh* VI. xxx. 7, 384 (= *CJ* XII. xxiii. 7 §6), 8+9, 385, 22, 419, 23, 422, all addressed *CSL*. EVECTIONES: *CTh* VIII. v. 12, 362, exceptis igitur vobis nulli evectionem licebit facere de cetero. sed ut necessitates publicae impleantur vicariis denas vel duodenas evectiones manu mea perscriptas ipse permittam, praesidibus vero binas annuas faciat vestra sublimitas, quibus ad separatas provinciarum secretasque partes necessariis ex causis officiales suos dirigere possint. sed his quoque nostra etiam mansuetudo evectiones singulas dabit, ut ad nos referre possint cum id fieri necessitas quaedam exegerit; cf. *Not. Dig. Or.* ii. 72, praefectus praetorio orientis evectiones annuales non habet sed ipse emittit,

iii. 33, praefectus praetorio Illyrici ipse emittit, xi. 53, magister officiorum ipse emittit (in the emperor's name), xiii. 35, comes largitionum quotiens usus exegerit, xiv. 15, comes rerum privatarum quotiens usus exegerit. The *magistri militum* (v–ix), the proconsul of Achaea (xxi), the vicar of Pontica (xxv), the *comites* of Egypt and Isauria (xxviii, xxix), and *duces* (xxx–xlii) have the number of their *evectiones* recorded. The prefect of the city had the right of issuing *evectiones* in 364 (*CTh* VIII. v. 19) but later lost it (*CTh* VIII. v. 55, *PU* 396).

75. The following constitutions illustrate bureaucratic promptitude or dilatoriness:

Maj. *Nov.* ii, 458, dat. vi id. Mart. Rav. acc. v id. ss. Rav.	1 day
Val. III, *Nov.* xxi. 2, 446, dat. vii kal. Ian. Rom. acc. vi kal. Ian. Rom. prop. v kal. Ian. in foro Traiani	2 days
Val. III, *Nov.* xix, 445, dat. vi id. Dec. Romae, pp. prid. id. Dec. in foro Traiani	4 „
Val. III, *Nov.* xxxi, 451, dat. prid. kal. Feb. Romae, acc. iii non. Feb. Romae, prop. in foro Traiani.	4 „
Val. III, *Nov.* xxv, 447, dat. iii. non. Iun. Rom. prop. in foro Traiani v id. Iun.	6 „
Val. III, *Nov.* x, 441, dat. x kal. Mart. Rav. accepta prid. id. Mart. ubi sup.	22 „
Anth. *Nov.* i, 468, dat. x kal. Mart. Romae, accep. id. Mart. Romae	23 „
Val. III, *Nov.* xxiii, 447, dat. iii id. Mart. Rom. acc. vi kal. April. Rom. prop. in foro Traiani viii id. April.	24 „

NICOMEDIA TO CONSTANTINOPLE: *CTh* VI. iv. 32, 397, dat. vi kal. Iul. Nicomedia, acc. prid. kal. Aug. Constp.

76. SYMMACHUS AND HONORIUS: *Coll. Avell.* 14, 15, 16, 33: another journey from Ravenna to Rome is Val. III, *Nov.* xxvii, 449, dat. xv kal. Iul. Rav. pp. in foro Traiani xiii kal. Aug. (33 days), cf. also *CTh* XI. xxxvi. 16, *PU* 364, dat. viii. id. Octob. Altino, acc. xvi kal. Nov. (9 days), VIII. xviii. 1, 315 (S), dat. xv kal. Aug. Aquil. recitata aput Vettium Rufinum *PU* in senatu non. Sept. (49 days).

FROM MILAN TO ROME:

CTh IX. vii. 3, 342, dat. prid. non. Dec. Med. pp. Romae xvii kal. Ianuar.	12 days
„ VI. x. 2 and vi. xxii. 5 +xxvi. 2, *PU* 381, dat. iv. kal. April Med. acc. xii kal. Mai.	22 „
„ VI. xxxv. 13, *PU* 386, dat. prid. non. Iul. Med. acc. iiii kal. Sept.	54 „
„ XIII. i. 1, 356, dat. iv. non. Dec. (at Milan) acc. Rom. viii id. Feb.	66 „

FROM ROME (MILAN) TO CONSTANTINOPLE (NICOMEDIA) AND VICE VERSA:

CTh VI. iv. 8 and 9, 356, dat. iii id. April. Med. lecta ab Araxio procons. die vi id. Mai.	29 days
„ XIV. xxiv. 1, 328, dat. kal. Mar. Nicomediae, acc. viii id. April. Romae	36 „
„ XIV. i. 1, 360 (S), dat. vi kal. Mar. Constanp. acc. id. Mai. Rom.	80 „

CONSTANTINOPLE TO HISPALIS: *CTh* III. v. 6, 336, dat. id. Iul. Constantp. accepta xiiii k. Mai. Hispali. SARDICA TO CORDUBA: *CTh* IX. i. 1, 316, dat. prid. non. Dec. Serdicae, accepta v non. Mart. Corduba.

The double dated constitutions to Africa are as follows:

CTh XI. xix. 1, 321, dat. xv kal. Mai. Sirmi, accep. xv kal. Iun. Karthag.	31 days
„ I. iii. 1, pc. Afr. 383, dat. xvi kal. Iul. Verona, accepta prid. kalend. Aug.	45 „
„ XI. xxx. 5+6, 316, dat. id. Aug. Arelato, pp. id. Octob. Theveste	61 „
„ XI. xxx. 33, 364, dat. prid. id. Sept. Aquil. acc. xviii kal. Dec. Tacapis	63 „
„ XI. vii. 8, 356 (S), dat. iiii non. Sept. Dinummae, acc. prid. id. Nov. Karthag.	71 „
„ XI. xxxvi. 23, pc. Afr. 378, dat. iii kal. Feb. Trev. acc. vi kal. Mai.	86 „
„ XI. i. 13, 365, dat. xv kal. Nov. Parisis, acc. xv kal. Feb. Karthag.	92 „
„ VIII. x. 1, 313 (S), dat. vi id. Nov. Treviris, acc. xv kal. Mart. Carthagine	99 „
„ XI. vii. 9, 364, dat. iii id. Mai. Hadrianop. acc. viii kal. Octob. Karthag.	134 „
„ XI. xxviii. 1, 363, dat. vii kal. Nov. Antiochiae, acc. xv kal. April. Karthag.	143 „
„ XV. i. 1, pc. Afr. 357, dat. iiii non. Feb. Med. acc. viii id. Iul.	156 „
„ IX. xl. 1+XI. xxx. 2+xxxvi. 1, dat. iiii non. Nov. Trev. acc. xv kal. Mai. Hadrumeti	166 „
„ VIII. vii. 12, pc. Afr. 372, dat. iii kal. Iun. Nassonaci, acc. vi kal. Dec.	180 „
„ XI. xxxvi. 10, 360 (S), dat. xv kal. Feb. Constantinop. acc. x kal. Aug. Karthag.	186 „
Sirm. 12, 407, data vii kal. Decembr. Romae, proposita Carthagine in foro sub programmate Porphyrii proconsulis nonis Iuniis	192 „
CTh XVI. ix. 1, 335, dat. xii kal. Nov. Constantinop. pp. viii id. Mai. Cartg.	199 „
„ X. xvii. 3, 391, dat. xiii kal. Iul. Aquil. acc. id. Ian. Hadrumeti	208 „
„ XV. vii. 13, 414, dat. vi id. Feb. Rv. Constantio v.c. cons. acc. a tribuno volupt. x kal. Feb. Karthagine post cons.	349 „

The last constitution evidently went astray in the post, following the *tribunus voluptatum*, whose proper residence was at Rome, to Carthage, where he had gone on mission or on holiday.

Journeys from various cities of Illyricum to Rome include:

CTh VI. xxii. 1, *PU* 324 (S), dat. x kal. Feb. Sirmio, acc. non. April.	72 days
„ XI. xxx. 28, 359, dat. xiv kal. Iul. Singiduno, pp. x kal. Aug. Rom.	35 „
„ II. xvi. 2, 319 (S), dat. viii kal. Aug. Naisso, prop. Rom. non. Octobr.	74 „
„ XI. xxx. 18, 329 (S), dat. xiii kal. Iul. Serdicae, pp. vi kal. Aug. Rom.	48 „
„ VIII. xvi. 1, 320, dat. prid. kal. Feb. Serdicae, pp. kal. April. Rom.	60 „

„ XVI. X. I, *PU* 320, dat. xvi kal. Ian. Serdicae, acc. viii id.
Mar.   82 „
„ II. xvii. I, 324 (S), dat. v id. April. Thessal. pp. iii kal.
Iun. Rom.   52 „
Cf. also *CTh* VII. xxii. I, 319, dat. xiiii kal. Mart. Sirmio, acc. vii id. April.
Regio (50 days).

Journeys from Gaul to Italy and *vice versa* are as follows:
    CTh VI. xxviii. I, 379, dat. prid. non. Aug. Treviris, acc. vii id.
        Sept. Romae   34 days
    „ VI. xxxv. 7, PU 367, dat. xiiii kal. Dec. Treviris, acc. iiii
        id. Dec.   22 „
    „ VI. vii. I, PU 372, dat. iii non. Iul. Nasonaci, acc. iii non.
        Sept.   60 „
    „ XI. xxix. I, 312, dat. vi kal. Ian. Trev. acc. viii id. Feb.
        Regio   41 „
    MGH (*Ep.*) III, p. 15, data xv kalendas Maias (at Ravenna,
        418), accepta Arelate X kalendas Iunias   36 „
Miscellaneous journeys include Antioch to Tyre in 42 days (*CTh* XII. i. 52,
362), Noviodunum to Marcianopolis in 15 days (*CTh* X. xxi. I, 369), Sirmium
to Corinth in 32 days (*CTh* II. iv. I, 319) and Aquileia to Salernum in 29 days
(*CTh* VIII. iii. I, 364).

77. DEFENSOR: *CTh* I. xxix. I, 368 (S), 4, 368, *CJ* I. lv. 8, 409, Just. *Nov.* viii
not. §49, 535. CURATOR: *CTh* XII. i. 20, 331. Montius' gibe to the Caesar
Gallus, οὐδὲ λογιστὴν, ἀντεῖπεν, ἔξεστί σοι προχειρίσασθαι (Philostorgius, III. 28)
implies that *curatores civitatis* were officially appointed by the emperor.
EXACTOR: *Chr.* I. 44. OTHER MAGISTRATES: *P. Oxy.* 2110. From Cass. *Var.*
VII. 11, 12 (cf. Just. *Nov.* civ §2, 537) it appears that all *curatores* and *defensores*
were appointed by the crown in Ostrogothic Italy. For *probatoriae* see above
n. 4, cf. *CTh* VIII. vii. 7, 356 (S) = *CJ* XII. lvii. 2, nullus iudicum quemquam
sine sacra probatoria probare audeat vel provehere, *CJ* XII. xxxv. 17 (472?),
neminem in ullo numero equitum vel peditum vel in quolibet limite sine
nostri nominis sacra probatoria in posterum sociari concedimus, consuetudine
quae hactenus tenuit antiquata, quae magisteriae potestati vel ducibus probatorias militum facere vel militibus adiungere licentiam tribuebat, ut ii
tantum in numeris vel limitibus militent qui a nostra divinitate probatorias
consequuntur.

78. CONSTANTINE'S LAW: *CTh* I. xvi. 3, 319, cum sex menses transcurrerint,
breves omnium negotiorum ab officio tuo descripti commeent ad scrinia
eminentissimae praefecturae, ut his recensitis et ad scrinia nostra perlatis
pandatur quis iudicum et in quibus discingendis causis fidelem operam
praestiterit. For appeals see ch. XIV, n. 26.

79. See ch. XIII, n. 99. Cf. Josh. Styl. 42, *CTh* XI. xxviii. 3, 401, post consulatum vero mansuetudinis nostrae, id est a prima indictione, in consulatum
Olybrii et Probini, omnium reliquorum exactionemsu spendi oportere censemus, donec admoniti ordinarii iudices nominatorios breves absque ulla con-
scribtos fraude transmittant, quibus aperte liqueat quae penes minuscularios,
quae penes curiales debita, quae etiam in defectis domibus habeantur.

80. *CTh* XI. i. 13, vic. Afr., 365, placuit per singulos quosque annos reliqua
eorum qui Romae consistentes in Africa possident missis brevibus indicari,
eosdemque compelli ut procuratores instructos ad officium tuae sinceritatis

pro celebranda solutione transmittant. ut autem nihil de transmissione ac pervectione obscuritatis oriatur, tabularios praefecti annonae Africae, sed et urbis Romae, ad officium quod sollertiae tuae paret deduci praecipimus, conlaturos aput acta quid transmissum, quid pervectum sit. cuius rei indicia manere et perferri ad scrinia nostra debebunt, eo nihilo minus curando ut plena instructio ad officium inlustris praefecturae praetorianae deferatur.

81. PROVINCIAL QUADRIMENSTRUI BREVES: *CTh* I. x. 7, 401, breves etiam quadrimenstruos ad officium palatinum noverint dirigendos, aurumque exactum ad sacras largitiones sine ulla dilatione mittatur, XII. i. 173, 410, hoc etiam observando ut quadrimenstruis quoque brevibus qui ad excellentiae tuae officium (so correctly in *CJ* x. xxii. 1) sollemniter diriguntur celebratae describtionis dispunctio societur, vi. 27, 400, *CJ* I. xlii. 1, οἱ ἄρχοντες καὶ αἱ τούτων τάξεις ἀνυπερθέτως μετὰ τῆς ἀληθείας καὶ ἀκριβείας ἐκπεμπέτωσαν τὰ τετραμηνιαῖα βρέβια, x. xxiii. 3, 468, quadrimenstruis brevibus per idoneum tractatorem eorundem titulorum super commendandis ratiociniis publicis periculo rectorum provinciarum ad sacratissimam urbem transmittendis, Cass. *Var*. XII. 2, 16. DUCAL QUADRIMENSTRUI BREVES: *CTh* XI. xxv. 1, 393, quotienscumque quadrimenstrui breves ab apparitoribus ducianis ad sedem vestrae celsitudinis destinantur, parilis notitia provinciali quoque tradatur officio, ut priusquam ad iudicium vestrum examinanda mittantur, ibidem sub utrorumque praesentia conferantur; cf. *SEG* IX. 356, xiv, τοῖς αὐτοῖς λόγῳ τετραμηνιακῶν ὁμοίως νο(μίσματα)δ′, and *CJ* I. xlii. 2 for similar *breves* from unit commanders to the *dux*. BREVIA OF MAGISTRI MILITUM: *CTh* VII. iv. 24, 398, excellentia tua erogationis per susceptores factae modum quantitati brevium conferri perficiat, ita ut ex quo die numeris datum sit diligentius exploretur, ac si quid amplius actuarios vel optiones accepisse constiterit quam brevium datorum scriniis nostris veritas continet, memorati in duplum reddere compellantur . . . nam ad inlustres quoque magistros utriusque militiae sacri apices cucurrerunt, quibus provida sanctione decrevimus ut breves ante indictionis principium summa fide ac veritate confecti ad nostra scrinia dirigantur, secundum quos a susceptoribus erogatio celebretur.

82. See ch. XIII, n. 98 (*canonicarii*), ch. XIII, n. 59 (*palatini*) ch. XIX, n. 106 (*discussores*). JULIAN: Amm. XVII. iii. 6 (cited above in n. 18).

83. See pp. 128–9, 174–5, 579, 593, 597.

84. GRATIAN'S LETTER: *Coll. Avell.* 13 §§1, 7, nostrorum videlicet iudicum socordia fretus, qui privatae gratiae imperialia praecepta condonant et religionem quam nos iure veneramur, quia fortasse ipsi neglegunt, inquietari patienter accipiant, cf. also *Sirm.* 14, 409, dubium non est conïventia iudicum fieri et culpabili dissimulatione inultum relinqui quod ad turbandam quietem publicam in contemptum Christianae religionis, quam debito cultu veneramur, sub publica testificatione commissum addiscimus et pariter non punitum.

85. The story is reconstructed by R. G. Salomon in *JEA* XXXIV (1948), 98 ff. The documents are published in this article and in *JEA* XV (1929), 96–102, and *P. Cairo*, 67029.

86. *V. Porph.* 26–7, 51.

87. Th. II, *Nov.* xvii. 2 §3, 444, sed vir inlustris quidem cuiuscumque temporis quaestor, si oblatae petitioni subscripserit vel etiam responsum dederit, virque inlustris comes rerum privatarum, si vel instrui permiserit vel petitionem si qua insinuetur admiserit, indignationem nostri numinis sustinebunt ceterisque

fient vindictae temeritatis exemplum. memoriales vero, qui excipienda eiusmodi rescripta vel implenda curaverint, et palatinos, qui instruxerint vel gesta admissae petitionis ediderint, bonorum proscriptione puniri decernimus; Val. III, *Nov.* xix §3, 445, vir spectabilis magister scrinii, qui interdicta supplicantibus responsa praebuerit, quinque librarum auri multam sacro aerario nostro cogatur inferre. memorialis quoque cuiuslibet scrinii, qui adversum vetita rescriptum fuerit executus, spoliatus militia quinquennii relegatione plectatur. Cf. *CJ* IV. lix. 1 (Leo against the grant of monopolies), 1. xxiii. 7 (Zeno on the issue of rescripts). For the prior annulment of rescripts contrary to law see, for example, Th. II, *Nov.* v. 2 §1, 439, legis temeratores quinquaginta librarum auri poena coercentes, tam videlicet petitorem quam officium quod petitionem concedit admitti, licet adnotatio nostra, licet divina pragmatica contra vetitum proferatur, vi §4, 438, quod si ulla processerit instructio, non sacra adnotatio, non divina pragmatica habeat locum contra generalem nostri numinis sanctionem, viii pr., 439, xvii. 1 §3, 439, xvii. 2 §5, 444.

XIII. FINANCE (pp. 412–13)

For the *res privata* the best comprehensive book is R. His, *die Domänen der Römischen Kaiserzeit*, Leipzig, 1896. For the *largitiones* I have derived much help from an unpublished thesis by my former pupil J. P. C. Kent, 'The office of the *comes sacrarum largitionum*' (London, 1951). On the financial role of the praetorian prefecture I have found no substantive work except on the assessment and levy of the *iugatio* and *capitatio*, on which the best and most recent book is A. Déléage, *La Capitation du Bas-Empire*, Macon, 1945.

1. The evidence as to title is ambiguous; *FIR* I². 94 (314), super itaque omnibus tam ad praefectos nostros quam etiam et praesides et rationalem et magistrum privatae scripta direximus, *CIL* III. 12044 = 13569, tam praefectis nostris quam etiam praesidibus provinciarum, rationali quoque et private magistro, *ILS* 1214, rationali privatae, *CTh* VIII. vii. 6 (probably Constantine), de largitionalibus comitatensibus et officialibus rationalis rerum privatarum. The earliest attested *comes* is Orion, *CTh* x. x. 8, ad Orionem com. r.p., 346 (S), cf. xiv. 2, Orioni v.c., 348. In *CTh* x. viii. 2, ad Priscum rationalem, 319, ne principali liberalitate praeventa dominium quis rei alienae affectet, iubemus, quotiens iure suadente aliquorum bona ex officio tuo fuerint occupata, breves eorum plenissimos ad virum perfectissimum comitem et amicum nostrum mitti, the reference is to the *CRP*. OFFICIUM: *Not. Dig. Or.* xiv, *Occ.* xii: that the first *scrinium*, to which the *primicerius* and *secundicerius totius officii* belonged, was the *exceptores* is proved by *CTh* VI. xxx. 5, 383.

2. DIOCESAN MAGISTRI REI PRIVATAE: *P. Beatty Panop.* 1, lines 205, 227, *Chr.* 1. 178, τοῦ διασημοτάτου μαγίστρου τῆς πριονάτης, (Egypt), *CTh* x. i. 4, ad Dometium Dracontium mag. privatae rei Afric., 320 (cf. XI. xix. 1, ad Dometium Dracontium, 324), *CIL* III. 18, Val. Epifanius v.p. mag. privat. Aeg. et Lib. (Constantine), Ath. *Apol. Const.* 12, καὶ ῾Ρουφῖνος καὶ Στέφανος, ὧν ὁ μὲν καθολικός, ὁ δὲ μάγιστρος ἦν ἐκεῖ (in Egypt c. 350). *Magistri* (*rei privatae*) are often thus linked with *rationales* (*rei summae*), e.g. Lact. *Mort. Pers.* vii. 4, *CJ* III. xxii. 5, 294, *CTh* x. i. 2, 319, XII. i. 14 (326–54), Firm. Mat. *Math.* IV. xxi. 9. It is

impossible to trace the change of title from *magister* to *rationalis*, for from an early date *rationales* appear to deal with matters concerning the *res privata*, e.g. *CJ* x. x. 1, 292, *CTh* x. viii. 1, 313, xi. 1, 317, i. 2, 319, viii. 2, 319, XII. vi. 2+vii. 1, 325, II. xxv. 1 (325). LIST OF RATIONALES REI PRIVATAE: *Not. Dig. Occ.* xii. 6–16; for their judicial powers see p. 486, for *Caesariani*, p. 600.

3. PROCURATORES: *Not. Dig. Or.* xiv. 7, *Occ.* xii. 17–25. EGYPT: *P. Oxy.* 2267, complaints of an ἐπίτροπος τῶν δεσποτικῶν κτήσεων νομοῦ 'Οξυρυγχίτου καὶ Κυνοπολίτου ἄνω (these two cities were often combined for fiscal purposes, cf. *P. Oxy.* 1909) against Diodotus τοῦ γενομένου καθολικοῦ τῶν δεσποτικῶν πραγμάτων (the *rationalis rei privatae Aegypti*), mentioning Evagrius, ὁ λαμπρότατος κόμης τῶν δεσποτικῶν (*CRP* 361, Amm. XXII. iii. 7). See *Chr.* I. 179 for another ἐπίτροπος δεσποτικῶν κτήσεων under a διασημότατος καθολικός. Under Diocletian there was a provincial *procurator rei privatae* (*P. Beatty Panop.* 1, line 365, ὁ κράτιστος ἐπίτροπος πριουάτης Θηβαίδος). In Africa Constantine authorised payments παρὰ 'Ηρακλείδα τοῦ ἐπιτρόπου τῶν ἡμετέρων κτημάτων; the area under his control is not stated (Eus. *HE* x. 6).

4. *Procuratores* are coupled with *rationales* in *CTh* XI. vii. 11, 365, x. ii. 1, 378, with *actores* in x. iv. 1, 326 (S), with *conductores* in XVI. v. 21, 392. They are also mentioned in XI. xvii. 1, 367, I. xxxii. 7, 388, XVI. x. 13, 395, x. i. 17, 420. Cf. also x. xxv. 1, 406, procuratores per singulas quasque provincias nobilissimarum puellarum filiarum mearum, and Th. II, *Nov.* xxiii, 443, a procuratore divinae domus, and *P. Oxy.* 1973, ἐπιτρόπῳ τῆς θειοτάτης οἰκίας (A.D. 420). GILDO'S ESTATES: *Not. Dig. Occ.* xii. 5, comes Gildoniaci patrimonii.

5. *Actores rei privatae* are associated with *procuratores* in *CTh* x. iv. 1, 326 (S), with *conductores* in XI. xvi. 12, 380, I. xi. 2, 398. They are subordinate to *rationales* in I. xi. 2, II. i. 11, XI. xix. 4, 398. They are also mentioned in I. i. 1 + XI. vii. 6, 349, x. iv. 2, 365, XII. xix. 1, 400, VII. xviii. 12, 403, Maj. *Nov.* ii §4, 458, and in *FIR* I². 108.

6. BASTAGA PRIVATA: *Not. Dig. Or.* xiv. 5, *Occ.* xii. 28–9. Cf. *SPP* xx. 82, which speaks of τὴν ὄχλησιν τὴν τῶν βασταγαρίων, which is expected τοῦ κυρίου μου καθολικοῦ ἐπιδημεῖν μέλλοντος τῇ πόλει; this may equally well refer to the *bastaga* of the *largitiones* GYNAECIA REI PRIVATAE: *Not. Dig. Occ.* xii. 26–7. PRAEPOSITI GREGUM ET STABULORUM: *Not. Dig. Or.* xiv. 6; see pp. 671, 706 for imperial horses.

7. COLLECTION OF RENT BY RATIONALES, ETC.: *CTh* XI. xix. 1 and *CJ* XI. lxii. 2, Dracontio, 321 (Dracontius was *magister rei privatae Africae*, cf. *CTh* x. i. 4, 320), *CTh* XII. vi. 2, 325, XI. vii. 1, 313 (S), v. xv. 20, 366. THEODOSIUS' LAW: *CTh* v. xiv. 31, 382 (S) saltuenses fundi iurisque patrimonii in Orientis regionibus siti turbata exactione dispositionis annuae maximo dicuntur dispendio fatigari et inmanissima opprimi mole reliquorum, eo, quod ad ordinarios sollicitatio transducta latiorem depraedandi praebuit facultatem. inlustris itaque auctoritas tua memoratos fundos ad rationalium curam praecipiat revocari. Cf. *CJ* XI. lxvi. 4 (383). VALENTINIAN II'S LAW: *CTh* I. xi. 2, 398, divae memoriae Valentiniano iuniori subreptum est, ut ordinariorum iudicum officiis actores seu conductores dominicos conveniendi licentia negaretur; et idcirco ad rationales privatae rei exigendorum fiscalium debitorum ex illo tempore cura translata est. HONORIUS' LAW: *CTh* I. xi. 1, 397, manentibus fideiussorum atque subsignationum meritis et possessoribus in eadem, qua nunc habentur, conductione durantibus ad palatinorum curam et ad rationalium officia omnium rerum nostrarum et totius perpetuarii iuris exactio revertatur

nihilque omnino de exactione reddita, hoc est perpetuarii iuris vel sacratissimae domus, ad ordinarios iudices pertineat. COMES ORIENTIS: *CTh* I. xiii. 1,
394, in officio comitis Orientis non amplius quam DC apparitores habeantur,
quos quidem publicis necessitatibus adeo novimus abunde suppetere, ut
per eos patrimonialium per Orientem possessionum maturetur exactio.
PROVINCIAL GOVERNORS: *CTh* VIII. viii. 5, 395, *CJ* XI. lxv. 5, 399, *CTh* I. v. 13,
400, XI. vii. 17, 408, Maj. *Nov.* vii §16, 458.

8. For the temple and civic lands, see pp. 732-3.

9. AFRICA: *CTh* XI. xxviii. 13, 422. For the *regiones*, etc., see ch. XIX, n. 4.
CAPPADOCIA: Just. *Nov.* xxx pr., 536, γῆ τε αὐτοῖς ἐστὶ πολλή τε καὶ θαυμαστὴ καὶ
οὕτως ἀρέσασα τῇ βασιλείᾳ, ὡς καὶ ἀρχὴν ἐπιστῆσαι ταῖς ἐκεῖσε κτήσεσιν ἰδίαν, τῆς
πολιτικῆς ἀρχῆς οὐκ ἐλάττω, μᾶλλον μὲν οὖν καὶ μείζω (πολιτικῆς of the better
Greek MSS is to be preferred to the 'Ponticae' of the *authentica*). If the office
of *comes domorum* was more important than that of the *praeses*, the area of the
land must have been considerably greater, for the *praeses* was responsible for
Caesarea.

10. Theod. *Ep.* (PG) 42, τοῦτο τῆς χώρας τὸ μέτρον πέντε μὲν μυριάδας ἔχει
ζυγῶν ἐλευθερικῶν, μύρια δὲ πρὸς τούτοις ἕτερα ταμιακά. The total assessment
was actually 62,000 iuga (see *Ep.* 47). For Avidius Cassius see SHA, *Ant. Phil.*
25, *Avidius Cassius*, 7.

11. FUNDI IURIS TEMPLORUM: *CJ* XI. lxx. 4 (397), *CTh* X. x. 32, 425, *CJ* XI. lxii.
14, 491. FUNDI IURIS REI PUBLICAE: *CTh* X. iii. 2, 372, *CJ* XI. lxxi. 2, 4 (383),
3 (395), lxii. 7, 386: both are coupled in *CTh* X. iii. 4, 383, *CJ* VII. xxxviii. 2,
387, *CTh* X. x. 24, 405, XI. xx. 6, 430, Marc. *Nov.* ii §1, 450. R. His (*Die
Domänen der Römischen Kaiserzeit*, 17 ff.) tries to distinguish *fundi patrimoniales*
from *rei privatae* but fails to establish his case.

12. Just. *Nov.* xxx §2-4, 536, *CTh* X. i. 11 (= XII. vi. 14), 367, ut perspicue
colonorum utilitatibus consulatur, decima indictione singulas tantum dependant
centesimas, qui reditus domui nostrae debitos quodannis iuxta consuetudinem
arcariis tradunt.

13. SHORT TERM LEASES: *CJ* XI. lxxi. 5 §6-7 (429), sane si quis non perpetuo
iure sed ad tempus locatam ab illustri viro comite rerum privatarum
possessionem videtur adeptus, non erit obstaculo principali largitati, si voluerit
in alterum donatione transferre quod ad definitum tempus alter forte conduxit.
si vero pro tali praedio ab altero conductore offeratur augmentum, sit in arbitrio
conductoris prioris, cui res ad tempus locata est, ut si ipse quod alter adiecit
obtulerit, maneat penes eum temporalis illa conductio; cf. *CJ* XI. lxvi. 3 (377),
vel iure perpetuo vel titulo conductionis, lxxi. 3 (395), loca omnia fundive rei
publicae propositis prius licenter edictis dehinc, ubi in eum canonis modum
contendentium augmenta succreverint, ut extendi ultra aut superari alterius
oblatione non possint, perpetuariis conductoribus locentur, lxxi. 4 (398-9),
congruit aequitati ut veteres possessores fundorum publicorum novis conductoribus praeferantur, si facta per alios augmenta suscipiant.

14. Perpetual leases were an old institution on civic lands, see Gaius, III. 145,
Dig. VI. iii. Emphyteutic tenures were also of long standing on private, civic
and imperial lands, but the technical term is not surely attested until Constantine (*CTh* XV. iii. 1, 319, *CJ* XI. lxii. 1, 313 (S), lxiii. 1, 319). By Justinian's
time the two concepts were synonymous, and *emphyteusis* the usual word; see
CTh I. xi. 1 (= *CJ* I. xxxiii. 2), perpetuarii <id est emphyteuticarii> iuris,

Dig. VI. iii, si ager vectigalis <id est emphyteuticarius> petatur, *CJ* v. lxxi. 13 (293), vectigale vel patrimoniale <sive emphyteuticum> praedium. For private emphyteutic leases see ch. XX, nn. 46-7.

15. For *emphyteusis* in Constantine's time see above, n. 14. HONORIUS' LAW: *CJ* XI. lxxi. 3 (cited in n. 13). OSTROGOTHIC ITALY: Cass. *Var.* VI. 8, habes quoque per provincias de perpetuario iure tributorum non minimam quantitatem.

16. INSECURITY QF PERPETUAL LEASES: *CTh* v. xv. 15, 364, enfyteutica praedia, quae senatoriae fortunae viris, praeterea variis ita sunt per principes veteres elocata, ut certum vectigal annuum ex his aerario penderetur, cessante licitatione, quae recens statuta est, sciat magnifica auctoritas tua a priscis possessoribus sine incremento licitandi esse retinenda, 16, 364, nequaquam enfyteuticos fundos ante commissi vitium ad alterum transire debere sancimus, *CJ* XI. lxii. 3, 365, quicumque possessiones ex emphyteutico iure susceperint, ea ad refundendum uti occasione non possunt, qua adserant desertas esse coepisse, tametsi rescripta per obreptionem meruerint. sed nec avelli eas ab his posse, nec si licitatio ab alio fuerit promissa, sed eas in perpetuum apud eos qui eas susceperint et eorum posteritatem remanere, nec si super hoc rescriptum fuerit adversus eos impetratum, *CTh* v. xiv. 33, 393, ius enfyteuticum, quo iuris patrimonialis vel rei publicae praedia possessoribus sunt adiudicata perpetuariis, ita inconcussum cum nostris tum maiorum nostrorum iussibus esse retinemus, ut, quod semel traditum fuerit, nec a nobis umquam possit nec ab alio aliis possidentibus occupari.

17. *CJ* XI. lxxi. 5 pr. §§1-4 (429).

18. *CJ* XI. lxxi. 5 §5-6 (429).

19. IUS PRIVATUM SALVO CANONE: *CJ* XI. lxii. 4, 368, fundi patrimoniales et qui ex emphyteutico iure ad domum nostram diversis generibus devoluti sunt, sic eis qui eos poposcerint cedant ut commissi metus esse non possit. neque enim magis commodamus nostra quam tradimus ea iure dominii, ita tamen ut ea quae in nostra possessione positi praestiterint et in posterum dissolvant, *CTh* v. xiii. 4 (368), provincialium opibus rei privatae possessiones concedimus, videlicet, ut de fundis ad eius dominium pertinentibus eligat unus quisque quem velit eumque perpetuo iure suscipiat, . . . si quis autem in annis singulis non solverit debitum, ex re ipsius cetera, quod in reliquis remansisse claruerit, sine aliquibus dependere cogetur indutiis. sane si quem postea minus idoneum factum esse constabit nec ita ut expedit rationem reddere pensionis, res, quas ex nostris rebus acceperat, ad alium idoneum iure quo sanximus transferentur: nec tamen decoctoris cuiusque reliquis qui novus accedit onerari, *CTh* v. xiv. 30, 386, quicumque defectum fundum patrimonialem exercuerit instruxerit fertilem idoneumque praestiterit, salvo patrimoniali canone perpetuo ac privato iure defendat velut domesticum et avita successione quaesitum sibi habeat, suis relinquat, neque eum aut promulgatione rescripti aut reverentia sacrae adnotationis quisquam a fructu inpensi operis excludat, *CTh* v. xiv. 34, 394, qui fundos patrimoniales iure privato salvo canone susceperunt, *CJ* XI. lxii. 9, 398, universi cognoscant nihil privato iure salvo canone fundis emptis cum patrimonialibus esse commune, ita ut ad eos numquam patrimonialium fundorum peraequator accedat, 10, 399, fundos patrimoniales eos dumtaxat qui salvo canone iure privato nostra liberalitate concessi sunt cum his patrimonialibus qui in condicione propria constituti sunt, illustris auctoritas tua iubebit exaequari, *CTh* v. xii. 2,

415, nulli penitus liceat sive salvo canonis servato iure sive cum imminutione canonis patrimonialis vel limitotrofos sive saltuenses per Orientem vel fundos patrimoniales postulare, Th. II, *Nov.* v. 2, 439, praecipimus itaque nulli iam in posterum licere patrimoniales seu limitotrofos vel saltuenses fundos qui per tractum Orientis positi sunt ad ius transferre privatum sive dempto sive salvo canone iuris fundorum immutatio postuletur. The grant of *ius privatum dempto canone* (*CTh* XI. xx. 5, 424, *Th.* II, *Nov.* v. 2, 439), which was equivalent to an outright sale or gift, was forbidden in 440 (Th. II, *Nov.* xix). MANU- MISSIONS: *CJ* XI. lxiii. 2, 367, libertates quas mancipiis ex fundis patrimonialibus atque emphyteuticis qui fundorum non sunt domini praestiterunt, rationales huiusmodi praecepti auctoritate rescindant, lxii. 12, 434, licentia eis concedenda etiam libertates mancipiis ex fundis patrimonialibus atque emphyteuticariis, cum fundorum sunt domini, praestare (this law refers to tenants who have obtained *ius privatum* by purchase or grant). On forfeiture upon *commissum* (failure to pay the rent at the due time) see the laws cited in note 16 and *CTh* v. xv. 18, 368, quotienscumque enfyteutici iuris praedia in vitium delapsa com- missi actis legitimis ac voci fuerint subicienda praeconis, super facto licitationis et augmento nostra perennitas consulatur, nec prius eius dominio, qui ceteros oblatione superavit, perpetuae firmitatis robur accedat, quam si super pensionis modo, conductoris nomine, enthecae quantitate nostrae tranquillitatis arbitrium fideli ratione consultum observanda praescripserit. Contrast v. xiii. 4 (cited above) for the security of tenure under *ius privatum salvo canone*.

20. For Valentinian's laws see n. 19. THEODOSIUS II: *CTh* v. xii. 3, 434: Possessores vel enfyteuticarii patrimoniales, qui fundos minime nunc usque conpararunt, eodem largitatis modo nequaquam ad eorum conparationem urgueantur, sed tamquam pretiis depensis sic eis nostri numinis beneficio potiantur, ut, quod iuris alter inferendo pretium consecutus est, hoc nostra liberalitate praedictus enfyteuticarius habeat.

21. RENTS: *CTh* XI. xvi. 1, 318 (S), patrimoniales fundos extraordinariis oneri- bus vel mediae aut tertiae portionis obsequiis fatigari non convenit, cum eosdem et auri speciem et frumenti plurimum modum constet persolvere, ita ut qui violare statuta temptaverit puniatur, *CJ* XI. lxii. 2 (321), patrimonialis fundi pensitationem aurariam sive frumentariam intra tempus omissam minorum dominio non nocere praecipimus nec ad fraudem iuris eorum evadere si quod sollemniter debetur paulo serius inferatur, *CTh* XII. vi. 2, 325, pro multis etiam et in diversis locis constitutis liceat simul auri pondus inferre, ita ut pro omnibus fundis securitas emissis cautionibus detur, ne separatim ab unoquoque auro exacto multis et adsiduis incrementis provincialium utilitas fatigetur. hoc quoque addimus, ut unusquisque quod debet intra anni metas, quo tempore voluerit, inferat, XI. xix. 3, 364, ab enfyteuticariis possessoribus annonariam quidem solutionem per quattuor menses ita statuimus procurari, ut circa ultimos anni terminos paria concludantur; aurum vero non ex die X kal. Dec. in prid. kalendarum Ianuariarum, sed per annum solidum, prout quisque pendere potuerit, inferetur, v. xv. 20, 366, placuit, ut enfyteuticorum fundorum patrimonialiumque possessores, quo voluerint, quo potuerint tempore et quantum habuerint pensionis paratum, dummodo non amplius quam in tribus per singulos annos vicibus, officio rationalis adsignent ac de suscepto ab eodem securitatem eodem die pro more percipiant, modo ut intra Ianuariarum iduum diem omnis summa ratiociniis publicis inferatur, XI. xvi. 13, 382, quandoquidem neque aurario canoni sub privilegiis aestimato aliquid ex ea iubentibus nobis praebitionum diversitate decutitur et pari cum

ceteris aestimari sorte non convenit quos praeter annonarias functiones aestimata perpetuo pensionum praerogativa nexuerint. For silver see Val. III *Nov.* xiii pr. 445, ita ut praedia domus divinae, quae a perpetuariis detinentur, simili modo octavam partem inferant etiam argentariae functionis. LAND TAX: *CTh* XI. xvi. 2, 323, ab extraordinariis omnibus fundi patrimoniales adque enfyteuticarii per Italiam nostram constituti habeantur immunes, ut canonica tantum et consueta dependant ad similitudinem per Africam possessorum, XI. xix. 2, 362, 3, 364, v. xiii. 4 (368), capitationis aut canonis, *CJ* XI. lxxv. 2 (370), rem privatam nostram levandorum provincialium causa canonicas necessitates ea condicione qua cunctos volumus sustinere, *CTh* v. xiv. 30, 386, tributa et canonem, *CJ* XI. lxxiv. 3 (404), *CTh* x. iii. 7, 417. It appears from *CTh* XI. i. 1 that in 360 the *res privata* did not pay the regular *canon* but it is implied by XI. xvi. 9 and XI. xix. 2 that in 359 and 362 it did pay. EXTRA-ORDINARIA, ETC.: *CTh* XI. xvi. 1, 318 (S), 2, 323, 5, 343, 9, 359, 12, 380, 13, 382, 17, 385, 20, 389 (S), XI. i. 36, 431; *CTh* XI. xix. 4, 398, is exceptional. ROADS: *CTh* XV. iii. 1, 319, 4, 399, 6, 423. RECRUITS: *CTh* VII. xiii. 2, 370, domum nostram ad exhibenda tironum corpora per eas provincias, a quibus corpora flagitantur, nolumus perurgueri: ceterum sinimus conveniri, in quibus pretia postulantur, ita ut ex certa praebitione redituum vicem concessionis istius repensemus, XI. xvi. 12, 380, VII. xiii. 12, 14, 397.

22. STATUS OF LESSEES: *CTh* v. xv. 15, 364, enfyteutica praedia, quae senatoriae fortunae viris, praeterea variis ita sunt per principes veteres elocata . . . x. v. 1, 398, quidquid divi parentis nostri Valentiniani senioris iussio de fundis privatae rei continebat, nostra etiam auctoritate firmamus. ut igitur ille praeceperat, ne consistoriani comites fideiussores in suscipiendis possessionibus darent, quod etiam divus Gratianus secutus est, custodiri oportet, x. iii. 2, 372, curialibus omnibus conducendorum rei publicae praediorum ac saltuum inhibeatur facultas: illo etiam observando, ne quis curialium vel de extraneis civitatibus fundos aut loca huiusmodi conductione suscipiat, *CJ* XI. lix. 5 (376-8), *CTh* x. iii. 4, 383, vel si voluntarius quis conductor non invenietur, tunc ad possessores antiquos, id est decuriones vel quoslibet alios, loca iuris praedicti adiunctis inutilibus revertantur. For cities leasing their lands to their decurions see Lib. *Or.* xxxi. 16, 17.

23. GIFTS AND BEQUESTS TO THE CROWN: *Liber Pont.* xxxiv, possessio Sybilles, donata Augusto; possessio Timialica, donata Augusto Constantino ab Ambrosio; possessio Agapi, quod donavit Augusto Constantino; possessio quod donavit Constantino Aug. Hybromius; possessio Hercoli quod donavit Augusto, Zonaras, XII. 1, ὅθεν νομίζεται καὶ μέχρι τοῦδε ταῖς διαθήκαις ἐγγράφεσθαι ὅτι καὶ τῷ βασιλικῷ ταμείῳ καταλιμπάνω τόδε. Cf. Malalas, 439–40, for an estate bequeathed to Justinian, the liabilities of which exceeded its assets.

24. NAVICULARII: *CJ* VI. lxii. 1, 326. DECURIONS: *CTh* v. ii. 1, 319, *CJ* VI. lxii. 4, 429. SOLDIERS: *CTh* v. vi. 1, 347. COHORTALES: *CJ* VI. lxii. 3, 349. FABRICENSES: Th. II, *Nov.* vi, 438. CLERGY: *CTh* v. iii. 1, 434.

25. BONA VACANTIA: Symm. *Rel.* 41.

26. REVOCATION OF THE LEX PAPIA POPPAEA: *CTh* VIII. xvi. 1, 320. MANICHEES, ETC.: *CTh* XVI. v. 7, 381, 9, 382, 17, 18, 389, 25, 395, 40, 407, 49, 410, 58, 415, 65, 428, *CJ* I. v. 15, 17, 18 §3 (527–9), 19, 529, 22, 531.

27. BONA DAMNATORUM: *CTh* IX. xlii. 2, 356, 4, 358, 6, 364, 8+9, 380, 24, 426.

28. PENAL CONFISCATION: *CTh* VII. xviii. 4, 380, 5, 381, 6, 382, 7, 383, 12, 403 (deserters), XVI. v. 3, 372, 4, 376, 8, 381, 12, 383, 21, 392, 30, 402 (S), etc. (heretical services), XVI. x. 12 §2, 392, *CJ*. I. xi. 8 (472) (pagan rites), *CTh* IX. xxi. 2, 321, 4, 329 (coining).

29. PENALTIES ON DELATORES: *CTh* X. x. 1, 313, 2, 312 (S), 3, 335, 4, 338, 8, 346 (S), 10, 365, 19, 387. PENALTY FOR THIRD INFORMATION: *CTh* X. x. 12, 380, 13, 380, 28, 418.

30. CONSTANTINE'S LAW: *CTh* X. x. 3, 335, omnes iudices invigilare praecipimus et delatores poenis adficere. apertissimi enim iuris est, ut, quod ex cuiuscumque patrimonio ceciderit in casum, et legibus et retro iuris ordine fisci advocatis agentibus vindicetur. RULES FOR PETITIO: *CTh* X. x. 7, 345, 8, 346 (S), qui largientibus nobis aliquid fuerint consecuti, cum delatoribus suis ad iudicia veniant, in iure consistant, negotia persequantur, ut adseveratio delatorum prodat fisco debitas facultates, 9, 364, 12, 380, qui cum ex praesenti die ut caducas poposcerit facultates ex consensu nostrae liberalitatis acceperit, non ante allegare rescribtum, non prius obtinere sententiam, non denique effectum exsecutionis debebit accipere, quam eum iudiciis introducat, a quo sibi id quod poposcerit delatum adserit esse patrimonium, 27, 418 (S), Th. II, *Nov.* xvii. 1, 439. BONA DAMNATORUM: Amm. XVI. viii. 11, inflabant itidem has malorum civilium bucinas potentes in regia, ea re ut damnatorum petita bona suis adcorporarent, *CTh* X. x. 15, 380, quisquis in crimine maiestatis deprehensus fuerit et punitus bonaque eius, sicut plectendi consuetudo criminis habet, fiscus invaserit, nullus easdem sub spe munificentiae principalis audeat proprio iuri poscere. qui contra legem id ausus fuerit sperare quod non licet, reus violatae legis habeatur. sed quoniam plerumque ita in nonnullis inverecunda petentum inhiatione constringimur, ut etiam non concedenda tribuamus, ne rescribto quidem nostro adversum formam latae legis loci aliquid relinquatur. si quid autem ex bonis talibus nostro iudicio, nullo tamen desiderante atque poscente, concedi cuiquam voluerimus, huiusmodi tantum valeat liberalitas, 23, 401, ne quis proscribtorum bona vel eorum, qui publicam videntur excepisse sententiam, intra biennium aestimet postulanda. abstineant facultatibus intra id temporis expetendis, ut aut proprias quis recipiat, si, ut nobis ingenitum est, duriores casus et tristiorem fortunam imperatoria humanitate molliamus, aut tum demum postulet, cum iam fiscalem potius quam proscribtorum expetisse noscatur, 29, 421, nullum patimur conpetitioni subiacere viventem, nisi quem crimini obnoxium capitalis sententia deportationi addixerit, ut ademptio facultatum poenam praemissae indignationis adcumulet. de quibus tamen, sicut divali sanctione decretum est, conpeti per biennium nihil iubemus. In Symm. *Ep.* v. 54, 66, there is a good instance of a form of vexatious *petitio*, the claim, long after the event, that property in private hands had originally been part of a confiscated estate.

31. GILDO: *CTh* IX. xlii. 16, 399, 19, 405. Cf. VII. viii. 9, 409, *Not. Dig. Occ.* xii. 5. STILICHO: *CTh* IX. xlii. 20-22, 408. HERACLIAN: Olymp. 23. Rufinus' estates were apparently kept by the crown (*CTh* IX. xlii. 14, 396). Of the estates confiscated by Tatian some were in 393 in the possession of the crown, but others had been granted to petitioners (*CTh* IX. xlii. 13).

32. COLLATIO DONATARUM POSSESSIONUM: *CTh* XI. xx. 1, 363, admodum nobis videtur absurdum et a nostrorum temporum tranquillitate submotum, ut ii, qui proscribtionis sortem pertulerunt, ad exemplum eorum, qui fundos donatos sacra liberalitate tenuerunt, auri atque argenti conlationi redderentur obnoxii, quae sub divae memoriae Constantio adscribta est, cum multum intersit inter

eum, qui principali munificentia perfruitur, et eos, qui propria recuperare meruerunt, 2, 364, 1 eos, qui rem paternam vel suam a fisco recuperare meruerunt, a conlatione auri atque argenti, quae adscribta est et his, qui aliquid a sacra liberalitate meruerunt, tutos defensosque servari praecipimus. SPECIAL LEVIES: *CTh* XI. xx. 4, 423, 5, 424.

33. *CTh* x. x. 32, 425, Th. II, *Nov.* xvii. 2, 444.

34. SALES OF STATE PROPERTY: *CTh* x. 1. 2, 319, v. xiii. 1+2, 341, x. ii. 1, 378, rationales vel ordinarii iudices earum domorum, quas procuratorum nequitia et rationalium neglegentia labi patitur in ruinas, instituant auctionem hastis habitis ex licitatione currente, 2, 398, ne domus ad nostrum patrimonium pertinentes, quae sunt in diversis urbibus, ex neglegentia nostro aerario adferant detrimentum, omnes licitatione habita volumus venundari, v. xvi. 32 (408–11), ne omni patrimonio domus aeternalis venditionibus denudetur, praeceptione praeteriti temporis antiquata distractionem volumus conquiescere, atque in domo aeternali universa praedia, quae ex promulgatae auctoritatis die reliqua fuerint, retineri.

35. CONSTANTINE: Eus. *HE* x. 6, ἔδωκα γράμματα πρὸς Οὖρσον τὸν διασημότατον καθολικὸν τῆς Ἀφρικῆς καὶ ἐδήλωσα αὐτῷ ὅπως τρισχιλίους φόλλεις τῇ σῇ στερρότητι ἀπαριθμῆσαι φροντίσῃ. ARCADIUS: *V. Porph.* 54, εὐθέως δὲ καὶ ὁ βασιλεὺς ἐκέλευσεν τοῖς ἐπάρχοις ληγατεῦσαι αὐτοῖς ἀπὸ δημοσίων Παλαιστίνης ἀνὰ χρυσοῦ λίτρας κ' (cf. below, τὴν ληγατιῶνα τῶν τεσσαράκοντα λιτρῶν). VALENTINIAN III: *CTh* XI. i. 36, 431, excepto patrimonio pietatis nostrae, cuius quidem reditus necessitatibus publicis frequentissime deputamus. . . .

36. RES PRIVATA OF THE EMPRESS: *CJ* XII. lix. 10 §3 (472), palatinorum rerum privatarum partis Augustae, x. xxxii. 64 (475–84), comitum privatarum nostrae vel Augustae partis, III. xxiv. 3 (485–6), cui nostra serenitas . . . res privatas nostrae pietatis vel serenissimae Augustae nostrae coniugis gubernandas iniunxit, x. xxxii. 66 (497–9), comitis privatarum nostrae vel piissimae Augustae partis. COMES PATRIMONII: *CJ* I. xxxiv. 1, τῆς ἰδικῆς ἐφευρεθείσης οὐσίας τῷ δημοσίῳ ἢ ἐφευρεθησομένης προβεβλήσθω ἢ καλείσθω κόμης τῆς ἰδικῆς κτήσεως κατὰ μίμησιν τοῦ κόμητος τῆς ἰδικῆς περιουσίας αὐτὴν διοικῶν· πᾶσι τοῖς ὑπ' αὐτὸν οὖσι γεωργοῖς ἢ παροίκοις ἢ ἐμφυτευταῖς τῶν αὐτῶν ὄντων προνομίων, ὧν οἱ ὑπὸ τὸν πραιπόσιτον καὶ τὸν κόμητα τῶν οἰκείων ἀπολαύουσι, καὶ παρὰ μόνῳ κόμητι τοῦ τῆς ἰδικῆς κτήσεως κινείτωσαν καὶ ἐναγέσθωσαν. οἱ δὲ τοῦ τῆς ἰδικῆς κτήσεως ταξεῶται τοῦ κόμητος τῆς ἁπανταχοῦ ἰδικῆς περιουσίας ἐχέτωσαν προνόμια, Joh. Lydus, *Mag.* II. 27, ὁ λεγόμενος πατριμώνιος, ἀντὶ τοῦ φύλαξ τῆς ἰδίᾳ πως ἀνηκούσης τῷ βασιλεῖ καὶ τυχὸν ἐκ προγόνων περιουσίας, ὃν καὶ αὐτὸν οὐ πρὶν ἀριθμούμενον Ἀναστάσιος ὁ πάντα ἔμφρων ἀνεστήσατο, διάκρισιν ὥσπερ εἰώθει περινοῶν τοῖς πράγμασιν ὅπως μὴ συγχύσει κάμνοιεν, Proc. *HA* xxii. 12, κἂν τοῖς παλατίνοις οἳ δὴ ἀμφί τε τοὺς θησαυροὺς καὶ τὰ πριβᾶτα καλούμενα τό τε πατριμώνιον ἐπιτελεῖν ἀεὶ τὴν ὑπουργίαν εἰώθασιν, cf. Malalas, 398, ὁ δὲ αὐτὸς βασιλεὺς ἐκούφισε τὴν λειτουργίαν τοῦ λεγομένου χρυσαργύρου πᾶσαν διαιωνίζουσαν ἀπὸ θείου τύπου, ἥτις ἐστὶ μεγάλη καὶ φοβερὰ φιλοτιμία, ἀντεισάξας ταῖς θείαις λαργιτιῶσι πρόσοδον ἀντ' αὐτοῦ ἐκ τῶν ἰδίων αὐτοῦ. I reject Stein's view that the *patrimonium* was abolished by Justinian: see *Historia* II (1954), 357–9.

37. VALENS: Them. *Or.* VIII. 112 c. JUSTIN II AND TIBERIUS: Greg. Tur. *HF* IV. 40, v. 19. For regular *petitiones* by palace officials see Amm. XXII. iv. 9, interrogatus tamen ille quid haberet ex arte compendii, vicenas diurnas respondit annonas totidemque pabula iumentorum, quae vulgo dictitant capita, annuum stipendium grave, absque fructuosis petitionibus multis,

CTh x. x. 34, 430, si quis ex his, qui sacro nostro cubiculo serviunt, ad petitionem caducorum ad fiscum pertinentium adspiraverit, cum impetrabile huius fuerit postulatum, lege, qua pars dimidia vindicatur aerario, protinus absolvatur primoque nutu nostrae clementiae statim integro perfruatur, nec laboret ad partis alterius, quae fisco videtur addicta, prorsus petitionem attingi, norma legis antea promulgatae in ceteris omnibus custodita. For gifts of gold in the *cubiculum* see *V. Porph.* 40, 53–4 and Joh. Eph. *V. SS. Or.* xxxvi.

38. DOMUS DIVINA IN AFRICA: *Not. Dig. Occ.* xii. 16. DOMUS DIVINA IN CAPPADOCIA: *Not. Dig. Or.* x. 2, xiv. 2, *CTh* vi. xxx. 2, 379, prisco iam nunc ordine revocato de palatino potius officio ad gerendum principatum officii comitis domorum per Cappadociam mittantur . . . ix. xxvii. 7, *CRP*, 390, unusquisque procurator praepositus gynaecei tabularius susceptor colonus vel quicumque se a comite domorum meminerit esse concussum, cum ipse cui pecuniam numeraverit administratione decesserit, intra anni spatia ad iudicium spectabilitatis tuae quidquid dederit repetiturus adcurrat, xi. xxviii. 9, 414, Musellio praeposito sacri cubiculi de titulis ad domum sacram pertinentibus, Just. *Nov.* xxx §6, 536.

39. *CJ* vii. xxxvii. 3, 531, Floro comiti rerum privatarum et curatori dominicae domus et Petro viro illustri curatori divinae domus serenissimae Augustae et Macedonio viro illustri curatori et ipsi dominicae domus. JUSTIN II: Just. *Nov.* cxlviii, 566, ἢ τοῦ μεγαλοπρεπεστάτου κουράτωρος τῶν οἰκιῶν. TIBERIUS: Just. *Nov.* clxiv, 574, οἵ τε ἐνδοξότατοι κουράτωρες τῶν θείων οἴκων, Tib. *Nov.* xii §§1–2 (Zacharia von Lingenthal, *Ius Graeco-Romanum*, III. 24–30), μηδένα τῶν ἐνδοξοτάτων ἢ μεγαλοπρεπεστάτων κουρατώρων τῶν θείων ἡμῶν ἢ τῆς εὐσεβεστάτης βασιλίδος οἴκων, οἷς συναριθμητέον τήν τε πατριμωνιαλικὴν τήν τε τῶν νέων ἐκκλησιῶν προεστῶσαν βασιλικὴν οἰκίαν. The *dominica domus* is mentioned side by side with the *res privata* and *patrimonium* in Just. *Nov.* lxix §4, 538, cii §1, 536, *Ed.* iv §2 (535–6), viii §2, 548. The institution of *curatores* may go back to the middle of the fifth century if Theodoret's letter (*Ep.* (Azema) 46) addressed Ἑλλαδίῳ κουράτωρι and styling him μεγαλοπρέπεια, refers to an imperial *curator domus divinae*. NAMED DOMUS: *IGC* 240+281 bis, Ἀλεξάνδρου τοῦ με[γαλο]πρεπ΄ κόμητ[ος] τῶν θίων πριονάτων, γενικοῦ κουράτορος τῶν προσ[ηκόν]των πραγμάτων Πλακιδίᾳ τῇ ἐπιφανεστάτῃ, cf. Malalas, 490, Ζήμαρχος ὁ ἀπὸ ἐπάρχων καὶ κουράτωρ τοῦ δεσποτικοῦ οἴκου τῶν Πλακιδίας; *IGLS* 528, τῷ θέῳ οἴκῳ τ(ῶ)ν Ὁρμίσδ(ο)υ π(ρον)οου(μ)έ(νω)ν ὑ(πὸ) Μάγνου τοῦ πανευφήμ(ου) ἀπὸ ὑπ(ά)των . . . κουρ(ά)τορος, cf. *Chron. Pasch.* 694, ἀπὸ ἐπάρχων γενόμενος πραιτωρίων καὶ λογοθέτης καὶ κουράτωρ τῶν Ὁρμίσδου, 696, κουράτορος γενομένου τῶν Ὁρμίσδου, Joh. Eph. *HE* vi. 28 (Hormisdas); *IGC* 308 bis, τῷ θίῳ οἴκῳ τῶν Μαρίνας προνοουμένων ὑπὸ Μάγνου τοῦ εὐδοξοτάτου κουράτορος, cf. Theophanes, A.M. 6053, Γεώργιον τὸν κουράτωρα τῶν Μαρίνης, 6057, τελευτᾷ Βελισάριος ὁ πατρίκιος ἐν Βυζαντίῳ καὶ ἡ τούτου περιουσία ἦλθεν εἰς τὸν δεσποτικὸν οἶκον τῆς Μαρίνης; Theoph. Sim. III. 3, Ἀριστόβουλος (ἦν δὲ ἄρα οὗτος τῆς βασιλικῆς οἰκίας προεστὼς τοῦ βασιλέως τοῦ Ἀντιόχου προσαγορευομένης), *Chron. Pasch.* 695, ὄντος ἐπάρχου πόλεως Λεοντίου τοῦ ἀπὸ κουρατόρων τῶν Ἀντιόχου, *V. Eutychii*, 76, Theoph. Sim. III. 3 (Antiochus). Other allusions to *curatores* include *A.C.Oec.* III. 86 (acclamations to a *curator* in 518), *MGH* (*Ep.*) III, 143, ad Megantem curatorem, *IGLS* 1905, τῶν ὑπὸ Λάζαρον τὸν ἐνδοξώτατον κουράτωρα (an estate of the late empress), Agath. v. 3, ἐπιμέλειαν τῶν βασιλέως οἴκων τε καὶ κτημάτων ἀρχὴν εἰληχότα · κουράτωρας δὲ τούτους καλοῦσι Ῥωμαῖοι, Malalas, 439–40 (a *curator* reports to Justinian on an estate bequeathed to the emperor). Private persons also had *curatores*, e.g. Hypatius in Sev. Ant. *Ep.* 1. 40, Belisarius in Theophanes, A.M. 6055: the Alexander of the first inscription

quoted above was a private *curator* of Placidia, who was also appointed *comes rei privatae* by Zeno (see Malchus, 13).

40. For the *patrimonium Italiae*, see ch. VIII, n. 44, IX, n. 45.

41. Iulius Antoninus, *v.p. rationalis*, who made dedications to Diocletian and Maximian at Nicomedia (*CIL* III. 325, *AE* 1947, 186), must be the chief *rationalis*. In *FIR* I². 94 (314) and *CIL* III. 12044 = 13569 (cited in n. 1), the *rationalis* is clearly the chief finance minister; it is not possible to distinguish the chief minister from diocesan officers in the early laws in the Code addressed to a *rationalis*. The earliest recorded *comes sacrarum largitionum* is Nemesianus, *Sb* 1005, ἀπὸ καθολικῶν [Αἰγύπ]του καὶ ἀπὸ ἡγεμόνων . . . καθολικὸς ὢν τῆς διοικήσεως, *CTh* XII. 1. 30, Nemesiano comiti, 340, XI. vii. 5, Nemesiano v.p. com. larg., 345. Next comes Domitianus who was *ex comite largitionum* in 353 (Amm. XIV. vii. 9) under Constantius II, and Marcellinus in 350 (Zos. II. 42, τῷ τοῦ ταμείου προεστηκότι) under Constans.

42. *Not. Dig. Or.* xiii. 21-34, *Occ.* xi. 87-99, *CTh* VI. xxx. 7 (= *CJ* XII. xxiii. 7), *CSL* (Or.) 384. For the dyeworks see *CTh* x. xx. 18, 436, septimum de scrinio exceptorum, sextum de scrinio canonum, quintum de scrinio tabulariorum ad bafia Foenices per certum tempus mitti praecipimus, ut fraus omnis eorum prohibeatur sollertia.

43. DIOCESAN RATIONALES: Lact. *Mort. Pers.* vii. 4, Eus. *HE* x. 6 (cited in n. 35), cf. *CJ* III. xxvi. 5, 315), *CTh* x. xi. 1, rationali[bus] Hispaniarum, 317, x. i. 2, ad Severum rationalem Africae, 319, x. xix. 1, ad Maximum rationalem Africae, 320, XII. vi. 2+vii. 1, ad Eufrasium rationalem trium provinciarum, 325, II. xxv. 1, Gerulo rationali trium provinciarum, 325 (S), XI. xxx. 14, Victori rationali urb. Rom. 327, *ILS* 1214, rationali vicario per Gallias, 1218, bis ration. urbis Romae et Africae, 6091, rationalem Asianae dioeceseos, *CIL* III. 17 (= 6585), Arrius Diotimus rat. Aeg., *Sb* 1002, Ἀντώνιος Θεόδωρος ὁ διασημότατος καθολικὸς τῆς Αἰγύπτου, *P. Oxy.* 1410 Μαγνίου Ρούφου τοῦ διασημ' καθολ' ἐπαρχείας Αἰγύπτου καὶ Λιβύης, *IGR* I. 1219, ὁ λαμπρότατος καθολικὸς Αἰγύπτου; *CIL* VIII. 7009, Florentinus v.p. rationalis Numid. et Mauret. (cf. 7007-8, 7010, Opt. *App.* x), *CTh* x. x. 5, Callepio rationali trium provinciarum, 340, x. viii. 4, ad Iuvenalem rationalem Numidiae, 346. COMITES LARGITIONUM (EAST): *Not. Dig. Or.* xiii. 5, comites largitionum per omnes dioceses, 12, comes et rationalis summarum Aegypti. RATIONALES SUMMARUM (WEST): *Not. Dig. Occ.* xi. 9-20. COMITES LARGITIONUM (WEST): *Not. Dig. Occ.* xi. 4, comes largitionum per Illyricum, 7, comes largitionum Italicianarum, 8, comes titulorum largitionalium per Africam, Amm. XXVII. vii. 5, Dioclis ex comite largitionum Illyrici, *CTh* I. v. 12, 399, per omnes provincias dioeceseos tuae per Africam largitionalium titulorum comitum submotis dispositionibus magnificentiae tuae huius tituli curam necessitatemque permittimus amotis palatinis omnibus, VI. xix. 1, 400, eos, qui consularitatis functi sunt dignitate, comitibus Italicianorum et Gallicianorum iure praeferimus, si quidem haud exiguus sit titulus meritorum regere et gubernare provincias, Aug. *Conf.* VI. 16, Romae adsidebat comiti largitionum Italicianarum. The *comites titulorum* of *CTh* I. x. 8, 428, are presumably the same. For the judicial functions of *rationales* etc. see pp. 485-6.

44. THESAURI: *Not. Dig. Or.* xiii. 10, *Occ.* xi. 21-37; *CJ* x. xxiii. 1, 383, omnem summam auri vel argenti reliquarumque specierum quae sacris largitionibus ex more penduntur statim ut exactio fuerit celebrata ad thesauros uniuscuiusque provinciae vel ad proximos referri . . . et thesaurorum praepositis consignari

praecipimus, ut exinde ad sacrum comitatum integer omnium titulorum numerus dirigatur, Amm XXII. iii. 7, hic idem Ursulus datis litteris ad eum qui Gallicanos tuebatur thesauros quidquid posceret Caesar procul dubio iusserat dari, XXIX. i. 26, Salia thesaurorum paullo ante per Thracias comes, Bas. *Ep.* 237, ἐγὼ καὶ διὰ τοῦ βικαρίου τῆς Θράκης ἐπέστειλα τῇ θεοσεβείᾳ σου καὶ διά τινος πραιποσίτου τῶν κατὰ Φιλιππούπολιν θησαυρῶν, Greg. Naz. *Or.* VII. 15, διέτριβε μὲν ἐν τῇ Βιθυνῶν, τὴν οὐ πολλοστὴν ἀπὸ βασιλέως διέπων ἀρχήν· ἡ δὲ ἦν ταμιεύειν βασιλεῖ τὰ χρήματα καὶ τῶν θησαυρῶν ἔχειν τὴν ἐπιμέλειαν (there follows an allusion to Nicaea), *CTh* I. xxxii. 3, 377, quicumque in largitionibus nostris quocumque nomine atque apparitione procurans nanctus fuerit administrationem ratiociniis obnoxiam, primum maxime idoneis satisdatoribus datis adfectatum munus incipiat; deinde abiens intra triginta dies in his thesauris, qui negotii sunt minoris, intra quinquaginta autem in his, qui maiorum sunt, chartas et ratiocinia cuncta restituat; plane conscriptum susceptoribus tradat, quid susceperit, quid erogaverit, quid in thesauris conditum maneat, VIII. vii. 14, 377, nullus thensaurensis vel officialis comitis thensaurorum . . . hi, qui nuper thensaurorum custodiam susceperunt, scriniarii etiam comitum thensaurorum vel ceteri thensaurenses, VIII. vii. 23, 426, comitum thensaurorum dioeceseos provectiones et ipsos thensaurenses vetus observatio principali dexterae reservavit, *CJ* XI. viii. 14 (426), XII. lix. 10 §4 (472).

45. LARGITIONALES CIVITATUM: *CTh* VI. xxxv. 3, 319, meritoque his iungimus largitionales urbium singularum, ne privilegio separentur quos dignitas propemodum similis copulavit, memorati namque palatinorum matriculis adtinentur, VIII. iii. 1, 364, eligendi autem erunt susceptores e diversis officiis, etiam ex largitionalibus civitatum, qui utique extra palatium degunt.

46. See pp. 826–7, 834–9 (*bastagae, comites commerciorum,* weaving and dyeing mills, *barbaricarii,* mines). COMES VESTIARII: *Not. Dig. Occ.* xi. 5; he is different from the *comes sacrae vestis* of *CTh* XI. xviii. 1, 412 (S), who was a eunuch of the bedchamber. MAGISTRI LINTEAE VESTIS, PRIVATAE: *Not. Dig. Or.* xiii. 14, 15, *CJ* XI. viii. 14 (426).

47. OCTAVAE: *CTh* IV. xiii. 6, 369, 8, 381, *CJ* IV. xlii. 2 (459–65), *IGC* 10, ὀκταβερήῳ καὶ ἀποθηκαρίῳ, Sophronius, *SS. Cyri et Ioh. Mir.* 1 (an ὀκταβάριος of Alexandria). The old rate of 25% (S. J. de Laet, *Portorium,* 333–9) seems to have already been reduced to 12½% by the time of Severus Alexander (*CJ* IV. lxv. 7). QUINQUAGESIMAE AND QUADRAGESIMAE: Symm. *Ep.* v. 62, quaestores ordinis nostri numquam ferarum suarum portorium contulerunt . . . nunc a fratre meo Cynegio quaestorio candidato quinquagesimae vectigal exigitur quod solos ursorum negotiatores utpote quaestui servientes oportet agnoscere, 65, quadragesimae portorium non recte poscitur a senatoribus candidatis. The collectors are called *publicani* in *Ep.* 62, *mancipes* in *Ep.* 65. On the civic *vectigalia* see ch. XIX, nn. 45–6, 49.

48. FARMING OF VECTIGALIA: *CTh* IV. xiii. 1. 321, penes illum vectigalia manere oportet, qui superior in licitatione extiterit, ita ut non minus quam triennii fine locatio concludatur nec ullo modo interrumpatur tempus exigendis vectigalibus praestitutum. quo peracto tempore licitationum iura conductionumque recreari oportet ac simili modo aliis conlocari. Cf. 4, 360 (S), praestatio vectigalis maximam continens utilitatem tanta debet diligentia custodiri, ut adsiduis licitationibus sumat augmentum. DECURIONS: *CJ* X. lvii. 1 (286–93), *CTh* XII. i. 97, 383. CONDUCTORES: *CJ* IV. lxii. 4 (336), *CTh* XI. xxviii. 3, 401, Aug. *Civ. Dei.* VII. 4. PRAEPOSITI: *CTh* XIII. v. 5, 326, I. xxxii. 3, 377, XIII.

v. 17, 386; for compulsion under the Principate see *Dig.* XXXIX. iv. 11 §5, XLIX. xiv. 3 §6, *CJ* IV. lxv. 5.

49. AURUM CORONARIUM: *CTh* XII. xiii. 1, 362, aurum coronarium munus est voluntatis, quod non solum senatoribus, sed ne aliis quidem debet indici, licet quaedam indictionum necessitas postulaverit; sed nostro arbitrio reservari oportebit, 2, 364, universi, quos senatorii nominis dignitas non tuetur, ad auri coronarii praestationem vocentur exceptis his, quos lex praeterita ab hac conlatione absolvit. omnes igitur possessores aut inter decuriones coronarium aurum aut inter senatores glebalem praestationem deinceps recognoscant, 3, 368, nullus exceptis curialibus, quos pro substantia sui aurum coronarium offerre convenit, ad oblationem hanc adtineatur, 5, 379, quae diversarum ordines curiarum vel amore proprio vel indulgentiarum laetitia vel rebus prospere gestis admoniti in coronis aureis signisque diversis obtulerint, in quacumque fuerint oblata materia, in ea suscipiantur, ne id, quod voluntate offertur, occasione obryzae incrementi, necessitatis iniuria insequatur. Cf. also 5, 384, 6, Satrapae Sofanenae, 387; *Lib. Or.* XVIII. 193, ὁ χρυσὸς δὲ οὗτος ἀνέμνησέ με χρυσῶν στεφάνων οὓς αἱ μὲν πόλεις ἔπεμπον διὰ πρέσβεων ἀλλήλας ὑπερβάλλουσαι τῷ σταθμῷ, χιλίων οὗτος στατήρων, δισχιλίων δὲ ἐκεῖνος, τούτων ὁ παρ' ἑτέρων ἕλκων πλέον, ὁ δὲ ἐπιτιμήσας τῷ μεγέθει σαφῶς εἰδὼς ὡς οὐκ ἄνευ πόνου τὰ τοιαῦτα συλλέγοιτο νομοθετεῖ τὸν στέφανον ἀπὸ στατήρων ἑβδομήκοντα φοιτᾶν. There is no formal proof that *aurum coronarium* was paid to the *largitiones*, but it seems natural that it should have been.

50. AURUM OBLATICIUM: *CTh* VI. ii. 16, 395, omnes senatores, qui in sacratissima urbe consistunt, licet habeant per longinquas provincias atque diversas possessiones, aurum oblaticium in urbe persolvant, quod a procuratoribus et actoribus suis ad urbem reditus perferuntur. sane his senatoribus, qui in provinciis larem fovent, per provincias censuales, qui plenam habent notitiam, immineant, quo cognoscant sine dilatione aurum profuturum aerario nostro quantocius inferendum, 20, 397, dudum praecepimus, ut aurum oblaticium senatores, qui in sacratissima urbe degunt, in urbe conplerent, ii vero, qui in provinciis larem foverent, per censualium officia in provinciis solverent. Sed quoniam cognovimus praedictum officium non posse exsecutioni sufficere, ad praedictum negotium auxilia congrua ab ordinariis iudicibus volumus ministrari, 25, 426, oblationem nobis amplissimi ordinis prompta liberalitate promissam partim remittimus vobis, partim patriae communi urbique largimur, Symm. *Ep.* II. 57, praefecti litterae ruperunt otium meum, quae bonae spei sollicita miscebant, speciatim praesentiam meam per ambiguum poposcerunt. non differo expectationem tuam. coactum in tractatum senatum commoneri sed et oblationem faciendam scriptis secretioribus indicavit. nihil publicatum, nihil lectum est, quantitas postulatae rei excessit opulentiam, re cognita vastum silentium cunctis stupor subitus imperavit, *Rel.* 13. Cf. *Rel.* 30, where two *palatini munerationum sacrarum* are suing the heirs of a deceased senator for arrears, 'quod oblativis functionibus eadem domus esset obnoxia'. This incidentally proves that *aurum oblaticium* went to the *largitiones*. CONSTANTINOPLE: *Them. Or.* III. 40c.

51. FOLLIS: Zos. II. 38, ἀπεγράψατο δὲ τὰς τῶν λαμπροτάτων οὐσίας, τέλος ἐπιθεὶς ᾧτινι φόλλιν αὐτὸς ἐπέθηκεν ὄνομα. EXEMPTIONS: *CTh* VI. ii. 13, 383, his tantum a necessitate huiusmodi segregandis, quos palatinae honore militiae et stipendiis adprobatos debita potius quam postulata senatorii ordinis societas advocaverit, 26, 428, praeter eos, qui notariorum nostrorum scholae praeclaro sunt sacrati collegio vel scriniorum praerogativa nostrorum aut etiam sacri con-

sistorii decurionum militia muniuntur, item qui e schola agentum in rebus expletis stipendiis ad principatum ducenae pervenerunt, togati quoque praetorianae atque etiam urbicariae praefecturae ceterique omnes, qui delatis sibi senatoriis dignitatibus fruuntur, pro suis viribus glebales tantum functiones agnoscant: palatinis sacrarum et privatarum largitionum, quoniam renuntiandum senatoriae dignitati adita nostra clementia crediderunt, senatoriis functionibus eximendis. Cf. vi. ii. 23, 414, xxvi. 14, 407 (*proximi scriniorum, comes dispositionum, magister admissionum*), xxiii. 1, 415, 4, 437, (*decuriones* and *silentiarii*), xxiv. 7, 414, 8, 9, 416, 10, 427, 11, 432 (*decemprimi* of *protectores* and *domestici*), xxv. i, 416 (*praepositi labarum*), xxvii. 6, 390, 22, 428 (*principes* of *agentes in rebus*), xiii. iii. 15, 393, 16, 414, 19, 428 (*archiatri*). RATE OF TAX: Hesychius, 5, τοῖς μὲν τοῦ πρωτίστου τέλους ὀκτὼ χρυσίου λίτραι, τοῖς δὲ τοῦ δευτέρου τέσσαρες, καὶ δύο τοῖς τρίτοις; pound of gold is a mistake for *follis*, cf. *CTh* vi. ii. 13, 383, duorum vero follium maneat cunctos indiscreta professio, etiam si possessiones forte non habeant, iv. 21 §6, 372, cum duos folles aut quattuor aut certe amplius in professionem habebunt. For the value of the *follis* see *JRS* xlix (1959), 35–6. Some passages in Libanius' letters (Lib. *Ep.* 252, φασὶ δὲ αὐτὸν καὶ χορηγὸν ἐνηνέχθαι τῆς τὰ μέγιστα δαπανώσης, ὁ δὲ οὔτε ταύτην οὔθ' ἣν δευτέραν νομίζετε δύναιτ' ἄν ἄρασθαι, φαίην δ' ἄν ὡς οὐδὲ τὴν τρίτην ἄνευ πόνου, καὶ ταῦτ' ἤν τις αὐτὸν κατὰ τὸν νόμον καλῇ, 1277, φησὶ τοίνυν ὁ Παγκράτιος μικρὰ ἔχων μεγάλα εἰσπράττεσθαι καὶ οὐκ ὀρθῶς ἐν τρίτοις ἠριθμῆσθαι) have been taken to refer to the three grades of the *follis*. The first passage, however, refers to the praetorship, which was also in three grades (*CTh* vi. iv. 5, 340), and so probably does the second. In Ep. 252 the first four sections refer to the *follis*, the last two to the praetorship; similarly in Ep. 251, §§6–9 refer to the *follis* (φορά), and §§10–12 to the praetorship (λειτουργία). RATE OF SEVEN SOLIDI: *CTh* vi. ii. 15, 393, quod ad eorum querimonias, qui se glebalia non posse ferre onera testabuntur, amplissimorum virorum consilio definitum est, scilicet ut septenos quotannis solidos pro sua portione conferret, qui praebitionem implere follium non valeret, eatenus . . . confirmamus, ut omnes, quibus est census angustia, contemplatis patrimonii sui viribus liberam habeant optionem, quatenus, si conlatio ista non displicet, a consortio amplissimi ordinis non retendant. sin vero grave, id est damnosum videtur, dignitatem senatoriam non requirant. ATTACHED TO LAND: *CTh* vi. ii. 21, 398, glebam possessionum, non personarum esse perspicimus, ac propterea necesse est, ut illis immineat exactio qui ex re eadem reditus consecuntur, 22, 401, a conlatione glebalis auri vel solidorum vii tituli ne domum quidem nostram immunem esse praecepimus; cf. 24, 417, si quis desertam possessionem sub peraequationis sorte perceperit, eum a praestatione glebae senatoriae, etiamsi antiquitus hoc onus fundum manebat, alienum esse praecepimus, xiv. iii. 10, 368, si autem a clarissimis viris aliquos acceperint fundos, sic praedicto corpori pareant, ut glebae, ex qua lucrata ea sunt corpora, nullum praeiudicium comparetur, and Syn. *Ep.* 38, ὅστις ἐκ προγόνων λαμπρότατος ὢν καὶ τὴν πατρῴαν βῶλον ὑποτελῆ τῇ συγκλήτῳ διαδεξάμενος, ἐπειδὴ γέγονεν ἡγεμών, ἀξιοῦται συντελεῖν ὥσπερ οἱ νεόβουλοι καὶ γενέσθαι διπλοῦς λειτουργός, τὸ μέν τι διὰ τὴν οὐσίαν τὸ δὲ δι' ἣν ἦρξεν ἀρχήν. DECLARATION: *CTh* vi. ii. 13, 383, quique consularitatis insignia fuerit adsecutus, dignitatis obeundae atque exercendae administrationis huius copiam non habeat, nisi propria adnotatione digesserit se senatorium nomen agnoscere et larem habitationemque vel sedes certas in provincia atque oppido conlocasse nihilque amplius quam certum professionis modum varias intra provincias possidere, cuius indicio palatinis scriniis quaesito quam primum omnis instructio facile declaret, quibus quantisve nominibus quove in modo perennis aerarii emolumenta subcreverint.

CENSUALES: *CTh* VI. ii. 17, 397, censuales nostros, quibus onerosa glebae adfirmatur esse exactio, ab ipso quidem negotio summovemus. sed quia praecipuam eis scimus harum rerum esse notitiam, et disquisitionis curam et rationem manifestae instructionis eis inponimus. Symmachus apparently refers to *censuales* in *Ep.* v. 55, nolo ex moribus ceterorum qui census senatorios tractant etiam huius ingenium quam commendo perpendas, and *Rel.* 30, Luciano monente qui census senatorios ante tractavit. ABOLITION: *CJ* XII. ii. 2 (450–55), glebam vel follem sive septem solidorum functionem sive quamlibet eiusmodi collationem tam circa personas quam circa res et praedia funditus iubemus aboleri, ut omnis huiusmodi sopita perpetuo conquiescat exactio.

52. COLLATIO LUSTRALIS: Zos. II. 38, cf. *Leg. Saec.* 117, *Chron. Pasch.* 525, *CTh* VII. xx. 2 §1, 326 (S), 3, 325 (S); Evagrius (III. 40–1) could not believe that the first Christian emperor created so wicked a tax. Quadrennial incidence in the fifth century is stated in Zosimus (II. 38) and Evagrius (III. 39) and Josh. Styl. 31 and *CJ* XI. i. 1 (498). Payment in gold and silver is recorded in *CTh* XIII. i. 1, 356, 4, 362, 6, 364, 8, 370, gold only in 9, 372, 11, 379, 13, 383 (S), 15, 386, 17, 399, 18, 400, 19, 403, 20, 410, 21, 418, Cass. *Var.* II. 26, 30, Josh. Styl. 31; the tax continued to be called *chrysargyrum* or *lustralis auri argentive conlatio* (*CTh* I. v. 14, 405). It is often called πραγματευτικόν (tax on merchants) in Greek, e.g. Basil, *Ep.* 88, *P. Lips.* 64, *PRG* v. 27. Procopius of Gaza (*Pan.* 13) enumerates those liable to the tax as craftsmen (αὐτουργοῦντες καὶ τῶν καθ' ἡμέραν ἐνδεεῖς καὶ ταῖς χερσὶ πᾶσαν ἐλπίδα πεποιημένοι τοῦ βίου), market gardeners (γεωργὸς περὶ τὰ δένδρα), fishermen (ἀλιεύς), merchants (ἔμπορός τις μετὰ χειμῶνα καὶ θάλασσαν καὶ τύχην ἀγρίαν μόλις τῆς γῆς ἐπιβάς) and prostitutes (αἱ ἐπὶ τῶν οἰκημάτων γυναῖκες). MONEY LENDERS: *CTh* XIII. i. 18, 400. PROSTITUTES: Zos. II. 38, Evagr. III. 39, Th. II, *Nov.* xviii, 439, *CJ* XI. xli. 7 (457–67). EXEMPTION OF DOCTORS AND TEACHERS: *Leg. Saec.* 116; OF LANDOWNERS AND PEASANTS: *CTh* XIII. i. 3, 361, 6, 364, 8, 370, 10, 374, 12, 384, 13, 383 (S); OF RURAL CRAFTSMEN: *CTh* XIII. i. 10, 374, colonos rei privatae vel ceteros rusticanos pro speciebus, quae in eorum agris gigni solent, inquietari non oportet. eos etiam, qui manu victum rimantur aut tolerant, figulos videlicet aut fabros, alienos esse a praestationis eius molestia decernimus, ut hi tantum, qui pro mercimonio et substantia mercis ex rusticana plebe inter negotiatores sunt, sortem negotiationis agnoscant, quos in exercendis agris ingenitum iam pridem studium non retinet, sed mercandis distrahendisque rebus institutum vitae et voluntatis inplicuit; OF PAINTERS: *CTh* XIII. iv. 4, 374; OF VETERANS: *CTh* VII. xx. 2 §1, 326 (S), fisco nostro quoque eadem epistula interdiximus, ut nullum omnino ex his inquietaret, sed liceat eis emere et vendere, 3, 325 (S), qui autem negotii gerendi habuerit voluntatem, huic centum follium summam inmunem habere permittimus, XIII. i. 2, 357 (S), praeter eos, quos manifesta probatio demonstrat sub armis militiae sacramenta tolerasse quosque, cum requiem sortirentur, in pecuniarum certo numero inmunitatem claruerit consecutos, universi, qui negotiandi videntur exercere sollertiam, ad onus conlationis adstringantur, VII. xx. 9, 366, XIII. i. 7, 369, 14, 385, eos, quos peractae militiae labor decurso stipendiorum ordine vel protectoris honore cumulavit vel honestae vel causariae missionis necessitate donavit, quindecim solidorum in mercimoniis omnibus inmunitatem habere iubemus, agnituros publicum munus, si ultra praestitutum legis nostrae modum emendis vendendisque rebus laxiore sumptu operam voluerint commodare; OF CLERGY: *Leg. Saec.* 117, *CTh* XVI. ii. 8, 343, 10, 346 (S), 14, 356 (S), XIII. i. 1, 356, negotiatores omnes protinus convenit aurum argentumque praebere,

clericos excipi tantum, qui copiatae appellantur, nec alium quemquam esse inmunem ab huius conlationis obsequio, XVI. ii. 15 §1, 360, clerici vero vel hi, quos copiatas recens usus instituit nuncupari, ita a sordidis muneribus debent immunes adque a conlatione praestari, si exiguis admodum mercimoniis tenuem sibi victum vestitumque conquirent; reliqui autem, quorum nomina negotiatorum matricula conprehendit eo tempore, quo conlatio celebrata est, negotiatorum munia et pensitationes agnoscant, quippe postmodum clericorum se coetibus adgregarunt, XIII. i. 11, 379, etsi omnes mercatores spectat lustralis auri depensio, clerici tamen intra Illyricum et Italiam in denis solidis, intra Gallias in quinis denis solidis inmunem usum conversationis exerceant. quidquid autem supra hunc modum negotiationis versabitur, id oportet ad functionem aurariam devocari, 16, 399; cf. Greg. Naz. *Ep.* 98 (a protest against imposing ζημίαν τὴν ἐκ τῶν τεχνῶν on a deacon).

53. ASSESSMENT OF THE TAX: Zonaras, XIV. 3, ἦν δὲ ὁ τοῦ χρυσαργύρου δασμὸς τοιοῦτος· ἅπαντες καὶ προσαῖται καὶ πένητες καὶ πᾶσα πόρνη καὶ ξύμπαντες ἀπελεύθεροι ἐν ἀγροῖς τε καὶ πόλεσι διατρίβοντες εἰσφέρειν ἠναγκάζοντο τῷ δημοσίῳ τέλος ἐτήσιον καὶ ὑπὲρ ἵππων καὶ ἡμιόνων καὶ βοῶν ὄνων τε καὶ κυνῶν ἐπράττετο φορολόγημα, ὑπὲρ ἀνθρώπων μέν ἑκάστου νόμισμα ἀργυροῦν, τὸ δ' αὐτὸ καὶ ὑπὲρ ἵππου ἡμιόνου τε και βοός, ὑπὲρ ὄνου δέ καὶ κυνὸς φόλλεις ἕξ. Cf. Lib. *Or.* XLVI. 22 (a cobbler pays on his tools) and *PSI* 884 (an assessment including a mill), *PRG* v. 28 (a μυλώναρχος assessed at 40 solidi). MATRICULA: *CTh* XVI. ii. 15 §1, 360 (cited in n. 52). MANCIPES: *CTh* XIII. i. 17, 399, a negotiatoribus aurum lustrale dependi non ignoramus et cum ad eos soleat distributionis cura recurrere, quos necessitas conlationis adstringit, non convenit municipes hoc onere subiacere. sciant igitur de corpore suo, sicut in omnibus fere civitatibus, mancipes eligere absque ulla aerarii nostri deminutione, a curialibus alienae functionis distributione reiecta, XII. vi. 29, 403, dudum praecepimus, ut ex corpore negotiatorum ad suscipiendam tuendamque aurariae nostrae rationem adponeretur idoneus, qui tamen fide omnium et periculo fuisset electus. Gregory of Nazianzus speaks of the tax as being imposed by the πολιτευόμενοι (decurions) in his day (*Ep.* 98). EDESSA: Josh. Styl. 31. Evagrius states that the tax went to the praetorian prefecture (III. 39, ἐπὶ τὴν πρώτην καὶ κορυφαίαν ἐσῆγον τῶν ἀρχῶν ἀνὰ τετραετηρίδα οἱ τοῦτον ἑκασταχοῦ συλλέγοντες, ὡς καὶ μέρος οὐκ ἐλάχιστον τῆς ἀρχῆς καθεστάναι καὶ τῶν εἰδικῶν σκρινίων τυχεῖν) but he is apparently wrong. The tax was administered by the prefecture, no doubt; of the constitutions in *CTh* XIII. i, de lustrali conlatione, all are addressed to the praetorian prefect, vicars and provincial governors, except 3 (the senate), 16 (*PU* on *corporati*) and 6 (*CSL*). But this last constitution proves that the tax flowed to the *largitiones*, as do *CJ* XI. xli. 7 (457–67), μηδεὶς πορνοβοσκείτω τοῦ λοιποῦ μηδὲ πόρος ἐντεῦθεν ταῖς λαργιτίοσιν εἰσαγέσθω, XI. i. 1 (498), ἑκατὸν δὲ λίτρας ὁρίζει πρόστιμον τῇ σχολῇ τῶν παλατίνων (Anastasius in the law abolishing the *chrysargyrum*), and Malalas, 398 (cited in n. 36); cf. also Bas. *Ep.* 88 (the tax goes τοῖς θησαυροῖς), Proc. Gaz. *Pan.* 13 (it went to ὁ τοῦ βασιλέως θησαυρός). The tax continued in the West in the sixth century, see Cass. *Var.* II. 26, 30.

54. AURUM TIRONICUM: Amm. XXXI. iv. 4, Soc. IV. 34, Soz. VI. 37, *CTh* VII. xiii. 2, 368, 7 §1, 375, 13, 397 (25 solidi), 14, 397, 18, 407, 20, 410 (30 solidi), Val. III, *Nov.* vi. 3, 444 (30 solidi): in P. *Lips.* 61, 62, the χρυσώνης, the provincial representative of the *largitiones*, gives receipts for χρυσὸς τιρώνων. Cf. Syn. *Ep.* 79 (an official collects arrears τοῦ στρατιωτικοῦ χρυσίου, τοῦ καλουμένου τιρωνικοῦ). HORSES: *CTh* XI. xvii. 3, 401, addressed to the praetorian prefects and the *CSL*. LEVY ON JEWS: *CTh* XVI. viii. 29, 429, Iudaeorum

primates qui in utriusque Palaestinae synedriis nominantur vel in aliis provinciis degunt, quaecumque post excessum patriarcharum pensionis nomine suscepere, cogantur exsolvere. in futurum vero periculo eorundem anniversarius canon de synagogis omnibus palatinis conpellentibus exigatur ad eam formam, quam patriarchae quondam coronarii auri nomine postulabant; quae tamen quanta sit, sollerti inquisitione discutias; et quod de occidentalibus partibus patriarchis conferri consueverat, nostris largitionibus inferatur. SILIQUATICUM: Val. III, *Nov.* xv (444) see also ch. XXI, n. 5. Fines are generally stated to go to the *fiscus* or *aerarium*, both ambiguous terms, but the *largitiones* are specified in *CTh* IX. xvii. 2, 349, XI. xvi. 7, 8, 356 (S), xxx. 58, 399, XIII. v. 38, 414, XV. vii. 6, 381, XVI. v. 54 §9, 414, Th. II, *Nov.* xxv §7, 444, *CJ* VII. lxii. 21, etc. They go regularly to the *res privata* in Justinian's laws, e.g. *CJ* I. v. 12 §16, 18 §11, x. 2, li. 14 §3, III. i. 13 §8, X. xxx. 4 §16, Just. *Nov.* cxii §2, cxvii §13, cxxiii §27, cxxiv §2-3, cxxviii §25.

55. MAXIMIN'S LEVY: *P. Cairo Isid.* 69, 127, *P. Oxy.* 1524, 1653, *P. Merton*, 31, *P. Cairo*, 57049 (*Chron. d'Ég.* 1952, 247), *P. Thead.* 33, cf. *Sb* 9253, ... ἀργύρῳ διδόναι [νομοθε]τουμένων ἑκάστην λίτραν εἰς η′ ἀτ̣ικὰς λογίζεσθαι, ἄκοντας δὲ μὴ ἀναγκάζεσθαι τὸ εἶδος διδόναι. τῶν γὰρ ἀτοπωτάτων ἐνόμισεν εἶναι ἡ ἔνθεος αὐτῶν τύχη ἀναγκαζομένους τινὰς εἰσφέρειν τὸν ἄργυρον συνωνεῖσθαι μὲν πλείονος τιμῆς τοῦτον, ἐλάττονος δὲ παρέχειν τῷ ἱερωτάτῳ ταμιείῳ. CONSTANTINE'S LEVY: *CTh* XI. ix. 2, 337, si quis fundum vel mancipia ob cessationem tributorum vel etiam ob vestium auri argentique debitum, quae annua exactione solvuntur, occupata convento debitore et aput iudicem interpellatione celebrata, cum solutio cessaverit, sub hasta distracta comparaverit. JULIAN'S LAW: *CTh* XI. xii. 2, 362, omnes omnino, quicumque capitationis indulgentiam immunitatemque meruerunt, non solum ex annonario titulo, verum etiam ex speciebus ceteris atque largitionibus excepti sunt immunesque erunt; neque enim praestanda dividimus. χρυσὸς ἀρουρατίονος: *P. Lips.* 62. Cf. also *P. Warren*, 7, for ἀργυρικῶν καθολικότητος levied on the village of Theadelphia. LAW OF HONORIUS: *CTh* XI. xxviii. 14, 423, quod de annonariis functionibus per urbicarias regiones clementia nostra concessit, etiam in largitionalibus titulis et enfyteuticis rei publicae praediis custodiri mandamus. Cf. also *CTh* XI. i. 35 + XII. vi. 32, 429, where *possessores* pay a gold and silver tax in which *palatini* and *comites aerarii* are interested. EGYPT: *Chr.* I. 180, εἰς μὲν ἐμβολὴν σίτου κανόνος ἀρτάβας ἑξήκοντα τρεῖς μετὰ τῶν τούτων ναύλων Ἀλεξανδρίας καὶ μεταφορᾶς καὶ παντοίων ἀναλωμάτων, καὶ ὑπὲρ κανονικῶν τὰ καὶ καταβαλλόμενα τῷ κατὰ καιρὸν ἐθνικῷ χρυσώνῃ χρυσοῦ κεράτια εἴκοσι δύο δημοσίῳ ζυγῷ, καί ὑπὲρ ἀρκαρικῶν τὰ καὶ καταβαλλόμενα τῷ κατὰ καιρὸν ἀρκαρίῳ ἤτοι ἐμβολάτορι χρυσοῦ κεράτια εἴκοσι δύο ἥμισυ ὀβρυζιακὰ εἰς δημοσίῳ κεράτια εἴκοσι τέσσαρα; cf. *P. Oxy.* 1887; both these are statements of taxes on land. ITALY: *P. Ital.* 2 (p. 182), in [can]on(e) praefect(orum) sol(idi) n(umero) MCLIIIS, in titul(is) largitional(ibus) sol(idi) n(umero) LXXXVS.

56. For the clothing factories see pp. 836-7. COMPULSORY PURCHASE OF VESTIS: *P. Cairo Isid.* 54, *P. Antinoop.* 39; cf. *P. Lond.* 1659 (a fourth century letter dealing with συνώνη of πάλλια, στιχάρια and χλάμυδες). LAW OF 377: *CTh* VII. vi. 3, 377, provinciae Thraciarum per viginti iuga seu capita conferant vestem, Scythia et Moesia in triginta iugis seu capitibus interim annua solutione dependant; per Aegyptum et Orientis partes in triginta terrenis iugis; per Asianam vero et Ponticam dioecesim ad eundem numerum in capitibus seu iugis annua vestis collatio dependatur, ita ut per Orientem provinciae in titulo auri comparaticii, quod per iugationem redditur, compensa-

tionis gratia perfruantur exceptis Osroene et Isauria; nam easdem constat aurum comparaticium minime redhibere. Other allusions to *vestis* as a tax on land are *CTh* XI. ix. 1, 323, vestes canonicas, 2, 337, ob cessationem tributorum vel etiam ob vestium auri argentique debitum, XIII. v. 14, 371, ita ut vestes adque equi ceteraeque canonicae species ab indictione eadem non negentur. EGYPTIAN SCHEDULE: *P. Oxy.* 1905, μερισμ(ὸς) ἀρουρ(ῶν) ιέ (ἔτους) ἰνδικτ(ίονος) οὕτως· ἔσθητος, τῶν (ἀρουρῶν) σμγ' χλάμ(υς) α' καὶ τῶν (ἀρουρῶν) ροε' στιχ(άριον) α' καὶ τῶν (ἀρουρῶν) Ατκε' πάλλ(ιον) α'. FRACTIONAL VESTES: *P. Lond.* 1259, *P. Oxy.* 1448 (a schedule of στιχάρια and πάλλια assessed on seventeen villages, nearly all fractional), *SPP* XX. 92, *P. Warren*, 7, *P. Oslo*. 119. *PSI* 781 is an account of commuted *vestis* (A.D. 341); *PRG* V. 61 looks like accounts of a *susceptor vestium* who bought *vestes* for cash. SUSCEPTORES VESTIUM: *CTh* VII. vi. 1 = XII. vi. 4, 365 (*principales* and *honorati* under Valentinian I's reformed system), XII. vi. 31, 412 (transferred from *curiales* to *officiales*); *P. Lips.* 45, 46, 58–60, are documents relating to curial ἐπιμεληταὶ ἔσθητος in A.D. 371 at Panopolis. *P. Oxy.* 1424, concerns a villager appointed by the village εἰς ἀπαίτησιν στιχαρίων καὶ παλλίων. That *vestis* came under the *largitiones* is shown by *CTh* VII. vi. 2, 368, omnem canonem vestium ex kalendis Sept. ad kal. April. nostris largitionibus tradi praecipimus, I. xv. 10, 379, vestes largitionales, VII. vi. 4, *CSL* 396, 5, 423.

57. *CTh* VII. vi. 4, 396, fortissimis militibus nostris per Illyricum non binos tremisses pro singulis chlamydibus sed singulos solidos dari praecipias, 5, 423, militaris adaeratio vestis a conlatoribus exigatur sacratissimis videlicet largitionibus inferenda, ita ut quinque eius partes fortissimis militibus erogentur in pretio, sexta vera portio a gynaeciariis clementiae nostrae absque ulla vel ipsorum vel publica incommoditate pro eadem contextione suscepta iunioribus gregariisque militibus in ipsa, quam maxime eos desiderare constitit, specie praebeatur, *PSI* 1264, ἀπὸ λόγου ἐξαργυρισμῶν τῶν νυνὶ κελευσθέντων ἐν χρυσῷ εἰσενεχθῆναι στιχαρ(ίων). As late as A.D. 420 four στιχάρια were levied in kind from a taxpayer (*P. Oxy.* 1136).

58. VECTIGALIA: *CTh* I. xv. 10, 379, vectigalia sane apud Karthaginem constituta vicariae praefecturae apparitio procuret; of the laws in *CTh* IV. xiii, de vectigalibus et commissis, no. 1 is addressed to a consular, nos. 4 and 7 to a proconsul, nos. 2 and 3 to Menander (a *comes provinciarum* or the like, see ch. III, n. 52), no. 5 to a vicar, no. 6 to the *comes Orientis* and only 8 and 9 (and XI. xii. 3) to the *CSL*. For the *aurum oblaticium, follis, collatio lustralis* and *vestis* see above, nn. 50, 51, 53, 56.

59. *CTh* VIII. 1. 12, 382, in provinciis singulis duo tabularii collocentur, quo ad unum fiscalis arcae ratiocinium, ad alterum largitionales pertinere tituli iubeantur, XII. vi. 30, 408, duos tabularios et susceptores totidem per universas provincias oportere constitui clementia nostra praecepit. super hoc autem admonuimus et praetorianam amplissimam praefecturam, quo sciret eos, qui aurum largitionale susceperunt, nihil cum arcae ratiociniis habere commune, *CJ* X. xxiii. 3 pr. §3, 468, praecepit nostra serenitas neque veloci cursui neque alii praeter veterem consuetudinem subiacere chartularios qui de cohortalibus officiis uniuscuiusque provinciae largitionales titulos retractare constituuntur . . . illud etiam generali forma sancimus, ut in omnibus provinciis tam nominatio specialium susceptorum largitionalium titulorum quam defensio tractatorum non tantum per viros clarissimos moderatores provinciarum sed etiam per viros spectabiles proconsules et praefectum Augustalem et laudabiles vicarios una cum eorum officiis, admonentibus semper necnon imminentibus palatinis, procuretur, cf. Val. III, *Nov*. vii. 3 §2, *CSL*, 447, provinciarum iudices

esse cogendos ut tabularios largitionalium titulorum ad amplitudinis tuae sedem cum ratiociniis instructionibusque transmittant. The two *tabularii* are called in the papyri χρυσώνης and ἀρκάριος (see *Chr.* I. 180, cited in n. 55). In Egypt the office of χρυσώνης dates back to Constantine's reign; see *P. Würtz.* 15, declaration, dated 341, from an ἐπιμελητὴς χρυσίου, stating that he had collected a fine of 2 oz. gold and delivered it to the χρυσώνης, with a copy of the receipt given by the χρυσώνης, dated 335. Χρυσῶναι appear in 375, collecting gold taxes (*Chr.* I. 187, *P. Flor.* 95, cf. *P. Lips.* 62–3, of 384–5, 388); these χρυσῶναι are decurions of the provincial metropolis, not officials, as provided in the law of 382. It would appear that the measure applied to all provinces in 382 by *CTh* VIII. I. 12 had been anticipated, in a rather different form, in Egypt half a century before. PALATINI: *CTh* VI. xxx. 1, 379, I. x. 1, 382 (S), 2, 385, VI. xxx. 10, 385, VIII. viii. 4, 386, 5, 6, 7, 395, I. v. 12, 399, 13, 400, x. 6, 7, 401, XI. vii. 17, 408, 18, 409, *CJ* I. xl. 10 (401), *CTh* VIII. viii. 9, 416, I. x. 8, 428, XII. vi. 32 §2, 429, Val. III, *Nov.* vii. 1, 440, 2, 442, Maj. *Nov.* ii §2, vii §16, 458. For the responsibility of the praetorian prefects, vicars and governors for *tituli largitionales* see *CJ* x. xxiii. 4, 468, praecipimus ut si forte delegatio quae ab amplissima praefectura in diversas provincias ex more quotannis emittitur minus contineat omnes largitionales titulos aut quomodo exactio eorum debet procedere, nihilominus competentem a viris spectabilibus tam proconsulibus quam vicariis et viro spectabili comite Orientis et praefecto Augustali necnon rectoribus provinciarum eorumque officiis et curialibus omnium largitionalium titulorum exactionem procurari.

60. Val. III, *Nov.* xv (444).

61. STIPENDIUM: Pan. Lat. III. I. 4, nam cum me aerarium publicum curare voluisti, . . . idque eo tempore quo exhaustae provinciae partim depraedatione barbarica partim non minus exitialibus quam pudendis praesidentum rapinis ultra opem imperatoris exposcerent, milites saepe anteactis temporibus ludo habiti praesens stipendium flagitarent (Mamertinus was *CSL*, Amm. XXI. viii. 1); Amm. XX. xi. 5, ibi tunc forte Ursulus praesens qui aerarium tuebatur dolore percitus exclamavit, en quibus animis urbes a milite defenduntur, cui ut abundare stipendium possit imperii opes iam fatiscunt, XXVI. viii. 6, Venustus quidem largitionum apparitor sub Valente multo ante Nicomediam missus ut aurum susceptum stipendii nomine militibus per Orientem diffusis viritim tribueret. For donatives see ch. XVII, n. 33. THE CARRIAGE: Symm. *Rel.* 20.

62. PROCURATORES MONETARUM: *Not. Dig. Or.* xiii. 18, *Occ.* xi. 38–44, *CTh* I. xxxii. 3, 377; Ammianus uses the term *praepositus* in XXII. xi. 9 but *procurator* in XXVIII. i. 29. MONETARII: *CTh* X. xx. 1, 317, monetarios in sua semper durare condicione oportet nec dignitates eis perfectissimatus tribui vel ducenae vel centenae vel egregiatus, 10, 380, edicimus, ne qua mulier splendidioris gradus monetarii adhaerens consortio decus nativae libertatis amittat. quod si quam ab hac praeceptione statutum nostrae perennitatis abduxerit, ea secundum auctoritatem senatus consulti Claudiani vel legitima admonita conventione discedat vel, si conplexui monetarii putaverit inhaerendum, non ambigat se et liberis praeiudicaturam et eius condicioni esse nectendam, 16, 426; Julian, *Misop.* 367d, δέδωκα οὖν ὑμῖν καὶ ἀπὸ τῶν ἐπιτροπευσάντων τοὺς θησαυροὺς τοὺς ἐμοὺς καὶ ἀπὸ τῶν ἐργασαμένων τὸ νόμισμα τοὺς πλουσιωτάτους ἑλομένοις ἔχειν. CHARCOAL: *CTh* XI. xvi. 15, 382, carbonis quoque, nisi eum, quem moneta sollemniter vel fabricatio secundum veterem morem poscit armorum, ab

huiusmodi viris praebitio desistat, 18, 390, carbonis ab eo inlatio non cogetur nisi vel monetalis cusio vel antiquo more necessaria fabricatio poscit armorum.

63. See pp. 838–9.

64. *CTh* XII. vi. 12, 366, nulla debet esse causatio, quin solidi ex quocumque titulo congregati, sicut iam pridem praecepimus, in massam obryzae soliditatemque redintegrentur, 13, 367, quotienscumque solidi ad largitionum subsidia perferendi sunt, non solidi, pro quibus adulterini saepe subduntur, sed aut idem in massam redacti aut, si aliunde qui solvit potest habere materiam, auri obryza dirigatur, pro ea scilicet parte, quam unusquisque dependit, ne diutius vel allecti vel prosecutores vel largitionales adulterinos solidos subrogando in conpendium suum fiscalia emolumenta convertant.

65. DIOCLETIAN'S COINS: H. Mattingly, *Roman Coins*², 217. SOLIDI: *CTh* XII. vi. 13, 367. SILVER COINS: *CTh* XV. ix. 1, 384, nec maiorem argenteum nummum fas sit expendere quam qui formari solet cum argenti libra una in argenteos sexaginta dividitur. Soz. v. 15, τῶν δημοσίων ἐριουργῶν καὶ τῶν τεχνιτῶν τοῦ νομίσματος, οἳ πλῆθος ὄντες καὶ ἐς δύο τάγματα πολυάνθρωπα διακεκριμένοι ἐκ προστάγματος τῶν πρὶν βασιλέων ἅμα γυναιξὶ καὶ οἰκείοις ἀνὰ τὴν Κύζικον διέτριβον, ἔτους ἑκάστου ἀποφορὰν τῷ δημοσίῳ κατατιθέντες, οἱ μὲν στρατιωτικῶν χλαμύδων, οἱ δὲ νεουργῶν νομισμάτων.

66. Anon. *de rebus bell.* iii, *CTh* IX. xxi. 1, 319, 2, 321, 3, 326, 4, 329, 5, 343, 9, 392 (S), 10, 393, si quis super cudendo aere vel rescribto aliquo vel etiam adnotatione nostra sibi eripuerit facultatem, non solum fructum propriae petitionis amittat, verum etiam poenam quam meretur excipiat.

67. MINTS: H. Mattingly, *Roman Coins*², 211–14, *Not. Dig. Occ.* xi. 38–44.

68. J. P. C. Kent in *Essays in Roman coinage presented to Harold Mattingly* (edd. R. A. G. Carson, C. H. V. Sutherland), pp. 198–204. For the later mints see W. Wroth, *Catalogue of the Imperial Byzantine Coins in the British Museum.* For the moneyers of the *largitiones* see *CTh* VI. xxx. 7 (= *CJ* XII. xxiii. 7 §9), 384, aurifices solidorum, and *P. Dip.* 120, palatinus sacrarum largitionum et monetarius auri.

69. I am convinced by Sture Bolin's analysis of the Diocletianic monetary system in *State and Currency in the Roman Empire to* 300 A.D., ch. XII.

70. See Bolin, *loc. cit.*

71. *Ec. Hist. Rev.* v (1953), 317–8, *JRS* XLIX (1959), 34. NEW COPPER ISSUES OF 348: R. A. G. Carson, P. V. Hill and J. P. C. Kent, *Late Roman Bronze Coinage*, 324–498, p. 41. LAW OF 356: *CTh* IX. xxiii. 1, 356. LAW OF 395: *CTh* IX. xxiii. 2. For a historical and metrological study of fifth century *minimi* (AE4) see H. L. Adelson and G. L. Kustas, 'A bronze hoard of the period of Leo I', *American Numismatic Society, Museum Notes* IX. 139–88.

72. For the temple treasures see ch. III, n. 33. THE TREMISSIS: J. W. E. Pearce, *Roman Imperial Coinage*, IX. xxvi, 205. THE SILVER COINS: ibid. XXVI, ff.

73. SILVER PRICES: *P. Thead.* 33, *P. Oxy.* 1653; cf. Bolin, op. cit., pp. 311–3 (4 *aurei* per lb. under Diocletian); *Sb* 6086, cf. *Num. Zeitschr.* N.F. VI (1913), 161 ff., 219 ff. (4 solidi per lb. in the early fourth century); *CTh* XIII. ii. 1, 397, iubemus, ut pro argenti summa, quam quis thensauris fuerat inlaturus, inferendi auri accipiat facultatem, ita ut pro singulis libris argenti quinos solidos inferat. In the early fifth century the rate was apparently 4 solidi,

CTh VIII. iv. 27, 422, pro singulis libris argenti quas primipilares viris spectabilibus ducibus sportulae gratia (cf. law 9) praestant, quaterni solidi praebeantur, si non ipsi argentum offerre sua sponte maluerint. This may however have been a special concession; 5 solidi was the official rate in the reign of Justinian (*CJ* x. lxxviii. 1). It is significant that the accession donative is constantly stated to be 5 solidi plus one pound of silver until Tiberius Constantine, who by converting the silver at 4 solidi to the pound made it 9 solidi (Joh. Eph. *HE* III, 11). The amount in the treasuries under Leo is stated separately in gold and silver by Joh. Lydus, *Mag.* III. 43 and Candidus, 2 (Proc. *BV* I. vi. 2, estimates the total in terms of gold). The concentration on gold began under Valentinian and Valens (see p. 148).

74. See *Ec. Hist. Rev.* v. (1953), pp. 307–9: to the documents there cited may be added *P. Oxy.* 2267, where 3,200 myriads are equated with 7 solidi under Evagrius *CRP*, who was executed in 361 (Amm. XXII. iii. 7).

75. One may conjecture that *centenionales* were so called because they were originally tariffed at 100 denarii.

76. Val. III, *Nov.* xvi, 445, hoc ergo edicto agnoscat universitas capitale manere supplicium, si quisquam vel domini patris mei Theodosii vel sacrarum necessitudinum nostrarum vel superiorum principum solidum aureum integri ponderis refutandum esse crediderit vel pretio minore taxaverit . . . quo praecepto etiam illud in perpetuum volumus contineri, ne umquam intra septem milia nummorum solidus distrahatur emptus a collectario septem milibus ducentis; cf. *Ec. Hist. Rev.* v (1953), pp. 309–10. For the *follis* see *JRS* XLIX (1959), pp. 34–8.

77. For payment of *stipendium et donativum* in denarii see ch. XVII, n. 31 and for the transformation of the *capitatio* ch. II, nn. 49 and 50. VALENS' LAW: *CTh* IX. xxi. 7, 369, quidquid ex auro hominum privatorum in monetis publicis reppereris figuratum, id omne nostris scias largitionibus vindicandum, si quidem ipse se dignum condemnatione iudicavit, quisquis aurum proprium non coactus monetis fiscalibus sponte credidit inferendum. He mitigated this judgment five years later; *CTh* IX. xxi. 8, 374, solitae moderationis arbitrio superiorem sententiam mitigamus, qua omne aurum, quod a privatis pro figuratione monetis dicebatur inlatum, fisci iusseramus commodis vindicari, ut pro omni summa, quae brevibus tenetur inserta, binae per singulas libras omissa frustratione unciae conferantur.

78. PECUNIA IN USU PUBLICO CONSTITUTA: *CTh* IX. xxiii. 1, 356. VALENTINIAN I'S LAW: *CJ* XI. xi. 2 (371–3), pro imminutione quae in aestimatione solidi forte tractatur omnium quoque specierum pretia decrescere oportet.

79. Symm. *Rel.* 29, vendendis solidis, quos plerumque publicus usus exposcit, collectariorum corpus obnoxius est, quibus arca vinaria statutum pretium subministrat. huic hominum generi taxationis exiguae vilitate nutanti divus frater numinis vestri tantum pro singulis solidis statuit conferendum quantum aequitas illius temporis postulabat, ddd. imppp., sed paulatim auri enormitate crescente vis remedii divalis infracta est, et cum in foro venalium rerum maiore summa solidus censeatur, nummulariis pretia minora penduntur. petunt igitur de aeternitate vestra pro ratione praesenti iusta definitionis augmenta, qui iam tanto oneri sustinendo pares esse non possunt. The curious title of provincial gold buyer (ἐθνικὸς χρυσώνης) borne by the *tabularius titulorum largitionalium* in the Egyptian provincial offices (see n. 59) suggests that his

original function was to buy solidi against issues of copper from the money changers of the provinces. For a forced purchase of gold from the cities of Egypt in the early fourth century see P. Oxy. 2106.

80. P. Grierson, *JRS* XLIX (1959), 73–80.

81. P. Grierson, loc. cit. Justinian's change in the exchange rate is recorded by Proc. *HA* XXV. 11, 12, τῶν γὰρ ἀργυραμοιβῶν πρότερον δέκα καὶ διακοσίους ὀβολούς, οὓς φόλλεις καλοῦσιν, ὑπὲρ ἑνὸς στατῆρος χρυσοῦ προίεσθαι τοῖς ξυμβάλλουσιν εἰωθότων, αὐτοὶ ἐπιτεχνώμενοι κέρδη οἰκεῖα ὀγδοήκοντα καὶ ἑκατὸν μόνους ὑπὲρ τοῦ στατῆρος δίδοσθαι τοὺς ὀβολοὺς διετάξαντο. That the *follis* was the XL (M) piece is proved by the Slavonic version of Malalas (M. Spinka and G. Downey, *The Chronicle of John Malalas*, p. 121, 'forty silver pieces which the Antiochenes call one *follis*').

82. For the silver coins see W. Wroth, *Catalogue of the Coins of the Vandals, Ostrogoths and Lombards in the British Museum*, xxii, 8–9, 11–15, 115–16.

83. Both points are made by Marcellinus Comes, 498 (*Chron. Min.* 11. 95); nummis quos Romani teruncianos vocant, Graeci follares, Anastasius princeps suo nomine figuratis placabilem plebi commutationem distraxit.

84. PECUNIA: Aug. *Serm.* 127 §3, ad aliquid ergo magnum et pretiosum comparandum parares aurum vel argentum vel pecuniam, vel fructus aliquos pecorum aut frugum. BUYING AND SELLING SOLIDI: Anon. *de Rebus Bell.* iii. 1, ementis enim eundem solidum fraudulenta calliditas et vendentis damnosa necessitas difficultatem quandam ipsis contractibus intulerunt, ne rebus possit interesse simplicitas, Aug. *Serm.* 389 §3, cum solidum, ut assolet, vendidisset, centum folles ex pretio solidi pauperibus iussit erogari, *CTh* IX. xxii. 1 (see below), Symm. *Rel.* 29 (cited in n. 78), *CTh* XII. vii. 2 (see below), Val. III, *Nov.* xvi (cited in n. 75). LARGE AND SMALL SOLIDI: *CTh* IX. xxii. 1, 343 (S), omnes solidi, in quibus nostri vultus ac veneratio una est, uno pretio aestimandi sunt atque vendendi, quamquam diversa formae mensura sit. nec enim qui maiore habitu faciei extenditur, maioris est pretii aut qui angustiore expressione concluditur, minoris valere credendus est, cum pondus idem existat. ZYGOSTATAE: *CTh* XII. vii. 2, 363, emptio venditioque solidorum, si qui eos excidunt aut deminuunt aut, ut proprio verbo utar cupiditatis, adrodunt, tamquam leves eos vel debiles nonnullis repudiantibus inpeditur. ideoque placet quem sermo Graecus appellat per singulas civitates constitui zygostaten, qui pro sua fide at queindustria neque fallat neque fallatur, ut ad eius arbitrium atque ad eius fidem, si qua inter vendentem emptoremque in solidis exorta fuerit contentio, dirimatur.

85. PACHOMIUS: *V. Pach.* 33–4. HYMETIUS: Amm. XXVIII. i. 17–8. For violent fluctuations in the prices of corn and other agricultural products see the interesting figures given in Josh. Styl. 26, 39, 43, 45, 46, for a succession of years in Mesopotamia.

86. ANTIOCH: Julian, *Misop.* 369.

87. COMMUTATION RATES: at 40 *modii*, Val. III, *Nov.* xiii §4, 445, *P. Cairo*, 67320; at 10 *artabae*, *P. Oxy.* 1909, 1920, *SEG* VIII. 355 (in *P. Oxy.* 1907 the rate is as high as 9⅙ *artabae*). EGYPTIAN MARKET PRICES: A. C. Johnson and L. C. West, *Byzantine Egypt: Economic Studies*, 176–8. MESOPOTAMIA: Josh. Styl. 26. ITALY: Anon. Val. 73. Contrast Cass. *Var.* x. 27, XII. 27–8, where in Liguria during a scarcity the market price rises to 10 *modii* for the solidus,

and the government sells wheat from the public granaries at 25 *modii* to the solidus.

88. MEAT: Val. III, *Nov.* xiii §4, 445 (Numidia), xxxvi §2, 452 (Italy), *P. Cairo*, 67320 (cf. *JHS* LXXI (1951), 271), *P. Oxy.* 1920 (Egypt).

89. OIL: *P. Oxy.* 1753, 1920, 2052, *P. Baden*, 95. WINE: Val. III, *Nov.* XIII §4, 445, *P. Cairo*, 67320.

90. ANNONA RATES: Val. III, *Nov.* xiii §4, 445, *CJ* I. xxvii. 1 §§22–38, 534, Just. *Ed.* xiii §18, 539. RATION SCALES: *P. Oxy.* 1920, 2046, 2196; cf. ch. XVII, n. 44. 80 LB. OF BREAD FROM 1 ARTABA: *P. Oxy.* 1920.

91. THE BARRISTER'S SERVANT: *P. Strassb.* 40. THE NUNS AT OME: Greg. *Ep.* VII. 23.

92. UNIFORMS: *CTh* VII. vi. 4, 396, *PRG* v. 61, D5. CLOTHES: Joh. Moschus, 116, 192, *V. Mel.* 8, *P. Strassb.* 40. BLANKETS: *V. Joh. Eleem.* 21, Greg. *Ep.* VII. 23.

93. MONKS: *Itin. Hier. Theodosius*, 20. THE BATH ATTENDANT: *V. Joh. Eleem.* 1. In *P. Oxy.* 2008, a rent collector received a salary of 3 solidi 8 carats, but he no doubt had perquisites. For wages rates in the building trade see ch. XXI, n. 82. CHILDREN: *Lex Vis.* IV. iv. 3; cf. *CJ* VII. vii. 1, 530. From Malalas, 439–40, it appears that Eulalius, a rich man who had been ruined (he died worth only 564 solidi), thought 15 *folles* a day (equivalent to 30 solidi a year at the rate of 180 *folles* to the solidus) an adequate income to maintain his three daughters until they married, when they were to get 10 lb. gold each as dowry.

94. For *annona* see ch. XII, n. 14. From Just. *Nov.* viii, *Notitia*, it appears that those who received *dignitates* paid a fee τῇ τάξει τῶν ἐνδοξοτάτων ἐπάρχων ὑπὲρ προστάγματος. This was probably a warrant entitling him to draw his *annona* (cf. Joh. Lydus, *Mag.* III. 30, τὸ πρόσταγμα τῶν ἀννονῶν). Cf. also for distribution of *annonae CTh* I. v. 5, 355, inter cetera solita perpetrari plerique dividere arbitrio suo annonarias species deteguntur, quod nulli omnino fas est praeter sublime fastigium praefecturae. nullus igitur iudex sine auctoritate tua in speciebus annonariis erogandis habeat facultatem, 6, 357 (S), nullum patimur praefectorum in aliena dioecesi emolumenta annonaria erogare, 7 (357), citra nostra praecepta nulli annonas cognoscas esse praebendas. From Just. *Ed.* xiii §§4–6 and 7–8, it is clear that the Augustal prefect of Egypt was responsible to the praetorian prefect of the East for collecting the corn for Constantinople and the freight money *(ναῦλα)*. Many earlier laws in *CTh* XIII. v addressed to the praetorian prefects show that they were responsible for the shipment of the corn and the emoluments of the *navicularii*; note especially laws 14, 371, 32, 409. For the *cursus publicus* see ch. XII, n. 14; cf. *CTh* VIII. v. 31, 376 (S) *(annonae* of staff), 34, 377 (levy of animals), 60, 400, XI. i. 9, 365 (fodder). For the arms factories and public works see ch. XII, nn. 8, 14.

95. From *CJ* x. xxiii. 4, 468, it appears that by this date at any rate the *tituli largitionales* were fixed by 'prisca et inveterata consuetudo'.

96. SCRINIA: Joh. Lydus, *Mag.* III. 5 (cited below), *CJ* XII. xlix. 10 (485–6) (mentioning the *numerarii, adiutores* and *chartularii* of the *scrinia* of Oriens, Asiana, Pontica and Thrace), 13 (mentioning the three ταβουλάριοι—i.e. *numerarius, adiutor* and *chartularius*—of the *scrinia* of Oriens, Pontus, and arms). The two *numerarii* of each *scrinium* are recorded in Bas. *Ep.* 142–3. TRACTA-

TORES: Bas. *Ep.* 144 (the earliest mention), *CJ* I. xlii. 1, XII. xlix. 10 §1 (485–6), 13 §§1–2, lx. 6 pr. (485–6), Just. *Nov.* xxviii pr., 535, cxxviii §1, 545, *Ed.* iv §1; cf. Joh. Lydus, *Mag.* III. 68, Malalas, 400. Though the language is sometimes ambiguous it is clear in most of these passages that there was one τρακτευτής for each province at Constantinople. In *Nov.* xxviii pr. Justinian remarks that the separation of Helenopontus and Pontus Polemoniacus was so incomplete that they still had one *tractator* between them (ὡς εἰς τὴν παροῦσαν ἡμέραν ἐνὶ τρακτευτῇ τῶν δημοσίων φόρων τε καὶ διατυπώσεων χρῆσθαι τὰς χώρας ἀμφοτέρας). For τρακτευταί in the provinces see below. CURAE EPISTULARUM: *Not. Dig. Or.* ii. 67, Joh. Lydus, *Mag.* III. 4–5 κοῦρα ἐπιστολάρουμ Ποντικῆς δύο. ἀλλ' ἴσως ἄν τις οὐκ ἔξω λόγου πύθοιτο τὴν αἰτίαν ἐπιζητῶν, τίνος χάριν πασῶν τῶν διοικήσεων ἐχουσῶν τοὺς καλουμένους κοῦρα ἐπιστολάρουμ τὸ πόλεως σκρινίον τό τε τῶν ὅπλων καὶ ἔργων οὐκ εἴληχε, 21, μεθ' ὃν οἱ τῶν διοικήσεων κοῦρα ἐπιστολάρουμ, οἳ τὰς μὲν ἐπὶ τοῖς δημοσίοις φοιτώσας ψήφους γράφουσι μόνον, τὸ λοιπὸν καταφρονούμενοι. οἱ δὲ λεγόμενοι τρακτευταὶ τὴν ἐγνωσμένην αὐτοῖς διδασκαλίαν ὑποτιθέντες τῷ προστάγματι τὴν ὅλην ὑφήρπαζον ἐξουσίαν. THE MILITARY AND CORN PURCHASE DEPARTMENTS: Joh. Lydus, *Mag.* III. 38, τοῖς δὲ σκρινιαρίοις προστέθεινται καὶ οἱ σίτου στρατιωτικοῦ οἱονεὶ ἀννωνιακοῦ προεστηκότες φροντίσματος, οὐχ ὅτι καὶ αὐτοὶ μέρος ἐτύγχανον τῆς παλαιᾶς ὄψεως τοῦ δικαστηρίου, ἀλλ' ὅτι τῶν στρατηγικῶν παρωθηθέντων σκρινιαρίων καὶ τούτων συνέβη ἀποτελεσθῆναι τὸν κατάλογον ... τοῦ γε μὴν σιτωνικοῦ ἀνέκαθεν ὑπὸ τὴν πολιαρχίαν τελοῦντος, δυνάμει δὲ καὶ αὐθεντίᾳ τοῦ βδελυροῦ Καππαδόκου ... ἀφαιρεθέντος ... μόνος Γαβριήλιος πολιαρχῶν ἀποκατέστησεν ἐκείνῳ τῷ δικαστηρίῳ. As the list of *scrinia* given in III. 5 is evidently meant to be complete, these two departments, which had recently been transferred from the offices of the *magister militum* and *praefectus urbi*, were evidently not entitled *scrinia*. For the former cf. Just. *Ed.* xiii. §13, διὰ τοῦ σκρινιαρίου τῆς σῆς ὑπεροχῆς ὃν ἐκ τοῦ τὰ στρατιωτικὰ διοικεῖν στρατιωτὸν καλοῦσιν Αἰγύπτιοι (evidently the provincial representative of the military department of the praefecture). The σιτωνικόν is presumably the fund mentioned in *CTh* XIV. xvi. 1, 409, 3, 434. GENERAL AND SPECIAL BANKS: Just. *Ed.* xiii §§9, τῶν εἰς ἑκατέραν τράπεζαν εἰσφερομένων τοῦ δικαστηρίου τῆς σῆς ὑπεροχῆς, τήν τε ἰδικὴν καὶ τὴν γενικήν, 12, ταῖς εἰσπράξεσι τῆς γενικῆς καὶ ἰδικῆς τραπέζης, 21, τὸν τῆς ἰδικῆς καὶ γενικῆς τραπέζης τοῦ δικαστηρίου τῆς σῆς ὑπεροχῆς, *Nov.* cxlviii §1, cf. Joh. Lydus, *Mag.* III. 36, λογοθέται [τῆς τε ἰδικῆς ?] καὶ γενικῆς τραπέζης διοικηταί, Evagr. III. 39 (cited in n. 53). The *arca* of the prefects is apparently first mentioned in 382 (see n. 124), next in 392; *CTh* VII. iv. 19, officiorum annonas dispositione providentissima his provinciis distributas, quae nec transvectioni publicae nec arcae possunt aliquod deferre conpendium, conprobamus.

97. ILLYRICUM: *Not. Dig. Or.* iii. 26, numerarii quattuor, in his auri unus, operum alter, 28, cura epistularum, *CJ* XII. xlix. 12, numerarius scrinii Macedoniae et scrinii Daciae et scrinii operum et scrinii auri, Sim. Metaphr. *S. Demetrii Miracula* I. xii. 97, τὴν ἔντιμον στρατίαν τοῦ Δακικοῦ καλουμένου σκρινίου τῶν ὑπερλάμπρων ὑπάρχων τοῦ Ἰλλυρικοῦ στρατευόμενος. GAUL: *Not. Dig. Occ.* iii. 44, 46. ITALY: ibid. ii. 49, 511; it had a *scrinium curae militaris*, Cass. *Var.* XI. 24. AFRICA: *CJ*. I. xxvii. 1 §§22–3, 36–7; it had no *curae epistularum*.

98. VICARS: *Not. Dig. Or.* xxiii. 21–2, xxiv. 26–7, xxv. 32–3, *Occ.* xx. 19, 22, xxi, 19, 22, xxii. 43, 46, xxiii. 19, 62. PRAEFECTUS ANNONAE AFRICAE: *Not. Dig. Occ.* ii. 41, *CTh.* XI. xxx. 4+XIII. v. 2+3, 314 (S), XIII. v. 12, 369, ix. 2 (372), cf. I. xii. 7, 400 (S), xv. 10, 379. PRAEFECTUS ANNONAE ALEXANDRIAE: *CTh.* XII. vi. 3, 349, *Chr.* I. 433 (A.D. 380), *P. Oxy.* 2408 (A.D. 397), *P. Ryl.* 652. The office is not mentioned in *Not. Dig. Or.*, perhaps because it had been

suppressed; it had certainly vanished by the time of Justinian, being conspicuously absent in *Ed.* xiii. PRAEFECTIANI IN THE PROVINCES: Amm. XVII. iii. 6, *CTh* XII. x. 1, 364 (S), I. xvi. 5, 365 (S), VIII. viii. 4, 386, 5, 395, 9, 416, Maj. *Nov.* vii §16, 458. They are called *canonicarii* in Maj. *Nov.* ii §2, 458, *CJ* x. xix. 9, 496, Cass. *Var.* XI. 38, XII. 4, 7, 13, 16, Just. *Nov.* cxxviii §5, 545. *Τρακτευταί* in the provinces are clearly recorded in Just. *Ed.* xiii §§9–12, 27, *V. Eutych.* 68, συνέβη πάντας τοὺς τὴν ἐπαρχίαν τοῦ Πόντου διοικοῦντας, τρακτευτὰς φημὶ καὶ αὐτὰς τῶν δημοσίων, ἔτι γε μὴν καὶ τὰ τῆς μοδερατοριανῆς τάξεως ἐμπεπιστευμένους, ὁρμᾶσθαι τοὺς πάντας ἐκ τῆς Ἀραβισσηνῶν πόλεως, and perhaps in Cyr. Scyth. *V. Sabae*, 54, οἱ κατὰ καιρὸν τρακτευταὶ καὶ βίνδικες τῶν κατὰ Παλαιστίνην δημοσίων, 73, κελεύσας τοῖς τρακτευταῖς Παλαιστίνης χρυσίον ὑπουργῆσαι εἰς τὴν οἰκοδομήν. Most of the *τρακτευταί* mentioned in the sixth century seem to be local officials (e.g. *P. Cairo*, 67329), but the μεγαλοπρεπέστατος τρακτευτής of *P. Flor.* 303 must be a *praefectianus* (cf. the περίβλεπτοι τρακτευταί of *IGLS* 316 in Syria). Ἐξπελλευταί: *CJ.* x. xix. 9, 496, Just. *Nov.* cxxviii §6, 545; the title also applied in sixth century Egypt to local officials (*P. Flor.* 291, *P. Lond.* 1038, 1703, *P. Cairo*, 67054, 67105).

99. JULIAN AND FLORENTIUS: Amm. XVII. iii. 2, cumque Florentius praefectus praetorio cuncta permensus, ut contendebat, quidquid in capitatione deesset ex conquisitis se supplere firmaret, talium gnarus animam prius amittere quam hoc sinere fieri memorabat . . . ob quae praefecto praetorio ferri non posse clamante se repente factum infidum, cui Augustus summam commiserit rerum, Iulianus eum sedatius leniens, scrupulose computans et vere, docuit non sufficere solum verum etiam exuberare capitationis calculum ad commeatuum necessarios apparatus. CONSTANTIUS II's LAW: *CTh* XI. xvi. 7, 356, 8, 357 (S) placet nullum omnino iudicem de cetero provincialibus inferendum aliquid indicere, ut ea tantum sedulo cunctorum studio pensitentur, quae canonis instituti forma complectitur vel nostra clementia decernit inferenda vel delegatione sollemniter sanciente vel epistulis praecedentibus. sed si quid urguere forsitan coeperit, referri ad celsitudinem tuam statuimus et auctore te fieri et eo persoluto referri ad scientiam nostram, ut nobis iubentibus roboretur. de ceteris quae prospici oportet ante plurimum temporis, insinuetur nobis tempore indictionis ex more promendae. quippe suggerit ratio eius omnia serie contineri; cf. I. xxviii. 1, 361, praesertim cum ea tantum solvi oporteat, quae vel in delegatione manu nostrae mansuetudinis adnotantur vel a praefectura pro rerum necessitatibus postulantur. JULIAN's LAW: *CTh* XI. xvi. 10, 362, nihil provincialibus indici sine nostra scientia fas est neque rursus ex his quae sunt indicta referri. omnia igitur, quae consuetudo vel dispositio nostra amplectitur, hoc est cursum publicum, translationes, itinerum sollicitudines ceteraque similia cuncti possessores implere pariter compellantur. VALENS' LAW: *CTh* XI. xvi. 11, 365, nihil a provincialibus extraordinaria patimur indictione deposci. caveat igitur magnifica auctoritas tua, ne praeter ea, quae a mansuetudine nostra patuerit indicta, tenuiorum oneret functionem; ut, si quis usurpatoria temeritate amplius aliquid fuerit conatus exigere, obnoxius quadrupli repetitione teneatur. quae severitas iussionis ad ordinariorum iudicum officiorumque terrorem debebit excurrere, ut, si eorum vel gratiosa coniventia vel ignobili dissimulatione temeritas admiserit curialis, eos quoque damni similis poena castiget. GRATIAN's LAW: *CTh* XI. vi. 1, 382, nihil superindictorum nomine ad solas praefecturae litteras quisquam provincialis exsolvat neque ullius omnino indictionis titulis etiam sollemnis immineat, nisi eum nostro confirmata iudicio et imperialibus nexa praeceptis sedis amplissimae deposcat indictio et cogat exactio.

100. Most early laws (*CTh* XI. xvi. 1, 318 (S), 2, 323, 4, 328, 9, 359, 12, 380, 13, 382) mention only *extraordinaria*, which appear to include everything beyond the indiction; cf. *tit. cit.* 2, 323, ab extraordinariis omnibus fundi patrimoniales adque enfyteuticarii per Italiam nostram constituti habeantur immunes, ut canonica tantum et consueta dependant ad similitudinem per Africam possessorum; 13, 382, privatae rei nostrae privilegiis permanentibus nihil extra ordinem praedia iure perpctuo consignata sustineant neque adiectis saepius ac praeter primum delegationis canonem postulatis adficiantur impendiis. Law 5 (343, privatas res nostras ab universis muneribus sordidis placet esse immunes neque earum conductores nec colonos ad sordida vel extraordinaria munera vel superindictiones aliquas conveniri), goes into more detail, and law 6 (346) mentions *temonaria onera* as well as *extraordinaria*; in XV. ii. 1, 330, both *super-indicta* and *extraordinaria* are mentioned. THE LAWS OF 382 AND 390: *CTh* xi. xvi. 15, 18, ac ne in occulto lateat quae sit, munerum enumeratio sordidorum vocabulis ipsis signata respondet. eius igitur patrimonium, quem ab his obsequiis lex nostra defendit, cura conficiendi pollinis non habebit; nullam excoctionem panis agnoscet; nulla pistrinis obsequia dependet; operas atque artifices non praebebit; excoquendae ab eo calcis sollicitudo cessabit; non conferendis tabulatis obnoxia, non lignis, indultam quoque materiem sub eadem exceptione numerabit; nulla paraveredorum et parangariarum praebitione pulsabitur exceptis his, quas Raetiarum limes, expeditiones Illyricae, quas pastus translatio militaris vel pro necessitate vel pro sollemnitate deposcunt; carbonis ab eo inlatio non cogetur, nisi vel monetalis cusio vel antiquo more necessaria fabricatio poscit armorum; nullam sollicitudinem publicarum aedium vel sacrarum constituendarum reparandarumve suscipiet; nulla pontium vel viarum constructione retinebitur; temonis sive capituli onera non sentiet; allectis atque legatis nihil in sumptuum conlatione numerabit. After this date *sordida munera* are generally mentioned as well as *extraordinaria* or *superindicta* or both, e.g. VI. xxvi. 14, 412, XVI. ii. 40, 411 (S). On roads see *CTh* xv. iii. 3, 387, 4, 399, 6, 423. For superindictions voted by city councils see *CTh* XI. xvi. 11 (cited in n. 99) and xv. i. 33, 395, praecipua nobis cura est, ne aut provinciales nostri superindictionibus praegraventur aut opera publica pereant vetustate conlabsa. singuli igitur ordines civitatum ad reparationem moenium publicorum nihil sibi amplius noverint praesumendum praeter tertiam portionem eius canonis, qui ex locis fundisque reipublicae quotannis conferri solet, sicut divi parentis nostri Valentiniani senioris deputavit auctoritas.

101. JULIAN: Amm. XVI. v. 14, quod profuerit anhelantibus extrema penuria Gallis hinc maxime claret, quod primitus partes eas ingressus pro capitibus singulis tributi nomine vicenos quinos aureos repperit flagitari, discedens vero septenos tantum munera universa complentes. INCREASE OF INDICTION: Them. *Or.* viii. 113, ἀεὶ γὰρ ἐπεδίδου τὸ μέγεθος τῶν εἰσφορῶν ὅσα ἔτη, καὶ τὸ παρελθὸν ἔτος ἀεὶ τοῦ παρόντος κουφότερον ἦν, καὶ βαρύτερον ἀμφοῖν τὸ προσδοκώμενον. ταύτην τὴν κακὴν αὔξησιν καταλαβόντες πρῶτον μὲν ἐστήσατε ἀπροσδοκήτως, καὶ τρεῖς ἐφεξῆς ἐνιαυτοὺς οὐ προὔβη τὸ νόσημα, ὥσπερ εἰώθει, τῷ τετάρτῳ δὲ τὴν ἴσην μοῖραν παρελύσατε τῆς βαρύτητος, καὶ ἀνεγνώσθη γράμματα ἀπιστούμενα, λειτουργήσεις ἐλάττους τόσους καὶ τόσους μεδίμνους καὶ οἴνου κοτύλας, καὶ τὰ λοιπὰ ἐξ ἴσης ἀποδέοντα τοῦ συνήθους . . . οἱ μὲν ἀεὶ κατὰ χοίνικα προστιθέντες ἔλαθον ἐν τεσσεράκοντα ἔτεσιν εἰς διπλάσιον τὰς εἰσφορὰς περιστάντες, σοὶ δέ, εἰ κατὰ γνώμην ἐκβαίνοι τὰ μέτρα τῆς ἐπανόδου, ἐξ ἡμισείας εἰς νέωτα λειτουργήσομεν. HONORIUS' LAW: *CTh* XI. v. 2, 416, omnes omnino quocumque ex titulo possidentes quod delegatio superindicti nomine videtur amplexa velut canonem cogantur inferre, et ne

qua sit dubietas, hac aperta definitione decernimus, ut id potius canonis vocabulo postuletur. nulla igitur domus vel sacri patrimonii vel enfyteutici iuris vel hominum privatorum, etiamsi privilegium aliquod habere doceantur, ab hac necessitudine seiuncta sit, quae iam non extraordinarium, ut hactenus, sed ipsis facientibus canonicum nomen accepit.

102. *CTh* XI. xxviii. 7, 413, 12, 418, XI. i. 33, 424, Val. III, *Nov.* xiii, 445.

103. See ch. II, n. 45.

104. See ch. II, n. 46.

105. See ch. II, nn. 49–50.

106. For Theadelphia and Hermopolis see *JRS* XLIII (1953), 58–64. For Cyrrhus, Theod. *Ep.* (*PG*) 42, 47.

107. REGISTRATION OF CHANGE OF OWNERSHIP: *Chr.* I. 180, *P. Oxy.* 1887, *P. Würtz.* 18, 19, *P. Warren*, 3, *P. Cairo*, 67048, 67117–8, *P. Nessana*, 24, *P. Michael.* 33, *P. Ital.* 10–11 (p. 292), actores Pierii v.i.d. certum est nobis per praesentem Amantium decemprimum atque Gregorium v.d. chartarium traditionem nobis factam praediorum ss. nullo contradicente, et parati sumus singulis annis pro eadem praedia fiscalia competentia solvere. unde rogamus uti iubeatis a polypthicis publicis nomen prioris dominii suspendi et nostri dominii adscribi. NO CONVEYANCES SINE CENSU: *CTh* XI. iii. 1, 313 (S), 2, 327, III. i. 2, 337, XI. iii. 3, 363, omnes pro his agris quos possident publicas pensitationes agnoscant nec pactionibus contrariis adiuventur, si venditor aut donator aput se conlationis sarcinam pactione inlicita voluerit retinere, etsi necdum translata sit professio censualis, sed aput priorem fundi dominum forte permaneat, dissimulantibus ipsis, ut non possidentes pro possidentibus exigantur. SABINUS: *Sb* 7623, 7669–72, *P. Thead.* 54. 5, *P. Corn.* 19, 20 (298–302), *BGU* 917 (342), 1049 (348). JOHN: *P. Cairo*, 67117 (524), 67097, 67140, 67329, 67118 (547), *P. Lond.* 1686 (565), *P. Michael.* 42 (566). CENSITORES, ETC., BY REQUEST: *CTh* VI. iii. 2, 396, 3, 396, XIII. x. 8, 383, exaequationes censuum, quas consensus provinciarum, quas nostra responsa, quas censorum et peraequatorum officia, quas auctoritates denique ordinariorum et amplissimorum iudicum necessaria emendatione vel constitutione probaverant, inconcussa aeternitate permaneant; XIII. xi. 4, 393, qui fundum aliquem, velut afanticorum mole depressum, cupit aliquatenus relevari, omne nihilominus patrimonium suum admisso patiatur inspectore censeri. quod quidem etiam ad singularum civitatium legationes convenit custodiri, ut scilicet omne territorium censeatur; VI. iii. 2, 396, si curia sibi censitorem vel peraequatorem voluerit postulare, sibi postulet, non senatui; 3, 396, sin vero curiales censitorem vel peraequatorem suis terris voluerint postulare, ab eorum petitione sit senatus alienus; XIII. xi. 9, 398 (legati Hierapolitanae civitatis), 15, 417 (possessionum dominus), 17, 417 (speciali impetratione diversis petitionibus), XI. i. 31, 412, X. iii. 7, 417, illut quoque pari diligentia statuimus, ut, si quis etiam rescribtum de nostris altaribus meruerit alium inspectorem loca debere discutere, subreptio ista vacuetur et illut valeat, quod probatissimi peraequatoris generalis electio, non specialis et gratiosa forsitan definivit ambitio, XI. xx. 5 pr., 424, 6 pr., 430, Th. II, *Nov.* xxvi §1, 444, nullique deinceps copia relinquitur inspectores sibi specialiter expetendi, nisi secundum sanctionem nostram, quae ad viri inlustris et consularis Florenti suggestionem emissa est, ex communi civitatis aut provinciae desiderio postuletur, *CJ* X. xvi. 13 pr., 496, ἐὰν μὲν αἰτήσῃ ἐπαρχία ἢ πόλις κουφισμὸν λαβεῖν ψυχικῆς συντελείας ἢ ἐπόπτην ἢ ἐξισωτὴν πεμφθῆναι, ἀναφερέσθω μὲν ἡ

δέησις αὐτῶν εἰς βασιλέα, καὶ ἐξ ἐπιλογῆς αὐτοῦ ὁ ἐπιτήδειος πρὸς τοῦτο πεμπέσθω ὅρκον πρότερον διδούς. . . . ὁ δὲ καθεὶς ἄνθρωπος δεήσεις περὶ τοιούτων ἐννοιῶν μὴ ἐπιδιδότω· μήτε δὲ κουφισμὸς ἢ μείωσις διηνεκῶς ἢ προσκαίρως μήτε ἐποψία μήτε ἐξίσωσις γινέσθω χωρὶς βασιλικῆς ἐγγράφου κελεύσεως. Theodoret (*Ep.* (*PG*) 42-7) pleads that a *peraequatio* of the territory of Cyrrhus made twelve years before be not rescinded. Basil (*Ep.* 198) alludes to a *peraequator* of Nicaea. Libanius (*Ep.* 1363) speaks of Julianus as conducting a *peraequatio* at Nicomedia and the same man acted at Nazianzus (Greg. Naz. *Or.* xix, *Ep.* 67-8). Basil, *Ep.* 83, 284, 312-3, are concerned with the activities of *censitores*.

108. CONSCRIPTION LAWS: *CTh* VII. xiii. 6, 370, circa eos enim legis iubemus valere beneficium, qui indigenas atque ipsius provinciae finibus innutritos vel adfixos censibus vel adcrescentibus suis obtulerint iuniores; neque enim convenit illum inmunitate gaudere, qui vana oblatione vagi atque fugitivi vel veterani filii statum futurae conventionis inviserit. quod hactenus decernimus custodiri, ut oblatus numerus ex adcrescentibus primitus repareturur ac, si conpensatio non potuerit convenire neque ex minoribus modus, qui oblatus fuerit, quiverit reparari, ita demum de publicis fascibus hi, qui ex superfluo veniunt, eximantur; 7 §3, 375, et quia publica utilitas quoque cogitanda est, ne sub hac indulgentia insertae capitationis numerus minuatur, ex incensitis adque adcrescentibus in eorum locum, qui defensi militia fuerint, alios praecipimus subrogari. LIABILITY FOR COLONI: *CTh* v. xvii. 1, 332, *CJ* xi. xlviii. 8 (371), 23 §5 (531-4). VILLAGES: *CTh* xiii. x. 7, 371, sicubi <in aliqua metrocomia de> subscribtorum modo sorte fatali morientibus de scribto aliquid fuerit inminutum contraque in vicina vel contermina eius vel in eodem <territorio> vel ubilibet simili substantia ratione nascendi ultra conscribtorum numerus adcreverit, modus censuum int<er u>tra<m>que servetur, ut ex eo, qui superest, ille qui defuerit suppleatur. I restore *metrocomia* because of the *querimonia defensorum vel plebeiorum* (not *possessorum*).

109. SCHEDULE OF VESTES: *CTh* VII. vi. 3 (cited in n. 56).

110. *CTh* XI. v. 3, 436, cum omnis hoc Aegyptiaci tractus possessoribus conducibile videatur, ut ante kal. Mai. praedelegatio manifestetur in locis, ne per ignorantiam conlatores ad anni prioris exemplum ante delegationem missam ea cogantur exsolvere, quae postmodum indebita missa delegatione forsitan provocavit eventus; scriniariis videlicet sedis excelsae modis omnibus ordinata salubriter impleturis, ita ut Augustaliani officii et cohortalis et defensoris discrimine in locis celeberrimis per dimenstruum tempus ad omnium perveniat notionem. Just. *Nov.* cxxviii §1, 545, ὅσα πρὸς ὠφέλειαν τῶν ἡμετέρων ὑποτελῶν ὁρᾷ σπουδάζοντες διαπράττεσθαι καὶ τὸν παρόντα τίθεμεν νόμον, δι᾽ οὗ θεσπίζομεν, κατὰ τὸν Ἰούλιον ἤτοι Αὔγουστον μῆνα μιᾶς ἑκάστης ἐπινεμήσεως τὰς μερικὰς διατυπώσεις τῶν συντελειῶν τῆς μελλούσης ἐπινεμήσεως ἐν τῷ δικαστηρίῳ τῶν ἑκάστης διοικήσεως ἐνδοξοτάτων ἡμῶν ἐπάρχων πραττομένων ὑπομνημάτων φανεροῦσθαι, σημαινούσας τὸ ὁπόσον ἐν ἑκάστῃ ἐπαρχίᾳ ἤτοι πόλει ὑπὲρ ἑκάστου ἰούγου ἢ ἰουλίων ἢ κεντουρίων ἢ ἄλλῳ οἱῳδήποτε ὀνόματι τοῦτο μὲν ἐν εἴδει τοῦτο δὲ ἐν χρυσίῳ δημοσίων ἕνεκεν ἐπίκειται, φανερούσας δὲ καὶ τῶν εἰδῶν τὴν ἀποτίμησιν κατὰ τὴν τράπεζαν καὶ τὴν ἐν ἑκάστῳ τόπῳ κρατοῦσαν συνήθειαν, καὶ τί ἐξ αὐτῶν εἰς τὴν ἄρκαν εἰσφέρεσθαι ἢ ἐν ἑκάστῃ ἐπαρχίᾳ δίδοσθαι ἢ δαπανᾶσθαι προσήκει. οὕτω δὲ συντιθεμένας τὰς τοιαύτας διατυπώσεις τοῖς τῶν ἐπαρχιῶν ἄρχουσιν εὐθέως πέμπεσθαι ἐν προοιμίοις ἑκάστης ἐπινεμήσεως, καὶ δι᾽ αὐτῶν προτίθεσθαι ἐν ταῖς ὑπ᾽ αὐτοὺς καθεστώσαις πόλεσιν ἐντὸς τοῦ Σεπτεμβρίου μηνὸς ἢ Ὀκτωβρίου. Some modern authors assume that the praetorian prefecture merely fixed totals for provinces or cities, and that it was left to the provincial or local authorities to share out the total between the taxpayers. The Novel cited

above is formal proof that in the sixth century the prefecture fixed the rate per *iugum*, etc., in detail, and the passage cited from Themistius in n. 101 shows that this was the practice in the fourth century. Additional assessments of various kinds were often apportioned (the technical term is μερισμός) on *capita* (see *JRS* XLVII (1957), 93) or on the taxpayers in proportion to their assessments (e.g. Cyr. Scyth. *V. Sabae*, 54).

111. The evidence for curial tax collectors is so enormous as to be not worth collecting; I have given some in my *Greek City*, p. 333, nn. 106–7. VILLAGE COLLECTORS AND THE PRAEPOSITUS PAGI: *P. Amh.* 139, *P. Cairo Isid.* 125, *P. Oxy.* 2124, 2232, *P. Thead.* 50, *PSI* 1106–7, *Sb* 7757; cf. *BGU* 21, *P. Amh.* 140, *P. Lond.* 1249, *P. Cairo Isid.* 71–3 for the corporate responsibility of the village; also tax receipts given by curial collectors to the village authorities, e.g. *P. Michael.* 21, *P. Cairo Isid.* 54. The evidence on villages is so far as I know confined to Egypt. EXACTOR CIVITATIS: *Greek City*, p. 332, n. 104, J. D. Thomas, 'The Office of Exactor in Egypt', *Chron. d'Egypte*, XXXIV (1959), 124–40. VALENTINIAN AND VALENS: *CTh* VIII. iii. 1, 364, vii. 8, XII. vi. 4, 5, 6, 7, 9, 365. See also pp. 146, 729. PONTIC LAW: *CTh* XI. vii. 12, 383. LANDS OF SENATORS: *CTh* VI. iii. 2, 3, 396, 4, 397. Cf. Cass. *Var.* II. 24–5 for senators' arrears under Theoderic. VINDICES: Joh. Lydus, Mag. III. 49, (Marinus) τὰ μὲν βουλευτήρια πασῶν παρέλυσε τῶν πόλεων, ὑπεμπολῶν τοὺς ὑπηκόους παντὶ ὡς ἔτυχεν, εἰ μόνον αὐτῷ τὸ πλέον ὑπόσχοιτο, καὶ ἀντὶ τῶν ἀνέκαθεν στηριζόντων τὰ πράγματα βουλευτῶν προχειρίζεται τοὺς λεγομένους βίνδικας ('Ιταλοῖς θεὸν ἀποκαλεῖν), οἳ παραλαβόντες τοὺς συντελεῖς οὐδὲν πολεμίων ἧσσον τὰς πόλεις διέθηκαν, Malalas, 400, Μαρῖνον τὸν Σύρον, ὅστις τοὺς πολιτευομένους ἅπαντας ἐπῆρε τῆς βουλῆς, καὶ ἐποίησεν ἀντ' αὐτῶν τοὺς λεγομένους βίνδικας εἰς πᾶσαν πόλιν τῆς 'Ρωμανίας, Evagr. III. 42, περιεῖλεν δὲ καὶ τὴν τῶν φόρων εἴσπραξιν ἐκ τῶν βουλευτηρίων, τοὺς καλουμένους βίνδικας ἐφ' ἑκάστῃ πόλει προβαλλόμενος, εἰσηγήσει φασὶ Μαρίνου τοῦ Σύρου, Just. *Ed.* xiii §14, τὸν κατὰ καιρὸν βίνδικα τῆς 'Αλεξανδρέων, §15, Ποταμῶνος τηνικαῦτα τῶν δημοσίων τῆς 'Αλεξανδρέων προεστῶτος κατὰ τὸ τοῦ βίνδικος σχῆμα, *Nov.* xxxviii. pr., τοὺς ὀλεθρίους μισθωτὰς οὓς δὴ βίνδικας καλοῦσι, cxxviii §5, εἴτε ἄρχοντες εἶεν εἴτε πολιτευόμενοι εἴτε ἐξάκτωρες εἴτε βίνδικες εἴτε κανονικάριοι ἢ ἄλλοι τινές, §8, οἱ πολιτευόμενοι ἤγουν ἐξάκτωρες ἢ βίνδικες ἢ ταξεῶται. *Vindices* of Tripolis and Anazarbus are mentioned in Sev. Ant. *Ep.* I. 9, 27, and of Antioch in *Chron. Pasch.* 626 (A.D. 532).

112. *CTh* XII. vi. 9, 365, verum in provinciis Africae tua sinceritas hoc ab his officium iubeat amoveri atque eos susceptores specierum annonariarum manere, quos ad hanc necessitatem vetus consuetudo constringit, maxime cum, si susceptores de curia dati aliquid vel neglegentia vel fraude decoxerint, ad redintegrationem specierum, sicuti moris est, ordo qui creaverit possit artari, *PSI* 684, τὰ δύο με[γαλο]φυῆ ἤδικτα ὦν τὸ μὲν προστάττει μηδένα βουλευτικὸν φρόντισμα ὑπεισελ[θεῖν] ἄνευ ὀνομασίας τῆς βουλῆς, τὸ δὲ ἄλλο κατ' ἀναλογί[αν] τῆς ἑκάστου ὑποστάσεως τοὺς πολιτευομένους τὰς [πολιτι]κὰς λειτουργίας ἐκ[τε]λ[εῖν], ὥστε ἢ Ταυρῖνον ἐξωθεῖσθαι τῆς ἐξακτορ[ίας ἄνευ τ]οῦ βουλευτηρίου κ[ατα]σταθέντα κατὰ τὴ[ν θ]εί[αν διάταξιν] καὶ τὰ μεγαλοφυῆ ἤδικτα ἢ ἀναμερισμὸν γενέσ[θαι κ]ατ' ἀ[να]λογίαν τῆς ἑκάστου ὑποστάσεως εἰ εὑρεθείη [κα]τὰ γνώμην τῆς βουλῆς ὀνομασθείς.

113. COMPULSOR: Maj. *Nov.* ii §2, 458, hinc est, quod vetus providentia dispositioque maiorum, quam in omnibus sequimur atque reparamus, provincialibus iudiciis exequenda commisit, quibus adnitentibus per singularum municipes civitatum moderatione tractabili fiscalium tributorum celebraretur inlatio: quam si acerbius humilis notusque compulsor pro sui conpendii utilitate tractasset, confestim depraedationibus vexatorum aditu audituque facilis provinciae cognitor subveniret, vii §14, 458, conpulsor

tributi nihil amplius a curiali noverit exigendum quam quod ipse a possessore susceperit, qui ad hoc tantummodo perurguendus est pariter ut
exigat et publicum debitorem ostendat atque convincat, Marc. *Nov.* ii §2, 450,
curialis exactor vel cohortalis conpulsor, cf. *Chr.* i. 281, 424 (letters from
provincial governors to civic authorities sending or threatening to send an
official to extract arrears). For the duties of the *canonicarii* of the praetorian
prefect see n. 98. EXTORTION: Val. iii, *Nov.* i. 3 §2, 450, ubi trepidam provinciam talis discussor adierit stipatus calumniarum ministris, superbit elatus
inter obsequia sumptuosa, expetit adminicula provincialis officii, scholares
etiam saepe coniungit, ut multiplicato et hominum numero et officiorum,
quantum avaritiae libuerit, terror extorqueat. prima sunt venientis exordia,
ut proferat et revolvat super diversis numerosisque titulis terribiles iussiones:
praetendit minutarum subputationum caligines inexplicabili obscuritate
confusas, quae inter homines versutiarum nescios hoc amplius agunt, quo
minus intellegi possunt. securitates expetunt annorum serie et vetustate
consumptas, quas servare nescit simplicitas et fiducia nihil debentis. re vera
enim aut, quoquomodo pereunt, quasi iusta contingit occasio depraedandi
aut, si extant, redimendum est, ut ferantur accepto. ita fit, ut apud inprobum
rei arbitrum merito noceat chartula, cum perit, nihil proficiat non perisse.
innumerae deinde clades, saeva custodia, suspendiorum crudelitas et universa
tormenta, quae interea, laetus et crudelitatis pertinax, egregius quaesitor
expectat, Maj. *Nov.* ii §2, 458, nunc vero canonicarios superioris militiae
auctoritate terribiles et in provincialium viscera et damna desaevientes nec
arguere quisquam apud provincialium iudicem potest, cum resupinae adpari-
turae et totum sibi de superioris cinguli fastidio blandienti potestas provincialis
examinis subiecta famuletur nec de longinquis provinciae regionibus cum
magno sumptuum expensarumque detrimento ad comitatum nostrum venire
audeat ille qui queritur, cui sub duro patientiae gemitu tolerabilior videtur
depraedatio saevientis quam sub magno observationis incommodo sustinendus
impetrandae ultionis eventus. On the conversion of arrears into private debts
see *CTh* XI. xxviii. 10, 415, Marc. *Nov.* ii §2, 450, ne qua liberalitatem nostram
caligo fraudis valeat inpedire, etsi in privatum contractum vel in cautionem
debitum publicum transisse vel novatum esse dicatur aut si quis curialis
exactor vel cohortalis conpulsor pro obnoxio se intulisse commemoret,
nihilominus liberalitas nostra firma permaneat, Maj. *Nov.* ii §1, 458, ut quidquid
ex praeteritis indictionibus usque in praesentem undecimam reliquorum est,
quod vel apud possessorem residet vel in privatum, ut fieri interveniente
versutia adsolet, nexum emissa curialibus vel canonicariis vel quibuslibet aliis
cautione migravit, penitus non petatur. Cf. Greg. *Ep.* i. 42, qui dum de suo
unde dare debeant non habent, ab actionariis publicis mutuo accipiunt et
gravia commoda pro eodem beneficio persolvunt.

114. *CTh* XI. xix. 3, 364, i. 15, 367 (S), unusquisque annonarias species pro
modo capitationis et sortium praebiturus per quaternos menses anni curriculo
distributo tribus vicibus summam conlationis implebit. si vero quisque uno
tempore omnia sua debita optat expendere, proprio in adcelerandis necessitatibus suis utatur arbitrio, Maj. *Nov.* ii §3, 458, et quia totum pro remedio
possessoris serenitas nostra constituit, quem tributorum gratia solvendorum
fruges suas sub opportunitate vendentem volumus per temporis intervalla
refoveri, trina per annum vice singularum indictionum quantitas speranda
solvatur et quadrimenstruis inlationibus annuae functionis celebretur exactio,
CJ x. xvi. 13 §§5–7, Cass. *Var.* II. 24, XI. 7, XII. 2, 16, Greg. *Ep.* i. 42, prima
illatio burdationis.

115. In *Ed.* xiii §18 Justinian assumes that the *annona* of the *dux* and the *praeses* and of their *officia* and of the local troops ought to be provided from the revenues of Libya, and, as they did not suffice, transferred the cities of Menelaites and Mareotes to that province. CURSUS PUBLICUS: *CTh* XI. i. 9, 365, tabulariorum fraudes se resecasse per suburbicarias regiones vir clarissimus Anatolius consularis missa relatione testatus est, quod pabula, quae hactenus ex eorum voluntate atque arbitrio ad mutationes mansionesque singulas animalibus cursui publico deputatis repente atque inprovise solebant convehi, nunc in consilio ratione tractata pro longinquitate vel molestia itineris ab unoquoque oppido certo ac denuntiato tempore devehi ordinavit. quod iubemus, ut etiam per omnes Italiae regiones pari ratione servetur. LIMITANEI: *CTh* XI. i. 11, 365, pro loco ac proximitate possessionum annona ad limitem transvehatur. quae iussio haut difficile capit effectum, si tabularii metu praesentium tormentorum a consuetis fraudibus arceantur, VII. iv. 15, 369, sicut fieri per omnes limites salubri prospectione praecipimus, species annonarias a vicinioribus limiti provincialibus ordinabis ad castra conferri, XI. i. 21, 385, nemo possessorum ad instruendas mansiones vel conferendas species excepta limitaneorum annona longius delegetur, sed omnis itineris ac necessitatis habita ratione, *CJ* XI. lx. 1, 385, Tiberianus ad possibilitatem singulorum quorumque locorum intuens statuit certas possessiones, quae ad limitem frumenta conveherent. quocirca generali lege sancimus Tiberiani dispositionem oportere servari.

116. The letters cited are *Chr.* I. 419, 420. PRAEPOSITI HORREORUM: *CTh* VII. iv. 1, 325, XII. i. 49 §2, 361, vi. 5, 8, 365, 24, 397, 33, 430. In Egypt these officials do not appear, their place being taken by διαδόται, distributors of *annona*, who took over the goods at the place of collection from the ἐπιμεληταί and conveyed them to their destination, and presumably distributed them to the quartermasters of the troops. See *Chr.* I. 422–3, *P. Oxy.* 1115; the letters cited in the text refer to διαδόται.

117. PRIMIPILI PASTUS: *CTh* VIII. iv. 6, 358, primipilaribus, qui ad pascendos milites sollemniter ad limitem destinantur, gravia sustinentibus detrimenta hoc modo credidimus consulendum, ut duces, qui multa eis extorquere firmantur, nomine munerum vel sportulae nihil amplius percipiant quam percipiebant patre nostro perennis memoriae regente rem publicam, ita ut species a primipilaribus ipsa praestetur nec in nummum aurumve dirigatur, ne super immensitate pretiorum necessitas conquerendi exsurgat. hac igitur remota iniuria idonei mittantur, qui ex more susceptis omnibus alimoniis militaribus easdem pervehere contendant, actis apud rectorem provinciae conficiendis, per quae designabitur, quantus specierum modus in usum alimoniae militaris a primipilaribus praebeatur et quid ob munera ducibus mittenda vel sportulam, cuius habet notitiam officium praesidale, iv. 9, 368, secundum divi Juliani statuta sportula duci in quinquaginta libras argenti non ab uno primipilari, sed ab universis pariter inferatur nihilque amplius duces sportulae sollemnis praetextu conentur exculpere, 17, 385 (S), cum ante placuisset, ut a primipilaribus secundum dispositionem divi Gratiani species horreis erogandae comitatensibus militibus ex more deferrentur, limitaneis vero pretia darentur, nunc placuit, ut aurum ad officium inlustris per Illyricum praefecturae cum certa taxatione, id est pro octogenis libris laridae carnis, pro octogenis etiam libris olei et pro duodenis modiis salis singuli solidi perferantur, 19, 396, in speciebus primipilaribus adaerandis eadem pretiorum taxatio servetur, quae in venalibus publicis poterit repperiri, 27, 422, pro singulis libris argenti, quas primipilares viris spectabilibus ducibus sportulae gratia praestant, quaterni

solidi praebeantur, si non ipsi argentum offerre sua sponte maluerint. That *primipilares* were retired *officiales* appears from many laws, e.g. *CTh* XII. i. 11, 325, VIII. vii. 6 (326–54), iv. 7, 361, 8, 364, 10, 365, vii. 12, 13, 372, XII. i. 79, 375, VII. xxii. 11, 380, 1. vi. 8, 382, VIII. iv. 13, 382, 16, 389, XVI. v. 61, 423, *CJ* XII. lvii. 13 (442), 14, 471, I. iii. 27, 466. The *primipilatus* was already a heavy financial charge as early as the reign of Caracalla; *CJ* VII. lxxiii. 1, cf. VIII. xiv. 4 (Carus), IV. ix. 1, XXXI. 11, XII. lxii. 3, 4 (Diocletian). Two inscriptions from Oescus in Dacia throw a dubious light on the earlier history of the institution; *AE* 1957, 287, pro salute adq. incolumitate dd. nn. Aug. Fl. Euforbius primipilarius leg. V Mac. ex Asia civitate Focia post pastum militum, 288 (similar except that the *primipilarius* is 'ex provincia Suria Palestina'). Legion V Macedonica was stationed at Oescus (*Not. Dig. Or.* xlii. 33), and it would appear that centurions of the legions at this time (286–93 or 340–50?) performed the *pastus* for their own units or armies; or was the retired *princeps officii* officially posted *primipilus* of the legion which he supplied? CALLINICUM: Lib. *Ep.* 21.

118. DELEGATORIAE: *CTh* VII. iv. 20, 393, nulli militarium pro his annonis, quae in provinciis delegantur, repudiata ad tempus specierum copia et inopiae occasione captata pretia liceat postulare, 22, 396, neque scholae neque vexillationes comitatenses aut palatinae neque legiones ullae neque auxilia, qualeslibet ad provincias delegatorias de specierum praebitione pertulerint, audiantur, si pretia poscant ultra ea, quae generali lege divi patris senioris Valentiniani constituta sunt. OPINATOR: *P. Oxy.* 2114, *CTh* VII. v. 1, 399, opinatores, quibus species in diversis provinciis delegantur, ut pretium maiore taxatione deposcant, contra omnem consuetudinem nullis consistentibus familiis excoctionem panis efflagitant, VII. iv. 26, 401, opinatoribus nullum sit cum provinciali commercium, ita ut a iudicibus vel officio provinciali omnis summa debiti postuletur intra anni spatium conferenda, XI. vii. 16, 401, missi opinatores cum delegatoriis iudicibus eorumque officiis insistant, ut intra anni metas id quod debetur accipiant; nihil his sit cum possessore commune, cui non militem, sed exactorem, si sit obnoxius, convenit imminere, VII. iv. 34, 414, XI. i. 34, XII. i. 186, 429; in Aug. *Ep.* 268, an *opinator* collects arrears in gold from a taxpayer. For the palatine *officia* see *CTh* VII. iv. 19, 392 (S), officiorum annonas dispositione providentissima his provinciis distributas, quae nec transvectioni publicae nec arcae possunt aliquod deferre compendium, conprobamus (the *officia* here mentioned are obviously not the provincial and diocesan offices, about which there was no question); VII. iv. 35, 423, annonas omnes quae universis officiis atque sacri palatii ministeriis et sacris scriniis ceterisque cunctarum adminiculis dignitatum adsolent delegari quasque ii, qui ad earum exactionem mittuntur, pro cupiditate ac libidine sua graviter ex provincialium visceribus eruebant, ad similitudinem militum, quibus aerariae praebentur annonae, adaerari praecipimus. In Cass. *Var.* XI. 33, 35–7 we have *delegatoriae* authorizing the payment of their emoluments to the retiring *princeps*, *cornicularius* and *primiscrinius* of the praetorian prefecture from the revenues of Samnium, Campania and an unnamed province.

119. For the commutation of military *annona* see pp. 629–30. In the East the commutation of their *annonae* by provincial governors was still at the end of the fourth century unofficial and illicit (*Lib. Or.* LVII. 51, τοὺς ἀποδέκτας ἐπλεονέκτησεν ἐν ταῖς τιμαῖς ὧν βασιλεὺς ταῖς ἀρχαῖς ἐκ τῶν παρὰ τῆς γῆς αὐτῷ προσιόντων δίδωσι), and in the West even the salary of the praetorian prefect was at the same period still calculated in kind; see Symm. *Ep.* IV. 19, on behalf of Flavian,

son of the Flavian who was praetorian prefect under Eugenius, who 'solvere salarium patris iussus est, taxatione pretiorum graviter exaggerata', 51, also on behalf of Flavian, who 'paterni salarii aestimationem iubetur exsolvere'. Cf. also Symm. *Ep.* III. 33, on behalf of Marcianus, who had also held office under the tyrant, and is too poor 'ut annonarum pretia possit exsolvere'. The commutation of taxes began as an abuse and is prohibited in certain cases in *CTh* XI. i. 8, 364 (species urbis Romae), XI. ii. 2, 364 (S), 1, 365 (vinum urbis Romae). In *CTh* XI. iv. 1, 372, however, it is assumed that landtax may be paid 'vel in pretiis vel in speciebus aut auro'. In *CTh* XI. i. 19+XI. ii. 4, 384, it is ordained on the one hand that 'non sunt pretia specierum sed ipsae quae postulantur species inferendae', and on the other hand some tax is envisaged as being paid 'sub praestatione auraria'. According to Greg. Tur. *V. Patrum*, ii. 1, Magnus Maximus conceded 'ut Arverna civitas quae tributa in specie triticea ac vinaria dependebat in auro dissolveret, quia cum gravi labore poenu inferebantur imperiali'. *CTh* XI. vii. 14, 393, speaks of a *collatio auri* collected by a curial *susceptor*; these may however be *tituli largitionales* on land (see n. 55), and not commutation of *annona*, and so may be the 'inlatio auri vel argenti' paid by *possessores* in *CTh* XI. i. 32, 412. On the other hand it is clear that *annona* was being commuted in Africa by 401 from *CTh* XII. vi. 28, 401, si apochae ad susceptores nomine militum deferantur, nihil ex ea pecunia intra provinciam tibi creditam prorogetur, quam sub testificatione gestorum ad instructionem provinciae Numidiae vel Mauretaniae oportet integram pervenire, ut illic devotissimus miles emolumenta sibi debita ex integro consequatur; cf. XI. i. 34, 429, numquam dissimulatione iudicum pro compulsore aut opinatore Africanus possessor mittatur in praedam, sed quattuor mensum ab edicti publicati die indutiis datis aurum a possessore Capitolio studio spontaneae devotionis sancimus inferri: ultra id tempus si tarditas adferatur, tunc militi debiti postulati delegandam esse rationem. From Val. III, *Nov.* xiii, 445, it appears that all landtax in Numidia and Mauretania, including military *annona*, was already in 445 regularly paid in gold, and from Maj. *Nov.* ii §3 (cited in n. 114) it appears that in Italy by 458 all landtax was paid in money. Compulsory purchase is first mentioned in *CTh* XI. xv. 1, 361, and carefully regulated in XI. xv. 2, 384. For *coemptio* in Italy under the Ostrogoths and Justinian see Cass. *Var.* XII. 22, commeantium igitur attestatione didicimus Istriam provinciam a tribus egregiis fructibus sub laude nominatam divino munere gravidam vini olei vel tritici praesenti anno fecunditate gratulari, et ideo memoratas species in tot solidos date pro tributaria functione qui vobis de praesenti prima indictione reputentur. reliqua vero propter solemnes expensas relinquimus devotae provinciae. sed quoniam nobis in maiore summa sunt quaerenda quae diximus, tot solidos de arca nostra transmisimus, 23, atque ideo experientiam tuam . . . ad Istriam provinciam iubemus excurrere, ut in tot solidos vini, olei vel tritici species de tributario solido debeas procurare, in aliis vero tot solidis quos a nostro arcario percepisti tam a negotiatoribus quam a possessoribus emere maturabis; cf. II. 26, 38, and Ennod. *V. Epiph.* 358, Boeth. *Consol.* I. 4, for complaints about *coemptiones* under Odoacer and Theoderic; Just. *App.* vii §26. Under Maurice even the corn for feeding Rome was obtained by *coemptio* from Sicily; see Greg. *Ep.* I. 2, IX. 115, on the *sitonicum*, and I. 42, which shows that the *burdatio* (the regular land tax, it would appear) was collected in gold, since the *coloni* had to sell their crops to pay it.

120. For commutation of *annonae* see pp. 397, 566. COMMUTATION OF LANDTAX: *CTh* XI. i. 37, 436, quicumque per adnotationem nostram in auro voluerit tributa dependere, communicata aestimatione quinquennii, sterilitatis ac

fecunditatis pro foro rerum venalium habita ratione, ex eadem summa, quae eiusdem quinquennii perpensis frugibus colligitur, partem quintam pro annis singulis solvere compellantur; cf. *CTh* XI. xx. 6 pr., 430, Th. II, *Nov.* xxvi §§2, 3, 444, which speaks of estates which are *adaerata* (*levius*) by special grant, and Theod. *Ep.* (*PG*) 42, μυρίων γὰρ καὶ πεντακισχιλίων ζυγῶν ἐπὶ τοῦ μεγαλοπρεποῦς τῆς μνήμης Ἰσιδώρου χρυσοτελῶν γενομένων. ANASTASIUS: Malalas, 394, ὁ δὲ θειότατος βασιλεὺς Ἀναστάσιος ἐποίησε χρυσοτέλειαν τῶν ἰούγων τοῖς συντελεσταῖς πᾶσι διὰ τὸ μὴ ἀπαιτεῖσθαι τὰ εἴδη καὶ διατρέφεσθαι ὑπὸ τῶν στρατιωτῶν, *CJ* X. xxvii. 1, 491, 2 §§5–10 (491–505), μηδείς ποτε χωρὶς μεγάλης ἀνάγκης ἐπιταττέσθω τοῖς κτήτορσιν συνωνήν, καὶ ὅτε δὲ γίνεται, κατὰ θείαν μόνον κέλευσιν γινέσθω, ἐφ᾽ ᾧ τε τὸ τῆς συνωνῆς χρυσίον ἐκ τῆς συντελουμένης παρὰ τῶν κτητόρων ἐν χρυσῷ συντελείας παρακατέχεσθαι, ἐὰν ὅλως τὰ τῆς οἰκείας αὐτῶν συντελείας ἀρκῇ πρὸς τὴν συνωνήν. ἐὰν δὲ μὴ χρεωστῶσι δημόσια οἱ τὴν συνωνὴν ἐπιταγέντες ἢ μέρος χρεωστῶσιν, ἐν νομίσμασιν εὐστάθμοις πρότερον τὸ χρυσίον λαμβανέτωσαν καὶ οὕτως τὸ εἶδος ἀπαιτείσθωσαν . . . καὶ ὅτε δὲ κατὰ θείαν κέλευσιν γένηται ἐπιταγὴ συνωνῆς, ἕκαστος τῶν κτητόρων πρὸς τὴν ἀναλογίαν τῶν ζευγῶν ἤτοι ζυγοκεφαλῶν ὑποκείσθω τῇ συνωνῇ, μηδενὸς αὐτῆς ἐξαιρουμένου. . . . ἀλλὰ ταῦτα χωρὶς τῆς Θρακικῆς διοικήσεως νενομοθέτηται. ἐν Θρᾴκῃ γάρ, ἐπειδὴ οὐκ εἰς ὁλόκληρον εἰσφέρεται τὰ δημόσια, διὰ τὸ προφάσει τῶν βαρβαρικῶν ἐφόδων ἐλαττωθῆναι τοὺς γεωργοὺς καὶ μὴ ἀρκεῖν τὴν ἐν εἴδεσι συντέλειαν τοῖς κατ᾽ αὐτὴν ἱδρυμένοις στρατιώταις, καὶ πάντων μᾶλλον ἀποτρέφεσθαι εἰς αὐτὴν στρατιωτικὰ τάγματα ἀνάγκη ἐστὶ συνεχὴς πάνυ γίνεσθαι, ἐπειδὴ μὴ ἐνδέχεται δίχα συνωνῆς ἀποτρέφεσθαι τοὺς ἐν αὐτῇ στρατιώτας· ἐν ἐκείνῃ τοίνυν τῇ διοικήσει ἡ μέχρι σήμερον κρατείτω συνήθεια, ὑποκειμένων καὶ τῶν ἐμπόρων τῇ συνηθείᾳ, πρότερον μέντοι καὶ τοῖς συντελεσταῖς καὶ τοῖς ἐμπόροις καταβαλλομένου τοῦ τῆς συνωνῆς χρυσίου ἐν εὐστάθμοις νομίσμασι καὶ ὀβρύζοις, καὶ οὕτως αὐτῶν ἀπαιτουμένων ἀδιαστρόφως καὶ ἀζημίως τὸ εἶδος εἰσφέρειν. For the abuses of *coemptio* see Proc. *HA* xxiii. 11–4, and Agath. IV. 22.

121. Just. *Ed.* xiii §18, λήψεται δὲ καὶ αὐτὸς τὰς ἀφωρισμένας αὐτῷ σιτήσεις, ὑπὲρ μὲν τῶν ἐν εἴδει ἀννόνων ἐνενήκοντα καὶ καπίτων ἑκατὸν εἴκοσι νομίσματα χίλια πέντε τέταρτον, ὑπὲρ δὲ τῶν ἐν χρυσῷ ἀννόνων πεντήκοντα καὶ καπίτων πεντήκοντα νομίσματα τετρακόσια, *Nov.* cxxviii §1, σημαινούσας τὸ ὁπόσον ἐν ἑκάστῃ ἐπαρχίᾳ ἤτοι πόλει ὑπὲρ ἑκάστου ἰούγου ἢ ἰουλίων ἢ κεντουρίων ἢ ἄλλῳ οἱῳδήποτε ὀνόματι τοῦτο μὲν ἐν εἴδει τοῦτο δὲ ἐν χρυσίῳ δημοσίων ἕνεκεν ἐπίκειται, φανερούσας δὲ καὶ τῶν εἰδῶν τὴν ἀποτίμησιν κατὰ τὴν τράπεζαν καὶ τὴν ἐν ἑκάστῳ τόπῳ κρατοῦσαν συνήθειαν. WARRANTS: *P. Cairo*, 67050–1, 67320 (see pp. 672–3); on the other hand there are warrants which do not specify any rates of *adaeratio* (*P. Cairo*, 67321, *P. Lond.* 1663, *Sb* 8028, *P. Erlangen*, 55), and may have been payable in kind. In *P. Flor.* 377, the owner or agent of a group of estates lately belonging to Olybrius of glorious memory protests that all the taxes of the eighth indiction have been paid in full, and submits a γνῶσις τῶν συντελουμένων δημοσίων εἰς διαφόρους στρατιωτικὰς διαταγάς. The payments are for the *annona* of the *dux*, his *princeps* and his *officium*, and are all reckoned in wheat (102,030½ *modii*), barley (68,688 *modii*), chaff (87,500 baskets), and wine and meat (252,994 *lb.*).

122. AERARIAE ANNONAE: *CTh* VII. iv. 34, 414, 35, 423, 36, 424, Just. *Ed.* xiii §18. MARKET RATE: *CTh* VII. iv. 28, 406, 32, 412, 36, 424. SPECIAL RATES: *CTh* VII. iv. 30, 31, 409. PARTICULARES DELEGATIONES: *CJ* I. lii. i, 439. SPECIAL RATE FOR THE PRAETORIAN PREFECT: *CTh* VII. iv. 32, 412. MIXTURE OF ANNONAE: *CTh* VII. iv. 36, 424, si quando tribuni sive comites vel praepositi numerorum per provincias annonas voluerint, hoc est quas pro dignitate sua consequuntur, in aere percipere, non aliis eas pretiis, nisi quae in foro rerum venalium habentur, adaerandas esse cognoscant. si alias annonas, quae non suae dignitatis

erunt, sed alio modo, dum tamen licito, suis commodis adquisitas in auro sibi dari   duces sive tribuni voluerint, illis pretiis contenti sint, quae in forma aerariarum annonarum universis militibus sollemni observatione praebentur, Just. *Ed.* xiii §18 (cited in n. 120).

123. *CTh* XI. i. 37 (cited in n. 119). Just. *Nov.* cxxviii §1 (cited in n. 121).

124. ASSESSMENTS IN GOLD: Val. III, *Nov.* xiii, 445. ARCA: *CTh* VIII. i. 12, 382, VII. iv. 19, 392 (S), VIII. viii. 5, 395, XII. vi. 30, 408, and thereafter regularly in remissions of arrears (XI. xxviii. 6, 9, 16, 17, etc.). In the literary sources the *arca* is first mentioned to my knowledge in 384 (Amb. *Ep.* 17 §3). THE TREASURIES UNDER LEO: Candidus, 2, ἦσαν γάρ, ὡς οἱ ταῦτα ἐφανέρωσαν κεχειρικότες, διὰ μὲν τῶν ὑπάρχων χρυσίου λίτραι τετρακισμύριαι πρὸς ἑπτακισχιλίαις· διὰ δὲ τοῦ κόμητος τῶν θησαυρῶν ἑπτακισχίλιαι πρὸς μυρίαις.

125. FORTS BUILT BY PRAESIDES: *ILS* 6886, 9352, *CIL* III. 6661, 14149, VIII. 2572, 8712, *AE* 1931, 82, 1942-3, 81. FORTS BUILT BY DUCES: *ILS* 762, cf. 773-5; in *AE* 1933, 170-1, a pair of inscriptions claim that a fort in Arabia was built by Flavius Archelaus, *v.c. comes et praeses*, in 349, and by Flavius Silvinianus, *v.p. dux*, who held office at the same time (see Wadd. 2194, *Princeton Exp. Syria*, 224). This is obviously not co-operation and may indicate a conflict of claims. The transfer of responsibility for forts from the *praeses* to the *dux* was perhaps made about this date. For civic buildings see pp. 736-7. GRANARIES AND POST-STATIONS: *CJ* x. xxvi. 2, 364, cum ad quamlibet urbem mansionemve acces-seris, protinus horrea inspicere te volumus, ut devotissimis militibus effloratae et incorruptae species praebeantur.   nam si per incuriam officii gravitatis tuae sartorum tectorum neglecta procuratione aliqua pluviis infecta perierint, iam ad damnum tuum referentur. ROADS AND BRIDGES: *CTh* XV. iii. 5, 412, anti-quatis omnibus vel personalibus rescriptis vel per adnotationes elicitis per Bithyniam ceterasque provincias possessores et reparationi publici aggeris et ceteris eiusmodi muneribus pro iugorum numero vel capitum, quae possidere noscuntur, adstringi cogantur. LABOUR AND MATERIALS: *CTh* XI. xvi. 15, 382, operarum atque artificum diversorum, excoquendae etiam calcis obsequia nulla de talibus adiumenta poscantur; materiam, lignum atque tabulata except-orum virorum patrimonia non praebeant, 18, 390, operas atque artifices non praebebit; excoquendae ab eo calcis sollicitudo cessabit; non conferendis tabulatis obnoxia, non lignis, indultam quoque materiem sub eadem exceptione numerabit. Cf. Lact. *Mort. Pers.* vii. 8, huc accedebat infinita quaedam cupiditas aedificandi, non minor provinciarum exactio in exhibendis operariis et artificibus et plaustris, omnibus quaecumque sint fabricandis operibus necessaria. LEVY OF LABOURERS FROM VILLAGES: *PSI* 162 (baths at Alexandria), 87, 689, *Sb* 7676, *P. Cairo Isid.* 81, *P. Oxy.* 1426 (Trajan's canal), *PSI* 873, *P. Oxy.* 895 (unspecified work at Babylon), 1425 (the same at Pelusium). For the change to free hired labour see the account of the building of Dara by Anastasius in Zach. Myt. *Chron.* VII. 6; cf. Joh. Moschus, 37. AUDIT OF PUBLIC WORKS: *CJ* x. xxx. 4, Just. *Nov.* xvii §4, cxxviii §18.

126. NUMIDIA AND MAURETANIA: Val. III, *Nov.* xiii pr., 445, hunc tributi modum ab his magnitudo tua sperandum esse cognoscat, ut retractis septem partibus octavam tam privatae quam enfyteuticae glebae possessor agnoscat, pro qua octava omnibus titulis ad unum redactis, quos possessor vel quivis quolibet nomine praestare consueverant, quattuor milia ducentos tantum solidos et mille ducentas militares annonas et ducentum capitum Numida provincialis exsolvat . . . has autem militares annonas cum provinciales pro longinqui

difficultate itineris in adaeratione persolverint, unius annonae adaeratio quattuor per annum solidis aestimetur, §5, Mauri vero Sitifenses servatis omnibus privilegiis dudum sibi a retro principibus indultis pro omnibus titulis totius annonae nomine quinque milia solidorum et quinquaginta capitum in annonis ducis consueto tempore annua functione dependant. EGYPT: Just. *Ed.* xiii §8, οἷα καὶ τῆς εὐτυχοῦς σιτοπομπίας εἰς ὀκτακοσίας μυριάδας συνιούσης; the *artaba* is the unit used elsewhere in the edict, e.g. §§6, 24. REVENUES OF OXYRHYNCHUS, ETC.: *P. Oxy.* 1907, 1909, *P. Cairo*, 67057.

127. Proc. *HA* xix. 8. ἐπὶ μέντοι Ἰουστίνου ἔτη ἐννέα τὴν αὐτοκράτορα ἀρχὴν ἔχοντος, τούτου Ἰουστινιανοῦ ξύγχυσίν τε καὶ ἀκοσμίαν τῇ πολιτείᾳ προστριψαμένου, τετρακισχίλια κεντηνάρια ἐς τὴν βασιλείαν εἰσκομισθῆναι οὐδενὶ νόμῳ.

128. Val. III, *Nov.* xxxiv §2, 451, ex titulo vicenarum siliquarum, quae per singulas centurias exiguntur. In Val. III, *Nov.* v §4, 440, we hear of 'septem solidis per millenas nuper indictis' in Italy. If the *millena* was 12½ *iugera*, as is implied by the equation 'iug. quinquaginta p. M IIII' in *CIL* x. 407, the Italian rate of taxation under Valentinian III was crippling, 13½ *siliquae* per *iugerum*, almost twice the Egyptian rate under Justinian, 7⅔ carats per *arura*. ANTAEOPOLIS: *P. Cairo*, 67059 (cf. *JHS* LXXI (1951), 271–2). For fees see n. 137.

129. On the *capitatio* see ch. II, nn. 47, 48. EDICT OF ZOTICUS: Zachariae von Lingenthal, Ἀνέκδοτα, 274, edict. xxiv, ὅπως ἂν εἰς τὸν τῶν ὁμοδούλων περιέλθῃ τρόπον, οἰκίαν . . . οὐκ ἀπογράφεσθαι οὐδὲ πολιτικὴν σίτησιν ἢ κῆπον οὐκ ἀπογεγραμμένον οὐδὲ ἄλλο παντελῶς οὐδέν, ᾧ μή τι γεῖκον τέλος ἢ ψυχικὸν προσγέγραπται. ὥστε μηδένα εὐλαβεῖσθαι ὑπὲρ ὁμοδούλων ἢ ὁμοκήνσων ἐπιβολῆς ἐπὶ οἰκίᾳ ἢ ἄρτοις ἢ ἑτέρῳ τινι μὴ ἐγγεγραμμένῳ τῷ κήνσῳ. HONORIUS'S LEVY: *CTh* XI. xx. 3, 405 (S).

130. EDESSA: Josh. Styl. 31. EGYPTIAN CITIES: *P. Oxy.* 1909.

131. See pp. 537–9.

132. *CTh* VI. xxxv. 2, 319 (S) (*memoriales* excused *repraesentatio equorum*), XIII. iii. 2, 320 (S) (*archiatri* excused *equorum praestatio*), VII. xxiii. 1, 369, quicumque honorariis codicillis habetur ex comite, tres protinus equos, qui digni sunt comprobari, curet offerre, quicumque autem eodem ex praeside factus indulto, duos pari devotione mox tradat. ita enim promptius instruitur usus armorum. quod munus in posterum ea lege novetur, ut quinto quoque anno, hoc est magis aliquando quam saepe, similis recurrat exactio, XIII. v. 15, 379, quisquis naviculariorum codicillis optaverit ornari, praebitioni equorum intellegat se esse subdendum, VI. xxvi. 3, 382, obsecundatoribus sacrorum scriniorum, quorum mentibus ingeniisque committimus, quidquid in alios quoque perennium saepe proferimus sanctionum, equorum ad militare subsidium ab honoratis proxime venire iussorum missam facimus; cf. 14, 412 (*scrinia* excused *equorum tironumque praestatio*), 15, 410 (*scrinia* excused *equorum indictio*), VII. xiii. 15, 402, ad conlationem iuniorum eos tantum oportet adtineri, quos constat dignitates legitimas beneficiis consecutos, non tamen si iusta privilegia suffragantur, 18, 407, iuniorum conlatione, vel qui proxime in pretio ab honoratis pro rerum necessitate petiti sunt vel si umquam tale aliquid rei publicae ratio flagitaverit, inmunes haberi oportere decernimus, qui militiae praerogativa ad tribunatus praepositurasve pervenerint, 20, 410, tirones tricenis solidis aestimatos ab omnibus officiis iudicum Africae, exemplo praecedentis temporis, postulamus; quod simul etiam ab honoratis memoratarum provinciarum nec non Sardiniae Siciliae et Corsicae, XI. xviii. 1, 412 (S)

(list of 'qui a praebitione tironum et equorum excusantur'), VI. xxiii. 2, 423 (*silentiarii* excused *tironum et equorum praestatio*), VII. xiii. 22, 428 (*sacerdotales* of Africa excused *praebitio tironum*), Val. III, *Nov.* vi. 3, 444 (details of a commuted levy of *tirones*).

133. TAX IMMUNITY: *CTh* XI. i. 1, 360 (S), praeter privatas res nostras et ecclesias catholicas et domum clarissimae memoriae Eusebii exconsule et exmagistro equitum et peditum et Arsacis regis Armeniorum nemo ex nostra iussione praecipuis emolumentis familiaris iuvetur substantiae. Datianus enim vir clarissimus patricius, qui hanc olim gratiam fuerat consecutus, auferri sibi id cum tanta instantia depoposcit, cum quanta alii poscere consuerunt. ideoque omnes pensitare debebunt quae manu nostra delegationibus adscribuntur, nihil amplius exigendi. For the very temporary immunity of the *res privata* and the lands of the church mentioned in this law see above n. 21 and ch. XXII, n. 65; the church of Thessalonica received immunity under Theodosius II (*CTh* XI. i. 33, 424, sacrosancta Thessalonicensis ecclesia civitatis excepta, ita tamen ut aperte sciat propriae tantummodo capitationis modum beneficio mei numinis sublevandum nec externorum gravamine tributorum rem publicam ecclesiastici nominis abusione laedendam). LOW ASSESSMENT: *CTh* XI. xx. 6, 430, ita ut omnium, quae praedicto tempore atque etiam sub inclytae recordationis avo nostro in terrena sive animarum discribtione relevata sunt usque ad quadringentorum iugorum sive capitum quantitatem pars dimidia publicis censibus adiungatur, ut, si quidem usque ad quadringenta iuga vel capita relevatio facta est, dimidia tantum pars fisco reddatur, si vero amplius aliquid relevatum est, usque ad ducentorum iugorum vel capitum aput beneficium consecutos relevatio firma permaneat, reliqua omnia publicis censibus refundantur. EXTRAORDINARIA AND SORDIDA MUNERA: *CTh* XI. xvi. 15, 382, 18, 390, 23, 412.

134. Amm. XVI. v. 15, denique eum adusque imperii finem et vitae scimus utiliter observasse ne per indulgentias quas appellant tributariae rei concederet reliqua. norat enim hoc facto se aliquid locupletibus additurum, cum constet ubique pauperes inter ipsa dictorum initia solvere universa sine laxamento compelli; cf. *CTh* XI. vii. 4, 328 (S), quoniam subclamatione vestra merito postulastis, ne qua his, qui praestationes fiscales differunt, reliquorum laxitas proveniret, specialiter praecipimus observari, ut res eorum, qui fiscalibus debitis per contumaciam satisfacere differunt, distrahantur.

135. *CTh* XI. xxviii. 3, 401, 9, 414, 16, 433, Marc. *Nov.* ii, 450, Val. III, *Nov.* i. 1, 438, 3, 450, Maj. *Nov.* ii, 458, Just. *Nov.* cxlvii, 553, τούτου χάριν ἐπὶ τὰς παρούσας θείας ἡμῶν ἤλθομεν δωρεάς, δι' ὧν θεσπίζομεν ἀφεῖσθαι πάντας τοὺς ἡμετέρους ὑποτελεῖς ἐλλειμμάτων παντοίων ὀφειλομένων παρ' αὐτῶν ἀπὸ τῆς τοῦ προτέρου κύκλου πρώτης ἐπινεμήσεως καὶ αὐτῆς, εἰς ἣν τὰς προτέρας ἡμῶν συνεκλείσαμεν δωρεάς, μέχρι τῆς ἄρτι παρελθούσης ἑβδόμης ἐπινεμήσεως καὶ αὐτῆς, ὡς εἶναι εἴκοσι δύο ἐτῶν ἐφεξῆς τὴν εἰς τοὺς ὑπηκόους παρ' ἡμῶν γινομένην φιλοτιμίαν, καὶ μηδεμίαν ἐλλειμάτων εἴσπραξιν εἶναι πρὸς ἐκείνους ἀναγομένων τοὺς χρόνους, cxlviii, 566.

136. Val. III, *Nov.* i. 3 §2, 450, securitates expetunt annorum serie et vetustate consumptas, quas servare nescit simplicitas et fiducia nihil debentis, *CJ* x. xxii. 3, 456, quicumque de provincialibus et collatoribus decurso posthac quantolibet annorum numero, cum probatio aliqua ab eo tributariae solutionis exposcitur, trium cohaerentium sibi annorum apochas securitatesque protulerit, superiorum temporum apochas non cogatur ostendere, neque de praeterito ad illationem functionis tributariae coartetur.

137. WEIGHTS AND MEASURES: *CTh* XII. vi. 19, 383, 21, 386, XI. viii. 3, 409, Maj. *Nov.* vii §15, 458. CURRENCY: Maj. *Nov.* vii §14, 458. DOUBLE PAYMENT: *CTh* XII. vi. 27, 400, for actual cases see the complaints of Aphrodito (pp. 407-8) and Greg. *Ep.* I. 42, cognovimus etiam rusticos burdationem quam iam ab eis exactam Theodosius minime persolverat iterum dedisse, ita ut in duplo exacti sunt. SPORTULAE: *CTh* XII. vi. 3, 349, susceptores centesimae dimidium, annotatores vero ceterorumque officiorum diversos homines, quos rationibus constat obnoxios esse, alterum dimidium habere censuimus, 14, 367, singulas tantum dependant centesimas, qui reditus domui nostrae debitos arcariis quotannis iuxta consuetudinem tradunt, 15, 369, in epimetris autem eam consuetudinem sinceritas tua faciat observari, ut in aridis quidem fructibus centesimam levandi dispendii causa a possessore susceptor accipiat, laridi vero et vini vicesimam consequatur, 21 §1, 386, et submotis, quae contra utilitatem populorum omnium hactenus gesta sunt, frumenti quinquagensimas, hordei quadragensimas, vini et laridi vicensimas susceptoribus dari praecipimus. The various fees and perquisites of the collectors are richly documented in the papyri; see A. C. Johnson and L. C. West, *Byzantine Egypt: Economic Studies*, 289 ff. COST OF COLLECTION: Maj. *Nov.* ii §2, 458, praefectiani si quidem atque palatini vel aliarum potestatum adparitores conpetentium titulorum exactione suscepta contra veterem morem per provincias discurrentes enormibus exactionibus possessorem curialemque concutiunt et ita omnia pro arbitrio suae depraedationis extorquent, ut, cum aliqua pars certa vel minima publicis compendiis inferatur, duplum aut amplius in sportulis avidus et praepotens executor accipiat, vii §16, 458, inter haec etiam officiorum pro laborum merito non est commoditas neglegenda. et quia per rectores provinciarum exigi omnem canonem tam ad arcam praefecturae pertinentem quam sacris vel privatis largitionibus inferendum, sed et binos per iugum vel millenam solidos remunerationibus deputatos compelli debere praecipimus, possessori non putamus onerosum, quem a multis molestiis et sportularum et numerosis mutaturae dispendiis liberamus, si semissem solidi per iuga singula seu singulas millenas amplius iubeamus inferri, qui pro ordinatione nostra inter diversa officia dividatur. ita ergo praedicta summa inter compulsores, ut diximus, partienda est, ut palatinus siliquam mediam pro siliquatico solidi <medii ad similitudinem> remunerationis binorum solidorum, exactor siliquam, quattuor autem siliquas tam curialis quam officium provinciale percipiat, officium sane praefectorum sex semis siliquas consequatur. BINA ET TERNA: Cass. *Var.* III. 8, VII. 20-22. TAX OF SEVEN SOLIDI: Val. III, *Nov.* v §4, 440.

138. COMPULSORES: *CJ* x. xix. 9, 496. SPORTULAE: Zachariae von Lingenthal, Ἀνέκδοτα, p. 271, edict xiii, ὥστε τοὺς ὑποτελεῖς τὰ δημοσία κατατιθέναι, ὡς αἱ μερικαὶ δηλοῦσι διατυπώσεις, καὶ πρὸς τούτοις λόγῳ παντοίας τῶν τὰ δημόσια πραττόντων παραμυθίας καὶ τοῦ λεγομένου διαζημίου καὶ καθ' ἕκαστον ἰοῦγον κεράτιον ἓν καὶ μηδὲν περαιτέρω . . . ἀλλὰ τὸ ἐκ τοῦ κερατίου συναγόμενον καὶ ταξεώτας καὶ βουλευτὰς καὶ σκρινιαρίους τῶν ἐπάρχων καὶ κανονικαρίους τῶν λαργιτιόνων καὶ πᾶν πρόσωπον συνηθείας κομιζόμενον μερίζεσθαι.

139. BANKRUPTCY OF THE WEST: Val. III, *Nov.* xv pr., 444. MARCIAN'S RESERVE: Joh. Lydus, *Mag.* III. 43. ANASTASIUS'S RESERVE: Proc. *HA* xix. 7. For the effect of the landtax on agriculture see pp. 819-21.

Of the many histories of Roman Law I have found H. F. Jolowicz, *Historical Introduction to the Study of Roman Law*[2], Cambridge, 1952, the most useful from my standpoint. On procedure M. A. von Bethmann-Hollweg, *Der Römische Civilprozess*, III, Bonn, 1866, is still the most comprehensive work.

1. For the bulk of the juristic sources see *CJ* I. xvii. 2 §1, 533.

2. *CTh* I. iv. 1, 321 (S), 2, 328 (S), 3, 426.

3. DECRETA: *CTh* IV. xx. 3, 386, apud acta imp. Theodosius A. dixit, VIII. xv. 1 (a dialogue between Constantine and a litigant), XI. xxxix. 5, 362, pars actorum habitorum apud imperatorem Iulianum Augustum Mamertino et Nevitta conss. X kal. april. Constantinopoli in consistorio: adstante Iovio viro clarissimo quaestore, Anatolio magistro officiorum, Felice comite sacrarum largitionum, et cetera. imp. Iulianus dixit, 8, 381, pars actorum habitorum in consistorio apud imperatores Gratianum, Valentinianum et Theodosium cons. Syagri et Eucheri die iii kal. Iul. Constantinopoli in consistorio. imp. Theodosius A. dixit. RESCRIPTS: nearly all the laws of Diocletian and his colleagues in the Codex Justinianus (all those listed on pp. 494–7 of Krüger's edition except those few whose addressee is noted) are rescripts to private persons, and many others are cited in *Fragmenta Vaticana, Collatio, Consultatio*, etc.; rescripts of Constantine are found in *Fr. Vat.* 33, 34, 36, 273–4, 287, of Valentinian I in *Consult.* IX. 2, 5, 6. On the publication of rescripts see *Hermes*, LV (1920), 1–42. *Consult.* IX. 2, a private rescript, was 'dat. viii id. Feb. alleg. non. kal. April. in basilica Thermarum Commodianarum', and IX. 4, a rescript to a *relatio* of the consular of Picenum, was 'alleg. iiii kal. Mai. Flavia Fanestri in secretario'; that is, they were cited in court during trials and copied from the court record by the editor who added them to the Codex Hermogenianus. For rescripts to *relationes* see also ch. XI, n. 60.

4. RESCRIPTS CONTRARY TO THE LAW: *CTh* I. ii. 2, 315, 3, 317 (S), *CJ* I. xix. 7, 426, cf. *CTh, Gesta senatus* 5, ut ad preces nullae leges promulgentur rogamus, dictum xxi. RESCRIPTS AND DECRETA DENIED FORCE OF LAW: *CTh* I. ii. 11, 398, *CJ* I. xiv. 2, 3 §1, 426; RESTORED: *CJ* I. xiv. 12, 529.

5. *CJ* I. xiv. 3, 426, leges ut generales ab omnibus aequabiliter in posterum observentur, quae vel missa ad venerabilem coetum oratione conduntur vel inserto edicti vocabulo nuncupantur, sive eas nobis spontaneus motus ingesserit sive precatio vel relatio vel lis mota legis occasionem postulaverit. nam satis est edicti eas nuncupatione censeri vel per omnes populos iudicum programmate divulgari vel expressius contineri, quod principes censuerunt ea, quae in certis negotiis statuta sunt, similium quoque causarum fata componere. sed et si generalis lex vocata est vel ad omnes iussa est pertinere, vim obtineat edicti; interlocutionibus, quas in uno negotio iudicantes protulimus vel postea proferemus, non in commune praeiudicantibus, nec his, quae specialiter quibusdam concessa sunt civitatibus vel provinciis vel corporibus, ad generalitatis observantiam pertinentibus. On the promulgation of laws see ch. XII, n. 15. Theoderic ordered his edict to be posted for 30 days (Cass. *Var.* IX. 19–20).

6. Lib. *Or.* I. 145; the law of Valentinian referred to is *CTh* IV. vi. 4, 371. *CTh* XII. i. 158, 398, vaccillare per Apuliam Calabriamque plurimos ordines

civitatum comperimus, quia Iudaicae superstitionis sunt et quadam se lege, quae in Orientis partibus lata est, necessitate subeundorum munerum aestimant defendendos. itaque hac auctoritate decernimus, ut eadem, si qua est, lege cessante, quam constat meis partibus esse damnosam, omnes, qui quolibet modo curiae iure debentur, cuiuscumque superstitionis sint, ad complenda suarum civitatum munia teneantur.

7. *CJ* I. xxvi. 2, 235, formam a praefecto praetorio datam, et si generalis sit, minime legibus vel constitutionibus contrariam, si nihil postea ex auctoritate mea innovatum est, servari aequum est. For surviving edicts of the prefects see Just. *Nov.* clxvi, clxviii, and Zachariae von Lingenthal, 'Ανέκδοτα, 227-278; cf. *PSI* 684, where τὰ μεγαλοφυῆ ἤδικτα (as opposed to ἡ θεία διάταξις) are probably edicts of the praetorian prefects.

8. The *decreta* cited in n. 3 are clearly copied from the record of the consistory. For rescripts also see n. 3.

9. See Jors in *PW* s.v. *Codex Gregorianus* and *Hermogenianus*, and G. Rotondi, *Scritti Giuridici* I. 118-146. The Gregorianus contained two laws later than 291 (*Coll.* VI. iv, xv. iii) and the Hermogenianus seven of Valentinian (*Consult.* IX. 1-7), which are presumably later additions.

10. Laws from the Gregorianus are cited by book and title in, for example, the *Epitome Codicum Gregoriani et Hermogeniani Wisigothica* (FIR II², pp. 655 ff.). For the Hermogenianus see *Schol. Sin.* iii (FIR II², p. 639).

11. See Seeck, *Reg.* 1-18.

12. *CTh* I. i. 5, ad senatum, 429. The quotation in the text is from Th. II, *Nov.* i §1.

13. *CTh* I. i. 6, 435.

14. EXCLUSIVE VALIDITY OF THE CODE: Th. II, *Nov.* i, 438, *CTh, gesta senatus.* MUTUAL EXCHANGE OF LAWS: Th. II, *Nov.* i §5, 438, his adicimus nullam constitutionem in posterum velut latam in partibus Occidentis aliove in loco ab invictissimo principe filio nostrae clementiae perpetuo Augusto Valentiniano posse proferri vel vim legis aliquam obtinere, nisi hoc idem divina pragmatica nostris mentibus intimetur. quod observari necesse est in his etiam, quae per Orientem nobis auctoribus promulgantur; cf. *CTh* I. i. 5, 429, in futurum autem si quid promulgari placuerit, ita in coniunctissimi parte alia valebit imperii, ut non fide dubia nec privata adsertione nitatur, sed ex qua parte fuerit constitutum, cum sacris transmittatur adfatibus in alterius quoque recipiendum scriniis et cum edictorum sollemnitate vulgandum; Th. II, *Nov.* ii, 447, Val. III, *Nov.* xxvi, 448, Anth. *Nov.* ii, iii, 468.

15. The Breviarium is published in G. Haenel, *Lex Romana Visigothorum*, Leipzig, 1849, the *Lex Romana Burgundionum* in FIR II², pp. 713 ff., the Edict of Theoderic, ibid., pp. 683 ff.

16. THE FIRST CODE: *CJ const.* Haec, Summa. THE DIGEST: *CJ* I. xvii. I (= *Dig. const.* Deo auctore), 2 (= *Dig. const.* Tanta), *Dig. const.* Omnem. THE SECOND CODE: *CJ const.* Cordi.

17. IUS ITALICUM: *CJ* VII. xxv. 1 (530-1), xxxi. i, 531; cf. *Inst.* II. vi. pr. LATINITAS: *CJ* VII. vi. 1, 531; cf. *Inst.* I. v §3.

18. On the collections of Justinian's novels see H. F. Jolowicz, *Historical Introduction to the Study of Roman Law*², 506–9. A good example of a codifying statute is *Nov.* xxii on the law of marriage.

19. The *iuridicus Alexandriae* survived under the later empire, *Chr.* II. 96, *CJ* I. lvii. 1, 469. So also did the two *legati* of the proconsul of Africa (*Not. Dig. Occ.* xviii. 3, cf. *CTh* I. xii. 1, 313 (S), 3, 313, 6, 398), the *legatus almae Karthaginis* (*ILS* 1220, 6809, Aug. *c. Cresc.* IV. 3, *Coll. Carth.* I. i, II. i, III. i, Mansi, IV. 51, 167, 181) and the *legatus Numidiae* (*ILS* 1240, *AE* 1933, 155); cf. also *ILS* 637, 5518, 5714, 5907, 9353, 9357. We also hear of a *legatus in provincia Achaea* in the late fourth century (*ILS* 1281) and a *legatus provinciae Asiae* under Constantine (*ILS* 2942). IUDICES PEDANEI: *CJ* III. iii. 2, 294, placet nobis praesides de his causis, in quibus, quod ipsi non possent cognoscere, antehac pedaneos iudices dabant, notionis suae examen exhibere, ita tamen ut, si vel per occupationes publicas vel propter causarum multitudinem omnia huiusmodi negotia non potuerint cognoscere, iudices dandi habeant potestatem (quod non ita accipi convenit, ut etiam in his causis, in quibus solebant ex officio suo cognoscere, dandi iudices licentia permissa credatur). IUDEX SACRARUM COGNITIONUM: *ILS* 1211, L. Aelio Helvio Dionysio c.v. iudici sacrarum cognitionum totius Orien. praesidi Syriae Coeles; cf. also 2941, corr. Italiae Transpadanae, cognoscenti vice sacra.

20. For the institution of *defensores* see pp. 144–5. Their judicial functions are defined in *CTh* I. xxix. 2, 365, 5, 370, 7, 8, 392, IX. ii. 5 + XI. viii. 3, 409. The limit of 50 solidi is given in the Justinianic interpolation in *CJ* I. lv. 1, that of 300 solidi in Just. *Nov.* xv §3, 535.

21. EPISCOPAL JURISDICTION: *CTh* I. xxvii. 1, 318 (S), *Sirm.* 1, 333, *CJ* I. iv. 7, 398, *CTh* I. xxvii. 2, 408. For the jurisdiction of the Jews see *CTh* II. i. 10, 398, *CJ* I. ix. 15, 415.

22. SILVANUS: Soc. VII. 37. JUDICIAL ASSESSORS: Cyr. Scyth. *V. Euthymii*, 3, *V. Sabae*, 75; in both passages he describes a lay advocate *(σχολαστικός)* as τὸ ἐπισκοπεῖον κρατῶν καὶ τῷ ἐπισκόπῳ συνεδρεύων; Zach. Myt. *Chron.* VII. 1, also speaks of the *scholasticus* of a church, and Greg. *Ep.* III. 18 is addressed to 'Theodorum virum eloquentissimum consiliarium nostrum'. AUGUSTINE'S COMPLAINTS: Aug. *En. in Ps.* CXVIII. xxiv. 3, cf. Poss. *V. Aug.* 19. Theodoret gives a pleasant picture of the judicial work of Abraham, bishop of Carrhae, in *Hist. Rel.* xvii. For the records of an actual case see *Chr.* II. 98, cf. *Sb* 7449 (a request for the bishop's jurisdiction): Amb. *Ep.* 82 is an equitable judgment on a case which was referred to him from the court of the praetorian prefecture by the counsel of both parties.

23. PRAETORIAN PREFECTS: *CTh* XI. xxx. 16, 331, a proconsulibus et comitibus et his qui vice praefectorum cognoscunt, sive ex appellatione sive ex delegato sive ex ordine iudicaverint, provocari permittimus, ita ut appellanti iudex praebeat opinionis exemplum et acta cum refutatoriis partium suisque litteris ad nos dirigat. a praefectis autem praetorio, qui soli vice sacra cognoscere vere dicendi sunt, provocari non sinimus, ne iam nostra contingi veneratio videatur. It is usually assumed that this law for the first time granted in-appellable jurisdiction to the praetorian prefects, but more probably it for the first time allowed appeals against *vice sacra iudicantes*, except for the praetorian prefects (see ch. II, n. 1). PRAEFECTUS URBIS ROMAE: *CTh* XI. xxx. 11, 321, sublimitatem tuam qui cognitionibus nostram vicem repraesentas, 13, 18, 329 (S), etc., *ILS* 692, 1213, 1220–1, 1240–1, etc. PROCONSUL OF AFRICA: *CTh* XI.

xxx. 3, 315, appellationum causas, quae per vos in auditorio nostro, quibus vicem nostri mandamus examinis, diiudicantur, xxxvi. 3, 315 (S), etc., *ILS* 1228, 1232, 1240–1, etc.; for the proconsuls of Asia and Campania see *ILS* 751, 1220, 1227, 5702. VICARS: *CTh* XI. xxx. 16 (cited above), *ILS* 733, 4152. COMITES PROVINCIARUM: *CTh* XI. xxx. 16 (cited above), xxxiv. 1, 331, contra comitum ceterorumque sententias qui vice nostra iudicaverint, *ILS* 1231, comiti Orientis, Aegypti et Mesopotamiae, iudici sacrarum cognitionum, 1237, comiti per Orientem, Aegypti et Mesopotamiae, per easdem vice sacra iudicanti. PREFECT OF CONSTANTINOPLE: *CTh* I. vi. 1, 361, cum appellatio interposita fuerit per Bithyniam, Paphlagoniam, Lydiam, Hellespontum, Insulas etiam ac Phrygiam Salutarem, Europam ac Rhodopam et Haemimontum, praefecturae urbi iudicium sacrum appellator observet. In *CTh* XI. xxx. 30, 363 (S), the judges of appeal are listed as 'praefectos urbi seu proconsules seu comites Orientis seu vicarios', in IX. xl. 15, 392, as 'proconsules, comites Orientis, praefecti Aug., vicarii', in XI. xxx. 57, 398, as 'sive proconsule, comes Orientis, Augustalis, vicarii'. SUPPLICATIO: *CJ* I. xix. 5,365, Th. II, *Nov.* xiii, 439.

24. The range of the appellate jurisdiction of the proconsul of Africa is inferred from Val. III, *Nov.* xiii §12, 445, quicumque etiam intra provincias Africanas ad ius nostrum pertinentes a cuiuslibet iudicis sententia provocaverint, quoniam decreti antiquitus cognitoris cessat officium, inlustris urbanae praefecturae examine ex appellatione se noverint iurgaturos, sed quia transmarinae regionis sunt, indutias tempori annum debere praestari (the proconsulate of Africa was in abeyance owing to the Vandal conquest). Cf. also *CTh* XI. xxx. 62, 405, in negotiis, quae ex appellatione descendunt, veterem consuetudinem volumus custodiri, illud addentes, ut, si quando a gentilibus vel a praefectis eorum fuisset interposita provocatio, sacrum sollemniter, hoc est proconsularis cognitionis, praestoletur examen.

25. PREFECT OF ROME: *Dig.* I. xii. 1 §4, quidquid igitur intra urbem admittitur ad praefectum urbi videtur pertinere; sed et si quid intra centesimum miliarium admissum sit ad praefectum urbi pertinet, Cass. *Var.* VI. 4, *CTh* XI. xxx. 27, ad Taurum *PPO*, 357, de Sardinia Sicilia Campania Calabria Brittiis et Piceno Aemilia et Venetia et ceteris interpositas appellationes laudabilis sublimitas tua more sollemni debebit audire competenti appellatione terminandas. nec vero ulla poterit esse confusio. praefectus enim urbis nostra responsione conventus praedictis cognitionibus temperandum sibi esse cognovit, *CTh* I. vi. 2, ad Symmachum [*PU*], 364, sacrae definitionis ius magnificentiae tuae detulimus, cum ab urbis Romae vicario interposita provocatio nostrae cognitionis opperiri videbitur dignitatem, 3,364, si quando provocatio interposita adversus sententias vicariae potestatis nostrae cognitionis videatur arbitrium opperiri, nulla itineris fatigatione laedatur; sed vir magnificus praefectus urbi rite sollemnibus ordinatis vicem nostram sustinens sacrae disceptationis arbitrium suscepto litis examine terminabit. *CTh* XI. xxx. 61, 400, virtually annulled this jurisdiction, which Symmachus (*Rel.* 38) exercised. For the concurrent jurisdiction of the prefect and the vicar and the resultant quarrels see *CTh* XI. xxx. 36, 374, and Symm. *Rel.* 23. PREFECT OF CONSTANTINOPLE: *CTh* I. vi. 1 (cited in n. 23), 10, 380 (S), sacrum iudicium praefecti urbis aeternae paucis dabat reddebatque regionibus: et ideo huic Bithyniam atque Paphlagoniam nec non Phrygiam Salutarem credidimus deputandas, ut appellationes suas ad illud mittant examen illudque expectent iudicium in sacrae cognitionis eventu.

26. INSISTENCE ON RIGHT OF APPEAL: *CTh* XI. xxx. 4, 314 (S), 15, 329, 16, 331, 20, 347 (see *Historia* IV (1955), 229 for the date), 22, 343, 25, 355, 29, 362, 30,

363 (S), 32, 365 (S), 33, 364, 58, 59, 399, 60, 400. CONFESSED OR MANIFEST
CRIMES: *CTh* XI. xxxvi. 1, 313 (S), 4, 339, 7, 344, 14, 361, 18, 364 (S), 31, 392, 32,
396. FISCAL DEBTS: *CTh* XI. xxxvi. 6, 342, 8, 347, 9, 353, 10, 360 (S), 12, 355, 13,
358, 18, 364 (S), 19, 370 (S), 21, 374, 27, 383, 30, 385, 32, 396, cf. xxx. 14, 327,
21, 340. APPEALS A PRAEIUDICIO: *CTh* XI. xxxvi. 1, 313 (S), 2, 315, 3, 315 (S),
5, 341, 11, 356 (S), 15, 365 (S), 16, 364, 18, 364 (S), 30, 385.

27. The judicial arrangements in Africa and Italy are inferred from the
administrative organisation. THE QUAESTOR EXERCITUS: Just. *Nov.* xli, 537.
SICILY: Just. *Nov.* civ, 537.

28. Just. *Nov.* xxiii. This law is probably to be dated to 3 Jan. 535; the limit
on appeals has probably been emended from 500 solidi to 10 lb. gold in the
text (see Stein, *Bas-empire* II. 805 ff.). The limit of 500 solidi is given in *Nov.*
xxiv–xxxi (18 May 535–18 March 536), that of 10 lb. gold in *Nov.* ciii (1 July
536).

29. APPELLATE JURISDICTION OF PROCONSULS, ETC.: Just. *Nov.* xxx §10, xxxi §1,
ciii §1, 536.

30. Just. *Nov.* xxiii §3, 536, evenit, ut super minimis causis maximi nostri
iudices inquietentur et homines propter minimas causas magnis fatigentur
dispendiis, ut forsitan totius litis aestimatio ad sumptus iudiciales non sufficeret.

31. CURATORES AQUARUM: Frontinus, *de aquis*, 127. PROCURATORS: Tac. *Ann.*
XII. 60, *Dig.* 1. xvi. 9 pr. For the disciplinary jurisdiction of magistrates over
their *apparitores* see Plut. *Cato Minor*, 16, Cic. *pro Cluentio*, 126. The jurisdiction
over soldiers by their commanders was embodied in the *ius gladii*; see my *Studies
in Roman Government and Law*, 59–63.

32. FORUM REI: *CJ* III. xiii. 2, 293, *CTh* II. i. 4, 364; for criminal cases see
CJ III. xv. 1, 196, *CTh* IX. i. 1, 316.

33. Aug. *Conf.* vi. 16; cf. *CTh* XI. xxx. 28, 359, si a rationali vel comite vel
alio, qui curam fiscalis commodi gerit, fiscale debitum postulante fuerit pro-
vocatum, ad eos, qui vice nostra huiusmodi cognitionibus praesident, appella-
tores intra diem tricensimum perducantur; 39, 381 (an appeal against a *comes
aerarii nostri* handled by the *CSL*).

34. *CJ* III. xxvi. 5, 315, ad fiscum pertinentes causas rationalis decidat, omnibus
concussionibus prohibendis.

35. In two laws (*CTh* XI. xxxvi. 8, 347, X. i. 6, 348) a provincial governor (the
consular of Syria) deals with fiscal debts, elsewhere the judge of first instance
is always a *rationalis* (*CTh* X. i. 7, 357, XI. xxx. 14, 327, 18, 329 (S), 28, 359,
41, 383, 45, 385, 49, 389, 68, 429, xxxvi. 29, 385) or *comes* (see n. 33). Earlier
laws on appeals about fiscal debts are addressed to the *PPO* (*CTh* XI. xxxvi. 6,
342), the *PU* (XI. xxx. 18, 329 (S), xxxvi. 9, 353, 18, 364 (S), 21, 374) or a
proconsul of Africa (XI. xxxvi. 10, 360 (S), 13, 358), and *CTh* XI. xxx. 28, 359,
directs that such appeals go 'ad eos qui vice nostra huiusmodi cognitionibus
praesident'. In *CTh* XI. xxx. 39, 381, 45, 385, xxxvi. 29, 385, xxx. 46 + xxxvi.
30, 385, xxxvi. 32, 396, appeals go to the *CSL* or *CRP*. In XI. xxx. 41, 383, the
old rule is restored temporarily. In XI. xxx. 49, 389, minor cases go on appeal
to the *PU* at Rome, major cases to the *CRP*. In XI. xxx. 68, 429, a limited
jurisdiction is allowed to the proconsul of Africa. Claims for *caduca*, etc., are
judged by provincial governors in *CTh* X. x. 7, 345, xii. 2, 368, X. 20, 392,
viii. 5, 435. The rules for a trial before the *CRP* are laid down in *CTh* X. x.

27, 418 (S), 30, 421, 31, 422, for the delegation of a case by the *CRP* to a *rationalis* see Symm. *Rel.* 41. In *CTh* x. x. 32, 425, such cases may come either before the *CRP* or provincial governors. By Th. II, *Nov.* xvii. 2 §4, 444, all jurisdiction about *caduca* was transferred to the praetorian prefects, but this clause is not reproduced in *CJ* x. xii. 2, and in *CJ* x. xi. 8 (undated) claims are judged by the *CRP* in Constantinople (§4) and by the governors in the provinces (§8).

36. CONDUCTORES AND COLONI REI PRIVATAE: *CJ* III. xxvi. 6, 343, 7, 349, 8, 358. COLONI OF THE DOMUS DIVINA: *CJ* III. xxvi. 11, 442. ACTORES AND PROCURATORES REI PRIVATAE: *CTh* x. iv. 1, 326 (S), II. i. 1, 349, cf. I. xi. 2 and II. i. 11, 398.

37. COURTS OF THE PRAEFECTI ANNONAE: *CTh* XI. xxx. 4, 314 (S), xxix. 2, 319, *CJ* III. xi. 3, 318. JURISDICTION OF THE PRAEFECTUS ANNONAE ROMAE: *CTh* XIV. xvii. 6, 370 (*panis gradilis*), iii. 5, 364 (*pistores*), OF THE PRAEFECTUS ANNONAE AFRICAE: *CTh* XIII. v. 38, 414, ix. 2, 372, 3, 380 (shipwrecks), XIII. v. 12, 369 (*navicularii*), cf. XIII. v. 2, 314 (S), where in a conflict of claims between the *pistores* and *navicularii* jurisdiction is reserved to the *PU*. JURISDICTION OF THE PRAEFECTUS ANNONAE OF CONSTANTINOPLE: *CJ* XII. xix. 12 §1, ita ut, si de civilibus annonis vel tutela seu curatione vel novi operis nuntiatione litem eos subire contigerit, in maiore quidem iudicio ad similitudinem sumptuum, quos in iudicio eminentiae tuae dependere praecepti sunt, apud virum autem clarissimum praefectum annonae seu fisci patronum urbicariae magnificae praefecturae vel architectos pro modo eorum, quae super arbitris et litibus apud eos exercendis superius statuta sunt, solventes expensas nihil amplius agnoscere seu dependere cogantur. COURT OF THE PRAEFECTUS VIGILUM OF ROME: *CTh* I. ii. 1, 313 (S), II. x. 1+2, 319, XV. xiv. 3, 313 (S); OF CONSTANTINOPLE: Just. *Nov.* xiii, 535. CORPORATI OF ROME AND CONSTANTINOPLE: *CTh* I. x. 4, 391, *CJ* XI. xvii. 2, 397, *CTh* I. vi. 11, 423. BUILDING LAWS OF CONSTANTINOPLE: *CJ* VIII. x. 12 §8, 474-491, 14, 532, XII. xxiii. 12, 424-5.

38. Th. II, *Nov.* iv pr., 438, opem atque auxilium nostrae clementiae limitaneorum poscit utilitas, qui adeo quorundam querimoniis vel exhibitionibus diversorum iudicum dicuntur adflicti, ut inter privatam vitam et militarem scientiam neutri nascantur. adde, quod usum armorum dediscere compelluntur observatione fori civilis officii et in vita peregrinantur aliena expertes litium, actionum ignari, quas inverecunda facundia et doctrina popularis instituit, *CJ* XII. v. 3, 467-470, cubic larios tam sacri cubiculi mei quam venerabilis Augustae, quos utrosque certum est obsequiis occupatos et aulae penetralibus inhaerentes diversa iudicia obire non posse, xvi. 4, 474-491, ne ad diversa tracti viri devoti silentiarii iudicia sacris abstrahi videantur obsequiis, *CJ* III. xiii. 6, 413, magisteriae potestati inter militares viros vel privato actore in reum militarem etiam civilium quaestionum audiendi concedimus facultatem, praesertim cum id ipsum e re esse litigantium videatur constetque militarem reum nisi a suo iudice nec exhiberi posse nec, si in culpa fuerit, coerceri.

39. *CTh* II. i. 2, 355, definitum est provinciarum rectores in civilibus causis litigia terminare, etsi militantes exceperint iurgia vel moverint. ne igitur usurpatio iudicia legesque confundat aut iudicibus ordinariis adimat propriam notionem, ad provinciarum rectores transferantur iurgia civilium quaestionum. in criminalibus etiam causis, si miles poposcerit reum, provinciae rector inquirat. si militaris aliquid admisisse firmetur, is cognoscat, cui militaris rei cura mandata est, *CJ* III. xiii. 6, 413, Th II, *Nov.* iv, 438 (*limitanei*), vii. 1, 439, 2, 3, 440 (all soldiers) ; *CJ* III. xxiii. 2, xxv. 1, which conflate these three laws,

show that for fiscal debts even *milites armati* were subject to ordinary juris-diction. A striking instance of the usurpation of civilian jurisdiction by military courts is the group of *libelli* addressed to Flavius Abinnaeus, the prefect of the Ala V Praelectorum at Dionysias under Constantius II, which all end: εἶτα γραφέντα ὑπὸ ἡμῶν εἰς γνῶσιν τοῦ κυρίου μου δοῦκος ἀνενίκης, αὐτοῦ γάρ ἐστι τὰ τοιαῦτα τολμῶντας ἐκδικεῖν (*P. Abinn.* 44–57): a soldier is accused in one only (48) of all these *libelli* and in nearly all both parties are civilians. Cf. also *P. Oxy.* 1101, an edict of Tatian, prefect of Egypt under Valens, forbidding civilians to bring suits against civilians before military *praepositi*.

40. The jurisdiction of *magistri militum* is referred to in *CTh* IX. ii. 2, 365, and *CJ* III. xiii. 6, 413; that of *duces* over *limitanei* is inferred from Anastasius's law, *CJ* XII. xxxv. 18, 492, which extends it to *comitatenses*.

41. *CJ* XII. lix. 8 (467–470), VII. lxii. 38, 529.

42. *Cohortales* might appeal against the governor in private suits, *CTh* XI. xxxvi. 17, 371 (S). PRAEFECTIANI: *CJ* XII. lii. 3 §2, 444, scriniariis autem exceptoribus ceterisque, qui in officio tui culminis merent, cum in legione prima adiutrice nostra militant, audientiam tantummodo in causis in quibus pulsantur tuae celsitudinis deputamus. in provinciis vero commorantes rectoribus earum eos respondere iubemus, nisi publicum officium aliquod eis iniunctum sit. DUCIANI: *CJ* XII. lix. 8, 467–470. OFFICIALS OF MAGISTRI MILITUM: *CTh* I. vii. 4, 414, Th. II, *Nov.* vii. 4, 441, *CJ* XII. liv. 5, 491–518.

43. *CTh* VI. xxix. 3, ad agentes in rebus, 359, per id tempus quo cursus tuendi sollicitudinem sustinetis, condemnationes praefectorum praetorio erga eos solos inritae sunt futurae, qui servaverint honestatem; erga eos vero, qui inhoneste et contra decus saeculi vel honorem militiae versabuntur, non solum condemnatio mansura est, verum etiam, si ad nostrae serenitatis notitiam culpabilia gesta pervenerint, in eos erit acrius vindicandum. A conflict of jurisdiction over *palatini* in the provinces is revealed by Symm. *Ep.* II. 44, to Flavian PPO, palatinos iniuriae reos, quos de Brittiis celsitudo tua praecepit exciri, miles de praetorio missus exhibuit. sed cum sacro auditorio eadem causa conpeteret, dominus meus parens noster praefectus urbi auctoritate iuris et fiducia tui personas sibi ad negotium vindicavit.

44. Val. III, *Nov.* vii. 1, 440, 2, 442.

45. Th. II, *Nov.* vii. 1, 439, 2, 440, cf. also *CJ* III. xiii. 7, 502.

46. CUBICULARII: *CJ* XII. v. 3 (467–470). SILENTIARIES: XII. xv. i. 4 (474–491). SACRA SCRINIA: XII. xix. 12. AGENTES IN REBUS: XII. xx. 4 (457–470). PALATINI: XII. xxiii. 12 (424–5). CASTRENSIANI: XII. xxv. 3 (467–470), 4, 474. DECANI: XII. xxvi. 2, 444. SCHOLARES: XII. xxix. 2, 474, 3. Symm. *Rel.* 38 suggests that a *strator* could claim the jurisdiction of the *magister officiorum* in 384–5. That *domestici* enjoyed *praescriptio* from as early as 439 appears from Th. II, *Nov.* vii. 1 pr., 439; that they came under their *comites* emerges from Just. *Ed.* viii, 548, where the vicar of Pontica is made representative of the *comites domesticorum* (§1) in order that he may have jurisdiction over *domestici* in the diocese (§3).

47. *Dig.* I. ix. 11, L. i. 23. *CTh* IX. i. 1, 316, quicumque clarissimae dignitatis virginem rapuerit vel fines aliquos invaserit vel in aliqua culpa seu crimine fuerit deprehensus, statim intra provinciam, in qua facinus perpetravit, publicis legibus subiugetur neque super eius nomine ad scientiam nostram referatur nec fori praescriptione utatur. omnem enim honorem reatus excludit, cum

criminalis causa et non civilis res vel pecuniaria moveatur. Justinian's version
(*CJ* III. xxiv. 1) substitutes for 'clarissimae dignitatis' the words 'non illustris
sed tantum clarissima dignitate praeditus'. GRATIAN'S LAW: *CTh* IX. i. 13, 376;
for the *quinquevirale iudicium* see also *CTh* II. 1. 12, 423, Sid. Ap. *Ep.* I. 7 §9
(reading 'Vviris' for 'Xviris'), Cass. *Var.* IV. 22. THEODOSIUS II: *CJ* XII. i. 16,
442-4. ZENO: *CJ* III. xxiv. 3, 485-6, cf. XII. i. 17, 485-6, for other judicial
privileges of *illustres*. CIVIL CASES: *CTh* II. i. 4, 364, *CJ* III. xxiv. 2, 376, senatores in pecuniariis causis, sive in hac urbe sive in suburbanis degunt, in iudicio
tam praetorianae quam urbicariae praefecturae nec non magistri officiorum
(quotiens tamen ad eum nostrae pietatis emanaverit iussio), in provinciis vero
ubi larem fovent aut ubi maiorem bonorum partem possident et adsidue
versantur respondebunt.

48. *CTh* XVI. ii. 12, 355, 41 (= *Sirm.* 15), 411 (S), 47 (= *Sirm.* 6), 425, Val.
III, *Nov.* xxxv pr. §§1-2, 452. That an appeal lay from a court of bishops to a
secular judge is shown by *CTh* XI. xxxvi. 20, 369, quoniam Chronopius ex
antistite idem fuit in tuo, qui fuerat in septuaginta episcoporum ante, iudicio
et eam sententiam provocatione suspendit, a qua non oportuit provocare,
argentariam multam, quam huiusmodi facto sanctio generalis inponit, cogatur
expendere.

49. Gelasius, *Ep.* 23.

50. *CJ* I. iii. 22, 430 (S), cf. Just. *Nov.* cxxiii §8, 546; *CJ* I. iii. 25, 456, 32, 472.
JUSTINIAN ON MONKS: Just. *Nov.* lxxix, 539; ON CLERGY: *Nov.* lxxxiii, 539.
In *Nov.* cxxiii §21, 546, the same rule is applied to monks as to clergy.

51. Symm. *Rel.* 41.

52. *CTh* I. xvi. 1, 313 (S), quicumque extraordinarium iudicium praefectorum
vel vicariorum elicuerit vel qui iam consecutus est, eius adversarios et personas
causae necessarias minime ad officium praefectorum vel vicarii pergere aut
transire patiaris, Opt. *App.* v, equidem gentes minora interdum iudicia refu-
gientes, ubi iustitia citius deprehendi potest, magis ad maiora iudicia auctoritate
interposita, ad appellationem se conferre sunt solitae, *CJ* III. xiii. 4, 331, nemo
post litem contestatam ordinariae sedis declinet examen, nec prius praefecti
praetorio aut comitis Orientis vel alterius spectabilis iudicis imploret auxilium,
sed appellatione legibus facta ad sacrum auditorium veniat, *CTh* II. i. 6, 385,
exceptis his, quibus extra ordinem subvenitur, omnes iacturam litis incurrant,
qui non ante in proprio foro iurgaverint, siquidem possint venire ad altioris
iudicis notionem, cum iudicatum quod displicet appellatione excluserint,
CJ III. xiii. 5, 397, in criminali negotio rei forum accusator sequatur. is vero,
qui suam causam sive criminalem sive civilem sine caelesti oraculo in vetito
vocabit examine aut exsecutionem poposcerit militarem, actor quidem propositi
negotii actione multetur, reus vero pro condemnato habeatur, *CTh* II. i. 9, 397,
si quis neglectis iudicibus ordinariis sine caelesti oraculo causam civilem ad
militare iudicium crediderit deferendam, praeter poenas ante promulgatas
intellegat se deportationis sortem excepturum, *CJ* I. xlvi. 2, 416, praecipimus,
ne quando curiales vel privatae condicionis homines ad militare exhibeantur
iudicium vel contra se agentum actiones excipiant vel litigare in eo cogantur,
Th. II, *Nov.* iv, 438, Marc. *Nov.* i, 450; note especially §2, has ergo ob causas
nullum adversarium suum a proximis vel longinquis partibus, non per sacros
adfatus, non per magnificentissimorum vel inlustrium iudicum sententias
volumus exhibere, nisi forsitan aut propter potestatem adversarii aut ipsius
rei difficultatem aut publici debiti molem deficiente rectore provinciae specta-

bilis iudicis, qui in locis vel proximo deget, vel amplissimae potestatis vel aliorum maiorum iudicum auxilium postuletur; cf. *CTh* I. xv. I, 325, ne tua gravitas occupationibus aliis districta huiusmodi rescriptorum cumulis oneretur, placuit has solas causas gravitati tuae iniungere, in quibus persona potentior inferiorem aut minorem iudicem premere potest aut tale negotium emergit, quod in praesidali iudicio terminari fas non est, vel quod per eosdem praesides diu tractatum apud te debeat terminari. For an actual case of *exhibitio* see the *libellus* of Sophronius in *A. C. Oec.* II. i. 219. Wishing to sue a protégé of the all powerful patriarch Dioscorus, Sophronius went straight to Constantinople and obtained τοὺς θείους τύπους, ἔτι δὲ καὶ τὰς μεγίστας ἀποφάσεις τῶν μεγάλων καὶ ἐξοχωτάτων ἐπάρχων, εἰκότως δὲ καὶ τὸν ταῦτα συνεκβιβάζοντα, φημὶ δὴ τὸν αἰδεσιμὸν Θεόδωρον τὸν ἐκ τῆς μεγίστης τάξεως.

53. VICAR OF PONTICA: Just. *Ed.* viii, 548. PROHIBITION OF EXHIBITIO: Just. *Nov.* lxix §4, 538.

54. Just. *Nov.* lxix §§2-3, 538.

55. Malalas, 384.

56. *CJ* III. i. 13, 530, properandum nobis visum est, ne lites fiant paene immortales et vitae hominum modum excedant, cum criminales quidem causas iam nostra lex biennio conclusit et pecuniariae causae frequentiores sunt et saepe ipsae materiam criminibus creare noscuntur, praesentem legem super his orbi terrarum ponendam, nullis locorum vel temporum angustiis coartandam ponere. censemus itaque omnes lites super pecuniis . . . non ultra triennii metas post litem contestatam esse protrahendas. APPEALS: *CJ* VII. lxiii. 2, 440, tempora fatalium dierum pro saeculi nostri beatitudine credidimus emendenda ubique dilationum materias amputantes. et primi quidem fatalis diei tempora post appellationem, sive a viro clarissimo rectore provinciae sive a specta- bili iudice fuerit appellatum, sex mensuum esse iubemus. quod si primo fatali die lapsus est appellator, tricesimum primum diem alterum volumus esse fatalem. quod si eo quoque appellator exciderit, tertium similiter totidem diebus intermissis fatalem observari decernimus. quod si tertius quoque lapsus fuerit temporalis, quartum etiam fatalem post tricesimum primum diem similiter observari decernimus. quod si ita contigerit, ut quattuor fatalibus diebus qui appellavit exciderit, tunc intra trium alium mensum spatium a nostro numine reparationem peti praecipimus; 5 §1, 529, sancimus itaque, si quidem ab Aegyptiaco vel Libyco limite vel Orientali tractu usque ad utrasque Cilicias numerando vel Armeniis et gentibus et omni Illyrico causa fuerit more appellationum transmissa, primum semestre spatium in antiqua definitione permanere et nihil penitus neque deminui neque adcrescere. sin autem ex aliis nostri imperii partibus sive Asianae sive Ponticae sive Thraciae dioeceseos lis provocatione suspensa in hanc regiam urbem perveniat, pro semestri spatio trium tantummodo mensum spatium eis indulgeri: aliis trium mensum spatiis, id est nonaginta tribus diebus simili modo sequentibus sive semestre tempus sive tres priores menses secundum locorum definitionem, quam designavimus. sed et aliis tribus mensibus, qui ex reparatione ab aula concedi solent, in suo robore duraturis et prioribus accedentibus, ut partim annale numeretur, partim novem mensum spatium consequatur. et cum antea in fine cuiusque temporis unus fatalis dies ex antiquis legibus constitutus est et saepe eveniebat (cum multae sunt occasiones mortales appellationum) vel aegritudine vel spatii prolixitate vel per alias causas, quas nec dici nec enumerari facile sit, eundem diem fatalem non observari et lites expirare et huiusmodi luctuosis infelicitatibus

patrimonia hominum titubare, propter hoc fortunae relevantes insidias sancimus non in unum diem fatalem standum esse in posterum, sed sive ante quartum diem fatalis luminis et ipsum fatalem sive post quinque dies, ex quo ortus fatalis effluxerit, appellator venerit et litem instituendam curaverit et eam in competens iudicium deduxerit, legi videri satisfactum. The older procedure is referred to in *CTh* XI. xxx. 63, 405, ubi vero in longioribus ac remotis provinciis eadem litis ac dilationis ratio pensabitur, ad eorum instar, quos a rectoribus provinciarum eorumque sententiis convenit appellare, sex mensum temporalis dies, trium reparationis nomine dilatio praebeatur. There are also frequent allusions to the three months allowed for *reparatio*, *CTh* XI. xxxi. 1, 364, 3, 368, 4, 369, 5, 6, 370 (S), 7, 379; law 9, 423, allows four months in some cases and alludes to *secunda reparatio*, first grudgingly permitted by law 2, 365.

57. *CJ* VII. lxiii. 5 §4, 529.

58. Two months with another month for *reparatio* was usual in appeals from lesser judges, *CTh* XI. xxx. 10, 320, xxxi. 1, 364, 3, 368, 8, 392; longer delays are permitted by *CTh* XI. xxxi. 9, 423, *CJ* VII. lxiii. 2 §§4-6, 440. FISCAL CASES: *CTh* XI. xxx. 41, 383, 45, 46, 385, 64, 412. CONSULTATIONES: *CTh* XI. xxx. 34, 364, si quisquam ausus consultationem sequi circa limina palatii nostri comitatumve fuerit deprehensus, aestimatae litis, quae in controversiam venit, medietatem in auro atque argento fisci viribus inferre cogetur, 47, 386, cum antea sit constitutum, ut consultationem iudicis ad comitatum sacrum missam litigatorum nemo sequeretur, hoc integra deliberatione sancimus, ut, si ad consultationem anno decurso non fuerit aliqua ratione responsum, litigatores quorum interest collectis omnibus gestis et ipsius relationis exemplis veniendi ad comitatum nostrae serenitatis habeant liberam facultatem, 54, 395, 66, 419, *CJ* VII. lxiii. 3, 518, 5 §§2, 3, 529, in his autem casibus in quibus biennium constitutum est, quatenus more consultationum in regia urbe sub communi audientia florentissimorum nostri palatii procerum ventilentur, biennii metas unius anni terminis coartamus, ut intra eum et gesta colligere et ea viris devotis epistularibus tradere et refutatorios libellos, si voluerint, offerre et litem in sacrum nostrum consistorium introducere cogantur: nulli licentia deneganda victrici parti, si voluerit, secundum quod iam constitutum est, et praemature causam inducere neque annali spatio expectato. si tamen in sacro nostro consistorio lis exordium ceperit, etsi non fuerit in eodem die completa, tamen perpetuari eam concedimus, cum iniquum sit propter occupationes florentissimi ordinis, quas circa nostrae pietatis ministeria habere noscitur, causas hominum deperire.

59. Just. *Nov.* xlix pr. §2, 537, sed plurimi interpellaverunt nos, dicentes se quidem denuntiasse appellantibus, et voluisse litem examinari, non tamen ab ipsis iudicibus impetrare valuisse propter quasdam forsan inevitabiles occupationes. alii vero etiam ventorum immensitatem accusaverunt, et quia navigare non licuisset de provincia, contrariis flantibus ventis, per terram vero venire non valentes propter inopiam, aut certe quia in insula commanentes aliter, nisi per mare, venire non poterant, et propterea non valuerunt examinare usque ad finem negotium neque secundo anno, et quidam tempestatum acerbitatem, alii languorem inevitabilem, quae omnia ex ipsis agnoscimus rebus nobis insinuatis. PROVINCIAL GOVERNORS: Lib. *Or.* XLV. 17 ff. The usual excuse for *reparatio* was that the judge could not hear the case because of 'aegritudo vel occupatio actuum publicorum', *CTh* XI. xxxi. 9, 423, cf. 2, 365, 3, 368, 4, 369. For the consistory see *CJ* VII. lxiii. 5 §3, 529 (cited in

n. 58), Just. *Nov.* xxiii §2, 535, ad hoc sancimus, si quando lis speratur in nostrum inferri consistorium, si forte contigerit imperatoriam maiestatem occupatam publicis causis ex mundanis provisionibus non posse convocare patres, quatenus causa agitetur, non ex hoc litem periclitari. quod enim vitium est litigantium, si culmen imperatorium occupetur? For the delays which a *relatio* might cause see Lib. *Ep.* 1235, δίκης δὲ αὐτῷ γενομένης ἐν ᾗ πόλεμός τις ἐξεφάνη νόμων, εἶδε μὲν ὁ κράτιστος Σέκουνδος (the praetorian prefect), ὡς οἶμαι, τὰ τοῦδε τοὺς ἑτέρους τρέποντα, νομίσας δὲ μακρῷ βέλτιον βασιλέως γνώμη τὸν ἀγῶνα λυθῆναι τῶν νόμων γράψας ἐρωτᾷ τὸν τότε κρατοῦντα (Jovian) τί χρὴ δρᾶν. ὁ δὲ μέλλων ἀποκρίνεσθαι ᾤχετο. μετὰ ταῦτα ἀσχολία τοῖν βασιλέοιν (Valentinian and Valens) καὶ πλῆθος πραγμάτων.

60. For the dilatory wiles of lawyers see Amm. xxx. iv. 13, qui inter sollicitudines iudicum per multa distentas, irresolubili nexu vincientes negotia, laborant, ut omnis quies litibus implicetur, et nodosis quaestionibus de industria iudicia circumscribunt, quae cum recte procedunt, delubra sunt aequitatis: cum depravantur, foveae fallaces et caecae: in quas si captus ceciderit quisquam, non nisi per multa exsiliet lustra, ad usque ipsas medullas exsuctus. UNNECESSARY RELATIONES: *CTh* XI. xxxix. 1, 325, xxx. 13, 329 (S), xxxix. 2, 333, 1. v. 4, 342, XI. xxx. 55, 399 (S).

61. *CTh* I. xvi. 7, 331, cessent iam nunc rapaces officialium manus, cessent, inquam: nam nisi moniti cessaverint, gladiis praecidentur. non sit venale iudicis velum, non ingressus redempti, non infame licitationibus secretarium, non visio ipsa praesidis cum pretio. aeque aures iudicantis pauperrimis ac divitibus reserentur. absit ab inducendo eius qui officii princeps dicitur depraedatio; nullas litigatoribus adiutores eorundem officii principum concussiones adhibeant; centurionum aliorumque officialium parva magnaque poscentium intolerandi inpetus oblidantur eorumque, qui iurgantibus acta restituunt, inexpleta aviditas temperetur.

62. *CTh* I. xxix. 5, 370, utili ratione prospectum est, ut innocens et quieta rusticitas peculiaris patrocinii beneficio fruatur, ne forensis iurgii fraudibus fatigata, etiam cum ultionem posceret, vexaretur; dum aut avarior instruitur advocatus aut obsessor liminis maioribus princeps praemiis exoratur, dum acta ab exceptoribus distrahuntur, dum commodi nomine amplius ab eo qui vicerit intercessor exposcit quam redditurus est ille qui fuerit superatus.

63. *FIR* I². 64.

64. Justinian's law on *sportulae*, which is lost in *CJ* III. ii, de sportulis et sumptibus in diversis iudiciis faciendis et de exsecutoribus litium, is referred to in *Inst.* IV. vi. 25, *Nov.* xvii §3, 535, lxxxii §7, lxxxvi §9, 539, cxxiv §3, 545. In *P. Cairo*, 67031, an edict of the governor of the Thebaid on *sportulae*, there appear to be allusions to Justinian's law (τῷ φιλανθρώπῳ σκόπῳ τῶν εὐσεβεστ᾽ καὶ γαληνοτάτων [βασιλέων]; the plural refers to Justinian and Theodora).

65. SPECIAL SCALES FOR AGENTES IN REBUS: *CJ* XII. xxi. 8, 484, cf. xx. 6 §3; FOR CASTRENSIANI: *CJ* XII. xxv. 4, 474; FOR SCHOLARES: *CJ* XII. xxix. 3 (474-91); FOR SACRA SCRINIA: *CJ* XII. xix. 12 (497-518); FOR CLERGY: *CJ* I. iii. 25 §2, 456, 32 §5, 472, *Leg. Saec.* 118.

66. *CJ* I. iii. 25 §2, 456. Joh. Lydus, *Mag.* III. 25, πόθεν γὰρ ἔμελλον λαμβάνειν, τῆς μὲν ἀρχαίας συνηθείας ἐχούσης ἑπτὰ καὶ τριάκοντα χρυσίνους παρέχεσθαι τῇ τάξει ὑπὲρ μονομεροῦς ἐντεύξεως πρὸς τῶν ὁπωσοῦν εἰσβαλλόντων ἐν τοῖς τότε μεγίστοις δικαστηρίοις, τὸ δὲ λοιπὸν χαλκοῦ κάρτα μετρίου (οὐ γὰρ χρυσίου), ὥσπερ εἰς ἔλαιον, οἰκτρῶς καὶ οὐδὲ συνεχῶς ἐπιδιδομένου;

67. TRIALS SINE SCRIPTIS: Just. *Nov.* xvii §3, 535, sit tibi quoque tertium studium lites cum omni aequitate audire, et omnes quidem breviores et quaecumque maxime vilium sunt ex non scripto decidere et iudicare et liberare homines alterna contentione, et non permittere ultra quam continetur sacra nostra constitutione occasione causalium expensarum damnificari, si tamen sufficientes in datione consistunt. alioquin etiam gratis lites audire et non permittere ex negligentia de provincia cui praesides ad hanc currere felicissimam civitatem et nobis molestum esse. From *P. Cairo*, 67031, it would appear that the *sportulae* were at half rate when the case was tried *sine scriptis*. The edict seems to distinguish an αἰτίαν ἄγραφον, as against ταῖς ἐγγράφοις ἐντεύξεσιν, and lays down two fees; οὐδὲν πλέον τῶν δύο κερατίων ὀφείλων καταθεῖναι ἐπὶ τὸν ὑπομιμνήσκοντα, and κεράτια τέσσαρα καταβαλέτω ἐπὶ τὸν ὑπομιμνήσκοντα. ALEXANDER: Josh. Styl. 29.

68. On the promotion of barristers see n. 97.

69. BARRISTERS AS DEFENSORES: *CTh* I. xxix. 1, 3, 368 (S), *P. Oxy.* 902, 1882–3, *PSI* 790, *P. Cairo Preis.* 7, *P. Cairo*, 67329, *BGU* 1094. Lib. *Ep.* 1353 appears to refer to a retired barrister who has been appointed *defensor* of a city.

70. On assessors see Lact. *Mort. Pers.* xxii, iudices militares humanitatis litterarum rudes sine adsessoribus in provincias inmissi, *CJ* I. li. 1, 286, 2, 320, 3, 399 (S), *CTh* I. xxxiv. 1, 400, 2, 422, *CJ* I. li. 10, 439. SALARIES: *CJ* I. xxvii. 2 §§22, 25, 28, 31, 34, 534 (African *duces*), Just. *Nov.* xxiv §6, xxv §6, xxvi §5, xxvii §2, xxviii §3, xxix §2, xxxi §1 (*spectabiles iudices*), xxx §6 (proconsul of Cappadocia), cii §2 (*moderator* of Arabia), *Ed.* xiii §4 (Augustal prefect), *CJ* I. xxvii. 1 §21 (*Ppo* of Africa). RANK: *CTh* VI. xv. 1, 413, Sid. Áp. *Ep.* I. 3, unde te etiam par fuerit privilegio consiliorum praefecturae, in quae participanda deposceris, antiquati honoris perniciter sarcire dispendium, ne si extra praerogativam consiliarii in concilium veneris solas vicariorum vices egisse videare. Cf. *CJ* I. li. 11, 444, for other privileges of assessors of the *Ppo*, *PU*, *mag. mil.*, and *mag. off.*

71. ALYPIUS: Aug. *Conf.* VI. 16 (cited in n. 74), VIII. 13, mecum erat Alypius otiosus ab opere iuris peritorum post assessionem tertiam, expectans, quibus iterum consilia venderet. TATIANUS: *ILS* 8844, Τατιανὸς μετὰ δικανικὴν [τοῖς] ἄρχουσιν συνκαθεσθείς, ἡγεμόνι, βικαρίῳ, ἀνθυπά[τῳ], δυσίν τ᾽ ἐπάρχοις. Cf. *CJ* I. li. 12 (450 or 455), liceat omnibus iudicibus illustri praeditis potestate consiliarios sibi eosdem secundo ac tertio et saepius iniungere, quia qui semel recte cognitus est, ob hoc solum non debet, quod iam probatus est, improbari. According to *CJ* I. li. 14, 529, a barrister might resume his practice after being an assessor.

72. Just. *Nov.* lxxxii, 539; cf. also *CJ* II. vii. 25 pr., 519.

73. On judicial corruption and *suffragia* see pp. 396, 399.

74. Aug. *Conf.* VI. 16, et ter iam adsederat mirabili continentia ceteris, cum ille magis miraretur eos, qui aurum innocentiae praeponerent. temptata est quoque eius indoles non solum inlecebra cupiditatis sed etiam stimulo timoris. Romae adsidebat comiti largitionum Italicianarum. erat eo tempore quidam potentissimus senator, cuius et beneficiis obstricti multi et terrori subditi erant. voluit sibi licere nescio quid ex more potentiae suae, quod esset per leges inlicitum; restitit Alypius. promissum est praemium: inrisit animo. praetentae minae: calcavit mirantibus omnibus inusitatam animam, quae hominem tantum et innumerabilibus praestandi nocendique modis ingenti fama celebratum vel

amicum non optaret vel non formidaret inimicum. ipse autem iudex, cui consiliarius erat, quamvis et ipse fieri nollet, non tamen aperte recusabat, sed in istum causam transferens ab eo se non permitti adserebat, quia et re vera, si ipse faceret, iste discederet.

75. Lib. *Or.* LI, LII, *CTh* I. xvi. 13, 377, ne quis domum iudicis ordinarii postmeridiano tempore ex occasione secreti ingredi familiariter affectet eiusdem dumtaxat provinciae, sive notus iudici sive etiam ignotus, gesti tamen honoris auctoritatem praeferens, xx. 1, 408, honorati, qui lites habere noscuntur, his horis, quibus causarum merita vel fata penduntur, residendi cum iudice non habeant facultatem: nec meridianis horis a litigatoribus iudices videantur.

76. LETTERS TO JUDGES: Lib. *Ep.* 56, 105, 110, 1168–9, 1237–8, 1249, 1398, Basil, *Ep.* 107, 109, 177–90, Greg. Nyss. *Ep.* 7, Greg. Naz. *Ep.* 22–4, 105, 146–8, Symm. *Ep.* I. 69, II. 87, VII. 108–9, Ennod. *Ep.* VIII. 23. GREAT MEN ON THE BENCH: Lib. *Or.* LII. 4 ff. TRANSFER OF LITIGATION TO POTENTES: *CJ* II. xiii. 1, 293, *CTh* II. xiv. 1, 400, xiii. 1, 422.

77. Marc. *Nov.* i pr. §§1, 2, 450, videtis enim agmina, videtis catervas adeuntium infinitas non solum a finitimis provinciis, verum extremo orbis Romani limite confluentes et adversum suos adversarios conquerentes. quod profecto nullatenus accidisset, si in locis integritas vel severitas iudicum floruisset. ne igitur huiusmodi flagitia etiam ulterius porrigantur, ne quis desertis laribus suis aut certe dulcibus pignoribus per incognitas mundi partes diutius pervagetur, hoc consultissimo edicto statuendum pariter et omnibus declarandum pietas nostra decernit. quicumque civilem actionem vel certe criminalem accusationem adversariis suis intendere moliuntur, viros clarissimos adeant provinciarum rectores et expositis querimoniis insinuatisque desideriis suis paratissimum promptissimumque posthac subsidium iuris expectent. illi noxiae potentiae vim legum benignam obponant, illi divitiis integram mentem obiciant. non illos supercilium, quod hoc tempore nullum est, terrebit, non effeminabit mentem severam quilibet census oblatus. sed unicuique, non altiore suspecta, non despecta humiliore fortuna, nostrae mandatorum non inmemores pietatis et antiquo et nostro iure succurrent et querimonias suas probantibus aut indemnitate servata aut legitima vindicta consulent subsecuta. has ergo ob causas nullum adversarium suum a proximis vel longinquis partibus, non per sacros adfatus, non per magnificentissimorum vel inlustrium sententias volumus exhibere, nisi forsitan aut propter potestatem adversarii aut ipsius rei difficultatem aut publici debiti molem deficiente rectore provinciae spectabilis iudicis, qui in locis vel proximo deget, vel amplissimae potestatis vel aliorum maiorum iudicum auxilium postuletur.

78. For the quaestor and *magistri scriniorum* see pp. 367–8; their duties are set out in *Not. Dig. Or.* xii, xix, *Occ.* x, xvii (cited in ch. XII, n. 3).

79. For *relationes* and for legislation arising from them see p. 349. For *preces* or *libelli* and rescripts and for legislation arising from them see p. 350.

80. *CTh* VIII. xv. 1 (Constantine), XI. xxxix. 5 (Julian), 8 (Theodosius), cf. also IV. xx. 3 (Theodosius). Cf. the account given of Julian's behaviour as a judge in Amm. XVIII. i. 2–4 and XXII. x. 1–5.

81. *CJ* VII. lxii. 32, 440, praecipimus ex appellationibus spectabilium iudicum, quae per consultationes nostri numinis disceptationem implorant, non nostram ulterius audientiam expectari, ne nostris occupationibus, quibus pro utilitate mundi a singulorum nonnumquam negotiis avocamur, aliena fraudari commoda

videantur. sed si a proconsulibus vel Augustali vel comite Orientis vel vicariis fuerit appellatum, virum illustrem praefectum praetorio, qui in nostro est comitatu, virum etiam illustrem quaestorem nostri palatii sacris iudiciis praesidentes disceptationem iubemus adripere eo ordine, ea observatione, isdem temporibus, quibus ceterae quoque lites fatali die post appellationem in sacris auditoriis terminantur. For the dress and other formalities see Just. *Nov.* cxxvi §1, 546. John Lydus (*Mag.* II. 17) describes a trial in the good old days, πάσης τῆς βουλῆς προτρεχούσης ἐν τοῖς λεγομένοις σιλεντίοις; from this passage it appears that the emperor was not normally present, but that his portrait was carried before the praetorian prefect.

82. Marc. *Nov.* v pr., 455. For Justinian's allusions to his personal jurisdiction see ch. XI, n. 59. DELEGATION OF APPEALS: *CJ* VII. lxii. 34, 520–24, 37, 529.

83. *CTh* XI. xxxix. 5, 362, pars actorum habitorum apud imperatorem Julianum Augustum Mamertino et Nevitta conss. X kal. April. Constantinopoli in consistorio: adstante Iovio viro clarissimo quaestore, Anatolio magistro officiorum, Felice comite sacrarum largitionum. MAGISTRI SCRINIORUM: *CJ* XII. ix. 1, 444, viris spectabilibus magistris omnium sacrorum scriniorum nostrae benevolentiae liberalitas tribuenda est, qui nostrae quodammodo adsidere maiestati videntur. For *comites consistoriani* see n. 85.

84. Marc. *Nov.* v pr., 455, nuper cum de testamento clarissimae memoriae feminae Hypatiae, quae inter alios virum religiosum Anatolium presbyterum in portione manifesta bonorum suorum scripsit heredem, amplissimo senatu praesente tractaret pietas mea, Just. *Nov.* lxii §1, 537.

85. For the choice of quaestors and *magistri scriniorum* see p. 387. The rank and privileges of *comites consistoriani* are defined in *CTh* VI. xii. 1, 399, *CJ* xii. x. 2 (491–518), Cass. *Var.* VI. 12. That many were honorary appears from *CTh* VI. xxii. 8 §1, 425, quin et de consistorianis comitibus hoc nobis universi placere cognoscant, ut his, qui vel absentes sunt facti vel testimonialibus tantum adepti sunt dignitatem, praecedant qui admitti intra consistorii arcanum meruerunt et actibus interesse et nostra adire responsa; cf. *CJ* x. xxx. 3, 442, which suggests that many lived in the provinces, and Val. III, *Nov.* vi. 3, 444, which exempts from a levy of recruits imposed on *comites consistoriani* and other *honorati* 'pro excubiis praesentibus viginti consistorianos comites'. HONOUR FOR BARRISTERS: *CJ* II. vii. 8, 440, 23, 506. CODE COMMISSIONS: *CTh* I. i. 5, 429, 6, 435; cf. Th. II, *Nov.* i §7, 438.

86. BAR CLASSED AS MILITIA: *CJ* II. vii. 14, 469; cf. *CTh* I. xxix. 1, 368 (S), aut forensium stipendiorum egere militiam. Barristers were accorded the military privilege of *peculium castrense* in the Eastern parts in 422 (*CTh* II. x. 6) and the privilege was confirmed in the West in 442 (Val. III, *Nov.* ii. 2 §4). CONSTANTINE'S RULE: *CTh* II. x. 1 + 2, 319, iussione subversa, qua certus advocatorum numerus singulis tribunalibus praefinitus est, omnes licentiam habeant, ut quisque ad huius industriae laudem in quo voluerit auditorio pro ingenii sui virtute nitatur . . . destituuntur negotia et temporibus suis excidunt, dum advocati per multa officia et diversa secretaria rapiuntur; ideoque censuimus, ne hi, qui semel protestati fuerint, quod apud te causas acturi sunt, apud alium iudicem agendi habeant potestatem. ANTIOCH: Lib. *Or.* XI. 191. COMES REI PRIVATAE: *CJ* II. vii. 20, 497; this law appears to be a conflation of two, referring to the advocates of the *CRP* and of the proconsul of Asia. PRAEFECTUS VIGILUM: *CTh* II. x. 1 + 2, 319.

87. PRIORES ADVOCATI OF PPO ORIENTIS AND PU CONST.: Th. II, *Nov.* x. 1 pr., 439, *CJ* II. vii. 7, 439, 15, 472, 16, 474, 26 pr., 524.

88. AFRICANS: Val. III, *Nov.* ii. 3, 443. PROVINCIAL BARRISTERS: Val. III, *Nov.* ii. 2 §2, 442.

89. The twenty years rule was abolished by Th. II, *Nov.* x. 2, 439, eloquentia non ut aliae res senio deterioratur. nullus enim eius est finis, nisi exercitationis eius cottidianae studium denegetur. unde advocationem certo tempore artare litigatoribus noxium, grave iudicantibus aestimantes constitutionem abrogamus, quae XX annorum curriculis silentium imperat advocatis. It appears to have been introduced about 388 (Lib. *Ep.* 857, ῥήτωρ ὢν ἀγαθὸς οὑτοσὶ Διόγνητος καὶ πολλοῖς σεσωκὼς καὶ ψυχὰς καὶ τὰ ὄντα, ἔπειτα νόμῳ τῷ περὶ τοῦ χρόνου σιγᾶν ἠναγκασμένος συμφοράν τε ἡγεῖται τὸ μὴ τὰ αὑτοῦ ποιεῖν ἄχθος τε τῆς γῆς αὐτὸν καλῶν οὐ παύεται). It was soon revoked (Lib. *Ep.* 916, νῦν καλῶς εἰργάσθαι συγχωρῶ τὸν περὶ τοῦ νόμου λόγον, ἐπειδὴ σὺ ταῦτα περὶ αὑτοῦ καὶ λέγεις καὶ γράφεις. οὐ μέντοι μετὰ τὴν λύσιν τοῦ κωλύοντος νόμου λέγειν ἐγράφη μελέτης εἵνεκα, ἀλλ᾽ αὐτὸ τοῦτ᾽ ἀγωνιζόμενος ἀεὶ λέγειν ἐξεῖναι τοῖς δυναμένοις λέγειν), but must have been re-enacted. The limit was reimposed by Val. III, *Nov.* ii. 4, 454, dudum laxata lex exceptis inlustribus foris ceteris ac provincialibus perpetuitatem concesserat actionis. sed nunc adcrescente pube et litterariae indolis iuventute aditi exoratique sumus, ne sub aliorum perpetuitate succedentium studiorum fervor evanescat. quis enim se ei officio novus professor inserat, quod veteranus insederit, ut non sit tam auctor quam observator alterius: cf. ii. 2 §2, quibus ad agendum viginti annos, non ut adpropinquare vicesimum, sed ut explere fas sit, legis huius auctoritate decernimus. For the paucity of barristers see Val. III, *Nov.* xxxii §8, 451.

90. NUMERUS CLAUSUS FOR BAR OF THE PPO ORIENTIS: Th. II, *Nov.* x. 1, 439, *CJ* II. vii. 8, 440, 11, 460; OF THE PPO ILL.: *CJ* II. vii. 17, 474 (there is no reason to prefer the figure 150 of the inferior MSS); OF THE PU: tit. cit. 26, 524; OF THE PRAEF. AUG.: tit. cit. 13, 468; OF COM. OR.: tit. cit. 22, 505; OF PRAESES SYRIAE II: tit. cit. 24, 517.

91. BIENNIAL TERM: *CJ* II. vii. 13, 468 (*praef. Aug.*), 22, 505 (*com. Or.*), 24, 517 (*praeses Syriae* II). ANNUAL TERM: *CJ* II. vii. 8, 440 (PPO *Or.* and *PU*), 12, 463 (PPO *Ill.*, extended to two years). TWO PATRONI FISCI OF PPO OR.: *CJ* II. vii. 10, 452.

92. SALARY: *CJ* II. vii. 26 §4, 524 (*PU*), 25 pr., 519 (PPO *Or.*). PRIVILEGES: *CJ* II. vii. 8, 440, 23, 506, 25, 519 (PPO *Or.*), cf. 13, 468 (*praef. Aug.*), 20, 497 (*CRP* and proconsul of Asia).

93. STATUTI AND SUPERNUMERARII: *CJ* II. vii. 11, 460, 13, 468. HEIRS OF PATRONI FISCI: *CJ* II. vii. 15, 472, 22 §6, 505, 24 §6, 517. PURCHASE OF SENIORITY: *CJ* II. vii. 26 §1, 524, interdicenda quoque cunctis licentia praevertendi progressus seriem, quam ipsius temporis ordo suppeditat, et ut in mercatorum contractibus loca permutandi et adhuc tirones iam interesse veteribus; cf. 27, 524, nemo excepta Menandri fisci patroni persona speret de cetero permutationum saltibus superiore gradu captato fruiturum. IDLE ADVOCATES DISBARRED: *CJ* II. vii. 26 §2, 524, 29 (531–4.)

94. *CJ* II. vi. 6 §4, 370 (S), apud urbem autem Romam etiam honoratis, qui hoc putaverint eligendum, eo usque liceat orare, quousque maluerint, videlicet ut non ad turpe compendium stipemque deformem haec adripiatur occasio, sed laudis per eam augmenta quaerantur. POSTUMIANUS: Macr. *Sat.* I. 2.

CELSUS: Symm. *Rel.* 23. AMBROSE: Paul. *V. Amb.* 5. Cf. also *ILS* 1272, Symm. *Ep.* II. 42, V. 41, for *viri clarissimi* who were barristers, and *ILCV* 87, recording Floridus, who was urban praetor, assessor to the *vicarius urbis*, governor of Liguria, assessor at Rome again, and finally 'publica post docuit Romani foedera iuris'; he was evidently a serious lawyer.

95. MAXIMUM OF 100 SOLIDI: *Dig.* L. xiii. 1 §12. EXCESSIVE FEES, ETC.: *CJ* II. vi. 5, 325, *CTh* II. x. 4, 326, VIII. x. 2, 344; cf. the case of Heliodorus cited in n. 98. FEES IN PROVINCIAL COURTS: *FIR* I². 64; similar fees are also prescribed in *Ed. Diocl.* vii. 72–3, advocato sive iurisperito mercedis in postulatione ∗ ducentos quinquaginta, in cognitione∗ mille (equivalent to 2½ and 10 *modii*). ADVOCATES AS SACERDOTES PROVINCIAE: *CTh* XII. i. 46, 358.

96. Val. III, *Nov.* ii. 2 §2, 442.

97. Val. III, *Nov.* ii. 2 §1, 442, neque enim oportet eos, quos semel adsciveris in seminarium dignitatum, non ita ad omnia esse defaecatos, ut idcirco digni universis honoribus habeantur, quod advocati esse meruerunt. ANASTASIUS: Joh. Lydus, *Mag.* III. 50. AEDESIUS: *ILS* 4152. MAXIMINUS: Amm. XXVIII. 1. 6. Other examples of the promotion of barristers include Ambrose (Paul. *V. Amb.* 5), his brother Satyrus (Amb. *de exc. Sat.* 25, 49), Festus of Tridentum (Amm. XXIX. ii. 22), Tatian (*ILS* 8844), Domnio (Lib. *Ep.* 861–2, an *advocatus fisci* who became proconsul of Asia), Theodorus (Lib. *Ep.* 1125, a lawyer who became governor), and *Princeton Exp. Syria*, 560, ἐπὶ Φλ' Ἀρκαδίου Ἀλεξάνδρου τοῦ λαμπροτάτου σχο' καὶ ἡγεμόνος, Eventius (*AE* 1953, 200, qui causas oravit meruitque pater conscriptus haberi, nec longo post aevo dixit iura Viennae), and Germanus of Auxerre (*V. Germani*, 1).

98. HELIODORUS: Lib. *Or.* LXII. 46–9. RHETORIC AND LAW: Lib. *Or.* II. 43–4; cf. his complaints in *Ep.* 1170, 1203, that nowadays a barrister has to know some law.

99. *CJ* II. vii. 11 §2, 460, iuris peritos etiam doctores eorum iubemus iuratos sub gestorum testificatione depromere, esse eum, qui posthac subrogare voluerit, peritia iuris instructum; 22 §4, 505, 24 §4, 517, nec de cetero quemquam, antequam per statuta tempora legum eruditioni noscatur inhaesisse, supra dicto consortio sociari. THE LEGAL COURSE: *Dig. const.* Omnem, §§1–5; in §7 the teaching of law was prohibited at Alexandria, Caesarea or anywhere else save the two capitals and Berytus. SEVERUS AND ZACHARIAS: Zach. *V. Sev.* pp. 11–12, 46–47. Agathias also studied both at Alexandria and Berytus (Agath. II. 15). In the West, though a legal education was not an official qualification for the bar, Germanus of Auxerre went to Rome to study law (*V. Germani*, 1), and Alypius, after a rhetorical training at Carthage, went on to Rome for law (Aug. *Conf.* VI. 11–3). It would appear from Lib. *Or.* LIV. 7–12 that a young barrister starting his career was much dependent on the goodwill of the governor (which it no doubt normally was expensive to obtain), and from Lib. *Or.* LXII. 41–2, that it was necessary for him to tip the officials of the court liberally.

100. COHORTALES: *CTh* VIII. iv. 30, 436, Th. II, *Nov.* x. 1 pr., 439, *CJ* II. vii. 8, 440, 17, 474, 21, 500.

101. *CJ* II. vii. 2, 378, qui necessario patriae suae debent municipio functiones, eos decurionibus adgregatos nolumus evagari, permittentes tamen, ut in negotiis causidicorum fungantur officiis et in civitatibus propriis subeant munia curiarum.

102. RELEASE FROM CURIA DENIED TO BARRISTERS: *CTh* XII. i. 46, 358, cum nulla umquam iura patronis forensium quaestionum vacationem civilium munerum praestituerint, 98, 383, eos quoque, qui advocationis obtentu curialia onera declinant, agere universa compellat, 116, 387, omnes, qui ex origine decurionum ad perorandas causas laudum atque industriae amore ducuntur, reddant patriae, cui nati sunt, debitas functiones nec sese superflui nominis praerogativa defendant, quando quidem facilius parere muniis possint, si necessitatem publicam eo tempore, quo student causis, industriae favore toleraverint. EXEMPTION OF HIGH COURT BARRISTERS IN THE WEST: Val. III, *Nov.* ii. 2 §§1 and 3, 442, xxxiii §7, 451; IN THE EAST: *CTh* XII. i. 188, 436, Th. II, *Nov.* x. 1, 439, *CJ* x. xxxii. 67 §2, 529. These laws may be renewals of an old privilege, for Libanius (*Ep.* 293) wrote to Modestus (praetorian prefect of the East under Valens) protesting against the imposition of curial burdens on two of his advocates and alluding to νόμον παλαιὸν βοηθοῦντα ῥήτορσιν ἐπὶ τῆς ἀρχῆς.

103. PREFERENCE FOR SONS OF ADVOCATES: *CJ* II. vii. 11, 460, 22 §5, 505, 24 §5, 517, 26 pr., 524. Admission fees are alluded to in the last three laws ('gratis et sine sumptibus', 'gratis videlicet et sine ullo suffragio').

104. THE DIGEST COMMISSION: *CJ* I. xvii. 2 §9, 533.

105. NOTARIES AND DECURIONS: *CTh* IX. xix. 1 + XII. i. 3, 316. THE NOTARIES OF APHRODITO: *P. Cairo*, 67283.

106. Just. *Nov.* xliv. 536, cf. lxxiii §7, 538. In *Sb* 9219, a μισθωτὴς ταβελλιόνων ʽΕρμοπολίτου certifies a deed of sale in A.D. 319. For the fees of notaries see *Ed. Diocl.* vii. 41, tabellioni in scriptura libelli bel tabularum in versibus n. centum * x.

107. Priscus, 8 (pp. 86–88). Augustine (*Ep.* 153 §24) also regards judicial *sportulae* as justifiable.

108. *Sb* 8246, *Chr.* II. 96. Cf. *P. Thead.* 14, for another record of a case in which an interpreter appears.

109. Symm. *Rel.* 38.

110. FREEDMEN: *CTh* IV. x. 2, 423. ADSCRIPTICII: *CJ* XI. i. 2, 396. HONESTIORES AND HUMILIORES: Cardascia, *Rev. Hist. de Droit*, XXVIII (1950), 305–37, 461–85.

111. TORTURE: *CJ* IX. xli. 8, 286–93, milites neque tormentis neque plebeiorum poenis in causis criminum subiungi concedimus, etiamsi non emeritis stipendiis videantur esse dimissi, exceptis scilicet his, qui ignominiose sunt soluti. quod et in filiis militum et veteranorum servabitur. oportet autem iudices nec in his criminibus, quae publicorum iudiciorum sunt, in investigatione veritatis a tormentis initium sumere, sed argumentis primum verisimilibus probabilibusque uti. et si his veluti certis indiciis ducti investigandae veritatis gratia ad tormenta putaverint esse veniendum, tunc id demum facere debebunt, si personarum condicio pateretur, 11, 290, divo Marco placuit eminentissimorum quidem nec non etiam perfectissimorum virorum usque ad pronepotes liberos plebeiorum poenis vel quaestionibus non subici, si tamen propioris gradus liberos, per quos id privilegium ad ulteriorem gradum transgreditur, nulla violati pudoris macula adspergit. in decurionibus autem et filiis eorum hoc observari vir prudentissimus Domitius Ulpianus in publicarum disputationum libris ad perennem scientiae memoriam refert, *CTh* ix. xxxv. 1, 369, 2, 376, 3, 377,

6, 399. CONSTANTINE'S RULE: *CTh* IX. xl. 1, 314, qui sententiam laturus est, temperamentum hoc teneat, ut non prius capitalem in quempiam promat severamque sententiam, quam in adulterii vel homicidii vel maleficii crimen aut sua confessione aut certe omnium, qui tormentis vel interrogationibus fuerint dediti, in unum conspirantem concordantemque rei finem convictus sit et sic in obiecto flagitio deprehensus, ut vix etiam ipse ea quae commiserit negare sufficiat. APPEAL BARRED BY CONFESSION: *CTh* XI. xxxvi. 1, 313 (S), 4, 339, 7, 348 (S).

112. Opt. *App.* ii (pp. 201-3).

113. Jerome, *Ep.* 1.

114. *Sirm.* 14, 409, ignorari ab his potuisse non credimus, quod commissum in civitatibus publice memoratur, quod iugis et magistratuum et ordinum cura, stationarii apparitoris sollicitudo, quae ministra est nuntiorum atque indicium, absentiae exhibet potestatum, . . . ut, si quisquam in hoc genus sacrilegii proruperit, ut in ecclesias catholicas inruens sacerdotibus et ministris vel ipsi cultui locoque aliquid importet iniuriae, quod geretur, litteris ordinum, magistratuum et curatoris et notoriis apparitorum, quos stationarios appellant, deferatur in notitiam potestatum, ita ut vocabula eorum, qui agnosci potuerint, declarentur. STATIONARII: Aug. *En. in Psalm.* xciii. 9, Opt. 1. 14, 27, *Passio Philippi*, 3, *Acta Agapae*, etc. 3, προκαθίσαντος Δουλκιτίου ἡγεμόνος ἐπὶ τοῦ βήματος, ᾿Αρτεμίσιος κομενταρήσιος εἶπεν· ὁποίαν νοτωρίαν περὶ τῶν παρεστώτων τούτων ὁ ἐνθάδε στατιωνάριος ἀπέστειλεν πρὸς τὴν σὴν τύχην εἰ κελεύεις ἀναγιγνώσκω (there follows the report from Κάσανδρος βενεφικιάριος); *Acta Saturnini*, etc. 2 (they are arrested 'a coloniae magistratibus atque ab ipso stationario milite'); *CTh* VIII. iv. 2, 315, V. 1, 315, VII. xx. 2, 326 (S), VI. xxix. 1, 355, *Sirm.* 14, 409, *P. Harris*, 91, *P. Brem.* 83 (στατιωνάριος), *P. Oxy.* 2187 (ὁ στατίζων βενεφικιάριος or ὁ ἐπίσταθμος), 65, *P. Cairo Isid.* 63, *Aegyptus*, 1951, 323 (ὁ στατίζων βενεφικιάριος), *P. Cairo Isid.* 62 (ὁ στατίζων). INSCRIPTIO: *CTh* IX. 1. 5, 320 (S), 8, 9, 366, 11, 368 (S), 14, 383, 19, 423. WARRANT BY GOVERNORS: *CTh* IX. ii. 4, 390, neminem iudicio exhibendum esse praecipimus, nisi de cuius exhibitione iudex pronuntiaverit. ARREST BY LOCAL AUTHORITIES: *CTh* IX. ii. 5, 409, defensores civitatum, curatores, magistratus et ordines oblatos sibi reos in carcerem non mittant, sed in ipso latrocinio vel congressu violentiae aut perpetrato homicidio, stupro vel raptu vel adulterio deprehensos et actis municipalibus sibi traditos expresso crimine prosecutionibus arguentium cum his, a quibus fuerint accusati, mox sub idonea prosecutione ad iudicium dirigant. In the Justinianic version of this law (*CJ* I. lv. 7) the words 'curatores, magistratus et ordines' are omitted, and in *CJ* IX. iv. 6, 529, only *defensores* are empowered to imprison accused persons. STATIONARII AND PRISONS: *CTh* VIII. iv. 2, 315, stationariis primipilarium, quorum manifesta sunt loca, coram mandatum est, ut, si extra modum aliquid extorserint, sciant se capite puniendos; praeterea ne carcerem habeant neve quis personam pro manifesto crimine apud se habeat in custodia, VI. xxix. 1, 355, memorati igitur curiosi et stationarii vel quicumque funguntur hoc munere crimina iudicibus nuntianda meminerint et sibi necessitatem probationis incumbere, non citra periculum sui, si insontibus eos calumnias nexuisse constiterit. cesset ergo prava consuetudo, per quam carceri aliquos immittebant.

115. MONTH'S GRACE FOR ACCUSED: *CTh* IX. ii. 3, 380, 6, 409. Augustine (*Ep.* 113-6) protested to the consular of Numidia and to the official who effected the arrest (and invoked the aid of the bishop of Cirta) in a case where

this rule was not observed, the victim being the *conductor* of an estate and his accuser its owner, a wealthy and influential man. CONDITIONS IN PRISONS: Lib. *Or.* XLV.

116. CONDITIONS IN PRISONS: *CTh* IX. iii. 1, 320, 7, 409. RULES FOR SPEEDY TRIAL: *CTh* IX. iii. 6, 380, *CJ* IX. iv. 6, 529. GENERAL PARDONS: *CTh* IX. xxxviii. 3, 367, 4, 370 (S), 6, 381, 7, 384, 8, 385, *Sirm.* 8, 386.

XV. SENATORS AND *HONORATI* (pp. 523–7)

On the later Roman senate there is no comprehensive work later than C. Lécrivain, *Le sénat romain depuis Dioclétien à Rome et à Constantinople*, Paris, 1888.

1. Symm. *Ep.* I. 52, orationem meam tibi esse complacitam nihilo setius gaudeo quam quod eam secunda existimatione pars melior humani generis senatus audivit, Pan. Lat. IV. 35 §2, sensisti, Roma, tandem arcem te omnium gentium et terrarum esse reginam, cum ex omnibus provinciis optimates viros curiae tuae pigneraris, ut senatus dignitas non nomine quam re esset illustrior, cum ex totius orbis flore constaret. Constantius II, in his speech recommending Themistius for election to the senate of Constantinople (Them. *Or.*), gives χρημάτων εὐκλεία, κτημάτων περιουσία, πόνοι δημόσιοι, λόγων δεινότης, and above all ἀρετή, as qualifications. The omission of birth is strange, and one may wonder whether χρημάτων has not replaced some such word as προγόνων.

2. Symm. *Or.* VIII.

3. Symm. *Or.* VI.

4. Symm. *Rel.* 5.

5. Symm. *Or.* VII.

6. See pp. 6–7, 19, 24, 48–9.

7. See pp. 7–8, 46–9.

8. See pp. 104–5.

9. CORRUPT GRANTS OF EQUESTRIAN RANK TO CURIALES: *CTh* VI. xxxviii. 1 (313–37), XII. i. 5, 317, VI. xxii. 1, 324 (S), XII. i. 26, 338, 36, 343, 41, 353, 42, 354, 44, 358; XII. i. 26, 36, 41 and 44 also refer to the *comitiva*. NUMERARII AND ACTUARII: *CTh* VIII. i. 6, 362, 10, 365; in *CTh* VIII. v. 36, 381, *mancipes* of the *cursus publicus*, and in I. xxxii. 5, 386, former procurators of the *res privata* enjoy the perfectissimate. *CTh* VIII. iv. 3 + X. vii. 1 + X. xx. 1 + XII. i. 5, 317, record all four grades of the equestrian order (perfectissimatus vel ducenae vel centenae vel egregiatus). The egregiate is last mentioned in *CTh* VI. xxii. 1, 324 (S), sive perfectissimi sunt sive inter egregiorum ordinem locumque constiterint. THREE GRADES OF PERFECTISSIMATE: *CTh* VI. xxx. 7 §§2, 3, 4, 5, 7, 8, 11–13, 15–17, 384.

10. See pp. 106–7.

11. See pp. 132–6.

12. *Honorati* means strictly those who have received a *honor* or *dignitas*. The term sometimes denotes or includes senators (*CTh* VI. xxvii. 20, 21, 426, XVI. v. 54 §4, 414, Val. III, *Nov.* xi, 443, *CJ* XII. iii. 1, 426), but senators are sometimes distinguished from (lesser) *honorati* (*CTh* VII. xiii. 7 §2, 375, sive senator, honoratus, principalis, decurio vel plebeius, IX. xxx. 1, 364, exceptis senatoribus et honoratis). Usually in a provincial context *honorati* are ranked above decurions and *possessores* (*CTh* IX. xxvii. 6, 386, XVI. ii. 43, 418, Val. III, *Nov.* xv. 5, 444, Maj. *Nov.* iii, 458, *CJ* I. iv. 19, 505, iv. 8, 409, XI. xxxii. 3, 469). *Not. Dig. Or.* xliv shows a *praeses* as *clarissimus*, but *Not. Dig. Occ.* xlv as *perfectissimus*; the latter is presumably an uncorrected anachronism, but implies that *praesides* had only recently acquired the clarissimate in the West, perhaps after the basic text of the Notitia was drafted c. 408. By this date most *praesides* were no doubt already *clarissimi* by birth or special grant; the latest recorded *praesides perfectissimi* seem to be Flavius Felix Gentilis of Mauretania Sitifensis (*CIL* VIII. 20266, A.D. 379–83), Flavius Benedictus of Tripolitania (*IRT* 103, 571, A.D. 378): also Flavius Sexio, *corrector* of Apulia and Calabria (*CIL* IX. 333, A.D. 379–95). The earliest example of a *clarissimus tribunus* that I can find is in 419 (*Coll. Avell.* 16 §4, habito cum v.c. tribuno Sereniano tractatu; he seems to be an ordinary regimental tribune, cf. the soldiers (*contubernales*) mentioned in §§ 5 and 6). The next example that I can trace is in 431–2 (*A.C.Oec.* I. iv. pars ii, 170, ammirandissimus et clarissimus tribunus Euricianus; he is an officer serving under Titus, the *vicarius* of the *magister militum per Orientem*). That the perfectissimate was still bestowed in the sixth century is implied by the retention of *CTh* VI. xxxviii. 1 (313–37) as *CJ* XII. xxxii. 1. *Equites Romani* seem also to have survived at Rome (*CTh* VI. xxxvii. 1 = *CJ* XII. xxxi. 1, 364). GRANT OF COMITIVA TERTII ORDINIS TO DECURIONS: *CTh* XII. i. 127, 392, cf. 75, 371, and 109, 385, where the grade is not specified; TO PATRONI OF GUILDS: *CTh* XIV. iv. 9, 417, 10, 419.

13. THE CONSULATE: *CTh* VI. vi. 1, 382; for the patriciate see Zos. II. 40.

14. See pp. 142–4.

15. In *CJ* X. xxxii. 63, 471–4, Doctitius, though the son of an *illustris*, born during or after his father's illustrious office, is only *vir clarissimus*; cf. also n. 17 below. It is probable that illustrious rank was always conferred by *codicilli* of some office, active, titular or honorary. This is assumed by such laws as *CTh* VI. xxii. 7, 383, and 8, 425, and *CJ* XII. viii. 2, 441 on precedence, which could not have been graded otherwise. In Cass. *Var.* VI. 11, formula illustratus vacantis, the rank actually conferred in the text is the *comitiva domesticorum vacans*. By Cassiodorus's day the rank of *spectabilis*, which had ceased to carry a seat in the senate, was conferred without office, like that of *clarissimus* (Cass. *Var.* VII. 37, 38); but the earlier laws on precedence suggest that in the days when *spectabiles* were still senators and their precedence mattered, the rank was conferred by an active, titular or honorary office.

16. For the fiscal privileges of senators see ch. XIII, n. 133, for their judicial privileges ch. XIV, n. 47. Cf. also *CJ* XII. i. 15 (426–42), clarissimis vel spectabilibus universis ad genitale solum vel quolibet alio et sine commeatu proficiscendi et ubi voluerint commorandi habitandive permittimus facultatem, *CTh* XII. i. 187, 436, where *spectabiles* of curial origin have to perform their civic duties in person, but *illustres* do so by proxy, *CJ* XII. ii. 1, 450, nemo ex clarissimis et spectabilibus qui in provinciis degunt ad praeturam postea

devocetur: maneat unusquisque domi suae tutus atque securus et sua dignitate laetetur. That by Justinian's day only *illustres* were senators is proved by the interpolation in *Dig.* I. ix. 12 §1, senatores autem accipiendum esse eos qui a patriciis et consulibus usque ad omnes illustres descendunt; quia hi soli in senatu sententiam dicere possunt. Certain laws in the Code have been emended to fit the new definition, e.g. *CJ* XII. i. 10 = *CTh* IX. xxxv. 3, severam indagationem per tormenta quaerendi a clarissimo (*CTh* senatorio) nomine submovemus; since not only senators in Justinian's sense but all *clarissimi* were still immune from torture. It appears from Cass. *Var.* VI. 16 that *notarii,* who were all *clarissimi* or *spectabiles,* did not enter the senate until they reached the *primiceriatus,* or more probably retired from it with the *illustratus vacans.* In *Var.* VI. 12, *comites primi ordinis,* who were *spectabiles,* entered the consistory but are not said to enter the senate. In *Var.* VIII. 17, Opilio, son of a *CSL,* is presented to the senate on being appointed *CSL* himself in words which suggest that he is a new member (quapropter, patres conscripti, favete vestris alumnis et nostris favete iudiciis. secundo ad vestram curiam venit qui ex senatore natus est et aulicis dignitatibus probatur honoratus). The only exception to the rule is the *vicarius urbis,* who though *spectabilis* was admitted to the senate (*Var.* VI. 15); Cassiodorus underlines the anomaly. Cf. *ILCV* 204, sumpsisti illustrem sed iam grandaevus honorem, antiquo factus more senator eras.

17. That sons of all grades ranked as *clarissimi* is proved by *CJ* XII. i. 11, 377, senator vel alius clarissimus privatos habeat filios, editos quippe, antequam susciperet dignitatem: quod non solum circa masculos dignoscitur constitutum, verum etiam circa filias simili condicione servandum. cum autem paternos honores invidere filiis non oportet, a senatore vel solo clarissimo susceptum in clarissimatus sciendum est dignitate mansurum. In this law the words 'vel alius clarissimus' and 'vel solo clarissimo' are probably interpolations. HIERIUS'S FAMILY: Just. *Nov.* clix, 555.

18. CODICILS OF EQUESTRIAN RANK: *CTh* XII. i. 5, 317, si vero decurio suffragio comparato perfectissimatus vel ducenae vel centenae vel egregiatus meruerit dignitatem declinare suam curiam cupiens, codicillis amissis suae condicioni reddatur, VI. xxxviii. 1 (313–37), codicillis perfectissimatus fruantur qui impetraverint, si abhorreant a condicione servili vel fisco aut curiae obnoxii non sint vel si pistores non fuerint. CODICILS OF HONORARY EQUESTRIAN POSTS: *CTh* XI. i. 41, 353, ex comitibus et ex praesidibus universi ceterique, qui sine administratione adumbratarum dignitatum codicillos honorarios meruerint, VIII. v. 23, 365, qui in provinciis codicillis comitivae et praesidatus aut rationum epistulis honorariis nixi. CODICILS OF COMITIVA: *CTh* VI. xxi. 1, 425, *CJ*. XII. xlix. 12 (491–518) (first class); *CTh* VI. xxvi. 17, 416 (second class); XIV. iv. 9, 417, 10, 419 (third class); XII. i. 41, 353 (*ex comitibus*), VII. xxiii. 1, 369 (*ex comite*); VIII. v. 23, 365 (*comitivae*). For the tendency of the *comitiva* and equestrian rank to become hereditary see *CTh* XII. i. 14 (326–54).

19. SENATORIAL RANK HEREDITARY: *CTh* VI. ii. 13, 383, si quis, senatorium consecutus nostra largitate fastigium vel generis felicitate sortitus, Symm. *Rel.* 45, devotione et more commonitus magistratuum nomina, quibus varias functiones designationum tempore amplissimus ordo mandavit, ad aeternitatis vestrae perfero notionem, ut muneribus exhibendis aut subeundis fascibus destinatos cognitio imperialis accipiat. his copulati sunt, quos senatui vestro recens ortus adjecit. In *Or.* VIII also Symmachus speaks of Valerius Fortunatus as a senator before he had held the quaestorship (adque ita noster hic

quaestorius candidatus non magis ut senator obtinuit quam ut pauper evasit) and indeed from infancy (primis aevi sui annis senator esse desierat). But the classification of *illustres, spectabiles, senatores* and *clarissimi* in *CTh* XVI. v. 52, 412, shows that there were *clarissimi* who were not members of the senate, and these could only be sons of senators not yet enrolled. The rule limiting senatorial status to sons born after their fathers' promotion is first enunciated in *CTh* XII. i. 58, 364, and elaborated in law 74, 371. It is reaffirmed in general terms (not only for senators of curial origin) in *CJ* XII. i. 11 of 377 (cited in n. 16). The old rule that all sons of a senator inherited his rank seems to have been inadvertently preserved in *Dig.* L. 1. 22 §5, senatores et eorum filii filiaeque, quoquo tempore nati nataeve, itemque nepotes pronepotes ex filio, origini eximuntur, licet municipalem retinent dignitatem, cf. *Dig.* 1. ix. 5, senatoris filium accipere debemus non tantum eum qui naturalis est, verum adoptivum quoque; neque intererit a quo vel qualiter adoptatus fuerit, nec interest, iam in senatoria dignitate constitutus eum susceperit an ante dignitatem senatoriam. It is implied in Symm. *Or.* VIII that entry to the senate was conditional on the quaestorship; Fortunatus's mother renounced his rank because she feared the expenses of the *quaestura* and Fortunatus himself, having recovered his hereditary rank (integrato natalium splendore), is promptly *quaestorius candidatus*.

20. Lib. *Or.* XLII. 6, χρῆται δὴ τῷ περὶ ταῦτα νόμῳ Θαλάσσιος, καθ' ὃν γράμματα τῆς σῆς δεξιᾶς λαβὼν ταῦτ' εἰς τὴν βουλὴν εἰσέπεμψε τῶν παρ' ἐκείνης τευξόμενα, cf. *Ep.* 86, οὐκ ἄρα διὰ σπουδῆς μόνον πληροῖς τὸ βουλευτήριον βουλευτῶν, ἀλλ' ἤδη καὶ εὔδοντι κύρτος. Κέλσος γὰρ ὁ τῶν μὲν παρ' ἡμῖν ἄριστος, τῶν δὲ ἐκεῖ μετὰ σὲ τοῦτο ἀκοῦσαι πρέπων, αὐτόματος ἐπ' ἀγαθῶν συνέδριον ἀγαθός . . . . ἔφθη δὲ αὐτὸν ἡ περὶ αὐτοῦ δέλτος, ἐφ'ἧ τὰ εἰωθότα πράξεις παρατηρῶν ὅπως μέτριον ἔσται τὸ ἀνάλωμα. CODICILLI CLARISSIMATUS AND ALLEGATIO: *CTh* XII. i. 42, 354, si quis autem clarissimae meruerit infulas dignitatis nec indulti muneris gratiam codicillorum allegatione percipit, XII. i. 180, 416, licet augeri coetum amplissimum cupiamus, cuius consortio gratulamur, tamen, si quis functionibus involutus et nexibus municipalis ordinis innodatus codicillos clarissimatus potuerit impetrare, nec suscipiendos eos tua sublimitas nec penitus allegandos esse cognoscat. Cf. 183, 418, elicitis codicillis clarissimatus, and 74 §5, 371, ceterum suae potestatis et nullis per provincias functionibus obligati, si vel longae militiae labore vel proximis erga nos . . . iuvantibus codicillos senatorios reportaverint, nisi vitiis aut actae vitae obprobriis amplissimo ordine deprehendantur indigni, indepti semel clarissimatus dignitatem perpetuo manebunt in ordine senatorum. IURATORES AND LAUDATORES: Symm. *Or.* VII, Lib. *Or.* XLII. 45–6.

21. SPEECHES: Symm. *Or.* VI, VII, VIII (*Or.* V concerns an election to the praetorship, and not apparently an admission to the senate). ELECTIONS: Symm. *Ep.* VII. 96 (to Longinianus), dignumque esse praedico qui nostro ordini copuletur; sed adicienda est ei praerogativa militiae ut beneficio allectionis utatur. his quippe tantum munia relaxari divalia statuta voluerunt quos honor castrensis illuminat, III. 38 (to Hilarius), inter haec tamen mala valetudinis meae amicis negotium dedi ut pignus commune consultu patrum viris consularibus iungeretur. habita est ratio meritorum tuorum: nihil enim gratiae meae dico delatum. acta amplissimi ordinis Datiano honesto viro tradidi, quae ubi in manus tuas venerint amicitiae me satisfecisse pronuntiato, IX. 118, hospitem tuum Faustinum senatus amplissimus in societatem recepit. tanta apud nos testimonii tui antiquitas fuit ut differri quae velis instar iniuriae sit. tibi igitur acceptum ferat studium totius ordinis; nam ut

beneficio sacro debet dignitatis impetrationem, ita tuo decreti nostri celeri-tatem. REJECTIONS: Lib. *Or.* XLII. 6 ff. *CTh* XII. i. 74 (cited in n. 20) also envisages rejection by the *amplissimus ordo* on the score of *vitia*.

22. CONSULARES: *CTh* VI. ii. 13, 383, quique consularitatis insignia fuerit adsecutus, dignitatis obeundae atque exercendae administrationis huius copiam non habeat, nisi propria adnotatione digesserit se senatorium nomen agnoscere et larem habitationemque vel sedes certas in provincia atque oppido conlocasse nihilque amplius quam certum professionis modum varias intra provincias possidere. VICARS: *CTh* VI. iv. 15, 359, meministis profecto, patres conscripti, nec ullius temporis avellet oblivio, quod Facundus ex proconsule et Arsenius ex vicariis praetorum insignibus splenduerunt, nec quisquam horum putavit esse praeturam intra propriam dignitatem. quid autem illustrius his repperitur exemplis? debuerat profecto res ista, debuerat alios etiam commonere pro-consulari ac vicariae praefecturae praeditos potestate non esse praeturam minorem propriis meritis. DUCES: Amm. Marc. XXI. xvi. 2, nec sub eo dux quisquam cum clarissimatu provectus est; erant enim, ut nos quoque memini-mus, perfectissimi.

23. Cass. *Var.* VI. 14, formula de referendis in senatu, cf. IV. 3–4, V. 3–4, 40–1, VIII. 9–10, 16–17, 18–19; in VIII. 13–14, it is said of Ambrosius, who had already been *CRP* and is now appointed quaestor, 'de illo enim non debet dubitari qui a vestro ordine in prima dignitate meruit approbari'; similarly in VIII. 21–2, of Cyprian, former *CSL*, now promoted to the patriciate, 'securus ad vos redit qui iam honores in libertatis aula reposuit'. Cf. also I. 41, III. 33, IV. 25, where the *PU* is requested to carry out 'quae circa referendos curiae priscus ordo designavit' for candidates who have apparently not held illustrious offices, and IV. 29, where he is reproved for delaying the admission of a candidate. In the East also Anastasius implies that a retired *praepositus sacri cubiculi* might not be elected to the senate (*CJ* XII. v. 5, iubemus duobus viris illustribus praepositis utriusque sacri cubiculi tam nostrae pietatis quam nostrae serenissimae coniugis, post finitam militiam si senatorio fuerit consortio sociati, licere, etc.).

24. QUAESTORS: *CTh* VI. iv. 1, 329 (S), XII. i. 58, 364, VI. iv. 27, 395, Symm. *Ep.* v. 62, VII. 76, IX. 145, *ILS* 1223–6, 1229–30, 1238, 1243, 1259, 1262, 1264, 1268–9, 1283 (Anicius Glabrio Faustus, cos. 438), 1285 (Rufius Praetextatus Postumianus, cos. 448). AEDILES: Auson. *de feriis Rom.* 31. TRIBUNES OF THE PLEBS: *CTh* XII. i. 74 §3, 371, his verae dignitatis titulis et iudicibus adiungendis, qui proprium decus senatorum indepti praeturae insignibus fuerint et honoribus ampliati, vel quos veteris tribunorum plebis appellatione respersos umbra nominis nobis annuentibus constiterit populo praefuisse. PRAETORS: *CTh* VI. iv, passim, *CJ* I. xxxix. 2 + XII. ii. 1, 450, Joh. Lydus, *Mag.* II. 30, περὶ τοῦ Κωνσταντιανοῦ καὶ Ἰουστινιανοῦ πραίτορος, Boethius, *Consol.* III. 4, atqui praetura, magna olim potestas, nunc inane nomen est et senatorii census gravis sarcina. SUFFECT CONSULS: *CTh* VI. iv. 1 (cited in n. 27), *ILS* 1230, 1243, consuli, praetori, quaestori (neither man was *consul ordinarius*), Symm. *Ep.* VI. 40, illud ante omnia interpretatio tristis horrescit, quod natali urbis suffectum consulem currus quo vehebatur evolvit per ferociam bigarum quae triumphum vehebant.

25. Ausonius (*Gratiarum Actio*, 16) classifies consuls as 'viros gloriae militaris', 'viros nobilitatis antiquae' and 'viros fide inclytos et officiis probatos'. For Eastern and Western consuls see Mommsen, *Ges. Schr.* VI. 363–87, and *JRS* LII (1962), 126.

26. HONORARY CONSULATE: *CJ* XII. iii. 3 §1 (474–6), cf. 2, 452, for the 100 lb. gold paid by ordinary consuls. Law 4 allows honorary consuls to hold the ordinary consulate and thereby to gain precedence as if they had held it on becoming honorary consuls; this implies that honorary consuls ranked below ordinary. From Greg. *Ep.* II. 36 we learn that 'filius meus dominus Venantius nepos quondam Opilii patricii . . . chartas exconsulatus petiit, pro quibus triginta auri libras transmisit ut ei debeant comparari'. Gregory instructs his *apocrisiarius* in Constantinople to see to it 'quatenus oblatis in sacella consuetudinibus honores mereatur accipere'. The 30 lb. gold are evidently a *suffragium*, additional to the statutory fee of 100 lb. gold.

27. *CTh* VI. iv. 1, 329 (S), religiosis vocibus senatus amplissimi persuasi decernimus, ut quaestores ea praerogativa utantur, qua consules et praetores, ita ut, si quis intra annum sextum decimum nominatus fuerit absens, cum editio muneris celebratur, condemnationis frumentariae nexibus minime teneatur, quoniam memoratae aetati placet hoc privilegium suffragari.

28. PRECEDENCE OF EX-CONSULS: *CTh* VI. vi. 1, 382, *CJ* XII. iii. 1, 426, Val. III, *Nov.* xi. 443: the last law refers to Gratian's law as the last enactment on the subject, and the second law must therefore be Eastern, not as Seeck (*Reg.* 137) suggested Western: *ad senatum urbis Constantinopolitanae* is paralleled by Th. II, *Nov.* xv. 1. Justinian (*Nov.* lxii §2, 537) altered senatorial precedence, giving priority to patricians over consulars. Only six patricians are known from the fourth century (see W. Ensslin, *Mélanges Bidez* I. 361, A. Piganiol, *Empire Chrétien*, 314–15), viz. Julius Constantius (Ath. *Apol. c. Ar.* 76), Optatus (Zos. II. 40, *P. Lond.* 1913), Taurus (*AE* 1934, 159), Datianus (*CTh* XI. i. 1, Philostorgius, VIII. 8), Petronius (Amm. XXVI. vi. 7, *CTh* VII. xxii. 7) and perhaps Salutius Secundus (*Chron. Pasch.* 555). In the first half of the fifth century they became commoner both in the West, where besides the *magistri militum* (see ch. XI, n. 50) several praetorian prefects, such as Dardanus (*ILS* 1279), Maximus (Val. III, *Nov.* xix), Albinus (Val. III, *Nov.* xxi–xxiii) and Firminus (Val. III, *Nov.* xxxi), received the honour, and in the East, where we know of two praetorian prefects, Anthemius (*CTh* IX. xxxiv. 10, XII. xii. 14) and Aurelian (*CTh* VII. vii. 4), and one master of the offices, Helio (*CTh* VI. xxvii. 20, VIII. viii. 14). At the council of Chalcedon (*A. C. Oec.* II. i. 334) six patricians attended, perhaps all there were at the time, Anatolius (*mag. mil.* and *cos.*), Florentius (*Ppo* and *cos.*), Nomus (*mag. off.* and *cos.*), Senator (*cos.*), Protogenes (*Ppo* and *cos.*) and Augarus (*Ppo*). ZENO'S LAW: *CJ* XII. iii. 3; from Just. *Nov.* lxii §2, 537, si qui autem illustri dignitate decorati sunt, liceat eis patriciatus codicillos accipere, etsi non consulares vel praefectorii existant, quod constitutio divae memoriae Zenonis irrite postulabat, it appears that 'aut magistri militum aut magistri officiorum' have been interpolated in the Code version of Zeno's law.

29. *CTh* VI. xiii. 1 + xiv. 3 + xv. 1 + xvi. 1 + xvii. 1 + xx. 1, 413.

30. *CTh* VI. xxii. 7, 383, cf. 5 and 6, 381.

31. *CJ* XII. viii. 2, 441; codicils *inter agentes* are first mentioned in *CTh* VI. xxii. 8, 425.

32. For *extraordinaria* and *sordida munera* see ch. XIII, n. 133; for jurisdictional privileges see ch. XIV, n. 47.

33. See pp. 741–3.

34. In *CTh* VI. xx. 1, 413, technicians rewarded by the *comitiva primi ordinis* (carrying the *consularitas*) may refuse the honour 'ne conlationis onus sustineant

vel frequentare senatum aliosque huiuscemodi conventus qui honoratorum frequentiam flagitant compellantur'. For provincial assemblies see *CTh* XII. xii. 12 §1, 392, ad provinciale concilium in una frequentiore totius provinciae urbe cunctos volumus convenire, qui primatum honorantur insignibus, exceptis praefectoriis, cf. xiii. 1, 392 (very eminent persons may send representatives if they do not wish to attend personally); *honorati* (and *curiales*) who failed to attend the diocesan council of the Seven Provinces at Arles were fined 3 lb. gold (*MGH* (*Ep.*) III. 13–15). COMMEATUS: *CJ* XII. i. 15 (cited in n. 16), 18, iubemus salvo honore, qui per evocationem sacrae revocatoriae defertur, durante licere cunctis tam maiores quam minores potestates gerentibus nec non etiam honorariis illustribus sive ex hac urbe regia, principali videlicet praecedente consensu, profecti fuerint, sive in provinciis habitantes sacratissimum, suis scilicet poscentibus negotiis, petere maluerint comitatum, sine sacra quoque revocatoria ad hanc regiam urbem pervenire, Cass. *Var.* VII. 36, formula commeatalis (for absence from Rome).

35. SUSCEPTOR VESTIUM: *CTh* XII. vi. 4, 365. PROCURATIO CURSUS: *CTh* VIII. v. 23, 365. OTHER TASKS: *CTh* I. x. 8, 428, xxix. 4, 368, XIII. v. 22, 393, *CJ* X. xxx. 3, 442, Val. III, *Nov.* xv §5, 444. That such tasks were unpopular is shown by laws which forbid their imposition on favoured classes such as senators (*CJ* XII. i. 14, 426), notaries (*CTh* VI. x. 1, 380, *CJ* XII. vii. 2, 474) and advocates (Th. II, *Nov.* x. 1 §4, 439). Cf. also Lib. *Ep.* 1482, 1484, asking release for Apellion, who has been ordered by an imperial letter to act as *censitor* in Thrace, *Or.* XLVI. 4, where Florentius penalises an advocate by sending him off περὶ μέτρα γῆς, and Basil, *Ep.* 281, asking Modestus, the praetorian prefect, to release Helladius (described as πρωτεύων) τῆς ἐπὶ τῇ ἐξισώσει φροντίδος. In another letter (*Ep.* 299) Basil suggests the motives which might induce a man to seek the office of *censitor*, the opportunity to benefit his friends and harm his enemies, and financial gain. The offices were paid (*CTh* XIII. xi. 8, 396).

36. For these financial charges see pp. 430–1.

37. *CTh* VI. iv. 1 (cited in n. 27). From Symm. *Rel.* 8, nullo enim dissentiente decretum est quis modus censuum semel aut saepius fungendis <muneribus obnoxius sit>, and Symm. *Or.* VIII, nam certe potuerat convenientem censibus suis, ut nunc facimus, petere quaesturam. sed hoc quoque ut gravissimum timuit, quo minus nihil est, Seeck inferred that poor senators could perform once only (*semel* as opposed to *saepius* for the quaestorship and praetorship and perhaps suffect consulate), and that the one performance would be the quaestorship. PRAETORIAN GAMES AT CONSTANTINOPLE: *CTh* VI. iv. 5, 340, etc. SYMMACHUS AND PETRONIUS: Olymp. 44.

38. Symm. *Rel.* 8.

39. Symm. *Ep.* IV. 8, ceterum quid praerogativae habeat non video, cum etiam censuales absentium munera illic solent exhibere, quorum mediocritatem volumus aemulari; cf. *Rel.* 23 §2, cum pro diligentia quae debet omnibus inesse iudicibus argenti publici ratio quaereretur quod censualium editores munerum contulerunt, inter ceteras fraudes repertum est quosdam functionibus absolutos sumptum debitum rei publicae non dedisse et ut fallacia ista tegeretur ex alieno argento tantundem censualibus falsis titulis imputatum quantum conferre debuerant. AEDESIUS: Symm. *Ep.* IX. 126. SHARING OF EXPENSES: *CTh* VI. iv. 21 §6, 372.

40. *CTh* VI. iv. 1, 329 (S), 4, 7, 354 (S), 18, 365.

41. *CTh* VI. iv. 5, 340, 13, 361, 25, 384 (cf. 20, 372, for four praetors), 29, 396, 30, 396, 33, 398.

42. *CTh* XV. ix. 1, 384, *CJ* XII. iii. 2, 452, Just. *Nov.* cv, 536, Proc. *HA* xxvi. 12–15. Justinian in 521 spent 4000 lb. gold (*Chron. Min.* II. 101–2), but this caused a sensation.

43. TEN YEARS: *CTh* VI. iv. 13 §2, 361, in potestate censualium denominatio non sit, sed ante decennium legitimo senatus consulto praetores designati editionem praeturasque ipsas senatus arbitrio sortiantur; 21 pr., 372, 22, 373, Symm. *Or.* v. 4. LATER RULE: *CTh* VI. iv. 34, 408.

44. ROME: I cannot accept Seeck's theory (*Hermes* XIX (1884), 186 ff.), based on a fanciful restoration of *ILS* 1222, that Constantine restored the elections to the senate in 336. There is no evidence that the senate ever lost the right of electing the lesser magistrates, and the use of the term *nominatus* of quaestors, praetors and (suffect) consuls in *CTh* VI. iv. 1, 329 (S), suggests that all these magistrates were elected in 329 (cf. VI. iv. 8, 356, for the use of *nominatio*). CONSTANTINOPLE: *CTh* VI. iv. 8 + 9 + 10, 356, 14 + 15, 359, 12 + 13, 361.

45. *CTh* VI. iv. 15, 359.

46. CONSTANTINOPLE: *CTh* VI. iv. 22 pr. §1, 2, 373, ante X annos cuiuslibet editionis praetorem nominari et intra quinque menses designatum iussimus commoneri, ut aut editurus praestet adsensum aut, si praeferet contrariam voluntatem, futuri examinis iudicium non moretur. nam intra septem menses adcelerandae cognitionis terminus constitutus dilationis licentiam imperio fundatae definitionis excludit; cf. law 34, from which it appears that these rules were enacted by Valens. ROME: *CTh* VI. iv. 21 pr., 372, fingamus enim posse fieri, ut designati primo et secundo vel tertio anno subterfugere inquirentium sollicitudinem possint; certe septem reliquis haut dubie poterunt repperiri. ROUND UP OF SENATORS: *CTh* VI. iv. 4, 354 (S), 7, 354 (S), Symm. *Ep.* IX. 126, cf. 134.

47. *CTh* VI. iv. 26, 393, nominandorum praetorum sollicitudinem inlustris magnificentia tua ad officium censuale sciat esse revocandam. Nomination by the *censuales* had been denounced as an abuse in 361 (*CTh* VI. iv. 13 §2).

48. That *adlectio* meant exemption from the games is proved by *CTh* VI. iv. 10, 356, et quicumque forsitan impetraverit pretio functorum coetibus adgregari, indulta ei cessent; allectionis quaerendus est honor; that the *consularitas* meant the same thing is shown by Symm. *Rel.* 5, dignum est igitur aeternitate numinis vestri Celsum genere eruditione voluntate laudabilem adiudicare nobilibus pignore dignitatis, cum praerogativa scilicet consulari, ne sumptum eius magis quam magisterium quaesisse videamur, non sine avaritiae nota, si ab eo munia publica postulamus qui spondet gratuita praecepta; cf. Symm. *Ep.* VII. 96 (cited in n. 21) which links *adlectio* with the *consularitas*; incidentally this letter and III. 38 (also cited in n. 21) show that *adlecti* had to be elected by the senate like other candidates for admission. EXEMPTION BY CODICILLI: *CTh* VI. iv. 23, 373, ab illis editionis peti ordinem non debere iustitia pariter et consuetudo declarat, qui consulares ac praetorios codicillos suo excellenti merito ac nostro sunt beneficio consecuti, cf. VI. iv. 10, 356, secernimus enim ab his, patres conscripti, quibus meriti suffragatio conciliat nostra beneficia et quicumque cessante suffragio inlustribus meritis praetorii vel aliam meruerit dignitatem, praesidio muneris nostri perpetuo perfruatur. ADLECTIO FOR RETIRED PALATINI: *CTh* VI. xxiii. 1, 415 (*decuriones* or *silentiarii*), xxiv. 7, 414, 8, 9, 416, 10, 427,

xxv. 1, 416 (*protectores* and *domestici*), xxvi. 7, 8, 396 (*sacra scrinia*), xxvii. 5, 386 (*agentes in rebus*), xxx. 19, 408, 24, 425 (*palatini*). All these except the *decuriones* are *inter consulares*, and it would seem that those admitted to higher grades of the senatorial order were normally ineligible for *adlectio*: in *CTh* vi. xxvii. 22, 428, *principes* of the *agentes in rebus* lost their immunity when raised from *consulares* to *ex vicariis*, and in vi. xxvi. 13, 407, immunity from the praetorship is specially granted to the *proximi* of the *scrinia*, who were *ex vicariis*; so too for *silentiarii* in vi. xxiii. 4, 437. It is declared by Symmachus (*Ep.* vii. 96, cited in n. 21) that *adlectio* was a privilege reserved to palatine civil servants. No such law is extant, but exemption from the praetorship is given to all ex-*palatini* who enter the senate in *CTh* vi. ii. 19, 397, and this law or the earlier law to which it alludes may have confined the privilege to them. In *CTh* vi. xxxv. 7, 367, *adlectio* is granted to *comites* and *tribuni*: the first part of the law, which gives some privilege to retired *palatini*, evidently does not refer to *adlectio* since some of the recipients are only *perfectissimi*; the privilege is perhaps that of *prosecutoriae*. EXEMPTION OF DUCES: *CTh* vi. iv. 28, 396 (cf. xxvi. 13); of curial senators, Th. II, *Nov.* xv. 1, 439.

49. Theod. *Ep.* (Azema) 33 (Euthalius), 52 (Theocles). *SPP* xx. 127 alludes to one Flavius Alypius, τῷ λαμπροτάτῳ ἀπὸ πραίτορος γεουχοῦντι, in A.D. 463; the praetorship must have imposed, before Marcian's law, on this obscure Egyptian landowner, a mere *clarissimus*.

50. CONSTANTINOPLE: *CJ* I. xxxix. 2 + xII. ii. 1, 450, xII. xvi. 5 §3 (497–9), liberos insuper eorum, qui dignitate virorum spectabilium comitum seu tribunorum decorati sunt vel fuerint, nullatenus nolentes administrationem praeturae suscipere seu peragere; the silence of Justinian on praetorian games suggests that they had lapsed. ROME: Boethius, *Consol.* III. 4 (cited in n. 24).

51. Lib. *Ep.* 731.

52. For honorific titles see P. Koch, *die Byzantinischen Beamtentitel von 400 bis 700* (pp. 45–58 for *magnificentissimi*, pp. 58–73 for *gloriosissimi*). ORDO SALUTATIONIS: *FIR* I². 64. LAW OF VALENTINIAN II: *CTh* vi. xxiv. 4, 387.

53. Lib. *Or.* xxvII. 42, xxvIII. 22, *CTh* xII. i. 127, 392, xIV. iv. 10, 419, Th. II, *Nov.* xv. 1 §1, 439.

54. Lib. *Or.* LI. 4 ff., 33, LII. 4 ff., 46, *CTh* I. xvi. 13, 377, xx. 1, 408.

55. *CTh* xII. i. 150, 395, Th. II, *Nov.* xv. 1 §§1, 2, 439.

56. Salv. *Gub. Dei*, vII. 92, illud gravius ac magis intolerabile, quod hoc faciunt et privati, isdem ante honoribus functi. tantum eis indeptus semel honor dat beneficii ut semper habeant ius latrocinandi.

57. Jer. *Ep.* 108 §§1-4 (Gracchi, Scipios, Julii), cf. 77 §2 (Fabii), Rut. Nam. *de red. suo*, I. 271–2 (Valerius Publicola); the fifth century Gallic senators Polemius and Leo more modestly claimed descent from the historian Tacitus and from Fronto (Sid. Ap. *Ep.* IV. 14, vIII. 3).

58. SENATORS TRANSFERRED FROM ROME TO CONSTANTINOPLE: *CTh* vi. iv. 11, 357, si quos in urbe Roma perfunctos esse claruerit magistratibus, ad nulla editionum genera devocentur. urbis autem Romae curiam callide declinantes clarissimo praeditos nomine per Achaiam, Macedoniam totumque Illyricum iussimus quaeri raro vel numquam sedem dignitatis propriae frequentantes, quibus locorum grata confinia possint esse iucunda, ut carens mora longinquae

peregrinationis debeat dignitas concupisci. We know of one senator thus transferred, Olympius, from Lib. *Ep.* 70, 251-2, 265. LIBANIUS ON THE SENATE OF CONSTANTINOPLE: Lib. *Or.* XLII. 22, and for individual senators, 23-6.

59. See pp. 740 ff.

60. *CJ* x. xxxii. 64 (475-84), 66 (497-9), Just. *Nov.* lxx. 538. We know of two actual cases in the reign of Leo, the father of Dorotheus and Irenaeus and the father of Hesychius (*CJ* x. xxxii. 61, 63).

61. *Curiales* who have obtained honorary offices are expelled from the senate by *CTh* XII. i. 74, 371, and 73, 373, they are forbidden to obtain *codicilli clarissimatus* in XII. i. 180, 416, 183, 418, and are denied titular or honorary illustrious posts in Th. II, *Nov.* xv. 2, 444. They nonetheless obtain them in Just. *Nov.* lxx, 538.

62. NOTARII: *CTh* VI. x. 2, 381, 3, 381. PROXIMI: *CTh* VI. xxvi. 2, 381, 4, 386. OTHER CLERKS OF THE SACRA SCRINIA: *CTh* VI. xxvi. 16, 410 (S). PRINCIPES OF AGENTES IN REBUS: *CTh* VI. xxvii. 5, 386, 21, 426. SILENTIARII: *CTh* VI. xxiii. 1, 415, 4, 437. DOMESTICI AND PROTECTORES: *CTh* VI. xxiv. 7, 414, 8, 416, 9, 416. PALATINI: *CTh* VI. xxx. 19, 408, 24, 425, cf. VI. ii. 26, 428. PRAEFECTIANI: *CJ* XII. xlix. 12, 491-518, cf. Joh. Lydus, *Mag.* III. 30, where John on his retirement is addressed as λαμπρότατος.

63. See pp. 571-85.

64. See pp. 513-4.

65. ARCHIATRI: *CTh* XIII. iii. 2, 326, 12, 379, 15, 393, VI. xvi. i, 413, XIII. iii. 19, 428. PROFESSORS OF CONSTANTINOPLE: *CTh* VI. xxi. 1, 425. LIBANIUS: Julian, *Ep.* 27, Eun. *V. Soph.* XVI. 2, cf. Lib. *Or.* I. 125, II. 8; the rhetor Prohaeresius was given the rank of praetorian prefect by Constantius II (Eun. *V. Soph.* x. 7), and Evagrius was given codicils of the quaestorship and the praetorian prefecture in recognition of his literary works (*Evagr.* VI. 24). CELSUS: Symm. *Rel.* 5. CLAUDIAN: *ILS* 2949. PROFESSORS OF LAW: *CJ Const.* Haec §1, *Const.* Summa §2, *Dig. Const.* Tanta (= *CJ* I. xvii. 2) §9, *Inst. Const.* Imperatoriam §3. Architects also often achieved senatorial rank, see Symm. *Ep.* v. 76, *Rel.* 25, Cyriades, v.c. comes et mechanicus, *IGR* III. 887 (Auxentius, cf. Symm. *Rel.* 25), *IGLS* 348, Ἰσιδώρου τοῦ μεγαλοπρ' ἰλλουστρίου καὶ μηχανικοῦ. AUGUSTINE: Aug. *Conf.* VI. 9.

66. See pp. 641-3.

67. PAEONIUS: Sid. Ap. *Ep.* I. 11 §§5-7. Sidonius himself boasted that his family had held illustrious offices for four generations and claimed a seat in the senate as his hereditary right; Sid. Ap. *Ep.* I. 3, i nunc et legibus me ambitus interrogatum senatu move, cur adipiscendae dignitati hereditariae curis pervigilibus incumbam; cui pater, socer, avus, proavus praefecturis urbanis praetorianisque, magisteriis palatinis militaribusque micuerunt.

68. THE SONS OF TAURUS: Syn. *de Prov.* proem. TAURUS, SON OF AURELIAN: Syn. *Ep.* 31. For Philip's family see J. Keil, *Anz. Ak. Wien*, 1942, pp. 185 ff.; add to his evidence Joh. Lydus, *Mag.* III. 50 (Anthemius, son of the emperor), and Proc. *HA* xii. 1-4 (Zeno, grandson of the emperor, a very wealthy man, appointed Augustal prefect under Justinian). Evagrius (III. 28) mentions one Mammianus of Antioch who in Zeno's reign rose from a workman to a senator (ἐξ ἐπιδιφρίων ἐπίσημον ἄνδρα γενέσθαι καὶ τῆς συγκλήτου βουλῆς μετασχεῖν) and endowed his native city with many fine buildings. He later

(v. 18) records one Anatolius of Antioch, who likewise rose from a workman to offices and wealth under Tiberius Constantine.

69. STILICHO AND SERENA: Zos. IV. 57. ARCADIUS AND BAUTO'S DAUGHTER: Philostorgius, XI. 6. THE FAMILY OF AREOBINDUS: Theophanes, A.M. 5997, cf. *V. Dan.* 80, for Dagalaifus under Zeno, and Nicephorus, p. 103 (Teubner) for the marriage of Areobindus and Anicia Juliana. HORMISDAS: Zos. II. 27, Amm. XVI. x. 16, XXIV. i. 2, ii. 4, v. 4; his son Hormisdas, XXVI. viii. 12. PUSAEUS: Amm. XXIV. i. 9.

70. The eunuch Eutherius settled at Rome when he retired (Amm. XVI. vii. 7); this was considered unusual for a eunuch, but it is implied that for other parvenus it was a common practice. ROMAN JEALOUSY OF MILAN: Symm. *Ep.* VI. 52.

71. FORI PRAESCRIPTIO: *CTh* IX. i. 1, 316, cf. *CTh* IX. i. 13 + *CJ* III. xxiv. 2, 376. GAMES: *CTh* VI. iv. 2, 327. CLARISSIMI IN ILLYRICUM: *CTh* VI. iv. 11, 357. AURUM OBLATICIUM: *CTh* VI. ii. 16, 395.

72. ILLUSTRES IN AFRICA: *CTh* XVI. v. 52, 412, cf. 54, 414. For Sidonius's visits to Rome see C. E. Stevens, *Sidonius Apollinaris*, pp. 29, 95.

73. CURIAL DUTIES: *CTh* XII. i. 187, 436. LEAVE OF ABSENCE: *CJ* XII. i. 15 (426–42). THE PRAETORSHIP: *CJ* I. xxxix. 2 + XII. ii. 1, 450. PROVINCIAL ILLUSTRES IN THE EAST: *CJ* III. xxiv. 3, 485–6, XII. i. 18 (cited in n. 34).

74. ROME: Olymp. 44, *V. Mel.* 15. CONSTANTINOPLE: Joh. Lydus, *Mag.* III. 48 (for Vibianus's praetorian prefecture see *CJ* I. iii. 26, II. vii. 11).

75. See above nn. 37, 42.

76. *CTh* VI. ii. 15, 393, quod ad eorum querimonias, qui se glebalia non posse ferre onera testabantur, amplissimorum virorum consilio definitum est, scilicet ut septenos quotannis solidos pro sua portione conferret, qui praebitionem implere follium non valeret, eatenus . . . confirmamus, ut omnes, quibus est census angustia, contemplatis patrimonii sui viribus liberam habeant optionem, quatenus, si conlatio ista non displicet, a consortio amplissimi ordinis non retendant. sin vero grave, id est damnosum videtur, dignitatem senatoriam non requirant. For Libanius's assistants see Lib. *Or.* XXXI. 11.

77. ARMY OFFICERS: Lib. *Or.* XLVII. 28. TECHNICIANS: *CTh* VI. xx. i, 413. PALATINE CIVIL SERVANTS: *CTh* VI. ii. 26, 428, cf. xxx. 19, 408, and 24, 425.

78. MELANIA: *V. Mel.* 11–2, cf. 18–21, 37. THEOCLES: Theod. *Ep.* (Azema) 52. DEFENSORES SENATUS: *CTh* I. xxviii. 1, 361, 2, 364, 3, 376, 4, 393, VI. iii. 2, 3, 396; the institution appears to have been confined to the Eastern parts.

79. TRADE: *CJ* IV. lxiii. 3 (408–9), nobiliores natalibus et honorum luce conspicuos et patrimonio ditiores perniciosum urbibus mercimonium exercere prohibemus, ut inter plebieum et negotiatorem facilius sit emendi vendendique commercium. PROBUS: Amm. XXVII. xi. THE ANICII ETC.: Amm. XVI. viii. 13.

80. See pp. 381–3.

81. POSTUMIANUS: *ILS* 1285. FAUSTUS: *ILS* 1283; his first praetorian prefecture was in 438 (*CTh Gesta senatus*, Val. III, *Nov.* i. 1), his second in 442 (Val. III, *Nov.* ii. 2). PETRONIUS: *ILS* 807–9, Sid. Ap. *Ep.* I. 13 §3.

82. ALBINUS: *ILS* 1238.

83. SENATOR: *A.C.Oec.* II. i. 334, Priscus, 4, Theod. *Ep.* (*PG*) 44, 93. OTIUM: Th. II, *Nov.* xv. 1, 439, nam etsi otio frui vos quodam tempore patiamur, ne labore videamini fatigari continuo, non tamen ideo cura vos deserit optime regendae rei publicae. According to Sidonius (*Ep.* II. 13 §4) Petronius when he became emperor 'perspexit pariter ire non posse negotium principis et otium senatoris'.

84. Amm. XIV. vi, XXVIII. iv.

85. For Melania's clothes and plate see *V. Mel.* 19. For Symmachus's villas see Seeck in *MGH* (*AA*) VI, p. xlv, xlvi. SLAVES: Joh. Chrys. *Hom. in Matth.* lxiii (*PG* LVIII. 608). See also *V. Olymp.* 5, for Olympias' three houses at Constantinople and her fifty *cubiculariae*.

86. PINIANUS'S TOWN HOUSE: *V. Mel.* 14. The villa near Enna is described in G. V. Gentili, *The Imperial Villa of Piazza Armerina*. There is no solid foundation for the author's view that the villa was imperial: that it belonged to the Symmachi is suggested by the *subscriptio* of a text of Livy, 'Nicomachus Flavianus v.c. III praefect. urbis emendavi apud Hennam' (see H. Bloch in *Paganism and Christianity in the fourth century* (ed. A. Momigliano), p. 215).

87. Symm. *Ep.* IV. 8 (Stilicho), IV. 58–60, 62–3, V. 56, 82–3, VII. 82, IX. 12, 18–21, 23–4 (Spanish horses), IV. 7, VII. 48, 105–6, IX. 22, 25 (*evectiones*), II. 76, V. 59, VII. 122, IX. 15, 16, 144 (African beasts and hunters), VII. 121, IX. 132, 135, 137, 142 (Dalmatian bears), VI. 43, IX. 141, 151 (crocodiles), II. 77 (Scottici canes), IV. 12, VII. 59 (leopards), VI. 33, 42 (actors and charioteers), IV. 46 (gladiators).

88. For the scholarly activities of great Roman nobles see H. Bloch, op. cit., pp. 213–17. Sidonius Apollinaris in his latter years came to regard literary studies as the only surviving hallmark of nobility, now that official rank had gone; *Ep.* VIII. 2, nam iam remotis gradibus dignitatum, per quas solebat ultimo a quoque summus quisque discerni, solum erit posthac nobilitatis indicium literas nosse.

XVI. THE CIVIL SERVICE (p. 564)

For the offices of the *sacrum cubiculum* and for those under the disposition of the *magister officiorum* there are two useful monographs, J. E. Dunlap, *The Office of the Grand Chamberlain in the later Roman and Byzantine Empires*, and A. E. R. Boak, *The Master of the Offices in the later Roman and Byzantine Empires*, New York and London, 1924. For the praetorian prefecture E. Stein, *Untersuchungen über das officium der Prätorianerpräfectur seit Diokletian*, Vienna, 1922, is basic. On the urban prefecture of Rome there is W. G. Sinnigan, *The Officium of the Urban Prefecture during the Later Roman Empire*, Rome, 1957.

1. For the civil service under the Principate see my *Studies in Roman Government and Law*, pp. 157–64. CAELIUS SATURNINUS: *ILS* 1214.

2. Op. cit. pp. 164-6. For *stratores* and *beneficiarii* of *rationales* see *CTh* IX. iii. 1, 320, VIII. iv. 7, 361; for *Caesariani* see n. 88.

3. Op. cit. pp. 165-6.

4. Op. cit. pp. 165-6.

5. COMMUTATION OF ANNONAE: *CTh* VII. iv. 35, 423; *capitus* as well as *annonae* is mentioned in Amm. XXII. iv. 9, *CJ* I. xxvii. 1 §§22-39, 2 §§20-34, 534. VESTIS: *CTh* VI. xxx. 11, 386. For *probatoriae* see ch. XII, n. 4. LEGIO I ADIUTRIX: *CJ* XII. xxxvi. 6, lii. 3 (444), Joh. Lydus, *Mag.* III. 3, et <coll> ocare eum in legione prima adiutrice nostra. For the survival of the rank *speculator* see Ath. *Apol. c. Ar.* 8, 83, *P. Oxy.* 1193, 1214, 1223, *P. Cairo Isid.* 127, *P. Oslo.* 88, *P. Erlangen*, 105, *P. Harris*, 133, *PRG.* V. 61, *CTh* VIII. iv. 16, 389, of centurion (for *princeps*), *CTh* I. xvi. 7, 331, *AE* 1946, 227, *P. Oxy.* 1261, 1424, *P. Flor.* 320; for his *vitis*, Joh. Lydus, *Mag.* II. 19. For the primipilate see p. 549.

6. MAGNUS MAXIMUS: Zos. IV. 37, Amb. *Ep.* 24 §2. MAMAS: Cyr. Scyth. *V. Theodosii*. As castration was illegal on Roman soil, eunuchs had to be imported (see pp. 851-2), and eastern lands were the only available source; Eutherius (Amm. XVI. vii. 5) and Narses (Proc. *BP* I. xv. 31) were both Armenians, and so too apparently was Eutropius (Claud. *in Eutrop.* I. 47); Gelanius, *castrensis* of Leo, was a Syro-Persian from Mesopotamia (*V. Dan.* 28, cf. 25). ABASGI: Proc. *BG* IV. iii. 15-20, Evagr. IV. 22. Eutherius's story (Amm. XVI. vii. 5, natus in Armenia sanguine libero captusque a finitimis hostibus etiam tum parvulus abstractis geminis Romanis mercatoribus venumdatus ad palatium Constantini deducitur) is probably typical. GIFTS OF EUNUCHS: *CJ* XII. v. 4, 473; the same law declares them free.

7. The Notitia Dignitatum records only one *praepositus*, *primicerius* and *castrensis* in both East and West and the last served both the emperor and empress. (*Not. Dig. Or.* xvii. 7-8, *Occ.* xv. 8-9). Eudoxia, however, had her own *castrensis* in 400 (*V. Porph.* 36-40), and *CJ* XII. v. 3 (467-70) and 5 (492-7) mention separate *cubicula* and *praepositi*; cf. *V. Eutych.* 85, Καλοποδίῳ τῷ πριμικηρίῳ Αὐγούστης. CUBICULARIAE: *A.C. Oec.* I. iv. pars ii. 224 (of Pulcheria), *CJ* XII. v. 4 §6, 473 (of servile origin). COMES SACRAE VESTIS: *CTh* XI. xviii. 1, 412 (S), non praepositum vel primicerium sacri cubiculi, non castrensem, non comitem sacrae vestis, non ceteros cubicularios. COMES DOMORUM: *CJ* XII. v. 2, 428 (S), hac nostrae mansuetudinis aeterna lege sancimus, ut omnes cubicularii, qui de nostro cubiculo exeunt, antequam primum locum obtineant, excepto castrensi et comite domorum his privilegiis perfruantur; the post was presumably first given to a eunuch after the *domus divina* was transferred from the *res privata* to the *cubiculum* (see pp. 425-6). SPATHARIUS: Theod. *Ep.* (*PG*) 110, *Chron. Pasch.* 590, *V. Dan.* 31 (Chrysaphius under Theodosius II), *V. Dan.* 56 (Hylasius under Leo.) SACELLARIUS: Joh. Ant. 214. 4, Παῦλον τὸν ἐκ δούλων γενόμενον αὐτοῦ σακελλάριον (under Zeno), Sev. *Ep.* 1. 17 (under Anastasius). CASTRENSIS: *CTh* X. xiv. 1, ad Mygdonium castrensem palatii, 346 (S), Ath. *Hist. Ar.* 15, *Apol. c. Ar.* 36 (Hesychius in 343), *Not. Dig. Or.* xvii, *Occ.* xv. Gelanius is described as καστρήσιος τῆς θείας τραπέζης of Leo in *V. Dan.* 25 and under Justinian we find a καστρησιανὸς τῆς θείας τραπέζης. It may be that the office of *castrensis* was split after the time of the Notitia, and there were several co-ordinate *castrenses* for different departments, or that there were subordinate departmental *castrenses* under the chief *castrensis*. Nothing is known of the function of the *primicerius* as his chapter is missing in *Not. Dig. Or.* and defective in *Not. Dig. Occ.* xiv., and he is rarely mentioned elsewhere (cf. *CTh*

xi. xviii. 1, cited above, *V. Eutychii*, 85, Calopodius, and Joh. Ant. 201. 2, Heraclius, the murderer of Aetius). Eusebius was *praepositus* throughout Constantius II's reign (Soc. II. 2, Soz. III. 1, Amm. xiv. x. 5, xi. 21, xv. iii. 2, xvi. viii. 13, xx. ii. 3). For Chrysaphius see above. Narses was *sacellarius* in 530 (Proc. *BP* I. xv. 31) and still in 538 (*BG* II. xiii. 16). Advancement by seniority to *comes domorum*, *castrensis* and *primicerius* is implied by *CJ* xii. v. 2 (cited above); for the two-year term see the story of Theodore in Joh. Eph. *V. SS. Or.* lvii.

8. For Eusebius, Eutropius and Chrysaphius see pp. 127, 177-8, 180. EUTHERIUS: Amm. xvi. vii. 5, 6, xx. viii. 19. GALLICANUS: Amb. *Ep.* 24. AMANTIUS: *V. Porph.* 36-40. CYRIL'S BRIBES: *A.C.Oec.* I. iv. pars i. 224, 293. ARSACIUS: Ath. *Hist. Ar.* 10. HESYCHIUS: Ath. *Hist. Ar.* 15, *Apol. c. Ar.* 36.

9. For Eutropius's sale of offices see Claud. *in Eutrop.* I. 192 ff. FEES IN THE CUBICULUM: Just. *Nov.* viii, notitia, 535. EUSEBIUS'S PETITIONES: Amm. xvi. viii. 13. PETITIONES OF CUBICULARII: *CTh* x. x. 34, 430. ANTIOCHUS AND CALOPODIUS: *CJ* I. ii. 24 §11 (530), γίνονται δὲ εἰς σκρίνιον τῆς ᾿Ανατολῆς χαρτουλάριοι ιε΄, εἰς τὸ ᾿Ασιανῆς ις΄, εἰς τὸ Πόντου ιε΄, εἰς τὸ ἐνοικίων ιε΄, εἰς τὸ Θράκης η΄, εἰς τὸ τοῦ ᾿Αντιόχου ς΄, εἰς τὸ τοῦ Καλοποδίου ς΄, εἰς τὸ τοῦ ἀναλώματος ι΄, εἰς τὸ τῶν ληγάτων θ΄. Calopodius must be the *praepositus* of Leo mentioned in *V. Dan.* 49, cf. 89; the name is rare and seems peculiar to eunuchs (*A.C.Oec.* II. i. 311, *Chron. Pasch.* 620, Theophanes, A.M. 6024, Malalas, 490, *V. Eutychii*, 85). The identification of Antiochus with the eunuch of that name who was highly influential in the earlier part of Theodosius II's reign (Theophanes, A.M. 5900, 5905, 5936, Malalas, 361) is more speculative.

10. PRIVILEGES OF RETIRED CUBICULARII: *CJ* xii. v. 2, 428. THEODORE: Joh. Eph. *V. SS. Or.* lvii.

11. RANK OF PRAEPOSITUS: *CTh* vi. viii. 1, 422; OF CASTRENSIS: *CTh* vi. xxxii. 1, 416, and 2, 422, viro spectabili com. et castrensi sacri palatii; OF COMES DOMORUM: *CJ* III. xxvi. 11, 442, viri spectabilis comitis domorum; OF CHARTULARIES: Just. *Nov.* viii, notitia, 535. Theodosius II deprived retired *praepositi* of senatorial rank (Malalas, 361), but their degradation was brief; two appear among the senators at the Council of Chalcedon (*A.C.Oec.* II. 1, 334-5); for their later membership of the senate see *CJ* III. xxiv. 3 (485-6), xii. v. 5, (492-7).

12. Amm. xvi. vii. 4-7.

13. On Eutropius's consulate see Claud. *in Eutrop.* I. 1 ff. He was also made patrician (Zos. v. 17, Claud. *in Eutrop.* II. 561). Antiochus, *praepositus* under Theodosius II, was also a patrician, but after his fall this honour was debarred to *praepositi* (Malalas, 361). Under Zeno's law (*CJ* xii. iii. 3 (474-6)) they were also debarred, but Justinian by *Nov.* lxii §2, 537, made them eligible again as *illustres*. Narses was not only patrician but honorary consul (*ILS* 832).

14. *Not. Dig. Or.* xvii, *Occ.* xv; *ministeriales* and *paedagogiani* in *CTh* viii. vii. 5, 326-54, a *paedagogianus* in Amm. xxix. iii. 3. The *curae palatiorum* under the *castrensis* are not to be confused with the *cura palatii* who ranked as a *tribunus scholae* (see ch. XII, n. 16). WIVES OF CASTRENSIANI: *CJ* xii. xxv. 3 (467-70), 4, 474. JULIAN'S BARBER: Amm. xxii. iv. 9. MERCURIUS: Amm. xv. iii. 4. HYPERECHIUS: Amm. xxvi. viii. 5. GRADING AND PROMOTION: *CTh* vi. xxxii. 1, 416, 2, 422. SINECURES: *P. Cairo*, 67126; for the purchase of *militiae* by *argentarii* see Just. *Nov.* cxxxvi, 535, *Ed.* vii. 542, ix (undated).

15. THIRTY SILENTIARIES AND THREE DECURIONS: *CTh* VI. xxiii. 4 §1, 437, sub hac videlicet definitione, ut triginta tantummodo numero haec privilegia consequantur, decuriones quoque tres, quos numquam plures fieri inveterata consuetudo permisit: the wording of the law suggests that this establishment was exceeded in fact. They are described by Procopius (*BP* II. xxi. 2) as βασιλεῖ μὲν ἀεὶ ἐν παλατίῳ τὰ ἐς τὴν ἡσυχίαν ὑπηρετοῦντα (σιλεντιαρίους 'Ρωμαῖοι καλοῦσιν οἷς ἡ τιμὴ αὕτη ἐπίκειται). They are first mentioned in Philostorgius, VII. 7 (under Constantius II) and in *CTh* VIII. vii. 5 (326-54), ii dumtaxat qui ministeriales et paedagogiani et silentiarii et decuriones exsistunt; cf. Ath. *Apol. c. Ar.* 56 and Amm. xx. iv. 20 for *decuriones* in 346 and 360. Their attendance at the consistory is attested by *CTh* VI. ii. 26, 428, aut etiam sacri consistorii decurionum militia muniuntur. Cf. Const. Porph. *Cer.* 87-90. In Cyr. Scyth. *V. Sabae*, 51, οἱ ἐπὶ τῶν θυρῶν σιλεντιάριοι (who appear to occupy τὸ λεγόμενον σιλεντιαρίκιν) admit Saba and his fellow monks to the palace, but do not seem to enter the *cubiculum*, where the *cubicularii* are in charge. The silentiaries do not appear in the Notitia Dignitatum; they were perhaps recorded in the lost or defective pages of the *praepositus sacri cubiculi*, cf. *CJ* XII. xvi. 4 (474-491), v. lxii. 25, 499, both addressed to the *praepositus* and dealing with the silentiaries, and Const. Porph. *Cer.* I. 86, where newly appointed silentiaries are presented by the *praepositus*. EUSEBIUS: Ath. *Apol. c. Ar.* 56. JOHN: *A.C.Oec.* II. i. 459, 489, Zach. Myt. *Chron.* III. 1. EUSTATHIUS: *A.C.Oec.* II. i. 406. MAGNUS: *A.C.Oec.* II. i. 138-9, 177-8, 181; cf. 'v.c. Aphthonius decurio sacri palatii vestri', who conveyed to Symmachus the 'caelestis praeceptio' about the disputed papal election in 419 (*Coll. Avell.* 18, 19). Other decurions appear carrying imperial letters to the popes (*Coll. Avell.* 83 §24). Leo sent a silentiary as envoy to the Goths (Malchus, 2), and silentiaries carry letters to the patriarch of Alexandria under Leo (Zach. Myt. *Chron.* IV. 6) and to the bishop of Ephesus under Theodosius II (*A.C.Oec.* II. i. 405).

16. HONOURS AND PRIVILEGES: *CTh* VI. xxiii. 1, 415, 4 §§1-2, 437; the sixth century rules are shown by the interpolated versions of these laws in *CJ* XII. xvi. 1 and 3; cf. also Const. Porph. *Cer.* I. 84. Their fiscal privileges include immunity from *angariae* and other *sordida munera* and superindictions, *CTh* VI. xxiii. 3, 432, 4 pr., 437. GUBAZES: Proc. *BP* II. xxix. 31. PAUL: Agath. v. 9.

17. PURCHASE OF POSTS: *CJ* XII. xvi. 5 §1, 497-9, nec ipsam militiam vel suffragium, quodcumque pro ea vel ab isdem viris devotis silentiariis vel a parentibus eorum vel quolibet alio datum est vel fuerit, ab his patimur in successionem defunctorum parentum conferri seu nomine collationis in medium easdem offerri pecunias vel his imputari; III. xxviii. 30 §3, 528, exceptis solis viris spectabilibus silentiariis sacri nostri palatii, quibus praestita iam specialia beneficia tam de aliis capitulis quam de pecuniis super memorata militia a parentibus eorum datis, ne in legitimam portionem eis computentur, rata esse praecipimus; Const. Porph. *Cer.* I. 86. The same chapter mentions the four silentiaries of the empress. From a comparison of Amm. xx. iv. 20 and Julian, *Ep. ad Ath.* 285B it would appear that in 360 Julian Caesar's wife had a personal decurion. In 577 we find a decurion as *dux Augustalis* of the Thebaid (*Sb* 7439).

18. *CTh* VI. xxxv. 7, 367, qui intra consistorii secreta veneranda notariorum funguntur officio. Notaries are first recorded under Licinius (Suidas, s.v. Αὐξέντιος). Libanius's chief complaints against the notaries (ὑπογραφεῖς, cf. Zos. v. 40, τῶν βασιλικῶν ὑπογραφέων οὓς τριβούνους καλοῦσι) and the art of shorthand (σημεῖα) are *Or.* II. 44, 46, 58, XVIII. 131-4, XLII. 23-5, LXII. 10-11, 15, 51. Themistius (*Or.* VII. 86bc) speaks of the usurper Procopius as ἐν

ὑπογραφέως ἀεὶ μοίρᾳ διαβιοὺς ἐκ τοῦ μέλανος καὶ τῆς καλαμίδος. MARIANUS: Eus. *V. Const.* IV. 44. PAULUS: Amm. XIV. v. 6. PENTADIUS: Amm. XIV. xi. 21. HILARIUS AND DIOGENIUS: Ath. *Hist. Ar.* 48. SPECTATUS: Amm. XVII. v. 15. PROCOPIUS: Amm. XVII. xiv. 3. GAUDENTIUS: Amm XVII. ix. 7, XXI. vii. 2. DECENTIUS: Amm. XX. iv. 2. For the promotion of notaries see pp. 127-8.

19. For notaries employed on special missions see Amm. XXVIII. ii. 5 (Syagrius ordered to seize a fort), vi. 12 (Palladius sent to report on the complaints of the Tripolitanians), XXX. iii. 2 (Paternianus sent to report on the invasion of Illyricum), Symm. *Rel.* 18 (a notary sent to supervise the shipment of corn from Africa to Rome), 26 (Aphrodisius sent to supervise public works at Rome). For promotion of notaries see Amm. XXI. iv. 2, Philagrium notarium, Orientis postea comitem, XXVI. v. 14, Neoterium, postea consulem tunc notarium, XXVIII. i. 12, Leonem notarium, postea officiorum magistrum, ii. 5, Syagrium tunc notarium, postea praefectum et consulem, Paul. *V. Amb.* 31, Johannes tunc tribunus et notarius, qui nunc praefectus est. PROCOPIUS: Amm. XVII. xiv. 3, XXVI. vi. 1 ff., ix. 8. IOVIANUS: Amm. XXV. viii. 18. BASSIANUS: Amm. XXIX. ii. 5. FAUSTINUS: Amm. XXX. v. 11. THEODORUS: Amm. XXIX. i. 1.

20. *CTh* VI. x. 2, 381, 3, 381. In Symm. *Rel.* 23 and 26 (of 384-5) *tribuni et notarii* are styled *viri clarissimi*.

21. NUMBERS OF NOTARII: Lib. *Or.* II. 58. CLAUDIAN: *ILS* 2949. PETRONIUS: *ILS* 809. MARCELLINUS: *Coll. Carth.* I. iv (Mansi, IV. 52), cf. Aug. *Ep.* 134, 151 (brother of Apringius proconsul). Other young nobles who served were Postumianus (*ILS* 1285), Junius Quartus Palladius (*AE* 1928, 80) and the father of Sidonius Apollinaris, son of a praetorian prefect and destined to become praetorian prefect himself (Sid. Ap. *Ep.* V. 9, cf. III. 12, Zos. VI. 4, 13). NOTARII IN THE PROVINCES: Val. III, *Nov.* vi. 3, 444, idcirco inlustres vacantes per omnes nostras provincias constitutos ternos tirones in adaeratione debere persolvere: comites quoque consistorianos vel primi ordinis nec non tribunos et notarios, sed et eos, qui administrationes ordinarias in provinciis gubernarunt, dare singulos oportere: tribunos vero vacantes sive comites secundi vel tertii ordinis omnesque clarissimos tertiam partem tironis agnoscere, ita ut unius tironis pretium triginta solidis taxetur, exceptis Afris, qui hostili necessitate sedibus suis nuper expulsi sunt: pro excubiis autem praesentibus viginti consistorianos comites, triginta notarios immunes esse debere. The *viri tribunicii* mentioned by Augustine (*Civ. Dei*, XXII. viii) in Africa and Sidonius (*Ep.* I. 3, IV. 24, VII. 11) in Gaul were probably men who had served, at any rate nominally, in the *notarii*; cf. *V. Germani*, 15, for a 'vir tribuniciae potestatis' in Britain.

22. ARISTOLAUS: *A.C.Oec.* I. i. pars iv. 6, 8. DAMASCIUS: *A.C.Oec.* II. i. 373, 378. EULOGIUS: *A.C.Oec.* II. i. 72-3. AGENTES IN REBUS AS SECRETARIES OF THE CONSISTORY: *CJ* XII. xxxiii. 5 §4, 524, excipiendis videlicet nec deducendis in hanc perpetuo conservandam legem pragmaticam eis, qui binas militias simul compositas et sociali nexas consortio fuerint adsecuti, ut in viris dicatissimis scholaribus atque candidatis fieri moris est nec non in viris devotis laterculensibus et pragmaticariis vel a secretis contigit, quos memorialium etiam aut agentum in rebus adornat cingulum, et si qui simili stipendiorum iunguntur copula, *A.C.Oec.* II. i. 70, 92, 94, etc. ὁ καθωσιωμένος μαγιστριανὸς καὶ σηκρητάριος τοῦ θείου κονσιστωρίου. ZENO'S LAW: *CJ* XII. vii. 2, 474. SLOW PROMOTION: Joh. Lydus, *Mag.* III. 9, οἱ ταχυγράφοι πολλῶν ἐτῶν δέονται, καθάπερ οἱ τριβοῦνοι, πρὸς τὸ διανύσαι τὴν στρατείαν. καὶ γὰρ εἰς πλῆθός εἰσιν ὥσπερ ἐκεῖνοι. PURCHASE OF POSTS: *CJ* II. vii. 23 §2, 506, et postquam tale deposuerint officium, si quidem

filios ingenuos habeant, eos clarissimorum notariorum inseri consortio tribunorum, sacras solitas epistulas sine quadam suffragii solutione percepturos.

23. RANK OF PRIMICERIUS: *CTh* VI. x. 4, 425, cf. *CJ* XII. vii. 2, 474, Cass. *Var*. VI. 16. DUTIES: *Not. Dig. Or.* xviii, Occ. xvi. FEES: Just. *Nov*. viii, notitia, 535. PRAGMATICARII AND LATERCULENSES: *CJ* XII. xx. 5 §1, 457-70, illi quoque sunt ab hac liberalitate nostrae mansuetudinis excludendi, qui, cum scholae eidem socientur, in sacris scriniis, quibus vir spectabilis primicerius et tertiocerius praesunt, adiuvantes eos publicarum chartarum tractatibus occupantur et duobus officiis operam suam adhibere non possunt, XII. xxxiii. 5 §4, 524 (cited in n. 22), I. xxxi. 5 §2, 527, ad haec quadrimenstruos breves eorundem scholarium cura tuae sublimitatis et pro tempore viri excellentissimi magistri officiorum conscribi volumus et eos sacro scrinio laterculi praestari ibi deponendos, ut semper notitia eorundem scholarium certa sit neque publico damnum aliquod infligatur. Another law of Leo (*CJ* IV. lix. 1, 473) mentions τὸν περίβλεπτον σεκουνδοκήριον ἢ τερτιοκήριον τῶν λαμπροτάτων τριβούνων as concerned with the illicit grants of monopolies, which would be made no doubt by a *pragmatica*; the *secundocerius* perhaps had the option of serving as *adiutor* or as head of the *scrinium pragmaticarum*.

24. Referendaries are first mentioned in *CJ* I. l. 2, mandata impp. Theodosii et Valentiniani AA. missa ad Antiochum pp. per referendarium, 427 (Constantinople); cf. also *A.C.Oec.* II. i. 177, Μακεδονίου τοῦ περιβλέπτου τριβούνου νοταρίου καὶ ῥεφερενδαρίου (A.D. 449) *V. Dan.* 76 (under Basiliscus), *CJ* IV. lix. 1, 473, I. xv. 2, 527, *A.C.Oec.* III. 29 (536). Their duties are described in Cass. *Var*. VI. 17, Proc. *BP* II. xxiii. 6, *HA* xiv. 11, their numbers and rank as *notarii* in Just. *Nov*. x, 535, Const. Porph. *Cer*. I. 86. An ex-referendary appears to be Augustal *dux* of the Thebaid in P. Cairo, 67002, ἐπὶ τῆς ἀρχῆς τοῦ ἐνδοξ̄ Κύρου τοῦ ῥεφερενδαρίου.

25. See ch. XII, n. 4. For their service in the court of appeal see Just. *Nov*. xx, 536; the *epistolares* and *libellenses* did this work.

26. PROBATORIAE: *CJ* XII. lix. 10, 472; see also ch. XII, n. 4. COMMISSIONS: *CTh* I. viii. 1, 415, 2 and 3, 424. LATERCULENSIS: *CJ* XII. xix. 13 §1 (518-27), 15 §1, 527, praeterquam si quis eorum vel ad laterculensis gradum in scrinio sacrae memoriae vel ad secundum locum in duobus aliis scriniis, id est sacrarum epistularum sacrorumque libellorum et cognitionum, provectus fuerit; Just. *Nov*. xxxv §1, 535, licentia primatibus tantummodo adiutoribus data in sua loca alios subrogandi, id est in scrinio quidem memoriae tertium primum locum optinenti et laterculensis nomen ineunti, in aliis autem duobus scriniis, id est epistularum et libellorum, in secundum gradum venientibus et melloproximatum ingredientibus.

27. NUMBERS: *CJ* XII. xix. 10, 470. RATE OF PROMOTION: *CTh* VI. xxx. 3, 379 (three years), xxvi. 6, 396, xxxiv. 1, 405 (two years), xxvi. 11, 397, 17, 416 (one year).

28. *CJ* XII. xix. 7, 443, 11 (492-7).

29. *CJ* XII. xix. 13, 15, 527, Just. *Nov*. xxxv, 535.

30. CURIALES: *CTh* VI. xxvi. 1, 362, xxxv. 14, 423, *CJ* X. xxxii. 67 §3, 529; there are also two laws of uncertain date earlier than 362 which give exemption to *curiales* after 20 years' service (*CTh* VI. xxvii. 1) or after completing their service (*CTh* VI. xxxv. 3). An early example (probably under Diocletian) of a

curialis enrolled in the *sacra scrinia* is *AE* 1961, 308, Aur. Valerino exceptori impp. in officio memorie qui aput civitatem Nicomediensium fati munus complevit . . . Aurelius Leontis vir docen. et dec. col. Salon. ex curatoribus eiusdem civitatis filio. JOHN CHRYSOSTOM: *Harvard Theol. Rev.* XLVI (1953), 171–3. POLYCHRONIUS: *CTh* VIII. iv. 21, 410. John Lydus (*Mag.* III. 26) originally intended to enlist in the *memoriales* and thus exploit his knowledge of Latin.

31. PROXIMI: *CTh* VI. xxvi. 2, 381, 4, 386, 17, 416, *CJ* XII. xix. 8, 444, cf. *A.C.Oec.* II. i. 149, 177, τοῦ περιβλέπτου κόμητος καὶ προξίμου τοῦ θείου σκρινίου τῶν λιβέλλων καὶ θείων κογνιτιόνων. OTHER CLERKS: *CTh* VI. xxvi. 7, 396, 8, 396, 16, 410 (S).

32. SCRINIUM DISPOSITIONUM: *Not. Dig. Or.* xi. 16, *Occ.* ix. 11, *CTh* VI. xxvi. 1, 362, *CJ* XII. xix. 11 (492–7). MAGISTER: *CTh* VI. xxvi. 2, 381. COMES: *CTh* VI. xxvi. 10, 397, 14, 412 (S), *CJ* XII. xix. 8, 444.

33. NUMBERS OF AGENTES IN REBUS: Lib. *Or.* II. 58, *CTh* VI. xxvii. 23, 430, *CJ* XII. xx. 4, 457–70.

34. Libanius uses such phrases as ἀγγελιαφόροι (Or. xviii. 135) or τὰς ἀγγελίας οἱ φέροντες (Or. II. 58, cf. XLVIII. 7, φέρει τὰς βασιλέως ἐντολάς) for the *agentes in rebus*; cf. also Or. LXII. 14, διακονοῦντες ταῖς βασιλέως ἐπιστόλαις ἃς ἐκ τῶν βασιλείων ἀνάγκη φερέσθαι πανταχοῖ τῆς γῆς, and the description of Aristophanes' career in Or. XIV. 13–14. The first known *curiosus* occurs in 335, Ath. *Apol. c. Ar.* 75, Φλαβίῳ Παλλαδίῳ δουκηναρίῳ παλατίνῳ κουριώσῳ, cf. 73, Παλλαδίῳ τῷ κουριώσῳ τοῦ Αὐγούστου. The official title was originally, it would seem, *praepositus cursus publici* (*ILS* 5905, Fl. Valeriano ducenario agente in reb. et pp. cursus publici, A.D. 340–50), and *curiosus* and *curagendarius* were popular slang (*CTh* VI. xxix. 1, 355, ii quos curagendarios sive curiosos provincialium consuetudo appellat). APPOINTED BY SENIORITY: *CTh* I. ix. 1, 359, ad ducenam etiam et centenam et biarchiam nemo suffragio, sed per laborem unusquisque perveniat, usus omnium testimonio: principatum vero adipiscatur matricula decurrente, ita ut ad curas agendas et cursum illi exeant, quos ordo militiae vocat et labor. DUTIES: *CTh* VI. xxix. 2, 357. REPORTS: *CTh* VI. xxix. 4, 359, etenim cuncti ita agere debebitis, quatenus labore atque ordine ad cursum regendum et ad curas agendas iudicio scholae et ordinis merito dirigamini, ita ut nihil vestri principis ex his, quae geri in re publica videritis, notitiae subtrahatis, scientes poenis eum debitis subiugari, qui tantum facinus ausus fuerit perpetrare. General police duties are implied in *CTh* VI. xxix. 1, 355, and in Libanius's strictures on the *curiosi*, whom he styles πευθῆνες (Or. IV. 25, XVIII. 135 ff.). NUMBERS: *CTh* VI. xxix. 2 §1, 357 (two), 8, 395 (one), 10, 412 (no limit): the second law is preserved in *CJ* XII. xxii. 4, and the *curiosi* thus limited to one per province in the sixth century. Their abolition in 414 (*CTh* VI. xxix. 11, 414) was probably a temporary concession to the African provinces, with which this law is concerned (cf. the *iunctae*, *CTh* VII. iv. 3, viii. 12). CURIOSI OF PORTS: *CTh* VI. xxix. 10, 412, 12, 415; cf. the *agens in rebus* stationed at Clysma who controlled the Indian trade (*Itin. Hier. Petrus Diaconus*, *CSEL* XXXIX. 116). THE CHIEF INSPECTOR: *Not. Dig. Or.* xi. 50–1, curiosus cursus publici praesentalis unus, curiosi per omnes provincias, *Occ.* ix. 44–5; cf. Pall. *Dial.* p. 11, ὑπὸ τοῦ κουριώσου τῆς πόλεως.

35. ADIUTOR AND HIS SUBADIUVAE: *Not. Dig. Or.* xi. 41–3, ix. 41–2, cf. *A.C.Oec.* II. i. 217, διὰ τοῦ καθωσιωμενοῦ μαγιστριανοῦ Σενήρου τοῦ γενομένου σουβαδιούβα τῆς σχολῆς καθωσιωμένων μαγιστριανῶν. SUBADIUVAE FABRICARUM: *Not. Dig. Or.*

xi. 44–9, *Occ.* ix. 43, *CJ* XII. xx. 5 (457–70.) It appears from this law that the *subadiuvae fabricarum* were very senior, holding the office, it would seem, in the year preceding their *principatus*. Other *subadiuvae* might be quite junior, not yet *centenarii* (*CJ* XII. xx. 4, 457–70); presumably the *adiutor* had a free choice in selecting his *subadiuvae*. For the high seniority of the *adiutor* see *CTh* VI. xxvii. 20, 426, *A.C.Oec.* II. i. 207, τοῦ μεγαλοπρεπεστάτου βοηθοῦ τοῦ ἐνδοξοτάτου μαγίστρου (A.D. 451).

36. On this complex problem see Stein, *Zeitschr. Sav. Stift. Rom. Abt.* XLI. (1920), 195–239, and W. G. Sinnigan, *The Officium of the Urban Prefecture during the Later Roman Empire*, 14 ff. I do not entirely agree with these authorities, but I have no clear-cut solution of my own. It is a priori probable that *principes* who served illustrious officers would rank higher than those who served *spectabiles* and from the Codes it appears that some *principes* achieved proconsular rank in 410 (*CTh* VI. xxviii. 7), whereas others reached only that of vicars in 426 (VI. xxvii. 20, 21), preferred to remain consulars in 428 (*CTh* VI. xxvii. 22) and rose to the vicariate again in 440 (*CJ* XII. xxi. 5). The latter and humbler class, however, seem, like the former and grander, to have ceased to belong to the *schola* of the *agentes in rebus* when they took the *principatus*. The Notitia Dignitatum, it is true, speaks of them as *ducenarii* in nearly all cases (*Or.* xxi–xxv, xxviii, *Occ.* xviii–xx, xxii, xxiii, but *ex ducenariis* in *Occ.* xxi). The terminology of the Codes is inconsistent, but in three laws it is specifically stated that *principes* (of lower rank) received the *principatus* after termination of service (*CTh* VI. xxvii. 20, 426, qui ex agentum in rebus numero militiae ordine et labore decurso ducenae dignitatis meruerit principatum, 21, 426, quicumque impleto militiae suae ordine ac labore finito ad ducenae pervenerit principatum VI. ii. 26, 428, qui ex schola agentum in rebus expletis stipendiis ad principatum ducenae pervenerunt), and in another of 440 these inferior *principes* receive the *principatus* 'post ducenam' (*CJ* XII. xxi. 5). It also appears from VI. xxvii. 8, 396, that *ducenarii* on taking the *principatus* vacated their places in the *agentes in rebus*. I would therefore argue that the distinction drawn by Stein between the higher *principes* who were *ex agentibus in rebus* and the lower who were still members of the *schola* is invalid, and that the conclusion he drew from it falls to the ground.

I would suggest on the basis of *CTh* VI. xxvii. 20 and 21 (cited above) that the *principatus* of the *spectabiles iudices* was styled *principatus ducenae*, no doubt because it was the office upon which *ducenarii* entered immediately on terminating their service: they were as we have seen frequently spoken of as *ducenarii* still at this stage. That the upper class of *principes* were styled *principes agentum in rebus* is suggested by the contrasting phraseology of *CJ* XII. xxi. 5 and 6, the former of which certainly applies to the lower class, the latter probably to the higher; *CTh* VI. xxviii. 7 (=*CJ* XII. xxi. 3), which certainly refers to the higher class, also uses the term *principes agentes* (or *agentum*) *in rebus*. But it is doubtful whether this phrase was always confined to the higher class. Under the titles 'de principibus agentum in rebus' in the Codes there are some laws which refer to the lower class (e.g. *CTh* VI. xxviii. 1, addressed to the *vicarius urbis*, and 8, circulated not only to the praetorian and urban prefects but to the *spectabiles iudices*, and *CJ* XII. xxi. 5). What remains unclear to me is how it was decided which *agentes in rebus* were to hold the lower and which the higher *principatus*. There is nothing to suggest that holders of the *principatus ducenae* were promoted to *principes agentum in rebus*.

37. PROMOTION BY SENIORITY: *CTh* I. ix. 1+VI. xxix. 4, 359, VI. xxvii. 4, 382, 1. ix. 2, 386, VI. xxvii. 14, 404. SPECIAL PROMOTIONS: *CTh* VI. xxvii. 3, 380, cf. 7 and 9, 396, I. ix. 3, 405. APPOINTMENT OF ADIUTOR: *CTh* I. ix. 1, 359, adiutor praeterea, in quo totius scholae status et magistri securitas constituta est, omni schola testimonium praebente, idoneus probitate morum ac bonis artibus praeditus nostris per magistratum obtutibus offeratur, ut nostro ordinetur arbitrio; cf. for his responsibilities VI. xxvii. 3, quod in posterum custodiendum ita ratum sit, ut periculum se et adiutor et subadiuvae subituros esse cognoscant, si huius sanctionis nostrae normam umquam etiam insequentibus magistris desierint intimare, and for the part of the *schola* in controlling promotion, VI. xxvii. 4, in schola agentum in rebus nemo facile sub nostra quoque adnotatione speciali prorumpat, nisi sub maiore scholae parte, quisque advenerit, probandus adsistat, qualis moribus sit, unde domo, quam officiorum originem ac sortem fateatur. novi quinquennio vacent a primi quoque honoris auspiciis; ante missionibus crebris futuris parent prodanturque nominibus; dehinc per singulos gradus iusta et firma praecedentium dimissione succedant. sane sic militantibus probeque in actu rei publicae diversatis singulorum graduum, quos meruerint, non negamus accessum, ita ut ipsis quoque sit praecedentium ordo venerabilis ac sub maiore parte scholae etiam de huius gradu bonorum adtestatio et consensus accedat.

38. ARPAGIUS: *ILS* 9043. GAUDENTIUS: Amm. xv. iii. 8, XVII. ix. 7. Cf. also *Coll. Avell.* 188, 218, and 199–201, where Eulogius is described first as *magistrianus* or *agens in rebus* and later as *tribunus et notarius*. Another Eulogius, of Oxyrhynchus, died a μαγιστριανός (P. Oxy. 1960; in 1876, 1958, 1961–2, he is described as καθοσ᾿ παλατινός), but his sons Martyrius and Apphous became *vv. cc. tribuni et notarii* (P. Oxy. 1891, 1959–62, 1994); the family seem to have been considerable landowners. PROMOTION OF PRINCIPES: *CTh* VI. xxvii. 2, 380, agentes in rebus, si principatus sorte deposita forsitan provinciae gubernacula isdem non evenerint, par erit salutationis loco his quidem, qui praesidatum gesserint, cedere, sed eos, qui rationales fuerint, praevenire; xxviii. 13, 403. THEODORE: *A.C.Oec.* II. i. 211–12. The honorary *principatus* is first mentioned in *CTh* VI. xxvii. 16, 413, cf. 19, 417 (20 years), xxviii. 8, 435. SUBADIUVAE FABRICARUM: *CJ* XII. xx. 5 §2 (457–70), quod si morbo vel aetatis senio capti vel imperiti huiusmodi rerum vel quocumque alio vitio praepediti per se memorati officii curam subire nequiverint, consideratis praecedentibus eorum laboribus per substitutum chartularium eiusdem scrinii, cui praefuturus est ipse, idoneum et tam moribus optimis praeditum quam scientiam peritiamque rerum habentem electione sua suarumque periculo facultatum praefatum munus eos implere praecipimus.

39. GRATUITIES: *CTh* VIII. xi. 1, 364, 2, 365, 3, 365 (S), 4, 383, 5, 389, *CJ* XII. lxiii. 2, 530, cf. Salv. *Gub. Dei.* v. 30 and Barsanuphius, p. 62ᵃ, ἄνθρωποί τινες ὑπατίαν ἔδωκαν · δὸς καὶ σύ. None of these sources give any clue to who were the recipients, but that they were, as might be expected, *agentes in rebus*, appears from Lib. Or. XIV. 14, ἐπαινούμενος δὲ τῶν πόνων τὰ προτεινόμενα κέρδη διεωθεῖτο, καὶ οὐκ ἔστιν ὅστις ἐπιδείξει τοῦτον οὐκ ἐπιμελητὴν ὁρέων, οὐκ ἄγγελον ὑπάρχων, οὐ νίκης μηνυτήν, οὐκ ἄλλο τῶν τοιούτων ὑπηρετηκότα οὐδέν, ὅ τὰς μὲν πόλεις ἀπώλλυε, τοὺς δὲ δοκοῦντας διακονεῖν μετ᾿ ἀμαξῶν χρυσὸν ἀγουσῶν ἀπέπεμπεν.

40. *CTh* VI. xxix. 5, 359, in his dumtaxat provinciis, in quibus cursus a provincialibus exhibetur, quoniam avaritiae occurri paene iam non potest, singulos solidos per singulas raedas, id est quas quadrigas vel flagella appellant, percipiatis per id tempus, quo curarum et cursus tuendi sollicitudinem sustinebitis.

MESSALA: *V. Mel.* 52. For the misbehaviour of *curiosi* see *CTh* VI. xxix. 8, 395, 12, 415, and Libanius on the πευθῆνες (see n. 34).

41. FEES OF PRINCIPES: *CTh* VI. xxviii. 1, 379, 3, 386, 4, 387, 5, 395, 6, 399, Val. III, *Nov.* xxviii, 449. For the fees of the *cornicularius* see Joh. Lydus, *Mag.* III. 24.

42. NOMINATIONS BY HIGH OFFICIALS: *CTh* VI. xxvii. 8, 396. CURIALES: Lib. *Or.* XIV (Aristophanes), XVIII. 135, XLVIII. 7, *CTh* VI. xxvii. 1, 326–54, 16, 413, *CJ* x. xxxii. 67 §3, 529; *CTh* VI. xxvii. 2, 363, in which Julian allowed exemption from the *curia* to *agentes* after only three years' service, and to all those discharged in the current year, must be an exceptional indulgence, granted in compensation for the large-scale dismissals whereby he reduced the numbers of the corps. OFFICIALS: *CTh* VI. xxxiv. 1, 405 (*mensores*), I. xv. 11, 380 (*vicariani*), *CJ* XII. xxi. 7, 468 (*cohortales*), *CTh* VI. xxvii. 3, 380, 4, 382 (*officia* in general). HEREDITARY TENURE: *CTh* VI. xxvii. 8 §2, 396, sed et sumentibus ducenariis principatum hanc tribuimus facultatem, ut his pro se liberos ac fratres suos in eadem militia serenitatis nostrae nutu liceat conlocare.

43. ABSENTEES AND PURGES: *CTh* I. ix. 3, mag. off. (Or.), 405, VI. xxvii. 15, mag. off. (Occ.), 412, 18 and 17, mag. off. (Or.), 416 (S), 23, mag. off. (Or.), 430. CIVIL EMPLOYMENTS OF AGENTES: Th. II, *Nov.* vii. 1, 439, *CJ* XII. xx. 5 pr. Cf. *P. Oxy.* 904, where a fifth-century *agens in rebus* has contracted with a citizen of Oxyrhynchus to serve in his place as *riparius* of the city.

44. The belief that the *agentes in rebus* constituted a secret police seems to be based on Aurelius Victor, who wrote of them under Constantius II (*Caes.* xxxix. 44): qui, quum ad explorandum annuntiandumque qui forte in provinciis motus existerent instituti viderentur, compositis nefarie criminationibus, iniecto passim metu, praecipue remotissimo cuique, cuncta foede diripiebant. This testimony receives some support from a law of Constantius II (*CTh* VI. xxix. 4, cited in n. 34) and two instances in Ammianus (XV. iii. 8, XVI. viii. 9), both in the same reign.

45. *Not. Dig. Or.* xi. 17, officium ammissionum, *Occ.* ix. 14, ammissionales, *CTh* VI. xxxv. 3, 326–54, 7, 367, *CJ* XII. lix. 10, 472; the senior clerk was styled *proximus admissionum*, as in the *sacra scrinia* (Amm. XXII. vii. 2). MAGISTER ADMISSIONUM: Amm. XV. v. 18, *CTh* XI. xviii. 1, 412 (S), VI. ii. 23, 414. COMES ADMISSIONUM AND DECURIO: Const. Porph. *Cer.* I. 84, cf. Joh. Lydus, *Mag.* II. 17. The ceremonial functions of the *admissionales* are described in Const. Porph. *Cer.* I. 87–9.

46. LAMPADARII: *Not. Dig. Or.* xi. 12, Val. III, *Nov.* xxx, 450, *CJ* XII. lix. 10, 472.

47. DECANI: *CTh* VI. xxxiii. 1, 416, *CJ* XII. xxvi. 2, 444, lix. 10, 472, *V. Porph.* 39, 40; *decani* execute minor missions outside the palace in Amb. *Ep.* 20 §4, *V. Hypatii*, 119, and *A.C.Oec.* I. iv. pars ii. 155. CANCELLARII: *Not. Dig. Occ.* ix. 15, *CTh* VI. xxvii. 1 (326–54), *CJ* XII. lix. 10, 472, <can>cellariorum, mensorum, lampadariorum eorum qui sacris scriniis deputati sunt, decanorum partis Augustae, cursorum partis Augustae. According to Philostorgius, II. 4, the empress Fausta was executed for adultery with a *cursor*.

48. MENSORES: *Not. Dig. Or.* xi. 12, *CTh* VI. xxxiv. 1, 405, *CJ* XII. lix. 10, 472. The regulations on *metata* are given in *CTh* VII. viii, Th. II, *Nov.* xxv and *CJ* XII. xl; *mensores* of the imperial household are mentioned in *CTh* VII. viii. 4, 394, 5, 398.

49. INTERPRETERS: *Not. Dig. Or.* xi. 52, *Occ.* ix. 46. VIGILANS: Priscus, 7 and 8.

50. *CTh* VI. xxx. 7 (= *CJ* XII. xxiii. 7), 384; cf. the abbreviated lists in *Not. Dig. Or.* xiii. 21–34, *Occ.* xi. 87–99.

51. NO TRANSFERS: *CTh* VI. xxx. 5, 383; the rule no doubt applied to *largitionales* also. RATE OF PROMOTION: *CTh* VI. xxx. 3, 379 (three years), 14, 396 (two years), 21, 416 (one year); for the *mittendarii* see laws 8 and 9, 385, 22, 419, 23, 422. For the duties of the four senior *exceptores* see *Not. Dig. Or.* xiii. 22, 32–4, *Occ.* xi. 88, 98–9. *CTh* VI. xxx. 7 §2, 384.

52. FIGURES OF ESTABLISHMENT: *CTh* VI. xxx. 7, 384, 13, 395, officium, quod sublimitatis tuae iussionibus obsecundat, eas tantummodo teneat dignitates, quas divae recordationis Valentis constitutio conprehendit, 15, 399, 16, 399, 17, 399; that supernumeraries received no emoluments is enacted by *CTh* VI. xxx. 11, 386, olim statuimus, ut ultra definitas dignitates nullus nec annonas nec strenas perciperet. sed quia plerosque de diversis palatinis officiis sub occasione indepti honoris strenas et vestes ceteraque sollemnia ultra statutum numerum percepisse cognovimus, et id quod ex superfluo praebitum est exigi facias et deinceps ultra statutas dignitates nihil praeberi permittas.

53. *Curiales, cohortales* and *collegiati* are all mentioned in the purge of 399 (*CTh* VI. xxx. 16); for *cohortales* see also I. x. 5, 400, VIII. iv. 24, 412, for *curiales* VI. xxvii. 1, VIII. vii. 6, 326–54, XII. i. 38, 357 (S), 120, 389, VI. xxxv. 14, 423. HONOURS OF PRIMICERII: *CTh* VI. xxx. 19, 408, VI. ii. 26, 428, *CJ* XII. xxiii. 13, 428.

54. ESTABLISHMENT: *CTh* VI. xxx. 16, 399. ORGANISATION: *Not. Dig. Or.* xiv. 8–14, *Occ.* xii. 30–38, *CTh* VI. xxx. 5, 383; this law proves that as in the *largitiones* the senior *scrinium*, whose chief was *primicerius totius officii*, was that of the *exceptores*. HONOURS OF PRIMICERII: *CTh* VI. xxx. 24, 425, ii. 26, 428, *CJ* XII. xxiii. 14 (428).

55. The privileges of *palatini* are set out in *CTh* VI. xxxv, de privilegiis eorum qui in sacro palatio militant, and many laws in other titles of the Codes. For their jurisdictional privileges see pp. 489–90.

56. *CTh* VII. i. 14, mag. off., 394, quicumque infantes vel pueri militare coeperunt, sterni eos inter ultimos iussimus, ita ut ex eo tempore, ex quo parere coeperint, locum sibi incipiant vindicare, ut laborum suffragiis incrementa militiae consequantur. MARCELLUS'S CHILDREN: Lib. *Ep.* 362; for Musonius see *CTh* VIII. v. 8, 356 (S). In two other letters (*Ep.* 875–6) Libanius writes on behalf of one of his pupils whom his father, Marianus, had enrolled in some palatine office when he was still at his primary school (ἔτι μὲν ἐν συλλαβαῖς τὸν νέον ὄντα τοῦτον ὁ πατὴρ Μαριανὸς τῆς ἐν τοῖς βασιλείοις ἀγέλης ποιεῖ, πρὸ δὲ τῆς παρ᾽ ἡμῖν διατριβῶν ἐγγραφεὶς εἰς συμμορίαν τινὰ τῶν ἐν τοῖς βασιλείοις), and has now (after his rhetorical studies) come to the time when he must take up his duties.

57. The basic study is E. Stein, *Untersuchungen über das Officium der Prätorianer-präfectur seit Diokletian* (Vienna, 1922). I have made some minor criticisms in my *Studies in Roman Government and Law*, 213–6.

58. That the *commentariensis* was still in 331, as in the Principate, the junior *promotus* is proved by *CTh* VIII. i. 2, ne ii, qui procul ab officio sublimitatis tuae sunt, nullum meritum per sedulitatem vel obsequia praeferentes locum possint laborantibus debitum inrepere, exceptores placet pro loco et ordine suo ad commentarios accedere et eorum administrationi subrogari ceteris propulsatis, ita ut inter exceptores, prout quisque locum tempore adipisci

meruerit, ordine et merito consequatur; the law is probably addressed to a praetorian prefect (*sublimitas tua*). The *princeps, cornicularius* and *commentariensis* appear still to be the only judicial *promoti* in all offices in *CTh* VIII. xv. 3, 364, princeps cornicularius commentariensis numerarius et ordinarii per singula officia possessionum adque aedium nec non etiam mancipiorum comparationem sciant sibi esse praeclusam; 5, 368 (S), patronos etiam fisci ab his contractibus iubemus inhiberi et qui principatum officiorum gerunt seu corniculum quique commentariensium nomine exosa miseris claustra custodiunt; tabularios quoque provinciarum et urbium singularum pari condicione constringimus; identidem numerarii praefecturae vel vicariae potestatis observent. In a provincial *officium* these three officers share all the judicial fees (*FIR* I². 64). The *adiutor* first appears under that name in Symm. *Rel.* 23 §7 (in the office of the urban prefect in 384), and under the title of *primiscrinius* in *CTh* VIII. viii. 2 (in the office of the *vicarius urbis* in 379) and 4 (in the office of the praetorian prefect in 386). The identity of the *adiutor* and the *primiscrinius* is proved by a comparison of the *officia* of the praetorian prefects in the Notitia with Joh. Lydus, *Mag.* III. 4 (cf. 9, 11–2) and Cass. *Var.* XI. 18–22, where the *adiutor* occupies the same place in the one as the *primiscrinius* in the other. He was also sometimes styled the *subadiuva* (*CJ* I. xxvii. 1 §24, 534, in scrinio primiscrinii quod est subadiuvae, cf. Joh. Lydus, *Mag.* II. 16, III. 8). Stein (op. cit. 57 ff.) held that the *adiutor* was in origin the principal assistant of the *princeps* and *cornicularius*, who, he believed, had a joint *scrinium* originally, and later had no *adiutores*. I believe that he originated as the principal assistant of the *princeps*, who certainly had *adiutores* in 331 (*CTh* I. xvi. 7) and 365 (*CTh* VIII. iv. 10), and that the *cornicularius* always retained *adiutores*. My reasons are (a) that in the Notitia the military *officia*, which have no *cornicularii*, nevertheless have *adiutores*, (b) that in the acts of the *Collatio Carthaginiensis* of 411 there appear *adiutores cornicularii, commentariorum* and *subadiuvarum* (Mansi, IV. 181), (c) that it is not clear in Joh. Lydus, *Mag.* III. 9, that the *cornicularius* had no *adiutores*; he only says that, as each principal officer had three *adiutores*, there were six in the *scrinia* of the *ab actis, commentariensis* and *primiscrinius*, since there were two holders of each of these posts (but only one *cornicularius*). A subordinate *ab actis* already existed under the Principate (*ILS* 2384, com(entariensis) ab actis civilib(us)); the ἀβάκτης of P. *Flor.* 71, line 509 (mid fourth century), is probably a similar subordinate. The earliest evidence for a principal officer so styled is the Notitia Dignitatum. DUTIES OF COMMENTARIENSIS: *CTh* IX. xl. 5, 364, VIII. xv. 5, 368, IX. iii. 5, 371, 6, 380, 7, 409, Basil, *Ep.* 286, *Acta Agapae, etc.* 3, *Acta Claudii, etc.* 2, *Acta Crispinae*, 1, Joh. Lydus, *Mag.* III. 16, 17; of *ab actis*, Joh. Lydus, *Mag.* III. 20, 27; of *primiscrinius, CTh* VIII. viii. 2, 379, 4, 386, Joh. Lydus, *Mag.* III. 11, 12; of *cura epistularum*, Cass. *Var.* XI. 23, Joh. Lydus, *Mag.* III. 5, 21; of *regendarius*, Joh. Lydus, *Mag.* III. 21 (his title is wrongly given as *regerendarius* in the Notitia). ADIUTORES: Joh. Lydus, *Mag.* III. 9, cf. 16, 20, *CTh* IX. iii. 5, 371 (of *commentariensis*), *CJ* II. vii. 26 §3, 524 (of *ab actis*). CHARTULARII: Joh. Lydus, *Mag.* III. 17, 27.

59. For the survival of the grade of *speculator* see above, n. 5. For *beneficiarius* see my *Studies in Roman Government and Law*, p. 209, n. 110. DEPUTATI AND AUGUSTALES: *CTh* VIII. vii. 8, 365, praefecturae corniculorios, qui annis singulis ex numero deputatorum exeunt, Joh. Lydus, *Mag.* III. 9–10, cf. 6, 16, 20, Cass. *Var.* XI. 30.

60. Joh. Lydus, *Mag.* III. 4, τῶν οὖν ἄλλων πάντων ἀδιουτώρων ὄντων, ὁ ὕπαρχος δι᾿ οἰκείας ὑποσημειώσεως δίδωσι τῷ πρὸς τὴν στρατείαν ἐρχομένῳ εἰς ὃν αὐτὸς ἕλοιτο ταχθῆναι κατάλογον. αἱ δὲ προσηγορίαι τῶν πάντων καταλόγων τῆς τάξεως αὗται· ὁ

κορνικουλάριος, etc.; 6, πολλῆς δὲ οὔσης ὑπὲρ ἀριθμὸν τῆς τῶν ταχυγράφων πληθύος, καὶ οὐ μικρὰς ἐχούσης ἀφορμὰς ἐπὶ κέρδους ἐργασίας, οἱ τούτων καὶ λογικώτεροι καὶ πρὸς τὴν ὑπηρεσίαν ἀρκοῦντες ἐν πεντεκαίδεκα συναγωγαῖς, ἃς καλοῦσι σχολάς, συλλεγόμενοι, οἱ τὴν οὖσαν αὐτοῖς πεῖραν τοῖς πράγμασιν ἐπιδειξάμενοι ἐπὶ τὸ τάγμα τῶν Αὐγουσταλίων, εἴγε ἄρα θέλουσι, παρίασι καὶ εἰς τὸ τοῦ κορνικουλαρίου πλήρωμα καταντῶσι, μετὰ μέντοι τὴν λεγομένην βοηθοῦραν· οἱ μένοντες ἐπὶ τῆς δέλτου εἰς τὸ τοῦ πριμισκρινίου ἀναφέρονται πλήρωμα. I take ὑπὲρ ἀριθμόν to be technical and to imply that the new entrants of ch. 4 are *supernumerarii*; those who make good are then enrolled in the fifteen *scholae*, and of these some eventually pass into the *Augustales*, others remain on the roll of *exceptores* (Stein interprets this otherwise, op. cit. pp. 52 ff.). Synesius (*Ep.* 61) in order to identify Asterius, a fairly junior *exceptor* (ταχύγραφος) of the praetorian prefecture, explains that he was third or fourth (now perhaps first) in a group (συμμορία), of which a well-known civil servant, Marcus, was chief. This, as Stein argues, indicates that the fifteen *scholae* were each in charge of a high official, and he suggests that the fifteen *deputati* were their heads. But it is also possible that the heads of the *scholae*, as of the κατάλογοι, were the fifteen principal officers, enumerated by Lydus (*Mag.* III. 4) as one *cornicularius*, two *primiscrinii*, two *commentarienses*, two *regendarii*, two *curae epistularum* of Pontica (and presumably six more for Asiana, Oriens and Thrace): it is not clear why the two *ab actis* are absent from the list — perhaps the arrangement dated from before their creation. SELECTION OF CHARTULARII: Joh. Lydus, *Mag.* III. 17, 27. SELECTION AND LATER PROMOTION OF ADIUTORES: Joh. Lydus, *Mag.* II. 18 (nine years' seniority), III. 6, 9-10, 16, 20.

61. DUPLICATION OF OFFICES: Joh. Lydus, *Mag.* III. 4, cf. 9, 16, 20. RETIREMENT OF CORNICULARIUS AND PRIMISCRINIUS: Cass. *Var.* XI. 18-21, *CJ* XII. xlix. 12 (491-518). For the scheme of promotion in the Italian prefecture see the ingenious argument in Stein, op. cit. pp. 31 ff., based on Cass. *Var.* XI. 18-30. SLOWNESS OF PROMOTION: Joh. Lydus, *Mag.* III. 9, cf. 30.

62. Joh. Lydus, *Mag.* III. 35, *CTh* VIII. i. 8, 363, iubemus omnes numerarios, non eos modo, quos plebe confusa vulgus abscondit, sed primos etiam et magistros eorum, officii sedis amplissimae, tum autem iudicum ceterorum, solutos penitus militaribus sacramentis condicionales etiam fieri, ne dignitas fraudibus faciat umbraculum; 11, 365, super numerariis celsissimi officii tui aliter est nostra sententia quam divae memoriae Julianus duxerat sanciendum. ille lege proposita numerarios omisso cingulo, condicionis conscios vilioris necessitati publicae obsecundare praecepit: nos, qui malumus obsequia hominum esse voluntaria quam coacta, sumere cingulum et militiae ordinem tenere numerarios iubemus, cum, si in aliquo fraudium scelere fuerint deprehensi, nullo modo possint a corporali iniuria vindicari.

63. For the financial *scrinia* see pp. 449-50. DUPLICATION OF NUMERARII: Basil, *Ep.* 142-3. TERM OF OFFICE: *CTh* VIII. i. 8, 363 (five years), 17, 433 (three years). ADIUTORES AND CHARTULARII: *CJ* XII. xlix. 10 (485-6). For *tractatores*, *canonicarii*, etc. see pp. 449-51.

64. *CJ* I. xxvii. 1 §§29-35, cf. *Not. Dig. Or.* ii. 71, iii. 32, *Occ.* ii. 55, iii. 50, Joh. Lydus, *Mag.* III. 7, Cass. *Var.* XI. 31-2, *A.C.Oec.* I. iv. pars ii. 203 (*singulares*); Joh. Lydus, *Mag.* III. 8, 16, 20 (*cursores, nomenclatores, praecones, applicitarii, clavicularii*); Val. III, *Nov.* xxii §4, 446 (*mensores*).

65. *CJ* I. xxvii. 1 §§22-39, 534.

66. For judicial *sportulae* see pp. 496-9. INCOMES: Joh. Lydus, *Mag.* III. 27

(*chartularius*), 11. 18 (*adiutor*), 111. 24 (*cornicularius*). BONUSES: Cass. *Var.* XI. 33-7. For fiscal *sportulae*, etc., see pp. 467-8.

67. CURIALES: *CTh* VIII. vii. 6, 326-54; there are no other specific references to *curiales*, but they are frequently debarred for *militiae* in general terms. COHORTALES: *CTh* VIII. iv. 23, 412, quia plurimi consuetam proconsularem ceterorumque iudicum fugientes militiam diversis palatinis seu inlustrium potestatum officiis se sociasse dicuntur, decernimus omnes absolutos cingulo militiae ad propriam functionem reduci. Joh. Lydus, *Mag.* III. 26. VIVENTIUS: *CTh* VIII. vii. 10, 369. HONOURS OF RETIRING OFFICIALS: *CTh* VIII. vii. 8, 365, 9, 366 (*cornicularii*), i. 13, 382 (*numerarii*), *CJ* XII. xlix. 12 (491-518), Cass. *Var.* XI. 18, 20. It is generally assumed that the dignity of *tribunus praetorianus* is identical with that of *tribunus et notarius*, but it was probably lower. Certainly the grade of *tribunus praetorianus militaris* was lower, for it was given to retired *largitionales* and *privatiani* as a consolation when they renounced senatorial rank (see above n. 53). The title was presumably a survival from the time when there was still a praetorian guard; other similar obsolete posts preserved as honorific distinctions were *tribunus vigilum militaris* (*CJ* XII. liv. 4) and *tribunus urbanicianus* (*CTh* VI. xxvii. 8). In Justinian's day the *cornicularius* was a *comes* and *clarissimus* during his year of office (Joh. Lydus, *Mag.* III. 4, 30) and presumably rose to be *spectabilis* on retirement. POLYCARP AND MARINUS: Joh. Lydus, *Mag.* III. 36. PETER BARSYMES: Proc. *HA* xxii. 3-6. Marathonius, a *numerarius* of the praetorian prefecture, retired a wealthy man (Soz. IV. 27, ὃς ἀπὸ ψηφιστῶν δημοσίου τῶν ὑπὸ τοὺς ὑπάρχους στρατιωτῶν, πλοῦτον πολὺν συλλέξας, ἐπειδὴ τῆς στρατείας ἐπαύσατο συνοικίας νοσούντων καὶ πτωχῶν ἐπεμελεῖτο).

68. On the prefects of the city see W. G. Sinnigan, *The Officium of the Urban Prefecture during the Later Roman Empire*, Rome, 1957. The chief financial officials of the urban prefecture were apparently called *primiscrinii* at first (Sym. *Rel.* 34 §6, *CTh* XIV. iv. 10, 419), later *numerarii* (Maj. *Nov.* iv §1, 458); cf. *Not. Dig. Occ.* iv. 25, primiscrinius sive numerarius. It is confusing that the *adiutor* (*Not. Dig. Occ.* iv. 21, Symm. *Rel.* 23 §7) is also sometimes styled *primiscrinius* (*Coll. Avell.* 16, 31). For the *censuales* see p. 431. For the *officia* of vicars, etc., we have very little information save the Notitia; the *Acta* of the *Collatio Carthaginiensis* show that in the proconsular office of Africa the *cornicularius*, *commentariensis* and *subadiuva* (i.e. *adiutor*) had their *adiutores* (see n. 58). A *nomenclator* of the *vicarius urbis Romae* is recorded in *CIL* VI. 9687. ESTABLISHMENTS: *CTh* I. xiii. 1, 394 (*comes Orientis*), xv. 5, 365, 12, 386 (vicars), 13, 389 (vicar of Asiana), Just. *Ed.* xiii §2 (Augustal prefect), *CTh* I. xii. 6, 398 (proconsul of Africa).

69. Just *Ed.* xiii 4, οἱ δέ γε αὐτῷ παρεδρεύοντες quinque librarum auri λήψονται ἐκ τῶν αὐτῶν καὶ ἑτέρους mille solidos καὶ ἡ κατ᾽ αὐτὸν τάξις, καίτοιγε πρότερον τὴν τρίτην αὐτῶν ἔχουσα ποσότητα.

70. PRINCIPES: *Not. Dig. Or.* xx. 10, xxi. 6, xxii. 34, xxiii. 16, xxiv. 21, xxv. 27, xxvi. 17, *Occ.* xviii. 5, xix. 16, xx. 17, xxi. 17, xxii. 41, xxiii. 17. HONOURS OF CORNICULARII: *CTh* VIII. vii. 16, 385; *vicariani* are omitted in the Justinianic version (*CJ* XII. liii. 1). CORNICULARIUS OF THE VICAR OF PONTICA: *CTh* I. xv. 11, 380. RECRUITMENT: *CTh* VIII. vii. 6, 326-54 (*curiales*), I. xii. 4, proc. Afr., 393 (*curiales* and *plebeii*), 6, 398 (*curiales* and *collegiati*), xv. 12, 386 (*curiales*). PROBATORIAE: *CTh* VIII. vii. 21, 426, *CJ* XII. lix. 10, 472.

71. For the general scheme of provincial *officia* see *Not. Dig. Or.* xliii, xliv, *Occ.* xliii-xlv, also *Or.* xxix (the *comes et praeses* of Isauria, who had a normal

praesidial *officium*), xxxvii. 43–51 (the praesidial *officium* of the *dux Arabiae*). For the addition of the *adiutor* and the *ab actis* see n. 58. The *a libellis* appears in *Not. Dig. Or.* xx. 17, xxi. 13 (proconsuls), xliii. 12 (consulars), xxix. 16 (*comes et praeses Isauriae*) and xxxvii. 50 (*praeses Arabiae*) and Seeck is therefore right in restoring it at xliv. 13 (other *praesides*). A *libellensis* appears in *FIR* I². 64 (consular of Numidia, 361–3), but as the office is not recorded anywhere in *Not. Dig. Occ.* it cannot have been an established post. SUBCLERICAL GRADES: *P. Oxy.* 1837, 1880–1, *PSI* 1365, *P. Lond.* 1679, 1797, *P. Flor.* 291, *P. Cairo*, 67054, 67103, 67282, 67291 (*singulares*); *P. Oxy.* 1901 (σχολὴ κουρσόρων, σχολὴ πραικόνων), 1958 (*cursores*); *ILS* 8881 (δρακωνάριος ἐξ ὀφικίου τοῦ λαμπροτάτου ἡγεμόνος), Theod. *Ep. (PG)* 59, 133 (*draconarii*). *P. Oxy.* 2050 also records κυεσσωνάριοι (*quaestionarii*; cf. *de Mirac. S. Steph.* II. 5, for *quaestionarii* of the proconsul of Africa), κλαουικουλάριοι (*clavicularii*) and κουροπερσονάριοι (*curae personarum*), presumably attached to the *commentariensis* (cf. Joh. Lydus, *Mag.* III. 16). *Stratores* are attested only for proconsuls (*CTh* XIII. xi. 6, 394 (S)). PRINCIPES DE EODEM OFFICIO: *Not. Dig. Or.* xxix. 10, xxxvii. 44, xliii. 6, xliv. 7, *Occ.* xliv. 7, xlv. 7; FROM THE OFFICIUM OF THE PU OR PPO ITALIAE: *CTh* I. vi. 8, 382, apparitoribus tuis stationes, quas habuere antiquitus, statuimus esse reddendas. igitur pristino more servato ad omnes provincias, quas vel divi Constantini constitutio dederat vel Probus vir illustris permissa sibi a patre nostro potestate reddiderat, praecelsa sinceritas tua principes destinabit; qui sane meminerint nihil morae in his, quae primipili nomine res poscuntur, esse faciendum; *Not. Dig. Occ.* xliii. 6.

72. The title *tabularii* is used in *CTh* VIII. i. 1, 319, but *numerarii* in laws 4, 334, 6, 362, 7, 362, 8, 363; *tabularii* is restored in law 9, 365 and used in 12, 382. *Numerarii* are recorded in *Not. Dig. Or.* xliii, xliv, *tabularii* in *Occ.* xliii–xlv. TORTURE: *CTh* VIII. i. 4, 334, 6, 362. In *CTh* VIII. i. 7, 362, Julian mentions a previous law which made *numerarii condicionales*; that this meant loss of military status is shown by law 11, which restores their *cingulum* and *militiae ordo* to *numerarii* of the praetorian prefecture, who had also been made *condicionales* and 'solutos penitus militaribus sacramentis' by law 8. I infer that *numerarii* did recover their military status from the omission of the laws making them *condicionales* from the Codex Justinianus. TERM OF OFFICE: *CTh* VIII. i. 4, 334 (two years), 6, 362 (five years), 9, 365 (three years); the last law remained the rule, being reproduced as *CJ* XII. xlix. 2. TWO TABULARII: *CTh* VIII. i. 12, 382.

73. NUMBERS AND PAY: *CJ* XII. lvii. 9, 396 (S), Just. *Nov.* xxiv. §1 and notitia, xxv §1 and notitia, xxvi §2 and notitia, xxvii notitia, xxviii §§3, 4, xxix §2, *CJ* I. xxvii. 1 §40. In Just. *Nov.* cii §2 the *officium* of the *moderator* of Arabia is allotted two lb. gold only instead of the usual five, but I suspect that the figure is corrupt. For the fees see pp. 496–9 (judicial), pp. 467–8 (revenue collection).

74. *CTh* VII. xxii. 3, 331, ii, qui ex officialibus quorumcumque officiorum geniti sunt, sive eorundem parentes adhuc sacramento tenentur sive iam dimissi erunt, in parentum locum procedant. There is no later allusion to a hereditary obligation on sons of officials other than *cohortales*. In *CTh* VIII. iv. 8, 364, the rule is partially relaxed for those 'in proconsulum consularium correctorum vel praesidum officiis'. In VIII. vii. 16, 385, the words 'vel sponte initiatus est vel suorum retinetur consortio maiorum' refer back to the two groups earlier mentioned in the law, (*a*) the offices of praetorian and urban prefects and vicars and (*b*) provincial *officia*. Similarly in VIII. vii. 19, 397, the words 'cui nati sunt ordo' refer only to *cohortales*, who were liable to the *mancipatus*. The hereditary obligation of the *cohortales* is on the other hand often mentioned, e.g. VIII. iv. 13, 382, XII. i. 79, 375, VIII. iv. 28, 423, 30, 436, and the

same rules were applied to *cohortales* and *curiales*; cf. *CJ* xii. xxi. 7, 468, with x. xxxii. 67 §3, 529. During the fourth century all officials, including *praefectiani*, were forbidden to move to other offices during their period of service (*CTh* viii. vii. 16, 385, 19, 397), but this rule was later relaxed for all but *cohortales*; it was still applied in 412 to officials of proconsuls (*CTh* viii. iv. 23, proc. Afr., 24, *CSL* (Occ.), 412), but in the Notitia the note 'quibus non licet ad aliam transire militiam sine annotatione clementiae principalis' applies only to *cohortales* (*Or.* xliii. 13, xliv. 14, *Occ.* xliii. 13, xliv. 14, xlv. 14), and in Val. iii, *Nov.* xxii §1, 446, *praefectiani* are expressly allowed to migrate to other *militiae*. RULES ON PROPERTY: *CTh* viii. iv. 7, 361 (the church), *CJ* vi. lxii. 3, 349 (intestacy), *CTh* viii. iv. 16, 389 (premature retirement). For the *primipili pastus* see ch. XIII, n. 117.

75. For the bar see pp. 513–4, for the church pp. 924–5. For the higher ministries see nn. 30, 42, 53, 67, cf. general allusions to *militia clarior* (*CTh* viii. iv. 8, 364), *maius privilegium militiae* (law 22, 412). *Dignitates* are mentioned in *CTh* viii. iv. 29, 428, 30, 436, *CJ* xii. lvii. 13, 442, 14, 471 (specifying provincial governorships), the senate in *CTh* viii. iv. 14, 383, qui relicto principatus officio quod gerebat ad senatoriae dignitatis nomen ambiit, propriae redditus militiae plumbatis coercendus est. This law was evidently elicited by an actual case. It might refer to the *princeps* of the *comes Orientis*, who though an *ex ducenariis* of the *agentes in rebus* was not at this date entitled to senatorial rank after retirement, still less during service, but the severity of the punishment suggests that the man concerned was of humbler status, and his presumption more heinous, that is, that he was the *princeps* of a provincial *officium*. ANNULMENT OF SPECIAL GRANTS: *CTh* viii. iv. 29, 428, *CJ* xii. lvii. 13, 442, 14, 471. ADVOCATI FISCI: *CJ* ii. vii. 8, 440. PRINCIPES OF AGENTES IN REBUS: *CJ* xii. xxi. 7, 468.

76. CURIALES: *CTh* viii. vii. 6, 326–54, iv. 8 §1, 364, xii. i. 96, 383, 134, 393; cf. viii. vii. 17, 385, exceptores omnes iudicibus obsequentes, qui nec militiam sustinent neque a fisco ullas consequuntur annonas, absque metu navare coeptis operam, etiamsi decuriones sint, minime prohibemus, dummodo munia propriae civitatis agnoscant et peracto secundum morem exceptionis officio ad propriam sibi curiam redeundum esse non nesciant. SONS OF VETERANS: *CTh* vii. xxii. 6, 349, 9, 380 (cf. xii. i. 83); vii. xxii. 7, 8, 10 and 12 speak of *officia* in general. MERCHANTS: *CJ* xii. lvii. 12 §3, 436.

77. TRIPOLITANIA: *CTh* xii. i. 133, 393. FLAVIUS POUSI: *P. Oxy.* 1901. OFFICIALS OF THE THEBAID: *P. Flor.* 71, lines 60, 160, 509, 515, 546, 550, 604, 612, 625, 680, 697, 707, 713; other landowning *cohortales* are recorded in *PSI* 1077–8, *P. Zill.* 7. SONS OF PRIMIPILARES: *CTh* vii. xxii. 11, 380; at Edessa, capital of Osrhoene, this was the regular rule, *CTh* xii. i. 79, 375, 105, 384.

78. *P. Lips.* 36, 45–55, 58–61, 64.

79. There are two drafts of the petition (*P. Lips.* 34, 35), both much corrected and inconsistent in their facts and figures. LEASES: *P. Lips.* 17, 20–23. INHERITANCE SUIT: *P. Lips.* 33. COMPLAINT AGAINST SHEPHERDS: *P. Lips.* 37.

80. All these facts are drawn from the Notitia Dignitatum; a convenient table of the military offices will be found on p. 336 of Seeck's edition. I infer that the *cornicularius* was a later addition from his ranking below the *commentariensis* in *Occ.* xxvi, xxviii, xxx, xxxi; he appears with normal precedence only in *Occ.* xxiv (*comes Africae*). The *numerarius* and *primiscrinius* are mentioned in Anastasius' regulations for the ducal *officium* of Libya (*SEG* ix. 356), and *primiscrinii*

and *scriniarii* in his regulations for the ducal *officium* of Arabia (*Princeton Exp. Syria*, 20, 562); in the latter it would appear that the term of office for *primiscrinii* was five years. Both mention a σουβσκριβενδάριος, but in the former he is on the personal staff of the *dux* and not a member of the *officium*. Of the subclerical grades *singulares* are recorded in *Sb* 7439, 8029, *draconarii* and a *schola semissalium vel equitum (τῆς σχολῆς τῶν σημισαλίων ἢ ἐκύτων)* in *Princeton Exp. Syria*, 20.

81. COMES AEGYPTI: *Not. Dig. Or.* xxviii. 48, principem de schola agentum in rebus ducenarium qui adorata clementia principali cum insignibus exit. EASTERN DUCES: *Not. Dig. Or.* xxxi. 69, xxxii. 46, xxxiv. 50, xxxv. 36, xxxvi. 38, xxxvii. 37, xxxviii. 40, principem de schola agentum in rebus. That the distinction means something is suggested by *CTh* VI. xxviii. 8, *mag. off.* (Or.), 435, which was circulated to the praetorian and urban prefects and to those *spectabiles iudices* only who are recorded in the Notitia to have had *ducenarii* as *principes*. DANUBIAN DUCES: *Not. Dig. Or.* xxxix. 37, xl. 38, xli. 41, xlii. 45, principem de eodem officio qui completa militia adorat protector, *Not. Dig. Occ.* xxxii. 61, xxxiii. 67, xxxiv. 42 (also Belgica II, xxxviii. 11), principem de eodem corpore (or *officio*). OTHER WESTERN MILITARY OFFICES: *Not. Dig. Occ.* vii. 112–14. (mag. equ. per Gallias), xxv, xxvi, xxviii–xxxi, xxxv–xxxvii, xl, xli; for Stilicho's establishment of the system see pp. 174–5.

82. *Not. Dig. Or.* v. 67, officium autem suprascriptae magisteriae in praesenti potestatis in numeris militat et in officio deputatur (cf. viii. 54, ix. 49), vi. 70, officium autem suprascriptae magisteriae in praesenti potestatis cardinale habetur (cf. vii. 59): Th. II, *Nov.* vii. 4, 441, which was circulated to both *praesentales* and applied to all five *magistri*, implies, especially in §2, that their *apparitores* were established civil servants, and in *CJ* xii. lix. 10, notitia, the *officia* of all the *magistri* (except that of Thrace, whose omission is probably accidental) received *probatoriae* in the ordinary way. NUMBERS: Th. II, *Nov.* vii. 4, 441; for the *statuti* see *CJ* I. xxix. 3, 476–85, XII. liv. 5, 491–518, and the Justinianic interpolation in *CJ* I. xxix. 2 (= *CTh* I. vii. 4).

83. OFFICIUM OF LIBYA: *SEG* IX. 356 §§2 (establishment), 8 (seconded soldiers), 14 (personal staff). AFRICAN OFFICIA: *CJ* I. xxvii. 2 §§20–34, 534.

84. *SEG* IX. 356 §§1 (service in regiments forbidden), 2 (*annonae* and *capitus*), 14 (fees). In Just. *Ed.* xiii §18 the *officium* of the *dux* of the other Libya is stated to get νομίσματα ρπζ ἥμισυ (187½ solidi). The figure is impossibly small, and should probably be emended to τπζ ἥμισυ (387½), which would be equivalent to 40 *annonae* and 40 *capitus* in kind on the same scale as those allotted to the *dux*.

85. *CJ* I. xxvii. 2 §§20–34, 534.

86. PRINCIPES AND NUMERARII: *CJ* XII. liv. 4, 443 (S). REMIGIUS: Amm. XV. v. 36, rationarius apparitionis armorum magistri, cf. XXVII. ix. 2, XXVIII. vi. 8, 30, XXIX. v. 2, XXX. ii. 10. LEO: Amm. XXVI. i. 6, sub Dagalaifo magistro equitum rationes numerorum militarium tractans, cf. XXVII. i. 12, XXX. ii. 10, v. 10. JOHN: Joh. Lydus, *Mag.* III. 57, οὗτος ὥρμητο μέν, ὡς ἔφην, ἐξ ἐκείνης, τοῖς δὲ τῆς στρατηγίδος ἀρχῆς σκρινιαρίοις συναριθμούμενος, δολερῶς οἷα Καππαδόκης παρεισδύς, οἰκειοῦται τῷ βασιλεῖ, καὶ κρείττονα πίστεως ἐπαγγειλάμενος πρᾶξαι ὑπὲρ τῆς πολιτείας εἰς λογοθέτας προῆλθεν. εἶτ᾽ ἐκεῖθεν, ὥσπερ κατ᾽ ἐπιβάθραν, ἐπὶ τοὺς λεγομένους ἰλλουστρίους ἀνελθών, καὶ μήπω γνωσθεὶς ὁποῖός τίς ἐστι τὴν φύσιν, ἀθρόως εἰς τὴν ὕπαρχον ἀνηρπάσθη τιμήν. SECUNDUS: Soc. VI. 3, Pall. *Dial.* p. 28, Ἰωάννης οὗτος τὸ μὲν γένος ἦν Ἀντιοχεύς (κεκοίμηται δὲ), υἱὸς γεγονὼς τῶν διαπρεψάντων εὐγενῶς παρὰ τῇ τάξει τοῦ στρατηλατοῦ τῆς Συρίας, cf. Joh. Chrys. *de Sacerdotio*, I. 5. Cf. *PSI* 176, for a στρατηλατιανός who owns land. Th. II, *Nov.* vii. 4 §2, 441, probari

autem adparitores magisteriae potestatis neque curiales neque cohortales neque censibus volumus adscriptos, cf. *CTh* XII. i. 175, 412 (*curiales*).

87. *P. Cairo*, 67312. Other *duciani* who are landowners appear in *P. Hamb.* 23 (*exceptor*), *P. Zill.* 6 (*scriniarius*), *Sb* 8029 (*singularis*).

88. For the *largitionales civitatum* and the *thesaurenses* see pp. 428–9. CAESARIANI: *CJ* x. i. 5 (285–93), *CTh* x. vii. 1, 317, viii. 2, 319, IX. xlii. 1 §4, 321, x. i. 5, 326, vii. 2, 364, Bruns, *Fontes*[7], 95, Amm. XXVIII. ii. 13. In *CJ* IX. xlix. 9 (=*CTh* IX. xlii. 1) Caesarianis is glossed 'id est catholicianis', that is officials of a *rationalis* (καθολικός). The laws speak of them only in relation to the business of the *res privata* (confiscations).

89. For the minor *officia* of the capitals see pp. 691–2. TITLES OF MUNICIPAL OFFICIALS: *CTh* VIII. ii, de tabulariis, logografis et censualibus, VIII. iv. 8, 364, subscribendarii vero, tabularii, diurnarii, logografi, censuales; *scribae* are mentioned in VIII. ii. 1, 341, 3, 380, XI. viii. 3, 409, cf. also VIII. ii. 3, vii. 6, XI. iv. 1 for *logografi*, and VIII. ii. 4 for *censuales*. *P. Cairo*, 67353 records τὸν δημόσιον σκρίβαν καὶ ταβουλάριον καὶ δημέκδικον τῆς. . . 'Αντινοέων πόλεως. The λογόγραφοι of *P. Amh.* 82, appear not to be civil servants but decurions performing a curial *munus*: their duty was to attend the court of the provincial governor. TABULARIUS CIVITATIS: *CTh* XIII. x. 1, 313, 8, 383, Symm. *Ep.* IX. 10 (assessments), *CTh* XI. i. 2 +vii. 1, 313 (S), XII. vi. 27, 400 (accounts); the *tabularii* of *CTh* XI. i. 9 and 11 may also be municipal. EXCLUDED FROM ARMY AND CIVIL SERVICE: *CTh* VIII. ii. 1, 341, 3, 380. ELIGIBLE FOR CURIA: *CTh* VIII. iv. 8 §§1–2, 364, ii. 2, 370. PROHIBITION OF SLAVES: *CTh* VIII. ii. 5, 401. The allusion in this law to *tabularii* who were appointed *solidis provinciis* is puzzling; they can hardly have been the regular *tabularii* of the provincial *officia*, who were certainly established civil servants; perhaps they kept the accounts of the provincial *concilia*. DECURIONS IN MUNICIPAL OFFICES: *CTh* VIII. ii. 4, 384. CLERKS OF THE DEFENSOR: Just. *Nov.* xv §3, 535, *P. Oxy.* 1108. For *stationarii* see ch. XIV, n. 114, and also *CTh* IV. xiii. 2 and 3, 321 (octroi), VIII. v. 1, 315 (postal warrants).

90. *CTh* VIII. ix. 1, 335, XIV. i. 1, 360 (S), 2, 386, 3, 389, 4, 404, 5, 407, 6, 409, Cass. *Var.* V. 21, 22. For their earlier history see my *Studies in Roman Government and Law*, 153–8, and for their later functions and development Sinnigan, *The Officium of the Urban Prefecture*, 78 ff. SCRIBA IN AFRICA: Mansi, IV. 51, 167, 181; cf. also *CTh* XIV. i. 6, 409, in eos sane, qui contra divalia statuta venisse dicuntur, spectabilis vic. Afric. vindictam ferre curabit. 'QUAESTOR' OF PROCOS. ACHAEAE: *Not. Dig. Or.* xxi. 9. SCRIBA OF PRAETOR OF CONSTANTINOPLE: Joh. Lydus, *Mag.* II. 30.

91. Joh. Lydus, *Mag.* I. 14–5, II. 6, 13, III. 22.

92. Joh. Lydus, *Mag.* II. 12, III. 42, cf. 68 (Latin), III. 3, 12 (*formulae*).

93. For interdepartmental feuds see pp. 353–4, and Joh. Lydus, *Mag.* II. 10, III. 23, 40 (the master of the offices), III. 35 (the financial officials).

94. For the rigid rule of seniority, varied only by graft, see *CTh* VIII. i. 1, 319, dudum sanximus ut nullus ad singula officia administranda ambitione perveniat, vel maxime ad tabularios, nisi qui ex ordine vel corpore officii uniuscuiusque est; VI. xxix. 4, 359, cesset omnis ambitio atque suffragium in schola vestra, etenim cuncti ita agere debetis quatenus labore atque ordine ad cursum regendum et ad curas agendas iudicio scholae et ordinis merito dirigamini; VI. xxvii. 4, 382, sane sic militantibus probeque in actu rei publicae diversatis singulorum graduum quos meruerint non negamus accessum, ita ut ipsis quoque sit praece-

dentium ordo venerabilis; 14, 404, nullus de schola agentum in rebus de cetero locum mortui conetur invadere, sed is qui ordine stipendiorum et laborum merito ad gradum militiae sequebatur, statim atque illum fata subduxerint, in eius praemia percipienda succedat, omni subreptione cessante; 19, 417, ideoque sancimus ut nullus ex his emendicato suffragio ad honorem principatus audeat adspirare, nisi quem ordo militiae ac laborum testimonium ad hunc honoris gradum provexerit . . . hos sane qui quoquomodo per ambitionem sine ullo stipendiorum suffragio memoratam principatus adepti sunt dignitatem, post eos qui laborum merito consecuti sunt numerari decernimus; *Princeton Exp. Syria*, 20, 562, ὥστε ἕκαστον τῶν δουκικῶν καὶ σκρινιαρίων καὶ ὀφφικιαλίων τὴν ἐν ταῖς μάτριξιν ὀρδιινατίονα φυλάττειν, καὶ μηδένα βαθμὸν ἢ νῦν ἢ μετὰ ταῦτα ἐναλλάττειν παρὰ τὴν τάξιν τῆς μάτρικος. The allusions to *labores* in these laws probably mean no no more than regular attendance at the office, and would bar the promotion of notorious absentees. Further evidence of graft is afforded by letters written by great men to ministers of state on behalf of officials serving under them, e.g. Symm. *Ep.* I. 60, Romanus familiaris meus aulicis etiam nunc paret officiis utpote sacri administer aerarii, sed instrumenta probitatis in quemvis usum publici honoris excoluit. quare dignitas illi est promiscua cum plurimis, honestas aequa cum paucis. quod eo memorandum putavi ut a te quoque pro ratione vitae non pro gradu militiae censeatur, II. 63, IV. 37, Paulus amicus meus iamdiu aerario sacro militat, sed non pro gradu militiae spectandus tibi, nam probitate morum suorum mediocritatem vincit officii, nec despexeris hominem, si numerum stipendiorum eius examines; sed tardiores processus habet verecundia quae facit ut intra merita honoris sui haereat, VII. 123, in viro optimo et amicissimo meo Petrucio Romana simplicitas est. taceo quod illum longa militia et inculpata cohonestat, minora enim cetera facit morum eius inspectio, Lib. *Ep.* 82, 136, 1000, 1505.

95. See Seeck's articles in *PW.* s.v. *cancellarius* and *domesticus*. They are first attested in Amm. xv. vi. 1 (*domesticus* of *magister militum* in 355), *CIL* VI. 1770 (*cancellarius*, probably of *tribunus fori suarii*, in 363). FUNCTIONS OF CANCELLARIUS: Joh. Lydus, *Mag.* III. 37, Cass. *Var.* XI. 6, Agath. I. 19; OF DOMESTICUS: *CJ* I. li. 4, 404, domesticus iudicis a publicis actibus arceatur, Malchus, 16, τοὺς προαγωγέας τῶν λημμάτων τῆς ἀρχῆς, οὓς δομεστίκους καλοῦσι 'Ρωμαῖοι. PURCHASES AND MARRIAGES: *CTh* III. vi. 1+VIII. xv. 6, 380, *CJ* I. liii. 1, 528 (*domestici* of provincial governors). PROHIBITION OF OUTSIDERS: *CTh* I. xxxiv. 3, 423, nullus iudicum ad provinciam sibi commissam quemquam secum ducere audeat, cui domestici vel cancellarii nomen imponat, nec profectum ad se undecumque suscipiat, ne famae nota cum bonorum publicatione plectatur. periculo enim primatium officii cancellarios sub fide gestorum electos iudicibus adplicari iubemus, ita ut post depositam administrationem per continuum triennium nec militiam deserant et provincialibus praesentiam sui exhibeant, quo volentibus sit accusandi eos facilitas. The last clause implies that *cancellarii* were to be drawn from the *officium*, and the Justinianic version (*CJ* I. li. 8) adds 'ex eodem officio'. It is also implied in *CTh* VIII. i. 16, 417, that *domestici* were normally members of the *officium* and Justinian's version (*CJ* I. li. 6) again adds 'officiis eorum connumeratus'. Symmachus mentions two of his *domestici*, both civil servants; Asellus evidently served him as urban prefect in 384–5 (*Ep.* IX. 57, cum igitur Asellus domesticus noster in urbanis castris militiae stipendia sine offensione confecerit), Firmus (*Ep.* III. 67, Firmum domesticum meum militiae stipendiis cum honestate perfunctum) presumably when he was proconsul of Africa in 373–5: both men must have been comparatively junior when chosen as *domestici*, for the letters, written on their final retirement from their official

career, are of much later date. CANCELLARII OF PPO OR.: Joh. Lydus, *Mag.* III. 36–7; OF PPO AFR.: *CJ* I. xxvii. 1 §21, 534 (grouped with *consiliarii* above the *officium* proper); OF PPO ITAL.: Cass. *Var.* XI. 6 (personal choice, not by seniority). PROVINCIAL CANCELLARII IN ITALY: Cass. *Var.* XII. 1, cf. I. 35, XI. 10, 14, 36–7, 39, XII. 3, 10, 12, 14–5. Further references to *domestici* include Isid. Pel. *Ep.* I. 300 (of *PPO*, the sole allusion), Proc. *BV* I. iv. 7, Joh. Ant. 201. 6 (of *mag. mil.*), Amm. XXX. ii. 11 (of *mag. off.*), XXVIII. vi. 21, Orosius, VII. xlii. 11 (of *comes Africae*), *A.C.Oec.* I. iv. pars ii. 224–5 (of *praep. sac. cub.*, *mag. off.* and quaestor), Malalas, 410 (of *praep. sac. cub.*), *V. Hypatii*, 74, cf. 72 (of *cubicularius*), Th. II, *Nov.* xxi, 441 (of *tribunus scholae*), *CJ* I. xlii. 2, XII. xxxvii. 19 pr. §4 (491–518) (of other tribunes), *CTh* VI. xxviii. 8, 435 (of *principes*). *Cancellarii* are also recorded in *CIL* XI. 317, VI. 8401 (*PPO Ital.* and *PU Rom.*, both late sixth century), *IGLS* 687 (*PPO Or.*, A.D. 422), *V. Germani*, 38 (*mag. mil.*), *IGLS* 530 (*comes Orientis*). The *domestici* of military officers are more prominent, the *cancellarii* of civil, but both categories seem to have possessed both officials, e.g. the *dux Libyae* in *SEG* IX. 356 §14, and provincial governors in *CJ* I. li. 3, 399. The *domesticus* is conspicuously absent from the African prefecture in *CJ* I. xxvii. 1, 534, and from the Eastern and Italian prefectures in Lydus and Cassiodorus, but this may be because he was a strictly personal assistant; he is attested once for a praetorian prefect (see above).

96. For decrepit seniors see *CTh* VI. xxvii. 16, 413, 19, 417, *CJ* XII. xx. 5 §2 (457–70), Joh. Lydus, *Mag.* III. 9.

97. PRICE OF PROBATORIAE: Joh. Lydus, *Mag.* III. 67. ENTRY FEES: *CJ* XII. xix. 7 §2, 444. For purchase of places in the palatine ministries see nn. 17, 22, 28–9. For the same practice in the praetorian prefecture see Joh. Lydus, III. 66, εἰκότως οὖν οὐδεὶς ἐπὶ στρατείαν ἀπήγγελλε, τὸ πρὶν εἰωθὸς ὑπὲρ χιλίους κατ᾽ ἔτος ἕκαστον ταχυγράφους στρατευομένους τοῖς παυομένοις τῶν πόνων καὶ μάλιστα τῷ λεγομένῳ ματρικουλαρίῳ—ἀντὶ τοῦ τῶν καταλόγων φύλακι—πόρον οὐ μικρὸν περιποιεῖν. This appears to mean that in the good old days the great influx of recruits used to enrich the officials who retired and in particular the establishment officer. This implies the same system as prevailed in the *sacra scrinia*, where retiring clerks sold their places to newcomers, who also had to pay a fee to the establishment officer.

98. Proc. *HA* xxiv. 30–1, *CJ* XII. xix. 11 (492–7), maxime cum viros etiam pro tempore spectabiles eorundem proximos scriniorum, si quis eorum ante completum proximatus actum morte praeventus sit, ad heredes successoresque suos residui temporis proximatus solacia sine quadam imminutione transmittere non dubitetur. Cf. the more generous rule for *domestici*; *CTh* VI. xxiv. 11, 432, *CJ* XII. xvii. 4 (527–534).

99. SINECURES: Joh. Lydus, Mag. III. 21, μετὰ δὲ τὸν αβ ἄκτις ὁ ῥεγενδάριος ἐπὶ τῆς φροντίδος τῶν συνθημάτων τοῦ δημοσίου δρόμου τεταγμένος ἔτι καὶ νῦν λέγεται μέν, πράττει δὲ οὐδέν, τοῦ μαγίστρου τῆς αὐλῆς τὴν ὅλην ὑφελομένου τοῦ πράγματος ἐξουσίαν. μεθ᾽ ὃν οἱ τῶν διοικήσεων κοῦρα ἐπιστολάρουμ, οἳ τὰς μὲν ἐπὶ τοῖς δημοσίοις φοιτώσας ψήφους γράφουσι μόνον, τὸ λοιπὸν καταφρονούμενοι· οἱ δὲ λεγόμενοι τρακτευταί, τὴν ἐγνωσμένην αὐτοῖς διδασκαλίαν ὑποτιθέντες τῷ προστάγματι, τὴν ὅλην ὑφήρπαζον ἐξουσίαν, μάλιστα ἐξ ὅτου τὴν ἀρχὴν ἑαυτοῖς ἐθάρρουν περιποιεῖν οἱ σκρινιάριοι.

100. ABSENTEEISM: *CTh* VII. xii. 2, 379, VI. xxvii. 15, 412, *CJ* XII. vii. 2 §2, 474, xvii. 3, c. 450. EUSEBIUS: Symm. *Ep.* IV. 43, IX. 59.

101. EGERSIUS: *V. Hypatii*, 117–8. PLURALISM: *CJ* XII. xxxiii. 5, 524.

102. For *sportulae* see pp. 467–8 (financial), pp. 496–9 (judicial). For financial extortion see pp. 457–8 and for corrupt drafting of illegal petitions p. 410.

103. THEODERIC'S PENSIONS: Proc. *HA* xxvi. 27–8.

104. Majorian (*Nov.* ii §2) contrasts the 'humilis notusque compulsor' of the provincial office with 'canonicarios superioris militiae auctoritate terribiles et in provincialium viscera et damna desaevientes'.

105. The double fine on the magistrate and his *officium* is almost standard in the sanctions of the Codes. For the role of the *officium* as a check on their chief see especially *CTh* i. vi. 9, 385, si quis igitur iudicum fuerit repertus, qui supercilium suum principali aestimet iudicio praeferendum, quinque libras auri eius officium, nisi formam nostrae sanctionis suggesserit, decem ipse fisci viribus inferre cogatur; VII. xvii. 1, 412, etiam sublimitatis tuae officio quinquaginta libras auri condemnationi subiciendo, si non per singulos annos aut conpletum numerum aut certe neglegentia praetermissum magisteriae potestati suggesserit; IX. xl. 15, 392, officia vero eorundem isdem, quibus iudices sui, dispendiis subiacebunt, si in suggestione cessaverint ac non praeceptum legis ingesserint atque iniecta manu, ne rei auferantur, obstiterint ac nisi id quod fuerit constitutum in effectum exsecutionemque perduxerint; XI. xxix. 5, 374, quod si qui iudicum posthac non ita observaverit cuncta in relationibus dirigendis, quae iam pridem statuta sunt, eo crimine tenebitur una cum officio, quod ordinem servandorum suggerere neglexerit, quo tenentur, qui sacrilegium admiserint; xxx. 34, 364, ipse quidem notabili sententia reprehensus X librarum auri condemnatione quatietur, officium vero eius, quod non suggesserit nec commonuerit de relationis necessitate, viginti libris auri fiat obnoxium; XIII. v. 16, 380, apparitione quoque sua ultimo supplicio deputanda, cuius monitio hanc debet sollicitudinem sustinere, ut iudices prava forsitan indignatione succensos ab inlicitis tempestiva suggestione deducat; XIV. iii. 21, 403, quod si non statim officium gravitatis tuae in ipsis inceptis occurrerit, sed in suggestione cessaverit, in singulis familiis librarum auri decem multa feriatur; XVI. v. 46, 409, officium quoque suum, quod saluti propriae contempta suggestione defuerit, punitis tribus primatibus condemnatione viginti librarum auri plectendum.

XVII. THE ARMY (p. 608)

The standard work on the later Roman army is R. Grosse, *Römische militär-geschichte von Gallienus bis zum Beginn der byzantinischen Themenverfassung*, Berlin, 1920. On the early development of the army the latest book is D. van Berchem, *L'armée de Dioclétien et la réforme constantinienne*, Paris, 1952. For the sixth century army there is a useful article by A. Muller, 'das Heer Justinians', *Philologus*, LXXI (1912), 101–38, and for Egypt, J. Maspéro, *Organisation militaire de l'Égypte byzantine*, Paris, 1912.

1. See pp. 52–60.

2. See pp. 97–101. In Isauria the offices of *dux* or *comes rei militaris* and *praeses* seem to have been generally united from the middle of the fourth century at

least (Amm. XIX. xiii. 2, *ILS* 740, *Not. Dig. Or.* xxix), but were not formally amalgamated until 535 (Just. *Nov.* xxvii). Military and civil powers may also have been regularly united in Mauretania Caesariensis (*Not. Dig. Occ.* xxx). In Arabia, however, the union (*Not. Dig. Or.* xxxvii) was temporary; there is a separate governor in Hierocles (721.12), Just. *Nov.* viii, notitia, 535, and Nov. cii, 536. In Tripolitania again there was a temporary union in 393 (*CTh* XII. i. 133, duci et correctori limitis Tripolitani); by 399 there was a separate *praeses* again (*CTh* XI. xxx. 59, cf. *Not. Dig. Occ.* i. 100, xxxi). For later combinations of powers in Egypt and Asia Minor see pp. 280–2.

3. See pp. 124–6.

4. *Not. Dig. Or.* v–ix, xxviii–xlii. VICARII OF MAGISTRI MILITUM: *CTh* XV. xi. 1, Mauriano com. domestic. et vices ag. mag. mil., 414; *A.C.Oec.* I. iv. pars ii. 200, Flavius Titus gloriosissimus comes devotissimorum domesticorum, implens locum magistri militiae potestatis; Sev. *Ep.* I. 15, 45 (τοποτηρητής of *mag. mil. Or.*), *Coll. Avell.* 186, una cum magistri militum vicario Candido comite (at Thessalonica; he was presumably *vicarius* of the *mag. mil. Illyr*). INCREASE IN MILITARY COMMANDS: *CJ* XII. lix. 10, notitia, 472. CONTROL OF MAGISTRI OVER DUCES AND LIMITANEI: *CTh* VII. xvii. 1, 412, Th. II, Nov. iv, 438, xxiv, 443. POWERS OF MAGISTER OFFICIORUM: Th. II, *Nov.* xxiv, 443; cf. ch. XIV, n. 41, for later conflicts of jurisdiction with the *magistri militum*.

5. *Not. Dig. Occ.* v–vii, xxiv–xlii; see Appendix II, Table IV.

6. *Numerus* had in the Principate been used technically for irregular barbarian formations, as opposed to the regular *cohortes* and *alae* (see G. L. Cheesman, *The Auxilia of the Roman Imperial Army*, 85 ff.) and one of the later *numeri* in Britain (*Not. Dig. Occ.* xl. 47, numeri Maurorum Aurelianorum) is evidently such a unit which had survived, but the others (xl. 22–31, xxviii. 13, 15, 20, 21, and xxxv. 32 in Raetia) bear titles common among formations of later date. For the general use of *numerus* see *Not. Dig. Or.* xviii. 5, *Occ.* vii. 1, and inscriptions and literary authorities.

7. Cohors XI Chamavorum and Ala I Iberorum (*Not. Dig. Or.* xxxi. 61 and 46) are recorded under Diocletian in *P. Beatty Panop.* 2, lines 292 and 37, and this increases the probability that the other barbarian cohorts and *alae* recorded in the oriental ducates in the Notitia (Abasgi, Alamanni, Franci, Iuthungi, Quadi, Sarmatae, Sugambri, Tzanni, Vandali, see the indices of *alae* and *cohortes* in Seeck's edition) date from Diocletian. For Constantine and the barbarians see p. 98.

8. SUBSIDIES: Amm. XXV. vi. 10, nos autem Saracenos ideo patiebamur infestos quod salaria muneraque plurima a Iuliano ad similitudinem praeteriti temporis accipere vetiti, questique apud eum solum audierant, imperatorem bellicosum et vigilantem ferrum habere non aurum, Proc. *BP* I. xix. 32, τότε δὴ ὁ βασιλεὺς οὗτος αὐτοῖς τε καὶ Βλέμυσιν ἔταξε δίδοσθαι ἀνὰ πᾶν ἔτος ῥητόν τι χρυσίον ἐφ᾿ ᾧ μηκέτι γῆν τὴν Ῥωμαίων λῄσωνται; Th. II, *Nov.* xxiv §2, 443, de Saracenorum vero foederatorum aliarumve gentium annonariis alimentis nullam penitus eos decerpendi aliquid vel auferendi licentiam habere concedimus; Proc. *BV* II. xxi. 17 (Antalas, a Moorish chief, rebels because τὰς σιτήσεις αἷς αὐτὸν βασιλεὺς ἐτετιμήκει Σολόμων ἀφείλετο), *BG* III. xxxiii. 8–9 (the Gepids ravage Roman territory, διὸ δὴ βασιλεὺς αὐτοῖς τὰς συντάξεις οὐκέτι ἐδίδου ἅσπερ εἴθιστο σφᾶς ἀνέκαθεν πρὸς Ῥωμαίων κομίζεσθαι). INSIGNIA: Proc. *BV* I. xxv. 3–7 (Moors), *Aed.* III. i. 17–23 (Armenian satraps), Malalas, 412–3, Agath. III. 15 (Lazi). PHYLARCHS: Malchus, 1 (Amorcesus asks Leo Ῥωμαίοις ὑπόσπονδος γενέσθαι καὶ

φύλαρχος τῶν κατὰ Πετραίαν ὑπὸ Ῥωμαίοις ὄντων Σαρακηνῶν, i.e. of Palestine III), Cyr. Scyth. V. Euthymii, 10 (Aspebetus), Proc. BP I. xix. 10 (Justinian appoints Abocharabus φύλαρχον τῶν ἐν Παλαιστίνῃ Σαρακηνῶν); cf. xvii. 46, οὐδεὶς δὲ οὔτε Ῥωμαίων στρατιωτῶν ἄρχων, οὓς δοῦκας καλοῦσιν, οὔτε Σαρακηνῶν τῶν Ῥωμαίοις ἐνσπόνδων ἡγούμενος, οἳ φύλαρχοι ἐπικαλοῦνται; Malalas, 435 (Justinian writes τοῖς δουξὶ Φοινίκης καὶ Ἀραβίας καὶ Μεσοποταμίας καὶ τοῖς τῶν ἐπαρχιῶν φυλάρχοις), 446 (the phylarch of Palestine), Just. Nov. cii §1, 536 (the moderator of Arabia is to yield μήτε τῷ περιβλέπτῳ δουκὶ μήτε τῷ φυλάρχῳ), Ed. iv §2 (555–6, the governor of Phoenice Libanensis to yield μήτε τοῖς περιβλέπτοις δουξὶ μήτε τοῖς λαμπροτάτοις φυλάρχοις). CROCUS: Epit. Caes. xli. 3. MAVIA: Soc. v. 1, cf. IV. 36, Soz. VII. 1, cf. VI. 38; cf. Amm. XXXI. xvi. 5.

9. See pp. 156–8.

10. FOEDERATI PROMOTED TO AUXILIA: Orosius, VII. xl. 7, cum barbaris quibusdam qui quondam in foedus recepti atque in militiam allecti Honoriaci vocabantur. For the drafting of limitanei into the comitatus under Honorius see Appendix II. For the disbanding of the surviving limitanei see V. Severini, 20, per idem tempus quo Romanum constabat imperium multorum milites oppidorum pro custodia limitis publicis stipendiis alebantur, qua consuetudine desinente simul militares turmae sunt deletae cum limite. Batavino utcumque numero perdurante, ex quo perrexerant quidam ad Italiam extremum stipendium commilitonibus allaturi, cf. 4, for the troops at Favianae.

11. SCHOLAE: Not. Dig. Or. xi. 3–10, Occ. ix. 3–8. STRENGTH: Proc. HA xxiv. 15 (3500 for 7 regiments). UNDER CONSTANTINE: CTh XIV. xvii. 9, 389, annonas civicas in urbe Constantinopolitana scholae scutariorum et scutariorum clibanariorum divi Constantini adseruntur liberalitate meruisse. Lact. Mort. Pers. xix. 6, Daia vero sublatus nuper a pecoribus et silvis, statim scutarius, continuo protector, mox tribunus, implies that the Scutarii were a select corps under Diocletian. SERGIUS AND BACCHUS: Anal. Boll. XIV (1895), 375–7. UNDER CONSTANTIUS II, ETC.: Amm. XIV. vii. 9, XVI. iv. 1, XX. viii. 13, XXVII. x. 12 (Scutarii and Gentiles), XXII. xi. 2, XXV. x. 9, XXVI. i. 4 (I and II Scutarii), XIV. xi. 21, XXVII. ii. 6 (Armaturae), XXXI. xii. 16 (Sagittarii); there are many other references to Scutarii. CANDIDATI: Amm. XV. v. 16, XXV. iii. 6, XXXI. xiii. 14, xv. 8, Jerome, V. Hilar. 22; they do not appear in the Notitia as a separate corps, and were probably a select group of scholares; under Justinian the militiae of candidatus and scholaris were held in plurality by ancient custom (CJ XII. xxxiii. 5 §4, 524). From Const. Porph. Cer. I. 86 it appears that the candidati numbered forty.

12. For Sergius and Bacchus see n. 11. Tribunes of the scholae named by Ammianus include Agilo and Scudilo (XIV. x. 8), both Alamans, Bainobaudes (XIV. xi. 14), Mallobaudes (XIV. xi. 21), Arinthaeus (XV. iv. 10), Malarich (XV. v. 6), Nestica (XVII. x. 5), Gomoarius (XXI. viii. 1), Balchobaudes (XXVII. ii. 6), Barzimeres (XXX. i. 11), and Bacurius (XXXI. xii. 16), an Iberian; as against these are Valentinian (XXV. x. 9) and Equitius (XXVI. i. 4), both Pannonians, and Romanus and Vincentius (XXII. xi. 2); but Roman names are not decisive, cf. Silvanus the Frank (XV. v. 33). Among other ranks Gaudentius (XXVI. v. 14), Salvius and Lupicinus (XXVII. x. 12) and Sallustius (XXIX. i. 16) as against Natuspardo (XXVII. xi. 16) and the candidatus Laniogaisus (XV. v. 16); cf. also the unnamed Alaman deserter in XVI. xii. 2 and another unnamed Alaman in XXXI. x. 3, and a Frankish candidatus in Jerome, V. Hilar. 22. JULIAN'S OFFER: Amm. XX. viii. 13. ARMENIANS: Proc. HA xxiv. 16.

13. THEODERIC AND THE SCHOLAE: Proc. *HA* xxvi. 27–8. From Cass. *Var.* vi. 6 it appears that the corps was not formally disbanded. THE DECAY OF THE SCHOLAE IN THE EAST: Proc. *HA* xxiv. 17, Agath. v. 15.

14. EXCLUSION OF SLAVES: *CTh* VII. xiii. 8, 380, 11, 382, xviii. 9 §3, 396, *CJ* XII. xxxiii. 6, 529. EXCEPTIONAL ENROLMENT: Symm. *Ep.* VI. 58, 62, 64, *CTh* VII. xiii. 16, 406. FREEDMEN: *CTh* IV. x. 3, 426. INNKEEPERS, ETC.: *CTh* VII. xiii. 8, 380, cf. *CJ* XII. xxxiv. 1 (528–9). CURIALES: *CJ* XII. xxxiii. 2 (285–293), *CTh* XII. i. 10, 325, 13, 326, VII. xiii. 1 (326–54), XII. i. 38, 357 (S) (condoned after 5 years' service), 56, 362 (S) (condoned after 10 years' service), VII. i. 6, 368 (condoned after 5 years), XII. i. 88, 382 (condoned after 5 years), 9, 383 (condoned after 15 years), VII. ii. 1, 383, 2, 385, XII. i. 113, 386, 154, 397, VII. xx. 12, 400, XII. i. 147 and 181, 416 and *CJ* XII. xxxiii. 4 (472–3). COHORTALES: *CTh* VIII. iv. 4, 349, vii. 12+13, 372, 19, 397, VII. xx. 12 §3, 400, VIII. iv. 28, 423, *CJ* XII. xxxiii. 4 (472–3). COLONI: *CJ* XII. xxxiii. 3 (395–402), cf. XI. xlviii. 18, 426 and XII. xliii. 1, nullus tiro vagus aut veteranus aut censibus obnoxius ad militiam accedat, which is Justinian's adaptation of *CTh* VII. xiii. 6 §1, 370.

15. MARCIAN: Evagr. II. 1. LAW OF 406: *CTh* VII. xiii. 17. SONS OF SOLDIERS AND VETERANS: *CTh* VII. xxii. 1, 313 (S), 2, 326, 5, 333, 4 (= XII. i. 35), 343 (S), VII. i. 5, 364, 8, 365, xxii. 7, 365, 8, 372, 9 and 10, 380, cf. 12, 398, xx. 12, 400. Gregory Nazianzen asked Ellebich, the *magister militum*, for the release of the son of a soldier who had become a reader in the church (*Ep.* 225). Cf. also *P. Abinn.* 19 (cited in n. 20). MARTIN: Sulp. Sev. *V. Mart.* 2; cf. *CTh* VII. xxii. 5, 333, veteranorum filii vel eorum, qui praepositi vel protectores fuerunt, vel ceterorum, qui quemlibet gradum militiae tenuerunt. VAGI: *CTh* VII. xviii. 10, 400, protectores, qui ad inquisitionem vagorum per provincias diriguntur, nullas in retinendis fugitivis dumtaxat indigenis iniurias possessoribus parent, quia hoc illis tantum permittitur, ut desertores veteranorum filios ac vagos et eos, quos militiae origo consignat, ad dilectum iuniorum provocent; 17, 412, omnes tribunos, qui per Africam vagorum et desertorum requirendorum sumpserunt officium; cf. VII. xiii. 6, 370, VIII. ii. 3, 380, VII. xx. 12, 400. A *protector* is sent to round up sons of veterans in *CTh* VII. xxii. 2, 326.

16. CONSCRIPTION ANNUAL: Amm. XXXI. iv. 4, ut conlatis in unum suis et alienigenis viribus invictum haberet exercitum et pro militari supplemento quod provinciatim annuum pendebatur thesauris accederet auri cumulus magnus; cf. *CTh* VII. xviii. 14, 403, hac tamen condicione servata, ut ab his iunioribus, qui proxima indictione praesenti tempore conferuntur, supplicio temperetur, quia per provinciales intra praescriptum legibus tempus ad ea signa, quibus destinati fuerant, redhibendi sunt, ne possessores redhibitionis damna percellant propter eos, qui necdum paene auspicati militiam fugerunt. sed ut in his patientiam tenemus, ita omnes, qui ultra memoratam indictionem et nostrae beneficia sanctionis castra et militiam deseruere, condemnationibus obnoxios esse praecipimus. COMMUTATION OF RECRUITS: *CTh* VII. xiii. 2, 370, domum nostram ad exhibenda tironum corpora per eas provincias, a quibus corpora flagitantur, nolumus perurgueri: ceterum sinimus conveniri, in quibus pretia postulantur, ita ut ex certa praebitione reditum vicem concessionis istius repensemus; 7 §1, 375, quem ordinem, cum corpora postulantur, conveniet custodiri. sin vero aurum fuerit pro tironibus inferendum, unumquemque pro modo capitationis suae debitum redhibere oportet. CURIAL CONSCRIPTION OFFICERS: *Chr.* 1. 466, ἐπὶ παρουσίᾳ Θέων[ος] ἐπιμελητοῦ τιρόνων τῆς αὐτῆς Ἡρακ-

[λ]εοπολιτῶν (πόλεως); Theon and his colleague Cyril are not specifically called decurions, but evidence for the responsibility of the councils is afforded by *Chr.* I. 465, βουλῆς οὔσης, πρντ' 'Ασκληπιάδου 'Αχιλλέως γυμ' βουλ', Εὐτρύγιος ἀπὸ λογιστῶν εἶπεν· τῆς ἐξουσίας τοῦ κυρίου μου τοῦ λαμ' δουκὸς Φλ' 'Αρτεμίου εὐτυχῶς ἐπιδημησάσης τοῖς αὐτόθι, ἀνεδιδάξαμεν αὐτοῦ τὴν ἀρετήν, ὡς τῶν νεολέκτων τῶν στρατευθέντων ὑφ' ἡμῶν ἐκ παραλογισμοῦ ἀνενεγκόντων ὡς μὴ πληρωθέντων τοῦ συμφώνου τοῦ πρὸς αὐτούς, etc., and *P. Oxy.* 1190 (a letter from the στρατηγός, that is *exactor civitatis*, of Oxyrhynchus to the two *praepositi* of the fifth *pagus*, stating that the *dux* has demanded recruits and instructing them to see that they are produced). Cf. *P. Lips.* 34V, 62, for curial ὑποδεκταὶ χρυσοῦ τιρόνων. Arrears of recruits were collected by official *exactores* (*P. Lips.* 55, Φλαονίῳ 'Ισιδώρῳ βενεφικιαρίῳ τάξεως ἡγεμονίας Θηβαίδος ἀπαιτητῇ τιρόνων Κωνσταντίνης καὶ Διοκλητιανοῦ πόλεως.). CAPITULA: *CTh* VII. xiii. 7 §1, 375, illud etiam similiter definitum est, ut ii tantum a consortibus segregentur, quorum iugatio ita magna est, ut accipere non possit adiunctum, cum pro suo numero in exhibendo tirone solus ipse respondeat. inter quos vero possessionis exiguae necessitas coniunctionem postulat, functionis annorum et praebitionis vicissitudo servetur, quippe ut senatores ceterique, qui primo anno et suo et consortis nomine tironem dederint, insequenti vice habeantur immunes illique in praebitione succedant, a quorum conventione fuerit ante cessatum. quem ordinem, cum corpora postulantur, conveniet custodiri. sin vero aurum fuerit pro tironibus inferendum, unumquemque pro modo capitationis suae debitum redhibere oportet; cf. XI. xxiii. 1, 361, protostasiae munus hactenus senatores inposita necessitate sustentent, ut isdem senatorum census implendae necessitatis contemplatione socientur nec cuiusquam alterius iuga aut capita senatorum censibus adgregentur, cum protostasiae munus ita debeant sustinere, ut ad eum numerum, quem ipsi censuali sorte sustentant, senatorum tantum censibus nexis eandem necessitatem debeant explicare; xvi. 14, 382, totius capitulariae sive, ut rem quam volumus intellegi communi denuntiatione signemus, temonariae functionis fieri iubemus exsortes, ita ut eorum uniuscuiusque adscriptio excusetur, non ut onus alterius excipiat, si etiam eius summae sit, ut recipere possit adiunctos, sed aut suum tantum munus agnoscat aut, si conplacito opus est, magis alteri ipse societur quam eidem alter adnectatur. Other allusions to the system are *CJ* x. lxii. 3, 285–93, xlii. 8 (293–305), *Acta Maximiliani*, i. 1, *CTh* XI. xvi. 6, 346, VI. xxxv. 3, 352 (S), XI. xxiii. 2, 362, VII. xviii. 3, 380, XI. xvi. 15, 382, 18, 390, xxiii. 3 and 4, 396, VI. xxvi. 14, 412 (S). For villages see *Chr.* I. 466–7.

17. VALENS' LAW: *CTh* VII. xiii. 7, 375, cf. *Chr.* I. 466 for the villager. For the abuse of the system see Anon. *de rebus bell.* iv, Soc. IV. 34. RECRUITS TO BE CENSITI: *CTh* VII. xiii. 6, 370.

18. LEVIES FROM HONORATI: *CTh* VII. xiii. 15, 402, 18, 407 (commuted), 20, 410 (commuted for 30 solidi), XI. xviii. 1, 412 (S) (commuted, list of exemptions), VI. xxvi. 14, 412 (exemption), xxx. 20, 413 (exemption), xxiii. 2, 423 (exemption), VII. xiii. 22, 428 (exemption), Val. III, *Nov.* vi. 3, 444 (details of commuted levy).

19. AGE: *CTh* VII. xxii. 2, 326 (20–25), xiii. 1, 326–54 (19), xxii. 4 (=XII. i. 35), 343 (S), iam dudum sanximus, ut veteranorum filii, qui post sedecim annos militiae munus subire non possunt vel armis gerendis habiles non exstiterint, curiis mancipentur. As decurions were not enrolled under 18 or recruits under 19, 'post sedecim annos' must mean sixteen years after they became liable to the call-up. HEIGHT: *CTh* VII. xiii. 3, 367, cf. i. 5, xxii. 8; for the old limit see Veg. I. 5. BRANDING: *Acta Maximiliani*, i. 5, Veg. I. 8, Aug. *c. Ep. Parm.* II. 29, cf. *CTh* x. xxii. 4, 398, stigmata, hoc est nota publica, fabricensium brachiis

ad imitationem tironum infligatur, ut hoc modo saltem possint latitantes agnosci.

20. Veg. I. 7, dum indicti possessoribus tirones per gratiam aut dissimulationem probantium tales sociantur armis, quales domini habere fastidiunt. DECURIONS: *CTh* VII. xiii. 1 (326–54), ii. 1, 383, 2, 385. IDENTIFICATION DISC: *Acta Maximiliani* ii. 6, ego Christianus sum, non licet mihi plumbum collo portare. For *probatoriae* see n. 143. POSTING TO UNITS: *CTh* VII. xxii. 8, 372, etenim hi, quibus vel corporis robur vel statura defuerit, qui comitatensi digni possint esse militia, ripensi poterunt copulari (this law refers to sons of veterans), *CTh* VII. xiii. 7 §3, 375, ipsorum etiam, qui militaturi sunt, privilegiis accedentibus facilius devotio provocatur, videlicet ut universi, qui militaria sacramenta susceperint, eo anno, quo fuerint numeris adgregati, si tamen in suscepto labore permanserint, immunes propriis capitibus mox futuri sint. conpletis vero quinque annorum stipendiis qui comitatensibus numeris fuerit sociatus, patris quoque et matris nec non et uxoris suae capitationem meritis suffragantibus excusabit. ii vero, qui in ripa per cuneos auxiliaque fuerint constituti, cum proprio capite uxorem suam tantum post quinque annos, ut dictum est, praestent immunem, si tamen eos censibus constiterit adtineri (ordinary conscripts), cf. P. *Abinn.* 19, υἱός ἐστιν στρατιώτου καὶ ἔδωκεν τῷ ὄνομα αὐτοῦ ἵνα στρατευθῇ. ἐὰν οὖν δύνῃ παραφῖναι αὐτὸν ὀπίσω, ἔργον καλὸν ποιεῖς . . . ἐὰν δὲ πάλιν στρατευθῇ ἵνα συντήρῃς αὐτὸν ἵνα μὴ ἔλθῃ ἔξω μετὰ τῶν ἐκλεγωμένων ἐς κωμίδατον (letter to Abinnaeus, *praepositus* of an *ala* of *limitanei*). SONS OF EQUITES: *CTh* VII. xxii. 2 §§1–2, 326.

21. IMMUNITY FROM POLL TAX: *FIR* I². 93 (reading in line 13, ut idem milites nostri militiae quidem suae tempore quinque [m] < annorum stipendiis completis quattuor > capita iuxta statutum nostrum ex censu adque a praestationibus sollemnibus annonariae pensitationis excusent); *CTh* VII. xx. 4 pr. §3, 325, xiii. 6 pr., 370, 7 §3, 375.

22. SELF-MUTILATION: *CTh* VII. xxii. 1, 313 (S), xiii. 4, 367, 5, 368, 10, 381, Amm. XV. xii. 3. RECRUITS UNDER GUARD: *V. Pachomii*, 4, *Chr.* I. 469. DESERTION OF RECRUITS: *CTh* VII. xviii. 4, 380, 6, 382, 9 §1, 396, 14 §1, 403.

23. Amm. XV. xii. 3, cf. *CTh* VII. xiii. 5, *Ppo Gall.*, 368.

24. EXEMPTION OF RES PRIVATA: *CTh* VII. xiii. 2, 370, XI. xvi. 12, 380, VII. xiii. 12 and 14, 397; OF SENATORS: *CTh* VII. xiii. 13, 14, 397. For the annual conscription see n. 16. VALENS AND THE GOTHS: Amm. XXXI. iv. 4, Soc. IV. 34. SPECIAL LEVIES OF RECRUITS: Val. III, *Nov.* vi. 1, 440, reparandi feliciter exercitus cura conferre debere tirones possessorem censuimus: 2, 443. The latest Eastern laws are *CTh* XI. xxiii. 3 and 4, 396. THRACIAN RECRUITS: Pall. *Dial.* p. 57. SABA'S FATHER: Cyr. Scyth. *V. Sabae*, 1.

25. Amm. XX. iv. 4, illud tamen nec dissimulare potuit nec silere, ut illi nullas paterentur molestias qui relictis laribus Transrhenanis sub hoc venerant pacto ne ducerentur ad partes umquam Transalpinas.

26. PRISONERS: Zos. V. 26. DEDITICII: Amm. XX. viii. 13, *CTh* VII. xiii. 16, 406. LEVIES OF RECRUITS: Amm. XVII. xiii. 3, XXVIII. v. 4. LAETI: Pan. Lat. VIII. 21 §1, Amm. XVI. xi. 4, XX. viii. 13, Laetos quosdam cis Rhenum editam barbarorum progeniem, XXI. xiii. 16, Zos. II. 54, γένος ἕλκων ἀπὸ βαρβάρων, μετοικήσας δὲ εἰς Λετούς, ἔθνος Γαλατικόν. TERRAE LAETICAE: *CTh* XIII. xi. 10, 399, quoniam ex multis gentibus sequentes Romanam felicitatem se ad nostrum

imperium contulerunt, quibus terrae laeticae administrandae sunt, nullus ex his agris aliquid nisi ex nostra adnotatione mereatur. PRAEFECTI LAETORUM: *CTh* VII. XX. 10, 369, si quis praepositus fuerit aut fabricae aut classi aut laetis, *Not. Dig. Occ.* xlii. 33–70. The Sarmatian *laeti* were probably settled in Italy by Constantine (Anon. Val. 32, sed servi Sarmatarum adversum omnes dominos rebellarunt, quos pulsos Constantinus libenter accepit, et amplius trecenta milia hominum mixtae aetatis et sexus per Thraciam, Scythiam, Macedoniam, Italiamque divisit). ALAMANS IN ITALY: *CTh* VII. XX. 12, 400, quisquis igitur laetus Alamannus Sarmata vagus vel filius veterani aut cuiuslibet corporis dilectui obnoxius et florentissimis legionibus inserendus. *Laeti* are apparently alluded to as 'corpora publicis obsequiis deputata' in Sev. *Nov.* ii, 465.

27. Vitalianus, a soldier in the *auxilium palatinum* of the Heruli, was to all appearances a Roman (Amm. xxv. x. 9), and so was Vetranio, commander of the *legio comitatensis* of the Tzanni (Amm. xxv. i. 19). FRAOMARIUS: Amm. XXIX. iv. 7. THE GOTHS: Amm. XXXI. xvi. 8.

28. Amm. XIV. x. 8 (Latinus, etc.), XVI. xii. 2 (the deserter), XXXI. x. 3 (the Lentiensis), XXIX. iv. 7 (Hortarius).

29. Jerome, *V. Hilar.* 22, Amm. XVIII. ii. 2.

30. Amm. XV. v. 16.

31. *P. Beatty Panop.* 2 gives the following figures for *annona*, *stipendium*, *salgamum* and *donativa* for the birthday (22 Dec. 299) and *dies imperii* (20 Nov. 299) of Diocletian and for the third consulate of Constantius and Maximian (1 Jan. 300). I have added in the last two columns hypothetical analyses of the figures. It should be noted that the papyrus covers only payments made from 1 Feb. to 27 Feb. 300; other donatives and other instalments of *stipendium* and *annona* and *salgamum* were doubtless paid during the rest of the year.

	Lines	Unit	Nature of payment	Amount of payment	Number of recipients	Rate of payment
A	36 ff.	ala I Iberorum	stipendium, 1 Jan. 300	73,500 den.	367½	× 200
B	,,	,,	annona, 1 Sept.–31 Dec. 299	23,600 den.	354	× 66⅔
C	57 ff.	legio III Diocletiana	stipendium, 1 Jan. 300	343,300 den.	1,716½	× 200
D	161 ff.	equites sagittarii	donativum, 20 Nov. 299	302,500 den.	242	× 1,250
E	,,	,,	donativum, 22 Dec. 299	302,500 den.	242	× 1,250
F	168 ff.	ala II Herculia dromedariorum	donativum, 20 Nov. 299	53,750 den.	211	× 250
G	,,	,,	donativum, 22 Dec. 299	53,750 den.	211	× 250
H	180 ff.	vexillatio of legio II Traiana	donativum, 20 Nov. 299	1,386,250 den.	1,109	× 1,250
I	186 ff.	vexillatio of various Eastern legions	donativum, 20 Nov. 299	2,496,250 den.	1,981	× 1,250
J	192 ff.	,,	donativum, 22 Dec. 299	2,496,250 den.	1,981	× 1,250

Lines	Unit	Nature of payment	Amount of payment	Number of recipients	Rate of payment
K 197 ff.	praepositus of equites promoti of legio II Traiana	stipendium, 1 Jan. 300	18,000 den.	1	× 18,000
L „	„	donativum, 20 Nov. 299	2,500 den.	1	× 2,500
M „	„	donativum, 22 Dec. 299	2,500 den.	1	× 2,500
N 204 ff.	equites promoti of legio II Traiana	donativum, 1 Jan. 300	93,12 <5> den.	149	× 625
O 245 ff.	vexillatio of legio III Diocletiana	salgamum, 1 Sept.–31 Dec. 299	8,280 lb. oil and sext. salt.	1,035	× 8 per month
P 259 ff.	lanciarii of legio II Traiana	donativum, 20 Nov. 299	1,097,500 den.	878	× 1,250
Q „	„	donativum, 22 Dec. 299	1,097,500 den.	878	× 1,250
R 266 ff.	„	donativum, 1 Jan. 300	526,875 den.	843	× 625
S 285 ff.	„	salgamum, 1 Nov. and 31 Dec.	3,596 lb. oil and sext. salt.	899	× 4 per month
T 291 ff.	cohors XI Chamavorum	stipendium, 1 Jan. 300	65,500 den.	524	× 125
U „	„	annona, 1 Sept.–31 Dec. 299	32,866 den.	493	× 66⅔

An analysis of P–S and A–B and T–U shows that in the same regiment the number of recipients varied according to the type of payment, and perhaps to the period in which it was made. There might be more or less men on strength in different accounting periods (probably of four months). Some payments (perhaps *annona* and *salgamum*) might be made to all at a uniform rate per head. In others (certainly *stipendium* and probably *donativum*) N.C.O.s received multiple payments (1½ or 2 or more times as much as privates). It is also possible that some payments, e.g. *donativa,* were made only to men who had served some probationary period. Owing to these variables it is difficult to extract any certain rates of payment from the figures.

Donatives are the simplest. An officer received 2,500 denarii for the birthday or accession day of an Augustus (L,M). On the same occasions ordinary soldiers in legions and vexillations evidently received 1,250 denarii, for 1,250 is the highest common factor of D–E, H–J, P–Q, and the resulting strengths are in themselves plausible, and some of them prime numbers. A comparison of P–Q and R shows that the donative for the consulates of Caesars was half this rate, 625, and N, yielding a prime number, confirms this. F–G shows that *alae* (and cohorts) received a much lower donative; 250 is the only plausible figure, and this for a major occasion when front line troops got 1,250. Since 299 was not a quinquennial year the accession and birthday donatives must have been annual; the consular donatives would of course be occasional.

For *annona* the key is U, where the odd figure 32,866 can hardly represent anything but 493 men at 66⅔ denarii for the four monthly period, i.e. 200 denarii a year; the same rate is plausible in B. *Stipendium* was probably paid in three instalments as under the Principate (cf. *P. Oxy.* 1047, recording the payment to an officer of a *stipendium* of 36,000 denarii on 1 Sept. together with a donative of 2,500 denarii on 25 July for Constantine's *dies imperii*). A comparison of A–B and T–U suggests that *cohortales* received about twice as much in *stipendium* as in *annona,* and *alares* (being cavalrymen they were better paid) about three times as much: rates of 125 (i.e. 375 a year) for *cohortales* and 200 (i.e. 600 a year) for *alares* yield plausible strengths. For the *stipendium* of legionaries C appears to be decisive: any higher rate than 200 (600 a year) involves fractions less than a half, and so far as we know the half *stipendium* (for a *sesquiplicarius*) was the lowest fraction used.

32. *Ed. Diocl.* pr. PAY UNDER JULIAN: Amm. xx. viii. 8, cuius iracundiae nec dignitatum augmenta nec annuum merentis stipendium id quoque inopinum accessit, quod ad partes orbis eoi postremas venire iussi homines adsueti glacialibus terris, separandique liberis et coniugibus egentes trahebantur et nudi; cf. XVII. ix. 6, et erat ratio iusta querellarum. inter tot enim rerum probabilium cursus articulosque necessitatum ancipites sudoribus Gallicanis miles exhaustus nec donativum meruit nec stipendium iam inde ut Iulianus illo est missus, ea re quod nec ipsi quod daret suppetere poterat usquam nec Constantius erogari more solito permittebat; Greg. Naz. *Or.* IV. 82–4 (he speaks of gold, but this would be on the special occasions). The gold *stipendium* which Silvanus paid out in 355 in Constantius's name (Amm. xv. vi. 3) must have been a delayed tricennial donative of 353, and the gold *stipendium* which Valens was about to pay in 365 (Amm. XXVI. viii. 6) must likewise have been a delayed accession donative. A more doubtful case is the *stipendium* or *donativum* which Valentinian paid to the African troops (Amm. XXVIII. vi. 12, 17, 19); equally ambiguous are Ursulus's and Mamertinus's remarks (see n. 34). It is hard to prove that *stipendium* was not paid at any date, but certainly by Justinian's time pay was reckoned exclusively in *annonae* and *capitus* (e.g. in *CJ* I. xxvii. 1 and 2, 534).

33. ACCESSION DONATIVE: Amm. xx. iv. 18, Const. Porph. *Cer.* I. 91–4, Joh. Eph. *HE* III. 11. QUINQUENNIAL DONATIVE: Zach. Myt. *Chron.* VII. 8, Proc. *HA* xxiv. 27–9.

34. URSULUS: Amm. xx. xi. 5. MAMERTINUS: Pan. Lat. III. 1. VENUSTUS: Amm. XXVI. viii. 6. PALLADIUS: XXVIII. vi. 12. In Syn. *Ep.* 18, a decurion of Alexandria brings χρυσίον ὡς ὑμᾶς (i.e. to Pentapolis) νομὴν στρατιώταις.

35. These garments are often mentioned in records of the clothing levy, e.g. *P. Cairo Isid.* 54, *P. Oxy.* 1424, 1448, 1905, *P. Lips.* 59, 60, *PRG* v. 61, also in *Ed. Diocl.* xix. 1, 2, xxv. 28–30. For the responsibility of the *largitiones* see ch. XIII, n. 56. BOOTS: *PSI* 886 (levy), *CTh* XII. i. 37, 344 (calcarienses). COMMUTATION: *CTh* VII. vi. 4, 396, 5, 42?. RECRUITS' CLOTHING MONEY: *CTh* VII. xiii. 7 §2, 375, cf. *P. Lips.* 34V and 34–5.

36. See pp. 834–6.

37. For the *tribunus (comes) stabuli* see ch. XII, n. 16. STRATORES: *CTh* VI. xxxi. 1, 365, VIII. viii. 4, 386, Amm. XXIX. iii. 3, cf. XXX. v. 19 for a *strator* serving as an imperial groom under the *tribunus stabuli*. In the reign of Maurice Longinus *v.c. strator* carried an imperial decree to Italy (Greg. *Ep.* III. 61), and another *strator* was cured by Theodore of Syceon (*V. Theod. Syc.* 129). *Stratores* apparently held the usual noncommissioned grades (CIL v. 374, cent. stabuli dm., 1880, ducenario princeps stabuli dominici). COMMUTATION: *CTh* XI. xvii. 1, 367, XI. i. 29 and xvii. 2 and 3, 401; commutation had already begun under Constantius II (Pan. Lat. III. 9, ipso enim tempore levati equorum pretiis enormibus Dalmatae). The levy of horses is also mentioned in *CTh* XI. ix. 1, 323, XIII. v. 14, 371, XI. xvi. 12, 380. Horses were also obtained by special levies on *honorati*, *CTh* VI. xxxv. 2, 319 (S), XIII. iii. 2, 320 (S), VII. xxiii. 1, 369, XIII. v. 15, 379, VI. xxvi. 3, 382, 15, 410, VI. xxvi. 14 and XI. xviii. 1, 412, VI. xxiii. 2, 423.

38. For collection of *annona* see pp. 456 ff. *Actuarii* and *optiones* are often coupled together, e.g. *CTh* VII. iv. 24, 398, Marc. *Nov.* ii §3, 450, *CJ* x. xxii. 3, 456. From *CTh* VII. iv. 1, subscribendario et optione, it appears that *subscribendarius* was equivalent to *actuarius*, and from *CJ* I. xlii. 2, τοῦ ἀκτουαρίου καὶ τῶν ὀπτιόνων, XII. xxxvii. 19 pr. §4, ὑπομνηματοφυλάκων καὶ ὀπτιόνων, that actuaries and ὑπομνηματοφύλακες were identical. In *CTh* VIII. i. 3, 333, the *actuarius* is graded above the *annonarius*, who is probably equivalent to the *optio*. STATUS AND PAY OF ACTUARIES: *CTh* VIII. I. 3, 333, 5, 357, 10, 365; from XII. i. 125, 392, submoto privilegio militari, quo sibi actuarii blandiuntur, eum, qui evidenter ostenditur curiali patre genitus, mox necessariis atque origini suae debitis functionibus mancipari praecipimus, it would appear that *actuarii* were still not recognised as military personnel in 392, and this rule was confirmed in *CJ* XII. xlix. 9 (472–3).

39. DELIVERY OF ANNONA: *CTh* VII. iv. 15, 369, sicut fieri per omnes limites salubri prospectione praecipimus, species annonarias <in> vicinioribus limit-<um part>ibus a provincialibus ordinabis ad castra conferri. et in <ulterior-ibus> castris constituti milites duas alimoniarum partes ibidem de conditis sumant nec amplius quam tertiam partem ipsi vehere cogantur: this appears to be the sense of this corrupt law. Cf. P. *Abinn.* 26, οὕτως γὰρ ἐκέλευσεν ὁ κύριός μου ὁ δοὺξ ὅλας τὰς ἀννώνας τοῦ ἐνιαυτοῦ ἐγκλῖσαι ἐπὶ τὰ κάστρα ἐξ ἐντυχίας τῶν ἀκτουαρίων τῆς ἄνω Θηβαΐδος, καὶ ἐκέλευσεν μετὰ τὴν σύγκλισιν τοῦ σίτου ὀφφ' ἀποσταλῆναι καὶ συνθεωρῆσαι τὸν ἐν ἀθέτῳ σιτόκριθον (letter to Abinnaeus from his actuary; the rest of the letter is concerned with making the *exactor civitatis* and other curial officials complete their deliveries). DISTRIBUTION OF ANNONA: *CTh* VII. iv. 11, 364, susceptor antequam diurnum pittacium authenticum ab actuariis susceperit, non eroget. quod si absque pittacio facta fuerit erogatio, id quod expensum est damnis eius potius subputetur . . . . nec prius de horreis species proferantur et maxime capitationis, quam, ut dictum est, ad diem pittacia authentica fuerint prorogata; 13, 365, actuarii per singulos vel ut multum binos dies authentica pittacia prorogent, ut hoc modo inmissis pittaciis species capitum annonarumve ex horreis proferantur. quod nisi fuerit custoditum, actuarius et susceptor, sed et officium iudicantis, quod non institerit huic iussioni, statutae obnoxium tenebitur; 17, 377, fortissimi ac devotissimi milites, familiae quoque, sed et ceteri quibuscumque praediti dignitatibus annonas et capitum singulis diebus aut certe competenti tempore, id est priusquam annus elabatur, de horreis consequantur, aut si perceptionem suam ac si debitam studio voluerint protelare, id, quod competenti tempore minime perceperint, fisci nostri commodis vindicetur. Cf. 16, 368, which seems to give actuaries 30 days grace to issue overdue *pittacia*. PRAEPOSITI HORREORUM: *CTh* VII. iv. 1, 325, XII. i. 49, 361, vi. 5 and 8, 365, 24, 397, 33, 430. For *primipili* see p. 459.

40. RATIONS DRAWN FROM GRANARIES: *CTh* VIII. iv. 17, 385 (S), cum ante placuisset, ut a primipilaribus secundum dispositionem divi Gratiani species horreis erogandae comitatensibus militibus ex more deferrentur; cf. VIII. i. 10, 365 (actuaries of *palatini, comitatenses* and *pseudocomitatenses* draw their own rations *ex horreorum conditis*) and VII. iv. 5, 360 (S) (*expeditionalis annona* is drawn *ex horreis*). DELEGATORIAE AND OPINATORES: *CTh* VII. iv. 20, 393, nulli militarium pro his annonis quae in provinciis delegantur, repudiata ad tempus specierum copia et inopiae occasione captata pretia liceat postulare; 22, 396, neque scholae neque vexillationes comitatenses aut palatinae neque legiones ullae neque auxilia, qualeslibet ad provincias delegatorias de specierum praebitione pertu-lerint, audiantur, si pretia poscant ultra ea, quae generali lege divi patris senioris Valentiniani constituta sunt; v. 1, 399, opinatores, quibus species in diversis

provinciis delegantur, ut pretium maiore taxatione deposcant, contra omnem consuetudinem nullis consistentibus familiis excoctionem panis efflagitant; XI. vii. 16, 401, missi opinatores cum delegatoriis iudicibus eorumque officiis insistant, ut intra anni metas id quod debetur accipiant; nihil his sit cum possessore commune, cui non militem, sed exactorem, si sit obnoxius, convenit imminere; VII. iv. 26, 401, opinatoribus nullum sit cum provinciali commercium, ita ut a iudicibus vel officio provinciali omnis summa debiti postuletur intra anni spatium conferenda; XI. i. 34 and XII. i. 186, 429. *Opinatores* are frequently mentioned as receiving *stipendium, annona*, etc., for their units in *P. Beatty Panop.* 2, lines 41, 166, 174, 184, 190, etc.; also in *P. Oxy.* 2114, Aug. *Ep.* 268, and *CTh* VII. iv. 34, 414.

41. PRAETORIAN PREFECTS: Amm. XIV. x. 3–4 (354), XVII. viii. 1 (358), XVIII. ii. 3–4 (359). DEPUTY PRAETORIAN PREFECTS: *CJ* XII. viii. 2 §4, 441, cur enim aut vir magnificus Germanus magister militum vacans appellatur, cui bellum contra hostes mandavimus? aut cur excellentissimus Pentadius non egisse dicitur praefecturam, cuius illustribus cincti dispositionibus vice praetorianae praefecturae miles in expeditione copia commeatuum abundavit. Cf. Proc. *BP* I. viii. 5, χορηγὸς δὲ τῆς τοῦ στρατοπέδου δαπάνης Ἀπίων Αἰγύπτιος ἐστάλη, Theophanes, A.M. 5997, ὕπαρχος τότε τοῦ στρατεύματος ὢν καὶ τῆς δαπάνης καὶ τῆς ἐποψίας πάντων προεστηκώς (he is wrongly styled *Ppo Or.* in Malalas, 398), Proc. *BV* I. xi. 17, Ἀρχέλαος, ἀνὴρ ἐς πατρικίους τελῶν, ἤδη μὲν τῆς αὐλῆς ἔπαρχος ἔν τε Βυζαντίῳ καὶ Ἰλλυριοῖς γεγονώς, τότε δὲ τοῦ στρατοπέδου καταστὰς ἔπαρχος. οὕτω γὰρ ὁ τῆς δαπάνης χορηγὸς ὀνομάζεται.

42. *CTh* VII. iv. 24, 398, VIII. i. 14, 398, 15, 415.

43. Aur. Victor, *Caes.* xxxiii. 13, genus hominum praesertim hac tempestate nequam, venale, callidum, seditiosum, habendi cupidum atque ad patrandas fraudes velandasque quasi ab natura factum, annonae dominans eoque utilia curantibus et fortunis aratorum infestum, prudens in tempore his largiendi quorum vecordia damnoque opes contraxerit. POPULARITY OF ACTUARIES: Amm. XX. v. 9, XXV. x. 7.

44. EXPEDITIONALIS ANNONA: Amm. XVII. viii. 2, *CTh* VII. iv. 4, 361 (S), 5, 360 (S), 6, 360. NEW WINE: *CTh* VII. iv. 25 (= *CJ* XII. xxxvii. 10), 398. Wheat, meat and wine are tariffed as constituents of *annona* in Val. III, *Nov.* xiii §4, 445. Oil is recorded in the Theodosian Code only in VIII. iv. 17, 385 (S), as a constituent (with meat and salt) of *primipilares species*. The ration scales may be tabulated as follows:

P. Oxy. 2046	Bread	Meat	Wine	Oil	Wood
(a) Bucellarii (26)	3 lb.	1 lb.	1 sest.	$\frac{1}{10}$ sest.	2 lb.
(b) Scythae (14)	3 lb.	2 lb.	2 sest.	$\frac{1}{8}$ sest.	2 lb.
(c) Tribune's men (4)	3 lb.	2 lb.	2 sest.	$\frac{1}{8}$ sest.	—
(d) Bucellarii and Scythae (13)	3 lb.	2 lb.	2 sest.	$\frac{1}{8}$ sest.	—
P. Oxy. 1920					
(e) Scythae ($41\frac{5}{6}$)	4 lb.	1 lb.	2 sest.	$\frac{1}{8}$ sest.	100 lb. for all
(f) σύμμαχοι (58)	3 lb.	$\frac{1}{2}$ lb.	1 sest.	$\frac{1}{10}$ sest.	200 lb. for all

The *bucellarii* (see pp. 666–7) and σύμμαχοι (i.e. messengers, cf. Liberatus, *Brev.* 23, per portitores literarum velocissimos quos Aegyptii symmachos vocant) were not regular soldiers. In the second part of *P. Oxy.* 2046, 54 *annonae* and 50 *capitus* and 34 *annonae* and 27 *capitus* are equated with rations on scale (b) for

54 and 34 men, and fodder for 50 and 27 horses on the scale of $\frac{1}{10}$ *artaba* of barley and $\frac{1}{6}$ load of hay for each horse. *P. Oxy.* 2013–4 confirms the scale of 1 lb. meat a day for soldiers. *P. Oxy.* 2196 gives a ration—it is not clear for whom—as at (*b*) and (*d*) above.

45. *CTh* xi. xvi. 15, 382, 18, 390 (cura conficiendi pollinis, panis excoctio, pistrini obsequium), vii. v. 1, 399 (excoctio panis), 2, 404 (excoctio bucellati), Josh. Styl. 54, 70, 77.

46. CAPITUS DRAWN FROM HORREA: *CTh* vii. iv. 13, 365, 17, 377. This must have been barley, recorded in *P. Beatty Panop.* 1, lines 392 ff., as being delivered to an *ala*. HAY AND CHAFF: *CTh* vii. iv. 9, 364, e vicensimo non amplius lapide milites sibi iubemus paleas convectare, cf. laws 7, 362, and 23, 396; we find curial collectors of chaff in Egypt, e.g. *Chr.* I. 419, οὐ θέλομεν γὰρ ἄχυρον, μήπως μὴ λήμφθῃ καὶ ἀναγκάσθωμεν τὴν τιμὴν διαγράψαι, 422 (receipts from a διοδότης to an ἐπιμελητής for wine, meat and chaff). NO FODDER UNTIL AUGUST: *CTh* vii. iv. 8, 362, militibus ad kalendas Augustas capitatio denegetur, ex kalendis Augustis praebeatur. PASTURE: Th. II, *Nov.* xxiv §4, 443, agros etiam limitaneos universis cum paludibus, *CTh* vii. vii. 3, 398, 4 and 5, 415.

47. PRIMIPILI: *CTh* viii. iv. 6, 358, 17, 385 (S), 19, 396. LIMITANEI: *CTh* vii. iv. 14, 365, riparienses milites mensibus novem in ipsa specie consequantur annonam, pro tribus pretia percipiant, cf. law 22 for the prices 'quae generali lege divi patris senioris Valentiniani constituta sunt'.

48. COMITATENSES IN THE EAST: *CTh* vii. iv. 18 and 20, 393, 21, 396, 28, 406; the last two laws do not specifically mention *comitatenses* but probably refer to them. LIMITANEI OF PALESTINE: *CTh* vii. iv. 30, 409. For rates of commutation p. 461.

49. COMITATENSES IN THE WEST: *CTh* vii. iv. 22, 396, cf. v. 1, 399. OPINATORES COLLECT GOLD: *CTh* xi. i. 34, 429, Aug. *Ep.* 268. ANNONA AND CAPITUS IN AFRICA: Val. III, *Nov.* xiii §§3–4, 445, has autem militares annonas cum provinciales pro longinqui difficultate itineris in adaeratione persolverint, unius annonae adaeratio quattuor per annum solidis aestimetur. ne vero necessitatis occasione in expeditione militi constituto carioris cuiquam vendere liceat, pretia necessariarum rerum sub hoc modo, quo annonam adaeravimus, iubemus inferri: id est tritici ad singulos solidos Italicos modios quadraginta et carnis pondo ducenta septuaginta, vini sextarios Italicos ducentos.

50. FAMILIES: *CTh* vii. i. 3, 349, quicumque militum ex nostra auctoritate familias suas ad se venire meruerint, non amplius quam coniugia, liberos, servos etiam de peculio castrensi emptos neque adscriptos censibus ad eosdem excellentia tua dirigi faciat. RATIONS FOR FAMILIES: *CTh* vii. i. 11, 392, ii, qui inter adcrescentes matriculis adtinentur, tamdiu alimoniam a parentibus sumant, quoad gerendis armis idonei fuerint aestimati, ita ut cesset super eorum nomine praebitio fiscalis annonae; iv. 17, 377, fortissimi ac devotissimi milites, familiae quoque, sed et ceteri quibuscumque praediti dignitatibus annonas et capitum singulis diebus aut certe competenti tempore, id est priusquam annus elabatur, de horreis consequantur; Lib. *Or.* II. 39; *CTh* vii. iv. 28, 406, 31, 409. A law addressed to Stilicho in 399 (*CTh* vii. v. 1) seems to imply that *familiae* received rations in the West also.

51. The forts of the *limitanei* are depicted in the illustrations to the chapters of *comites rei militaris* and *duces* in the Notitia and the ruins of many still survive. *Limitanei* are associated with *castra* in Th. II, *Nov.* xxiv §§1–2, 443, *CJ* I. xxvii.

2 §8, 534, and are sometimes called *castellani* (*CTh* VII. xv. 2, 423) or *castrenses* (*CTh* XVI. v. 65 §3, 428, *SEG* IX. 356 §§11, 14). For the *comitatenses* see Zos. II. 34. EXEMPTIONS FROM BILLETING: *CTh* VII. viii. 8, 400 (*fabricenses*), XIII. iii. 3, 333, 10, 370, 16, 414, 18, 427 (doctors and teachers), iv. 4, 374 (painters), XVI. ii. 8, 343 (clergy); shops are excluded by *CTh* VII. viii. 5 §1, 398, *CJ* XII. xl. 10 §6 (450-55); also synagogues by *CTh* VII. viii. 2, 368; Josh. Styl. 86 shows that inns were liable. The aristocracy also enjoyed exemptions in Constantinople (*CTh* VII. viii. 16, 435, *CJ* XII. xl. 10, 450-5). RULE FOR DIVISION: *CTh* VII. viii. 5, 398. SALGAMUM: *CTh* VII. ix. 1, 340, 2, 361, 3, 393, 4, 416; cf. Malalas, 437, (Justinian) ἐδωρήσατο τὸ Γοτθικὸν ξυλέλαιον, κουφίσας τοὺς ὑποτελεῖς ἐκ τοῦ βάρους. Why the 'soldier's wood and oil' should have been called *salgamum* (literally 'pickles') is obscure; the word is used in Diocletian's time (*P. Beatty Panop.* 2. lines 245 ff., 285 ff.) to denote a regular issue of oil and salt to troops. CENATICUM: *CTh* VII. iv. 12, 364. BATHS: *CTh* VII. xi. 1, 406, 2, 417.

52. Josh. Styl. 86, 93-6.

53. F. C. Burkitt, *Euphemia and the Goth*, 129-153. The soldier is called a Goth, but 'Goth' is the usual Syriac colloquialism for a soldier. The historical details in §4 are correct and the story rings true.

54. Syn. *Ep.* 129.

55. SURGEONS: Amm. XVI. vi. 2, Dorus quidam ex medico scutariorum. CHAPLAINS: Cyr. Scyth. *V. Sabae*, 9, Theod. *Ep.* (Azema) 2, cf. Soz. I. 8, Eus. *V. Const.* IV. 18-19 and Pelagius I (*PL* LXIX. 416). See my article in *Harvard Theol. Rev.* XLVI (1953), 249 ff. *P. Nessana*, 35, records the ἐκκλησία τοῦ κάστρου and its priest.

56. LEAVE: *CTh* VII. xii. 1, 323, i. 2, 353 (for the date see *Historia* IV (1955), 232-3). For corrupt grant of leave see n. 86.

57. GRAFT IN PROMOTION: *P. Abinn.* 59. TIRONES: Anon. *de rebus bell.*, v. 5, scilicet ut centeni aut quinquageni iuniores, extra hos qui in matriculis continentur, habeantur in promptu armis exerciti et minori utpote tirones stipendio sublevati, in locum amissorum si res ita tulerit subrogandi: *tiro* is also recognised as a grade by Jerome (see below). SEMISSALIS: *ILS* 2800, *P. Amh.* 148, *CJ* I. xxvii. 2 §§22-34, 534. NON-COMMISSIONED GRADES (OLD UNITS): *P. Beatty Panop.* 2, 60, 174, 183, 190, 195, 206, 264, 269, 289 (centurions), 41 (decurions), *ILS* 9206, centurionis legionis secunde Flavie Virtutis, cf. n. 127 for sixth century evidence. NON-COMMISSIONED GRADES (NEW UNITS): Jerome, *c. Joh. Hierosol.* 19, finge aliquem tribuniciae potestatis suo vitio regradatum per singula militiae equestris officia ad tironis vocabulum devolutum. numquid ex tribuno statim fit tiro? non, sed ante primicerius, deinde senator, ducenarius, centenarius, biarchus, circitor, eques, deinde tiro. The grades from *ducenarius* to *eques* are found in the *agentes in rebus* (*CJ* XII. xx. 3 (457-70)), those of *primicerius, ducenarius, centenarius, biarchus, circitor* (and *semissalis*) in the military offices of Africa (*CJ* I. xxvii. 2 §§22-34, 534). From the *scholae* we have *primicerius* (*ILS* 9213, *CJ* XII. xxix. 2, 474), *senator, ducenarius, centenarius* (Th. II, *Nov.* xxi, 441, *ILS* 8883, *CIL* III. 14188, VI. 32948, *AE* 1891, 104) and *biarchus* (*CIL* VI. 32949). These grades are also found among the *stratores* (see n. 37) and in the *fabricae* (see ch. XXI, n. 26). Otherwise they occur only, so far as I have traced them, in *vexillationes* and *auxilia* (I have omitted units whose classification is unknown):

P. Ital. 16, ILS 2806	primicerius	Felices Theodosiani	aux.
ILS 9481a	,,	Mattiaci Sen.	aux.
P. Abinn. 42	,,	unnamed	vex.
ILS 2796	senator	Heruli	aux.
ILS 2804	,,	Equites Bracchiati	vex.
BGU 316	,,	Constantiaci	aux.
ILS 2797	ducenarius	Batavi Sen.	aux. or vex.
P. Abinn. 42	,,	unnamed	vex.
CIL III. 14704	,,	unnamed	vex.
ILS 2798	centenarius	Bracchiati	aux. or vex.
CIL v. 8745	,,	Ebores	aux.
CIL v. 8758	,,	Comites Sen. Sagittarii	vex.
CIL III. 14406a	,,	Cataphractarii	vex.
AE. 1891, 106	,,	,,	vex.
CIL XIII. 1848	,,	,, Sen.	vex.
AE 1912, 44	,,	Sagittarii	vex.
SPP xx. 139, Sb 4753	,,	Leontoclibanarii	vex.
P. Würtz. 17	biarchus	Equites Clibanarii	vex.
BGU 316	,,	Cataphractarii	vex.
ILS 2805	,,	VIII Dalmatae	vex.
ILS 2799	,,	Batavi Sen.	aux. or vex.
ILS 2804	,,	Bracchiati	vex.
CIL v. 8755	,,	Leones Sen.	aux.
AE 1946, 42	,,	Scutarii	vex.
ILS 9209	circitor	Cataphractarii	vex.
AE 1912, 192	,,	,,	vex.
CIL v. 6784	,,	,,	vex.
AE 1919, 18	,,	XII Cataphractarii	vex.
CIL XIII. 3457	,,	Dalmatae	vex.
CIL XIII. 7298, AE 1882, 113–4	,,	Catharenses	aux.(?)

The earliest record of a *circitor* is in 326 (*CTh* VII. xxii. 2); the earliest *biarchus* is perhaps 'Val. Victorinus biarcus qui militavit in sacro palatio . . . qui in proelio Romanorum Calcedonia contra aversarios decessit', presumably in 324 (*AE* 1922, 72). CAMPIDOCTOR: Veg. I. 13, II. 23 (duties), Amm. XV. iii. 10, XIX. vi. 12, Pall. *Dial.* p. 13, *ILS* 2803, *CIL* VIII. 4354, *P. Lond.* 113. 5(a), *MAMA* I. 168, Const. Porph. *Cer.* I. 91–3. DRACONARIUS: Amm. XX. iv. 18, Veg. I. 20, II. 7, 13, *ILS* 2805, *CIL* III. 1433², *P. Lond.* 113. I, *MAMA* I. 218, *SPP* xx. 135, Joh. Moschus, 20.

58. RATES OF PAY: *CJ* I. xxvii. 2 §§22–34, 534; it seems likely that the *numerarius* in these lists ranked as *senator*. For a *circitor's* earlier scale see *CTh* VII. xxii. 2, 326. SLOW PROMOTION: Anon. *de rebus bell.* v. 2–3, militaris ordo, stipendiis aliquot peractis, ubi ad quinque vel eo amplius annonarum emolumenta pervenerit, ne haec diutius percipiens rempublicam gravet, honesta missione donatus vacans sibi otio gaudeat absolutus. in cuius locum posterior succedens totum numerum per certa temporum spatia expensis gravissimis relevabit. quod si numerosior miles de sequentibus scholis in decedentium locum vocatur, hic quoque pari liberalitate alio donatus abscedat, vel ad alium ordinem cui miles deest locum suppleturus accedat. quae res non solum expensis gravidam rem-

publicam recreabit, sed etiam curas imperatoriae provisionis imminuet. animabit etiam plures ad militiam, quos ab ea stipendiorum tarditas prohibebat.

59. TRANSFERS FORBIDDEN: *CTh* VII. i. 18, 400. TESTIMONIALES EX PROTECTORI-BUS: *CTh* VII. xx. 5, 328, veterani protectoria dignitate cumulati aut qui honores varios pro meritis suis consecuti sunt; in law 8, 364, the veteran 'qui ex protectore dimissus erit' is contrasted with those 'qui honestas missiones sive causarias consequuntur'; cf. also XIII. i. 14, 385; their abuse is forbidden in *CTh* VII. xxi. 1, 320 (S), VIII. vii. 2, 353 (S), 3, 352 (S), VII. xx. 12, 400, xxi. 4, 408.

60. DISCHARGE: *FIR* I². 93, *CTh* VII. xx. 4, 325. Memorius (*ILS* 2788) served 42 years, 28 of them in the ranks; Derdius (*ILS* 2789) served 40 years, retiring *ex tribuno*; Sindia (*ILS* 2796) died as *senator* at 60, and Adabrandus (*ILS* 9213) at the same age as *primicerius*.

61. CAUSARIA MISSIO: *CTh* VII. xx. 4, 325.

62. POLL-TAX: *FIR* I². 93, *CTh* VII. xx. 4, 325. MARKET DUES, ETC.: *CTh* VII. xx. 2, 326 (S), XIII. i. 2, 360, VII. xx. 9, 366, XIII. i. 7, 369, 14, 385. CURIA: *CTh* VII. xx. 2, 326 (S), cf. *Dig*. XLIX. xviii. 2, 5 §2.

63. ALLOTMENTS AND BONUSES: *CTh* VII. xx. 3, 325 (S), 8, 364; in law 11, 386 (S), a general licence is given to veterans to occupy waste lands. In Anon. *de rebus bell*. v. 4, it is assumed that the land will be in the frontier provinces.

64. For the origins of the *protectores* see p. 53. The title *domesticus* is first certainly attested in 354 by Ammianus (XIV. x. 2) and in 357 by *CTh* XII. i. 38, but is used by the author of *Vita Numeriani*, 13, and Aur. Victor, *Caes*. XXXIX. 1, in describing Diocletian's rank before his accession. The use of the word is anachronistic no doubt, but if, as I believe, the Historia Augusta was written not later than Constantine's reign, *domestici* must have existed by then. Our authorities rarely draw any distinction between *protectores* and *protectores domestici*, often using the former term to denote the latter, but *CTh* VI. xxiv. 5, 392, and 6, 395, 8 and 9, 416, clearly show that they were two separate corps. That the *protectores* were commanded by the *magistri militum* is suggested by *CTh* VI. xxiv. 5, 392, and 6, 395; the former law about the *domestici* is addressed to Addaeus as *comes domesticorum*, the latter about the *protectores* to Addaeus as *mag. mil.* (*per Orientem*). It is also suggested by *CTh* XII. i. 38, 357 (S), which deals with *curiales* who 'domesticorum seu protectorum se consortio copularunt, scholari etiam quidam nomen dederunt militiae aut palatinis sunt officiis adgregati'. The *magistri militum, comes domesticorum* and *magister officiorum* (with the *CSL* and *castrensis*) are instructed to take action. The second was responsible for the *domestici* and the third for the *scholares*; the *magistri militum* can only be concerned with the *protectores*. That the *comites domesticorum* commanded the *domestici* only is proved by *Not. Dig. Or*. xv, *Occ*. xiii. PRAESENTALES AND DEPUTATI: *CTh* VI. xxiv. 5, 392 (S), omnes, qui domesticorum iniuncti nomini numquam nostris obsequiis inhaeserunt neque certis quibusque officiis deputati publicas exsecuti sunt iussiones, protinus matriculis eximantur; cf. 1, 362, scias senum capitum domesticis per singulas quasque scholas, quinquagenis iussis in praesenti esse, iuxta morem debere praestari; *CJ* II. vii. 25 §3, 519, XII. xvii. 4 (527-34) (praesentales); *Not. Dig. Or*. xv, *Occ*. xiii (deputati). Ammianus Marcellinus was seconded to Ursicinus, *magister militum*, in 353 (XIV. ix. 1) and again in 355 and 356 (XV. v. 22, XVI. x. 21). *CTh* VI. xxiv. 9, 416, proves that the *protectores* (in the Eastern parts at any rate) were all on one roll with a single *primicerius*; cf. Amm. XVIII. iii. 5, ex primicerio

protectorum (but Ammianus does not always distinguish *protectores* and *domestici*). The same is proved of the *domestici* by Amm. xxv. v. 4, domesticorum ordinis primus (Jovian), xxvii. x. 16, domesticorum omnium primus (Valerian), and strongly implied by *CTh* vi. xxiv. 7. The *domestici* are spoken of as a single corps by Julian (*Ep.* 22, τῷ τῶν οἰκείων συντάγματι), and in Amm. xxvi. v. 3, *CTh* vi. xxiv. 3, 364, as a single *schola*. The term *schola* is, however, probably untechnical, for *CTh* vi. xxiv. 1 (cited above) proves that the *domestici* were in 362 divided into more than two *scholae*, and I take *AE* 1939, 45, protectori de scola seniore peditum, and *ILS* 9204, Fl. Concordius protector divinorum laterum et prepositus iuniorum, to refer to the *domestici protectores*; they are probably early inscriptions, before the title *domestici* had come in. By Justinian's time the *equites* and *pedites* were completely separate *scholae*, each with its own order of seniority (*CJ* xii. xvii. 2, 4, 5). *CTh* vi. xxiv. 8+xxv. 1 shows that by 416 in the East there was more than one *schola* of the *domestici*, and that each had its *primicerius*. This law does not however make it clear whether the *decemprimi* were the ten seniors of the whole body of the *domestici* or of each *schola*, and law 10, 427, praeter primicerios protectorum domesticorum decem primi scholarum, clarifies this point. Law 11, 432, appears to speak of one *primicerius* and one body of *decemprimi*, but is probably to be interpreted, as in the Justinianic version (*CJ* xii. xvii. 2), 'utriusque scholae'. The duplication of the office of *comes domesticorum* is first mentioned in 409, when Attalus appointed Athaulf ἡγεμὼν τῶν ἱππέων δομεστικῶν καλουμένων (Soz. ix. 8), but as it is recorded in both *Not. Dig. Or.* xv and *Occ.* xiii was probably already the established rule.

65. NUMBERS: *CTh* vi. xxiv. 1, 362 (cited in n. 64). SPECIAL DUTIES: *CTh* vii. xxii. 2, 326, xviii. 10, 400 (recruits), viii. v. 30, 368, vii. xvi. 3, 420 (traffic control), ix. xxvii. 3, 382, Amm. xiv. vii. 12, xv. iii. 10, xxix. iii. 8, v. 7, Symm. *Rel.* 36 (arrest and custody of prisoners), xviii. vii. 6 (defence of Euphrates), cf. xviii. vi. 21 (Ammianus is sent to obtain intelligence from the satrap of Corduene), xxvi. v. 14 (Masaucio sent with others by Valentinian to secure Africa).

66. Const. Porph. *Cer.* i. 86, δομέστικοι δὲ καὶ προτίκτορες οὕτως. πάλαι μὲν ἀπὸ προσκυνήσεως μόνης ἦν ἡ στρατεία αὐτῶν. νῦν δὲ προβατωρείαν ποιεῖ ὁ δεσπότης, καὶ προσάγει αὐτὸν ὁ δηκουρίων ἀτραβατικὸν φοροῦντα χλανίδιν, ἢ ἐν κονσιστωρίῳ μετὰ τὸ πάντα πραχθῆναι, ἢ ἀνιόντος αὐτοῦ εἰς τὸ ἱππικὸν ἵσταται ἐμπρὸς τοῦ δέλφακος, καὶ λέγει ἐπὶ μὲν τῶν προτικτόρων· «ἀδοράτορ προτέκτορ», ἐπὶ δὲ τῶν δομεστίκων· «ἀδοράτορ προτέκτορ δομεστίκους». καὶ λαμβάνει τὴν προβατωρίαν παρὰ τοῦ δεσπότου, καὶ φιλεῖ τοὺς πόδας καὶ ἐξέρχεται, cf. *Not. Dig. Or.* xxxix. 37, xl. 38, xli. 41, xlii. 45 principem de eodem officio qui completa militia adorat protector, *CTh* vi. xxiv. 3, 364, viii. vii. 4 (326-54), 8, 365, 9, 366, 16, 385, vi. xxiv. 4, 387, x. xxii. 3, 390; for *testimoniales* see n. 59.

67. *ILS* 2781 (Thiumpus), 2777 (Baudio), 2783 (Marcus), cf. 2788 (Memorius); Amm. xxv. x. 9 (Vitalianus), xxx. vii. 2-3 (Gratian). Maximinus's rapid promotion is criticised by Lactantius, *Mort. Pers.* xix. 6, statim scutarius, continuo protector, mox tribunus, postridie Caesar. Cf. Paul. *Ep.* 25 §8, in hac militia soletis in votis habere hanc officii promotionem ut protectores efficiamini.

68. P. *Abinn.* 1.

69. Amm. xiv. x. 2 (Herculanus), xxv. v. 4 (Jovian), *ILS* 2813 (Hariulfus), cf.

Amm. XXVI. v. 13 (Masaucio, son of Cretio *comes Africae*) and XXVI. x. 1 (Marcellus a relative of Procopius), and Pall. *Hist. Laus.* liv (Paulus, the son of Innocentius, γενόμενος τῶν ἐπιδόξων τῶν ἐν τῷ παλατίῳ ἐν ταῖς ἀρχαῖς Κωνσταντίου τοῦ βασιλέως, is now δομεστικὸν στρατευόμενον). CURIALES: *CTh* XII. i. 38, 357 (S), cf. VII. xxi. 2 (326–54), si quis de paganis vel decurionibus ambierit ad honores protectoriae dignitatis, nec tempus nec stipendia ei post hanc legem computanda sunt, and XII. i. 88, 382. OFFICIALS: *CTh* VIII. vii. 9, 366, 16, 385. Besides the *cornicularii* of prefects (*CTh* VIII. vii. 8, 365, 9, 366, cf. Symm. *Ep.* III. 67), those of vicars were in 385 allowed to adore the purple (*CTh* VIII. vii. 16); also the *principes* of the *duces* of Scythia, Dacia and Moesia I and II (see n. 66), and retired *primicerii* of *fabricae* (*CTh* x. xxii. 3, 390).

70. *CTh* VI. xxiv. 2+3, 364, domesticorum filios vel propinquos parvos vel inpuberes domesticorum coetibus adgregamus, ita ut non solum matriculis inserantur, verum etiam annonarum subsidiis locupletentur. quaternas etenim annonas eos, quos armis gestandis et procinctibus bellicis idoneos adhuc non esse constiterit, in sedibus iubemus adipisci his condicionibus, ut annonae, quae amplius insumuntur vel per tractorias deferuntur, recidantur. sicuti variis itineribus protectorum domesticorum schola comprehensos ad eam venire perspicimus, ita etiam sportularum diversa esse debebit insumptio. grave enim admodum est viros post emensum laborem, qui nullius rei cupidiores fuere quam gloriae, huiuscemodi erogationibus fatigari; eos tamen penitus solummodo inter quinos et denos solidos sportularum nomine primatibus distribuere praecipimus. eos autem, qui vel suffragio vel potentium gratia sacram purpuram adorare pervenerint, quinquagenos solidos volumus insumere.

71. *ILS* 2781 (Thiumpus), 2788 (Memorius), *P. Abinn.* 1 (Abinnaeus), Amm. XXX. vii. 2–3 (Gratian), XXV. x. 9 (Vitalianus, cf. Zos. IV. 34), XVIII. ix. 3 (Aelianus), cf. XVIII. iii. 5, Valentinus ex primicerio protectorum tribunus . . . ducis in Illyrico meruit potestatem. Teutomeres, a *domesticus* in 353 (Amm. XV. iii. 10), is probably the Tautomedes, *dux Daciae*, of *CTh* xv. i. 13. At an earlier date Constantius Chlorus was 'protector primum, exin tribunus, postea praeses Dalmatiarum' (Anon. Val. 1). *Princeton Exp. Syria*, 213, records an ἔπαρχος ἀπὸ προτήκτορος, and *ILCV* 1574 a man who though he was enrolled in the *protectores* at the age of 18 and served 37 years died only *ex tribunis*. REGULAR PROMOTION OF PROTECTORES: Amm. XVI. x. 21, provectis e consortio nostro ad regendos milites natu maioribus, adulescentes eum sequi iubemur, quicquid pro re publica mandaverit impleturi.

72. ABSENTEES: *CTh* VI. xxiv. 5, 392 (S), 6, 395, Symm. *Ep.* II. 74, Valentinianus protector dudum patrocinio culminis tui per me traditus adque commissus domesticis occupationibus adtinetur atque ideo magnopere poposcit obeundum sibi aliquod negotium per suburbanas provincias impetrari. quare, decus nostrum, familiari meo desideratum munus excude aut impetra commeatum, quo possit a militari nota sub hac impetratione defendi. Synesius complains of the slowness of promotion in the *domestici*, which was no doubt due to the inflation of the corps by absentees (*Ep.* 75, Θεοδόσιος ὁ βασιλέως ὑπασπιστὴς σύνοικος, ἕνεκα μὲν τοῦ χρόνου καὶ τῆς ἐν τῇ στρατείᾳ προσεδρίας, κἂν ἐπροστάτησε πάλαι· αἱ δὲ σπουδαὶ πλέον δύνανται τῶν ἐνιαυτῶν).

73. *CTh* VI. xxiv. 7, *PU Rom.*, 414, 8 and 9, *Ppo Or.*, 416, 10, *Ppo Or.*, 427, 11, *PU Const.*, 432.

74. *CJ* XII. xvii. 3 (c. 450). Proc. *HA* xxvi. 27–8; the 'domestici protectores equitum et peditum qui nostrae aulae videntur iugiter excubare', who complained

that their salaries were paid in short weight solidi (Cass. *Var.* I. 10) were presumably these pensioners.

75. For tribunes of the *scholae*, vexillations, legions and *auxilia* in the *comitatus* see Grosse, *Röm. Militärgeschichte*, 146–7, and for *praepositi*, op. cit. 143–5. The titles of the commanders in the *limitanei* are given in the Notitia. TRIBUNUS VACANS: Amm. XV. iii. 10, XVI. xii. 63, XVIII. ii. 2, XXXI. xiii. 18, cf. XV. v. 22, XVIII. vii. 6.

76. Lact. *Mort. Pers.* xviii. 10, erat tunc praesens iam pridem a Diocletiano factus tribunus ordinis primi. VALENTINIAN'S PROMOTION: Amm. XXV. x. 9, cf. XVI. xi. 6. For the promotion of tribunes of the *scholae* see ch. XII, n. 16.

77. *CTh* VI. xiii. 1, 413; cf. *A.C.Oec.* I. i. pars vii. 68, τῷ περιβλέπτῳ κόμητι καὶ πραιποσίτῳ Ἰακώβῳ τῆς τετάρτης σχολῆς (σκουταρίων). For ordinary tribunes see ch. XV, n. 12.

78. LATERCULUM MINUS: *CTh* I. viii. 1, 415, 2 and 3, 424; the units concerned are listed in *Not. Dig. Or.* xxviii, xxxi–xxxviii, xl, under the heading 'et quae de minore laterculo emittuntur'. The other commands were presumably issued from the *laterculum maius*, which appears among the insignia of the *primicerius notariorum* in both East and West. Only in the East, however (*Not. Dig. Or.* xviii. 5), is it stated that he 'scolas etiam et numeros tractat', and this implies that the Western *primicerius* had lost this function—to the *magister militum* (Paul. *V. Amb.* 43).

79. *P. Abinn.* 1.

80. DECURIONS GET COMMISSIONS: *CTh* VII. xxi. 2 (326–54), Lib. *Or.* XLVIII. 42, xlix. 19. PUSAEUS: Amm. XXIV. i. 9. FRAOMARIUS: Amm. XXIX. iv. 7. HERACLIUS: *ILS* 2786. CHEILAS: Syn. *Ep.* 110; cf. Zos. v. 9 (Bargus, the sausage seller).

81. LAW OF HONORIUS: *CTh* VII. xx. 13, 407 (S). Veg. II. 7, tribunus maior per epistulam sacram imperatoris iudicio destinatur, minor tribunus pervenit ex labore. For *vicarii* see n. 158. MARCIAN: Evagr. II. 1, Proc. *BV* I. iv. 2–7. CONON: Cyr. Scyth. *V. Sabae*, 1, 9, 25.

82. SCHOLARES: *CTh* VII. iv. 34, 414, his scholaribus, quibus laborum intuitu regendos numeros dederimus, de aerariis annonis singulos solidos per opinatores, caballationis quoque rationem pro administrato tempore debitam, quando militibus erogatur, sine mora praeberi oportet, vel, si quis eorum antequam accipiat in fata concesserit, quod ex utraque causa ei debebatur, heredibus eius restitui.

83. ARBETIO: Amm. XV. ii. 4, XVI. vi. 1, a gregario ad magnum militiae culmen evectus. MAURUS: Amm. XX. iv. 18, cf. XXXI. x. 21. For Gratian, Vitalianus and Memorius see n. 71, and for Abinnaeus *P. Abinn.* 1. Other ranker officers are Laniogaisus (Amm. XV. v. 16, Laniogaeso vetante, tunc tribuno, quem dum militaret candidatus solum adfuisse morituro Constanti supra retulimus), and Claudius and Sallustius (Amm. XXIX. iii. 7, ex Iovianorum numero adusque tribunatus dignitates progressos).

84. STIPENDIUM: *P. Beatty Panop.* 2, line 201, *P. Oxy.* 1047. ANNONAE AND CAPITUS: *CTh* VI. xxiv. 1, 362, 2, 364 (*domestici*), Val. III, *Nov.* xiii §5, 445 (*dux*

of Mauretania), Just. *Ed.* xiii §18, λήψεται δὲ καὶ αὐτὸς τὰς ἀφωρισμένας αὐτῷ σιτήσεις, ὑπὲρ μὲν τῶν ἐν εἴδει ἀννόνων ἐνενήκοντα καὶ καπίτων ἑκατὸν εἴκοσι νομίσματα χίλια πέντε τέταρτον, ὑπὲρ δὲ τῶν ἐν χρυσῷ ἀννόνων πεντήκοντα καὶ καπίτων πεντήκοντα νομίσματα τετρακόσια (*dux* of Libya). It is natural to assume that the round sum represents the official salary, particularly as the figure of 50 agrees with that specified for the *dux* of Mauretania, and for a civil office of equivalent rank, the Augustal prefect (Just. *Ed.* xiii §3). The *annonae* and *capitus* in kind must be legalised perquisites.

85. STELLATURA: SHA, *Pesc. Nig.* 3, *Sev. Alex.* 15, *CTh* VII. iv. 28 §1, 406, (= *CJ* XII. xxxvii. 12), semper (*Just.* septem) dierum, per quas resistentes tribuni emolumenti gratia sollemniter stillaturae nomine consequuntur species, non aliter adaerentur, nisi ut in foro rerum venalium distrahuntur. THE TWELFTH: Th. II, *Nov.* xxiv §2, 443, quibus cum principe castrorumque praepositis pro laborum vicissitudine limitanei tantum militis duodecimam annonarum partem, distribuendam videlicet inter eos magisteriae potestatis arbitrio, deputamus, *SEG* IX. 356 §6, ὥστε τὴν δωδεκάτην μοῖραν μὴ ἐκ τῶν προτέρων διδομένων ἐκ [τοῦ] δημοσίου πᾶσαν παρακατέχεσθαι, ἀλλ' αὐτῶν τῶν κατὰ μέρος διδομένων· τὴν μὲν δοδεκάτην κατὰ ἀναλογίαν ἔχειν ἕκαστον τῶν προσώπων, οἷς ἡ τοιαύτη ἀφώρισται παραμυθία, τὰ δὲ λοιπὰ μέρη τοὺς γενναιοτάτους κομίζεσθαι στρατιώτας· ὁμοίως ἑκάστους τούτων κατὰ ἀναλογίαν τῶν ἐκ τοῦ δημοσίου δοθέντων καὶ κομιζομένους καὶ μὴ τοὺς μὲν ἀποπληροῦσθαι τὴν αὐτῶν παραμυθίαν, τοὺς δὲ στρατιώτας χρεωστῖσθαι, *Princeton Exp. Syria*, 20, 562, ὥστε [τὸν δοῦκα μ]όνα λαμβάνειν τὰ ἀφωρισμένα αὐτῷ κατὰ τὸ ἀρχαῖον ἔθος ὑπὲρ ἀννωνῶν καὶ καπίτων ἐκ τοῦ δημοσίου καὶ ἐκ τοῦ μέρους τῆς δω[δεκάτ]ης. GIFT OF ANNONAE: *CTh* VII. iv. 29, 407, si quas sub gratia donationis a militibus auferunt quam merentur annonas duces seu tribuni, iuxta nummaria defixa pretia sine ulla dubitatione percipiant; 36, 424, si quando tribuni sive comites vel praepositi numerorum per provincias annonas voluerint, hoc est quas pro dignitate sua consequuntur, in aere percipere, non aliis eas pretiis, nisi quae in foro rerum venalium habeantur, adaerandas esse cognoscant. si alias annonas, quae non suae dignitatis erunt, sed alio modo, dum tamen licito, suis commodis adquisitas in auro sibi dari duces sive tribuni voluerint, illis pretiis contenti sint, quae in forma aerariarum annonarum universis militibus sollemni observatione praebentur.

86. RATIONS OF DEAD SOLDIERS: Them. *Or.* x. 136b, τῶν φυλάκων δὲ ἐλαττοῦσθαι τὸν ἀριθμόν, ὅπως ἂν γίνοιτο κέρδος αὐτοῦ ἡ μισθοφορὰ τῶν ἐκλειπόντων; cf. Lib. *Or.* XLVII. 31, τοσοῦτον δὲ τὸ παρὰ τῆς τροφῆς τῶν λόχων· οἷς ἔνι ζῶντα ποιεῖν τὸν οἰχόμενον ἐσθίειν τε αὐτοῖς ἐν τῷ τοῦ τεθνεῶτος ὀνόματι. SALE OF EXTENDED LEAVE: Syn. *Ep.* 129, ὥσπερ γὰρ ὄντος νόμου, τὰ τῶν στρατιωτῶν εἶναι τῶν στρατηγῶν, ἃ πάντες εἶχον λαβών, ἀντέδωκεν αὐτοῖς ἀστρατίαν, καὶ τὸ μὴ συντετάχθαι, βαδίζειν ἐπιτρέψας, ᾗ τις ᾤετο θρέψεσθαι; cf. *P. Abinn.* 33, in which Clematius asks Abinnaeus to give indefinite leave to Ision, a *promotus* of his unit, to act as Clematius' agent *(ὅπως συγχωρήσῃς τούτῳ τοῖς πράγμασιν ἡμῶν προσέχειν, δυναμένου σου ὅπου τις ἀνάγκη κατεπίγει τοῦτον μετακαλέσασθαι καὶ πάλιν εὐθέως ποιῆσαι, ὡς προεῖπον, τοῖς πράγμασιν ἡμῶν προσέχειν)*: cf. also n. 95. CUSTOMARY PERQUISITES: Syn. *Ep.* 62, ὑπερεῖδε κερδῶν, ἃ δοκεῖν εἶναι νόμιμα πεποίηκεν ἡ συνήθεια; *SEG* IX. 356 §4, ὥστε μὴ ἐξεῖναι τῷ νῦν ἢ κατὰ καιρὸν δουκὶ κομίζεσθαί τι παρὰ τῶν στρατιωτῶν ὑπὲρ τῆς μὲν καλουμένης εὐμενείας, οὔσης δὲ ἐξ ἔθους οὐκ ἀγαθοῦ κακῆς συνηθείας. For the large total of perquisites see n. 84.

87. ILLEGAL COMMUTATION: *CTh* VII. iv. 1, 325, 17, 377.

88. LEGAL COMMUTATION: *CTh* VII. iv. 10, ad Symmachum *PU*, 364, protectores fori rerum venalium iuxta veteris moris observantiam in annonarum suarum

commoda pretia consequantur, 28, 406, 29, 407, 36, 424 (all cited in n. 85), *CJ* I. lii. 1, 439, omnibus tam viris spectabilibus quam viris clarissimis iudicibus, qui per provincias sive militarem sive civilem administrationem gerunt . . . in praebendis solaciis annonarum hic fixus ac stabilis servabitur modus, ut ea pro annonis et capitu dignitati suae debitis pretia consequantur, quae particularibus delegationibus soleant contineri. The *dux* of Libya appears to draw his salary in cash *annonae* and his perquisites in commuted *annonae* in kind (see n. 84).

89. PECULATION BY OFFICERS: Them. *Or.* x. 135d—36d, Lib. *Or.* II. 37–9, Syn. *Ep.* 131. PALLADIUS: Amm. XXVIII. vi. 17 ff.

90. SOLDIERS' SLAVES: Sulp. Sev. *V. Mart.* 2, *CTh* VII. xxii. 2 §2, 326, *Chr.* II. 271.

91. SLAVES: *CTh* VII. i. 3, 349, quicumque militum ex nostra auctoritate familias suas ad se venire meruerint, non amplius quam coniugia liberos, servos etiam de peculio castrensi emptos neque adscriptos censibus ad eosdem excellentia tua dirigi faciat; xiii. 16, 406, praecipue sane eorum servos, quos militia armata detentat, foederatorum nihilominus et dediticiorum, quoniam ipsos quoque una cum dominis constat bella tractare; cf. Them. *Or.* x. 135d. FREE SERVANTS: *CTh* VII. i. 10, 367, plerique milites secum homines condicionis ingenuae propinquitate simulata vel condicione lixarum frequenter abducunt.

92. THE SCHOLAE: Th. II, *Nov.* xxi, 441.

93. SOLDIERS OWN LAND: *CTh* VII. xx. 4 pr., 325, comitatenses et ripenses milites atque protectores suum caput, patris ac matris et uxoris, si tamen eos superstites habeant, omnes excusent, si censibus inditi habeantur. quod si aliquam ex his personis non habuerint vel nullam habuerint, tantum pro suo debent peculio excusare, quantum pro iisdem, si non deessent, excusare potuissent, ita tamen, ut non pactione cum alteris facta simulato dominio rem alienam excusent, sed vere proprias facultates; VII. i. 3, 349 (cited in n. 91).

94. For desertion by recruits see n. 22. Of the 17 laws in *CTh* VII. xviii, de desertoribus et occultatoribus eorum, seven (2–8) fall between 379 and 383 and five (11–15) in 403 and 406.

95. *CTh* VII. i. 12, 384, 15, 396, 16 and 17, 398, *CJ* XII. xxxv. 15, 458.

96. *CTh* VII. xviii. 16, 413.

97. SHA, *Sev. Alex.* 58.

98. Even sons of officers had to serve (see n. 15); that sons of veterans and ordinary conscripts were drafted to either service is proved by *CTh* VII. xxii. 8, 372, xiii. 7 §3, 375, *P. Abinn.* 19 (cited in n. 20). ALLOTMENTS: *CTh* VII. xx. 3, 320, is addressed 'ad universos veteranos', and 8, 364, grants them 'omnibus benemeritis veteranis'; cf. Anon. *de rebus bell.* v. 4.

99. The *annonae* of *limitanei* are specifically mentioned in *CTh* VII. iv. 14, 365, 15, 369, 30, 409, Th. II, *Nov.* xxiv, 443, and in the sixth century in Proc. *HA* xxiv. 12–4, Just. *Nov.* xl, 536. In Anastasius's regulations for the *dux* of Arabia (*Princeton Exp. Syria*, 20) there are very fragmentary sections dealing with τὴν ῥόγαν, which was apparently paid by an ἠρογάτωρ in three four-monthly instalments. There is also an allusion to payments (?) ὑπὲρ βέστεως.

100. See App. II, Table VII.

101. FUNDI LIMITROPHI: *CJ* XI. lxii. 8, 386, *CTh* V. xii. 2, 415, Th. II, *Nov.* v. 2, 439, 3, 441.

102. BURGARII: *CTh* VII. xiv. 1, 398, in burgariis eadem volumus observari, quae de mulionibus lex nostra praecepit, ut ii quoque, qui intra Hispanias vel in quibuscumque locis ausi fuerint burgarios vel sollicitare vel receptare, eodem modo teneantur, similisque eos, qui publicis vestibus deputatos sollicitaverint vel receperint, et de coniunctione et de agnatione et de peculiis et de cunctis rebus quas in illis deprehendimus poena cohibeat.

103. GENTILES: *CTh* VII. xv. 1, 409, terrarum spatia, quae gentilibus propter curam munitionemque limitis atque fossati antiquorum humana fuerant provisione concessa, quoniam comperimus aliquos retinere, si eorum cupiditate vel desiderio retinentur, circa curam fossati tuitionemque limitis studio vel labore noverint serviendum ut illi, quos huic operi antiquitas deputarat. alioquin sciant haec spatia vel ad gentiles, si potuerint inveniri, vel certe ad veteranos esse non inmerito transferenda, ut hac provisione servata fossati limitisque nulla in parte timoris esse possit suspicio. For the archaeological remains see J. Baradez, *Vue aérienne de l'organisation romaine dans le Sud algérien: Fossatum Africae*, Paris, 1949. COMITATENSES: *Not. Dig. Occ.* vii. 140-52, 179-98 (see App. II). PRAEPOSITI LIMITUM: *Not. Dig. Occ.* xxv, xxx, xxxi.

104. THE FIRST PRAEPOSITUS LIMITIS: *IRT* 880. PRAEFECTI: Amm. XXIX. v. 21, 35, *CTh* XI. xxx. 62, procos. Afr., 405, in negotiis, quae ex appellatione descendunt, veterem consuetudinem volumus custodiri, illud addentes, ut, si quando a gentilibus vel a praefectis eorum fuisset interposita provocatio, sacrum sollemniter hoc est proconsularis cognitionis praestoletur examen; Aug. *Ep.* 199 §46, sunt enim apud nos, hoc est in Africa, barbarae innumerabiles gentes, in quibus nondum esse praedicatum evangelium ex his, qui ducuntur inde captivi et Romanorum servitiis iam miscentur, cotidie nobis addiscere in promptu est. pauci tamen anni sunt, ex quo quidam eorum rarissimi atque paucissimi, qui pacati Romanis finibus adhaerent, ita ut non habeant reges suos, sed super eos praefecti a Romano constituantur imperio, et illi ipsi eorum praefecti Christiani esse coeperunt. TRIBUNI and DECURIONES: Aug. *Ep.* 46, in Arzugibus, ut audivi, decurioni, qui limiti praeest, vel tribuno solent iurare barbari iurantes per daemones suos; qui ad deducendas bastagas pacti fuerint vel aliqui ad servandas fruges ipsas, singuli possessores vel conductores solent ad custodiendas fruges suscipere quasi iam fideles epistulam decurione mittente vel singuli transeuntes, quibus necesse est per ipsos transire.

105. MACAE: *SEG* IX. 356 §11, ὥστε τοὺς καστρησιανοὺς μετὰ πάσης ἐπιμελίας παραφυλάττιν, καὶ μὴ σ[υνω]νῆς χάριν τινὰ παρειέναι ἐπὶ τοὺς βαρβάρους μήτε τὰ ἀλλάγματα πρὸς αὐτοὺς τιθ[έν]αι· ἀλλὰ φυλάττιν αὐτοὺς καὶ τὰς ὁδοὺς ἐπὶ τῷ μήτε Ῥωμαίους μήτε Αἰγυπιλίο[υς μ]ήτε ἕτερόν τ<ι>να δίχα [πρ]οστάγματος τὴν πάροδον ἐπὶ τοὺς βαρβάρους ποιεῖν· [το]ὺς δὲ ἐκ τοῦ ἔθνου[ς τ]ῶν Μακῶν διὰ γραμμάτων τοῦ λα(μπροτάτου) πραιφέκτου συγχωρῖσθαι ἐπὶ τὰ χωρία [Πε]νταπόλεως παραγίνεσθαι. MARCOMANNI: *Not. Dig. Occ.* xxxiv. 24, tribunus gentis Marcomannorum, xxxv. 31, tribunus gentis per Raetiam deputatae. These Marcomanni are probably those mentioned in Paul. *V. Amb. 36.*

106. UNNIGARDAE: Syn. *Ep.* 78, δέονται γὰρ δὴ σοῦ μὲν δι' ἡμῶν, βασιλέως δὲ διὰ σοῦ δέησιν, ἢν εἰκὸς ἡμᾶς ἦν, ἐκείνων σιωπώντων, ποιήσασθαι, μὴ καταλεγῆναι τοὺς ἄνδρας ἀριθμοῖς ἐγχωρίοις. ἀχρεῖοι γὰρ ἂν ἑαυτοῖς τε καὶ ἡμῖν γένοιντο, τῶν βασιλικῶν δωρεῶν ἀφηρημένοι, εἰ μήτε ἵππων ἕξουσι διαδοχήν, μήτε ὅπλων παρασκευήν, μήτε δαπάνην ἀγωνισταῖς ἄνδρασιν ἀρκοῦσαν. μὴ σύ γε, ὦ μετ' αὐτῶν ἀριστεύων, μὴ περιίδῃς τοὺς στρατιώτας εἰς ἀτιμοτέραν τάξιν χωροῦντας.

107. LAW ON MANICHEES: *CTh* XVI. v. 65 §3. The last law on sons of veterans is *CTh* VII. xxii. 12, 398; for later practice see nn. 145-6.

108. *CTh* VII. xv. 2, 423, quicumque castellorum loca quocumque titulo possident, cedant ac deserant, quia ab his tantum fas est possideri castellorum territoria, quibus adscripta sunt et de quibus iudicavit antiquitas. quod si ulterius vel privatae condicionis quispiam in his locis vel non castellanus miles fuerit detentator inventus, capitali sententia cum bonorum publicatione plectatur. Th. II, *Nov.* xxiv §4, 443, agros etiam limitaneos universis cum paludibus omnique iure, quos ex prisca dispositione limitanei milites ab omni munere vacuos ipsi curare pro suo compendio atque arare consueverant, et si in praesenti coluntur ab his, firmiter ac sine ullo concussionis gravamine detineri, et si ab aliis possidentur, cuiuslibet spatii temporis praescriptione cessante ab universis detentoribus vindicatos isdem militibus sine ullo prorsus, sicut antiquitus statutum est, conlationis onere volumus adsignari.

109. Th. II, *Nov.* iv §1, 438, xxiv, 443.

110. For the regiments of Philae, Syene and Elephantine see n. 127. MAURI: *P. Ryl.* 609 (*vexillatio*), cf. *BGU* 21, *SPP* xx. 98, *P. Zill.* 5, *P. Lond.* 999, 1313, *P. Čairo,* 67091, for Mauri at Hermopolis from 340 to 538; in *Not. Dig. Or.* xxxi. 23–4, the Cuneus Equitum Maurorum Scutariorum is placed at Lycopolis and a Cuneus Equitum Scutariorum at Hermopolis. VERONENSES: *P. Ital.* 22. TARVISIANI: *ILS* 2809. HIPPONIENSES REGII: *ILS* 2811; cf. the Ravennates, Mediolanenses, Cadisiani, Salonitae (*P. Ital.* 20, 23, *P. Dip.* 122, *ILS* 2808, *PSI* 247).

111. THE GOLDEN GATE INSCRIPTION: *ILS* 9216, cf. *Not. Dig. Or.* vi. 50 for the Cornuti. LEONES CLIBANARII: *P. Amh.* 148, *SPP* xx. 131, 135, 139. BISELECTI: *P. Cairo,* 67057. NUMIDAE JUST.: *P. Cairo,* 67321, *P. Lond.* 1663, *Sb* 8028. FELICES PERSO-ARMENII: *P. Dip.* 122. EQUITES PERSO-JUST.: *ILS* 2810. ELECTI: *ILS* 9211. BISELECTI: *CIL* VIII. 17414. PRIMI FELICES JUST.: *CIL* VIII. 9248. V MACEDONICA: *P. Cairo,* 67002 (Μακεδόνες), *PRG* III. 10 (Κυνταυοί); cf. *Not. Dig. Or.* vii. 39, xxviii. 14. ARMIGERI: *P. Oxy.* 1888, cf. *Not. Dig. Or.* v. 35, vii. 26. DACI: *SPP* xx. 139, cf. *Not. Dig. Or.* vi. 43. SCYTHAE: *P. Oxy.* 1920, 2046, *P. Cairo,* 67002, 67057, *P. Grenf.* II. 95, cf. *Not. Dig. Or.* vi. 44. TRANSTI-GRITANI: *SPP* xx. 131, 139, *BGU* 369, *Chr.* I. 471, cf. *Not. Dig. Or.* vii. 58. TERTIO DELMATAE: Just. *Ed.* iv §2, cf. *Not. Dig. Or.* vii. 27. IV PARTHICA: Theoph. Sim. II. 6, cf. *Not. Dig. Or.* xxxv. 24. REGII: Proc. *BG* I. xxiii. 3, cf. *Not. Dig. Or.* vi. 49. ARMENII: *P. Ital.* 22, 23, cf. *Not. Dig. Or.* vi. 31. DACI: *P. Ital.* 18–9, cf. *Not. Dig. Or.* vi. 43. FELICES THEODOSIANI: *P. Ital.* 16, cf. *Not. Dig. Or.* vi. 62. PRIMI THEODOSIANI: *ILS* 2806, cf. *Not. Dig. Or.* v. 64. The Theodosiaci stationed at Rome (*P. Ital.* 17, Greg. *Ep.* II. 45) may be identical with one of these units, but are more probably the Equites Theodosiaci of *Not. Dig. Or.* vi. 33 or viii. 27. The Theodosiaci of Nessana in Palestine (*P. Nessana,* 15) are no doubt the Balistarii Theodosiaci of the Eastern field army (*Not. Dig. Or.* vii. 57).

112. See pp. 271, 273–4, 292.

113. See pp. 280–2.

114. SCHOLAE: Proc. *HA* xxiv. 15–23, Agathias, v. 15, cf. *CJ* I. xxxi. 5, 527 (*probatoriae*), IV. lxv. 35 §1, 530 (eleven *scholae*), XII. xxix. 2, 474 (*primicerii* given rank of *comes clarissimus*). Eutychius's father Alexander, though τῇ τοῦ σχολαρίου τετιμημένος στρατίᾳ, saw active service under Belisarius (*V. Eutychii,* 7).

115. PROTECTORES AND DOMESTICI: Proc. *HA* xxiv. 24–6, cf. *V. Theod. Syc.* 25, 45, for *protectores* at Ancyra. PURCHASE OF PLACES: *CJ* II. vii. 25 §3, 519, Const.

Porph. *Cer.* I. 86, πάντων δὲ τῶν ἀγοραζόντων τόπους καὶ συμβολαῖα ἔξωθεν παρὰ τῶν πιπρασκόντων γίνεται πρὸς τούτοις καὶ σύμβολα γίνεται. MENANDER'S CAREER: Menander, I.

116. Joh. Lydus, *Mag.* I. 47, ἀδωράτορας οἱ ῾Ρωμαῖοι τοὺς ἀπομάχους καλοῦσιν; *CIL* v. 8747, *CIG* 9449 (protector), *P. Ital.* 17, *P. Dip.* 122 (adorator). The Codex Justinianus ignores the privileges given to the *primicerius* and *decemprimi* of the *protectores* by *CTh* VI. xxiv. 9; perhaps the corps had ceased to exist, and the title alone survived (as proved by Const. Porph. *Cer.* I. 86).

117. EXCUBITORES: Joh. Lydus, *Mag.* I. 16, Proc. *HA* VI. 1–5 (Justin enlists and serves in Isauria), *BV* II. xii. 17 (they serve in Africa). JUSTIN: Const. Porph. *Cer.* I. 93, Anon. Val. 76, Malalas, 410, cf. Proc. *HA* VI. 11, Evagr. IV. 1. TIBERIUS: Theoph. Sim. III. 11. MAURICE: Joh. Eph. *HE* VI. 14, Greg. *Ep.* III. 61. For *excubitores* in action at Constantinople see Malalas, 394, *Chron. Pasch.* 606, 608; in service abroad, Joh. Eph. *HE* VI. 14, Greg. *Ep.* I. 16, IX. 5, 89.

118. SCRIBONES: *Lib. Pont.* lxi. 4 (first mention in 545), Theoph. Sim. I. 4, ἄνδρα τῶν σωματοφυλάκων τοῦ βασιλέως ὑπερφερόμενον, ὃν σκρίβωνα τῇ Λατινίδι φωνῇ ῾Ρωμαῖοι κατονομάζουσιν (cf. Suidas, s.v. σκρίβα), Agathias, III. 14, τῶν ἀμφὶ τὰ βασίλεια δορυφόρων οὓς δὴ σκρίβωνας ὀνομάζουσιν; Theophylact's phrase implies an officer of the guards and this is confirmed by Mansi, x. 855, venit quidam scribo nomine Sagoleva cum multis excubitoribus (A.D. 653). SPECIAL MISSIONS: *Lib. Pont.* lxi. 4, lxxv. 2, Greg. *Ep.* IX. 4, Theoph. Sim. VII. 3 (arrests); Agathias, III. 14 (official enquiry); Theoph. Sim. I. 4 (envoy); Greg. *Ep.* II. 38 (recruits); V. 30 (distribution of pay); Theoph. Sim. VIII. 5 (equipment of fleet). Other *scribones* are mentioned by Gregory in *Ep.* V. 29 (apparently at Salona), and IX. 57, 63, 73, 77, 78, X. 15, and in *V. Eutychii*, 70, Joh. Moschus, 174.

119. *Comitatenses* is used (in distinction from *limitanei*) in Julianus's summary of Just. *Nov.* xli. *Milites* (στρατιῶται) are usually contrasted with *foederati* (see nn. 133–4), sometimes also with *limitanei* (Just. *Nov.* ciii §3) or with *scholares* (Just. *Nov* cxvii. §11), but the term is also used in a wider sense to include *foederati* and *scholares* (*CJ* IV. lxv. 35 §1, 530, milites autem appellamus eos, qui tam sub excelsis magistris militum tolerare noscuntur militiam quam in undecim devotissimis scholis taxati sunt, nec non eos, qui sub diversis optionibus foederatorum nomine sunt decorati; Proc. *BG* I. v. 2, στρατιώτας ἐκ μὲν καταλόγων καὶ φοιδεράτων τετρακισχιλίους, ἐκ δὲ ᾽Ισαύρων τρισχιλίους μάλιστα ἔχοντα; III. xxxiii. 13, τινὲς δε αὐτῶν (the Heruls) καὶ ῾Ρωμαίων στρατιῶται γεγένηνται ἐν τοῖς φοιδεράτοις καλουμένοις ταττόμενοι. *Numerus* (ἀριθμός, κατάλογος) is used to denote a regiment of *comitatenses* as opposed to *scholares* or *foederati* in Just. *Nov.* cxvi, cxvii §11, Proc. *BG* I. v. 2 (cited above), *BV* II. iii. 4, XV. 50. BARBARIANS IN THE NUMERI: Proc. *BG* I. xvii. 17, ἦλθον δὲ αὐτοῖς αὐτόμολοι δύο καὶ εἴκοσι, βάρβαροι μὲν γένος, στρατιῶται δὲ ῾Ρωμαῖοι, ἐκ καταλόγου ἱππικοῦ, οὗπερ ᾽Ιννοκέντιος ἦρχεν; xxvii. 1–2, Μαρτῖνος δὲ καὶ Βαλεριανὸς ἦκον, ἑξακοσίους τε καὶ χιλίους στρατιώτας ἱππεῖς ἐπαγομένω. καὶ αὐτῶν οἱ πλεῖστοι Οὖννοί τε ἦσαν καὶ Σκλαβηνοὶ καὶ ῎Ανται, οἳ ὑπὲρ ποταμὸν ῎Ιστρον οὐ μακρὰν τῆς ἐκείνῃ ὄχθης ἵδρυνται. VANDALS: Proc. *BV* II. xiv. 17, cf. *BP* II. xxi. 4; Ostrogoths were similarly used in the East (Proc. *BP* II. xiv. 10, cf. xviii. 24–5, xxi. 4). PERSIANS: Proc. *BP* II. xix. 24–5, cf. *BG* III. iii. 10–11, *ILS* 2810, *P. Dip.* 122.

120. The contrast is most marked in *BG* III. vi. 2, Κόνων γὰρ ἐνταῦθα ἐφύλασσε, ῾Ρωμαίων τε καὶ ᾽Ισαύρων χιλίους ἔχων, cf. *BP* I. xviii. 5, *BG* I. v. 2, X. 1, II. v. 1,

xii. 26-7, xxiii. 2, xxvii. 5 ff., III. x. 19 ff., xx. 4 ff., xxxvi. 7 ff. (Isaurians), *BP*
II. xxi. 4, *BG* II. v. 1, xii. 26-7, III. vi. 10 (Thracians), *BP* II. xxi. 4, *BG* III. x.
2, xi. 11-14 (Illyrians), *BP* II. xxi. 2, xxiv. 12, *BG* III. vi. 10, xxvii. 3, 10, IV. xi.
57 (Armenians). Thracians and Armenians are called στρατιῶται in *BG* III. vi.
10, Illyrians in *BG* III. x. 2, xi. 11, Thracians and Illyrians in *BG* III. xii. 4. For
recruiting in Illyricum and Thrace see n. 144. The Isaurians in *BP* I. xviii. 5,
38-40, were raw recruits, mostly from Lycaonia; Saba's father, a Cappadocian,
was posted to an Isaurian regiment (see n. 123).

121. BELISARIUS'S ARMIES: Proc. *BV* I. xi. 2 (Africa), *BG* I. v. 2 (Italy). REIN-
FORCEMENTS FROM ILLYRICUM: Proc. *BG* II. xxviii. 2, III. x. 2, xi. 11-4; FROM
THRACE: *BG* III. xxxix. 18. For individual regiments see n. 111. WESTERN
REGIMENTS IN THE EAST: *PSI* 247 (Salonitae at Oxyrhynchus), *P. Cairo*, 67321,
P. Lond. 1663, *Sb* 8028 (Numidae in the Thebaid), *CIL* VIII. 17414, *P. Cairo*,
67057 (Biselecti in Africa and the Thebaid).

122. *CJ* XII. xxxv. 18, 492.

123. ISAURI: Cyr. Scyth. *V. Sabae*, 1, 9, 25, cf. *Not. Dig. Or.* vii. 56. ARMIGERI:
P. Oxy. 1888, cf. *Not. Dig. Or.* vii. 26. SCYTHAE: *P. Oxy.* 1920, 2046, *P. Cairo*,
67002, 67057, *P. Grenf.* II. 95, cf. *Not. Dig. Or.* vi. 44. LOAN CONTRACT: *SPP* xx.
139, cf. *Not. Dig. Or.* vi. 43 (Daci), vii. 58 (Transtigritani), *P. Amh.* 148 (Leones
Clibanarii at Arsinoe in 487), *P. Lond.* 113. 5(a) (Transtigritani at Arsinoe in
498). John of Maiuma (*Pleroph.* 27) mentions the Daci at Alexandria under
Zeno. See also n. 121 for Western regiments stationed in Egypt.

124. PENTAPOLIS: *SEG* IX. 356 §§5, 7, 8, 12. LIBYA: Just. *Ed.* xiii §18. PHOENICE:
Just. *Ed.* iv §2, cf. *Not. Dig. Or.* vii. 27. PALMYRA: Malalas, 426. PALESTINE:
Just. *Nov.* ciii §3. The Theodosiaci of Nessana in Palestine (*P. Nessana*, 15) are
not recorded in the Notitia among the *limitanei* and are probably the Balistarii
Theodosiaci, *pseudocomitatenses* of the *mag. mil. Or.* (*Not. Dig. Or.* vii. 57). In
Arabia similarly Justinian assigned to the moderator τῶν καταλόγων τῶν ἰδρυμένων
ἐκεῖσέ τινα (Just. *Nov.* cii §2). BOSPORUS: Malalas, 432.

125. LIMITANEI: *CJ* I. xxxi. 4+xlvi. 4+XI. lx. 3 (= Th. II, *Nov.* xxiv, 443).
THE DANUBE: Just. *Nov.* xli, 536. THE EAST: Proc. *HA* xxiv. 12-14, Malalas,
426 (Phoenice), 430 (Armenia), Just. *Nov.* ciii §3 (Palestine), Theoph. Sim. II. 6
(Syria), *Princeton Exp. Syria*, 20, 562 (Arabia). PENTAPOLIS: *SEG* IX. 356 §§11, 14.

126. V MACEDONICA: *P. Cairo*, 67002 (Macedonians), *PRG* III. 10 (Quintani), cf.
Not. Dig. Or. xxviii. 14. For the Mauri see n. 108. LEASE: *SPP* xx. 98.

127. The dossier is published partly in *P. Monac.*, partly in *P. Lond.* v. 1719-37.
Flavius Patermuthis is styled στρατιώτης in *P. Lond.* 1730 (585), 1732 (586),
P. Monac. 10 (586), 12 (590-1), 13-14 (594), *P. Lond.* 1736 (611), 1737 (613).
LEGION OF SYENE: *P. Lond.* 1722, 1728, *P. Monac.* 4-5, 8, 15, 16. LEGION OF
PHILAE: *P. Monac.* 16. Cf. *Not. Dig. Or.* xxxi. 35, milites miliarenses, Syene, 37,
legio prima Maximiana, Filas, 64, cohors prima felix Theodosiana, apud
Elephantinem. ORDINARII: *P. Monac.* 2, 3, 8, 16. CENTURIONS: *P. Lond.* 1722,
1727, 1729, 1731, 1734, *P. Monac.* 8, 9.

128. PATERMUTHIS: *P. Monac.* 10, στρατιώτῃ ἀριθμοῦ Ἐλεφαντίνης, ναύτῃ τῷ
ἐπιτηδεύματι, *P. Lond.* 1736-7, στρατιώτης ἀριθμοῦ Ἐλεφαντίνης, ναύτης ἀπὸ Συήνης,
P. Monac. 7, 9, 14, *P. Lond.* 1727 (ναύτης only), *P. Monac.* 12, 13 (στρατιώτης
only). JOHN: *P. Lond.* 1730, στρατιώτης ἀριθμοῦ Συήνης, ὁρμώμενος ἀπὸ τῆς αὐτῆς,

ναύτης τὸ ἐπιτήδευμα, 1728, στρατιώτης τείρων λεγίωνος Συήνης (584–5), P. Monac. 7, 9, 14 (στρατιώτης in 583, 585, 594). THE PROBATORIA: Chr. I. 470.

129. LEASE OF BAKERY: SPP xx. 131. THE PIOUS SOLDIER: Moschus, 73.

130. LIMITANEI IN AFRICA: CJ I. xxvii. 2 §8, 534.

131. The word σύμμαχοι (or cognate terms) is used in BV I. xi. 11 and BG I. v. 4 of Huns, in BG IV. xxvi. 12 of Lombards, in BG II. xiv. 34 of Heruls, in BV II. xiii. 20, 28, 30 of Moors; ἔνσπονδοι of the Tetraxite Goths in Aed. III. vii. 13. Heruls, Huns and Gepids are associated with the Lombards in BG IV. xxvi. 13. Heruls are very frequently mentioned, and Moors appear in the East in BP II. xxi. 4.

132. FEDERATES: Proc. BV I. xi. 3–4, ἐν δὲ δὴ φοιδεράτοις πρότερον μὲν μόνοι βάρβαροι κατελέγοντο, ὅσοι οὐκ ἐπὶ τῷ δοῦλοι εἶναι, ἅτε μὴ πρὸς Ῥωμαίων ἡσσημένοι, ἀλλ᾿ ἐπὶ τῇ ἴσῃ καὶ ὁμοίᾳ ἐς τὴν πολιτείαν ἀφίκοιντο. φοίδερα γὰρ τὰς πρὸς τοὺς πολεμίους σπονδὰς καλοῦσι Ῥωμαῖοι. τὸ δὲ νῦν ἅπασι τοῦ ὀνόματος τούτου ἐπιβατεύειν οὐκ ἐν κωλύμῃ ἐστὶ, τοῦ χρόνου τὰς προσηγορίας ἐφ᾿ ὧν τέθεινται ἥκιστα ἀξιοῦντος τηρεῖν, ἀλλὰ τῶν πραγμάτων ἀεὶ περιφερομένων, ᾗ ταῦτα ἄγειν ἐθέλουσιν ἄνθρωποι, τῶν πρόσθεν αὐτοῖς ὠνομασμένων ὀλιγωροῦντες, cf. BG III. xxxiii. 13, τινὲς δὲ αὐτῶν καὶ Ῥωμαίων στρατιῶται γεγένηνται ἐν τοῖς φοιδεράτοις καλουμένοις ταττόμενοι. In BG IV. v. 13–14, Procopius uses φοιδέρατοι, in the old sense of the Ostrogoths before their migration to Italy. CJ I. v. 12 §17, 527, Γότθους πολλάκις τοῖς καθωσιωμένοις ἐγγράφομεν φοιδεράτοις.

133. FEDERATES AND COMITATENSES: Proc. BV I. xi. 2, πεζοὺς μὲν στρατιώτας μυρίους, ἱππέας δὲ πεντακισχιλίους, ἔκ τε στρατιωτῶν καὶ φοιδεράτων συνειλεγμένους, II. iii. 4 (ὅσοι ἄλλοι φοιδεράτων ἄρχοντες ἦσαν contrasted with ὅσοι τῶν ἱππικῶν καταλόγων ἦρχον), xv. 50 (ἡγεμόνες φοιδεράτων contrasted with those καταλόγου ἱππικοῦ and πεζῶν), BG I. v. 2, στρατιώτας ἐκ μὲν καταλόγων καὶ φοιδεράτων τετρακισχιλίους, ἐκ δὲ Ἰσαύρων τρισχιλίους μάλιστα ἔχοντα, cf. BG III. xxxiii. 13 (cited in n. 132); CJ IV. lxv. 35 §1, milites autem appellamus eos, qui tam sub excelsis magistris militum tolerare noscuntur militiam quam in undecim devotissimis scholis taxati sunt, nec non eos, qui sub diversis optionibus foederatorum nomine sunt decorati, Just. Nov. cxvi, 542, et milites quidem ad numeros suos transmittant in quibus militant, foederatos vero ad proprios optiones, cxvii §11, 542, quod autem a nobis sancitum est de his qui in expeditionibus sunt et in militiis constituti, sive milites sint sive foederati sive scholares sive alii quidam sub alia quacumque militia armata constituti, melius ordinare perspeximus. et iubemus quantoscumque annos in expedito manserint, sustinere horum uxores, licet nec litteras nec responsum aliquod a suis maritis susceperint. si qua vero ex huiusmodi mulieribus suum maritum audierit mortuum, neque tunc ad alias eam venire nuptias sinimus, nisi prius accesserit mulier per se aut per suos parentes aut per aliam quamcumque personam ad priores numeri et cartularios, in quo huius maritus militabat, et eos seu tribunum, si tamen adest, interrogaverit . . . si vero scholaris fuerit ille de cuius morte dubitatio est, a primis scholae et actuario, si autem foederatus, ab optione eius memoratam depositionem accipere eius uxorem.

134. AUDIT: Just. Nov. cxlvii §2, 553, tam militares quam foederaticas discussiones. REGIMENTS: Just. Nov. cxlviii §2, 566, τὰ τοῖς στρατιωτικοῖς τάγμασιν ἢ φοιδερατικοῖς ἐπιδοθέντα. OFFICERS: Proc. BV I. xi. 5, xix. 13, II. iii. 4, vii. 11, xv. 50. OPTIONES: CJ IV. lxv. 35 (cited in n. 133), Nov. cxvi, cxvii §11 (cited in n. 133).

135. TOLERATION OF ARIANISM: *CJ* i. v. 12 §17. That federates were not under the command of the *magistri militum* appears from the wording of *CJ* iv. lxv. 35 (cited in n. 133). COMES FOEDERATORUM: Malalas, 364 (Areobindus, cos. 434), Theophanes, AM. 6005 (Patriciolus, father of Vitalian), Proc. *BG* iii. xxxi. 10 (Artabanes). FEDERATES IN PALESTINE: Just. *Nov.* ciii §3, 536.

136. Olymp. 7, ὅτι τὸ βουκελλάριος ὄνομα ἐν ταῖς ἡμέραις Ὁνωρίου ἐφέρετο κατὰ στρατιωτῶν οὐ μόνων Ῥωμαίων, ἀλλὰ καὶ Γότθων τινῶν· ὡς δ' αὕτως καὶ τὸ φοιδεράτων κατὰ διαφόρου καὶ συμμιγοῦς ἔφερετο πλήθους. *CTh* vii. xiii. 16, 406, praecipue sane eorum servos, quos militia armata detentat, foederatorum nihilo minus et dediticiorum, quoniam ipsos quoque una cum dominis constat bella tractare.

137. UNNIGARDAE: Syn. *Catastasis* 11, Οὐννιγάρδαι μετὰ Ἀνυσίου Ῥωμαϊκαὶ χεῖρές εἰσιν. ἄνευ δὲ τούτου καὶ τοὺς τεσσαράκοντα τοὺς παρόντας ἐπαινεῖν μὲν ἔχω τῆς ῥώμης, ἐγγυήσασθαι δὲ τῆς γνώμης οὐ βούλομαι; *Ep.* 78, οὐδὲν ἂν γένοιτο Πενταπόλει λυσιτελέστερον τοῦ τοὺς ἀγαθοὺς καὶ ἄνδρας καὶ στρατιώτας Οὐννιγάρδας προτετιμῆσθαι πάντων στρατιωτῶν, οὐ τῶν ἐγχωρίων λεγομένων μόνον, ἀλλὰ καὶ ὅσοι πώποτε κατὰ συμμαχίαν εἰς τούσδε τοὺς τόπους ἀφίκοντο. . . . δέονται γὰρ δὴ σοῦ μὲν δι' ἡμῶν, βασιλέως δὲ διὰ σοῦ δέησιν, ἣν εἰκὸς ἡμᾶς ἦν, ἐκείνων σιωπώντων, ποιήσασθαι, μὴ καταλεγῆναι τοὺς ἄνδρας ἀριθμοῖς ἐγχωρίοις. ἀχρεῖοι γὰρ ἂν ἑαυτοῖς τε καὶ ἡμῖν γένοιντο, τῶν βασιλικῶν δωρεῶν ἀφῃρημένοι, εἰ μήτε ἵππων ἕξουσι διαδοχήν, μήτε ὅπλων παρασκευήν, μήτε δαπάνην ἀγωνισταῖς ἄνδρασιν ἀρκοῦσαν. TITUS: *V. Dan.* 60–64.

138. RUFINUS: Claud. *in Ruf.* ii. 76 ff. STILICHO: Zos. v. 34. AETIUS: Joh. Ant. 201.4–5. ASPAR: Malalas, 371. VALERIAN: Th. ii, *Nov.* xv. 2, 444. LEO'S LAW: *CJ* ix. xii. 10, 468. JOHN THE CAPPADOCIAN: Proc. *BP* i. xxv. 7. PRIVATE BUCELLARII: *Chr.* i. 471, P. Oxy. 156, P. Erlangen, 67.

139. OATH: Proc. *BV* ii. xviii. 6. NUMBERS: Proc. *BG* iii. i. 18–20 (Belisarius), xxvii. 3 (Valerian), Agathias, i. 19 (Narses). Lesser commanders who had δορύφοροι include Martin (Proc. *BV* i. xi. 30), Peter (*BP* ii. xxvi. 26) and Theodore (*BV* ii. xviii. 1). The *bucellarii* of P. Oxy. 2046 probably belonged to Athanasius, *dux* of the Thebaid (cf. P. Oxy. 1920). Justinian had a δορύφορος when he was only a *candidatus* (Proc. *BG* iii. xxxviii. 5).

140. ORIGINS OF BUCELLARII: *BV* i. xvii. 1 (Armenian), *BG* iii. xxxvi. 16 (Cilician), *BG* i. xxviii. 23 (Pisidian), i. xxix. 20 (Cappadocian), ii. x. 19 (Isaurian), *BV* ii. xxviii. 3, *BG* ii. ii. 10, xiii. 14, iii. xi. 37 (Thracians), *BV* ii. x. 4, *BG* i. xvi. 1, ii. i. 21, ii. 10, xiii. 14, iii. xxx. 6 (Huns), *BG* ii. ii. 10, iii. xi. 37 (Persians). MAJOR DOMO: Proc. *BG* ii. xviii. 8, iii. xxxvi. 16, Agathias, i. 19, ii. 8. OPTIO: Proc. *BV* i. xvii. 1. Δορύφοροι IN COMMAND OF SPECIAL DETACHMENTS: *BP* i. ix. 13 (1,000 men), ii. xix. 15 (1,200 men, mostly ὑπασπισταί), xxi. 2 (1,000 men), *BV* i. xix. 23 (800 ὑπασπισταί), xxiii. 5 (22 ὑπασπισταί), ii. xix. 6, *BG* i. vii. 34 (500 men), xxvii. 4, 11 (200 and 300 ὑπασπισταί), ii. ii. 3 (100 ὑπασπισταί), 10 (600 cavalry), vii. 27 (800 ὑπασπισταί), iii. xi. 19 (1,000 men), xxxvi. 1 (3,000 men), etc. Δορύφοροι BECOME OFFICERS: Proc. *BP* i. xii. 21 (Belisarius and Sittas), *BG* iii. xiv. 1 (Chilbudius), xxxvi. 16 (Paul), *BP* i. xviii. 6 (Peter, of Justinian), *BG* iii. xxxviii. 5 (Asbadus, also of Justinian), *BV* ii. x. 4 (Aigan, of Belisarius), Theoph. Sim. i. 14 (Stephanus, of Tiberius Constantine).

141. The figures given for the African expeditionary force (Proc. *BV* i. xi) are 10,000 πεζοὶ στρατιῶται and 5,000 cavalry, selected from στρατιῶται (under 4 commanders) and φοιδέρατοι (under 9 commanders), 400 Heruls and 600 Huns. ITALIAN EXPEDITIONARY FORCE: *BG* i. v. 2. REINFORCEMENTS: *BG* ii. v. 1, xiii. 16–8, iii. vi. 10, x. 1–3 (cf. ii. xxviii. 2).

142. GERMANUS: *BG* III. xxxix. 9–10, 16–20. NARSES: *BG* IV. xxvi. 8–13. Cf. the analysis of the Roman army in Lazica in Agathias, III. 20, where of seven groups one only (the Heruls and Lombards) are barbarian allies.

143. *CJ* XII. xxxv. 17, 472, neminem in ullo numero equitum vel peditum vel in quolibet limite sine nostri numinis sacra probatoria in posterum sociari concedimus, consuetudine quae hactenus tenuit antiquata, quae magisteriae potestati vel ducibus probatorias militum facere vel militibus adiungere licentiam tribuebat, ut ii tantum in numeris vel in limitibus militent, qui a nostra divinitate probatorias consequuntur. viros autem eminentissimos pro tempore magistros militum nec non etiam viros spectabiles duces, si supplere numeros pro his qui fatalibus sortibus decrescent necessarium esse putaverint, veritate discussa per suggestionem suam nostrae mansuetudini declarare, qui et quanti et in quo numero vel limite debeant subrogari, ut ita demum, prout nostrae sederit maiestati, divina subnotatione subnixi militiam sortiantur.

144. PROHIBITIONS ON SLAVES, ETC.: *CJ* XII. xxxiii. 2, 3, 4, xliii. 1, 2; cf. *P. Ryl.* 609. RECRUITING CAMPAIGNS: *BG* III. x. 1–3 (544), cf. xii. 4, xxxix. 16 (549). Theodoret implies that soldiers were mainly volunteers even in the mid-fifth century in *Ep.* (PG) 144, where he writes to the στρατιῶται of the garrison of Cyrrhus, οἱ μὲν γὰρ ναυτικόν, οἱ δὲ πολεμικὸν αἱροῦνται βίον, καὶ οἱ μὲν ἀθλητικόν, οἱ δὲ γεωργικόν.

145. For recruitment and conditions in fifth and sixth century Egypt, see J. Maspéro, *Organisation militaire de l'Égypte byzantine*, Paris, 1912. THE TWO BROTHERS: *SPP* XX. 131. PAULACIS: *P. Ital.* 22. Among the Theodosiaci of Nessana in Palestine recruitment was also local and service often hereditary (*P. Nessana*, 15, 22, 29). The family of Dios is described in *P. Monac.* 1 (574), where he is called a ναύτης, and is said to have had his son John συνεργαζόμενον αὐτῷ τῇ ναυτικῇ τεχνῇ, but to have paid a solidus for his *probatoria* (νομισμάτιον ἐν ζυγῷ Συήνης ὅπερ δέδωκέν σοι ὁ μνημονευθεὶς ἡμῶν πατὴρ Δῖος ὑπὲρ στρατευσιμοῦ τοῦ υἱοῦ σοῦ; cf. *SEG* IX. 356 §12, for the meaning of τὸ στρατευσιμόν). For Paeion see *P. Monac.* 4, line 55 (581), and for John, son of Jacob, n. 128.

146. *Chr.* I. 470, *P. Ryl.* 609, [Flavius Cons]tantinius Theofanes comes et vir inlustris comes devotissimorum virorum domesticorum et rei militaris Thebaici limitis Flavio [. . . .]rte sive Theodoti viro devotissimo tribuno Hermupoli degenti. . . . . eridero sacra iussione domini nostri Anastasii piissimi ac triumfatoris semper Augusti [e qua n]umeris supplementi caus[a] i[u]niores robustis corporibus adsociarentur Heracleon fil[ium] Constantinii [ortum e] civitati Hermupolitana in vexillatione prudentiae tuae pro tempore credita edictio mea militare praecipit [eiusq]ue nomen si ex genere oritur militari et neque curialis nec praesidalis est nec invecillo corpore [. . . . .] is nec censibus adscribtos matriculis eiusdem numeri inseri facito annonas ei ex die iduum [. . . . .]m Sabiniano et Theodoro viris clarissimis consulibus ministrari curaturus cum ceteris [. . . .] libus suis muniis militaribus operam navaturo ita tamen si octavum decimum annum [pereg]isse dinoscitur.

147. For the accession and quinquennial donative see n. 33. ANNONA: Val. III, *Nov.* xiii §3, Just. *Ed.* xiii §18, *CJ* I. xxvii. 1 §§22 ff., 2 §§22 ff. ARMS AND CLOTHING ALLOWANCE: Theoph. Sim. VII. 1, ὁ δὲ τύπος ἔβουλετο τριτταῖς μοίραις συντάττεσθαι τὴν ἐπίδοσιν, δι' ἐσθῆτος καὶ ὅπλων καὶ χαράγματος χρυσίου; cf. Proc. *BG* III. i. 8, ἵππου δὲ ἢ τόξου ἢ ἄλλου ὁτουοῦν στρατιώτου ἐν τῇ μάχῃ ἀπολωλότος ἕτερον ἀντ' αὐτοῦ πρὸς Βελισαρίου αὐτίκα ὑπῆρχεν.

148. CLOTHING FACTORIES: *CJ* XII. xxxix. 4. STUD FARMS: Proc. *BV* I. xii. 6, βασιλεὺς ἵπποις ὅτι μάλιστα πλείστοις τὸν στρατηγὸν ἐνταῦθα ἐδωρεῖτο ἐκ τῶν βασιλικῶν ἱπποφορβίων, ἃ οἱ νέμονται ἐς τὰ ἐπὶ Θράκης χωρία, *BG* IV. xxvii. 8 (Thrace), Theoph. Sim. III. 1 (Asia Minor), ἱπποφορβοῖς τοιγαροῦν προσομιλεῖ τοῖς τὰς ἵππους τὰς στρατιωτικὰς περιβόσκουσι. FABRICAE: *CJ* XI. x. 7 (467–72), Just. *Nov.* lxxxv, 539.

149. PALESTINE: *CTh* VII. iv. 30, 409. LIBYA: *SEG* IX. 356 §11, ὥστε τοὺς καστρησιανοὺς μετὰ πάσης ἐπιμελίας παραφυλάττιν, καὶ μὴ σ[υνω]νῆς χάριν τινὰ παρειέναι ἐπὶ τοὺς βαρβάρους μήτε τὰ ἀλλάγματα πρὸς αὐτοὺς τιθ[έν]αι. TRANSPORT OF FOOD-STUFFS: *CJ* XII. xxxvii. 4.

150. For the land tax and συνώνη see pp. 460–1. *CJ* XII. xxxvii preserves many laws which deal with rations in kind, e.g. nos. 1, 5, 6, 7, 10. In *Sb* 9455 (late fifth or early sixth century) the two *optiones* of the Leontoclibanarii give a μονορεκαῦτον to the ἐπιμελητής of Heracleopolis [λόγῳ τροφ]ημῶν τοῖς ἡμετέροις κοντουβελανίοις (*contubernalibus*) ὑπὲρ πρώτης καὶ δευτέρας καὶ τρίτης τετραμήνου for 2370 *artabae* of wheat. At Faran in the Sinai peninsula there were under Justin II 'octingentas condomos militantes in publico cum uxoribus suis, annonas et vestes de publico accipientes de Aegypto, nullum laborem habentes qui nec habent ibi eo quod totum harena sit, et praeter singulis diebus habentes singulos equos Saracenos qui capitum paleos et hordeum de publico accipiunt' (*Itin. Hier. Antoninus*, 40). DELEGATORIAE: *P. Cairo*, 67320–1, *P. Lond.* 1663, *Sb* 8028, *P. Erlangen*, 55. FORMARIAE: *P. Cairo*, 67050–1.

151. COMMUTATION: *CJ* XII. xxxvii. 19 pr., ἐὰν στρατιῶται ὑφεστῶτες μὴ ὦσιν ἐν ταῖς οἰκείαις ἀγγαρείαις, ἀλλ' ἢ εἰς βοήθειαν ἠφορίσθησαν προσώποις τισὶν ἢ κατὰ ἄφεσιν ἀπελύθησαν, μὴ λαμβάνειν τὰς ἀννόνας αὐτῶν τὸν ὑπομνηματοφύλακα ἐν εἴδει διὰ τὸ μὴ φθείρεσθαι, ἀλλ' ἐν χρυσῷ, . . §1, εἰ δὲ καὶ στρατιώτης ἐξαργυρίσαι βουληθείη τὰς παρεχομένας αὐτῷ ἀννόνας, λήψεται τὰ χρήματα κατὰ τὴν τράπεζαν. . . . εἰ δὲ καὶ ὁ ὑπομνηματοφύλαξ ἀγοράσῃ παρὰ στρατιώτου τὰς ἀννόνας αὐτοῦ καὶ αὐτὸς λαμβάνει αὐτὰς παρὰ τοῦ συντελεστοῦ ὡς ἐκχωρηθείσας αὐτῷ, πάλιν κατὰ τὴν τράπεζαν λαμβάνειν αὐτόν, εἰ μὴ παρὰ τὸ εἶδος βούλεται ὁ συντελεστὴς προσαγαγεῖν.

152. The details of commutation are given in *P. Cairo*, 67050–1, 67320.

153. BELISARIUS: Proc. *BG* I. xxv. 3. TROOPS IN TRANSIT: Just. *Nov.* cxxx, 545; *P. Oxy.* 1920, 2046.

154. DEPUTY PRAETORIAN PREFECTS ON THE EASTERN FRONT: Josh. Styl. 54, 70, 77, 93, 99, Proc. *BP* I. viii. 5, II. x. 2, Just. *Nov.* cxxxiv §1, 556, solum vero iubemus esse loci servatorem praefecturae in Osroena et in Mesopotamia, et si necessitas vocaverit, in aliis locis tempore expeditionis pro nutrimentis eius destinatos, et hoc quidem per nostram iussionem; FOR AFRICA: *BV* I. xi. 17, xv. 13, xvii. 16, II. xvi. 2, cf. I. xiii. 12–20 (John the Cappadocian).

155. ACTUARY'S COMMISSION: Just. *Nov.* cxxx pr., 545. ACTUARY'S ACCOUNTS: *P. Cairo*, 67145.

156. ANASTASIUS'S LAW: *CJ* XII. xxxvii. 16.

157. LEAVE: *CJ* XII. xxxvii. 16 §§2–4, I. xxvii. 2 §9, 534.

158. See n. 57 for grades of *comitatenses* and centurions and decurions. OTHER GRADES OF LIMITANEI: *Chr.* I. 470 (*primicerius, ordinarii, adiutor*), *P. Monac.* 3, 8, 16 (*ordinarii*), 8, 13, 14 (*adiutor*), 8, 13–16, *P. Lond.* 1722, 1724, 1733–4, cf.

PRG III. 10, *MAMA* I. 216 (*Augustales*), BGU 369 (*Flavialis*), P. *Monac.* 14 (*draconarius*), 15 (*campidoctor*), 9 (ἰατρός), P. *Lond.* 1722 (τυμπανάριος), 1722–3, 1731, 1733, 1736, P. *Monac.* 1, 12 (*actuarius*). For *Augustales* and *Flaviales* see Veg. II. 7. *Vicarii* are coupled with tribunes in *CJ* I. xlii. 2, XII. xxxvii. 19 pr. §4 (both probably of Anastasius), XII. xlii. 1 (where they are interpolated in a law of Constantine), III. xiii. 5 (these are probably interpolated in a law of 397). They are mentioned by Vegetius (III. 4, 6) and frequently in papyri, e.g. *P. Cairo*, 67002, 67009, 67057, *PSI* 1366, P. *Oxy.* 1883. It is significant that in the Patermuthis documents *vicarii* or *ex vicariis* frequently appear as witnesses etc. together with other ranks (P. *Lond.* 1722, 1724, 1727, 1733, P. *Monac.* 8, 9, 10), but only one *ex tribunis* is mentioned, and he is τοποτηρητὴς τοῦ λίμιτος, apparently a regional commander (P. *Monac.* 6). This suggests that the *vicarii* were rankers, resident in the place; the tribunes were perhaps absentees. That tribunes were often not to be found with their regiments is suggested by Just. *Nov.* cxvii §11, nisi prius accesserit mulier per se aut per suos parentes aut per aliam quamcumque personam ad priores numeri et cartularios, in quo huius maritus militabat, et eos seu tribunum, si tamen adest, interrogaverit.

159. ANASTASIUS'S REGULATIONS: *SEG* IX. 356 §7, ὥστε ἰνσπεσίμον συνοδιακοῦ μὴ καταζητῖσθαι ὡς ἀσθενεῖς ἢ ἀ[χ]ρείους τοὺς πρώτους ἑκάστου ἀριθμοῦ καὶ κάστρου, τουτέστιν, εἰ μὲν [ἑ]κατὸν εἶεν ἄνδρες, τοὺς πρώτους πέντται, εἰ δὲ διακόσιο[ι τ]οὺς [πρώτου]ς δέκα· τὴν δὲ αὐτὴ[ν ἀ]ναλ[ο]γείαν καὶ ἐ[πὶ τ]οῖ[ς] πλίοσιν καὶ ἐπὶ τοῖς ἐλάττοσιν ἀνδράσιν φυλάττεσθαι; cf. Proc. *HA* xxiv. 2–4.

160. JUSTINIAN: Proc. *HA* xxiv. 8. MAURICE'S LAWS: Theoph. Sim. VII. 1; the second seems to be identical with *CJ* XII. xlvii. 3 (from the Basilica) and I have used this text to supplement Theophylact.

161. For promotion of *bucellarii* see n. 140. BARBARIAN OFFICERS: Proc. *BG* III. xxiii. 6, Agathias, III. 21, IV. 15 (Huns), Proc. *BG* IV. ix. 5, Agathias, I. 14 (Heruls), Proc. *BG* III. vi. 10 (Iberian), IV. xxv. 11 (Goth), IV. viii. 15 (Gepid), Agathias, III. 21 (Anta), III. 6 (three barbarians).

162. STELLATURA: *CJ* XII. xxxvii. 12. THE TWELFTH: *CJ* I. xlvi. 4, *SEG* IX. 356 §6, *Princeton Exp. Syria*, 20. PAYMENTS FOR LEAVE: *CJ* I. xxvii. 2 §9. ANNONAE OF DEAD SOLDIERS: Proc. *HA* xxiv. 5–6.

163. SALARY OF DUX OF LIBYA: Just. *Ed.* xiii §18 (see n. 84).

164. ARREARS IN THE EAST: Proc. *HA* xxiv. 13, *BP* II. vii. 37; no garrison is recorded at Beroea in the Notitia, but in Maurice's reign a unit of *limitanei* was stationed there (Theoph. Sim. II. 6). ARREARS IN AFRICA: Proc. *BV* II. xv. 55, xvi. 5, xviii. 9; IN ITALY: *BG* III. vi. 6–7, xi. 13–16, xxxvi. 7–26, IV. xxvi. 5–6.

165. ALEXANDER: Proc. *BG* III. i. 28–33; cf. for auditors in general Proc. *HA* xxiv. 5–11, Agathias, V. 14.

166. MAURICE'S ECONOMIES: Theoph. Sim. III. 1 ff., VIII. 6 ff.

167. PAULACIS: P. *Ital.* 22. TSITAS: P. *Dip.* 122. SORTES VANDALORUM: Proc. *BV* II. xiv. 8–10. The papyri record several soldiers who owned land in Egypt (P. *Michael.* 43, *PSI* 296) and in Palestine (P. *Nessana*, 16, 21, 24).

168. Joh. Lydus, *Mens.* I. 27, ὅτι ἐπὶ τοῦ Διοκλητιανοῦ ἡ πᾶσα τῶν Ῥωμαίων στρατιὰ μυριάδες ἦν ὀκτὼ καὶ τριάκοντα καὶ ἐννακισχίλιοι καὶ ἑπτακόσιοι καὶ τέσσαρες, ναυτικὴ δὲ δύναμις ἡ ἐπὶ τῶν ἐπικαίρων χωρίων ναυλοχοῦσα ἐπί τε τοῖς ποταμοῖς ἐπί τε τῇ θαλάσσῃ τετρακισμύριοι καὶ πεντακισχίλιοι καὶ πεντακόσιοι ἑξήκοντα καὶ δύο.

ὅτι πρὸς τοῦτον τὸν ἀριθμὸν ὁ μέγας Κωνσταντῖνος ἐπὶ τῆς ἀνατολικῆς βασιλείας τὸν
στρατὸν διέθηκεν, ὡς ἑτέρας τοσαύτας μυριάδας στρατοῦ προστεθῆναι τῇ Ῥωμαϊκῇ
πολιτείᾳ. Zos. II. 15, συναγαγὼν δυνάμεις ἔκ τε ὧν ἔτυχεν ἔχων δορικτήτων
βαρβάρων καὶ Γερμανῶν καὶ τῶν ἄλλων Κελτικῶν ἐθνῶν, καὶ τοὺς ἀπὸ τῆς Βρεττανίας
συνειλεγμένους, εἰς ἐννέα που μυριάδας πεζῶν ἅπαντας καὶ ὀκτακισχιλίους ἱππέας
(Constantine) . . . Ῥωμαίων μὲν καὶ Ἰταλῶν εἰς ὀκτὼ μυριάδας αὐτῷ συνεμαχοῦν,
καὶ Τυρρηνῶν ὅσοι τὴν παραλίαν ἅπασαν ᾤκουν, παρείχοντο δὲ καὶ Καρχηδόνιοι στράτευμα
μυριάδων τεσσάρων, καὶ Σικελιῶται πρὸς τούτοις, ὥστε εἶναι τὸ στράτευμα πᾶν ἑπτα-
καίδεκα μυριάδων, ἱππέων δὲ μυρίων πρὸς τοῖς ὀκτακισχιλίοις (Maxentius), Agathias,
v. 13, τὰ γὰρ τῶν Ῥωμαίων στρατεύματα, οὐ τοσαῦτα διαμεμενηκότα ὁπόσα τὴν
ἀρχὴν ὑπὸ τῶν πάλαι βασιλέων ἐξευρῆται, ἐς ἐλαχίστην δέ τινα μοῖραν περιελθόντα,
οὐκέτι τῷ μεγέθει τῆς πολιτείας ἐξήρκουν. δέον γὰρ ἐς πέντε καὶ τεσσαράκοντα καὶ
ἑξακοσίας χιλιάδας μαχίμων ἀνδρῶν τὴν ὅλην ἀγείρεσθαι δύναμιν, μόλις ἐν τῷ τότε εἰς
πεντήκοντα καὶ ἑκατὸν περιειστήκει. καὶ τούτων αἱ μὲν ἐν Ἰταλίᾳ ἐτετάχατο, αἱ δὲ
κατὰ τὴν Λιβύην, ἕτεραι δὲ ἐν Ἱσπανίᾳ, καὶ ἄλλαι περὶ τοὺς Κόλχους, καὶ ἄλλαι κατὰ
τὴν Ἀλεξάνδρου καὶ Θήβην τὴν Αἰγυπτίαν. ἐκάθηντο δὲ ὀλίγοι καὶ πρὸς τὰ ἑῷα τῶν
Περσῶν ὅρια.

169. See App. II.

170. COHORTES MILIARIAE: *Not. Dig. Or.* xxxvii. 31, xxxviii. 27, 29, 30. ALAE
MILIARIAE: *Not. Dig. Or.* xxxiv. 32, 36, xxxvii. 25, 28; cf. xxxi. 35, milites
miliarenses. In *P. Beatty Panop.* (see n. 30) the cohors XI Chamavorum seems
to number c. 500, and the ala I Iberorum c. 360, the ala II Herculia Drome-
dariorum only 211. Libanius speaks of an ἴλη ὁπλιτῶν (a cohort?) in Diocletian's
day as numbering 500 men (*Or.* XI. 159 ff., xx. 18).

171. VEXILLATIONES MILIARIAE: *ILS* 531, 2726. In *P. Beatty Panop.* (see n. 30)
a *vexillatio* of Legio Traiana seems to number c. 1100, and its *lanciarii* c. 875,
a *vexillatio* of Legio III Diocletiana c. 1000, a *vexillatio* of several legions nearly
2,000, and Legio III Diocletiana (the main body, after deduction of contingents)
c. 1700. All these figures are actual strengths, no doubt below establishment.

172. SUBDIVISION OF LEGIONS: *Not. Dig. Or.* xxxix. 28–35, xl. 29–35, xlii. 30–9,
Occ. xxxii. 44–8, xxxiii. 51–7, xxxiv. 25–7, 37–41, xxxv. 17–9, 21–22. Cf. legio III
Diocletiana in *Or.* xxviii. 18, xxxi. 31, 33, 38. For detachments of legions in the
comitatus see App. II, Table IX.

173. SCHOLA: Proc. *HA* xxiv. 15, 19 (3,500 in the seven old *scholae*, 2,000 in the
four new, cf. *Not. Dig. Or.* xi. 4–10, *CJ* iv. lxv. 35). VEXILLATIO: Joh. Lydus,
Mag. 1. 46. In *P. Beatty Panop.* (see n. 30) the number of the Equites Sagittarii
seems to be only about 250 and of the *promoti* of Legio II Traiana c. 150.
Ammianus (XVIII. viii. 2) speaks of 'duarum turmarum equites circiter septin-
genti, ad subsidium Mesopotamiae recens ex Illyrico missi'. These again are
actual strengths, and no doubt below establishment. On the other hand
Zosimus (III. 3) speaks of an ἴλη ἑξακοσίων ἱππέων under Julian Caesar. In
Justinian's reign the Numidae Justiniani numbered 508 (*P. Cairo*, 67321,
P. Lond. 1663, *Sb* 8028).

174. Amm. XVIII. ix. 3–4, cuius oppidi praesidio erat semper quinta Parthica
legio destinata cum indigenarum turma non contemnenda. sed tunc ingruentem
Persarum multitudinem sex legiones raptim percursis itineribus antegressae
muris adstitere firmissimis. Magnentiaci et Decentiaci quos post consummatos
civiles procinctus, ut fallaces et turbidos ad orientem venire compulit imperator,
ubi nihil praeter bella timetur externa, et Tricensimani Decimanique Fortenses

et Superventores atque Praeventores cum Aeliano iam comite, quos tirones tum etiam novellos hortante memorato adhuc protectore erupisse a Singara Persasque fusos in somnum rettulimus trucidasse complures. aderat Comitum quoque Sagittariorum pars maior, equestres videlicet turmae ita cognominatae, ubi merent omnes ingenui barbari, armorum viriumque firmitudine inter alios eminentes; xix. ii. 14, intra civitatis ambitum non nimium amplae legionibus septem et promiscua advenarum civiumque sexus utriusque plebe et militibus aliis paucis ad usque numerum milium viginti cunctis inclusis (Amida); xx. iv. 2, Decentium tribunum et notarium misit auxiliares milites exinde protinus abstracturum Aerulos et Batavos cumque Petulantibus Celtas et lectos ex numeris aliis trecentenos, hac specie iussos adcelerare, ut adesse possint armis primo vere movendis in Parthos; xxxi. x. 13, qua difficultate perpensa, velut murorum obicibus opponendi per legiones singulas quingenteni leguntur armati, usu prudenter bellandi comperti; xxxi. xi. 2, atque ilico ut oblatae occasionis maturitas postulabat, cum trecentenis militibus per singulos numeros lectis Sebastianus properare dispositus est; Zos. v. 45, ἔδοξε τῷ βασιλεῖ πέντε τῶν ἀπὸ Δελματίας στρατιωτικὰ τάγματα, τῆς οἰκείας μεταστάντα καθέδρας, ἐπὶ φυλακῇ τῆς ῾Ρώμης ἐλθεῖν. τὰ δὲ τάγματα ταῦτα ἐπλήρουν ἄνδρες ἑξακισχίλιοι; VI. 8, ἐξ τάγματα στρατιωτῶν προσωρμίσθησαν, πάλαι μὲν ἔτι περιόντος Στελίχωνος προσδοκώμενα, τότε δὲ πρὸς συμμαχίαν ἐκ τῆς ἑῴας παραγενόμενα, χιλιάδων ἀριθμὸν ὄντα τεσσάρων.

175. See App. II, Table XV.

176. Agathias, v. 13 (cited in n. 168). Procopius's statement (HA xxiv. 13) that Justinian deprived the *limitanei* of τὸ τῆς στρατείας ὄνομα is borne out by the definition of *miles* in CJ iv. lxv. 35 (530).

177. JULIAN'S PERSIAN EXPEDITION: Zos. III. 12–13, ἔδοξεν οὖν ὀκτακισχιλίους καὶ μυρίους ὁπλίτας αὐτόθι καταλειφθῆναι, στρατηγεῖν δὲ τούτων Σεβαστιανὸν καὶ Προκόπιον, αὐτὸν δὲ ἅμα τῇ πάσῃ δυνάμει διὰ τοῦ Εὐφράτου χωρῆσαι, διχῇ διελόντα τὴν σὺν αὐτῷ στρατιάν, ὥστε πανταχόθεν, εἴ τινες τῶν πολεμίων φανεῖεν, εἶναι τοὺς τούτοις ἀνθισταμένους, καὶ μὴ ἐπ᾽ ἀδείας τὰ προσπεσόντα καταδραμεῖν. ταῦτα ἐν Κάρραις διαθεὶς (ἡ δὲ πόλις διορίζει ῾Ρωμαίους καὶ ᾽Ασσυρίους) ἠβουλήθη τὸ στρατόπεδον ἐξ ἀπόπτου τινὸς θεωρῆσαι χωρίου, ἄγασθαι δὲ τὰ πεζικὰ τάγματα καὶ τὰς τῶν ἱππέων ἴλας. ἦσαν δὲ ἅπαντες ἄνδρες πεντακισχίλιοι καὶ ἑξακισμύριοι. BARBATIO AND JULIAN: Amm. XVI. xi. 2, parte alia Barbatio post Silvani interitum promotus ad peditum magisterium ex Italia iussu principis cum XXV milibus armatorum Rauracos venit; xii. 2, Scutarius perfuga, qui commissi criminis metuens poenam transgressus ad eos post ducis fugati discessum armatorum tredecim milia tantum remansisse cum Iuliano docebat—is enim numerus eum sequebatur—barbara feritate certaminum rabiem undique concitante, Libanius (*Or.* XVIII. 49) gives the figures as 30,000 and 15,000. STILICHO: Zos. v. 26, ἀναλαβὼν ὁ Στελίχων ἅπαν τὸ ἐν τῷ Τικήνῳ τῆς Λιγυστικῆς ἐνιδρυμένον στρατόπεδον (ἦν δὲ εἰς ἀριθμοὺς συνειλεγμένον τριάκοντα) καὶ ὅσον οἷός τε γέγονε συμμαχικὸν ἐξ ᾽Αλανῶν καὶ Οὔννων περιποιήσασθαι.

178. ANASTASIUS: Proc. BP I. viii. 4, στράτευμα γὰρ τοιοῦτό φασιν οὔτε πρότερον οὔτε ὕστερον ἐπὶ Πέρσας ῾Ρωμαίοις ξυστῆναι, Josh. Styl. 54, cf. the figures of bread baked in 54, 70, 77. JUSTINIAN IN THE EAST: Proc. BP I. xiii. 23, xviii. 5, 11. xxiv. 16; Agathias's (III. 8) figure of 50,000 men in Lazica in 554 is incredible, especially as Procopius (BG IV. xiii. 8) records only 12,000 in the same theatre in 551. ILLYRICUM: Marcell. Com., a. 499, Proc. BG III. xxix. 3. AFRICA: Proc. BV I. xi. 2, 11–2, 19. ITALY: BG I. v. 2–4, III. iii. 4, Agathias, II. 4.

A good recent book on Rome in the later empire is A. Chastagnol, *La préfecture urbaine à Rome sous le bas-empire* (Paris, 1960), which deals with all aspects of the administration. There is no parallel work on Constantinople.

1. CLOTHING FACTORY AT ROME: *Not. Dig. Occ.* xi. 51.

2. The *Notitia Urbis Constantinopolitanae* (cited as *Not. Const.*) is printed in Seeck's *Notitia Dignitatum*, pp. 229–43. The *Notitia Regionum Urbis XIV* (cited as *Not. Rom.*) and the closely parallel document, the *Curiosum Urbis Regionum XIV*, are published by H. Jordan in *Topographie der Stadt Rom in Alterthum*, ii. 551–74, and by A. Nordh in *Libellus de regionibus urbis Romae, Acta Inst. Rom. Regni Sueciae*, iii (1949), 73–106. There is also a Syriac translation of the Breviarium or summary of this document in Zacharias of Mytilene (*Chron.* x. 6), which despite many fantastic mistranslations is sometimes useful, having apparently been taken from a rather fuller and more accurate version of the Breviarium than our own Latin text; a Latin translation is given in Jordan, op. cit. ii. 575–7, Nordh, op. cit. 42–6. At Constantinople the numbers of *domus* given in the regions add up to the right total. At Rome the numbers of *domus* and *insulae* given region by region and in the total do not tally precisely, but the variations are not significant.

3. For the *praefectus urbi* see p. 380, and for his judicial duties pp. 481–2, 486, 490–1. His overriding control of the city is implied by *Not. Dig. Occ.* iv. and stated by Symm. *Rel.* 17, cum ad praefecturam urbanam civilium rerum summa pertineat, minoribus officiis certa quaedam membra creduntur.

4. *CTh* i. vi. 6, 368, illustris sinceritas tua quasi in speculis tuebitur, quemadmodum singuli, quibus intra urbem Romam publicum munus iniungimus, credito sibi famulentur officio: et si aliquis indignum administratione se gesserit, referre non differat, ut veritate comperta continuo alium idoneum vel tuae celsitudinis testimonio vel nostro dirigamus arbitrio; Sym. *Rel.* 17, *CTh* i. vi. 9, 385, disputari de principali iudicio non oportet: sacrilegii enim instar est dubitare, an is dignus sit, quem elegerit imperator. si quis igitur iudicum fuerit repertus, qui supercilium suum principali aestimet iudicio praeferendum, quinque libras auri eius officium, nisi formam nostrae sanctionis suggesserit, decem ipse fisci viribus inferre cogatur; Symm. *Rel.* 22 (*tribunus fori suarii*), 27, cf. *CTh* xiii. iii. 9, 370 (*archiatrus*).

5. CONFLICTS WITH THE PRAEFECTUS ANNONAE: *CTh* i. vi. 5, 365(S), studentibus nobis statum urbis et rationem annonariam aliquando firmare in animo subiit eiusdem annonae curam non omnibus deferre potestatibus. ac ne praefectura urbis abrogatum sibi aliquid putaret, si totum ad officium annonarium redundasset, eidem praefecturae sollicitudinis ac diligentiae necessitatem mandamus, sed non ita, ut lateat officium annonariae praefecturae, sed ut ambae potestates, in quantum sibi est negotii, tueantur annonam sitque societas muneris ita, ut inferior gradus meritum superioris agnoscat atque ita superior potestas se exserat, ut sciat ex ipso nomine, quid praefecto debeatur annonae; 7, 376, suis partibus annonae praefectura moderatur, sed ita, ut ex veterum more praefecto urbis per publicum incedente honoris eius et loci gratia expensio panis habeatur. eatenus tamen praefecturam annonae cedere volumus dignitatis fastigio, ut curandi partibus non cedat. neque tamen apparitoribus urbanae praefecturae

annonarium officium inseratur, sed apparitorum aemulatione secreta ministerio suo annonae praefectura fungatur, non ut potentiae subiecta, sed ut negotii sui diligens tantumque se a contemptu vindicans, quantum non pergat in contumeliam superioris. praefectura autem urbis cunctis, quae intra urbem sunt, antecellat potestatibus, tantum ex omnibus parte delibans, quantum sine iniuria ac detrimento alieni honoris usurpet.

6. CONSULARIS AQUARUM: *Not. Dig. Occ.* iv. 11, *CTh* VIII. vii. 1, 315 (the same man is called *curator aquarum et Miniciae* in *CIL* VI. 37133), XV. ii. 1, 330, *ILS* 1223-4 (the same man is called *curator* in 8943), 2941, 5791; other *curatores* in *ILS* 643, 702, 1211. CURATOR RIPARUM, ETC.: *ILS* 1217, 1223, 1225 (the same man is *consularis* in 1224); *comes* in *Not. Dig. Occ.* iv. 6. CURATOR OPERUM: *Not. Dig. Occ.* iv. 12, 13, *ILS* 1211, 1223-5 (the same man is called *curator operum publicorum, consularis operum publicorum* and *curator operum maximorum*); *praefectus operum maximorum* in *ILS* 1250. CURATOR STATUARUM: *Not. Dig. Occ.* iv. 14, *ILS* 1222. CURATOR HORREORUM GALBIANORUM: *Not. Dig. Occ.* iv. 15.

7. PRAEFECTUS ANNONAE: *Not. Dig. Occ.* iv. 3, *CJ* III. xi. 3, 318, *CTh* XI. xxix. 2, III. i. 1+XIV. iii. 1, 319, XIV. xxiv. 1, 328, XV. 2, 366, xvii. 3, 368, 6, 370, iii. 14, 372, 15, 377, *CJ* I. xxiii. 5, 385, *CTh* I. xii. 7, 399, XIV. iii. 21, 403, *ILS* 687, 707, 726, 805, 1214, 1228, 1231, 1257, 1272, 5694, 9355, Cass. *Var.* VI. 18. PRAEFECTUS VIGILUM: *Not. Dig. Occ.* iv. 4, *CTh* I. ii. 1, 313(S), II. x. 1+2, 319, XV. xiv. 3, 313 (S), *ILS* 700, 765, Cass. *Var.* VII. 7. COMES FORMARUM: *Not. Dig. Occ.* iv. 5, *CIL* VI. 1765, Cass. *Var.* VII. 6; the *procurator aquarum* is last recorded c. 300 in *ILS* 2941. COMES PORTUS: *Not. Dig. Occ.* iv. 7, *ILS* 1250 (*comes portuum*), Cass. *Var.* VII. 9. CENTENARIUS PORTUS: *Not. Dig. Occ.* iv. 16.

8. TRIBUNUS FORI SUARII: *ILS* 722, Symm. *Rel.* 22, *Not. Dig. Occ.* iv. 10: cf. Zos. II. 9, Λουκιανόν, ὃς τοῦ χοιρείου κρέως ἦν χορηγὸς ὃ τὸ δημόσιον ἐπεδίδου τῷ 'Ρωμαίων δήμῳ. The *tribunus* in *CIL* VI. 1771 must be the *tribunus fori suarii*. TRIBUNUS RERUM NITENTIUM: *Not. Dig. Occ.* iv. 17, cf. Amm. XVI. vi. 2; the *formula comitivae Romanae* (Cass. *Var.* VII. 13) refers to him or the *curator statuarum*. TRIBUNUS VOLUPTATUM: *ILCV* 110, Cass. *Var.* VII. 10 (*formula tribuni voluptatum*), cf. VI. 19, at cum lascivae voluptates recipiant tribunum, hoc non meretur habere primarium? The office does not appear in *Not. Dig. Occ.* iv, and appears to be first mentioned in *CTh* XV. vii. 13, Diogeniano v. c. trib. volupt., mimas diversis adnotationibus liberatas ad proprium officium summa instantia revocari decernimus, ut voluptatibus populi ac festis diebus solitus ornatus deesse non possit. dat. VI Id. Feb. Ravennae Constantio v. c. cons.; acc. a tribuno volupt. X Kal. Feb. Karthagine post cons. Honorii VIIII et Theodosii V AA (corrected by Seeck to 'post cons. ss.'). Under the Ostrogothic kingdom there were *tribuni voluptatum* in other large cities (Cass. *Var.* V. 25, Milan), but Diogenianus was probably not *tribunus voluptatum* of Carthage (which would have been mentioned in the title), but the *tribunus voluptatum*, probably recently created, of the capital, temporarily visiting Carthage (hence no doubt the long delay in delivering the letter; it must have been kept at Rome to await his return, and finally, when he did not come back in the autumn, sent on to Carthage in mid-winter).

9. MAGISTER CENSUS: *Not. Dig. Occ.* iv. 8, *CTh* XIV. ix. 1, 370. RATIONALIS VINORUM: *Not. Dig. Occ.* iv. 9.

10. OFFICIA: *CTh* VIII. vii. 1, 315, XV. ii. 1, 330 (of *cos. aquarum*), I. vi. 5, 365 (S), 7, 376 (of *praef. annonae*), Cass. *Var.* VII. 13 (of *comitiva Romana*). COURTS: *CTh* II. x. 1+2, 319 (of *praef. vigilum*), XI. xxix. 2, 319, *CJ* III. xi. 3, 318, Cass.

Var. VI. 18 (of *praef. annonae*). The *praef. vigilum* is a *v.p.* in *ILS* 765 (under Valentinian I), and the *praef. annonae* in *ILS* 687, 1214 (under Constantine): otherwise most recorded office holders are senators (e.g. *ILS* 1211, 1217, 1223–5, 1228, 1231, 1250, 1257, 1272). For the army surgeon see Amm. XVI. vi. 2.

11. FIRST PREFECT: *Chr. Min.* I. 239, Soc. II. 41. MAGISTER CENSUS: *CJ* I. iii. 31, 472, VIII. liii. 32, 496, I. ii. 17 §2 (Anastasius), VI. xxiii. 23, 524, IV. lxvi. 3 §3, 530, Joh. Lydus, *Mag.* II. 30, ἐκ τῆς φάλαγγος οὖν τῶν ἐν τῇ ˊΡώμῃ πραιτόρων τὸν τουτηλάριον προχειρίζεται <καὶ τὸν φιδεικομμισσάριον>, τὸν μὲν Κωνσταντιανὸν τὸν δὲ μάγιστρον τοῦ κήνσου ἐπιφημίσας, οἱονεὶ ἄρχοντα τῶν ἀρχετύπων συμβολαίων, ὅτι κῆνσον μὲν τὴν ἀπογραφὴν τῶν ἀρχείων, ῥέγεστα δὲ <τῶν πραττομένων> λέγουσι. καὶ σκρίβαν μὲν ἐκείνῳ (ἀντὶ τοῦ ὑπογραφέα), κηνσουᾶλες δὲ τούτῳ (ἀντὶ τοῦ ἀρχειοφύλακας) ὑπηρετεῖσθαι διώρισε. PRAEFECTUS ANNONAE: *CJ* XII. xix. 12 §1 (Anastasius), ita ut si de civilibus annonis vel tutela seu curatione vel novi operis nuntiatione litem eos subire contigerit, in maiore quidem iudicio ad similitudinem sumptuum, quos in iudicio eminentiae tuae dependere praecepti sunt, apud virum autem clarissimum praefectum annonae seu fisci patronum urbicariae magnificae praefecturae vel architectos pro modo eorum, quae super arbitris et litibus apud eos exercendis superius statuta sunt, solventes expensas nihil amplius agnoscere seu dependere cogantur; Just. *Nov.* lxxxviii §2, 539, ὁρῶμεν γὰρ σφόδρα συχνάζον τοῦτο ἐπὶ τῆς βασιλίδος ταύτης μάλιστα πόλεως, καί τινας παραγγέλλοντας τοῖς χορηγοῦσι τὸ δημόσιον σιτηρέσιον ἢ καὶ ψήφους ποριζομένους παρὰ τοῦ τῶν ἀννόνων ὑπάρχου, βουλομένους ἀναρτηθῆναι τὴν χορηγίαν. PRAEFECTUS VIGILUM and PRAETOR PLEBIS: Malalas, 479, Just. *Nov.* xiii, 535, Proc. *HA* xx. 7–12, Joh. Lydus, *Mag.* II. 29. QUAESITOR: Just. *Nov.* lxxx, 539, Proc. *HA* xx. 7–12, Joh. Lydus, *Mag.* II. 29.

12. *ILS* 722, domino nostro Fl. Claudio Constantino fortissimo ac beatissimo Caesari, Fl. Ursacius v.p., tribunus cohortium urbanarum X XI et XII et fori suari; Symm. *Rel.* 42, urbanarum dudum cohortium miles, *CTh* VI. xxvii. 8, 396 (*tribuni urbaniciani*).

13. LEONTIUS: Amm. XV. vii. 2–5. TERTULLUS: Amm. XIX. x. 2–3. VIVENTIUS: Amm. XXVII. iii. 11–13. THE ELDER SYMMACHUS: Symm. *Rel.* 23, 31. THE YOUNGER SYMMACHUS: *Coll. Avell.* 16, 32.

14. CHRYSOSTOM'S ARREST: Pall. *Dial.* p. 57.

15. POLICE OF CONSTANTINOPLE: *Not. Const.* ii. 21–6, curatorem unum qui totius regionis sollicitudinem gerat, vernaculum unum, velut servum in omnibus et internuntium regionis, . . . vicomagistros quinque quibus per noctem tuendae urbis cura mandata est (cf. lin. 19–22, etc.). John Chrysostom (*Hom. in Act.* xxvi. 4) alludes to τοὺς νυκτερινοὺς φύλακας of Constantinople, who περίασιν ἐν κρυμῷ βοῶντες μεγάλα καὶ διὰ τῶν στενωπῶν βαδίζοντες. POLICE OF ROME: *Not. Rom.* vicomag. XLVIII, curat. II (in each region); in the Syriac Breviarium the *vicomagistri* are said to guard the city. CURATORES REGIONUM: SHA, *Sev. Alex.* 33, *ILS* 1209, 1216, *CIL* VI. 31958. PRIORES, PRIMATES, MAIORES REGIONUM: *Coll. Avell.* 14, admonui etiam corporatos, officio quoque interminatus sum, ac maiores deterrui regionum, ne quis quietem urbis vestrae perturbare temptaret, 21, monemus sane ut regionum primatibus evocatis disciplinae publicae quietique prospicias . . . in regionum quoque priores intelligent vindicandum, 31, primates vero regionum nisi spiritum plebis inconditae domuerint et frenarint sciant se raptos ultimo iudicio esse subdendos,

32, inrumpentibus corporatis et maioribus regionum qui praeceptis imperialibus serviunt.

16. VIGILES: *CIL* VI. 31075, descriptio fer[iarum] quae in cohorte [. . .] Cl. Mamertino e[t Fl. Nevitta] coss. matronae cum carpentis, sifon[arii], falc[arii], unc[inarii]; cf. also *CIL* XIV. 231, Fl. Honorio n. p. et Fl. Eubodio conss. Flaviis Adeodato cent. coh. VII et Cr[ispino] coh. II. TRIBUNI VIGILUM: *CJ* XII. liv. 4, 443. COLLEGIATI: *Not. Const.* ii. 25, collegiatos viginti quinque qui e diversis corporibus ordinati incendiorum solent casibus subvenire (cf. iii. 21, etc.); Joh. Lydus, *Mag.* I. 50, ὅτι δὲ ἀληθὴς ὁ λόγος ἐστί, καὶ νῦν τοιούτου τινὸς ἀεὶ συμβαίνοντος ἀνὰ τὴν πόλιν οἱ τυχὸν ἐπικαίρως ἐξ αὐτῶν εὑρισκόμενοι βοῶντες τῇ πατρίῳ Ῥωμαίων φωνῇ, omnes collegiati οἷον εἰπεῖν "πάντες ἑταῖροι συνδράμετε"; Symm. *Rel.* 14, per alios fortuita arcentur incendia; *CTh* XIV. viii. 2, 369 *(centonarii)*. There is no mention of firefighting in Just. *Nov.* xiii (in §4 the *praetor plebis* is only to prevent looting when a fire occurs) or in Cass. *Var.* VII. 7.

17. MAINTENANCE: *CTh* XV. ii. 1, 330, Cass. *Var.* VII. 6; cf. *CJ* XI. xliii. 6 §1, 440, 10 §2 (474-491), for the rule against trees. The *caespes formensis* of Val. III, *Nov.* v §4, 440, is the land subject to the duty of cleaning the aqueducts. AQUEDUCT OF VALENS: Them. *Or.* XI. 151; OF THEODOSIUS I: *CTh* VI. iv. 29, 30, 396 (payments by praetors). PAYMENTS BY CONSULS: *CJ* XII. iii. 2 §3, 452, 3 §1, 4 §1 (476-84). AQUEDUCT TAXES: *CJ* XI. xliii. 7 (445-7), ad reparationem aquaeductus huius almae urbis omnia vectigalia, quae colligi possunt ex universis scalis huius inclitae urbis et ex operariis qui Cyzicenii dicuntur, ad refectionem eiusdem aquaeductus procedere; the fund was under a special *arcarius* (*CJ* XI. xliii. 8 (474-91), separatus vero arcarius aurum aquaeductus suscipiat gloriosissimorum consulum liberalitate vel ex aliis titulis ad aquas publicas pertinentibus collectum vel postea colligendum). ROMAN AQUEDUCT FUND: Symm. *Rel.* 20, ex formarum conditis. AQUARII: *CJ* XI. xliii. 10 §§4, 5 (474-91), universos autem aquarios vel aquarum custodes, quos hydrophylacas nominant, qui omnium aquaeductuum huius regiae urbis custodiae deputati sunt, singulis manibus eorum felici nomine nostrae pietatis impresso signari decernimus, ut huiusmodi adnotatione manifesti sint omnibus nec a procuratoribus domorum vel quolibet alio ad usus alios avellantur vel angariarum vel operarum nomine teneantur. quod si quem ex isdem aquariis mori contigerit, eum nihilo minus qui in locum defuncti subrogatur signo eodem notari praecipimus, ut militiae quodammodo sociati excubiis aquae custodiendae incessanter inhaereant nec muneribus aliis occupentur; Cass. *Var.* III. 31, mancipia formarum servitio principum provisione deputata.

18. AQUA HADRIANA: *CJ* XI. xliii. 6, 440. LACUS: *Not. Rom.* PRIVATE SUPPLY BY LICENCE: *CTh* XV. ii. 5, 389, 6, 395, *CJ* XI. xliii. 5, 6, 440, 9 (474-91), 11 (506-18). DIAMETER OF PIPES: *CTh* XV. ii. 3, 382.

19. On the arrangement under the Principate see D. van Berchem, *Les distributions de blé et d'argent à la plèbe romaine sous l'empire* (Geneva, 1939). GRADUS and PANES GRADILES: *CTh* XIV. xvii. 2-6. The number of recipients was probably the same for bread as for pork, for which see n. 35. THE RATION: *CTh* XIV. xvii. 5, 369, civis Romanus, qui in viginti panibus sordidis, qui nunc dicuntur ardinienses, quinquaginta uncias comparabat, triginta et sex uncias in bucellis sex mundis sine pretio consequatur. EXCLUSION OF UNQUALIFIED PERSONS: *CTh* XIV. xvii. 5, 369, 6, 370.

20. DISTRIBUTION STARTED: *Chron. Min.* I. 234. GRADUS: *Not. Const.* ii. 20, iii. 18, etc. NUMBER OF RECIPIENTS: Soc. II. 13, ἐζημίωσε δὲ τὴν πόλιν, ἀφελὼν τοῦ

σιτηρεσίου τοῦ παρασχεθέντος παρὰ τοῦ πατρὸς αὐτοῦ ἡμερησίου ὑπὲρ τέσσαρας μυριάδας· ὀκτὼ γὰρ ἐγγὺς μυριάδες ἐχορηγοῦντο πρότερον τοῦ σίτου ἐκ τῆς Ἀλεξανδρέων κομιζομένου πόλεως; that 80,000 rations (ἄρτοι) are meant is indicated by the *Vita Pauli* (*PG* CIV. 124), ἣν δὲ τὸ ὅλον τῆς δωρεᾶς ἡμερήσιοι ἄρτοι μυριάδες ὀκτώ. THEODOSIUS'S INCREMENT: *CJ* XI. xxv. 2, 392, cf. *CTh* XIV. xvii. 14, 402, xvi. 2, 416. SALE OF TICKETS PROHIBITED: *CTh* XIV. xvii. 7, 372, vendendi de reliquo popularibus annonam consuetudinem derogamus, ut huiusmodi celebrata venditio omni careat firmitate. verum si quis urbe abeundum esse crediderit, panes ceteraque quae percipit in horreorum conditis reserventur, poscentibus iuxta legem eiusdem ordinis hominibus deferenda. quin lege proposita etiam quae fuerint fortasse distractae, ad originem propriam iusque revocamus, si quidem iustum est, ut in perpetuum suum quisque detineat et per succedaneas vices proprius ordo teneat, ut palatinus palatini, militis vero militaris, popularem annonam popularis exposcat nec alter alterius sibi expetens diversorum ordinum valeat miscere rationem: lapse on death is implied by law 8, 380, si quis ex schola defecerit mortemque obierit, non ab alio corpore vacantes flagitentur annonae, sed ipsis scholis cessurae dividendaeque perdurent, if these *annonae* were classified as *populares*. It appears from laws 9 (quod alii eas putarunt tamquam proprias distrahendas, alii per successionum gradus hereditarium ius venire) and 10 (quicumque perceptarum annonarum emolumenta vel in heredes proprios iure sanguinis transfuderunt vel in extraneos distractionis titulo transcripserunt) of the same title that by 389 and 392 the inheritance and sale of *annonae civicae* was permitted normally, and this term seems to cover *populares* (see n. 22). ANNONAE CIVICAE HELD BY CHURCHES: *CJ* I. ii. 14 pr., 470, 17 §1 (Anastasius), Just. *Nov.* vii §1, 535; cf. *V. Olymp.* 7, *Anal. Boll.* XVI (1897), 45, Joh. Eph. *HE* II. 41, for gifts of πολιτικοὶ ἄρτοι to churches.

21. PANES AEDIUM AT CONSTANTINOPLE: *CTh* XIV. xvii. 1, 364, quia comperimus nonnullos venditis aedibus panes earum penes se retinere, nulli liceat, ut aedes sequantur annonae. sane si qui ex huiusmodi titulo caduci sint panes, fisci viribus vindicentur; cf. 11 and 12, 393, si quae speciatim annonae domus in hac urbe habentibus divae memoriae Constantini vel Constantii largitate concessae sunt atque in heredes proprios iure successionis vel in extraneos venditionis titulo transierunt, erogatione solita ministrentur, 13, 396; law 12 seems to make old *panes aedium* freely alienable, but 13 restricts the grant of new *annonae* (in this class presumably) to house owners. PANES AEDIFICIORUM AT ROME: *CTh* XIV. xvii. 5, 369. GRANT OF ANNONAE TO STATE EMPLOYEES: *CTh* XIV. ix. 2, 372.

22 The term *civ cae* (*annonae*) is used to describe rations granted to builders of houses (*CTh* XIV. xvii. 11, 13), to holders of posts (laws 9 and 10), and to individuals unconditionally (law 10); these last are probably to be identified with *panes populares* (a term only used in *CTh* XIV. ix. 2+xvii. 7, 372) and not o be made into yet another category. The word *civicae* was probably therefore used to denote any rations connected with the city, as opposed to *militares annonae*; it is applied to the *annonae* held by the churches (see n. 20), which were not allowed to hold military *annonae* (*CJ* I. ii. 20 (528–9), μηδὲ ἀπὸ θείου τύπου ἢ ἀρχικῆς προστάξεως ἢ οἱουδήποτε δικαστηρίου στρατιωτικὴ σίτησις εἰς εὐκτηρίους οἴκους ἢ κληρικοὺς ἢ μοναστήρια μεταγέσθω, ὡς ἐλλειπόντων δῆθεν τοῖς ἀριθμοῖς σωματείων), and in what appears to be an inclusive sense in Just. *Nov.* lxxxviii §2, 539. THE ANNONAE OF THE SCHOLAE: *CTh* XIV. xvii. 8, 380, 9, 389, 10, 392 (= *CJ* XI. xxv. 1), 11, 393, 12, 393.

23. PRAEFECTUS ANNONAE AFRICAE: *CTh* XI. i. 13, 365, I. xv. 10, 379 (collection of *canon*), XIII. ix. 2, 372 (shipment to Portus); he was under the disposition of the *Ppo. It. (Not. Dig. Occ.* ii. 41), who was ultimately responsible for filling the granaries of Rome (cf. Symm. *Ep.* I. 61, thanking Probus, *Ppo. It.* and Cass. *Var.* VI. 18, triticeas quidem copias praefectura praetoriana procurat). There are many other allusions to Africa (e.g. Symm. *Rel.* 18, *Ep.* IV. 54, VII. 68). Supplies were sometimes drawn from Sardinia (Symm. *Ep.* IX. 42) and Spain (*CTh* XIII. v. 4, 324), and under Theoderic Spain was apparently the main source (Cass. *Var.* v. 35). For the collection and shipment from Egypt the main authority is Just. *Ed.* xiii; the *praefectus Augustalis* is here responsible, the *praefectus annonae Alexandriae* (see ch. XIII, n. 98) having apparently ceased to exist. The figure of 8,000,000 is given in §8 of the Edict (the unit implied is *artabae*, see ch. XIII, n. 126). I have based my calculations on the fact that one *artaba* made 80 lb. of bread (*P. Oxy.* 1920), and one *modius* therefore 24, so that a daily ration of 3 lb. would require 45 *modii* a year, rather more than the standard ration of 10 *artabae* or 40 *modii*. THE ROMAN CANON UNDER SEVERUS: SHA, *Severus*, 23.

24. CORN FUND OF CONSTANTINOPLE: *CTh* XIV. xvi. 1, 409, 3, 434, cf. Joh. Lydus, *Mag.* III. 38 for John's attempt to annex τὸ σιτωνικόν.

25. SACCARII: *CTh* XIV. xxii. 1, 364, omnia, quaecumque advexerint privati ad Portum urbis aeternae, per ipsos saccarios vel eos, qui se huic corpori permiscere desiderant, magnificentia tua iubeat comportari et pro temporum varietate mercedes considerata iusta aestimatione taxari, ita ut, si claruerit aliquem privatum per suos adventicias species comportare, quinta pars eius speciei fisco lucrativa vindicetur. MENSORES AND CAUDICARII: *ILS* 1272, hinc etiam factum est, ut mensores nos Portuenses, quib. vetus fuit cum caudicariis diuturnumq. luctamen, voti conpotes abiremus, ut utrumq. corpus et beneficio se et victoria gratuletur adfectum, *CTh* XIV. iv. 9, 417, ad excludendas patronorum caudicariorum fraudes et Portuensium furta mensorum unus e patronis totius consensu corporis eligatur, qui per quinquennium custodiam Portuensium suscipiat conditorum, clandestinum ad collegas digma missurus, ne quid ex specie fraus occulta vectorum pessimae qualitatis immutet, cf. also XIV. xv. 1, 364 (cited in n. 31), and for the *caudicarii* XIV. iii. 2, 355. CATABOLENSES: *CTh* XIV. iii. 9, 10, 370.

26. In *Not. Rom.* the *pistrina* recorded region by region come to 274; the total is wrongly given as 254 in the Breviarium, but correctly in the Syriac version, which also states that public bakeries are meant. PISTORES CALLED MANCIPES: *CTh* XIV. iii. 18, 386, Soc. v. 18, cf. *CTh* XIV. xvii. 3, 368 (*conductores*). ANIMALS AND SLAVES: *CTh* XIV. iii. 7, 364 (cited in n. 29). CONVICTS: *CTh* IX. xl. 3, 319, 5, 6 and 7, 364. KIDNAPPING: Soc. v. 18. WATER-MILLS: *CTh* XIV. xv. 4, 398, Proc. *BG* I. xix. 19 ff. As a result of the change to watermills it would appear that the processes of milling, which had to be carried out on the Janiculum, and of baking, which went on in the old bakeries, were separated, and that a separate guild of *molendinarii* was instituted; see *CIL* VI. 1711, Claudius Iulius Ecclesius Dynamius v.c. et inl. urbi praefectus dicit: amore patriae compulsi, ne quid diligentiae deesse videatur, studio nostro adici novimus, ut omnium molendinariorum fraudes amputentur, quas subinde venerabili populo atque universitati fieri suggerentibus nobis agnovimus, et ideo stateras fieri praecepimus, quas in Ianiculo constitui nostra praecepit auctoritas; unde hoc programmate universitatem nosse decernimus frumenta cum ad haec loca conterenda detulerint, consueta fraudibus licentia quo modo

possit amoveri: primo pensare non differant, deinde postquam fregerint, propter fidem integrae observationis adhibitis isdem ponderibus agnoscant nihil sibi abstulisse licentiam fraudatorum. accipere autem secundum constitutum brevem molendinarios tam in Ianiculo quam per diversa praecipimus per modium unum nummos III, ita quod si quis eorum inlicita praesumptione farinam crediderit postulandam, deprehensus et multae subiaceat et fustiario supplicio se noverit esse subdendum. illud autem humanitas nostra propter corporatorum levamen adicit ut, si qui voluntate propria, non compulsus, sed donandi animo farinam offerre voluerit, habeat qui accipit liberam facultatem.

27. TRAJAN'S PRIVILEGES: Gaius, I. 34, *Fr. Vat.* 233, 235, 237. PROPERTY OF PISTORES: *CTh* XIII. v. 2, 315, XIV. iii. 1, 319, 2, 355, 3, 364, 13, 369, 14, 372, 21, 403.

28. DECURIAE: *CTh* XIV. iii. 18, 386. THE CHURCH: *tit. cit.* 11, 365. VOTE OF THE GUILD: *tit. cit.* 8, 365, cf. 21, 403. IMPERIAL RESCRIPT: *tit. cit.* 6, 364, 20, 398, cf. 21, 403. RECRUITS FROM AFRICA: *tit. cit.* 12, 370, ad Claudium proc. Afric., secundum parentis nostri Constantini divale praeceptum omnibus lustris pistores ex officio, quod ei corpori constat addictum, ad urbem sacratissimam destinentur. in quo illud convenit praecaveri, ne quis hanc, quae personalis est, functionem pretio putet esse taxandam. veniant suo tempore, quos causa constringit et ita veniant, ut eos officium, quod tibi paret, pistorum patronis atque annonae praefecto apud publica monumenta consignet; 17, 380, iudices Africanos laudabilis sinceritas tua huiusmodi interminatione conterreat, ut, nisi tempore solito debitos pistores venerabilis Romae usibus dirigere curaverint, sciant se ipsos quinquaginta argenti librarum officiumque eorum pari condemnatione multandum; cf. Val. III, *Nov.* xxxiv §4, 451, for *praedia pistoria* in Africa.

29. The bakeries seem to have been occupied in rotation by seniority, see *CTh* XIV. iii. 7, 364, post quinquenni tempus emensum unus prior e patronis pistorum otio et quiete donetur, ita ut ei qui sequitur officinam cum animalibus servis molis fundis dotalibus, pistrinorum postremo omnem enthecam tradat atque consignet; law 8, 365, ne illud quidem cuiquam concedi oportet, ut ab officina ad aliam possit transitum facere, presumably refers to jumping the queue by illicit transfers. FUNDI DOTALES: *CTh* XIV. iii. 7 (cited above), 13, 369, non ea sola pistrini sint vel fuisse videantur, quae in originem adscripta corpori dotis nomen et speciem etiam nunc retentant, sed etiam ea, quae ex successione pistorum ad heredes eorum vel quos alios devoluta noscuntur, 19, 396, pistores urbis aeternae praetermissa veteri consuetudine fundis vel praediis ad nihilum redactis, quae eorum corpori solacia certa praebebant, Cass. *Var.* VI. 18, pistorum iura . . . quae per diversas mundi partes possessione latissima tendebantur. Estates might be assigned to the guild corporately by *CTh* XIII. v. 2, 315, and apparently by XIV. iii. 21, 403.

30. BANKRUPTS: *CTh* XIV. iii. 15, 377. SENATORS: *tit. cit.* 4, 364; cf. Amm. XXVII. iii. 2, Terentius enim humili genere in urbe natus et pistor ad vicem praemii, quia peculatus reum detulerat Orfitum ex praefecto, hanc eandem provinciam correctoris administraverat potestate.

31. PANIS OSTIENSIS ATQUE FISCALIS: *CTh* XIV. xix. 1, 398. CHEAP CORN: *CTh* XIV. xv. 1, 364, ne pessimus panis populi Romani usibus ministretur, sola (solita?) ducentena milia modiorum frumenti integri atque intemerati iuxta priscum morem mensores et caudicarii levioribus pretiis pistoribus venundare

cogantur. This is a very puzzling law. The *mensores* and *caudicarii* must presumably have acted as government agents, being debited with the value of the corn imported (less that required for the free distribution?) and authorised to sell it, part at fixed prices, the rest for what it would fetch: some such arrangement would explain their anxiety to palm off rotten corn on the bakers (see n. 25). The figure is very odd too. Does it mean that 200,000 *modii* (presumably per annum) were to be sold by each guild or to each baker? In the first case the amount is so small as hardly to help the bakers, in the latter, if the bakers really numbered 274, far too great. Perhaps the number of bakers had by this date greatly diminished. ARCA FRUMENTARIA: *CTh* XII. xi. 2, 386.

32. COMES HORREORUM: *CJ* XI. xvi. 1 (457–65); five *horrea* are recorded in the *Not. Const.* (vi. 15–17, x. 6, 9) besides the *horrea olearia*. BAKERS: *Not. Const.* ii. 18–19, iii. 17 etc.; the totals by regions come to 21 public and 114 private, those in the summary are 20 and 120 (xvi. 40–41). MANCIPES: *CTh* XIV. xvi. 2, 416, 3, 434, *CJ* XI. xvi. 1 (457–65).

33. OIL ISSUE: SHA, *Severus*, 18, populo Romano diurnum oleum gratuitum ei iucundissimum in aeternum donavit, Symm. *Rel.* 35, frumenti cotidianus usus in facili est; olei tantum species victum plebis tenuiter invecta sollicitat. cuius rei v.c. praefectus annonae, partium suarum diligens executor, praetorianae amplissimae praefecturae, ut ipse adserit, dudum fecit indicium missis de more brevibus. . . . ut quam primum iudices Africanos super hac specie Romanis horreis inferenda divinus sermo destimulet. nam properato opus est priusquam reliquum profligat diurna praebitio; cf. *Rel.* 14, frugis et olei baiulos, and for the *canon olearius*, *CTh* XIV. xv. 3, 397. MENSAE OLEARIAE: *CTh* XIV. xxiv. 1, 328; their number is recorded in the Syriac Breviarium. ARCA OLEARIA: *CTh* XII. xi. 2, 386. For Constantinople there is only the very obscure law, *CTh* XIV. xvii. 15, 408, and the *horrea olearia* (*Not. Const.* vi. 13).

34. BUTCHERS' GUILDS: Symm. *Rel.* 14, hic lanati pecoris invector est, ille ad victum populi cogit armentum, hos suillae carnis tenet functio, cf. *CTh* XIV. iv. 10 §1, 419, for the *pecuarii*. PORK ISSUE: SHA, *Aurelianus*, 35. SEVERUS AND THE SUARII: *Fr. Vat.* 236–7. PROPERTY OF SUARII: *CTh* XIV. iv. 1, 334, 5, 389, 7, 397, 8, 408. PROHIBITION OF HONORES, MILITIAE AND THE CHURCH: *CTh* XIV. iv. 8, 408.

35. DISTRIBUTION OF PORK: *CTh* XIV. iv. 10 §3, 419, per quinque autem menses quinas in obsoniis libras carnis possessor (this must be wrong, perhaps inserted from the line below) accipiat, ne per minutias exigui ponderis amplius fraus occulta decerpat, §5, quattuor milia sane obsoniorum, amputatis superfluis ac domus nostrae perceptionibus, diurna sublimitas tua decernat, quibus copiis populus animetur. Recipients get their ration of 5 lb. once a month, 4,000 issues are made daily, and therefore 120,000 monthly. These figures tally with Val. III, *Nov.* xxxvi §2, 452, ita ut centum quinquaginta diebus obsoniorum praebitionem sine ulla causatione singulis annis a se noverint procurandam, quae quantitas in tricies sexies centenis viginti novem milibus libris cum duarum decimarum ratione colligitur. The 4,000 rations of 5 lb. daily for 150 days (5 months) come to 3,000,000 lb., to which must be added two allowances of 10%, making 3,000,000 + 300,000 + 330,000 = 3,630,000: I do not understand by what arithmetical error the imperial accountants reached the curious figure of 3,629,000. PROVINCES LIABLE TO THE LEVY: *CTh* XIV. iv. 3, 363 (Campania), 4, 367 (Lucania and Bruttium), Val. III, *Nov.* xxxvi §1, 452 (Campania, Samnium, Lucania), Cass. *Var.* XI. 39 (Lucania had provided pork, Bruttium beef). There

is no allusion to the pork supply of Constantinople except *CTh* VIII. vii. 22, 426, suarii etiam et optiones per omnes regiones urbis Constantinopolitanae: the *suarii* appear to have been officials appointed by *probatoriae*.

36. CONSTANTINE'S LAW: *CTh* XIV. iv. 2, 324, in arbitrio suo possessor habeat, ne suario pecuniam solvat, quod ideo permissum est, ne in aestimando porcorum pondere licentia suariis praebeatur. quod si iuste porcos suarius aestimaverit, huic pecuniam possessor, cui pensitationis utriusque copia est indulta, numerabit. ne autem suario in suscipienda pecunia detrimenti aliquid adferatur, singulis quibusque annis ea pretia porcinae possessor adnumeret, quae usus publicae conversationis adtulerit. et quoniam non semper nec in omnibus locis una est forma pretiorum, pro diversitate locorum et temporum in specie pretia danda sunt, nisi ipsa porcina praestetur. iudices autem regionum monendi sunt, ut per singulos annos ad scientiam tuam referant, quae in quibus locis sunt pretia porcinae, ut instructione hac a tua gravitate perpensa tunc demum suarii per diversa proficiscantur et pretia suscipiant, quae in his regionibus versari cognoveris. queri enim suarii non poterunt, quia nihil interest, carius an vilius comparent, cum, quantum pretium daturi sunt, a possessore accipiant; et possessores erunt moderati in specie distrahenda, cum se sciant, quanto maiora pretia pro carne poposcerint, tanto plus suariis soluturos. JULIAN'S LAW: *CTh* XIV. iv. 3, 363; by this the whole levy was compulsorily commuted at the prices prevailing in the provinces where the levy was made. For the edict of Turcius Apronianus and Valentinian I's law see n. 37, and for Valentinian III's law see n. 38. HONORIUS'S LAW: *CTh* XIV. iv. 10, 419; this also prescribes commutation. WEIGHING OF PIGS: *CTh* XIV. iv. 4 §2, 367, quibus in rebus illud quoque a decessore tuo salubriter institutum est, quo suariis aestimandi licentia denegetur pondusque porcorum trutinae examine, non oculorum libertate quaeratur, ita videlicet, ut ne volenti quidem possessori tradere animal liceat, cuius modum non prius ponderatione certa deciderit suarius. animal vero a possessore tradendum ob digeriem prius unius noctis tantum ieiunitate vacuetur.

37. VALENTINIAN I'S LAW: *CTh* XIV. iv. 4, 367, per singulas et semis decimas, quibus suariorum dispendia sarciuntur, damnum, quod inter susceptionem et erogationem necessario evenit, vini, hoc est septem et decem milium amphorarum perceptione relevetur (§§1 and 2 deal with commutation of the wine levy and the weighing of pigs), §3, illud quoque salubris Constantinianae legis forma compescat, videlicet ut cum possessore, cui commodioris pretii beneficia indulta a veteribus principibus praerogativa providit, proprium ordo decidat ac transigat isque ordo suariis, quibuscum habet vini emolumenta communia, aut legitimum pretium, id est Romani fori, cui carnem fuerat inlaturus, tradat, aut carnem debitam subministret. TURCIUS APRONIANUS'S EDICT: *CIL* VI. 1771, cum suarios damnis videremus adfectos et eos etiam ordines, qui suariam faciunt, providimus his levamen ex titulo canonico vinario, ut viginti quinque milia amforum annua consequantur, sub ea divisione, ut duae partes suariis, tertia vero his ordinibus proficiat, qui suariam recognoscunt, ita ut idem ordines iuxta consuetudinem tam proprium quod appellatur quam annonas exsolvant et moderatione adhibita perinde a possessore suscipiant adque accipere sunt soliti. I do not profess to understand all this, but I would prefer to read 'praeter' instead of 'per' in the first sentence of the law, translating: 'besides the 15 % whereby the expenses of the *suarii* are made good, the loss which inevitably occurs between collection and distribution is to be relieved by a grant of 17,000 amphorae of wine'. The allowance of 15 % is mentioned again in §4, where it is implied that the *ordo*, if it delivered pigs in kind, had to supply a 15 % supplement (in kind). According to §3, if money was paid, the *ordo*

paid the *suarii* the higher Roman price, but the *possessor* paid the *ordo* the lower local price. The difference between the two prices appears to be called the *proprium*, and was met by the *ordo* out of its share of the wine grant. Similarly if the *ordo* paid in kind, it would presumably supply the 15 % supplement from the wine grant. The 15 % supplement was apparently later increased to the *duae decimae* of Val. III, *Nov.* xxxvi §2.

38. Val. III, *Nov.* xxxvi, 452.

39. *CTh* xiv. iv. 3, 363, ea pretia, quae in Campania per singulos annos repperiuntur, suariis urbis Romae debent solvi, ita ut periculo suariorum populo porcinae species adfatim praebeatur. et quia officialibus pro omni supplicio sufficit direptorum restitutio, quidquid ultra senos folles per singulas libras claruerit flagitatum, id fisci viribus protinus vindicetur. exactio autem nummaria non per officium tuum vel ipsos suarios sed per officiales consularis iuxta praeceptum nostrae mansuetudinis competentem sortiatur effectum. nam quia maiorum potestatum officiales solent esse provincialibus perniciosi, per ordinarios iudices adque curias etiam hanc exactionem convenit celebrari; *CIL* vi. 1771, interdicentes ne enormia illa indebitaque praestentur, quae tam tribunus quam patroni diversi et varia consequebantur officia; contra quod interdictum si qui ausi fuerint de communi largiri, et scribae quidem ceterique poenae subiaceant; *CTh* xiv. iv. 10 §4, 419, primiscrinii quoque tam inlustris urbanae sedis quam spectabilis vicariae potestatis, nisi anno militiae finali institerint, ad supplendam summam praeteritae dissimulationis artentur, ut ex propriis facultatibus debita suariae functionis exsolvant, quae neglexerunt flagitare dum militabant, privilegia etiam militiae perdituri.

40. VINA FISCALIA: SHA, *Aurelianus*, 47–8. WINE LEVY: *CTh* xi. ii. 1 and 2, 365, 3, 377, *CIL* vi. 1771, ex titulo canonico vinario. *CIL* vi. 1784–5 are apparently regulations for the wine levy, fixing fees for the various persons concerned in receiving and storing the wine, the drawers (austoribus in cupa una numm. XXX), the tally clerks (tabulariis in singulis apocis numm. XX), the cooper (exasciatori in cupa una numm. X), the porters who carried the barrels from the docks to the temple of the Sun (falancariis qui de ciconiis ad templum cupas referre consueverint), the nightwatchmen (custodibus cuparum), and the tax accountants (professionariis de ciconiis statim ut advenerit vinum in una cupa numm. CXX); the wine evidently arrived in jars, supplied by the taxpayer, and was transferred to casks after tasting (de ampullis placuit ut post degustationem possessori reddantur). REDUCED PRICE: *CTh* xi. ii. 2, 365, in tantumque populi usibus profutura provisionis nostrae emolumenta porreximus, ut etiam pretio laxamenta tribuantur. sanximus quippe, ut per vini singulas qualitates detracta quarta pretiorum, quae habentur in foro rerum venalium, eadem species a mercantibus comparetur.

41. PAYMENTS IN WINE: *CIL* vi. 1771, *CTh* xiv. iv. 4, 367 (*suarii*), vi. 3, 365, statum urbis aeternae reformare cupientes ac providere publicorum moenium dignitati iubemus, ut calcis coctoribus vectoribusque per singulas vehes singuli solidi praebeantur, ex quibus tres partes inferant possessores, quarta ex eius vini pretio sumatur, quod consuevit ex arca vinaria ministrari. ARCA VINARIA: Symm. *Rel.* 29 (*collectarii*), 34, *Ep.* ix. 150 (debt to the *largitiones*), *CTh* xiv. vi. 3, 365 (money payment to *calcis coctores*), cf. also Anon. Val. 67, ad restaurationem palatii, seu ad recuperationem moeniae civitatis singulis annis libras ducentas de arca vinaria dari praecepit.

42. THERMAE: *Not. Const.* ii. 13, iii. 10, vi. 7, 10, viii. 17, x. 8, xi. 10, xiv.

10, xv. 16, xvi. 25. PRIVATE BATHS: *Not. Rom.* (the regional and grand totals do not tally), *Not. Const.* ii. 17, iii. 16, etc. (the total in the regions agrees with the summary). MANCIPES SALINARUM: *CTh* XIV. v. 1, 370, quidquid erga mancipes, qui thermarum exhibitionem Romae curant, in exercitio conpendiisque salinarum scitis priorum principum cautum est, aeterna sanctione firmamus, Symm. *Ep.* IX. 103, totis viribus adiuvandi sunt communis patriae corporati, praecipue mancipes salinarum, qui exercent lavacra lignorum praebitione. NAVICULARII: *CTh* XIII. v. 13, 369, ad Olybrium PU, sicut olim de linteonibus et naviculariis divus Constantinus instituit, ita nunc ex omnibus sexaginta ad praesentis necessitatis teneantur impensas, quos tamen idoneos et communis delectus adseruit et facultatum inspectio comprobavit et sententia tuae sublimitatis adstruxit. quibus, si quem aut necessitas fatalis aut inopia repentina aut aliquis casus inviderit, ex vocationibus obnoxiis oportebit idoneum subrogari. sed sollicita inspectione prospiciatur, ne a quoquam amplius postuletur quam necessitas exegit lavacrorum vel instituta iamdudum forma praescripsit; Symm. *Rel.* 44; the same guild is probably referred to in *CTh* XIII. v. 11, 365, ad Symmachum PU, and Val. III, *Nov.* xxix, 450, Epitynchano PU, publicis commodis et sacratissimae urbis utilitatibus amica suggestio magnitudinis tuae clementiam nostram more solitae provisionis admonuit, ut naviculariorum corpori per tot detrimenta lassato remedia praestaremus (they are called in the title *navicularii amnici*).

43. LUDI: *Not. Rom.*, ludum matutinum, ludum magnum, *CTh* xv. xii. 3, 397. WILD BEASTS: *CTh* xv. xi. 1, 414, 2, 417.

44. STABLES: *Not. Rom.*, stabula IV factionum. RACE HORSES: *CTh* xv. x. 1, 371, Palmatis adque Hermogenis equis, quos in curulis certaminis sorte vel contentionis incertum vel annorum series vel diversa ratio debiles fecit, ex horreis fiscalibus alimoniam praeberi decrevimus, equos vero Hispani sanguinis vendendi solitam factionariis copiam non negamus. illud quoque sinceritas tua praecipiat observari, ne Graecorum equorum nomina, qui hinc missi fuerint, commutentur; vii. 6, 381, equos, quos ad sollemne certamen vel mansuetudinis nostrae largitio subministrat vel diversorum ex amplissimo ordine magistratuum, hactenus ad copiam providendos serenitas nostra decrevit, ut, quidquid illud est, quod palmarum numero gloriosum et celebratis utrimque victoriis nobile congregatur, spectaculis potius urbanae plebis inserviat quam praedae atque compendio deputetur. quisquis igitur ex eo, quod vel serenitas nostra vel ordinarii consules vel praetores in huiuscemodi tribuunt voluptates, quamlibet commodis conpendioque privato derivandam duxerit esse iacturam, unius auri librae condemnatione multatus largitionibus nostris cogatur esse munificus; x. 2, 381, equos voluptatibus profuturos nequaquam Campanorum populus adsequatur, quam si duo milia modiorum fabae per singulas factiones stabulorum in urbe venerabili necessaria antiqua et sollemni praebitione contulerint. ACTUARII EQUORUM CURULIUM AND THYMELAE: *CTh* VIII. vii. 22, 426. For the *tribunus voluptatum* see n. 8.

45. See pp. 537–9.

46. PROFESSORS: Suet. *Vesp.* 18, Symm. *Ep.* I. 79, Priscianus frater meus cum primis philosophorum litteratura et honestate censendus senatu auctore salarii emolumenta consequitur. super eius annonis dicitur orta dubitatio, cui si nihil talis compendii optimatium voluntas ante tribuisset, eruditio tua fructum ferre deberet. scis enim bonas artes honore nutriri atque hoc specimen florentis esse reipublicae, ut disciplinarum professoribus praemia opulenta pendantur. quaeso

igitur, ne hac inquietudine aut illius minuatur utilitas aut amplissimo ordini censendi auctoritas derogetur; Cass. *Var.* IX. 21, qua de re, patres conscripti, hanc vobis curam, hanc auctoritatem propitia divinitate largimur, ut successor scholae liberalium litterarum tam grammaticus quam orator nec non et iuris expositor commoda sui decessoris ab eis quorum interest sine aliqua imminutione percipiat et semel primi ordinis vestri ac reliqui senatus amplissimi auctoritate firmatus, donec suscepti operis idoneus reperitur, neque de transferendis neque de imminuendis annonis a quolibet patiatur improbam quaestionem, sed vobis ordinantibus atque custodientibus emolumentorum suorum securitate potiatur, praefecto urbis nihilo minus constituta servante. et ne aliquid pro voluntate praebentium relinquatur incertum, mox sex menses exempti fuerint, statutae summae consequantur praedicti magistri mediam portionem, residua vero anni tempora cum annonarum debita redhibitione claudantur; Just. *App.* vii §22, 552, ut annona ministretur medicis et diversis. annonam etiam, quam et Theodoricus dare solitus erat et nos etiam Romanis indulsimus, in posterum etiam dari praecipimus, sicut etiam annonas, quae grammaticis ac oratoribus vel etiam medicis vel iurisperitis antea dari solitum erat, et in posterum suam professionem scilicet exercentibus erogari praecipimus, quatenus iuvenes liberalibus studiis eruditi per nostram rempublicam floreant. STUDENTS: *CTh* XIV. ix. 1, 370.

47. Lib. *Or.* 1. 35 (appointment by the emperor on advice from the senate), 37 (salary); from 1. 80 it appears that the salary was fixed by a decree of the senate. UNIVERSITY OF CONSTANTINOPLE: *CTh* XIV. ix. 3, 425, VI. xxi. 1, 425.

48. ARCHIATRI OF ROME: *CTh* XIII. iii. 8, 368, exceptis portus Xysti virginumque Vestalium quot regiones urbis sunt, totidem constituantur archiatri. qui scientes annonaria sibi commoda a populi commodis ministrari honeste obsequi tenuioribus malint quam turpiter servire divitibus. quos etiam ea patimur accipere, quae sani offerunt pro obsequiis, non ea, quae periclitantes pro salute promittunt. quod si huic archiatrorum numero aliquem aut condicio fatalis aut aliqua fortuna decerpserit, in eius locum non patrocinio praepotentium, non gratia iudicantis alius subrogetur, sed horum omnium fideli circumspectoque delectu, qui et ipsorum consortio et archiatriae ipsius dignitate et nostro iudicio dignus habeatur. de cuius nomine referri ad nos protinus oportebit; 9, 370, si qui in archiatri defuncti est locum promotionis meritis adgregandus, non ante eorum particeps fiat, quam primis qui in ordine repperientur septem vel eo amplius iudicantibus idoneus adprobetur, ita ut, quicumque fuerit admissus, non ad priorum numerum statim veniat, sed eum ordinem consequatur, qui ceteris ad priora subvectis ultimus poterit inveniri. hisque annonarum compendia, quae eorum sunt meritis dignitatique praestanda, tua sinceritas iuxta dispositionem prius habitam faciat ministrari; 13, 387, Symm. *Rel.* 27, Cass. *Var.* VI. 19, Just. *App.* vii §22 (cited in n. 46).

49. THE ARCHITECT OF ROME: Cass. *Var.* VII. 15. There were also official architects at Constantinople; *CJ* XII. xix. 12 §1 (Anastasius).

50. BUILDING LABOUR: Symm. *Rel.* 14, sunt qui fabriles manus augustis operibus adcommodent. BRICKS: Cass. *Var.* I. 25, dudum siquidem propter Romanae moenia civitatis, ubi studium nobis semper impendere infatigabilis ambitus erit, portum Licini deputatis reditibus reparari iussio nostra constituit, ut XXV milia tegularum annua illatione praestaret: simul etiam portubus iunctis, qui ad illa loca antiquitus pertinebant, qui nunc diversorum usurpatione suggeruntur invasi. LIME: *CTh* XIV. vi. 1, 359, ex omnibus praediis, quae iam dudum praesta-

tioni calcis coeperunt obnoxia adtineri, coctoribus calcis per ternas vehes singulae amphorae vini praebeantur, vecturariis vero amphora per bina milia et nungenta pondo calcis. quin etiam volumus non personas, sed ipsos fundos titulo huius praestationis adstringi. vecturarios etiam ex quattuor regionibus trecentos boves praecipimus dari; 2, 364, 3, 365, statum urbis aeternae reformare cupientes ac providere publicorum moenium dignitati iubemus, ut calcis coctoribus vectoribusque per singulas vehes singuli solidi praebeantur, ex quibus tres partes inferant possessores, quarta ex eius vini pretio sumatur, quod consuevit ex arca vinaria ministrari: illud addentes, ut non amplius quam terna milia minores vehes annuae postulentur. huius autem vehationis ita sit ratio partita, ut mille quingenta onera formis, alia sartis tectis annua deputentur, ita ut nulli iudicum seu officiorum excoquendae calcis licentia relinquatur, sub eo statuto, ut, qui in hac usurpatione fuerit, austeritatem vigoris publici ferre cogatur. hoc autem excepto a Tarracinensis praestationis canone suggera, quae vetusto praeberi fari ac Portus usibus more consuevit. a curialibus vero Tuscis nungentarum vehum, quas inferre per singulos annos cogebantur, sarcinam sub ea condicione praecipimus amoveri, ut, si quando necessitas novi operis extiterit, id ipsum in notitiam nostram suggestionibus iudicum perferendum quid addendum vel quatenus inferendum sit, nostrae deliberationis moderamine sanciatur. ex supra dicto autem numero vehationis medietatem, quam sartis tectis iussimus deputari, separatim conveniet adscribi, ita ut praefecti urbi officium ad suam partem hanc curam pertinere cognoscat; cf. Val. III, *Nov.* v §4, 440, confirming the immunity of *caespes ar*<*en*>*ensis, calcarius et vecturarius.* PRAEPOSITUS CALCIS: Cass. *Var.* VII. 17. Lime surplus to public requirements could be supplied to private persons (*CTh* XIV. vi. 4, 382, ut caementorum et calcis in urbe venerabili copiae minime derogetur, quisquis ex his quippiam sibi deferendum qualibet caelestis indulgentiae definitione contenderit, nihil prorsus accipiat, nisi quod cunctis moenibus fabricationique Romanae super-fluere ac redundare constiterit. cf. Cass. *Var.* VII. 17).

51. CONTRIBUTIONS BY PRAETORS: *CTh* VI. iv. 13, 361; cf. n. 17 for payments for the aqueducts. LIME BURNING: *CTh* XIV. vi. 5, 419.

52. AERARIUM SATURNI: *ILS* 1233. AERARIUM POPULI ROMANI: Symm. *Rel.* 37, ad vos igitur salutaria numina convolamus et opem largam populi Romani imploramus aerario, cum iam diu nihil solitorum vectigalium decretae provinciae contulerunt atque ideo iustus est metus, ne cessantibus subsidiis necessaria deserantur, quae hactenus personae tenues alieno, ut queruntur, aere tolerarunt. super hoc etiam reverendus ordo consultus, cum per se mederi adfectis rebus nequiret, opem vestrae perennitatis oravit. edita ratio est vectigalium, quae Hispaniensis atque Alexandrinus invehere debuit commeatus; expensionum quoque titulos competentes officii cura digessit: quaeso, ut omnibus, quae cohaerent, libenter inspectis utilitati publicae velox remedium porrigatis. SPECIAL TREASURIES: *CTh* XII. xi. 2, 386, tam oleariae arcae quam frumentariae, Symm. *Rel.* 20, ex arca quaestoria itemque ex formarum conditis; for the *arca vinaria* see n. 41. PUBLIC WORKS: Amm. XXVII. iii. 10, aedificia erigere exoriens nova, vel vetusta quaedam instaurans, non ex titulis solitis parari iubebat inpensas sed, si ferrum quaerebatur aut plumbum aut aes aut quicquam simile, apparitores inmittebantur, qui velut ementes diversa raperent species, nulla pretia persolvendo; *CTh* XV. i. 48, 411, nihil ex his, quae instaurationi ornati-busque singulis deputavit antiquitas, nullius colore occasionis auferri volumus. igitur a futuro proximo consulatu universa praedictae urbi debitorum vecti-galium inlibata augmenta pervaleant; cf. tit. cit. 12, 364, annonas quoque horreis antiquitus deputatas. It is not clear whether the *Romanis fabricis deputata*

pecunia of Cass. *Var.* I. 21, II. 34, was regular revenue or a special grant. Cf. also Just. *App.* vii §25 (cited in n. 56).

53. Symm. *Rel.* 40.

54. For the *arca frumentaria* and the aqueduct fund see nn. 31, 17.

55. Cass. *Var.* XI. 39. For the conditions of Rome see the *formulae* of the urban administrators (VI. 4, 15, 18, 19, VII. 6–7, 9–10, 13) and for the corn supply v. 35, XI. 5, XII. 11, for the games I. 20, 27, 30–3, and for the public buildings I. 21, II. 34, III. 30–1, IV. 51. Anon. Val. 67, donavitque populo Romano et pauperibus annonas singulis annis, centum viginti milia modios, presumably refers to an increase of the *annona* made by Theoderic; the figure suggests that he maintained the number of the *plebs frumentaria* at 120,000, adding one *modius* to the annual ration.

56. Just. *App.* vii §22, 554, annonam etiam quam et Theodericus dare solitus erat et nos etiam Romanis indulsimus, §25, consuetudines etiam et privilegia Romanae civitatis vel publicarum fabricarum reparationi vel alveo Tiberino vel foro aut portui Romano sive reparationi formarum concessa servari praecipimus, ita videlicet ut ex isdem tantummodo titulis, ex quibus delegata fuerunt, praestentur. For the administration of Rome and the corn supply in Gregory the Great's time see ch. X, n. 29, and ch. XIII, n. 119.

XIX. THE CITIES (pp. 712–13)

In this chapter I largely rely on my own two books, *The Cities of the Eastern Roman Provinces*, Oxford, 1937 (cited as *CERP*), and *The Greek City from Alexander to Justinian*, Oxford, 1940 (cited as *Greek City*). I have also derived much profit from P. Petit, *Libanius et la vie municipale à Antioche au IVe siècle après J.-C.*, Paris, 1955. There are no comparable studies for the West.

1. The rules on *origo* and *incolatus* are given in *Dig.* L. i, *CJ* x. xxxix, xl, *CTh* XII. i. 12, 325.

2. The Notitia Galliarum is printed in Seeck's *Notitia Dignitatum*, 261–74. There can be no doubt that it is a civil register, not a list of bishoprics, as in the province of Viennensis it ignores the ecclesiastical province of Arles (see pp. 882, 890). In date it appears to be roughly contemporary with the Notitia Dignitatum, with whose list of provinces it agrees. The eight units which are not *civitates* are seven *castra* (i. 6, 7, ix. 6–9, xv. 9) and one *portus* (ix. 10). For the date, character and reliability of Hierocles and Georgius Cyprius see *CERP*, App. III, 502–509. Their lists for the dioceses of Thrace, Asiana, Pontica, Oriens and Egypt are set out with other evidence in the tables in *CERP*, App. IV, 510–540. I have based my statistical statements in this and the following paragraphs on these tables, as interpreted and explained in the general body of the book. For the dioceses of Dacia and Macedonia I use the plain text of Hierocles.

3. For the villages of Arabia see *CERP*, 284–91; cf. 282, 294 for other villages in Oriens. A village is also recorded in Lycia (pp. 109–10) and four in Egypt

(p. 348). The δῆμοι appear only in Phrygia Salutaris and Pamphylia (*CERP*, App. IV, Table xii. 20–23, xviii. 5, 7, 11, 12, 32, 33).

4. There are only two χωρία, the Patrimonial and the Milyadic (in Caria and Pamphylia; Table x. 29, xviii. 17), two κλῆροι (in Phrygia Salutaris; Table xii. 6, 7), and two κτήματα (in Caria and Pamphylia; Table xii. 31, xviii. 28). Groups of *regiones* occur in Bithynia (*CERP*, 161–2, 166–7, 169), Cappadocia (*CERP*, 184–191) and Palestine (*CERP*, 282, cf. 274–5); their probable origins as royal land are discussed in these passages. There are also six other isolated *regiones* (*CERP*, 65, 109, 123, 137, 145, 347) whose origin is matter of conjecture. Apart from the κλίμα Νεστικόν in Macedonia I (Hierocles, 640, 8, κλίμα Μεντικὸν καὶ Ἀκόντισμα; Acontisma was on the Nestus), the κλίματα are all in Oriens (*CERP*, 139–140, 226, 269, 283, 294–5). There are two *saltus* in Thessaly (Hierocles, 643, 1, 2), one in Pontus (*CERP*, 172–3); the remainder are all in Oriens (*CERP*, 369, 282–3, 289–91, 294).

5. For Alexandria see *CERP*, 305–6.

6. *CERP*, 10–22 (Thrace), 157–62 (Pontus), 177–83 (Cappadocia), 274–91 (Herodian kingdom), 316 ff. (Egypt).

7. Number of the Gallic *civitates*: Strabo, 192 (sixty), Tac. *Ann.* III. 44 (sixty-four). Cenabum of the Carnutes (Caes. *BG* VII. 11, VIII. 5, Strabo, 191) is identified with the Civitas Aurelianorum by the evidence of the itineraries: the town was presumably made a city by Aurelian. Bononia is equated with Gessoriacum by the Peutinger Table, and Gessoriacum is stated to be a town of the Morini by Pliny, *Hist. Nat.* IV. 102, 122; the name Bononia, which no doubt was given to it when it became a city, is first recorded under Constantine (Pan. Lat. VI. 5), and the old name is still used under Constantius I as Caesar (Pan. Lat. VIII. 6, 14). Icolisma is first mentioned by Ausonius (*Ep.* xv), and seems to have already been a city then, since Tetradius taught there as a *grammaticus*. Cabillonum and Matisco are said to be towns of the Aedui in Caes. *BG* VII. 90. For Gildas on Britain see Stevens in *EHR* 1937, 193ff.

8. AFRICA: Pliny, *Hist. Nat.* V. 29–30. There is a list of African bishoprics in J. Mesnage, *L'Afrique Chrétienne*, Paris, 1912. For bishops on estates see *Coll. Carth.* I. 181–2, *V. Mel.* (L), 21; for the *municipium Tulliense*, Aug. *de cura gerenda pro mortuis*, 15.

9. The Bordeaux Itinerary is published in O. Cuntz, *Itineraria Romana*, I.

10. MACEDONIA: Pliny, *Hist. Nat.* IV. 33.

11. *CERP*, 64 ff. (Asia), 107–10 (Lycia), 134 ff. (Galatia).

12. *CERP*, 122–3 (the Gauls), 157 ff. (Bithynia and Pontus), 177 ff. (Cappadocia).

13. TERRITORIES OF ANTIOCH, APAMEA AND CYRRHUS: *CERP*, 270. ARABIAN CITIES: ibid. 287–8.

14. EGYPT: *CERP*, 344 ff.; for Nilopolis and Heracleopolis see *P. Oxy.* 1909.

15. TYMANDUS: *ILS* 6090. ORCISTUS: *ILS* 6091.

16. See the index of *CERP* s.v. Anastasiopolis, Arcadiopolis, Basilinopolis, Constantia, Constantine, Diocletianopolis, Eudocias, Eudoxias, Eudoxiopolis, Helenopolis, Julianopolis, Justiniana, Justinianopolis, Leontopolis, Marciana, Marcianopolis, Maximianopolis, Pulcherianopolis, Theodorias, Theodosiana,

Theodosiopolis, Valentia, Valentinianopolis, Verinopolis, Zenonopolis. Add from Hierocles Constantiana of Scythia, Diocletianopolis of Thessaly, Pulcheriopolis of Epirus Nova. The second—and very small—city named after Theodora has recently been discovered in Cyrenaica (*SEG* XVIII. 768). Dynastic names are very rare in the West, Constantina Cirta and Arelate, Gratiana in Moesia and Gratianopolis (Cularo).

17. *Greek City*, 86 ff.; for the individual cases see *CERP* under the names.

18. *ILS* 6090, ut autem sic uti ceteris civitatibus ius est coeundi in curiam, faciendi etiam decreti et gerendi cetera quae iure permissa sunt, ipsa quoque permissu nostro agere possit, et magistratus ei itemque aediles, quaestores quoque et si qua alia necessaria facienda sunt, creare debebunt. quem ordinem agendarum rerum perpetuo pro civitatis merito custodiri conveniet. numerum autem decurionum interim quinquaginta hominum instituere debebis. deorum autem immortalium favor tribuet, ut auctis eorum viribus atque numero maior eorum haberi copia possit (cf. above, isdem maxime pollicentibus quod apud se decurionum sufficiens futura sit copia).

19. BASILINOPOLIS: *A.C.Oec.* II. i. 418, ὥσπερ Ταττάϊος καὶ Δωρὶς ῥεγεῶνές εἰσιν ὑπὸ Νίκαιαν, οὕτως ἦν πρὸ τούτου καὶ Βασιλεινούπολις ὑπὸ τὴν Νίκαιαν. βασιλεύς τις Ἰουλιανὸς ἢ οὐκ οἶδα τίς πρὸ αὐτοῦ ἐποίησεν αὐτὴν πόλιν καὶ λαβὼν ἀπὸ Νικαίας πολιτευομένους κατέστησεν ἐκεῖ, καὶ τὸ ἔθος ἀπὸ τότε ἕως νῦν τοῦτο κρατεῖ, ἐὰν λείψῃ ἐν Βασιλεινουπόλει πολιτευόμενος ἀπὸ Νικαίας πέμπεται ἐκεῖ καὶ πάλιν ἀπὸ Βασιλεινουπόλεως μεθίσταται ἐν Νικαίᾳ. καὶ πρότερον οὖσα ῥεγεὼν πάλιν μετὰ ταῦτα ἐγένετο πόλις. PODANDUS: Basil, *Ep.* 75, πολλῶν μὲν καὶ πρότερον αὐτῆς ἀφαιρεθέντων τῶν πολιτευομένων, νῦν δὲ σχεδὸν ἁπάντων ἐπὶ τὴν Ποδανδὸν μετοικισθέντων. This letter was written at the time when Valens divided Cappadocia into two provinces, and it may be inferred that the transformation of the *regio* of Podandus into a city was part of the plan.

20. THE AEDUI: Pan. Lat. v. 3. CYRENE: Syn. *Catastasis* I. ANTIOCH: Lib. *Or.* XI. 42 ff., Malalas, 28–30.

21. POPULAR ASSEMBLIES: *CTh* XII. v. 1, 325 (S), ii magistratus, qui sufficiendis duumviris in futurum anni officium nominationes impertiunt, periculi sui contemplatione provideant, ut, quamvis populi quoque suffragiis nominatio in Africa ex consuetudine celebretur, tamen ipsi nitantur pariter ac laborent, quemadmodum possint ii, qui nominati fuerint, idonei repperiri. nam aequitatis ratio persuadet, nisi idonei fuerint nominati, ipsos, quorum est periculum, adtineri. Cf. *IRT* 564, 566, 574, 578, 595, where honours are said to have been given 'suffragiis populi et decurionum decreto'. See Soc. VII. 13 for the prefect of Egypt doing official business in the theatre; Joh. Chrys. *Hom. in Matth.* xix. 9, for the reading of imperial letters in the theatre; cf. Lib. *Or.* I. 157, where the consular of Syria breaks up Libanius's audience by summoning them to hear imperial letters.

22. THE ASSEMBLY AT OXYRHYNCHUS: *Chr.* I. 45.

23. CONSTANTINE'S EDICT: *CTh* I. xvi. 6, 331, iustissimos autem et vigilantissimos iudices publicis adclamationibus conlaudandi damus omnibus potestatem, ut honoris eis auctiores proferamus processus, e contrario iniustis et maleficis querellarum vocibus accusandis, ut censurae nostrae vigor eos absumat; nam si verae voces sunt nec ad libidinem per clientelas effusae, diligenter investigabimus, praefectis praetorio et comitibus, qui per provincias constituti sunt, provincialium nostrorum voces ad nostram scientiam referentibus.

24. On this topic see R. Browning, *JRS* XLII (1952), 13 ff., who cites much evidence from Libanius and John Chrysostom.

25. *CERP* 334, 341-2; the evidence is *P. Oxy.* 1116, 1627, *P. Flor.* 39, *PSI* 86, 1108, 1232, *P. Lips.* 65, *Sb* 4513. The police functions of the ἐπιμεληταὶ τῶν φυλῶν at Antioch (Lib. *Or.* XXIII. 11, XXIV. 26, XXXIII. 35-6) suggest that the tribes of Antioch were used as in Egypt.

26. That 100 was the standard number for *coloniae* and *municipia* is fairly certain; see Cic. *de lege Agraria* II. 96 (Capua), *ILS* 5670 (Cures), 6121 (Canusium), 6579 (Veii). But peregrine *civitates* sometimes had larger councils, e.g. Thuburbo Maius (*ILA* 266). SYRIAN CITIES: Lib. *Or.* II. 33. TYMANDUS: *ILS* 6090. ANTIOCH: Lib. *Or.* XLVIII. 3.

27. See below n. 40.

28. TYMANDUS: *ILS* 6090. In Egypt the *exegetes* is last recorded in 294 (*P. Oxy.* 891), the *cosmetes* in 347 (*P. Antinoop.* 31), gymnasiarchs in 370 (*P. Oxy.* 2110), and *archiereis* in 386 (*CTh* XII. i. 112). Cf. *Sb* 9219 (ἀρχιερεύς, ὑπομνηματόγραφος and γυμνασίαρχος at Alexandria in 319), *P. Amh.* 82 (ἀρχιερεύς and γυμνασίαρχος at Arsinoe), *CPR* 247 (γυμνασίαρχος at Heracleopolis in 346). *Prytaneis* are frequently mentioned; they are often styled προπολιτευόμενος.

29. *Riparii* are frequently mentioned in the papyri (see Oertel, *die Liturgie*, 284-6; they appear first in 346, P. Oxy. 897); that they existed in other provinces of Oriens is implied by *Chr.* I. 469, a letter of C. Valerius Eusebius, *comes* Orientis (cf. *ILS* 8947) addressed ῥιπαρίοις κατὰ πόλιν ἀπὸ Θηβαίδος ἕως Ἀντιοχείας; but eirenarchs are recorded at Gaza (*V. Porph.* 25), and Libanius speaks of εἰρηνοφύλακες at Antioch (*Or.* XLVIII. 9) and εἰρήνης φύλαξ at Elusa (*Ep.* 101-2); this title is no doubt due to Libanius's Atticism, but is more likely to have been suggested by εἰρηνάρχης than by *riparius*. EIRENARCHS: *CTh* XII. xiv. 1, 409. Νυκτοστράτηγοι are frequently mentioned in the papyri; they date from the third century (see Oertel, *die Liturgie*, 281-3). At Antioch a νυκτέπαρχος is recorded (Pall. *Dial.* p. 97, Malalas, 396-7). PRAEPOSITUS PAGI: Eus. *HE* IX. 1 (the edict of Sabinus), γράψαι τοιγαροῦν πρὸς τοὺς λογιστὰς καὶ τοὺς στρατηγοὺς καὶ τοὺς πραιποσίτους τοῦ πάγου ἑκάστης πόλεως ἡ σὴ ἐπιστρέφεια ὀφείλει ἵνα γνοῖεν περαιτέρω αὐτοῖς τούτου τοῦ γράμματος φροντίδα ποιεῖσθαι μὴ προσήκειν, *CTh* VII. iv. 1, 325. VIII. xv. 1 (a law of Constantine), AGRIPPINA DIXIT: τῷ τόπῳ ἐκείνῳ οὐκ ἐπαγάρχει; AGRIPPINA DIXIT: τοῦ τόπου ἐκείνου πραιπόσιτος οὐκ ἦν, XII. vi. 8, 365, iuxta inveteratas leges nominatores susceptorum et eorum, qui ad praeposituram horreorum et pagorum creantur, teneantur obnoxii, si minus idonei sint qui ab iisdem fuerint nominati, nec quicquam ex eorum substantia celebrata per interpositam personam emptione mercentur, and perhaps XII. i. 49 §2, 361, praepositi horreorum iique, qui suscepturi sunt magistratum, praepositi etiam pagis seu susceptores diversarum specierum (reading 'pagis' for 'pacis'); Basil (*Ep.* 3) mentions a πάγαρχος in Cappadocia. For their date (in Egypt from 307-8) see Boak, *Mélanges Maspéro*, II. 125-9, and for their functions ch. XIII, n. III (appointment of village officials and finance) and Oertel, *die Liturgie*, 301-2.

30. For the earlier history of the *curator* see Liebenam, *Philologus*, 1897, 290 ff., Kornemann, *PW* IV. 1806 ff. There is a full account of the λογιστής in Egypt by Rees, *J. Jur. Pap.* VII-VIII (1953-4), 83 ff. For their general police functions see Eus. *HE* IX. 1 (the edict of Sabinus), Opt. *App.* I, *CTh* XVI. ii. 31 (= *Sirm.* 14), 409. *Curatores* were still appointed by imperial *epistula* in 331 (*CTh* XII. i. 20, nullus decurionum ad procurationes vel curas civitatum accedat, nisi

omnibus omnino muneribus satisfecerit patriae vel aetate vel meritis. qui vero
per suffragium ad hoc pervenerit administrare desiderans, non modo ab expetito
officio repellatur, sed epistula quoque vel codicilli ab eo protinus auferantur et
ad comitatum destinetur), but had apparently ceased to be so by Justinian's
reign (no fees are recorded in Just. *Nov.* viii). In Ostrogothic Italy they were
however appointed by royal *epistula* (Cass. *Var.* VII. 12) and continued to
require imperial confirmation in Sicily after Justinian's reconquest (Just. *Nov.*
lxxv, 537). In 353 (Philostorgius, III. 28) Montius taunted the Caesar Gallus,
οὐδὲ λογιστὴν ἐξεστί σοι προχειρίσασθαι.

31. The *defensor* first appears in Egypt in 332 (*P. Oxy.* 1426) and 336 (*P. Oxy.*
901, *Sb* 6294); in Arabia in 322 (Wadd. 2238-40). He appears as a judge in 340
(*Sb* 8246). VALENTINIAN: *CTh* I. xxix. 1, 368, 2, 365, 3, 368, 4, 368, 5, 370. For
a history of the *defensor* in Egypt see Rees, *J. Jur. Pap.* VI (1952), 73 ff.

32. DEFENSOR NOMINATED BY THE COUNCIL: *CTh* I. xxix. 6, 387; APPOINTED BY
THE PRAETORIAN PREFECT: Just. *Nov.* viii. notitia 37, 535; BY THE KING: Cass.
Var. VII. 11. OPPRESSION BY DEFENSORES: *CTh* I. xxix. 7, 392. WEAKNESS OF
DEFENSORES: Just. *Nov.* xv, 535.

33. The evidence of the papyri and the codes on the election of curial *susceptores*,
etc., is collected in my *Greek City*, pp. 333-4, notes 106, 108, 109, that on the
exactor civitatis on p. 332, note 104; see also J. D. Thomas, *Chron. d'Égypte*,
XXXIV (1959), 124 ff. For Thamugadi see below n. 40.

34. *CJ* x. xxxii. 2 (285-93), observare magistratus oportebit, ut decurionibus
sollemniter in curiam convocatis nominationem ad certa munera faciant eamque
statim in notitiam eius qui fuerit nominatus per officialem publicum perferre
curent, habituro appellandi, si voluerit, atque agendi facultatem apud praesidem
causam suam iure consueto: quem si constiterit nominari minime debuisse,
sumptus litis eidem a nominatore restitui oportebit; *CTh* XII. i. 8, 323, decuriones
ad magistratum vel exactionem annonarum ante tres menses vel amplius
nominari debent, ut, si querimonia eorum iusta videatur, sine impedimento in
absolvendi locum alius subrogetur; 28, 339, constitutionibus perspicue definitum
est kalendis Martiis nominationes fieri, ut splendidorum honorum munerumque
principia primo tempore procurentur; 84, 381, in nominationibus a singulis
quibusque ordinibus celebrandis dudum expressae quantitatis modum eatenus
volumus custodiri, ut eorum in duabus, quae concilio adesse debent, partibus
numerus derogetur, quos aut obtentus debilitatis alienat aut senectus pigra
remoratur aut clericatus obsequia vindicarunt aut crimen desertionis absentat,
ut ex reliquo numero duabus tertiis supputandis.

35. CURATOR: *CTh* XII. i. 20, 331 (cited in n. 30). EXACTOR: *Chr.* I. 44,
Αὐρήλιος Εὐλόγειος Ἀνδρέω ἔναρχος πρύτανις προπολιτευόμενος τῆς Ἀρσινοϊτῶν
πόλεως Φλ' Ἀβενναίῳ ἀπὸ ἐπάρχων εἴλης χαίριν. ἀπαντοῦντί σοι ἐν τῷ ἱερῷ κομιτάτῳ
ἐντέλλομαί σοι καὶ ἐπιτρέπω κατὰ τήνδε τὴν ἐντολὴν ὅπως ἐπιστολὴν ἐξακτορίας ἐπ'
ὀνόματός μου ἐνέγκῃς παρὰ τῆς θιότητος τῶν δεσποτῶν ἡμῶν αἰωνίων Αὐγούστων,
ἐ[μοῦ ἐπι]γιγνώσκοντος εἴ τι ἂν ἁπαξαπλῶς ἀναλώσῃς εἰς τὴν αὐτὴν ἐπιστολὴν τῇ σῇ
πίστι.

36. EXEMPTION FOR AGE: *Dig.* L. iv. 3 §§6, 12, v. 1 §3, 2 §1, 8 pr., vi. 3, *CJ* x.
xxxii. 10, 294, l. 3 (285-93); for ill-health, *Dig.* L. v. 2 §§6-7, 13 pr., *CJ* x. li. 1
(Gordian), 2, 3, 4 (Diocletian). PERICULUM NOMINATORIS: *Dig.* L. i. 11, 13,
15 §1, 17 §§14-5, iv. 14 §4, *CJ* XI. xxxiv. 1, 2, xxxvi. 2 (Gordian), 3 (Carus), 4
(Diocletian), *CTh* XII. vi. 1, 321, v. 1, 325 (S). Nomination by magistrates of their

successors is implied by *CTh* XII. v. 1, 325 (S), (cited in n. 21); the *prytanis* nominates in *Chr.* I. 420, II. 95, *P. Oxy.* 2110. FINANCIAL RESPONSIBILITY OF THE COUNCIL: *PSI* 684 (cited in ch. XIII, n. 112).

37. EIRENARCHS: *CJ* x. lxxvii. 1, 409, irenarchae, qui ad provinciarum tutelam quietis ac pacis per singula territoria faciunt stare concordiam, a decurionibus iudicio praesidum provinciarum idonei nominentur.

38. *P. Oxy.* 2110.

39. The old *cursus honorum* is confirmed by *CJ* x. xliii. 2 (285–93). IMMUNITY OF DUOVIRALES: *CTh* XII. i. 21, 335, quoniam Afri curiales conquesti sunt quosdam in suo corpore post flamonii honorem et sacerdotii vel magistratus decursa insignia praepositos compelli fieri mansionum, quod in singulis curiis sequentis meriti et gradus homines implere consuerunt, iubemus nullum praedictis honoribus splendentem ad memoratum cogi obsequium, ne nostro fieri iudicio iniuria videatur; v. 2, 337, sacerdotales et flamines perpetuos atque etiam duumvirales ab annonarum praeposituris inferioribusque muneribus immunes esse praecipimus. quod ut perpetua observatione firmetur, legem hanc incisam aeneis tabulis iussimus publicari. ALBUM ORDINIS: *Dig.* L. iii.

40. The text (*CIL* VIII. 2403 + 17824, partly reproduced in *ILS* 6122) has been greatly improved by L. Leschi in *REA* L (1948), 71 ff.

41. *Principales* are mentioned as important and responsible members of the *curia* in *CTh* XII. i. 77, 372, nec vero a duumviratu vel a sacerdotio incipiat, sed servato ordine omnium officiorum sollicitudinem sustineat, quod nec his deferri per gratiam aut conivente iudice patimur, qui advocationis praerogativa nituntur; nec vero principalium vel sacerdotalium, cum nullam curialium officiorum agnoverint functionem, in honores primos inrepant; 79, 375, si quos curiales patrocinio principalium invenerint excusari; XIII. xi. 10, 399, conludio principalium vel defensorum vel subrepticiis rescriptis; VIII. v. 59, 400, periculo civitatis sive defensoris et principalium civitatum; X. xxv. 1, 406; XVI. v. 40 §8, 407, defensores quoque et principales urbium singularum; Maj. *Nov.* vii §18, 458. OPPRESSION OF LESSER DECURIONS: *CTh* XI. xvi. 4, 328, extraordinariorum munerum distributio non est principalibus committenda, ideoque rectores provinciarum monendi sunt, ut eam distributionem ipsi celebrent manuque propria perscribant atque encauto nomina adnectant, ea forma servata, ut primo a potioribus, dein a mediocribus atque infimis quae sunt danda praestentur; XII. iii. 2, 423, quoniam de constitutione inclytae recordationis avi nostri de alienandis praediis curialium promulgata dubitatum est, utrum soli principales sine decreti interpositione collegarum possessiones emere vetentur an omnibus comparandorum huiuscemodi fundorum copia sine praedicta observatione negata sit, generali sanctione decernimus, ut, si curialis praedium urbanum aut rusticum vendat cuiuscumque condicionis emptori, apud rectorem provinciae idoneas causas alienationis alleget; Symm. *Ep.* IX. 10, sed principalibus et tabulariis liberum est alios a dispendio vindicare, aliis indebitum munus imponere.

42. DECEMPRIMI IN SICILY: *ILS* 8843, *P. Ital.* 10–11, col. iii. 13, iv. 8, 9, v. 1. TEN PRINCIPALES IN AFRICA: *CTh* XVI. v. 52, 412, 54, 414 (*principales = decem primi curiales*); IN EGYPT: *P. Oxy.* 2110. *Decemprimi* are also mentioned in *CTh* IX. xxxv. 2, 376 (addressed to *Ppo Galliarum*) and XVI. ii. 39, 408 (*Ppo It.*). FIVE PRIMATES OF ALEXANDRIA: *CTh* XII. i. 190, 436. PRINCIPALES IN GAUL: *CTh* XII. i. 171, 412 (S), placuit principales viros e curia in Galliis non ante discedere,

quam quindecennium in ordinis sui administratione compleverint, per quae annorum moderata curricula impleant patriae gratiam. et quamvis cunctos deceat revocari, qui brevi tempore videntur elapsi, sectandam tamen moderationem esse censuimus, ut eos tantum ad declinatas necessitates nunc redire iuberemus, qui ante hoc recessisse sexennium deteguntur. nec quemquam convenit constituta salubriter annorum spatia recusare, quando expletis omnibus splendoris et honoris ornamenta succedunt. sane quoniam principalem locum et gubernacula urbium probatos administrare ipsa magnitudo deposcit, sine ordinis praeiudicio consensu curiae eligendos esse censemus, qui contemplatione actuum omnium possint respondere iudicio. eum vero, qui usque ad secundum evectus locum administrationem aut aetate implere aut debilitate nequiverit, suffragium meritorum et transactae testimonium vitae, tamquam primus constituto tempore curiam rexerit, obtinere conveniet. HONOURS OF PRIMUS CURIAE: *CTh* XII. i. 189 (= *CJ* X. xxxii. 56), 436.

43. *Greek City*, 241 ff.; Arcadius Charisius is cited in *Dig*. L. iv. 18 §5.

44. CIVIC LANDS RESTORED BY JULIAN: *CTh* X. iii. 1, *CJ* XI. lxx. 1, 362, Amm. XXV. iv. 15, Lib. *Or*. XIII. 45. In *Or*. XXXI. 16, delivered c. 360, Libanius speaks of Antioch as still possessing large quantities of civic land, and in 359 the proconsul of Achaea allocated building materials for civic works at Chalcis ἐκ τῶν πολειτικῶν προσόδων (*IG* XII. ix. 907); so the confiscation must have taken place in Constantius's last years. In *Or*. L. 5, delivered in 385, Libanius again speaks of lands which had been bequeathed to the city in the past and were under its control; these are presumably the restored third or bequests during the past twenty years. Cf. W. Liebeschütz, *Byz. Zeitschr*. LII (1959), 344 ff. for a different explanation of the problem. CIVIC TAXES RESTORED BY JULIAN: Amm. XXV. iv. 15. TEMPLE LANDS CONFISCATED BY CONSTANTINE: Lib. *Or*. XXX. 6, 37, LXII. 8; BY VALENTINIAN AND VALENS: *CTh* V. xiii. 3, X. i. 8, 364.

45. PART OF THE RENTS RESTORED: *FIR* I². 108, [quod ex red]itibus fundorum iuris re[i publicae, quo]s intra Asiam diversis quibusque civitatibus ad instaurand[am mo]enium fac[iem . . . . pr]o certis [partibu]s habita aestimatione concensimus capere quidem urbes singulas beneficii nostri uberem fructum et pro [temporum r]efers felici[tate nostror]um a foedo [recentiu]m squalore ruinarum in antiquam sui faciem nova reparatione consurgere, verum non integram gra[tiam con]cessi ad urbes singulas benefic[ii nostri perv?]enire, si quidem pro partibus praestitis reditus civitatibus potius [qua]m ipsi cum reditibus fundi fuerint restitu[end]i et ministrandi, idem reditus ab acto[ri]bus [pr]ibatae rei nostrae et diu miserabiliterque poscantur et vix aegreque tribuantur atque id quod amplius e[x i]sdem fundis super statutum canonem colligatur, et isdem civitatibus pereat eorundemque actorum fraudibus devoratum nihil tamen aerario nostro adiciat augmenti possitque a curialibus vel excultione maiore vel propensiore diligentia nonnullus praestitionis cumulus ad gratiam concessionis accedere, igitur cuncta diligenti coram investigatione perspeximus. A THIRD OF THE RENTS RESTORED: *CTh* IV. xiii. 7, 374, ex reditibus rei publicae omniumque titulorum ad singulas quasque pertinentium civitates duae partes totius pensionis ad largitiones nostras perveniant, tertia probabilibus civitatum deputetur expensis; XV. i. 18, 374, si civitatis eius res publica tantum in tertia pensionis parte non habeat, quantum coeptae fabricae poscat impendium, ex aliarum civitatum rei publicae canone praesumant, tertiae videlicet portionis; V. xiv. 35, 395, restaurationi moenium publicorum tertiam portionem eius canonis, qui ex locis fundisve rei publicae annua praestatione confertur, certum est satis posse sufficere. de vectigalibus itaque publicis, quae semper ex integro nostri

aerarii conferebant expensas, nihil omnino decerpi nomine civitatum permittimus; xv. i. 32, 395, ne splendidissimae urbes vel oppida vetustate labantur, de
reditibus fundorum iuris rei publicae tertiam partem reparationi publicorum
moenium et thermarum subustioni deputamus; 33, 395, singuli igitur ordines
civitatum ad reparationem moenium publicorum nihil sibi amplius noverint
praesumendum praeter tertiam portionem eius canonis, qui ex locis fundisque
rei publicae quotannis conferri solet, sicut divi parentis nostri Valentiniani
senioris deputavit auctoritas. A THIRD OF THE TAXES RESTORED: *CTh* IV. xiii.
7, 374; since the law is placed in the title *de vectigalibus et commissis* it must refer
(*inter alia*) to civic taxes. ALL CIVIC TAXES TO THE STATE: *CTh* v. xiv. 35, 395;
vectigalia publica should mean civic taxes.

46. URBAN LANDS: *CTh* x. iii. 5, 400, aedificia, hortos atque areas aedium
publicarum et ea rei publicae loca, quae aut includuntur moenibus civitatum
aut pomeriis sunt conexa, vel ea quae de iure templorum aut per diversos petita
aut aeternabili domui fuerint congregata, vel civitatum territoriis ambiuntur,
sub perpetua conductione, salvo dumtaxat canone, quem sub examine habitae
discussionis constitit adscriptum, penes municipes, collegiatos et corporatos
urbium singularum conlocata permaneant omni venientis extrinsecus atque
occulte conductionis adtemptatione submota; xv. i. 41, 401, omnia aedificia
publica sive iuris templorum intra muros posita vel etiam muris cohaerentia,
quae tamen nullis censibus patuerit obligata, curiales et collegiati submotis
competitoribus teneant atque custodiant . . . . si quando a quopiam vacans
locus aut area postulatur, consultius ad ordinarios iudices nostri mittantur
affatus, ut, si neque usui neque ornatui civitatis adcommodum videtur esse quod
poscitur, periculo ordinis et provincialis officii absque ullius gratiae conludio
competitori sub gestorum testificatione tradantur. pensiones autem, quae
deinceps sublatae a competitoribus fuerint, rationabiliter inpositas reparationi
iubemus proficere civitatis, exceptis videlicet pensionibus praeteriti temporis,
quae iam sollemniter sacro privatoque debentur aerario. CIVIC TAXES: *CJ* IV.
lxi. 13, 431, exceptis his vectigalibus, quae ad sacrum patrimonium nostrum
quocumque tempore pervenerunt, cetera rei publicae civitatum atque ordinum
aestimatis dispendiis quae pro publicis necessitatibus tolerare non desinunt,
reserventur, cum duas portiones aerario nostro conferri prisca institutio
disposuerat: atque hanc tertiam iubemus adeo in dicione urbium municipumque
consistere, ut proprii compendii curam non in alieno potius quam in suo
arbitrio noverint constitutam. designatae igitur consortium portionis eatenus
iuri ordinum civitatumque obnoxium maneat, ut etiam locandi quanti sua
interest licentiam sibi noverint contributam.

47. Th. II, *Nov.* xxiii §1, 443, omnibus itaque consiliis diu nostro animo
volutatis nullam salubriorem causam revocandae pristinae beatitudinis invenI-
mus, quam si praedia tam urbana quam rustica nec non etiam tabernae, quae
ad ius civile pertinent et a quibusdam quolibet modo intra triginta annos abhinc
retro numerandos detentae sunt, universis civitatibus adsignentur exceptis
videlicet tantum his, quae vel a procuratore divinae domus vel a viro inlustri
comite rerum privatarum iussu nostrae clementiae vel communi consensu
civitatum cum scripturae interpositione distractae sunt. nemo igitur quodcumque
memorati iuris praeter civitates, quas suis volumus opibus frui, sibi deinceps
existimet possidendum, ne propositum nostrae pietatis offendat, quod divinitus
nobis in mentem venisse confidimus; Marc. *Nov.* iii, 451, si qui vel ex titulo
donationis vel ex emptione sive ex alio quolibet titulo possessiones iuris civilis,
tantummodo quae huius iuris esse vere probantur, cuiuslibet civitatis et praecipue

huius aeternae urbis, cui maiorem debemus favorem, tam civilis, ut dictum est, iuris quam etiam agonotheticas possessiones, ex consulatu Auxonii et Olybrii dempto civili canone acceperunt, impositum praediis canonem iuxta fidem publicorum monumentorum civitati, ad quam praedia pertinuerunt, praebere iubeantur: ex praesenti quoque quarta indictione, cessante praeteriti temporis canonis exactione, manente penes eos successoresque eorum et detentatores inlibato dominio. nam si privatis viris debita non patimur denegari, multo magis praebenda sunt civitatibus quae iure debentur, cum sufficiat possessoribus, quod apud eos dominium in perpetuum ex nostra liberalitate permaneat. si quae tamen possessiones iuris civilis canonem privatis largitionibus in praesenti praebent vel numquam ademptum vel postea impositum, ad hanc pragmaticam iussionem non pertinebunt, sed privato aerario canonem, quem nunc agnoscunt, inferre ex more debebunt, dominio firmiter apud eos successoresque eorum et detentatores pari modo permanente. For a property of the second category see *SPP* xx. 143, a receipt for half a solidus rent given by the ὑποδέκτης λαργιτιωναλικίων καὶ δεσποτικῶν προσόδων to the agent of Theodotus, *comes Aegypti*, ὑπὲρ ἱερίου ἐρήμου καλουμένου Ἀμμῶνος ... διαπραθέντος σοὶ κατὰ τὸν θῖον νόμον σωζομένου τοῦ κανόνος παρὰ τοῦ λαμπροτάτου καὶ περιβλέπτου τριβούνου καὶ νοταρίου Καπετολίνου. The deserted temple of Ammon within the walls of Hermopolis must have once belonged to the city. Cf. also *CJ* xi. lxx. 6, 480.

48. *CJ* xi. xxxii. 3, 472, si qua hereditatis vel legati seu fideicommissi aut donationis titulo domus aut annonae civiles aut quaelibet aedificia vel mancipia ad ius inclitae urbis vel alterius cuiuslibet civitatis pervenerunt sive pervenerint, super his licebit civitatibus venditionis pro suo commodo inire contractum, ut summa pretii exinde collecta ad renovanda sive restauranda publica moenia dispensata proficiat. APHRODISIAS: Just. *Nov*. clx.

49. BONA VACANTIA: *CJ* x. x. 1, 292. ESTATES OF DECURIONS DYING INTESTATE: *CTh* v. ii. 1, 319, *CJ* vi. lxii. 4, 429; ABSCONDING: *CTh* xii. i. 139, 394, 143-4, 395; TAKING ORDERS: *CTh* xii. i. 49, 361, 59, 364, 123, 391, 163, 399, 172, 410. THE QUARTER: *CJ* x. xxxv. 1, 428, Th. 11, *Nov*. xxii. 2, 443, *CJ* x. xxxv. 3, 528; raised to three-quarters by Just. *Nov*. xxxviii, 535. NEW CIVIC TAXES: *CJ* xiv. lxi. 10 (400-3, cited in n. 50). We know of civic taxes at Alexandria (*CTh* xiv. xxvii. 2, 436, ex dinummio vectigali memoratae civitatis; Just. *Ed*. xiii §15, τὸν τοῦ ἐξαγωγίου τίτλον) and at Mylasa (*CIL* iii. 7151-2 = *IGC* 241). This document concerns τὸ λιμενικὸν τέλος τῆς Πασσαλιητῶν κώμης τῆς Μυλασέων πόλεως, which was τῇ πολιτείᾳ ἤτοι τῷ δημοσίῳ λυσιτελὲς καὶ τοῖς χρείοις τῆς αὐτῆς πόλεως (i.e. went partly to the *largitiones*, partly to the city). In a constitution addressed to Eudoxius the emperor, following his suggestion, declares μηδενὶ τὸ μνημονευθὲν τέλος ἢ αἰτεῖν ἐξεῖναι ἢ εἰς ἴδια κέρδη δύνα[σθαι ...] There follows a letter from Flavius Eudoxius, *CSL*, to the governor of Caria, which states that there had been much litigation in his court between the attorney of Domninus, the *cubicularius*, and the decurions of Mylasa. We may take it that Domninus had petitioned for the tax and had been rebuffed.

50. *FIR* I². 108 speaks of 'id quod amplius ex isdem fundis super statutum canonem colligatur'. CIVIC LANDS OF ANTIOCH: Julian, *Misop*. 370D-371A; Lib. *Or*. xxxi. 16-7. The allocation of civic taxes to those performing liturgies is implied by *CJ* iv. lxi. 10, 400-3, vectigalia, quaecumque quaelibet civitates sibi ac suis curiis ad angustiarum suarum solacia quaesierunt, sive illa functionibus curialium ordinum profutura sunt seu quibuscumque aliis earundem civitatum usibus designantur, firma his atque ad habendum perpetua manere praecipimus.

51. PANOPEUS: Pausanias, x. iv. 1. ANTIOCH: Lib. *Or*. xi. 133 ff., 245 ff., 267.

52. POLICE: Lib. *Or.* XLVIII. 9, καὶ μείνη παρὰ τοῖς εἰρηνοφύλαξιν ὁ τῶν κορυνηφόρων μισθός, *Chr.* I. 404 (nomination to a νυκτοστράτηγος by a γνωστὴρ ε′ φυλῆς of a man to serve τῇ σῇ ἐπιεικείᾳ πρὸς ἐνιαύσιον χ[ρόνον] ὑπὲρ τῆς δημοτικῆς αὐτο[ῦ λ]ι[το]υργίας), 474 (list of νυκτοφύλακες), 476 (complaint by the two νυκτοστράτηγοι to the two *riparii* that they have failed to supply to them τοὺς δημοσίους καὶ τοὺς ἐφοδευτάς), PRICE CONTROL: *P. Oxy.* 83, 85, *PSI* 202, *P. Antinoop.* 38, Lib. *Or.* IV. 26-35, XXVII. 23-9. BUILDERS AT SARDIS: *IGC* 322.

53. ALEXANDRIA: *Chron. Pasch.* 514, Proc. *HA* xxvi. 41 (given by Diocletian), *CTh* XIV. xxvi. 2 (increased in 436), Just. *Ed.* xiii §§4, 6, 26; Alexandrian corn rations (ἄρτοι) are mentioned in Ath. *Hist. Ar.* 63, *Chr.* II. 96 (where they are part of an inheritance) and *Sb* 9023 (where they appear to be attached to a house). ANTIOCH: Lib. *Or.* xx. 7, Just. *Nov.* vii §8, 535, δηλαδὴ τῆς ὁμοίας παρατηρήσεως καὶ ἐπὶ τῆς ἐκποιήσεως τῶν πολιτικῶν σιτήσεων παραφυλαττομένης, καθὰ πολλάκις εἴπομεν, διότι τοιαύτας εἶναι σιτήσεις οὐ μόνον ἐπὶ τῆς βασιλίδος ταύτης πόλεως, ἀλλὰ καὶ ἐπὶ τῆς μεγάλης Ἀλεξανδρείας καὶ ἐπὶ τῆς Θεουπολιτῶν εἶναι μεμαθήκαμεν; the corn dole at Antioch perhaps originated from a private benefaction made in A.D. 181 (Malalas, 289-90, *Chron. Pasch.* 490). For Carthage the only evidence is the very obscure law, *CTh* XIV. xxv. 1, 315, dealing with *aeneum frumentum*; from the position of the law in the code I infer that this *frumentum Carthaginiense* was an institution analogous to the *frumentum Alexandrinum* of the next title. LIBANIUS AND THE BAKERS: Lib. *Or.* XXIX. BASIL AND THE LANDLORDS: Greg. Naz. *Or.* XLIII. 35. Σιτωνία: *CJ* x. xxvii. 3 (Anastasius), I. iv. 26, 530, Just. *Nov.* cxxviii §16, 545. Σιτωνικὰ χρήματα: *CJ* x. xxvii. 2 §12 (Anastasius), x. xxx. 4, 530, cf. *Chron. Pasch.* 585.

54. WATER SUPPLY: Lib. *Or.* XI. 246-7; funds for maintenance of aqueducts are mentioned in *CJ* I. iv. 26, x. xxx. 4, 530, Just. *Nov.* cxxviii §16, 545. CORVÉES: Lib. *Or.* XLVI. 21. STREET LIGHTING: Amm. XIV. i. 9, Lib. *Or.* XI. 267, XXII. 6, XXXIII. 35-7, Proc. *HA* xxvi. 7.

55. BATHS AT ANTIOCH: Lib. *Or.* XI. 245 (cf. XIX. 62 for the eighteen φυλαί). HEATING OF BATHS FROM CIVIC FUNDS: *CTh* XV. i. 32, 395, *CJ* I. iv. 26, 530, Just. *Nov.* clx, *Ed.* xiii §14; FROM SPECIAL FUNDS: *CJ* x. xxx. 4, 530; BY LITURGY: Lib. *Or.* I. 272, II. 34, XXVI. 5-6, XXVIII. 6, XXXV. 4, XLIX. 10.

56. SALARIES OF PROFESSORS AND DOCTORS: *CTh* XIII. iii. 1, 321, Lib. *Or.* XXXI. 19 ff., Proc. *HA* xxvi. 5-7. GAMES FROM ENDOWMENTS: Marc. *Nov.* iii, 451 (*agonotheticae possessiones*), Proc. *HA* xxvi. 6 (θεωρητικά); BY LITURGY: Julian, *Misop.* 371A, *P. Oxy.* 2110, *CTh* XV. v. 1, 372, ix. 2, 409, Lib. *Or.* XXVII. 13, XXVIII. 7, XXXIII. 14, XXXV. 4, 13-4, XLIX. 10, LIV. 45.

57. CORVÉE LABOUR: Lib. *Or.* XLVI. 21, L, passim. PAYMENTS FOR CRAFTSMEN AND MATERIALS: *Chr.* I. 48, 197, Lib. *Or.* L. 3.

58. REPAIRS FROM CIVIC FUNDS: *FIR* I². 108, *CTh* XV. i. 18, 374, V. xiv. 35, XV. i. 32, 33, 395, Th. II, *Nov.* xxiii, 443, *CJ* I. iv. 26, x. xxx. 4, 530, Just. *Nov.* cxxviii §16, 545, clx; BY SPECIAL LEVIES: *CTh* XV. i. 23, 384, 34, 396, 49, 412; also implied by laws 5, 338, 7, 361, and 33, 395. Procopius's *Aedificia* gives a long catalogue of dilapidated civic buildings restored by Justinian.

59. All kinds of civic expenditure appear to be covered by civic funds in *CJ* I. iv. 26, x. xxx. 4, 530, and Just. *Nov.* cxxviii §16, 545. Procopius (*HA* xxvi. 6 ff.) similarly implies that Justinian's alleged confiscation of civic funds brought all municipal expenditure to a standstill.

60. For games at Antioch see ch. XXIV, n. 67. CAECILIANUS AND INGENTIUS:

Opt. *App.* II. CURMA: Aug. *de cura gerenda pro mortuis*, 15. Libanius (*Or.* XLVIII. 37-8, XLIX. 8) stresses the inequality between the richer and poorer decurions of Antioch.

61. ORIGO AND DOMICILIUM: see n. 1. FREE BIRTH: *CJ* x. xxxiii. 1 (285-93); cf. Maj. *Nov.* vii §2, 458, quorum progeniem ita dividendam esse censemus, ut quotquot fuerint masculini sexus filii patrem sequantur feminis praedii domino relinquendis: illa discretione servata, ut, si ex colonabus nati sunt, curiis inserantur, si ex ancillis editi, collegiis deputentur, ne materni sanguinis vilitate splendor ordinum polluatur. RETIREMENT TO COUNTRY ESTATES: *CTh* XII. xviii. 2, 396. ALIENATION OF ESTATES: *CTh* XII. iii. 1, 386, 2, 423, *CJ* x. xxxiv. 3 (Zeno), cf. also *CTh* XII. i. 72, 370, si quis negotiator fundos comparaverit et ut aliquorum possessor praediorum vocetur ad curiam, 96, 383, concessum curialibus provinciae Mysiae, ut, si quos e plebe idoneos habent, ad decurionatus munia devocent, ne personae famulantium facultate locupletes onera, pro quibus patrimonia requiruntur, obscuritate nominis vilioris evadant.

62. *CTh* XII. i. 33, 342, quoniam sublimitas tua suggessit multos declinantes obsequia machinari, ut privilegia rei privatae nostrae colonatus iure sectantes curialium nominationes declinent, sancimus, ut, quicumque ultra XXV iugera privato dominio possidens ampliorem ex re privata nostra iugerationis modum cultura et sollicitudine propria gubernaverit, omni privilegiorum vel originis vel cuiuslibet excusationis alterius frustratione submota curiali consortio vindicetur. illo etiam curiae similiter deputando, qui minus quidem quam XXV iugerorum proprietatem habeat, ex rebus vero nostris vel parvum vel minorem iugerationis modum studio cultionis exercet; note that the law arises from a suggestion made by the *comes Orientis*. Val. III, *Nov.* iii §4, 439, illam quoque partem dispositio nostra non praeterit, ut, quisquis civis vel incola deinceps in nullo obnoxius, cuius tamen substantia trecentorum solidorum non exuperet quantitatem, fuerit repertus, habeat adipiscendi clericatus liberam facultatem. eum vero, cuius patrimonium maiore quam definivimus aestimatione censebitur, liceat curiae secundum vetera statuta sociari, exceptis his qui sacris scriniis nostris et agentum in rebus scholae militant et aliis qui continuatae militiae observatione desudant, ut multis provisionum generibus ordinum numerus suppleatur nec tamen desint ministri venerandae religionis obsequiis; for land values see p. 822.

63. AGE LIMIT: *CTh* XII. i. 7, 320, filios decurionum, qui decem et octo annorum aetate vegetantur, per provinciam Carthaginem muneribus civicis adgregari praecipimus. neque enim opperiendum est, ut solvantur familia et sacris explicentur, cum voluntates patrum praeiudicare non debeant utilitatibus civitatum; 19, 331, quoniam nonnulli diversarum civitatum curiales intemperanter minores, quibus publica tutela debetur, ad curiae consortium devocarunt, ut septem vel octo annorum constitutos nonnullos nominasse firmentur, decernimus, ut omnino nullus in curiam nominationibus devocetur nec functionum obsequia subire cogatur, nisi qui decimum et octavum annum aetatis fuerit ingressus; cf. Basil, *Ep.* 84 (a protest against the enrolment of the four-year-old grandson of a retired decurion). NOMINATION OF OUTSIDERS: *CJ* XII. xxxiii. 2 (285-93), non tantum decurionum filiis, sed omnibus in fraudem civilium munerum nomina armatae militiae dantibus fraudem prodesse displicuit; *CTh* XII. i. 10, 325, quoniam diversis praestitimus, ut legionibus vel cohortibus deputentur vel militiae restituantur, quisquis huiusmodi beneficium proferat, requiratur, utrum ex genere decurionum sit vel ante nominatus ad curiam, ut, si quid tale probetur, curiae suae et civitati reddatur; 13, 326, ut qui derelicta curia militaverit, revocetur ad curiam, non solum si originalis sit,

sed et si substantiam muneribus aptam possidens ad militiam confugerit vel beneficio nostro fuerit liberatus; XVI. ii. 3, 329 (S), cum constitutio emissa praecipiat nullum deinceps decurionem vel ex decurione progenitum vel etiam instructum idoneis facultatibus atque obeundis publicis muneribus opportunum ad clericorum nomen obsequiumque confugere; 6, 329 (S), cui nulla ex municipibus prosapia fuerit neque ea est opulentia facultatum, quae publicas functiones facillime queat tolerare.

64. SPECIAL ENROLMENT OF PLEBEII: *CTh* XII. i. 53, 362, placuit etiam designare, quae corpora sint, in quibus nominationis iuste sollemnitas exercetur. decurionum enim filios necdum curiae mancipatos et plebeios eiusdem oppidi cives, quos ad decurionum subeunda munera splendidior fortuna subvexit, licet nominare sollemniter; 137, 393, omnes, qui municipibus genere aut actu tenentur obnoxii, a militia vel a quibuslibet retrahi mandamus officiis, nec rescripta aut adnotationes ad munerum fugam prodesse permittimus. incolas etiam et vacantes, qui tamen idonei sunt, iubemus adstringi; 179, 415, vacantes quoque et nulla veterum dispositione ullius corporis societati coniunctos curiae atque collegiis singularum urbium volumus subiugari; Val. III, *Nov.* iii §4, 439. MOESIA: *CTh* XII. i. 96, 383 (cited in n. 61). TRIPOLITANIA: *CTh* XII. i. 133, 393, quicumque ex numero plebeiorum praesentibus singularum ordinibus civitatum agro vel pecunia idonei comprobantur, muniis curialibus adgregentur. qui vero nullam rei familiaris substantiam habent, militare in apparitorum numero non vetentur.

65. BASTARDS: Th. II, *Nov.* xxii. 2, 445, *CJ* V. xxvii. 1, 470, SONS OF VETERANS: *CTh* VII. xxii. 1, 313 (S), 2, 318 (S), XII. i. 15, 327, VII. xxii. 5, 333, XII. i. 32, 341, 35, VII. xxii. 4, 343, XII. i. 18 (326-53), VII. xxii. 7, 365, 11, 380, XII. i. 83, 380, 89, 382. DELINQUENT OFFICIALS: *CTh* XII. i. 66, 365, ordinibus curiarum, quorum nobis splendor vel maxime cordi est, non adgregentur nisi nominati, nisi electi, quos ipsi ordines coetibus suis duxerint adgregandos, nec quis ob culpam, ob quam eximi deberet ex ordine, mittatur in curiam; 108, 384, ne quis officialium curiae poenae specie atque aestimatione dedatur, nisi si quis forte curiam defugiens ob hoc coeperit militare, ne ingenitis fungatur officiis. omnes itaque omnino iudices tuae censurae subditos admonebis, ne quis aestimet curiae loco supplicii quemquam deputandum, cum utique unumquemque criminosum non dignitas debeat, sed poena comitari; *CJ* XII. lvii. 13, 442, 14, 471. UNFROCKED CLERGY: *CTh* XVI. ii. 39, 408.

66. EQUESTRIAN RANK AND COMITIVA: P. *Oxy.* 1204, *CTh* VI. xxxviii. 1, 317, XII. i. 5, 317, VI. xxii. 1, 324 (S), XII. i. 26, 338, 41, 339 (S), 36, 343, 42, 346 (S), 44, 358.

67. The earliest prohibitions of decurions entering the senate are *CTh* XII. i. 29, 340, 42, 346 (S), addressed to the councils of Cirta and Caesena; *CTh* XII. i. 14 and 18 are of uncertain date but probably fall in Constantius II's reign. LAW OF CONSTANTIUS II: *CTh* XII. i. 48, 361, si qui forte decuriones munia detrectantes ad senatus nostri sese consortium contulerunt, exempti albo curiae propriis urbibus mancipandi sunt. qui vero praetorum honore perfuncti sunt residentes in senatu, redhibere debebunt quae ex rationibus fisci aut urbium visceribus abstulerunt, ita ut omnibus deinceps adipiscendi honoris huiusce aditus obstruatur. LAWS OF VALENTINIAN AND VALENS: *CTh* XII. i. 57, 58, 364, 74, 371, in his, qui ex curiis ad senatus consortia pervenerunt, haec forma servetur, ut, si perfunctus quispiam muneribus et filii subole nixus fuerit, quem senatorio necdum adepto honore suscepit, filium suum curiae functionibus tradat, ipse optata clarissimatus dignitate potiatur. quod si ei gemina vel numerosa suboles erit, tunc discrimen promptae dudum divalis legis adhibendum est, ut de

duobus eius liberis aut pluribus sortiendi unius filii ad collegium senatus habeat optionem, ita ut ei, qui cum patre vel post patrem ad consortium senatus legetur, divisione cum fratribus per sortem successionis patrimonii idonea solius glebae substantia congregetur. plane si qui curialis factus senator et unius filii posteritate subnixus ipsum senatui poposcerit conecti seque promittat ad curiae munera regressurum, eiusmodi captio minime admittatur. ceterum si de numero curialium factus senator filium non habebit, quem functionibus patriae heredem generis ac munerum derelinquat, glebae senatoriae brevibus eximatur circa eos forma data, qui intra annos XI consulatus Constantii decimi et Iuliani III amplissimi ordinis participasse collegium monstrabuntur: ceterum anteriore tempore adscitos ipsa aequum est antiquitate defendi; cf. *CTh* XII. i. 90, 383, for the date 360.

68. ILLYRICUM: *CTh* XII. i. 82, 380, 93, 382. THEODOSIUS'S NEW RULES: *CTh* XII. i. 111, 386, 118, 387, 122, 390, ii quibus detulimus splendidos magistratus quosque etiam ornavimus insignibus dignitatum, si non habent curiam, cui aut necessitudinis foedere aut nexu sanguinis teneantur, in splendidissimum ordinem senatorium et illam nobilissimam curiam cooptentur. is vero ratio diversa sit, qui statim ut nati sunt, curiales esse coeperint. ii namque praerogativa quidem concessae dignitatis utantur atque eos praestiti honoris splendor exornet, sed maneant in sinu patriae et veluti dicati infulis mysterium perenne custodiant; sit illis piaculum inde discedere. de filiis vero eorum ut in avitis curiis debeant permanere, adfatim cautum est, cum adempta sit patribus licentia discedendi; 129, 392; 130, 132, 393; Libanius describes the change of policy in *Or.* XLIX. 5-6. WESTERN LAWS: *CTh* XII. i. 110, 385; 155, 397, quia receptum in splendidissimum ordinem submoveri dignitatibus non oportet, quisquis emensus curialia onera honorum vel administrationis vel quarumcumque aliarum dignitatum infulas impetraverit, ipse quidem decoretur insignibus, sed liberi omnisque successio paternae dignitatis obiectu curialia vincula non exuant, nisi forte quis iam senatore susceptus consortio curiae nobilioris adnectitur. inlustrium quoque virorum liberos, si non otio et torpore degeneri paternam exuere virtutem, fas erit excusari. in his tamen, qui ante expletas curialium munerum functiones meruerint dignitates, speciali humanitate tribuimus, ut, quae illis imponentur a patria, per substitutos praebere, si maluerint, non vetentur, nec agentis persona quaeratur, dummodo debiti non negetur officii. LAWS OF ARCADIUS AND THEODOSIUS II: *CTh* XII. i. 159, 398 (referred to in law 160, 404 (S)), 180, 416, 183, 418.

69. *CTh* XII. i. 187, 436, qui ante hanc legem spectabilium vel inlustrium quocumque modo sortiti sunt dignitatem, parto semel honore et privilegiis perfruantur. si qui vero postea ex decurionibus vel subiectis curiae ad spectabilium gradum processerint, per se tam curialia quam senatoria subeant munera eorumque liberi post senatoriam suscepti dignitatem patrum obstringantur exemplo. quod si qui inter inlustres etiam viros locum occupaverint non laborioso administrationis actu, sed honorario titulo dignitatis, senatui quidem per se respondeant, curiae vero per substitutos suarum periculo facultatum satisfaciant; quorum liberos et post eorum inlustrem dignitatem progenitos non solum senatorum, sed etiam decurionum munia per se, non per subrogatos, subire conveniet; Th. II, *Nov.* xv. 1, 439; 2, 444.

70. ZENO'S LAW: *CJ* x. xxxii. 64, cf. 66 (497-9); 67, 529.

71. MILITIA PALATINA: *CTh* XII. i. 5, 317, 22, 336 (full immunity), 31, 341, 38, 357 (S) (five years), VI. xxvi. 1, 362 (full immunity for *sacra scrinia*), XII. i. 88, 382 (thirty years), 100, 383, 120, 389, 154, 397, 147, 416 (no immunity), VI. xxxv. 14,

423 (fifteen years), XII. i. 188 (=*CJ* x. xxxii. 55), 436 (no immunity). Probably of the reign of Constantius II are VI. xxvii. 1 (twenty years for *agentes in rebus*), VIII. vii. 5 (fifteen years for various ministries), 6 (twenty-five years for *palatini* and *praefectiani* and *vicariani*). This immunity of *vicariani* had been abolished by 386 (*CTh* I. xv. 12). Officials of the *magistri militum* enjoyed no immunity (*CTh* XII. i. 175, 412, Th. II, *Nov.* vii. 4, 441).

72. PRINCIPES OF AGENTES IN REBUS: *CTh* VI. xxvii. 16, 413. PROXIMI SCRINIORUM: *CJ* x. xxxii. 67, 529.

73. PROVINCIAL OFFICIA: *CTh* XII. i. 22, 336, 31, 341, 42, 346, 96, 383, 134, I. xii. 4, 393, 6, 398. FORFEITURE OF PROPERTY: *CTh* XII. i. 139, 394, 161, 399.

74. THE ARMY: *CJ* XII. xxxiii. 2 (285-93) (contrast x. xlviii. 2 (285-93), which gives immunity to *ex protectoribus* and *ex praepositis*), *CTh* XII. i. 10, 325, 13, 326, VII. xiii. 1 (326-54), VII. ii. 1, 383, 2, 385, XII. i. 113, 386, 154, 397, VII. xx. 3 §3, 400, XII. i. 147, 181, 416, *CJ* XII. xxxiii. 4, 472. These laws all impose an absolute ban. By *CTh* XII. i. 38, 357 (S), five years' service gives immunity, by law 56 of 363 ten years, by law 88 of 382 five years, by law 95 of 383 fifteen years. FICTIVE MILITARY SERVICE: *CTh* VII. xxi. 3, 396, quicumque ex protectoribus aut domesticis honorarias missiones meruerint, sub hac norma penes eos dignitas maneat, ut neque municeps curiam neque collegiatus obsequium propriae urbis effugiat. Decurions were also forbidden to become *fabricenses*, *CTh* XII. i. 37, 344, 81, 380, x. xxii. 6, 412.

75. CONDUCTORES VECTIGALIUM: *CJ* x. lvii. 1 (285-93), non alios a muneribus et honoribus vacationem habere, quam qui mancipatum suo nomine vectigal a fisco conducunt, certum est. quare eos, qui ab his quaedam exercenda accipiunt, nullis privilegiis esse munitos haud dubii iuris est; *CTh* XII. i. 97, 383, scias excepta dioecesi Aegyptiaca ubique servandum esse, ne usquam penitus in susceptionem vel minimi vectigalis decurio conductor accedat, sed eorum professionibus et personis omnis haec diversarum locationum summa credatur, qui ad exhibendam publicis rationibus fidem periculo et fortunae coguntur et vitae; in Egypt κονδουκτορίαι were treated as regular curial liturgies (P. Oxy. 2110). LEASE OF CROWN LANDS: *CTh* XII. i. 33, 342, 114, 386. Decurions were often excluded from leasing or managing crown land; *CTh* XII. i. 30, 340, x. iii. 2, 372, *CJ* XI. lxxiii. 1, 401, *CTh* XI. vii. 21, 412 (except old civic and sacred lands of their own city, *CTh* x. iii. 4, 383), but in Egypt a decurion was πραιπόσιτος πατριμωνιαλίων in 322 (*Chr.* I. 437). NAVICULARII: *CTh* XIII. v. 5, 329 (S), 14, 371, 16, 380; these laws allow immunity, which is abolished by XIII. v. 19, 390, quae de naviculariis et curialibus ordinasti maneant inlibata et perpetua; sint perpetuo navicularii, quia, qui merito esse debeant, providisti. ac si, cum obierint, subolem non relinquent, quilibet in eorum facultatibus qualibet ratione successerit, auctoris sui munus agnoscet. manebit vero in ordine curiali et ei filius in officium curiale succedat; XII. i. 134, 393, 149+XIII. v. 25, 395. Libanius (*Ep.* 705) suggests that Megistus, the agent of Bassiana, might be given immunity by being enrolled ἐν τοῖς κομίζουσιν ἀπ' Αἰγύπτου σῖτον.

76. THE BAR: *CTh* XII. i. 188, 436, Th. II, *Nov.* x. 1, 439, *CJ* II. vii. 8, 440, 21, 500, x. xxxii. 67, 529. For the West see Val. III, *Nov.* ii. 2, 442. See also pp. 513-14.

77. PROFESSORS AND DOCTORS: *CJ* x. liii. 5 (293-305), *CTh* XIII. iii. 1, 321, 3, 333 (= *CJ* x. liii. 6), 16, 414 (= *CJ* x. liii. 11).

78. THE CHURCH: Eus. *HE* x. 7, *CTh* XVI. ii. 1, 313, 2, 313 (S), qui divino cultui ministeria religionis impendunt, id est hi, qui clerici appellantur, ab omnibus omnino muneribus excusentur, ne sacrilego livore quorundam a divinis obsequiis avocentur; 6, 326, neque vulgari consensu neque quibuslibet petentibus sub specie clericorum a muneribus publicis vacatio deferatur, nec temere et citra modum populi clericis conectantur, sed cum defunctus fuerit clericus, ad vicem defuncti alius allegetur, cui nulla ex municipibus prosapia fuerit neque ea est opulentia facultatum, quae publicas functiones facillime queat tolerare, ita ut, si inter civitatem et clericos super alicuius nomine dubitetur, si eum aequitas ad publica trahat obsequia et progenie municeps vel patrimonio idoneus dinoscetur, exemptus clericis civitati tradatur. opulentos enim saeculi subire necessitates oportet, pauperes ecclesiarum divitiis sustentari; 3, 329 (S), 7, 330, 9, 349.

79. Surrender of property is first mentioned in *CTh* XII. i. 49, 361. VALENTINIAN AND VALENS: *CTh* XII. i. 59+XVI. ii. 17, 364, XVI. ii. 19, 370 (allows immunity after ten years), 21, 371 (allows immunity to those ordained before 364). THEODOSIUS I: *CTh* XII. i. 104, 383, 115, 386, 121, 390, 123, 391. LATER LAWS IN THE EAST: *CTh* IX. xlv. 3, 398, XII. i. 163, 399, 172, 410, *CJ* I. iii. 21, 442; IN THE WEST: Val. III, *Nov.* iii, 439, xxxv §§3-5, 452, Maj. *Nov.* vii §7, 458.

80. JUSTINIAN'S LAWS ON THE CLERGY: *CJ* I. iii. 52, 531, Just. *Nov.* vi §1, 535, cxxiii §§1, 4, 15, 546, cxxxvii §2, 565. MONKS: *CTh* XII. i. 63, 370, Val. III, *Nov.* xxxv §3, 452.

81. PATRONAGE OF POTENTIORES: *CTh* XII. i. 6, 318 (S), praecipimus itaque, ne decuriones in gremia potentissimarum domorum libidine ducente confugiant. . . . . igitur si legis latae die repperietur quisquam patrimonium suum alienasse atque in dominum servulae contulisse, ordini liceat diligenter inquirere, ut ita rei publicae civitatis quod de facultatibus supra dicti fuerit deminutum, in pecunia sarciatur; 50, 362, et quoniam ad potentium domus confugisse quosdam relatum est curiales, ut tam foeda perfugia prohibeantur, multam statuimus, ut per singula capita singulos solidos dependat, qui ad potentis domum confugerit et tantundem qui receperit multae nomine inferat; 76, 371, 92, 382, 146, 395, Th. II, *Nov.* ix, 439, Maj. *Nov.* vii §§1-6, 458.

82. Sale of estates to purchase offices is mentioned in Lib. *Or.* XXVIII. 22, XLVIII. 11; the abstention of decurions from marriage in *Or.* II. 72, XLVIII. 30; their marrying their daughters to 'soldiers' in *Or.* XLVIII. 30.

83. CONTROL OF SALES: *CTh* XII. iii. 1, 386 (cf. Lib. *Or.* XLVIII. 37 ff.), 2, 423, *CJ* x. xxxiv. 3 (Zeno), Just. *Nov.* xxxii, 535; cf. Cass. *Var.* VII. 47.

84. THE RULE OF THE QUARTER: *CJ* x. xxxv. 1, 428. OBLATIO CURIAE: Th. II, *Nov.* xxii. 1, 442, 2, 443, *CJ* v. xxvii. 4, 470. JUSTINIAN'S LAWS: *CJ* x. xxxv. 3, 528, Just. *Nov.* xxxviii, 536, lxxxvii, ci, 539.

85. Maj. *Nov.* vii, 458, curiales nervos esse rei publicae ac viscera civitatum nullus ignorat.

86. For the perquisites of the leading decurions see Lib. *Or.* XLVIII. 4, XLIX. 8-9; cf. n. 41 for the *principales*.

87. BURDENS OF A DECURION: Lib. *Or.* XXV. 43, *Dig.* L. iv. 1 (Hermogenian), 18 (Arcadius Charisius). The list given by these authorities is not exhaustive; it appears for instance from Symm. *Ep.* IX. 48 that the decurions were responsible for allotting billets (*metata*).

88. For the privileges of *honestiores* see my *Roman Government and Law*, pp. 64–5; they are still recorded in the Digest and the Justinian Code, and still existed in the fifth and sixth centuries (see *CJ* II. xv. 2, 439, Just. *Nov.* xlv pr., 537). FLOGGING OF DECURIONS: *CTh* XII. i. 39, 349, 47, 359, IX. xxxv. 2, 376, XII. i. 80, 380, 85, 381, 117, 387, IX. xxxv. 6, 399, cf. Lib. *Or.* XXVII. 13, 42, XXVIII. 4 ff., esp. 22, LIV. 51, *Ep.* 994, and *CTh* XII. i. 75, 371, 127, 392, 190, 436, Th. II, *Nov.* xv. 1, 439, where the *comitiva* or senatorial rank are regarded as protection against the *iniuriae* of provincial governors.

89. Th. II, *Nov.* xv. 1, 439.

90. Th. II, *Nov.* xv. 2, 444.

91. Libanius (*Or.* XXXII. 8) objected to the enrolment of his son Cimon on the council of Antioch on the ground that it was reduced in number and wealth, and the burden was unfairly distributed. For the latter abuse see also *CTh* XI. xvi. 4, 328, XII. i. 140, 148, 399, 173, 409 (S).

92. Cass. *Var.* IX. 4.

93. Just. *Nov.* xxxviii pr., 535.

94. VALERIAN: Th. II, *Nov.* xv. 2, 444. DOROTHEUS, IRENAEUS AND DOCTITIUS: *CJ* X. xxxii. 61, 63. ZENO'S LAW AND ANASTASIUS'S AMENDMENT: *CJ* X. xxxii. 64, 66. JUSTINIAN ON THE HONORARY ILLUSTRATE: Just. *Nov.* lxx, 538.

95. Proc. *IL* 1 *adm.* 17 15 Justinian in *Nov.* cxxi (535) tells the story of a curial family of Tarsus which must have been it not opulent comfortably off. Demetrius had borrowed 500 solidi, and his son and grandsons had paid back capital and interest to the amount of 949 solidi.

96. Libanius's aversion from technical terms often makes his meaning obscure, but he mentions ἀρχαί (*dignitates*) in *Or.* XLVIII. 11, 13; the senate with *militia* (surely in this context *palatina*) in XVIII. 146, τῶν μὲν εἰς τὰ στρατιωτῶν τῶν δὲ εἰς τὸ μέγα συνέδριον; *agentes in rebus* (ἀγγελιάφοροι) and *curiosi* (πευθῆνες) in XVIII. 135; *agentes in rebus* again in XLVIII. 7, οὗτος ὁπλίτης καὶ σιωπᾶται· ἐκεῖνος φέρει τὰς τοῦ βασιλέως ἐντολάς, ἅπτεται δ' οὐδείς (ὁπλίτης probably denotes *protector domesticus*); military officers in XLIX. 19, λοχῶν ἡγησαμένους ἀνθρώπους καὶ στρατιώταις ἐπιτάξαντας. For Latin and the law see *Or.* I. 214, XLIII. 4–5, XLVIII. 22 ff., XLIX. 27 ff., LXII. 21–3.

97. Lib. *Or.* XLVIII, XLIX, passim. For Antoninus of Ephesus see Pall. *Dial.* pp. 89–90.

98. For the individual cases see Lib. *Or.* XLVIII. 11–13; for the two excuses, XLVIII. 8, XLIX. 13 ff., 21 ff.; for bribery, XLVIII. 14; for collusion, XLVIII. 28 ff. Penalties on councils which fail to reclaim their members are threatened in *CTh* VII. ii. 2, 385, ordines etiam urbium noverint, si cuiquam praestitisse se gratiam doceantur ac non vera actis promendo per mendacium quemquam abire permiserint, se periculo subiacere; XII. i. 110, 385, et ne colludio forte municipum quae sunt iussa frustrentur, sciant singularum ordines civitatum XXX libras auri se esse multandos, nisi ad reposcendos proprios sedulis institerint querellis; 113, 386, etc. It is worthy of note that Libanius himself, who was in the abstract so firm on maintaining the strength of the councils, in practice frequently supported individual claimants for immunity (*Ep.* 150, 245, 336, 374–6, 705, 789, 870, 902–9, 1393, 1524).

99. For the survival of civic spirit at Antioch see ch. XXIV, n. 67. For the West evidence is less abundant, but Symmachus speaks highly of the local aristocracy

of Beneventum (*Ep.* I. 3, et urbs cum sit maxima, singuli eius optimates visi sunt mihi urbe maiores, amantissimi literarum morumque mirabiles. deos magna pars veneratur, privatim pecuniam pro civitatis ornatu certatim fatigant), and inscriptions (e.g. *IRT* 564, 567, 569, 595) praise decurions for lavish games. VOLUNTARY MAGISTRATES: *CTh* XII. i. 177, 413, *CJ* x. xliv. 3, 465, 4 (528–9). A very exceptional case is that of Menander of Corinth, who on becoming a senator allowed his son Aristophanes to remain a decurion (Lib. *Or.* XIV. 6).

100. RUIN DUE TO CIVIC LITURGIES: Lib. *Or.* LIV. 22, 45; liturgies of course often caused temporary financial embarrassment to their holders, who, having their capital mostly in land, found difficulty in raising large sums in cash suddenly and had to sell some land (cf. Aug. *En. in. Ps.* cxlvii. 7, non enim illi tantum qui talia (sc. munera) edunt damno feriuntur, sed maiori damno percutiuntur qui talia libenter intuentur. illorum arca auro exinanitur . . . . plangunt plerique editores vendentes villas suas; *PSI* 944, complaint of the wife of a βουλευτής who has got into debt διὰ τὰ λειτουργήματα and alienated her dowry). But this does not mean that they could not make up the expenditure later from income, and buy more land. RUIN DUE TO TAX COLLECTION: Lib. *Or.* XLIX. 2 (the Persian war), Theod. *Ep.* (*PG*) 42 (Cyrrhus), Lib. *Or.* XLVII. 7–10 (patronage), Cass. *Var.* II. 25, proinde factum est ut curiales, quibus nos volumus esse prospectum, imminentium sollicitudine coacti, gravia damna sentirent, et, si dici fas est, cum alienis debitis sub truculentis compulsoribus urgerentur, possessionum quoque suarum amissione privati sunt; this resulted from senators' failing to pay their taxes.

101. OPPRESSION BY DECURIONS: Salv. *Gub. Dei*, v. 18, 27 ff. EXTRAORDINARY LEVIES: *CTh* XI. xvi. 4, 328, XII. i. 173, 409 (S). EXACTORES: *CTh* XII. vi. 22, 386, non perpetui exactores in continuata vexandorum provincialium potestate veluti concussionum dominatione teneantur, sed per annos singulos iudiciaria sedulitate mutentur, nisi aut consuetudo civitatis aut raritas ordinis eos per biennium esse compellat. THE SONS OF AGENANTIA: Cass. *Var.* IX. 4, quapropter inlustris magnificentia tua Agenantiam uxorem Campaniani viri disertissimi in Lucania provincia constitutam filiosque eorum de albo curiae suae faciat diligenter abradi, ut ventura posteritas nesciat fuisse quod vetatur obicere, quia calumnia non praesumitur, ubi aliqua probatio non habetur. proinde in possessorum numero potius collocentur passuri nihilominus molestias quas ipsi aliis ingerebant. ad tributa enim solita turbabuntur; faciem compulsoris horrebunt—a potestatibus iussa prius venisse nesciebant—, et votiva ignorantia fatigati formidare delegata incipient per quae antea timebantur. nam et ex ea parte bonis moribus vixisse probandi sunt, quando patiuntur inter illos otiosi vivere, quorum se non cognoscunt odia meruisse. alioquin non paterentur sub illis esse, quos se cognoscebant malis actibus incitasse; cf. IX. 2, erigite colla, depressi; sublevate animos, malorum sarcinis ingravati: date studium recuperare quae vos male cognoscitis amisisse. unicuique civi urbs sua res publica est. administrate civitatum sub consentanea voluntate iustitiam. ordines vestri aequabiliter vivant. nolite gravare mediocres, ne vos merito possint opprimere potiores. poena ista peccati est, ut unusquisque in se recipere possit quod in alterum protervus exercuit. vivite iuste, vivite continenter, quia vix audet quisquam in illos excedere, quibus culpas non potest invenire. JUSTINIAN ON CURIALES: *CJ* I. iii. 52 §1, 531.

102. TRANSFER OF GAMES: *CTh* XV. v. 1, 372, 3, 409, Lib. *Or.* XXXIII. 21. TRANSFER OF COLUMNS, ETC.: *CTh* XV. i. 14, 365, 37, 398.

103. FAMINES: Lib. *Or.* I. 205 ff., 226 ff., XXIX. 2 ff. GAMES: *CTh* xv. ix. 2, 409, cf. Lib. *Or.* XXXIII. 14 ff. For public works see *CTh* xv. i, passim, where provincial governors are always assumed to be responsible and the city councils are mentioned in two laws only out of fifty-three, nos. 33 and 34, 395–6.

104. ELECTION OF DEFENSOR: *CJ* I. lv. 8, 409, defensores ita praecipimus ordinari, ut sacris orthodoxae religionis imbuti mysteriis reverentissimorum episcoporum nec non clericorum et honoratorum ac possessorum et curialium decreto constituantur: de quorum ordinatione referendum est ad illustrissimam praetorianam potestatem, ut litteris eiusdem magnificae sedis eorum solidetur auctoritas; 11 (= I. iv. 19), 505, iubemus eos tantummodo ad defensorum curam peragendam ordinari, qui sacrosanctis orthodoxae religionis imbuti mysteriis hoc imprimis sub gestorum testificatione, praesente quoque religiosissimo fidei orthodoxae antistite, per depositiones cum sacramenti religione celebrandas patefecerint. ita enim eos praecipimus ordinari, ut reverentissimorum episcoporum nec non clericorum et honoratorum ac possessorum et curialium decreto constituantur; *MAMA* III. 197A, Ἴνδακος ὁ ὁσιώτατος ἐπίσκοπος τῆς Κο[ρυκιωτ]ῶν πόλεως κὲ ὁ ὑπ' αὐτῷ τεταγμένος εὐ[αγ]ὴς [κλῆρος οἵ] τε κτίτορες κὲ οἰκήτορες τῆς αὐ[τῆς] πόλεως περὶ δι]αφόρων κεφαλαίων ἱκέτε τῆς ἡμετέ[ρας κατέστησαν] γαληνότατος ὢν ἐφε[ξῆς ἃ τῇ σῇ ὑπεροχῇ ἀνή]κοντα συνίδαμεν [θείῳ τύπῳ περιλήψαμεν· διὰ] τοῦτο θεσπίζομεν τὸν [γινόμενον κατ]ὰ κερὸν ἔκδικον ὀφίλοντα ἱρημέ[νην πόλιν τηρεῖν ἀσι]νῆ κὲ τὸν ταύτης ἔφορον μηδα[μῶς τῇ προστασί]ᾳ τίνων αὐθεντίαν ἢ ἐξου[σίαν ἐχόντων ἐμὶ] τούτῳ προχ...[...εθ.., ἀλλὰ [τοῦ λοιποῦ τῇ ψή]φῳ κὲ δοκιμασίᾳ τοῦ τε νῦν κὲ [τοῦ κατὰ κερὸν] θεοφιλεστάτου ταύτης ἐπισκόπου κὲ τοῦ ὑ[π' αὐτῷ τεταγμένου] εὐαγοῦς κλήρου κὲ τῶν [ἐν πᾶσι τοῖς κτίτορ]σι κὲ οἰκήτορσι λογάδων τ[ὴν τῶν ἰρημένων γί]νεσθε προβολὴν μηδεν[ὸς τολμήσοντος τῶν] τῆς κατὰ χώραν [τάξεως πρω]τ[ευόντων ἢ τῶν κα]λουμένων ὠρδιναρίων ἐπικ[λήσεσιν . . . μ]ήτ[ε ἀ]ξιώσεσι[ν ἤτοι] ἐντεύξεσιν [ἢ γραφ]ομένες τ[ὸν τῆ]ς πόλεως ἔκδικον [ἢ τὸν ταύτης ἔφορον] . . . ; the title ἔφορος is otherwise unknown, and is perhaps equivalent to *curator*. The σιτώνης was also elected by the same body (*CJ* I. iv. 17, 491–505). In Just. *Nov.* cxxviii §16, 545, the *pater* and σιτώνης are elected by the bishop and landowners. For the equivalence of *curator* and *pater civitatis* see *CJ* I. iv. 26, 530, VIII. xii. 1 (485–6), x. xxvii. 2 (Anastasius), xxx. 4, 530, XII. lxiii. 2, 530, Just. *Nov.* clx, where the *pater* is responsible for civic finance, and *CJ* I. iv. 25, 529, 26, 530, v. 12, 527, III. ii. 4, 530, xliii. 1, 529, VIII. li. 3, 529, Just. *Nov.* lxxxv, 539, where the *defensor* and *pater* are the two chief magistrates of a city.

105. DEFENSOR: Just. *Nov.* xv, 535. LOCI SERVATORES: *Nov.* xvii §10, 535, xxviii §4, xxix §2, 535, cxxviii §20, 545, cxxxiv, 556; cf. *SEG* VII. 873–4 (Gerasa), [ἐπὶ Φλ. Ἀνασ]τασίου τοῦ μεγαλοπρε' καὶ ἐνδοξ' κομ' κ'δουκὸς κ' ἀρχ' τὸ β' κ' Φλ. Σερ[γίου τοῦ καθως' μ]αγιστριανοῦ καὶ τοποτηρητοῦ, P. Cairo, 67279, Δῖος ὁ λαμπρ' καγκελλάριος τῆς τοποτηρεσίας ἐπιλαβόμενος τῆς Ἀνταιοπολιτῶν, Ἑλλαδίος ὁ λαμπρ' σκρινιάριος τοποτηρητὴς γενάμενος, *BGU* 669, τῷ μεγαλοπρ' καὶ περιβλε' Φλ. Μαρκέλλῳ καγκ' καὶ τοποτηρ' (Hermonthis). In the West there is perhaps an allusion to the office in *Greg. Ep.* III. 49, de Bonifacio vero quaedam gravis ad nos accusatio pervenit, cuius scelera volumus utrum vera sint ut fraternitas tua (the bishop of Lilybaeum) cum loci servatore praetoris examinet. Cf. *IRT* 834–5, 839–40, 843 (tombs of the family of Stefanus *loki serbator* at Lepcis).

106. ZENO'S REFORM: *CJ* VIII. xii. 1, (485–6). On the *vindices* see ch. XIII, n. III. POTAMO'S SCHEME: Just. *Ed.* xiii §15. JUSTINIAN'S MANDATES: Just. *Nov.* xvii §4, cf. xxiv §3, xxv §4, xxvi §4, xxx §8 (535–6). JUSTINIAN'S REFORM: Just. *Nov.* cxxviii §16, 545. Procopius's allegation (*HA* xxvi. 6–11) that Justinian confiscated the civic revenues appears to be unfounded; it is of course possible

that before 545 they mostly went into the pockets of provincial governors.
DISCUSSORES: *CJ* I. iv. 26, x. xxx. 4, 530, Just. *Ed.* xii, 535, the mandates cited
above, and *Nov.* cxxviii §§17-8, 545.

107. Joh. Lydus, *Mag.* I. 28, τὸ γὰρ μηδένα τῶν ἀρχόντων ἑτέρᾳ παρὰ τὴν ἐν ἑορταῖς
στολῇ χρήσασθαι πᾶσίν ἐστι γνωριμώτατον· καὶ οὐκ ἐπὶ τῆς ῾Ρώμης μόνης ἀλλὰ μὴν
κἂν ταῖς ἐπαρχίαις τοῦτο κρατῆσαν αὐτὸς ἐγὼ διαμέμνημαι, ἕως ἂν τὰ βουλευτήρια
διῷκουν· τὰς πόλεις, ὧν ἀπολομένων συνεξωλίσθε τοῖς ἐν γένει τὰ ἐν εἴδει. Evagr. III. 42,
περιεῖλε δὲ καὶ τὴν τῶν φόρων εἴσπραξιν ἐκ τῶν βουλευτηρίων, τοὺς καλουμένους
βίνδικας ἐφ᾽ ἑκάστῃ πόλει προβαλλόμενος . . . ὅθεν κατὰ πολὺ οἵ τε φόροι διερρύησαν,
τά τε ἄνθη πόλεων διέπεσεν· ἐν τοῖς λευκώμασι γὰρ τῶν πόλεων οἱ εὐπατρίδαι πρόσθεν
ἐνεγράφοντο, ἑκάστης πόλεως τοὺς ἐν τοῖς βουλευτηρίοις ἀντὶ συγκλήτου τινὸς ἐχούσης
τε καὶ ὁριζομένης.

108. Mansi, IX. 277-8.

109. For the *comes civitatis* and *tribunus civitatis* see pp. 257-8, 260-2, 313.

110. ITALY: Cass. *Var.* II. 24-5, VII. 47, IX. 2, 4, XII. 8, Greg. *Ep.* IV. 26. SPAIN:
the Breviarium includes *CTh* XII. i. 1, 12, 19, 20, 47, 55, 124, 151, 170, Th. II,
Nov. ix, xv. 1, xxii. 1 and 2, Maj. *Nov.* vii.

111. MUNICIPAL ACTA: *P. Ital.* 4-5, 7 (557, Reate), 8, 10-11 (489, Syracuse), 12,
14-5, 21; those not specified all come from Ravenna, the latest being 21, of
625 A.D. NOTARIAL FORMULAE: *MGH* (*Leg.*), V. 4, 28, 97, 136, 161, 170, 176, 202,
209 (Merovingian Gaul), 587 (Visigothic Spain). BERTRAM'S WILL: J. M.
Pardessus, *Diplomata, chartae, epistulae, leges ad res Gallo-Francicas spectantia*,
no. 230.

112. FLIGHT OF COLLEGIATI: *CTh* XII. i. 146, 395, VII. xxi. 3, 396, XII. i. 156,
XIV. vii. 1, 397 (this law is in the Breviarium), de retrahendis collegiis vel
collegiatis iudices competentes dabunt operam, ut ad proprias civitates eos,
qui longius abierunt, retrahi iubeant cum omnibus, quae eorum erunt, ne
desiderio rerum suarum loco originario non valeant adtineri. de quorum
agnatione haec forma servabitur, ut, ubi non est aequale coniugium, matrem
sequatur agnatio, ubi vero iustum erit, patri cedat ingenua successio; I. xii. 6,
398, VI. xxx. 16, 17, 399, VII. xx. 12, XII. xix. 1, 400, destitutae ministeriis
civitates splendorem, quo pridem nituerant, amiserunt: plurimi siquidem
collegiati cultum urbium deserentes agrestem vitam secuti in secreta sese et
devia contulerunt. sed talia ingenia huiusmodi auctoritate destruimus, ut,
ubicumque terrarum repperti fuerint, ad officia sua sine ullius nisu exceptionis
revocentur. de eorum vero filiis, qui tamen intra hos proxime quadraginta annos
docebuntur fuisse suscepti, haec forma servabitur, ut inter civitatem et eos,
quorum inquilinas vel colonas vel ancillas duxerint, dividantur, ita ut in ulteriorem gradum missa successio nullam calumniam perhorrescat; 2, 3, 400, XIV.
vii. 2, 409 (S), Val. III, *Nov.* xxxv §3, 452 (in the Breviarium), Maj. *Nov.* vii.
§§2-8, 458 (in the Breviarium), *Ed. Theod.* 64.

113. See C. R. Kraeling, *Gerasa, City of the Decapolis*, 65-6, 171 ff.

114. DELEGATIONS OF CITIES: *CTh* XII. xii. 7, 380, 8, 382, 11, 386, 15, 416.
There are allusions to embassies sent by Antioch in 351, 359-60, 362, 363, 364
and 365 (Lib. *Ep.* 114, 551-2, 439-41, 449, 697, 704, 1184-6, 1432, 1499, 1505).

115. *C. Ilib.* can. 55, sacerdotes qui tantum coronas portant nec sacrificant
nec de suis sumptibus aliquid ad idola praestant, placuit post biennium accipere
communionem. TEMPLE AT HISPELLUM: *ILS* 705, cum igitur ita vos Tusciae

adsereretis esse coniunctos, ut instituto consuetudinis priscae per singulas annorum vices a vobis atque praedictis sacerdotes creentur, qui apud Vulsinios Tusciae civitatem ludos scenicos et gladiatorum munus exhibeant, sed propter ardua montium et difficultates itinerum saltuosa impendio posceretis, ut indulto remedio sacerdoti vestro ob editiones celebrandas Vulsinios pergere necesse non esset, scilicet ut civitati, cui nunc Hispellum nomen est quamque Flaminiae viae confinem atque continuam esse memoratis, de nostro cognomine nomen daremus, in qua templum Flaviae gentis opere magnifico nimirum pro amplitudine nuncupationis exsurgere, ibidemque is sacerdos, quem anniversaria vice Umbria dedisset, spectaculum tam scenicorum ludorum quam gladiatorii muneris exhibere, manente per Tusciam ea consuetudine, ut indidem creatus sacerdos apud Vulsinios ut solebat editionum antedictarum spectacula frequentare: precationi ac desiderio vestro facilis accessit noster adsensus. nam civitati Hispello aeternum vocabulum nomenque venerandum de nostra nuncupatione concessimus, scilicet ut in posterum praedicta urbs Flavia Constans vocetur; in cuius gremio aedem quoque Flaviae, hoc est nostrae gentis, ut desideratis, magnifico opere perfici volumus, ea observatione perscripta, ne aedis nostro nomini dedicata cuiusquam contagiose superstitionis fraudibus polluatur; consequenter etiam editionum in praedicta civitate exhibendarum vobis licentiam dedimus; scilicet ut, sicuti dictum est, per vices temporis sollemnitas editionum Vulsinios quoque non deserat, ubi creatis e Tuscia sacerdotibus memorata celebritas exhibenda est.

116. ELECTION OF SACERDOTES: *CTh* XII. i. 148, 399 (S), cum super ordinando sacerdote provinciae publicus esset ex more tractatus, idem nostra auctoritate decretum est, ut ad subeunda patriae munera dignissimi et meritis et facultatibus eligantur nec huiusmodi nominentur, qui functiones debitas implere non possint. ASIARCH, ETC.: *CJ* I. xxxvi. 1, 465 (Syriarchia), v. xxvii. 1, 336, sacerdotii, id est Phoenicarchiae vel Syriarchiae, ornamenta; *CTh* VI. iii. 1, 393 (Syriarch), XII. i. 103, 383 (Syriarch), xv. ix. 2, 409 (cited below); cf. also *SEG* XVIII. 745 for a Libyarch. PROVINCIAL GAMES: *ILS* 705, *CTh* XV. v. 1, 372, sacerdotiorum editiones; ix. 2, 409, exceptis alytarchis Syriarchis agonothetis itemque Asiarchis et ceteris quorum nomen votiva festivitatis sollemnitas dedicavit; the title *agonothetes* recurs in *CTh* XII. I. 109, 385. IMPERIAL SUBVENTION: Lib. *Ep.* 970–1, 1147–8, 1459; W. Liebeschütz (*Historia* VIII (1959), 113–26) has demonstrated that these letters refer to the Syriarchia. ENDOWMENTS: Marc. *Nov.* iii, 451, agonotheticas possessiones. LEVIES: *CTh* VI. iii. 1, 393, si quid Syriarchiae a senatoriis possessionibus annua conlatione confertur iubemus aboleri. HYMETIUS: *ILS* 1256, quod studium sacerdotii provinciae restituerit ut nunc a competitoribus adpetatur quod antea formidini fuerit.

117. The *sacerdotium* was a *munus patrimonii* (*CJ* x. xlii. 8, 293–305), but was supposed to be voluntary (*CTh* XII. i. 103, 383, voluntate propria unusquisque Syriarchiae munus suscipere debet, non necessitate imposita; 166, 400, iuxta veterem morem Mecilianus legatus adstruxit, ut sacerdotum filii inviti ad sacerdotium non cogantur. antiquam igitur consuetudinem laudabilitas tua praecipiat custodiri, ita ut neque ullus indebite teneatur et tamen idonei sacerdotes deesse non possint). IMMUNITIES OF SACERDOTALES: *CTh* XII. i. 21, 335, v. 2, 337, i. 75, 371; also VII. xiii. 22, 428 (excused recruits). IMPERIAL TITLES: *CTh* XII. i. 75, 371, 109, 385 (*ex comitibus*), Bruns, *Fontes*[7], 97b (senators). *Sacerdotales* are spoken of as *curiales* of the highest rank in *CTh* XII. i. 77, 372, XVI. v. 52, 412, 54, 414. CHOSEN FROM ADVOCATES: *CTh* XII. i. 46, 358, a solis praecipimus advocatis eorumque consortio dari provinciae sacerdotem. nec aliquis arbitretur ita esse advocationis necessitatem impositam sacerdotio, ut et

ab eo munerum oppidaneorum functio secernatur, cum nulla umquam iura patronis forensium quaestionum vacationem civilium munerum praestituerint; from the decurions of the metropolis or other cities: Bruns, *Fontes*[7], 97b, 375, ex sententia denique factum est, quod divisis officiis per quattuor civitates, quae metropolis apud Asiam nominantur, lustralis cernitur edi[tio?] constituta, ut, dum a singulis exhibitio postulatur, non desit provinciae coronatus nec gravis cuiquam erogatio sit futura, cum servatis vicibus quinto anno civitas praebeat editorem. nam et illud quoque libenter admisimus quod in minoribus municipiis generalis, quos popularis animi gloria maior attollit, facultatem tribui edendi muneris postulasti, videlicet ut in metropoli Efesena alia e civitate Asiarchae sive alytarchae procedant ac sic officiis melioribus nobilitate conten-dant. unde qui desideriis sub seculi nostri felicitate ferventibus gaudiorum debeamus fomenta praestare celebrandae editionis dedimus potestatem, adversum id solum voluntatem contrariam ref[eren]tes, ne suae civitatis obliti eius in qua ediderint munera, curiae socientur, Feste carissime ac iucundissime. laudata ergo experientia tua nostri potius praecepta sequatur arbitrii, ut omnes qui ad hos honores transire festinant, cunctas primitus civitatis suae restituant functiones, ut peractis curiae muneribus ad honorem totius provinciae debito favore festinent percepturi postmodum, si tamen voluerint, senatoriam digni-tatem, ita tamen, ut satisfacientes legi in locis suis alteros deserant substitutos. ceterum nequaquam ad commodum credimus esse iustitiae, ut expensis rebus suis laboribusque transactis veluti novus tiro ad curiam transeat alienam, cum rectius honoribus fultus in sua debeat vivere civitate; *CTh* XII. i. 174, 412, curiales etiam sacerdotio provinciae, sed et filios reddi praecipimus propriae civitati; 176, 413, exceptis his, qui Karthaginiensi curiae munus sacerdotii transegerunt, omnes, quicumque ex aliis provinciis atque civitatibus hoc honore decorantur, ad proprias urbes redire praecipimus; . . . . inhiberi autem etiam illas occasiones praesenti auctoritate censemus, ne comparatis sacerdotalis aliquis subito aedibus domicilium se habere confingat, cum specialiter statuisse videamur, ut quisque illo redeat, unde eum ducere originem constat; XVI. x. 20 pr., 415, sacerdotales paganae superstitionis competenti coercitioni subiacere praecipimus, nisi intra diem kalendarum Novembrium de Karthagine decedentes ad civitates redierint genitales, ita ut simili quoque censurae per totam Africam sacerdotales obnoxii teneantur, nisi de metropolitanis urbibus discesserint et remearint ad proprias civitates. LEO AND THE SYRIARCHIA: *CJ* I. xxxvi. 1, 465, titulos, qui alytarchiae et Syriarchiae muneribus in prima Syria deputati sunt, per officia tam viri spectabilis comitis Orientis quam viri clarissimi rectoris provinciae flagitari praecipimus. alytarchiae quidem ludi cura viri spectabilis comitis Orientis et eius officii, Syriarchiae vero sollicitudine viri clarissimi moderantis provinciam eiusque apparitionis exerceantur, nullique penitus curialium, nec si voluerint, idem munus vel honorem subeundi licentia permit-tatur. The alytarchia was the Antiochene Olympia, a civic festival, see W. Liebeschütz, *Historia* VIII (1959), 113–26.

118. For the complaints of provincial delegations and the laws issued in response to them see p. 356. In *IG* VII. 24 a decision on the amounts and dates of the contributions to the two ὁρρεοπραιποσιτίαι of Scarphaea and Corinth by the several cities of Achaea διετυπώθη μεταξὺ τῶν Ἑλληνίδων πόλεων ἐς ταὐτὸ συνελθουσῶν ἐν τῇ Κορινθίων μητροπόλει. DIOCESAN CONCILIA: *CTh* XII. xii. 9, 382, sive integra dioecesis in commune consuluerit sive singulae inter se voluerint provinciae convenire: *MGH* (*Ep.*) III. 13–5 (the Seven Provinces, 418); *CTh* XI. i. 33, 424, implies a delegation from the diocese of Macedonia, including the province of Achaea. RULES FOR RECEPTION OF DELEGATIONS: *CTh* XII. xii.

1, 355, in Africanis provinciis universis conciliis liberam tribuo potestatem, ut congruente arbitrio studii condant cuncta decreta aut commodum quod credunt consulant sibi, quod sentiunt eloquantur decretis conditis missisque legatis. nullus igitur obsistat coetibus dictator, nemo conciliis obloquatur; 3, 4, 364, iuxta legem divi Constantini nihil post tractatum habitum civitatum voluntate mutetur sive mutiletur, sed integrae atque inlibatae civitatum petitiones ad magnificentissimae sedis tuae notitiam perferantur, ut sit examinis tui, quaenam ex his auxilio tuo implenda protinus, quae clementiae nostrae auribus intimanda videantur; 9, 382, 10, 385, quotienscumque ex diversis provinciis ad sacrum mansuetudinis nostrae comitatum legationes, quas instruxere decreta, necesse erit commeare, in auditorio quidem celsitudinis tuae universa tractentur, sed ita, ut nullum finem capiat ordo gestorum inlibataque rerum decisio singularum nostro auditui sententiaeque servetur, ita ut deinceps excellentia tua, cum in consistorio mansuetudinis nostrae secundum consuetudinem ex decretis petitiones legatorum de nostris scriniis recitantur, motum proprii arbitrii ratione decursa sententiis, quas pandimus, referat; 12, 392, si quod extraordinarium concilium postulatur, cum vel ad nos est mittenda legatio vel vestrae sedi aliquid intimandum, id, quod inter omnes communi consilio tractatuque convenerit, minime in examen cognitoris ordinarii perferatur. provincialium enim desideria, quibus necessaria saepe fortuitis remedia deposcuntur, vobis solis agnoscere atque explorare permittimus, nobis probationem ac iudicium reservamus; 14, 408, omnium legationum provincialium instructiones apud sublimitatem tuam actis legi pensarique praecipimus, ut, quae digna nutu vel indulgentia nostrae clementiae probabuntur, eligere et referre ad nos sublimitas tua non ambigat. nam remedia fessis quibusque necessaria nostro arbitrio decernentur. USE OF CURSUS PUBLICUS: *CTh* XII. xii. 9, 382.

119. COMPOSITION OF CONCILIA: *CTh* XII. xii. 12, 392, ad provinciale concilium in una frequentiore totius provinciae urbe cunctos volumus convenire, qui primatum honorantur insignibus, exceptis praefectoriis, quos dignitatibus ampliatos indignum a consiliantibus praeteriri, indignius vero ad publicum cum honoris iniuria devocari; unde honestum esse censemus de singulis quae tractanda erunt intra domos suas eos consuli, ut nec plebi mixta dignitas inclinetur nec eius, cuius praesentiae copia deerit, probatum in re publica consilium neglegatur; scilicet ut in loco publico de communi utilitate sententia proferatur atque id, quod maioris partis probarit adsensus, sollemnis firmet auctoritas; 13, 392, provinciale concilium quo tempore iniri debeat, cum adsensu omnium atque consilio propria auctoritate definiat, ita ut ipse conventus in una opulentiore totius provinciae urbe absque ullius iniuria celebretur. inde quod in consilium communia vota deducunt, vel in aede publica vel in aliqua fori parte tractetur, ad quam omnium possit esse concursus, ne quid dispositio paucorum tegat, quod in communem utilitatem expetat sollicitudo cunctorum. si quis autem eorum virorum, quos emeritos honor a plebe secernit, provincialium extraordinario cupit interesse concilio, pro suo loco atque ordine servata reverentia dignitatis vel ad eum locum, in quo cunctorum desideria possit agnoscere, ire debebit vel procuratoribus destinatis sententiae suae promere voluntatem, modo ut, quod voluerit paucorum voluntas, publica convocetur auctoritas; *MGH* (*Ep.*) III. 13-5, 418, unde inlustris magnificentia tua et hanc praeceptionem nostram et priorem sedis suae dispositionem secuta, id per Septem Provincias in perpetuum faciet custodiri, ut ab Idibus Augustis quibuscumque mediis diebus in Idus Septembres in Arelatensi urbe noverint honorati vel possessores, iudices singularum provinciarun annis singulis concilium esse servandum; ita ut de Novempopulana et secunda Aquitanica,

quae provinciae longius constitutae sunt, si earum iudices occupatio certa retinuerit, sciant legatos iuxta consuetudinem esse mittendos. qua provisione plurimum et provincialibus nostris gratiae nos intelligimus utilitatisque praestare, et Arelatensi urbi, cuius fidei secundum testimonia atque suffragia parentis patriciique nostri multa debemus, non parum adicere nos constat ornatui. sciat autem magnificentia tua, quinis auri libris iudicem esse multandum, ternis honoratos vel curiales, qui ad constitutum locum intra definitum tempus venire distulerint. The delegates chosen by the *concilia* comprise senators, *comites* and *sacerdotales* (CTh XI. i. 34, XII. i. 186, 429, Val. III, *Nov.* xiii, 445, CIL VIII. 27, IRT 588). From Sid. Ap. *Ep.* I. 6, non nequiter te concilii tempore post sedentes censentesque iuvenes inglorium rusticum, senem stantem latitabundum pauperis honorati sententia premat, it would appear that only *honorati* had seats and could make proposals and that the others stood in the background (and perhaps voted).

120. Just. *App.* vii §12, 554, *Nov.* cxlix, 569, clxi, 574.

XX. THE LAND (pp. 767–8)

There is an excellent survey of late Roman agriculture, especially on the technical side, by C. E. Stevens in the *Cambridge Economic History*, vol. I, ch. ii. E. R. Hardy, *The Large Estates of Byzantine Egypt* (New York, 1931), gives a good account, based on the papyri, of the management of large estates, especially those of the Apion family. The colonate is exhaustively discussed, with a full summary of the earlier literature, by R. Clausing, *The Roman Colonate* (New York, 1925). Later contributions to this subject include C. Saumagne, *Byzantion* XII (1937), 487–581, F. L. Ganshof, *Antiquité Classique* XIV (1945), 261–77, A. Segrè, *Traditio* V (1947), 103–33, and myself in *Past and Present* XIII (1958), 1–13.

1. On the techniques of Roman agriculture see C. E. Stevens, *Cambridge Economic History*, vol. I, chap. ii.

2. SEED AT ONE ARTABA THE ARURA: *P. Tebt.* 108, 375, *BGU* 171, 538, 918, *PSI* 31, *Sb* 7196, *Chr.* I. 362. A yield of tenfold is implied by *P. Tebt.* 49 (failure to cultivate $2\frac{1}{4}$ *arurae* is estimated to involve a loss of 20 *artabae*), *BGU* 1217 (81,540 *arurae* yield 834,500 *artabae* of cereals, mainly wheat) and *PSI* 400 (an offer by a prospective bailiff to give the landlord 10 *artabae* for each *arura* sown). A list of Egyptian land leases from Diocletian to the Arab conquest is given in Johnson and West, *Byzantine Egypt: Economic Studies*, 80–93. ITALY: Columella, II. 9 (rate of sowing), III. 3 (yield), Varro, *de re rustica*, I. 44, Pliny, *Hist. Nat.* XVIII. 198–200, Palladius, *de re rustica*, XII. 1 (rate of sowing). SICILY: Cic. *II Verr.* III. 112 (rate of sowing and yield). CYRENAICA: Hyginus, *de condicione agrorum* (*Corpus Agrimensorum Romanorum*, p. 86), where an area equal to a *iugerum* is called a *medimnus*.

3. ASSESSMENT OF ARABLE, VINEYARD AND OLIVES: *Leges Saeculares*, 121 (*FIR* II². 795–6). For Egyptian leases see n. 2.

4. SPANISH HORSES: *CTh* xv. x. 1, 371, Symm. *Ep.* IV. 7, 58–60, 63, v. 82–3, VII. 48, 82, IX. 12, 18, 20–2. CAPPADOCIAN HORSES: *CTh* xv. x. 1, 371 (*equi Palmati* came from the Villa Palmati near Tyana, *Itin. Burd.* 577. 6, O. Cuntz, *Itineraria Romana*, I. 93). WOOL PRICES: *Ed. Diocl.* xxv. 1–9. PAPAL RANCHES IN SICILY: Greg. *Ep.* II. 38. SALTUS ERUDIANUS: *P. Ital.* 3; for perquisites of fruit, etc., in Egyptian leases see the list cited in n. 2.

5. See ch. XIII.

6. RURAL AND URBAN RENTS OF THE ROMAN CHURCH: *Lib. Pont.* xxxiv, xxxv, xxxix, xlii, xlvi.

7. See pp. 732–4 and pp. 893–9 for the estates and revenues of the cities and churches.

8. For senators see pp. 554–7, for decurions pp. 738–9.

9. COHORTALES OF SYRIA: *CTh* VIII. iv. 11, 365. PRINCIPES OF OSRHOENE: *CTh* XII. i. 79, 375, 105, 384; for civil servants see also pp. 569, 572, 596, 599. SOLDIERS: *CTh* VII. i. 3, 349, quicumque militum ex nostra auctoritate familias suas ad se venire meruerint, non amplius quam coniugia liberos, servos etiam de peculio castrensi emptos neque adscriptos censibus ad eosdem excellentia tua dirigi faciat (*servi adscripti censibus* were agricultural slaves); cf. also pp. 648, 678–9. BARRISTERS: *CJ* II. vii. 22 §1, 505, 24 §1, 517, ad haec eos, qui, prout statutum est, fisci patroni deposuerint officium, postea quoque non prohiberi singulos tam pro se quam pro iugali sua et socero et socru nec non genero et nuru liberisque propriis, colonis et servis ad se pertinentibus advocationis fungi officio; these laws refer to barristers of quite humble courts (those of the *comes Orientis* and the *praeses* of Syria II). PROFESSORS AND DOCTORS: *Lib. Or.* XLVII. 13, *Ep.* 776, 1089–90, *P. Cairo*, 67151.

10. CLERGY: *CTh* XVI. ii. 15, 360, de his sane clericis, qui praedia possident, sublimis auctoritas tua non solum eos aliena iuga nequaquam statuet excusare, sed etiam pro his, quae ipsi possident, eosdem ad pensitanda fiscalia perurgeri. DAMASUS: *Lib. Pont.* xxxix. REMIGIUS: see below n. 36. AUGUSTINE'S CLERGY: Aug. *Serm.* 355–6. Cf. Amb. *Off.* I. 184, (a priest) ab omni usu negotiationis abstinere debet agelluli sui contentus fructibus, si habet, si non habet, stipendiorum suorum fructu. RAVENNATE CLERGY: *P. Dip.* 118, *P. Ital.* 21. See also the wills of Gregory Nazianzen (*PG* XXXVII. 389–96) and Caesarius of Arles (*PL* LXVII. 1139–42), and *C. Sard.* can. 12.

11. For *navicularii* see pp. 827–9. In Joh. Moschus, 188, we meet two brothers who were ἀργυροπρᾶται at Constantinople and owned inherited land in Syria. HERMOPOLIS REGISTER: *P. Flor.* 71, analysed in *JRS* XLIII (1953), 58 ff., for the craftsmen see p. 61. RAVENNATE DOCUMENTS: *P. Ital.* 14–15, *P. Dip.* 113, 117.

12. See preceding note.

13. THEADELPHIA REGISTER: *P. Princeton*, 134, analysed in *JRS* XLIII (1953), 63 ff. A similar distribution of land may be inferred at Caranis from *P. Cairo Isid.* 9, 11, where the πολῖται appear to have numbered 22, and to have paid under 1,000 *artabae* in tax, while the κωμῆται were about 130, and paid over 7,000 *artabae*: the average peasant's holding, it may be noted, is larger than the average townsman's. RENTAL OF PATAVIUM: *P. Ital.* 3.

14. Salvian, *Gub. Dei*, v. 27-35, cf. pp. 451-2, 466-8, for false assessments, remissions of arrears and *extraordinaria*.

15. THEADELPHIA: *P. Thead*. 17. GAUL: Salvian, *Gub. Dei*, v. 43. It is hardly necessary to cite the many constitutions forbidding landlords to harbour runaway *coloni*.

16. Just. *Nov*. xxxii, xxxiii, xxxiv, 535.

17. Lib. *Or*. XLVII. 1-16.

18. EGYPT: *CTh* XI. xxiv. 1, 360, colonorum multitudinem indicasti per Aegyptum constitutorum ad eorum sese, qui variis honoribus fulciuntur, ducum etiam patrocinia contulisse; 3, 395 (addressed to the *comes Aegypti*), quicumque ex officio tuo vel ex quocumque hominum ordine vicos in suum detecti fuerint patrocinium suscepisse, constitutas luent poenas. More general laws are 2, 368, 4, 399, censemus, ut, qui rusticis patrocinia praebere temptaverit, cuiuslibet ille fuerit dignitatis, sive magistri utriusque militiae sive comitis sive ex proconsulibus vel vicariis vel Augustalibus vel tribunis sive ex ordine curiali, etc., and 5, 399.

19. *CTh* XI. xxiv. 6, 415, Valerii, Theodori et Tharsacii examinatio conticiscat, illis dumtaxat sub Augustaliano iudicio pulsandis, qui ex Caesarii et Attici consulatu possessiones sub patrocinio possidere coeperunt. quos tamen omnes functionibus publicis obsecundare censemus, ut patronorum nomen extinctum penitus iudicetur. possessiones autem adhuc in suo statu constitutae penes priores possessores residebunt, si pro antiquitate census functiones publicas et liturgos, quos homologi coloni praestare noscuntur, pro rata sunt absque dubio cognituri. metrocomiae vero in publico iure et integro perdurabunt, nec quisquam eas vel aliquid in his possidere temptaverit, nisi qui ante consulatum praefinitum coeperit procul dubio possidere, exceptis convicanis, quibus pensitanda pro fortunae condicione negare non possunt. et quicumque in ipsis vicis terrulas contra morem fertiles possederunt, pro rata possessionis suae glebam inutilem et conlationem eius et munera recusent. ii sane, qui vicis quibus adscripti sunt derelictis, et qui homologi more gentilicio nuncupantur, ad alios seu vicos seu dominos transierunt, ad sedem desolati ruris constrictis detentatoribus redire cogantur, qui si exsequenda protraxerint, ad functiones eorum teneantur obnoxii et dominis restituant, quae pro his exsoluta constiterit. et in earum metrocomiarum locum, quas temporis lapsus vel destituit vel viribus vacuavit, ex florentibus aliae subrogentur. arurae quoque et possessiones, quas curiales quolibet pacto publicatis apud acta provincialia desideriis suis vel reliquerunt vel possidere alios permiserunt, penes eos, qui eas excoluerunt et functiones publicas recognoscunt, firmiter perdurabunt, nullam habentibus curialibus copiam repetendi. quidquid autem in tempus usque dispositionis habitae a viro inlustri decessore sublimitatis tuae ecclesiae venerabiles, id est Constantinopolitana atque Alexandrina, possedisse deteguntur, id pro intuitu religionis ab his praecipimus firmiter retineri, sub ea videlicet sorte, ut in futurum functiones omnes, quas metrocomiae debent et publici vici pro antiquae capitationis professione debent, sciant procul dubio subeundas. nequaquam cefalaeotis, irenarchis, logografis chomatum et ceteris liturgis sub quolibet patrocinii nomine publicis functionibus denegatis, nisi quid ex his quae exigenda sunt vel neglegentia vel contemptus distulerit. metrocomias possidere nostro beneficio meruerunt, et publicos vicos committere compellantur.

20. In Egyptian documents of the Principate the word ὁμόλογος appears to be used as an equivalent of λαογραφούμενος, entered on the census, see Wilcken, *Grundzüge*, 59–60.

21. *CJ* XI. liv. 1, 468 (citing Marcian's law), 2, μηδεὶς κωμήταις προστασίαν ὑπισχνείσθω μηδὲ δεχέσθω γεωργοὺς ἐπὶ τούτῳ ὑπόσχεσιν προσόδων ἢ ἕτερον κέρδος λαμβάνων ... οἱ κωμῆται, εἰ μὲν δοῦλοι εἶεν, τοῖς δεσπόταις ἀποδοθήσονται σωφρονισθέντες, οἱ δὲ ἐλεύθεροι κ' λίτρας προστιμῶνται καὶ τύπτονται μετὰ δέκα τῶν πρωτευόντων τῆς κώμης καὶ διηνεκῶς ἐξορίζονται, ἐν ᾧ γνώμῃ πάντων ἐστασίασαν.

22. Salvian, *Gub. Dei.* v. 38 ff.

23. GRANTS TO VETERANS: *CTh* VII. xx. 3, 320, 8, 364, Anon. *de rebus bell.* v. 4.

24. From *CTh* v. xvi. 34, 425, verum quotiens alicui colonorum agrum privati patrimonii nostri placuerit venundari, non unus tantum, qui forte consortibus suis gravis ac molestus existat, sed alii quoque duo vel plures ex simili origine ac iure venientes in supradicta emptione socientur, it appears that *coloni* of the *res privata* sometimes bought crown lands. MELANIA'S ESTATES: *V. Mel.* (L), 15.

25. VILLAGES OF LANDLORDS AND OF FREEHOLDERS: Lib. *Or.* XLVII. 4, 11, Theod. *Hist. Rel.* xiv, xvii.

26. The estates of the church are mentioned in *V. Theod. Syc.* 75–6. MANCIAN TENURES: C. Saumagne in *Tablettes Albertini, Actes privées du l'époque Vandale* (Paris, 1952), 97 ff.

27. HERMOPOLIS: *JRS* XLIII (1953), 59–60, 63–4.

28. For the Apion estates see n. 34. Their contribution to the ἐμβολή was c. 140,000 *artabae*; the total contribution of the Oxyrhynchite and Cynopolite was 350,000 *artabae* (*P. Oxy.* 1909).

29. For recruits from Illyricum, Thrace and Asia Minor see p. 668. For the ineligibility of *adscripticii* as recruits p. 614.

30. SPAIN: *V. Mel.* 19, 37, Pan. Lat. II. 9 (Theodosius), Orosius, VII. xl. 5–6 (Didymus and Verinianus); cf. also Symmachus's many horsebreeding friends (see n. 4). AFRICA: Symm. *Ep.* VII. 66, Aug. *Ep.* 58 (Pammachius and other Roman senators), *V. Mel.* 20 ff. (Pinianus), *Not. Dig. Occ.* xii. 5, *CTh* VII. viii. 7, 400, 9, 409 (Gildo).

31. For the *res privata* see pp. 412 ff. CHURCH OF ROME: Lib. *Pont.* xxxiv, xxxv, xxxix, xlii, xlvi; for the sixth century see n. 45. CHURCH OF CONSTANTINOPLE: *CJ* I. ii. 24 §11, 530 (cited in ch. XVI, n. 9), cf. *CTh* XI. xxiv. 6, 415 (cited in n. 19) for Egypt. CHURCH OF RAVENNA: *P. Ital.* 12 (Forum Cornelii), 13 (Urbinum, Luca), 18–9 (Agubium), 20 (Ariminum), Simplicius, *Ep.* 14 (Bononia), Greg. *Ep.* XI. 8 (Sicily); it is probable that *P. Ital.* 3 (accounts of two estates in Patavium) belongs to the Ravennate archives. CHURCH OF MILAN: Greg. *Ep.* I. 80, XI. 6, Cass. *Var.* II. 29. ANTINOOPOLIS: *P. Flor.* 71, lines 747–52. NICAEA: *CJ* XI. lxx. 6, 480.

32. SYMMACHUS: Symm. *Ep.* VI. 11 (Samnium), 12 (Apulia), 66, IX. 52 (Sicily), VII. 66 (Mauretania); for his villas see pp. xlv–vi of Seeck's edition. MELANIA: *V. Mel.* 11–12, 19–21, 37. PAULINUS OF PELLA: Paul. *Euch.* 498 ff., 575 ff. (Burdigala), 413 ff. (Achaea, etc.), he also had an estate at Massilia (516 ff.); for his father's vicariate see line 26. Olympias owned estates in Thrace,

Bithynia, Galatia and Cappadocia (*V. Olymp.* 5), and Proba of the Roman family of the Anicii owned lands in Asia (*A.C.Oec.* I. ii. 90). Basil's family, which was probably not senatorial, held land in three provinces (Greg. Nyss. *V. Macr.* 965, καὶ τρισὶν ἄρχουσιν ὑπετέλει διὰ τὸ ἐν τοσούτοις ἔθνεσιν αὐτῆς κατεσπάρθαι τὴν κτῆσιν. In Greg. *Ep.* IX. 88 the rectors of the patrimony in Sicily, Campania, Bruttium and Calabria are instructed to protect the estates of Romanus, ex-praetor of Sicily (see n. 45).

33. BERTRAM'S WILL: J. M. Pardessus, *Diplomata Chartae Epistulae Leges ad res Gallo-Francicas spectantia*, no. 230.

34. P. *Oxy.* 127R, συντελεῖ ὁ ἔνδοξ(ος) οἶκ(ος) ᾿Οξυρυγχ(ιτῶν) ὑ(πὲρ) ἐμβολῆς σί(του) καν(κέλλῳ) (ἀρταβῶν) (μυριάδας) η καὶ ζωιη (ἥμισυ) . . . συντελεῖ ὁ ἔνδοξ(ος) οἶκ(ος) τῆς Κυνῶν ὑ(πὲρ) ἐμβολῆς σί(του) καν(κέλλῳ) μυριάδ(ας) ε καὶ βω [. . .]. For the rate of ἐμβολή see P. *Cairo*, 67057.

35. The land registers of Magnesia (Kern, *Inschr. von Magnesia am Maiander*, no. 122), Tralles (*BCH* 1880, 336-8), Hermopolis (P. *Flor.* 71) and other places are discussed in *JRS* XLIII (1953), 49 ff.

36. ANTINOOPOLITES: P. *Flor.* 71, lines 521, 566, 599, 747-51. LETOIUS OF ANTIOCH: Theod. *Hist. Rel.* xiv. REMIGIUS'S WILL: *MGH* (*Scr. Rer. Merov.*) III. 336-47; for a defence of its authenticity and an analysis of its contents see *Rev. Belge Phil. Hist.* XXXV (1957), 356 ff. SMALL HOLDINGS AT HERMOPOLIS: *JRS* XLIII (1953), 60.

37. FUNDI OF THE ROMAN CHURCH: *Lib. Pont.* xxxiv. RAVENNATE FUNDI: P. *Dip.* 116 (1½ oz. for 5⅓ solidi = 42⅔ solidi), 117 (2 oz. for 20 = 120), 118 (4 oz. for 133 = 399), 121 (6 oz. for 14 = 28), 122 (6 oz. for 24 = 48), 124 (1 oz. for 6 = 72). The Sicilian *fundi* in P. *Ital.* 1 have rentals of 52, 147 and 200 solidi, those in P. *Ital.* 10-1 of 18, 15¾ (part only), and 7 (part only). The rentals of the two Paduan estates in P. *Ital.* 3 total between 40 and 45 solidi each. Other fractions of *fundi* appear in P. *Ital.* 8, 14-15, 20, 22, 23, P. *Dip.* 111, 114-5, 120.

38. MASSAE OF ROMAN CHURCH: *Lib. Pont.* xxxiv. The three Sicilian *massae* in P. *Ital.* 1 have rents of 756, 500 and 445 solidi, and the *massa Pyramitana* at Syracuse in P. *Ital.* 10-1 of more than 480 solidi. In P. *Ital.* 13, the moiety of the two *massae* in Urbinum and Luca yields only 100 solidi. The *massa* at Signia is recorded in P. *Ital.* 17. A *massa* comprising ten *fundi* is recorded in Greg. *Ep.* XIV. 14.

39. For Bertram's will see above n. 33. For rounding off estates see also Sid. Ap. *Ep.* III. 5.

40. MELANIA'S LARGE ESTATES: *V. Mel.* (L) 18, 21. AFRICAN SALTUS: Agennius Urbicus, *de controversiis agrorum* (*Corp. Agr. Rom.*, p. 45). Augustine (*c. Lit. Pet.* II. 184, cf. *Ep.* 66) mentions a *fundus emphyteuticus* of the *res privata* which had eighty inhabitants.

41. PAULINUS'S ESTATES: Paul. *Euch.* 413 ff., pars ubi magna mihi etiamnunc salva manebat materni census, complures sparsa per urbes Argivas atque Epiri veterisque novaeque, per quas non minima numerosis farta colonis praedia diffusa nec multum dissociata quamvis profusis dominis nimiumque remissis praebere expensas potuissent exuberantes. SENATORIAL ESTATES AT MAGNESIA: *JRS* XLIII (1953), 52-3. The Apion estates were divided into groups, each

managed by a προνοητής, described in such terms as κτήματος Ματρέου καὶ τῶν ἐν ταῖς κώμης 'Επισήμου καὶ 'Αδαίου καὶ τῶν ἐξωτικῶν αὐτῶν τόπων τῶν διαφερόντων τῇ ὑμῶν ὑπερφυείᾳ (P. Oxy. 136); οἴκων Τερύθεως καὶ Θεαγένους καὶ Εὐτυχιάδος καὶ ἄλλων ἐξωτικῶν τόπων (P. Oxy. 2019); Παγγουλεείου σὺν τοῖς ἄλλοις μέρεσι καὶ Μαργαρίτου καὶ 'Αμβιοῦτος καὶ Μαιουμᾶ καὶ ἄλλων ἐξωτικῶν τόπων (P. Oxy. 999); κτημάτων Πεζούλιος (and five other names) μετὰ καὶ τῶν ἐξωτικῶν τόπων. Cf. also P. Oxy. 1910v, accounts of a προνοητής, in which the receipts are itemized as λήμματα Θαήσιος (evidently a κτῆμα), four much smaller amounts ἐν κώμῃ (four names), and ὑπὲρ τοῦ κτήματος Πλακίτου; P. Oxy. 1912, a similar account with four entries labelled ἐποικίου (four names), and one ἐν κώμῃ Πέτνῃ. The Apions are thus stated to be owners of κτήματα and ἐποίκια, but never of κῶμαι; they only own land ἐν κώμαις.

42. SYRIAN VILLAGES: Lib. Or. XLVII. 4, 11, Theod. Hist. Rel. xiv, xvii. EGYPTIAN VILLAGES: CTh XI. xxiv. 6, 415 (cited in n. 19); cf. n. 41 for the Apion holdings in villages. LEO'S LAW: CJ XI. lvi. 1, 468, in illis, quae metrocomiae communi vocabulo nuncupantur, hoc adiciendum necessario nostra putavit humanitas, ut nulli extraneo illic quoquo modo possidendi licentia tribuatur: sed si quis ex isdem vicanis loca sui iuris alienare voluerit, non licere ei nisi ad habitatorem adscriptum eidem metrocomiae per qualemcumque contractum terrarum suarum dominium possessionemque transferre: sciente persona extranea, quod, si contra vetitum se huic negotio immiscere vel illio possidere temptaverit, quicumque contractus initus fuerit, carebit effectu et contractu soluto, si quid praestitum est, hoc tantum reddetur. The laws against patronage usually speak of vici; the communal responsibility of the village is stressed in CJ XI. liv. 2 (cited in n. 21). A concrete case is Aphrodito, which ultimately put itself under the protection of Theodora (P. Cairo, 67019, 67283).

43. For the administrative hierarchy of the res privata see pp. 412-4.

44. For land tenures in the res privata see pp. 416-9.

45. THE PATRIMONY OF GAUL: Greg. Ep. III. 33, VI. 6 (Dynamius), V. 31 (Aregius), VI. 51 (the bishop of Arles), VI. 5-6, 10, 49-53, 56-7, IX. 221, XI. 43-4 (Candidus, presbyter). AFRICA: Greg. Ep. I. 73-4 (Hilarius, notarius). DALMATIA: Greg. Ep. II. 23, III. 22, 32 (Antoninus, subdiaconus); cf. Gelasius, fr. 2, Vigilius, Ep. ad Rusticum et Sebastianum (PL LXIX. 46), iterum Thessalonica ad Dalmatias patrimonii regendi causa remissus es, ex qua provincia frequenti te auctoritate monuimus ut non ante discederes nisi omnes secundum pollicitationem tuam tam de Dalmatiarum patrimonio quam de Praevalitano colligeres pensiones. SICILY: Greg. Ep. I. 1-3, 9, 18, 38, etc. (Peter, subdiaconus). On his recall the Sicilian patrimony was divided into a Syracusana pars and a Panormitana pars (II. 38). His successors in the Syracusana pars were Cyprian, diaconus (IV. 6, 15, V. 7, VII. 38; he appears to have had a general responsibility for all Sicily, his Panormitan colleague being subordinate to him); Romanus, defensor (IX. 29-31; his sphere is defined as the territories of Syracuse, Catana, Agrigentum and Messana); and Adrian, notarius (XIII. 22-3, 25, 37). Between Cyprian and Romanus John, bishop of Syracuse, administered the Syracusana pars (IX. 22). In the Panormitana pars Peter was followed by Benenatus, notarius (II. 38, III. 27), and Fantinus, defensor (IX. 23, 39, 40, 172, XIV. 4, 5). APPIA: Greg. Ep. XIV. 14 (Felix, subdiaconus). CAMPANIA: Greg. Ep. V. 28 (dealing with action taken in Campania 'a dilectissimo filio nostro Petro diacono, tunc autem subdiacono et rectore patrimonii'). This is the only explicit reference to

the rector of the Campanian patrimony, but many letters on Campanian business are addressed to Peter, *subdiaconus Campaniae* (III. 1, 5, 19, 23, 34-5, 39), and also to Anthemius, *subdiaconus* (*Campaniae* in IX. 136, 142, 144, 163, X. 7, XI. 53, XIII. 29, 31); Peter, when rector of Sicily, is similarly addressed as *subdiaconus Siciliae* in I. 42, 67, 71. We may therefore postulate a patrimony of Sardinia from III. 36 (Sabino, defensori Sardiniae) and IX. 203, XIV. 2 (Vitali, defensori Sardiniae), and of Corsica from XI. 58 (Bonifatio, defensori Corsicae). Further evidence is afforded by two circular letters, IX. 88, Romano defensori, Anthemio subdiacono, Sabino subdiacono, Sergio defensori a paribus, and IX. 110, Romano defensori, Fantino defensori, Sabino subdiacono, Hadriano notario, Eugenio notario, Felici subdiacono, Sergio defensori, Bonifatio defensori a paribus. Of these Romanus, Fantinus, Anthemius, Felix and Boniface are known to have been rectors of the *Syracusana pars*, the *Panormitana pars*, Campania, Appia and Corsica respectively, and Sabinus is called *rector patrimonii* in XIV. 9 (his district was Bruttium, as appears from IX. 122, 124-7, X. 2). It is therefore reasonable to infer that the others were also *rectores patrimoniorum*. Eugenius, *notarius*, deals with church lands in Tuscia in IX. 96, Sergius, *defensor*, deals with affairs in Calabria (VIII. 9, IX. 169, 200; his district was perhaps the 'Apuliae provinciae patrimonium' of Pelagius I, *Ep.* 64); Hadrian was later rector of the *Panormitana pars*, but his post at the time of *Ep.* IX. 110 is not known. It is possible that Pantaleon, *notarius*, was rector of a Ligurian patrimony (XI. 6, 14) and Castorius of a Venetian (V. 25, IX. 168). *Ep.* III. 21 is addressed to the three sons of Urbicus, 'quondam defensorem de patrimonio Savinensi atque Cartiolano, quod eius fuerat curae commissum'. Under Pelagius I (*Ep.* 83) the bishop of Cingulum had the management 'massarum sive fundorum per Picenum ultra XI positorum'.

46. ACTORES OR ACTIONARII: Greg. *Ep.* I. 9, 42, 53, 71, II. 38, VI. 42, IX. 137, 192; cf. IX. 41-2, 145, for *actores* of the church of Syracuse. CONDUCTORES: I. 42, iubemus etiam, ut hoc experientia tua summopere custodiat, ut per commodum conductores in massis ecclesiae numquam fiant, ne dum commodum quaeritur conductores frequenter mutentur. ex qua mutatione quid aliud agitur, nisi ut ecclesiastica praedia numquam colantur? II. 38, greges vero equarum quos valde inutiliter habemus omnes volo distrahi, et tantummodo quadringentos iuniores servari ad foetum, ex quibus quadringentis singuli conductoribus singulae condomae dari debent; V. 31, conductoribus massarum sive fundorum per Galliam constitutis; XIII. 37, XIV. 5. GREGORY AND EMPHYTEUTIC LEASES: I. 70, multi vero hic veniunt, qui terras aliquas vel insulas in iure ecclesiae nostrae in emphyteusin sibi postulant dari. et aliquibus quidem negamus, aliquibus vero iam concessimus. THE CONSTANTINOPOLITAN CHURCH AND EMPHYTEUTIC LEASES: *CJ* I. ii. 24 §12, 530, καὶ λαμβάνουσι λόγῳ συνηθειῶν ἐπὶ μὲν τοῖς ἐμφυτευτικοῖς συμβολαίοις πεντηκοστάς, ἐπὶ δὲ τοῖς μισθωτικοῖς καὶ λοιποῖς συναλλάγμασιν ἑκατοστήν. Emphyteusis by churches is regulated by *CJ* I. ii. 17 §§1, 3 (Anastasius), 24 §5, 530, Just. *Nov.* vii §§3, 7, 535, cxx §§1, 5, 6, 8, 544. Examples are *P. Cairo*, 67298-9, *PRG* III. 43, *P. Lond.* 483, *PSI* 176, *P. Michael.* 41, *P. Dip.* 95, 132.

47. ADMINISTRATION OF THE APION ESTATES: E. R. Hardy, *The large estates of Byzantine Egypt*, 80-93, and for φροντισταί, 133. The title ἀντιγεοῦχος (*P. Oxy.* 153, 156, 943, 1844-54, 1859-61, 1867, etc.) is paralleled by the Latin *vice-dominus* (see ch. VIII, n. 44). LAURICIUS: *P. Ital.* 1. Private owners are envisaged as granting emphyteutic leases in *CJ* IV. lxvi. 1 (Zeno), 2, 529, 3, 530, 4 (531-4), but emphyteutic tenants of private owners do not appear in other laws, whereas

procuratores, actores and *conductores* are frequently mentioned. In Egypt I can find one emphyteutic lease by a private owner (*P. Giss.* 106), as against many by churches (see n. 46).

48. For the titles of the agents of the Apion family see especially the correspondence in *P. Oxy.* 1844 ff. SERENUS THE DEACON: *P. Oxy.* 136, cf. 2239 for a similar contract. SERVILE ACTORES AND PROCURATORES: *CTh* IV. xii. 5, 362, ut libera mulier, sive procuratori sive actori privato sive alii cuilibet servili condicione polluto fuerit sociata, non aliter libertate amissa nexu condicionis deterrimae adstringatur, nisi trinis fuerit denuntiationibus ex iure pulsata; VII. xviii. 2, 379, actor eius fundi, in quo alienigena vel idoneus militiae vel ante iam traditus latuerit, ultima flammarum animadversione consumatur. hoc interim nos constituisse sufficiat, nam si parum profecerit in servos interminatio constituta, in dominos peccatum deinceps emendatura decernet; XVI. v. 65 §3, 428, de procuratore, qui hoc nesciente domino fecerit, decem librarum auri multam vel exilium, si sit ingenuus, subituro, metallum vero post verbera, si servilis condicionis sit, Maj. *Nov.* vii §4, 458, si quis actor procuratorve domino nesciente susceperit curialem et non intra annum propriae restituerit civitati, si ingenuus probabitur, collegiis adplicetur, si servus est, fustuario supplicio interficiendum se esse cognoscat. CLERGY AS PROCURATORES: Pall. *Dial.* pp. 86–7 (Antoninus), *C. Carth.* I, can. 6, *C. Hippon.* can. 15, *C. Carth.* III, can. 5, *A.C.Oec.* II. i. 353–5. CURIALES AS PROCURATORES: *CTh* XII. i. 92, 382, si quis procurationem facultatum suarum curiali crediderit esse mandandam, totius dignitatis exceptione depulsa patrimonium eius quod crediderat curiali proscriptio fiscalis invadat. ille vero, qui immemor libertatis et generis infamissimam suscipiens vilitatem existimationem suam servili obsecundatione damnaverit, deportationis incommodo subiugetur; Th. II, *Nov.* ix §1, 439. *Fabricenses* and soldiers were also forbidden to be *procuratores*; *CTh* x. xxii. 5, 404, *CJ* IV. lxv. 31, 458. In *BGU* 303, we find a μεγαλοπρεπέστατος τριβοῦνος acting as ἀντιγεοῦχος, and Lauricius employed the tribune Pyrrhus in a similar capacity (*P. Ital.* 1). Theodore of Syceon, as bishop of Anastasiopolis, employed a *protector* (*V. Theod. Syc.* 76).

49. SERVILE CONDUCTORES: Gelasius, fr. 28, Ampliatus conductor, quem non solum servum constat esse ecclesiae sed ita eius rationibus a multis temporibus implicatum ut, etiamsi esset ingenuus, donec ratiocinia cuncta deduceret modis omnibus obnoxius haberetur; Pelagius I, *Ep.* 84, de rusticis qui possunt conductores vel coloni esse si capillum relaxaris, nulla erit ratio quae me circa te placare praevaleat; *CTh* XVI. v. 21, 392, conductorem eius fundi, si ingenuus est, decem libras fisco nostro inferre praecipimus, si servili faece descendens paupertate sui poenam damni ac vilitate contemnit, caesus fustibus deportatione damnabitur. CURIALES AS CONDUCTORES: Th. II, *Nov.* ix, 439, non dubium est in legem committere eum, qui verba legis amplexus contra legis nititur voluntatem, nec poenas insertas legibus evitabit, qui se contra iuris sententias scaeva praerogativa verborum fraudulenter excusat. curiales ne ad procurationem rerum alienarum accederent, cautum est providentissima sanctione, cuius in fraudem conducendi eos sibimet usurpare licentiam sublimitatis tuae suggestione comperimus. quos licet pristinae legis laqueis inretiri cernamus— conductionem namque speciem esse procurationis certissimum est—adtamen ne sub fraudis suae velamine legis lateant contemptores neve eis fucata suae calliditatis excusatio relinquatur, hac perpetuo lege valitura sancimus conducendi quoque fundos alienos licentiam curialibus amputari, locatas res fisci viribus vindicari. SOLDIERS AND OFFICIALS AS CONDUCTORES: Th. II, *Nov.* vii.

I, 439, iuratur in militiae sacramenta, ut necessitates publicae procurentur, sed suggestione culminis tui comperimus quosdam ideo tantum sortiri militiam, ut alienorum praediorum idonei possint fieri conductores. quod nisi numinis nostri fuerit auctoritate correctum, in contumeliam aulae divinae proficiet, si iisdem privilegiis muniantur qui in privatis negotiis occupantur, quibus iure militiae servientes obsequiorum praemiis gloriantur. quare praesenti lege sancimus omnes omnino domesticos, agentes in rebus et quaecumque alia praetenditur militiae dignitas, sub moderatoribus provinciarum functionibus publicis respondere, nulla fori praescriptione valitura, si hac qui exiguntur debita publica uti temptaverint; *CJ* IV. lxv. 31, 458, 35, 530. CLERGY AS CONDUCTORES: *C. Hippon.* can. 15, *C. Carth.* III, can. 5, *A.C.Oec.* II. i. 353–5, *C. Arel.* II, can. 14, si quis clericus pecuniam dederit ad usuram, aut conductor alienae rei voluerit esse, aut turpis lucri gratia aliquod negotiationis exercuerit, depositus a communione alienus fiat.

50. The three laws *CTh* VII. xiii. 12–4, 397, taken in conjunction suggest that many senators were lessees of imperial land. Cf. *CTh* V. xv. 15, 364, enfyteutica praedia, quae senatoriae fortunae viris, praeterea variis ita sunt per principes veteres elocata, ut certum vectigal annuum ex his aerario penderetur. For the virtual equivalence of *procuratores* and *conductores* see Th. II, *Nov.* ix §1, 439 (cited in n. 49). Responsibility is laid on the *procurator* or *conductor* in *CTh* XVI. vi. 4, 405, *Sirm.* 16, 408, *CTh* XVI. v. 52, 412, *CJ* I. v. 8, 455; more usually the *procurator* or *actor* is alone mentioned. APION ESTATES: E. R. Hardy, *op. cit.* 113–32.

51. VINTAGE: Joh. Chrys. *Hom. in Matth.* lxi. 3 (peasants), Josh. Styl. 52 (townsmen). HARVEST: Rufinus, *Hist. Mon.* xviii (his Latin version gives 80 modii, the Greek original σίτου ἀρτάβας δεκάδυο ὡς τεσσαράκοντα τοὺς παρ' ἡμῖν μοδίους καλουμένους, which is more plausible); cf. Joh. Moschus, 183, and Greg. Tur. *Glor. Conf.* 1, for a landlord collecting seventy men for the harvest.

52. FREE LABOURERS: Joh. Moschus, 154. Permanent hired labourers seem also to be the subject of *CPR* 233 (A.D. 314), where a lady obtains an order from the governor of the Thebaid, ὁ πραιπόσιτος τοῦ πάγου τῆς συνήθους γεωργείας ἔχεσθαι τοὺς σοὺς μ[ισθωτὰς] καταναγκάσει . . . ὑπὲρ τοῦ μὴ εἰς χερσίαν τραπῆναι τὸ χωρίον· ἧς ὁ κίνδυνος εἰς τοὺς μισθωτὰς, εἰ παρίδοιεν τὴν τούτου καλλιέργειαν. SLAVES: *JRS* XLIII (1953), 56–7; for a slave-run estate on Samos see Joh. Moschus, 108.

53. *V. Mel.* (L), 18; in ch. 10–1 it is implied that not only their suburban villas near Rome, but their estates generally were manned by slaves. SLAVES ON THE PAPAL ESTATES AND THEIR NEIGHBOURS: Gelasius, *Ep.* 20, 21, fr. 23, 28, Pelagius I, *Ep.* 64, 84. SPAIN: Orosius, VII. xl. 5–6, duo fratres iuvenes nobiles et locupletes Didymus et Verinianus . . . servulos tantum suos ex propriis praediis colligentes ac vernaculis alentes sumptibus nec dissimulato proposito absque cuiusquam inquietudine ad Pyrenaei claustra tendebant; *C. Hisp.* I, can. I, *C. Tol.* IV, can. 74 (slaves of the church), *Lex Vis.* V. vii. 16, XII. ii (*servi fiscales*). REMIGIUS: *Rev. Belg. Phil. Hist.* XXXV (1957), 372–3; rural slaves of the church are mentioned in several Gallic councils, e.g. *C. Agath.* can. 7, *C. Epaon.* can. 8, *C. Aurel.* IV, can. 9, 32, *C. Elus.* can. 6, *C. Rem.* can. 13.

54. LEVY OF COLONI: *CTh* VII. xiii. 13, 14, 397. LEVY OF SLAVES: Symm. *Ep.* VI. 58, iuniorum dilectus urbanis familiis imperatus, 62, 64, in usum militarem petita servitia.

55. See *Econ. Hist. Rev.* IX (1956–7), 192–5.

56. For slave prices see p. 852. RADAGAESUS'S MEN: Orosius, VII. xxxvii. 16.
PRISONERS AS COLONI: Pan. Lat. VIII. 9 §§3-4, arat ergo nunc mihi Chamavus
et Frisius et ille vagus, ille praedator exercitio squalidi ruris operatur et frequentat
nundinas meas pecore venali et cultor barbarus laxat annonam. quin etiam si
ad dilectum vocetur, accurrit et obsequiis teritur et tergo cohercetur et servire
se militiae nomine gratulatur, *CTh* v. vi. 3, 409, Scyras barbaram nationem
maximis Chunorum, quibus se coniunxerunt, copiis fusis imperio nostro
subegimus. ideoque damus omnibus copiam ex praedicto genere hominum
agros proprios frequentandi, ita ut omnes sciant susceptos non alio iure quam
colonatus apud se futuros nullique licere ex hoc genere colonorum ab eo,
cui semel adtributi fuerint, vel fraude aliquem abducere vel fugientem suscipere,
poena proposita, quae recipientes alienis censibus adscriptos vel non proprios
colonos insequitur. opera autem eorum terrarum domini libera utantur ac
nullus sub acta peraequatione vel censui . . . acent nullique liceat velut donatos
eos a iure census in servitutem trahere urbanisve obsequiis addicere, licet
intra biennium suscipientibus liceat pro rei frumentariae angustiis in quibuslibet
provinciis transmarinis tantummodo eos retinere et postea in sedes perpetuas
conlocare, a partibus Thraciae vel Illyrici habitatione eorum penitus prohibenda
et intra quinquennium dumtaxat intra eiusdem provinciae fines eorum traduc-
tione, prout libuerit, concedenda, iuniorum quoque intra praedictos viginti
annos praebitione cessante. ita ut per libellos sedem tuam adeuntibus his qui
voluerint per transmarinas provincias eorum distributio fiat. Cf. Amm. XXVIII.
v. 15, XXXI. ix. 4, Lib. *Or.* LIX. 83-5.

57. *CTh* v. xiii. 4, 368, si quid adiecerit sumptus cura sollertia, quidquid
mancipiorum vel pecoris adcreverit, capitationis aut canonis augmenta non
patiatur. ITALIAN FAMINE: Amb. *Off.* III. 46-8.

58. SALE OF RURAL SLAVES: *CTh* XI. iii. 2, 327, mancipia adscripta censibus
intra provinciae terminos distrahantur et qui emptione dominium nancti
fuerint, inspiciendum sibi esse cognoscant; *CJ* XI. xlviii. 7, 371, quemadmodum
originarios absque terra, ita rusticos censitosque servos vendi omnifariam
non licet; *Ed. Theod.* 142, liceat unicuique domino ex praediis, quae corporaliter
et legitimo iure possidet, rustica utriusque sexus mancipia, etiamsi originaria
sint, ad iuris sui loca transferre, vel urbanis ministeriis adplicare, ita ut et illis
praediis adquirantur, ad quae voluntate domini migrata fuisse constiterit, et
inter urbanos famulos merito censeantur: nec de eiusmodi factis atque
ordinationibus, velut sub oppositione originis, quaestio ulla nascatur. alienare
etiam supradictae conditionis homines liceat dominis, absque terrae aliqua
portione, sub scripturae adtestatione, vel cedere, vendere cui libuerit, vel
donare. SERVI QUASI COLONI: *Dig.* XV. iii. 16, XXXIII. vii. 12 §3, 20 §1, Pelagius I,
Ep. 84, nec enim eiusdem aestimationis est artifex et ministerialis puer contra
rusticum vel colonum . . . vide ergo ne tales des homines qui vel continere casas
vel colere possint (see also n. 49).

59. AMPLIATUS: Gelasius, fr. 28. CELERINUS: Pelagius I, *Ep.* 64.

60. RENEWAL OF FIVE YEAR LEASES: *Dig.* XIX. ii. 13 §11, 14. EGYPTIAN LEASES:
A. C. Johnson, *Roman Egypt* (*Economic Survey of Ancient Rome*, II), 81 ff. HEREDI-
TARY LEASES: *ILS* 6870, col. iii, lines 28-9 (Africa), Keil and Premerstein,
Denkschr. Ak. Wien LVII (1914-15), 55, line 46 (Lydia).

61. I have set out my theory of the colonate in *Past and Present*, 1958, 1-13,
where I give my reasons for believing it to have originated as a by-product
of Diocletian's census.

62. That peasant freeholders were originally tied is proved by *P. Cairo Isid.* 126, of 308–9, citing an imperial order that strangers found in the villages be returned to their own villages under a penalty of five *folles*, ibid. 128, of 314, a receipt by village officials for fugitives returned, and *P. Thead.* 16–7, of 332, a petition by villagers to the prefect of Egypt for the repatriation of their fellow villagers who had absconded. Later laws enforcing this rule are very rare; *CTh* x. xii. 2, 368, which rules that vagrants, if slaves or *coloni*, are to be restored to their owners or landlords, quisquis autem plebeium se adserit esse vel liberum . . . ad ea loca ex quibus eum esse claruerit remittatur, and *CTh* XI. xxiv. 6 §3, 415, ii sane qui vicis quibus adscripti sunt derelictis, et qui homologi more gentilicio nuncupantur, ad alios seu vicos seu dominos transierunt, ad sedem desolati ruris constrictis detentatoribus redire cogantur. CHAINING OF COLONI: *CTh* v. xvii. 1, 332, apud quemcumque colonus iuris alieni fuerit inventus, is non solum eundem origini suae restituat, verum super eodem capitationem temporis agnoscat. ipsos etiam colonos, qui fugam meditantur, in servilem condicionem ferro ligari conveniet, ut officia, quae liberis congruunt, merito servilis condemnationis compellantur implere. PROPERTY OF COLONI: *CTh* v. xix. 1, 365, non dubium est colonis arva, quae subigunt, usque adeo alienandi ius non esse, ut, et si qua propria habeant, inconsultis atque ignorantibus patronis in alteros transferre non liceat. TAXES OF COLONI: *CTh* XI. i. 14, 371 (S), penes quos fundorum dominia sunt, pro his colonis originalibus, quos in locis isdem censos esse constabit, vel per se vel per actores proprios recepta compulsionis sollicitudine implenda munia functionis agnoscant. sane quibus terrarum erit quantulacumque possessio, qui in suis conscripti locis proprio nomine libris censualibus detinentur, ab huius praecepti communione discernimus; eos enim convenit propriae commissos mediocritati annonarias functiones sub solito exactore cognoscere. COLONI DEBARRED FROM SUING MASTERS: *CJ* XI. i. 2, 396, coloni censibus dumtaxat adscripti, sicuti ab his liberi sunt, quibus eos tributa subiectos non faciunt, ita his, quibus annuis functionibus et debito condicionis obnoxii sunt, paene est ut quadam servitute dediti videantur. quo minus est ferendum, ut eos audeant lite pulsare, a quibus ipsos utpote a dominis una cum possessionibus distrahi posse dubium non est. quam de cetero licentiam submovemus, ne quis audeat domini in iudicio nomen lacessere, et cuius ipsi sunt, eiusdem omnia sua esse cognoscant. cum enim saepissime decretum sit, ne quid de peculio suo cuiquam colonorum ignorante domino praedii aut vendere aut alio modo alienare liceret, quemadmodum contra eius personam aequo poterit consistere iure, quem nec propria quidem leges sui iuris habere voluerunt et adquirendi tantum, non etiam transferendi potestate permissa, domino et adquirere et habere voluerunt? sed ut in causis civilibus huiusmodi hominum generi adversus dominos vel patronos et aditum intercludimus et vocem negamus exceptis superexactionibus, in quibus retro principes facultatem eis super hoc interpellandi praebuerunt, ita in criminum accusatione quae publica est non adimitur eis propter suam suorumque iniuriam experiendi licentia.

63. *CJ* XI. liii. i, 371, colonos inquilinosque per Illyricum vicinasque regiones abeundi rure, in quo eos originis agnationisque merito certum est immorari, licentiam habere non posse censemus. inserviant terris non tributario nexu, sed nomine et titulo colonorum, ita ut, si abscesserint ad aliumve transierint, revocati vinculis poenisque subdantur; lii. 1, 393, per universam dioecesim Thraciarum sublato in perpetuum humanae capitationis censu iugatio tantum terrena solvatur. et ne forte colonis tributariae sortis nexibus absolutis vagandi et quo libuerit recedendi facultas permissa videatur, ipsi quidem originario

iure teneantur, et licet condicione videantur ingenui, servi tamen terrae ipsius cui nati sunt aestimentur nec recedendi quo velint aut permutandi loca habeant facultatem, sed possessor eorum iure utatur et patroni sollicitudine et domini potestate.

64. COLONI OF PALESTINE: *CJ* xi. li. 1, 386, cum per alias provincias, quae subiacent nostrae serenitatis imperio, lex a maioribus constituta colonos quodam aeternitatis iure detineat, ita ut illis non liceat ex his locis quorum fructu relevantur abscedere nec ea deserere quae semel colenda susceperunt, neque id Palaestinae provinciae possessoribus suffragetur, sancimus, ut etiam per Palaestinas nullus omnino colonorum suo iure velut vagus ac liber exsultet, sed exemplo aliarum provinciarum ita domino fundi teneatur, ut sine poena suscipientis non possit abscedere: addito eo, ut possessionis domino revocandi eius plena tribuatur auctoritas. GALLIC COLONI: *CTh* xi. i. 26, 399, omni amoto privilegio beneficiorum possessores sublimitas tua praecipiet universos muneribus adstringi, earum scilicet provinciarum, ex quibus orta querimonia est aut in quibus haec retinendae plebis ratio adscriptioque servatur. nullum gratia relevet, nullum iniquae partitionis vexet incommodum, sed pari omnes sorte teneantur; ita tamen, ut, si ad alterius personam transferatur praedium, cui certus plebis numerus fuerit adscriptus, venditi onera novellus possessor compellatur agnoscere, cum plebem constet non tam hominibus quam praediis adscribendam neque auferendam ab eo, cui semel posthac deputata fuerit. For different systems of registration see *JRS* XLIII (1953), 50 ff.

65. *CTh* xi. i. 14, 371 (S), cited in n. 62.

66. For the census registers see *JRS* XLIII (1953), 50 ff. For the absence of regular censuses see pp. 454–5. TAX ON ABSCONDING COLONI: *CTh* v. xvii. 1, 332 (cited in n. 62), *CJ* xi. xlviii. 8, 371, omnes profugi in alieno latebras collocantes cum emolumentis tributariis, salva tamen moderatione, revocentur, scilicet ut si, apud quos homines reperiuntur, alienos esse noverant fugitivos et profugis in lucrum suum usi sunt, hoc est sive excoluerunt agros fructibus dominis profuturos sive aliqua ab isdem sibi iniuncta novaverunt nec mercedem laboris debitam consecuti sunt, ab illis tributa quae publicis perierunt functionibus exigantur. ceterum si occultato eo profugi, quod alieni esse videntur, quasi sui arbitrii ac liberi apud aliquem se collocaverunt aut excolentes terras partem fructuum pro solo debitam dominis praestiterunt cetera proprio peculio reservantes, vel quibuscumque operis impensis mercedem placitam consecuti sunt, ab ipsis profugis quaecumque debentur exigantur: nam manifestum est privatum iam esse contractum; *CTh* xiii. x. 7, 371, hoc autem ut rite celebretur, auctoritas tua iudicibus tantum, id est rectoribus provinciarum, permittat potestatem, ita ut iidem, cum querimonia defensorum vel plebeiorum ad eos fuerit nuntiata, exhibitis partibus secundum fidem rerum coram cognoscant ac stabilitatem census finita altercatione componant, eos tantum, qui mortui videbuntur, ex adcrescentibus repleturi. ceterum illos, qui relictis censibus aufugerunt, ad excusationem pertinere non est aequum, quando quidem eum, qui videbitur aufugisse, constat esse revocandum. RULES ON CONSCRIPTION: *CTh* vii. xiii. 6, 370, quod hactenus decernimus custodiri, ut oblatus numerus ex adcrescentibus primitus reparetur ac, si compensatio non potuerit convenire neque ex minoribus modus, qui oblatus fuerit, quiverit reparari, ita demum de publicis fascibus hi, qui ex superfluo veniunt, eximantur; 7, 375, et quia publica utilitas quoque cogitanda est, ne sub hac indulgentia insertae capitationis numerus minuatur, ex incensitis adque adcrescentibus in eorum locum, qui defensi militia fuerint, alios praecipimus subrogari.

67. That outsiders who settled on an estate were not tied is clear from Val. III, *Nov.* xxxi §5, 451.

68. Transfer of *coloni* from one *fundus* to another is allowed in *CJ* XI. xlviii. 13 §1, 400, illud etiam servandum est, ut, si quando utriusque fundi idem dominus de possessione referta cultoribus ad eam colonos quae laborabat tenuitate transtulerit, idemque fundi ad diversorum iura dominorum qualibet sorte transierint, maneat quidem facta translatio, sed ita, ut praedii eius dominus, a quo coloni probantur fuisse transducti, translatorum agnationem restituat; Val. III, *Nov.* xxxv §18, 452, si forte duorum praediorum unus dominus atque possessor ex referto originariis et colonis agro ad alterum rus aliquos homines propria voluntate et ordinatione transtulerit, ita id maneat, ut, sive venditione seu donatione seu quolibet alio modo ad diversos dominos res utraque pervenerit, translatos originis iure et titulo revocari non liceat. TRIBUTARII: *CTh* x. xii. 2 §2, 368, si quis etiam vel tributarius repperitur vel inquilinus ostenditur, ad eum protinus redeat, cuius se esse profitetur; *CJ* XI. xlviii. 12, 396 ('vel tributarios vel inquilinos' is probably a Justinianic interpolation). In *CTh* XI. vii. 2, 319, unusquisque decurio pro ea portione conveniatur, in qua vel ipse vel colonus vel tributarius eius convenitur et colligit; neque omnino pro alio decurione vel territorio conveniatur, *tributarius* appears to be distinguished from *colonus*, and may mean a tax-paying (i.e. rural) slave. INQUILINI: *CJ* XI. xlviii. 6, 365 (S), omnes omnino fugitivos [adscripticios] colonos vel inquilinos; *CTh* x. xii. 2, 368 (cited above), *CJ* XI. liii. 1, 371, colonos inquilinosque per Illyricum; *CTh* XII. xix. 1, 400, inquilinas vel colonas vel ancillas; 2, 400, colonatus . . . aut inquilinatus quaestionem; *CJ* XI. xlviii. 13, 400, inter inquilinos colonosve, quorum quantum ad originem pertinet vindicandam indiscreta eademque paene videtur esse condicio, licet sit discrimen in nomine; *CTh* v. xviii. 1, 419, colonus originalis vel inquilinus, *CJ* III. xxvi. 11, 442, domorum nostrarum colonus aut inquilinus aut servus; Val. III, *Nov.* xxvii, 449, de originariis et colonis, inquilinis ac servis; xxxv, 452, nullus originarius inquilinus servus vel colonus; Sev. *Nov.* ii, 465, inquilinus vel colonus. In *CJ* III. xxxviii. 11 (= *CTh* II. xxv. 1, 325) 'vel colonorum adscripticiae condicionis seu inquilinorum' is a Justinianic interpolation, and so probably is 'vel tributarios vel inquilinos' in *CJ* XI. xlviii. 12, 396. None of these passages is inconsistent with the meaning of *inquilinus* in the classical lawyers, tenant of a house. The *casarii* (cotters) of *CTh* IX. xlii. 7, 369, quotve mancipia in praediis . . . quot sint casarii vel coloni, may be identical with them. ORIGINALES: *CJ* XI. lxviii. 1, 325, xlviii. 7, 371 (S), *CTh* x. xx. 10, 380, *CJ* XI. xlviii. 11, 396 (S), *CTh* v. xviii. 1, 419, Val. III, *Nov.* xxvii, 449, xxxi, 451, xxxv, 452, Maj. *Nov.* vii, 458, Theod. *Ed.* 21, 48, 56, 63–8, 80. CENSIBUS ADSCRIPTI, ETC.: *CJ* XI. I. 2, 396 (S), I. iii. 16, 409, *CTh* v. vi. 3, 409, x. xx. 17, 427, v. iii. 1, 434, Th. II, *Nov.* vii. 4, 441, also applied to rural slaves in *CTh* XI. iii. 2, 327, VII. i. 3, 349, *CJ* XI. xlviii. 7, 371. *Adscripticius* appears first in *CJ* I. xii. 6, 466, ἐνυπόγραφος in *A.C.Oec.* II. i. 353 §17, in 451. For the equivalence of *origo* and *census* see *CTh* XI. i. 14, 371 (S), pro his colonis originalibus quos in locis isdem censos esse constabit, *CJ* XI. xlviii. 6, 366, omnes omnino fugitivos [adscripticios] colonos vel inquilinos . . . ad antiquos penates ubi censiti atque educati natique sunt, provinciis praesidentes redire compellant. Sidonius Apollinaris uses all the above terms (except *adscripticius*) in *Ep.* v. 19, nutricis meae filiam filius tuae rapuit: facinus indignum quodque nos vosque inimicasset, nisi protinus scissem te nescisse faciendum. sed conscientiae tuae purgatione praelata petere dignaris culpae calentis impunitatem. sub condicione concedo: si stupratorem pro domino iam patronus originali solvas inquilinatu.

mulier autem illa iam libera est, quae tum demum videbitur non ludibrio addicta sed assumpta coniugio, si reus noster, pro quo precaris, mox cliens factus e tributario plebeiam potius incipiat habere personam quam colonariam.

69. LONGI TEMPORIS PRAESCRIPTIO: *CTh* v. xviii. 1, 419, Val. III, *Nov.* xxvii, 449; the rule had been applied in Gaul in 400, *CTh* XII. xix. 2, 3.

70. Val. III, *Nov.* xxxi, 451.

71. Salvian, *Gub. Dei*, v. 44, iugo se inquilinae abiectionis addicunt, 45, fiunt praeiudicio habitationis indigenae.

72. *CJ* XI. xlviii. 19 (Anastasius), τῶν γεωργῶν οἱ μὲν ἐναπόγραφοί εἰσιν καὶ τὰ τούτων πεκούλια τοῖς δεσπόταις ἀνήκει, οἱ δὲ χρόνῳ τῆς τριακονταετίας μισθωτοὶ γίνονται ἐλεύθεροι μένοντες μετὰ τῶν πραγμάτων αὐτῶν· καὶ οὗτοι δὲ ἀναγκάζονται καὶ τὴν γῆν γεωργεῖν καὶ τὸ τέλος παρέχειν. τοῦτο δὲ καὶ τῷ δεσπότῃ καὶ τοῖς γεωργοῖς λυσιτελές, 22 §3, 531, 23 §1 (531–4).

73. JUSTINIAN'S LAW: *CJ* XI. xlviii. 24 (the old rule is stated in Just. *Nov.* liv), Just. *Nov.* liv pr. §1, 537. ILLYRICUM: Just. *Nov.* clxii §2, 539; six months later the original ruling was reversed by Just. *App.* i, but this law seems in turn to have been abrogated. AFRICA: Just. II, *Nov.* vi, Tib. *Nov.* xiii.

74. Ἐναπόγραφοι γεωργοί IN EGYPT: *P. Oxy.* 135, 137, 1896, 1979, 1982–3, 1985, 1988–91, 2479, *P. Lond.* 774 5, 777–8, *P.SI* 59, 61–2, 180, *P. Amh.* 149, *P. Iand.* 48 (all of the Apion estates), *P. Oxy.* 1900, 2238 (of the church). The earliest example is in 497 (*P. Oxy.* 1982).

75. *CJ* XI. xlviii. 21, 530, quae etenim differentia inter servos et adscripticios intellegetur, cum uterque in domini sui positus est potestate, et possit servum cum peculio manumittere et adscripticium cum terra suo dominio expellere? For *adscripticii* and military service see p. 614, for ordination and admission to monasteries, pp. 921, 931.

76. For the rights of free *coloni* see *CJ* XI. xlviii. 19 (Anastasius), 23 §§1–3 (531–4), Just. *Nov.* clxii §2, 539, οὐκ ἐξελεύσονται δὲ τοῦ χωρίου, ἀλλὰ τοῦτο γεωργήσουσιν, οὐδὲ ἔσται αὐτοῖς ἄδεια τοῦτο μὲν ἀπολιμπάνειν ἕτερα δὲ περινοστεῖν ἀλλότρια, πλὴν εἰ μὴ κύριοι γένοιντο κτήσεώς τινος ἰδίας, ἱκανῆς οὔσης ἀσχολεῖν αὐτοὺς περὶ αὐτὴν καὶ μὴ συγχωρούσης καὶ ἕτερα γεωργεῖν, εἰς ἐκείνην τε μετασταῖεν. The prohibitions against military service, ordination and the monastic life applied specifically to *adscripticii*, and not to *coloni liberi*.

77. For Egyptian leases see above n. 2. The formula ἐφ' ὅσον βούλει χρόνον did not, as some suppose, bind the applicant for the lease to stay on until the landlord released him; it is equally common in leases of houses and rooms, and must clearly assume the lessee's willingness as well as the lessor's.

78. ITALY: Pliny, *Ep.* IX. 37. AFRICA: *FIR* I². 100, *col.* i–iii, 101, *col.* iii, 102. For Egyptian leases see above n. 2. The Digest mentions the *partiarius colonus* only once (XIX. ii. 25 §6).

79. FORMS OF RENT: *CJ* XI. xlviii. 5, 365 (S), domini praediorum id quod terra praestat accipiant, pecuniam non requirant, quam rustici optare non audent, nisi consuetudo praedii hoc exigat. For Egyptian leases see n. 2, and for the Apion estates the accounts in *P. Oxy.* 1911–12, 2195–6, which show receipts in corn and gold, and *P. Oxy.* 1896, which shows a rent in wine, but cf. *P. Oxy.* 1915, where the rents on arable and vineyards are all in gold. SEQUESTRATION

OF RENT: *CJ* XI. xlviii. 20 §§1-2, 529, sin autem hoc coloni minime facere voluerint vel potuerint, tunc idem reditus per officium iudicis annui exigantur per solita tempora, in quae etiam dominis dependebantur, et deponantur in aede sacra, id est in cimeliarchio civitatis, sub qua possessio sita est, vel si localis ecclesia ad susceptionem pecuniarum idonea non sit, in metropolitana ecclesia, ut remaneant cum omni cautela et post plenissimam definitionem vel dominis dentur vel colonis restituantur. sin autem reditus non in auro, sed in speciebus inferuntur, vel in totum vel ex parte, interim per officium iudicis fructus vendantur et pretia eorum secundum praedictum modum deponantur.

80. GOLD RENTS: Greg. *Ep.* v. 7, quod ita quoque fieri volo, ut si quis ex eis conversus fuerit, si solidum pensionem habet, tremissis ei relaxari debeat, si tres vel quattuor, unus solidus relaxetur; II. 3, sed et terrulam ecclesiae nostrae vicinam sibi, quam solidum unum et tremisses duos pensitare asserunt, require; si ita est libellario nomine ad summam tremissis unius habere concede; IX. 194, hac tibi auctoritate praecipimus, ut ad tres siliquas aureas factis libellis ei vineolam ipsam locare debeas. PURCHASE OF CORN FROM COLONI: Greg. *Ep.* I. 42, cognovimus rusticos ecclesiae vehementer in frumentorum pretiis gravari, ita ut instituta summa eis in comparatione abundantiae tempore non servetur, et volumus, ut iuxta pretia publica omni tempore, sive minus sive amplius frumenta nascantur, in eis comparationis mensura teneatur: cf. I. 70, quinquaginta vero auri libris nova frumenta ab extraneis compara et in Sicilia in locis, in quibus non pereant, repone, ut mense Februario illic naves quantas possumus dirigamus et eadem ad nos frumenta deferantur.

81. FUNDI OF PATAVIUM: *P. Ital.* 3. For *excepta* see Greg. *Ep.* I. 42, super iusta ergo pondera praeter excepta et vilicilia nihil aliud volumus a colonis ecclesiae exigi; v. 31, visum autem nobis est, ut consuetudinaria excepta eius utilitati debeatis inferre; IX. 78, proinde excepta quae de possessione potuerunt in eius utilitate verti, ea te volumus eius magnitudini annis singulis offerre, id est porcos XX, qualiter ipse praevideris, verbices XX et gallinas LX. quae omnia in exceptis volumus reputari; Agnellus, *Lib. Pont. Eccl. Rav.* 60.

82. ROMAN SENATORS: Olymp. 44, ὅτι πολλοὶ οἶκοι ῾Ρωμαίων προσόδους κατ᾽ ἐνιαυτὸν ἐδέχοντο ἀπὸ τῶν κτημάτων αὐτῶν ἀνὰ τεσσαράκοντα χρυσοῦ κεντηνάρια, χωρὶς τοῦ σίτου καὶ τοῦ οἴνου καὶ τῶν ἄλλων ἁπάντων εἰδῶν, ἃ εἰς τρίτον συνέτεινεν, εἰ ἐπιπράσκετο, τοῦ εἰσφερομένου χρυσίου. LAURICIUS: *P. Ital.* I, line 30, spec(ies) per [id quod] domui nostrae necessatur, si navis fuerit inventa quae ad Ravennatem portum feliciter oportuno tempore disponat, transmitte, et ne forte non invenias qui Ravenna veniat, ad urbem mittatur et in horreo nostro consignetur. For hoarding by landlords in famines see Julian, *Misop.* 368C-370C, Greg. Naz. *Or.* XLIII. 34-5.

83. PAYMENT OF TAXES: *CTh* XI. i. 14, 371 (S) (cited in n. 62), *CJ* XI. xlviii. 20 §3, 529, haec de reditibus definientes ad publicas transeamus functiones. et si quidem coloni more solito eas dependant, ipsi maneant in pristina consuetudine, nullo praeiudicio dominis generando, qui et quiescentibus colonis et non contradicentibus ad publicum tributarias functiones minime inferebant. sin autem moris erat dominos totam summam accipere et ex ea partem quidem in publicas vertere functiones, partem autem in suos reditus habere, tunc, si quidem fideiussor a colonis detur, eundem fideiussorem dominis sine praeiudicio litis tantam summam inferre, quantam tributa publica faciunt, ut a dominis publicis rationibus persolvatur: nullo ex hoc colonis praeiudicio generando. For Egyptian leases see above n. 2, and for the Apions, E. R. Hardy, *op. cit.* 50-9

84. LABOUR SERVICES IN AFRICA: *FIR* I². 100, col. iv, 103, col. iii. Labour services may be referred to in *CJ* XI. xlviii. 8, 371, ut si, apud quos homines reperiuntur, alienos esse noverant fugitivos et profugis in lucrum suum usi sunt, hoc est sive excoluerunt agros fructibus dominis profuturos sive aliqua ab isdem sibi iniuncta novaverunt nec mercedem laboris debitam consecuti sunt, ab illis tributa quae publicis perierunt functionibus exigantur; 22 §3, 531, quod per multos annos neque agrum coluit neque aliquid colonarii operis celebravit. SYRIA: Joh. Chrys. *Hom. in Matth.* lxi. 3.

85. *P. Ital.* 3.

86. This conjecture is based on the fact that the home farm (locus qui adpellatur saltus Erudianus, per Maximum vilicum) is followed by 'col(onica) s(upra) s(cripta) per Iohannem, Vigilium et Bassum'. This *colonica*, which unlike the others has no name of its own but is called by the same name as the home farm, probably was originally part of it.

87. For wage labour on the Apion estates see E. R. Hardy, *op. cit.* 122-32.

88. MONEY SURCHARGE: Greg. *Ep.* I. 42, cognovimus etiam, in aliquibus massis ecclesiae exactionem valde iniustissimam fieri, ita ut libram septuagenum ternum semis quod dici nefas est exigantur et adhuc neque hoc sufficit, sed insuper aliquid ex usu iam multorum annorum exigi dicuntur. quam rem omnimodo detestamur et amputari de patrimonio funditus volumus. sed tua experientia sive in hoc quod per libram amplius, sive in aliis minutis oneribus et quod ultra rationis aequitatem a rusticis accipitur, penset et omnia in summam pensionis redigat, ut, prout vires rusticorum portant pensionem integram et pensantem libram septuagenum binum persolvant; *P. Oxy.* 1915, lines 22-3. RECEIPT MEASURES: Greg. *Ep.* I. 42, valde autem iniustum et iniquum esse perspeximus, ut a rusticis ecclesiae de sextariaticis aliquid accipiatur, ut ad maiorem modium dare compellantur, quam in horreis ecclesiae infertur. unde praesenti admonitione praecipimus, ut plus quam decem et octo sextariorum modium numquam a rusticis ecclesiae frumenta debeant accipi: XIII. 37, Salerio siquidem cartulario nostro narrante cognovimus, quia modius ad quem coloni ecclesiae frumenta dare compellebantur viginti et quinque sextariorum inveneris; *P. Oxy.* 136, lines 27-9, προσομολογῶ δὲ λημματίσαι τῇ ὑμῶν ὑπερφυείᾳ ὑπὲρ παραμυθείας τοῦ παραλημπτικοῦ μέτρου τῶν ἀρταβῶν ἑκατὸν ἀρτάβας δέκα πέντε. CORN PRICES: Greg. *Ep.* I. 42 (cited in n. 80). COMMODA NUPTIARUM: Greg. *Ep.* I. 42, pervenit etiam ad nos, quod de nuptiis rusticorum immoderata commoda percipiantur. de quibus praecipimus, ut omne commodum nuptiarum unius solidi summam nullatenus excedat. si qui sunt pauperes etiam minus dare debent, si qui autem divites praefati solidi summam nullatenus transgrediantur. quod nuptiale commodum nullatenus volumus in nostra ratione redigi, sed utilitati conductorum proficere; cf. IX. 128, Petrus, quem defensorem fecimus, quia de massa iuris ecclesiae nostrae quae Iutelas dicitur oriundus sit, experientiae tuae bene est cognitum. et ideo quia ita circa eum benigni debemus existere, ut tamen ecclesiae utilitas non laedatur, hac tibi praeceptione mandamus, ut eum stricte debeas commonere ne filios suos quolibet ingenio vel excusatione foris alicubi in coniugio sociare praesumat, sed in ea massa, qua lege ex condicione ligati sunt, socientur. SERENUS'S CONTRACT: *P. Oxy.* 136, cf. 2239, where another agent pays 30 solidi λόγῳ εἰσβατικοῦ, receiving a salary of 6 solidi, 36 artabae of wheat and 24 of barley and 80 cnidia of wine καὶ πάσας τὰς συνηθείας ἃς εἴωθεν ὁ αὐτὸς ἐπικείμενος κατὰ τὸ ἔθος παρὰ τῶν γεωργῶν.

89. RENT RESTRICTION: *CJ* XI. l. 1, 325, quisquis colonus plus a domino exigitur, quam ante consueverat et quam in anterioribus temporibus exactus est, adeat iudicem, cuius primum poterit habere praesentiam, et facinus comprobet, ut ille, qui convincitur amplius postulare, quam accipere consueverat, hoc facere in posterum prohibeatur, prius reddito quod superexactione perpetrata noscitur extorsisse; 2 §4, 396, sed ut in causis civilibus huiusmodi hominum generi adversus dominos vel patronos et aditum intercludimus et vocem negamus exceptis superexactionibus, in quibus retro principes facultatem eis super hoc interpellandi praebuerunt, ita in criminum accusatione quae publica est non adimitur eis propter suam suorumque iniuriam experiendi licentia; cf. also XI. xlviii. 23 §2 (531–4), caveant autem possessionum domini, in quibus tales coloni constituti sunt, aliquam innovationem vel violentiam eis inferre. si enim hoc approbatum fuerit et per iudicem pronuntiatum, ipse provinciae moderator, in qua aliquid tale fuerit perpetratum, omnimodo provideat et laesionem, si qua subsecuta est, eis resarcire et veterem consuetudinem in reditibus praestandis eis observare. For the Paduan *fundi* see *P. Ital.* 3.

90. See above n. 2. RENTS OF FIVE ARTABAE: *PSI* 34, *P. Lond.* 1012, *Sb* 7167, *SPP* II, p. 33, *CPR* 41, *P. Jena*, 3; OF SEVEN: *P. Flor.* 320; OF SIX: *SPP* XX. 105, *BGU* 1092; OF FOUR: *P. Lips.* 19, 20. MONEY RENTS: *P. Lond.* 1006 (19½ carats), *Sb* 9461 (14½ carats), *P. Lond.* 1036 (13½ carats), *P. Oxy.* 1126 (13 carats), *Sb* 5139, *PER* 35 (9½ carats), *SPP* XX. 142 (3¼ carats).

91. *P. Oxy.* 1915.

92. AURELIUS SACAON: *P. Thead.* 6–9, 22–3, *P. Strassb.* 43. COLONI OF RES PRIVATA: *CTh* v. xvi. 34, 425. For Ampliatus and Celerinus see above n. 59. PETER: Greg. *Ep.* IX. 128 (cited in n. 88).

93. COLONI IN CIVIL SERVICE: Th. II, *Nov.* vii. 4 §2, 441, probari autem apparitores magisteriae potestatis neque curiales neque cohortales neque censibus volumus adscriptos, Val. III, *Nov.* xxvii pr. §1, 449, diuturno excubiarum labore perfunctis inpingi contumeliosam status conperimus quaestionem et, quos verecundiae adtestatione, natalium splendore conspicuos praeclara scriniorum officia probaverunt, naevo erubescendae obiectionis urgueri, emeritos aulicis honoribus viros trahi ad laqueos vilissimi colonatus. For the church see pp. 921–2.

94. COLONI OWNING STOCK: Greg. *Ep.* XIII. 37, et ideo volumus cum omni fide, omni puritate considerato timore omnipotentis Domini reducta ad memoriam districtione beati Petri apostoli per unamquamque massam colonos pauperes et indigentes experientiam tuam describere atque ex eis pecuniis quae in fraudibus sunt inventae vaccas, oves porcosque comparare et singulis colonis pauperioribus ea distribuere. For *coloni* owning slaves see above n. 36 (Remigius's will) and Greg. *Dial.* I. 1.

95. ITALIAN FAMINE: Amb. *Off.* III. 45 ff. In Ostrogothic Italy too a famine is remedied by the sale of corn from the local state granaries, Cass. *Var.* x. 27, quapropter industriosae Liguriae devotisque Venetis copia subtracta dicitur esse de campis, sed nunc nascatur in horreis, quia nimis impium est plenissimis cellis vacuos esurire cultores. atque ideo illustris magnitudo vestra . . . Liguribus, quos tamen indigere cognoscitis, tertiam portionem ex horreis Ticinensibus atque Dertonensibus per solidum viginti quinque modios distrahi censitote. Venetis autem ex Tarvisiano atque Tridentino horreis ad definitam

superius quantitatem item dari facite tertiam portionem, cf. XII. 27 (Datianus, bishop of Milan, requested to arrange the sale of the corn in Liguria). SYRIAN FAMINE: Lib. *Or.* XXVII. 6, 14. The same thing happened in an earlier famine in Syria in Julian's reign; Julian, *Misop.* 369D, καὶ οὐχ ἡ πόλις μόνον ἐπὶ τοῦτο συρρεῖ, οἱ πλεῖστοι δὲ καὶ ἐκ τῶν ἀγρῶν συντρέχουσιν, ὃ μόνον ἐστὶν εὑρεῖν πολὺ καὶ εὔωνον, ἄρτους ὠνούμενοι; he subsequently speaks of τὸν ὑπὸ τῶν πλουσίων ἀποκεκλεισμένον ἐν ταῖς ἀποθήκαις σῖτον.

96. MESOPOTAMIAN FAMINES: Pall. *Hist. Laus.* xl, Soz. III. 16, Josh. Styl. 39 ff.

97. TAX COLLECTORS: Theod. *Hist. Rel.* xvii, Amm. XXII. xvi. 23, erubescit apud eos si qui non infitiando tributa plurimas in corpore vibices ostendat. SOLDIERS: Lib. *Or.* XLV. 5. PRIVATE BUCELLARII: *CJ* IX. xii. 10, 468, *Chr.* I. 471, *P. Klein. Form.* 344, *P. Oxy.* 156, *PSI* 953, *BGU* 963. PRIVATE PRISONS: *CJ* IX. v. 1, 486, iubemus nemini penitus licere per Alexandrinam splendidissimam civitatem vel Aegyptiacam dioecesin aut quibuslibet imperii nostri provinciis vel in agris suis aut ubicumque domi privati carceris exercere custodiam; *PSI* 953. Cf. also E. R. Hardy, *op. cit.* 60–73.

98. CIRCUMCELLIONS: Aug. *Ep.* 108 §18, 185 §15, Opt. III. 4, cf. Aug. *Ep.* 58.

99. BACAUDAE: Aur. Victor, *Caes.* xxxix. 17, Eutrop. IX. 20, Pan. Lat. IX. 4, X. 4 (under Maximian), *Chron. Min.* I. 660 (435–7), *V. Germani*, 28, 40 (442), *Chron. Min.* II. 24–5, 27 (in Spain). The rebellion of 417 is inferred from Rut. Nam. *de red. suo*, I. 213–6. They were still active in Salvian's day (*Gub. Dei*, v. 24–6). For their courts see E. Thompson, *Past and Present* II (1952), 18–9.

100. PERTINAX: Herodian, II. iv. 6. AURELIAN AND CONSTANTINE: *CJ* XI. lix. 1, cum divus Aurelianus parens noster civitatum ordines pro desertis possessionibus iusserit conveniri et pro his fundis, qui invenire dominos non potuerunt quos praeceperamus, earundem possessionum triennii immunitate percepta de sollemnibus satisfacere, servato hoc tenore praecipimus, ut, si constiterit ad suscipiendas easdem possessiones ordines minus idoneos esse, eorundem agrorum onera possessionibus et territoriis dividantur.

101. IMPERIAL LANDS: *CTh* XI. i. 4, 337, si quis ab enfyteuticariis seu patrimoniali possessore privati iuris quippiam comparaverit, cuius substantia alias possessiones sustentare consueverat, et succisis quasi quarundam virium nervis reliqua lababuntur, earum possessionum onera subiturus est, quae penes distractores inutiles permanebunt; *CJ* XI. lix. 3, 364, quicumque deserta praedia meruerint sub certa immunitate, ad possessionem impetratorum non prius sinantur accedere, quam vel fideiussoribus idoneis periculo curialium datis vel fundis patrimonii sui maxime utilibus obligatis idonea cautione firmaverunt susceptam a se possessionem nullo detrimento publico relinquendam; lxii. 3, 365, quicumque possessiones ex emphyteutico iure susceperint, ea ad refundendum uti occasione non possunt, qua adserant desertas esse coepisse, tametsi rescripta per obreptionem meruerint; 5, 377, si qui a prioribus colonis vel emphyteuticariis destitutum patrimonialem fundum a peraequatore vel censitore susceperint, perpetuo eundem atque inconcusso iure possideant, nec quisquam secundus petitor accedat; lix. 5, 378, qui utilia rei publicae loca possident, permixtione facta etiam deserta suscipiant; 6, 383, ut quisque conductor fuerit inventus possessor fundi, qui ex publico vel templorum iure descendit, huic ager iungatur inutilior: *CTh* v. xiv. 30, 386, quicumque defectum fundum patrimonialem exercuerit instruxerit fertilem idoneumque praestiterit, salvo patrimoniali canone perpetuo ac privato iure defendat velut domesticum et

avita successione quaesitum sibi habeat, suis relinquat, neque eum aut promulgatione rescripti aut reverentia sacrae adnotationis quisquam a fructu impensi operis excludat. ceterum eos, qui opimas ac fertiles retinent terras aut etiamnunc sibi aestimant eligendas, pro defecta scilicet portione summam debiti praesentis iubemus implere: eos etiam, qui enfyteuticario nomine nec ad plenum idoneas nec omnimodis vacuas detinent, sic ex illis quoque, quae praesidio indigent, iustam ac debitam quantitatem debere suscipere, ut indulto temporis spatio post biennium decretum canonem solvendum esse meminerint. hi autem, qui proprio voluntatis adsensu nunc quod diximus elegissent neque sibi nunc opimum aliquid et conducibile vindicarent, sed tantum nuda et relicta susceperunt, triennii immunitate permissa debitum canonem inferant; CJ XI. lxii. 7, 386, quicumque ad emphyteusin fundorum patrimonialium vel rei publicae iussu nostri numinis venerit, is si redundantia fortunarum idoneus fuerit ad restituenda, quae desertis forte possessionibus requirentur, patrimonium suum publicis implicet nexibus. si vero minor facultatibus probabitur, datis fideiussoribus idoneis ad emphyteusin accedat; CTh v. xiv. 33, 393, 34, 394, qui fundos patrimoniales iure privato salvo canone susceperunt, hanc omnes sine ullius exceptione personae propositam intellegant optionem, ut aut ea loca, quibus minor est soli fecunditas, cum his, ex quibus fructus uberes capiunt, suscipere et tenere non abnuant, aut, si eorum refugiunt sterilitatem, opimioribus cedant; Th. II, Nov. xxvi §4, 444, verum et si quis ex auctoritate nostri numinis vel praeceptis amplissimae praefecturae de fundis patrimonialibus steriles sub certi canonis pollicitatione suscepit, firmiter eum volumus possidere sub eiusdem tantum canonis solutione, quem nostrae maiestatis auctoritas aut praeceptum magnificae tuae sedis per annos singulos solvendum esse praescripsit, nullamque eos discriptionem aut adiectionem aut innovationem in posterum sustinere, quoniam nimis absurdum est eos, qui nobis hortantibus aut magnifica praefectura fundos inopes atque ieiunos magno labore impenso aut exhausto patrimonio vix forte meliorare potuerint, utpote deceptos inopinatum onus suscipere illudque velut quadam circumventione deposci, quod si se daturos praescissent, fundos minime suscipere aut etiam colere paterentur.

102. VETERANS: CTh VII. xx. 11, 368, commoneat tua sinceritas hac sanctione veteranos, ut loca absenti⸱⸱m squalida et situ dissimulationis horrentia, de solida fructuum indemnitate securi, quantum vires uniuscuiusque patientur, exerceant. namque decernimus, ut his, qui soli relicti terras sulcaverint, sine molestia praeiudicioque dominorum proventuum emolumenta quaerantur nihilque illis, qui messium tempus adsolent aucupari, agratici nomine deferatur. GRANT OR SALE OF DESERTED LANDS: CTh v. xi. 8, 365, quicumque possidere loca ex desertis voluerint, triennii immunitate potiantur. qui vero ex desertis nonnihil agrorum sub certa professione perceperunt, si minorem modum professi sunt, quam ratio detentae possessionis postulat, usque ad triennium ex die latae legis in ea tantum possessione permaneant, quam ipsi sponte obtulerunt; exacto autem hoc tempore sciant ad integrae iugationis pensitationem se esse cogendos. itaque qui hoc sibi incommodum iudicarit, e vestigio restituat possessionem, cuius in futurum onera declinat; 9, 365 (cited in n. 104); 11, 386; CJ XI. lix. 8 (388–92), qui agros domin ocessante desertos vel longe positos vel in finitimis ad privatum pariter publicumque compendium excolere festinat, voluntati suae nostrum noverit adesse responsum: ita tamen, ut, si vacanti ac destituto solo novus cultor insederit, ac vetus dominus intra biennium eadem ad suum ius voluerit revocare, restitutis primitus quae expensa constiterit facultatem loci proprii consequatur. nam si biennii fuerit tempus emensum,

omni possessionis et dominii carebit iure qui siluit; 11, 405 (S), locorum domini intra sex menses edictis vocati revertantur. qui si adfuerint, et propria teneant et ea quae ex praeterito contraxerint debita redhibere cogantur. sin vero impares esse earum rerum tributis propria confitentur absentia nec adesse voluerint, penes eos, qui haec susceperint et certum quem tributorum canonem promittunt, proprietas possessionis intemerata permaneat, ut, postquam ea exsolverint, sciant sibi inquietudinem submovendam nec subreptione cuiusquam competitionis loca quae tenuerunt auferenda. quibus etiam illud indulsimus, ut ex eo tempore, ex quo primum loca de quibus agitur coeperint possidere, tributa poscantur; *CTh* XIII. xi. 13, 412, loca, quae praestationem suam implere non possunt, praecipimus adaequari, ut, quid praestare possint, mera fide et integra veritate scribatur, id vero quod impossibile est e vasariis publicis auferatur. et primo quidem veteribus dominis adscribi praedia ipsa conveniet, quorum si personae eorumve heredes non potuerint repperiri, vicinos vel peregrinos volentes, modo ut sint idonei, dominos statuendos esse censemus. in tantum autem omnium animos beneficiis provocamus, ut id, quod defectae possessioni inspectoris arbitrio adscribitur, biennii immunitate relevetur, ut nec idonea praedia alterius glebae sarcina in posterum praegraventur.

103. LAW SUIT AT CARANIS: *FIR* III². 101, *Sb* 8246. LEASES BY VILLAGES: *P. Gen.* 66–7, 69–70 (ἀπὸ ὀνομάτων ἀπόρων); cf. *Sb* 7675 (ἀπὸ τῶν διαφερόντων τῇ κώμῃ ἀπὸ ὀνόματος ᾿Ακελ Κασιανοῦ; the tenants pay the taxes but no rent). LEVIES FOR INSOLVENT NAMES: *Pap. Roll,* xiv. 8, *P. Thead.* 41. LEVY AT JERUSALEM: Cyr. Scyth. *V. Sabae,* 54, καὶ νῦν δυσωπούμεν ὑμας κουφίσαι τὴν ἐλευθεόπολιν περισσοπρακτίαν τῇ τε ἁγίᾳ ᾿Αναστάσει καὶ τοῖς τῆς ἁγίας πόλεως κτήτορσιν ἐκ τῶν ἀπόρων καὶ δυσπράκτων προσώπων. τίς δὲ ἡ αἰτία γέγονεν τῆς τοιαύτης περισσοπρακτίας, ἐρῶ. οἱ κατὰ καιρὸν τρακτευταὶ καὶ βίνδικες τῶν κατὰ Παλαιστίνην δημοσίων ἑκατὸν χρυσίου λίτρας ἐξ ἀπόρων προσώπων καὶ δυσπράκτων ἀνυσθῆναι μὴ δυναμένας εἰσπραττόμενοι ἠναγκάσθησαν ἐπιρρῖψαι τὴν τούτων εἴσπραξιν τοῖς κατὰ τὰ ῾Ιεροσόλυμα συντελεσταῖς κατ' ἀναλογίαν τῆς ἑκάστου δυνάμεως. Διαγραφή: Proc. *HA* xxiii. 17–21, τὰ δὲ τῶν διαγραφῶν ὡς συντομώτατα φράσαντι ἀπηλλάχθαι τῇδέ πῃ ἔχει. ζημίαις πολλαῖς ἄλλως τε καὶ ὑπὸ τοὺς χρόνους τούτους περιβάλλεσθαι τὰς πόλεις ἦν ἀνάγκη· . . . . ταύτας οἱ τὰ χωρία ἔχοντες ἀπέτινον, τίμημα κατατιθέντες κατὰ λόγον τῆς ἐγκειμένης ἑκάστῳ φορᾶς. οὐκ ἄχρι δὲ τούτων αὐτοῖς τὸ κακὸν ἔστη, ἀλλὰ καὶ τοῦ λοιμοῦ ξύμπασαν περιλαβόντος τήν τε ἄλλην οἰκουμένην καὶ οὐχ ἥκιστα τὴν τῶν ῾Ρωμαίων ἀρχήν, τῶν τε γεωργῶν ἀφανίσαντος μέρος τὸ πλεῖστον, καὶ ἀπ' αὐτοῦ ἐρήμων ὡς τὸ εἰκὸς τῶν χωρίων γεγενημένων, οὐδεμιᾷ φειδοῖ ἐχρήσατο ἐς τοὺς τούτων κυρίους. φόρον γὰρ τὸν ἐπέτειον οὔποτε ἀνίει πραττόμενος οὐχ ἥπερ ἑκάστῳ ἐπέβαλλε μόνον, ἀλλὰ καὶ γειτόνων τῶν ἀπολωλότων τὴν μοῖραν.

104. PERAEQUATIO OF A LANDLORD'S FARMS: *CTh* XIII. xi. 4, 393, qui fundum aliquem, velut afanticorum mole depressum, cupit aliquatenus relevari, omne nihilominus patrimonium suum admisso patiatur inspectore censeri. quod quidem etiam ad singularum civitatum legationes convenit custodiri, ut scilicet omne territorium censeatur, quotiens defectorum levamen exposcitur, ut squalida atque ieiuna in culta atque opima compensent; 15, 417, si qui aliarum possessionum dominus desertum praedium suum inspici forte voluerit, universa loca quae possidet etiamsi idonea sunt, peragrari patietur, ut sarcina destitutae possessionis, in quantum inspectio deprehenderit, possit melioribus sociari peraequatoque omni patrimonio nihil de desertis postea conqueratur. tantum enim his praediis aperta et absoluta levamenta praestamus, quorum aut domini omnino non extant aut paupertate mediocres ipsa tantum praedia habere monstrantur. HEIRS: *CTh* XI. i. 17 (= *CJ* XI. lix. 4), 371, heredes

scripti etiam pro minus idoneis fundis fiscale onus cogantur agnoscere, vel si renuntiandum hereditati putent, cedant his omnibus rebus, quas ex isdem bonis quocumque titulo et iure perceperint. PERAEQUATIO OF CITIES: *CTh* XIII. xi. 4, 393 (cited above), cf. 9, 398, qui per impotentiam fundos opimos ac fertiles occuparunt, cum quaestuosis uberibusque pro rata portione suscipiant infecundos. quoniam itaque legati Hieropolitanae civitatis succisos esse prosecuti sunt, huiusmodi possessionum retentatores cum opimis fundis et minus idoneos suscipiant, quo eiusmodi aequalitate servata et ante dictae curiae vires possint in posterum respirare et fisci indemnitas custodiri. For the allocation of estates by a *peraequator* see n. 105. ITALY IN 365: *CTh* v. xi. 9, 365, per Italiam afanticiae iugerationis onere consistentibus patrimoniis superfuso unumquemque tributarium adiectionem alieni debiti baiulare non dubium est; ideoque deserta iugatio, quae personis caret, hastis subiciatur, ut licitationis competitione futuros dominos sortiatur.

105. THE LAW OF 412: *CTh* XI. i. 31, possessor Africanus pro destitutis possessionibus cogitur tributa dependere. quod ne accidat, hac definitione sancimus nullum possessorem neque munificum praedium pro alienis debitis vel destitutione esse detinendum neque eorum praediorum depectione praegravari, quae ex isdem bonis, quae retinent, nequaquam esse monstrantur; XIII. xi. 13, loca, quae praestationem suam implere non possunt, praecipimus adaequari, ut, quid praestare possint, mera fide et integra veritate scribatur, id vero quod impossibile est e vasariis publicis auferatur. et primo quidem veteribus dominis adscribi praedia ipsa conveniet, quorum si personae eorumve heredes non potuerint repperiri, vicinos vel peregrinos volentes, modo ut sint idonei, dominos statuendos esse censemus. in tantum autem omnium animos beneficiis provocamus, ut id, quod defectae possessioni inspectoris arbitrio adscribitur, biennii immunitate relevetur, ut nec idonea praedia alterius glebae sarcina in posterum praegraventur. *Peraequatores* nevertheless still allocate deserted lands to outsiders in *CTh* VI. ii. 24, 417, si quis desertam possessionem sub peraequationis sorte perceperit, eum a praestatione glebae senatoriae, etiamsi antiquitus hoc onus fundum manebat, alienum esse praecepimus, XIII. xi. 16, 417, competitionis obreptione seclusa apud eum possessio firma permaneat, cui a peraequatore semel eam traditam fuisse constiterit . . . si quis vero privatus aut obligatam sibi possessionem, quae deserta huc usque permansit, aut ex aliquo titulo deberi sibi iure confirmat, allegationes suas sine mora vel per se vel per aliam personam legibus ordinatam apud spectabilitatem tuam publicare debebit, ita ut, si aequitatis ratione suadente ad petitorem fuerit translata possessio, is, qui eam a peraequatore susceperat, rei melioratae receptis sublevetur expensis . . . quod si quis eo tempore, quo peraequator praedium alicui addicit, de suo iure vel per se vel per homines suos non crediderit actitandum, duorum mensum curriculis evolutis in perpetuum conquiescat; perhaps the transfer was theoretically voluntary. THE EDICT OF DEMOSTHENES: Just. *Nov.* clxvi. GUARANTEE IN CONVEYANCES: *P. Cairo*, 67169. It was presumably to cover a possible ἐπιβολὴ ὁμοδούλων that in a transfer of tax liability following a conveyance (*P. Nessana*, 24) it was stipulated that if the purchaser defaulted, the vendor became liable *(ἐν μηδενὶ καταβλαπτομένου ἢ κλινομένου τοῦ δημοσίου λόγου· εἰ γὰρ ἀπορηθείη, ὅπερ μὴ γένοιτο, τὸ ἐκλαβὸν πρόσωπον, τὸν πρωτότυπον . . .).* Ἐπιβολὴ ὁμοκήνσων: *CJ* I. xxxiv. 2 (Anastasius), τὰ τῆς ἰδικῆς κτήσεως κτήματα . . . μὴ δεχέσθωσαν ἀπόρων ἢ ὁμοκήνσων ἐπιβολήν (as patrimonial estates acquired at all recently might well become liable to ἐπιβολὴ ὁμοδούλων arising from transactions some generations back, it seems likely that Anastasius would have exempted them from this burden also and that

ὁμοδούλων has fallen out before ἤ); Just. *Nov.* clxviii (an edict of Zoticus, praetorian prefect of the East under Anastasius; only fragments survive), τὰς τῶν ὁμοδούλων ἐπιφορὰς ὁ νόμος οἶδε καὶ τῶν ὁμοκήνσων; τινῶν μὲν ἀπὸ τῶν ὁμοκήνσων ἡ ζήτησις ἐπὶ τὰ ὁμόδουλα φέρεται καὶ οὕτως ἐπάγεται τοῖς ταῦτα κεκτημένοις, τινὰ δὲ ἀρχὴν παρὰ τῶν ὁμοδούλων λαμβάνει καὶ φέρεται ἐπὶ τὰ ὁμόκηνσα; Just. *Nov.* cxxviii §§7, 8, 545, εἴ ποτε δὲ συμβαίη ἐπιβολὴν οἱασδήποτε κτήσεως ὁμοδούλων ἢ ὁμοκήνσων γενέσθαι, ἐξ ἐκείνου τοῦ χρόνου κελεύομεν τὸν τὴν ἐπιβολὴν δεχόμενον ἀπαιτεῖσθαι ὑπὲρ αὐτῆς τὰ δημόσια, ἐξ οὗ παρεδόθη αὐτῷ ἡ ἐπιβαλλομένη κτῆσις; . . . εἴ ποτε δὲ συμβαίη δεσπότην οἱασδήποτε κτήσεως ἢ μὴ φαίνεσθαι ἢ πρὸς τὴν τῶν δημοσίων καταβολὴν μὴ ἀρκεῖν, ὥστε διὰ τοῦτο τὴν τῆς ἐπιβολῆς ἀνάγκην γενέσθαι, κελεύομεν παραχρῆμα ταύτην παραδίδοσθαι τοῖς ὁμόδουλα ἢ ὁμόκηνσα χωρία κεκτημένοις μετὰ πάντων τῶν ἐν αὐτῇ εὑρισκομένων γεωργῶν καὶ πεκουλίων αὐτῶν καὶ ἐνθηκῶν καὶ καρπῶν καὶ ζῴων καὶ πάντος ἄλλου instructov καὶ instrumentov τοῦ ἐκεῖσε εὑρισκομένου. The meaning of ὁμόκηνσα is never explained in our surviving sources, but etymologically it should mean property on the same census list, just as ὁμόδουλα means property under the same ownership. If the government could find no suitable owner of ὁμόδουλα, it is difficult to see what alternative it had except to allocate a deserted estate to a neighbouring landlord in the same census district, i.e. territory. From Justinian's Novel it is clear that the actual estate was allocated to a new owner, and that ἐπιβολὴ ὁμοκήνσων was not a synonym for ἐπιγραφή, whereby the tax burden of an abandoned estate was distributed among the owners of ὁμόκηνσα. Procopius complains bitterly about ἐπιβολή (*HA* xxiii. 15–6, τὸ δὲ τῆς ἐπιβολῆς ὄνομα ὄλεθρός τίς ἐστιν ἀπρόοπτος ἐξαπιναίως τοῖς τὰ χωρία κεκτημένοις ἐπιγενόμενος πρόρριζόν τε αὐτοῖς ἐκτρίβων τὴν τοῦ βίου ἐλπίδα. χωρίων γὰρ τὸ τέλος τῶν ἐρήμων τε καὶ ἀπόρων γεγενημένων, ὧν δὴ τοῖς τε κυρίοις καὶ τοῖς γεωργοῖς ἤδη τετύχηκεν ἢ παντάπασιν ἀπολωλέναι, ἢ γῆν πατρῴαν ἀπολιποῦσι τοῖς ἐγκειμένοις σφίσι διὰ ταῦτα κακοῖς τρύχεσθαι, οὐκ ἀπαξιοῦσιν ἐπιφέρειν τοῖς οὔπω διεφθαρμένοις παντάπασι).

106. *CTh* XI. i. 12, 365, quisquis ex desertis agris veluti vagos servos liberalitate nostra fuerit consecutus, pro fiscalibus pensitationibus ad integram glebae professionem, ex qua videlicet servi videantur manere, habeatur obnoxius. id etiam circa eos observari volumus, qui ex huiusmodi fundis servos ad possessiones suas transire permiserint; Just. *Nov.* xvii §14, 535, ἀλλὰ καὶ τοὺς εἰσδεχομένους ἀλλοτρίους γεωργοὺς οὕτω μισήσεις, οὕτως ἀναγκάσεις θᾶττον ἀποδοῦναι τοὺς ληφθέντας κακῶς, ὡς, εἰ μέχρι πολλοῦ μειναῖεν ἀπειθοῦντες, ἅπαν ὅσον ἄπορον τῆς ἐπαρχίας ἐστί, τοῦτο ταῖς ἐκείνων κτήσεσιν ἐπιθήσεις.

107. JUSTINIAN'S MANDATES: Just. *Nov.* cxxviii §§7–8, 545; for complaints under Justin II and Maurice see n. 112.

108. ANTIOCH: Julian, *Misop.* 370D–371A, γῆς κλήρους οἶμαι τρισχιλίους ἔφατε ἀσπόρους εἶναι καὶ ᾐτήσασθε λαβεῖν, λαβόντες δ' ἐνείμασθε πάντες οἱ μὴ δεόμενοι. τοῦτο ἐξετασθὲν ἀνεφάνη σαφῶς. ἀφελόμενος δ' αὐτοὺς ἐγὼ τῶν ἐχόντων οὐ δικαίως, καὶ πολυπραγμονήσας οὐδὲν ὑπὲρ τῶν ἔμπροσθεν, ὧν ἔσχον ἀτελεῖς, οὓς μάλιστα ἐχρῆν ὑποτελεῖς εἶναι, ταῖς βαρυτάταις ἔνειμα λειτουργίαις αὐτοὺς τῆς πόλεως. καὶ νῦν ἀτελεῖς ἔχουσιν οἱ καθ' ἕκαστον ὑμῖν ἐνιαυτὸν ἱπποτροφοῦντες γῆς κλήρους ἐγγὺς τρισχιλίους; the statement in 362C that Antioch was μυρίους κλήρους γῆς ἰδίας κεκτημένη must mean that the Antioch territory comprised 'countless' not 'ten thousand' *iuga*, for the much smaller city of Cyrrhus was assessed at 50,000 *iuga* of private land, and its total territory including imperial lands came to 62,000 *iuga* (Theod. *Ep.* (*PG*) 42, 47). FUNDI REI PUBLICAE IN ASIA: *FIR* I². 108, hac sane quia ratione plenissima, quot intra Asiam rei publicae iuga esse videantur cuiusque qualitatis quantumve annua praestatione dependant,

mansuetudo nostra instructa cognovit, offerendam experientiae tuae credidimus optionem, ut, si omnem hanc iugationem, quae est per omnem diffusa provinciam, id est sex milia septingenta triginta sex semis opima atque idonea iuga, quae praeter vinum (sic; an engraver's error for VIII M (octo milia) or some other figure) solidorum ad fixum semel canonem tria milia extrinsecus solidorum annua praestare referuntur, sed et septingenta tria deserta et iam defecta ac sterilia iuga, quae per illa, quae idonea diximus, sustinentur, suscipere propria praestatione non abnuis, petitis maiestas nostra consentiat. CAMPANIA: CTh XI. xxviii. 2, 395, quingenta viginti octo milia quadraginta duo iugera, quae Campania provincia iuxta inspectorum relationem et veterum monumenta chartarum in desertis et squalidis locis habere dinoscitur, isdem provincialibus concessimus et chartas superfluae discriptionis cremari censemus.

109. IMPERIAL LANDS IN AFRICA: CTh XI. xxviii. 13, 422, unde secundum fidem polyptychorum per provinciam proconsularem novem milia duas centurias iugera centum quadraginta unum in solvendo et quinque milia septingentas centurias iugera centum quadraginta quattuor semis in removendis, per provinciam vero Byzacenam in praestanda functione septem milia quadringentas sexaginta centurias iugera centum octoginta, septem milia sescentas quindecim vero centurias iugera tria semis in auferenda constat adscripta; Val. III, Nov. xxxiv §2, 451, igitur intra Numidiam provinciam ex desertis locis, de quibus, sicut celsitudinis tuae suggestio loquitur, nihil emolumenti accedit, honoratis et possessoribus, quos praediximus, XIII milia fere centuriarum sub quinque annorum vacatione concedimus. CYRRHUS: Theod. Ep. (PG) 42, τοῦτο τῆς χώρας τὸ μέτρον πέντε μὲν μυριάδας ἔχει ζυγῶν ἐλευθερικῶν, μύρια δὲ πρὸς τούτοις ἕτερα ταμιακά . . . . μυρίων γὰρ καὶ πεντακισχιλίων ζυγῶν ἐπὶ τοῦ μεγαλοπρεποῦς τῆς μνήμης Ἰσιδώρου χρυσοτελῶν γενομένων, οὐκ ἐνεγκόντες τὴν ζημίαν οἱ ἐκ τῆς κομητιανῆς τάξεως πράκτορες, ἀπωδύραντο μὲν πολλάκις, ἱκέτευσαν δὲ δι' ἀναφορῶν τὸν ὑψηλὸν ὑμῶν θρόνον, δισχιλίων αὐτοὺς καὶ πεντακοσίων ἀπόρων ἀπαλλάξαι ζυγῶν. καὶ προσέταξαν οἱ πρὸ τῆς ὑμετέρας μεγαλοφυΐας ταύτας πιστευθέντες τὰς ἡνίας, ἀπολυθῆναι μὲν τοῖς ἀθλίοις πολιτευομένοις τὴν ἄπορον ἰουγατίωνα, ἀντιδοθῆναι δὲ τοῖς κομητιανοῖς ἰσάριθμα ἕτερα; 47, τῷ ὄντι γὰρ βαρυτάτην μὲν ἀπογραφὴν ὑπὲρ πάσας τῆς ἐπαρχίας τὰς πόλεις ἡ ἡμετέρα πόλις ἐδέξατο· πάσης δὲ πόλεως κουφισθείσης, μεμένηκεν αὕτη μέχρι καὶ τήμερον ὑπὲρ ἓξ μυριάδων καὶ δισχιλίων εἰσφέρουσα ζυγῶν.

110. OWNERS RECLAIM AMELIORATED LAND: CTh VII. xx. 11, 368 (cited in n. 102), CJ XI. lix. 8 (388–92), qui agros domino cessante desertos vel longe positos vel in finitimis ad privatum pariter publicumque compendium excolere festinat, voluntati suae nostrum noverit adesse responsum: ita tamen, ut, si vacanti ac destituto solo novus cultor insederit, ac vetus dominus intra biennium eadem ad suum ius voluerit revocare, restitutis primitus quae expensa constiterit facultatem loci proprii consequatur. nam si biennii fuerit tempus emensum, omni possessionis et dominii carebit iure qui siluit. CIVITAS AEDUORUM: Pan. Lat. v. 6.

111. For the census lists see JRS XLIII (1953), 53–6.

112. RESTOCKING LAND WITH SLAVES: CTh V. xiii. 4, 368. COMPLAINTS OF AFRICAN LANDOWNERS: Just. II, Nov. vi, suggessit autem tua magnitudo, maximam partem possessorum Africanae provinciae precibus suis intimare desolatos agros remansisse, cum divina lex promulgata fuisset, constituens creatos ex libera matre et adscripticio marito liberos esse. LANDS OF THE CARALITAN CHURCH: Greg. Ep. IX. 203, dictum etiam nobis est, quod rustici possessionis eiusdem Caralitanae ecclesiae rura propria deserentes in privatorum

possessionibus culturam laboris adhibeant. ex qua re agitur ut possessiones ecclesiae proprio in aliis occupato cultore depereant atque ad tributa sua persolvenda idoneae non existant. It is perhaps significant that these complaints are made after the great plague, to which Procopius attributes the depopulation of estates and their consequent abandonment (*HA* xxiii. 20, οὐκ ἄχρι δὲ τούτων αὐτοῖς τὸ κακὸν ἔστη, ἀλλὰ καὶ τοῦ λοιμοῦ ξύμπασαν περιλαβόντος τήν τε ἄλλην οἰκουμένην καὶ οὐχ ἥκιστα τὴν τῶν Ῥωμαίων ἀρχήν, τῶν τε γεωργῶν ἀφανίσαντος μέρος τὸ πλεῖστον, καὶ ἀπ᾽ αὐτοῦ ἐρήμων ὡς τὸ εἰκὸς τῶν χωρίων γεγενημένων, οὐδεμιᾷ φειδοῖ ἐχρήσατο ἐς τοὺς τούτων κυρίους). For slaves and *coloni* left on deserted land, see n. 106.

113. OVERTAXATION: Lact. *Mort. Pers.* vii. 3, adeo maior esse coeperat numerus accipientium quam dantium, ut enormitate indictionum consumptis viribus colonorum, desererentur agri et culturae verterentur in silvam. CIVITAS AEDUORUM: Pan. Lat. v. 5–7. CARANIS: *FIR* III². 101, *Sb* 8246. ANTIOCH: Julian, *Misop.* 370D–71A.

114. For assessment systems see pp. 453-4.

115. TAX LIST OF ANTAEOPOLIS: *P. Cairo*, 67057, cf. Johnson and West, *Byzantine Egypt: economic studies*, 275 ff. and *JHS* LXXI (1951), 271–2.

116. LANDS OF RAVENNATE CHURCH: *P. Ital.* 2.

117. Symmachus's complaints that agriculture did not pay (*Ep.* I. 5, sed res familiaris inclinata a nobis usque quaque visenda est, non ut quaestuum summa ditescat, sed ut spes agri voluntariis dispendiis fulciatur. namque hic usus in nostram venit aetatem, ut rus, quod solebat alere, nunc alatur) need not be taken very seriously, seeing that he drew some 1500 lb. gold a year in rents (Olymp. 44). EGYPTIAN LAND PRICES: *PSI* 66 (1¼ *arurae* for 4 solidi), *Sb* 4661 (1 *arura* for 4 solidi), *SPP* xx. 121 (8 *arurae* for 40 solidi), *P. Cairo*, 67169 (1 *arura* for 6 solidi).

118. ITALIAN LAND PRICE: *P. Dip.* 114; cf. Columella, III. 3, for prices under the Principate.

119. SYRIAN VILLAGES: G. Tchalenko, *Villages antiques de la Syrie du nord*, Paris, 1953.

XXI. TRADE (p. 824)

1. STILICHO'S BLOCKADE: *CTh* VII. xvi. 1, 408, hostis publicus Stilicho novum atque insolitum reppererat, ut litora et portus crebris vallaret excubiis, ne cuiquam ex Oriente ad hanc imperii partem pateret accessus. huius iniquitate rei moti et ne rarior sit diversarum mercium commeatus, praecipimus hac sanctione, ut litorum desistat ac portuum perniciosa custodia et eundi ac redeundi libera sit facultas. Γαλλοδρόμοι: *V. Joh. Eleem.* 35. Σπανοδρόμοι: Pall. *Hist. Laus.* xiv. IMPORTS OF GAUL: Greg. Tur. *HF* v. 5 (papyrus, oil), VII. 29, *Glor. Conf.* 64 (wines), cf. Sid. Ap. *Carm.* xvii. 15 for wines of Gaza, Sarepta, Chios and Falerii in late fifth century Gaul. FOREIGN MERCHANTS IN SPAIN: *Lex Vis.* XI. iii. 2, 3, 4, cf. *V. SS. Patr. Emerit.* 5. Cf. also Jacob the Jew, who was instructed to visit Gaul as well as Africa (see below n. 105).

2. For the currency see pp. 438 ff. THE REPUTATION OF THE SOLIDUS: Cosmas Indicopleustes, II. 116A, cf. XI. 448CD. MEROVINGIAN SOLIDI: Greg. *Ep.* VI. 10, pergens auxiliante domino Deo nostro Iesu Christo ad patrimonium quod est in Galliis gubernandum volumus ut dilectio tua ex solidis quos acceperit vestimenta pauperum vel pueros Anglos, qui sint ab annis decem et septem vel decem et octo, ut in monasteriis dati Deo proficiant, comparet, quatenus solidi Galliarum, qui in terra nostra expendi non possunt, apud locum proprium utiliter expendantur.

3. For roads see *CTh* xv. iii. Bridges are specifically mentioned in XI. xvi. 15, 382, 18, 390, XV. i. 36, 397, XVI. ii. 40, 412, XV. iii. 6, 423, and harbours in *CJ* I. iv. 26 pr., X. xxx. 4 pr., 530, Just. *Nov.* xvii §4, 535. For maintenance of harbours see also Lib. *Or.* XI. 159, *CTh* x. xxiii. 1, 369 (Seleucia), *CTh* XIV. xxvii. 2, 436 (Alexandria).

4. For *vectigalia* see pp. 429–30. We know of a 5 per cent. *teloneum* at Rusicada and Chulla in Numidia (Val. III, *Nov.* xiii §1, 445), a *portorium* at Passala, a village of Mylasa (*IGC* 241), and a *dinummium vectigal* at Alexandria (*CTh* XIV. xxvii. 2, 436, perhaps identical with τὸν τοῦ ἐξαγωγίου τίτλον of Just. *Ed.* xiii §15). There was an imperial control station at Abydos, which Justinian converted into a customs station (*IGC* 4 = *OGI* 521, Proc. *HA* xxv. 3, 5, Agath. v. 12, Symeon Metaphr. *S. Demetrii Acta*, I. ix. 71). That maritime customs were levied at many ports is suggested by the immunity given to *navicularii* (*CTh* XIII. v. 5, 326, 17, 386, 23, 393, 24, 395) and the law forbidding illicit grants of immunity (*CTh* XI. xii. 3, 365). Octroi dues are suggested by *CTh* IV. xiii. 2, 321, universi provinciales pro his rebus, quas ad usum proprium vel ad fiscum inferunt vel exercendi ruris gratia revehunt, nullum vectigal a stationariis exigantur. ea vero, quae extra praedictas causas vel negotiationis gratia portantur, solitae praestationi subiugamus, and 3, 321, rusticanos usibus propriis vel culturae ruris necessaria revehentes vectigal exigi non sinimus: capitali poena proposita stationariis et urbanis militibus et Tertiis Augustanis, quorum avaritia id temptari firmatur. pro ceteris autem rebus, quas quaestus gratia comparant vendituri, solitum eos oportet vectigal agnoscere. The immunity granted to veterans probably applied to such dues (*CTh* VII. xx. 2, 326 (S), where *vectigalia* are coupled with market dues) as well as to *portoria* (*CTh* VII. xx. 9, 366).

5. SILIQUATICUM: Val. III, *Nov.* xv, 444–5, cf. Cass. *Var.* II. 4, 12, 26, 30, III. 25, IV. 19, V. 31.

6. MONOPOLIES: *CJ* IV. lix. 1, 473, 2, 483; *monopolium* is coupled with *siliquaticum* in Cass. *Var.* II. 4, 26, 30. ARMS MONOPOLY: Just. *Nov.* lxxxv, 539. SILK MONOPOLY: Proc. *HA* xxv. 13–26, cf. *Ec. Hist. Rev.* XIII (1960), 191–2; there was a regular imperial monopoly of raw silk imported from Persia (*CJ* IV. xl. 2 (383–92), comparandi serici a barbaris facultatem omnibus, sicut iam praeceptum est, praeter comitem commerciorum etiamnunc iubemus auferri; Just. *App.* v, χρὴ τὴν μέταξαν τοὺς κομμερκιαρίους πρὸς τοὺς βαρβάρους πραγματεύεσθαι ιε´ νομίσμασι τὴν λίτραν καὶ μεταπωλεῖν τοῖς μεταξαρίοις ἢ τοῖς ἄλλοις οὐ πλέον καθαρὰν δίχα σφηκώματος ἢ ἄλλης προσθήκης ἢ ῥύπου. εἰ δέ τις πρὸς βαρβάρους μὴ ὢν κομμερκιάριος πραγματεύσηταί τι καὶ μέταξαν ἐκεῖθεν ἀγάγῃ, δύναται αὐτὴν ἀφαιρεῖσθαι ὁ κομμερκιάριος, καὶ ὁ πραγματευσάμενος δημεύεται καὶ διηνεκῶς ἐξορίζεται. εἰ δὲ ὁ κομμερκιάριος ἢ ὁ μεταξάριος ὑπὲρ τὸ ῥηθὲν ποσὸν πωλήσῃ ἢ ἀγοράσῃ, ὁμοίως τιμωρεῖται) JUSTINIAN'S ALLEGED MONOPOLIES: Proc. *HA* xx. 1–5, xxvi. 18 ff.

7. For *octavae* see ch. XIII, n. 47. COMITES COMMERCIORUM: *Not. Dig. Or.* xiii. 6–9, *CJ* IV. xl. 2 (383–92) (cited in n. 6); cf. for *commerciarii, Princeton Exp. Syria*, 20, 562, ἀπὸ κομμερκιαρίου [γ]ε τὸν ἐν [Μεσο]ποταμίᾳ καὶ ἀπὸ τοῦ Κλύσ[ματος τ]ὸν ἐν Παλ[αισ]τίνῃ, Just. *App.* v. (cited in n. 6), Joh. Moschus, 186 (at Tyre). CLYSMA: *Itin. Hierosol. Petrus Diaconus*, 116, Clesma autem ipsa in ripa est, id est super mare, nam portus est ibi clausus qui intro castro ingreditur mare. qui portus mittit ad Indiam vel excipit venientes naves de India; alibi enim nusquam in Romano solo accessum habent naves de India nisi ibi. IOTABE: Malchus, 1, Theophanes, A.M. 5990. NISIBIS: Petr. Patr. 14. CALLINICUM: *CJ* IV. lxiii. 4, 409, mercatores tam imperio nostro quam Persarum regi subiectos ultra ea loca, in quibus foederis tempore cum memorata natione nobis convenit, nundinas exercere minime oportet, ne alieni regni, quod non convenit, scrutentur arcana. nullus igitur posthac imperio nostro subiectus ultra Nisibin Callinicum et Artaxata emendi sive vendendi species causa proficisci audeat nec praeter memoratas civitates cum Persa merces existimet commutandas; in 562 trade was confined to Nisibis on the Persian side and Dara on the Roman (Menander, 11). HIERON: Proc. *HA* xxv. 2, 4. THE DANUBE: Them. *Or.* x. 135C, *ILS* 775. PROHIBITED EXPORTS: *CJ* IV. xli. 1, 368 (S) (wine and oil), lxiii. 2, 374 (gold), xli. 2 (455–7), arms), *Totius Orbis Descr.* 22, has enim duas species, hoc est aeramen et ferrum, non licet hostibus dare; cf. for iron, Lib. *Or.* LIX. 66–7.

8. DIOCESAN GUILDS: *CTh* XIII. v. 7, 334 (Oriens and *Alexandrinus stolus*), 8, 336 (Hispaniae), 10, 364, ix. 3, 380, v. 36+37+ix. 6, 412 (Africa), v. 32, 409 (*Alexandrina* and *Carpathia classis*). MEMBERSHIP HEREDITARY AND ATTACHED TO LAND: *CTh* XIII. v. 1, 314, 3, 314 (S), si quis navicularius per obreptionem vel quacumque ratione immunitatem impetraverit, ad excusationem eum admitti nullo modo volumus. sed et si quis patrimonium naviculario muneri obnoxium possidet, licet altioris sit dignitatis, nihil ei honoris privilegia, in hac parte dumtaxat, opitulentur, sed sive pro solido sive pro portione huic muneri teneatur. nec enim aequum est, ut patrimonio huic functioni obnoxio excusato commune onus non omnes pro virili sustineant portione; vi. 1, 326, alienationes possessionum a naviculariis factas fugiendi muneris gratia praeiudicare vobis non sinimus. ideoque volumus, ut comparatores supra scriptarum possessionum interpellato praefecto annonae ad id obsequium compellantur, cui se obnoxios esse fecerunt; 2, 365, 4, 367, naviculariae facultates naviculario corpori reddantur, si bona rite retinentes subire eorum onera nolint, quorum possessione fruuntur. ceterum si sponte cognoscunt naviculariam functionem sine exceptione potioris vel cuiuscumque, bona ad se transmissa sine inquietudine possideant, cum pro rata ex parte debitis fungantur officiis; 6, 372, 7, 375, in his, quae navicularii vendunt, quoniam intercipere contractum emendi vendendique fas prohibet, emptor navicularii functionem pro modo portionis comparatae subeat, res enim oneri addicta est, non persona mercantis. neque navicularium ilico iubemus fieri eum, qui aliquid comparavit, sed eam partem quae empta est pro suo modo ac ratione esse munificam; v. 19, 390, 20, 392, 27, 397, vi. 8, 399. LIABILITY OF THE RES PRIVATA: *CTh* XIII. vi. 3, 370, sed et si est quidquam naviculario iuri obnoxium, quod domus nostrae proprietatem spectat, tolerare praecipimus navicularias functiones; 5, 367, domum etiam mansuetudinis nostrae in his, quae naviculario nomine obnoxia sunt, agnoscere praecipimus debitam functionem; OF THE CHURCH: Aug. *Serm.* 355 §5. LANDS RECLAIMED: *CTh* XIII. vi. 2, 365, 4, 367, 6, 372, etc. NO PRESCRIPTION: *CTh* XIII. vi. 3, 370, 5, 367 (except for 50 years, *CTh* XIII. vi. 10, 423). ENROLMENT OF NAVICULARII: *CTh* XIII. v. 14, 371.

9. FREIGHT: *CTh* XIII. v. 7, 334, et ad exemplum Alexandrini stoli quaternas in frumento centesimas consequantur ac praeterea per singula milia singulos solidos, ut his omnibus animati et nihil paene de suis facultatibus expendentes cura sua frequentent maritimos commeatus; cf. 36, 412, for *centesimae,* and *AE* 1947, 148-9, for Diocletian's tariff. In Justinian's time the rate was one solidus for 100 *artabae* (Just. *Ed.* xiii §8), that is 10 per cent. From Cass. *Var.* v. 35, ut, quia naucleri ducentos octoginta solidos in triticum et in naulis septingentos quinquaginta octo solidos accepisse perhibentur, si apud vos facti veritas innotescit, in summam ratione collecta, ab eis mille triginta octo solidorum quantitas inferatur, it appears that Theoderic paid the *navicularii* who brought corn from Spain to Italy partly in gold and partly in corn (here commuted to gold), but the rates cannot be calculated. PRIVILEGES: *CTh* XIII. v. 5, 326, navicularios omnes per orbem terrarum per omne aevum ab omnibus oneribus et muneribus, cuiuscumque fuerint loci vel dignitatis, securos vacuos immunesque esse praecipimus, sive decuriones sint sive plebei seu potioris alterius dignitatis, ut a conlationibus et omnibus oblationibus liberati integris patrimoniis navicularium munus exerceant; 7, 334, pro commoditate urbis, quam aeterno nomine iubente deo donavimus, haec vobis privilegia credidimus deferenda, ut navicularii omnes a civilibus muneribus et oneribus et obsequiis habeantur immunes et ne honores quidem civicos, ex quibus aliquod incommodum sentiant, subire cogantur. ab administratione etiam tutelae, sive legitimae sive eius, quam magistratus aut provinciae rectores iniungunt, habeantur immunes. et vacatione legis Iuliae et Papiae potiantur, ut etiam nullis intervenientibus liberis et viri ex testamento uxorum solidum capiant et ad uxores integra voluntas perveniat maritorum. de proprietate etiam vel hereditate vel qualibet alia civili causa pulsati ne ex rescripto quidem nostro ad extraordinarium iudicium evocentur, sed agentibus in suo foro respondeant; 16, 380; for immunity from customs see especially *CTh* XIII. v. 24, 395, ne qua causatio vectigalium nomine relinquatur, hoc observari decernimus, ut nulla omnino exactio naviculariis ingeratur, cum sibi rem gerere probabuntur, sed a praestatione vectigalium habeantur immunes. TAX REBATE: *CTh* XIII. v. 14, 371, excusandis videlicet pro denum milium modiorum luitione quinquagenis numero iugis in annonaria praestatione dumtaxat, ita ut vestes atque equi ceteraeque canonicae species ab indictione eadem non negentur. ad conficienda vero competentia navigia a provincialibus cunctis primitus materiae postulentur, reparationem deinceps per singulos annos isdem naviculariis ex concessa iugorum immunitate curaturis; cf. 32, 409, solaciis pro mercedula praestitis ex tributariae pensitationis immunitate vel ex eo, quod vocatur φιλικόν, nec non etiam aliis, quae tuae cognitionis limavit examen.

10. EXPEDITIONALES PORTUS: *CTh* XIII. ix. 2, 372, v. 35, 412; cf. Lib. *Or.* LIV. 47, ἡ ναῦς αὕτη τὴν σωτηρίαν ἔφερε καὶ βασιλεῖ καὶ στρατιώταις καὶ πόλεσι ταῖς ὑπὲρ ἄλλας. DATES OF SAILING: *CTh* XIII. ix. 3 §3, 380. TWO YEARS' GRACE: *CTh* XIII. v. 21, 392, 26, 396. LOSSES BY STORM: *CTh* XIII. ix. 1, 372, 2, 372, 3, 380, 4, 391, 5, 397, 6, 412. Cf. XIII. v. 32, 409.

11. STATUS OF NAVICULARII: *CTh* XIII. v. 5, 326, navicularios omnes per orbem terrarum per omne aevum ab omnibus oneribus et muneribus, cuiuscumque fuerint loci vel dignitatis, securos vacuos immunesque esse praecipimus, sive decuriones sint sive plebei seu potioris alterius dignitatis; 14, 371, et sunt corpora, de quibus navicularii ex indictione quinta decima constituendi sunt iuxta sacram iussionem ita: ex administratoribus ceterisque honorariis viris praeter eos, qui intra palatium sacrum versati sunt, de coetibus curialibus et

de veteribus idoneis naviculariis et de ordine primipilario. et de senatoria dignitate ut, si qui voluerint freti facultatibus, consortio naviculariorum congregentur; in P. Oxy. 87 a decurion is a *navicularius* (ναυκλήρου θαλαττίου ναυκληρίου). Libanius asks that one Megistus be enrolled ἐν τοῖς κομίζουσιν ἀπ' Αἰγύπτου σῖτον to avoid curial services (Ep. 705), and begged for an imperial office for his bastard son, who feared τά τε πλοῖα καὶ τὸν σῖτον καὶ τὴν θάλασσαν τάς τε ἐν τῷ βουλεύειν πληγάς (Ep. 959; the *curia* and the *navicularia functio* are presumably alternatives). There are other complaints about the imposition of σιτηγία in Or. LIV. 40–1, 47, Ep. 210, 349–50, 1414, 1496; of the persons concerned one, Julianus, was a *honoratus*, the others mostly of curial station (see W. Liebeschütz, Rhein. Mus. civ (1961), 242–56, who doubts if the letters all refer to the *navicularia functio*). In CTh XIII. ix. 2, 372, half the crew have to be produced in the investigation of a shipwreck, in law 3 of 380, the master and two or three sailors, or in case of total loss the *affectiones naviculariorum*, interpreted by CJ XI. vi. 3 as the children of the sailors or masters. In Paul. Ep. 49, the *navicularius* Secundinianus sends his ship from Sardinia to Rome, but does not sail on it himself. SLEEPING MEMBERS: CTh XIII. vi. 7, 375, neque navicularium ilico iubemus fieri eum, qui aliquid comparavit, sed eam partem quae empta est pro suo modo ac ratione esse munificam. nec enim totum patrimonium ad functionem navicularii muneris occupandum erit, quod habuerit qui rei exiguae mercator accessit, sed illa portio, quae ab initio navicularii fuit, ad pensionem huius functionis sola tenenda est, residuo patrimonio, quod ab hoc vinculo liberum est, otioso et immuni servando. domos vero, quarum cultu decus urbium potius quam fructus adquiritur, ubi a naviculariis veneunt, pro tanto modo ad hanc pensionem obligari placet, quantum habebant emolumentum, cum pecunia mutuarentur. The church of Hippo would, however, have had to run a ship and employ sailors to man it (Aug. Serm. 355 §5). CHARTER OF SHIPS: CTh XIII. vii. 1, 399, 2, 406, Th. II, Nov. viii, 439.

12. For the earlier history of the *navicularii* see Suetonius, *Claudius*, 18–9, Gaius, I. 32, Ulpian, III. 6, Tac. Ann. XIII. 51, and for their immunity from civic burdens Dig. L. ii. 9 §1, iv. 5, v. 3, vi. 1, 5 §§3–9, 13.

13. For the *caudicarii* and *lintriones* see pp. 698–9, 705. THEODERIC'S DROMONES: Cass. Var. IV. 15, v. 16–20; the boat service on the Po (Cass. Var. II. 31) already existed in 467 (Sid. Ap. Ep. I. 5, Ticini cursoriam (sic navigio nomen) escendi . . . Brixillum dein oppidum, dum succedenti Aemiliano nautae decedit Venetus remex, tantum, ut exiremus, intravimus, Ravennam paulo post cursu dexteriore subeuntes). NILE BOATS: P. Oxy. 1048, a list of river craft (λουσώρια and πλοῖα), with their cargoes of corn; two boats belong to a *clarissimus*, five to decurions, three to owners of unspecified rank. GUARANTEES: Chr. I. 434 (five ναυκληροκυβερνηταί and one κυβερνητὴς πλοίου καθολικῆς ἐκκλησίας), P. Oxy. 2347 (κυβερνητὴς of a private πλοῖον Ἑλληνικόν). RECEIPTS FOR CARGOES: P. Goodspeed, 14 (ναυκληροκυβερνητὴς πλοίου ἰδίου Ἑλληνικοῦ), P. Flor. 75 (ναυκληροκυβερνητὴς), P. Oxy. 1260 (κυβερνητὴς of a private πλοῖον Ἑλληνικόν), P. Amh. 138 (κυβερνητὴς πλοίου ταμιακοῦ), P. Cairo Preis. 34 (ναύκληρος πλοίου δημοσίου τῆς Μαξιμιανουπόλεως); cf. also Chr. I. 46 (κυβερνητὴς πλοίου δημοσίου).

14. There is a good account of the system in E. J. Holmberg, Zur Geschichte des Cursus Publicus (Upsala, 1933). CURSUS VELOX AND CLABULARIS: CTh VIII. v. 62, 401, usurpationem cursus publici penitus iussimus amputari, scilicet ut excepta magnitudine tua praesumendi velocis et clavularii cursus nullus habeat potestatem; Joh. Lydus, Mag. III. 61, νόμος ἄνωθεν ἐκράτησε πλατὺν

ἅμα καὶ ὀξὺν δρόμον ἐνιδρύσθαι ταῖς ἐπαρχίαις, ὧν ὁ μὲν πλατὺς ὀχήμασιν ἐχρῆτο, ὁ δὲ ὀξὺς ὑποζυγίοις ἵπποις· βεραίδους αὐτοὺς οἱ κρατοῦντες ὠνόμασαν, Mens. I. 31–2, κλαβουλάριος ὀχηματικός· κλάβον γὰρ τὸν οἴακα καλοῦσιν. βῆλωξ, ὀξύς, ὃς καὶ βεραιδαρικὸς ἔτι καὶ νῦν λέγεται. βεραίδους δὲ Ἰταλοῖς εἶναι δοκεῖ τοὺς ὑποζυγίους ἵππους . . . ὅπερ ἐστίν, ἕλκειν τὸ ὄχημα· ὅθεν καὶ δασύνουσι γράφοντες τὸ ῥαίδας ὄνομα ἐκ τοῦ ῥαδίως ἐπιρρήματος παρηγμένον· οἱ γὰρ βεραίδους τοὺς ῥαίδας ἐκτὸς λέγοντες σφόδρα πλανῶνται. The term *cursus velox* is also used in CJ x. xxiii. 3, 468; *cursus clabularis* in CTh VI. xxix. 5, 359, in his dumtaxat provinciis, in quibus cursus a provincialibus exhibetur, quoniam avaritiae occurri paene iam non potest, singulos solidos per singulas raedas, id est quas quadrigas vel flagella appellant, percipiatis per id tempus, quo curarum et cursus tuendi sollicitudinem sustinebitis. e cursu vero clavulari singulas angarias, in his scilicet stationibus, in quibus cursus est conlocatus, ad exhibendam humanitatem venientibus excusetis; VIII. v. 23, 26, 365, CJ XII. l. 22 (Leo); ὀξὺς δρόμος in *Proc. HA* xxx. 2, *Chr.* I. 405, 437, *P. Oxy.* 2115. I agree with Holmberg (*op. cit.* 60) that the *cursus velox* supplied not only riding and pack horses (*veredi* and *parhippi*), but also carriages and carts drawn by horses or mules, while the *cursus clabularis* handled only ox wagons (*angariae*). This is strongly suggested by *CTh* VI. xxix. 5 (cited above), and is supported by John Lydus (see above). John's definition of *veredi* is, however, inaccurate, for *veredi* were saddle horses and their use for pulling carts is forbidden in *CTh* VIII. v. 24, 365. Julian's definition of *parhippi* in *CTh* VIII. v. 14, 362, et quamquam, quid sit parhippus, et intellegere et discernere sit proclive, tamen, ne forte interpretatio depravata aliter hoc significet, sublimitas tua noscat parhippum eum videri et habendum esse, si quis usurpato uno vel duobus veredis, quos solos evectio continebit, alterum tertiumve extra ordinem commoveat, is apparently a laboured joke, for he himself (Julian, *Ep.* 20, 31, 76) and later emperors (*CTh* VIII. v. 29, 367, 49, 389) issued warrants which made express provision for *parhippi*, and in VIII. v. 22, 365, *parhippus* is equated with *avertarius* (baggage animal). TEAMS: *CTh* VIII. v. 8, 356, octo mulae iungantur ad raedam aestivo videlicet tempore, hiemali decem; birotis trinas sufficere iudicavimus. LOADS: *CTh* VIII. v. 8, 356 (S), statuimus raedae mille pondo tantummodo superponi, birotae ducenta, veredo triginta; non enim ampliora onera perpeti videntur; 17, 364, vehiculis nihil ultra mille librarum mensuram patiemur imponi, ita ut veredarii sat habeant, quod his triginta libras equis vehere concessimus; 28, 368, quod iam Gallis prodest, ad Illyricum etiam Italiaeque regiones convenit redundare, ut non amplius raeda quam mille pondo subvectet, angariae mille quingenta sufficiant, veredo ultra triginta nullus imponat; 30, 368, perspicue sanxeramus, ut in carpentis raedarum mensuram subditam nullus excederet, nemo amplius raedae quam mille pondo, angariae quam mille quingenta, veredo quam triginta auderet imponere; 47, 385, raedae mille librarum onus imponi debet, carro sescentarum nec amplius addito eo, ut aurum ceteraeque species largitionales non ad libidinem prosecutorum vel susceptorum, sed aptis oneri ac ponderi vehiculis deferantur . . . et quoniam veredorum quoque cura pari ratione tractanda est, sexaginta libras sella cum frenis, triginta quinque vero averta non transeat; Justinian's version of this law raises the limit for *veredi* to 60 lb., and allows this to be exceeded if the load is a *centenarium* sack of gold. Theoderic fixed a maximum of 100 lb. (Cass. *Var.* IV. 47, V. 5). TRANSPORT OF GOLD AND SILVER: *CTh* VIII. v. 47, 385, 48, 386, si aurum sacrarum largitionum vel argentum ad comitatum nostrum destinatur, una raeda quingentis auri libris, mille vero argenti, si vero privatarum, auri trecentis, quingentis vero argenti libris oneretur; this law also directs that henceforth ordinary clothing should be conveyed by ship or ox wagon, and only *delicatae vestes* for the use of the court carried by *raeda* (see n. 16); cf. also laws 18 and 20, 364, for transport by *carpentum* of *largitionales species*, and *CJ* xii. l. 23 (Anastasius), Proc. *HA* xxx. 2 (the *cursus velox* used for conveying taxes). EUSEBIUS'S SCRIPTURES: Eus. *V. Const.* iv. 36.

15. For the system of *evectiones* see p. 402. ISSUED TO THOSE INVITED TO COURT: Soc. i. 25 (Constantine to Arius), Julian, *Ep.* 12, 20, 31, 39, 76; TO BISHOPS FOR COUNCILS: Amm. xxi. xvi. 18, ut catervis antistitum iumentis publicis ultro citroque discurrentibus per synodos, quas appellant, dum ritum omnem ad suum trahere conantur arbitrium, rei vehiculariae succideret nervos; cf. the protest of the Eastern bishops at Sardica, cursusque ipse publicus attritus ad nihilum deducitur (*CSEL* lxv. 64); TO PROVINCIAL DELEGATIONS: *CTh* viii. v. 32, 371, xii. xii. 9, 382; TO THE HIGHEST OFFICES: *CTh* viii. v. 44, 384 (cf. Amm. xx. viii. 22, for the family of the praetorian prefect Florentius); TO PRIVATE PERSONS: Symm. *Ep.* i. 21, iv. 7, vii. 48, 105–6, ix. 22. MELANIA'S JOURNEY: *V. Mel.* 52.

16. TEAM: *CTh* viii. v. 11, 360 (cited below). LOAD: *CTh* viii. v. 30, 368 (cited in n. 14). USES OF THE WAGON POST: *CTh* viii. v. 16, 363, sane angariarum cursum submoveri non oportet propter publicas species, quae ad diversos portus deferuntur; 48, 386, lineae vel amictoria, quibus hactenus onerari raedae solebant, nec ulterius raedis, sed angariis vel navibus dirigantur et si alicubi repertae fuerint huiusmodi species, thensauris eius urbis, in qua deprehensae fuerint, deputentur, per angarias, ubi facultas fuerit, destinandae; reliquae vero delicatae vestes, sed et linteamen amictorum nostrorum usibus necessarium raedis sub mille librarum ponderatione mittantur; *CJ* xii. l, 22 (Leo), in transitu fortissimorum militum (quando nostra serenitas disposuerit ex aliis ad alia eos loca deduci, evectionesque animalium secundum consuetudinem a nostra fuerint aeternitate consecuti) et in armorum tam confectione quam translatione servata consuetudine, in profectione quin etiam legatorum; xi. x. 7 §1 (Leo), quotiens sane in translatione armorum angariae necessariae fuerint, sublimitas tua litteras ad eminentissimam iubeat dirigi praefecturam et numerum ei armorum et ex quo loco transferenda sunt indicare, ut continuo super praebendis angariis pro numero eorum quae transferuntur armorum praeceptione sua viros clarissimos provinciae moderatores conveniat, ut secundum missam a sublimitate tua notitiam naves vel angariae confestim de publico praebeantur; *CTh* viii. v. 11, 360, ne qua posthac legio amplius quam duas angarias et hoc eorum, si qui aegri sunt, causa usurpare conetur, cum ad destinata proficiscitur, ita tamen, ut pro singulis angariis bina tantum boum paria consequantur; Amm. xx. iv. 11, textu ad comitatum perlato lectoque Iulianus contemplans rationabiles querelas, cum familiis eos ad orientem proficisci praecepit, clabularis cursus facultate permissa; Maj. *Nov.* vii §13, 458, itaque provinciali iudici non solum faciendarum evectionum nulli tribuatur facultas, verum ne ipsi quidem, cum ad alteram pergere coeperit civitatem, plus quam unam sibi angariam et duos paraveredos alteramque angariam officio suo et paraveredos duos liceat postulare. USE BY PRIVATE PERSONS: *CTh* viii. v. 15, 363, mancipum cursus publici dispositio proconsulis forma teneatur, neque tamen sit cuiusquam tam insignis audacia, qui parangarias aut paraveredos in civitatibus ad canalem audeat commovere, quo minus marmora privatorum vehiculis provincialium transferantur, ne otiosis aedium cultibus provincialium patrimonia fortunaeque lacerentur; Symm. *Ep.* ix. 25, oro praeterea, ut equorum tractoriis, quas vir inlustris Theodorus emisit, con-

firmationem per epistulam praestes, ne mutato iudice beneficii lentescat auctoritas. *Tractoriae* are also mentioned in *CTh* VIII. v. 9, miranda sublimitas tua nullos evectioni dies addendos esse cognoscat nec passim raedarum tractorias vel evectiones birotum faciat; *CJ* XII. l. 22 §1 (Leo), tractorias videlicet animalium super memoratis causis nulli alii iudici, cuiuscumque sit dignitatis, nisi tuo tantummodo culmini faciendi licentiam patere decernimus; and two obscure laws in the title *CTh* VIII. vi, de tractoriis et stativis, from which it would appear that they were given to soldiers on discharge, presumably to convey their families and effects to their homes, and to those 'qui animalia atque equos sacro usui necessarios prosequuntur'. The document preserved in Opt. *App.* VIII is probably a *tractoria*. The word is used in Aug. *Ep.* 59 to denote a summons to an episcopal council.

17. The Antonine Itinerary and Bordeaux Itinerary are published in O. Cuntz, *Itineraria Romana*, I (Leipzig, 1929). Procopius (*HA* XXX. 3) says that there were from five to eight stations for a day's journey.

18. MAINTENANCE OF STATIONS: *CTh* VIII. v. 34, 377, nam ut stabula impensis publicis extruantur, contra rationem est, cum provincialium sumptu citius arbitremur et utilius adparanda; *CJ* XII. l. 7, 377, stabula autem ut impensis publicis extruantur, contra rationem est, cum provincialium sumptu, in quorum locis stabula constituta sunt, citius arbitremur apparanda et utilius tam publico quam his, quos stercus animalium pro suo solacio habere concedimus; cf. Symm. *Ep.* II. 27, sed licet publicae rei absolutione laeteris, volo te adversum incerta muniri, videlicet ut sub actorum confectione vel tuorum, si adhuc retines potestatem, vel vicariae praefecturae, quae tibi poscenti aequa non deerit, diligentiae tuae ratio digeratur, quae possit ostendere, quot numero animalia conlocaris, et quo apparatu instruxeris mansiones, et quantum in titulis fiscalibus exigendis tua cura promoverit. MANCIPES (EXHIBITIO CURSUS): *CTh* VIII. vii. 6 (326–54) (*primipilares*), 7, 356 (S) (*officiales*), iv. 7, 361 (*officiales rationalis*), 8, 364 (*officiales*), v. 23, 365, ad procurationem clavularii cursus eligendi sunt ex eo hominum genere, qui in provinciis codicillis comitivae et praesidatus aut rationum epistulis honorariis nixi ab omnium se civilium et publicorum officiorum ministerio removerunt, 26, 365, cursus mancipes clavularii ex quo genere hominum debeant ordinari, apertissima lege decrevimus. quorum si praedictae numerus functioni non potuerit occurrere, curiales ad hoc munus sunt vocandi, vii. 9, 366, qui de ordinariorum officiis iudicum vel amplitudinis tuae, exceptis his, qui cornicularii honore perfuncti sunt vel his, qui secundum legem purpuram nostram adorarunt, inter protectores domesticos vel scholares militant, ad eius, quod declinare temptaverunt, muneris functionem et ad necessitates constringantur mancipatus, v. 34, 377, iam vero mancipum non ab ordine nec a magistratibus accipienda videntur obsequia, sed ab officio proconsulari qui missione donantur, vel ex aliis officiis, quos idoneos atque emeritos esse constiterit. non enim improbabilis haec dispositio est, cum et in suburbicariis regionibus haec consuetudo servetur, 35, 378 (*militans* or *decurio*), 46, 385 (*officiales*), vii. 16, 385 (*officiales*), v. 51, 392 (*curiales*), vii. 19, 397 (*officiales* including *praefectiani*), iv. 23, 412 (*officiales*), *Chr.* I. 437 (a decurion nominated εἰς κονδουκτορίαν τοῦ ὀξέος δρόμου), P. Oxy. 2115, Φλάυιος Εὐλόγιος λογιστὴς ᾿Οξυρυγχίτου λογογράφῳ κονδουκτορίου τῆς αὐτῆς πόλεως χαίρειν. ἐπειδὴ ἐν τῷ ἐπιστάλματι τῶν κονδουκτόρων τοῦ ὀξέου δρόμου ἔνκιτοι καὶ ἡ ἐπονυμία τοῦ υἱοῦ Ζεφυρίου Παιανίου ὑπὲρ ἡμίσους στάβλου καὶ διε[. . .]. TERMS OF SERVICE: *CTh* VIII. v. 36, 381, mancipibus supra lustrale tempus cura non immineat mancipatus: nec intra triginta dies . . . amplius cuiquam

liceat ex mutatione discedere. quod si quis supra praescriptum numerum dierum ab statione, quam receperit, excesserit, capitali animadversione puniatur. idcirco enim quinquennio devoluto eos honorem perfectissimatus manere praecipimus omniumque aliarum necessitatum immunitate fovemus, ut tempus procurationis impositae sollerti fide et integritate succedant; cf. 42, 382, for the five years' tenure. For the duties of a *manceps* see *CTh* VIII. v. 23, 24, 365, 35, 378, 53, 395, 60, 400, VI. xxix. 9, 412. Cf. Greg. Naz. *Ep.* 126 (a plea for Nicobulus, who suffers from ill health and is unequal τῇ τοῦ δρόμου φροντίδι καὶ τῇ τῆς μονῆς προσεδρίᾳ).

9. NUMBER OF ANIMALS: Proc. *HA* xxx. 4, cf. *CTh* VIII. v. 35, 378, a nullo umquam oppido aut frequenti civitate, mansione denique atque vico uno die ultra quinque veredorum numerus moveatur . . . si tamen necessitas maior coegerit, super sollemnem numerum iubemus admitti quos aut sacras litteras ferre constiterit aut habere in evectionibus adnotatum, ut aliqua de causa instantius ire iubeantur, quod vel spectabilis viri officiorum magistri vel sinceritatis tuae litteris oportebit adscribi, ut exstet evidens causa, quae praescriptum legis excedat. in vehiculis etiam hac volumus ratione moderari, ne supra assium numero raeda moveatur; 40, 382, sane ut etiam agendi itineris possit esse moderatio, seni veredi, singulae etiam raedae per dies singulos dimittantur. REPARATIO CURSUS: *Pap. Roll,* I. 21–2, II. 18–9, IV. 24 payments εἰς λόγον ἀποτρίπτων κτηνῶν δημοσίων, II. 13, 17, IV. 22, *CTh* VIII. v. 34, 377, quia in omnibus aliis provinciis veredorum pars quarta reparatur, in proconsulari provincia tantum detur, quantum necessitas postulaverit et quidquid absumptum non fuerit, hoc nec pro debito habeatur nec a provincialibus postuletur. non dubitamus autem plus quam quartam ad reparationem necessariam non esse iumentorum; cf. 42, 382, reparationis conlatione ab officialium persona submota idoneos mancipes constitutos quinquennii tempus implere praecipimus.

20. FODDER: *CTh* VIII. v. 23, 365, qui viri et evectiones commeantium exactissima cura inspicere debebunt et animalibus alimenta, quae fiscus noster suggerit, ministrare; XI. i. 9, 365, tabulariorum fraudes se resecasse per suburbicarias regiones vir clarissimus Anatolius consularis missa relatione testatus est, quod pabula, quae hactenus ex eorum voluntate atque arbitrio ad mutationes mansionesque singulas animalibus cursui publico deputatis repente atque improvise solebant convehi, nunc in consilio ratione tractata pro longinquitate vel molestia itineris ab unoquoque oppido certo ac denuntiato tempore devehi ordinavit. quod iubemus, ut etiam per omnes Italiae regiones pari ratione servetur; VIII. v. 60, 400, animalia publica, dum longe maiore ac periniquo pretio pabula aestimantur, per mancipes atque apparitores aperte vexantur. ne id contingat, sublimitas tua disponat, ut neque pabula mutationibus desint neque provinciales ultra, quam iustitiae sinit ratio, praegraventur.

21. STAFF: *CTh* VIII. v. 31, 370, nec mulionibus nec carpentariis nec mulomedicis cursui publico deputatis mercedem a quoquam sinceritas tua siverit ministrari, cum iuxta publicam dispositionem annonas et vestem, quam isdem credimus posse sufficere, consequantur; 34 §1, 377, praeterea in singulis mutationibus arbitramur ternis veredis muliones singulos posse sufficere; 37, 382, 50, 390 (*hippocomi*), 53, 395 (*muliones*), 58, 398, si quis mulionem mutationibus deputatum vel sollicitatione vel receptione subtraxerit, per singula capita humana X libras argenti inferre cogatur. et ne sollicitatoribus et occultatoribus sit ullum in aliqua excusatione perfugium, nec mutari quemquam per compensationis simulationem vel absolvi sub aetatis aut debilitatis

alicuius obtentu licebit. ideoque iudex, qui sibi hoc vindicaverit ut servum publicum liberet, unam libram auri per homines singulos, officium quoque eius, si legem supprimendo consenserit, simili poena multetur. haec in futurum mansuetudo nostra constituit. in praeteritum autem hoc statuisse sufficiat, ut, si muliones publici repperti fuerint licet senes aut debiles, cum uxoribus suis et omni peculio atque agnatione retrahantur. *Hippocomi* are also mentioned in Proc. *HA* xxx. 4, *V. Hypat.* 97.

22. BLUDGEONS: *CTh* VIII. v. 2, 316. That *paraveredi* were an additional burden over and above the cost of post appears from *CTh* VIII. v. 64, 403, comperimus provinciales et pabula et pecuniam pro equorum cursualium sollemni ratione conferre et extrinsecus paraveredorum onere praegravari. provinciarum igitur rectores procurent, ne umquam cursus publicus veniat in querellam et occasio deceptionis curiales animalia indebita praestare compellat. The provision of *parangariae* and *paraveredi* was a *sordidum munus*, *CTh* XVI. ii. 10, 353, 14, 357, XI. xvi. 15, 382, 18, 390, VI. xxiii. 3, 432, 4, 437. They are also mentioned in *CTh* VIII. v. 3, 339 (S), 6, 354, 7, 360, 59, 400, 63, 401, Maj. *Nov.* vii §13, 458, *CJ* XII. l. 23 (Anastasius).

23. JULIAN AND SARDINIA: *CTh* VIII. v. 16, 363, in provincia Sardinia, in qua nulli paene discursus veredorum seu paraveredorum necessarii esse noscuntur, ne provincialium status subruatur, memoratum cursum penitus amputari oportere decernimus, quem maxime rustica plebs, id est pagi, contra publicum decus tolerarunt. excellens igitur auctoritas tua officio praesidali necessitatem tolerandae huiusmodi exhibitionis imponat, aut certe, si hoc existimant onerosum, suis animalibus uti debebunt, quotiens eos commeare per provinciam necessitas publica persuaserit. sane angariarum cursum submoveri non oportet propter publicas species, quae ad diversos portus deferuntur. proinde considerata rerum necessitate pro locorum situ atque itineris qualitate tantum numerum angariarum collocari oportere decernas, quantum necessarium esse adhibitae plenissime deliberationes suaserint. LEO AND ORIENS: *CJ* XII. I. 22, cursum clavularem ab omni Orientali tractu nec non ab his civitatibus aliarum regionum, quarum instructio tui culminis meminit, tolli amputarique decernimus, ita tamen, ut in transitu fortissimorum militum (quando nostra serenitas disposuerit ex aliis ad alia eos loca deduci, evectionesque animalium secundum consuetudinem a nostra fuerint aeternitate consecuti) et in armorum tam confectione quam translatione servata consuetudine, in profectione quin etiam legatorum animalium dominis, qui ea solent accepta mercede locare, praebenda pensio arcae tui culminis imputetur. JUSTINIAN: Proc. *HA* xxx. 1-11, Joh. Lydus, *Mag.* III. 61. Procopius states that throughout the East, except on the road to the Persian frontier, the number of stations was reduced to one per day's journey (there having previously been from five to eight). John says that the *cursus velox* was entirely abolished in Asiana (through which the strategic road did not pass).

24. BASTAGAE: *Not. Dig. Or.* xiii. 19, xiv. 5, *Occ.* xi. 78-85, xii. 28-9. REPLACE-MENT OF ANIMALS: *CTh* x. xx. 4, 368 (= *CJ* XI. viii. 4), quod ad praesens remedium pertinet, decimum (*CJ* 'quintum') animal bastagariis pro reparatione praebeatur. STATUS OF BASTAGARII: *CTh* x. xx. 11, 384 (= *CJ* XI. viii. 8), aeternam fiximus legem, ne umquam bastagariis militiam vel suam deserere liceat vel aliam, antequam eam impleverint, subreptiva impetratione temptare.

25. FABRICAE: *Not. Dig. Or.* xi. 18-39, *Occ.* ix. 16-39. BARBARICARII: *Not. Dig. Occ.* xi. 74-77; in *Not. Dig. Or.* xi. 45-9, the four *subadiuvae* who con-

trolled the *barbaricarii* of Oriens, Asiana, Pontica and Thrace with Illyricum are recorded (cf. also *CJ* XII. xx. 5 (Leo), in unoquoque scrinio fabricarum et barbar<icari>orum), but no list of factories is given. *CTh* x. xxii. 1, 374, mentions the factories of Antioch and Constantinople, and shows that they were then under the *CSL*. For the control of the *Ppo, mag. off.* and *CSL* see ch. XII, n. 8.

26. FABRICENSES: Cass. *Var.* VII. 19, formula ad praefectum praetorio de armorum factoribus, Just. *Nov.* lxxxv §3, 539, ut per sacrum nostrum rescriptum in illis statuantur locis in quibus sunt publicae fabricae, quatenus ipsi operantes arma et de fisco annonas accipiant; *CTh* x. xxii. 4, 398, stigmata, hoc est nota publica, fabricensium brachiis ad imitationem tironum infligatur, ut hoc modo saltem possint latitantes agnosci; VII. xx. 10, 369, *ILS* 699, *CIL* v. 8721, VI. 1696, Amm. XXIX. iii. 4 (*praepositus fabricae*); Amm. XIV. vii. 18, ix. 4, XV. v. 9 (*tribunus fabricae*); *CTh* x. xxii. 3, 390 (*primicerius fabricae*); *CIL* v. 8754, 8757 (*biarchus fabricensis*). HEREDITARY: *CTh* x. xxii. 4, 398. DECURIONS FORBIDDEN TO SERVE: *CTh* XII. i. 37, 344, 81, 380, x. xxii. 6, 412. FABRICENSES AS CONDUCTORES: *CTh* x. xxii. 5, 404, *CJ* XI. x. 7 (Leo). JOINT RESPONSIBILITY: Th. II, *Nov.* vi, 438, fabricensium corpus invenit necessitas dura bellorum, quod immortalitatis genere principum scita custodit, ne deficiente principio successus generis laberetur: hoc enim armat, hoc nostrum ornat exercitum. hinc iure provisum est artibus eos propriis inservire, ut exhausti laboribus immoriantur cum subole professioni cui nati sunt. denique quod ab uno committitur, totius delinquitur periculo numeri, ut constricti nominationibus suis sociorum actibus quandam speculam gerant, et unius damnum ad omnium transit dispendium. universi itaque velut in corpore uniformi uni decoctioni, si ita res tulerit, respondere coguntur.

27. SUPPLY OF METAL: *CTh* x. xxii. 2, 388, omnibus fabricis non pecunias pro speciebus, sed ipsas species sine dilatione inferri, in perpetuum servanda hac forma praecipimus, ut venae nobilis et quae facile deducatur ignibus seu liquescat ferri materies praebeatur, quo promptius adempta fraudibus facultate commodo publico consulatur; Claudian, *de Bello Getico*, 535–9, at nunc Illyrici postquam mihi tradita iura meque suum fecere ducem, tot tela, tot enses, tot galeas multo Thracum sudore parari inque meos usus vectigal vertere ferri oppida legitimo iussu Romana coegi; for the *scrinium armorum* see ch. XIII n. 96. SUPPLY OF CHARCOAL: *CTh* XI. xvi. 15, 382, 18, 390, carbonis ab eo inlatio non cogetur, nisi vel monetalis cusio vel antiquo more necessaria fabricatio poscit armorum. VALENTINIAN AND THE PRAEPOSITUS: Amm. XXIX. iii. 4. WORKING RATE: *CTh* x. xxii. 1, 374, cum senae per tricenos dies ex aere tam apud Antiochiam quam apud Constantinopolim a singulis barbaricariis cassides, sed et bucculae tegerentur, octo vero apud Antiochiam cassidas totidemque bucculas per dies triginta et tegerent argento et deaurarent, apud Constantinopolim autem tres solas, statuimus, ut Constantinopoli quoque non octonas singuli cassidas per tricenos dies, sed senas sic pari numero bucculamrum auro argentoque condecorent.

28. HADRIANOPOLIS: Ath. *Hist. Ar.* 18, Amm. XXXI. vi. 2. CAESAREA: Greg. Naz. *Or.* XLIII. 57.

29. LINYPHIA, ETC.: *Not. Dig. Occ.* xi. 45, 73, xii. 26–7, *SEG* XVI. 417 (Heraclea), Soz. v. 15 (Cyzicus), Greg. Naz. *Or.* XLIII. 57 (Caesarea), Amm. XIV. ix. 7, *Itin. Hier. Antoninus*, 2 (Tyre), *CTh* x. xx. 8, 374 (Scythopolis), 18, 436 (bafia Foenices), Lib. *Ep.* 1362 (Cyprus); for *baphia* and *gynaecia* of the *res privata*

see also *CTh* I. xxxii. I, 333. CALCARIENSES: *CTh* XII. i. 37, 344, hoc et in calcariensibus et fabricensibus et argentariis observetur, ut, quicumque obnoxii officiis vel muneribus civilibus ex supra dictis fabricis fuerint, curiae restituti nec impetrato rescripto liberentur.

30. PROCURATORES: *Not. Dig. Occ.* xi. 45–73, xii. 26–7, *CTh* I. xxxii. I, 333, 3, 377, *CJ* XI. viii. 14, 426. WORKERS: Eus. *V. Const.* II. 34 (enslaved Christians), *CTh* x. xx. 2, 357 (S), 9, 380 (*mancipia*), 5, 371, 7, 372 (*familiae*), 3, 365 (SC. Claudianum, cf. 10, 379, on the *monetarii*); they appear as a hereditary caste in *CTh* x. xx. 15, 425, 16, 426, 17, 427. MURILEGULI: *CTh* x. xx. 14, 424 (*dignitates*); Just. *Nov.* xxxviii §6, 535 (*curiales*).

31. CYZICUS: Soz. v. 15. CAESAREA: Greg. Naz. *Or.* XLIII. 57. For the quota system see Soz. loc. cit., τῶν δημοσίων ἐριουργῶν καὶ τῶν τεχνιτῶν τοῦ νομίσματος· οἳ πλῆθος ὄντες, καὶ εἰς δύο τάγματα πολυάνθρωπα διακεκριμένοι, ἐκ προστάγματος τῶν πρὶν βασιλέων ἅμα γυναιξὶ καὶ οἰκείοις ἀνὰ τὴν Κύζικον διέτριβον, ἔτους ἑκάστου ῥητὴν ἀποφορὰν τῷ δημοσίῳ κατατιθέντες, οἱ μὲν στρατιωτικῶν χλαμύδων, οἱ δὲ νεουργῶν νομισμάτων.

32. LEVIES OF WOOL AND FLAX ON VILLAGES: *P. Thead.* 34, 37, *P. Hibeh*, 219, cf. *Sb* 7756, *P. Oxy.* 1428, 2154. LEVIES ON CORPORATI: *CTh* x. xx. 8, 374, XI. i. 24, 395. MURILEGULI: *CTh* x. xx. 14, 424.

33. *CTh* VII. vi. 5, 423, militaris adaeratio vestis a conlatoribus exigatur sacratissimis videlicet largitionibus inferenda, ita ut quinque eius partes fortissimis militibus erogentur in pretio, sexta vero portio a gynaeceariis clementiae nostrae absque ulla vel ipsorum vel publica incommoditate pro eadem contextione suscepta iunioribus gregariisque militibus in ipsa, quam maxime eos desiderare constitit, specie praebeatur.

34. MARBLE: *CTh* x. xix. 1, 320, 2, 363, 8, 376, 10, 382, 11, 384, 13, 393. THE THREE GREAT STATE QUARRIES: *CTh* XI. xxviii. 9, 414, 11, 416. CONVICT LABOUR: Eus. *Mart. Pal.* 8, 9, Just. *Nov.* xxii §8, 535. CORVÉES: *Chr.* I. 391, *P. Thead.* 34–6, *Sb* 2267, *SPP* xx. 76, *P. Lips.* 85–6.

35. CONVICTS: Eus. *Mart. Pal.* 7, 13. OBLIGATIONS OF METALLARII: *CTh* x. xix. 3, 365, perpensa deliberatione duximus sanciendum, ut, quicumque exercitium metallorum vellet adfluere, is labore proprio et sibi et rei publicae commoda compararet. itaque si qui sponte confluxerint, eos laudabilitas tua octonos scripulos in balluca cogat exsolvere; quidquid autem amplius colligere potuerint, fisco potissimum distrahant, a quo competentia ex largitionibus nostris pretia suscipient; 4, 367, ob metallicum canonem, in quo propria consuetudo retinenda est, quattuordecim uncias ballucae pro singulis libris constat inferri; 12, 392, per annos singulos septeni per hominem scripuli largitionibus inferantur ab aurilegulis non solum in Pontica dioecesi, verum etiam in Asiana. HUNT FOR MINERS: *CTh* x. xix. 5, 369, 6, 369, 7, 370, 9, 378, 15, 424; all these laws presume that *metallarii* were bound to their *origo*, and the last deals with their children. THRACIAN MINERS AND THE GOTHS: Amm. XXXI. vi. 6.

36. COMES METALLORUM: *Not. Dig. Or.* xiii. 11. PROCURATORES METALLORUM: *CTh* I. xxxii. 5, 386, cum procuratores metallorum intra Macedoniam Daciam Mediterraneam Moesiam seu Dardaniam soliti ex curialibus ordinari, per quos sollemnis profligetur exactio, simulato hostili metu huic se necessitati sub-

traxerint, ad implendum munus retrahantur ac nulli deinceps licentia laxetur prius indebitas expetere dignitates, quam subeundam procurationem fideli sollertique exactione compleverint. METALLICA LOCA: *CTh* x. xix. 15, 424, qui vero metallica loca praedictae obnoxia functioni emisse perhibentur, isdem procul dubio, quae auctores eorum implere consueverant, muniis subiacebunt. nam de his, qui ad census annonarios transierunt, observandum est, ut illi, qui ante quinquennium tantummodo nexibus privatorum videntur impliciti, sine dubio ad originem propriam redire cogantur, ex aequo cum publicis fundis eorum subole dividenda et unico filio metallariorum origini vindicando, omni tamen ceteris in futurum huiuscemodi licentia arte praeclusa.

37. LEVY OF IRON: Basil, *Ep.* 110, ἐλεεινῇ ἀγροικίᾳ τὴν σωτηρίαν χαρίσασθαι, καὶ τοῖς τὸν Ταῦρον οἰκοῦσι τὸν σιδηροφόρον φορητὴν προστάξαι γενέσθαι τὴν τοῦ σιδήρου συντέλειαν. LEVY OF COPPER: *CTh* XI. i. 23, 393, aerariae praestationis adiectio, quam citra priscam consuetudinem provincialium umeris Tatianus inposuit, a cunctis penitus salubri moderatione removenda est; xxi. 2, 396, aeris pretia, quae a provincialibus postulantur, ita exigi volumus, ut pro viginti quinque libris aeris solidus a possessore reddatur; 3, 424, perpetuo sancimus generalique decreto, ne cui deinceps ex praecepto comitivae sedis vel per oraculum sacrum vel per divinas adnotationes numinis nostri in nummo vel in specie, nisi ita publica necessitas postularit, propria liceat tributa persolvere, sed ut magis aut ipsam speciem, si hoc usus exegerit, aut aurum, quod aestimatio certa constituit pro centenario aeris, huiusmodi possessor exsolvat. AURARIA AERARIA ATQUE FERRARIA PRAESTATIO: *CTh* XI. xx. 6, 430.

38. LEVIES AND CORVÉES FOR PUBLIC WORKS: *CTh* XI. xvi. 15, 382, 18, 390, operas atque artifices non praebebit; excoquendae ab eo calcis sollicitudo cessabit; non conferendis tabulatis obnoxia, non lignis, indultam quoque materiem sub eadem exceptione numerabit.

39. Lact. *Mort. Pers.* xxxi. 5, quid vestis omnis generis? quid aurum? quid argentum? nonne haec necesse est ex venditis fructibus comparari? unde igitur haec, o dementissime tyranne, praestabo, cum omnes fructus auferas?

40. For commutation of taxes and payments, and for *coemptio* see pp. 460–1.
COEMPTIO FROM MERCHANTS: *CJ* x. xxvii. 2, §§10–11 (Anastasius), ἐν ἐκείνῃ τοίνυν τῇ διοικήσει ἡ μέχρι σήμερον κρατείτω συνήθεια, ὑποκειμένων καὶ τῶν ἐμπόρων τῇ συνηθείᾳ, πρότερον μέντοι καὶ τοῖς συντελεσταῖς καὶ τοῖς ἐμπόροις καταβαλλομένου τοῦ τῆς συνωνῆς χρυσίου ἐν εὐστάθμοις νομίσμασι καὶ ὀβρύζοις, καὶ οὕτως αὐτῶν ἀπαιτουμένων ἀδιαστρόφως καὶ ἀζημίως τὸ εἶδος εἰσφέρειν, τοῦ δὲ ταῦτα παραβαίνοντος τοῖς αὐτοῖς ἐπιτιμίοις ὑποκειμένου. βέλτιον γὰρ ἀντὶ τῆς ἰδιωτικῆς ἐμπορείας μᾶλλον τοῖς στρατιώταις καὶ τοὺς ἐμπόρους χορηγεῖν τὰς ἀναγκαίας αὐτῶν ἀποτροφάς; Just. *App.* vii §26, 554, ut per negotiatores coemptiones fiant. super haec cognovimus, Calabriae vel Apuliae provinciae possessoribus pro coemptionibus non inferendis superindicticium titulum impositum esse pro unaquaque millena; unde coemptiones per negotiatores annis singulis exerceri, in praesenti vero negotiatoribus specierum coemptiones recusare temptantibus tam superindicticium titulum quam coemptionis onus provinciae possessoribus imminere; cum abunde mercatores sint, per quos possit exerceri coemptio, sancimus magnitudine tua haec examinante, si possibile sit per negotiatores species comparatas inferri, collatores provinciae nullatenus praegravari, cum superindicticio titulo semel eis imposito coemptionis etiam onus inferre sit impossibile.

41. ROMAN SENATORS: Olymp. 44. LAURICIUS: *P. Ital.* I. CHURCH OF RAVENNA: *P. Ital.* 3; the document appears to belong to the archives of the Ravennate church. For allocation of these *excepta* to the bishop see Agnellus, *Lib. Pont. Eccl. Rav.* 60. GREGORY'S SUPPLIES OF CORN: Greg. *Ep.* I. 42, cf. I. 70, where the *rector* of the Sicilian patrimony is directed to buy corn from outside as well. GREGORY'S SUPPLIES OF TIMBER: Greg. *Ep.* IX. 124–7. BERTRAM: Pardessus, *Diplomata chartae epistolae leges ad res Gallo-Francicas spectantia,* no. 230. SHIPS OF ALEXANDRIAN CHURCH: *Chr.* I. 434 (a Nile boat), *V. Joh. Eleem.* 10, 28 (sea-going ships); Gregory in *Ep.* I. 70 speaks of sending a ship to Sicily, and instructs the *rector* of the Sicilian patrimony to protect 'naves . . . quae commendatae ecclesiae sanctae semper fuerunt'.

42. LAND TRANSPORT CHARGES: *Ed. Diocl.* xvii. 3–5, cf. i. 1, for the price of wheat, and Pliny, *Hist. Nat.* XVIII. 66 for its weight. Camels, it may be noted, were used even in western Europe; see Ennod. *Ep.* v. 13 for Ostrogothic Italy and Greg. Tur. *HF* VII. 35 for Merovingian Gaul. SEA TRANSPORT CHARGES: *AE* 1947, 148–9.

43. POSTUMIANUS: Sulp. Sev. *Dial.* I. 1, 3, 6. GREGORY: Greg. Naz. *de vita sua,* 124 ff. MARK: *V. Porph.* 6, 26–7, 34, 37, 55, 57.

44. Syn. *Ep.* 4.

45. Veg. IV. 39, cf. the dates given to *navicularii* in *CTh* XIII. ix. 3, 380 (1 April to 15 October). The fact that even imperial messengers did not cross from Italy to Africa during the winter months (see p. 403) shows that the seas really were closed. For the disasters which befell a cornship compelled to sail from Sardinia to Rome in winter see Paul. *Ep.* 49.

46. CORNSHIPS: Th. II, *Nov.* viii, 439 (2000 *modii*), Gaius, I. 32 (10,000 *modii* under Claudius), cf. *CTh* XIII. v. 14, 371, where the unit for remission of tax to *navicularii* is 10,000 *modii*. BELISARIUS'S FLEET: Proc. *BV* I. xi. 13. ALEXANDRIAN SHIP: *V. Joh. Eleem.* 10. For the two largest ships see Joh. Moschus, 83, 190. For ancient ships see L. Casson, *TAPA* LXXXI (1950), 43–56, LXXXII (1951), 136–48.

47. THE RHINE ARMY SUPPLIED FROM BRITAIN: Amm. XVIII. ii. 3, horrea quinetiam exstrueret pro incensis ubi condi posset annona a Britannis sueta conferri, Zos. III. 5, Julian, *Ep. Ath.* 279D, Eunap. 12, Lib. *Or.* XVIII. 83. QUAESTOR EXERCITUS: Just. *Nov.* xli, 536. THE UPPER DANUBE: *Not. Dig. Occ.* XXXV. 21–2, praefectus legionis tertiae Italicae transvectioni specierum deputatae, *CTh* XI. xvi. 15, 382, exceptis his quibus ex more Raeticus limes includitur vel expeditionis Illyricae pro necessitate vel tempore utilitas adiuvatur, 18, 390.

48. PRICE OF WHEAT AT ANTIOCH: Julian, *Misop.* 369D; see pp. 445–6 for other prices. JULIAN'S IMPORTS: Julian, *Misop.* 369AB. CAESAREA: Greg. Naz. *Or.* XLIII, 34–5. For civic σιτωνία see p. 735.

49. Proc. *HA* xxx. 5–6, 11. Joh. Lydus, *Mag.* III. 61.

50. For special vintages see above n. 1; cf. *Totius Orbis Descr.* 29, similiter aliae civitates Ascalon et Gaza in negotiis eminentes et abundantes omnibus bonis mittunt omni regioni Syriae et Aegypti vinum optimum, *V. Porph.* 58 (Egyptian wine merchants at Gaza). CAPPADOCIANS BUY SYRIAN WINE: Joh. Eph. *V. SS. Or.* viii. AFRICAN OIL EXPORTS: *Totius Orbis Descr.* 61, paene ipsa omnibus gentibus usum olei praestare potest. OIL IMPORTED AT MARSEILLES: Greg. Tur. *HF* v. 5.

51. HORTULANI OF CONSTANTINOPLE: Just. *Nov.* lxiv, 538.

52. For the pork supply of Rome see pp. 702–4. For Bertram's will see J. M. Pardessus, *Diplomata Chartae Epistolae Leges ad res Gallo-Francicas spectantia*, no. 230.

53. WOOL PRICES: *Ed. Diocl.* xxv. 1–9.

54. USE OF CURSUS PUBLICUS FOR MARBLE TRANSPORT: *CTh* VIII. v. 15, 363 (cited in n. 16); cf. Cass. *Var.* III. 10, atque ideo magnitudini tuae praesenti ammonitione declaramus, ut marmora, quae de domo Pinciana constat esse deposita, ad Ravennatem urbem per catabolenses vestra ordinatione dirigantur. TIMBER: Greg. *Ep.* IX. 124–7 (for Rome), VIII. 28, IX. 175, X. 21 (for Eulogius). Libanius's friend Severus of Lycia apparently regularly sold his timber (*Ep.* 1383, ξύλων ἡρπασμένων ἃ ἦν αὐτῷ πρόσοδος καὶ ὅθεν εἰσέφερέ τε καὶ τἆλλα διῴκει). He sent some timber to Libanius at Antioch, refusing payment for it (*Ep.* 1191).

55. SALE OF MARBLE: *CTh* X. xix. 1, 320, 8, 376, 11, 384. GREGORY'S CHAPEL: Greg. Nyss. *Ep.* 25.

56. *CTh* XIII. i. 10, 374, colonos rei privatae vel ceteros rusticanos pro speciebus, quae in eorum agris gigni solent, inquietari non oportet. eos etiam, qui manu victum rimantur aut tolerant, figulos videlicet aut fabros, alienos esse a praestationis eius molestia decernimus, ut hi tantum, qui pro mercimonio et substantia mercis ex rusticana plebe inter negotiatores sunt, sortem negotiationis agnoscant, quos in exercendis agris ingenitum iampridem studium non retinet, sed mercandis distrahendisque rebus institutum vitae et voluntatis implicuit; Lib. *Or.* XI. 230, τοῦτο μὲν κῶμαι μεγάλαι καὶ πολυάνθρωποι πόλεων οὐκ ὀλίγων πλέον πολυανδρούμεναι καὶ χειροτέχναις, ὥσπερ ἐν ἄστεσι, χρώμεναι, κοινούμεναι πρὸς ἀλλήλας ‹τὰ› σφῶν αὐτῶν διὰ τῶν πανηγύρεων καλοῦσαί τε ἐν μέρει παρ' αὐτὴν ἑκάστη καὶ καλούμεναι καὶ τοῖς αὐτοῖς εὐθυμούμεναί τε καὶ χαριζόμεναι καὶ κερδαίνουσαι, ὧν μὲν περίεστι μεταδιδοῦσαι, ὧν δὲ ἐνδεῖ προσλαμβάνουσαι, τὰ μὲν διατιθέμεναι, τὰ δὲ ὠνούμεναι.

57. APHRODITO: *P. Cairo*, 67283 (petition), 67288 (tax list), cf. 67110 (lease of pottery).

58. On the cloth industry in the Roman Empire see *Ec. Hist. Rev.* XIII (1960), 183–92. DOMESTIC WEAVING: Pelagius I, *Ep.* 84, viros qui forte gynaecaeo utiles esse possunt concedas illis, ita tamen ut pro artificii ipsorum merito in agricolis compensetur ecclesiae; nec enim eiusdem aestimationis est artifex et ministerialis puer contra rusticum vel colonum. FLORENTIUS'S CASULA: Aug. *Civ. Dei*, XXII. viii. 9.

59. *Ed. Diocl.* xxvi, xxvii, xxviii; cf. *Totius Orbis Descr.* 31, Scythopolis igitur, Laodicia, Byblus, Tyrus, Berytus omni mundo linteamen emittunt.

60. *Ed. Diocl.* loc. cit.

61. *Ed. Diocl.* xix. 'vestis Laodicena' and 'Norica' are noted in *Totius Orbis Descr.* 42, 57.

62. For levies of clothing see pp. 433–4.

63. ANTIOCHENES: *V. Mel.* (G) 8, (L) 8. Cf. also *P. Fouad*, 74, a letter asking the recipient to buy at Alexandria στιχάριον Ἀντιοχήσιον ἔμπλουμον ἀπὸ ὀλίγης χρήσεως ἕως τιμῆς κερατίων ι' πλέον ἔλαττον. For high-quality linen and woollen clothes see above nn. 59–61.

64. The price of raw silk is given in *Ed. Diocl.* xxiii. 1a, as 12,000 denarii a pound, sixty times that of the very best wool (ibid. xxv. 9) and equivalent to nearly a quarter of a pound of gold. In Just. *App.* v. the price is fixed at 15 solidi. Finished silk fabrics, especially if dyed purple, were enormously more expensive; see SHA, *Aurelianus*, 45, libra enim auri tunc libra serici fuit, and *Ed. Diocl.* xxiv. 1a, where μεταξόβλαττα is priced at 150,000 denarii per lb., three times its weight in gold. For the trade in oriental spices, perfumes, etc. see *Totius Orbis Descr.* 35 (cited in n. 80); *PSI* 1264, a list of government deliveries to Alexandria from the Thebaid, including 136 lb. pepper from Antaeopolis and 70 lb. pepper and sundry quantities of malabathrum, nard, myrrh etc. from Lycopolis sent by the ὑποδεκτὴς ἀρωματικῶν; *P. Antinoop.* 32, official receipts from Diospolis of the Thebaid, including sundry quantities εἰδῶν ἀρωματικῶν. These documents suggest that there was a government monopoly of the imported raw materials (as with silk), and they were landed on the Red Sea coast and carried across the desert to the upper Nile. GAZAN WINE: Sid. Ap. *Carm.* xvii. 15, Cass. *Var.* XII. 12, Greg. Tur. *HF* VII. 29, *Glor. Conf.* 64, Isid. *Etym.* xx. iii. 7. PEPPER AT ROME: Zos. v. 41; cf. *PSI* 1264, for its import.

65. For agricultural slaves see pp. 793–4; workers in the state factories, the post and the mints, nn. 21, 30 above and ch. XIII n. 62; in private industry n. 86 below; as bailiffs etc. pp. 790–1; as commercial agents, Joh. Moschus, 79.

66. SENATORIAL SLAVE HOUSEHOLDS: Amm. XIV. vi, XXVIII. iv, Joh. Chrys. *Hom. in Ep.* 1 *ad Cor.* xl. 5; Olympias had fifty *cubiculariae* (*V. Olymp.* 6). ATHANASIUS: *A.C.Oec.* II. i. 217–8; John Chrysostom (*Hom. in Hebr.* xxviii. 4) accepts two slaves as the basic minimum for a lady. LIBANIUS'S LECTURERS: Lib. *Or.* XXXI. 11. SOLDIER'S SLAVES: *CTh* VII. xxii. 2 §2, 326, i. 3, 349, xiii. 16, 406, *FIR* III². 135, Sulp. Sev. *V. Mart.* 2. ARISTOCRATIC HERMITS: Greg. Nyss. *V. Macr.* 968 (Basil's brother Naucratius keeps one slave), *V. Caesarii*, 1. 5 (Caesarius, two years after becoming a monk, travels to Marseilles 'cum uno tantum famulo'), Joh. Eph. *V. SS. Or.* xliv (the *comes* Tribunus keeps two slaves).

67. PROHIBITION OF CASTRATION: Amm. XVIII. iv. 5, horum et similium taedio iuvat veterem laudare Domitianum, qui licet patris fratrisque dissimilis memoriam nominis sui inexpiabili detestatione perfudit, tamen receptissima inclaruit lege qua minaciter interdixerat ne intra terminos iuris dictionis Romanae castraret quisquam puerum; quod ni contigisset, quis eorum ferret examina, quorum raritas difficile toleratur? *CJ* IV. xlii. 1 (Constantine), 2 (Leo), Romanae gentis homines sive in barbaro sive in Romano solo eunuchos factos nullatenus quolibet modo ad dominium cuiusdam transferri iubemus: poena gravissima statuenda adversus eos, qui hoc perpetrare ausi fuerint, tabellione videlicet, qui huiusmodi emptionis sive cuiuslibet alterius alienationis instrumenta conscripserit, et eo, qui octavam vel aliquod vectigalis causa pro his susceperit, eidem poenae subiciendo. barbarae autem gentis eunuchos extra loca nostro imperio subiecta factos cunctis negotiatoribus vel quibuscumque aliis emendi in commerciis et vendendi ubi voluerint tribuimus facultatem; Just. *Nov.* cxlii, 558. For imperial eunuchs see pp. 566 ff., for those in private households, Amm. XIV. vi. 17, Jerome, *V. Hilar.* 14, Claud. *in Eutrop.* 1. 60 ff., Pall. *Hist. Laus.* xxxv, lxi, *CJ* XII. v. 4 (Leo), Cyr. Scyth. *V. Sabae*, 69. EUTHERIUS: Amm. XVI. vii. 5. ABASGI: Proc. *BG* IV. iii. 12–21, Evagr. IV. 22.

68. CASUALTIES IN CASTRATION: Just. *Nov.* cxlii, 558. PRICES OF EUNUCHS AND OTHER SLAVES: *CJ* VII. vii. 1, 530, ne autem quantitas servilis pretii sit incerta, sed manifesta, sancimus servi pretium sive ancillae, si nulla arte sunt imbuti, viginti solidis taxari, his videlicet, qui usque ad decimum annum suae venerunt aetatis, in decem tantummodo solidis ponendis: sin autem aliqua arte praediti sunt exceptis notariis et medicis, usque ad triginta solidos pretium eorum redigi sive in masculis sive in feminis. sin autem notarius sit vel medicus sive masculus sive femina, notarius quidem usque ad quinquaginta, medicus autem usque ad sexaginta taxetur. sin vero eunuchi sint servi communes maiores decem annis, si quidem sine arte sint, in quinquaginta solidos computentur, sin autem artifices, usque ad septuaginta: minores etenim decem annis eunuchos non amplius triginta solidis aestimari volumus; *FIR* III². 135 (18 solidi), Pall. *Hist. Laus.* xxxvii (20 solidi), *V. Joh. Eleem.* 22 (30 solidi). AURUM TIRONICUM: *CTh* VII. xiii. 13, 397, Symm. *Ep.* VI. 64 (25 solidi, 5 lb. silver). LOWER PRICES OF SLAVES: *MGH* (*Scr. Rer. Mer.*) III. 339 (14 solidi), *C. Matisc.* 1, can. 16 (12 solidi), Greg. Tur. *HF* III. 15 (12 solidi), *Tablettes Albertini*, II. 26 (p. 117), as interpreted by Grierson, *JRS* XLIX (1959), 73 ff. (1 solidus, 700 *folles*), *Archiv Pap.* III. 415 ff. (4 solidi). In *Lex Rom. Burg.* II. 6 the compensation for the murder of an unskilled slave (a ploughman or swineherd) is fixed at 30 solidi, but there may be a penal element in this high price. In *CJ* VI. i. 4, 317, compensation for an escaped slave is fixed at 20 solidi; the figure may well be a Justinianic interpolation.

69. For *laeti* see p. 620; for prisoners as *coloni*, ch. XX, n. 56. Some, however, of the Sciri were sold (Soz. IX. 5), and so were many of Radagaesus's followers (Orosius, VII. xxxvii. 16). OFFICERS AND THE SLAVE TRADE: Them. *Or.* x. 136b, Amm. XXXI. iv. 9–11. SYMMACHUS AND FLAVIAN: Symm. *Ep.* II. 78, pars hominum compendiis et quaestibus gaudent, me votiva delectat expensio. itaque avidus civicae gratiae quaestoriis filii mei sumptibus studeo aliud genus largitatis adicere, ut curulibus stabulis urbis aeternae etiam quina mancipia largiamur. et quoniam servorum per limitem facilis inventio et pretium solet esse tolerabile, quam maxime te deprecor, ut per homines strenuos viginti iuvenes praedicto negotio congruentes iubeas comparari. in quam rem . . . solidos ad te misi habita aestimatione hominum quorum non forma sed aetas et sanitas eligenda est.

70. EXPOSED CHILDREN: *CTh* v. ix. 1, 331, quicumque puerum vel puellam, proiectam de domo patris vel domini voluntate scientiaque, collegerit ac suis alimentis ad robur provexerit, eundem retineat sub eodem statu, quem apud se collectum voluerit agitare, hoc est sive filium sive servum eum esse maluerit: omni repetitionis inquietudine penitus submovenda eorum, qui servos aut liberos scientes propria voluntate domo recens natos abiecerint; 2, 412, *CJ* VIII. li. 3, 529, Just. *Nov.* cliii, 541. SANGUINOLENTI: *Fr. Vat.* 34, 313, cum profitearis te certa quantitate mancipium ex sanguine comparasse, cuius pretium te exsolvisse dicis et instrumentis esse firmatum, hoc a nobis iam olim praescriptum est, quod, si voluerit liberum suum reciperare, tunc in eius locum mancipium domino dare aut pretium quo valuisset numeraret. etiamnunc, si a suis parentibus certo pretio comparasti, ius dominii possidere te existimamus. nullum autem ex gentilibus liberum adprobari licet; *CTh* v. x. 1, 329 = *CJ* IV. xliii. 2, secundum statuta priorum principum si quis a sanguine infantem quoquo modo legitime comparaverit vel nutriendum putaverit, obtinendi eius servitii habeat potestatem: ita ut, si quis post seriem annorum ad libertatem eum repetat vel servum defendat, eiusdem modi alium praestet aut pretium, quod potest valere, exsolvat; *Lex Vis.* IV. iv. 3.

71. PROHIBITION OF SALE OR PLEDGE OF CHILDREN: *CJ* VIII. xvi. 6, 293, IV. x. 12, xliii. 1, 294, *CTh* III. iii. 1, 391, *Cod. Euric.* 299. Cf. *CTh* XI. xxvii. 2, 322 (children's allowances), Zos. II. 38, Lib. *Or.* XLVI. 23 (the *chrysargyron*), Val. III, *Nov.* xxxiii, 451 (the famine), Ruf. *Hist. Mon.* 16 (the tax payer), *P. Cairo*, 67023 (Martha), cf. Cass. *Var.* VIII. 33, praesto sunt pueri ac puellae diverso sexu et aetate conspicui, quos non fecit captivitas esse sub pretio, sed libertas: hos merito parentes vendunt, quoniam de ipsa famulatione proficiunt; *P. Iand.* 62 (a borrower pledges his sister ἐ[φ᾿ ᾧ α]ὐτὴν πᾶσαν δουλικὴν [ἔχειν] χρείαν).

72. SELF SALE: *CJ* VII. xvi. 5, sed nec hoc ad praescriptionem operatur, quod venditionis tempore maior viginti annis fuit, cum aetatis adlegatio non alias possit praescriptionem adversus civem Romanum accommodare, quam is participandi pretii gratia consensum servituti dedisse probetur; xviii. 1, dispar causa est eius, qui dissimulata condicione sua distrahi se passus est, et eius, qui pretium participatus est. nam superiori quidem non denegatur libertatis defensio, posteriori autem, et si civis Romanus sit et participatus est pretia, libertas denegatur; *Cod. Euric.* 300, Pall. *Hist. Laus.* xxxvii, *V. Joh. Eleem.* 22.

73. REDEMPTION OF CAPTIVES BY THE CHURCH: *CJ* I. ii. 21, 529, Just. *Nov.* vii §8, 535, cxx §10, 544, cf. *Nov.* lxv, 538, cxx §9, 544, for the churches of Moesia; for actual examples see for instance Amb. *Off.* II. 136-9, Soc. VII. 21, Victor Vit. I. 25. POSTLIMINIUM: *CJ* VIII. l. 2, 6, 7, 8, 15, 17 (Diocletian), *CTh* v. vii. 2, 408 (S), diversarum homines provinciarum cuiuslibet sexus condicionis aetatis, quos barbarica feritas captiva necessitate transduxerat, invitos nemo retineat, sed ad propria redire cupientibus libera sit facultas. quibus si quicquam in usum vestium vel alimoniae impensum est, humanitati sit praestitum, nec maneat victualis sumptus repetitio: exceptis his, quos barbaris vendentibus emptos esse docebitur, a quibus status sui pretium propter utilitatem publicam emptoribus aequum est redhiberi. ne quando enim damni consideratio in tali necessitate positis negari faciat emptionem, decet redemptos aut datum pro se pretium emptoribus restituere aut labore obsequio vel opere quinquennii vicem referre beneficii, habituros incolumem, si in ea nati sunt, libertatem. MARIA: Theod. *Ep.* (*PG*) 70.

74. INDENTURES: *P. Oxy.* 1122, *P. Reinach*, 103, *Sb* 4490, 4739, *P. Strass.* 40.

75. The eunuchs Eutherius and Eutropius were sold by merchants; Amm. XVI. vii. 5, natus in Armenia sanguine libero captusque a finitimis hostibus etiam tum parvulus abstractis geminis Romanis mercatoribus venundatus ad palatium Constantini deducitur; Claudian, *in Eutrop.* I. 58-9, inde per Assyriae trahitur commercia ripae; hinc fora venalis Galata ductore frequentat (Galata was evidently a slang term for a slave dealer, cf. Amm. XXII. vii. 8, illis enim sufficere mercatores Galatas, per quos ubique sine condicionis discrimine venundantur); for Atalous and Maria see *Archiv. Pap.* III. 415 ff., Theod. *Ep.* (*PG*), 70. JEWISH SLAVE MERCHANTS: Greg. *Ep.* IX. 104.

76. VILLAGE FAIRS: Theod. *Hist. Rel.* vii (Immae), Cass. *Var.* VIII. 33 (Consilinum), *OGI* 262 (Baetocaece, third century), cf. Lib. *Or.* XI. 230 (cited in n. 56), *CJ* IV. lx. 1, qui exercendorum mercatuum aut nundinarum licentiam vel veterum indulto vel nostra auctoritate meruerunt, ita beneficio rescripti potiantur, ut nullum in mercatibus atque nundinis ex negotiatorum mercibus conveniant, vel in venaliciis aut locorum temporali quaestu et commodo privata exactione sectentur, vel sub praetextu privati debiti aliquam ibidem concurrentibus molestiam possint inferre. APOLLONIUS: Pall. *Hist. Laus.* xiii.

77. WINE MERCHANT: *P. Cairo*, 67283. ABRAHAM: Theod. *Hist. Rel.* xvii. CARRIERS: Lib. *Or.* L. 4, *CJ* XII. l. 22 (Leo), animalium dominis qui ea solent accepta mercede locare.

78. For corn merchants see above n. 40, and for Caesarea, Greg. Naz. *Or.* XLIII. 34.

79. CONSTANTINOPLE: Them. *Or.* IV. 61a. ANTIOCH: Lib. *Or.* XI. 20 (wine and oil), 263–4 (imports), cf. *Not. Dig. Or.* xi. 21–2, *CTh* x. xxii. 1, 374, for the two arms factories, and *V. Mel.* 8, for cheap Antiochene clothes.

80. ALEXANDRIA: SHA, *Saturninus*, 8, civitas opulenta, dives, fecunda, in qua nemo vivat otiosus. alii vitrum conflant, aliis charta conficitur, omnes certe linyphiones aut cuiuscumque artis esse videntur et habentur; *Totius Orbis Descr.* 35–6, haec cum Indis et barbaris negotia gerit merito; aromata et diversas species pretiosas omnibus regionibus mittit. sed et in hoc valde laudanda est quod omni mundo sola chartas emittit, quam speciem licet vilem sed nimis utilem et necessariam in nulla provincia nisi tantum apud Alexandriam invenies abundare.

81. For corvées see above n. 38. For the grant of such corvée labour to the church, see Constantine's letter to Macarius, bishop of Jerusalem, on the building of the Church of the Holy Sepulchre (Eus. *V. Const.* III. 31, καὶ περὶ μὲν τῆς τῶν τοίχων ἐγέρσεώς τε καὶ καλλιεργίας Δρακιλιανῷ τῷ ἡμετέρῳ φίλῳ, τῷ διέποντι τὰ τῶν ἐπαρχιῶν μέρη, καὶ τῷ τῆς ἐπαρχίας ἄρχοντι, παρ᾽ ἡμῶν τὴν φροντίδα ἐγκεχειρίσθαι γίνωσκε. κεκέλευται γὰρ ὑπὸ τῆς ἐμῆς εὐσεβείας, καὶ τεχνίτας καὶ ἐργάτας, καὶ πάνθ᾽ ἅπερ εἰς οἰκοδομὴν ἀναγκαῖα τυγχάνειν παρὰ τῆς σῆς καταμάθοιεν ἀγχινοίας, παραχρῆμα διὰ τῆς ἐκείνων προνοίας ἀποσταλῆναι.) BUILDING LABOUR: Joh. Moschus, 37 (the bishop), 134 (a monk). ISAURIANS: *V. Sym. Jun.* 201, πλήσιον τῆς Ἀντιόχου ἐν τῇ λεγομένῃ Ἀπάτῃ Ἰσαύρων ἐργαστήριον ἦν χειροτεχνούντων ἐν ταῖς οἰκοδομίαις καὶ λατομίαις τῶν τῆς πόλεως τείχεων, Theophanes, A.M. 6051 (Isaurians working at St. Sophia at Constantinople).

82. DARA: Zach. Myt. *Chron.* VII. 6. LABOURERS IN EGYPT: *V. Dan. Scet.* 9, *V. Joh. Eleem.* 36. THE MONK: Joh. Moschus, 134. A *colonus* of the Roman church who had worked three years on building a house was paid only 14⅔ solidi in all; but he complained that he had been bilked (Greg. *Ep.* IX. 43).

83. For the *chrysargyron* see pp. 431–2. CORVÉES: Maj. *Nov.* vii §3, 458, quibus illud provisio nostrae serenitatis adiungit, ut collegiatis operas patriae alternis vicibus pro curialium dispositione praebentibus extra territorium civitatis suae habitare non liceat; cf. *CTh* XII. xix. 1, 400, destitutae ministeriis civitates splendorem, quo pridem nituerant, amiserunt; plurimi siquidem collegiati cultum urbium deserentes agrestem vitam secuti in secreta sese et devia contulerunt; XIV. xxvii. 2, 436 (Alexandria), Lib. *Or.* XLVI. 21 (Antioch). FABRI, CENTONARII AND DENDROPHORI: *CTh* XIV. viii. 1, 315.

84. CURSUS PUBLICUS: *CTh* XI. x. 1, 369, operarum praebitionem, quae inlicite a provincialibus hactenus expetita est, sinceritas tua cessare praecipiat. nullum autem, qui caupona vel propola vel tabernaria lucrum familiare sectetur, cum animalia, quibus prosecutio debeatur, advenerint, si collegiati numero impares videbuntur, ab hoc obsequio esse patiatur. melius enim est, ut otiosorum sit ista sedulitas, quam ipsas quoque perdat urbes tristis abductio rusticorum; Lib. *Or.* XLVI. 19; *Chr.* I. 405, (ἁλιαδίτου ἤτοι γραμματηφόρου τοῦ ὀξέως δρόμου), 437 (ὀνηλάται of the ὀξὺς δρόμος), 46 (ἔθος ἐστὶν τοῦ παρασχεθῆναι πρὸς [ὑπ]ηρεσίαν

τοῦ αὐτοῦ δημοσίου πλοίου [ἐκ] τῆς πόλεως ναύτην ἕνα. πολλάκις τοίνυν διεστιλάμην Εὐστοχίῳ συστά[τῃ] τῆς νυνὶ λιτουργούσης φυλῆς ὥστε ναύτην παρασχεῖν ὑπὲρ το[ῦ ἐνεστῶτος] ἐνιαυτοῦ).

85. For declarations by guilds see ch. XIX, n. 52. THE BUILDERS OF SARDIS: *IGC* 322. ZENO'S LAW: *CJ* IV. lix. 2, 483. For the bakers of Antioch see p. 735.

86. THALASSIUS'S FACTORY: Lib. *Or.* XLII. 21, καὶ μαχαιρῶν δή τινων ἐμέμνητο κἀκ τούτων ὄνομα περιῆπτε καὶ τὴν ἐκβολὴν ἐντεῦθεν ἐποιεῖτο. ὁ δὲ μαχαίρας μὲν οὐδεπώποτε εἰργάσατο, οὐδ' ἔμαθε τὴν τέχνην, οὐδ' εἶχεν, ἀλλ' οὐδὲ ὁ πατὴρ οὐδέτερον. οἰκέται δὲ ἦσαν αὐτῷ ταῦτα ἐπιστάμενοι, καθάπερ Δημοσθένει τῷ Δημοσθένους πατρί. καὶ οὐδὲν ἐκώλυσε τὸν υἱὸν Δημοσθένους τὸν Δημοσθένη τὸ εἶναι τοιούτους αὐτοῖς οἰκέτας οὔτε προστῆναι τῶν Ἑλληνικῶν πράξεων οὔτε ῥύσασθαι πόλεις οὔτε ἀντιτάξασθαι πρὸς τὴν Φιλίππου καὶ ῥώμην καὶ τύχην οὔτ' αἴτιον γενέσθαι τῇ πόλει στεφάνων καὶ κηρυγμάτων ἀπολαῦσαι. εἶχον δὲ οὐ δεσπότας τῶν ἐν ταῖς τέχναις Ἀθηναίων τινὰς μόνον λέγειν, ἀλλὰ καὶ αὖ τοὺς ἀπὸ τεχνῶν ἥκοντας ἰσχύσαντας. THE MOESIAN CITIES: *CTh* XII. i. 96, 383, concessum curialibus provinciae Mysiae, ut, si quos e plebe idoneos habent, ad decurionatus munia devocent, ne personae famulantium facultate locupletes onera, pro quibus patrimonia requiruntur, obscuritate nominis vilioris evadant.

87. CAECILIANUS: Opt. *App.* ii.

88. It is clear from *CTh* XII. i. 50, 362, et ab auri atque argenti praestatione, quod negotiatoribus indicitur, curiae immunes sint, nisi forte decurionem aliquid mercari constiterit, and from law 96 (cited in n. 86) that *negotiatores* were not normally decurions; they were only liable to become so if they bought land (*CTh* XII. i. 72, 370). In *CTh* XVI. v. 52, 412, they are classed between decurions and *plebeii*. SHOPS AND STALLS AT ANTIOCH: Lib. *Or.* XXXIII. 35ff., XXVI. 20-21.

89. JOHN OF LYCOPOLIS: Pall. *Hist. Laus.* XXXV. APPRENTICESHIPS AND CONTRACTS OF SERVICE: *PSI* 287, *P. Aberdeen*, 59, *P. Lond.* 1706, *P. Iand.* 43, *P. Cairo*, 67305, *SPP* XX. 219, *Sb* 4503, 9456, ἐπειδὴ ἔσχον σὲ εἰς τὸ ἐμὸν ἐργαστήριον ἐν τάξει μισθίου καὶ ἀναχωρήσαντος σοῦ τῆς πρὸς ἐμὲ παραμονῆς. PAUL AND THE BUILD-ERS: *P. Ryl.* 654.

90. For these laws see ch. XIX, n. 112.

91. The story is told in Proc. *HA* XXV. 13–26. For my interpretation of it, see *Ec. Hist. Rev.* XIII (1960), 191–2.

92. WOOL PRICES: *Ed. Diocl.* XXV. 1–9. FLAX PRICES: *Ed. Diocl.* XXVI. 4–12. It is perhaps significant that the edict gives wage rates for spinners only for silk and purple wool (XXIV. 14-6) and puts the wages of silk weavers and of weavers of fine wool fabrics in the same section (XX. 9–11, 12–3). CAECILIANUS: Opt. *App.* ii. THE WEAVER OF APHRODITO: *P. Cairo*, 67116.

93. IMMUNITIES OF SKILLED CRAFTS: *CTh* XIII. iv. 2, 337 = *CJ* X. lxvi. 1. GERONTIUS THE WOOD CARVER: Theod. *Ep.* (Azema) 38. GREGORY AND THE BUILDERS: Greg. Nyss. *Ep.* 25.

94. THE GOLDSMITH'S APPRENTICE: Joh. Moschus, 200. THE JERUSALEM SILVERSMITH: Cyr. Scyth. *V. Sabae*, 78. SILVERSMITHS ETC. FORBIDDEN TO BE COHORTALES: *CJ* XII. lvii. 12, 436, sed etiam cunctos, qui diversarum rerum negotiationibus detinentur, trapezitas scilicet vel gemmarum argentique

vestiumve venditores, apothecarios etiam ceterosque institores aliarum mercium quibuscumque ergasteriis adhaerentes iubemus a provincialibus officiis removeri, ut omnis honor atque militia contagione huiusmodi segregetur.

95. THE ARGENTARII OF CONSTANTINOPLE: *CJ* VIII. xiii. 27, 528, XII. xxxiv. 1 (528-9), Just. *Nov.* cxxxvi, 535, *Ed.* vii, 542, ix. For saleable offices see pp. 572, 574, 576-7. FLAVIUS ANASTASIUS: *P. Cairo*, 67126.

96. ARLES: *MGH (Ep.)*, III. 14, ac plane praeter necessitates publicas etiam humanae ipsi conversationi non parum credimus commoditatis accedere, quod in Constantina urbe iubemus annis singulis esse concilium. tanta enim loci opportunitas, tanta est copia commerciorum, tanta illic frequentia commeantium ut quicquid usquam nascitur illic commodius distrahatur; neque enim ulla provincia ita peculiari fructus sui felicitate laetatur ut non haec propria Arelatensis soli credatur esse fecunditas. quidquid enim dives Oriens, quidquid odoratus Arabs, quidquid delicatus Assyrius, quod Africa fertilis, quod speciosa Hispania, quod fortis Gallia potuit habere praeclarum, ita illic adfatim exuberat quasi ibi nascantur omnia quae ubique constat esse magnifica. ALEXANDRIA: *V. Joh. Eleem.* 27.

97. For clothing merchants who aspired to be *cohortales*, see above n. 94. AURELIUS PSATES: *P. Paris*, 20, 21, 21 bis, 21 ter., *Sb* 4503-5. The *metaxarii* of Constantinople, like the *argentarii*, bought *militiae* (*CJ* VIII. xiii. 27, 528).

98. PROCOPIUS'S FRIEND: Proc. *BV* I. xiv. 7. PETER OF ALEXANDRIA: *ILS* 7564. GEORGE OF ANTIOCH: *P. Ital.* 4-5.

99. PANTOPOLAE: Val. III, *Nov.* v, 440. ORIENTALS AT RAVENNA: Sid. Ap. *Ep.* I. 8, *P. Ital.* 16 (Marinus), 20 (John the Syrian), *P. Dip.* 114 (Julian the *argentarius*), 121 (Peter).

100. ORIENTALS IN GAUL: Greg. Tur. *HF* VIII. 1 (Orleans), VII. 31 (Euphronius), x. 26 (Eusebius), VI. 5 (Priscus). Salvian (*Gub. Dei*, IV. 69) mentions Syrian traders in Gaul at an earlier date.

101. VETERAN AND CLERICAL TRADERS: *CTh* XIII. i. 11, 379, 13, 383 (S). THE GREEK MERCHANT OF VIMINACIUM: Priscus, 8 (p. 86). ANTONINUS: Amm. XVIII. v. 1. ELIAS AND THEODORE: Joh. Eph. *V. SS. Or.* xxxi.

102. FLEET OF THE ALEXANDRIAN CHURCH: *V. Joh. Eleem.* 28; that persons of influence (*potiores*) endeavoured to secure exemption for their ships from compulsory charter by the government on the score of their *dignitates*, and that humble persons sought their patronage and affixed their *tituli* to their ships, appears from *CTh* XIII. vii. 1, 399, cunctis per Aegyptum intimetur viginti librarum auri multae esse subdendos eos, qui naves suo nomine vel defensione a transvectionibus publicis excusare temptaverint, publica iactura navium quoque dominis feriendis, qui neglectis necessitatibus publicis potiorum voluerunt patrociniis excusari; 2, 406, multi naves suas diversorum nominibus et titulis tuentur. cui fraudi obviantes praecipimus, ut, si quis ad evitationem publicae necessitatis titulum crediderit adponendum, sciat navem esse fisco sociandam; Th. II, *Nov.* viii, 439, ideo calcatam legem, quae de navigiis non excusandis olim fuerat promulgata, suggestione tuae sublimitatis edocti humanis sensibus saluberrima repetere scita compellimur ac iubemus, nullam navem ultra duorum milium modiorum capacitatem ante felicem embolam vel publicarum specierum transvectionem aut privilegio dignitatis aut religionis

intuitu aut praerogativa personae publicis utilitatibus excusari posse sub-
tractam; this last law implies that churches commonly owned ships. The
relations between the *magister navis* and the owner (*dominus*) or *exercitor* (the
man who chartered a ship from the owner and operated it at his own risk) are
set out in *Dig.* xiv. i; cf. *CJ* iv. xxv. 4, 293. For the merchant who entrusted
his ship to his brother see *V. Joh. Eleem.* 26.

103. For the rules of average see *Dig.* xiv. ii, de lege Rhodia de iactu. HILARION:
Jerome, *V. Hilar.* 35. THE JEWEL MERCHANT: Joh. Moschus, 203.

104. THE FAIR OF AEGAE: *Itin. Hier.*, *Theodosius* 32, in provincia Cilicia Aegea
dicitur civitas, ubi XL dies commercia geruntur et nemo de eis aliquid requirit;
si post XL dies inventus fuerit negotium gerere, fiscalia reddit; Theod. *Ep.*
(*PG*) 70. Similar merchants' fairs are recorded at Batnae (Amm. xiv. iii. 3,
Batnae municipium in Anthemusia conditum Macedonum manu priscorum
ab Euphrate flumine brevi spatio disparatur, refertum mercatoribus opulentis,
ubi annua sollemnitate prope Septembris initium mensis ad nundinas magna
promiscuae fortunae convenit multitudo ad commercanda quae Indi mittunt
et Seres aliaque plurima vehi terra marique consueta) and Edessa (Greg. Tur.
Glor. Mart. 32, in supradicta igitur urbe, in qua beatos artus diximus tumulatos,
adveniente festivitate, magnus adgregatur populorum coetus, ac de diversis
regionibus cum votis negotiisque venientes, vendendi comparandique per
triginta dies sine ulla thelonei exactione licentia datur).

105. THE ATHENIAN MERCHANT: Syn. *Ep.* 52. JACOB THE JEW: *Doctrina Jacobi*,
v. 20.

106. W. Ashburner, *The Rhodian Sea Law* (Oxford, 1909), II, 16, εἶναι τὴν
χιλιάδα τοῦ μοδισμοῦ χρυσίνων πεντήκοντα μετὰ πάσης τῆς ἐξαρτίας αὐτοῦ καὶ εἰς
συμβολὴν ἐρχέσθω, τοῦ δὲ πλοίου τοῦ παλαιοῦ χρυσίνων τριάκοντα, cf. the commentary on pp. 63–5.

107. NAUTICUM FOENUS: *Dig.* xxii. ii; *CJ* iv. xxxiii. 2, 286, traiecticiam pecuniam,
quae periculo creditoris datur, tamdiu liberam esse ab observatione communium
usurarum, quamdiu navis ad portum appulerit, manifestum est; 3, 286, cum
dicas pecuniam te ea lege dedisse, ut in sacra urbe tibi restitueretur, nec incertum
periculum, quod ex navigatione maris metui solet, ad te pertinuisse profitearis,
non dubium est pecuniae creditae ultra licitum te usuras exigere non posse.
JUSTINIAN'S RULE: *CJ* iv. xxxii. 26 §2, 528.

108. Just. *Nov.* cvi, 540, cx, 541. Pope Gregory (*Ep.* ix. 108) describes an
obscure transaction, which looks like an evasion of Justinian's law. The
passage runs: Maurus praesentium portitor in quadringentis se solidis quasdam
merces a Felice viro magnifico asserit suscepisse atque promisisse sex siliquas
per solidum lucri causa persolvere pretii; qua lucri quantitate in uno congesta
duas se cautiones, id est unam de quadringentis quinquaginta et alteram de
quinquaginta solidis, emisisse spondens certo tempore quod debeat exsolvere.
sed quia, ut perhibet, in eisdem mercibus passus est non leve dispendium et
restitutis quadringentis decem solidis, quod reliquum lucri est, implere
compellitur atque ex hoc maiori se necessitati ac potius desperationi ingemit
subiacere et propterea aliquo sibi subveniri petit auxilio. I interpret this as
meaning that Maurus borrowed 400 solidi from Felix (a wealthy landowner,
see *Ep.* ix. 41–2, 90–1) to buy a cargo, and entered into bonds to repay him
500 solidi (concealed interest at 25 per cent.); he had not apparently suffered
shipwreck but merely done badly on his venture.

109. Joh. Moschus, 186 (Tyre), 189 (Ascalon).

110. THE POOR ALEXANDRIAN: Joh. Moschus, 75. JOHN AND THE SHIPPER: *V. Joh. Eleem.* 10.

111. *V. Joh. Eleem.* 26.

112. Joh. Moschus, 193.

113. Pall. *Hist. Laus.* xiv; Ruf. *Hist. Mon.* 16.

114. *CJ* IV. lxiii. 3 (408–9), nobiliores natalibus et honorum luce conspicuos et patrimonio ditiores perniciosum urbibus mercimonium exercere prohibemus, ut inter plebeium et negotiatorem facilius sit emendi vendendique commercium; cf. also *CTh* XIII. i. 5, 364, potiorum quoque homines vel potiores ipsos, si tamen his mercandi cura est, ad necessitatem pensitationis adhibeas, praesertim cum potiorum quisque aut miscere se negotiationi non debeat aut pensitationem debeat, quod honestas postulat, primus agnoscere.

115. On the *collatio lustralis* see pp. 431–2.

116. Lib. *Or.* XLVI. 22–3.

117. *CTh* XIII. i. 20, 410, functiones, quas conferentium frequentia extenuata debilitat, ad stabilitatem revocandae sunt, ut, quod simul et sub una conventione petebatur, sub parva ac minima contributione absque consensu conferentium praebeatur. hoc in lustralis auri conlatione in perpetuum decernimus observari, illud videlicet praecaventes, ne quis a nostra clementia vectigal huiusmodi audeat postulare. For the Egyptian guild see *PSI* 1265.

118. Zos. II. 38.

119. See p. 465.

XXII. THE CHURCH (pp. 873–5)

The most useful and comprehensive book of which I know on the organisation and discipline of the church is Joseph Bingham, *The Antiquities of the Christian Church*, London, 1726.

1. *A.C.Oec.* I. i. pars vii. 118–22. Cf. Innocent, *Ep.* 24, for earlier claims by Antioch over Cyprus.

2. For the powers of bishops see W. Telfer, *The office of a bishop*, London, 1962.

3. For the election of bishops see below pp. 914 ff., and for provincial councils, n. 15.

4. THEODORE OF MOPSUESTIA: H. B. Swete, *Theodori Episcopi Mopsuestiae in Epistulas B. Pauli Commentarii*, II. 124–5. SCYTHIA: Soz. VII. 19, ἀμέλει Σκύθαι πολλαὶ πόλεις ὄντες ἕνα πάντες ἐπίσκοπον ἔχουσι, *CJ* I. iii. 35 §2 (Zeno), ταῦτα δὲ γενικῶς διατάξαντες καὶ εἰς νοῦν εἰληφότες τὴν κατάστασιν τῶν ἁγιωτάτων ἐκκλησιῶν

τῶν διακειμένων ὑπὸ Τόμιν τῆς τῶν Σκυθῶν ἐπαρχίας καὶ ὅτι οὐκ ἐγχωρεῖ τὰς αὐτὰς ἀγιωτάτας ἐκκλησίας συνέχεσι βαρβάρων ἐπιδρομαῖς καταβλαπτομένας ἢ καὶ ἄλλως πως πενίᾳ συζώσας ἑτέρως διασώζεσθαι, εἰ μὴ διὰ τῆς τοῦ θεοφιλοῦς ἐπισκόπου Τόμεως, ἥτις ἐστὶ καὶ τοῦ ἔθνους μητρόπολις, τυγχάνοιεν προμηθείας, θεσπίζομεν ὑπεξαιρεῖσθαι τῆς παρούσης θείας νομοθεσίας καὶ μηδαμῶς αὐτὰς ὑπάγεσθαι τῇ ταύτης ἀνάγκῃ, ἀλλ' ἐπὶ τοῦ οἰκείου σχήματος μένειν.

5. GREGORY THAUMATURGUS: Basil, *de spiritu sancto*, 74. CANON AGAINST BISHOPS OF SMALL CITIES: *C. Sard.* can. 6, μὴ ἐξεῖναι δὲ ἁπλῶς καθιστᾶν ἐπίσκοπον ἐν κώμῃ τινὶ ἢ βραχείᾳ πόλει, ᾗ τινι καὶ εἷς μόνος πρεσβύτερος ἐπαρκεῖ· οὐκ ἀναγκαῖον γὰρ ἐπισκόπους ἐκεῖσε καθίστασθαι, ἵνα μὴ κατευτελίζηται τὸ τοῦ ἐπισκόπου ὄνομα καὶ ἡ αὐθεντία. ἀλλ' οἱ τῆς ἐπαρχίας, ὡς προεῖπον, ἐπίσκοποι ἐν ταύταις ταῖς πόλεσι καθιστᾶν ἐπισκόπους ὀφείλουσιν, ἔνθα καὶ πρότερον ἐτύγχανον γεγονότες ἐπίσκοποι· εἰ δὲ εὑρίσκοιτο οὕτω πληθύνουσά τις ἐν πολλῷ ἀριθμῷ λαοῦ πόλις, ὡς ἀξίαν αὐτὴν καὶ ἐπισκοπῆς νομίζεσθαι, λαμβανέτω; Leo, *Ep.* 12 §10.

6. EUROPE: *A.C.Oec.* I. i. pars vii. 122, ἔθος ἐκράτησεν ἀρχαῖον ἐπὶ τῆς Εὐρωπαίων ἐπαρχίας ἕκαστον τῶν ἐπισκόπων καὶ δύο καὶ τρεῖς ἔχειν ὑφ' ἑαυτὸν πόλεις, ὅθεν ὁ μὲν τῆς Ἡρακλείας ἐπίσκοπος ἔχει τήν τε Ἡράκλειαν καὶ τὸ Πάνιον καὶ Ὀρνοὺς καὶ Γάνον, τέσσαρας πόλεις τὸν ἀριθμόν, ὁ δὲ τῆς Βύζης ἐπίσκοπος ἔχει τήν τε Βύζην καὶ Ἀρκαδιούπολιν, ὁ δὲ Κοίλων ὁμοίως ἔχει τήν τε Κοῖλα καὶ Καλλίπολιν, ὁ δὲ Σαυσαδίας ἐπίσκοπος ἔχει τήν τε Σαυσαδίαν καὶ Ἀφροδισιάδα. MITYLENE: Hierocles, 686. 5-9, *A.C.Oec.* II. i. 450, ἐπίσκοπος Λέσβου Τενέδου Ποροσελήνης Αἰγιαλῶν. MAREOTES: Soc. I. 27, Ath. *Apol. c. Ar.* 85, ὁ Μαρεώτης, καθὰ προεῖπον, χώρα τῆς Ἀλεξανδρείας ἐστί, καὶ οὐδέποτε ἐν τῇ χώρα γέγονεν ἐπίσκοπος οὐδὲ χωρεπίσκοπος, ἀλλὰ τῷ τῆς Ἀλεξανδρείας ἐπισκόπῳ αἱ ἐκκλησίαι πάσης τῆς χώρας ὑπόκεινται. ἕκαστος δὲ τῶν πρεσβυτέρων ἔχει τὰς ἰδίας κώμας μεγίστας, καὶ ἀριθμῷ δέκα που καὶ πλέονας; that Mareotes was legally a city is proved by the official letter quoted in the same chapter (ἐπιστολὴ τοῦ καθολικοῦ. Φλάονιος Ἡμέριος ἐξάκτορι Μαρεώτου χαίρειν), which shows that it had an *exactor civitatis*; it is also listed as a city in Georgius Cyprius, 725. HIPPO: Aug. *de cura gerenda pro mortuis*, 15. Cf. Hilarus, *Ep.* 14, cum ecclesia illius municipii in qua ante fuerat ordinatus semper huius civitatis (sc. Barcino) ecclesiae fuisse dioecesis constet.

7. NEWLY FOUNDED CITIES: *C. Chalc.* can. 17 (*A.C.Oec.* II. i. 357), εἰ δέ τις ἐκ βασιλικῆς ἐξουσίας ἐκαινίσθη πόλις ἢ αὖθις καινισθείη, τοῖς πολιτικοῖς καὶ δημοσίοις τύποις καὶ τῶν ἐκκλησιαστικῶν παροικιῶν ἡ τάξις ἀκολουθείτω. ANTARADUS: Soz. II. 5, Eus. *V. Const.* IV. 39, Hierocles, 716, 5-7, *A.C.Oec.* II. v. 44, episcopus Aradi et Constantiae. TERMESSUS: Hierocles, 680, 1-2, *A.C.Oec.* I. i. pars ii. 63, pars vii. 114, ἐπίσκοπος πόλεως Τερμησοῦ καὶ Εὐδοκιάδος, II. i. 146, ἐπίσκοπος τῆς κατὰ Τερμισσὸν καὶ Εὐδοκιάδα καὶ Ἰοβίαν ἁγίας τοῦ Θεοῦ ἐκκλησίας; by 458 Termessus and Eudocias were separate bishoprics (*A.C.Oec.* II. v. 60). ISAURA: *CJ* I. iii. 35 §3 (Zeno), κατὰ δὲ τὸν αὐτὸν τρόπον ὑπεξαιρεῖσθαι τῶν ἐπὶ τοῦ παρόντος νενομοθετημένων βουλόμεθα καὶ τὴν ἔναγχος πολισθεῖσαν κατὰ τὸ Ἰσαύρων ἔθνος πρὸς τιμὴν καὶ θεραπείαν τοῦ καλλινίκου μάρτυρος Κόνωνος πόλιν, τουτέστι τὴν Λεοντοπολιτῶν, ὥστε καὶ αὐτήν, ὥσπερ νῦν ἔχει σχήματος, διαμένειν διὰ τὸ (πολλῶν σφόδρα φιλονεικηθέντων, εἴτε αὐτὴν προσήκει ἰδιαζόντως τυχεῖν ἐπισκόπου, εἴτε ὑπὸ τὴν φροντίδα καὶ πρόνοιαν τοῦ θεοφιλεστάτου ἐπισκόπου τῆς Ἰσαυροπόλεως συντελεῖν) δεδόχθαι πόλιν μὲν αὐτὴν εἶναι καὶ τῶν πολιτικῶν ἀνελλιπῶς καὶ εἰς πλῆρες ἀπολαύειν δικαίων, ὑπὸ δὲ τὴν φροντίδα τοῦ μνημονευθέντος ἐπισκόπου διὰ παντὸς διαμένειν. GAZA: Soz. II. 5, V. 3, ἐπεὶ δὲ εἰς τὴν βασιλείαν παρῆλθεν Ἰουλιανός, δίκην ἔλαχον οἱ Γαζαῖοι τοῖς Κωνσταντιεῦσι. καὶ δικαστὴς καθίσας αὐτός, προσένειμε Γάζῃ τὴν Κωνσταντίαν, ἀμφὶ τοὺς εἴκοσι σταδίους διεστῶσαν. καὶ τὸ ἐξ ἐκείνου τῆς προτέρας ἀφαιρεθεῖσα προσηγορίας, παραθαλάττιον μέρος τῆς

Γαζαίων πόλεως ὀνομάζεται. κοινοὶ δὲ αὐτοῖς πολιτικοὶ ἄρχοντες, καὶ στρατηγοὶ καὶ τὰ δημόσια πράγματα. μόνα δὲ τὰ περὶ τὴν ἐκκλησίαν εἰσέτι καὶ νῦν δύο πόλεις δείκνυσιν. ἑκατέρα γὰρ ἰδίᾳ ἐπίσκοπον καὶ κλῆρον ἔχει, καὶ πανηγύρεις μαρτύρων, καὶ μνείας τῶν παρ' αὐτοῖς γενομένων ἱερέων, καὶ ὅρους τῶν πέριξ ἀγρῶν, οἷς τὰ ἀνήκοντα ἑκατέρᾳ ἐπισκοπῇ θυσιαστήρια διορίζεται. τῶν οὖν καθ' ἡμᾶς ἐπισκόπων τις τῆς Γαζαίων πόλεως, τετελευτηκότος τοῦ προεστῶτος τῆς Μαϊουμιτῶν ἐκκλησίας, ἐσπούδασεν ἀμφοτέρους τοὺς κλήρους ὑφ' ἑαυτὸν ποιῆσαι, μὴ θεμιτὸν εἶναι λέγων, μιᾶς πόλεως δύο ἐπισκόπους προεστάναι. ἀντειπόντων δὲ τῶν Μαϊουμητῶν, διέγνω ἡ τοῦ ἔθνους σύνοδος, καὶ ἕτερον ἐχειροτόνησεν ἐπίσκοπον.

8. In Africa new bishoprics seem to have been regularly created as the Christian communities increased (C. Carth. II. 5, III. 42, 46, Cod. Can. Eccl. Afr. 98). MAREOTES: Ath. Apol. c. Ar. 37, 85, Soc. II. 20. CITIES OF EUROPE: A.C.Oec. I. i. pars vii. 122–3. TENEDOS: A.C.Oec. I. i. pars vii. 137–8. ZENO'S LAW: CJ I. iii. 35. It is only possible to test the correspondence of cities and bishoprics if we possess both civil and ecclesiastical provincial lists which are contemporary and reliable. These conditions exist only for the patriarchate of Antioch where we have on the one hand Hierocles and Georgius Cyprius and on the other the sixth century Notitia Antiochena (published by Honigmann in Byz. Zeitschr. XVIII (1925), 60 ff. and defended by him as a genuine sixth century document in Traditio V (1947), 151 ff.). This shows two cities, Nicopolis and Dium, which are not bishoprics. I have endeavoured to work out as far as possible the correspondence of cities and bishoprics in the Eastern provinces in CERP, pp. 381–2, 402, 407, 410, 418, 429, 434, 440, 445, 459, 466, 468, 483–4, 486–7, 489. In the West we possess a civil register for Gaul only: there is no early notitia of bishoprics, but in Les Fastes Épiscopaux de l'ancienne Gaule Duchesne has worked out a fairly complete list from signatures at councils and other sources.

9. CAESAREA OF CAPPADOCIA: CERP, p. 186. NICAEA: A.C.Oec. II. i. 418, ἐγὼ δὲ δείκνυμι Βασιλεινούπολιν ἀεὶ ὑπὸ Νίκαιαν γενομένην· καὶ γὰρ ῥεγεὼν ἦν αὐτῆς . . . ὥσπερ Ταττάϊος καὶ Δωρὶς ῥεγεῶνές εἰσιν ὑπὸ τὴν Νίκαιαν, οὕτως ἦν πρὸ τούτου καὶ Βασιλεινούπολις ὑπὸ τὴν Νίκαιαν. HELEARCHIA: PG XXVI. 808, Ἀγαθὸς Φραγόνεως καὶ μέρους Ἐλεαρχίας τῆς Αἰγύπτον, Ἀμμώνιος Παχνεμουνέως καὶ τοῦ λοιποῦ μέρους τῆς Ἐλεαρχίας, A.C.Oec. I. i. pars ii. 7, 27, 60, etc. The four regiones of Jericho, Amathus, Livias and Gadara were all represented at the council of Jerusalem in 536 (Mansi, VIII. 1171–6) and the saltus of Gerara at Chalcedon (A.C.Oec. II. i. 58, etc.). At Chalcedon there were also bishops of the regiones of Lagania, Mnizus, Trocnades and Paralus (A.C.Oec. II. i. 59–60), while the saltus of Eragiza and the clima of Iabruda are recorded in the Notitia Antiochena. VILLAGE BISHOPRICS IN ARABIA: Soz. VII. 19, ἐν ἄλλοις δὲ ἔθνεσιν ἐστὶν ὅπῃ καὶ ἐν κώμαις ἐπίσκοποι ἱεροῦνται, ὡς παρὰ Ἀραβίοις καὶ Κυπρίοις ἔγνων.

10. BACATHA: Epiph. adv. Haer. lviii. 1, ἐν Βακάθοις τῆς Φιλαδελφηνῆς χώρας, A.C.Oec. III. 80, 188. MARATHAS: V. Dan. 2, Notitia Antiochena. CYPRUS: Soz. VII. 19 (cited in n. 9). In Cyrenaica Synesius mentions village bishoprics at Hydrax and Palaebisca, Erythrum (Ep. 67), and Olbia (Ep. 76), and bishops of Barca, Olbia, Dysthis, Erythrum and Tesila attended the councils of Ephesus in 431 and 449 (A.C.Oec. I. i, pars ii. 60, pars vii. 88, 115–6, II. i. 81), while Philostorgius (apud Nicetas Choniata, Thesaurus, 7) mentions a bishop of Boreum. The Notitia Antiochena records bishoprics of Chonochora, Harlana and Coradea, probably villages of Damascus, Rachla and Porphyreon, probably in the territory of Sidon, and Sarepta, probably in that of Tyre. PHILAE: Not. Dig. Or. xxxi. 37, PG XXVI. 808. SYENE AND ELEPHANTINE: Not. Dig. Or.

xxxi. 34, 64-5, *Chr.* i. 6. BABYLON: *Not. Dig. Or.* xxviii. 15, *A.C.Oec.* ii. i. 81.
SCENAE MANDRON: *Not. Dig. Or.* xxviii. 26, *A.C.Oec.* ii. v. 17. SYRIAN
FORTRESSES: *Not. Dig. Or.* xxxii. 19, 31, xxxiii. 25, 27, 28 and the *Notitia
Antiochena.* SASIMA: Greg. Naz. *de vita sua*, 439-50, *Ep.* 48-50: it is recorded
as a *mansio* in *Itin. Burd.* 577. 4 (Cuntz, *Itin. Rom.* i. 9). AFRICA: *Coll. Carth.* i.
181-2, Alypius episcopus ecclesiae catholicae dixit: scriptum sit istos omnes in
villis vel in fundis esse episcopos ordinatos, non in aliquibus civitatibus.
Petilianus episcopus dixit: sic etiam tu multos habes per omnes agros dispersos.
Among the African sees there are many whose titles seem to denote rural
estates (see pp. 715-16).

11. For Gregory the Great's suppression of Italian sees see p. 312
GINDARUS: Theod. *Hist. Rel.* ii, ἐν τοῖς περὶ Γίνδαρον χωρίοις, κώμη δὲ αὕτη
μεγίστη τελεῖν ὑπὸ τὴν Ἀντιόχειαν τεταγμένη, *Patr. Nic. Nom.* no. 69, Mansi,
II. 1307; it appears at no later council, nor in the *Notitia Antiochena.* HYDRAX
AND PALAEBISCA: Syn. *Ep.* 67. RESAPHA: *Not. Dig. Or.* xxxiii. 27, *A.C.Oec.*
I. iv. 162-3, pervasit vero et martyrium sancti et boni victoris Sergii martyris
quod sub Hieropolitana erat ecclesia et noviter illic contra morem ordinavit
episcopum; *A.C.Oec.* ii. i. 351, 428, Georgius Cyprius, 883, Σεργιούπολις ἤτοι
Ἀναστασιούπολις, ἡ σήμερον Ῥαττάφα, ἔνθα ἐμαρτύρησεν ὁ ἅγιος Σέργιος. Similarly
Evaria, a military post (*Not. Dig. Or.* xxxii. 19) which was a bishopric in 451
(*A.C.Oec.* ii. i. 59), was made a city in 573 (Joh. Eph. *HE* iii. 40), and Ana-
sartha, also a military post and bishopric in 451 (*A.C.Oec.* ii. i. 57), was made a
city by Theodora (Malalas, 444).

12. BOUNDARY DISPUTES: *C. Chalc.* can. 17 (*A.C.Oec.* ii. i. 357), τὰς καθ᾿ ἑκάστην
ἐκκλησίαν ἀγροικικὰς παροικίας ἢ ἐγχωρίους μένειν ἀπορασαλεύτους παρὰ τοῖς
κατέχουσιν αὐτὰς ἐπισκόποις, καὶ μάλιστα εἰ τριακονταετῆ χρόνον ταύτας ἀβιάστως
διακατέχοντες ᾠκονόμησαν. εἰ δὲ ἐντὸς τῶν τριάκοντα ἐτῶν γεγένηταί τις ἢ γένοιτο
περὶ αὐτῶν ἀμφισβήτησις, ἐξεῖναι τοῖς λέγουσιν ἠδικῆσθαι περὶ τούτων κινεῖν
παρὰ τῇ συνόδῳ τῆς ἐπαρχίας; Gelasius, *fr.* 17, territorium etiam non facere
dioecesim olim noscitur ordinatum, 18, 19.

13. In the West *chorepiscopi* are recorded only at Salona (*CIL* iii. 9547, depositio
Eugrafi chorepiscopi), Corduba in the early seventh century (*C. Hisp.* ii,
can. 7, chorepiscopos vel presbyteros, qui tamen iuxta canones unum sunt),
and in Gaul in 439 (*C. Reg.* can. 3); in the last case the office was specially
created for an irregularly consecrated bishop, and canon 9 of Nicaea, which
ruled that reconciled Novatian bishops should rank as priests or *chorepiscopi*,
was cited as a precedent. SIGNATURES AT NICAEA: *Patr. Nic. Nom.* nos. 60,
68, 88, 99-103, 182, 185, 187, 189, 201, 203; AT CHALCEDON: *A.C.Oec.* ii. i. 58,
60, 63, 268-9, 272-3, 283, 287, 329-30, 333, 449. *Chorepiscopi* are mentioned
in *C. Ancyr.* can. 13, *C. Neocaes.* can. 14, *C. Nic.* can. 8, *C. Ant.* can. 8, 10.

14. *C. Laod.* can. 57, ὅτι οὐ δεῖ ἐν ταῖς κώμαις καὶ ἐν ταῖς χώραις καθίστασθαι
ἐπισκόπους, ἀλλὰ περιοδευτάς. τοὺς μέντοι ἤδη προκατασταθέντας μηδὲν πράττειν
ἄνευ γνώμης τοῦ ἐπισκόπου τοῦ ἐν τῇ πόλει. BASIL'S FIFTY CHOREPISCOPI: Greg.
Naz. *de vita sua*, 447, ὁ πεντήκοντα χωρεπισκόποις στενούμενος, cf. Bas. *Ep.* 53-4,
142-3, 290. Athanasius (*Apol. c. Ar.* 85, cited in n. 6) speaks of *chorepiscopi* as
a normal institution in Egypt. Theodoret had two at Cyrrhus (*Ep.* (*PG*) 113).
Other instances are Greg. Naz. *Ep.* 152 (Nazianzus), Pall. *Hist. Laus.* xlviii
(Cappadocia), *A.C.Oec.* I. i. pars vii. 104-5 (Philadelphia), Sev. Ant. *Ep.* i. 37-8
(Chalcis), Cyr. Scyth. *V. Euthymii*, 16 (Jerusalem), *Narr. de ob. Theod. Hierosol.*
pp. 15, 55, 57 (Antioch), Joh. Eph. *V. SS. Or.* viii, xi (Anzitene), *IGLS*

1940–1, 2159. Theodoret (*Hist. Rel.* xxvi) describes the office of a περιοδευτής as ὃς τηνικαῦτα πολλὰς περιώδευσε κώμας τοῖς κατὰ κώμην ἱερεῦσιν ἐπιστατῶν, cf. *A.C.Oec.* III. 146, περιοδευτὴς τῶν ἁγίων ἐκκλησιῶν ἐπὶ χωρίων τῆς πρώτης Συρίων ἐπαρχίας. Both χωρεπίσκοποι and περιοδευταί are mentioned in *CJ* I. iii. 38 §2 (Anastasius), 41 §19, 528, and the two terms are equated in Sev. Ant. *Ep.* I. 37–8. For other περιοδευταί see *A.C.Oec.* I. i. pars ii. 59, II. i. 458, *Narr. de ob. Theod. Hierosol.* p. 57, *IGLS* 130, 332, 389, 421, 460, 634, 733, 1405, 2517.

15. PROVINCIAL COUNCILS: *C. Nic.* can. 5; cf. *C. Ant.* can. 20, *Can. Apost.* 36. CONSECRATION OF BISHOPS: *C. Nic.* can. 4.

16. *C. Ant.* can. 9, τοὺς καθ᾿ ἑκάστην ἐπαρχίαν ἐπισκόπους εἰδέναι χρὴ τὸν ἐν τῇ μητροπόλει προεστῶτα ἐπίσκοπον καὶ τὴν φροντίδα ἀναδέχεσθαι πάσης τῆς ἐπαρχίας, διὰ τὸ ἐν τῇ μητροπόλει πανταχόθεν συντρέχειν πάντας τοὺς τὰ πράγματα ἔχοντας.

17. MINIMUM OF THREE BISHOPS: *C. Arel.* I, can. 20, cf. *C. Carth.* III, can. 39, *C. Reg.* can. 2; this rule was not received in the East, see *Can. Apost.* I, ἐπίσκοπος χειροτονείσθω ὑπὸ ἐπισκόπων δύο ἢ τριῶν.

18. AFRICAN PRIMATES: *Cod. Can. Eccl. Afr.* 86, ut matricula et archivus Numidiae et apud primam sedem sit, et in metropoli, id est Constantina. Bishops of many different sees are recorded as primates of Numidia, e.g. Secundus of Tigisa (Aug. *c. ep. Parm.* I. 5), Megalius of Calama (Poss. *V. Aug.* 8), Xanthippus of Tagaste (Aug. *Ep.* 59). For the same practice in the Mauretanias see Aug. *Ep.* 59, 209 §8. Gregory the Great (*Ep.* I. 72, 75) tried to alter the rule but failed.

19. Innoc. *Ep.* 24, nam quod sciscitaris utrum divisis imperiali iudicio provinciis ut duae metropoleis fiant, sic duo metropolitani episcopi debeant nominari, non vere visum est ad mobilitatem necessitatum mundanarum dei ecclesiam commutari, honoresque aut divisiones perpeti quas pro suis causis faciendas duxerit imperator. The same view was taken by Gregory Nazianzen, *Ep.* 185, τὴν μὲν οὖν περὶ τῶν παροικιῶν ἀμφισβήτησιν δηλαδὴ αὐτὸς διαλύσεις κατὰ τὴν ἐν σοὶ τοῦ πνεύματος χάριν καὶ τὴν τῶν κανόνων ἀκολουθίαν· ἐκεῖνο δὲ μὴ ἀνεκτὸν φανήτω τῇ σῇ εὐλαβείᾳ τὸ δημοσίοις δικαστηρίοις τὰ ἡμέτερα στηλιτευέσθαι.

20. HONORIAS ETC.: Just. *Nov.* xxviii §2, 535, xxix §1, 535. The province of Theodorias, recorded in Georgius Cyprius, is ignored in the *Notitia Antiochena.*

21. For Bacatha and Marathas see above n. 10. MASSILIA: *C. Taurin.* can. 1.

22. JERUSALEM: *C. Nic.* can. 7, ἐπειδὴ συνήθεια κεκράτηκε καὶ παράδοσις ἀρχαία, ὥστε τὸν ἐν Αἰλίᾳ ἐπίσκοπον τιμᾶσθαι, ἐχέτω τὴν ἀκολουθίαν τῆς τιμῆς, τῇ μητροπόλει σωζομένου τοῦ οἰκείου ἀξιώματος. ARLES: *C. Taurin.* can. 2.

23. NICOMEDIA AND NICAEA: *A.C.Oec.* II. i. 416–21.

24. BERYTUS: *A.C.Oec.* II. i. 462–9.

25. SIDE METROPOLIS IN 431: *A.C.Oec.* I. i. pars vii. 112. I infer that Pamphylia was already by 458 divided into two ecclesiastical provinces, as in the episcopal notitiae, from the fact that the letter of Epiphanius of Perge to Leo (*A.C.Oec.* II. v. 60) is signed by fourteen bishops who are all in the later province of Perge, and none in the later province of Side (the letter of Amphilochius of Side is not preserved). The province of Resapha is first recorded in the *Notitia*

Antiochena; for its possible creation by Anastasius see Georgius Cyprius, 883 (cited in n. 11). In 451 Resapha was still a suffragan of Hierapolis and none of its later suffragans existed (see *A.C.Oec.* ii. i. 350–1).

26. *C. Nic.* can. 6, τὰ ἀρχαῖα ἔθη κρατείτω τὰ ἐν Αἰγύπτῳ καὶ Λιβύῃ καὶ Πενταπόλει, ὥστε τὸν Ἀλεξανδρείας ἐπίσκοπον πάντων τούτων ἔχειν τὴν ἐξουσίαν, ἐπειδὴ καὶ τῷ ἐν τῇ Ῥώμῃ ἐπισκόπῳ τοῦτο σύνηθές ἐστιν· ὁμοίως δὲ καὶ κατὰ Ἀντιόχειαν καὶ ἐν ταῖς ἄλλαις ἐπαρχίαις τὰ πρεσβεῖα σώζεσθαι ταῖς ἐκκλησίαις. καθόλου δὲ πρόδηλον ἐκεῖνο, ὅτι, εἴ τις χωρὶς γνώμης τοῦ μητροπολίτου γένοιτο ἐπίσκοπος, τὸν τοιοῦτον ἡ μεγάλη σύνοδος ὥρισε μὴ δεῖν εἶναι ἐπίσκοπον· ἐὰν μέντοι τῇ κοινῇ πάντων ψήφῳ, εὐλόγῳ οὔσῃ καὶ κατὰ κανόνα ἐκκλησιαστικόν, δύο ἢ τρεῖς δι᾽ οἰκείαν φιλονεικίαν ἀντιλέγωσι, κρατείτω ἡ τῶν πλειόνων ψῆφος.

27. Synesius in *Ep.* 67 speaks of Ptolemais as τὴν μητροπολῖτιν ἐκκλησίαν, and he called provincial councils (*Ep.* 13); for his incapacity to consecrate bishops see *Ep.* 67, 76.

28. *PG* x. 1565, magni episcopi ac patris nostri Petri honorem, ex quo cuncti per spem quam habemus in domino Jesu Christo pendemus. *A.C.Oec.* ii. i. 309, οἶδεν ὁ θεοφιλέστατος ἀρχιεπίσκοπος Ἀνατόλιος ὅτιπερ τοιοῦτο ἔθος κεκράτηκεν ἐν τῇ Αἰγυπτιακῇ διοικήσει ὥστε πάντας τοὺς ἐπισκόπους ὑπακούειν τῷ Ἀλεξανδρείας ἀρχιεπισκόπῳ.

29. For the Latin versions of the Nicene canons preserved at Carthage see *Eccl. Occ. Mon. Iur. Ant.* I. 120–1: cf. also Ruf. *HE* i. 6, ut apud Alexandriam et in urbe Roma vetusta consuetudo servetur, ut vel ille Aegypti vel hic suburbicariarum ecclesiarum sollicitudinem gerat. In Sicily Gregory the Great entrusted some of the functions of a metropolitan to the rector of the local patrimony (*Ep.* i. 1, 18) and himself consecrated the bishops (*Ep.* ii. 24); he sometimes appointed the bishop of Syracuse as papal vicar (*Ep.* ii. 8). Lucifer of Caralis is called ὁ ἀπὸ μητροπόλεως τῆς Σαρδινίας in Ath. *Hist. Ar.* 33, *Apol. de fuga*, 4 and the bishop of Caralis is specifically styled metropolitan in Greg. *Ep.* i. 47, and consecrated his own bishops (*Ep.* iv. 29).

30. Bishops from Syria, Phoenice, Palestine, Arabia, Cilicia (and even some from Cappadocia) assembled in 385 to elect a successor to Philogonius of Antioch (Opitz, *Athanasius Werke*, iii. i. 36, no. 18); the council which elected Euphronius included Aetius of Lydda (Palestine), Narcissus of Neronias (Cilicia) and Theodore of Sidon (Phoenice) as well as Theodotus of Laodicea and Alphaeus of Apamea (Eus. *V. Const.* iii. 62); and the Council of Constantinople claimed that οἵ τε τῆς ἐπαρχίας καὶ τῆς ἀνατολικῆς διοικήσεως συνδραμόντες κανονικῶς ἐχειροτόνησαν Flavian (Theod. *HE* v. 9). On the right of the bishop of Antioch to consecrate see Innocent, *Ep.* 24, itaque arbitramur, frater carissime, ut sicut metropolitanos auctoritate ordinas singulari, sic et ceteros non sine permissu conscientiaque tua sinas episcopos procreari, in quibus hunc modum recte servabis ut longe positos litteris datis ordinari censeas ab his qui nunc eos suo tantum ordinant arbitratu, vicinos autem si aestimas ad manus impositionem tuae gratiae statuas pervenire. That the bishops of Antioch did not, despite this ruling, have any voice in the election of suffragans is shown by the dispute between Photius of Tyre and Eustathius of Berytus (*A.C.Oec.* ii. i. 462–9). THE CYPRIOT CASE: *A.C.Oec.* i. i. pars vii. 118–22. On his jurisdiction contrast *C. Ant.* can. 14, εἴ τις ἐπίσκοπος ἐπί τισιν ἐγκλήμασι κρίνοιτο, ἔπειτα συμβαίη περὶ αὐτοῦ διαφωνεῖν τοὺς ἐν τῇ ἐπαρχίᾳ ἐπισκόπους, τῶν μὲν ἀθῶον τὸν κρινόμενον ἀποφαινόντων, τῶν δὲ ἔνοχον, ὑπὲρ ἀπαλλαγῆς πάσης ἀμφισβητήσεως ἔδοξε τῇ ἁγίᾳ συνόδῳ τὸν τῆς μητροπόλεως ἐπίσκοπον

ἀπὸ τῆς πλησιοχώρου ἐπαρχίας μετακαλεῖσθαι ἑτέρους τινὰς τοὺς ἐπικρινοῦντας καὶ τὴν ἀμφισβήτησιν διαλύσοντας, τοῦ βεβαιῶσαι σὺν τοῖς τῆς ἐπαρχίας τὸ παριστάμενον, and *A.C.Oec.* II. i. 428–42, where Domnus, patriarch of Antioch, takes cognizance of a dispute between the metropolitan of Hierapolis and one of his suffragans and calls a council to decide the issue.

31. From *Ep.* 72 we learn that Cyprian held a council of African bishops and communicated their decisions to those of Numidia and Mauretania, from *Ep.* 73 that he held a council of 71 bishops from Africa and Numidia, and in his works (pp. 435–61) are preserved the acts of a council of 87 bishops from Africa, Numidia and Mauretania. For the election of Caecilian see Opt. 1. 18 ff.

32. *C. Const.* 1, can. 2, τοὺς ὑπὲρ διοίκησιν ἐπισκόπους ταῖς ὑπερορίοις ἐκκλησίαις μὴ ἐπιέναι, μηδὲ συγχέειν τὰς ἐκκλησίας· ἀλλὰ κατὰ τοὺς κανόνας τὸν μὲν Ἀλεξανδρείας ἐπίσκοπον τὰ ἐν Αἰγύπτῳ μόνον οἰκονομεῖν, τοὺς δὲ τῆς Ἀνατολῆς ἐπισκόπους τὴν Ἀνατολὴν μόνην διοικεῖν, φυλαττομένων τῶν ἐν τοῖς κανόσι τοῖς κατὰ Νικαίαν πρεσβείων τῇ Ἀντιοχέων ἐκκλησίᾳ, καὶ τοὺς τῆς Ἀσιανῆς διοικήσεως ἐπισκόπους τὰ κατὰ τὴν Ἀσίαν μόνην οἰκονομεῖν, καὶ τοὺς τῆς Ποντικῆς τὰ τῆς Ποντικῆς μόνον, καὶ τοὺς τῆς Θρᾴκης τὰ τῆς Θρακικῆς μόνον οἰκονομεῖν, 3, τὸν μέντοι Κωνσταντινουπόλεως ἐπίσκοπον ἔχειν τὰ πρεσβεῖα τῆς τιμῆς μετὰ τὸν τῆς Ῥώμης ἐπίσκοπον, διὰ τὸ εἶναι αὐτὴν νέαν Ῥώμην. In the imperial constitution (*CTh* XVI. i. 3, 381) enforcing the creed of the council, besides Nectarius of Constantinople and Timothy of Alexandria, two or three bishops are named as arbiters in the dioceses of Asiana, Pontica, Oriens and Thrace.

33. For the councils of Rome and Arles we have Constantine's letters in Eus. *HE* x. 5, for the council of Caesarea Theod. *HE* 1. 28, *P. Lond.* 1913, for that of Tyre, Eus. *V. Const.* IV. 42, Theod. *HE* 1. 29.

34. Pall. *Dial.* pp. 42 ff. esp. 48.

35. For challenges to Roman claims see Eus. *HE* v. 24, Cyprian, *Ep.* 67, 74, 75, Soz. III. 8. For the Eastern view that Rome's claims were partly based on her being the capital see Ath. *Hist. Ar.* 35, καὶ οὐχ ὅτι ἀποστολικός ἐστι θρόνος ἠδέσθησαν, οὐθ' ὅτι μητρόπολις ἡ Ῥώμη τῆς Ῥωμανίας ἐστί, Theod. *Ep.* (*PG*), 113, ἡ γὰρ αὐτὴ πασῶν μεγίστη καὶ λαμπροτάτη καὶ τῆς οἰκουμένης προκαθημένη καὶ τῷ πλήθει τῶν οἰκητόρων κυμαίνουσα· πρὸς δὲ τούτοις καὶ νῦν κρατοῦσαν ἡγεμονίαν ἐβλάστησε καὶ τῆς οἰκείας προσηγορίας τοῖς ἀρχομένοις μετέδωκε (then follow Peter and Paul).

36. *C. Sard.* can. 3, εἰ δὲ ἄρα τις ἐπισκόπων ἔν τινι πράγματι δόξῃ κατακρίνεσθαι καὶ ὑπολαμβάνει ἑαυτὸν μὴ σαθρὸν ἀλλὰ καλὸν ἔχειν τὸ πρᾶγμα, ἵνα καὶ αὖθις ἡ κρίσις ἀνανεωθῇ· εἰ δοκεῖ ὑμῶν τῇ ἀγάπῃ, Πέτρου τοῦ ἀποστόλου τὴν μνήμην τιμήσωμεν, καὶ γραφῆναι παρὰ τούτων τῶν κρινάντων Ἰουλίῳ τῷ ἐπισκόπῳ Ῥώμης, ὥστε διὰ τῶν γειτνιώντων τῇ ἐπαρχίᾳ ἐπισκόπων, εἰ δέοι, ἀνανεωθῆναι τὸ δικαστήριον καὶ ἐπιγνώμονας αὐτὸς παράσχοι· εἰ δὲ μὴ συστῆναι δύναται, τοιοῦτον αὐτοῦ εἶναι τὸ πρᾶγμα, ὡς παλινδικίας χρῄζειν, τὰ ἅπαξ κεκριμένα μὴ ἀναλύεσθαι, τὰ δὲ ὄντα βέβαια τυγχάνειν, 5, ἤρεσεν, ἵν' εἴ τις ἐπίσκοπος καταγγελθείη, καὶ συναθροισθέντες οἱ ἐπίσκοποι τῆς ἐνορίας τῆς αὐτῆς τοῦ βαθμοῦ αὐτὸν ἀποκινήσωσι, καὶ ὥσπερ ἐκκαλεσάμενος καταφύγῃ ἐπὶ τὸν μακαριώτατον τῆς Ῥωμαίων ἐκκλησίας ἐπίσκοπον, καὶ βουληθείη αὐτοῦ διακοῦσαι, δίκαιόν τε εἶναι νομίσῃ ἀνανεώσασθαι αὐτοῦ τὴν ἐξέτασιν τοῦ πράγματος, γράφειν τούτοις τοῖς συνεπισκόποις καταξιώσῃ τοῖς ἀγχιστεύουσι τῇ ἐπαρχίᾳ, ἵνα αὐτοὶ ἐπιμελῶς καὶ μετὰ ἀκριβείας ἕκαστα διερευνήσωσι καὶ κατὰ τὴν τῆς ἀληθείας πίστιν ψῆφον περὶ τοῦ πράγματος ἐξενέγκωσιν. εἰ δέ τις ἀξιῶν καὶ πάλιν αὐτοῦ τὸ πρᾶγμα ἀκουσθῆναι, καὶ τῇ δεήσει τῇ ἑαυτοῦ τὸν Ῥωμαίων

ἐπίσκοπον δόξειεν ἀπὸ τοῦ ἰδίου πλευροῦ πρεσβυτέρους ἀποστείλοι, εἶναι ἐν τῇ ἐξουσίᾳ αὐτοῦ τοῦ ἐπισκόπου, ὅπερ ἂν καλῶς ἔχειν δοκιμάσῃ καὶ ὁρίσῃ δεῖν, ἀποσταλῆναι τοὺς μετὰ τῶν ἐπισκόπων κρινοῦντας, ἔχοντάς τε τὴν αὐθεντίαν τούτου παρ᾽ οὗ ἀπεστάλησαν· καὶ τοῦτο θετέον. εἰ δὲ ἐξαρκεῖν νομίσῃ πρὸς τὴν τοῦ πράγματος ἐπίγνωσιν καὶ ἀπόφασιν τοῦ ἐπισκόπου, ποιήσει ὅπερ ἂν τῇ ἐμφρονεστάτῃ αὐτοῦ βουλῇ καλῶς ἔχειν δόξῃ. For Pope Zosimus's unsuccessful attempt to enforce these canons in the case of Apiarius see ch. VI, n. 89. ROMAN COUNCIL UNDER DAMASUS: Mansi, III. 624–7. GRATIAN'S LAW: *Coll. Avell.* 13 §11.

37. AMBROSE AT SIRMIUM: Paul. *V. Amb.* 11. POSITION OF SIRMIUM: *Gesta Conc. Aquil.* 16 (PL XVI. 921), caput Illyrici non nisi civitas est Sirmiensis. THE DEPOSITION OF TWO DACIAN BISHOPS: *Gesta Conc. Aquil.* (PL XVI. 916–49); that the two bishops came from the diocese of Dacia is shown by PL XVI. 948, in latere Daciae Ripensis et Moesia. In this instance Ambrose was acting under imperial authority, see the imperial constitution cited in the *Gesta* 3–4 (PL XVI. 916–17).

38. The whole dossier of papal, imperial and other letters bearing on the vicariate of Illyricum was cited at a Roman council in 521, and is printed in Mansi, VIII. 749–72.

39. *CTh* XVI. ii. 45, 421; the letters of Honorius and Theodosius are nos. xi and xii in Mansi, *loc. cit.*

40. THE VICARIATE OF ARLES: Zosimus, *Ep.* 1, 4–7, 10–11; it is ignored by Boniface, *Ep.* 12, Celestine, *Ep.* 4 §4.

41. HILARY: Leo, *Ep.* 10 (cf. Val. III, *Nov.* xvii, 445). RAVENNIUS: Leo, *Ep.* 65–6. CAESARIUS: Symmachus, *Ep.* 16. THE VICARIATE OF SPAIN: Simplicius, *Ep.* 21, Hormisdas, *Ep.* 24, 142.

42. Ephesus certainly enjoyed some form of primacy, which Palladius implies extended over all Asiana, when he says that John Chrysostom, in response to an appeal from the church of Ephesus and the bishops there assembled after the death of Antoninus, went to Ephesus ἐπὶ καταστάσει μάλιστα νενοσηκότων πραγμάτων ὅλης τῆς Ἀσιανῆς διοικήσεως (*Dial.* p. 88). John, however, summoned a council to elect Antoninus's successor from Lydia, Asia and Caria only, and some bishops from Phrygia attended voluntarily (*Dial.* p. 89). This suggests that the influence of Ephesus did not extend to the remoter provinces of Asiana. There was local indignation at Ephesus after Chalcedon at the loss of its prerogatives, and in the anti-Chalcedonian reaction under Basiliscus they were temporarily restored (Zach. Myt. *Chron.* IV. 5, v. 4, Evagr. III. 6). At the sixth ecumenical council of 680 the metropolitans of Ephesus and Caesarea signed as ἔξαρχος τῆς Ἀσιανῶν διοικήσεως and ἔξαρχος τῆς Ποντικῆς διοικήσεως respectively (Mansi, XI. 688–9), but this does not prove that either see enjoyed any special prerogatives at an earlier date: I know of no evidence that Caesarea held any special position except that its bishop enjoyed high precedence, and precedence does not imply powers. There is also, as far as I know, no evidence that Heraclea had any primacy in Thrace, except that its bishop had high precedence.

The suggestion of the imperial commissioners at Chalcedon that οἱ ὁσιώτατοι πατριάρχαι διοικήσεως ἑκάστης ἐπιλεξάμενοι ἕνα ἢ δεύτερον τῆς οἰκείας ἕκαστος διοικήσεως (*A.C.Oec.* II. i. 274) should form a committee to draw up the creed shows that they thought every diocese had an acknowledged head; but this layman's suggestion was not acted upon, doubtless because it ignored the facts.

It has also been argued from two canons of Chalcedon that the dioceses of Thrace, Asiana and Pontica had 'exarchs'. They run: εἰ δὲ πρὸς τὸν τῆς αὐτῆς ἐπαρχίας μητροπολίτην ἐπίσκοπος ἢ κληρικὸς ἀμφισβητοίη, καταλαμβανέτω ἢ τὸν ἔξαρχον τῆς διοικήσεως ἢ τὸν τῆς βασιλευούσης Κωνσταντινουπόλεως θρόνον καὶ ἐπ' αὐτῷ δικαζέσθω (canon 9, A.C.Oec. II. i. 356), εἰ δέ τις παρὰ τοῦ ἰδίου ἀδικοῖτο μητροπολίτου, παρὰ τῷ ἐξάρχῳ τῆς διοικήσεως ἢ τῷ Κωνσταντινουπόλεως θρόνῳ δικαζέσθω, καθὰ προείρηται (canon 17, A.C.Oec. II. i. 357). These canons were enacted before the creation of the patriarchate of Constantinople, and were evidently meant to be of general application throughout the Eastern church. They certainly cannot mean, as has been maintained, that in the patriarchate of Constantinople, cases went first to the 'exarchs' of Thrace, Pontica and Asiana, and by appeal to Constantinople; for in the first place the patriarchate did not yet exist, and in the second 'the exarch of the diocese' and 'the throne of Constantinople' are quite clearly alternative courts of equal status. Moreover on that interpretation the canons would ignore the other dioceses of the East. The most natural interpretation of their rather obscure wording is that the cases in question are to be referred to the head of the diocese (if any), or to the see of Constantinople (if the diocese had no head). The 'exarchs' would include the bishop of Antioch, who is often styled ἔξαρχος τῆς Ἀνατολικῆς διοικήσεως (A.C.Oec. II. i. 438, cf. 389, Perry, The Second Synod of Ephesus, 355). These canons, then, do not imply that every diocese had its 'exarch'; on the contrary they imply that in some dioceses Constantinople exercised the jurisdiction which elsewhere fell to the 'exarch'.

An instance of an imperial constitution in favour of Constantinople is given by Soc. VII. 28. The visiting synod is seen functioning under John Chrysostom (Pall. Dial. p. 83) and Flavian (A.C.Oec. II. i. 100–45) and its authority is confirmed in A.C.Oec. II. i. 465–6.

43. JOHN CHRYSOSTOM'S INTERVENTION IN ASIA: Pall. Dial. pp. 83 ff. Cf. also Syn. Ep. 66 (John Chrysostom consecrated a bishop at Basilinopolis in Bithynia).

44. JOHN CHRYSOSTOM'S SUCCESSORS: Soc. VII. 25 (Nicaea), 28 (Cyzicus), 37 (Philippopolis and Troas), 48 (Caesarea), cf. VII. 3 for a decision of Atticus about Synnada.

45. THE PATRIARCHATE OF CONSTANTINOPLE: A.C.Oec. II. i. 447–8 (the canon), 453–8 (the debate).

46. ANCYRA: A.C.Oec. II. i. 457. That Ancyra, metropolis of Galatia I, was the residence of the vicar of Pontica appears from Just. Nov. viii §3, 535, where the posts of governor of Galatia I and of vicar are united.

47. EPHESUS: A.C.Oec. II. i. 411–12.

48. THE PATRIARCHATE OF JERUSALEM: A.C.Oec. II. i. 364–6. JUVENAL'S EARLIER CLAIMS: A.C.Oec. I. i. pars. iii. 18–9.

49. PRIMA JUSTINIANA: Just. Nov. xi, 535, cxxi §3, 545. The title patriarch is first used (anachronistically) by Socrates (v. 8), writing about 440, to describe the bishops who were selected, several to each diocese, in 381 under CTh xvi. i. 3 to test the orthodoxy of the other bishops in their dioceses. At Chalcedon the title is applied to Pope Leo (A.C.Oec. II. i. 191, 211, 216, 218–9) and is used once by the imperial commissioners to denote the chief bishop of a diocese (see n. 42). An alternative term, which did not ultimately find favour,

was ἔξαρχος (see n. 42). The rule for consecrations is clearly laid down in
A.C.Oec. II. i. 448 for Constantinople, and the same rule applied to Oriens
(see above n. 30). For Alexandria see above n. 27. For Thessalonica the
rules are stated in Leo, *Ep.* 14 §5–6. Justinian's language in *Nov.* xi and cxxxi
§3 might be taken to mean that the archbishop of Justiniana Prima consecrated
all his bishops, but is compatible with the Thessalonican rule.

50. For the Apiarius case see ch. VI, n. 89.

51. On the finances of the church see my article in *JTS* 1960, 84–94. *Oblationes*
are mentioned as part of the church revenue in Simplicius, *Ep.* 1, Gelasius,
Ep. 14 §27, 15, 16, *C. Aurel.* 1, can. 14, 15, καρποφορίαι in *C. Gangr.* can. 7, 8,
A.C.Oec. II. i. 384, *CJ* 1. iii. 38.

52. There are vague allusions to first fruits and tithe in *Can. Apost.* 4, *Can.
Athan.* 3, 63, 82, 83, *Const. Apost.* vii. 29, viii. 30; in *Const. Apost.* ii. 25–6
(cf. 34–5) they are mentioned as a biblical institution worthy of imitation.
ACTUAL GIFTS OF TITHE: Cassian, *Coll.* XIV. vii. 1–3, XXI. i–viii, *V. Severini*, 17.
That tithe was not normally paid is proved by Joh. Chrys. *Hom. in Eph.* iv. 4,
Jerome, *Comm. in Mal.* iii, Aug. *Enarr. in Psal.* cxlvi. 17, *Serm.* 9 §19, 85 §5.
TITHE IN MEROVINGIAN GAUL: *C. Tur.* II, *Ep. ad plebem*, *C. Matisc.* II, can. 5.

53. *CJ* 1. iii. 38 §2, καὶ τοῦτο ἰδὲ θεσπίζομεν, ὥστε μηδένα τῶν θεοφιλεστάτων
ἐπισκόπων ἢ χωρεπισκόπων ἢ περιοδευτῶν ἢ κληρικῶν ἄκοντας τοὺς λαϊκοὺς συνελαύνειν
πρὸς τὴν τῶν καρποφοριῶν τῶν ἐν τοῖς τόποις καλουμένων ἀπαρχῶν ἤτοι προσφορῶν
ἔκτισιν ὥσπερ τι τέλος ταῦτα μεθοδεύοντας . . . μηδ' ἀφορισμοὺς τούτων ἕνεκα τῶν
αἰτιῶν ἢ ἀναθεματισμοὺς τούτοις ἐπάγειν καὶ τῆς τῶν ἁγίων μυστηρίων μεταλήψεως
καὶ αὐτοῦ τοῦ σεβασμίου καὶ σωτηριώδους βαπτίσματος, ὅπερ καὶ λέγειν ἀθέμιτον,
ἐντεῦθεν ἀποστερεῖν; §§3–4, καὶ γάρ ἐστι πρόδηλον, ὡς προσήκει μάλιστα ἕκαστον ἐκ
τῶν οἰκείων πόνων ἕκοντα τῷ θεῷ καὶ τοῖς ὑπηρετουμένοις αὐτῷ προσφέρειν, ἅπερ ἂν
αὐτὸς δοκιμάσοι, οὐ μὴν συνωθεῖσθαι πρὸς τοῦτο καὶ ἀναγκάζεσθαι καὶ ἀποροῦντα ἴσως
καὶ οὐδὲ τῶν ἐκ τῆς γεωργίας καρπῶν διά τινας συμβαινούσας οἷα εἰκὸς ἀφορίας ἀπολ-
αύοντα. διὰ γὰρ τοῦτο τὴν μὲν ἀνάγκην κωλύομεν, τὴν δ' αὐθαίρετον γνώμην τῶν προσφε-
ρόντων οὐ μόνον οὐκ εἴργομεν, ἀλλὰ καὶ ἀποδεχόμεθα.

54. EDICT OF GALLIENUS: Eus. *HE* VII. 13; OF MAXIMIN: ibid. IX. 10, εἴ τινες
οἰκίαι καὶ χωρία τοῦ δικαίου τῶν Χριστιανῶν πρὸ τούτου ἐτύγχανον ὄντα; OF
CONSTANTINE: X. 5, εἴτε κῆποι εἴτε οἰκίαι εἴθ' ὁτιονδήποτε τῷ δικαίῳ τῶν αὐτῶν
ἐκκλησιῶν διέφερον; OF LICINIUS: Lact. *Mort. Pers.* 48 §9, et quoniam iidem
Christiani non ea loca tantum, ad quae convenire consuerunt, sed alia etiam
habuisse noscuntur ad ius corporis eorum id est ecclesiarum, non hominum
singulorum, pertinentia, ea omnia lege quam superius comprehendimus, citra
ullam prorsus ambiguitatem vel controversiam iisdem Christianis id est corpori
et conventiculis eorum reddi iubebis, supra dicta scilicet ratione servata, ut
ii qui eadem sine pretio sicut diximus restituant, indemnitatem de nostra
benevolentia sperent.

55. BEQUESTS TO THE CHURCH LEGALISED: *CTh* XVI. ii. 4, 321. Constantine's
gifts to the churches of Rome and Italy are set out in *Lib. Pont.* xxxiv. MELANIA:
V. Mel. 21. RAVENNA DEEDS: *P. Ital.* 4–6, 12–24. FLAVIUS PUSI: *P. Oxy.* 1901;
cf. *P. Cairo*, 67151 (bequest of one *arura* by a doctor), *P. Gröningen*, 10 (bequest
by a retired officer of his whole estate, with a life interest in half to his widow).

56. INTESTATE CLERICS: *CTh* V. iii. 1, 434. ESTATES OF BISHOPS: *PG* XXXVII.
389–96 (Gregory's will), *PL* LXVII. 1139–42 (Caesarius's will), *Cod. Can. Eccl.*

Afr. 81, item constitutum est, ut si quis episcopus haeredes extraneos a consanguinitate sua vel haereticos etiam consanguineos aut paganos ecclesiae praetulerit, saltem post mortem anathema ei dicatur.

57. SCHEDULE OF BISHOP'S PROPERTY: *C. Ant.* can. 24, *Can. Apost.* 39, *C. Tarrac.* can. 12, *C. Ilerd.* can. 16, *C. Valent.* can. 2, 3. PROPERTY ACQUIRED BY BISHOPS: *C. Carth.* III. 49, placuit ut episcopi, presbyteri, diaconi vel quicumque clerici, qui nihil habentes ordinantur, et tempore episcopatus vel clericatus sui agros vel quaecumque praedia nomine suo comparant, tamquam rerum dominicarum invasionis crimine teneantur obnoxii, nisi admoniti ecclesiae eadem ipsa contulerint. si autem ipsis proprie aliquid liberalitate alicuius vel successione cognationis obvenerit, faciant inde quod eorum proposito congruit; *C. Agath.* can. 6, pontifices vero, quibus in summo sacerdotio constitutis ab extraneis dumtaxat aliquid aut cum ecclesia aut sequestratim aut dimittitur aut donatur, quia hoc ille qui donat pro redemptione animae suae, non pro commodo sacerdotis probatur offerre, non quasi suum proprium sed quasi dimissum ecclesiae inter facultates ecclesiae computabunt, quia iustum est, ut sicut sacerdos habet quod ecclesiae dimissum est, ita et ecclesia habeat quod relinquitur sacerdoti; *CJ* I. iii. 41 §§5–7, 528, Just. *Nov.* cxxxi §13, 545; Pelagius I, *Ep.* 33, Greg. *Ep.* IV. 36, VI. 1, IX. 194, XII. 14.

58. BISHOPS' POOR RELATIONS: *Can. Apost.* 37. IBAS: *A.C.Oec.* II. i. 384. CORRUPTION IN PAPAL ELECTIONS: *MGH (AA)* XII. 399 ff.

59. ALIENATION OF CHURCH PROPERTY: *CJ* I. ii. 14, 470, 17 (Anastasius), cf. Just. *Nov.* vii pr., 535.

60. JUSTINIAN'S LAWS: *CJ* I. ii. 24, 530, cf. Just. *Nov.* vii pr., 535; the nature of *ius colonarium* is explained in an ancient gloss to the Novel. The rules of the law of 530 are elaborated in Just. *Nov.* vii, 535; exchange with the crown is authorised in §2.

61. ALIENATION FOR FISCAL OR PRIVATE DEBTS: Just. *Nov.* xlvi, 537. SPECIAL LAWS FOR JERUSALEM AND MOESIA: Just. *Nov.* xl, 535, lxv, 538. PERPETUAL LEASES ALLOWED: Just. *Nov.* cxx §1 (houses), §6 (land), 544.

62. *CJ* I. ii. 24 §1, 530, τὰ μέντοι λοιπὰ συναλλάγματα, ὅσα ἐφεῖται τοῖς θεοφιλεστ-άτοις ἐπισκόποις τῆς αὐτῆς ἁγιωτάτης μεγάλης ἐκκλησίας ποιεῖν, ἐξεῖναι αὐτοῖς τίθεσθαι, πρὸς οὓς ἂν δοκιμάσωσι, δίχα τῶν ἐνδοξοτάτων ἢ μεγαλοπρεπεστάτων ἐμπράκτων ἀρχόντων ταύτης τῆς βασιλίδος πόλεως. πρὸς γὰρ τούτους κατ' οὐδένα τρόπον ποιεῖσθαι αὐτοὺς οἱανδήποτε ἔκδοσιν ἀκινήτων πραγμάτων, ἀλλὰ μηδὲ ἄλλου παρεντιθεμένου προσώπου ἐπὶ περιγραφῇ τῆς θείας ἡμῶν διατυπώσεως συγχωροῦμεν, εἴτε τινὰ οἰκειότητα οὗτος ἔχει πρὸς τὸν ἄρχοντα τὸν ἐπὶ τῇ ἐξουσίᾳ τελοῦντα, εἴτε δίχα παλαιᾶς οἰκειότητος νεωστὶ παρ' αὐτοῦ πρὸς τοῦτο παρείληπται; Just. *Nov.* vii §9, 535, ἐπειδὴ δὲ εἰκός τινας ἐπὶ παρακρούσει τοῦδε τοῦ νόμου πειρᾶσθαι πραγματικοὺς ἡμῶν τύπους λαμβάνειν τοιοῦτό τι πράττειν αὐτοῖς ἐπιτρέποντας, καὶ τοῦτο κωλύομεν ἐπὶ παντὸς προσώπου, μείζονός τε καὶ ἐλάττονος, εἴτε ἀρχὴν ἔχοι τινὰ εἴτε τῶν περὶ ἡμᾶς εἴη εἴτε τῶν ἄλλων τις τῶν εἰς δήμους τελούντων, §10, εἰ μέντοι βούλονταί τινα ὑπὸ τὴν ἑαυτῶν διοίκησιν ἔχειν οἱ θεοφιλέστατοι οἰκονόμοι ἢ οἱ τῶν ἄλλων ἡγούμενοι συστημάτων, μηδενὶ τῶν ἐν δυνάμει μηδὲ κατὰ θεῖον πραγματικὸν τύπον παρρησίαν εἶναι ἀναγκάζειν αὐτοὺς ἢ κατὰ μίσθωσιν ἢ κατὰ ἐμφύτευσιν ταῦτα ἐκδιδόναι, lv pr., 537, ἐπειδὴ δὲ ἔγνωμεν ὥς τινες τὸ τῆς προτέρας διατάξεως κεφάλαιον, ὅπερ ἐπὶ ἀμείψει διαφερόντως τοῖς εὐαγέσιν οἴκοις πραγμάτων πρὸς τὴν βασιλείαν ἐγράψαμεν, εἰς τὴν κατὰ τοῦ νόμου τέχνην ἔτρεψαν, ᾔτησαν δὲ ὥστε ἡμᾶς μὲν παρὰ τῆς ἁγιωτάτης ἐκκλησίας λαβεῖν, αὐτοῖς δὲ ταῦτα δοῦναι, ἐντεῦθεν δὲ ὡρμήθησαν πολλοὶ ταῖς ὁμοίαις αἰτήσεσι χρώμενοι τὴν θείαν περιγράφειν διάταξιν.

63. AFRICAN RULE: *Cod. Can. Eccl. Afr.* 33, item placuit ut presbyteri non vendant rem ecclesiae ubi sunt constituti, nescientibus episcopis suis; quomodo et episcopis non licet vendere praedia ecclesiae, ignorante concilio vel presbyteris suis. non habenti ergo necessitatem nec episcopo liceat matricis ecclesiae rem <nec presbytero rem> tituli sui usurpare. GALLIC CANONS: *C. Agath.* can. 7, quod si necessitas certa compulerit, ut pro ecclesiae aut necessitate aut utilitate vel in usufructu vel in directa venditione aliquid distrahatur, apud duos vel tres comprovinciales vel vicinos episcopos causa, qua necesse sit vendi, primitus comprobetur: et habita discussione sacerdotali eorum subscriptione quae facta fuerit venditio roboretur; aliter facta venditio vel transactio non valebit. sane si quod de servis ecclesiae bene meritos sibi episcopus libertate donaverit, collatam libertatem a successoribus placuit custodiri, cum hoc quod iis manumissor in libertate contulerit; quod tamen iubemus viginti solidorum numerum, et modum in terrula, vineola vel hospitiolo tenere. quod amplius datum fuerit, post manumissoris mortem ecclesia revocabit. minusculas vero res aut ecclesiae minus utiles peregrinis vel clericis salvo iure ecclesiae in usum praestari permittimus; 45, terrulas aut vineolas exiguas et ecclesiae minus utiles aut longe positas parvas episcopus sine consilio fratrum, si necessitas fuerit, distrahendi habeat potestatem; *C. Epaon.* can. 12, nullus episcopus de rebus ecclesiae suae sine conscientia metropolitani sui vendendi aliquid habeat potestatem, utili tamen omnibus commutatione permissa; *C. Mass.* quia multas domus ecclesiae Regensis absque ratione contra canonum statuta sine consilio sanctorum antistitum perpetuo iure distraxit. Cf. for parish priests *C. Agath.* can. 49, 53, *C. Epaon.* can. 7.

64. COMPENSATION FOR ALIENATIONS: *C. Agath.* can. 33, episcopus qui filios aut nepotes non habens alium quam ecclesiam relinquit haeredem, si quid de ecclesia non in ecclesiae causa aut necessitate praesumpsit, quod distraxit aut donavit irritum habeatur: qui vero filios habet, de bonis quae relinquit ab haeredibus eius indemnitatibus ecclesiae consulatur; *C. Aurel.* IV, can. 9, ut episcopus, qui de facultate propria ecclesiae nihil relinquit, de ecclesiae facultate si quid aliter quam canones eloquuntur obligaverit, vendiderit aut distraxerit, ad ecclesiam revocetur. sane si de servis ecclesiae libertos fecerit numero competenti, in ingenuitate permaneant, ita ut ab officio ecclesiae non recedant. Two actual cases are recorded in detail in *C. Mass.* and *C. Hisp.* I. PRESSURE BY THE GREAT: *C. Arvern.* I, can. 5, qui reiculam ecclesiae petunt a regibus, et horrendae cupiditatis impulsu egentium substantiam rapiunt, irrita habeantur quae obtinent, et a communione ecclesiae cuius facultatem auferre cupiunt excludantur; *C. Aurel.* IV, can. 25, si quis clericus aut laicus sub potentum nomine atque patrocinio res ad ius ecclesiae pertinentes contempto pontifice petere seu possidere praesumpserit, primum admoneatur quae abstulit civiliter reformare; *C. Paris.* III, can. I, competitoribus etiam huiusmodi frenos districtionis imponimus, qui facultates ecclesiae sub specie largitatis regiae improba subreptione pervaserint. Cf. Greg. Tur. *Virt. Jul.* 14, *Glor. Conf.* 70.

65. Church lands were apparently made tax free for a brief period after the council of Ariminum in 359; see *CTh* XI. i. 1, where they are immune on 18 Jan. 360, and *CTh* XVI. ii. 15, 30 June 360, in Ariminensi synodo super ecclesiarum et clericorum privilegiis tractatu habito usque eo dispositio progressa est ut iuga quae videntur ad ecclesiam pertinere a publica functione cessarent inquietudine desistente: quod nostra videtur dudum sanctio reppulisse. For the church of Thessalonica see *CTh* XI. i. 33, 424, sacrosancta Thessalonicensis ecclesia civitatis excepta, ita tamen ut aperte sciat propriae tantummodo capitationis modum beneficio mei numinis sublevandum, nec

externorum gravamine tributorum rem publicam ecclesiastici nominis abusione laedendam. IMMUNITY FROM EXTRAORDINARIA ETC.: *CTh* XI. xvi. 21, 22, 397, XVI. ii. 40, 412, XV. iii. 6, 423. The original grant of this immunity is not recorded, but must have been made before 360, when it is assumed in *CTh* XVI. ii. 15, universos namque clericos possessores dumtaxat provinciales pensitat-iones fiscalium recognoscere iubemus, maxime cum in comitatu tranquillitatis nostrae alii episcopi, qui de Italiae partibus venerunt, et illi quoque, qui ex Hispania atque Africa commearunt, probaverint id maxime iuste convenire, ut praeter ea iuga et professionem, quae ad ecclesiam pertinet, ad universa munia sustinenda translationesque faciendas omnes clerici debeant adtineri.

66. STATE SUBSIDY: Theod. *HE* I. 11, καὶ μέντοι καὶ γράμματα πρὸς τοὺς τῶν ἐθνῶν προστατεύοντας δέδωκεν ἄρχοντας, καθ᾽ ἑκάστην πόλιν χορηγεῖσθαι παρεγγυῶν ταῖς ἀεὶ παρθένοις καὶ χήραις καὶ τοῖς ἀφιερωμένοις τῇ θείᾳ λειτουργίᾳ ἐτήσια σιτηρέσια, φιλοτιμίᾳ μᾶλλον ἢ χρείᾳ ταῦτα μετρήσας. τούτων τὸ τριτημόριον μεχρὶ καὶ τήμερον χορηγεῖται. Ἰουλιανοῦ μὲν τοῦ δυσσεβοῦς πάντα καθάπαξ ἀφελομένου, τοῦ δὲ μετ᾽ ἐκεῖνον τὰ νῦν χορηγούμενα παρασχεθῆναι προστεταχότος, IV. 4, Soz. V. 5, *CJ* I. ii. 12, 451, ut pauperibus alimenta non desint, salaria etiam quae sacrosanctis ecclesiis in diversis speciebus de publico hactenus ministrata sunt iubemus nunc quoque inconcussa et a nullo prorsus imminuta praestari, cf. Ath. *Apol. c. Ar.* 18, Soc. II. 17, *A.C.Oec.* II. i. 213, Greg. *Ep.* X. 8, fertur itaque quod annonas atque consuetudines diaconiae, quae Neapolim exhibetur, eminentia vestra (sc. Johannes, praefectus praetorio Italiae) subtraxerit.

67. CHURCHES OF ALEXANDRIA: Epiph. *adv. Haer.* lxix. 1–2. CHURCH OF ROME: Ath. *Apol. c. Ar.* 20, ἔνθα Βίτων ὁ πρεσβύτερος συνῆγεν, Innocent, *Ep.* 25 §5, de fermento vero quod die dominica per titulos mittimus, superflue nos consulere voluisti; cum omnes ecclesiae nostrae intra civitatem sint constitutae, quarum presbyteri, qui die ipsa propter plebem sibi commissam nobiscum convenire non possunt, ideo fermentum a nobis confectum per acolythos accipiunt.

68. Early examples of endowed city churches are those founded by Constantine and others in Rome (*Lib. Pont.* xxxiv, xxxv, xxxviii, xxxix, xlii, xlvi). NO CONSECRATION WITHOUT ENDOWMENT: Gelasius, *Ep.* 34, fr. 21, Loewenfeld, *Ep. Pont. Rom. Ined.* 2, 15, Pelagius I, *Ep.* 86, Greg. *Ep.* II. 9, 15, IX. 58, 71, 180, Just. *Nov.* lxvii §2, 538, ἔπειτα μὴ ἄλλως αὐτὸν ἐκκλησίαν ἐκ νέου οἰκοδομεῖν, πρὶν ἂν διαλεχθείη πρὸς τὸν θεοφιλέστατον ἐπίσκοπον καὶ ὁρίσειε τὸ μέτρον ὅπερ ἀφορίζει πρός τε τὴν λυχνοκαΐαν καὶ τὴν ἱερὰν λειτουργίαν καὶ τὴν ἀδιάφθορον τοῦ οἴκου συντήρησιν καὶ τὴν τῶν προσεδρευόντων ἀποτροφήν; C. *Aurel.* IV, can. 33, si quis in agro suo aut habet aut postulat habere dioecesim, primum et terras ei deputet sufficienter et clericos qui ibidem sua officia impleant, ut sacratis locis reverentia condigna tribuatur; C. *Bracar.* II, can. 5, hoc tantum unusquisque episcoporum meminerit, ut non prius dedicet ecclesiam aut basilicam, nisi antea dotem basilicae et obsequium ipsius per donationem chartulae confirmatum accipiat: nam non levis est ista temeritas, si sine lumin-ariis vel sine sustentatione eorum qui ibidem servituri sunt, tamquam domus privata, ita consecretur ecclesia.

69. PELAGIUS'S RULING: Pelagius I, *Ep.* 17, sed si tanta est ecclesiae Sessulanae penuria ut parrochia esse non possit, eam potius titulum Nolanae ecclesiae constitue, ut tali dispositione habita nec de sacris quicquam ministeriis detra-hatur et competentia ibidem divini cultus per deputatos cardinales ecclesiae presbyteros ministeria celebrentur, et si quid est in caespite, per ecclesiae

Nolanae homines ut diligentius saltem fiscus solvere valeat, excolatur. Cf. Just. *Nov.* vi §8, 535, ἐν δὲ ἅπασι τοῖς ἔξω τόποις θεσπίζομεν, εἰ μὲν ὁ συστησάμενος ἐξ ἀρχῆς καὶ οἰκοδομήσας τὴν ἐκκλησίαν ὥρισε τὸ τῶν χειροτονουμένων μέτρον, οἷα πρὸς αὐτὸ καὶ τὴν δαπάνην περιστήσας, μὴ πρότερον χειροτονηθῆναί τινα κατὰ τὴν αὐτὴν ἐκκλησίαν, πρὶν ἂν εἰς τὸν ἀριθμὸν τὸν ἐξ ἀρχῆς ὁρισθέντα τὸ μέτρον αὐτοῦ περισταίη. εἰ δὲ μὴ τοῦτο γέγονεν, αὐτὴ δὲ ἡ τῆς πόλεως ἐκκλησία χορηγοίη τὰς σιτήσεις ἑαυτῇ τε καὶ ταῖς ἄλλαις ἐκκλησίαις, τηνικαῦτα μὴ προχείρως αὔξειν τοὺς ἐκεῖσε κληρικούς; cxx §6, 544, καὶ εἰ μὲν ἁγιώταται ὦσιν ἐκκλησίαι ἢ ἕτεροι εὐαγεῖς οἶκοι, ὧν τὴν διοίκησιν ὁ κατὰ τόπον ὁσιώτατος ἐπίσκοπος ἢ δι᾽ ἑαυτοῦ ἢ διὰ τοῦ εὐαγοῦς αὐτοῦ κλήρου ποιεῖται . . . εἰ δὲ πτωχεῖα ἢ ξενῶνες ἢ νοσοκομεῖα ἢ ἕτεροι εὐαγεῖς οἶκοι ὦσιν ἰδίαν διοίκησιν ἔχοντες.

70. ENDOWMENTS HELD BY TITULI: *MGH* (*AA*) xii, p. 450, pari etiam ecclesiarum per omnes Romanae civitatis titulos qui sunt presbyteri vel quicumque fuerint adstringi volumus lege custodes . . . quicumque tamen oblitus Dei et decreti huius immemor, cuius Romanae civitatis sacerdotes volumus religiosis nexibus devinciri, in constitutum praesens committens quidquam de iure titulorum vel ecclesiae superius praefatae quolibet modo . . . perpetuo iure, exceptis dumtaxat sub praefata conditione domibus, alienare tentaverit, donator, alienator ac venditor honoris sui amissione mulctetur. GREGORY'S GRANT TO S. PAUL'S: Greg. *Ep.* xiv. 14. It may be noted that he did not merely carmark the rents, but ordered the *rector* of the *patrimonium Appiae* to transfer these lands from his books to those of the *praepositi* of the basilica, who would henceforth be responsible for their management. Thus as Gregory says, licet omnia quae haec apostolica habet ecclesia beatorum Petri et Pauli, quorum honore et beneficiis adquisita sunt, deo sint auctore communia, esse tamen debet in administratione actionum diversitas personarum, ut in adsignatis cuique rebus cura adhiberi possit impensior. DONATION OF FLAVIA XANTHIPPE: *P. Ítal.* 17. Here the gift is made 'in omnes mansionarios essentibus et introeuntibus perenniter basilicae Dei genetricis Mariae quae appellatur ad praesepem'.

71. THE CHURCHES OF CONSTANTINOPLE: Just. *Nov.* iii §§1–2, 535, ἐν δὲ ταῖς ἄλλαις ἁπάσαις ἐκκλησίαις, ὧν τὴν χορηγίαν ἡ ἁγιωτάτη μεγάλη ἐκκλησία ποιεῖται, θεσπίζομεν τοὺς μὲν νῦν ὄντας μένειν ὁμοίως καὶ αὐτοὺς ἐπὶ σχήματος, τοῦ δὲ λοιποῦ μηδένα χειροτονεῖσθαι, πρὶν ἂν εἰς τὸ καλούμενον στατοῦτον ἑκάστης ἐκκλησίας, ὅπερ ἐξ ἀρχῆς ὥρισται παρὰ τῶν ταύτας οἰκοδομησαμένων, ὁ τῶν πρεσβυτέρων τε καὶ διακόνων, ἀρρένων τε καὶ θηλειῶν, καὶ ὑποδιακόνων καὶ ἀναγνωστῶν καὶ ψαλτῶν καὶ πυλωρῶν ἀριθμὸς περισταίη . . . ἀλλ᾽ οὐδὲ ἐν ταῖς ἐκκλησίαις ταῖς ἄλλαις, ὅσαι μὴ τὴν τροφὴν καὶ χορηγίαν ἔχουσιν ἐκ τῆς ἁγιωτάτης μεγάλης ἐκκλησίας, προσῆκόν ἐστι πλῆθος ἐπαφιέναι τῶν χειροτονουμένων ἐν αὐταῖς, οὐδὲ ὑπερβαίνειν τοῦ λοιποῦ τὸ τεταγμένον ἐξ ἀρχῆς καὶ ἐπ᾽ ἐκείναις μέτρον.

72. *C. Aurel.* iii, can. 5, si quae oblationes in quibuslibet rebus atque corporibus collatae fuerint basilicis in civitatibus constitutis, ad potestatem episcopi redigantur, et in eius sit arbitrio quid ad reparationem basilicae aut observantium ibi substantiam deputetur; de facultatibus vero parochiarum vel basilicarum in pagis civitatum constitutis singulorum locorum consuetudo servetur. LIBANUS: Theod. *Hist. Rel.* xvii. CHURCHES BUILT BY LANDOWNERS: Joh. Chrys. *Hom. in Act.* xviii. 4, Gelasius, *Ep.* 34–5, *C. Aurel.* iv, can. 33 (cited in n. 68). CHURCHES BUILT FOR PROFIT: *C. Bracar.* ii, can. 6, placuit ut si quis basilicam non pro devotione fidei, sed pro quaestu cupiditatis aedificat, ut quidquid ibidem oblatione populi colligitur medium cum clericis dividat, eo quod basilicam in terra sua ipse condiderit, quod in aliquibus locis usque

modo dicitur fieri; hoc ergo de cetero observari debet, ut nullus episcoporum tam abominabili voto consentiat, ut basilicam quae non pro sanctorum patrocinio, sed magis sub tributaria conditione est condita, audeat consecrare.

73. BASIL'S HOSPITALS: Greg. Naz. *Or.* xliii. 63. JUSTINIAN'S HOSPITAL: Cyr. Scyth. *V. Sabae*, 73. CHARITABLE INSTITUTIONS OWN PROPERTY: *CJ* I. ii. 17 §2 (Anastasius), Just. *Nov.* vii §1, 535, cxx §§1, 5-7, 544; independent institutions are clearly distinguished from those managed by the bishop in *Nov.* cxx §6, καὶ εἰ μὲν ἁγιώταται ὦσιν ἐκκλησίαι ἢ ἕτεροι εὐαγεῖς οἶκοι, ὧν τὴν διοίκησιν ὁ κατὰ τόπον ὁσιώτατος ἐπίσκοπος ἢ δι᾽ ἑαυτοῦ ἢ διὰ τοῦ εὐαγοῦς αὐτοῦ κλήρου ποιεῖται, κατὰ γνώμην αὐτοῦ καὶ συναίνεσιν γίνεσθαι τὸ τοιοῦτον συνάλλαγμα . . . εἰ δὲ πτωχεῖα ἢ ξενῶνες ἢ νοσοκομεῖα ἢ ἕτεροι εὐαγεῖς οἶκοι ὦσιν ἰδίαν διοίκησιν ἔχοντες, εἰ μὲν ἁγίους εὐκτηρίους οἴκους εἶναι συμβαίη, κατὰ γνώμην τοῦ πλείονος μέρους τῶν ἐκεῖσε λειτουργούντων κληρικῶν, οὐ μὴν ἀλλὰ καὶ τοῦ οἰκονόμου, εἰ δὲ ξενὼν ἢ πτωχεῖον ἢ νοσοκομεῖον ἢ ἕτερος εἴη εὐαγὴς οἶκος, τὸν προεστῶτα τούτων τὸ συνάλλαγμα ποιεῖσθαι.

74. OECONOMI: *C. Chalc.* can. 26 (*A.C.Oec.* II. i. 359); by the end of the sixth century the office had been introduced into some Western churches (Greg. *Ep.* III. 22, XIV. 2). From the functions assigned in hagiography to St. Laurence (cf. Aug. *Serm.* 302 §8, 303 §1) it has often been inferred that the archdeacon was the financial manager in Western churches, but there is no good evidence for this. In Gelasius, fr. 23-4, the archdeacon and a *defensor* are given special authority to restore the finances of the church of Volaterrae, but this is because the present bishop was not trustworthy; and the trouble was due to the mismanagement of earlier bishops. A bishop might of course delegate his powers to one of his clergy, as in Ennod. *V. Epiph.* 337, where the junior deacon Epiphanius is put in charge of the church finances. THE DIVIDEND UNDER CYPRIAN: Cyprian, *Ep.* 7, sumptus suggeratis ex quantitate mea propria quam apud Rogatianum compresbyterum nostrum dimisi, 39, ut et sportulis idem cum presbyteris honorentur et divisiones mensurnas aequatis quantitatibus partiantur.

75. THE ROMAN FOURFOLD DIVISION: Simplicius, *Ep.* 1, Gelasius, *Ep.* 14 §27, quattuor autem tam de reditu quam de oblatione fidelium, prout cuiuslibet ecclesiae facultas admittit, sicut dudum est rationabiliter decretum, convenit fieri portiones. quarum sit una pontificis, altera clericorum, pauperum tertia, quarta fabricis applicanda; 15, 16, cf. fr. 23, 24, Greg. *Ep.* XI. 56[a], cf. IV. 11, V. 12, 27, 48, VIII. 7, XIII. 46. RAVENNA: Agnellus, *Lib. Pont. Eccl. Rav.* 60. SPAIN: *C. Bracar.* I, can. 7, item placuit, ut ex rebus ecclesiasticis tres aequae fiant portiones, id est una episcopi, alia clericorum, tertia in recuperationem vel in luminaria ecclesiae. GAUL: *C. Aurel.* I, can. 14, antiquos canones relegentes priora statuta credidimus renovanda, ut de his quae in altario oblatione fidelium conferuntur, medietatem sibi episcopus vindicet, et medietatem dispensandam sibi secundum gradus clerus accipiat, praediis de omni commoditate in episcoporum potestate durantibus.

76. DIVISION AMONG THE CLERGY: Greg. *Ep.* VIII. 7, et quia inter alia de quarta portione clerus hoc tenendum statuit ut unam portionem hi qui in sacro loco sunt positi et reliquas duas clerus accipiat et latores praesentium Donatus presbyter nec non et Theodosianus atque Viator diacones aliorum quoque qui in sacrato sunt ordine constituti relationem ad nos deferentes conquesti sunt hoc contra antiquam consuetudinem in suo gravamine praeiudicialiter statutum, quippe quia de eadem quarta semper duas se partes et tertiam clerum se perhibent consecutum.

77. DIVIDENDS IN THE EAST: Sev. Ant. *Ep.* I. 57, cf. *Can. Apost.* 4, ἡ ἄλλη πᾶσα ὀπώρα εἰς οἶκον ἀποστελλέσθω, ἀπαρχὴ τῷ ἐπισκόπῳ καὶ τοῖς πρεσβυτέροις, ἀλλὰ μὴ πρὸς τὸ θυσιαστήριον. δῆλον δέ, ὡς ὁ ἐπίσκοπος καὶ οἱ πρεσβύτεροι ἐπιμερίζουσι τοῖς διακόνοις καὶ τοῖς λοιποῖς κληρικοῖς, and Just. *Nov.* iii §2, 535, where the clergy of the independent (and perhaps unendowed) churches of Constantinople are spoken of as τοὺς προσιόντας αὐτοῖς παρὰ τῶν εὐσεβούντων πόρους μεριζόμενοι. FINANCIAL DIFFICULTIES OF THE GREAT CHURCH ETC.: Just. *Nov.* iii pr. §1, 535, Sev. Ant. *Ep.* I. 8, 17. From *Nov.* iii pr. it appears that in the East founders of churches normally laid down an exact establishment of clergy and supplied endowments accordingly; this suggests that they specified fixed stipends payable from the endowment. THEODORE OF SYCEON'S SALARY: *V. Theod. Syc.* 78.

78. *CJ* I. ii. 17 §2, καὶ ἐπὶ μὲν τῶν ἐκκλησιῶν παρόντων τῶν οἰκονόμων καὶ τῶν ἐνδημούντων κληρικῶν, ἐπὶ δὲ τῶν μοναστηρίων δεῖ παρεῖναι τοὺς ἡγουμένους καὶ τοὺς ἄλλους μονάχους, ἐπὶ δὲ τῶν πτωχείων τοῦ διοικητοῦ καὶ τῶν ὑπουργούντων καὶ τῶν πτωχῶν, ἐπὶ δὲ τῶν ξενώνων τοῦ διοικητοῦ καὶ τῶν εὑρισκομένων πάντων ὑπουργῶν τῆς διοικήσεως καὶ ὁμοίως ἐπὶ τῶν ὀρφανοτροφείων, ὥστε κρατεῖν τὸ τοῖς πλείοσιν ἀρέσκον· συναινοῦντος καὶ τοῦ ἐπισκόπου τῶν τόπων, ἐν οἷς τοῦτο σύνηθες ἐπιγίνεσθαι. So also in Just. *Nov.* cxx §6, 544, the financial administrators of churches and institutions could grant perpetual emphyteutic leases, having taken an oath before the bishop that the lease would not be detrimental to their finances.

79. AFRICAN RULE: *Cod. Can. Eccl. Afr.* 33 (cited above in n. 63); cf. the Roman council of 502 cited in n. 70, *C. Epaon.* can. 7, quidquid parochiarum presbyteri de ecclesiastici iuris possessione distraxerint inane habeatur et vacuum, in venditorem comparantis actione vertenda. EPISCOPAL CONTROL OF LOCAL ENDOWMENTS: *C. Aurel.* I, can. 15, de his quae parochiis in terris, vineis, mancipiis atque peculiis quicumque fideles obtulerint antiquorum canonum statuta serventur, ut omnia in episcopi potestate consistant; de his tamen quae in altario accesserint, tertia fideliter episcopis deferatur; *C. Carp.*, hoc nobis iustum et rationabile visum est, ut si ecclesia civitatis eius cui episcopus praeest ita est idonea ut Christo propitio nihil indigeat, quidquid parochiis fuerit derelictum, clericis qui ipsis parochiis deserviunt vel reparationibus ecclesiarum rationabiliter dispensetur; si vero episcopum multas expensas et minorem substantiam habere constiterit, parochiis quibus largior fuerit collata substantia, hoc tantum quod clericis vel sartis tectis rationabiliter sufficiat reservetur: quod autem amplius fuerit, propter maiores expensas episcopus ad se debeat revocare, ita tamen ut nihil de facultatula ipsa vel de ministerio clerici loci ipsius licentiam habeant minuendi; *C. Aurel.* III, can. 5 (cited in n. 72), *C. Aurel* v, can. 15 (Childebert's hospital), *C. Tol.* III, can. 19, multi contra canonum constituta sic ecclesias quas aedificaverint postulant consecrari, ut dotem quam ei ecclesiae contulerint censeant ad episcopi ordinationem non pertinere, quod factum et in praeterito displicet et in futurum prohibetur; sed omnia secundum constitutionem antiquam ad episcopi ordinationem et potestatem pertineant; *C. Tol.* IV, can. 33, pro qua re constitutum est a praesenti concilio, episcopos ita dioeceses suas regere, ut nihil ex earum iure praesumant auferre, sed iuxta priorum auctoritatem conciliorum tam de oblationibus quam de tributis ac frugibus tertiam consequantur; quod si amplius quidpiam ab eis praesumptum extiterit, per concilium restauretur, appellantibus aut ipsis conditoribus, aut certe propinquis eorum, si iam illi a saeculo decesserunt. noverint autem conditores basilicarum in rebus, quas eisdem ecclesiis conferunt, nullam potestatem habere, sed iuxta canonum constituta sicut ecclesiam ita et dotem eius ad ordinationem episcopi pertinere.

80. THE BISHOP'S THIRD OF PAROCHIAL OFFERINGS: *C. Aurel.* I, can. 15 (cited in n. 79), *C. Tarrac.* can. 8, multorum casuum experientia magistrante reperimus nonnullas dioecesanas esse ecclesias destitutas; ob quam rem id constitutione decrevimus, ut antiquae consuetudinis ordo servetur, et annuis vicibus ab episcopo dioeceses visitentur, ut si qua forte basilica reperta fuerit destituta, ordinatione ipsius reparetur; quia tertia ex omnibus per antiquam traditionem ut accipiatur ab episcopis novimus statutum; *C. Bracar.* II, can. 2, placuit ut nullus episcoporum, cum per suas dioeceses ambulat, praeter honorem cathedrae suae, id est duos solidos, aliquid aliud per ecclesias tollat, neque tertiam partem ex quacumque oblatione populi in ecclesiis parochialibus requirat; sed illa tertia pars pro luminariis ecclesiae vel recuperatione servetur, ut singulis annis episcopo inde ratio fiat; nam si tertiam partem illam episcopus tollat, lumen et sacra tecta abstulit ecclesiae; *C. Tol.* IV, can. 33 (cited in n. 79).

81. THE ROMAN CLERGY IN THE THIRD CENTURY: Eus. *HE* VI. 43. CONSTANTINE'S DONATIONS: *Lib. Pont.* xxxiv. AGORIUS PRAETEXTATUS AND DAMASUS: Jerome, *c. Joh. Hierosol.* 8. THE LUXURY OF THE POPES: Amm. XXVII. iii. 14–15, neque ego abnuo, ostentationem rerum considerans urbanarum, huius rei cupidos ob impetrandum, quod appetunt, omni contentione laterum iurgare debere, cum id adepti, futuri sint ita securi ut ditentur oblationibus matronarum, procedantque vehiculis insidentes circumspecte vestiti, epulas curantes profusas adeo ut eorum convivia regales superent mensas. qui esse poterant beati re vera, si magnitudine urbis despecta, quam vitiis opponunt, ad imitationem antistitum quorundam provincialium viverent, quos tenuitas edendi potandique parcissime, vilitas etiam indumentorum et supercilia humum spectantia perpetuo numini verisque eius cultoribus ut puros commendant et verecundos.

82. ANTIOCH: Joh. Chrys. *Hom. in Matth.* lxvi. 3. HIPPO: Aug. *Ep.* 126 §7. ALEXANDRIA: *A.C.Oec.* I. iv. 222–5, *V. Joh. Eleem.* 45.

83. Just. *Nov.* cxxiii §3, 546. RAVENNA: Agnellus, *Lib. Pont. Eccl. Rav.* 60. ANASTASIOPOLIS: *V. Theod. Syc.* 78. MELOE: Sev. Ant. *Ep.* I. 4 (cf. I. 23 for Musonius's see).

84. For comparative figures see ch. XII, n. 65 (governors), ch. XIV, n. 70 (assessors), ch. XVII, nn. 33, 35, 147 (soldiers), ch. XXIV, n. 59 (doctors), ch. XXIV, n. 39 (professors). PENSIONS FOR DEPOSED BISHOPS: *A.C.Oec.* II. i. 414 (Ephesus), ii. 113 (Antioch).

85. Of the minor orders subdeacons, acolytes, exorcists, readers and door-keepers already existed at Rome in the mid third century (Eus. *HE* VI. 43). Subdeacons, readers and acolytes are attested in Africa at the same period (Cyprian, *Ep.* 23, 29, 34, 35, 45, 47, etc.). The ceremonies whereby members of these orders and also singers (*cantores*) were ordained are described in *Stat. Eccl. Ant.* 5–10 (an African document of the early fifth century); the ceremonies give some indication of their ritual duties. Acolytes do not seem to have existed in the Greek-speaking churches (the ἀκόλουθοι of Just. *Nov.* lix §§2, 3 are professional mourners at funerals and not acolytes). The other orders are attested in the East from the fourth century, e.g. *CTh* xvi. ii. 7, 330 (readers and subdeacons), *C. Ant.* can. 10 (exorcists, readers and subdeacons), *C. Laod.* can. 15, 23, 24, 26 (subdeacons, exorcists, doorkeepers and singers). *Fossores* appear among the clergy of Cirta in 305 (Opt. *App.* i) and *fossarii* are the lowest clerical order in the pseudo-Jeromian *De septem ordinibus ecclesiae* (*PL* xxx. 150–1): cf. also *ILCV* 1316–23. *Copiatae* are classed as *clerici* in *CTh*

XIII. i. 1, 356, XVI. ii. 15, 360; their function appears from Epiph. *Expos. fid.* 21 κοπιαταὶ οἱ τὰ σώματα περιστέλλοντες τῶν κοιμωμένων, and Just. *Nov.* lix §2; they are mentioned with *lecticarii* at Antioch in S. G. F. Perry, *The Second Synod of Ephesus,* 296, 325. PARABALANI: *CTh* XVI. ii. 42, 416, 43, 418, parabalani qui ad curanda debilium aegra corpora deputantur. For the *decani* and *lecticarii* who conducted funerals at Constantinople see below, n. 98. For the functions of deaconesses see Epiph. *adv. Haer.* lxxix. 3, *Expos. fid.* 21, Just. *Nov.* vi §6, 535, *Stat. Eccl. Ant.* 12. There were several attempts to abolish them in Merovingian Gaul, *C. Araus.* I, can. 26, *C. Epaon.* can. 21, *C. Aurel.* II, can. 18. For regular promotion from lower to higher orders see below n. 104; that salaries were graded by orders is implied by *C. Aurel.* I, can. 14 (cited in n. 75). STIPENDS OF PRIESTS AND DEACONS: Gelasius, fr. 10; for a possible explanation see *JTS* XI (1960), p. 92.

86. *C. Aurel.* III, can. 18, de his vero clericorum personis quae de civitatensis ecclesiae officio monasteria, dioeceses vel basilicas in quibuscumque locis positas, id est sive in territoriis sive in ipsis civitatibus suscipiunt ordinandas, in potestate sit episcopi, si de eo quod ante de ecclesiastico munere habebant eos aliquid aut nihil exinde habere voluerit: quia unicuique facultas suscepti monasterii, dioecesis vel basilicae debet plena ratione sufficere. GREGORY, BISHOP OF MUTINA: Simplicius, *Ep.* 14. Similarly Musonius of Meloe contrasts the rich *diaria* of the Antiochene clergy with his wretched episcopal salary (Sev. Ant. *Ep.* 1. 4).

87. POPE CORNELIUS'S LETTER: Eus. *HE* VI. 43. PRIESTS AND DEACONS IN AFRICA: Cyprian, *Ep.* 1. In *Ep.* 41, cumque ego vos pro me vicarios miserim, ut expungeretis necessitates fratrum nostrorum sumptibus istis, si qui vellent etiam suas artes exercere, additamento quantum satis esset desideria eorum iuvaretis, Cyprian is probably speaking of the lower clergy. READERS AT CIRTA: Opt. *App.* i.

88. For clerical immunity from the *collatio lustralis* see ch. XIII, n. 52; cf. Basil, *Ep.* 198, καὶ γὰρ εἰ καὶ πολυάνθρωπόν πως εἶναι δοκεῖ τὸ ἱερατεῖον ἡμῶν, ἀλλὰ ἀνθρώπων ἀμελετήτως ἐχόντων πρὸς τὰς ὁδοιπορίας διὰ τὸ μήτε ἐμπορεύεσθαι μήτε τὴν ἔξω διατριβὴν αἱρεῖσθαι, τὰς δὲ ἑδραίας τῶν τεχνῶν μεταχειρίζεσθαι τοὺς πολλούς, ἐκεῖθεν ἔχοντας τὴν ἀφορμὴν τοῦ ἐφημέρου βίου. BAN ON CLERICAL TRADE: Val. III, *Nov.* xxxv §4, 452, iubemus ut clerici nihil prorsus negotiationis exerceant; si velint negotiari sciant se iudicibus subditos clericorum privilegio non muniri, *C. Arel.* II, can. 14, cf. *C. Aurel.* III, can. 27. ALEXANDRIA AD ISSUM: Sev. Ant. *Ep.* 1. 32. JERUSALEM: Cyr. Scyth. *V. Sabae,* 78. ALEXANDRIA: *V. Joh. Eleem.* 44A. Sidonius Apollinaris (*Ep.* VI. 8) mentions a humble merchant who was a *lector*.

89. THEODORE: *A.C.Oec.* II. i. 211–12. MARINUS AND ELEUTHERIUS: Sev. Ant. *Ep.* 1. 17, VII. 6, cf. 1. 8 and Just. *Nov.* iii pr. §§2–3, 535. THE JUDGMENT OF FELIX IV: Agnellus, *Lib. Pont. Eccl. Rav.* 60; if the priests and deacons got two-thirds of the clergy's share, as they claimed at Catana (Greg. *Ep.* VIII. 7), 21 persons would have shared 2000 solidi.

90. COLONI PRIESTS OF CHURCHES ON ESTATES: *CTh* XVI. ii. 33, 398, ecclesiis quae in possessionibus ut adsolet diversorum, vicis etiam vel quibuslibet locis sunt constitutae, clerici non ex alia possessione vel vico sed ex eo ubi ecclesiam esse constiterit eatenus ordinentur ut propriae capitationis onus ac sarcinam recognoscant, *CJ* I. iii. 16, 409, quisquis censibus fuerit adnotatus, invito agri domino ab omni temperet clericatu, adeo ut etiam, si in eo vico, in quo noscitur

mansitare, clericus fuerit, sub hac lege religiosum adsumat sacerdotium, ut et capitationis sarcinam per ipsum dominum agnoscere compellatur et ruralibus obsequiis quo maluerit subrogato fungatur, ea scilicet immunitate indulta, quae certae capitationis venerandis ecclesiis relaxatur, Just. *Nov.* cxxiii §17, adscripticios autem in ipsis possessionibus quarum sunt adscripticii clericos et praeter voluntatem dominorum fieri permittimus, ita tamen ut clerici facti impositam sibi agriculturam adimpleant; cf. Gelasius, *Ep.* 21, for a slave priest on his owner's estate, and *P. Lond.* 778 for a deacon who is an ἐναπόγραφος γεωργός. There is an interesting passage in Barsanuphius (p. 351) on the question whether the clergy in villages should be liable τῇ κοσμικῇ λειτουργίᾳ τῇ τε σωματικῇ καὶ τῇ χρηματικῇ. For *capitatio* see below n. 101. ENDOWMENTS OF PAROCHIAE: Greg. *Ep.* II. 9, IX. 58, 71, 180. For the bishop's third see above n. 80. CATHEDRATICUM: Gelasius, fr. 20, cathedraticum etiam non amplius quam vetusti moris esse constiterit ab eius loci presbytero noveris exigendum, Pelagius I, *Ep.* 32, 33, sed aliud eum cavere districte fecimus ut non amplius de parochiis suis quam binos solidos annuos sub qualibet occasione praesumat accipere, *C. Bracar.* II, can. 2, placuit ut nullus episcoporum, cum per suas dioeceses ambulat, praeter honorem cathedrae suae, id est duos solidos, aliquid aliud per ecclesias tollat, *C. Tol.* VII, can. 4. For other exactions of bishops on parishes see *C. Tol.* III, can. 20, Pelagius I, *Ep.* 32, illud te modis omnibus volumus custodire, ne quis episcoporum Siciliae de parrochiis ad se pertinentibus nomine cathedratici amplius quam duos solidos praesumat accipere neque compellere presbyteros aut clerum parrochiarum suarum supra vires suas eis convivia praeparare.

91. SILVANUS OF CIRTA AND MAJORINUS: Opt. *App.* i. BASIL'S CHOREPISCOPI: Bas. *Ep.* 53–4. ANTONINUS OF EPHESUS: Pall. *Dial.* pp. 84, 90–1. Ibas of Edessa was also accused of simony (*A.C.Oec.* II. i. 383). The earliest denunciation of simony in general terms seems to be in *Ep. ad Gallos*, 10, meritis enim et observandae legis ad istiusmodi dignitatis artem accedant, non Simonis pecunia vel gratia quis poterit pervenire aut favore populi: non enim quid populus velit sed quid evangelica disciplina perquiritur. plebs tunc habet testimonium, quoties ad digni alicuius meritum reprehendens aurem favoris impetit.

92. SIMONY CONDEMNED AT CHALCEDON: *A.C.Oec.* II. i. 354 (can. 2); AT ARLES: *C. Arel.* II, can. 54; also at the council of Constantinople in 459 (Mansi, VII. 911–6), of Rome in 499, 501, 502 (*MGH* (*AA*) XII. 399 ff., cf. Cass. *Var.* IX. 15), of Orleans in 533 (*C. Aurel.* II, can. 3, 4) and 549 (*C. Aurel.* V, can. 10), of Tours in 567 (*C. Tur.* II, can. 27). Imperial laws begin with *CJ* I. iii. 31, 472. For obtaining orders or promotion therein by patronage see the cases cited in n. 89, and also Felix IV's judgment on Ravenna, 'clerici vero vel monachi ad indebitum obtinendum ordinem vel locum potentium patrocinia non requirant, per quae aut non faciendo ingratus aut faciendo iniustus videatur episcopus' (Agnellus, *Lib. Pont. Eccl. Rav.* 60). For graft and intimidation in episcopal elections see *C. Arvern.* I, can. 2, non patrocinia potentum adhibeat, non calliditate subdola ad conscribendum decretum alios hortetur praemiis, alios timore compellat, *C. Aurel.* V, can. 10, ut nulli episcopatum praemiis aut comparatione liceat adipisci, 11, nec per oppressionem potentium personarum ad consensum faciendum cives aut clerici, quod dici nefas est, inclinentur. For the scandals of papal elections see the proceedings under Odoacer and Theoderic (*MGH* (*AA*) XII. 399 ff.), and Cass. *Var.* IX. 15.

93. INSINUATIVA: Just. *Nov.* lvi, 537, cxxiii §16, 546. FEES OF ASSISTANTS OF ORDAINING BISHOP: Just. *Nov.* cxxiii §16, 546, sed neque clericum cuiuscumque

gradus dare aliquid ei a quo ordinatur aut alii cuilibet personae permittimus, solas autem praebere eum consuetudines his qui ordinanti ministrant ex consuetudine accipientibus, unius anni emolumenta non transcendentes. in sancta vero ecclesia, in qua constituitur sacrum complere ministerium, nulla penitus propriis conclericis dare pro sua insinuatione, neque ob hanc causam propriis emolumentis aut aliis portionibus hunc privari.

94. CONSECRATION FEES: *A.C.Oec.* II. i. 457 (Eusebius's complaint), Just. *Nov.* cxxiii §3, 546 (Justinian's regulations).

95. Loewenfeld, *Ep. Pont. Rom. Ined.* 22.

96. NUMBERS OF CLERGY: Eus. *HE* VI. 43 (Rome), Opt. *App.* i (Cirta). CONSTANTINE'S LAW: *CTh* XVI. ii. 6, 326. THE CANON OF CHALCEDON: *A.C.Oec.* II. i. 355 (can. 6), μηδένα δὲ ἀπολελυμένως χειροτονεῖσθαι μήτε πρεσβύτερον μήτε διάκονον μήτε ὅλως τινὰ τῶν ἐν τῷ ἐκκλησιαστικῷ τάγματι, εἰ μὴ ἰδικῶς ἐν ἐκκλησίᾳ πόλεως ἢ κώμης, ἢ μαρτυρίῳ ἢ μοναστηρίῳ ὁ χειροτονούμενος ἐπικηρύττοιτο.

97. NUMBERS OF CLERGY: *A.C.Oec.* III. 103–6 (Apamea), Agnellus, *Lib. Pont. Eccl. Rav.* 60 (Ravenna), Just. *Nov.* iii §1, 535 (Constantinople). Cf. n. 100 for Edessa.

98. PARABALANI: *CTh* XVI. ii. 42, 416, 43, 418. DECANI: *CJ* I. ii. 4, 409, 18 (Anastasius), Just. *Nov.* xliii, 536, lix, 537; the history of the institution is given in the proem of the last novel. Cf. *P.Iand.* 154.

99. For the *oeconomus* see above n. 74; for managers of the papal patrimonies see ch. XX, n. 45. SACRISTS: Soz. v. 8, *A.C.Oec.* II. i. 129, οἱ εὐλαβέστατοι πρεσβύτεροι Μέμνων ὁ σκευοφύλαξ καὶ 'Επιφάνιος, 387, διάκονος ἀπὸ κειμηλιοφυλάκων. KEEPERS OF THE ARCHIVES: *A.C.Oec.* III. 59, διάκονος νοτάριος καὶ χαρτοφύλαξ. Besides the heads of the endowed hospitals etc. (see above n. 73) we find hospitallers on the staff of cathedral churches, like the priest Isidore (Pall. *Dial.* p. 35), ξενοδόχον 'Αλεξανδρείας. In the East notaries and *defensores* (ἔκδικοι, ἐκκλησιέκδικοι) held all the canonical orders concurrently with their office (e.g. *A.C.Oec.* II. i. 164, 206, 209, ἀναγνώστης καὶ νοτάριος, 153, 221, 428, διάκονος καὶ νοτάριος, 204, ἀρχιδιάκονος τῆς βασιλευούσης Κωνσταντινουπόλεως νέας 'Ρώμης καὶ πριμικηρίος νοταρίων, 82, πρεσβύτερος 'Αλεξανδρείας καὶ πρῶτος νοταρίων, 102, πρεσβύτερος καὶ ἔκδικος). In the West they seem to be regarded almost as minor orders by Gelasius (*Ep.* 14 §2, continuo lector vel notarius aut certe defensor effectus, post tres menses existat acolythus), but in Val. III, *Nov.* xxxv §5, 452, *defensores ecclesiae* are distinguished from *clerici*, though closely associated with them, and from Zosimus, *Ep.* 9 §3 (sane ut etiam defensores ecclesiae qui ex laicis fiunt supradicta observatione teneantur si meruerint esse in ordine clericatus) it appears that they might when appointed be laymen or clerics (in minor orders), and often, perhaps normally, took minor orders. Cf. the letter of appointment in Greg. *Ep.* v. 26, ut si nulli condicioni vel corpori teneris obnoxius nec fuisti clericus alterius civitatis aut in nullo tibi canonum obviant statuta, officium ecclesiae defensoris accipias; in another letter of appointment (Greg. *Ep.* IX. 97) the conditional clause does not appear, because Vitus was already a cleric of the Roman church (*Ep.* IX. 118). *Notarii* similarly held minor orders (e.g. *A.C.Oec.* III. 52, 136, 152, ἀναγνώστης καὶ σεκουνδοκήριος νοταρίων τοῦ ἀποστολικοῦ θρόνου τῆς πρεσβυτέρας 'Ρώμης). *Defensores* were often promoted to be subdeacons and deacons, and went on doing the same kind of administrative work as hitherto, but were no longer styled *defensores* (e.g. Boniface in Greg. *Ep.* VIII. 16, XIII. 41, and Peter in VI. 24,

1, 1. 3, v. 28 etc.). Both *notarii* and *defensores* at Rome were organised in *scholae* (Greg. *Ep*. VIII. 16). For the duties of *notarii* see *Lib. Pont*. xxxvi and Agnellus, *Lib. Pont. Eccl. Rav.* 60. For those of *defensores* see Just. *Nov.* lxxiv §4, 538, cxvii §4, 542 (registration of marriages), *A.C.Oec.* II. i. 102, 132–5, 157 ff. (service of a summons to an accused person), III. 168, πρεσβύτερος καὶ ἐκκλησιέκδικος καὶ ἐπὶ τῶν φυλακῶν, *A.C.Oec.* II. i. 358 (*C. Chalc.* can. 23), *CJ* I. iii. 41 §26, 528, Just. *Nov.* cxxxiii §5, 539 (disciplinary measures against clergy and monks), cf. *V. Joh. Eleem.* 24 (the ἐκκλησιέκδικος of Alexandria flogs a monk), *V. Dan.* 19 (the ἔκδικος ἅμα δεκάνοις arrests Daniel), Loewenfeld, *Ep. Pont. Rom. Ined.* 34–5 (two *defensores* sent to arrest a bogus bishop), Pelagius I, *Ep.* 27, omnimoda enim et illius habitus et istius officii diversitas est. illic enim quies, oratio, labor manuum, at hic causarum condicio, conventiones, actus, publica litigia, et quaecumque vel ecclesiastica instituta vel supplicantium necessitas poscit. Both *notarii* and *defensores* were extensively used in the administration of the Roman patrimony (see ch. XIII, n. 45). These clerical *defensores* have no connection with the barristers who were appointed *defensores ecclesiae* in Africa in 407 (*Cod. Can. Eccl. Afr.* 97, *CTh* xvi. ii. 38, 407).

100. CLERGY OF EDESSA: *A.C.Oec.* II. i. 386, ἔστιν ὁ κλῆρος ἡμῶν μικρῷ πρὸς διακοσίων ὀνομάτων ἢ καὶ πλειόνων· οὐδὲ γὰρ σώζω τὸν ἀριθμόν: contrast the testimonial to Ibas παρὰ παντὸς τοῦ κλήρου τῆς Ἐδεσσηνῶν μητροπόλεως with its 65 signatures (*A.C.Oec.* II. i. 394–6). CLERGY OF CARTHAGE: Victor Vit. III. 34, universus clerus ecclesiae Carthaginis, caede inediaque maceratus, fere quingenti et amplius, inter quos quam plurimi erant lectores infantuli.

101. Immunity from *collatio lustralis*, see ch. XIII, n. 52. IMMUNITY FROM CAPITATIO: *Leges saeculares*, 117 (FIR II². 794), beatus rex Constantinus . . . liberavit κληρικοὺς omni tributo ut neque argentum capitis dent neque χρυσάργυρον, *CTh* xvi. ii. 10, 346 (S), quod et coniugibus et liberis eorum et ministeriis, maribus pariter ac feminis, indulgemus, quos a censibus etiam iubemus perseverare immunes, 14, 356 (S), omnibus clericis huiusmodi praerogativa succurrat, ut coniugia clericorum ac liberi quoque et ministeria, id est mares pariter ac feminae, eorumque etiam filii immunes semper a censibus et separati ab huiusmodi muneribus perseverent, Greg. Naz. *Ep.* 67, τοὺς περὶ ἐμὲ κληρικοὺς ὅσους παρῃτησάμην τῆς ἀπογραφῆς ἐλευθέρωσον . . . ἄλλαις μὲν πόλεσι πάντας τοὺς περὶ τὸ βῆμα δοθῆναι, ἡμῖν δὲ μηδὲ τοὺς σύνοντας καὶ θεραπεύοντας, Bas. *Ep.* 104, τοὺς τῷ θεῷ ἡμῶν ἱερωμένους πρεσβυτέρους καὶ διακόνους ὁ παλαιὸς κῆνσος ἀτελεῖς ἀφῆκεν· οἱ δὲ νῦν ἀπογραψάμενοι, ὡς οὐ λαβόντες παρὰ τῆς ὑπερφυοῦς σου ἐξουσίας (sc. Modestus, *Ppo Or.*) πρόσταγμα, ἀπεγράψαντο πλὴν εἰ μή πού τινες ἄλλων εἶχον ὑπὸ τῆς ἡλικίας τὴν ἄφεσιν· δεόμεθα οὖν . . . συγχωρηθῆναι κατὰ τὸν παλαιὸν νόμον τῆς συντελείας τοὺς ἱερατεύοντας, καὶ μὴ εἰς πρόσωπον τῶν νῦν καταλαμβανομένων γενέσθαι τὴν ἄφεσιν (οὕτω γὰρ εἰς τοὺς διαδόχους ἡ χάρις μεταβήσεται, οὓς οὐ πάντως συμβαίνει τοῦ ἱερατεύειν ἀξίους εἶναι) ἀλλὰ κατὰ τὸν ἐν τῇ ἐλευθέρᾳ ἀπογραφῇ τύπον κοινήν τινα συγχώρησιν κληρικῶν γενέσθαι. In these texts the immunity appears to be universal, but in *CTh* xvi. ii. 33, 398 (cited in n. 90), the rural clergy have to pay *capitatio*, and in *CJ* I. iii. 16, 409 (also cited in n. 90), immunity is limited to a fixed number. IMMUNITY FROM HOSPITIUM, PARANGARIA AND MUNERA PERSONALIA: *CTh* xvi. ii. 8, 343, 10, 346 (S), 14, 356 (S), 24, 377. LIABILITY TO LAND TAX: *CTh* xvi. ii. 15, 360 (cited in n. 65). For immunity from the *curia* see pp. 745–6.

102. PROHIBITION OF MIGRATION: *C. Arel.* I, can. 2, 21, *C. Nic.* can. 15, 16, *C. Sard.* can. 15, etc.

103. Siricius, *Ep.* 1 §§9–10. Zosimus, *Ep.* 9 §3.

104. Zosimus, *Ep.* 9 §1, si enim officia saecularia principem locum non vestibulum actionis ingressis sed per plurimos gradus examinato temporibus deferunt, quis ille tam arrogans, tam impudens invenitur ut in caelesti militia, quae pensius ponderanda est et sicut aurum repetitis ignibus exploranda, statim dux esse desideret cum tiro non ante fuerit? PETER OF APAMEA: *A.C.Oec.* III. 94, cf. Sev. Ant. *Ep.* I. 32, for the subdeacons of Alexandria ad Issum.

105. CYRIL AND THE AGENS IN REBUS: *A.C.Oec.* II. i. 211–12; for Felix IV's warning see above n. 92, and for Severus of Antioch, n. 89.

106. ORDINATION OF CLERGY ON ESTATES: *CTh* XVI. ii. 33, 398, *CJ* I. iii. 16, 409 (cited in n. 90). PRESENTATION OF CLERGY BY FOUNDER OR PATRON: *C. Araus.* I, can. 10, si quis episcoporum in alienae civitatis territorio ecclesiam aedificare disponit, vel pro fundi sui negotio aut ecclesiastica utilitate vel pro quacumque sua opportunitate, permissa licentia aedificandi, quia prohibere hoc votum nefas est, non praesumat dedicationem, quae illi omnimodis reservatur in cuius territorio ecclesia assurgit, reservata aedificatori episcopo hac gratia, ut quos desiderat clericos in re sua videre, ipsos ordinet is cuius territorium est, vel si ordinati iam sunt ipsos habere acquiescat; *C. Aurel.* IV, can. 7, ut in oratoriis domini praediorum minime contra votum episcopi, ad quem territorii ipsius privilegium noscitur pertinere, peregrinos clericos intromittant, nisi forsitan quos probatos ibidem districtio pontificis observare praeceperit; Just. *Nov.* lvii §2, 537. Cf. Gelasius, *Ep.* 41, where the pope agrees to ordain a monk presented by the landlord for the church on his estate.

107. EUTHALIUS: Theod. *Ep.* (Azema) 33; other instances will be given below of men who took orders after pursuing a secular career. INFANT CLERGY: Siricius, *Ep.* 1 §9, Zosimus, *Ep.* 9 §3. COUNCIL OF MOPSUESTIA: Mansi, IX. 179–83.

108. PINIANUS: Aug. *Ep.* 125–6. FORCIBLE ORDINATION OF CHILDREN: Maj. *Nov.* xi, 460.

109. TRANSLATION OF BISHOPS: *C. Nic.* can. 15, *C. Ant.* can. 21, Soc. VII. 36.

110. LAYMEN NOT TO BE CONSECRATED: *C. Sard.* can. 10, Siricius, *Ep.* 1 §§9–10, Innocent, *Ep.* 37 §5, Zosimus, *Ep.* 9 §1, Celestine, *Ep.* 4 §3, Leo, *Ep.* 12 §4, 14 §§3, 6, Just. *Nov.* vi §1, 535.

111. SIDERIUS: Syn. *Ep.* 67. Gregory of Nyssa (*Ep.* 17) wrote to the Nicomedians deploring the preference given to birth, wealth and rank in the choice of bishops; the apostles, he says, were not consuls, *magistri militum* or praetorian prefects, or famous rhetoricians or philosophers.

112. *V. Theod. Syc.* 58, 78–9.

113. AMBROSE: Paul. *V. Amb.* 6 ff. CYRUS: Malalas, 361–2. BASSIANUS: *A.C.Oec.* II. i. 405. EXCOMMUNICATION OF BISHOPS WHO REFUSED SEES: *C. Ant.* can. 17.

114. AUGUSTINE: Poss. *V. Aug.* 8, Aug. *Ep.* 31; Augustine later realised that his consecration was contrary to the canons of Nicaea (the allusion is to *C. Nic.* can. 8, ἵνα μὴ ἐν τῇ πόλει δύο ἐπίσκοποι ὦσιν), but he nevertheless had his successor preelected (but not consecrated) during his own lifetime (Aug. *Ep.* 213). ROMAN COUNCIL OF 465: Hilarus, *Ep.* 14–6: the practice had been condemned earlier by *C. Ant.* can. 23. PORPHYRY OF GAZA: *V. Porph.* 11–12.

115. *C. Anc.* can. 18, εἴ τινες ἐπίσκοποι κατασταθέντες καὶ μὴ δεχθέντες ὑπὸ τῆς παροικίας ἐκείνης, εἰς ἣν ὠνομάσθησαν, ἑτέραις βούλοιντο παροικίαις ἐπιέναι καὶ βιάζεσθαι τοὺς καθεστῶτας καὶ στάσεις κινεῖν κατ᾽ αὐτῶν, τούτους ἀφορίζεσθαι, *C. Ant.* can. 18, cf. 16, εἴ τις ἐπίσκοπος σχολάζων ἐπὶ σχολάζουσαν ἐκκλησίαν ἑαυτὸν ἐπιρρίψας ὑφαρπάζοι τὸν θρόνον δίχα συνόδου τελείας, τοῦτον ἀπόβλητον εἶναι, καὶ εἰ πᾶς ὁ λαός, ὃν ὑφήρπασεν, ἕλοιτο αὐτόν. THE METROPOLITAN OF ACHAEA: Leo, *Ep.* 13. SISINNIUS: Soc. VII. 28.

116. AMBROSE: Paul. *V. Amb.* 6–7. MARTIN: Sulp. Sev. *V. Mart.* 9.

117. BASSIANUS: *A.C. Oec.* II. i. 408.

118. ELECTION OF DAMASUS: Amm. XXVII. iii. 12, *Coll. Avell.* 1. ELECTION OF BONIFACE: *Coll. Avell.* 14 ff.

119. PARISH PRIESTS AS ELECTORS: Gelasius, fr. 4, plebs Clientensis data nobis petitione deflevit diu se sine rectoris proprii gubernatione dispergi; ac, sicut asseritur, is qui a vobis iam probatus dicitur a paucis et tenuibus putatur eligendus, quum ad vos pertineat universos assidua admonitione compellere, ut omnes in unum quem dignum sacerdotio viderint et sine aliqua reprehensione consentiant. et ideo, fratres carissimi, diversos ex omnibus saepe dicti loci paroeciis presbyteros, diaconos et universam turbam vos oportet saepius convocare. POPULAR ELECTIONS AT OLBIA AND HYDRAX AND PALAEBISCA: Syn. *Ep.* 67, 76; so at Gaza the few Christian laity deliberated with the clergy on the choice of a bishop (*V. Porph.* 11). Even in large towns like Caesarea (Greg. Naz. *Or.* XVIII. 33) and Alexandria (Ath. *Apol. c. Ar.* 6) the people are spoken of as demanding a candidate and demonstrating in his favour. In Roman elections the *plebs sancta* (*Coll. Avell.* 1 §5), the *populus Romanus* (ib. 4), or the *Christiana plebs* (ib. 17 §2) are said to take part. CLERUS, ORDO ET PLEBS: Boniface, *Ep.* 12, Celestine, *Ep.* 4 §5; Leo adds the *honorati* in *Ep.* 10 §6, and substitutes them for the *ordo* in *Ep.* 40. Cf. Greg. Naz. *Ep.* 41, καὶ ἱερατικοῖς γράφω καὶ μοναστικοῖς, καὶ τοῖς ἐκ τοῦ ἀξιωματικοῦ καὶ βουλευτικοῦ τάγματος καὶ τοῦ δήμου παντός. The respective roles of the various classes are well put in Theod. *HE* IV. 20 (on the election of Athanasius's successor Peter), πάντων συμψήφων γεγενημένων καὶ τῶν ἱερωμένων καὶ τῶν ἐν τέλει καὶ ἀξιώμασι καὶ ὁ λαὸς δὲ ἅπας ταῖς εὐφημίαις ἐδηλοῦν τὴν ἡδόνην. EXCLUSION OF THE POPULACE: *C. Laod.* can. 13, περὶ τοῦ μὴ τοῖς ὄχλοις ἐπιτρέπειν τὰς ἐκλογὰς ποιεῖσθαι τῶν μελλόντων καθίστασθαι εἰς ἱερατεῖον. Gregory Nazianzen (*Or.* XVIII. 35) held that the clergy and the monks should have the sole or at least a predominant voice in episcopal elections, and that they should not be entrusted τοῖς εὐπορωτάτοις τε καὶ δυνατωτάτοις ἢ φορᾷ δήμου καὶ ἀλογίᾳ. The role of the people is also minimised in *Ep. ad Gallos,* 10 (cited in n. 91).

120. Leo, *Ep.* 14 §5, ita ut si in aliam forte personam partium se vota diviserint, metropolitani iudicio is alteri praeferatur qui maioribus et studiis iuvatur et meritis, tantum ut nullus invitis et non petentibus ordinetur. Sid. Ap. *Ep.* IV. 25 (Cabillonum), VII. 9 (Bituriges).

121. THREE CANDIDATES PROPOSED BY THE BISHOPS: *C. Arel.* II, can. 54, placuit in ordinatione episcopi hunc ordinem custodiri ut primo loco venalitate vel ambitione submota tres ab episcopis nominentur de quibus clerici vel cives erga unum eligendi habeant potestatem. THREE CANDIDATES ELECTED BY THE CLERGY AND PEOPLE: Sev. Ant. *Ep.* I. 18, 30, 39 (where he speaks of the rule as a sacred law, confirmed by the emperor), 46, *CJ* I. iii. 41 pr., 528.

122. ATHANASIUS: Philostorg. II. 11; for another hostile account of his election see Soz. II. 17. BASSIANUS: *A.C.Oec.* II. i. 405.

123. CONSTANTINE AND ANTIOCH: Eus. *V. Const.* III. 62.

124. NECTARIUS: Soz. VII. 8 (for a different account see Soc. V. 8). JOHN CHRYSOSTOM: Pall. *Dial.* pp. 29–30, Soc. VI. 2, Soz. VIII. 2. NESTORIUS: Soc. VII. 29. SISINNIUS: Soc. VII. 26. MAXIMIAN: Soc. VII. 35. PROCLUS: Soc. VII. 40. ELECTION OF 449: Leo, *Ep.* 53, πρότερον μὲν ἐπέτρεψε τῷ κατ' αὐτὴν εὐλαβεστάτῳ κλήρῳ τοὺς ἐπιτηδειοτέρους εἰς ἐπιστασίαν μετὰ δοκιμασίας ψηφίσασθαι, τὴν ἐπιλογὴν ἑαυτῷ τοῦ πάντων ἐκκρίτου ταμιευσάμενος. εἶτα . . . ἔδοξε λοιπὸν τοῖς κρατοῦσι τῶν ὅλων ἐπιτραπῆναι κλήρῳ τὴν ἐπιλογὴν τοῦ πρωτεύοντος. MENAS: *A.C.Oec.* III. 135, 153. On Menas's death there was much intrigue (*V. Eutych.* 23, ἀγὼν ἄφατος καὶ σπουδὴ ἄμετρος τοῖς πολλοῖς ἦν εἰς τὸ προβάλλεσθαι τοὺς μὴ ἀξίους τῆς ἀρχιεροσύνης), but it was directed to securing the support of the emperor's advisers (ibid. 23, ὑποσχέσεσι καὶ δωροδοκίαις βουλομένοις πεῖσαι τοὺς δυναστὰς τοῦ βασιλέως), and Justinian made his own choice and obtained the formal assent of the clergy and senate (ibid. 24). Gregory the Great (*Ep.* VII. 6) gives Maurice the entire credit for the choice of Cyriacus.

125. For the appointment of royal favourites and ministers by the Frankish kings see Greg. Tur. *HF* v. 45, VI. 7, 38, VIII. 20, 22, 39 etc., and for their sale of bishoprics Greg. Tur. *V. Patr.* VI. 3.

126. IMPERIAL LAWS ON THE ORDINATION OF SLAVES: *CTh* IX. xlv. 3, 398, Val. III, *Nov.* xxxv §3, 452, *CJ* I. iii. 36, 484, Just. *Nov.* cxxiii §17, 546.

127. THE CHURCH ON THE ORDINATION OF SLAVES: *Lib. Pont.* xliv, Leo, *Ep.* 4 §1, *C. Aurel.* I, can. 8, *C. Aurel.* III, can. 26, *C. Aurel.* v., can. 6, cf. also Sev. Ant. *Ep.* I. 35.

128. ORDINATION OF COLONI: *CJ* I. iii. 16, 409, Val. III, *Nov.* xxxv §3, 452, *CJ* I. iii. 36, 484, Just. *Nov.* cxxiii §17, 546, Leo, *Ep.* 4 §1, Gelasius, *Ep.* 14 §14, *C. Aurel.* III, can. 26.

129. RULES ON SLAVES AND COLONI: Val. III, *Nov.* xxxv §6, Gelasius, *Ep.* 20–23.

130. Just. *Nov.* cxxiii §4, 546.

131. ROMAN GUILDS: *CTh* XIV. iii. 11, 365 (bakers), Val. III, *Nov.* xx, 445. WESTERN COLLEGIATI: Val. III, *Nov.* xxxv §§3, 5, 452, Maj. *Nov.* vii §3, 458. In the East *murileguli* were forbidden to take orders by *CTh* IX. xlv. 3, 398. ALBINUS: Loewenfeld, *Ep. Pont. Rom. Ined.* 39.

132. VICTRICIUS: Paul. *Ep.* 18. MARTIN: Sulp. Sev. *V. Mart.* 2. Two other soldiers, one of whom became a priest and the other a bishop, are recorded in Zach. Myt. *Chron.* VII. 6. EVASION OF MILITARY SERVICE THROUGH ORDINATION: Bas. *Ep.* 54, *CTh* VII. xx. 12 §2, 400.

133. *C. Carth.* III, can. 49, ut episcopi presbyteri diaconi vel quicumque clerici qui nihil habentes ordinantur et tempore episcopatus vel clericatus sui agros vel quaecumque praedia nomine suo comparant, etc. AETIUS: Philostorgius, III. 15. Cf. *C. Carth.* III, can. 44, where a bishop brings up a very poor boy and ordains him *lector*, and another bishop then, contrary to the canons, makes him deacon.

134. AMBROSE: Paul. *V. Amb.* 3–7. NECTARIUS: Soc. v. 8, Soz. VII. 8. ARSACIUS: Soc. VI. 19, Soz. VIII. 23. For Paulinus's birth, wealth and rank see

Amb. *Ep.* 58 §§1–3, Aus. *Ep.* 20, 24, lines 64–5, 115–16; it appears from Paul. *Carm.* 21, line 395, that he was consular of Campania. P. Fabre, *Essai sur la chronologie de l'oeuvre de saint Paulin de Nole* (Paris, 1948) dates his conversion to 389, his ordination as priest to 394, and his consecration as bishop to between 408 and 416.

135. Siricius, *Ep.* 6 §1, ut tales videlicet ad ecclesiasticum ordinem permitterentur accedere quales apostolica auctoritas iubet non quales dico, vel eos qui cingulo militiae saecularis adstricti olim gloriati sunt. qui posteaquam pompa saeculari exultaverunt aut negotiis rei publicae optaverunt militare aut mundi curam tractare, adhibita sibi quorundam manu et proximorum favore stipati, hi frequenter ingeruntur auribus meis ut episcopi esse possint; Innocent, *Ep.* 37 §3, sed designata sunt genera de quibus ad clericatum pervenire non possunt, id est, si quis fidelis militaverit, si quis fidelis causas egerit, hoc est, postulaverit, si quis fidelis administraverit. CAESARIUS: Symmachus, *Ep.* 15 §11, illud etiam pari supplicatione deposcimus, ut de laica conversatione, qui in singulis iudicum officiis meruerint aut certe rexerint sub aliqua potestate provincias, nisi multo ante tempore praemissa conversatione legitima et vita examinata, nullus aut clericus aut episcopus ordinetur. Cf. also *Ep. ad Gallos*, 10, eos praeterea qui saecularem adepti potestatem ius saeculi exercuerint immunes a peccato esse non posse manifestum est. dum enim et gladius exeritur aut iudicium confertur iniustum aut tormenta exercentur per necessitatem causarum aut parandis exhibent voluptatibus curam aut praeparatis intersunt . . . multum sibi praestant si non episcopatum adtectent, sed propter haec omnia agentes poenitentiam certo tempore impleto mereantur altaribus sociari. GERMANUS OF AUXERRE: *V. Germani*, 1, 2; as he had previously practised at the bar of the prefecture it is clear that the post described by his Merovingian biographer as 'ducatus culmen et regimen per provincias' was a provincial governorship. SIDONIUS APOLLINARIS: Greg. Tur. *HF* II. 21. CHRYSANTHUS: Soc. VII. 12. THALASSIUS: Soc. VII. 48. EPHRAEM: Evagr. IV. 6.

136. LAWYERS: *C. Sard.* can. 10, Innocent, *Ep.* 3 §4, quantos enim ex his qui post acceptam gratiam in forensi exercitatione versati sunt et obtinendi pertinaciam susceperunt adscitos ad sacerdotium esse comperimus? e quorum numero Rufinus et Gregorius perhibentur. quantos ex aliqua militia, qui cum potestatibus oboedirent severa necessario praecepta sunt executi? quantos ex curialibus, qui dum parent potestatibus, quae sibi sunt imperata fecerunt? quantos qui voluptates et editiones populo celebrarunt . . . ? quorum omnium neminem ne ad societatem quidem ordinis clericorum oportuerat pervenire, §6, ne quispiam qui post baptismum militaverit ad ordinem debeat clericatus admitti, neque qui causas post acceptum baptismum egerint, aut qui post acceptam dei gratiam administraverint. PROFESSORS: Soc. II. 46, Soz. VI. 25 (the elder Apollinaris, a *grammaticus*, and the younger, a *rhetor*, were priest and reader), Evagr. I. 9 (Eusebius bishop of Dorylaeum had been a rhetor). MAMERTINUS: *V. Severini*, 4. AMBROSE: Paul. *V. Amb.* 5. GERMANUS: *V. Germani*, 1. ALYPIUS: Aug. *Conf.* VI. 16, VIII. 13. SEVERUS: Zach. *V. Sev.* pp. 46 ff., 92. ZACHARIAS: Zach. *V. Sev.* pp. 47 ff., 95, cf. also 81 (a former *scholasticus* is priest). SEVERUS'S FOUR LAWYERS: Sev. Ant. *Ep.* 1. 5.

137. OFFICIALS: Siricius, *Ep.* 5 §2, item si quis post remissionem peccatorum cingulum militiae saecularis habuerit ad clerum admitti non decet; *C. Tol.* 1, can. 8, si quis post baptismum militaverit et chlamydem sumpserit vel cingulum, etiam si gravia non admiserit, si ad clerum admissus fuerit diaconi dignitatem non accipiat; Innocent, *Ep.* 2 §2 (the same rule as Siricius, *Ep.* 5§ 3), 3 §§4, 6

(cited in n. 136). CAESARIUS: Symmachus, *Ep.* 15 §11 (cited in n. 135). Even before Siricius a council held in Illyricum c. 375 had ruled that priests and deacons should be ordained from among the (lower) clergy καὶ μὴ ἀπὸ τοῦ βουλευτηρίου καὶ στρατιωτικῆς ἀρχῆς (Theod. *HE* IV. 9).

138. RETIRED OFFICIALS ALLOWED TO TAKE ORDERS: *CJ* I. iii. 27, 466. EUTHALIUS: Theod. *Ep.* (Azema) 33. THEODORE: *A.C.Oec.* II. i. 211-2. Cf. also the imperial notary Theodulus, who became bishop of Mutina (Paul. *V. Amb.* 35); Eleusius, a former palatine official, bishop of Cyzicus (Soz. IV. 20); Marathonius, a former *numerarius* of the praetorian prefecture, bishop of Nicomedia (Soz. IV. 20, 27). The sons of higher officials were of course allowed to take orders, as did John Chrysostom, son of a member of the *officium* of the *magister militum per Orientem* (Pall. *Dial.* p. 28).

139. COHORTALES: *CTh* VIII. iv. 7, 361, *CJ* I. iii. 27, 466, 52, 531, Just. *Nov.* cxxiii §15, 546 (the words quoted are in §1 of this law).

140. STEPHEN OF LARISSA: *Stephani ad Bonifacium Libellus* (PL LXV. 34), mihi enim in saeculari vita antea provincialis ordo militiae, mediocriter sicut erat meam vitam humiliter transibam. MAURICE'S LAW: Greg. *Ep.* III. 61, 64.

141. LAWS ON CURIALES AND THE CHURCH: Eus. *HE* X. 7, *CTh* XVI. ii. 1, 313, 2, 319, 3, 329 (S), 6, 329 (S), 7, 330, 9, 349, XII. i. 49, 361, 59+XVI. ii. 17, 364, XVI. ii. 19, 370, XII. i. 99, 104, 383, 115, 386, 121, 390, 123, 391, IX. xlv. 3, 398, XII. i. 163, 399, Val. III, *Nov.* iii, 439, *CJ* I. iii. 21, 442, Val. III, *Nov.* xxxv §§3, 5, 452, Maj. *Nov.* vii §7, 458, *CJ* I. iii. 52, 531, Just. *Nov.* cxxiii §15, 546.

142. A council held in Illyricum c. 375 banned the ordination of *curiales* (see above n. 137). Ambrose's complaints are in *Ep.* 18 §13, 40 §29; Theodosius's law is *CTh* XII. i. 121.

143. Innocent, *Ep.* 3 §4 (cited in n. 136), §6, neque de curialibus aliquem venire ad ecclesiasticum ordinem posse qui post baptismum vel coronati fuerint vel sacerdotium quod dicitur sustinuerint et editiones publicas celebraverint. nam et hoc de curialibus est cavendum ne eidem qui ex curialibus fuerint aliquando a suis curiis, quod frequenter videmus accidere, reposcantur, 2 §12, praeterea frequenter quidam e fratribus nostris curiales vel quibuslibet publicis functionibus occupatos clericos facere contendunt; quibus postea maior tristitia cum de revocandis eis aliquid ab imperatore praecipitur quam gratia de adscito nascitur. constat enim eos in ipsis muniis etiam voluptates exhibere, quas a diabolo inventas esse non dubium est, et ludorum vel munerum apparatibus aut praeesse aut interesse, 37 §3, de curialibus autem manifesta ratio est, quoniam etsi inveniantur huiusmodi viri qui debeant clerici fieri, tamen quoniam saepius ad curiam repetuntur, cavendum ab his est propter tribulationem quae saepe de his ecclesiae provenit.

144. JUSTINIAN: *CJ* I. iii. 52 §1, 531, Gelasius, *Ep.* 15, Greg. *Ep.* IV. 26.

145. CONSTANS'S LAW: *CTh* XVI. ii. 9, 349, curialibus muneribus atque omni inquietudine civilium functionum exsortes cunctos clericos esse oportet, filios tamen eorum, si curiis obnoxii non tenentur, in ecclesia perseverare. EPISCOPAL FAMILIES: *ILCV* 1030, 1806. CHRYSANTHUS: Soc. VII. 12. SEVERUS'S FAMILY: Zach. *V. Sev.* p. 11.

146. The old rule is given in *Const. Apost.* VI. 17, cf. *C. Anc.* can. 10.

147. Clerical continence is ordered by *C. Ilib.* can. 33, and advocated by Eus. *Dem. Ev.* I. 9, Cyr. Hierosol. *Catech.* XII. 25 (for priests). NICAEA: Soc. I. 11, Soz. I. 23. GANGRA: *C. Gangr.* can. 4.

148. CLERICAL CONTINENCE: Siricius, *Ep.* 1 §7, 5 §3, Innocent, *Ep.* 2 §9, 6 §1, *Ep. ad Gallos*, 3, Leo, *Ep.* 14 §4, 167 §3, *C. Carth.* II, can. 2, *Cod. Can. Eccl. Afr.* 70, *C. Taur.* can. 8, *C. Araus.* I, can. 22, *C. Tur.* I, can. 1, 2, *C. Agath.* can. 9, *C. Aurel.* III, can. 2, *C. Tol.* I, can. 1.

149. Jerome, *C. Vig.* 2, Epiph. *adv. Haer.* XLVIII. 9, *Can. Apost.* 5. ANTONINUS: Pall. *Dial.* p. 84. SYNESIUS: Syn. *Ep.* 105. NO RULE OF CONTINENCE IN THE EAST: Soc. v. 22.

150. *CJ* I. iii. 41 §§2-4, 528, 47, 531, Just. *Nov.* vi §1, 535, cxxiii §1, 546, cxxxvii §2, 565. Cf. Pelagius I, *Ep.* 33, illud consultius iudicavimus faciendum ut congrua providentia causam propter quam principalis constitutio habentem filios et uxorem ad episcopatus prohibet ordinem promoveri, salva dispositione consilii muniremus. qua de re summo studio ab eodem Syracusanae urbis episcopo, priusquam a nobis eum contingeret ordinari, huiusmodi exegimus cautionem, per quam et suam fateretur quantula esset praesentis temporis habita rerum descriptione substantiam, et nihil umquam per se aut per filios et uxorem sive per quamlibet propinquam aut domesticam vel extraneam forte personam de rebus usurparet ecclesiae. et universa episcopatus quaesita tempore ecclesiae suae dominio sociaret, nihil ultra id quod modo descriptum est suis filiis vel heredibus relicturus.

151. For early monasticism see P. de Labriolle in *Hist. de l'Église*, III, 299-369, where there is a full bibliography.

152. EUSTATHIUS: Soz. III. 14. BASIL'S RULES: Basil, *Regulae fusius tractatae*, *Regulae brevius tractatae* (*PG* XXXI. 889-1306). The story of the early monastic settlement near Constantinople is told in *V. Hypatii*, 58, 60-1, 66, 70-1, cf. Soz. VI. 40, Theod. *HE* IV. 34 for the date of Isaac.

153. ATHANASIUS'S INFLUENCE IN THE WEST: Jerome, *Ep.* 127 §5. MARTIN: Sulp. Sev. *V. Mart.* 7. HONORATUS: Hilarius Arel. *de vita S. Honorati*, 15 ff. (*PL* L. 1256 ff.). CASSIAN: Gennadius, *de script. eccl.* 61. AMBROSE: Aug. *Conf.* VIII. 15. AUGUSTINE: Poss. *V. Aug.* 5, 11.

154. PACHOMIUS'S FOUNDATIONS: *V Pachom.* 6, Pall. *Hist. Laus.* xxxii; the figure of 3000 for the Tabennesiot order comes from Soz. VI. 28, Ruf. *Hist. Mon.* 3, the figure of 7000 from *V. Pachom.* 6; Cassian, *Inst.* IV. 1, gives 5000. NITRIA: Pall. *Hist. Laus.* vii, xiii. SCETIS: Joh. Moschus, 113. ALEXANDRIA: Pall. *Hist. Laus.* vii. ANTINOOPOLIS: Pall. *Hist. Laus.* lviii, lix. OXYRHYNCHUS: Ruf. *Hist. Mon.* 5. ARSINOE: Ruf. *Hist. Mon.* 18. MONASTERY BY THE RED SEA: *V. Hypatii*, 140; at Thecoa, Joh. Maium. *Pleroph.* 25; at Amida, Joh. Eph. *V. SS. Or.* 35; elsewhere in Syria, ib. 14, 15. NUMBER OF MONASTERIES AT CONSTANTINOPLE AND CHALCEDON: *A.C.Oec.* III. 260-2.

155. MARCIAN'S PROPOSAL: *A.C.Oec.* II. i. 353; canon 4 on slaves, *A.C.Oec.* II. i. 355. LAWS ON SLAVES AND COLONI: Val. III, *Nov.* xxxv §3, 452, *CJ* I. iii. 36, 37, 484, Just. *Nov.* v §2, 535, cxxiii §35, 546. MAURICE'S LAWS: Greg. *Ep.* III. 61, 64, cf. VIII. 10, X. 9.

156. EGYPTIAN MONKS WORK IN THE HARVEST: Ruf. *Hist. Mon.* 18, Joh. Moschus, 183; WORK AT HANDICRAFTS: Pall. *Hist. Laus.* xxxii; SELL PRODUCTS: Joh. Moschus, 194. PACHOMIAN HOUSES: *V. Pachom.* 7, cf. 25 (mat weaving), 35 (shoemaking), Pall. *Hist. Laus.* xxxii (surplus to charity, cf. Cassian, *Inst.* X. 22, *Coll.* XVIII. 7).

157. MONASTIC ENDOWMENTS IN EGYPT: *P. Cairo*, 67170, 67299, *P. Lond.* 483, *P. Giss.* 56, *PRG* III. 48, etc. SYRIAN MONKS WORK FOR THEIR LIVING: Joh. Chrys. *Hom. in Matth.* lxxii. 4. THEODOSIUS'S MONASTERY: Theod. *Hist. Rel.* x.

158. HYPATIUS'S MONASTERY: *V. Hypatii*, 67, 76, 120. Cassian, *Inst.* x. 22–3, hinc est quod in his regionibus nulla videmus monasteria tanta fratrum celebritate fundata, quia nec operum suorum facultatibus fulciuntur ut possint in eis iugiter perdurare, et si eis subpeditare quoquo modo valeat sufficientia victus alterius largitate, voluptas tamen otii et pervagatio cordis diutius eos in loco perseverare non patitur. MONASTIC SLAVES NOT TO BE FREED: *C. Epaon.* can. 8, mancipia vero monachis donata ab abbate non liceat manumitti. iniustum enim putamus ut monachis quotidianum rurale opus facientibus servi eorum libertatis otio potiantur. Monasteries are regularly mentioned among the bodies prohibited to alienate their endowments, e.g. *CJ* I. ii. 17 §2 (Anastasius), Just. *Nov.* vii §1, 535.

159. VALENS AND THE MONKS: Cassian, *Coll.* XVIII. 7. MONASTIC REBELLION IN PALESTINE: *A.C.Oec.* II. i. 483–6, Zach. Myt. *Chron.* III. 3 ff., Evagr. II. 5.

160. CANONS ON MONASTIC DISCIPLINE: *A.C.Oec.* II. i. 353 (Marcian's proposal), 355 (can. 4), *C. Agath.* can. 27, *C. Aurel.* I, can. 19. THE PRIVILEGE OF LERINS: Mansi, VII. 907–8. PRIVILEGE OF CAESARIUS'S NUNNERY: Hormisdas, *Ep.* 150. In Africa two councils in 525 and 534 (Mansi, VIII. 648–56, 841–2) granted monasteries immunity from episcopal control, following the precedent of Lerins. In the East bishops often appointed inspectors or controllers of the monks in their diocese, e.g. Theod. *Ep.* (*PG*) 113, 116–7, ἔξαρχον τῶν παρ' ἡμῖν μοναζόντων, Cyr. Scyth. *V. Euthymii*, 16, χωρεπίσκοπον καὶ τῶν μοναχῶν ἀρχιμανδρίτην, *V. Sabae*, 30, ἀρχιμανδρίτας καὶ τῶν μοναχῶν ἐξάρχους, *V. Eutych.* 18, ἀναδέχεται τὴν φροντίδα ἤτοι ἡγεμονίαν ὅλου τοῦ ὑπὸ τὴν μητρόπολιν μοναχικοῦ συστήματος, ὅθεν καὶ καθολικὸς ὠνομάζετο, Just. *Nov.* v §7, οἵ τε ἀρχιμανδρῖται καλούμενοι, cxxxiii §4, ὁ τῶν μοναστηρίων ἔξαρχος. IMPERIAL LEGISLATION ON MONKS: *CJ* I. iii. 43, 529 (no mixed houses), 46, 530 (election of abbots), Just. *Nov.* v, 535 (common life is ordered in §3), cxxxiii, 539, cxxiii §§33 ff., 546 (repetition of the above rules).

161. See pp. 82, 86 ff.

162. JUSTINIAN ON CLERICAL DICING: *CJ* I. iv. 34, 534.

163. NESTORIUS ON HERETICS: Soc. VII. 29. MARTIN: Sulp. Sev. *Chron.* II. 50, *Dial.* III. 13. AUGUSTINE: Aug. *Retract.* II. v; for an account of Augustine's change of mind see G. G. Willis, *Augustine and the Donatist Controversy*, pp. 127 ff. SOCRATES ON NESTORIUS: Soc. VII. 29; he also expresses approval of Atticus's tolerance and tells with pleasure the ignominious end of a persecuting bishop of Synnada (VII. 2–3). PROCOPIUS ON THE HERETICS: Proc. *HA* xi. 21–3. For the Donatists see pp. 81–2; the Donatist slogan 'quid imperatori cum ecclesia?' is quoted in Opt. III. 3. A plea for *libertas* is made in Hilary, *Liber I ad Constantium*; cf. the synodical letter of the Council of Sardica in *CSEL* LXV. 181 ff., Hosius's letter in Ath. *Hist. Ar.* 44, and Athanasius's own remarks in *Hist. Ar.* 52.

164. GELASIUS ON THE TWO POWERS: Gelasius, *Ep.* 12 §2, duo quippe sunt, imperator auguste, quibus principaliter mundus hic regitur, auctoritas sacrata pontificum et regalis potestas. in quibus tanto gravius est pondus sacerdotum,

quanto etiam pro ipsis regibus hominum in divino reddituri sunt examine rationem. nosti etenim, fili clementissime, quod licet praesideas humano generi dignitate, rerum tamen praesulibus divinarum devotus colla submittis. CONSTANTIUS'S ALLEGED REMARK: Ath. *Hist. Ar.* 33, ἀλλ᾽ ὅπερ ἐγὼ βούλομαι τοῦτο κανών, ἔλεγε, νομιζέσθω· οὕτω γάρ μου λέγοντος ἀνέχονται οἱ τῆς Συρίας λεγόμενοι ἐπίσκοποι. ἢ τοίνυν πείσθητε ἢ καὶ ὑμεῖς ὑπερόριοι γενήσεσθε.

XXIII. RELIGION (pp. 938–41)

The best general works on the topics covered by this chapter are Gaston Boissier, *La fin du Paganisme*[3], Paris, 1898, and Samuel Dill, *Roman Society in the last century of the Western Empire*[2], London, 1910.

1. See pp. 91–2, 113–4, 167–9.

2. LAWS AGAINST PAGANISM: *CTh* XVI. x. 19, 407 (S), cf. *Cod. Can. Eccl. Afr.* 58, instant etiam aliae necessitates religiosis imperatoribus postulandae, ut reliquias idolorum per omnem Africam iubeant penitus amputari; nam plerisque in locis maritimis atque possessionibus diversis adhuc erroris istius iniquitas viget: ut praecipiant et ipsas deleri, et templa eorum, quae in agris vel in locis abditis constituta nullo ornamento sunt, iubeantur omnino destrui, *CTh* XVI. x. 20, 415, 23, 423, 25, 435, *CJ* I. xi. 7, 451, 8, 472, 9 (a law of Anastasius, cf. *P. Oxy.* 1814), μηδενὶ δὲ ἐξέστω μήτε ἐν διαθήκῃ μήτε κατὰ δωρεὰν καταλιμπάνειν ἢ διδόναι τι προσώποις ἢ τόποις ἐπὶ συστάσει τῆς τοῦ Ἑλληνισμοῦ δυσσεβείας, εἰ καὶ μὴ τοῦτο ἰδικῶς τοῖς τῆς βουλήσεως ἢ διαθήκης ἢ δωρεᾶς περιέχοιτο ῥήμασιν, ἄλλως δὲ σὺν ἀληθείᾳ καταληφθῆναι παρὰ τῶν δικαζόντων δύναται.

3. PAGANS EXCLUDED FROM MILITIAE: Zos. V. 46, *CTh* XVI. x. 21, 416; FROM THE BAR: *CJ* I. iv. 15 (= II. vi. 8), 468; FROM PROFESSORSHIPS: *CJ* I. v. 18 §4, xi. 10 §2, Malalas, 451, Agath. II. 30. The other disabilities are imposed by *CJ* I. v. 18; baptism is ordered by *CJ* I. xi. 10, cf. Malalas, 449, Theophanes, A.M. 6022.

4. THE MISSION IN ASIA: Joh. Eph. *V. SS. Or.* xl, xliii, xlvii, *HE* II. 44, III. 36–7. HELIOPOLIS: Joh. Eph. *HE* III. 27 ff. CARRHAE AND THE NUSAIRI: *Encyclopedia of Islam*, II. 270, III. 964–5. Other examples of the survival of paganism in the sixth century are to be found in Sophronius, *Narr. de mir. SS. Cyri et Johannis*, 30, 32 (at Alexandria), and *V. Sym. Jun.* 160–3, 169, 174 ff., 201–4, 217–8, 220, 237 (at Antioch and Apamea).

5. PAGANISM AT TARRACINA: Greg. *Ep.* VIII. 19; AT TYNDARIS: III. 59; IN SARDINIA: IV. 23, 25–7, 29, V. 38, IX. 204, XI. 12. SPAIN: Mart. Bracar. *de correctione rusticorum*, C. Tol. III, can. 16. GAUL: C. *Arel.* II, can. 23, C. *Aurel.* II, can. 20, C. *Aurel.* IV, can. 15, 16, C. *Tur.* II, can. 22, C. *Autis.* can. 1, 3, 4, C. *Rem.* can. 14, Greg. Tur. *V. Patr.* VI. 2, *HF* VIII. 15; cf. *V. Caesarii*, II. 18, daemonium quod rustici Dianam appellant (near Arles).

6. The quotation is from Symm. *Rel.* 3 §9. For paganism among senators, see p. 163 (the altar of Victory), 168–9 (support for Eugenius), Zos. IV. 59, V.

41. THE UNIVERSITIES OF ALEXANDRIA AND BERYTUS: Zach. *V. Sev.* pp. 15 ff., 57 ff.; OF ATHENS: Agath. II. 30.

7. PERSECUTION OF PAGANS IN 529: Malalas, 449, Theophanes, A.M. 6022; IN 546: *Rev. Or. Chrét.* II (1897), 481–2 (a fragment of John of Ephesus); IN 578: Joh. Eph. *HE* III. 30 ff.

8. PAGANS IN GAUL: Sulp. Sev. *V. Mart.* 12–15, *Dial.* II. 4, III. 8. THE ANAUNI: Vigilius Tridentinus, *Ep.* 1, 2. PAGANS ON ITALIAN ESTATES: Maximus Taurin. *Serm.* 101–2.

9. PAGANS ON ESTATES: Joh. Chrys. *Hom. in Act.* XVIII. 4; cf. *V. Hypatii.* 103, 124–5, for the survival of rural paganism near Constantinople in the early fifth century. ABRAM: Theod. *Hist. Rel.* xvii. THALALAEUS: ib. xxviii.

10. MAVIA: Soc. IV. 36. ASPEBETUS: Cyr. Scyth. *V. Euthym.* 10. BLEMMYES AND NOBADAE: Priscus, 21, Proc. *BP* I. xix. 34–7; cf. *Sb* 1169–70 (pagan dedications at Philae in 452). CONVERSION OF THE NOBADAE: Joh. Eph. *HE* IV. 6 ff. AUGILA: Proc. *Aed.* VI. ii. 14–20. THE MOORS: Proc. *BV* I. viii. 15 ff., II. viii. 9 ff., *Aed.* VI. iii. 10. THE GOTHS: J. Zeiller, *Les origines chrétiennes dans les provinces danubiennes,* 440 ff. THE FRANKS: Greg. Tur. *HF* II. 29–31.

11. CALAMA, MADAURA AND SUFES: Aug. *Ep.* 50, 91, 232; for the early conversion of rural Africa see W. H. C. Frend, *The Donatist Church,* pp. 87 ff.

12. EDESSA: *CAH* XII, 493 ff. CARRHAE: *Itin. Hierosol., S. Silvia,* 20. 8, and above n. 4. ANTIOCH: Julian, *Misop.* 357D; a generation later John Chrysostom estimated that there were 100,000 Christians (*Hom. in Matth.* lxxxv. 4) out of a total population of 200,000 (*Laud. Ign. Mart.* 4). APAMEA: Lib. *Ep.* 1351, Soz. VII. 15. HELIOPOLIS: Theod. *HE* IV. 22, Joh. Eph. *HE* III. 27. MAIUMA: Soz. II. 5, V. 3. GAZA: Jerome, *V. Hilar.* 20, *V. Porph.* 11, 19, 26 ff.

13. RESISTANCE AT ALEXANDRIA AND OTHER CITIES: Soz. VII. 15. The Sardinian pagans paid a regular *praemium* to the governor to induce him to turn a blind eye to their cult (Greg. *Ep.* v. 38).

14. APOSTATES: *CTh* XVI. vii. 1, 381, 2, 383, 3, 383, 4+5, 391, 6, 396, 7, 426. PAGAN HOPES UNDER ZENO: Zach. *V. Sev.* p. 40, cf. *V. Isaiae,* p. 7, for Christian fears of a restoration of paganism at this time.

15. JOSEPH: Epiph. *adv. Haer.* XXX. 11–12. JEWISH REVOLT IN GALILEE: Soc. II. 33, Soz. IV. 7, Aur. Victor, *Caes.* xlii. 10.

16. SAMARITAN REVOLT UNDER MARCIAN: *A.C.Oec.* II. i. 486, 488; IN 529: Malalas, 445–7, Proc. *HA* xi. 24–30; AT THE END OF JUSTINIAN'S REIGN: Malalas, 487.

17. JEWISH MERCHANTS: Greg. *Ep.* IX. 104, Greg. Tur. *HF* IV. 12, VI. 5. JEWISH COLONI: Lib. *Or.* XLVII. 13, Greg. *Ep.* v. 7. SAMARITANS IN UPPER EGYPT: *Sb* 9278; AT ROME: Cass. *Var.* III. 45; AT CATANA AND SYRACUSE: Greg. *Ep.* VI. 30, VIII. 21.

18. The most important passages on the Jewish patriarchs and their *apostoli* are Origen, περὶ ἀρχῶν, iv. 1, Epiph. *adv. Haer.* xxx. 4–11, Pall. *Dial.* p. 90; for the lapse of the office in 429 see *CTh* XVI. viii. 29 (cited below). TITLES OF JEWISH CLERGY: *CTh* XVI. viii. 1, 315 (maioribus eorum et patriarchis), 2, 330 (patriarchis vel presbyteris), 4, 331 (hiereos et archisynagogos et patres

synagogarum), 13, 397 (archisynagogis patriarchisque ac presbyteris), 14, 399 (archisynagogi sive presbyteri), *IGLS* 1319 (three ἀρχισυνάγωγοι, one γερουσίαρχος and two or more πρεσβύτεροι). PAYMENTS TO THE PATRIARCH: Epiph. *adv. Haer.* XXX. 11, τὰ ἐπιδέκατα καὶ τὰς ἀπαρχάς, *CTh* XVI. viii. 14, 399, superstitionis indignae est, ut archisynagogi sive presbyteri Iudaeorum vel quos ipsi apostolos vocant, qui ad exigendum aurum atque argentum a patriarcha certo tempore diriguntur, a singulis synagogis exactam summam atque susceptam ad eundem reportent, 17, 404, 29, 429, Iudaeorum primates, qui in utriusque Palaestinae synedriis nominantur vel in aliis provinciis degunt, quaecumque post excessum patriarcharum pensionis nomine suscepere, cogantur exsolvere. in futurum vero periculo eorundem anniversarius canon de synagogis omnibus palatinis compellentibus exigatur ad eam formam, quam patriarchae quondam coronarii auri nomine postulabant; quae tamen quanta sit, sollerti inquisitione discutias; et quod de occidentalibus partibus patriarchis conferri consueverat, nostris largitionibus inferatur. RANK OF PATRIARCHS: *CTh* XVI. viii. 8, 392, 11, 396, 13, 397 (illustris), 15, 404 (spectabilis), 22, 415 (Gamaliel's prefecture).

19. PROTECTION OF SYNAGOGUES: *CTh* XVI. viii. 9, 393, 12, 397, 20, 412, 21, 420 (S), 25, 26, 27, 423. NO NEW SYNAGOGUES: *CTh* XVI. viii. 22, 415, 25, 27, 423, Th. II, *Nov.* iii §§3, 5, 438 (repairs allowed). This last law deals with both Jews and Samaritans, and presumably covers the latters' synagogues. DESTRUCTION OF SAMARITAN SYNAGOGUES: *CJ* I. v. 17.

20. PROHIBITION OF PROVOCATIVE JEWISH RITES: *CTh* XVI. viii. 18, 408, cf. 21, 420 (S). TARRACINA: Greg. *Ep.* II. 6. JUSTINIAN'S REGULATION OF SYNAGOGUES: Just. *Nov.* cxlvi, 553.

21. NO BILLETING IN SYNAGOGUES: *CTh* VII. viii. 2 (= *CJ* I. ix. 4), 368. CURIAL IMMUNITY OF JEWISH CLERGY: *CTh* XVI. viii. 3, 321, 2, 330, 4, 330 (S), 13, 397; WITHDRAWN IN THE WEST: *CTh* XII. i. 99 (= *CJ* I. ix. 5), 383, cf. 158, 398; it is not clear whether 165 (= *CJ* I. ix. 10), 399, was intended to revoke the immunity in the East. SABBATH RESPECTED: *CTh* II. viii. 26 + VIII. viii. 8 + XVI viii. 20 (=*CJ* I. ix. 12), 412. JEWISH JURISDICTION: *CTh* II. i. 10 (= *CJ* I. ix. 8), 398, XVI. viii. 22, 415; for price control see *CTh* XVI. viii. 10 (= *CJ* I. ix. 9), 396, and for the right of the Jewish authorities to excommunicate, *CTh* XVI. viii. 8, 392.

22. MIXED MARRIAGES PROHIBITED: *CTh* III. vii. 2 = IX. vii. 5 (= *CJ* I. ix. 6), 388. SLAVES OF JEWS: *CTh* XVI. ix. 1, 335, 2, 339, 3, 415, 4, 417, 5, 423, *CJ* I. x. 2 (Justinian).

23. LEVIES ON JEWS: Julian, *Ep.* 25. SEIZURE OF PATRIARCHAL DUES: *CTh* XVI. viii. 14, 399, 29, 429 (cited above in n. 18).

24. JEWISH CLAIM TO CURIAL IMMUNITY: *CTh* XVI. viii. 3, 321, XII. i. 158, 398 (cf. XVI. viii. 13, 397), 165, 399.

25. JEWS AT MAGONA: *Ep. Severi*, 4, 14, 17. WESTERN JEWS EXPELLED FROM AGENTES IN REBUS: *CTh* XVI. viii. 16, 404; EXPELLED FROM ARMY AND DEBARRED FROM CIVIL SERVICE: *CTh* XVI. viii. 24, 418.

26. EASTERN JEWS DEBARRED FROM PUBLIC SERVICE: Th. II, *Nov.* iii §§2, 5–6, 438; FROM THE BAR: *CJ* I. iv. 15 (= II. vi. 8), 468. Justinian's version of Th. II, *Nov.* iii (*CJ* I. ix. 18) adds *pater civitatis* to the list of banned offices. JEWS AND SAMARITANS DEPRIVED OF CURIAL PRIVILEGES: Just. *Nov.* xlv, 537.

27. CIVIL DISABILITIES OF JEWS AND SAMARITANS: *CJ* I. v. 12, 527, 13, 18, 19, 529, 21, 531, Just. *Nov.* xlv §1, 537, cxxix, 551, cxliv, 572.

28. The Jews are already called a *feralis* or *nefaria secta* in *CTh* XVI. viii. 1, 315, and Constantine's language is much more violent in his letter of 325 on Easter (Eus. *V. Const.* III. 18). *CTh* XVI. viii. 4, 330 (S), 10, 396, 23, 416, ix. 3, 415, are all addressed to the Jewish community or its leaders, and all favourable to their claims; XVI. viii. 8, 392, and 26, 423, allude to the *Iudaeorum querellae* and their *miserabiles preces*. Theodoric in Italy maintained the rules of Roman law on the protection of synagogues (Cass. *Var.* IV. 43, v. 37) and their repair (ib. II. 27) and protected Jewish rights (ib. IV. 33).

29. AMBROSE AND THE SYNAGOGUE: Paul. *V. Amb.* 22–3, Amb. *Ep.* 40, 41. It was the local bishop who instigated the burning of the synagogue at Callinicum (Amb. *Ep.* 40); Cyril, bishop of Alexandria, destroyed the synagogues and expelled the Jews from his city (Soc. VII. 13), and Severus, bishop of Iammona, led the attack on the synagogue of Magona (*Ep. Severi*, 9–10). Symeon Stylites, like Ambrose, bullied Theodosius II into withdrawing his order that the synagogues of Antioch, recently seized by the Christians, should be restored to the Jews (Evagr. I. 13). GALLIC AND SPANISH COUNCILS: *C. Aurel.* III, can. 13, *C. Aurel.* IV, can. 30, 31 (Christian slaves of Jews), *C. Matisc.* I, can. 13, ne Iudaei Christianis populis iudices deputentur aut telonarii esse permittantur, 14 (Jews confined at Easter), 16 (Christian slaves of Jews redeemed for 12 solidi each), *C. Tol.* III, can. 14 (Christian slaves of Jews, Jews in public office), *C. Narb.* can. 9 (chanting at Jewish funerals forbidden), *C. Par.* v, can. 15, ut nullus Iudaeorum qualemcumque militiam aut actionem publicam super Christianis aut petere a principe aut agere praesumat, *C. Rem.* can. 11 (sale of Christian slaves to Jews, Jews in public office). GREGORY THE GREAT'S POLICY TOWARDS JEWS: Greg. *Ep.* I. 34, II. 6, IX. 38, 195 (protection of synagogues), XIII. 15 (protection of Jewish cult), I. 45 (against forcible baptism), III. 37, IV. 9, 21, VI. 29, 30, VIII. 21, IX. 104 (Christian slaves of Jews).

30. SEVERUS OF IAMMONA: *Ep. Severi.* AVITUS OF ARVERNI: Greg. Tur. *HF* v. 11. CHILPERIC: ibid. VI. 17. THE BISHOPS OF NARBO AND ARLES: Greg. *Ep.* I. 45. KING SISIBUT: Isid. *Chron.* 416, *Hist. Goth.* 60 (*Chron. Min.* II. 291, 480); cf. *C. Tol.* IV. can. 57. HERACLIUS: *Doctrina Iacobi*, I. 2.

31. THE JEWS DURING THE PERSIAN INVASIONS: *Doctrina Iacobi*, IV. 7, v. 12; cf. Theophanes, A.M. 6101, 6106. THE JEWS AND THE ARABS: *Doctrina Iacobi*, v. 16.

32. On Constantine and the Donatists see pp. 81–2. At the council of Nicaea terms were offered to the Melitians (Soc. I. 9), Novatians and Paulianists (*C. Nic.* can. 8, 19). The first persecution edict against heretics followed shortly after (Eus. *V. Const.* III. 64–5).

33. The existence of Manichees in the Eastern half of the empire is implied by the imperial laws against them and by the many anti-Manichaean treatises written by Eastern theologians, but specific evidence is hard to find; see *V. Porph.* 85–91 (Antioch and Gaza), Proc. *HA* xi. 26 (Palestine), Malalas, 423; Coptic Manichaean texts have been found in Egypt. For Africa the evidence is abundant from *Coll.* xv. 3 (Julianus, the proconsul of Africa, reports their presence to Diocletian) to Augustine (*Conf.* IV. 1, v. 3 ff., and his anti-Manichaean works), and down to the end of the sixth century (Greg. *Ep.* II. 37). For Rome there is *Lib. Pont.* xxxiii (Miltiades), Aug. *Conf.* v. 19,

Leo, *Ep.* 7, *Serm.* 16 §4, Val. III, *Nov.* xviii, 445; according to Pope Gregory (*Ep.* v. 7) they were common in Sicily. MARCIONITES: Epiph. *adv. Haer.* xlii. 1. PRISCILLIANISTS: Leo, *Ep.* 15, C. *Bracar.* 1; these show that the sect still flourished in Spain in the fifth and sixth centuries, but it is nowhere else mentioned (the 'Priscillianistae' of *CTh* xvi. v. 40, 407, 43, 407, 48, 410, 59, 423, 65, 428, were evidently Montanists, so called from their devotion to the prophetess Priscilla). MONTANISTS: Epiph. *adv. Haer.* xlviii. 14; it would appear from *CTh* xvi. v. 40, 407, that they also existed in Rome, where no doubt every heresy was to be found; Procopius (*HA* xi. 23) implies that they existed only in Phrygia. Socrates, who took a strong interest in the Novatians (see below nn. 42-3), does not seem to know of any other communities except those which he describes in northwestern Asia Minor.

34. The works are Epiphanius, κατὰ αἱρεσέων or πανάριον, Philastrius Brixiensis, *Liber de haeresibus*, Augustine, *de haeresibus ad Quodvultdeum*, and Theodoret, αἱρετικῆς κακομυθίας ἐπιτομή; Augustine's introductory letter to his work is *Ep.* 222. The longest official list of heresies is in *CTh* xvi. v. 65 (= *CJ* I. v. 5), 428.

35. EUSTATHIANS: *C. Gangr.*, synodical letter and canons. MONTANISTS: Aug. *de Haer.* 26, 27, cf. Epiph. *adv. Haer.* xlviii. 14. OPHITAE: Epiph. *adv. Haer.* xxxvii, Aug. *de Haer.* 17, Theod. *Haer. Fab. Comp.* I. 14. ADAMIANI: Epiph. *adv. Haer.* lii, Aug. *de Haer.* 31.

36. THE MARCIONIST: Theod. *Haer. Fab. Comp.* I. 24. ABELONII: Aug. *de Haer.* 87.

37. The normal penalties were decreed in Constantine's first edict of persecution (Eus. *V. Const.* III. 64-5) and many later laws, *CTh* xvi. v. 3, 4, 8, 12, etc. FINE ON HERETICAL CLERGY: *CTh* xvi. v. 21, 392. DEPORTATION OF MONTANIST CLERGY: *CTh* xvi. v. 57, 415. FINES ON RECUSANT DONATISTS: *CTh* xvi. v. 52, 412, 54, 414. CIVIL DISABILITIES OF MANICHEES: *CTh* xvi. v. 7, 381, 9, 382, 18, 389, 40, 407, 65 §3, 428, Val. III, *Nov.* xviii §3, 445; OF EUNOMIANS: *CTh* xvi. v. 17, 389, 23, 394, 25, 27, 395, 36, 399, 49, 410, 58, 415.

38. HERETICS DEBARRED FROM MILITIA: *CTh* xvi. v. 29, 395, sublimitatem tuam investigare praecipimus, an aliqui haereticorum vel in scriniis vel inter agentes in rebus vel inter palatinos cum legum nostrarum iniuria audeant militare, quibus exemplo divi patris nostri omnis et a nobis negata est militandi facultas, 42, 408, eos qui catholicae sectae sunt inimici intra palatium militare prohibemus, ut nullus nobis sit aliqua ratione coniunctus, qui a nobis fide et religione discordat, 48, 410, Montanistas et Priscillianistas et alia huiuscemodi genera nefariae superstitionis per multiplicata scita divalia diversa ultionum supplicia contemnentes ad sacramenta quidem militiae, quae nostris obsecundat imperiis, nequaquam admitti censemus: si quos vero ex his curialis origo vel ordinum nexis aut cohortalinae militiae inligat obsequiis et functionibus, his adstringi praecipimus, ne sub colore damnatae religionis eliciant vacationis cupitae sibi suffragia, 58 §7, 415, 61, 423 (Eunomians), 65 §3, 428, nulla his (sc. Manichaeis) penitus praeter cohortalinam in provinciis et castrensem indulgenda militia, Val. III, *Nov.* xviii §4, 445 (Manichees), *CJ* I. v. 8 §6, 455 (monophysites). HERETICS EXCLUDED FROM THE BAR: *CJ* I. iv. 15 (= II. vi. 8), 468.

39. THE DEATH PENALTY: *Coll.* xv. 3 §6 (Manichees), *CTh* xvi. v. 9 §1, 382, ceterum quos Encratitas prodigiali appellatione cognominant, cum Saccoforis sive Hydroparastatis refutatos iudicio, proditos crimine, vel in mediocri

vestigio facinoris huius inventos summo supplicio et inexpiabili poena iubemus adfligi, *CJ* I. v. 11, 510, 12 §3, 527 (Manichees). Priscillian was put to death by Maximus, but not on the formal charge of heresy but for magic (*maleficium*); see Sulp. Sev. *Chron.* II. 50. JUSTINIAN'S LAWS AGAINST HERETICS: *CJ* I. v. 12, 527, 13, 14, 18, 19, 529, 20, 530, 21, 22, 531.

40. SURVIVAL OF DONATISTS: Greg. *Ep.* I. 72, 75, 82, II. 46, IV. 32, 35, VI. 34, 59, 61; OF MELITIANS: Theod. *Haer. Fab. Comp.* IV. 7, *Sb* 5174, 5175; for later references see H. I. Bell, *Jews and Christians in Egypt*, pp. 42–3.

41. RURAL HERETICS: Proc. *HA* xi. 21–3; Theod. *Ep. (PG)* 81, cf. *Hist. Rel.* xxi, xxii. THE QUARTODECIMANS: *A.C.Oec.* I. i. pars vii. 100–105. DONATISTS SPEAK PUNIC: Aug. *Ep.* 66, 108 §14, 209 §3. CIRCUMCELLIONS: Aug. *c. Gaud.* I. 32, Poss.*V. Aug.* 10. PETILIAN THE BARRISTER: Aug. *c. Litt. Pet.* iii. 19. CRESCONIUS THE GRAMMARIAN: Aug. *Retract.* II. 26. SCALE OF FINES: *CTh* XVI. v. 52, 412, cf. 54, 414.

42. RURAL NOVATIANS: Soc. IV. 28, V. 10.

43. MARCIAN: Soc. IV. 9, V. 21. SISINNIUS: Soc. VI. 22. PAUL: Soc. VII. 17. CHRYSANTHUS AND ABLABIUS: Soc. VII. 12.

44. EPICUREANS: Julian, *frag. Epist.* 301C, μήτε ᾽Επικούρειος εἰσίτω λόγος μήτε Μυρρώνειος. ἤδη μὲν γὰρ καλῶς ποιοῦντες οἱ θεοὶ καὶ ἀνῃρήκεσαν ὥστε ἐπιλείπειν καὶ τὰ πλεῖστα τῶν βιβλίων. For the strongly religious, not to say superstitious, tone of Neoplatonism the works of Julian and Eunapius's Lives of the Sophists are witnesses.

45. For the cult of the martyrs see H. Delehaye, *Les origines du culte des martyrs*[2] Brussels, 1933.

46. LUCILLA: Opt. I. 16. BABYLAS: Soz. V. 19. Hilary, *de Trin.* XI. 3, hunc apostolorum et martyrum per virtutum operationes loquuntur sepulchra. Basil, *Or. in S. Mamantem*, passim.

47. GERVASIUS AND PROTASIUS: Amb. *Ep.* 22, Paul. *V. Amb.* 14, Aug. *Civ. Dei*, XXII. viii. 2, *Conf.* IX. 16. VITALIS AND AGRICOLA, AND NAZARIUS AND CELSUS: Paul. *V. Amb.* 29, 32–3. DAMASUS: *Lib. Pont.* xxxix, multa corpora sanctorum requisivit et invenit, cf. Damasus, *Epigrammata*, 27, 49, 80.

48. Sulp. Sev. *V. Mart.* 11.

49. AFRICAN CANON: *Cod. Can. Eccl. Afr.* 83. INVENTION OF ST. STEPHEN ETC.: *Ep. Luciani* (PL XLI. 807–18). Sozomen records a number of other spectacular finds, Habakkuk and Micah near Eleutheropolis (VII. 29), the Forty Martyrs at Constantinople (IX. 2) and Zachariah, also near Eleutheropolis (IX. 17).

50. ANTONY: Ath. *V. Ant.* 91. HILARION: Jerome, *V. Hilar.* 46, Soz. III. 14. SYRIAN HERMITS: Theod. *Hist. Rel.* iii (shrine built two years in advance), x, xiii, xvi (battle between villages), xxi (Jacob).

51. WESTERN OBJECTION TO TRANSLATION: Greg. *Ep.* IV. 30, in Romanis namque vel totius occidentis partibus omnino intolerabile est atque sacrilegium si sanctorum corpora tangere quisquam fortasse voluerit, cf. Hormisdas, *Ep.* 77. TRANSLATIONS TO CONSTANTINOPLE: Jerome, *c. Vigil.* 5, *Chron. Min.* I. 238–9. TRAFFIC IN RELICS: Aug. *de opere monachorum*, 36, alii membra martyrum si tamen martyrum venditant; the traffic was forbidden in the East by *CTh* IX. xvii. 7, 386, humatum corpus nemo ad alterum locum transferat, nemo martyrem distrahat, nemo mercetur.

52. Theod. *Graec. Aff. Cur.* VIII. 62–9. The cures of SS. Cyrus and John are recounted by Sophronius, *Narr. de mir. SS. Cyri et Johannis.* St. Martin's patronage of Tours is illustrated by many stories in Gregory's *Historia Francorum* and *de Virtutibus S. Martini:* notable is the immunity of the city of Tours from taxation, which was granted and respected by the Frankish kings from fear of St. Martin (Greg. Tur. HF IX. 30). For S. Demetrius's protection of Thessalonica see Symeon Metaphrastes, *S. Demetrii Martyris Acta.*

53. See H. Delehaye, op. cit., 404 ff.

54. Julian, *Misop.* 344A, τοῖς περὶ τοὺς τάφους καλινδουμένοις γραδίοις, controverted by Greg. Naz. *Or.* IV. 69, 70, Cyr. Alex. *c. Iulianum,* X. FAUSTUS THE MANICHEE: Aug. *c. Faust.* XX. 21; cf. *Serm.* 273 for a vigorous defence of the cult of martyrs. VIGILANTIUS: Jerome, *c. Vigil.* 4, 6, 8.

55. PAGAN MIRACLES: Eun. *V. Soph.* V. 2, VII. 2.

56. For the system of *libelli* see Aug. *Civ. Dei,* XXII. viii. 20–1; an actual libellus is preserved in Aug. *Serm.* 322. CATALOGUES OF MIRACLES: *de miraculis S. Stephani protomartyris* (PL XLI. 833–54), Aug. *Civ. Dei,* XXII. viii.

57. SEVENTY MIRACLES IN TWO YEARS: Aug. *Civ. Dei,* XXII. viii. 20. The miracle narrated in the text is in the Evodian collection (II. 3).

58. Aug. *Ep.* 78.

59. Greg. Nyss. *Or. de deitate Filii et Spiritus Sancti* (PG XLVI. 557).

60. ARIUS'S THALEIA: Ath. *de Syn.* 15, *Or. c. Arianos,* i. 4. Augustine's remarks on his *Psalmus contra partem Donati* are in *Retract.* I. 20. It was a counterblast to Donatist songs composed by Cresconius (Aug. *Ep.* 55 §34, Praedestinatus, I. 44). In Egypt songs of Melitius are mentioned in the Canons of Athanasius (12). For the addition to the Trisagion see Zach. Myt. *Chron.* VII. 7, 9.

61. I have dealt more fully with this topic in *JTS* X (1959), 280–98. The story of Theoderic and the deacon is in Theodore Lector, II. 18.

62. HUNNERIC'S PUBLIC DEBATE: Victor Vit. II. 39 ff. EURIC'S ATTITUDE: Sid. Ap. *Ep.* VII. 6 §6, sed, quod fatendum est, praefatum regem Gothorum, quamquam sit ob virium merita terribilis, non tam Romanis moenibus quam legibus Christianis insidiaturum pavesco. tantum, ut ferunt, ori, tantum pectori suo catholici mentio nominis acet, ut ambigas, ampliusne suae gentis an suae sectae teneat principatum. ad hoc armis potens acer animis alacer annis hunc solum patitur errorem, quod putat sibi tractatuum consiliorumque successum tribui pro religione legitima, quem potius assequitur pro felicitate terrena.

63. For the Donatists see *JTS* X (1959), 282–6.

64. EGYPTIAN REVOLT UNDER MARCUS: Cassius Dio, LXXII. 4. THE PROPHESY OF THE POTTER: *P. Oxy.* 2332.

65. It has been urged by Stein (*Hist. du Bas-Empire,* II. 164) that the riots which accompanied the installation of Dioscorus II, a monophysite appointed by Anastasius, show that the Egyptians were hostile to the imperial government even when it was on their side in the theological controversy. The incident is related in Theophanes, A.M. 6009 and Malalas, 401 and fr. 41. It appears that the Alexandrians insisted on Dioscorus being elected and consecrated by the local clergy and bishops in due form, which shows that they

were jealous of the canonical rights of the see, and that they next day lynched the Augustal prefect, according to Malalas because of a shortage of bread, according to Theophanes because he praised Anastasius. Even if the latter version is correct, the story will hardly bear the weight which Stein gives to it; Dioscorus was accepted as patriarch.

66. For anti-Chalcedonian feeling at Ephesus see Zach. Myt. *Chron.* IV. 5, V. 4, Hormisdas, *Ep.* 75.

67. See V. Inglisian, 'Chalkedon und die Armenische Kirche', in A. Grillmeier and H. Bacht, *Das Konzil von Chalkedon* (Würtzburg, 1953) II. 361-417.

68. MONOPHYSITISM IN PALESTINE: *A.C.Oec.* II. i. 483 ff., Evagr. II. 5, Zach. Myt. *Chron.* III. 3 ff.; AT THESSALONICA: Hormisdas, *Ep.* 100. THE JOURNEYS OF JAMES BARADAEUS: Joh. Eph. *V. SS. Or.* i, cf. the similar journeys of John of Hephaestopolis (Joh. Eph. *V. SS. Or.* xxv). For monophysite communities in various parts of Asia Minor see Joh. Eph. *HE* I. 14, 39, II. 52, IV. 19, V. 6, *V. SS. Or.* xlvi, Joh. Maium. *Pleroph.* 21, 28, 44-6, 64, 80, 82, 83, 85.

69. THE CIRCUMCELLIONS: Opt. III. 4, Aug. *Ep.* 108 §18, 185 §15.

70. PAMMACHIUS AND HIS DONATIST TENANTS: Aug. *Ep.* 58.

71. The importance of φιλανθρωπία in pagan morals is discussed by G. Downey, *Historia* IV (1955), 199 ff. For the Hellenic virtue of forgiveness (especially of one's enemies) see Lib. *Or.* XV. 22 ff., XIX. 12-13, XLIII. 18, *Ep.* 75, 256, 823, 1120, 1397, 1414.

72. See Lib. *Or.* XI. 134-8, Aug. *c. Acad.* I. 2 for the liberality expected of decurions.

73. Amb. *Off.* II. 109.

74. Julian, *Ep.* 49.

75. On Christian teaching on almsgiving see E. F. Bruck, *Kirchenväter und Sozialen Erbrecht* (Berlin, 1957).

76. On homosexual practices see Lib. *Or.* XXXVIII. 8-11, XXXIX. 5-6 and especially LIII. 6 ff.; Joh. Chrys. *adv. opp. vit. mon.* III. 8. DIOCLETIAN ON INCEST: *Coll.* VI. 4, 295. INCEST IN MESOPOTAMIA: Just. *Nov.* cliv (535-6).

77. For the *lex Iulia de adulteriis* see *Dig.* XLVIII. v. The remark on the chastity of husbands is from Ulpian (*Dig.* XLVIII. v. 14 §5). FREQUENCY OF DIVORCE: Jerome, *Ep.* 123 §9. CONCUBINES: Paulus, *Sent.* II. xx. 1, eo tempore quo quis uxorem habet concubinam habere non potest, *CJ* v. xxvi. 1, 326, nemini licentia concedatur constante matrimonio concubinam penes se habere.

78. CONCUBINES: Aug. *Serm.* 392 §2, concubinas vobis habere non licet, audiat Deus si vos surdi estis, audiant angeli eius si vos contemnitis. concubinas vobis habere non licet. et si non habetis uxores, non licet vobis habere concubinas; *C. Tol.* I, can. 17, si quis habens uxorem fidelis concubinam habeat, non communicet: ceterum is qui non habet uxorem et pro uxore concubinam habeat, a communione non repellatur, tantum ut unius mulieris aut uxoris aut concubinae, ut ei placuerit, sit coniunctione contentus; in *C. Aurel.* III, can. 9, men who have had a wife and a concubine successively are debarred from holy orders as *bigami*, but are not otherwise penalised. AUGUSTINE ON ADULTERY: Aug. *de Serm. Dom. in Monte*, I. 43 ff., but cf. *Retract.* I. 18. REMARRIAGE AFTER

DIVORCE: Origen, *Comm. in Matth.*, xiv. 23, *C. Arel.* I, can. 10, Epiph. *adv. Haer.* lix. 4, Aug. *de adult. coniug.* I. 28, *de bono coniug.* 7, *de fide et oper.* 35, *Cod. Can. Eccl. Afr.* 102, *C. Venet.* can. 2.

79. *CTh* III. xvi. 1, 331, 2, 421.

80. Th. II, *Nov.* xii, 439, Val. III, *Nov.* xxxv §11, 452, *CJ* v. xvii. 8, 449, 9, 497.

81. JUSTINIAN'S LAW ON DIVORCE: *CJ* v. xvii. 10, 528, Just. *Nov.* xxii §§3–19, 536, cxvii §§8–15, 542 (§8 forbids divorce by consent and §13 gives the penalties for divorce without due cause), cxxvii §4, 548, cxxxiv §11, 556 (equalizing the penalty for husbands and wives). JUSTIN II'S LAW: Just. *Nov.* cxl, 566. THE EGYPTIAN DIVORCE: *Chr.* II. 297.

82. *Cod. Can. Eccl. Afr.* 102, placuit ut secundum evangelicam et apostolicam disciplinam neque dimissus ab uxore neque dimissa a marito alteri coniungatur, sed ita maneant aut sibimet reconcilientur; quod si contempserint, ad poenitentiam redigantur, in qua causa legem imperialem petendum est promulgari. Asterius Amas. *Hom.* 5 (*PG* XL. 228).

83. PROSTITUTION AND THE COLLATIO LUSTRALIS: Zos. II. 38; Evagrius (III. 41) refused to believe that Constantine could have been the author of so wicked a tax. CONSTANTINE ON BARMAIDS: *CTh* IX. vii. 1, 326. FLORENTIUS'S LAWS: *CTh* xv. viii. 2, 428, Th. II, *Nov.* xviii, 439; the first law is addressed to Florentius and probably inspired by his *suggestio*. LEO'S LAW: *CJ* XI, xli, 7.

84. THEODORA AND THE CONVENT OF REPENTANCE: Malalas, 440–1, Proc. *Aed.* I. ix. 5–10, *HA* xvii. 5–6. JUSTINIAN'S LAW: Just. *Nov.* xiv, 535.

85. PROHIBITION OF MIXED BATHING: *Const. Apost.* I. 6, 9, *C. Laod.* can. 30. Jerome, *Ep.* 14 §10, sed qui in Christo semel lotus est, non illi necesse est iterum lavare. AUGUSTINE'S NUNS: Aug. *Ep.* 211 §13. Barsanuphius, p. 336. Cf. Jerome, *Ep.* 107 §11, mihi omnino in adulta virgine lavacra displicent, quae seipsam debet erubescere et nudam videre non posse. si enim vigiliis et ieiuniis macerat corpus suum et in servitutem redigit, si flammam libidinis et incentiva ferventis aetatis extinguere cupit continentiae frigore . . . cur e contrario balnearum fomentis sopitos ignes suscitat? For Sisinnius see Soc. VI. 22.

86. It would be a Herculean task to assemble all the Christian diatribes against all forms of games. Typical among the Latins are Lactantius, *Div. Inst.* VI. 20, *Epit.* 58, Augustine, *de symbolo*, 3–5, Salvian, *Gub. Dei*, VI passim. Among the Greeks John Chrysostom is particularly insistent (e.g. *Hom. de Lazaro*, VII. 1–2, *de Anna*, IV. 1–2, *contra ludos et theatra*, passim). The pagan associations of the games are stressed by Lactantius (*Div. Inst.* VI. 20 ad fin.) and Salvian (*Gub. Dei*, VI. 12, 60). ACTORS AND CHARIOTEERS: *Const. Apost.* VIII. 32, *C. Ilib.* can. 62, *C. Arel.* I, can. 4, 5, *C. Carth* III, can. 35, *C. Arel.* II, can. 20; cf. Jerome, *V. Hilar.* 16.

87. PROHIBITION OF GLADIATORS IN THE EAST: *CTh* xv. xii. 1, 325, Eus. *V. Const.* IV. 25, Lib. *Or.* I. 5; in the West, Theod. *HE* v. 26; gladiatorial games still went on at Rome when Augustine was a young man (*Conf.* VI. 13), cf. also *CTh* xv. xii. 3, 397. *Venationes* were still going on in the West in the middle of the fifth century (Salv. *Gub. Dei*, VI. 10–11); banned by Anastasius (Josh. Styl. 34, Proc. Gaz. *Pan.* 15–6) they continued in the East under Justinian (*Nov.* cv §1, 536, *CJ* XI. xli. 5, in which 'bestias histriones' has been interpolated by the Justinianic editors into *CTh* xv. v. 3).

88. MIMES BANNED BY ANASTASIUS: Josh. Styl. 46, Proc. Gaz. *Pan*. 15–6; for their survival see Just. *Nov*. cv §1, 536, *CJ* XI. xli. 5 (see n. 87). THE MAIUMA: *CTh* xv. vi. 1 (= *CJ* XI. xlvi. 1), 396, 2, 399; John Chrysostom is very severe on this feast (*Hom. in Matth*. vii. 6).

89. *V. Hypatii*, 107–9.

90. The first quotation is from Joh. Chrys. *Hom. in Genesim*, xliii. 1. For laudation of the monastic life see *Hom. in Matth*. lv. 5, lxviii. 3, lxix. 3–4, lxxii. 3–4, *Hom. in Ep*. I *ad Tim*. xiv. 3–5, and above all the three books *Adversus oppugnatores vitae monasticae*. The second quotation is from 1. 7 of this work, and the advice to all Christians to become monks in 1. 8. GREGORY THE GREAT: Greg. *Ep*. III. 61.

91. LATE BAPTISM: Basil, *Hom*. XIII, Greg. Naz. *Or*. XL, Greg. Nyss. *de baptismo;* *Const. Apost*. VI. 15, Joh. Chrys. *Hom. in Joh*. xviii. 1, *Hom. in Act*. i. 6, 8, *Hom. in Ep*. II *Cor*. ii. 6.

92. CONSTANTIUS II: Soc. II. 47. THEODOSIUS I: Soc. V. 6, Soz. VII. 4. AMBROSE: Paul. *V. Amb*. 9. SATYRUS: Amb. *de excessu fratris sui Satyri*, I. 43 ff. JUNIUS BASSUS: *ILS* 1286. THE ELDERLY ROMAN: *ILCV* 1483. Cf. Orosius, VII. xxxiii. 7 (Theodosius *comes*) cf. Pall. *Hist. Laus*. xi (Rufinus).

93. Zach. *V. Sev*. p. 11.

94. There is an excellent and fully documented account of penance in J. Bingham, *Antiquities of the Christian Church*, book xviii. PENANCE ALLOWED ONCE ONLY: Amb. *de Poenitentia*, II. 10, Aug. *Ep*. 153 §7, Siricius, *Ep*. 1 §5, *C. Arel*. II, can. 21, *C. Venet*. can. 3, *C. Turon*. I, can. 8, *C. Aurel*. I, can. 11. RULES TO BE OBSERVED AFTER PENANCE: Siricius, *Ep*. 1 §5, de his ... qui acta poenitentia tamquam canes et sues ad vomitus pristinos et volutabra redeuntes et militiae cingulum et ludicras voluptates et nova coniugia et inhibitos denuo appetivere concubitus, quorum professam incontinentiam generati post absolutionem filii prodiderunt, Leo, *Ep*. 167 §10 (no litigation), §11 (no trade), §12 (no *militia*), §13 (chastity, with indulgence for young men), *C. Arel*. II, can. 21 (marriage forbidden). DEATH BED PENANCE: Innocent, *Ep*. 6 §2, et hoc quaesitum est, quid de his observare oporteat, qui post baptismum omni tempore incontinentiae voluptatibus debiti in extremo fine vitae suae poenitentiam simul et reconciliationem communionis exposcunt; Leo, *Ep*. 108, 167 §7, de his qui in aegritudine poenitentiam accipiunt et cum revaluerint agere eam nolunt, §9, de his qui dolore nimic perurgente rogant dari sibi poenitentiam et cum venerit presbyter daturus quod petebant, si dolor parum perquieverit, excusant et nolunt accipere quod offertur, *Stat. Eccl. Ant*. 76, si supervixerit ... subdatur statutis poenitentiae legibus quamdiu sacerdos qui poenitentiam dedit probaverit, *C. Araus*. I, can. 3, *C. Epaon*. can. 36. WARNINGS AGAINST POSTPONING PENANCE: Aug. *Serm*. 393, Caesarius, *Serm*. 60, 61, 63.

95. Soc. V. 19, Soz. VII. 16. *C. Tol*. III, can. 11, quoniam comperimus per quasdam Hispaniarum ecclesias non servandum canonem sed foedissime pro suis peccatis homines agere poenitentiam, ut quotiescumque peccare libuerit toties a presbyteris se reconciliari expostulent; ideo pro coercenda tam execrabili praesumptione id a sancto concilio iubetur ut secundum formam canonum antiquorum detur poenitentia.

96. *C. Arel*. I, can. 7, de praesidibus qui fideles ad praesidatum prosiliunt, placuit ut cum promoti fuerint litteras accipiant ecclesiasticas communicatorias,

ita tamen ut in quibuscumque locis gesserint, ab episcopo eiusdem loci cura illis agatur, et cum coeperint contra disciplinam agere, tum demum a communione excludantur. similiter et de his qui rempublicam agere volunt.

97. Amb. *Ep.* 25. Innocent, *Ep.* 6 §3.

98. Basil, *Ep.* 188 §13. A similar view is voiced by Lactantius (*Div. Inst.* VI. xx. 15–7) and by Paulinus of Nola (*Ep.* 25 §3). Under Diocletian there were some Christian conscientious objectors such as Maximilianus and Marcellus (Krüger, *Ausgewählte Martyrerakten*[3], nos. 19, 20), but the first Council of Arles condemned such conduct (*C. Arel.* 1, can. 3, de his qui arma proiiciunt in pace placuit abstineri eos a communione).

99. *Ep. ad Gallos*, 10; cf. 4, de eo qui militaverit iam fidelis militiae saecularis notitia est quod utatur publica libertate. quis enim potest illum custodire? quis negare vel spectaculis interfuisse vel pecuniae utilitate impulsam a violentia et iniustitia immunem esse non potuisse? BAN ON HOLY ORDERS: Siricius, *Ep.* 5 §2, Innocent, *Ep.* 37 §3, Symmachus, *Ep.* 15 §11 (cited in ch. XXII, n. 135). On penance see above n. 94. AUGUSTINE TO CAECILIANUS: Aug. *Ep.* 151 §14. PAULINUS ON PUBLIC SERVICE: Paul. *Ep.* 25, 25*.

XXIV. EDUCATION AND CULTURE (pp. 987-8)

On the subject of education and literary culture I rely heavily on H. I. Marrou, *A history of education in Antiquity*, London, 1956, and *Saint Augustin et la fin de la culture antique*[2], Paris, 1958.

1. GREEK AT SCHOOL: Aug. *Conf.* 1. 20–3; for an estimate of Augustine's Greek scholarship see H. I. Marrou, *Saint Augustin et la fin de la culture antique*[2], Paris, 1958, 27–46, 631–7. PAULINUS: Paul. *Euch.* 72 ff., 113 ff. SYMMACHUS: Symm. *Ep.* IV. 20.

2. SIDONIUS: Sid. Ap. *Ep.* IV. 12. FULGENTIUS: *V. Fulg.* 4–5. GRATIAN'S LAW: *CTh* XIII. iii. 11, 376; nevertheless Ausonius records several Greek grammarians of Bordeaux (*Prof.* viii, xiii, xxi) and declares that the rhetor Alethius was versed in Greek as well as in Latin (*Prof.* ii).

3. On the survival of Greek learning in the West see P. Courcelle, *Les lettres grecques en Occident de Macrobe à Cassiodore*[2], Paris, 1948. PRAETEXTATUS: *ILS* 1259, tu namque quidquid lingua utraque est proditum cura soforum, porta quis caeli patet, vel quae periti condidere carmina, vel quae solutis vocibus sunt edita, meliora reddis quam legendo sumpseras; he translated Themistius's commentary on Aristotle's *Analytics* (Boeth. *comm. in Arist.*, secunda editio, I. 1). For the other scholars their extant works are witness. CASSIAN: Gennadius, *de script. eccl.* 61, Cassianus natione Scytha. DIONYSIUS: Cass. *Inst.* 23, fuit enim nostris temporibus et Dionysius monachus, Scytha natione sed moribus omnino Romanus, in utraque lingua valde doctissimus.

4. Cassian, *Inst.* v. 39. Cf. Jerome's complaint (Aug. *Ep.* 172), grandem Latini sermonis in ista provincia (Palestine) notariorum patimur penuriam.

5. LATIN FORMULAE IN JUDICIAL RECORDS: *Chr.* II. 96–7, *P. Lips.* 38, 40, *P. Zilliacus*, 4, *Sb* 5357, *P. Thead.* 13, *PSI* 1309, *P. Ryl.* 653–4, 702, *P. Oxy.* 1876–9, *P. Cairo*, 67329; in the last document Latin is used even in the court records of a *defensor civitatis* in the sixth century. LATIN IN THE PRAETORIAN PREFECTURE OF THE EAST: Joh. Lydus, *Mag.* II. 12, III. 42; cf. III. 3 and 12 for fragments of Latin formulae. Latin was still preserved in the *scrinium Europae* until the time of John the Cappadocian (ibid. III. 68).

6. ABINNAEUS DOCUMENTS: *P. Abinn.* 1, 2; in 16 an officer signs a letter dictated in Greek 'et te per multos annos bene valere'. LETTER OF THE COMES THEBAIDOS: *P. Ryl.* 609. Cf. also *SPP* xx. 285–7 (military accounts in Latin in 398).

7. JUDGMENTS IN GREEK: *CJ* VII. xlv. 12, 397; this law was, curiously enough, addressed by Honorius to the proconsul of Africa. WILLS IN GREEK: Th. II, *Nov.* xvi §8, 439, illud etiam huic legi perspicimus inserendum ut quoniam Graece iam testari concessum est legata quoque ac directas libertates, tutores etiam Graecis verbis liceat in testamentis relinquere. For the citation of an imperial constitution in Greek see *Sb* 8246.

8. LATIN AND LAW: Lib. *Or.* II. 43–4, XLVIII. 22–3. For the transition to Greek in the schools of Berytus see Collinet, *Histoire de l'école de droit de Beyrouth*, 211 ff. and for Greek translations of and commentaries on the Corpus Iuris, Jolowicz, *Historical Introduction to Roman Law²*, pp. 512–3.

9. CONSTANTINE'S GREEK: Eus. *V. Const.* IV. 35; he delivered his formal oration opening the Council of Nicaea in Latin (op. cit. III. 13), but from the same chapter and from Eusebius' letter in Theod. *HE* I. 12 it is plain that he followed the debate in Greek, cf. also *CTh* VIII. xv. 1, where he argues with a Greek speaking litigant. Valens knew no Greek (Them. *Or.* IX. 126b). RUFINUS: Lib. *Ep.* 865; Festus of Tridentum, consular of Syria and proconsul of Asia, knew no Greek (Lib. *Or.* I. 156). Libanius often complains that owing to its advantages in public life Latin is ousting traditional Greek education (*Or.* I. 214, 234, *Ep.* 951, 957, cf. Greg. Nyss. *Ep.* 14).

10. LATIN SCHOOLBOOKS FROM EGYPT: *Corpus pap. Lat.* 1–8, 21–2, 58–62, 277–81. YOUNG MEN SENT TO BERYTUS AND ROME: Lib. *Or.* XLVIII. 22.

11. LACTANTIUS: Jerome, *de viris illustr.* 80; Paul, who became Novatian bishop of Constantinople in 419, had previously taught Latin literature (Soc. VII. 17). Libanius (*Ep.* 363) mentions a Latin grammarian, Celsus, who taught at Antioch. THE UNIVERSITY OF CONSTANTINOPLE: *CTh* XIV. ix. 3, 425. PRISCIAN: Cass. *de orthogr.* 12, ex Prisciano grammatico, qui nostro tempore Constantinopoli doctor fuit. JOHN: Joh. Lydus, *Mag.* III. 29. Pope Gregory complained that in his day there was no one in Constantinople who could translate Latin into Greek idiomatically (Greg. *Ep.* VII. 27).

12. STRATEGIUS: Amm. XV. xiii. 1; for his *comitiva* see Ath. *Hist. Ar.* 15, *Apol.* c. *Ar.* 36. SUBSTANTIA: Jerome, *Ep.* 15 §§3–4. ROMAN LEGATES AT EPHESUS: *A.C.Oec.* II. i. 191, Ἵλαρος διάκονος τῆς Ῥωμαίων ἐκκλησίας εἶπεν. κοντραδικιτουρ, ὅ ἐστιν ἀντιλέγεται; cf. 190, where he speaks ἑρμηνεύοντος αὐτὸν Φλωρεντίου ἐπισκόπου Λυδῶν.

13. On Syriac literature see A. Baumstark, *Geschichte der Syrischen Literatur*, Bonn, 1922. For Syriac schools see below, n. 52. Uranius, bishop of Himeria in Osrhoene, had to use an interpreter (*A.C.Oec.* II. i. 98–9, 184, 190, 193, 382), and of the Edessene clergy eighteen signed the testimonial to Ibas in Syriac (*A.C.Oec.* II. i. 394–6).

14. On Coptic literature see J. Leipoldt, *Geschichte der Koptischen Literatur*, Leipzig, 1907. We know of an Egyptian bishop, Calosirius of Arsinoites, who knew no Greek (*A.C.Oec.* II. i. 185).

15. For the Gothic scriptures see J. Zeiller, *Les origines chrétiennes dans les provinces danubiennes*, 465 ff. THE RAVENNATE DEED: *P. Dip.* 119.

16. Sulp. Sev. *Dial.* I. 27. Jerome, *Comm. in Ep. Gal.* ii.

17. *Ep. Severi*, 15.

18. PUNIC: Aug. *Ep.* 66, 108 §14, 209 §3; in *Ep.* 84 §2 *Punica* must surely be read for *Latina*, for Hippo had no shortage of Latin speaking clergy; cf. also *in Ep. Joh. ad Parthos*, ii. 3, *Serm.* 167 §4, proverbium notum est Punicum quod quidem Latine vobis dicam quia Punice non omnes nostis, and Jerome, *Ep.* 130 §5, stridor linguae Punicae. For the resemblance of Punic to Hebrew see Aug. *Serm.* 113 §2, *c. litt. Pet.* II. 239.

19. THRACIAN: Greg. Nyss. *c. Eunom.* xii (*PG* XLV. 1045), Joh. Chrys. *Hom. hab. in eccl. Pauli* (*PG* LXIII. 501). MONASTERY OF THE BESSI: Sym. Metaphr. *V. Theod. Coenob.* 37; cf. *Itin. Hierosol. Antoninus*, 37 (Bessic spoken at the monastery of Sinai). One of Auxentius's disciples τῇ γλώττῃ μὲν βάρβαρος ὑπῆρχεν ἐκ τῆς Μυσίας ὁρμώμενος (*V. Auxentii*, 57); in Greek of this period Μυσία nearly always means Moesia, and the language was no doubt Thracian or Illyrian.

20. GALATIAN: Jerome, *Comm. in Ep. Gal.* ii, Cyr. Scyth. *V. Euthymii*, 55. CAPPADOCIAN: Basil, *de Spir. Sancto*, 74, καὶ Καππαδόκαι δὲ οὕτως λέγομεν ἐγχωρίως. LYCAONIAN: *V. Marthae*, 41 (*AASS* Mai. v. 413C). ISAURIAN: Holl, *Hermes* XLIII (1908), 243 (quoting an unpublished fuller version of *V. Sym. Jun.*).

21. SYRIAC SPOKEN BY PEASANTS: Joh. Chrys. *Hom. ad pop. Ant.* xix. 1. PUBLIUS OF ZEUGMA: Theod. *Hist. Rel.* v. MACEDONIUS AND THALELAEUS: ibid. xiii, xxviii. PROCOPIUS: Eus. *Mart. Pal.* 1 §1. ELUSA: Jerome, *V. Hilar.* 25. GAZA: *V. Porph.* 66–8. Daniel the Stylite, who came from Marathas near Samosata, could speak Syriac only (*V. Dan.* 2–3, 10, 14, 17, 28).

22. E. Maier-Leonhard, Ἀγράμματοι (Frankfurt, 1913), provides lists of literate and illiterate persons (pp. 23–24, 56–64) and classifies them by rank and profession (pp. 76–8); of those who act as scribes nine (nos. 382, 389, 411, 418, 436, 450, 469, 471, 473) are clergy.

23. INTERPRETERS AT TRIAL: *Sb* 8246. MONKS: Ruf. *Hist. Mon.* 7, ad fin. BILINGUAL EDICT: *P. Cairo*, 67031.

24. See above n. 18 for Punic and n. 23 for Coptic. The linguistic situation in Palestine is described in *Itin. Hierosol.*, *S. Silvia*, 47, et quoniam in ea provincia pars populi et graece et siristi novit, pars etiam alia per se graece, aliqua etiam pars tantum siriste, itaque quoniam episcopus licet siriste noverit tamen semper graece loquitur et numquam siriste, itaque ergo stat semper presbyter qui episcopo graece dicente siriste interpretatur, ut omnes audiant quae exponantur. lectiones etiam quaecumque in ecclesia leguntur, quia necesse est graece legi, semper stat qui siriste interpretatur propter populum ut semper discant.

25. Aug. *Retract.* I. 19.

26. SCHOOLMASTERS' PAY: *Ed. Diocl.* vii. 66, magistro institutori litterarum in singulis pueris menstruos (denarios) L, cf. 70, 71 for grammarians and rhetors;

UNPRIVILEGED STATUS: *Dig.* L. v. 2 §8, qui pueros primas litteras docent immunitatem a civilibus muneribus non habent.

27. PROTOGENES: Theod. *HE* IV. 18. SIMEON AND SERGIUS: Joh. Eph. *V. SS. Or.* v. SYLLABUS OF PRIMARY SCHOOLS: Aug. *Conf.* I. 20, adamaveram enim Latinas, non quas primi magistri, sed quas docent qui grammatici vocantur. nam illas primas, ubi legere et scribere et numerare discitur, non minus onerosas poenalesque habebam quam omnes graecas; cf. I. 22 for the tables.

28. FEES OF GRAMMARIANS AND RHETORS: *Ed. Diocl.* vii. 70, grammatico Graeco sibe Latino et geometrae in singulis discipulis menstruos (denarios) ducentos, 71, oratori sibe sofistae in singulis discipulis menstruos (denarios) ducentos quinquaginta. AUGUSTINE SENT TO MADAURUS: Aug. *Conf.* II. 5. AETIUS: Philostorgius, p. 45. John Chrysostom (*de sacerdotio,* I. 5) stresses the expense of a rhetorical education.

29. PRIVILEGES OF PROFESSORS: *CTh* XIII. iii. 1, 321, 3, 333, XI. xvi. 15, 382, 18, 390, XIII. iii. 16+17, 414. For the professors of the capitals see ch. XVIII, nn. 46–7. Gratian, by an exceptional measure, evidently inspired by Ausonius, gave salaries from imperial funds (*e fisco*) to professors in the metropoleis (*CTh* XIII. iii. 11, 376, cited in n. 30). Justinian provided from public funds for two rhetors and two grammarians in Africa, presumably at Carthage (*CJ* I. xxvii. 1 §42, 534). MUNICIPAL SALARIES: *CTh* XIII. iii. 1, 321, mercedes etiam eorum et salaria reddi praecipimus. In *CTh* XIII. iii. 11 (see n. 30), the clause 'nec vero iudicemus, liberum ut sit cuique civitati suos doctores et magistros placito sibi iuvare compendio' must, I think, refer to cities other than the metropoleis, where the salaries were paid 'e fisco'. See also Pan. Lat. IX. 11, salarium me liberalissimi principes ex huius rei publicae viribus in sexcenis milibus nummum accipere iusserunt (cf. 14, denique etiam salarium te in sexcentis milibus nummum ex rei publicae viribus consequi volumus), and Proc. *HA* xxvi. 5–7, where professorial salaries are mentioned as a normal civic expense.

30. Municipal chairs can be identified where the professor was appointed by the city council, as at Milan (Aug. *Conf.* v. 23), Nicomedia, Nicaea, Athens (Lib. *Or.* I. 48, 83) or Apamea (Lib. *Ep.* 1366), or where a salary was paid, as at Antioch (Lib. *Or.* XXXI. 19), Apamea (Lib. *Ep.* 1391), Carthage (*CJ* I. xxvii. 1 §42) or Gaza (Proc. Gaz. *Ep.* 50). GRATIAN'S LAW: *CTh* XIII. iii. 11, 376, per omnem dioecesim commissam magnificentiae tuae frequentissimis in civitatibus, quae pollent et eminent claritudine, praeceptorum optimi quique erudiendae praesideant iuventuti: rhetores loquimur et grammaticos Atticae Romanaeque doctrinae. quorum oratoribus viginti quattuor annonarum e fisco emolumenta donentur, grammaticis Latino vel Graeco duodecim annonarum deductior paulo numerus ex more praestetur, ut singulis urbibus, quae metropoles nuncupantur, nobilium professorum electio celebretur, nec vero iudicemus, liberum ut sit cuique civitati suos doctores et magistros placito sibi iuvare compendio. Trevirorum vel clarissimae civitati uberius aliquid putavimus deferendum, rhetori ut triginta, item viginti grammatico Latino, Graeco etiam, si qui dignus repperiri potuerit, duodecim praebeantur annonae.

31. LIBANIUS'S STUDENTS: Lib. *Or.* LXII. 27–8; cf. Petit, *Les Étudiants de Libanius,* pp. 112–5.

32. LENGTH OF COURSE: Petit, op. cit. pp. 63–6.

33. STUDIES AT ALEXANDRIA: Amm. XXII. xvi. 17–8, Greg. Naz. *Or.* VII. 6–7.

According to Gregory Nazianzen Basil studied not only grammar and rhetoric but philosophy, astronomy, geometry, arithmetic and theoretical medicine at Athens (*Or.* XLIII. 23). PHILOSOPHY AND LAW AT CONSTANTINOPLE: *CTh* XIV. ix. 3, 425; AT ROME, Symm. *Rel.* 5 (philosophy), Lib. *Or.* XLVIII. 22 (law). LEGAL COURSE AT BERYTUS: *Dig. const.* Omnem. CERTIFICATE OF STUDY: *CJ* II. vii. 11 §2, 460, 22 §4, 505, 24 §4, 517. LAW TEACHING LIMITED TO ROME, CONSTANTINOPLE AND BERYTUS: *Dig. const.* Omnem §7.

34. PRIVATE TEACHERS BANNED AT CONSTANTINOPLE: *CTh* XIV. ix. 3, 425.

35. TAVIUM: Lib. *Ep.* 1080. ILERDA: Auson. *Prof.* 23. AUGUSTINE'S CAREER: Poss. *V. Aug.* 1, Aug. *c. Acad.* II. 3, *Conf.* IV. 2, V. 14, 22–3. LIBANIUS'S CAREER: Lib. *Or.* I. 31 ff.

36. For Rome and Constantinople see pp. 707–8, JULIAN'S LAW: *CTh* XIII. iii. 5, 362.

37. LIBANIUS'S CAREER: Lib. *Or.* I. 48 ff.

38. LIBANIUS AS A STUDENT: Lib. *Or.* I. 5, 8–9, 11–25. AUGUSTINE'S DIFFICULTIES: Aug. *Conf.* II. 5, *c. Acad.* II. 3. Rusticus after learning rhetoric in Gaul was sent to Rome to complete his studies (Jerome, *Ep.* 125), and Ennodius' nephew Parthenius was also sent to Rome, presumably from Ticinum (Ennod. *Ep.* V. 9–12, VI. 1, 23, VII. 30–1). Basil studied at Caesarea and then at Constantinople and Athens (Greg. Naz. *Or.* XLIII. 13–4).

39. LIBANIUS'S START AT ANTIOCH: Lib. *Or.* I. 101, *Ep.* 405; he had done much better at Constantinople, where he quickly acquired a class of 80 (*Or.* I. 37). LIBANIUS'S ASSISTANTS: Lib. *Or.* XXXI. 8 ff. SALARIES: *CTh* XIII. iii. 11, 376, *CJ* I. xxvii. 1 §42, 534.

40. GERONTIUS: Lib. *Ep.* 1391. LIBANIUS'S LOSS OF 1500 SOLIDI: Lib. *Or.* I. 61.

41. KIDNAPPING AT ATHENS: Lib. *Or.* I. 16–22, Eunap. *V. Soph.* IX. 2, X. 1, Greg. Naz. *Or.* XLIII. 15-16. BILKING OF FEES: Aug. *Conf.* V. 22, Lib. *Or.* XLIII.

42. THE ATHENIAN PHILOSOPHER: Symm. *Rel.* 5. PROFESSORS AT CONSTANTINOPLE: *CTh* VI. xxi. 1, 425. LIBANIUS'S HONOURS: Julian, *Ep.* 27, Eunap. *V. Soph.* XVI. 2. Prohaeresius was also granted an honorary prefecture (op. cit. X. 7) and Isocasius the rank of quaestor (Malalas, 369). For honours accorded to professors of law see ch. XV, n. 65.

43. For the syllabus and methods of late classical education see H. I. Marrou, *A History of Education in Antiquity*, pp. 160–75, 274–91. The verse inscriptions from Gerasa are published in C. H. Kraeling, *Gerasa, City of the Decapolis*, 476–85.

44. The declamations cited are Lib. *Decl.* III, XXI, XLIII.

45. For Augustine see H. I. Marrou, *St. Augustin et la fin de la culture antique*[2], 345.ff. JEROME'S DREAM: Jerome, *Ep.* 22 §30.

46. *Const. Apost.* I. 6. DESIDERIUS: Greg. *Ep.* XI. 34.

47. JEROME: *Ep.* 21 §13. Gregory Nazianzen vigorously defends secular education, ἣν οἱ πολλοὶ Χριστιανῶν διαπτύουσιν ὡς ἐπίβουλον καὶ σφαλερὰν καὶ Θεοῦ πόρρω βάλλουσαν (*Or.* XLIII. 11). He nevertheless rebukes Gregory of Nyssa for his addiction to rhetoric as causing scandal to the faithful (*Ep.* 11).

48. Tertullian, *de Idololatria*, 10. For Julian see pp. 121–2. Among the eminent Christian professors who were deprived of their chairs were Prohaeresius at Athens (Eunap. *V. Soph.* x. 8), and Victorinus at Rome (Aug. *Conf.* VIII. 10).

49. Soc. III. 16, Soz. v. 18.

50. Jerome, *Ep.* 22 §30.

51. Basil, *Reg. Brev.* 292. Marrou (*History of Education in Antiquity*, 332–3) states that the council of Chalcedon forbade monasteries to educate secular children, but I cannot trace any such prohibition. That girls were sent to nunnery schools in the West is suggested by Caesarius, *Reg. Virg.* 5, nobilium filiae sive ignobilium ad nutriendum aut docendum penitus non accipiantur.

52. *C. Tol.* II, can. 1, *C. Tol.* IV, can. 24, *C. Vas.* II, can. 1, hoc enim placuit, ut omnes presbyteri qui sunt in parochiis constituti, secundum consuetudinem quam per totam Italiam satis salubriter teneri cognovimus, iuniores lectores quantoscumque sine uxore habuerint, secum in domo ubi ipsi habitare videntur recipiant, et eos quomodo boni patres spiritualiter nutrientes psalmos parare, divinis lectionibus insistere et in lege domini erudire contendant, ut et sibi dignos successores provideant et a domino praemia aeterna recipiant. cum vero ad aetatem perfectam pervenerint, si aliquis eorum pro carnis fragilitate uxorem habere voluerit, potestas ei ducendi coniugium non negetur. We know only of the school of Nisibis, in Persian territory; Cass. *Inst. praef.*, Junilius, *de partibus divinae legis, praef.*, vidisse me quemdam Paulum nomine, Persam genere, qui in Syrorum schola in Nisibi urbe est edoctus, ubi divina lex per magistros publicos, sicut apud nos in mundanis studiis grammatica et rhetorica, ordine et regulariter traditur.

53. Augustine's syllabus is the *de Doctrina Christiana*, Cassiodorus's the *de Institutione Divinarum Litterarum* and the *de Artibus ac Disciplinis Liberalium Litterarum*.

54. Pan. Lat. II. 1 §3, Sulp. Sev. *Dial.* I. 27.

55. For Dioscorus's verses see J. Maspéro, 'un dernier poète grec d'Égypte', *REG* XXIV (1911), 426–81.

56. For scientific thought see S. Sambursky, *The Physical World of Late Antiquity*, London, 1962. The inventor is the anonymous author of *de rebus belliciis*, published with translation and commentary by E. A. Thompson, *A Roman Reformer and Inventor*.

57. PRIVILEGES OF DOCTORS: *CJ* x. liii. 5 (293–305), *CTh* XIII. iii. 1, 321, 3, 333, 16+17, 414. ARCHIATRI SACRI PALATII: *CTh* XIII. iii. 2, 354, 4, 362, 12, 379, 14, 387, 15, 393, VI. xvi. 1, 413, XIII. iii. 16, 414, 18, 427, 19, 428; Caesarius was promoted *comes thesaurorum* (Greg. Naz. *Or.* VII. 10, 15), Vindicianus to vicar (compare *CTh* x. xix. 9 with XIII. iii. 12 and Marcellus Empiricus, ed. Helmreich, p. 21).

58. ARCHIATRI OF ROME: *CTh* XIII. iii. 8, 368, 9, 370, 13, 387, Symm. *Rel.* 27.

59. SALARIES OF PUBLIC DOCTORS: *CTh* XIII. iii. 1, 321. DOCTORS AT CARTHAGE: *CJ* I. xxvii. 1 §41, 534. PHOEBAMMON: *P. Cairo*, 67151. Valentinian's rules are in *CTh* XIII. iii. 8, 368.

60. MEDICAL CERTIFICATES: *P. Oxy.* 896, 983, *BGU* 928, *P. Lips.* 42, *P. Reinach*, 92, *P. Soc. Ath.* 34, *Sb* 6003.

61. MEDICINE AT ALEXANDRIA: Greg. Naz. *Or.* VII. 6–7, Greg. *Ep.* XIII. 44. TEACHING OF PUBLIC DOCTORS: *CTh* XIII. iii. 3, 333, beneficia divorum retro principum confirmantes medicos et professores litterarum, uxores etiam et filios eorum ab omni functione et ab omnibus muneribus publicis vacare praecipimus nec ad militiam comprehendi neque hospites recipere nec ullo fungi munere, quo facilius liberalibus studiis et memoratis artibus multos instituant.

62. FEES OF SURVEYORS AND ARCHITECTS: *Ed. Diocl.* vii. 70 (see n. 28,) 74, architecto magistro per singulos pueros menstruos (denarios) centum. CONSTANTINE ON ARCHITECTS: *CTh* XIII. iv. 1, 334, architectis quam plurimis opus est; sed quia non sunt, sublimitas tua in provinciis Africanis ad hoc studium eos impellat, qui ad annos ferme duodeviginti nati liberales litteras degustaverint. quibus ut hoc gratum sit, tam ipsos quam eorum parentes ab his, quae personis iniungi solent, volumus esse immunes ipsisque qui discent salarium competens statui.

63. CYRIADES: Symm. *Rel.* 25, 26, *Ep.* v. 76; his predecessor on the job, Auxentius (cf. *IGR* III. 887) held the same rank; cf. *V. Hypatii*, 126, κόμης τοὔνομα Ἐλπίδιος ἀρχιτέκτων τοῦ βασιλέως. ISIDORE JUNIOR: *IGLS* 348–9. ANTHEMIUS: Agathias, v. 6 ff.

64. WAGES OF PAINTERS: *Ed. Diocl.* vii. 8, 9. PRIVILEGES OF PAINTERS: *CTh* XIII. iv. 4, 374.

65. SHORTAGE OF ARCHITECTS AND CRAFTSMEN: *CTh* XIII. iv. 1, 334 (cited in n. 62), 2, 337, artifices artium brevi subdito conprehensarum per singulas civitates morantes ab universis muneribus vacare praecipimus, si quidem ediscendis artibus otium sit adcommodandum; quo magis cupiant et ipsi peritiores fieri et suos filios erudire.

66. CLOSING OF BATHS AND SUSPENSION OF GAMES: Lib. *Or.* xx. 6, Joh. Chrys. *Hom. ad pop. Ant.* XIV. 6, XVII. 2. TREVIRI: Salvian, *Gub. Dei*, VI. 82–9.

67. AUGUSTINE AND ALYPIUS: Aug. *Conf.* III. 2–3, VI. 11–13. THE COUNCIL OF ANTIOCH: Lib. *Or.* XXXV. 4, 13–14, XLVIII. 6, 9, XLIX. 27; see LIV. 22 for a decurion who ruined himself by producing chariot races. Libanius's letters about games include 113, 217–9, 381, 439–40, 544–5, 552, 586–8, 598–9, 663, 843, 970–1, 1017, 1038, 1148, 1167, 1179–83, 1189, 1231–2, 1243, 1278–9, 1399, 1400, 1459, 1509, 1520.

68. CONVICTS AS GLADIATORS: *CTh* IX. xviii. 1, 315, xl. 2, 316, XV. xii. 1, 325, IX. xl. 8, 365, 11, 366; Symmachus's Saxons (*Ep.* II. 46) were presumably prisoners of war. VOLUNTEERS: *CTh* XV. xii. 2, 357, universi, qui in urbe Roma gladiatorium munus impendunt, prohibitum esse cognoscant sollicitandi auctorando milites vel eos, qui palatina sunt praediti dignitate, sex auri librarum multa imminente, si quis contra temptaverit. sponte etiam ad munerarium adeuntes per officium sublimitatis tuae ad magistros equitum ac peditum aut eos, qui gubernant officia palatina, oneratos ferreis vinculis mitti conveniet, ut huius legis statuto palatii dignitas a gladiatorio detestando nomine vindicetur. Symmachus also alludes in *Ep.* II. 46 to volunteers ('ut auctoramento lectos longus usus instituat'). WILD BEASTS: *SEG* XIV. 386 (prices), Lib. *Ep.* 1399 (popularity), 217–9 (beasts and hunters from Phoenicia), 544, 586–8, 598–9 (beasts from Bithynia), 1231–2, 1399, 1400 (beasts from Asia and Hellespont). HUNTERS: Lib. *Ep.* 217 (from Phoenicia), 1509 (from Pamphylia). BEROEA: Lib. *Or.* XXXIII. 21–5. LIBANIUS'S NEPHEW: Lib. *Ep.* 217–9, cf. 1520 for another

imperial ban on killing beasts. See also ch. XVIII, n. 43, and ch. XXIII, n. 87 for other references to *venationes*.

69. *CTh* xv. vii. 3, 376, non invidemus, sed potius cohortamur amplectenda felicis populi studia, gymnici ut agonis spectacula reformentur (addressed to the proconsul of Africa). THE ANTIOCHENE OLYMPIA: Lib. *Or.* x (deploring the vulgarisation of the athletic contests). IMMUNITY OF VICTORS: *CJ* x. liv. 1 (286–93), athletis ita demum, si per omnem aetatem certasse, coronis quoque non minus tribus certaminis sacri, in quibus vel semel Romae seu antiquae Graeciae, merito coronati non aemulis corruptis ac redemptis probentur, civilium munerum tribui solet vacatio. ATHLETES FROM OTHER PROVINCES: Lib. *Ep.* 843, 1183 (Egypt), 1179–82 (Asia and Bithynia); in 1179 Libanius asks for the use of the *cursus publicus* to carry athletes from Asia to Antioch, and in 1180 he mentions the money awards offered by the *athlothetes* in addition to the crowns (cf. 663). In *Ep.* 1278–9 Libanius praises two young Egyptian athletes, Horus and Phanes, in terms which show that they belonged to the upper classes. Cassian (*Inst.* v. 12) uses the rules of athletic contests as an analogy, but the passage may be drawn from a literary source and not from real life.

70. CHARIOTEERS AND MAGICIANS: Lib. *Or.* xxxv. 13. HORSES TRAINED IN BITHYNIA: Lib. *Ep.* 381; BOUGHT IN SPAIN: Symm. *Ep.* IV. 62. CIVIC LEASES FOR HORSE BREEDERS: Julian, *Misop.* 370D–371A. For a famous charioteer of Constantinople under Anastasius and Justin I, who was honoured with statues in the Hippodrome and epigrams in the Anthology, see A. A. Vasiliev, 'the monument of Porphyrios in the Hippodrome at Constantinople', *Dumbarton Oaks Papers* IV (1948), 27–49; contrast Sabinus at Rome, who got a pension of 12 solidi a year only (Cass. *Var.* II. 9).

71. What little we know about the circus factions in the Principate, which is mostly derived from inscriptions from Rome, is collected in Ruggiero, *Dizionario Epigrafico*, s.v. factio. I am not convinced by the modern theory that the factions of the later empire were political or religious groups.

72. ANASTASIUS AND THE REDS: Malalas, 393; cf. 386 for the four colours at Constantinople under Zeno. For the stables of the four factions at Rome see ch. XVIII, n. 44. In Malalas, 386, dancers are assigned to the factions, and in Proc. *HA* ix. 2, 5, Acacius, θηριόκομος τῶν ἐν κυνηγεσίᾳ θηρίων, and Asterius the dancer belong to the Greens.

73. Proc. *BP* I. xxiv. 2–6.

74. Jerome, *V. Hilar.* 20.

75. Libanius's defence of the mime is in *Or.* LXIV. ACTORS: *C. Ilib.* can. 62, *C. Arel.* I, can. 5, de theatricis, et ipsos placuit quamdiu agunt a communione separari, *C. Carth.* III, can. 35, ut scaenicis et histrionibus ceterisque huiusmodi personis, vel apostaticis conversis vel reversis ad dominum gratia vel reconciliatio non negetur, *C. Arel.* II, can. 20; *CTh* xv. vii. 1, 371, 2, 371, 4+5, 380, 8, 381, 9, 381, 13, 413, *CJ* v. iv. 29, 1. iv. 33, 534, Just. *Nov.* li, 536. John Chrysostom (*Hom. in Matth.* lxvii. 3) tells the story of a famous actress who entered a nunnery and remained there despite the efforts of the prefect to force her to go on the stage again.

76. For the *maiuma* see ch. XXIII, n. 88. For the Gerasene *maiuma* see Kraeling, *Gerasa, City of the Decapolis*, pp. 470–1.

77. Libanius's *Antiochicus* (*Or.* XI) was probably delivered in 360 (for his later speeches at the Olympia see *Or.* I. 184, 222). THE BANQUET AT THE OLYMPIA: Lib. *Or.* LIII. 9 ff.; for the presents see §16 of this speech and *Or.* XXXVIII. 5.

78. Symm. *Ep.* IV. 18.

79. ARVANDUS: Sid. Ap. *Ep.* I. 7 §5. RICIMER AND ANTHEMIUS: Ennod. *V. Epiph.* 343 ff. For the welcome given to Justinian's armies in Africa see Proc. *BV* I. xvi. 11, xvii. 6, xx. 1; in Italy, *BG* I. viii. 2, xiv. 5, II. vii. 35–6; the discontent at the new fiscal regime, *BV* II. viii. 25, *BG* III. i. 32–3. Though Gregory the Great was at times moved to anger against the emperor and the exarch by their apparent neglect of Rome and Italy, there is no trace in his correspondence that either he or his fellow-countrymen regarded the government of Constantinople as in any sense a foreign occupying power.

80. THE MOORISH CHIEF: *ILS* 859, pro sal. et incol. reg. Masunae gent. Maur. et Romanor. He is probably identical with the Massonas of Proc. *BV* II. xiii. 19. Cf. *AE* 1945, 97, the tomb of Masties *dux* (cf. Proc. *BV* II. xiii. 19, xx. 31), 'qui numquam periuravi neque fide fregi neque de Romanos neque de Mauros'.

81. Zos. VI. 5.

82. Zos. VI. 10.

83. For the Bacaudae see pp. 811–2. BRITISH APPEAL TO AETIUS: Gildas, 20. ARMORICAN CONTINGENT WITH AETIUS: Jordanes, *Get.* 191.

84. R. H. Charles, *The Chronicle of John Bishop of Nikiu.*

XXV. THE DECLINE OF THE EMPIRE (pp. 1025–34)

1. Jerome, *Comm. in Ezech.* i, praef. Claudian, *de cos. Stil.* III. 159–60. Amm. XIV. vi. 3. Lact. *Div. Inst.* VII. 25.

2. Aug. *Serm.* 105, §§12–3, 296 §7, ecce quando faciebamus sacrificia diis nostris, stabat Roma, florebat Roma. modo quia superavit et abundavit sacrificium dei vestri, et inhibita sunt et prohibita sacrificia deorum nostrorum, ecce quid patitur Roma.

3. For the numbers of the barbarians see pp. 194–6.

4. See pp. 684–5.

5. For Britain and Armorica see Zos. VI. 5, 10. J. Sundwall, *Weströmische Studien*, 8–26, has made much of the fact that in the first half of the fifth century administrative posts in Gaul were mostly filled by senators of Gallic domicile, and sees in this fact a separatist tendency which culminated in Avitus's election. But it does not seem very significant that Gallic (and Italian) senators should prefer to serve near their homes, and no reader of Sidonius Apollinaris could imagine that he did not regard himself as a Roman in the fullest sense, and

Avitus as a real Roman emperor. GILDO AND MASCAZEL: Amm. XXIX. v. 6, 21, 24, Zos. v. 11.

6. See pp. 965–9 and *JTS* x (1959), 280–98. JEWISH HOSTILITY TO THE EMPIRE: Proc. *BG* I. x. 24–5 (Naples), *Doctrina Jacobi*, iv. 7, v. 12, 16 (the East).

7. See pp. 284, 289, 310–1, 314–5.

8. See pp. 649–54, 661–3.

9. See pp. 621–3.

10. The theory which I am combating is that of F. W. Walbank, *The Decline of the Roman Empire in the West* (London, 1946).

11. See pp. 848–50.

12. See pp. 465, 871–2.

13. See pp. 812–23.

14. The strongest exponent of the depopulation theory is A. E. R. Boak, *Man-power Shortage and the Fall of the Roman Empire in the West* (London, 1955); cf. M. I. Finley's critical discussion of the work in *JRS* XLVIII (1958), 156–64.

15. For Rome and Constantinople see p. 698. ALEXANDRIA: Proc. *HA* xxvi. 41–3; I assume that the figure μυριάδας ἐς διακοσίας ἐπετείους μεδίμνων represents the whole *annona* of the city; 2,000,000 *medimni* are equivalent to nearly 4,000,000 *artabae*, and the *annona* of Constantinople amounted to 8,000,000 *artabae*. ANTIOCH: Lib. *Ep.* 1119 (150,000), Joh. Chrys. *Laud. Ign. Mart.* 4 (200,000); there are higher figures, e.g. Malalas, 420 (250,000 killed in the earthquake of 526), Proc. *BP* II. xiv. 6 (300,000 killed on the same occasion). EGYPT: Jos. *Bell. Jud.* II. 385, πεντήκοντα πρὸς ταῖς ἑπτακοσίαις ἔχουσα μυριάδας ἀνθρώπων, δίχα τῶν 'Αλεξάνδρειαν κατοικούντων, ὡς ἔνεστιν ἐκ τῆς καθ' ἑκάστην κεφαλὴν εἰσφορᾶς τεκμήρασθαι; I take this figure to include both sexes and all ages, since the Roman census in Egypt included women and infants. CIVITAS AEDUORUM: Pan. Lat. v. 11, septem milia capitum remisisti, quintam amplius partem nostrorum censuum . . . remissione ista septem milium capitum viginti quinque milibus dedisti vires. This gives a total of 32,000 *capita*. For reasons which I do not understand all French commentators on the passage insist that the *caput* of Gaul was a fiscal unit comprising both land and population, but in 5 the orator says that the Aedui could not complain of the *novi census acerbitas*, 'cum et agros qui discripti fuerint haberemus et Gallicani census communi formula teneremur', and in 6, 'habemus enim, ut dixi, et hominum numerum qui delati sunt et agrorum modum'. This surely means that the assessment was in two schedules, *homines* and *agri*. In 12 the orator declares that, as a result of the remission, 'liberi parentes suos cariores habent et mariti coniuges non gravate tuentur et parentes adultorum non paenitet filiorum'. This surely means that the *capita* remitted were on the schedule of *homines*, which included both sexes and grown-up children. Two laws addressed to the praetorian prefect of the Gauls (*CTh* XIII. x. 4, 368, 6, 370) confirm that the *capitatio plebeia* was paid by both sexes and that children became liable before the age of twenty, and a third law (*CTh* XI. i. 26) shows that in some provinces the *plebs* was attached to estates. For the area of the Aeduan territory see A. Déléage, *La Capitation du Bas-empire*, 210; the calculation is made on the assumption that the *castra* of Matisco and Cabillonum, separately recorded in the Notitia Galliarum, were at this date still part of Aeduan territory, and makes

the area 1,335,902 hectares. The area of Gaul is given by J. Beloch, *die Bevölkerung der griechisch-römischen Welt*, 448–9, as 63,559,830 hectares.

16. A. R. Burn, *Past and Present*, IV (1953), 1–31.

17. For the colonate see pp. 795–803. PREFERENCE FOR AURUM TIRONICUM: *CTh* VII. xiii. 12–4, 397. MINERS MOVE TO THE LAND: *CTh* X. xix. 7, 373, 9, 378. COLLEGIATI MOVE TO THE LAND: *CTh* XII. xix. 1, 400, Maj. *Nov.* vii §3, 458, *Ed. Theod.* 69. Some *coloni*, it is true, entered the civil service (Th. II, *Nov*, vii. 4 §2, 441, Val. III, *Nov.* xxvii §1, 449), and some enrolled themselves in *curiae* and *collegia* (*CTh* XII. xix. 2, 400), but in every other law of which I know fugitive *coloni* are still working on the land.

18. THE PLAGUE: ZOS. I. 26, 37, 46.

19. For rents and taxes see pp. 807–8, 820–1. CONSTANTINE'S ALIMENTARY LAWS: *CTh* XI. xxvii. 1, 315, 2, 322. For the sale of children see pp. 853–4.

21. *JRS* XLII (1953), 55–6.

20. See pp. 810–1.

22. See pp. 695 ff. for Rome and Constantinople, and p. 735 for the other cities.

23. See pp. 556–7.

24. See pp. 737 ff.

25. See pp. 895 ff., 931–2.

26. Palladius, *de re rustica*, VII. 2, cf. Pliny, *Hist. Nat.* XVIII. 296.

27. IRRIGATION MACHINES: *P. Oxy.* 137, 192, 194, 202, 1982–91, 2244, etc. WATER-MILLS: *Ed. Diocl.* xv. 54, Palladius, *de re rustica*, I. 42; AT ROME: *CTh* XIV. xv. 4, 398, *CIL* VI. 1711, Proc. *BG* I. xix. 19–22. Water-mills are mentioned as a normal thing at Dijon by Greg. Tur. *HF* III. 19, but as something exceptional in *V. Patr.* xviii. 2. Cassian (*Coll.* I. 18) uses a water-mill as a simile. For the archaeological evidence see L. A. Moritz, *Grain-mills and flour in classical antiquity*, 131–9.

28. Anon. *de rebus. bell.* praef. 7, docebimus igitur velocissimum liburnae genus decem navibus ingenii magisterio praevalere, ita ut hae per eam sine auxilio cuiusquam turbae obruantur, 9, hunc enim pontem, amnibus paludibusque necessarium, perpauci homines aut quinquaginta fere numero iumenta portabunt, vii, sciendum est autem quod hoc ballistae genus duorum opera virorum sagittas ex se non ut aliae funibus sed radiis intorta iaculatur. For Anthemius's scientific practical jokes see Agath. v. 7–8.

29. Auson. *Mosella*, 361–4, ille praecipiti torquens cerealia saxa volatu, stridentesque trahens per laevia marmora serras, audit perpetuos ripa ex utraque tumultus. This saw mill, to our knowledge unique, was near Trier, then an imperial capital, where skilled engineers would be numerous and the demand for building stone heavy.

30. For *Caesariani* and the factory, mint and postal workers see pp. 435, 600, 833, 866; for soldiers, civil servants and *fabricenses* pp. 594–5, 615, 835.

31. For *navicularii* see pp. 827–9, for the Roman guilds pp. 699 ff. The laws cited are *CTh* VII. xxii. 2, 326, XVI. ii. 9, 349.

32. See pp. 737 ff.

33. For agricultural workers see pp. 795 ff., for miners p. 838, for craftsmen p. 861.

34. I know of five laws only which order that the antecedents of recruits should be investigated before they are accepted, *CTh* VII. ii. 1, 383, 2, 385, xiii. 1 (326–53), for the army, x. xxii. 6, 412, for *fabricenses*, *CJ* II. vii. 11, 460, for lawyers.

35. For the preference conceded to sons of palatine civil servants and lawyers see *CTh* VI. xxiv. 2, 364, xxvii. 8, 396, *CJ* XII. xix. 7, 444, II. vii. 11, 460,13, 468, 22, 505, 24, 517.

36. See pp. 737 ff.

37. For a pessimistic view of the administration under the Principate see P. A. Brunt, *Historia* x (1961), 189–227. The imperial ideal is well expressed by a letter of Marcus Aurelius (from an unpublished African inscription, communicated to me by my pupil R. Duncan-Jones, of King's College). Exemplum codicillorum: Caesar Antoninus Aug. Domitio Marsiano suo salut. ad ducenariae procurationis splendorem iamdudum te provehere studens utor opportunitate quae nunc obtigit; succede igitur Mario Pudenti tanta cum spe perpetui favoris mei quantam conscientiam retinueris innocentiae diligentiae experientiae. vale, mi Marsiane karissime mihi. The high priority given to 'innocentia' suggests that it was valued, but perhaps rare.

38. For *suffragium* see pp. 393–6.

39. For the effect of the provincial governors' malpractices on the taxes see Just. *Nov.* viii pr., 535.

40. For these military abuses see pp. 644–6, 676–7.

41. For *sportulae* see pp. 467–8, 496–9.

42. For centralisation see pp. 403–6, and for inflation of numbers, sale of posts, etc., pp. 571 ff.

43. For corruption in the central secretariats see p. 410, and for the congestion of the central courts pp. 483–4. The figure of 25 per cent. is based on a tax rate of 7 solidi per *iugum* or *millena* (Val. III, *Nov.* v §4, 440) and *remunerationes* of 2½ solidi per *iugum* or *millena*, of which one-third went to the *curiales* and *cohortales* who really collected the tax, and two-thirds to the central offices (Maj. *Nov.* vii §16, 458, cf. p. 468).

44. The Notitia records 113 provinces (apart from the three proconsulates), which at 100 each (see ch. XVI, n. 73) gives 11,300 *cohortales*. There were 17 proconsuls, vicars etc. at 300 each, with a few variations up and down (see ch. XVI, n. 68), which gives 5,400 officials. There were 8 *magistri militum* at 300, and 25 *duces* at 40 (see ch. XVI, nn. 82–3), making 3,400. In the text I have allowed 1,600 for 7 *comites rei militaris* (omitting Isauria, Italia and Argentoratum, which had no *officia*, and including Hispania and Illyricum). We have no figure for the size of their *officia*, except that from Just. *Ed.* xiii §2, where the combined *officia* of the *praefectus Augustalis* and *dux Aegypti* come to 600, it may be inferred that the latter's *officium* had numbered 300. I suspect however that this is an exceptionally high figure; it seems unlikely that *comites* in general had *officia* of equal size to those of *magistri*. The praetorian prefectures are a guess (see pp

590–1) and so are the urban prefectures, on which we have no information at all. For the figures of the palatine ministries see ch. XVI, nn. 15, 21, 27, 33, 52, 54. The ministries mentioned total 2,284, and I have allowed an extra 216 for minor *officia* such as the *admissionales, lampadarii*, etc. I have not included domestic palace staff (*cubicularii* and *castrensiani*). The following table will clarify my calculations:

$$
\begin{aligned}
113 \text{ provinces} \times 100 &= 11,300 \\
12 \text{ vicars} + procos. \text{ } Achaiae + praef. \text{ } Aug. \times 300 &= 4,200 \\
comes \text{ } Orientis &= 600 \\
proconsul \text{ } Africae &= 400 \\
vicarius \text{ } Asianae &= 200 \\
25 \text{ } duces \times 40 &= 1,000 \\
8 \text{ } magistri \text{ } militum \times 300 &= 2,400 \\
7 \text{ } comites \text{ } rei \text{ } militaris \times 200(?) &= 1,400(?) \\
4 \text{ praetorian prefects} \times 1,000(?) &= 4,000(?) \\
2 \text{ urban prefects} \times 500(?) &= 1,000(?) \\
30+30 \text{ } notarii &= 60 \\
33+33 \text{ silentiaries} &= 66 \\
130+130 \text{ in the } sacra \text{ } scrinia &= 260 \\
1,174+1,248 \text{ } agentes \text{ } in \text{ } rebus &= 2,422 \\
546+446 \text{ } largitionales &= 992 \\
300+300 \text{ } privatiani &= 600 \\
admissionales, decani, lampadarii \text{ etc.} &= \text{?}
\end{aligned}
$$

$$30,900? + ?$$

The figures are of very various dates, but mostly of the fifth and sixth centuries, when it may be presumed that in general numbers had reached their maxima.

45. For *petitiones* see pp. 442–4 and for *suffragia* pp. 391–6. PRISCILLIAN: Sulp. Sev. *Chron.* II. 48. CYRIL: *A.C.Oec.* I. iv. 224. The two laws are Th. II, *Nov.* xvii. 2, 444, and *CJ* IV. lix. i, 473.

46. Marcian's pronouncement is in Marc. *Nov.* i pr., sciens quippe felicem fore rem publicam si a nolentibus et actus publicos repulsantibus regeretur. The same remark was made by Symmachus (*Rel.* 17) and was doubtless a commonplace.

47. ARVANDUS: Sid. Ap. *Ep.* I. 7. SERONATUS: ibid. VII. 7 §2.

48. BRITAIN AND ARMORICA: Zos. VI. 5. VALENTINUS: Zos. V. 15–6. SYNESIUS: Syn. *Ep.* 107–8, 113, 125, 129*, 131–2. PUDENTIUS: Proc. *BV* I. x. 22–4. TULLIANUS: Proc. *BG* III. xviii. 20–2, xxii. 1–5, 20–1.

49. SPAIN: Orosius, VII. xli. 4–5. AFRICA: Poss. *V. Aug.* 28, Val. III, *Nov.* xii and ii. 3, 443, xxxiv, 451, Theod. *Ep.* (*PG*) 29–36, 52–3, (Azema) 23.

50. Orosius, VII. xli. 7, Salvian, *Gub. Dei*, v. 21–3.

51. ADRIANOPLE: Amm. XXXI. vi. 2. ASEMUS: Priscus, 5. For the defence of the Civitas Arvernorum see C. E. Stevens, *Sidonius Apollinaris and his Age*, 141 ff., 197–207. In Syria the Antiochenes manned their walls (Proc. *BP* II. viii. 11, 17), but ransoms were offered by the citizens of Sura, Hierapolis, Beroea, Chalcis, Edessa, Carrhae and Constantina (*BP* II. v. 13, vi. 24, vii. 5, xii. 2, 34, xiii. 7, 8).

52. NAPLES: Proc. *BG* I. viii–x. Contrast *BV* I. xvi. 11 (Sullectum), xvii. 6–8 (between Sullectum and Carthage), xx. 1 (Carthage), *BG* I. v. 12, 18 (Sicily), vii. 10, 31 (Salona), viii. 2 (Southern Italy), xiv. 4–5 (Rome), xvi. 3–4 (Tuscia), II. vii. 35 (Milan), x. 5–6 (Ariminum). THE GREEK MERCHANT: Priscus, 8 (pp. 86–8).

53. Salvian, *Gub. Dei*, v. 36–7; the context indicates that he is talking about peasants. DIDYMUS AND VERINIANUS: Zos. VI. 4, Soz. IX. 11, Orosius, VII. xl. 5–6. TOTILA: Proc. *BG* III. xxii. 4. DESERTION OF TULLIANUS'S PEASANTS: ibid. III. xxii. 20–1. CYRENAICA: Syn. *Ep.* 122. MINERS: Amm. XXXI. vi. 6, quibus accessere sequendarum auri venarum periti non pauci, vectigalium perferre posse non sufficientes sarcinas graves, susceptique libenti consensione cunctorum, magno usui idem fuere ignota peragrantibus loca, conditoria frugum occulta et latebras hominum et receptacula secretiora monstrando; cf. *CTh* x. xix. 5, 369, 7, 373, for recent laws against miners. SLAVES: Amm. XXXI. vi. 5, per Thraciarum latus omne dispersi caute gradiebantur, dediticiis vel captivis vicos uberes ostendentibus, eos praecipue, ubi alimentorum reperiri satias dicebatur, eo maxime adiumento praeter genuinam erecti fiduciam, quod confluebat ad eos in dies ex eadem gente multitudo, dudum a mercatoribus venundati, adiectis plurimis, quos primo transgressu necati inedia, vino exili vel panis frustis mutavere vilissimis; Zos. v. 42.

54. RADAGAISUS: *CTh* VII. xiii. 17, 406, provinciales pro imminentibus necessitatibus omnes invitamus edicto, quos erigit ad militiam innata libertas. ingenui igitur, qui militiae obtentu arma capiunt amore pacis et patriae, sciant se denos solidos patratis rebus de nostro percepturos aerario, quibus tamen ternos ex summa supra dicta iam nunc solidos praeberi mandavimus, nam optimos futuros confidimus, quos virtus et utilitas publica necessitatibus obtulit. The law forbidding civilians to bear arms was the Lex Iulia de vi publica (*Dig.* XLVIII. vi. 1); the rule is mentioned as still operative in Synesius, *Ep.* 107–8, and in Priscus, 8 (p. 86), and was reinforced by Just. *Nov.* lxxxv, 539. GAISERIC: Val. III, *Nov.* ix, 440; singulos universosque hoc admonemus edicto, ut Romani roboris confidentia et animo, quo debent propria defensari, cum suis adversus hostes, si usus exegerit, salva disciplina publica servataque ingenuitatis modestia, quibus potuerint utantur armis nostrasque provincias ac fortunas proprias fideli conspiratione et iuncto umbone tueantur: hac videlicet spe laboris proposita, ut suum fore non ambigat quidquid hosti victor abstulerit; it is under the title 'de reddito iure armorum'.

55. See pp. 982–5.

56. Salvian, *Gub. Dei*, VI. 68, eversis Sardinia et Sicilia, id est fiscalibus horreis, atque abscissis velut vitalibus venis, Africam ipsam, id est quasi animam captivavere rei publicae, VII. 60, tam divitem quondam (before the Vandal invasion) Africam fuisse ut mihi copia negotiationis suae non suos tantum sed etiam mundi thesauros videatur implesse, VII. 8, nemini dubium est Aquitanos ac Novempopulanos medullam fere omnium Galliarum et uber totius fecunditatis habuisse. TRANSPORT OF ANNONA FROM AQUITANIA: Amm. XIV. x. 2, XVII. viii. 1. For the revenues of Egypt and Africa see pp. 462–3

57. I cannot claim to have made an exhaustive search, but I have spotted only four reused antique columns in northern France (in the apse of Senlis cathedral) and none in this country.

58. For senatorial incomes see pp. 554 ff., and for peasant proprietors pp. 778–81.

59. See pp. 177, 180, 205–7.

APPENDIX I

THE *LARGITIONES* AND THE *RES PRIVATA*

In general the addresses of the laws in the Codes agree with the demarcation of duties between the *largitiones* and the *res privata* which I have presented. There are however a few laws addressed to the *comes sacrarum largitionum* which concern the *res privata*. Various explanations are possible. (*a*) There may be a confusion in the manuscripts between *CSL* and *CRP*: this is almost demonstrable in (v) and (vi) below. (*b*) We know that the *CSL* sometimes deputised for the *CRP* (Th. II, *Nov.* xvii. 1, 439, suggestionem viri inlustris comitis sacrarum largitionum Marcellini, vicem agentis viri inlustris c.r.p.): a law on the *res privata* might therefore be addressed to the *CSL* when the office of *CRP* was temporarily vacant. (*c*) Many laws were given a wide circulation (see Seeck, *Regesten*, 4 ff.) being addressed not only to the minister primarily responsible, but to others for information; the redactors of the Codes have sometimes preserved a copy addressed to a minister only indirectly interested, and moreover omitted the clause of the law which did affect him; see (iii) and (iv) below. (*d*) There remain some cases when the government altered the normal arrangements, assigning functions or revenues which normally belonged to the one department to the other. For instance in Th. II, *Nov.* xvii. 2, 444, *caduca*, which usually went to the *res privata*, were divided between the *arca* of the prefects, the *largitiones* and the *res privata*. This experiment was evidently soon abandoned; the clause is omitted from the Justinianic version of the law (*CJ* x. xii. 2). In most cases such variations from the norm seem to have been short-lived.

The following laws dealing with the *res privata* are addressed to the *CSL*:

(i) *CTh* IX. xlii. 5, ad Felicem com. s.l., pp. Rom(ae) vii id. Mart. Mamertino et Nevitta conss. (9 March 362). Felix was certainly *CSL* on 23 March 362 (*CTh* XI. xxxix. 5) and early in 363 (Amm. xxiii. i. 5). He may have been *CRP* or *CSL* acting *CRP* on 9 March.

(ii) *CTh* x. ii. 1, com. largit., dat. vii kal. Octob. Valente vi et Valentiniano ii AA. conss. (25 Sept. 378). The address is obviously defective.

(iii) *CTh* xv. i. 32, Impp. Arcad(ius) et Honor(ius) AA. Eusebio com. s.l. ne splendidissimae urbes vel oppida vetustate labantur, de reditibus fundorum iuris rei publicae tertiam partem reparationi publicorum moenium et thermarum subustioni deputamus. dat. xi kal. Iul. Med(iolano) Olybrio et Probino conss.

(iv) *CTh* v. xiv. 35, Impp. Arcad(ius) et Hon(orius) AA. Hadriano c.s.l. restaurationi moenium publicorum tertiam portionem eius canonis, qui ex locis fundisve rei publicae annua praestatione confertur, certum est satis posse sufficere. de vectigalibus itaque publicis, quae semper ex integro nostri aerarii conferebant expensas, nihil omnino decerpi nomine civitatum permittimus. dat. viii id. Aug. Olybrio et Probino conss.

Law (iv) is probably addressed to the *CSL* because of the last sentence about the *vectigalia publica* (which is omitted in the Justinianic version, *CJ* XI. lxx. 3). I suspect that law (iii) originally contained a similar clause, omitted by the redactors of the Theodosian Code as irrelevant.

(v) *CJ* XI. lxxi. 4, Minervio comiti sacrarum largitionum (no date). Minervius is otherwise attested only as *CRP* (*CTh* VII. xiii. 14, 12 Nov. 397, I. xi. 1, 23 Dec. 397, *CJ* x. xvi. 10, 398). The title is probably an error.

(vi) *CTh* I. xi. 2+XI. xix. 4, Firmino com. s.l., dat. viiii k. Iun. Med(iolano) Honorio A. iv et Eutychiano consul. (24 May 398). *CTh* x. ii. 2, Firmino com. sac. larg., dat. kal. Novemb. Med(iolano) Honorio A. iiii et Eutychiano conss. (1 Nov. 398). Firminus is attested as *CRP* in *CTh* x. x. 22, 27 Oct. 398 and XII. vi. 25, 18 March 399. The title is very probably an error, for *CRP* was a junior post to *CSL*, and no one is known to have held the offices in the order *CSL*, *CRP*.

(vii) *CTh* IX. xlii. 19, Ursicino com. s.l., dat. xii kal. Mai. Rav(ennae) Stilichone ii et Anthemio conss. (20 April 405). Ursicinus is otherwise unknown and the title may be wrong.

(viii) *CJ* XI. lxii. 11, Probo comiti sacrarum largitionum, d. id. April. Ravennae Honorio viiii et Theodosio v AA. conss. (13 April 412). Probus is recorded as *CSL* on 29 Feb. 412 (*CTh* VIII. iv. 24) and on 10 Jan. 414 (*CTh* VII. viii. 11 = *CJ* VIII. xvi. 8). He was probably *agens vices CRP*.

(ix) I have left to the last the most difficult case, that of Germanianus who as *CSL* received one law (no. 5) on the *largitiones* and five (nos. 1–4, 6) on the *res privata*, viz.:

(1) *CTh* v. xv. 19, dat. v. k. Aug. Valentiniano et Valente AA. conss. (28 July, 365).

(2) *CJ* XI. lxii. 3, dat. viii k. Oct. Mediolani Valentiniano et Valente AA. conss. (24 Sept. 365).

(3) *CTh* VII. vii. 1, dat. v. k. Feb. Rem(is) <p.c.> Valentinian*i* et Valent*is* AA. (28 Jan. 366, see Seeck, *Reg.* 71).

(4) *CTh* v. xv. 20+*CJ* I. lvi. 2, dat. xiv k. Iun. Remis Gratiano n.p. et Dagalaifo conss. (19 May, 366).

(5) *CTh* x. xix. 4+XII. vi. 13, dat. vi id. Ian. Rem(is) Lupicino et Ioviano conss. (8 Jan. 367).

(6) *CJ* XI. lxiii. 2, pp. xiii k. Mai. Lupicino et Iovino conss. (19 April, 367).

Germanianus was preceded as *CSL* by Florentius who is attested in three laws, viz.:

(*a*) *CTh* XIII. i. 6, dat. vi. id. Sept. Divo Ioviano et Varroniano conss. (8 Sept. 364).

(*b*) *CTh* XI. xii. 3, dat. x. kal. Mart. Med(iolano) Valentiniano et Valente AA. conss. (20 Feb. 365).

(*c*) *CTh* XII. vi. 11, dat. xv kal. Oct. Mantebri Gratiano n.p. et Dagalaifo conss. (17 Sept. 366).

The date of (*c*) must be wrong, since it makes Florentius overlap Germanianus. Seeck's solution was to make the consulate a *propositum* and date the law 17 Sept. 365; he also dated (1) and (2) to the second consulate of Valentinian and Valens (368). It would be simpler to make (*c*) a postconsulate, and make the date 17 Sept. 367, so that Florentius would be reappointed *CSL* after Germanianus. During the same period Florianus is attested *CRP* on 12 Sept. 364 (*CTh* VIII. v. 20) and 25 May 365 (*CTh* XI. vii. 11) and then not until 13 Oct. 367 (*CJ* VI. iv. 2), 26 Feb. 368 (*CTh* v. xv. 18), 12 March, 368 (*CJ* XI. lxii. 4) and 29 March, 369 (*CTh* x. ix. 1). It is a tenable hypothesis that Florentius and Florianus were *CSL* and *CRP* respectively from 364 to the summer of 365, that Germanianus then took over both departments, but that after two years this experiment was abandoned, and Florentius and Florianus reappointed *CSL* and *CRP*. The first of Germanianus's laws suggests that the *largitiones* and *res privata* were temporarily amalgamated; *CTh* v. xv. 19, fundi enfyteutici patrimonialisque iuris in antiquum ius praestationemque redeant, ne quoquo modo exempti ab enfyteutico patrimonialique titulo veluti privato iure teneantur, rectoribus provinciarum et rationalibus monendis, ut sciant contra commoda largitionum nostrarum specialia non admittenda esse rescripta, his tantummodo exceptis, quos in re privata nostra secundam legem datam iam dudum in hoc nomine manere praecepimus.

A division of the revenues of emphyteutic estates between the *largitiones* and the *res privata* is suggested by the fragmentary law *CTh* v. xvi. 29, 395, ..n officium rei privatae canonis enfyteutici annonas sacris largitionibus pendantur, illud etiam, quod his fundis vel iuris rei publicae praeter antiquum canonem peraequatio imposuit, privatis largitionibus inferatur. The law is not reproduced in the Codex Justinianus and the arrangement, like that under Th. 11, *Nov.* xvii. 1, was probably shortlived.

It might be inferred from *CTh* iv. xiii. 7, proc. Afr., 374, ex reditibus rei publicae omniumque titulorum ad singulas quasque pertinentium civitates duae partes totius pensionis ad largitiones nostras perveniant, tertia probabilibus civitatum deputetur expensis, that the rents of the confiscated civic estates flowed to the *largitiones*. This law was however placed by the redactors of the Code in the title 'de vectigalibus et commissis' and must refer to the civic *vectigalia*. Either the word *vectigalium* has dropped out after *ex reditibus* or the context of the full law made it plain that the revenues in question were the civic taxes.

Three *comites rerum privatarum* receive laws which appear to concern the *largitiones*, viz.:

(1) Florianus in 364, *CTh* viii. v. 20, iuxta divi Iuliani consultissimam legem ad transferendas largitionum res necessarias conpetentia iudices evectionum subsidia perferant. This law was probably addressed to both the *CSL* and *CRP*, who were both concerned in the transport of the goods of their respective departments, and the redactors have omitted the clause referring to the goods of the *res privata*.

(2) Pancratius in 379, *CTh* xii. xiii. 4, quae diversarum ordines curiarum vel amore proprio vel indulgentiarum laetitia vel rebus prospere gestis admoniti in coronis aureis signisque diversis obtulerint, in quacumque fuerint oblata materia, in ea suscipiantur, ne id, quod voluntate offertur, occasione obryzae incrementi, necessitatis iniuria insequatur. Pancratius is styled *PU* in this law, but he was at the time *CRP*, as five other laws testify (*CTh* x. i. 12, vi. xxx. 2, x. x. 12, x. iii. 3, x. x. 14). Why he dealt with *aurum coronarium* is not clear unless he was *agens vices CSL*.

(3) Macedonius in 410, *CTh* vii. xiii. 20, tirones tricenis solidis aestimatos ab omnibus officiis iudicum Africae, exemplo praecedentis temporis, postulamus. Macedonius is otherwise unknown and the title may be wrong; otherwise he must have dealt with *aurum tironicum* as *agens vices CSL*.

There is a similar overlap of functions among the *rationales* of the two departments. In the first place there are many laws about the business of the *res privata* addressed to *rationales* at the time of Diocletian and Constantine, when on other evidence it would appear that the officers of the *res privata* were called *magistri*: examples are *CJ* x. x. 1, *CTh* x. viii. 1, x. xi. 1, x. viii. 2, Opt. *App.* x. There was however some fluidity in the use of the two titles (e.g. *CJ* iii. xxii. 5, *CTh* x. i. 2), and these cases cannot be pressed. Clearer examples are the laws addressed to Eufrasius and Gerulus and Callepius, *rationales III provinciarum*, for this post certainly was under the *CSL* (*Not. Dig. Occ.* xi. 14), and all the laws (*CTh* xii. vi. 2+vii. 1, 325, 11. xxv. 1, 325 (S), x. x. 5, 340) deal with concerns of the *res privata*. So too does *CTh* x. viii. 4, ad rationalem Numidiae, 346, although the *rationalis Numidiae* was under the disposition of the *CSL* (*Not. Dig. Occ.* xi. 16), and *CJ* iii. xxvi. 7, ad rationalem summae rei, 349.

The most plausible explanation is that *rationales* in the dioceses handled business for either department when convenience dictated. There was no representative of the *res privata* in the three islands of Sicily, Sardinia and Corsica, so the emperor wrote to the *rationalis summarum*, who was on the spot.

APPENDIX II

THE NOTITIA DIGNITATUM

The Notitia Dignitatum presents a number of unsolved and perhaps insoluble problems, but any historian of the later Roman empire must make the utmost possible use of so valuable a document, and in order to do so must take up a provisional position on the questions of its composition.

It is fairly generally agreed that the Notitia is an official document, in fact the 'notitia omnium dignitatum et administrationum tam civilium quam militarium' held by the *primicerius notariorum* (*Or.* xviii, *Occ.* xvi). Our copy was drawn up after 395 since it shows the empire divided as it was divided from that date and is the document held by the Western *primicerius*. The evidence for the last statement is as follows. First, our manuscript was preserved in the West. Secondly some chapters of the Eastern section are in summary form, omitting details which would not have interested the Western *primicerius*; there are no lists of *rationales, thesauri, bastagae*, mints and factories in the chapter of the *comes sacrarum largitionum* (*Or.* xiii), nor of *rationales* and *procuratores* in that of the *comes rei privatae* (*Or.* xiv). Thirdly, as we shall see, the Western section has been revised to a later date than the Eastern.

A document of this type is very difficult to maintain accurately. When an addition, deletion or alteration is made in one chapter, the consequential changes elsewhere may be neglected: old items from a much earlier date may thus be preserved in a document which is substantially later. There probably never was a time when the Notitia was completely up to date in all sections and contained no inconsistencies. On the other hand a few casual corrections may later be made in a document which is substantially earlier. In these circumstances it is difficult to fix any date for the document as a whole, or for either of its halves. The evidence, however, suggests that the Eastern section was revised fairly thoroughly at a date not long after 395, and thereafter left virtually untouched.

In the first place some of the sections on Illyricum, just taken over in 395, show signs of haste: in the Index (*Or.* i) the *duces, consulares* and *praesides* are not listed under the dioceses of Dacia and Macedonia but lumped together under Illyricum, and so too are the *fabricae* in *Or.* xi, and the *comites commerciorum* in *Or.* xiii. Secondly, the *correctores* of Augustamnica and Paphlagonia are not put in their proper place in the Index between *consulares* and *praesides*, but at the end. The title *corrector* of Augustamnica is first recorded in 393 (*CTh* I. vii. 2) and that of Paphlagonia in 395 (ibid. II. viii. 22). This alteration has led to certain errors. In the Index Augustamnica and Paphlagonia have been correctly deleted in the list of *praesides*, but they have also been deleted by excess of zeal from the list of provinces under the disposition of the praetorian prefect of the East (*Or.* ii). Thirdly, only one of the *magistri praesentales* and the *magister per Orientem* have an *officium cardinale*, consisting that is of regular civil servants (*Or.* vi, vii). The other three *magistri* have *officia* formed from soldiers seconded from their regiments (*Or.* v, viii, ix). This latter arrangement was clearly a temporary makeshift and implies that the commands concerned had only recently been established. It would appear that Theodosius when he marched against Eugenius left behind only the *magister per Orientem* and one *praesentalis*, and that when the Eastern armies returned in 395, Arcadius had to improvise staffs for the second *praesentalis* and the *magistri* of Thrace and Illyricum.

Fourthly, in the lists of military units there are no regiments which can be proved to have been raised after 395, and there are signs that some regiments raised shortly before that date were recent additions to the lists. Before arguing these points it is necessary to state certain general rules about the composition of the lists. In the lists of the *comitatus* under the disposition of the several *magistri militum*, the units are arranged in their classes (*vexillationes palatinae* and *comitatenses, legiones palatinae, auxilia palatina, legiones comitatenses, pseudocomitatenses*) and within each class by seniority, that is according to the date at which they were promoted to that class. Thus an old *vexillatio comitatensis*, promoted to be *palatina*, came lower on the list than a *vexillatio palatina* junior to it in the date of its formation, but senior as *palatina*. The same applied to *vexillationes* promoted from the *limitanei* into the *comitatus*, and to *legiones palatinae, comitatenses* and *pseudocomitatenses* and to infantry units promoted from the *limitanei*. These rules of seniority might, it seems, be varied as a penal measure, a unit losing so many places in seniority as a disgrace: at any rate there are some anomalies which it is very difficult to explain otherwise.

The only units which we can hope to date are those named after emperors or members of the imperial family. It is generally assumed that regiments were named only after reigning Augusti, or at least Caesars, but there is good reason to doubt this assumption. Libanius (*Or.* xix. 62) makes a clear allusion to the province of Honorias in a speech composed in 387, when he urges Theodosius not to take away from Antioch what he had given to a minor Paphlagonian city, that is the status of metropolis of a province. Honorius was born 9 Sept. 384, but did not become Augustus until 23 Jan. 393. If a new province could be named after a boy prince, surely so could a new regiment.

Under the tetrarchy the emperors frequently named units after their colleagues, and the practice continued down to the death of Valens, who called several units after his brother Valentinian and his nephew Gratian (*Or.* viii. 20-2, Augustenses, Valentinianenses, Gratianenses, a group it would seem named after Valens himself, as Augustus of the East, and his Western colleagues; *Or.* xxxi. 36, 39, Legio I and II Valentiniana in the Thebaid; *Or.* xxxvii. 30, Ala II Felix Valentiniana in Arabia; *Or.* xxxiv. 42, Ala II Gratiana in Palestine). No units named after Valens are recorded in the West, but so few Western regiments of this date survive at all that this is not significant. But from the accession of Theodosius I the practice seems to have ceased. No Theodosian (or Arcadian) units occur in the West, and in the East there are no units named after Valentinian II, and none named after Gratian except the Ala II Gratiana and the Gratianenses, probably created by Valens. This being so it is probable that the few Honoriani of the East were created by Theodosius I and named after his younger son.

One further point may be noted. The Notitia contains no unit named after a 'tyrant'. Usurpers certainly raised and named regiments, and these regiments were sometimes taken over by the legitimate emperors who succeeded them; an example are the Magnentiaci and Decentiaci employed by Constantius II in the East (Amm. xviii. ix. 3). These particular units were annihilated at Amida, but those that survived may well have been renamed by the legitimate emperors after themselves.

With these principles in mind we may look at the units named after Theodosius, Arcadius, and Honorius in the *comitatus* of the East (see Table I). It is fairly certain that the Felices Theodosiani, Felices Arcadiani Seniores and Juniores and Felices Honoriani Seniores and Juniores are a group raised simultaneously; their order indicates that they were raised by Theodosius I, and they might date anywhere between Honorius' birth (384) and Theodosius I's death (395). I to IV Theodosiani must be junior to them, but may well have been raised by Theodosius I. Similarly the Equites Theodosiani Seniores and Juniores must be junior to the Comites Arcadiani and Honoriani, but the second pair must have been raised before 395, and all four may be creations of Theodosius I. There is in fact no unit that must have been raised after Theodosius I's death.

Among the *limitanei* the units are not put in order of seniority, but newly raised units were sometimes so labelled ('nuper constituta') and were often entered provisionally out of place: thus new *alae* may be placed after the *equites* and *legiones* above the rubric 'et quae de minore laterculo emittuntur', or right at the end, after the *cohortes* (see Table II). Among such recent additions, there are in Egypt the Ala Theodosiana and the Ala Arcadiana, both labelled 'nuper constituta' and entered in the wrong place. To judge by the order of the names these two units must have been raised by Theodosius I. The Equites Felices Honoriani of the Thebaid, which must have been raised before 395, are also out of place, and so are the Ala Theodosiana and the Ala Felix Theodosiana of Armenia.

The army lists of the *limitanei* then suggest a date shortly after 395, and those of the *comitatus* are compatible with the same date. It would also be possible to date the latter to the reign of Theodosius II, assigning to him such units as I–IV Theodosiani, and Equites Theodosiani I and II, but this seems less likely. Theodosius I had strong reasons for raising new regiments, first to fill the gaps caused by the battle of Adrianople and the heavy fighting with the Goths which followed, and later for his campaign against Maximus and Eugenius. The earlier part of Theodosius II's reign was peaceful.

Two reasons have been suggested for dating the Eastern part of the Notitia substantially later than 395, the fact that the *praepositus sacri cubiculi* ranks immediately after the prefects and *magistri militum*, a position which, it is alleged, he only attained by *CTh* VI. viii. 1 in 422, and the entry 'tabularium dominarum Augustarum' in the chapter of the *castrensis* (*Or.* xvii. 8): there were two Augustae simultaneously only from 423. Neither argument is probant. *CTh* VI. viii. 1 gives *ex praepositis sacri cubiculi* equal rank with *ex praefectis* and *ex magistris militum*, that is, places them in the upper bracket of the *illustres*. The order in the Notitia need indicate no more than that the *praepositus* heads the second bracket, and there is no proof that he did not rank as high as this earlier than 422. *CTh* XI. xxviii. 9 (414), where he is mentioned in the distribution list of a law granting remission of arrears after the *comes sacrarum largitionum*, is not evidence; for this law was of primary interest to the *comes*, but of marginal import to the *praepositus*, whom it affected only 'de titulis ad domum sacram pertinentibus'. *CTh* VII. viii. 3 (384), which grants immunity from billeting to *ex praefectis, ex magistris militum, ex comitibus consistorianis* and *ex praepositis sacri cubiculi* in that order, probably gives the order of precedence prevailing in 384, but the *praepositus* may have risen in rank in the following decade. Eutropius, who probably already held the office in the last years of Theodosius I's reign, may well have secured its promotion.

The second argument is also invalid. In the early fifth century an Augusta had her own *cubiculum* with its appropriate officers. In 401 we meet with Amantius, *castrensis* of Eudoxia, Augusta from 400 to 404 (*V. Porph.* 37), and in the early 430s with Chryseros and Paulus simultaneously *praepositi sacri cubiculi*, the latter apparently of Pulcheria, Augusta from 414 (*A.C. Oec.* I. iv. 224). A decade later there is the quarrel between the two Augustae, Pulcheria and Eudocia, who was given the title in 423, and now claimed that she should have her own *praepositus* or take over Pulcheria's (Theophanes, A.M. 5940; the date is probably wrong). If the Notitia Orientis had been drawn up after 414 (or between 400 and 404), it would then show a *praepositus*, *castrensis* (and presumably *primicerius*) of the Augusta in addition to those of the Augustus.

It remains to account for the entry 'tabularium dominarum Augustarum'. I would conjecture that it was the strongminded and independent Eudoxia who first introduced the separate *cubiculum Augustae*, and that in the fourth century an Augusta had only her separate *tabularius*, and that this arrangement continued to be the rule in the West. The item 'tabularium dominae Augustae' would have been added to the Western notitia in 421, when Placidia became Augusta, and a corresponding item, 'tabularium dominarum Augustarum' may have been inserted then in the Notitia Orientis by the Western *primicerius*, who was aware that there were two Augustae in the East, but ignorant of—or not interested in—the organisation of the Eastern *cubiculum*. It is also possible that he may have found an item, 'tabularium dominae Augustae', retained by inadvertence in the Notitia Orientis, and mechanically corrected it when a second Augusta was created in the East. It is at any rate clear that this entry is a blunder.

A firm *terminus ad quem* is provided by *CTh* vi. xiii. 1 (413), which alludes to 'eos qui comites Aegypti vel Ponticae dioeceseos fuerint, quorum par dignitas est'. The second of these offices is not recorded in the Notitia, which must therefore be earlier than 413. Another but less conclusive piece of evidence points the same way. The Index records a *praeses* of Macedonia Salutaris (*Or*. 1. 125), but in the chapter of the praetorian prefect of Illyricum (*Or*. iii. 13 and 19) we read 'Epirus Nova et pars Macedoniae Salutaris' under the Macedonian diocese and 'Praevalitana et pars Macedoniae Salutaris' under the Dacian. Evidently the province had recently been suppressed when the Notitia was drawn up. Macedonia Salutaris was probably created about 386 and had been suppressed before 412 (F. Papazoglu, *Bull. Ac. Roy. Belg.* 5e ser. XLII (1956), 115).

There are various minor anomalies in the Eastern section (listed by Bury in *JRS* x (1920), 133–4). Most of them merely go to prove that the chancery of the later Roman Empire was not very meticulous in preserving perfect consistency; provinces are placed in different orders in different lists, and even the order of some *duces* is not the same in the Index and in the sequence of chapters. Some anomalies are more significant. The last line of the chapter of the *comes per Isauriam* runs 'dux Isauriae VI' (*Or*. xxix. 18). We know of a *comes* of Isauria as early as 353 and 359 (Amm. XIV. ii. 14, XIX. xiii. 2, *ILS* 740), but the title was doubtless in these cases personal. A *dux Isauriae* appears in 382 (*CJ* IX. xxvii. 1; the title is corrupt in the version of the law in *CTh* IX. xxvii. 3): we do not know, however, when the *dux Isauriae* was definitely upgraded to a *comes*.

In both the Eastern and Western sections there is the same anomaly, that the *primicerius notariorum* ranks before the *castrensis* in the Index but after him in the order of chapters. Evidently the precedence of these two offices had been changed at one time, but we do not know when. In both sections also the *magister officiorum* ranks before the quaestor, contrary to the rule prevailing earlier, as shown by *CTh* vi. ix. 1 (372), 2 (380), and later, as shown by the order of the titles 1. viii and ix in the Code (published in 438). Here again we do not know when and for how long the *magister officiorum* achieved his temporary precedence over the quaestor, but it may be reasonably conjectured that Rufinus, who was consul in 392 while he held the office and appears to have enlarged its powers, may have secured higher precedence for it.

To sum up, the Eastern part of the Notitia must be earlier than 413, when the office of *comes Ponticae* was already established, and need not be later than 395. Plausible dates for its transmission to the West would be either 395 or 408, when diplomatic relations were resumed after Stilicho's fall. The document was no doubt revised for the occasion, but not very thoroughly, and still contained many anomalies.

Prima facie one would expect that the Western section would have been revised for transmission to the East at the same time that the Eastern section was revised for transmission to the West. It has been claimed that it must be considerably earlier because it does not list the mint of Milan, which was important from 383 (Salisbury, *JRS* XVII (1927), 102 ff.): but this argument has been refuted (Kent in *Essays in Roman Coinage presented to Harold Mattingly*, 201). Its original date is all the more difficult to determine because it was corrected during the reign of Honorius. There is in the chapter of the *comes rei privatae* a *comes Gildoniaci patrimonii* (*Occ.* xii. 5; Gildo's rebellion was crushed in 398) and in the chapter of the *comes Africae* the *princeps* and *numerarii* of the *officium* are, in accordance with *CTh* I. vii. 3 (398), supplied from the *officium* of the *magisteria potestas* (*Occ.* xxv. 38, 41–2). The *tabularius dominae Augustae* (*Occ.* xv. 9) must have been inserted in 421 when Placidia was proclaimed Augusta.

There are, as in the Eastern section, various minor inconsistencies of no great moment (see Bury, *JRS* x (1920), 136–7). More significant is the omission of the chapter of the *vicarius Italiae*, who still appears in the Index; but we do not know when the office was suppressed. There is also a curious clerical error. The province of Valeria (in Illyricum) is missing from the Index and the chapter of the praetorian prefect of Italy, and this despite the fact that the *dux Valeriae* is protecting the province with a large army (*Occ.* xxxiii, cf. i. 42, v. 137). On the other hand the Italian Valeria, which is last recorded in 399 (*CTh* IX. xxx. 5) and is never mentioned again (it is omitted in *CTh* XI. xxviii. 7 of 413, and in Polemius Silvius), is recorded in the Index (*Occ.* i. 95) and under the praetorian prefect of Italy (*Occ.* ii. 25) and under the vicar of the city (*Occ.* xix. 14). It is fairly clear that a clerk ordered to delete Valeria deleted the wrong province. On this clerical error have been based great theories on the occupation of the Illyrican Valeria by the Huns.

In the chapters on the *magister peditum* and *magister equitum* (*Occ.* v, vi) and the *distributio numerorum* (*Occ.* vii) there are many indications of revision. But before discussing these it is necessary to consider the mutual relation of the lists of units given under the *magistri* and those given in the *distributio*, and in particular to discover whether they are contemporary or not. The lists do not tally as they should, some units appearing under the *magistri* but not in the *distributio*, and many in the *distributio* but not under the *magistri*. A few discrepancies can be explained by textual errors. Thus Seeck has restored the Attecotti Iuniores Gallicani (vii. 78) at v. 218 on the basis of the shield of that unit at v. 70, and to make up the stated number of *auxilia palatina*, and also the Equites Bracchiati Iuniores (vii. 170) at VI. 46 to make up the ten *vexillationes palatinae*. These are fairly certain emendations, and others could be suggested, but there remain a very large number of discrepancies which must have been in the original text. They are shown in Table III.

In some cases the *distributio* appears to list twice a unit only given once under the *magistri*. These duplications may be the result of clerical errors arising from the transfer of units from one army group to another, the unit being marked up in its new station but not deleted in its old place; these I have listed separately. But there are a large number of units in the *distributio* of which there is no trace in the chapters of the *magistri*. They include, as we shall see, one very late formation and many regiments which appear to be *pseudo-comitatenses*, drafted into the *comitatus* at a late date. The lists of the *magistri* contain few units not in the *distributio*. In some cases their omission in the latter may be due to textual errors (which it is impossible to check as there are no total numbers given in that chapter, and no shields). In others it may be due to clerical errors, a unit having on transfer to another army group been deleted in its original place and not entered in its new (this again is impossible to check). Or again the unit may really have ceased to exist, and been struck off his list by the local commander and in the *distributio*, but not deleted in the lists of the *magistri*.

So far it would seem that the *distributio* is more up to date than the chapters of the *magistri*. But there are discrepancies in the order of the units which suggest the reverse conclusion. In general the lists in the *distributio* observe the same order of precedence as those of the *magistri*. There are many minor discrepancies, which it would be a waste of labour to catalogue, since they are inexplicable and are no doubt due to simple clerical errors. But there are some which are significant.

The list of *legiones palatinae* shows first six units (v. 145–150), which are also the first six units in Italy (vii. 3–8), and then:

v. 151 (vii. 142)	Armigeri Propugnatores Seniores	2nd in Africa (after 1 *aux. pal.*)
v. 152 (vii. 82)	Lanciarii Sabarienses	19th in Gaul (after 16 *aux pal.* and 2 *leg. com.*)
v. 153 (vii. 28)	Octavani ⎫	26-7th in Italy
v. 154 (vii. 29)	Thebaei ⎬	(after 25 *aux. pal.*)
v. 155 (vii. 145)	Cimbriani	5th in Africa (after 1 *aux. pal.*, nos. 151 and 156 and 1 *leg. com.*)
v. 156 (vii. 143)	Armigeri Propugnatores Iuniores	3rd in Africa (after 1 *aux. pal.*, and no. 151

It is clear that these legions were originally *comitatenses* and are listed in their place as such in the *distributio*, but have later been promoted to be *palatinae* and are so listed, in order of promotion, under the *magister peditum*. Another instance of the same phenomenon is afforded by the three legions I, II, III Iulia Alpina. In the *distributio* I and III are listed in that order below the *legiones comitatenses* in Italy and II among the *pseudocomitatenses* in Illyricum. In the *magister*'s list III appears among the *comitatenses*, I and II among the *pseudocomitatenses*. Evidently all three legions are reckoned as *pseudocomitatenses* in the *distributio*, but III was later promoted to *comitatensis* and is so recorded in the *magister*'s list. In this respect then the lists of the *magistri* are more up to date than the *distributio*.

The best explanation of this apparent contradiction is that the two lists are contemporary, but, being kept for different purposes and based on different returns, tended to be out of date in different ways. The lists of the *magistri* were primarily intended to record the precedence of units in the whole army, which was presumably determined by the *magistri*. The *distributio* showed the actual strength of the several army groups and was presumably based on returns from their commanders. For this purpose precedence did not matter greatly, and although the original lists seem to have been drawn up in the correct order little trouble was taken to make alterations consequent on the upgrading of units. Nor were accessions always entered in their proper place.

Another feature of the *distributio* is that high ranking units often appear at the tail of the regional armies. The Gratianenses Iuniores and the Honoriani Marcomanni, the 32*nd* and 41–2*nd auxilia palatina* (v. 189, 198–9), are listed second and third from bottom in the Italian army below *legiones comitatenses* and *pseudocomitatenses*, and the Valentinianenses, the 33*rd auxilium palatinum*, appear in an appropriate position in Gaul, but among the *pseudocomitatenses* second from last in Illyricum. In these cases it would seem that a unit transferred from another army group has been entered at the end of its new group without regard to precedence.

In the *distributio*, as far as numbers went, the lists were kept more or less up to date. In the lists of the *magistri* on the other hand upgradings were sedulously recorded, but the addition of new units was often neglected, and, it may be suspected, units which had been destroyed were not always deleted.

The lists are then probably contemporary, but the *distributio* gives a more complete and accurate picture of the army at the date to which both lists were revised. Clues to this date are afforded by three (perhaps four) units. The last *vexillatio comitatensis* on the list of the *magister equitum* before the African units, which is also the last cavalry unit in Gaul, is the Equites Constantiani Felices or Constantiaci Feroces (vi. 62 = vii. 178). It figures after Honorian units and must have been named after Constantius III, who was Augustus 8 Feb. to 2 Sept., 421. The last *vexillatio palatina* in the *magister*'s list, which is also the last cavalry unit in Italy, is the Equites Constantes Valentinianenses Seniores (vi. 52) or Iuniores (vii. 165). It is a late addition to the latter list, coming after a *vexillatio comitatensis*. It may have been raised by Valentinian III in or after 425, but its name rather suggests an allusion to Constantius III and his son, born 2 July, 419. Second from last in the Italian infantry (vii. 36), but not yet entered in the list of the *magister peditum*, are the Placidi Valentinianici Felices, probably an *auxilium palatinum*, clearly named after Valentinian III in 420 or later.

The fourth unit which may be of late date is the Felices Valentinianenses (v. 203 = vii. 47), an *auxilium* which comes below eight Honoriani, but is senior to fourteen *auxilia*, including three Honoriani, the last of which is twelve places below it. If the Felices Valentinianenses were named after Valentinian III, they could not have been raised before 420, and Honorius died in 423; he would therefore have raised at least twelve new *auxilia* in three years. This is possible, but seems unlikely. An alternative explanation of the Felices Valentinianenses is that they were raised by Valentinian II, and were later degraded some twenty places. In the army of Illyricum the regiment is placed above the Mauri Honoriani Seniores, one of the units which precedes it in the list of the *magister peditum*. It is possible that the *distributio* has here preserved the original seniority of the units, but not much can be built on this argument, as the order in this part of the Illyrican army list is very irregular. Another possible instance of the degradation of a unit is the Equites Stablesiani Italiciani, who are first among the cavalry units of Africa (vii. 182), but last of the same group in the list of the *magister equitum* (vi. 82), thus losing twenty places. The Equites Caetrati of the same army have also gone down five places (vii. 187, vi. 74).

The military lists have then been revised after a fashion down to 420, perhaps to the end of Honorius' reign. The date is unlikely to be much later, since the units named after Valentinian III are so few.

There are notable discrepancies about the *comites rei militaris* between the *distributio* on the one hand and the Index, the chapter of the *magister peditum* and the chapters of the several *comites* on the other (see Table IV). The former records a *magister equitum Galliarum* and *comites* of Illyricum, Spain, Tingitania, Africa and Britain. The last three of these appear in other appropriate places, but the *magister equitum Galliarum* though listed in the Index has no chapter, and his *officium* is inserted in the *distributio*. The *comites* of Illyricum and Spain appear nowhere else; on the other hand there are chapters for three other *comites*, of the Saxon Shore, of Italy and of Argentoratum, and they appear in the Index and the chapter of the *magister peditum*.

If I am right in believing that the *distributio* is a working army list of about 420, all the offices mentioned in it must have then existed. The *comites* of Spain and Illyricum, I would suggest, are not recorded elsewhere because they were recent creations, perhaps regarded as provisional. In fact we first hear of a *comes Hispaniarum* in 420 (Hydatius, 74, *Chron. Min.* II. 20). It is more surprising that the *comes Illyrici* should be a recent creation, for we hear of Valens as commander of the military units in Dalmatia in 409 (Zos. v. 45), and his successor Generid was given a command which covered Dalmatia, Pannonia Superior, Noricum and Raetia (Zos. v. 46). We can only suppose that this command was abolished, to be revived c. 420. There had also been a *magister equitum per Gallias* down to 408, when Chariobaudes, who then held the post, was killed in the mutiny which preceded Stilicho's fall (Zos. v. 32). He had, however, withdrawn to Italy after Constantine's rebellion, and it may be that his post was now abolished. Constantius reconquered Gaul as *magister praesentalis* in 411, and we do not hear of a *magister equitum* of Gaul until after Valentinian III's accession. It would seem however that the post was restored c. 420.

The *comitivae Africae* and *Tingitaniae* were old established posts. So also was the *comitiva litoris Saxonici*, which does not appear in the *distributio* because it commanded no *comitatenses*. There had been a *comes Britanniarum*, Gratian, in the early fourth century, but the post was not permanently established (there was no *comes Britanniarum*, but only a *dux* and *comes litoris Saxonici* in 368; see Amm. XXVII. viii. 1). It must presumably have been re-established on a regular footing after Constantius' reconquest of Gaul from the tyrants.

The *comites Italiae* and *Argentoratensis*, who have no troops under their command and no *officia*, but only chapter headings and places in the Index and in the list of *comites rei militaris* subject to the *magister peditum*, must be vestigial relics of posts which had existed but had been suspended. The *comes Italiae*, whose zone was the 'tractus Italiae circa Alpes', would seem to date from a period when there was no *comes Illyrici* holding Raetia and Noricum, and thus guarding the northern approaches to Italy. The *comes Argentoratensis* would seem to belong to a time when the emperor's dominions in Gaul were reduced to little more than the province of Sequanica, and his furthest outpost was Argentoratum. The posts might have been established not long after Stilicho's death, and retained until the re-establishment of a *comes Illyrici* and a *magister Galliarum* made them superfluous.

There are also inconsistencies in the lists of *duces*. The Index states that there were twelve and names them. The chapters supply only eleven; Seeck restored a chapter for the missing *dux Germaniae* I, but his argument is very dubious. The chapter of the *magister peditum* states that there were ten *duces*, omitting those of Sequanica and the Tractus Armoricanus. This suggests that these two ducates were recent creations, which the clerks had omitted to insert in one chapter. The order of the *duces* in all these lists is very similar and down to Britain appears to be geographical (in the Index Pannonia I has been put in front of Pannonia II for the sake of neatness). The last entry, the *dux Moguntiacensis*, violates the geographical order, and again looks like a later addition. It is almost impossible that a *dux Germaniae I* and a *dux Moguntiacensis* can have existed simultaneously, and the former had perhaps ceased to exist, remaining only in the Index and Chapter V, and was replaced by the latter.

Something can be learned from the lists of the history of the Eastern *comitatus* in the reign of Theodosius and shortly afterwards, and of that of the Western *comitatus* under Honorius. In the East the Illyrican army looks a rather ill-assorted group hastily got together, including an unusually large number of *pseudocomitatenses*. These comprise, besides three Theodosian units, six named after towns in the interior of Illyricum, Timacenses, Bugaracenses, Scupenses, Ulpianenses, Merenses, Scampenses. They are perhaps old cohorts stationed in rearward areas, like those attached to the *dux Moesiæ II* in Rhodope and Thrace (*Or.* xl 44–9). The *pseudocomitatenses* of Oriens seem on the other hand to be mostly of earlier origin. Nos. 1 and 2 (I and II Armeniaca) and 6 and 7 (IV Italica and VI Parthica) were probably legions garrisoning the territories surrendered by Jovian to Persia; II Armeniaca is mentioned by Ammianus at Bezabda (xx. vii. 1), and V Parthica (destroyed) at Amida (xviii. ix. 3). No. 3 (Fortenses Auxiliarii) is a detachment from Valeria (*Occ.* xxxiii. 49) and No. 5 (I Italica) from Moesia II (*Or.* xl. 30–32). No. 8 (I Isaura Sagittaria) is the third legion once under the *comes Isauriae*, who still has II and III Isaura (*Or.* xxix. 7, 8). After the Balistarii Theodosiani (No. 9) come the Transtigritani (No. 10), probably raised from the Armenian satrapies annexed by Theodosius I.

In Table V I have analysed the units of the Eastern *comitatus* according to date, placing in the right hand columns regiments certainly Theodosian (or post-Theodosian) and in the left those presumably earlier, though the latter may include a few units raised by Theodosius early in his reign and not given dynastic names. It will be seen that of the army of 395 nearly one-fifth was Theodosian and over four-fifths earlier than his accession. This is unlikely to mean that he increased the army by a quarter. Some units were no doubt added to the *comitatus* to help form the new army of Illyricum in 395 (fairly certainly the 9 units of *pseudocomitatenses*), but the majority of the new units were probably replacements of losses incurred in the battle of Adrianople and later wars. If so approximately one-seventh of the *comitatus* was destroyed in these wars.

When we turn to the Western *comitatus* the situation is very different (see Table VI; I have used the *distributio* for this table, as giving a more complete picture of the army at the end of Honorius' reign than Chapters V and VI, but I have eliminated the seven units which I take to be duplicates; see Table III). By the end of Honorius' reign only 84 units survived of the army of the period prior to 395, that is, if the Western *comitatus* had then been of similar size to the Eastern, about one-third. The losses in the fighting against Alaric and Radagaesus, in the great barbarian invasions of Gaul, and in the wars between Honorius and the tyrants, must have been staggering. No doubt, too, the Western armies had been reduced before 395 by the campaigns in which Maximus and Eugenius were conquered.

The gaps have been filled partly by raising new units, partly by pulling in old units from the frontiers. The record is best among the *auxilia palatina*, which were evidently the crack troops of the West. Forty old *auxilia* existed and twenty new regiments were created; about a dozen of these are proved by their titles to have been barbarians, Attecotti, Marcomanni, Brisigavi, Moors.

Among the new cavalry units there are five regiments named after Honorius, Constantius III and Valentinian III, and one other apparently new formation, the Mauri Felices. The others are nearly all stationed in Africa (18) and Tingitania (2). They are all junior to the Constantiani Felices, raised in 421. It seems very unlikely that all these regiments were raised *de novo* between 421 and 423, and one is tempted to believe that they are local *limitanei* upgraded during these years. This suspicion is confirmed when one notes that nearly all the units bear titles common among the *equites* of the Eastern frontier armies (Sagittarii, Scutarii, Stablesiani, Promoti), and that one, IV Sagittarii, was already stationed in Africa in 371 (Amm. XXIX. v. 20). Two of the four British *vexillationes* also, the Cataphractarii Iuniores and Stablesiani (vii. 200, 203), appear to be upgraded local *limitanei*, being recorded under the *dux Britanniarum* (xl. 21) and the *comes litoris Saxonici* (xxviii. 17).

The six surviving palatine legions have been brought up to twelve by promoting six *legiones comitatenses*. To the remaining sixteen *legiones comitatenses* three new units have been added, two Honoriani (*Occ.* v. 239, 247) and the Propugnatores Iuniores (*Occ.* v. 240). For the rest the gaps have been filled by promoted *limitanei*, some of which have been graded as *comitatenses*, others as *pseudocomitatenses*. Many of the units have not been deleted from the frontier lists, and are thus duplicated (see Table VII).

It will be seen that in Gaul the great majority of the units have been transferred from the garrisons of Armorica, Moguntiacum, Belgica, Britain, Raetia and Spain. In Illyricum four units out of six come from Noricum and Pannonia II. In Italy one unit comes from Spain, another from Raetia, and the legions I and III Iulia Alpina must have formed the garrison of an Alpine province, perhaps the mysterious Gallia Riparensis, of which fragments survive in *Occ.* xlii. 13-17; the third legion of this group has moved on to Illyricum. The six African legions are junior to the Honoriani Felices Gallicani, and yet include III Augusta, which had been in Africa since the reign of Augustus, and five others with Constantinian names; II Flavia Virtutis is recorded in an African inscription probably of fourth century date (*ILS* 9206), and Ammianus mentions First and Second legions already stationed in Africa in 371 (Amm. XXIX. v. 18). These *legiones comitatenses* are clearly the local garrison upgraded. The same applies to the Fortenses of Tripolitania, and the Constantinian legion of Tingitania.

Apart then from the *auxilia palatina*, of which a substantial number of new units were raised, the great gaps in the western *comitatus* were almost entirely filled in Honorius' reign by upgrading *limitanei*: for the most part the reinforcement was a paper change only, the local *limitanei* remaining in their old areas. The losses in cavalry in Europe were largely left unfilled: it is notable that there was no regular cavalry in Spain or Illyricum, where presumably the *comites* had to rely on federates.

It is not possible to deduce much from the Notitia of the earlier history of the *comitatus*. It is evident from the large number of units, including such crack regiments as the palatine legions of the Herculiani and Ioviani, the *auxilia palatina* of the Batavi, Bracchiati and Petulantes, and the *vexillationes* of the Comites, Promoti, Batavi and Bracchiati, which are split between East and West, that the *comitatus* was at some time deliberately halved. This probably did not happen in 395, when Stilicho returned the old Eastern troops to Arcadius (so Claudian, *in Ruf.* II. 161-2, Eoa remittat agmina, supported by the fact that there are no Theodosiani or Arcadiani in the Western army). The next possible date is 365, when the *comitatus* was divided between Valentinian and Valens (Amm. XXVI. v. 3, militares partiti numeri). Shortly after Ammianus speaks of the 'Divitenses et Tungricani Iuniores' (xxvi. vi. 12), but before that date he never mentions a double regiment except for the 'numeri Moesiacorum duo' in 360 (xx. i. 3), and they are a rather special case, for the Moesiaci would have been detachments from the two legions of one of the Moesian provinces. On the other hand Ammianus strongly implies that the Heruli and Batavi, and Celtae and Petulantes, which Julian was ordered to surrender in 360, were the only regiments of those names (xx. iv. 2).

For the reasons given elsewhere (vid. sup., pp. 52–3, 97–8 and Table VIII) it seems likely that the three most senior *legiones palatinae*, the Lanciarii, Herculiani and Ioviani, and the two most senior *vexillationes palatinae*, the Comites and Promoti, go back to Diocletian's *comitatus*, and that the most senior *auxilia palatina*, including the Cornuti and Bracchiati and Batavi, with their homonymous *vexillationes palatinae*, which rank immediately below the Comites and Promoti, go back to Constantine's.

To turn to the *limitanei*, the legions are the units which are most readily identifiable and datable. Table IX shows that of the 34 legions of the Severan army 28 survive, and of the 6 absent XX Valeria still existed under Carausius and I Minervia, VIII Augusta and XXX Ulpia survived long enough to contribute detachments to the *comitatus*. To these have been added 7 undoubtedly Diocletianic legions (I Maximiana, III Diocletiana, I and V Iovia, II, III and VI Herculia), to which may be added a missing IV Iovia (to complete the numerical sequence). There are 10 others which are very probably Diocletianic, I Illyricorum, I Ponticorum, I Noricorum, I–III Isaura, I and II Armeniaca, and IV and VI Parthica, to which may be added the lost V Parthica, the three Flavian legions in Gaul, fairly certainly raised by Constantius I as Caesar (perhaps as Augustus), and II Flavia Constantia of the Thebaid, which was probably named after him as senior Caesar, the two Augusti having a legion each already in Egypt. The six legions with Constantinian names in Africa and Tingitania may have been raised by Constantine, but it would be very odd that Maximian, who fought serious wars in Africa, should have left no legions to garrison it, and it may be that these legions were originally his, and were renamed by Alexander and Maxentius, and again by Constantine. So far we have counted 29 legions which belong with some probability to the Tetrarchy. The two Western legions named after Sol and Mars must date from before c. 320, and IV Martia and the Dianenses in the East from before 324. I and II Flavia Gemina cannot be firmly dated; they might be legions of Maximin or Licinius, renamed by Constantine, or legions of Constantine or Constantius II. The four Julian legions are presumably named after Constantine's sons, as Caesars or Augusti. There is no clue to the date of Legio Fortis. The only later additions are I and II Valentiniana and I Felix Valentis in the Thebaid.

As argued elsewhere (vid. sup. pp. 57–9) there is good reason for believing that the armies of the Eastern frontier provinces from the Thebaid to Armenia (with Isauria) and those of Britain and the Saxon shore, Spain and Tingitania remain in the Notitia much as Diocletian left them. Tables X and XI show a common basic structure of *equites* and legions, *alae* and cohorts, with certain local peculiarities, such as the *numeri* of Britain and the Saxon shore, and the remarkably uniform layout of the Eastern provinces from Palestine to Mesopotamia with their Equites Illyriciani and Indigenae: they also show the many Tetrarchic formations and the few later additions. In the Danubian province (Table XII) Raetia conforms to the Diocletianic scheme, but in the rest of the provinces this scheme is progressively overlaid, as one goes downstream, by another, which, as argued elsewhere, is probably Constantinian (vid. sup. p. 99). In the African provinces (Table XIII) there are besides the *equites* and legions (upgraded into the *comitatus*) only the *limites*, whose nature is discussed elsewhere (vid. sup. pp. 651-3). Finally in Gaul (Table XIV) there survive only scattered fragments, all (with three exceptions) labelled indiscriminately *milites*.

For the numerical calculations on pp. 680-3, Table XV, which can be checked from Tables V, VI, X–XIV, may be helpful.

TABLE I

THEODOSIAN UNITS IN THE COMITATUS

MAG. MIL. PRAES. I	MAG. MIL. PRAES. II	MAG. MIL. OR.	MAG. MIL. THRAC.	MAG. MIL. ILLYR.
vex. pal. (last) 32. Equ. Arcades	*vex. pal.* (last) 33. Equ. Theodosiani Sen.		*vex. pal.* (3 only) 25. Comites Arcadiani 26. Comites Honoriani 27. Equ. Theodosiani Iun.	
			vex. com. (last) 32. Equ. I Theodosiani	
aux. pal. (last 5) 62. Felices Honoriani Iun. 63. Victores 64. I Theodosiani 65. III Theodosiani 66. Felices Theodosiani Isauri	*aux. pal.* (last 4) 62. Felices Theodosiani 63. Felices Arcadiani Iun. 64. II Theodosiani 67. IV Theodosiani	*aux. pal.* (2 only) 36. Felices Arcadiani Sen. 37. Felices Honoriani Sen.		
		leg. com. (last) 47. I Flavia Theodosiana		
		pseudocom. (9th of 10) 57. Balistarii Theodosiani		*pseudocom.* (2nd, 7th, 8th of 9) 41. Felices Theodosiani Iun. 46. II Theodosiani 47. Balistarii Theodosiani Iun.

TABLE II
THEODOSIAN UNITS IN THE LIMITANEI

EGYPT (*or.* xxviii)

(last three above the rubric)
20. Ala Theodosiana nuper constituta
21. Ala Arcadiana nuper constituta
22. Ala II Armeniorum, Oasi Minori

THEBAID (*or.* xxxi)

(last two above the rubric)
40. Equ. Felices Honoriani, Asfynis
41. Ala I Abasgorum, Hibeos Oaseos Maioris†

(below the rubric)
55. Ala I Abasgorum, Oasi Maiore†
64. Cohors I Felix Theodosiana, apud Elephantinem

PALESTINE (*or.* xxxiv)

(last *ala*)
37. Ala Idiota constituta*

OSRHOENE (*or.* xxxv)

(last *ala*, after two cohorts)
34. Ala I Salutaria Duodecimo constituta*

MESOPOTAMIA (*or.* xxxvi)

(last Equites Illyriciani)
22. Equ. Felices Honoriani Illyriciani, Constantina

ARMENIA (*or.* xxxviii)

(last three above the rubric)
17. Ala Rizena, Aladaleariza
18. Ala Theodosiana, apud Auaxam
19. Ala Felix Theodosiana, Silvanis

(below the rubric)
25. Ala Castello Tablariensi constituta*
26. Ala I praetoria nuper constituta
32. Ala I Felix Theodosiana, Pitheae
33. Cohors I Theodosiana, Valentia

SCYTHIA (*or.* xxxix)

(last cavalry unit)
18. Cuneus equ. Arcadum, Talamonio

---

* An incomplete correction, 'nuper' having been deleted and the station inserted.

† The first (provisional) entry has not been deleted when the unit was entered in its proper place.

TABLE III

ADDITIONAL UNITS IN DISTRIBUTIO

vii.	17	Victores Sen.	*aux. pal.*	Italy
	36	Placidi Valentinianici Felices	,, ,,	,,
	73	Britones	,, ,,	Gaul
	155	Primani Iun.	*leg. com.*	Britain
	62	Catarienses	*pseudocom.*	Illyricum
	97	Balistarii	,, ,,	Gaul
	98	Defensores Iun.	,, ,,	,,
	99	Garronenses	,, ,,	,,
	100	·Anderetiani	,, ,,	,,
	101	Acincenses	,, ,,	,,
	104	Cursarienses Iun.	,, ,,	,,
	105	Musmagenses	,, ,,	,,
	107	Insidiatores	,, ,,	,,
	108	Truncensimani	,, ,,	,,
	109	Abulci	,, ,,	,,
	110	Exploratores	,, ,,	,,
	200	Equ. Catafractarii Iun.	*vex. com.*	Britain
	201	Equ. Scutarii Aureliaci	,, ,,	,,
	203	Equ. Stablesiani	,, ,,	,,
	204	Equ. Syri	,, ,,	,,

ADDITIONAL UNITS IN MAG. PED. AND MAG. EQU.

v.	183	Augustei	*aux. pal.*
	198–9	Honoriani Marcomanni Sen. *or* Iun.	,, ,,
	207	Exculcatores Iun. Britanniciani	,, ,,
	217	Felices Iun. Gallicani	,, ,,
	261	Taurunenses	*pseudo com.*
	262	Antianenses	,, ,,
vi.	75	Comites Iun.	*vex. com.*
	85	Cuneus Equ. Promotorum	,, ,,

DUPLICATED UNITS IN DISTRIBUTIO

v.	185	Victores Iun.	*aux. pal.*	vii.	{ 126	Spain	Victores Iun.
					{ 154	Britain	Victores Iun. Britanniciani
	190	Valentinianenses Iun.	*aux. pal.*		{ 61	Illyricum	Valentinianenses
					{ 71	Gaul	Valentinianenses
	241	Secunda Britannica	*leg. com.*		{ 84	Gaul	Secundani Britones
					{ 156	Britain	Secundani Iun.
	273	Septimani	*pseudo-com.*		{ 103	Gaul	Septimani Iun.
					{ 139	Tingitania	Septimani Iun.
vi.	59	Equ. Honoriani Taifali Iun.	*vex. com.*		{ 172	Gaul	Equ. Honoriani Iun.
					{ 205	Britain	Equ. Taifali
	60	Equ. Honoriani Sen.	*vex. com.*		{ 171	Gaul	Equ. Honoriani Sen.
					{ 202	Britain	Equ. Honoriani Sen.
	63	Equ. Scutarii	*vex. com.*		{ 181	Africa	Equ. Scutarii Sen.
					{ 207	Tingitania	Equ. Scutarii Sen.

TABLE IV

COMITES AND DUCES IN THE WEST

INDEX	MAG. PED. PRAES.	CHAPTERS	DISTRIBUTIO
5. Magister peditum in praesenti		v. Magister peditum praesentalis	—
6. Magister equitum in praesenti		vi. Magister equitum praesentalis	—
7. Magister equitum per Gallias		___	63, 166. Magister equitum Galliarum (*officium*, 111–117)
30. Comites rei militaris rex	126. Comites limitum infrascriptorum		
31. Italiae	127. Italiae	xxiv. Comes Italiae tractus Italiae circa Alpes (no *officium* or troops)	—
32. Africae	128. Africae	xxv. Comes Africae (*limitanei* and *officium*)	140, 179. Comes Africae
33. Tingitaniae	129. Tingitaniae	xxvi. Comes Tingitaniae (*limitanei* and *officium*)	135, 206. Comes Tingitaniae
34. Tractus Argentoratensis	130. Tractus Argentoratensis	xxvii. Comes Argentoratensis tractus Argentoratensis (no *officium* or troops)	—
35. Britanniarum	131. Britanniarum	xxix. Comes Britanniarum provincia Britannia (*officium* but no troops)	153, 199. Comes Britanniarum
36. Litoris Saxonici per Britannias	132. Litoris Saxonici per Britannias	xxviii. Comes Litoris Saxonici per Britanniam (troops and *officium*)	—
—	—	—	40. Comes Illyrici
—	—	—	118. Comes Hispaniarum

TABLE IV—*continued*

INDEX	MAG. PED. PRAES.	CHAPTERS	DISTRIBUTIO
37. Duces duodecim	133. Duces limitum infra scriptorum decem		
38. Limitis Mauretaniae Caesariensis	134. Mauretaniae Caesariensis	xxx. Dux et praeses prov. Maur. Caes.	
39. Limitis Tripolitani	135. Tripolitani	xxxi. Dux prov. Tripolitanae	
41. Pannoniae II	136. Pannoniae II	xxxii. Dux prov. Pann. II Ripariensis et Saviae	
42. Valeriae Ripensis	137. Valeriae Ripensis	xxxiii. Dux prov. Val. Rip.	
40. Pannoniae I et Norici Ripensis	138. Pannoniae I et Norici Ripensis	xxxiv. Dux prov. Pann. I et Nor. Rip.	
43. Raetiae I and II	139. Raetiae I et II	xxxv. Dux prov. Raet. I et II	
44. Sequanicae		xxxvi. Dux prov. Sequanici	
45. Tractus Armoricani et Nervicani		xxxvii. Dux tractus Arm. et Nerv.	
46. Belgicae II	140. Belgicae II	xxxviii. Dux Belgicae II	
47. Germaniae I	141. Germaniae I		
48. Britanniae	142. Britanniarum	xl. Dux Britanniarum	
49. Moguntiacensis	143. Moguntiacensis	xli. Dux Moguntiacensis	

TABLE V

EASTERN UNITS RAISED BEFORE AND AFTER 379

	BEFORE 379	AFTER 379	TOTAL	MAG. MIL. PRAES. I	MAG. MIL. PRAES. II	MAG. MIL. OR.	MAG. MIL. THRAC.	MAG. MIL. ILLYR.
vex. pal.	9	5	14	4+1 = 5	5+1 = 6	—	0+3 = 3	—
vex. com.	28	1	29	7+0 = 7	6+0 = 6	10+0 = 10	3+1 = 4	2+0 = 2
leg. pal.	13	0	13	6+0 = 6	6+0 = 6	—	—	1+0 = 1
aux. pal.	32	11	43	13+5 = 18	13+4 = 17	0+2 = 2	—	6+0 = 6
leg. com.	37	1	38	—	—	8+1 = 9	21+0 = 21	8+0 = 8
pseudocom.	8	12	20	—	0+1 = 1	8+2 = 10	—	0+9 = 9
Total	127	30	157	30+6 = 36	30+6 = 36	26+5 = 31	24+4 = 28	17+9 = 26

TABLE VI*

WESTERN UNITS RAISED BEFORE AND AFTER 395

	BEFORE 395	AFTER 395	TOTAL	ITALY	GAUL	ILLYRICUM	SPAIN	AFRICA	TINGITANIA	BRITAIN
vex. pal.	9	1	10	5+1 = 6	4+0 = 4	—	—	—	—	—
vex. com.	7	27	34	0+1 = 1	5+3 = 8	—	—	0+19 = 19	0+2 = 2	2+2 = 4
leg. pal.	12	—	12	8+0 = 8	1+0 = 1	—	—	3+0 = 3	—	—
aux. pal.	40	24	64	16+6 = 22	9+6 = 15	7+6 = 13	8+3 = 11	0+1 = 1	0+2 = 2	1+0 = 1
leg. com.	16	17	33	3+2 = 5	2+7 = 9	4+1 = 5	5+0 = 5	1+7 = 8	0+1 = 1	—
pseudocom.	—	28	28	0+2 = 2	0+21 = 21	0+4 = 4	—	—	—	—
Total	84	97	181	32+12 = 44	21+37 = 58	11+11 = 22	13+3 = 16	4+27 = 31	0+5 = 5	3+2 = 5

* In this table I have omitted the eight units which appear only in ch. v and vi (and not in vii), and have assigned the seven duplicated units in ch. vii to the first army in which they are named (see Table III).

BLE VII

LIMITANEI PROMOTED INTO THE WESTERN COMITATUS

DISTRIBUTIO	MAGISTER PEDITUM	ORIGIN OF UNITS
INTRA ITALIAM		
31. Septimani Iun.	242. Septimani Iun.	(from VII Gemina, Spain, xliii. 26)
34. I Iulia	257. I Alpina	⎱ (units from Gallia Riparensis?)
35. III Iulia	248. III Iulia Alpina	⎰
39. Pontaenenses	263. Pontinenses	(unit from Pons Aeni, Raetia)
INTRA ILLYRICUM		
58. Lanciarii Lauriacenses	259. Lanciarii Lauriacenses	(unit from Lauriacum, Noricum)
59. Lanciarii Comaginenses	260. Lanciarii Comaginenses	(unit from Comaginae, Noricum)
60. II Iulia	258. II Iulia Alpina	(unit from Gallia Riparensis?)
62. Catarienses		(unit from Moguntiacum, ILS 2626)
—	261. Taurunenses	= Aux. Ascarii, Tauruno (Pannonia II, xxxii. 43)
—	262. Antianenses	= Aux. Novensia, Antiana (Pannonia II, xxxii. 40)
INTRA GALLIAS		
84. (cf. 156) Secundani Britones	241. II Britannica	(from II Augusta, Britain, xxviii. 19)
85. Ursarienses	244. Ursarienses	= Mil. Ursarienses (Raetia, xxxv. 20)
86. Praesidienses	243. Praesichantes	= Aux. Praesidentia (Pannonai II, xxxii. 42)
87. Geminiacenses	246. Geminiacenses	(unit from Geminiacum, Belgica)
88. Cortoriacenses	245. Cortoriacenses	(unit from Cortoriacum, Belgica)
90. I Flavia Gallicana	264. I Flavia Gallicana Constantia	= Mil. I Flaviae, Constantia (Armorica, xxxvii. 20)
91. Martenses	265. Martenses	= Mil. Martenses (Armorica, xxxvii. 19)
92. Abrincateni	266. Abrincateni	= Mil. Dalmatae, Abrincatis (Armorica, xxxvii. 22)
93. Defensores Sen.	267. Defensores Sen.	= Num. Defensorum (Britain, xl. 27)
94. Mauri Osismiaci	268. Mauri Osismiaci	= Mil. Mauri Osismiaci (Armorica, xxxvii. 17)
95. I Flavia	269. I Flavia Metis	(from I Flavia, stationed at Metis, Belgica)
96. Superventores Iun.	270. Superventores Iun.	= Mil. Superventores (Armorica, xxxvii. 18)
97. Balistarii	—	= Mil. Balistarii (Moguntiacum, xli. 23)
98. Defensores Iun.	—	= Mil. Defensores (Moguntiacum, xli. 24)

(continued on p. 366)

TABLE VII—(continued)

DISTRIBUTIO	MAGISTER PEDITUM	ORIGIN OF UNITS
INTRA GALLIAS		
99. Garronenses	—	= Mil. Garronenses (Armorica, xxxvii. 15)
100. Anderetiani	—	= Mil. Anderetiani (Moguntiacum, xli. 17)
101. Acincenses	—	= Mil. Acincenses (Moguntiacum, xli. 25)
102. Cornacenses	272. Cornacenses	(unit from Cornacum, Pannonia II)
103. (cf. 139) Septimani Iun.	273. Septimani	(from VII Gemina, Spain, xliii. 26)
104. Cursarienses Iun.	—	= Mil. Ursarienses (Armorica, xxxvii. 21)
105. Musnagenses	—	—
106. Romanenses	274. Romanenses	—
107. Insidiatores	—	= Aux. Insidiatorum (Valeria, xxxiii. 50)
108. Truncensimani	—	(from XXX Ulpia of Germania I)
109. Abulci	—	= Numerus Abulcorum (Britain, xxviii. 20)
110. Exploratores	—	= Numerus Exploratorum (Britain, xxxiii. 21)
INTRA TINGITANIAM		
138. Constantiniani	271. Constantiaci	(from an African legion)
139. (cf.103) Septimani Iun.	—	(from VII Gemina, Spain)
INTRA AFRICAM		
146. Primani	249. I Flavia Pacis	⎫
147. Secundani	250. II Flavia Virtutis	⎪
148. Tertiani	251. III Flavia Salutis	⎬ (African legions)
149. Constantiniani	252. Flavia Victrix Constantina	⎪
150. Constantiaci	253. II Flavia Constantiniana	⎪
151. Tertio Augustani	254. Tertio Augustani	⎭
152. Fortenses	255. Fortenses	= Mil. Fortenses (Tripolitania, xxxi. 29)
INTRA BRITANNIAS		
155. Primani Iun.	—	(from I Adiutrix, Valeria, or I Noricorum, Noricum, or I Minervia?)
156. (cf. 84) Secundani Iun.	—	(from II Augusta, Britain, xxvii. 19)

TABLE VIII

SENIOR PALATINE REGIMENTS

MAG. PED. OCC.	MAG. MIL. PRAES. I OR.	MAG. MIL. PRAES. II OR.
legiones	*legiones*	*legiones*
145. *Ioviani Sen.*	42. *Lanciarii Sen.*	
146. *Herculiani Sen.*	43. *Ioviani Iun.*	
147. Divitenses Sen.	44. *Herculiani Iun.*	
148. Tungricani Sen.		
auxilia	*auxilia*	*auxilia*
158. Cornuti Sen.	49. Batavi Sen.	49. Regii
159. Brachiati Sen.	50. Brachiati Iun.	50. Cornuti
160. Petulantes Sen.	51. Salii	51. Tubantes
161. Celtae Sen.	52. Constantiani	52. Constantiniani
162. Heruli Sen.	53. Mattiaci Sen.	53. Mattiaci Iun.
163. Batavi Sen.		
164. Mattiaci Sen.		
165. Mattiaci Iun.		
MAG. EQU. OCC.		
vexillationes	*vexillationes*	*vexillationes*
43. *Comites Sen.*	28. *Equ. Promoti Sen.*	27. *Comites Sen.*
44. *Equ. Promoti Sen.*		28. Equ. Brachiati Iun.
45. Equ. Brachiati Sen.		29. Equ. Batavi Iun.
46. Equ. Batavi Sen.		
47. Equ. Cornuti Sen.		
48. Equ. Cornuti Iun.		

Note: Units which probably belonged to Diocletian's *comitatus* are italicised. The remainder may have formed part of Constantine's early *comitatus*.

TABLE IX

THE SEVERAN ARMY		THE NOTITIA DIGNITATUM					
Province	Legion	Commander	Legion	Station	Legions or detachments in the *comitatus*	Army group	Reference
Cyrenaica	none	dux Libyarum (*or.* xxx)	(page missing)	(page missing)			
Aegyptus	II Traiana	comes limitis Aegypti (*or.* xxviii)	II Traiana	Parembole (19)			
			III Diocletiana	Andropolis (18)			
			V Macedonica[1]	Memphis (14)			
			XIII Gemina[1]	Babylon (15)			
		dux Thebaidos (*or.* xxxi)	III Diocletiana[2]	Ombi (31) / Praesentia (33) / Thebae (38)	III Diocletiana Thebaeorum (com.)	Thracia	*or.* viii. 37
			II Flavia Constantia	Cusae (32)	II Flavia Constantia Thebaeorum (com.)	Oriens	*or.* vii. 45
			II Traiana[2]	Apollinopolis (34)			
			I Valentiniana	Coptos (36)	I Maximiana Thebaeorum (com.)	Thracia	*or.* viii. 36
			I Maximiana	Philae (37)			
			II Valentiniana	Hermonthis (39)	II Felix Valentis Thebaeorum (com.)	Oriens	*or.* vii. 46
					Thebaei (com.)	Italia	*occ.* vii. 29 (v. 154)

Province		dux (or.)			Oriens
Palaestina	X Fretensis VI Ferrata	dux Palaestinae (or. xxxiv)	X Fretensis[3]	Aila (30) —	
Arabia	III Cyrenaica	dux Arabiae (or. xxxvii)	III Cyrenaica IV Martia	Bostra (21) Betthoro (22)	
Phoenice	III Gallica	dux Phoenicis (or. xxxii)	III Gallica[4] I Illyricorum[4]	Danaba (30) Palmyra (31)	
Syria	IV Scythia XVI Flavia Firma	dux Syriae et Euphratensis (or. xxxiii)	IV Scythica XVI Flavia Firma	Oresa (23) Sura (28)	
Mesopotamia	I Parthica	dux Mesopotamiae (or. xxxvi)	I Parthica II Parthica[5]	Constantina (29) Cefa (30)	IV Italica (ps.) I Armeniaca (ps.) II Armeniaca (ps.) VI Parthica (ps.) } Oriens[6] or. vii. 49, 50, 54–5
	III Parthica	dux Osrhoenae (or. xxxv)	[III Parthica] IV Parthica	[Apatna] (25) Circesium (24)	
	IV Italica(?)	—	—	—	
Cappadocia	XV Apollinaris XII Fulminata	dux Armeniae (or. xxxviii)	XV Apollinaris XII Fulminata I Pontica[7]	Satala (13) Melitene (14) Trapezus (16)	

[1] Detachments from Dacia (q.v.).

[2] Detachments from Egypt (q.v.).

[3] A detachment of X Fretensis was destroyed in 359 at Amida (Amm. xviii. ix. 3, xix. viii).

[4] These two legions sent a vexillation to Egypt in 315–23 (ILS 8882).

[5] II Parthica was stationed in Italy under the Severi.

[6] These units were probably the garrison of Diocletian's Transtigritane conquests. V Parthica was destroyed in 359 (Amm. xviii. ix. 3, xix. viii) at Amida.

[7] Recorded at Trapezus under the tetrarchy (ILS 639).

TABLE IX—*continued*

| THE SEVERAN ARMY | | THE NOTITIA DIGNITATUM | | | | | |
Province	Legion	Commander	Legion	Station	Legions or detachments in the *comitatus*	Army group	Reference
Galatia	none	comes per Isauriam (*or.* xxix)	— II Isaura III Isaura	— —[8] —[8]	I Isaura Sagittaria (ps.)[8]	Oriens	*or.* vii. 56
Moesia Inferior		dux Scythiae (*or.* xxxix)	I Iovia	Noviodunum (32, 33) Aegissus (34) Platypegiae (35) Troesmis (29, 31)	Ioviani Sen. (pal.)[9]	Italia	*occ.* vii. 3 (v. 145)
			II Herculia	Axiupolis (30) Platypegiae (35)	Ioviani Iun. (pal.)[9] Herculiani Sen. (pal.)[9]	Praes. Or. Italia	*or.* v. 43 *occ.* vii. 4 (v. 146)
					Herculiani Iun. (pal.)[9]	Praes. Or.	*or.* v. 44
	I Italica	dux Moesiae II (*or.* xl)	I Italica	Novae (30, 31) Sexagintaprista (32)	I Italica (ps.) Primani (pal.)	Oriens Praes. Or.	*or.* vii. 53 *or.* vi. 45
	XI Claudia		XI Claudia	Durostorum (33) Transmarisca (34, 35)	Undecimani (pal.)	Praes. Or.	*or.* vi. 46
					Undecimani (com.)	Hispania	*occ.* vii. 134 (v. 234)
Moesia Superior	IV Flavia	dux Moesiae I (*or.* xli)	IV Flavia	Singidunum (30)	Moesiaci Sen. (pal.)[10]	Italia	*occ.* vii. 8 (v. 150)
	VII Claudia		VII Claudia	Viminacium (31) Cuppi (32)			

Region	Legion	Command (dux)	Legion (N.D.)	Forts / stations	Comitatensian unit	Region (army)	Reference
Dacia	V Macedonica	dux Daciae Ripensis (or. xlii)	V Macedonica[11]	Variana (31), Cebrus (32), Oescus (33), Sucidava (39), Aegeta (34), Transdrobeta (35), Burgus Novus (36), Zernae (37), Ratiaria (38)	V Macedonica (com.)	Oriens	or. vii. 39
	XIII Gemina		XIII Gemina[11]		Tertiodecimani (com.)	Thracia	or. viii. 38
		dux Pannoniae II Ripariensis et Saviae (occ. xxxii)	V Iovia[12]	Bononia (44), Burgenae (46), Onagrinum (48), AureusMons (45), Teutiborgium (47), Onagrinum (48)			
			VI Herculia[12]				
Pannonia inferior	I Adiutrix	dux Valeriae Ripensis (occ. xxxiii)	I Adiutrix	Brigetio (51)	Primani Iun.[13]	Britannia	occ. vii. 155
	II Adiutrix		II Adiutrix	Alisca (52), Florentia (53), Acincum (54), Tautantum (55), Cirpus (56), Lussonium (57)	Pannoniciani Sen. (pal.)[14]	Italia	occ. vii. 7 (v. 149)
					Pannoniciani Iun. (com.)[14]	Thracia	or. viii. 48
					Secundani (com.)[13]	Illyricum Or.	or. ix. 35

[8] There were three legions in Isauria in 353 (Amm. xiv. ii. 14).

[9] These detachments (or some of them) might also come from V Iovia and VI Herculia of Pannonia II (q.v.) or from III Herculia (Com. Illyr. Occ, Occ, Occ. v. 238 = vii. 54) and a presumed IV Iovia.

[10] Ammianus (xx. i. 3) mentions two numeri Moesiacorum in 360.

[11] There are detachments of both legions in Egypt (q.v.).

[12] See n. 9.

[13] These detachments may come from other First and Second legions.

[14] These detachments may come from Pannonia Superior.

TABLE IX—continued

THE SEVERAN ARMY		THE NOTITIA DIGNITATUM					
Province	Legion	Commander	Legion	Station	Legions or detachments in the comitatus	Army group	Reference
Pannonia Superior	X Gemina	dux Pannoniae I et Norici Ripensis (*occ.* xxxiv)	X Gemina	Vindobona (25) Arrabona (27)	X Gemina (com.)	Oriens	*or.* vii. 42
	XIV Gemina		XIV Gemina	Carnuntum (26) Arrabona (27)	Quartodecimani (com.)	Thracia	*or.* viii. 39
Noricum	II Italica		II Italica	Ioviacum (37) Lentia (38) Lauriacum (39) Adiuvense (40) Favianae (41)	Secundi Italiciani (com.)	Africa	*occ.* vii. 144 (v. 235)
			I Noricorum				
Raetia	III Italica	dux Raetiae I et II (*occ.* xxxv)	III Italica	Vallatum (17) Submuntorium (18) Cambodunum (19) Foetes (21) Terioli (22)	III Italica (com.)	Illyricum Occ.	*occ.* vii. 53 (v. 237)

Province	Legion	Command (dux)		Station	Field-army unit	Province	Reference
ania ior	I Minervia	dux Sequanici occ. xxxvi / dux Moguntiacensis (occ. xli)	II Flavia	Vangiones (20)	Minervii (com.)	Illyricum Or.	or. ix. 37
					Germaniciani Sen.[15] (com.)	Illyricum Or.	or. ix. 34
	XXX Ulpia		—	—	Truncensimani(ps.)[16]	Gallia	occ. vii. 108
ca	none	dux Belgicae II (occ. xxxviii)	—	—	I Flavia Mettis (ps.)[17]	Gallia	occ. vii. 95 (v. 269)
lunensis	none	dux Tractus Armoricani (occ. xxxvii)	I Flavia	Constantia (20)	I Flavia Constantia (com.)[18]	Oriens	or. vii. 44
					I Flavia Gallicana Constantia[18] (ps.)	Gallia	occ. vii. 90 (v. 264)
nania ior	VIII Augusta		—	—	Octavani (pal.)	Italia	occ. vii. 28 (v. 153)
	XXII Primigenia		— —		II Britannica (com.)	Gallia	occ. vii. 84 (v. 241)
unnia rior	II Augusta	comes litoris Saxonici (occ. xxviii)	II Augusta	Rutupiae (19)	Secundani Iun.	Britannia	occ. vii. 156
annia rior	XX Valeria Victrix[19] VI Victrix	dux Britanniarum (occ. xl)	— VI	— (18)			

[15] ...is detachment may come from Germania [superio]r.

[16] ...detachment of XXX was destroyed in 359 [at Am]ida (Amm. XVIII. ix. 3, XIX. viii).

[17] This legion is distinguished by its station, Mettis in Belgica I.

[18] This legion is distinguished by its station, Constantia in Lugdunensis II. The two entries under Armorica and among the pseudocom. of Gaul are probably duplicates.

[19] Last recorded on the coinage of Carausius.

TABLE IX—*continued*

THE SEVERAN ARMY			THE NOTITIA DIGNITATUM				
Province	Legion	Commander	Legion	Station	Legions or detachments in the comitatus	Army group	Reference
Hispania	VII Gemina	praepositura magistri peditum (*occ.* xlii)	VII Gemina	Legio (26)	VII Gemina (com.) Septimani Sen. (com.) Septimani Iun. (com.) Septimani Iun. (ps.)	Oriens Hispania Italia { Gallia Tingitania	*or.* vii. 41 *occ.* vii. 132 (v. 228) *occ.* vii. 31 (v. 242) *occ.* vii. 103, 139 (v. 273)
Mauretania Tingitana	none	comes Tingitaniae (*occ.* xxvi)	—	—	Constantiaci *or* Constantiniani (ps.)	Tingitania	*occ.* vii. 138 (v. 271)
Mauretania Caesariensis	none	dux Mauritaniae Caesariensis (*occ.* xxx)	—	—	I Flavia Pacis[20] II Flavia Virtutis	} Africa	*occ.* vii. 146–51 (v. 249–54)
Africa	none	dux Tripolitanae (*occ.* xxxi)	—	—	III Flavia Salutis		
Numidia	III Augusta	comes Africae (*occ.* xxv)	—	—	Flavia Victrix Constantina II Flavia Constantiniana Tertio Augustani		

[20] The Milites Pacenses under the dux Mogentiacensis (*occ.* xli, 5) and the Numerus Pacensium under the dux Britanniarum (*occ.* xl. 29) are perhaps detachments of I Flavia Pacis.

To judge by their numeration and titles the following legions of the *comitatus* may also have belonged to the frontier army of the early fourth century:

1. III Herculia	*com.*	Illyr. occ.	(*occ.* v. 238 = vii. 54)
2. I Flavia Gemina	*com.*	Thrac.	(*or.* viii. 40)
3. II Flavia Gemina	*com.*	Thrac.	(*or.* viii. 41)
4. Iulia Alexandria	*com.*	Thrac.	(*or.* viii. 51)
5. I Iulia Alpina	*pseud.*	Ital.	(*occ.* v. 257 = vii. 34)
6. II Iulia Alpina	*pseud.*	Illyr. occ.	(*occ.* v. 258 = vii. 60)
7. III Iulia Alpina	*com.*	Ital.	(*occ.* v. 248 = vii. 35)
8. I Martiorum	*com.*	Illyr. or.	(*or.* ix. 32, *ILS* 775)
9. Solenses Seniores	*com.*	Thrac.	(*or.* viii. 34)
Solenses Gallicani	*com.*	Thrac.	(*or.* viii. 50)
10. Dianenses	*com.*	Illyr. or.	(*or.* ix. 33)
	pal.	praes. or.	(*or.* v. 45)
11. Fortenses	*com.*	Hispania	(*occ.* v. 225 = vii. 130)
	com.	Africa	(*occ.* v. 255 = vii. 152)

No. 1 should be one of a pair (III Herculia, IV Iovia), filling the gap between I Iovia and II Herculia of Scythia and V Iovia and VI Herculia of Pannonia II; they perhaps belonged to Sequanica. Nos. 2 and 3 might be detachments from a pair of legions stationed in some province, probably Eastern; Cyrenaica is a possibility. No. 4's title suggests that it came from Egypt. For Nos. 5–7 see above p. 356. There are tile stamps of the third century in Upper Germany of LEG I MR (*CIL* XIII. 12105–11) and No. 8 is probably this legion or a detachment of it (cf. the Milites Martenses of the dux Moguntiacensis (*occ.* xli. 19) and of the dux Armoricae (*occ.* xxxvi. 19)). No. 9 (cf. *occ.* xl. 28, Numerus Solensium in Britain) looks like a detachment from a legion named after Sol, Constantine's favourite god in his pagan days, and No. 10 with its pagan name must have been raised before 324. No. 11 (cf. *occ.* xxxi. 29, milites Fortenses at Lepcis in Tripolitania, perhaps the parent legion) also has a name of early style.

TABLE X
THE EASTERN FRONTIER

PRO-VINCE	EQUITES ILLYRICIANI				EQUITES INDIGENAE		OTHER EQUITES	LEGIO-NES	ALAE	COHOR-TES	THEO-DOSIAN ADDI-TIONS
	DAL-MATAE	PRO-MOTI	SCUTA-RII	MAU-RI	PRO-MOTI	SAGIT-TARII					
Palestine (or. xxxiv)	1	1	1	1	2	4	2	1	5^1	11^2	1 *ala*
Arabia (or. xxxvii)	1	1	1	1	2	2	—	2	6^3	5	—
Phoenice (or. xxxii)	1	1	1	1	2	4	2	2	7^4	5^5	—
Syria (or. xxxiii)	1	1	1	1	2	4	—	1	2^6	4^7	—
Osrhoene (or. xxxv)	1	1	—	1	2	4	—	2	5^8	2	1 *ala*
Mesopotamia (or. xxxvi)	—	1	1	—	2	4	1	2	3^9	2^{10}	1 *equites*

[1] Constantiana, Valentiana.   [2] Valeria, Flavia, Gratiana.   [3] Constantiana, Valentiana, Valentiniana.   [4] Diocletiana.   [5] Herculia.   [6] Herculia.
[7] Valeria.   [8] Valeria, Diocletiana.   [9] two Flaviae.   [10] Valeria.

TABLE XI
OTHER ARMIES OF EARLY TYPE

PROVINCE	CUNEI EQUITUM	EQUITES	LEGIONES	ALAE	COHORTES	NUMERI	MILITES	THEODOSIAN ADDITIONS
Armenia (*or.* xxxviii)	—	2	3	6	9[1]	—	—	5 *alae* / 1 *cohors*
Egypt (*or.* xxviii)	—	2	4[2]	13[3]	9	—	—	3 *alae*
Thebais (*or.* xxxi)	2	6	8[4]	14[5]	10	—	1	1 *equites* / 1 *ala*
Britain (*occ.* xl) per lineam valli	1	—	—	5[6]	16	1	—	—
others	—	3[7]	1	—	—	10	—	—
Litus Saxonicum (*occ.* xxviii)	—	2	1	—	1	4	1	—
Spain (*occ.* xlii)	—	—	1	—	5[8]	—	—	—
Tingitania (*occ.* xxvi)	—	—	—	1[9]	7[10]	—	—	—

[1] Valentiana.   [2] Diocletiana.   [3] Herculia.   [4] Diocletiana, Maximiana, Flavia Constantia, I and II Valentiniana.   [5] Iovia, two Herculiae, Valeria.
[6] Herculia.   [7] Crispiani.   [8] Flavia.   [9] Herculia.   [10] Herculia.

TABLE XII

THE DANUBIAN FRONTIER

PROVINCE	CUNEI EQUITUM	EQUITES	AUXILIA	LEGIONES	CLASSES	ALAE	COHORTES	OTHERS
Scythia (or. xxxix)	7[1]	—	8[2]	7[3]	1	—	—	—
Moesia II (or. xl)	7	—	10[4]	6	1	—	3[5]	—
Moesia I (or. xli)	8[6]	—	8[7]	3	2	—	—	5 milites
Dacia (or. xlii)	9[8]	—	6	9	2	—	2	1 milites
Pannonia II (occ. xxxii)	6[9]	11	5	5[10]	5[11]	1	4[12]	1 milites
Valeria (occ. xxxiii)	5[13]	17[14]	5	8	1	—	6	—
Pannonia I (occ. xxxiv)	2	14	—	8	3	—	5	1 gens
Raetia (occ. xxxv)	—	3	—	5	—	3[15]	7[16]	1 milites 1 gens 1 numerus

[1] Arcades. [2] Constantini, two Constantiani, Gratianenses. [3] Herculia, Iovia. [4] Constantini, Constantiniani, [5] Valeria. [6] Constantiani, [7] Gratianenses [8] Constantiniani. [9] Constantiani, Constantes. [10] Iovia, Herculia. [11] two Flaviae. [12] Iovia. [13] Constantiani. [14] Flavianenses. [15] two Valeriae, Flavia. [16] three Valeriae, three Herculiae.

TABLE XIII
GAUL

PROVINCE	MILITES	EQUITES	CLASSES	COHORTES
Armorica (*occ.* xxxvii)	9*	—	—	1
Moguntiacensis (*occ.* xli)	11*	—	—	—
Belgica II (*occ.* xxxviii)	1	1	1	—
Sequanica (*occ.* xxxvi)	1	—	—	—

* Including one legion.

TABLE XIV
AFRICA

PROVINCE	LIMITES	MILITES
Africa (*occ.* xxv)	16	—
Mauretania (*occ.* xxx)	8	—
Tripolitania (*occ.* xxxi)	12	2

Note: There are also in *occ.* xlii eight *classes*, two *milites* and two cohorts in Italy and Gaul.

TABLE XV
NUMBERS

EASTERN COMITATUS

vex. pal.	14 × 500 =	7,000
vex. com.	29 × 500 =	14,500
leg. pal.	13 × 1,000 =	13,000
aux. pal.	43 × 500 =	21,500
leg. com.	38 × 1,000 =	38,000
pseudocom.	20 × 500 =	10,000
	Total	104,000

WESTERN COMITATUS

vex. pal.	10 × 500 =	5,000
vex. com.	34 × 500 =	17,000
leg. pal.	12 × 1,000 =	12,000
aux. pal.	64 × 500 =	32,000
leg. com.	33 × 1,000 =	33,000
pseudocom.	28 × 500 =	14,000
	Total	113,000

TABLE XV—*continued*

EASTERN LIMITANEI

Province	Legions × 3,000	Other units × 500	Total
Libya	2?	20?	16,000?
Egypt	2 + 2[1]	27	21,500
Thebaid	2 + 2[2]	35[3]	26,000
Palestine	1	29[4]	18,500
Arabia	2	19[5]	17,000
Phoenice	2	24	18,000
Syria	1	16	11,000
Osrhoene	2	17	14,500
Mesopotamia	2	15	13,500
Armenia	3	23[6]	22,000
Isauria	2	—	6,000
Scythia	2	16	14,000
Moesia II	2	21	16,500
Moesia I	2	23	17,500
Dacia	2	20	16,000
Total	29 + 4	305	248,000

[1] V Macedonica and XIII Gemina are reckoned at only 1,000 each.
[2] I and II Valentiniana are reckoned at only 1,000 each. Four detachments of Egyptian legions are omitted.
[3] Including one unit of 1,000 (no. 35).
[4] Including two *alae miliariae* (nos. 32, 36).
[5] Including two *alae* and one *cohors miliariae* (nos. 25, 28, 31).
[6] Including three *cohortes miliariae* (nos. 27, 29, 30).

WESTERN LIMITANEI

Province	Legions × 3000	Other units × 500	Total
Britain	1	36	21,000
Saxon Shore	1	8	7,000
Spain	1	5	5,500
Tingitania	—	8	4,000
Tripolitania	1	1	3,500
Pannonia II	2	33	22,500
Valeria	2	34	23,000
Pannonia I	4	25	24,500
Raetia	1	16	11,000
Sequanica	—	1	500
Moguntiacum	1	10	8,000
Belgica II	—	3	1,500
Armorica	1	9	7,500
Misc.	—	12	6,000
Total	15	201	145,000
Deduct duplicated units	—	20	10,000
Revised total	15	181	135,000

APPENDIX III

DIOCESES AND PROVINCES

In the table which follows I have set forth the main evidence for the diocesan and provincial structure of the empire from the Severi to the sixth century. The principal authorities are as follows:

(1) The Verona list, published by Mommsen (*Ges. Schr.* v. 561–88) and Seeck (in his edition of the Notitia Dignitatum). It seems to be, apart from a few later glosses and textual errors, an accurate account of the empire as it was between 312 and 314 (see Ch. II, n. 9).

(2) Festus's Breviarium. He dedicated it to Valens, and wrote it before 368, since he does not know of the new British province of Valentia.

(3) Ammianus's geographical excursuses. He published his history c. 391–5, but reproduced older material in these surveys (see Mommsen, *Ges. Schr.* VI. 393–425).

(4) The conciliar lists of the fourth century. That of Nicaea (325, covering the Eastern parts only) is reconstructed by Gelzer, *Patrum Nicaenorum Nomina* (Teubner), those of Sardica (343–4) have been collated by Feder (*Sb. Ak. Wien*, CLXVI (1910), no. v), that of Constantinople (381, covering the Eastern parts only) is printed in Mansi, III. 568–72. The lists as a whole conform to the contemporary secular provinces, and are of particular value since they show which cities belonged to each province.

(5) The Notitia Dignitatum. I would date the document basically to c. 408, with later revisions in the West down to 423 (see Appendix II).

(6) The Notitia Galliarum (printed in Seeck's edition of the Notitia Dignitatum). It conforms exactly to the Notitia Dignitatum, and is of a high value as listing the cities of each province.

(7) Polemius Silvius. He wrote in 448, but used out-of-date and inaccurate material for Illyricum and the East (Mommsen, *Ges. Schr.* VII. 633–67, *Chron. Min.* I. 532–42; text also in Seeck's Notitia Dignitatum).

(8) The conciliar lists of the Council of Chalcedon (451) and the Epistles of Leo (457). For the areas which they cover (Dacia, Macedonia, Thrace, Asiana, Pontica, Oriens, Egypt) they correspond very closely to the Notitia Dignitatum and give us lists of the cities in each province. The evidence is assembled by Schwartz in *A.C.Oec.* II. vi. 105–11.

(9) The Synecdemus of Hierocles (Teubner and E. Honigmann, *Le Synekdémus d'Hiérocles et l'opusculum géographique de Georges de Chypre*, Brussels, 1939, with full commentary). I have discussed the date of this list (which gives the cities of each province and the title of the governors for the Eastern empire) in my *Cities of the Eastern Roman Provinces*, 502–3, and still believe that it was based on a document of the latter part of Theodosius II's reign, with some later revision.

(10) The schedule to Just. *Nov.* viii, 535. It gives civil governors (graded by rank) for the provinces of the praetorian prefecture of the East.

(11) Georgius Cyprius (Teubner and Honigmann, op. cit.). This list, covering the dioceses of Oriens and Egypt only, resembles that of Hierocles (but omits the titles of governors). I have discussed its date in my *Cities*, 503–4; it falls in my opinion at the beginning of Justinian's reign.

(12) *CJ* I. xxvii. 1 (for Africa) and Justinian's later Novels.

DIOCESES AND PROVINCES
THE WESTERN PARTS

Severan provinces	THE VERONA LIST		NOTITIA DIGNITATUM					
	dioceses	provinces	dioceses	provinces	govs.	vicarii, etc.	rationales summarum	rationales sui privatae
Britannia Sup.	1 Britanniae	Britannia I	Britanniae	Britannia I	praes.	vicarius Britanniarum	Britanniarum	per Britannias
		Maxima Caesariensis		Maxima Caesariensis	cons.			
Britannia Inf.		Britannia II		Britannia II	praes.			
		Flavia Caesariensis		Flavia Caesariensis	praes.			
				Valentia	cons.			
Belgica	2	Belgica I		Belgica I	cons.		Galliarum	per Gallias
		Belgica II		Belgica II	cons.			
Germania Sup.		Sequania		Maxima Sequanorum	praes.			
Germania Inf.		Germania I		Germania I	cons.			
Lugdunensis		Germania II		Germania II	cons.			
	Galliae	Lugdunensis I		Lugdunensis I	cons.			
		Lugdunensis II		Lugdunensis II	praes.			
				Lugdunensis III	praes.			
				Lugdunensis Senonia	praes.			
Alpes Graiae		Alpes Graiae et Poeninae		Alpes Poeninae et Graiae	praes.			
Narbonensis	3 Viennensis	Viennensis	Septem Provinciae	Viennensis	cons.	vicarius Septem Provinciarum	Quinque Provinciarum	per Quinque Provincias
		Narbonensis I		Narbonensis I	praes.			
		Narbonensis II		Narbonensis II	praes.			
		Novempopuli		Novempopulana	praes.			
Aquitania		Aquitanica I		Aquitanica I	praes.			
		Aquitanica II		Aquitanica II	praes.			
Alpes Maritimae		Alpes Maritimae		Alpes Maritimae	praes.			

Baetica	4	Baetica	Hispaniae	Baetica	cons.	vicarius Hispaniarum	Hispaniae	per Hispanias
Lusitania		Lusitania		Lusitania	cons.			
Tarraconensis	Hispaniae	Carthaginiensis		Carthaginiensis	praes.			
		Tarraconensis		Tarraconensis	praes.			
		Callaecia		Callaecia	cons.			
Mauretania Tingitana		Mauretania Tingitania		Tingitania	praes.			
				Insulae Balearum	praes.			
Africa	5	Proconsularis Zeugitana	Africa	Africa	proc.	proconsul	Africae	per Africam
	Africa	Byzacena (Tripolit)ana		Byzacium	cons.			
				Tripolitania	praes.			
Numidia		Numidia Cirtensis		Numidia	cons.	vicarius Africae	Numidiae	
		Numidia Militiana						
Mauretania Caesarensis		Mauretania Caesariensis		Mauretania Caesariensis	dux et praes.			
		Mauretania Tabia (?)		Mauretania Sitifensis	praes.			

[1] Festus agrees with the Verona list; Polemius with the Notitia. Valentia was created in 369 (Amm. xxviii. iii. 7).

[2] Festus and Ammianus (xv. xi) agree with the Verona list; Polemius and the Notitia Galliarum (which distinguishes this diocese as Provinciae Gallicanae) agree with the Notitia.

[3] Ammianus (xv. xi; cf. xvii. i. 4, xxii. i. 2), Hilary (*de synodis*, proem) and Festus give one Narbonensis only; the two provinces reappear first in 381 (Mansi, iii. 615). Ammianus and Hilary also record one Aquitanica only, but Festus gives two. Polemius and the Notitia Galliarum (which calls this diocese Septem Provinciae) agree with the Notitia.

[4] Festus agrees with the Verona list; Polemius with the Notitia. Justinian (*CJ* i. xxvii. i, 534) joined Tingitania (under a consular) to Africa.

[5] The last items of the Verona list, Mauretania Tabia Insidiana, are corrupt, and probably refer to Sitifensis and Tripolitana. Festus and Polemius both agree with the Notitia. Justinian (*CJ* i. xxvii. i, 534) put Proconsularis, Byzacium and Tripolitania under consulars, and Numidia and Mauretania (one province) under *praesides*.

DIOCESES AND PROVINCES
THE WESTERN PARTS—continued

Severan provinces	THE VERONA LIST		NOTITIA DIGNITATUM					
	dioceses	provinces	dioceses	provinces	govs.	vicarii, etc.	rationales summarum	rationales rei privatae
Alpes Cottiae Raetia	6	Alpes Cottiae Raetia		Alpes Cottiae	praes.	vicarius Italiae	Italiae	per Italiam
				Raetia I	praes.			
				Raetia II	praes.			
		Venetia Histria		Venetia et Histria	cons.			
		Flaminia		Flaminia et Picenum Annonarium	cons.			
		—		Aemilia	cons.			
		—		Liguria	cons.			
(Italia)	Italia	Tuscia Umbria	Italia	Tuscia et Umbria	cons.	vicarius urbis Romae	urbis Romae	per urbem Romam et suburbicariam regionem
		Picenum		Picenum Suburbicarium	cons.			
		—		Campania	cons.			
		Apulia Calabria		Samnium	praes.			
		Lucania		Apulia et Calabria	corr.			
		—		Bruttii et Lucania	corr.			
				Valeria	praes.			
Sicilia		—		Sicilia	cons.		Trium Provinciarum	per Siciliam
Sardinia Corsica		—		Sardinia	praes.			
		Corsica		Corsica	praes.			

Noricum Pannonia Sup.	7		Noricum Ripariense Noricum Mediterraneum Pannonia Superior Valeria	Noricum Ripense Noricum Mediterraneum Pannonia I	praes. praes. praes.	Pannoniae I Valeriae et Norici Med. et Rip.	per Illyricum
Pannonia Inf. Dalmatia	Pannonia	Illyricum	Pannonia Inferior Savensis Dalmatia	Pannonia II Savia Dalmatia	cons. corr. praes.	Pannoniae II Dalmatiae et Saviae	

⁶ The Verona list is very defective. The heading runs: 'dioecensis Italiciana habet provincias numero xvi', but there follow only the nine provinces given in the table. The old provinces of Sicily and Sardinia can certainly be restored, and also Campania, attested in the late third century (CIL vi. 1418, x. 304, 6084). The list of provinces given in SHA, Triginta Tyranni, 24, Campania, Samnium, Lucania Bruttii, Apulia Calabria, Etruria atque Umbria, Picenum et Flaminia, probably refers to the position in the late third or early fourth century, and adds Samnium, but excludes Valeria. In the north Aemilia is recorded in 321 (CTh iv. xiii. 1). Liguria was in 332 (CTb xi. xvi. 2, cf. CIL x. 1125) united with Aemilia, but may have been separate earlier. This gives only fifteen unless Raetia was already divided, but the number xvi may well be corrupt or a miscount by the scribe. The Notitia Dignitatum wrongly retains Valeria. It is correctly omitted by Polemius, who otherwise agrees with the Notitia (see p. 351). Justinian attached Sardinia (under a praeses) to Africa (CJ i. xxvii. 1, 543), and placed Sicily under a praetor directly responsible to Constantinople (Just. Nov. civ, 537).

⁷ The Notitia wrongly omits Valeria. It is recorded by Festus and Polemius, who otherwise agree with the Notitia. Pannonia II is recorded by Hierocles in the diocese of Dacia.

DIOCESES AND PROVINCES
THE EASTERN PARTS

Severan provinces	THE VERONA LIST		NOTITIA DIGNITATUM				Hierocles	Justinian, *Nov.* viii	
	dioceses	provinces	dioceses	provinces	govs.	vicarii, etc.		provinces	govs.
Moesia Sup.	8	Praevalitana	Dacia	Praevalitana	praes.		praes.		
		Dardania		Dardania	praes.		praes.		
		Moesia Superior Margensis		Moesia I	praes.		praes.		
		Dacia		Dacia Ripensis	praes.		cons.		
				Dacia Mediterranea	cons.		cons.		
Macedonia	Moesiae	Macedonia	Macedonia	Macedonia	cons.		cons.		
				Macedonia Salutaris	praes.		praes.		
Epirus		Epirus Nova		Epirus Nova	praes.	vicarius Macedoniae	cons.		
		Epirus Vetus		Epirus Vetus	praes.		praes.		
		Thessalia		Thessalia	praes.		praes.		
Achaia		—		Achaia	proc.		proc.		
Creta (with Cyrene)		Creta		Creta	cons.		cons.		
Moesia Inf.	9	Moesia Inferior	Thracia	Moesia II	praes.		praes.	Moesia II	praes.
		Scythia		Scythia	praes.	vicarius Thraciarum	praes.	Scythia	praes.
		Thracia		Thracia	cons.		cons.	Thracia	cons.
Thracia	Thracia	Rhodope		Rhodope	praes.		praes.	Rhodope	cons.
		Haemimontus		Haemimontus	praes.		cons.	Haemimontus	cons.
		Europa		Europa	cons.		cons.	Europa	cons.

Diocese (Verona)	Verona list (10)	Province	Rank	Province	proconsul Asiae / vicarius Asianae	Rank	Province	Rank
Asia	Asia / Hellespontus	Asia / Hellespontus	proc. cons.	Asia / Hellespontus	proconsul Asiae	proc. cons.	Asia / Hellespontus	proc. cons.
	Insulae	Insulae	praes.	Insulae		praes.	Insulae	praes.
	Lydia	Lydia	cons.	Lydia		cons.	Lydia	cons.
	Caria	Caria	praes.	Caria		cons.	Caria	cons.
Asiana	Phrygia I	Phrygia Pacatiana	praes.	Phrygia Pacatiana	vicarius Asianae	cons.	Phrygia Pac.	comes
	Phrygia II	Phrygia Salutaris	cons.	Phrygia Salutaris		cons.	Phrygia Sal.	cons.
	Pamphylia	Pamphylia	praes.	Pamphylia		cons.	Pamphylia	cons.
		Lycia	praes.	Lycia		cons.	Lycia	cons.
Lycia Pamphylia	Pisidia	Pisidia	praes.	Pisidia		cons.	Pisidia	cons.
		Lycaonia	praes.	Lycaonia		cons.	Lycaonia	cons.

[8] In the Verona list 'Priantina', a dittography of 'Privalentina' which follows, has replaced Achaia. The diocese of Moesiae was probably split into Dacia and Macedonia before 327 (see ch. III, n. 66). Polemius agrees with the Verona list, but Festus gives two Daciae and omits Dardania. Some conciliar lists of Sardica give two Daciae and Dardania. Dacia was still undivided in 321 (CTb II. xix. 2). In the Notitia Macedonia Salutaris is given in the index, but in the chapter of the praetorian prefect of Illyricum it is split between 'Epirus Nova et pars Macedoniae Salutaris' in the Macedonian diocese and 'Praevalitana et pars Macedoniae Salutaris' in the Dacian. The Macedonia I and II of Hierocles represent a different division of Macedonia (see p. 350).

[9] Ammianus (XXVIII. iv), Festus and Polemius all concur. Justinian assigned Moesia and Scythia to the Quaestor Exercitus (Just. Nov. xli, 536). There was apparently no longer a vicar of Thrace in his reign (he is omitted in Nov. viii).

[10] The signatures of Nicaea show Asia united with Hellespontus (cf. ILS 1220–1), and only one Phrygia, but record Lycia, perhaps accidentally omitted from the Verona list. The signatures of Sardica agree with the Verona list except that they also add Lycia. Lycaonia was created shortly before 373 (Basil, Ep. 138). Polemius agrees with the Notitia. Justinian abolished the vicar of Asiana (Nov. viii §2, 535), assigned the Islands and Caria to the Quaestor Exercitus (Nov. xli, 536), and promoted the governor of Phrygia Pacatiana to comes and those of Lycaonia and Pisidia to praetor (Nov. viii §2, xxiv, xxv, 535).

DIOCESES AND PROVINCES
THE EASTERN PARTS—*continued*

Severan provinces	THE VERONA LIST		NOTITIA DIGNITATUM				Hierocles	Justinian, *Nov.* viii	
	dioceses	provinces	dioceses	provinces	govs.	vicarii, etc.		provinces	govs.
Bithynia Pontus	11	Bithynia		Bithynia	cons.		cons.	Bithynia	cons.
		Paphlagonia		Paphlagonia	corr.		corr.	—	—
				Honorias	praes.		praes.	Honorias	praes.
Galatia		Galatia		Galatia	cons.		cons.	Galatia I	comes
		Diospontus		Galatia Salutaris	praes.		praes.	Galatia II	praes.
				Helenopontus	praes.		cons.	Heleno-pontus	cons.
Cappadocia	Pontica	Pontus Polemoniacus	Pontica	Pontus Polemoniacus	praes.	vicarius Ponticae	praes.	—	cons.
		Cappadocia		Cappadocia I	praes.		cons.	Capp. I	cons.
		Armenia Minor		Cappadocia II	praes.		praes.	Capp. II	cons.
				Armenia I	praes.		praes.	Arm. I	praes.
				Armenia II	praes.		praes.	Arm. II	cons.
								Armenia Magna	cons.
								Nova Iustiniana	cons.
Cilicia	12	Isauria		Isauria	comes		praes.	(Isauria)	—
		Cilicia		Cilicia	cons.		cons.	Cilicia I	cons.
				Cilicia II	praes.		praes.	Cilicia II	praes.
Syria	Oriens	Syria Coele	Oriens	Syria	cons.	comes Orientis	cons.	Syria I	comes
								Theodo-rias	cons.
Mesopotamia		Augusta Euphratensis		Syria Salutaris	praes.		praes.	Syria II	cons.
		Osrhoena		Euphratensis	praes.		praes.	Euphrat.	praes.
		Mesopotamia		Osrhoena	praes.		praes.	Osrhoene	cons.
				Mesopotamia	praes.		praes.	Mesop.	praes.

Phoenice	Phoenice	comes Orientis	Phoenice	cons.	Phoenice	cons.	Phoenice	cons.
			Augusta Libanensis	praes.	Phoenice Libani	praes.	Phoenice Paral. (Phoenice Liban.)	—
Arabia	Arabia		Arabia	dux et praes.	Arabia	cons.	Arabia	praes.
Palaestina	Palaestina		Palaestina	cons.	Palestina	cons.	Palaestina I	cons.
	Arabia		Arabia	praes.	Palaestina II	praes.	Palaestina II	cons.
					Palaestina Salutaris	praes.	Palaestina III	praes.
Cyprus	Cyprus		Cyprus	cons.	Cyprus	cons.	Cyprus	cons.
Aegyptus	Aegyptus Iovia	praefectus Augustalis	Aegyptus Iovia	praes.	Aegyptus	Augustalis	Aeg. I	praes.
							Aeg. II	praes.
	Aegyptus Herculia		Aegyptus Herculia	corr.	Augustamnica	corr.	Augustamnica I	cons.
							Augustamnica II	praes.
					Arcadia	praes.	(Arcadia)	—
	Thebais		Thebais	praes.	Thebais	praes.	(Thebais)	—
							(Thebais)	—
	Libya Inferior		Libya Inferior	praes.	Libya Inferior	dux	(Libya)	—
Cyrenaica (with Creta)	Libya Superior		Libya Superior	praes.	Libya Superior	praes.	Libya Sup.	praes.

11 The signatures of Nicaea agree with the Verona list. Polemius adds Honorias. Cappadocia was divided in 371 (Greg. Naz. Or. xliii. 58) and Armenia before 386 (CTb XIII. xi. 2). Justinian abolished the vicar of Pontica and promoted the governor of Galatia I to comes (Nov. viii §3) and later united Paphlagonia and Honorias under a praetor of Paphlagonia (Nov. xxix, §35), and Helenopontus and Pontus Polemoniacus under a moderator of Helenopontus (Nov. xxviii, §35). Hence the rather careless deletion of the corrector of Paphlagonia and the praeses of Pontus Polemoniacus from the schedule of Nov. viii. He also promoted the consular of Cappadocia I to proconsul (Nov. xxx, §36). Finally he reorganised the Armenias, making Armenia Magna, not yet recognised as a province in Hierocles but already under a consular in Nov. viii, into Armenia I under a proconsul, renumbering the old Armenia I as II (under a praeses) and the old II as III (under a comes); and making the Satrapies Armenia IV (under a praeses). The province of Nova Justiniana in Nov. viii is otherwise unknown; it appears to have been in Pontica, and may have been a temporary name of the Satrapies.

12 See overleaf, pp. 390-1.

DIOCESES AND PROVINCES
THE EASTERN PARTS—continued

[12] The original diocese of Oriens was divided into Oriens and Aegyptus c. 367 (ch. V, n. 9.). In the last column I have used Georgius Cyprius to fill a few gaps in Just. *Nov.* viii, which gives civil governors only and thus omits some provinces under military governors. This certainly accounts for the omission of Isauria, and probably of Phoenice Libanensis in Oriens, and of the Upper Thebaid in Egypt, and probably of the other missing Egyptian provinces. The early history of the provinces of Oriens in the narrow sense is so complicated that it merits a supplementary table:

Verona List	Council of Nicaea	Ammianus (xiv. viii)	Polemius	Council of Constantinople	Notitia Dignitatum
Isauria	Isauria	Isauria	Isauria	Isauria	Isauria
Cilicia	Cilicia	Cilicia	Cilicia	Cilicia	Cilicia
					Cilicia II
Syria Coele	Syria Coele	Syria	Syria Coele	Syria Coele	Syria
					Syria Salutaris
Aug. Euphrat.		Euphrat.	Euphrat.	Aug. Euphrat.	Euphratensis
Osrhoene		Osrhoene	Osrhoene	Osrhoene	Osrhoene
Mesopotamia	Mesopotamia		Mesopotamia	Mesopotamia	Mesopotamia
Phoenice	Phoenice	Phoenice	Syria Phoenice	Phoenice	Phoenice
Aug. Liban.					Phoenice Liban.
Arabia	Arabia	Arabia	Arabia	Bostra	Arabia
Arabia				Arabia	Pal. Salutaris
Palaestina	Palaestina	Palaestina	Palaestina	Palaestina	Palaestina
					Palaestina II
Cyprus	Cyprus	Cyprus	Cyprus	Cyprus	Cyprus

The first Arabia is the northern half of the old province, whose capital was Bostra, the second the southern half, whose capital was Petra; the second province was revived c. 357–8 (Lib. Ep. 334–5, Jerome, Quaest. ad Gen. xvii. 30), and having been attached to Palestine was called Palestine III. Cilicia II and Syria Salutaris (together with Honorias) are attributed by Malalas, 365, to Theodosius II; his source must have said Theodosius I. There were already three Palestines in 409 (CTb vii. iv. 30). Justinian made the comes Orientis merely the governor of Syria I (Nov. viii §5, 535), promoted the governors of Arabia and Phoenice Libanensis to moderator (Nov. cii, 536, Ed. iv, 535–6) and that of Palestine I to proconsul (Nov. ciii, 536), and transferred Cyprus to the Quaestor Exercitus (Nov. xli, 536).

The early changes in the diocese of Egypt also deserve a supplementary table:

Verona List	Council of Nicaea	Ammianus (XXII. xvi)	Polemius
Aegyptus Iovia	Aegyptus	Aegyptus	Aegyptus
Aegyptus Herculia		Augustamnica	Augustamnica
			Arcadia
Thebais	Thebais	Thebais	Thebais
Libya Inferior	Libya Inferior	Libya	Libya Sicca
Libya Superior	Libya Superior	Pentapolis	Libya Pentapolis

Augustamnica was created in 341 (Ath. Index to Festal Letters, 13).

LIST OF COLLECTIONS AND PERIODICALS
CITED

Acta Inst. Rom. Regni Sueciae	*Acta Instituti Romani Regni Sueciae (Skrifter utgivna av Svenska Institutet i Rom)*
Aegyptus	*Aegyptus, rivista italiana di egittologia e di papirologia*
	American Numismatic Society, Museum Notes
Anal. Boll.	*Analecta Bollandiana*
	Antiquité Classique
Anz. Ak. Wien	*Anzeiger der Osterreichischen Akademie d. Wissenschaften (Phil.-Hist. Kl.)*
Ἀρχ Δελτ	*Ἀρχαιολογικὸυ Δελτίου*
Archiv Pap.	*Archiv für Papyrusforschung*
BCH	*Bulletin de correspondance hellénique*
BSA	*Annual of the British School at Athens*
Bull. Ac. Roy. Belg.	*Bulletin de l' Académie royale de Belgique (Classe des Lettres et des Sciences morales et politiques)*
Byz. Zeitschr.	*Byzantinische Zeitschrift*
CSEL	*Corpus Scriptorum Ecclesiasticorum Latinorum*
CSHB	*Corpus Scriptorum Historiae Byzantinae*
Chron. d'Égypte	*Chronique d'Égypte*
Denkschr. Ak. Wien	*Denkschriften der Osterreichischen Akademie d. Wissenschaften (Phil.-Hist. Kl.)*
EHR	*English Historical Review*
Econ. Hist. Rev.	*Economic History Review*
FHG	*Fragmenta Historicorum Graecorum*, C. Mueller, Paris, 1874–85
FIR	*Fontes Iuris Romani Ante-Iustiniani*, editio altera, by S. Riccobono and others, Florence, 1940, 1941, 1943 (3 vols.)
Gr. Schr.	*Die Griechischen Christlichen Schriftsteller der ersten drei Jahrhunderte, herausgegeben im auftrage der Kirchenväter-Commission der Preussischen Akademie der Wissenschaften*
Harvard Theol. Rev.	*Harvard Theological Review*
	Hermes
	Historia
JEA	*Journal of Egyptian Archaeology*
J. Eccl. Hist.	*Journal of Ecclesiastical History*
JHS	*Journal of Hellenic Studies*
J. Jur. Pap.	*Journal of Juristic Papyrology*
JRS	*Journal of Roman Studies*
JTS	*Journal of Theological Studies*

                        Klio

MGH (AA)	*Monumenta Germaniae Historica (Auctores Antiquissimi)*
„ *(Leg.)*	„ *(Leges)*
„ *(Concilia)*	„ *(Legum Sectio III, vol.* 1*)*
„ *(Ep.)*	„ *(Epistulae)*
„ *(Gest. Pont. Rom.)*	„ *(Gesta Pontificum Romanorum)*
„ *(Scr. rer. Lang.)*	„ *(Scriptores rerum Langobardicarum et Italicarum)*
„ *(Scr. rer. Merov.)*	*(Scriptores rerum Merovingicarum)*
Mansi	J.-D. Mansi, *Sacrorum Conciliorum nova et amplissima collectio*
Mém. Soc. Nat. Ant. de France	*Mémoires de la Société nationale des antiquaires de France*
Nachr. Ges. Gött. Wiss.	*Nachrichten der Gesellschaft der Wissenschaften zu Göttingen (Phil.-Hist. Kl.)*
Not. Scav.	*Notizie degli Scavi di Antichità*
Num. Chron.	*Numismatic Chronicle*
Num. Zeitschr.	*Numismatische Zeitschrift*
PG	J. P. Migne, *Patrologia Graeca*
PL	J. P. Migne, *Patrologia Latina*
PW(-K)	Pauly-Wissowa (-Kroll), *Real-Encyclopädie der classischen Altertumswissenschaft*
	Past and Present
	Philologus
REA	*Revue des Études Anciennes*
REG	*Revue des Études Grecques*
Rev. Belg. phil. hist.	*Revue Belge de philologie et d'histoire*
Rev. Hist.	*Revue Historique*
Rev. Hist. de droit.	*Revue Historique de droit français et étranger*
Rev. Or. Chrét.	*Revue de l'Orient Chrétien*
Rhein. Mus.	*Rheinisches Museum für Philologie*
Röm. Mitt.	*Mitteilungen des deutschen archäologischen Instituts, Römische Abteilung*
Sb. Ak. Wien	*Sitzungsberichte der Akademie der Wissenschaften in Wien (Philos.-Hist. Kl.)*
	Studi e Testi
	Studios de edad media de la corona de Aragon, sec. de Zaragoza
TAPA	*Transactions of the American Philological Association*
Traditio	*Traditio: Studies in ancient and medieval history, thought and religion*
Zeitsch. Sav. Stift. Rom. Abt.	*Zeitschrift der Savigny-Stiftung für Rechtsgeschichte, Romanistische Abteilung*

LIST OF SOURCES, WITH ABBREVIATIONS

A.C.Oec.	*Acta Conciliorum Oecumenicorum*	Ed. Schwartz, Berlin and Leipzig, 1922–
AE	*Année Épigraphique*	
	Acta Agapae	G. Krueger, *Ausgewählte Märtyrerakten³* (Tubingen, 1929), 95-100
	Acta Claudii	ibid., 106-9
	Acta Crispinae	ibid., 109-11
	Acta Eupli	*Studi e Testi*, XLIX (1928), 47 ff.
	Acta Marcelli	*Anal. Boll.* XLI (1923), 260 ff.
	Acta Maximiliani	G. Krueger, op. cit., 86-7
	Acta Saturnini	*Studi e Testi*, LXV (1935), 49 ff.
	Acta Sergii et Bacchi	*Anal. Boll.* XIV (1895), 375 ff.
Agath.	Agathias, *Historiarum libri V*	*CSHB*
	Agennius Urbicus, *de controversiis agrorum*	*Corpus Agrimensorum Romanorum*, C. Thulin, 1913 (Teubner)
Agnellus, *Lib.*	Agnelli qui et Andreas, *Liber*	*MGH (Scr. rer. Lang.)* 263-391
Pont. Eccl. Rav.	*Pontificalis Ecclesiae Ravennatis*	
	A. Alt, *Die griechischen Inschriften der Palestina Tertia westlich der 'Araba*, Berlin and Leipzig, 1921	
Amb. *c. Aux.*	Ambrose, *contra Auxentium*	*PL* XVI. 1007-18
„ *de exc. Sat.*	„ *de excessu fratris Satyri*	*CSEL* LXXIII. 209-325
„ *de ob. Theod.*	„ *de obitu Theodosii*	*CSEL* LXXIII. 371-401
„ *de ob. Val. Jun.*	„ *de obitu Valentiniani Iunioris*	*CSEL* LXXIII. 329-67
„ *Ep.*	„ *Epistulae*	*PL* XVI. 875-1286
„ *de Paen.*	„ *de Paenitentia*	*CSEL* LXXIII. 119-206
„ *Off.*	„ *de Officiis*	*PL* XVI. 23-184
Amm.	Ammianus Marcellinus	V. Gardthausen, 1874 (Teubner)
Anon. *de rebus bell.*	Anonymus *de rebus bellicis*	E. A. Thompson, *A Roman Reformer and Inventor*, Oxford, 1952
Anon. Val.	Anonymus Valesianus	V. Gardthausen, 1874 (Teubner)
Anth. *Nov.*	Anthemius, *Novellae*	*Codex Theodosianus*, vol. II, P. Meyer, Berlin, 1905
	Appian, *Syriaca*	L. Mendelssohn, 1879 (Teubner)
Asterius Amas. *Hom.*	Asterius of Amaseia, *Homiliae*	*PG* XL. 163-478
Ath. *Apol. c. Ar.*	Athanasius, *Apologia contra Arianos*	H. G. Opitz, *Athanasius Werke*, II. i. 87-168
„ *Apol. Const.*	„ *Apologia ad Constantium*	*PG* XXV. 595-642
„ *Apol. de fuga*	„ *Apologia de fuga sua*	Opitz, op. cit., II. i. 68-86
„ *Decr. Nic.*	„ *de decretis Nicaenae synodi*	Opitz, op. cit., II. i. 1-45
„ *de Synodis*	„ *de Synodis*	Opitz, op. cit., II. i. 231-78
„ *Fest. Ep.*	„ *Festal Epistles*	F. Larsow, *Die Fest-Briefe des heiligen Athanasius*, Leipzig, Gottingen, 1852
„ *Hist. Ar.*	„ *Historia Arianorum*	Opitz, op. cit., II. i. 183-230
„ *Or. I c. Arianos*	„ *Oratio I contra Arianos*	*PG* XXVI. 11-116
„ *V. Ant.*	„ *Vita S. Antonii*	*PG* XXVI. 837-976
Aug. *ad Don. post Coll.*	Augustine, *ad Donatistas post Collationem*	*CSEL* LIII. 97-162
„ *Brev. Coll.*	„ *Breviculus Collationis cum Donatistis*	*CSEL* LIII. 39-92

Aug. *c. Acad.*	Augustine, *contra Academicos*	*CSEL* LXIII. 3–81
„ *c. Cresc.*	„ *contra Cresconium*	*CSEL* LII. 325–582
„ *c. Ep. Parm.*	„ *contra Epistulam Parme-*	*CSEL* LI. 19–141
	niani	
„ *c. Faust.*	„ *contra Faustum*	*CSEL* XXV. 251–797
„ *c. Gaud.*	„ *contra Gaudentium*	*CSEL* LIII. 201–74
„ *Civ. Dei*	„ *de Civitate Dei*	*CSEL* XL
„ *c. Lit. Pet.*	„ *contra Litteras Petiliani*	*CSEL* LII. 3–227
„ *Coll. cum Maximino*	„ *Collatio cum Maximino*	PL XLII. 709–42
„ *Conf.*	„ *Confessiones*	*CSEL* XXXIII
„ *de adult. coniug.*	„ *de adulterinis coniugiis*	*CSEL* XLI. 347–410
„ *de bono coniug.*	„ *de bono coniugali*	*CSEL* XLI. 187–230
„ *de cura gerenda pro*	„ *de cura gerenda pro mortuis*	*CSEL* XLI. 621–59
mortuis		
„ *de doctrina Chris-*	„ *de doctrina Christiana*	PL XXXIV. 15–122
tiana		
„ *de fide et oper.*	„ *de fide et operibus*	*CSEL* XLI. 35–97
„ *de haer.*	„ *de haeresibus ad Quodvult-*	PL XLII. 21–50
	deum	
„ *de op. mon.*	„ *de opere monachorum*	*CSEL* XLI. 531–95
„ *de Serm. Dom. in*	„ *de Sermone Domini in Monte*	PL XXXIV. 1229–1308
Monte		
„ *de Symbolo*	„ *Sermo ad Catechumenos de*	PL XL. 637–60
	Symbolo	
„ *En. in Ps.*	„ *Enarrationes in Psalmos*	PL XXXVI, XXXVII
„ *Ep.*	„ *Epistulae*	*CSEL* XXXIV, XLIV, LVII
„ *in Ep. Joh. ad*	„ *in Joannis epistulam ad*	PL XXXV. 1977–2062
Parthos	*Parthos tractatus*	
„ *Ps. c. part. Don.*	„ *Psalmus contra partem*	*CSEL* LI. 3–15
	Donati	
„ *Retract.*	„ *Retractationes*	*CSEL* XXXVI
„ *Serm.*	„ *Sermones*	PL XXXVIII, XXXIX
Aur. Victor, *Caes.*	Aurelius Victor, *Liber de Caesaribus*	F. Pichlmayr, 1911 (Teubner)
Auson. *de feriis Rom.*	Ausonius, *de feriis Romanis*	*MGH* (*AA*), V
„ *Ep.*	„ *Epistulae*	„
„ *Gratiarum Actio*	„ *Gratiarum Actio dicta*	„
	domino Gratiano Augusto	
„ *Mosella*	„ *Mosella*	„
„ *Prof.*	„ *Commemoratio Profess-*	
	orum Burdigalensium	

BGU — *Aegyptische Urkunden aus den staatlichen Museen zu Berlin, Griechische Urkunden*, Berlin, 1892–1937

Barsanuphius — Βίβλος ψυχωφελεστάτη, περιέχουσα ἀποκρίσεις, διαφόροις ὑποθέσεσιν ἀνήκουσας, συγγραφεῖσα μὲν παρὰ τῶν ὁσίων καὶ θεοφόρων πατέρων ἡμῶν Βαρσανουφίου καὶ Ἰωάννου, ἐπιμελῶς δὲ διορθωθεῖσα καὶ τῇ τῶν ὁσίων βιογραφίᾳ . . . Soterios N. Schoinas, Volo, 1960

Basil, *de spiritu sancto*	Basil, *liber de spiritu sancto*	PG XXXII. 67–218
„ *Ep.*	„ *Epistulae*	PG XXXII. 219–1112
„ *Hom.*	„ *Homiliae*	PG XXXI. 164–617
„ *Hom. in S. Ma-*	„ *Homilia in S. Mamantem*	PG XXXI. 589–600
mantem		
„ *Reg. Brev.*	„ *Regulae brevius tractatae*	PG XXXI. 1079–1306
„ *Reg. Fus.*	„ *Regulae fusius tractatae*	PG XXXI. 889–1052
Boeth. *Consol.*	Boethius, *de Philosophiae Consolatione*	*CSEL* LXVII
„ *Comm. in Arist.*	„ *Commentarii in librum*	C. Meiser, 1877–80 (Teubner)
	Aristotelis περὶ ἑρμηνείας.	
Boniface, *Ep.*	(Pope) Boniface I, *Epistulae*	PL XX. 750–84
Bruns, *Fontes juris Romani*[7]	C. G. Bruns, *Fontes iuris Romani antiqui*	septimum ed. O. Gradenwitz, Tübingen, 1909
C. Agath.	*Concilium Agathense* (506)	Mansi, VIII. 319–36
C. Anc.	*Concilium Ancyranum* (314)	Mansi, II. 513–22
C. Ant.	*Concilium Antiochenum* (c. 326)	Mansi, II. 1308–20
C. Araus. I	*Concilium Arausicanum I* (441)	Mansi, VI. 434–41
C. Araus. II	*Concilium Arausicanum II* (529)	*MGH* (*Concilia*) 44–54

C. Arel. I	Concilium Arelatense I (314)	Mansi, II. 470–4
C. Arel. II	Concilium Arelatense II (452)	Mansi, VII. 875–85
C. Arvern. I	Concilium Arvernense I (535)	MGH (Concilia) 65–71
C. Aurel. I	Concilium Aurelianense I (511)	MGH (Concilia) 1–14
C. Aurel. II	Concilium Aurelianense II (533)	MGH (Concilia) 61–5
C. Aurel. III	Concilium Aurelianense III (538)	MGH (Concilia) 72–86
C. Aurel. IV	Concilium Aurelianense IV (541)	MGH (Concilia) 86–99
C. Aurel. V	Concilium Aurelianense V (549)	MGH (Concilia) 99–112
C. Autis.	Concilium Autissiodorense (578)	MGH (Concilia) 178–84
C. Bracar. I	Concilium Bracarense I (563)	C. W. Barlow, Martini episcopi Bracarensis opera omnia, New Haven, 1950
C. Bracar. II	Concilium Bracarense II (572)	ibid.
C. Carp.	Concilium Carpentoratense (527)	MGH (Concilia) 40–3
C. Carth. I–IV	Concilia Carthaginiensia	C. García Goldáraz, Los concilios de Cartago, Madrid, 1960
C. Chalc.	Concilium Chalcedonense (451)	A. C. Oec. II
C. Const. I	Concilium Constantinopolitanum (381)	Mansi, III. 557–64
C. Elus.	Concilium Elusanum (551)	MGH (Concilia) 113–15
C. Epaon.	Concilium Epaonense (517)	MGH (Concilia) 15–30
C. Gangr.	Concilium Gangrense (c. 362)	Mansi, II. 1101–5
C. Hippon.	Concilium Hipponense (393)	Bruns, Canones I. 134–9
C. Hisp. I	Concilium Hispalense I (590)	Mansi, X. 449–51
C. Hisp. II	Concilium Hispalense II (618)	Mansi, X. 555–68
C. Ilerd.	Concilium Ilerdense (523)	Mansi, VIII. 609–15
C. Ilib.	Concilium Iliberitanum (305)	Mansi, II. 1–19
C. Laod.	Concilium Laodicenum	Mansi, II. 563–74
C. Mass.	Concilium Massiliense (533)	MGH (Concilia) 60–1
C. Matisc. I	Concilium Matisconense I (581)	MGH (Concilia) 155–61
C. Matisc. II	Concilium Matisconense II (585)	MGH (Concilia) 163–73
C. Milev.	Concilium Milevitanum (402)	Bruns, Canones I. 176–81
C. Narb.	Concilium Narbonense (589)	Mansi, IX. 1013–18
C. Neocaes.	Concilium Neocaesariense (314)	Mansi, II. 539–43
C. Nic.	Concilium Nicaenum (325)	Mansi, II. 667–77
C. Paris. III	Concilium Parisiense III (557)	MGH (Concilia) 141–6
C. Paris. V	Concilium Parisiense V (615)	MGH (Concilia) 185–92
C. Reg.	Concilium Regense (439)	Mansi, V. 1189–94
C. Rem.	Concilium Remense (625)	MGH (Concilia) 202–6
C. Sard.	Concilium Sardicense (347)	Mansi, III. 5–21
C. Tarrac.	Concilium Tarraconense (516)	Mansi, VIII. 539–44
C. Taurin.	Concilium Taurinense (401)	Mansi, III. 860–2
C. Tol. I	Concilium Toletanum I (398)	Mansi, III. 997–1002
C. Tol. III	Concilium Toletanum III (589)	Mansi, IX. 977–99
C. Tol. IV	Concilium Toletanum IV (633)	Mansi, X. 611–41
C. Tol. VII	Concilium Toletanum VII (646)	Mansi, X. 763–70
C. Turon. I	Concilium Turonicum I (460)	Mansi, VII. 943–7
C. Turon. II	Concilium Turonicum II (567)	MGH (Concilia) 121–36
C. Valent.	Concilium Valentinum (524)	Mansi, VIII. 620–3
C. Vas. I	Concilium Vasense I (442)	Mansi, VI. 451–6
C. Vas. II	Concilium Vasense II (529)	MGH (Concilia) 55–8
C. Venet.	Concilium Veneticum (465)	Mansi, VII. 951–5
CIL	Corpus Inscriptionum Latinarum	
CJ	Codex Justinianus*	P. Krueger, Berlin, 1877
CPR	Corpus Papyrorum Raineri	C. Wessely, Vienna, 1895
CTh	Codex Theodosianus*	Th. Mommsen, Berlin, 1905
Caes. BG	Caesar, de bello Gallico	A. Klotz, 1952 (Teubner)
Caesarius, Serm.	Caesarius, Sermones	G. Morin, Corpus Christianorum, ser. Lat. 103, 104
„ Reg. Virg.	„ Regula ad Virgines	PL LXVII. 1107–20

* When a law in the Codes (or a Novel) is in my opinion correctly dated in the original text, I have given the date thus—CTh I. i. 1, 322. When I accept a date as emended by O. Seeck (Regesten der Kaiser und Päpste, Stuttgart, 1919) I have given Seeck's date followed by the letter S in brackets thus—CTh I. ii. 1, 313(S). When the date of a law is inferred I have placed it in brackets thus—CTh V. xv. 21 (368–70).

Can. Apost.	Canones Apostolorum	H. T. Bruns, Canones Apostolorum et Conciliorum (Berlin, 1839), I. 1–13
Can. Athan.	The Canons of Athanasius of Alexandria	W. Riedel and W. E. Crum, London, Oxford, 1904
Candidus	Candidus Isaurus, fragments	FHG IV. 135–7
Cass. de orthogr.	Cassiodorus, de orthographia	PL LXX. 1239–70
„ Inst.	„ Institutiones	R. A. B. Mynors, Cassiodori Senatoris Institutiones, 1937
„ Var.	„ Variae	MGH (AA) XII
Cassian, Coll.	John Cassian, Collationes	CSEL XIII
„ Inst.	„ de coenobiorum institutis	CSEL XVII
Cassius Dio	Cassius Dio, Historia Romana	U. P. Boissevain, Berlin, 1895
Celestine, Ep.	Pope Celestine I, Epistulae	PL L. 417–558
Chr. I	U. Wilcken, Chrestomathie, Berlin, 1912	
Chr. II	L. Mitteis, Chrestomathie, Berlin, 1912	
Chron. Min.	Chronica Minora	MGH (AA), IX, XI, XIII
Chron. Pasch.	Chronicon Paschale	CSHB
Cic. de lege agraria	Cicero, de lege agraria	C. F. W. Mueller, 1896 (Teubner)
„ pro Cluentio	„ pro Cluentio	C. F. W. Mueller, 1896 (Teubner)
„ II Verr.	„ Actio secunda in C. Verrem	C. F. W. Mueller, 1880 (Teubner)
Claudian, de bello Getico	Claudian, de bello Pollentino sive Gothico	MGH (AA) X
„ de bello Gild.	„ de bello Gildonico	„
„ de cos. Stil.	„ de consulatu Stilichonis	„
„ de IV cos. Hon.	„ de quarto consulatu Honorii	„
„ de VI cos. Hon.	„ de sexto consulatu Honorii	„
„ de III cos. Hon.	„ de tertio consulatu Honorii	„
„ Epigr.	„ Epigrammata	„
„ in Eutrop.	„ in Eutropium	„
„ in Ruf.	„ in Rufinum	„
„ Pan. Mallio Theodoro cos.	„ Panegyricus dictus Mallio Theodoro consuli	„
Cod. Can. Eccl. Afr.	Codex Canonum Ecclesiae Africanae	H. T. Bruns, Canones Apostolorum et Conciliorum (Berlin, 1839), I. 155–202
Cod. Euric.	Codicis Euriciani fragmenta	MGH (Leg.) I. i. 3–32
Coll.	Mosaicarum et Romanarum legum collatio	FIR II². 544–89
Coll. Avell.	Epistulae imperatorum pontificum aliorum . . . Avellana quae dicitur Collectio	CSEL XXXV
Coll. Carth.	Gesta Collationis Carthagine habitae	Mansi, IV. 51–275
Columella	Columella, de re rustica	H. B. Ash, E. S. Forster, E. Hoffner, 1941–55 (Loeb)
Const. Apost.	Apostolic Constitutions	F. X. Funk, Didascalia et Constitutiones Apostolorum, Paderborn, 1905
Const. Porph. Cer.	Constantine VII Porphyrogenitus, de ceremoniis aulae Byzantinae	CSHB
Consult.	Consultatio veteris cuiusdam iurisconsulti	FIR II.² 594–613
Corippus, Laud. Just.	Corippus, in laudem Justini Augusti	MGH (AA) III. 115–56
Corpus pap. Lat.	Corpus Papyrorum Latinarum	R. Cavenaile, Wiesbaden, 1956–8
	Cosmas Indicopleustes	E. O. Winstedt, The Christian Topography of Cosmas Indicopleustes, Cambridge, 1909
Cyprian, Ep.	Cyprian, Epistulae	CSEL III. 465–842
Cyr. Alex. c. Iulianum	Cyril of Alexandria, contra Iulianum libri decem	PG LXXVI. 509–1058
Cyr. Hierosol. Catech.	Cyril of Jerusalem, Catecheses	PG XXXIII. 331–1128

Cyr. Scyth. *V. Sabae*	Cyril of Scythopolis, *Vita Sabae*	⎫ Ed. Schwartz, *Texte und Unter-*
„ *V. Euthymii*	„ „ *Vita Euthymii*	⎬ *suchungen*, vol. 49. ii
„ *V. Theodosii*	„ „ *Vita Theodosii*	⎭
Damasus, *Epigrammata*	Pope Damasus I, *Epigrammata*	A. Ferrua, *Epigrammata Damasiana*, Rome, 1942
Dig.	Justinian, *Digesta seu Pandectae*	Th. Mommsen, Berlin, 1870
Doctrina Jacobi	*Doctrina Jacobi nuper baptizati*	N. Bonwetsch, *Abh. Ges. Gött. Wiss. (Phil.-Hist. Kl.)*, N.F. XII. 3 (1910)
Eccl. Occ. Mon. Iur. Ant.	*Ecclesiae Occidentalis Monumenta Iuris Antiquissima*	C. Turner, Oxford, 1899–1930
Ed. Diocl.	Diocletian, *Edict on Prices*	Tenney Frank, *Economic Survey of Ancient Rome*, V, 305–421
Ed. Theod.	*Edictum Theoderici regis*	*FIR* II.² 684–710
Ennod. *V. Epiph.*	Ennodius, *Vita Epiphanii episcopi Ticinensis ecclesiae*	*CSEL* VI
„ *Ep.*	„ *Epistulae*	„
„ *Pan.*	„ *Panegyricus dictus Theoderico regi*	„
Ep. ad Gallos	*Canones synodi Romanorum ad Gallos episcopos*	*PL* XIII. 1181–94
Ep. Luciani	*Epistula Luciani ad omnem ecclesiam*	*PL* XLI. 807–18
Ep. Severi	*Epistula Severi ad omnem ecclesiam*	*PL* XLI. 821–32
Epiph. adv. Haer.	Epiphanius, *adversus Haereses*	K. Holl, *Gr. Schr.* vols. 25, 31, 37
„ *Expos. Fid.*	„ *Brevis ac vera expositio fidei catholicae et apostolicae ecclesiae*	K. Holl, *Gr. Schr.* vol. 37
Epit. Caes.	*Epitome de Caesaribus*	F. Pichlmayr, 1911 (Teubner)
Eunap.	Eunapius of Sardis, *fragments*	*FHG* IV. 11–56
„ *V. Soph.*	„ „ *Vitae Sophistarum*	I. Giangrande, Rome, 1956
Eus. Dem. Ev.	Eusebius, *Demonstratio Evangelica*	I. A. Heikel, *Gr. Schr.* vol. 23
„ *HE*	„ *Historia Ecclesiastica*	Ed. Schwartz, *Gr. Schr.* vol. 9
„ *Laud. Const.*	„ *Oratio de laudibus Constantini*	I. A. Heikel, *Gr. Schr.* vol. 7
„ *Mart. Pal.*	„ *Liber de martyribus Palaestinae*	Ed. Schwartz, *Gr. Schr.* vol. 9
„ *V. Const.*	„ *de vita Constantini*	I. A. Heikel, *Gr. Schr.* vol. 7
Eutrop.	Eutropius, *Breviarium*	F. Ruehl, 1887 (Teubner)
Evagr.	Evagrius Scholasticus, *Historia Ecclesiastica*	J. Bidez and L. Parmentier, London, 1898
Firm. Mat. Math.	Julius Firmicus Maternus, *Mathesis*	W. Kroll and F. Skutsch, 1897 (Teubner)
„ *Prof. Rel.*	„ *de errore profanarum religionum*	K. Ziegler, 1907 (Teubner)
Fr. *Vat.*	*Fragmenta quae dicuntur Vaticana*	*FIR* II.² 464–540
Frontinus, de aquis	Julius Frontinus, *de aquis urbis Romae*	F. Krohn, 1922 (Teubner)
Gaius	Gaius, *Institutiones*	*FIR* II.² 9–192
	Galen, *de probis pravisque alimentorum succis*	C. G. Kuehn, *Medicorum Graecorum opera*, vol. 6, Leipzig, 1823
Gelasius	Gelasius, *Historia Ecclesiastica*	G. Loeschcke, M. Heinemann, *Gr. Schr.* vol. 28
Gelasius, *Ep.*	Pope Gelasius I, *Epistulae*	A. Thiel, *Epistulae Romanorum Pontificum* (Braunsberg, 1867), 287–483
„ *fr.*	„ „ *Fragments*	ibid. 483–510
Gennadius, *de script. eccl.*	Gennadius, "*Liber de scriptoribus ecclesiasticis*	*PL* LVIII. 1059–1120
Georgius Cyprius	Georgius Cyprius, *Descriptio orbis Romani*	H. Gelzer, 1890 (Teubner)
Gesta Conc. Aquil.	*Gesta Concilii Aquileiensis*	*PL* XVI. 916–39
Gildas, de exc. Brit.	Gildas, *de excidio et conquestu Britanniae*	*MGH (AA)* XIII. 25–85
Greg. Dial.	Pope Gregory I, *Dialogi*	*PL* LXXVII. 149–430
„ *Ep.*	„ „ *Epistulae*	*MGH (Ep.)*, I, II

Greg. Naz. *Or.*	Gregory of Nazianzus, *Orationes*	*PG* XXXV–XXXVI
„ *vit. sua*	„ „ *de vita sua*	*PG* XXXVII. 1029–1166
„ *Ep.*	„ „ *Epistulae*	*PG* XXXVII. 21–388
Greg. Nyss. *de deit. Fil.*	Gregory of Nyssa, *Oratio de deitate Filii et Spiritus Sancti*	*PG* XLVI. 553–76
„ *de bapt.*	Gregory of Nyssa, *de baptismo*	*PG* XLVI. 415–32
„ *c. Eunom.*	„ „ *contra Eunomium*	*PG* XLV. 247–1122
„ *Ep.*	„ „ *Epistulae*	W. Jaeger, *Gregorii Nysseni Opera* (Leiden, 1952–9) VII. ii
„ *V. Macr.*	„ „ *de Vita S. Macrinae*	ibid. VIII. i. 370–414
Greg. Tur. *Glor. Conf.*	Gregory of Tours, *Liber in gloria confessorum*	*MGH* (*Scr. rer. Merov.*) I.
„ HF	Gregory of Tours, *Historia Francorum*	„
„ *Virt. Jul.*	„ *Liber de virtutibus S. Juliani*	„
„ *Virt. Mart*	„ *Libri IV de virtutibus S. Martini*	„
„ *V. Patrum*	„ *Liber Vitae Patrum*	„
Herodian	Herodian, *ab excessu divi Marci libri VIII*	K. Stavenhagen, 1922 (Teubner)
Hesychius	Hesychius of Miletus, *fragments*	FHG IV, 145–77
Hierocles	Hierocles, *Synecdemus*	A. Burckhardt, 1893 (Teubner)
Hilarius Arel. *de vit. S. Hon.*	Hilarius of Arles, *Sermo de vita S. Honorati Arelatensis episcopi*	*PL* L. 1249–72
Hilarus, *Ep.*	Pope Hilarus, *Epistulae*	A. Thiel, *Epistulae Romanorum Pontificum* (Braunsberg, 1867), 127–70
Hilary, *Lib. I ad Const.*	Hilary of Poitiers, *Liber I ad Constantium*	*PL* X. 577–606
„ *de Trin.*	„ „ *de Trinitate*	*PL* X. 25–472
Hist. *Aceph.*	*Historia Acephala*	*PG* XXVI. 1443–50
Hormisdas, *Ep.*	Pope Hormisdas, *Epistulae*	A. Thiel, *Epistulae Romanorum Pontificum* (Braunsberg, 1867), 741–990
Hydatius	Hydatius, *Chronica*	*MGH* (*AA*) XI. 13–36
	Hyginus, *de condicione agrorum*	*Corpus Agrimensorum Romanorum*, C. Thulin, 1913 (Teubner)
IG	*Inscriptiones Graecae*	
IGC	H. Grégoire, *Recueil des inscriptions grecques chrétiennes d'Asie Mineure*, Paris, 1922	
IGLS	L. Jalabert and R. Mouterde, *Inscriptions grecques et latines de la Syrie*, Paris, 1929–	
IGR	R. Cagnat, *Inscriptiones Graecae ad res Romanas pertinentes*, Paris, 1901–27	
ILA	R. Cagnat and A. Merlin, *Inscriptions latines d'Afrique*, Paris, 1923	
ILCV	E. Diehl, *Inscriptiones Latinae Christianae Veteres*, Berlin, 1925–31	
ILS	H. Dessau, *Inscriptiones Latinae Selectae*, Berlin, 1892–1916	
IRT	J. M. Reynolds and J. B. Ward Perkins, *The Inscriptions of Roman Tripolitania*, Rome and London, 1952	
Innocent, *Ep.*	Pope Innocent I, *Epistulae*	*PL* XX. 463–612
Inst.	Justinian, *Institutiones*	P. Krueger, Berlin, 1877
Isid. *Chron.*	Isidore of Seville, *Chronicon*	*MGH* (*AA*) XI. 424–81
„ *Etym.*	„ *Etymologiae sive Origines*	W. M. Lindsay, Oxford, 1911
„ *Hist. Goth.*	„ *Historia Gothorum*	*MGH* (*AA*) XI. 267–95
„ *Hist. Vand.*	„ *Historia Vandalorum*	*MGH* (*AA*) XI. 295–300
Isid. Pel. *Ep.*	Isidore of Pelusium, *Epistulae*	*PG* LXXVIII. 177–1646
Itin. *Burd.*	*Itinerarium Burdigalense*	*CSEL* XXXIX; O. Cuntz, *Itineraria Romana*, Leipzig, 1929
Itin. *Hier.*	*Itinera Hierosolymitana*	*CSEL* XXXIX
Jerome, *Chron.*	Jerome, *Chronicle*	R. Helm, *Gr. Schr.* vol. 24
„ *c. Joh. Hierosol.*	„ *Liber contra Joannem Hierosolymitanum*	*PL* XXIII. 355–96

Jerome, *Comm. in Ep. Gal.*	„ *Commentaria in Epistulam ad Galatas*	PL XXVI. 307–438
„ *Comm. in Ezech.*	„ *Commentaria in Ezechielem*	PL XXV. 15–490
„ *c. Vig.*	„ *Liber contra Vigilantium*	PL XXIII. 339–52
„ *de viris illustr.*	„ *Liber de viris illustribus*	W. Herding, 1879 (Teubner)
„ *Ep.*	„ *Epistulae*	CSEL LIV–LVI
„ *Hom. in Matth.*	„ *Homilia in Evangelium secundum Matthaeum*	G. Morin, *Corpus Christianorum*, ser. Lat. 78
„ *V. Hilar.*	„ *Vita S. Hilarionis Eremitae*	PL XXIII. 29–54
Joh. Ant.	John of Antioch, *fragments*	FHG IV. 538–622; V. 27–38
„ *Exc. de ins.*	„ „ *Excerpta de insidiis*	C. de Boor, Berlin, 1905
Joh. Biclar.	John of Biclarum, *Chronica*	MGH (AA) XI. 211–20
Joh. Chrys. *adv. opp. vit. mon.*	John Chrysostom, *adversus oppugnatores vitae monasticae*	PG XLVII. 319–86
„ *c. lud.*	„ *Homilia contra ludos et theatra*	PG LVI. 263–70
„ *de Anna*	„ *Sermones de Anna*	PG LIV. 631–76
„ *de Sac.*	„ *de Sacerdotio*	PG XLVIII. 623–92
„ *Ep.*	„ *Epistulae*	PG LII. 529–742
„ *Hom. ad pop. Ant.*	„ *Homiliae de statuis ad populum Antiochenum*	PG XLIX. 15–222
„ *Hom. de Laz.*	„ *Homiliae de Lazaro*	PG XLVIII. 963–1054
„ *Hom. hab. in eccl. Pauli.*	„ *Homilia habita in ecclesia Pauli*	PG LXIII. 501–10
„ *Hom. in Act.*	„ *Homiliae in Acta apostolorum*	PG LX. 13–384
„ *Hom. in Ep. I ad Cor.*	„ *Homiliae in epistulam primam ad Corinthios*	PG LXI. 9–382
„ *Hom. in Ep. II ad Cor.*	„ *Homiliae in epistulam secundam ad Corinthios*	PG LXI. 382–610
„ *Hom. in Ep. I ad Tim.*	„ *Homiliae in epistulam primam ad Timotheum*	PG LXII. 501–600
„ *Hom. in Eph.*	„ *Homiliae in epistulam ad Ephesios*	PG LXII. 9–176
„ *Hom. in Gen.*	„ *Homiliae in Genesim*	PG LIII–LIV
„ *Hom. in Hebr.*	„ *Homiliae in epistulam ad Hebraeos*	PG LXIII. 9–236
„ *Hom. in Joh.*	„ *Homiliae in Joannem*	PG LIX
„ *Hom. in Matth.*	„ *Homiliae in Matthaeum*	PG LVII–LVIII
„ *Laud. Ign. Mart.*	„ *Laudatio in S. martyrem Ignatium Deiferum*	PG L. 587–96
Joh. Eph. *V. SS. Or.*	John of Ephesus, *Vitae Sanctorum Orientalium*	E. W. Brooks, *Patrologia Orientalis*, XVII. i; XVIII. iv; XIX. ii
„ *HE*	„ *Historiae ecclesiasticae pars tertia*	E. W. Brooks, *Corpus scriptorum christianorum orientalium (Scriptores Syri)* III. iii
Joh. Epiph.	John of Epiphania, *fragments*	FHG IV. 273–6
Joh. Lydus, *Mag.*	John Lydus, *de magistratibus populi Romani*	R. Wuensch, 1903 (Teubner)
„ *Mens.*	„ „ *de mensibus*	R. Wuensch, 1898 (Teubner)
Joh. Maiuma. *Pleroph.*	John Rufus, bishop of Maiuma, *Plerophoriae*	F. Nau, *Patrologia Orientalis*, VIII. 1
Joh. Moschus	John Moschus, *Pratum Spirituale*	PG LXXXVII. iii. 2851–3112
Jordanes, *Get.*	Jordanes, *Getica*	MGH (AA) V
„ *Rom.*	„ *Romana*	MGH (AA) V
Jos. *Bell. Jud.*	Flavius Josephus, *de Bello Judaico*	S. A. Naber, 1895 (Teubner)
Josh. Styl.	Joshua the Stylite, *Chronicle*	W. Wright, Cambridge, 1882
Julian, *Ep.*	Julian, *Epistulae*	F. C. Hertlein, 1875–6 (Teubner)
„ *Ep. ad Ath.*	„ *Epistula ad Athenienses*	„
„ *Frag. Ep.*	„ *Fragmentum epistulae*	„
„ *Misop.*	„ *Misopogon*	„
„ *Or.*	„ *Orationes*	„
Junilius, *de part. div. leg.*	Junilius, *de partibus divinae legis*	PL LXVIII. 15–42

Just. II, *Nov.*	Justin II, *Novellae*	C. E. Zachariae von Lingenthal, *Ius Graeco-Romanum* (Leipzig, 1856-84) III, 3-17
Just. *App.*	Justinian, *Appendix constitutionum dispersarum*	R. Schoell and W. Kroll, Berlin, 1895
„ *Ed.*	„ *Edicta*	„
„ *Nov.*	„ *Novellae*	„
Kern, *Inschr. von Magnesia am Maiander*	O. Kern, *Die Inschriften von Magnesia am Maiander*, Berlin, 1900	
Lact. *Div. Inst.*	Lactantius, *Divinae Institutiones*	*CSEL* XIX. 1-672
„ *Epit.*	„ *Divinarum institutionum epitome*	*CSEL* XIX. 675-761
„ *Mort. Pers.*	„ *de mortibus persecutorum*	*CSEL* XXVII. 171-238
Leg. *Saec.*	*Leges Saeculares*	FIR II.² 759-98
Leo, *Ep.*	Pope Leo I, *Epistulae*	PL LIV. 593-1218
„ *Serm.*	„ „ *Sermones*	PL LIV. 142-468
Lex Burg.	*Lex Burgundionum, liber constitutionum*	*MGH* (*Leg.*) I. ii. 36-116
„ *prima const.*	„ *prima constitutio*	*MGH* (*Leg.*) I. ii. 30-5
„ *extrav.*	„ *constitutiones extravagantes*	*MGH* (*Leg.*) I. ii. 117-22
Lex Rom. Burg.	*Lex Romana Burgundionum*	*MGH* (*Leg.*) I. ii. 123-63
„ *Theudi*	„ *Theudi regis*	*MGH* (*Leg.*) I. i. 467-9
„ *Vis.*	„ *Visigothorum*	*MGH* (*Leg.*) I. i. 38-456
Lib. *Decl.*	Libanius, *Declamationes*	R. Foerster,1903-22 (Teubner)
„ *Ep.*	„ *Epistulae*	„
„ *Or.*	„ *Orationes*	„
Lib. *Pont.*	*Liber Pontificalis* (*pars prior*)	*MGH* (*Gest. Pont. Rom.*) I
Liberatus, *Brev.*	Liberatus, *Breviarium causae Nestorianorum et Eutychianorum*	PL LXVIII. 969-1050
Loewenfeld, *Ep. Pont. Rom. Ined.*	S. Loewenfeld, *Epistulae Pontificum Romanorum Ineditae*, Leipzig, 1885	
MAMA	W. M. Calder, *Monumenta Asiae Minoris Antiqua*, Manchester, 1928-62	
Macr. *Sat.*	Macrobius, *Saturnalia*	F. Eyssenhardt, 1893 (Teubner)
Maj. *Nov.*	Majorian, *Novellae*	*Codex Theodosianus*, vol. II, P. Meyer, Berlin, 1905
Malalas	John Malalas, *Chronographia*	*CSHB*
„ *Exc. de Insid.*	„ „ *Excerpta de Insidiis*	C. de Boor, Berlin, 1905
Malchus	Malchus of Philadelphia, *fragments*	*FHG* IV. 112-32
Marc. *Nov.*	Marcian, *Novellae*	*Codex Theodosianus*, vol. II, P. Meyer, Berlin, 1905
Marcell. com.	Marcellinus comes, *Chronicon*	*MGH* (*AA*) XI. 60-104
Marcellus Empiricus	Marcellus Empiricus, *Liber de medicamentis*	G. Helmreich, 1889 (Teubner)
Mart. Bracar. *de corr. rust.*	Martin of Bracara, *de correctione rusticorum*	C. W. Barlow, *Martini episcopi Bracarensis opera omnia*, New Haven, 1950
Maximus Taurin. *Serm.*	Maximus of Turin, *Sermones*	PL LVII. 531-760
Menander	Menander Protector, *fragments*	*FHG* IV. 201-69
de Mirac. S. Stef.	*Libri II de miraculis S. Stefani*	PL XLI. 833-54
Narr. de ob. Theod. Hierosol.	*Narratio de obitu Theodosii Hierosolymitani*	E. W. Brooks, *Corpus scriptorum Christianorum orientalium* (*Scriptores Syri*), III. xxv
Nicephorus, *Op. Hist.*	Nicephorus, patriarch of Constantinople, *Opuscula Historica*	C. de Boor, 1880 (Teubner)
Nicetas Choniata, *Thesaurus*	Nicetas Choniata, *Thesaurus orthodoxae fidei*	*PG* CXXXIX-CXL
Not. *Const.*	*Notitia Urbis Constantinopolitanae*	O. Seeck, *Notitia Dignitatum*
Not. *Dig. Occ.*	*Notitia Dignitatum Occidentalis*	O. Seeck, Berlin, 1876
„ *Or.*	„ „ *Orientalis*	
Not. *Rom.*	*Notitia Regionum Urbis XIV*	*Acta Inst. Rom. Regni Sueciae*, III (1949), 73-106
Notitia *Ant.*	*Notitia Antiochena*	*Byz. Zeitschr.* XVIII (1925), 60 ff.

OGI	W. Dittenberger, *Orientis Graecae Inscriptiones Selectae*, Leipzig, 1903–5	
Olymp.	Olympiodorus of Thebes, *fragments*	*FHG* IV. 58–68
Opt.	Optatus Milevitanus	*CSEL* XXVI
Origen, *Comm. in Matth.*	Origen, *Commentaries in Matthew*	E. Klostermann, *Gr. Schr.* vol. 40
„ περὶ ἀρχῶν	„ *de Principiis*	P. Koetschau, *Gr. Schr.* vol. 22
Orosius	Orosius, *Historiarum adversus paganos libri VII*	C. Zangemeister, 1889 (Teubner)

P. Aberdeen — *Catalogue of Greek and Latin papyri and ostraca in the possession of the University of Aberdeen*, E. G. Turner, Aberdeen, 1939

P. Abinn. — *The Abinnaeus Archive; papers of a Roman officer in the reign of Constantius II*, H. I. Bell, V. Martin, E. G. Turner, D. van Berchem, Oxford, 1962

P. Amh. — *The Amherst Papyri*, B. P. Grenfell and A. S. Hunt, London, 1900–1

P. Antinoop. — *The Antinoopolis Papyri*, C. H. Roberts, London, 1950–

P. Baden — *Veroeffentlichungen aus den badischen Papyrus-Sammlungen*, W. Spiegelberg, F. Bilabel and others, Heidelberg, 1923–34

P. Beatty Panop. — (unpublished)

P. Bremen — *Die Bremer Papyri (Abhandlungen der Preussischen Akademie der Wissenschaften)*, U. Wilcken, Berlin, 1936

P. Cairo — *Catalogue générale des antiquités égyptiennes du Musée du Caire; Papyrus grecs d'époque byzantine*, J. Maspéro, Cairo, 1911–16

P. Cairo Isid. — *The Archive of Aurelius Isidorus*, A. E. R. Boak and H. C. Youtie, Ann Arbor, 1960

P. Cairo Preis. — *Griechische Urkunden des Aegyptischen Museums zu Kairo*, F. Preisigke, Strassburg, 1911

P. Corn. — *Greek Papyri in the library of Cornell University*, W. L. Westermann and C. J. Kraemer, Jr., New York, 1926

P. Dip. — *I papiri diplomatici*, Gaetano Marini, Rome, 1805

PER — *Mitteilungen aus der Sammlung der Papyrus Erzherzog Rainer*, Vienna, 1887. N.S. 1– Vienna, 1932

P. Erlangen — *Die Papyri der Universitätsbibliothek Erlangen*, W. Schubart, Leipzig, 1942

P. Flor. — *Papiri greco-egizii*, D. Comparetti and G. Vitelli, Milan, 1906–15

P. Fouad — *Les Papyrus Fouad I* (Publications de la Société Fouad I de Papyrologie, Textes et Documents, iii), A. Bataille, A. Guéraud, P. Jouguet and others, Cairo, 1939

P. Gen. — *Les Papyrus de Genève*, J. Nicole, Geneva, 1896–1900

P. Gen. Lat. — *Archives militaires du Ier siècle*, J. Nicole and C. Morel, Geneva, 1900

P. Giss. — *Griechische Papyri im Museum des oberhessischen Geschichtsvereins zu Giessen*, O. Eger, E. Kornemann and P. M. Meyer, Leipzig, 1910–12

P. Goodspeed — *Greek Papyri from the Cairo Museum together with papyri of Roman Egypt from American collections*, E. J. Goodspeed, Chicago, 1902

P. Grenf. — *New Classical Fragments and other Greek and Latin Papyri*, B. P. Grenfell and A. S. Hunt, Oxford, 1897

P. Groningen — *Papyri Groninganae: Griechische Papyri der Universitätsbibliothek zu Groningen nebst zwei Papyri der Universitätsbibliothek zu Amsterdam*, A. G. Roos, Amsterdam, 1933

P. Hamb. — *Griechische Papyrusurkunden der Hamburger Staats- und Universitätsbibliothek*, P. M. Meyer, Leipzig-Berlin, 1911–24

P. Harris — *The Rendel Harris Papyri of Woodbrooke College, Birmingham*, J. E. Powell, Cambridge, 1936

P. Hibeh — *The Hibeh Papyri*, B. P. Grenfell, A. S. Hunt and E. G. Turner, London, 1906–

P. Iand. — *Papyri Iandanae*, cum discipulis edidit C. Kalbfleisch, Leipzig, 1912–38

P. Ital. — *Die nichtliterarischen lateinischen Papyri Italiens aus der Zeit 445–700*, J. O. Tjäder, Lund, 1955

P. Jena — *Jenaer Papyrus-Urkunden*, F. Zucker and F. Schneider, Jena, 1926

P. Kalen — *Berliner Leihgaber griechischer Papyri*, T. Kalén, Uppsala, 1932

P. Klein. Form — *Griechische Papyrus-Urkunden kleineren Formats*, C. Wessely, Leipzig, 1904, 1908 (= *SPP*. vols. iii and viii)

P. Lips. — *Griechische Urkunden der Papyrussammlung zu Leipzig*, L. Mitteis, Leipzig, 1906

P. Lond. — *Greek Papyri in the British Museum*, F. G. Kenyon and H. I. Bell, London, 1893–1917

P. Lugd. Bat.   Papyri Graeci Musei Antiquarii Publici Lugduni-Batavi, C. Leemans, Leiden, 1885

P. Merton   A descriptive catalogue of the Greek papyri in the collection of W. Merton, H. I. Bell and C. H. Roberts, London, 1948, Dublin, 1959

P. Michael.   Papyri Michaelidae; being a catalogue of the Greek and Latin papyri, tablets and ostraca in the library of Mr. G. A. Michaelidis of Cairo, D. J. Crawford, Aberdeen, 1955

P. Monac.   Veroeffentlichungen aus der Papyrussammlung der K. Hof- und Staats-bibliothek zu München: Byzantinische Papyri, A. Heisenberg and L. Wenger, Leipzig and Berlin, 1914

P. Nessana   Excavations at Nessana, conducted by H. D. Colt, Jr.; vol. 3, Non-literary Papyri, C. J. Kraemer, Jr., Princeton, N.J., 1958

P. Oslo.   Papyri Osloenses, S. Eitrem and L. Amundsen, Oslo, 1925–36

P. Oxy.   The Oxyrhynchus Papyri, B. P. Grenfell, A. S. Hunt and others, London, 1898–

P. Paris   Notices et Textes des papyrus grecs du Musée du Louvre et de la Bibliothèque impériale (Notices et Extraits des manuscripts de la Bibl. Impériale et autres Bibl. 18. 2), J. A. Letronne and W. Brunet de Presle, Paris, 1865

P. Princeton   Papyri in the Princeton University collections, A. C. Johnson, H. B. van Hoesen, E. H. Kase, Jr., and S. P. Goodrich, Baltimore and Princeton, 1931–42

PRG   Papyri russischer und georgischer Sammlungen, G. Zereteli, O. Krueger and P. Jernstedt, Tiflis, 1925–35

P. Reinach   Papyrus grecs et démotiques recueillis en Égypte, T. Reinach, W. Spiegel-berg and S. de Ricci, Paris, 1905; Les papyrus Théodore Reinach, tom. ii, P. Collart, etc., Cairo, 1940

P. Ryl.   Catalogue of the Greek Papyri in the John Rylands library, Manchester, A. S. Hunt, J. de M. Johnson, V. Martin and C. H. Roberts, Manchester, 1911–52

PSI   Papiri greci e latini (Pubblicazioni della Societa Italiana per la ricerca dei Papiri greci e latini in Egitto), G. Vitelli, M. Norsa and others, Florence, 1912–

P. Soc. Ath.   Papyri Societatis Archaeologicae Atheniensis, G. A. Petropoulos, Athens, 1939

P. Strassb.   Griechische Papyrus der Kaiserlichen Universitäts- und Landesbibliothek zu Strassburg, F. Preisigke, Leipzig, 1912, 1920; continued as Papyrus grecs de la Bibliothèque nationale et Universitaire de Strassburg, by P. Collomp and his pupils, Paris, 1948

P. Tebt.   The Tebtunis Papyri, B. P. Grenfell, A. S. Hunt and others, London, 1902–38

P. Thead.   Papyrus de Théadelphie, P. Jouguet, Paris, 1911

P. Vars.   Papyri Varsovienses, G. Manteuffel, Warsaw, 1935

P. Vind.   Einige Wiener Papyri, E. Boswinkel, Leyden, 1942

P. Warren   The Warren Papyri (Pap. Lugd.-Bat. i), M. David, B. A. van Groningen and J. C. van Oven, Leyden, 1941

P. Würz.   Mitteilungen aus der Würzburger Papyrussammlung, U. Wilcken, Berlin, 1934

P. Zill.   Vierzehn Berliner griechische Papyri: Urkunde und Briefe, H. Zilliacus, Helsingfors, 1914

Pall. Dial.   Palladius, Dialogus de vita S. Joannis   P. R. Coleman-Norton, Cam-
                            Chrysostomi   bridge, 1928

  „ Hist. Laus.   „   Historia Lausiaca   Dom C. Butler, The Lausiac
                                                         History of Palladius, Cam-
                                                         bridge, 1904

Palladius, de re rust.   Palladius, de re rustica   J. C. Schmidt, 1895 (Teubner)
Pan. Lat.   Panegyrici Latini   W. Baehrens, 1911 (Teubner)
Pap. Roll   A papyrus roll in the Princeton collection, E. H. Kase, Jr., Baltimore,1933
                        J. M. Pardessus, Diplomata, chartae, epistulae, leges ad res Gallo-
                        Francicas spectantia, Paris, 1843–9
                        Passio Philippi   T. Ruinart, Acta Martyrum
                                                         (Ratisbon, 1859)

Patr. Nic. Nom.   Patrum Nicaenorum Nomina   H. Gelzer, 1898 (Teubner)
Paul. V. Amb.   Paulinus of Milan, Vita S. Ambrosii   PL XIV. 27–46
Paul. Carm.   Paulinus of Nola, Carmina   CSEL XXX
  „ Ep.   „   „ Epistulae   CSEL XXIX

Paul. Euch.	Paulinus of Pella, *Eucharisticus*	*CSEL* XVI. 291-314
Paulus, *HL*	Paulus diaconus, *Historia Lango-bardorum*	*MGH* (*Scr. rer. Lang.*) 45-187
Paulus, *Sent.*	Julius Paulus, *Sententiae*	*FIR* II.² 321-417
Pausanias	Pausanias, *Graeciae Descriptio*	F. Spiro, 1903 (Teubner)
Pelagius I. *Ep.*	Pope Pelagius I, *Epistulae*	P. M. Gasso and C. M. Batlle, *Pelagii I Papae epistulae quae supersunt*, Montserrat, 1956
Pelagius II, *Ep.*	Pope Pelagius II, *Epistulae*	*PL* LXXII. 703-50
	S. G. F. Perry, *The Second Synod of Ephesus*, 1881	
Petr. Patr.	Peter the Patrician, *fragments*	*FHG* IV. 184-91
Phil. Brix. *Haer.*	Philastrius Brixiensis, *Liber de haeresibus*	*CSEL* XXXVIII
Philostorgius	Philostorgius, *Historia Ecclesiastica*	J. Bidez, *Gr. Schr.* vol. 21
Photius, *Bibl.*	Photius, *Bibliotheca*	*PG* CIII, CIV. 9-356
Pliny, *Hist. Nat.*	Pliny the elder, *Historia Naturalis*	C. Mayhoff, 1875-1906 (Teubner)
Pliny, *Ep.*	Pliny the younger, *Epistulae*	M. Schuster, 1952 (Teubner)
„ *Paneg.*	„ „ *Panegyricus*	„
Plut. *Cato Minor*	Plutarch, *Cato Minor*	K. Ziegler, 1932 (Teubner)
Poss. *V. Aug.*	Possidius, *Vita S. Augustini*	*PL* XXXII. 33-66
Princeton Exp. Syria	*Princeton University Archaeological Expeditions to Syria in 1904-5 and 1909*, III. A, *Greek and Latin Inscriptions* E. Littmann, D. Magie, D. R. Stuart, Leyden, 1921	
Priscian, *Pan.*	Priscian of Caesarea, *Panegyricus*	*CSHB*
Priscus	Priscus of Panium, *fragments*	*FHG* IV. 71-110
Proc. *Aed.*	Procopius of Caesarea, *de aedificiis*	J. Haury, 1905-13 (Teubner)
„ *BG*	„ „ *Bellum Gothicum*	„
„ *BP*	„ „ *Bellum Persicum*	„
„ *BV*	„ „ *Bellum Vandalicum*	„
„ *HA*	„ „ *Historia Arcana*	„
Proc. Gaz. *Ep.*	Procopius of Gaza, *Epistulae*	*PG* LXXXVII. 2717-92
„ *Pan.*	„ „ *Panegyricus*	*PG* LXXXVII. 2793-826
Ruf. *HE*	Rufinus, *Historia Ecclesiastica*	*PL* XXI. 467-540
„ *Hist. Mon.*	„ *Historia Monachorum*	*PL* XXI. 391-462
Greek original	*Historia monachorum in Aegypto*	A. J. Festugière, Brussels, 1961
Rut. Nam. *de red. suo*	Rutilius Namatianus, *de reditu suo*	J. Vessereau and F. Préchac (Coll. Budé), Paris, 1933
Sb	*Sammelbuch griechischer Urkunden aus Aegypten*, F. Preisigke and others, Berlin, Strassburg, etc. 1913-	
SEG	*Supplementum Epigraphicum Graecum*	
SHA	*Scriptores Historiae Augustae*	E. Hohl, 1927 (Teubner)
SPP	*Studien zur Palaeographie und Papyruskunde*, C. Wessely, Leipzig, 1901-	
Salv. *Gub. Dei*	Salvian, *de gubernatione Dei*	*CSEL* VIII; *MGH* (*AA*) I
Schol. *Sin.*	*Scholia Sinaitica*	*FIR* II.² 638-52
de septem ord. ecclesiae	Pseudo-Jerome, *Ep. XII de septem ordinibus ecclesiae*	*PL* XXX. 148-62
Sev. *Nov.*	Severus, *Novellae*	*Codex Theodosianus, vol.* II, P. Meyer, Berlin, 1905
Sev. Ant. *Ep.*	Severus of Antioch, *Epistulae*	E. W. Brooks, *The Select Letters of Severus of Antioch*, London, 1903-4
Sid. Ap. *Carm.*	Sidonius Apollinaris, *Carmina*	P. Mohr, 1895 (Teubner)
„ *Ep.*	„ „ *Epistulae*	„
Simplicius, *Ep.*	Pope Simplicius, *Epistulae*	A. Thiel, *Epistulae Romanorum Pontificum* (Braunsberg, 1867), 127-214
Siricius, *Ep.*	Pope Siricius, *Epistulae*	*PL* XIII. 1131-94
Sirm.	*Constitutiones Sirmondianae*	*Codex Theodosianus*, vol. I, Mommsen, Berlin, 1905
Soc.	Socrates, *Historia Ecclesiastica*	*PG* LXVII. 33-841
Sophron. *Narr. de mir. Cyr. et Joh.*	Sophronius, *Narratio de miraculis SS. Cyri et Johannis*	*PG* LXXXVII. 3124-676

Soz.	Sozomen, *Historia Ecclesiastica*	J. Bidez and G. C. Hansen, *Gr. Schr.* vol. 50
Stat. Eccl. Ant.	*Statuta Ecclesiae Antiqua*	C. Munier, *Les Statuta Ecclesiae Antiqua*, Paris, 1960
Steph. ad Bon. Libell.	*Stephani ad Bonifacium Libelli*	PL LXV. 34–40
Strabo	Strabo, *Geographica*	A. Meineke, 1852 (Teubner)
Suet.	Suetonius, *Vitae duodecim Caesarum*	M. Ihm, 1923 (Teubner)
Suidas	Suidas, *Lexicon*	A. Adler, Leipzig, 1928
Sulp. Sev. *Chron.*	Sulpicius Severus, *Chronica*	*CSEL* I
,, *Dial.*	,, ,, *Dialogi*	,,
,, *V. Mart.*	,, ,, *Vita S. Martini*	
Sym. Metaphr. *S. Dem.*	Symeon Metaphrastes, *S. Demetrii*	PG CXVI. 1203–1462
Mirac.	*Miracula*	
V. Theod. Coenob.	,, *Vita et conversatio S. Theodosii coenobiarchae*	PG CXIV. 469–554
Symm. *Ep.*	Symmachus, *Epistulae*	*MGH (AA)* VI
,, *Or.*	,, *Orationes*	,,
,, *Rel.*	,, *Relationes*	,,
Symmachus, *Ep.*	Pope Symmachus, *Epistulae*	A. Thiel, *Epistulae Romanorum Pontificum* (Braunsberg, 1867), 642–734
Syn. *de Prov.*	Synesius, *de Providentia seu Aegyptius*	PG LXVI. 1209–82
,, *de Regno*	,, *de Regno*	PG LXVI. 1053–1108
,, *Catastasis*	,, *Catastasis*	PG LXVI. 1565–78
,, *Ep.*	,, *Epistulae*	PG LXVI. 1321–560
Tac. *Ann.*	Tacitus, *Annales*	E. Koestermann, 1960 (Teubner)
Tertullian, *de idol.*	Tertullian, *de idololatria*	PL I. 663–96
Th. II, *Nov.*	Theodosius II, *Novellae*	*Codex Theodosianus*, vol. II, P. Meyer, Berlin, 1905
Them. *Or.*	Themistius, *Orationes*	W. Dindorf, Leipzig, 1832
Theod. *Ep.* (*Azéma*)	Theodoret, *Epistulae*	Y. Azéma, Paris, 1955
,, *Ep.* (PG)	,, *Epistulae*	PG LXXXIII. 1173–485
,, *Graec. Aff. Cur.*	,, *Graecarum Affectionum Curatio*	J. Raeder, 1904 (Teubner)
,, *Haer. Fab. Comp.*	, *Haereticarum Fabularum Compendium*	PG LXXXIII. 335–556
,, *HE*	,, *Historia Ecclesiastica*	L. Parmentier, *Gr. Schr.* vol. 84
,, *Hist. Rel.*	,, *Historia Religiosa*	PG LXXXII. 1283–1496
Theodore Lector	Theodore Lector, *Excerpta Historiae Ecclesiasticae*	PG LXXXVI. i. 165–226
Theoph. Byz.	Theophanes of Byzantium, *fragments*	FHG IV. 270–1
Theoph. Sim.	Theophylactus Simocatta, *Historiae*	C. de Boor, 1887 (Teubner)
Theophanes	Theophanes, *Chronographia*	C. de Boor, Leipzig, 1883
Totius Orbis Descr.	*Totius Orbis Descriptio*	C. Mueller, *Geographi Graeci Minores*, vol. II
Tib. *Nov.*	Tiberius, *Novellae*	C. E. Zachariae von Lingenthal, *Ius Graeco-Romanum* (Leipzig, 1856-84), III. 17–31
Ulpian	Ulpian, *Liber singularis regularum*	FIR II.[2] 262–301
V. Auxentii	*Vita, conversatio et exercitatio S. Auxentii*	PG CXIV. 1377–1436
V. Caes.	*Vita S. Caesarii episcopi*	*MGH (Scr. rer. Merov.)* III. 457–501
V. Dan.	*Vita S. Danielis Stylitae*	*Anal. Boll.* XXXII (1913), 121–214
V. Dan. Scet.	*Vie de l'abbé Daniel le Scétiote*	L. Clugnet, Paris, 1901
V. Eutych.	*Vita et conversatio Eutychii, patriarchae Constantinopolitani*	PG LXXXVI. ii. 2273–389
V. Fulg.	*Vita S. Fulgentii episcopi Ruspensis*	PL LXV. 117–50
V. Germani	*Vita Germani episcopi Autissiodorensis*	*MGH (Scr. rer. Merov.)* VII. 247–83
V. Hilarii	*Vita S. Hilarii Arelatensis*	PL L. 1219–46

V. Hypatii	Callinicus, *Vita S. Hypatii*	ediderunt seminarii philologo-rum Bonnensis sodales, 1895 (Teubner)
V. Isaiae	*Vita Isaiae monachi*	E. W. Brooks, *Corpus Scriptorum Christianorum Orientalium (Scriptores Syri)*, III. xxv
V. Joh. Eleem.	*Vita Johannis Eleemosynarii, patriarchae Alexandriae*	*Anal. Boll.* XLV (1927). 19–73
V. Marcelli	*Vita et conversatio S. Marcelli, archimandritae monasterii Acoemetorum*	*PG* CXVI. 705–46
V. Marthae	*Vita S. Marthae*	*Acta Sanctorum*, Mai. v. 398–427
V. Mel.	*Vita S. Melaniae Junioris* (Greek)	*Anal. Boll.* XXII (1903), 7–49
V. Mel. (L)	*Vita S. Melaniae Junioris* (Latin)	*Anal. Boll.* VIII. (1889), 19–63
V. Olymp.	*Vita S. Olympiadis*	*Anal. Boll.* XV (1896), 409–23
V. Pach.	*Vita S. Pachomii*	F. Nau and J. Bousquet, *Patrologia Orientalis*, IV. v
V. Pauli	*Vita Pauli, episcopi Constantinopolitani confessoris*	*PG* CIV. 120–32
V. Porph.	*Vie de Porphyre, évèque de Gaza*	H. Grégoire and M. A. Kugener, Paris, 1930
V. SS. Patr. Emerit.	*Vitae Sanctorum Patrum Emeritensium*	*PL* LXXX. 117–64
V. Severini	Eugippius, *Vita S. Severini*	*CSEL* IX. ii
V. Sym. Jun.	*Vita S. Symeonis Junioris*	*PG* LXXXVI. ii. 2988–3216
V. Theod. Syc.	*Vita S. Theodori Syceotae*	Theophilus Ioannis, Μνημεῖα Ἁγιολογικά (Venice, 1884), 361–495
Val. III, *Nov.*	Valentinian III, *Novellae*	*Codex Theodosianus*, vol. II, P. Meyer, Berlin, 1905
	Varro, *de re rustica*	G. Goetz, 1912 (Teubner)
Veg.	Vegetius, *Epitoma rei militaris*	C. Lang, 1885 (Teubner)
	Victor Tonnennensis	*MGH (AA)* XI. 184–206
Victor Vit.	Victor Vitensis, *Historia persecutionis Africae*	*CSEL* VII; *MGH (AA)* III
Vigilius, *Ep. Encycl.*	Pope Vigilius, *Epistula Encyclica*	*PL* LXIX. 53–9
„ *Ep. ad Rust. et Seb.*	„ „ *Epistula ad Rusticum et Sebastianum*	*PL* LXIX. 43–51
Vigilius Tridentinus,*Ep.*	Vigilius of Tridentum, *Epistulae*	*PL* XIII. 549–58
Wadd.	W. H. Waddington. *Recueil des Inscriptions grecques et latines de la Syrei*, Paris, 1870 (= P. le Bas and W. H. Waddington, *Voyage archéologique en Grèce et en Asie Mineure*, III. 6, Pains. 1847–73).	
Zach. Myt. *Chron.*	The Chronicle of Zacharias of Mytilene	F. J. Hamilton and E. W. Brooks, London, 1899
„ *V. Sev.*	Zacharias of Mytilene, *Vita Severi*	M. A. Kugener, *Patrologia Orientalis*, II. i
	C. E. Zachariae von Lingenthal, ᾿Ανέκδοτα, Leipzig, 1843.	
Zonaras	Zonaras, *Epitome Historiarum*	L. Dindorf, 1868–75 (Teubner)
Zos.	Zosimus, *Historia Nova*	L. Mendelssohn, Leipzig, 1887
Zosimus, *Ep.*	(Pope) Zosimus, *Epistulae*	*PL* XX. 642–83

INDEX

Persons with two (or more) names, unless they are by general convention known by both (e.g. Sidonius Apollinaris), are indexed under their second (or last) name, which they in fact normally used. Holders of several offices are distinguished by the highest office which they are recorded to have held; thus references to Constantius, the patrician of Honorius, will be found under Constantius III, emperor. All references are to Volumes I and II.

INDEX